BRENDAN SIMMS

Three Victories and a Defeat

The Rise and Fall of the First British Empire, 1714–1783

PENGUIN BOOKS

PENGUIN BOOKS

Published by the Penguin Group
Penguin Books Ltd, 80 Strand, London WC2R 0RL, England
Penguin Group (USA) Inc., 375 Hudson Street, New York, New York 10014, USA
Penguin Group (Canada), 90 Eglinton Avenue East, Suite 700, Toronto, Ontario, Canada M4P 2Y3
(a division of Pearson Penguin Canada Inc.)
Penguin Ireland, 25 St Stephen's Green, Dublin 2, Ireland
(a division of Penguin Books Ltd)
Penguin Group (Australia), 250 Camberwell Road, Camberwell, Victoria 3124, Australia
(a division of Pearson Australia Group Pty Ltd)
Penguin Books India Pvt Ltd, 11 Community Centre, Panchsheel Park, New Delhi – 110 017, India
Penguin Group (NZ), 67 Apollo Drive, Rosedale, North Shore 0632, New Zealand
(a division of Pearson New Zealand Ltd)
Penguin Books (South Africa) (Pty) Ltd, 24 Sturdee Avenue, Rosebank, Johannesburg 2196, South Africa

Penguin Books Ltd, Registered Offices: 80 Strand, London WC2R 0RL, England

www.penguin.com

First published by Allen Lane 2007
Published in Penguin Books 2008
2

Copyright © Brendan Simms, 2007

The moral right of the author has been asserted

Typeset by Rowland Phototypesetting Ltd, Bury St Edmunds, Suffolk
Printed in Great Britain by Clays Ltd, St Ives plc

A CIP catalogue record for this book is available from the British Library

978-0-140-28984-8

www.greenpenguin.co.uk

Penguin Books is committed to a sustainable future
for our business, our readers and our planet.
The book in your hands is made from paper
certified by the Forest Stewardship Council.

For Anita

Contents

List of Illustrations   ix
List of Maps   xiii
Note on Dating and Quotations   xiv
Acknowledgements   xv

Introduction   1

I Imperial Apprenticeship

1 A Part of the Main: England in Europe, 1558–1697   9
2 Marlborough Country: Britain and the Empire,
   1697–1714   44

II Imperial Opportunities

3 Imperial Restoration, 1714–1715   79
4 Britain's New European Empire, 1716–1717   107
5 Preventive War in the Mediterranean and the Baltic,
   1718–1719   135

III Imperial Challenges

6 A Protestant Empire, 1721–1724   159
7 The Return of Charles V, 1725–1726   183
8 The Resurgence of France, 1727–1732   204

IV Imperial Visions

9   Imperial Retreat, 1733–1736   227

10 The Colonial Mirage, 1737–1739   247

11 Imperial Isolation, 1740–1742   274

V Imperial Recovery

12 The Empires Strike Back, 1742–1745   307

13 The American Empire Restores the Balance in the
    German Empire, 1745–1748   333

14 Imperial Pre-emptions, 1748–1752   355

VI Imperial Triumph

15 Transferring the Seat of Empire? 1753–1756   387

16 The Imperial Missions of William Pitt, 1757–1759   422

17 An Island Once Again, 1760–1763   463

VII Imperial Hubris

18 Imperial Retrenchments, 1763–1765   501

19 Imperial Pre-emptions, 1765–1767   532

20 Empire Adrift, 1768–1772   555

VIII Imperial Nemesis

21 Fighting for Europe in America, 1773–1777   579

22 Losing America in Europe, 1778–1779   615

23 The Partition of Britain, 1780–1783   636

    Conclusion   662
    Bibliography   685
    Notes   726
    Index   783

List of Illustrations

1 *Frederick V Elector Palatinate with his wife Elisabeth Stuart and their children* by a follower of Gerhard van Honthorst, c.1630 (Photo: Sotheby's/akg-images)   21

2 *John Churchill, 1st Duke of Marlborough* by Godfrey Kneller, c.1706 (copyright © National Portrait Gallery, London)   51

3 Playing card depicting the victory at the Battle of Höchstädt (Blenheim), English School (18th century) (Private collection. Photo: The Bridgeman Art Library)   55

4 *Johann Caspar von Bothmer* by John Faber (Photo copyright © Queen's Printer and Controller of HMSO, 1998. UK Government Art Collection)   81

5 The flag of the King-Elector George I (Courtesy Historisches Museum, Hanover)   91

6 *Count Andreas Gottlieb von Bernstorff* (Private collection)   119

7 *Charles Townshend, 2nd Viscount Townshend*, anon, after Godfrey Kneller, c.1715–20 (copyright © National Portrait Gallery, London)   121

8 *The Battle of Cape Passaro, 11 August 1718* by Richard Paton, 1767 (copyright © National Maritime Museum, London)   140

9 *An allegory of the power of Great Britain by land*, design for a decorative panel for George I's ceremonial coach, attributed to Sir James Thornhill, c.1718 (Yale Center for

British Art, Paul Mellon Collection. Photo: The Bridgeman
Art Library)   150

10 *Charles VI, Holy Roman Emperor, as Charles III King
    of Hungary* by Johann Georg Mentzel, 1730 (Photo:
    akg-images)   161

11 *Abraham Stanyan* by John Faber (copyright © National
    Portrait Gallery, London)   197

12 *Charles Wager* by John Faber (copyright © National
    Portrait Gallery, London)   201

13 *George II in his coronation robes*, engraving after Thomas
    Hudson, 1744 (Photo: Corbis)   206

14 *Horatio Walpole* by Christian Friedrich Zincke, c.1720–25
    (copyright © National Portrait Gallery, London)   220

15 *The Princesses Anne, Amelia & Caroline, daughters of
    George II* by Martin Maingaud, early 18th century (Photo:
    Sotheby's/akg-images)   230

16 *The solemnization of the marriage of Prince James Francis
    Edward Stuart and Princess Maria Clementina Sobieska at
    Montefiascone, 1 September 1719* by Agostino Masucci,
    c.1735 (Scottish National Portrait Gallery, Edinburgh.
    Photo: The Bridgeman Art Library)   233

17 *A Spanish coastguard boarding Captain Jenkins's ship and
    cutting off his ear*, English School (18th century), c.1731
    (Private collection. Photo: The Bridgeman Art Library)   248

18 *Henry St John, 1st Viscount Bolingbroke*, English School
    (18th century) (Private collection. Photo: The Bridgeman
    Art Library)   254

19 *Fan with a poem celebrating the victory at Porto Bello* by
    F. Chassereau, 1739 (copyright © National Maritime
    Museum, London)   277

20 *A prospect of the town and harbour of Carthagena, taken
    by the English under the brave Admiral Vernon*, English
    School (18th century), 1741 (Private collection. Photo: The
    Bridgeman Art Library)   285

21 *Admiral Nicholas Haddock*, English School (18th century),
   c.1742–3 (copyright © Greenwich Hospital Collection,
   National Maritime Museum, London)   287

22 *King George II at the Battle of Dettingen* by John Wootton,
   c.1743 (Courtesy of the Council, National Army Museum,
   London. Acquired with assistance of National Art
   Collections Fund. Photo: The Bridgeman Art Library)   316

23 *An actual survey of the Electorate, or face of the country
   whereon Hanover stands, with a view of Herenhaussen
   and the seats of manufactures*, 1743 (copyright © Trustees
   of the British Museum (BMC 2587))   327

24 *The landing of New England forces under Commodore
   Warren, Cape Breton*, engraving by John Bowles, after a
   painting by J. Stevens, c.1745 (Photo: The Art Archive/
   Eileen Tweedy)   345

25 *The attack on Berg-Op-Zoom, 4 a.m. 16 September
   1746* by Henri-Desiré van Blarenberghe, 1786 (Château
   de Versailles. Photo: Giraudon/The Bridgeman Art
   Library)   349

26 *Plan of the town of Ypres, Belgium* by Sebastian de
   Pontault Beaulieu, 1729 (Krigsarkivet, Stockholm)   357

27 *Baron Gerlach Adolf von Münchhausen*, engraving by Egid
   Verhelst, 1760 (Photo: akg images)   376

28 Map of Louisiana by J. B. Hommann, 18th century (Musée
   National de la Coopération Franco-américaine, Blérancourt.
   Copyright © Photo RMN)   393

29 *George II in the House of Lords*,1742 (copyright ©
   Hulton-Deutsch Collection/Corbis)   399

30 Staffordshire teapot depicting Frederick the Great,
   c.1757–8 (copyright © National Museum of Scotland,
   Edinburgh)   448

31 *The vanity of human glory*, 1760 (Library of Congress,
   Prints and Photographs Division)   453

32 *Sic transit gloria mundi*, satirical print depicting William

Pitt (copyright © Trustees of the British Museum, London
(BM 3913))   472

33 *A view of the House of Commons*, English School (mid
    to late 18th century) (Photo: Stapleton Collection/The
    Bridgeman Art Library)   485

34 *King George III with General Robert Ramsden* by David
    Morier, *c*.1765 (Photo: Sotheby's/akg-images)   522

35 *The Colonies reduced and its companion*, 1768 (Library of
    Congress, Prints and Photographs Division)   552

36 *President John Adams*, *c*.1770 (Photo: Corbis)   572

37 *The parricide, or a sketch of modern patriotism*, 1776
    (Library of Congress, Prints and Photographs Division)   595

38 *The Colossus*, satirical print depicting Benjamin Franklin,
    American School (18th century), *c*.1776 (American
    Antiquarian Society, Worcester, Massachusetts. Photo: The
    Bridgeman Art Library)   604

39 *A picturesque view of the state of the nation for February
    1778* (Library of Congress, Prints and Photographs Division)   619

40 *Jack England fighting the four confederates*, 1781 (Library
    of Congress, Prints and Photographs Division)   641

41 *The state tinkers* by James Gillray, 1780 (copyright
    © and courtesy of the Warden and Scholars of New College,
    Oxford. Photo: The Bridgeman Art Library)   656

42 *Das verstümmelte Britanien*, Dutch School, 1783 (Library
    of Congress, Prints and Photographs Division)   664

List of Maps

1 Europe in the Eighteenth Century   xviii–xix

2 The Empire in the Eighteenth Century   xx–xxi

3 Britain's Security Architecture in the Eighteenth Century   xxii–xxiii

4 British North America from Encirclement to Triumph,
   1713–1763   xxiv–xxv

5 British Interest in the Western Mediterranean   xxvi–xxvii

6 Imperial Retreat in North America, 1763–1783   xxviii–xxix

Note on Dating and Quotations

Until 1752, most Britons used the old Julian calendar, which was eleven days behind the newer Gregorian calendar in use throughout most of the rest of Europe. Very often, correspondence cited both dates, which is confusing. I have changed the dating to the newer style throughout except where the overlap between months was not clear with Older Style dates, which are thus marked ('OS').

This book makes extensive use of quotations from parliamentary debates. Most of these are taken from Cobbett's *Parliamentary history*, which is not a verbatim record in the style of Hansard today, but a compilation based on diverse pamphlet and other sources. The orations are usually rendered in indirect speech. To reproduce this directly would be too stilted, and so I have had recourse to a combination of brackets, elisions and quotation which faithfully renders the sense of what was reportedly said.

I have quoted extensively from a wide variety of sources: to avoid distracting inconsistency, spelling (and occasionally punctuation) has been modernized.

Acknowledgements

This book could not have been written without the help of others, living and dead. I hope that the reduced annotation – the original volume of which made even my indulgent publishers blench – will pay adequate tribute to most of the existing literature. All the same, I would like to single out here those who have most influenced me. These authors not only gave me a framework to follow, or sometimes to struggle against, but also helped to direct my archival researches. If this book is based on extensive archival records and contains some important fresh material, the author would never have got anywhere if he had not been guided to it by previous generations of historians.

My first and greatest debt is to the leading eighteenth-century international historian, Hamish Scott. He is the latest in a long line of historians from A. W. Ward through Sir Richard Lodge, Basil Williams, Richard Pares and D. B. Horn, who have stressed the importance of the European connection to British history in the eighteenth century. Hamish was kind enough to comment on the entire manuscript, and save me from excruciating error. He also helped me in too many other ways to record here. I thank my old friend Chris Clark, who commented in detail on the text from beginning to end. Whatever clarity the finished product possesses is to large degree his achievement. My interest in the 'Hanoverian connection' was first awakened by my PhD supervisor Tim Blanning, to whom I have had opportunity to express my gratitude in his Festschrift (Hamish Scott and Brendan Simms (eds.), *Cultures of power in Europe during the long eighteenth century*, Cambridge University Press, 2007). It has been sustained and refined by the colleagues who contributed to Brendan Simms and Torsten Riotte (eds.), *The Hanoverian dimension in British history, 1714–1837* (Cambridge, 2007), especially those concentrating on the period before

1783: Andrew Thompson, Nick Harding and my 'dynastic advisor', Clarissa Campbell Orr.

My understanding of the sixteenth- and seventeenth-century background was greatly increased by the work of R. B. Wernham, David Trim, J. H. Elliott, Jonathan Scott, Jonathan Israel, and many conversations with my colleagues John Adamson and Scott Mandelbrote. My treatment of George I is greatly dependent on his biographer Ragnhild Hatton and on the pioneering work of Wolfgang Michael. I was also helped by a number of other fine biographies, including Reed Browning on the Duke of Newcastle, and Marie Peters on William Pitt the Elder. The chapter on the Spanish depredations is heavily indebted to Philip Woodfine, and my views on colonial and maritime issues have been strongly influenced by Richard Pares. My understanding of colonial America profited immensely from reading Robert Tucker and David Hendricksen on the problem of imperial defence after 1763; Marc Egnal on the 'expansionists'; Theodore Draper on the *political* nature of the transatlantic divide; the comments of Gideon Mailer; and Gerald Stourzh on the geopolitics of Benjamin Franklin. The work of P. J. Marshall helped me to understand the problems of Empire after 1763. More generally, the work of Bob Harris for the mid eighteenth century and Stephen Conway for the later period has convinced me how important the European connection was for British social and cultural history.

I am also very aware of how much I owe those with whom I sometimes disagree. Jeremy Black is very much a 'Tory' to my 'Whig', but I would simply have been lost without his work on the early eighteenth century, to which I returned again and again. I think of Great Britain in less 'naval' terms than Nicholas Rodger, but his *Command of the ocean* is unlikely ever to be equalled. I stress the importance of 'Continental' strategies more than Daniel Baugh, but I have been greatly stimulated by his work on the 'blue water' policy. Likewise, this book stresses the 'European' focus and identity of eighteenth-century Britain, but engagement with the new imperial and 'Atlantic' history of David Armitage, Kathleen Wilson and others has helped me to clarify my thoughts. Although this book emphasizes the importance of the Hanoverian dimension to the development of British identity and xenophobia in the eighteenth century, the work of Linda Colley on Francophobia and anti-Catholicism must remain the starting point for any serious investigation.

I also received a great deal of practical help from librarians and archivists, and from assistants. I would have been sunk without the copying efforts of Jasper Heinzen, Geoffrey Dumbreck and Doohwan Ahn; and I am most grateful to the latter for accessing so many printed sources online. Miranda Long very kindly helped with those online sources as well as performing many other tasks, and I am most grateful to Hazel Dunn for assisting with the bibliography so efficiently.

Having said all this, all remaining mistakes are of course my own.

I also thank my colleagues at the Centre of International Studies at Cambridge for their support, company and intellectual stimulation. I am especially grateful to Jonathan Haslam, who led me in that direction. I could not have had two better Heads of Department: James Mayall and Christopher Hill, who gave me time to complete this project. The Chairman of the Degree Committee, my fellow historian Charles Jones, put me deeply in his debt. I am also hugely grateful to Wendy Cooke and Wendy Slaninka, and the irreplaceable Matthew Ham. All of them have made the Centre an excellent place to work.

My colleagues at Peterhouse provided the perfect environment in which to write. I am particularly grateful to the Master and Lady Wilson for the kindness shown to me and my family, and to James Carleton Paget, who dispensed advice and coffee. I also thank all those members of the Governing Body who have supported the teaching of History in recent times, especially Clare Baker, Tony Crowther, Simon Deakin, Adrian Dixon, Martin Golding, Richard Grigson, Sophie Jackson, Jack Klinowski, Andrew Lever, Scott Mandelbrote, Paul Midgeley, Roderick Munday, Andy Parker, Philip Pattenden, Ben Quash, Rob Ross Russell, Magnus Ryan, Chris Tilmouth, Mark Walters, and Philip Woodland.

Simon Winder at Penguin was the perfect editor: engaged, enthusiastic, and occasionally brutal. Jane Birdsell, my copy editor, imposed order on an unruly manuscript. My parents, David and Anngret Simms, maintained a keen interest in this project from start to finish.

Finally, I thank my wife Anita Bunyan, who not only submitted to the primacy of foreign policy, but also read and commented on many drafts. This book is for her.

Europe in the
Eighteenth Century

★ Barrier fortress

NORWAY

DENMARK

North
Sea

IRELAND

GREAT
BRITAIN

UNITED
PROVINCES

HANOVER   BR

London   The Hague

Elbe

Atlantic
Ocean

★★★ ★ AUSTRIAN
NETHERLANDS

Rhine

HOLY
E M

Seine

Versaillles • Paris   PALATINATE

Loire

LORRAINE   BAVARIA

F R A N C E   AUSTR

PIEDMONT-
SAVOY   • Milan

VENIC

Piacenza

Genoa •   • Parma

GENOA

SPAIN

TUSCANY   PAPAL
STATE

PORTUGAL

• Madrid   Barcelona   Toulon

CORSICA   Rome •

Balearic Is.

Minorca (Br.)

Ibiza   Majorca   SARDINIA   Tyrrhenian
Sea

Cartagena

Gibraltar (Br.)

M e d i t e r r a n e a n

Mers-el-Kebir

Melilla   • Oran   Algiers   Tunis •

The Empire in the Eighteenth Century

★   Barrier fortress

——   Boundary of the Holy Roman Empire

North Sea

DENMARK

ENGLAND

MECKLENBURG-SCHWERIN

BREMEN

VERDEN

UNITED PROVINCES

Osnabrück   • Hanover

• Hildesheim

MÜNSTER

• Paderborn

JÜLICH

BERG

• Waldeck

• Brussels

AUSTRIAN NETHERLANDS

COLOGNE

HESSE-KASSEL

SAXE-GOTHA

Rhine

HESSE-DARMSTADT

HESSE-HANAU

TRIER

MAINZ

PALATINATE

• Heidelberg

(Seat of Imperial Diet

Regensburg

Versailles

Seine

BADEN

WÜRTTEMBERG

FRANCE

LORRAINE

BAVARIA

• Munich

Loire

SWITZERLAND

Elbe

Spanish-sponsored
Jacobite invasion of
Scotland 1719

Jacobite Rising 1715

↑ ⚔ *To Culloden* 1746

Glasgow •
Edinburgh •

SCOTLAND

Londonderry •

ULSTER
Carrickfergus ⚔
1759   Belfast •

IRELAND

CONNAUGHT

• Galway   Drogheda •

LEINSTER
Limerick •   Dublin •

MUNSTER

Cork •   Wexford •

• Newcastle-
upon-Tyne

Irish Sea

Jacobite invasion
1745

Possible back door
to England

E N G L A N D

*North
Sea*

Cambridge •

<u>Cherbourg</u>   Battles involving
British troops

★   Barrier forts

Bristol •

London •

Dover •

<u>Bergen op Zoo</u>
1747

Plymouth •

Portsmouth •

Ostend •
Dunkirk •
Calais •   Bruges •

English Channel

Threatened French or
Franco-Spanish
invasion armadas
1744, 1759, 1779

Boulogne •

<u>Cherbourg</u>
⚔ 1758

Le Havre •

<u>Fontenoy</u> 1'

<u>Oudenarde</u> ⚔ Brussel
1708

Denain ⚔
1712

<u>Malplaquet</u>
1709

Brest •

<u>Quiberon</u>
1759

⚔ <u>St Malo</u>
1758

Bar le Duc
(Court of the
Pretender,
1712–1715

Paris/Versailles/
St Germain en Laye
(Court of the Pretender,
1689–1712)

F R A N C E

ENGLAND

**UNITED PROVINCES
(DUTCH REPUBLIC)**

Flushing •   **ZEALAND**

Dover •   *Narrow Seas*   Sluys

Dungeness •   Dunkirk •   ★ Knocke
★ Furnes   • Dendermonde

Calais •   ★★

Boulogne •   Ypres ★
Warneton
Menin   ★ Tournai   **AUSTRIAN
NETHERLANDS**

• Brussels

★ Namur

0		100		200 miles

0	100	200	300 kms

Britain's Security Architecture in the Eighteenth Century

Baltic Sea

DENMARK

● Copenhagen

Source of naval stores

● Danzig
● Elbing

BREMEN AND VERDEN
(To Hanover 1719)

BRANDENBURG – PRUSSIA

POLAND

Electorate
of Hanover

● Celle (British postal
intercept station)

Minden ✕
1759

Kunersdorf ✕
1759

✕ Hastenbeck
1757

Elbe

Krefeld
1758

✕
Vellinghausen
1761

Weser

Leuthen 1757

✕ *Lauffeldt* 1747

✕
Rossbach
1757

SILESIA (annexed
from Austria by Prussia
1740)

✕ *Rocoux* 1746
● Liège

AUSTRIAN
NETHERLANDS

Ramillies
1706

Rhine

✕ *Dettingen*
1743

HOLY ROMAN
EMPIRE

HABSBURG MONARCHY
(Austria)

LORRAINE

(Under French
influence from
1735; annexed
by France, 1766)

Blenheim
1704
✕

Vienna ●

SWITZERLAND

HUNGARY

VENICE

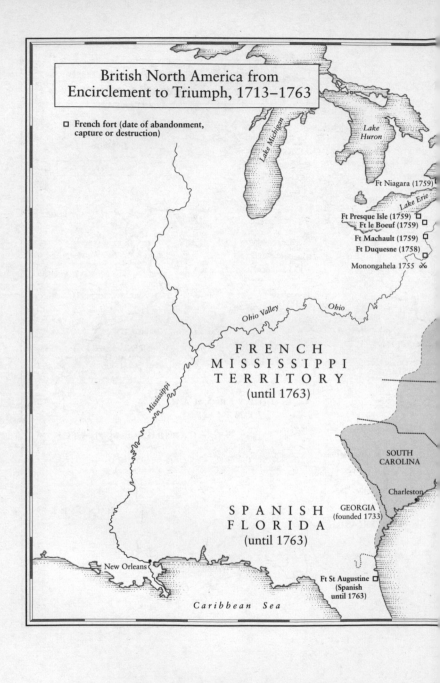

British North America from
Encirclement to Triumph, 1713–1763

□ French fort (date of abandonment,
capture or destruction)

Lake Michigan

Lake Huron

Ft Niagara (1759) □

Lake Erie

Ft Presque Isle (1759) □
Ft le Boeuf (1759) □
Ft Machault (1759) □
Ft Duquesne (1758) □
Monongahela 1755 ✕

Ohio Valley *Ohio*

F R E N C H
M I S S I S S I P P I
T E R R I T O R Y
(until 1763)

Mississippi

SOUTH
CAROLINA

Charleston

S P A N I S H   GEORGIA
F L O R I D A   (founded 1733)
(until 1763)

New Orleans

Ft St Augustine □
(Spanish
until 1763)

Caribbean Sea

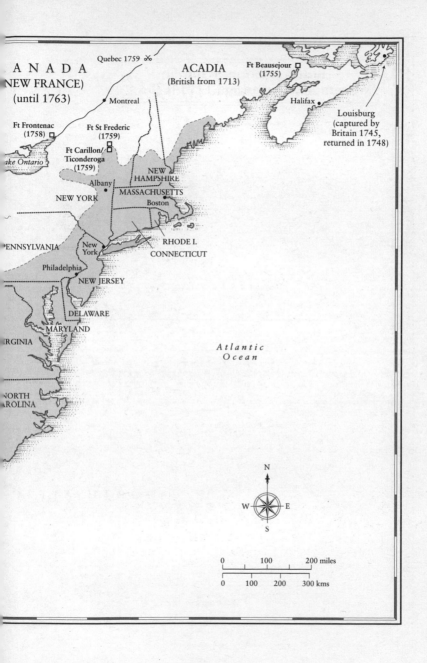

ANADA
NEW FRANCE)
(until 1763)

Quebec 1759 ✂

ACADIA
(British from 1713)

Ft Beausejour ☐
(1755)

Montreal

Halifax

Louisburg
(captured by
Britain 1745,
returned in 1748)

Ft Frontenac
(1758) ☐

Ft St Frederic
(1759)

Ft Carillon/
Ticonderoga
(1759) ☐

ake Ontario

NEW
HAMPSHIRE

Albany

NEW YORK

MASSACHUSETTS

Boston

New
York

RHODE I.

CONNECTICUT

PENNSYLVANIA

Philadelphia

NEW JERSEY

DELAWARE

MARYLAND

RGINIA

Atlantic
Ocean

NORTH
AROLINA

N

W — E

S

| 0 | 100 | 200 miles |
| 0 | 100 | 200 | 300 kms |

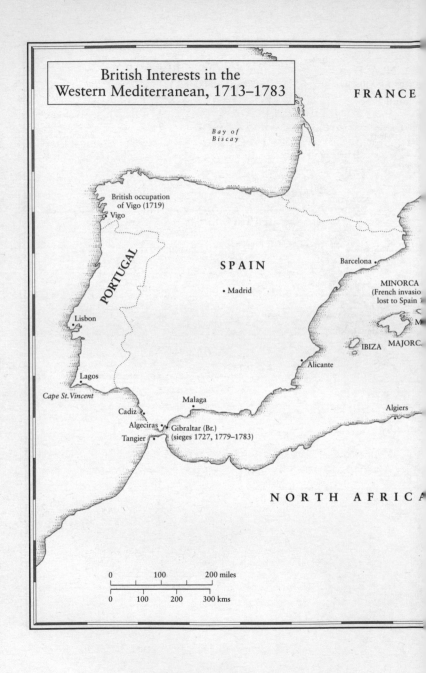

British Interests in the
Western Mediterranean, 1713–1783

FRANCE

Bay of Biscay

British occupation
of Vigo (1719)
Vigo

PORTUGAL

SPAIN

• Madrid

Barcelona •

MINORCA
(French invasio
lost to Spain

M

Lisbon

IBIZA MAJORC.

• Alicante

Lagos

Cape St.Vincent

Malaga

Cadiz

Algeciras • Gibraltar (Br.)
Tangier   (sieges 1727, 1779–1783)

Algiers

NORTH AFRICA

| 0 | 100 | 200 miles |

| 0 | 100 | 200 | 300 kms |

GERMAN EMPIRE

SWITZERLAND

VENICE

HABSBURG MONARCHY
(Austria)

• Milan

Venice

PIEDMONT–
SAVOY

• Piacenza
• Parma

• Genoa

D A L M A T I A

TUSCANY

• Leghorn

PAPAL
STATES

Toulon

ITALY

ELBA

Adriatic
Sea

(Naval battle
1744)

CORSICA
(To France 1768)

• Rome

KINGDOM OF THE
TWO SICILIES
(Austrian 1713–1735)

SARDINIA
(Austrian 1713–1720,
to Savoy after 1720.
Spanish invasion 1717)

(British naval
demonstration
off Naples 1742)

Naples

CORFU

Cagliari

T y r r h e n i a n
S e a

C A L A B R I A

Ionian
Sea

M
e
d
i
t
e
r
r
a
n

Messina

Palermo

Straits of Messina

Tunis

Syracuse

SICILY (Savoy 1713–1720.
Austrian 1720–1735.
Spanish invasion 1718)

e
a

Cape Passaro 1718

MALTA
(Knights of St John)

Tripoli

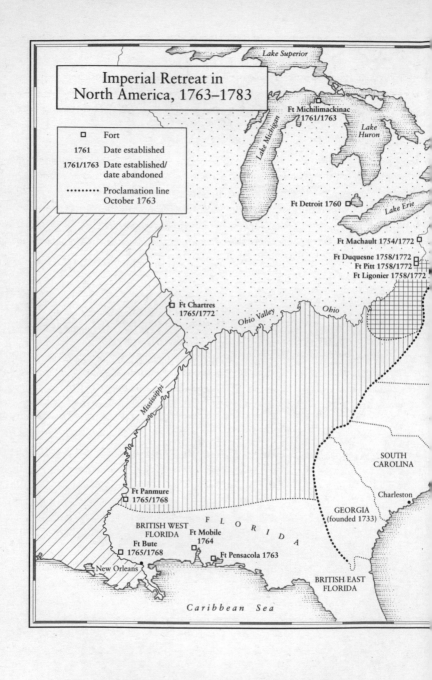

Imperial Retreat in North America, 1763–1783

Fort

1761 Date established

1761/1763 Date established/
date abandoned

········· Proclamation line
October 1763

Lake Superior

Ft Michilimackinac
1761/1763

Lake Huron

Lake Michigan

Ft Detroit 1760

Lake Erie

Ft Machault 1754/1772

Ft Duquesne 1758/1772
Ft Pitt 1758/1772
Ft Ligonier 1758/1772

Ft Chartres
1765/1772

Ohio Valley   *Ohio*

Mississippi

SOUTH
CAROLINA

Charleston

Ft Panmure
1765/1768

GEORGIA
(founded 1733)

F L O R I D A

BRITISH WEST
FLORIDA   Ft Mobile
1764
Ft Bute
1765/1768   Ft Pensacola 1763

New Orleans

BRITISH EAST
FLORIDA

Caribbean Sea

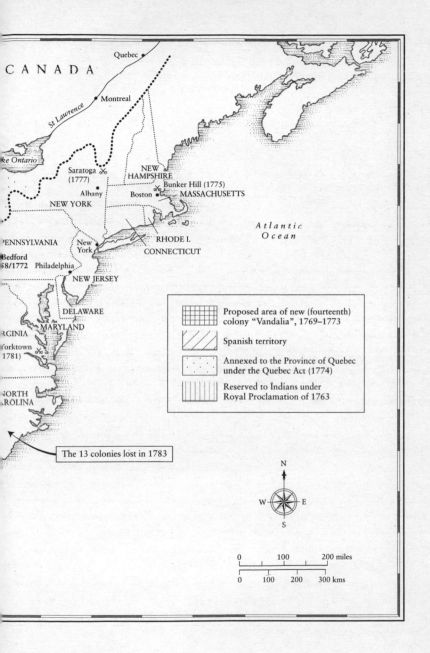

CANADA

Quebec •

St Lawrence

Montreal •

ke Ontario

Saratoga ⚔
(1777)

NEW
HAMPSHIRE

Bunker Hill (1775)

Albany

Boston •⚔ MASSACHUSETTS

NEW YORK

Atlantic
Ocean

PENNSYLVANIA

New
York

RHODE I.

Bedford
58/1772 Philadelphia

CONNECTICUT

NEW JERSEY

DELAWARE

MARYLAND

RGINIA

orktown ⚔
1781)

NORTH
ROLINA

Proposed area of new (fourteenth)
colony "Vandalia", 1769–1773

Spanish territory

Annexed to the Province of Quebec
under the Quebec Act (1774)

Reserved to Indians under
Royal Proclamation of 1763

The 13 colonies lost in 1783

N

W ✦ E

S

0   100   200 miles

0   100   200   300 kms

Introduction

'The history of England' in the eighteenth century, John Robert Seeley proclaimed in his classic *The expansion of England*, was 'not in England, but in America and Asia.' It was not: the history of eighteenth-century Britain was in Europe. From the Dutch invasion of 1688 through the Wars of Grand Alliance against Louis XIV, the French and Spanish-backed Jacobite revolts, the War of the Austrian Succession and the Seven Years War to the American War of Independence, the destiny of England – or Great Britain, as the composite state became known – was decided by events in Europe. It was European pressures which led to the Act of Union with Scotland in 1707. Between 1689 and 1702, England shared a sovereign – William III – with the Dutch. From 1714, Britain was dynastically and geopolitically linked to the European mainland through the Personal Union with Hanover. The apparatus of the 'fiscal-military state' – the Bank of England, the national debt, the stock market, the Royal Navy and the standing army – was primarily designed to sustain Britain's international role in Europe, not to defend against domestic rebellion. Much contemporary British political thought centred on Britain's position within the international state system. The discussion of European treaties, subsidies, wars and the balance of power generally also loomed large in the emerging public sphere. Trade with Europe far outstripped that with other continents until very late in the century.[1]

It should come as no surprise, therefore, that the question of Britain's position in Europe, and issues of grand strategy more generally, structured British politics and public political discourse throughout the period 1714–83. Foreign policy, rather than taxation, popular unrest, religion, elections or colonial expansion, was the central political preoccupation in eighteenth-century Britain. It was by far the largest single subject of debate in Parliament, at least in the first two-thirds of the century. Virtually all of the King's speeches at the opening of the session, which were written by his ministers, and approved by him, primarily concerned foreign policy. Foreign policy was central to shifting high-political fortunes, and especially to royal favour. Most ministries before 1760 rose or fell on the strength of their perceived performance in defence of Britain's European position; another fell towards the end of the American War for failing to hold off the Franco-Spanish alliance and to coerce the rebel colonists. For much of the eighteenth century, the main dividing line between Tory and Whig, and between establishment and radical Whigs, was the question of what role Britain should play in the international state system. Indeed, much of the current British debate on Europe would have struck an informed eighteenth-century observer as remarkably familiar, if slightly tame. Should Britain engage militarily, politically and financially with Europe? Or should she look to her maritime destiny and seek her future with America? Was Britain politically and psychologically part of Europe, or in some way an island apart? These were questions which exercised Britons some three hundred years ago as much as they do today. On the one hand, there were those who were convinced that British security and prosperity could only be achieved through engagement in Europe. On the other, there was a vocal but increasingly important minority, who believed that the nation's destiny lay in commercial, colonial and naval expansion. It is this strain which has been most audible in the past hundred and fifty years or so.[2]

The prevailing sense has been that English and then British history should be viewed in an insular and maritime context. In 1905, for example, Henrietta Marshall published a celebrated narrative for children, entitled *Our island story*. Borrowing from Shakespeare, in 1984 Arthur Bryant called the first volume of his 'History of Britain and the British people', *Set in a silver sea*. He entitled volume two, covering the period from the Tudors to the early nineteenth century, *Freedom's own island*. Even the subtitle was distinctly maritime: *The British oceanic expansion*. Of the nineteen chapters, at least seven – '[naval] Captains courageous', 'Preparations for invasion', 'The invincible Armada', 'Encompassed within wooden walls', 'Freedom's own island', 'Blockade, pursuit and victory', 'Neptune's generals' – had a naval theme. Only one – 'Waterloo' – referred unambiguously to armies, land warfare or Europe. Raphael Samuel, the radical founder of the 'History Workshop' (which pioneered 'history from below'), who could not have been more unlike Bryant in every other way, wrote an essay on British historiography entitled *Island stories*; there might be many stories, but he did not doubt that Britain's was primarily an *island* story. To underline the point, the jacket of volume two featured the white cliffs of Dover, as if they were a rampart to keep out foreign, that is European, influences.[3]

There is no doubt that the Eurosceptics have had the better tunes. The words of Britain's informal national anthem, written by James Thomson around 1740, famously announce that 'When Britain first, at heaven's command / Arose from out the azure main, / This was the charter of the land, / And guardian angels sung this strain: / "Rule Britannia, [Britannia] rule the waves; / Britons never [never] will be slaves.' There it is in a nutshell: British navalism, providentialism, patriotism and liberty in one stirring chorus. This theme was later elaborated by the American Alfred Thayer Mahan into a rousing narrative of British strategic success in his classic *The influence of sea power on history* (1890). More recently, Nicholas Rodger, the doyen of maritime historians, and Daniel Baugh have powerfully restated the navalist case. The Tudor historian David Starkey writes that 'the English Channel is much wider than the Atlantic', and in important ways always had been. The trend has been accentuated by the current preoccupation with the imperial or 'Atlantic' dimension to eighteenth-century British history. Kathleen Wilson has written of a 'sense of the people', which was primarily imperial and colonial. Peter Marshall even speaks of 'a nation defined by empire'. 'We are,' David Armitage has written, 'all Atlanticists now.'[4]

To resist this confection is not to deny the importance of the navy, commerce and overseas empire in the development of modern Britain since 1700, or even earlier. All these dimensions need to be taken into account. Rather, it is to question the connection between these factors, and to suggest that a forward policy in Europe best secured Britain's maritime predominance, whereas a narrow focus on ruling the waves was in fact the best way of losing them to her rivals. It is to recognize that the sea was not a bulwark at all. Rather it was a highway connecting Britain not only to the wider world, but more importantly to her immediate neighbours: a bridge, not a moat. 'Rule Britannia' had it wrong: the 'main' which mattered most to Britons was not the shimmering 'Spanish main' of unlimited colonial opportunity, but the European 'mainland' to which they belonged, politically, if not geographically. In short,

Britain's first and most important lines of defence lay not in her 'wooden walls', but in Europe itself.[5]

If eighteenth-century Britons were focused on Europe, their primary preoccupation there was with the 'Holy Roman Empire of the German Nation' (often referred to at the time simply as 'Germany' or more commonly 'the Empire'). In particular, they were concerned with the defence of the Low Countries: Flanders (which was part of the Holy Roman Empire) and the Dutch Republic. It was from Flemish ports that an invasion, by the Austrians, the French or (in earlier times) the Spanish, was most to be feared. It was from Dutch ports that William of Orange had staged his successful descent in 1688. Yet experience showed that the defence of Flanders, a territory over which British statesmen claimed a joint sovereignty, necessitated a much broader strategic design for Europe. The Low Countries could not be defended by British forces alone, even with the support of the local population; the assistance of other major powers was required. For much of our period that power was Austria, and it therefore made sense to intervene in central Europe, militarily and diplomatically, in order to secure to the House of Habsburg the necessary weight and resources to discharge that task.

Moreover, the security of Flanders was inseparable from that of northern and western Germany, from whence it could be outflanked. The security of Britain thus rested on the management of the broader political commonwealth to which Flanders and its hinterland belonged: the German Empire. In short, even if the main threat came from further south, from Spain and especially France, Britain's European policy was still first and foremost German policy. If the balance of power in Germany was overturned, then the European balance, and with it Britain's continental bulwarks, would soon be in mortal danger. This would have been true even if the King of England had not been the Elector of the north German territory of Hanover. But it was also clear that in order to secure the Holy Roman Empire, the Baltic, the Mediterranean and the Balkans would need attention as well. It made sense, for example, to distract the Austrians in south-eastern Europe when they were a threat to the Empire, and to relieve them of French-inspired distractions there when they were not. Britons found that they could not conceive of Germany without thinking of Europe as a whole, and they could not pursue a European policy without putting Germany at the heart of it.

The strategic and political centrality of the Holy Roman Empire to eighteenth-century Britons was embedded in a shifting mental map. Their horizons gradually spread ever further eastwards, northwards and southwards, as well as across the oceans. At the same time, British statesmen strove to maintain and deepen the cohesiveness of the United Kingdom and its overseas possessions upon which the effective exercise of military and financial muscle depended. The domestic divisions within the British Isles, between Jacobites and supporters of the Protestant Succession; between Whigs and Tories; between metropolis and colonial periphery; between king and ministers; and between individual ministers, were all part of this world-view. And no matter how hard they tried to insure against adversity, and anticipate events, British statesmen, parliamentarians and the public knew that any number of strategic wild cards – a diplomatic revolution, a lost battle, the sudden death of a monarch, a palace coup or a rebellion – might overturn all their calculations. For the individual, the price for failure in this environment might be loss of power, disgrace, imprisonment and even execution; for the state it could be partition and even extinction.

This is a book about Hanoverian Britain after the accession of George I in 1714. Yet in order to understand why he came to the throne in the first place, and why Britons cared so passionately about the European state system and their place in it, we need to delve more deeply into an earlier period of English history. Our European story begins in Tudor times, and gallops through the strategic and ideological controversies of the early Stuarts, the Protectorate, the later Stuarts, the arrival of William of Orange, to the eve of the Hanoverian Succession. It was in those one hundred and fifty years or so of strategic debate, civil strife, revolution, war and invasion that the assumptions with which Britons went into the eighteenth century were forged. It was then that they came to believe that the security of the realm would be determined not by their growing overseas empire, but by events in Europe and particularly in the Holy Roman Empire.

I

Imperial Apprenticeship

I

A Part of the Main: England in Europe, 1558–1697

No man is an island, entire of itself; every man is a piece of the continent,
a part of the main; if a clod be washed away by the sea, Europe is the less,
as well as if a promontory were, as well as if a manor of thy friends or of
thine own were; any man's death diminishes me, because I am involved
in mankind; and therefore never send to know for whom the bell tolls; it
tolls for thee.

John Donne (1572–1631), 'Meditation XVII' (1624)

John Donne's lines have traditionally been seen as a reflection on the human condition, written as he lay stricken with illness, listening to the sound of nearby church bells. What has been almost completely overlooked, however, is the strategic and ideological context in which they were penned. Donne was writing in 1624, at the height of the Thirty Years War in Germany and the seemingly irresistible surge of Catholic forces of the Holy Roman Emperor and his Spanish allies. It was only a few years earlier that the Protestant hero Frederick, Elector Palatine, had been ejected by Spanish troops from his principality along with his wife, Elizabeth, eldest daughter of King James I of England. To the fury and humiliation of public opinion in England, Frederick and Elizabeth were reduced to the status of princely Ancient Mariners, button-holing Protestant diplomats and courtiers with their tale of woe and expropriation. The King himself would do nothing, even though the fall of the Palatinate had taken a Protestant boot off the Spanish windpipe – the 'Spanish Road' along which their armies in Flanders were re-supplied. It would not be long, many feared, before the Catholic armies surged into the Dutch Republic and were within striking distance of England itself. The 'passing bell', as Sir Edward Sackville told the

House of Commons in 1621, 'now tolleth for religion and the state of the Palatinate; it is not dead, but dying'. Donne himself was keenly aware of these controversies. He had served on the Continent as a soldier, written a moving poem on the marriage of Frederick and Elizabeth, and recently participated in diplomatic missions in support of the Elector Palatine. Against this background 'No man is an island' is clearly a geopolitical lament. England, Donne argues, was no island but part of the Continent; the clods being washed away by the Spanish tide were her outer ramparts; and the bell was tolling not merely for European Protestants but for the European balance and thus for English liberties.[1]

The notion that the destiny and security of England was closely tied to events in Europe was a sixteenth-century commonplace. Most of her history in the Middle Ages, right down to the Hundred Years War with France, had been dominated by the European context. For hundreds of years, English kings and barons held vast lands in France. Moreover, because of the great wealth and prestige of the kingdom, many Englishmen believed that it was their mission to lead Europe. At the same time, the 'Jerusalem-centric' world-view of the time placed England firmly within but on the edge of Europe, or of 'Christendom' as it was then known. This made Englishmen all the more keen to get closer to the 'centre', to the south and east. Taken together, these beliefs sustained active engagement in Europe and on behalf of 'European' causes. Englishmen therefore accepted that their rulers would be absent for long periods of time: Norman kings such as William the Conqueror and Henry I were out of the kingdom for longer than they were in it, and Richard the Lionheart only spent about six months of his ten-year rule at home. The English nobility routinely went on and paid for crusades to liberate the Holy Land from the infidel. Medieval England, in short, was never an island: Normandy and Gascony were far closer to London than Wales or Scotland were.[2]

This was the world into which the founder of the modern English state, Henry VIII, burst in the early sixteenth century. He too was actively involved in wars on the Continent: his assault on the Church was driven in large part by the need to finance these ambitions. His principal aim was the reconstitution of England's position in France, lost in the previous century with the exception of an enclave at Calais. To that end, he pursued an active policy in Germany, where he sought to deny support to his principal adversary, the French King Francis I. Indeed, Henry put himself forward as a candidate for the title of Holy Roman Emperor in 1519, which he craved principally in order to forestall Francis. Henry soon fell out, however, with the successful candidate, Francis's arch-rival, the Habsburg Charles V. Henry's feud with the Pope originated in the fact that the pontiff had refused to release the King from Catherine of Aragon because he himself was the captive of Catherine's nephew, the Holy Roman Emperor and King of Spain, Charles V. At the peak of his powers, Charles ruled an empire stretching from the Iberian peninsula across Naples and Sicily, Bohemia, the hereditary Habsburg lands in Austria proper, Silesia, parts of Hungary and 'Burgundy'- Lorraine, Luxemburg and the Low Countries. Indeed, some Englishmen had looked with concern on Habsburg pretensions towards 'universal monarchy', that is total domination of Europe, long before they faced each other as Protestant and Catholic. Others consoled themselves with the fact that Spain encircled England's own rival France, which in turn was politically and dynastically linked to England's old adversary Scotland through the 'Auld Alliance'. To make matters worse, there were links between disaffected Irish magnates and the Habsburgs. Ireland and Scotland were therefore very much a European rather than a 'British' problem.[3]

In the course of the sixteenth century, the picture was complicated by the progress of the European Reformation, which led to the creation of separate national churches in England, Scotland and much of western and central Europe. Protestantism also established a strong presence in the northern Spanish Netherlands. Lutheranism or Calvinism was the state religion in many German principalities such as Saxony, Brandenburg-Prussia and Brunswick-Lüneburg. The rulers of France and the Habsburg lands remained resolutely Catholic, although there were many Protestant enclaves within their territories, especially the Huguenot communities of southern and western France. The struggles between Charles V and his European rivals eventually led to the partition of his empire in 1555 between the Spanish and Austrian Habsburgs. Both halves, particularly Spain, remained so powerful as to constitute a major threat to the balance of Europe in their own right; moreover, they tended to act in concert until well into the seventeenth century. All this mattered to England, because if the question of the religious settlement had a major bearing on how she interacted with Europe, the potential impact of Europe on the domestic politics of England was greater still.

Many therefore regarded Queen Mary's marriage to the future King Philip II of Spain in 1554 with alarm. In part, this was because they feared that her rigorous attempts to re-Catholicize the country would be backed by Habsburg troops. But it also reflected a feeling that England was conniving in the rise of a hegemon – Philip – who was proving every bit as dangerous to the European balance as Charles V. Moreover, Spain was gaining in European weight and fiscal staying power through her spectacular colonial expansion into the gold and silver mines of Central and South America. To the horror of some, instead of confronting Spain, Mary led England into war with France at Philip's side. These critics were even less impressed when English-ruled Calais fell to the French in 1558; not only was England fighting the wrong war, it was doing so ineffectively, while Spain was winning hers against France. Calais, whose name Mary famously said would be 'lying in her heart', was England's last remaining outpost on the Continent. Its loss first established the fatal link in the minds of Englishmen between popery and strategic incompetence which her Stuart successors (Protestant and Catholic) later found impossible to shake off. It was in this grim context of domestic turbulence and a looming 'universal monarch' that Queen Elizabeth came to the throne in 1558. The strategic debates and decisions of her reign set the tone for English and British grand strategy for the next 250 years.

To later generations, the Elizabethan age was that of Drake, Frobisher and Hawkins: a time when English seamen engaged and defeated Phillip II's shipping on the 'Spanish Main', that is on the high seas and in the colonies. Elizabeth's reign provides an irresistible vista of Protestantism, patriotism and plunder. To contemporaries, however, the battle for the Protestant Succession and the independence of England was part of a much broader European struggle, first against France and then to contain the pretensions of the Habsburgs towards 'universal monarchy'. For the first twenty years or so, Elizabeth pursued a pan-Protestant alliance of kingdoms, principalities and even republics in order to keep Catholic powers at bay. At first, France represented a mortal threat because Elizabeth's Catholic cousin Mary Stuart ('Queen of Scots') was married to Francis, heir to the French throne. In 1559, he menacingly adopted the arms of England on the strength of Mary's claim to the throne. England thus remained encircled by the Franco-Scottish alliance. For the moment, maintaining good relations with Spain made a great deal of sense, as did support for the Huguenots. Within a few years, however, Elizabeth had dealt with this problem by military intervention in Scotland, which banished the French influence for good. England's relations with her northern neighbour were re-fashioned, and the periodic Scottish incursions ceased, until the Civil War almost one hundred years later. This was a major change in England's European position. Not only would Scotland now be a major net contributor to English security, but the 'back door' into England had been closed. Only that through Ireland remained, and in time that would be slammed shut too.[4]

Moreover from the early 1560s France was roiled by the wars of religion, which were to continue intermittently for the next forty years or so, while Philip II went from strength to strength. The implications of this for English grand strategy were immense. On the one hand France was now a potential ally against Spanish domination; in that case, backing religious dissidents there could be counter-productive. On the other hand, the triumph of the Catholic party with Spanish help in 1572–3 would turn France into a satellite of Madrid, and thus throw the entire western coast of Europe into the hands of a single hostile power. This was the ultimate Elizabethan nightmare. It was to hedge against that outcome, and in order to show religious solidarity, that Elizabeth continued her military, financial and moral support for French Protestants. English troops were sent to Le Havre. The hope of recapturing Calais and thus a sally-port on the continent was also a major consideration. The English garrison at Le Havre was soon pinned against the sea, under constant attack and afflicted by the plague; it was eventually withdrawn. The first dispatch of English troops in support of a Protestant internationalist intervention to maintain the European balance had ended in fiasco; but they would be back.[5]

More importantly, Elizabeth now began to look to Calvinist communities in the Low Countries, and German Protestant powers more generally, as England's first line of defence. She increasingly realized that English security depended on the careful management of the balance in Germany and even further afield. Troops hired there could be deployed in support of the Huguenots, while the substantial anti-Habsburg constituency in the Holy Roman Empire diverted attention from France and the Low Countries. A new and more intense phase of this contest began in the 1560s with the Dutch revolt and its savage Spanish repression under the Duke of Alba. The English leadership had no objection to Philip's sovereignty, so long as the ancient liberties of the population were respected. Otherwise, England – whose principal trading partner was the Netherlands – would be vulnerable to economic blackmail by Spain. Moreover, Alba's arrival lodged a large, potentially hostile force in present-day Belgium, an area which Elizabeth's advisor William Cecil described as 'the very counterscarp of England'. The Queen and her councillors feared that the triumph of Alba would be followed by a cross-Channel attempt to reimpose Catholicism on England. Cecil's use of the term 'counterscarp' was well-chosen, and illustrates how many Englishmen viewed Europe as part of England's defensive system. In the military parlance of the time, the citadel was surrounded by ramparts and bastions, after which came the moat. On the far side of the moat lay the counterscarp, followed by the glacis and the outworks, which were the first line of defence. The 'counterscarp', in other words, was well within the inner perimeter. By this reckoning, the glacis and outworks of England lay not in Flanders, but in the buttresses which enabled the defence of that region, that is to say within the German Empire itself. It should come as no surprise therefore, that Elizabeth should have sought alliances among the Protestant German princes.[6]

Throughout the 1570s and early 1580s, England's European situation steadily deteriorated, as Spanish forces defeated the Turks at Lepanto and in 1580–81 overran Portugal. From 1580, France was once again convulsed by religious war, and was unable to contain Spain. Elizabeth now frantically dispatched envoys to the Protestant powers of Scandinavia – Denmark and Sweden – and northern Germany in search of support. She did manage to persuade the Danes to stop the sale of naval stores to Spain, an early example of the use of Continental diplomacy in pursuit of maritime security. It was not enough. Worse still, the triumph of the Catholic League in 1585 meant that France itself threatened to fall under Spanish influence, placing the entire western coast of Europe in enemy hands. The Spanish commander, the Duke of Parma, continued his inexorable advance in the Low Countries. The task of fighting universal monarchy thus devolved to Elizabeth, or so it seemed to those councillors who advocated a strategy of direct Continental intervention. Both the Earl of Leicester and Sir Francis Walsingham warned that once Philip had defeated the Dutch he would turn his attention to England, greatly strengthened by the resources of the Low Countries. The Dutch cause was thus England's cause. On this reading, the defence of Protestantism and English liberties in England demanded the defence of Protestantism and the European balance everywhere.

Not all of Elizabeth's councillors agreed. Her trusted advisor and Lord High Treasurer William Cecil, Lord Burghley, for example, though usually a supporter of German, Dutch, French and Scandinavian Protestant alliances, argued that the Dutch were despicable rebels against lawful authority, and that Philip might leave England alone so long as he was not provoked. 'If the Queen would meddle no more in the matters of the Netherlands,' he claimed, 'but most strongly fortify her kingdom ... gather money, furnish her navy with all provisions, strengthen her borders towards Scotland with garrisons, and maintain the ancient military discipline of England', then all would be well. Behind the Navy, 'the wall of England', Burghley argued, the nation could await all comers. Others, such as the Treasurer of the Navy John Hawkins and Sir Francis Drake, believed that Spain could be defeated through a purely maritime strategy focusing on her overseas possessions, commerce and navy – a 'blue water' policy, as it was dubbed by later generations. It was the beginning of a great strategic debate in English and later British history, which has rumbled on ever since.'

In retrospect, the naval and colonial enthusiasm in Elizabethan England seems like the start of a turn away from Europe towards an essentially maritime and global destiny. That was not how contemporaries saw it. To be sure, there were many agendas behind the sixteenth-century European expansion into the New World. For some, it was an opportunity to convert native peoples – or those that had survived the diseases brought by the colonists – and thus save souls. Others thought of exporting paupers and solving the problem of over-population. Others still were mesmerized by the prospect of fabulous wealth. But the principal reason why European states competed for a share of the New World was the fact that the colonial balance, or lack of it, was conceived as part of the overall European balance of power. In this context, Spanish hegemony in the Americas and the Pacific was a threat which could not be ignored. The prestige and fiscal muscle which Philip enjoyed as King of New Spain – which provided about 10 per cent of his revenues in the mid sixteenth century, rising to about 25 per cent by the end of his reign – was an important part of his European leverage. Thus Richard Hakluyt, in his celebrated 'Discourse of western planting' (1584), noted that 'with this great treasure', Charles V had 'got from the French King the Kingdom of Naples, the dukedom of Milan and all his other dominions in Italy, Lombardy, Piedmont and Savoy'. So when English mariners proposed to knock the Spanish king off his colonial perch, it was really the future of Europe, not that of the New World that they were concerned with.[8]

England thus went to war with Spain in 1585 not over the Pacific or the Caribbean but over events in France and the Netherlands. It was not a moment too soon. In the summer of 1585 the Duke of Parma captured Sluys, just a short step away from Flushing, which would be a viable base for an attack across the Channel. Now even Burghley was persuaded. Substantial forces under the Earl of Leicester were sent to the Low Countries to support the Dutch. He was accompanied with great fanfare by a roll-call of some of England's greatest noble families; the return to the Continent had begun. Parliament was consulted and a public debate ensued in 1586–7; the intervention was thus 'owned' by the political nation. Even so, the Armada, which Philip dispatched against England in 1588, was a very close thing. Because the Spanish transports and some warships were able to mass in the ports of Flanders, a substantial English squadron under Sir Henry Seymour, which was desperately needed to engage the Armada itself, was detached to watch Parma at Dunkirk. The only consolation was that the Dutch – suitably stiffened by English support – were holding firm to the north. Elizabeth's Continental intervention had thus contributed directly to the maritime security of England. Once the Spanish ships were through the Straits of Dover, they were on their own. What would have happened if the Armada had been able to shelter in Dutch ports, before making a fresh attempt, can only be guessed at. English Protestantism, and perhaps the independence of England itself, only survived through good luck and because Spain was forced to divide its efforts between Elizabeth and the Dutch. In late 1588, the 'Continental' strategy was further vindicated when a Spanish assault on the Dutch fortress of Bergen-op-Zoom was repulsed, largely by English forces; this showed that Spain could be beaten on land.[9]

What the late Tudor period had shown, therefore, was that the integrity of England depended on the independence of the Dutch, who could draw off enemy resources, and deny them the bases in Flanders from which to launch an invasion. In the early seventeenth century, English troops still held the 'cautionary towns' in the Low Countries, partly as security for Dutch debts, but also to secure the area in the English interest and to make sure that the Dutch would pull their military weight against Spain. This had implications for English views of Germany. Spanish attacks on Holland were now increasingly launched from the *east*, from bases in northern Germany; after 1609, the main threat to the Dutch came from there. Moreover, the re-supply of Philip's armies in Holland ran along the famous 'Spanish Road', a Habsburg-controlled lifeline connecting Flanders with his possessions in Northern Italy and thence to the Spanish heartland. It therefore became a preoccupation of English Continental diplomacy to disrupt this where possible. In short, the Netherlands and the Protestant German principalities were the crucial outworks of European Protestantism, and thus of England herself. It was there, rather than on the high seas, that England would be defended. Protestantism in one country – the theological and ecclesiological nub of Anglicanism – was not a practical proposition in strategic terms.[10]

England had also been taught a lesson about the nature of naval power. This was not just a matter of ship construction or the skill of English sailors. Naval security also depended on keeping the European coast from Gibraltar to the Dutch–German border out of the hands of a single European power; this in turn required the maintenance of an equilibrium between France and Spain. But the European state system mattered in other respects as well. The aftermath of the Battle of Lepanto, for example, had demonstrated that if Philip was not distracted in the Mediterranean he would be better able to pursue the war in the Low Countries. For this reason, Walsingham tried to persuade the Ottomans to attack the Habsburgs in Naples in 1580, and in 1583 an envoy was sent to Constantinople. The security of the realm required that English diplomacy think in ever broader terms. A few years later, Philip's absorption of Portugal was an object lesson in how shifts in the Continental balance could affect the naval balance. That coup gave him not only hundreds of miles of additional coastline, but also valuable galleons and experienced seamen. Spain became an Atlantic as well as a Mediterranean power. Finally, English decision-makers had taken on board the importance of the New World for the struggle in Europe and the Narrow Seas. Elizabeth sponsored Drake's voyages between 1577 and 1580 not as the first step towards an overseas empire of her own, but to reduce the flow of bullion to pay Philip's armies in Flanders.

The home front needs to be seen in this wider European context. If many English Protestants feared popery, it was not because of their Catholic recusant neighbours *per se* – these were fewer and fewer in number by 1600. Rather, they lived in terror of the Catholic Habsburgs, and the advance of the Counter-Reformation across Europe. As each bastion fell, they saw the enemy inch closer and closer to them. So defined, the 'Protestant interest' was not simply bigotry. It was from the beginning a primarily political and strategic concept, and it lost most of its overtly theological content as time went on. It was the 'popery' of 'universal monarchy', that is European domination, that Englishmen feared. Elizabeth's councillors were prepared to overlook the Catholicism of the French heir presumptive, the Duke of Anjou (although they hoped for his subsequent conversion) when they recommended him to the Queen as a husband. What mattered there was the strategic aim of securing French support against Spain. Likewise, the Huguenot Henri IV was a Protestant hero not only before, but *after* his conversion to Catholicism in order to take up the French crown. This was because the hopes of containing supposed Spanish and Austrian Habsburg designs against the European balance rested with him. Henry might have been denominationally a Catholic, but he was politically and strategically a Protestant.[11]

This was also the context in which Elizabethan policy towards Ireland and Scotland should be viewed. These areas posed problems which are best understood not within a 'British', 'archipelagic', or 'three kingdoms' framework, but as a part of England's European grand strategy. At the beginning of Elizabeth's reign, the principal threat still came from France, which, as one minister put it, had 'one foot in Calais and the other in Scotland'. England was effectively surrounded. Moreover Mary, Queen of Scots was not only married to the heir to the French throne, but also maintained her own claim to the crown of England. After the rise of Spain, the rapprochement with France and the elimination of Mary, Queen of Scots, the problem of Ireland loomed larger. In the hands of a hostile power it would be a back door to England, or at the very least contribute to her encirclement. It was for this reason that Spanish infiltration in Ireland had to be stopped, and the threat of Gaelic rebellion crushed for good. The brutality with which a papal-backed landing of Italians and Spaniards at Smerwick in 1579 was treated reflected this wider strategic unease. It came to the fore again with the revolt of the northern lords, O'Neill and O'Donnell, in the 1590s, which culminated in a Spanish landing at Kinsale in 1601.[12]

By and large, Elizabeth mastered the threats facing her, although it was a success that grew in the telling. Ireland was subdued; Scotland neutralized; and Spain was seen off. Her legacy in foreign policy after 1603, however, was more problematic. She had inherited a relatively strong bureaucratic apparatus, forged during the Tudor revolution in government, but by the early seventeenth century the English state, which had not undergone the absolutist transformations beginning else-where in Europe, was now relatively weak. At the same time, inflation eroded the Crown's income to the extent that it became impossible to wage war or intervene financially in Europe without the consent of Parliament. The royal prerogative in foreign policy was passed on unchallenged, and because the Queen had been prepared to listen to advice, and her policy vindicated, the constitutional issue that would have arisen in the event of disagreement had been effectively masked. Elizabeth had galvanized Parliament and the nation in the life-and-death struggle against Catholic Spain. This strategic consensus, which had been shaky to begin with, rapidly fragmented under the Stuarts.[13]

Throughout the early seventeenth century, English and 'British' poli-tics continued to be overshadowed, and to a considerable extent deter-mined, by developments in Europe. The first thing that King James I did on coming to the throne in 1603 was to end the war with Spain, which was already beginning to peter out towards the end of Elizabeth's reign. This was unpopular, if inescapable for financial reasons; it also caused outrage among the Dutch, who were left to soldier on alone until their own truce. Even more controversial was James's attempt to navigate between the two European camps. He sought a 'Spanish match' between his son and the King of Spain's daughter. This outraged popular and parliamentary opinion, and opened a whole can of worms concerning the succession, the future Queen's right to worship and the disabilities of English Roman Catholics. It was also an alarming straw in the wind as far as England's strategic orientation in Europe was concerned, put-ting in doubt James's commitment to Dutch independence, for example. The first choice any English monarch had had to make since the 1570s was that between Spain and the Netherlands. James would have pre-ferred to fudge it, but his preference was clearly for Madrid. His decision was so divisive, not merely in patriot Protestant opinion but within the court, that it needed a separate apparatus of secretaries and ambassadors to implement it.[14]

More encouragingly, from the perspective of Protestant intervention-ists, the new King appeared to embrace the Protestant cause in Germany. English troops were sent to repulse Catholic claims to the succession of Jülich-Cleves. This apparently minor north German principality was strategically vital because of its proximity to the Dutch eastern border. James's eldest son, Prince Henry, was a particularly enthusiastic advo-cate of intervention there. How the Stuarts might have fared had he lived and perhaps turned himself into a successful Protestant hero and 'patriot king', is one of the fascinating counterfactuals of seventeenth-century English history. Above all, James married his daughter Elizabeth to the Elector Palatine, a major figure in Germany, who held one of the seven crucial 'Electoral' votes needed to choose the Holy Roman Emperor. Some saw him leading a possible future Protestant candidature for the imperial crown of Germany, which would reduce Habsburg power. At the very least, a solid ally in the Palatinate, an important principality on the middle Rhine with a capital at Heidelberg, would be a bone in the throat of the 'Spanish Road'. It would both help the Dutch and render an invasion across the Channel more difficult. The Holy Roman Empire was thus central to English security.[15]

Instead, James's German gambit blew up in his face. The Protestant Bohemian nobility, outraged at the Austrian Habsburg attempt to impose Roman Catholicism on them, and taking advantage of the failing health of the Emperor Matthias, elected Frederick of the Palatinate as their king, rather than Matthias's heir Ferdinand, soon to be Emperor Ferdinand II (1619–37). This provoked a Spanish and Austrian Habs-burg attack on Frederick, followed by swift defeat at the battle of the White Mountain in Bohemia in 1620. English popular and parliamen-tary opinion overwhelmingly supported Frederick; James was much more equivocal. On the one hand he was conscious of his duty to his son-in-law and European Protestantism. On the other hand, he was genuinely aghast at Frederick's usurpation of the Bohemian crown, and at the prospect of losing the much sought-after Spanish match for his son Charles. Besides, as one observer remarked, there was not much

1. The fate of the Elector Palatine, champion of the Protestant cause in the Empire and Europe, who was married to James I's daughter, was the central issue in English politics in the 1620s and 1630s.

James could do unless 'his great fleet could fly thither over land';[16] this problem was to dog English and later British foreign policy long after Frederick was forgotten. Rather than intervene wholeheartedly in support of the Protestant cause in Germany, James was prepared to send troops to defend the Palatinate, but not Bohemia. To many, James was simply refusing to see that the battles in Germany and the Netherlands were connected. They saw the religious struggle for mastery in Germany being lost, especially once Spanish troops burst into the Palatinate, expelled Frederick and bestowed his Electoral title on the Catholic Duke of Bavaria. A European rampart had been breached. Counter-Reformation solidarity had found no Protestant echo, or so it seemed to many Englishmen. In those days, Bohemia was no far-off country of which they knew nothing.

The response was a barrage of pamphlets, petitions, plays, masques and entertainments lambasting James for having betrayed Frederick in order to curry favour with Spain. Parsons, poets and pub-goers lamented the abandonment of Continental Protestantism. The military passivity of James was unfavourably contrasted with the naval virtue of Elizabeth. Parliament too challenged the King, both demanding more decisive action and denying James the financial means to implement it. It now rejected the idea of 'forbidden areas' in foreign policy and national security, beyond the reach of parliamentary scrutiny. Reservations about the direction of royal foreign policy were articulated in terms of expenditure and the liberties of the subject, because there was no other way of expressing them. The royal prerogative was under serious attack for the first time, not because Englishmen had finally found their constitutional voices, but because they feared being overrun by continental Catholicism. As Sir John Davies told the House of Commons in 1620, 'the Palatinate is on fire; religion is on fire; and all other countries on fire . . . this is dangerous to the Low Countries, the United Provinces and the whole Protestant interest'. The danger was that the imperial commander in Germany, Tilly, would link up with the Spanish armies in Flanders. Together they might crush the Dutch rebels and then cross the Channel to extirpate English Protestantism and liberties. As Viscount St Albans remarked, 'If we suffer the Flemings to be ruined, they are our own outwork, and we shall remain naked and dismantled.' The creation of a Spanish 'Admiralty of the North' in Flanders in 1624, designed to deal with the Dutch, only increased the sense of anxiety in London. In short, the security of the realm was believed to be inseparable from the fate of the German Protestant bastions which shielded England's inner line of defence in Flanders.[17]

Those demanding active intervention on behalf of the Elector Palatine did not just shout from the sidelines; they suggested an alternative strategy. Many Members of Parliament and some influential figures at court believed that the Habsburg threat could be countered if the struggle was more broadly conceived than James would allow. An expedition to the Palatinate, if unsupported by other measures, might be a proportionate response but made no military sense whatever: any English force would simply be left stranded in the middle of the Holy Roman Empire. Instead, critics suggested that England make war on Spain in the Low Countries, closer to home; a substitute should be found, which could be exchanged for the Palatinate. At the same time, they demanded a vigorous naval campaign to cut off the flow of New World bullion on which so much of Spain's European power was believed to rest. Thus Sir Benjamin Rudyerd told the House of Commons in 1624 'that Spain itself is but weak in men, and barren of natural commodities'; it was 'his mines in the West Indies' which fuelled 'his vast ambitious desire of universal monarchy'. The connection made here between overseas empire, the security of England's Continental bulwarks and ultimately the safety of the realm was to resonate in English strategic discourse for the next one hundred and fifty years or so.[18]

All this was wrapped up in the language of hysteria and moral panic. English Puritans had contemplated James's retinue of underdressed Scotsmen, overdressed courtiers, and shapely page-boys with disdain. They recoiled at the sight of the heavily bejewelled Duke of Buckingham supplicating to Madrid for a Spanish bride, while turning his back on Protestant refugees from central Europe. A naval hero of Elizabethan times, Sir Walter Raleigh, was executed in 1618 for disobeying orders and attacking Spanish settlements in South America. Here James had been left with little choice, but to many Raleigh's martyrdom at Spanish insistence, and the death of his son in battle, contrasted favourably with the King's apparently decadent entourage. In short, as far as Puritan and patriot opinion was concerned, court and government (or, in contemporary parlance, ministry), presented an unwholesome vista of crypto-popery, homoerotic intensity and diplomatic incompetence. All this mattered because it reflected a contemporary sense of the enfeeblement of the nation, the sapping of martial will, and the suborning of the executive through cultural and physical corruption at a time of general European crisis. These moral panics were to recur at regular intervals at times of perceived external threat.

Charles I, who succeeded on the death of James I in 1625, was less vulnerable to such charges, and for a time it looked as if the new king might don the mantle of Protestant hero. After some comic and humiliating attempts to complete the Spanish match, he settled for the French Henrietta Maria instead. She was no less Catholic than the Infanta, and there were the usual complaints about arrangements for her private worship. That said, the marriage was actually desirable from the Protestant point of view, because it consolidated relations with the power best able to stem the Habsburg tide. Together with a commitment to secure Dutch independence, one of James's last acts as king in 1624, and the hire of Danish mercenaries, all this seemed to presage a concerted drive to roll back Habsburg power. But an attack on Cadiz in 1625 ended in complete fiasco, and invited further unwelcome comparisons with Drake's triumphs under Elizabeth. An attempt to send a mercenary army to restore Frederick and a war with France to relieve the embattled Huguenots at La Rochelle both ended in total failure. Above all, Charles was powerless in the face of the Catholic advance in Germany. In 1625, he had agreed to subsidize the King of Denmark and the princes of Lower Saxony against the Emperor, but very soon the Danish king too had been defeated. Another rampart of European Protestantism had been cast down. In short, even where Englishmen agreed with the direction of royal foreign policy, they despaired of its execution. In 1626, Parliament claimed its first scalp when the late King's favourite and chief foreign policy advisor, Buckingham, was impeached, largely for mismanaging the war and allegedly betraying England to France. It was to be the first of many dramatic impeachments over the next one hundred and fifty years or so, nearly all of them driven principally by concern over the decline of England's position in Europe.[19]

All this culminated in a series of Commons resolutions in late February 1628. The authors looked across to the Continent and saw 'a mighty and prevalent party . . . aiming at the subversion of all the Protestant Churches of Christendom'. They noted 'the weak resistance that is made against them'. Indeed, these critics spoke of 'their victorious and successful enterprises, whereby the Churches of Germany, France, and other places, are in a great part already ruined, and the rest in the most weak and miserable condition'. An exasperated King thereupon dissolved Parliament. In 1629 Charles made peace with Spain, and in 1630 with France. All these developments were connected. An active foreign policy cost money, and thus necessitated the involvement of Parliament, so Charles was resolved to avoid international conflict for the time being. For just over a decade, he ruled without Parliament, and kept a relatively low profile on the European stage. This was not because the King was uninterested in Continental affairs. On the contrary, he remained as ambitious as ever, but he now felt that the existing constitutional and fiscal arrangements in England made any sustained policy impossible.[20]

After all, Charles had called Parliament in order to declare 'the miserable afflicted estate of those of the reformed religion in Germany, France, and other parts of Christendom'. He was in no doubt of 'the distressed extremities of our dearest uncle, the King of Denmark, chased out of a great part of his dominions'. Nor did Charles entertain any illusions about 'the strength of that party which was united against us', including 'the Pope, the House of Austria and their ancient confederates' and even France. It was for all those reasons that the King had come to Parliament for 'a speedy supply of treasure, answerable to the necessity of the cause'. This had been agreed readily enough, the King continued, but the Commons had then been 'diverted by a multitude of questions raised amongst them touching their liberties and privileges'. The result was 'our foreign actions then in hand being thereby disgraced and ruined for want of timely help'. The primacy of foreign policy dictated that he would have to put England's domestic house in order first, as he saw it, so that he could in time cut the figure he wanted in the European state system.[21]

The trouble for Charles was that the European state system would not stand still while he tackled the governance of England. Throughout the 1620s and 1630s the Thirty Years War raged across Germany, with Continental Protestantism taking a terrific battering, at least until the mid 1630s. Charles did, and could do, next to nothing. Sometimes he made a virtue of his inaction, telling his subjects that he had spared them the horrors of war. On other occasions he gestured towards Protestantism, but his few attempts to keep the Palatine issue on the boil only underlined his own impotence. Englishmen breathed a sigh of relief when the Swedish King Gustavus Adolphus appeared on the scene on the Protestant side, but his triumphs were a further reproach to Charles. Moreover, Charles's subjects were cast into a despondency by Gustavus's death at the Battle of Lützen, from which they were only lifted by French military intervention against the Habsburgs in 1635. In that sense, the King of France was more 'Protestant' than their own monarch.

There was one area where the Stuarts showed considerable robustness and initiative: commerce, colonization and the Royal Navy. The Stuarts were keen supporters of the American project. James had been something of a pioneer: in 1607, he had sponsored the settlement of several hundred colonists at Jamestown, Virginia. Moreover, the Stuarts were quick to take on the emerging power which most threatened English interests on the high seas: the Dutch United Provinces. If James was sometimes criticized for not responding to the Dutch massacre of English merchants at Amboyna in the East Indies, his son was a staunch defender of English fisheries. Much of the intellectual spadework underpinning the idea of England's maritime dominance, such as John Selden's *Mare clausum*, was conducted under the Stuarts. Both Buckingham and Charles were mesmerized by naval and colonial glory, and sought to draw on the Elizabethan heritage, as they saw it. Buckingham put up a mural to Francis Drake at his residence of Newhall. In the 1630s Charles controversially sought to levy 'ship money' to guarantee England's naval security. Elderly Elizabethans were recalled to advise on policy. Discussions of grand strategy were peppered with references to 'as they did in Queen Elizabeth's time' and 'as Queen Elizabeth's time did truly show', and so on. But they had appropriated only part of the Elizabethan heritage, the colonial and naval glory, not the most important part, which dictated alliance with the Dutch and the defence of England on the far side of the Channel.[22]

None of this reconciled the political nation to the monarchy. Englishmen were grateful for these efforts, yet believed them essentially misdirected. The Dutch were certainly economic and imperial rivals; but they were also and much more importantly a crucial European bulwark of English security. Not all of Charles's critics were indifferent to the financial bottom line, though many were, but strategic arguments were much more important to them. From 1621, these concerns were heightened after the twelve-year truce lapsed and hostilities between Spain and the Dutch were resumed. The critics were therefore horrified when the King not only allowed the Spaniards to funnel bullion through England to their armies in the Netherlands, but also men. Charles even offered to hire out the Royal Navy to open Spain's lines of communications to Flanders by sea in the 1630s. It also seemed to them characteristic that Charles should try to levy unconstitutional 'ship money' to deter the Dutch, instead of applying to Parliament in the normal way for money to take on the Habsburgs in central Europe. When the Dutch finally retaliated by sending Admiral Tromp to destroy a Spanish fleet sheltering by the Downs in 1639, Englishmen were outraged at both the unavenged violation of their neutrality and the closeness of their king to the court of Spain. Nor had the issue of the Palatinate gone away: it continued to bubble throughout the decade before erupting again with renewed force in the early 1640s.[23]

Charles's critics gave him no credit for keeping England out of the devastation of the Thirty Years War. Rather, they had now formed the powerful impression that their monarch was strategically wrong-headed, inclined to absolutism and incompetent to boot. Whether the King really intended to destroy English liberties and impose Catholicism, or whether he was simply incapable of preventing Counter-Reformation Europe from doing so, was almost irrelevant. What was clear was that Charles was not the man to vindicate Protestantism at home by defending it in Europe. All this placed his critics in an impossible dilemma. They accepted the royal prerogative in foreign policy. As the Parliamentarian Oliver St John remarked in November 1637, the task of the King was 'not only to keep the peace at home, but to protect his wife and children and whole families from injury abroad'. For this reason, St John continued, 'he only hath power to make war and peace'. Indeed, the monarch had the sole right not only to declare war, but to determine the 'means of defence'. To be quite clear, he added that 'it is not in the power of the subject to order the way and means of defence, either by sea or by land, according as they think fit'. St John also accepted that the common defence should be paid for by the nation 'equally apportioned upon each person'. The main *constitutional* point at issue, therefore, was the extent to which the King would have to respect established liberties and conventions in extracting these resources from his subjects. The *political* reality was that many critics had lost confidence in the royal judgement of the European balance and the Protestant cause. It was this, rather than class interest or constitutional precocity, which drove them to question royal authority more generally.[24]

It is no accident, therefore, that the failure to support the Palatinate and European Protestantism featured highly in Parliament's Grand Remonstrance of 1641. So did issues of grand strategy as a whole, which dominated the first five articles of the Remonstrance. The domestic fear of 'papists in England' was seen in the context of a Spanish design to reintroduce Catholicism by force. The core of the grievance was expressed in article five, which charged that peace with Spain had been made 'without consent of Parliament, contrary to the promise of King James to both Houses, whereby the Palatine's cause was deserted and left to chargeable and hopeless treaties'. Continuing a long tradition in English political discourse, incompetence was interpreted as treason. The welfare of German Protestants was also central to Parliamentarian politics and rhetoric once the conflict was under way, for example in the Nineteen Propositions of 1642 and the subsequent Propositions of Uxbridge. The prosecutor's undelivered draft speech at the trial of Charles I began with the King's alleged failure to come to the aid of Continental Protestants. Two of the principal scourges of royal authority during the Civil War, Sir Dudley Digges and Sir Thomas Fairfax, had cut their teeth on behalf of the interventionist cause in the 1620s. The revolt against Charles was in its essence a revolt against Stuart foreign policy. The failure to grasp a foreign nettle led to the breakdown of consensus at home. In the end, Englishmen went to war with each other in 1642 because they had not done so effectively on behalf of the Protestant cause in Europe from 1618.[25]

Once the Civil War was over and Charles I beheaded it comes as no surprise to find the very first priority of the new Commonwealth regime to be the pursuit of a Protestant crusade in Europe. This was not a general declaration of war on Roman Catholicism and all Catholic powers, but a programme for the destruction of Habsburg claims to universal monarchy. Cromwell's natural allies were not only Protestant Sweden and Holland, but also Catholic France. England's war effort was to be underpinned by the revival of English commerce and naval power, through the Navigation Act of 1651, which reaffirmed and enforced the long-standing principle that English trade should be carried in English vessels. The Act excluded foreign shipping from importing goods from outside Europe to England; it also banned third countries from carrying European goods to England. Here Cromwell's strategy immediately snagged on the Dutch, who were not prepared to sink their colonial and commercial differences in the common cause, or so Cromwell saw it. As his principal foreign policy advisor, the Secretary of State, John Thurloe, complained, the United Provinces were incapable of thinking strategically or ideologically but 'always found it necessary for them to mingle therewith considerations of trade'. He added in disgust that 'The Hollanders had rather' Cromwell face the Catholic powers alone 'than that they should lose a tun of sack or a frail of raisins'. Far from putting colonial and commercial concerns first, Cromwell actually offered the Dutch to drop the Navigation Act in return for an anti-Habsburg alliance. In 1653–4 the Dutch were therefore worsted in battle by the English more in sorrow than in anger. Cromwell was also indifferent to the commercial costs of war with Spain, despite being warned of them. He saw himself as the vindicator not so much of England's maritime destiny as of European Protestantism.[26]

In 1655, somewhat behind schedule, the crusade was launched in earnest and hostilities with Spain begun. Expeditions were dispatched to the Caribbean, leading to the capture of Jamaica. The purpose behind this 'western design' however was not to carve out a new English empire overseas, but to unbolt the Spaniards from the colonial resources that would support their European hegemony. In 1658, a joint Franco-English army defeated the Spaniards at the Battle of the Dunes. The prize was control of Dunkirk. For the first time since the loss of Calais, England now had a Continental bridgehead from which to influence affairs in Europe. The Channel was now no dyke to keep out the European torrent, but a sluice gate through which England could inundate the Continent at will. Nothing came of this, because Cromwell died shortly after and the Protectorate collapsed within two years.[27]

Europe was bemused by the Commonwealth. The regicide of Charles I repelled even the Dutch. They were perplexed by Cromwell's preoccupations, particularly his support for Savoyard Protestants – recently described as 'the first humanitarian intervention'[28] – from which he gained no direct strategic benefit. To Continental courts, there was something anachronistic about the idea of a 'Protestant' foreign policy after the Treaty of Westphalia in 1648, in which Europeans had agreed to differ on matters of religion. Europe had moved on since the early seventeenth century: Spain was much less of a threat, and the Austrian Habsburgs, like most other European powers, were utterly exhausted. It was a sign of the times that the first European state to recognize the Protectorate, and to seek its alliance, had been Spain; truly the triumph of hope over experience. The Dutch had seen their independence internationally recognized, and had lost the appetite for further conflict with Spain. In fact the European state system of the 1650s was almost unique in that there was no identifiable hegemon against whom Europeans might have rallied. They failed to realize that for Cromwell the Thirty Years War was only just beginning. He was still eager to slay the 'universal monarch' threatening true religion. One thing, however, was not in doubt. The Cromwellian regime had shown in Ireland, where it had massacred thousands of Catholics at Drogheda and Wexford, in Spain and against the United Provinces, that it was capable of exceptional lethality. For a short period in the 1650s England ceased to be the laughing stock of Europe and became a valued alliance partner. English Republicans later drew comfort and confidence from this fact. They believed their cause was not only more godly, virtuous and less arbitrary than monarchy (the latter a very debatable point), but also a more effective vehicle for the articulation of national greatness.

The English monarchy was restored in 1660, for reasons almost entirely to do with domestic policy. Ten years of interregnum, instability and rule by Puritan busybodies had driven Englishmen to welcome the return of Charles II, the late King's son, who had last left the country in disguise to avoid being lynched by his own subjects. They had forgotten the ideological and strategic motivations that had led them to break with the Stuarts in the first place. The political nation was to regret the Restoration almost immediately for reasons which were primarily to do with grand strategy. Quite apart from his personal morality and suspect Anglicanism, Charles infuriated Englishmen with his incompetent and, most importantly, misdirected foreign policy. Very like his father during the 1620s, the new king lurched from one European alignment to another.

As far as the avatars of the 'Protestant interest' were concerned, Restoration foreign policy began on the wrong foot. In 1662 Charles married Catherine of Braganza, a Portuguese princess who brought with her a handsome dowry of cash and the two port towns of Tangier and Bombay. In return, Charles agreed to defend Portuguese independence against Spain. Charles may have thought that a short sharp war against Spain, the historic enemy of the past century, would consolidate the position of the monarchy. If so, he was soon disabused. The threat of 'universal monarchy' was no longer associated with Spain. Shortly after the dynamic young Louis XIV assumed sole responsibility for the government of France in 1661, the threat was widely perceived to come from Bourbon France. A new geopolitical paradigm was emerging in Europe, which Charles at first did not grasp, then did not act against, and finally sought to accommodate himself to. By the mid 1660s, in fact, it was clear that Louis was a huge threat to his neighbours, and to the European balance as a whole. In 1665 he launched the War of Devolution against Spain, and threatened to overrun the whole of the Spanish Netherlands (roughly the territory of present-day Belgium). He was menacing not merely the United Provinces but also England itself. The European outworks of the nation were once again under attack. At the same time, Louis pursued an aggressive policy of Counter-Reformation Catholicism and absolutism at home. All this was beginning to register with Protestant and patriot opinion in England. Thus when Charles sent English troops to Portugal, he thought he was defending his 'oldest ally' against hated Spain. In fact, he was undermining Spain at the very moment when the English political nation came to believe that she would be needed as a counterweight to France.[29]

To make matters worse, Charles sold Dunkirk to France in November 1662, in order to appease Louis and balance the books. To many Protestants and patriots, this was unforgivable. In the first place, the nation had paid a high price for the port, probably about 5,000 men dead. To flog it in order – as it was believed – to pay for the King's louche lifestyle, revolted many. To deliver it to the new universal monarch was even worse; that the money was going to Portugal so as further to damage one of Louis's enemies was worse still. Dunkirk was seen as part of England's European defensive system. As Sir William Lockhart, who was both governor of Dunkirk and ambassador to France, pointed out, the port was 'an excellent outwork for the defence of England'. Dunkirk was also, as Lockhart put it, a 'sally-port' through which England could burst forth against her enemies. Sir George Downing, who had served as ambassador to Holland, reacted to rumours of the sale in February 1662 in much the same way. 'I confess that I am such a doting fool in this point that I had rather . . . let his Majesty have . . . the little I have in the world . . . than that he should want wherewithal to maintaine this place [Dunkirk].' He went on to say that 'England was never considerable, I mean to say considerable indeed since it wanted a footing on this side of the water . . . and if this footing be lost, I doubt whether the youngest that is now alive will ever see England have any other.' England had forfeited her European bridgehead. Even the Great Elector of Brandenburg, Europe's premier Calvinist, taxed Charles for thus abandoning European Protestantism. Charles had made England an island again, and the political nation did not thank him for it.[30]

The outrage over Dunkirk contributed substantially to the fall of Charles's chief minister, the Earl of Clarendon, in 1667, the first of a number of Restoration impeachments driven by foreign policy. By the time that happened, the King had become obsessed with the Dutch. His hatred was primarily ideological and commercial. Charles took England to war with the United Provinces twice: in 1664–7 and again in 1672–4, in alliance with Louis. His critics took all this very badly. In part this was because the wars were hardly resounding successes. In June 1667,

Admiral de Ruyter cheekily sailed up the Thames and captured and burned the English flagship, the *Royal Charles*. The cry 'Dutch in the Medway' was an embarrassment to a nation and a monarchy which prided itself on its naval prowess, but not a fatal one. It was the strategic orientation, rather than the incompetence, which really worried Englishmen. War with the Dutch as a first step towards a Protestant crusade in Europe, as Cromwell had conceived it, was one thing. Furthering Louis's agenda, as Charles seemed determined to do, was quite another. Critics suspected that Charles had concluded a secret treaty with Louis at Dover in 1670, in which he promised to convert to Catholicism when the time was right. They would have been even more horrified had they known that in return the French King granted him a regular subsidy and undertook to support Charles's conversion with 6,000 men. In their minds, the link between the suborning of the King and the collapse of England's Continental outworks was a direct one. The worry was not simply for the Low Countries, but about French penetration of the Holy Roman Empire. Thus Sir Thomas Littleton warned Parliament in April 1675 of the 'enlargement' which Louis 'had made of his empire in Flanders, Germany, the Franche Comte and elsewhere'. In due course, the King's chief minister, Thomas Osborne, Earl of Danby was impeached for the failure to implement a sufficiently anti-French foreign policy.[31]

Throughout the 1670s and the early 1680s, therefore, the spectre of French universal monarchy became the main issue in English politics. It expressed itself as fear of 'popery', but the sentiment was political rather than theological. The public sphere erupted in pamphlets and petitions. Parliament could think of little else. 'Popish plots' were uncovered at home, not so much because Englishmen feared local Catholics, but because Louis's fifth columnists were believed to be ubiquitous. The failed attempt to exclude the King's brother James, Duke of York, who had converted to Catholicism, from the succession in 1680–81, was driven by these fears. In the parliamentary debate, for example, Sir Henry Capel argued that the Jesuits were conspiring to make Louis the 'universal monarch', by 'keeping this nation in this unsettled condition', and thus allowing him to 'take Flanders and Holland'. All the while, Louis was on the advance in Europe, slicing away at the Spanish Netherlands and penetrating the German Empire. By the early to mid 1680s, the French tide had seeped through Germany and was lapping at the borders of Holland *from the east*. It seemed to many Englishmen that the Protestant bastions defending England, which Charles I had so fatally neglected, were once again crumbling under his son.[32]

It was no consolation that the Restoration period had seen a leap in English colonial and naval power. During this time Samuel Pepys famously laid the foundations for the modern Royal Navy. It was at Charles's request that the preamble to the Articles of War stated that 'It is upon the Navy under the providence of God that the safety, honour and welfare of this realm do chiefly attend.' This played well with Englishmen's sense of their 'island' identity. Thus the first Earl of Shaftesbury, one of the major figures of Restoration politics, wrote in 1663 that 'when you consider that we are an island . . . we are no longer Freemen, being Islanders and Neighbours, if they master us at sea'. He went on to observe that 'there is not so lawful or commendable a jealousie in the world, as an *English man's*, of the growing greatness of any prince or state at sea'. The logic of this dictated, as it did for Shaftesbury, naval and commercial confrontation with the Dutch. The twenty years after 1660 were also a time of renewed overseas expansion. In addition to Tangier and Bombay, Charles's reign also saw the capture of New York, New Jersey and Delaware from the Dutch; one of the successes of the final war against the Dutch was putting the Dutch West India Company out of business in 1674. The East India Company also flourished, admittedly on the basis of a Cromwellian charter. But Parliament and the political nation were not much interested in these exotic white elephants. Eventually, after considerable expense had been invested in fortifying it, Tangier was blown up. 'It had better to have been done the first hour it was taken in dower from the Portuguese,' one MP commented. In time, Bombay would prove its worth, as Tangier might have; but for the moment, Englishmen had higher priorities in Europe, nearer to home. To that extent, the Stuarts and their foreign policy spoke to an important yet subordinate strand in the national psyche. Englishmen welcomed the growth of their naval power, but not if it was going to be used against the Protestant cause, and in support of Louis. It was the German Empire, not the English empire, they were worried about.[33]

Like his father and grandfather before him, therefore, Charles was accused of misreading the European state system. His critics lambasted not so much the military and naval record, which was in any case less disastrous than they gave him credit for, but the *strategic direction* of

English policy. In this sense, even the successes were failures, because each blow against Spain or the Dutch made Louis's breeze to blow. Given more resources, Charles might have crushed the Dutch, and delivered the European hegemony to France on a plate. It was this fear, not primarily parsimony or cussedness, which drove Parliament to limit the supply of money to the Crown. Confidence in the King was so low that he had to default on his creditors in 1672. Charles was not punished for it in his lifetime through a combination of luck, deception and charm. Englishmen fancied they could sniff out a papist, but many could not quite bring themselves to believe that this amiable bumbler would actually sell them to Louis. So long as Charles ruled, the strategic situation might be increasingly desperate, but it was not serious.

This changed with the accession of James II in 1685. The new king was not only openly Catholic, but set about increasing England's military preparedness. James saw his monarchical duty very much in strategic terms, but this led him in very different directions to his critics. He sought to open the army, Navy, universities and Parliament to non-Anglican talent – mainly Catholic, but also dissenting Protestants. Only in this way, he believed, could the energies of the nation be harnessed for the struggles which lay ahead. Protestants and patriots, on the other hand, saw in this only the hand of the French universal monarch. It seemed to them no accident that 1685 was also the year in which Louis revoked the Edict of Nantes, which had granted a measure of toleration to French Protestants. A wave of Huguenot refugees bearing terrible tales of persecution arrived in England. Their presence gave an immense boost to anti-French discourse, and many Huguenots were to become prominent advocates of the 'Protestant interest' in English and later British foreign policy. They joined forces with an English public sphere already profoundly suspicious of James, not least because he had been one of the architects of war against the Dutch.[34]

Parliament was suspended from November 1685, so the controversy perforce took place 'out of doors' – that is, beyond Westminster. The open debate on English grand strategy which had been in full swing since the early seventeenth century, despite periodic attempts by the executive to muzzle it, entered a new phase after 1680. A 'public sphere' was taking shape in which thousands of petitions and addresses competed with pamphlets and prints for the attention of the political nation and those who felt they should be part of it. The whole country, but especially London, was gripped by fear of 'popery' and 'universal monarchy'. Foreign policy was central to the emerging domestic polarity between Whigs and Tories. Both saw a dominant role for England on the European stage; they were bitterly divided on how this should be effected, and the direction which policy should take.[35]

The Whigs felt that James was doing nothing to stop the French advance on the Continent: England, in effect, was punching below its weight in Europe. On the contrary, the King demanded the recall of six English regiments serving in the Netherlands. To those worried for English liberties at home, this seemed ominous; for the even larger number also concerned about England's commitment to the 'Protestant' cause against universal monarchy, it was an outrage. In 1686, Louis's European enemies came together in the League of Augsburg: Austria, Spain, Sweden and Saxony agreed to stop the French tide. The Pope – alienated by Louis's treatment of the French Catholic Church and his failure to go on crusade against the Turks – gave secret support. Even the papacy, therefore, seemed more 'Protestant' in foreign policy than the entirely inactive King of England; this may have been unfair to James, but that is how it was perceived. The same vicious cycle which had hamstrung the early Stuarts was now repeated. Because they distrusted the King's judgement on foreign policy, critics blocked James at every turn, weakening him diplomatically and thus leading to further loss of prestige at home.

And yet, in so far as England was a commercial, colonial and maritime nation, James was very much in touch with it. In him, England had her first sailor king, certainly a brave one, and probably not a bad one either. He had been Governor of the Hudson's Bay and Royal Africa Companies: his vision was by no means confined to Europe. Some of the most systematic thinking about England's northern American colonies took place under James. Once the Dutch had been expelled from New England, he worried about possible French 'encirclement'. It was to escape the Bourbon embrace and pre-empt further French settlements, rather than in pursuit of some esoteric grail, that Englishmen sought the famous 'North-West Passage'. Failure to keep the French at bay by forestalling them in the Ohio Valley, James's Irish Governor of New York, Thomas Dongan, warned, would lead to his colonies being pressed against the coast and possibly destroyed. Moreover, crucial intellectual work about the importance of commerce, colonial expansion and naval dominance was done under the Stuarts by William Petty in the 1680s. 'Such as desire empire & liberty,' he wrote in the *Dominion of the sea*, 'let them encourage the art of ship-building.' The Stuarts, in other words, were very much in tune with English economic and colonial interests, narrowly conceived; it was the superstructure of strategic assumptions about Europe and England's place in it with which they were fatally out of step. If one sees England's historic destiny as lying primarily in naval and colonial expansion, then the unpopularity of the Stuarts is incomprehensible. In those terms they were much more in tune with the national mood than the Dutchman and the Germans who succeeded them. Only if it is grasped that critics believed that England's and later Britain's future would be decided by her European alliances, and the domestic structures needed to underpin them, does the path taken during the 'Glorious Revolution' make sense.[36]

Matters came to a head in 1688. In June of that year, a male heir was unexpectedly born to James: the hope of an eventual Protestant succession through his (adult) daughter Mary thus evaporated. In Ireland, James's deputy, Richard Talbot, Duke of Tyrconnell was assembling an army which Whigs feared would be used against them. More important from the strategic point of view, however, were developments in the German Empire and the Electorate. For in September 1688, Louis won over the ecclesiastical Elector of Cologne, who was strategically located in north-west Germany, not far from Flanders and the Dutch border. To the fury and despair of Austrians, the Dutch, the Catholic but anti-French Elector Palatine and the Whigs, he was abetted by James's diplomats in Austria. The Spanish Road (once a mortal threat, now a lifeline which would help declining Spain keep the French out of Flanders) had been cut. Worse still, French troops now threatened Holland from across the Rhine as well. The final Protestant bastion seemed about to fall.[37]

This, rather than the birth of young James, was the immediate trigger for the Glorious Revolution of 1688. In October, the Dutch Republic, Prussia, Hanover and Hesse-Kassel moved to a formal military coalition to contain Louis. Its leading spirit, the Dutch Stadholder, William III, believed that no time was to be lost. He had seen the dangers of an Anglo-French alliance in 1672–4. Who would speak for England when the final showdown with Louis loomed? William was determined that it should not be James, at least not in his present frame of mind.

Seven Whig peers, the guardians of the Protestant interest at home, but especially abroad, agreed. William was invited to take the English throne, on the strength of his marriage to James's daughter Mary, who had remained an Anglican. To be on the safe side, William brought with him hundreds of warships and more than 20,000 men; an alliance with Brandenburg covered his back in northern Germany. So began the greatest military, geopolitical and constitutional gamble in history. The old England had been – with the significant exception of the Commonwealth – too weak to fulfil its role in the European state system. It was now in grave danger of being entirely manipulated by Louis XIV. Confronted with this, the Dutch Stadholder and a strong-willed group of Whig grandees decided to wind up the old England and invent a new one.[38]

1688 was thus not about what European absolutism might do to English freedoms, but what England could do for the 'liberties of Europe', that is the balance of power. And if the restoration and redirection of English power had become a European necessity, most propertied Englishmen also believed that the maintenance of the European balance was essential to the preservation of their own liberty and security. It was the second English revolution of the century, and Englishmen were once again able to pursue a 'Protestant' foreign policy. The sequence here is important. Whigs had made the Revolution to pursue the Protestant foreign policy; they did not – as is sometimes assumed – undertake a Protestant foreign policy in order to protect the Revolution, although that imperative naturally followed. But this time, by contrast with Cromwell, they did not have to go forth in search of monsters to destroy. The enemy was clear in view. Louis was already at war with much of Europe. Now England entered the lists too, and joined the Grand Alliance in 1689. The first battles against Louis were fought in Ireland, whence James had fled after the Glorious Revolution. French-backed forces loyal to James – henceforth known as 'Jacobites' – were defeated at the Boyne in 1690 and again at Aughrim in 1691. The French navy was worsted at Barfleur in 1692. The main focus, however, was Flanders: the decisive theatre of the war, the barrier which England was determined should not fall to Louis. Throughout the 1690s, English troops fought there with determination and varying success. At the same time, English diplomacy was active on the Continent, cultivating allies and trying to end the Emperor's war with Turkey, in order to release imperial forces for service against France. Not all of these activities were crowned with success, but they gave English diplomats valuable experience in the interconnectedness of the various parts of the European balance.[39]

The strategic choice to confront Louis in 1688–9 led to a fundamental transformation of English society, politics, the military and above all of public finance. The energies unleashed then were to be a necessary (though not a sufficient) cause of Britain's eighteenth-century pre-eminence. The Revolution settlement was thus driven by the primacy of foreign policy. Power projection within Europe was not incompatible with English liberties but essential to their maintenance. In the Bill of Rights of 1689, a standing army was authorized, but only with the consent of Parliament. The rights of certain groups, especially Roman Catholics, were circumscribed for reasons of state security: they could not succeed to the throne, marry into the royal family, take seats in Parliament or even vote. Contemporary liberal opinion thought these restrictions perfectly reasonable. It was also comfortable with the idea that the security of Englishmen in a predatory world, as well as against domestic enemies, rested on mobilizing national energies against the common foe. In his famous 'Letter concerning toleration', for example, John Locke laid down that the principal task of the supreme power was to make provision 'for the security of each man's private possessions; for the peace, riches, and public commodities of the whole people; and, as much as possible, for the increase of their inward strength against foreign invasions'. In another treatise, he laid down that the 'first care and thought' of society must be 'how to secure themselves against foreign force'.[40]

The framers of the Revolution settlement realized that all this required a more sophisticated bureaucratic apparatus. Strong government – and a large state – were thus to become as English as roast beef and warm beer. A funded national debt was established. The Bank of England was founded in 1694. A stock market developed, whose fluctuating fortunes mirrored those of the nation's war with France. Regular taxes were voted for the war effort. Customs and excise officers, the foot-soldiers of the 'fiscal-military state', fanned out across the nation in ever greater numbers. In order to wage the struggle against France, therefore, Englishmen accepted and perfected some of the very instruments of governance and finance which they had so long denied the Stuarts. During the

Nine Years War from 1688–97, England spent a staggering £49,320,145, of which some £32 million came from income, but more than £16 million was raised in loans. But the Continental model they imported was Dutch and consensual rather than French and absolutist; it picked up where the highly successful Parliamentarian war effort had left off. It was no less 'European' than what the Stuarts had planned, or were accused of planning. But if Charles had merely agreed to call on French troops if needed, the Whigs had actually changed the regime with the support of 20,000 Dutch bayonets. The old England had been founded in 1066 by a Frenchman; the new England in 1688 by a Dutchman.[41]

Unlike European absolutist states, however, the English executive was subjected to regular scrutiny by Parliament and the public sphere; the basis of its legitimacy was very different. Parliament now met continuously. In 1694 the Triennial Act laid down that elections should take place every three years; soon many realized that this subjected the nation to more crippling expense and controversy than was strictly necessary. A year later, the Licensing Act was allowed to lapse, effectively ending censorship. There was an immediate boom in journalism to respond to the new appetite for commercial and diplomatic news. Between them Parliament and the public sphere could now hold the executive to account. The crucial link between political consensus and public credit, broken by the Stuarts, was restored for good. Parliament stood as collateral for the debts of the nation. Foreign policy remained a royal prerogative, but it was exercised in coordination with Parliament, which controlled the purse strings. But it was not just about money: even if it was kept in the dark about important details and treaties, the political nation now 'owned' English grand strategy in a way that had not been true since Elizabeth's time, and intermittently during the Civil War.[42]

As important as these structural changes was the emergence of a new strategic consensus. Not only was England's security once again to be defended in Europe – a restoration in foreign policy – but England was from now on to become the principal guardian of the European balance of power as a whole. Earlier generations had often claimed a national destiny to defend Continental Protestantism, but the idea that England should be the main motor of European unity in the face of French universal monarchy, and the vindicator of the 'liberties of Europe' was an innovation. Englishmen saw no contradiction between this mission and the choice of Catholic allies, such as the Holy Roman Emperor. As one Williamite propagandist put it in 1696, 'England should always make itself the head and protection of the whole Protestant interest.' It would achieve this by drawing on the Elizabethan tradition. 'By making all true Protestants, i.e. all true Christians, her friends,' he argued, 'she enabled England to make good her oldest maxim of state, which was to keep the balance of Europe equal and steady . . . Our allies of the Roman communion must allow this Protestant maxim to be truly Catholic, because their safety from the power of France was wrapped up in it together with our own.' The events of 1688–9 had shown that Louis was unable to intervene and perform his obligations under the Dover treaty because he was distracted by events in Germany. The League of Augsburg had stood midwife to the Glorious Revolution.[43]

Furthermore, Englishmen were increasingly convinced that the maintenance of England's maritime superiority depended on the preservation of the European balance of power, and – to a certain extent – vice versa. As we have seen, the contours of this doctrine had first become apparent under Elizabeth, when the Dutch had drawn off so much Spanish fire and the Royal Navy was deployed to cut the flow of American bullion to Parma's forces in the Low Countries. The Nine Years War confirmed that English naval superiority depended on drawing off French resources through land warfare in coordination with European allies. Louis was unable to capitalize on his naval victory at Beachy Head in July 1690, which left the south coast wide open to attack, because of his European commitments. Despite Parliament's intense interest in the naval war and naval expenditure, maritime and colonial considerations were subordinated to Continental affairs; indeed the Navy was largely inactive in the colonies in the 1690s. This was the Whig orthodoxy which was to dominate English and later British strategic thinking for a generation. It involved a strategic and conceptual revolution which most Englishmen accepted but a significant minority never came to terms with.[44]

By contrast, the Tory heresy was both more insular and more global. It was highly suspicious of the fiscal-military state, which it dismissed as a scheme to line the pockets of William's Whig and Dutch cronies. It sought to reduce and emasculate the standing army as an expensive luxury at best, and a vehicle for Whig or European-style tyranny at worst. Public credit was something of a dirty word; the same was true of the national debt. And if Tories could see a limited role for subsidy payments to European princes, especially to keep English troops out of combat, they were resolutely opposed to any expenditure in peacetime. Above all, the Tories rejected the idea of a standing commitment to the Continent. Thus from the 1690s both the Jacobites and the 'New Country Party' in Parliament attacked the Continentalist strategy which had bogged English troops down in Flanders. The European balance, the Tories felt, could look after itself, or it was no balance at all. They were prepared to support a strategy of 'descents' – amphibious raids – but not a substantial commitment to a European land war. Instead, Tory heretics, and the few Whig schismatics who agreed with them, called for a more commercial and colonial orientation to British policy. Instead of being entangled in the European thicket, they argued, Britain should press home her advantage against the French and Spanish overseas. In his *Discourses on the public revenue*, the MP Charles Davenant contrasted the cost of land forces with the rewards that a navalist strategy promised.[45]

This discourse was strongest outside government. All the same, it appealed to a number of William's ministers, who had supported the domestic revolution of 1688, but were uneasy at its strategic implications. Indeed, his first secretary of state (in charge of foreign affairs), Daniel Finch, Earl of Nottingham, was a High Church Tory who supported the Protestant Succession, and was a strong advocate of naval over Continental warfare. In a gesture towards this constituency, William chose a number of Tory admirals, such as Sir Cloudesley Shovell, Henry Killigrew, and Sir Ralph Delavall. Men such as Sir Edward Seymour, a Tory supporter of William and a Lord of the Treasury, and Laurence Hyde, first Earl of Rochester, pressed for a maritime strategy against France; the latter two wanted to starve Flanders of funds altogether and concentrate entirely on the naval war. The experience of the 1690s, however, did not vindicate them. Various fiascos showed its limitations even in the benign confines of the Mediterranean, and in 1690 a failed assault on the French colony of Quebec in Canada showed that there were no easy pickings there either. A few years later, Nottingham suggested a raid on the French coast. This, he argued, would be a crushing blow to Louis and would prop up William's position with English public opinion. It would guarantee, Nottingham claimed, nothing less than 'the establishment of their Majesties' throne, the perpetual security of this island, and the peace of Europe'. Men were diverted from Flanders to this end – much to William's unease and that of the Dutch. The attack on Brest went ahead in 1694 and was a complete disaster; it became clear that a maritime or colonial strategy did not provide all the answers. At the heart of the political divide between Whigs and Tories, therefore, were their differing views of England's position in Europe.[46]

All this had profound implications for Englishmen's sense of identity. Whereas the Whigs tended to confine their prejudices to Catholics and the French, the xenophobic exuberance of the Tories extended to the Dutch, the Spaniards, from the early eighteenth century the Hanoverians, and many other groups as well. Hostility to European entanglements, war and foreigners were mutually reinforcing elements of Toryism; domestically, it tended to stress the Dutchness of the Stadholder-King and his entourage. Williamite administrations recognized the potency of these arguments, and responded by 'nationalizing' the war against Louis XIV. Their propagandists portrayed the English as Israelites to be saved from universal monarchy and popish encirclement by France and its agents in Ireland and Scotland. This new national identity joined the people of England in a common project with the Dutch, German Protestants and many others to curb French pretensions towards universal monarchy. This was not a 'British' struggle – the term would have struck contemporaries as puzzling and possibly specious – but a European one.[47]

In other words, Europe was not just an 'other' against which English and later British identity was defined. To be sure, sixteenth- and seventeenth-century 'Englishness' was defined against the Continental enemy, first Spain and then France. But Europe was also *part* of that identity, and not only because so many Englishmen from the time of the immigration of the Angles, the Saxons, the Jutes, the Danes and the Normans through to the contemporary influx of Huguenots had come from across the Channel. One very important strand of Englishness was the sense of belonging to a broader European commonwealth, the 'main(land)'. The statesmen and diplomats who defended England's interests within the state system (the great powers of Europe and how they related to each other) felt this, but so did Members of Parliament, and many in the political nation and the public sphere. Europe mattered to them, and many saw themselves as not necessarily better, but more fortunate than their fellows across the Channel, whom they would redeem through their example and by their efforts. Hitherto Englishmen had spoken largely of 'Christendom' and the 'Protestant interest'. From now on, they would speak more of 'Europe', 'the liberties of Europe', and of the 'balance of power'. All these terms meant essentially the same thing. These Englishmen had a profound sense of their destiny and particularity, but there was no room in their world for a narrow chauvinism. How could there be, when they believed the safety of Protestantism abroad to be inextricably linked to the security of the Protestant Succession at home; and when English constitutional liberties were being defended in England's European outworks? On this reading, William was more of an 'Englishman' than the native dynasts, who had not scrupled – or so it was believed – to sell the nation to France. Indeed, English identity itself was not only a political construction, but a 'mongrel' one. As the great Whig partisan Daniel Defoe wrote in *The true-born Englishman* in 1701, ' 'tis impossible we should be true-born: and if we could, should have lost by the bargain'.[48]

Towards the end of the 1690s domestic pressure, war weariness and military stalemate compelled William, rather against his better judgement – and to the fury of his Austrian ally – to break off the war before Louis's power had been broken for good. All the same, the Treaty of Ryswick in 1697 was a triumph when measured against the spectre of universal monarchy threatening Europe in 1688. Louis was forced to back off from the Spanish Netherlands, and to recognize William as king of England. The colonial gains made at French expense were returned in exchange for concessions on dynastic and Continental matters closer to home. This was further proof of the centrality of the European balance in English thinking. The most important development at Ryswick, however, was the establishment of a formal Anglo-Dutch 'barrier' in the Spanish Netherlands, by which Dutch troops garrisoned a ring of fortresses designed to deter Louis's French troops from overrunning the Low Countries. The English security interest in Flanders, the old 'counterscarp', was now formally recognized as an integral part of the European balance and international law. Henceforth, London would pay ever more attention to the Holy Roman Empire within which the barrier was located and through which its defence would have to be organized.

2

Marlborough Country: Britain and the Empire, 1697–1714

A monument designed to perpetuate the memory of the signal victory obtained over the French and the Bavarians near the village of Blenheim on the banks of the Danube by JOHN, DUKE OF MARLBOROUGH, *the hero not only of his nation but of his age ... Who ... broke the power of* France: *when raised the highest, when exerted the most, rescued the Empire* from desolation, asserted and confirmed the liberties of Europe.

Inscription on the Column of Victory, Blenheim Palace, Oxfordshire

Nobody epitomized Britain's eighteenth-century commitment to Europe more than the supreme commander of the coalition forces on the Continent during the War of the Spanish Succession. The Duke of Marlborough was not just a brilliant tactician, but also a consummate master strategist and diplomat. In a series of stunning victories from 1704, he checked the French advance into Germany and the Low Countries. He maintained good relations with Britain's prickly Austro-Dutch allies, and in 1707 he pulled off perhaps the greatest coup of his career by persuading the Swedish king, Charles, to withdraw from Germany rather than pressing on and causing a fatal diversion to the allied war effort. He became a new type of English European hero, whose image was carefully burnished by Whig propagandists, and whose exploits fired the elite and popular imagination. Even though his war was ultimately waged to secure English liberties, it was principally fought not in the British Isles, on the high seas or in the colonies, but in the Low Countries, the Rhineland and South Germany. The Bavarian town of Blindheim – from which the more familiar name of Blenheim derives – was geographically remote. It was the furthest from the sea that English troops had ever been deployed in Europe – but strategically close to the minds of

Englishmen. In short, the 'Empire' whose rescue was later celebrated on the Column of Victory at his palace of Blenheim, was the Holy Roman Empire, not the British Empire. This chapter is thus the story of the development of Britain's eighteenth-century imperial mission: to maintain the balance of power in the German Empire, upon which the security of the Barrier in Flanders and the broader European balance depended.[1]

By 1700, the Whig project to contain the threat of French universal monarchy to the European balance and their own liberties was firmly established in England. Its roots, however, were still dangerously shallow. Much remained to be done on the near side of the Channel. The failure to grasp the constitutional thistle with Scotland in 1689 by pushing through an Act of Union there and then soon came back to haunt London. It led to a crisis in 1698, when the Scots embarked on their disastrous colonization of Darien on the Isthmus of Panama. This not only cut across William's pro-Spanish policy, but also conjured up the possibility of Anglo-Scottish colonial rivalry. At the very least, English and Scottish strategy was not yet 'joined up'. Nor was the fiscal-military complex firmly entrenched. Englishmen had made great efforts during the Nine Years War which followed the Revolution, but after the Treaty of Ryswick Parliament insisted on the disbandment of the standing army, even though the national credit was strong. Those who paid a land-tax specifically designed to pay for the war were heavily represented in both Houses, and it was natural that they should seek to slough off the burden as soon as possible. Moreover, it was feared that a permanent national debt would strengthen the executive and accentuate its tendency towards despotism. It was not only Jacobites and crypto-Catholics who believed that a large military on a permanent footing posed a greater threat to English liberties than Louis XIV.

William disagreed strongly, the more so as the question of the Spanish succession now loomed. The death of Carlos II without an heir was imminent; the most plausible candidate to succeed him was the French Bourbon, Louis XIV's grandson Philip of Anjou. This conjured up the spectre of a union between the French and Spanish crowns in due course. Not only would this add Spain itself to the Bourbon powerhouse, including her Mediterranean lands in Sicily and Naples, and her overseas empire, but also the all-important Spanish Netherlands. It would create an empire more formidable than that of Charles V, just across the

English Channel. The alternative, which was the Austrian Habsburg candidate, the Archduke Charles, was better, but by opening up the possibility of a reunification of the Spanish and German Habsburg lines, it too presaged a massive conglomerate inimical to the European balance. The logical solution was a partition of the Spanish empire in Europe and overseas, which was agreed with Louis XIV by treaty in 1698. A compromise candidate for the Spanish throne, the Prince of Bavaria, was found. Yet William's activism over the Spanish succession proved highly controversial in English politics. On the one hand, he was criticized for any solution which resulted in an increase of French territory: the three Whig peers involved in the partition were promptly impeached for neglecting their duty to the European balance. On the other hand, there were many who felt that they were being obliged to prepare for a hypothetical eventuality. They blamed William for creating problems where none really existed. In any case, the partition plan unravelled. The Bavarian died before it could be implemented. Moreover, Carlos himself and Spanish opinion were strongly opposed to any such division. His will stipulated that the entire Spanish Empire should fall to Philip of Anjou in the first instance; if he refused to accept it as a whole, the lot would pass to the Habsburg candidate. It was winner-take-all, and the Spanish king's death in November 1700 duly set the cat among the pigeons. Rather than risk losing the entire inheritance to Charles of Habsburg, Louis advised Philip to accept. '*Il n'y a plus de Pyrénées*,' he boasted ('There are no more Pyrenees').

Even then, war might have been avoided. There was still no majority in Parliament for another conflict. It sought to hobble William by demanding that his diplomacy, such as the partition treaties, be subjected to Parliament's approval. 'Out of doors', however, it was another matter. Many in the political nation and public sphere now believed that the final showdown with French universal monarchy was at hand. They were convinced that the failure to prepare for war and seek Continental alliances reflected a misguided strategy at best, and treason at worst. A wave of petitions now hit Westminster. The famous Kentish Petition of May 1701, for example, demanded that England aid her Dutch ally in good time; Parliament struck back by imprisoning the five gentlemen who presented it. Much the same argument was made in the 'Legion' memorial – Daniel Defoe was to write 'Our name is legion for we are many' – which claimed that Parliament no longer represented the will of the people in foreign policy. A struggle for the executive erupted, in which Parliament sought to slow down the slide to war through detailed scrutiny of royal policy, while extra-parliamentary opinion generally demanded more direct action to contain Louis. The old debates of the late Stuart period were thus reprised, but with the roles reversed: the King and popular opinion now supported the containment of France, while many in Parliament counselled caution or remained unconcerned. One way or the other, competing views of foreign policy once again threatened to tear the country apart in a constitutional crisis.[2]

William despaired at English indifference to the collapse of the partition treaties. 'I am troubled to the very bottom of my soul,' he wrote to a Dutch confidant in late 1700, 'to find ... that nearly everybody congratulates himself that France has preferred the will to the treaty, insisting that it is much better for England and for the whole of Europe.' He went on to lament that 'people here are perfectly unconcerned, and turn their thoughts but little to the great change which is happening in the affairs of the world. It seems as if it was a punishment of heaven that this nation should be so little alive to that which passes outside of its own island, although it ought to have the same interests and the same anxieties as the Continental nations.' William was not exaggerating. As the French threat loomed once more, some Tories did indeed cultivate an air of ignorance and insouciance. 'I am commenced so violent a Sportsman,' one Tory squire wrote in December 1700, 'that my satisfaction to continue in the country two months longer than usual has not been interrupted by the death of his Catholic majesty [the Spanish King], nor am I a jot concerned whether the widow accepts the handkerchief of Monsieur le Dauphin to dry up those tears [i.e. whether he is succeeded by a French candidate].' Indeed, he added, 'whether the original papers for partition of the Spanish monarchy be allotted to the politicians or to the tobacconists for the use of their best Virginia does not trouble my head'. The 1701 election, in which the Whigs called for war against France, produced a Tory majority still opposed to an intervention.[3]

Gritting their teeth, England and the United Provinces recognized Philip of Anjou as king of Spain. They were rewarded with economic decrees from Madrid directed against English and Dutch commerce. The lucrative *Asiento*, the right to trade in slaves with the Spanish New World, was awarded to France. In September 1701, James II died.

Despite his renunciation of the Jacobites at the Treaty of Ryswick, Louis recognized his son 'James III' as the rightful king of England. Of course he also occupied the Spanish Netherlands on behalf of Philip of Anjou. Dutch troops were expelled from the Barrier fortresses, and no compensation was offered to the Emperor. That was the last straw: the enemy was now once again in the counterscarp of England. Even if Louis had not intended to provoke, the threat of Europe's domination by a single power now loomed large once more. One pamphleteer wrote 'that the Succession in Spain is not a particular controversy between the Emperor and most Christian King, but a business of the utmost importance to all Europe . . . on which her liberty and slavery entirely depends'. He went on to claim that 'there is no way of restoring the balance of Christendom, which is so necessary for the common good, but by settling the whole monarchy of Spain' on the Austrian candidate. Finally, the author insisted that 'any kind of dismembering whatever', even if France did not directly profit, 'would prove sufficient to advance that crown to the universal monarchy'. Charles Davenant, who had only a few years earlier advocated an exclusively maritime strategy, argued in his *Essay upon the balance of power* in 1701 that the prospect of 'holding the balance of Europe . . . will make us patiently endure the Bloodshed, hazards, losses and expences of Treasure' necessary to maintain it.[4]

England now committed itself to a far-reaching geopolitical reordering of Europe. In June 1701 the House of Commons undertook to support William of Orange's efforts 'in conjunction with the Emperor and the Estates-General [the Netherlands], for the preservation of the liberties of Europe, the prosperity and peace of England, and for reducing the exorbitant power of France'. The terms of the Grand Alliance of September 1701 between England, the Emperor and Holland now committed the parties to 'use their utmost endeavours to recover the provinces of the Spanish Low Countries, that they may be a fence and a rampart, commonly called a barrier, separating and distancing France from the United Provinces.' It also envisaged the same role for 'the Duchy of Milan, with all its dependencies, as a fief of the Empire and contributing to the security of his Majesty's hereditary countries' – that is, as a rampart for Austria. Lastly, the Grand Alliance stipulated that 'the Kingdom of Naples and Sicily and the lands and islands upon the coasts of Tuscany in the Mediterranean that belong to the Spanish dominions' should also be constructed as a constraint on French power in Italy. One way or another the Grand Alliance was to shape not only British strategic discourse, but also domestic politics for much of the century.[5]

The approach of war drove the search for dynastic stability in England itself. For in July 1700, Princess Anne's last surviving child, William of Gloucester, died. As William and Mary had had no children, this threw the succession wide open once more. In order to forestall the return of the Stuarts, and the removal of England from the anti-French front, Parliament passed the Act of Settlement in 1701. This effectively excluded the Stuarts, even if they abjured Roman Catholicism. Instead, the succession was fixed on the Electress Sophia of Brunswick-Lüneburg (Hanover), and her descendants, so long as these were Protestant. Though only fiftieth in line to the throne, she had the indisputable merit of being a Protestant. She was also the daughter of James I's eldest daughter Elizabeth and Frederick Elector Palatine, the man for whom the Stuarts did not go to war in the 1620s and 30s. It was a neat symmetry. William III died in 1702, and was succeeded by Mary's sister Anne. She had little affection for the Hanoverians, and was upset by public discussions of her mortality, but there is no evidence that she ever wavered in her commitment to the settlement of 1701. The succession was secure. [6]

Thus began the last of the three Wars of Grand Alliance against Louis. It was the second struggle which England waged against the threat of French universal monarchy, though by no means the last. It was very much a national rather than a dynastic contest, which was 'owned' by the political nation. Parliamentary authorization for war was sought and obtained, on the grounds, as the supreme commander the Duke of Marlborough put it, that otherwise 'we shall never see a quiet day more in England'. English diplomats were once again dispatched to pursue the 'Protestant interest' in Europe. They fanned out across the Continent, and especially the German Empire, in search of allies and mercenaries; in October 1702, the Empire declared war on France. The Duke of Marlborough was sent to Germany and Flanders to confront the French armies. Most of the funding came from London, but at the beginning only about a fifth of his force was English; the rest came from across the coalition arrayed against Louis. Two-fifths were Dutch, the other two-fifths German mercenaries paid for by both England and the United Provinces. An allied army was also dispatched to Spain in order to press the claims of the Habsburg candidate, Archduke Charles, to the throne.

England recognized his succession to the whole Spanish Empire, partly because this was necessary to sustain his claim in the eyes of Spanish opinion, but also because it was believed to be the only way of dealing with an overmighty France. A strategy of encirclement was devised, to contain France on all sides of the compass: in Spain, in Flanders, in Germany, in Italy and on the high seas. The allies also stirred domestic unrest in France and Bourbon-held Spain: the Protestant Camisards rose in revolt in the Cevennes region of southern France, as did the Catholic Catalans against Philip of Anjou. Most Continental Protestants looked to Britain for leadership, and voluntary groups such as the Society for the Promotion of Christian Knowledge (SPCK) and the Society for the Propagation of the Gospel lobbied strenuously on their behalf, effectively becoming an arm of British foreign policy.[7]

At first all went well. Attacks on French commerce and colonies were launched, primarily to serve European purposes. Their aim, as one set of Admiralty instructions made clear, was to 'depriv[e] them of the supply of money and plate which they seem to rely on for the support of the war'. In 1702, for example, an Anglo-Dutch fleet attacked and destroyed a Spanish plate fleet in Vigo harbour, thus reducing the flow of New World silver to England's enemies. The orders for an attack on Havana in 1703 spoke of the intent to 'prejudice the family of Bourbon and advance the interests of the House of Austria'. In Europe itself, English arms, gold and diplomacy worked together in apparently unstoppable synergy: leadership of the Grand Alliance fell to London, not Vienna. The Methuen Treaty of 1703 initiated a long-standing alliance with Portugal; a year later English forces captured Gibraltar. But the main effort was made in Flanders and Germany. The first priority was to prevent Austria from being knocked out of the war at an early stage by a Franco-Bavarian-Savoyard pincer movement through South Germany and North Italy. Marlborough therefore struck south from Flanders into Germany, in order to establish a line of communication with Vienna. In 1704 he smashed a French army at Blenheim, and administered a decisive check to Louis. It was truly, as Marlborough's descendant Charles Spencer was later to write, a 'battle for Europe'. Not long afterwards, the Emperor rewarded Marlborough for his services with the Swabian territory of Mindelheim, taken from the vanquished Elector of Bavaria; on the strength of this Marlborough was subsequently made a prince of the Holy Roman Empire. The great English victory of Blenheim, therefore, was won in Germany, by a largely German army, under the command of a man who was to become a prince of the Holy Roman Empire, in order (ultimately) to place a German prince on to the throne of England.[8]

2. Marlborough was not only a British but also a European hero. The Emperor made him a prince of the Holy Roman Empire.

Meanwhile, the war drove the process of state formation in the British Isles. Clarifying the relationship between England and Scotland now became imperative for strategic reasons. English strategists sought to forestall attempts by foreign powers to deal directly with the Scots – or the Irish, for that matter. The danger of a separate Scottish path in foreign policy had been raised by the 'Act Anent Peace and War', which the Edinburgh parliament passed in 1703. It stipulated that after Anne's death, the consent of the Scottish parliament to treaties and declarations of war would be required. The Scots had been dragged into the Nine Years War and the War of the Spanish Succession without being consulted. Now they were signalling that they could not always be taken for granted. The implications for English grand strategy were potentially enormous. Moreover it became a matter of urgency to regulate the succession, which the Act of Settlement had decided for England, but the passing of which had reopened the Scottish debate. Offended at this unilateral move, the Scots had passed their own 'Act of Security' in 1703. Unlike the English measure – which by explicitly settling the succession on the House of Hanover had effectively excluded the Stuarts, even if Protestant – the Scottish Act left open the possibility that the Pretender might return if he abjured Roman Catholicism. England had retaliated in 1705 with the Aliens Act, which declared the Scots to be aliens unless they repealed the Act of Security. This reflected anxiety in London that the Act not only provided the Pretender with a base from which to unravel the English succession, but might also revive the 'Auld Alliance' between France and Scotland and thus the encirclement of England, which Elizabeth had banished in the sixteenth century.[9]

There was also a much broader strategic consideration. The war made ever greater demands on English and Scottish resources; it required more and more coordination. In this context the continuing colonial and economic rivalry with Scotland – which manifested itself in the continued application of the Navigation Acts to that country – was profoundly counter-productive. The Darien fiasco had shown that Scotland was a potential colonial rival; and in 1703, in the middle of a common war against Louis, the Edinburgh parliament legalized the wine trade with France. It therefore made sense to weld both halves closer together into a commercial and political whole. This would achieve imperial economies of scale to mutual benefit. The Scots would gain access to the burgeoning British overseas trade; in return they committed themselves completely and in perpetuity to the Protestant interest and the Liberties of Europe. If the coming together of England and Scotland was a 'union for Empire', it was still more a union against universal monarchy. The empire that was at stake here was the Holy Roman Empire.[10]

In April 1706, English and Scottish commissioners convened in London to discuss the terms of Union. Agreement was reached in July, and in January–February 1707 the measure was passed by both the London and the Edinburgh parliaments. Henceforth, the Scots would participate as equals in the English colonial trade, were granted generous representation at Westminster, and retained their separate legal system and religious establishment. In return they gave up their parliament, agreed to pay a proportion of the land tax, and – above all – they agreed to subsume their foreign policy into that of the new composite state. Some far-sighted observers recognized this as the start of a virtuous circle of Anglo-Scottish co-prosperity; most traders south of the border at first saw only the arrival of unwelcome competitors. They knew that the Union was not an economic proposition but a strategic gambit. The United Kingdom of Great Britain, as the new state came to be known, was thus a product of the European balance of power.[11]

Other attempts to bring the constitutional architecture of Britain and its dependencies into line with strategic imperatives were less successful. To be sure, the Protestant Succession had been secured in Ireland in the 1690s, and was not seriously contested during the War of the Spanish Succession. All the same, Ireland remained a worry, and its parliament a distraction. Plans for a Union in 1703 came to nothing. It would take another European conflict, a century later, to effect the Irish Union in 1801. Moreover, few had even begun to think of the constitutional architecture of the overseas empire and its strategic dimensions. For the moment, the American colonists were left to fend for themselves, paying for fortifications and levies out of their own revenues, under the direction of governors appointed by London. On the other side of the world the English East India Company, which was increasingly a branch of the state, paid for common defence out of its own budget. In time, London statesmen would regret this neglect. If the pressures of the European state system had forged the Union with Scotland, they were later to drive Britain and its thirteen American colonies to war and separation.[12]

War and foreign policy were also central to the burgeoning early-eighteenth-century British public sphere of pamphleteering, books and coffee-house debate, in which the nearly 50 per cent of the population who were literate could participate. Foreign news – often translated French or Dutch reports – generally took up the first page of a newspaper, and indeed dominated the press in general. Partisan sheets such as the Tory *Post Boy* (circulation of 4,000 per issue), and the Whig *Flying Post* (400 per issue) and the *Post Man* (3,000 per issue) widely disseminated news of the latest diplomatic and military developments. Most appeared three times a week. It is estimated that each issue was read by about 100 people after being displayed in coffee houses or handed around between friends. This means that there was a critical public of perhaps hundreds – certainly of tens – of thousands in Britain who followed developments in Europe very closely, partly in order to make informed decisions about trade and investments, but principally because of the national obsession with containing Louis and his designs for universal monarchy. Nowhere else in Europe, with the exception of the Dutch Republic, was there such a vibrant public sphere in which questions of foreign policy and grand strategy were the subject of intensive discussion. Joseph Addison satirized these obsessions in 1709, when he remarked that the situation of these armchair strategists was:

more hard than that of the soldiers, considering that they have taken more towns, and fought more battles. They have been upon parties and skirmishes, when our armies have lain still; and given the general assault to many a place, when the besiegers were quiet in their trenches. They have made us masters of several strong towns many weeks before our generals could do it; and completed victories, when our greatest captains have been glad to come off with a drawn battle ... It is impossible for this ingenious sort of men to subsist after a peace: every one remembers the shifts they were taken to in the reign of King Charles the Second, when they could not furnish out a single paper of news, without lightening up a comet in *Germany*, or a fire in *Moscow*.[13]

All this mattered, because it placed English – and after 1707, British – politicians under an obligation to justify their foreign policy to the public; and because foreign policy and grand strategy became the primary motor of party-political polarization under Queen Anne. Where one stood on the great strategic issues of the day tended to determine party-political allegiance.[14]

This public sphere was international, and thus also global in scope, but it was primarily European. At this point, it was still a commonplace that the main theatre of war was Flanders and Germany; it was there that France would primarily have to be contained. The Spanish and Italian theatres of war were also considered far more important than the naval and overseas struggle. It was not a time, therefore, of great English naval heroes. The captor of Gibraltar, Sir George Rooke, was reasonably well known, but Sir Cloudesley Shovell, the commander of the Mediterranean was hardly a household name. Most English observers, by contrast, were familiar with the great allied commanders such as Louis of Baden and Prince Eugene of Savoy. The darling of most Britons, of course, was the Duke of Marlborough. His cause was actively promoted by Whig pamphleteers such as Francis Hare, who from July 1704 also acted as chaplain and confidant to the Duke. Everybody knew about the victory at Blenheim, and at Ramilies two years later, but Marlborough was also famous for his diplomatic triumphs. The most spectacular of these was in 1707, when the Swedish king, Charles XII – fresh from triumphs against the Russians and Poles in the Baltic – threatened to burst on the western and central European scene. He had just worsted the King of Saxony-Poland and imposed the humiliating Treaty of Altranstädt on him. It appeared as if the Great Northern War was about to merge into the War of the Spanish Succession and thus into one great European conflagration.

3. A playing card depicting the great victory that became known as Blenheim, which banished the French from the Holy Roman Empire.

Marlborough recognized the danger at once. His fear was that Charles – who was an ally of France – might press on into Germany in support of Louis. In order to persuade him to remain neutral towards the Grand Alliance, Marlborough travelled in person to the Saxon town of Altranstädt in order to reason with Charles XII in 1707–8. To London's immense relief, the Swedish king was persuaded, leaving Germany in 1708, never to return. Here Marlborough showed himself as the consummate grand strategist with a view of the whole chessboard, not simply the military theatre for which he was immediately responsible. It was one of many educations which the War of the Spanish Succession offered to Britons in the interconnectedness of various parts of the

European state system. The lesson of the past century, and especially of the 1690s – that English security depended on an integrated understanding of the European system as a whole – was resoundingly confirmed.

For various reasons, 1706–7 proved to be the high point of Britain's war effort in Europe. Things began to go wrong thereafter. The Rakoczy rising of disaffected Hungarians, which had begun in 1703, continued to divert Austrian efforts from the main front against France. But the real bone of contention was the fate of British armies in Europe. Oudenaarde (1708) was a victory, but not a decisive one. It had been preceded by a crushing defeat of the Archduke Charles's forces at Almanza in Spain. Peace feelers were put out. While flexible in general, Louis remained stubborn on the Spanish question. The allies, in turn, were determined to unbolt Philip from the Spanish throne. In December 1707 the arch-Whig Lord Somers carried a resolution stipulating 'that no peace could be honourable or safe . . . if Spain and the Spanish West Indies were suffered to continue in the power of the House of Bourbon'. 'No peace without Spain' became henceforth the watchword. Peace negotiations at Gertruydenberg and The Hague in 1709–10 therefore petered out. This was partly because the Whig negotiators pitched their demands of Louis too high. He offered to surrender Alsace, and to recognize Charles as King of Spain; but the allies remained unpersuaded. They were mindful of Louis's bad faith on earlier occasions. They insisted on the immediate ejection of Anjou by French troops – an impossible demand – and the evacuation of Mons and Namur in Flanders as pledges of good behaviour.[15]

The continued determination to contain France was reflected in the Barrier Treaty with the United Provinces in 1709, which was designed to bolster Flanders against French incursions. The commercial terms, which allowed the Dutch a share of the South American trade, were not favourable to Britain. The strategic benefits, however, were massive: the Dutch agreed to garrison a string of fortresses in the Low Countries – including Maubeuge, Charleroi, Namur, Dendermonde, Ghent, Nieuport and Tournai – in order to deter a French attack on Flanders. The Dutch also promised to supply troops to defend the Protestant Succession in Britain itself if needed. These were the prizes to which economic concerns were sacrificed; indeed, the commercial clauses of the Barrier Treaty were primarily designed to put the Dutch in the financial position to fulfil their military obligations. The Whigs were thereby continuing the seventeenth-century Protestant and patriot discourse, which had always been prepared to forego commercial gain in search of ideological and strategic common ground with the Dutch. At the same time, Whig strategists looked beyond the Low Countries to the German Empire, in order prevent the barrier from being outflanked. As the western principalities of the Empire never tired of pointing out, Germany itself required a barrier, perhaps pivoting on the Alsatian fortresses of Schlettstadt, Colmar and Bitsch. This was the impulse behind Marlborough's efforts to keep the 'imperial' contingents in the allied armies up to strength. The Whigs were thus putting in place another key pillar of Britain's eighteenth-century geopolitical architecture in Europe: a holistic view of British security based on an interlocking series of barriers across western Germany and Flanders.[16]

Most Tories remained unconvinced by this strategy; in that respect not much had changed since the 1690s. Because many of them remained deeply sceptical of the Glorious Revolution, or at least of the entourage which had accompanied William to England, they were naturally inclined to despise the Dutch anyway. Their leader, Robert Harley, dismissed the Whig obsession with the Barrier as a 'remote' rather than an 'immediate' issue and considered the land war a waste of men and money. Tories were also outraged by the Barrier Treaties of 1709, which granted Holland important trading privileges at Britain's expense. Moreover, it was becoming clear to them that Louis XIV would not buckle under the allied assault, and that victory in Spain was a chimera. During the early years of the war, the Tories had fallen silent: they had been comprehensively discredited by their failure to anticipate the Spanish Succession crisis, and many of them agreed with Marlborough's Continental strategy. As British military fortunes in Europe waned, however, the Tory strategic analysis waxed. In September 1709 the hard-fought Battle of Malplaquet convinced many that a decisive victory in Flanders was remote. Its impact was more political and psychological than military. English casualties were not particularly high – some 600 fatalities and 1,300 wounded – but a public spoiled by a diet of victories now despaired. In November 1709 Henry Sacheverell gave a provocative sermon in St Paul's, attacking the government for tolerating Dissenters, a recognized code for a general assault on the ministry. His subsequent trial by Parliament inflamed the London mob, which rampaged through the City attacking the Bank of England and Dissenting meeting houses to cries of 'Sacheverell and peace'. Moreover, the war in Spain now began to go seriously wrong. In late 1710 the allied cause there suffered a double defeat: a British force under General James Stanhope was defeated at Brihuega and its commander captured; the Austrian expeditionary force of Archduke Charles was worsted at Villa Viciosa. But by then a war-weary public and monarch had pulled the rug from under the Whigs and their Continental strategy.[17]

Fed up with the mantra about staying the course against Louis, Anne sacked her Whig ministers and turned to the Tories under their leader, Robert Harley. If her hope had been to construct a more pliable ministry of moderate Whigs and Tories, she was sorely disappointed. In October 1710 Tory extremists formed the 'October Club' for a quick peace, even at the expense of Britain's allies. At the subsequent elections in late 1710 the Whigs were routed; withdrawal from the Continent was more popular than the Whig determination to fight on. The 'moneyed interest', by which Tories meant the fiscal-military complex supporting the war, came under sustained public attack. A blizzard of parliamentary enquiries into the conduct of the war, and even impeachments, seemed likely. The Tories were determined to wind down the land war and give greater priority to naval and colonial expansion. The new Secretary of State for the Northern Department, Henry St John, was a confirmed opponent of the war in Flanders, hated the Dutch and was a vocal Austrophobe to boot. A bitter high-political and public debate about the British commitment to Europe now erupted which was to set the tone for the rest of the eighteenth century.[18]

The first priority for the Tories was to knock Marlborough, the hero of Britain's European policy and the avatar of the Protestant cause, off the pedestal carefully constructed by Whig propagandists. There were to be many assassins, but none more effective than the writer and Tory polemicist Jonathan Swift. In his famous diatribe, *The conduct of the allies*, first published in November 1711, Swift sought to discredit both the course of British foreign policy and the domestic structures designed to underpin it. His work had the support not only of Henry St John, but also of the new chief minister Robert Harley, who was busy mobilizing the press against war and the former administration. It made an immediate impact. Like a handful of other eighteenth-century pamphlets on foreign policy, *The conduct of the allies* was not only the subject of general public discussion but was also frequently cited in parliamentary debates on grand strategy. Swift himself boasted that 'the House of

Commons have this day made many severe votes about our being abused by our allies; those who spoke drew all their arguments from my book, and their votes confirm all I writ.'[19]

Swift lampooned the idea that Britain was primarily responsible for the European balance of power. If the balance mattered as much as the Whigs claimed, he asked, why were its Continental beneficiaries – and here he had the hated Dutch specifically in mind – not pulling their weight? Surely there was nothing at stake in the war – apart from repelling the Pretender – which did not equally or more obviously concern other European powers. Why should Britain have to act as their advocate, and pay them for what they should be doing on their own account in any case? 'If a house be on fire,' Swift reasoned, 'it behoves all in the neighbourhood to run with buckets to quench it; but the owner is sure to be undone first, and it is not impossible that those at next door may escape by a shower from heaven, or the stillness of the weather, or some other favourable accident.' This was classic strategic Micawberism: there was no need to take a decision or to expose oneself for the common good, because something might turn up.

Moreover, Swift completely rejected the prevailing preoccupation with the security of the Low Countries. Of all of Louis's provocations in 1701, which included Philip's acceptance of the Spanish crown, and the occupation of Milan and Flanders, he would allow only recognition of the Pretender as something 'directly relating to us'. It was an astonishing statement which made sense only within a strategic framework in which the principal threat to British interests came not from France but the United Provinces. Indeed, maintaining the 'barrier' against Louis, Swift argued, only caused further damage. He wrote that making 'the Dutch in effect . . . entire Masters of all the Low Countries' would enable them to turn it into a trading and manufacturing powerhouse. 'And as they increase their trade,' he continued, 'it is obvious they will enlarge their strength at sea, and that ours must lessen in proportion.' Swift – and the Tories – were reverting to classic Stuart grand strategy. Because they conceived of Britain's national interest in primarily commercial terms, they saw the Dutch as mortal rivals, not partners against French universal monarchy. The seventeenth-century arguments about the right balance between ideological, economic and strategic considerations were being waged anew.

Swift attacked not only the substance but also the tone of Britain's

European policy. The early successes against France, he argued, had produced a fatal hubris among the Whigs. Swift lamented that '[O]ur victories early only served to lead us on to further visionary prospects, advantage was taken of the sanguinary temper which so many successes had wrought the nation up to; new romantic views were proposed, and the old, reasonable sober design was forgot.' Rather than settle for the excellent terms on offer at Gertruydenberg, he complained, Britain – at Dutch behest – had elected to fight on in the hope of total victory. Moreover, he argued, the consequences of this failed strategy for British domestic politics were wholly negative. The land war was being paid for by taxes on the landed interest, while the commercial lobbies linked to the ministry made fat profits. Swift lamented that 'the grossest impositions have been submitted to, for the advancement of private wealth and power, or in order to forward the more dangerous designs of a faction, to both which a peace would have put an end.' Swift, in fact, was fundamentally dismissive of the idea of public credit, which he thought specious insofar as it was not based on 'growth and product of land'. He therefore took aim at the fiscal-military complex: 'that set of people who are called the moneyed men; such as had raised vast sums by trading with stocks and funds, and lending upon great interest and premiums; whose perpetual harvest is war, and whose beneficial way of traffic must very much decline by a peace'. The classic Tory link between funny money and foreign war was thus made explicit.

Furthermore, Swift saw in the London public sphere simply an echo chamber in which arguments in support of Britain's true interests resonated unheard. 'It is the folly of too many,' he remarked, 'to mistake the echo of a London coffee house for the voice of the kingdom. The city coffee houses have been for some years filled with people whose fortunes depend upon the Bank, East India, or some other Stock.' In short, for Swift the whole fiscal-military complex which had developed to support the wars against Louis XIV was a racket designed to enrich foreign carpet-baggers and shady financiers. It was a system weighted against the 'landed interest', and perhaps less intuitively, Britain's maritime mission. He accused the ministry of spending 'all our vigour in pursuing that part of the war which could least' deliver a decisive result, that is the land war in Flanders. The naval war, he insisted, was 'the part of the war which was chiefly our province', and it was there that Englishmen could 'enrich' themselves; 'the sea,' he claimed, was Britain's 'element' and the 'perpetual maxims of our government' should be to privilege sea warfare over that on land. According to Swift's reading, the recent history of England was a retreat from her naval and commercial destiny. During the Nine Years War, he complained, 'the sea was almost entirely neglected, and the greatest part of six millions annually employed to enlarge the frontier of the Dutch, for the King was a general, not an Admiral, and although King of England, was a native of Holland'. There was, in short, something foreign and suspicious about the commitment to the European balance, at least if it involved Britain in a land war on the Continent; and perhaps even about land warfare in general.

Many rose to Marlborough's defence and that of the ministry, but none more doggedly than his chaplain, the Whig apologist Francis Hare. He argued that only the maintenance of a European balance of power would deter Versailles from overturning the Revolution settlement and restoring the Stuarts. This principle underlay his rejection of peace negotiations in 1709–10 with a French monarch whom he regarded as simply untrustworthy. Anyone who was familiar with Louis XIV's volte-face on the Spanish Partition Treaties and the Pretender in 1700–1701, the argument ran, could not regard his assurances with anything other than deep suspicion. 'France,' Hare wrote, 'has been guilty of the Breach of Publick faith on so many occasions, that it is hard to find an instance to the contrary.' Like many Whigs, but in contrast to Swift, Hare saw Britain not as a property in detached splendour, but as an end-of-terrace house whose tenants could not be indifferent to events next door, or even a few doors down. In *The allies and the late ministry defended*, Hare wrote that

'Twould be a pretty sight when a house is on fire, to have a consultation held in the neighbourhood what each should do towards extinguishing it, and if it should be seriously debated how many buckets and hands each should employ, and the council should in the end in this wise resolve, that the number of buckets and the hands should be in exact proportion to the nearness each was at to the house where the fire began.

The Channel, in other words, could not be relied on as a firebreak. The conflagration would have to be dealt with well before it had got out of control. But if Hare and the other Whig propagandists could soften Swift's blow, they were unable to parry it. *The conduct of the allies* – and its many imitators – had inflicted intellectual, rhetorical and political damage from which the interventionist camp never fully recovered before the end of the war. Marlborough himself, fearful of impeachment and for his personal safety, fled England for the United Provinces at the end of 1712.[20]

From 1710, the Tories put their alternative strategy into operation. Salvation would be sought not through European alliances or Dutch finance, but by concentration on overseas expansion and naval activism, a strategy later described as a 'blue water' policy. St John showed a profound interest in colonial and commercial matters, often consulting the Board of Trade on diplomatic issues. Because his ministry could not rely on credit from the Whig-dominated Bank of England and East India Company, Robert Harley encouraged the creation of the South Sea Company in 1711. For all the Swiftian rhetoric about the moneyed interest, the Company was actually much more of a governmental and monopolistic enterprise than its Whig rivals. The basis of its operations were trading privileges within the Spanish colonial empire, rather than European and Indian trade. This sent a strong signal of where Britain's strategic priorities would henceforth lie. A vigorous attack on Bourbon colonial possessions would now be the order of the day. The war and British finance would continue to work in synergy, only now the focus would be on maritime and colonial expansion, rather than the European balance.[21]

To Tory strategists, the security of the North American colonies was the pressing overseas concern. Here the French stronghold of Quebec on the St Lawrence River had long been a bone in the throat, which an attack in the 1690s had failed to dislodge. This was also the view of the nascent American and transatlantic public sphere. For the moment, this spoke with a faint voice, but its views on grand strategy were to become ever more important as the century progressed. In 1708 the Scottish-born Boston grandee, Samuel Vetch demanded the capture of Quebec in his memorandum to the London government, 'Canada Surveyed'. It was, he argued, the 'new Carthage'. A few years later the Bostonian Jeremiah Dummer, who resided in London as Agent for Massachusetts, called upon Britons to secure North America once and for all. He wrote of the 'necessity there is for dislodging the French at Canada, to secure our commerce and colonies on the northern continent'. Only this would secure New England from daily attack by the 'the French and Frenchified Indians'. Otherwise, the British colonists were 'in danger of being driven out of the country, if the French power increases'. All this was bad enough, but the even greater risk was that French penetration of the North American interior would allow Louis to link up his Canadian territories with French settlements on the Mississippi, thus encircling the twelve British colonies. By the construction of the settlements at Detroit and Mobile, Samuel Vetch warned, the French 'have surrounded and hemmed in betwixt them and the sea all the English governments upon the [American] continent'. This would sooner or later lead to the expulsion of the British. After the triumph of the Tories in 1710, these lobbyists saw their chance. In early January 1711 Dummer repeated his call for Canada – 'the American Carthage' – to be 'subdued'.[22]

For all these reasons British strategists turned their attention to the reduction of French Canada during 1710–11. The instructions for Robert Hunter, the Captain General and Governor, in February 1711 show just how successful American and Tory lobbyists had been in persuading the ministry. These noted that the French 'encircle all our plantations on the continent of North America, by which (if not prevented) they may in time dispossess us thereof'. The purpose of the expedition, therefore, was to 'remove' the French and secure to Britain a 'nursery of seamen' through the Newfoundland fisheries, and 'naval stores sufficient to serve all Europe'. Here colonial expansion was not simply an opportunistic programme to enrich Tory cronies, but a forward-looking strategy of pre-emption to secure the future of British North America. The old Stuart policy of forestalling French 'encirclement' was about to experience a revival. But the option for America was also a decision against Europe. In a separate letter to Hunter, St John set out the broader strategic framework within which the Quebec operation was conceived. He complained that Britain had 'exhausted itself' financially and militarily in defence of the Spanish crown and the Dutch Barrier 'as if we were defending provinces of our own'. It was 'now high time,' he said, 'to do something in particular for Britain'. The colonial vista which St John set out was to remain a staple of Tory strategic thinking and rhetoric for the rest of the century. 'If one supposes the French driven out from Canada,' he enthused, 'and the Queen mistress of the whole continent of North America, such a scene opens itself, that the man who is not charmed with it must be void of all sense of the honour, of the grandeur, and of the prosperity of his country.'[23]

The ground had been prepared carefully enough. A Mohawk

delegation of the 'Five Nations' Indians to London in 1710 was treated with great seriousness. They were courted by the government; treated to a performance of *Macbeth* at the Haymarket; had a copy of the Bible individually thrust into their hands by the Archbishop of Canterbury; and generally caused a popular surge of interest in all things American. The purpose behind this charade, of course, was strategic: to persuade the Mohawks to open the land corridor for an attack on the French colony of Quebec from the south. That was the easy bit: the operation itself, which went ahead in 1711, was a total disaster. The naval commander, Sir Hovenden Walker, blundered on to the rocks in the approaches to the city, lost hundreds of men through drowning, suffered an attack of nerves, and turned back. The land force under General Hill, hearing of this, did likewise. It was to be by no means the last eighteenth-century colonial and amphibious military fiasco. The whole episode did nothing to shake the Whig conviction that wars against European powers were to be fought and won in Europe.[24]

This was a bad start for Tory grand strategy and the 'blue water' policy, but it was in Europe that the impact of the new ministry was to be most lastingly felt. In 1710 Parliament for the first time refused to congratulate Marlborough on his campaign that year. In January 1711 the House of Lords censured the previous ministry and its commanders for the disasters in Spain. The war in Flanders was progressively starved of men and supplies; five battalions were withdrawn in order to support General Hill's attack on Quebec. In February Parliament repudiated the Barrier Treaty with the Dutch; the new treaty negotiated in January 1713 involved fewer fortresses and was commercially less beneficial to the United Provinces. The retreat from Europe had begun. That said, Tory policy towards Europe was not simply one of disengagement; it also reflected a profound shift in the balance itself. For in mid April 1711 the German emperor, Joseph I, died unexpectedly. He was succeeded as Holy Roman Emperor in October of that year by his brother Charles, the allied candidate for the Spanish throne. The Tories now saw the spectre of a united Austro-Spanish bloc which would certainly wreck the balance of power in the Mediterranean and might even lead to a revival of the empire of Charles V. 'By this accident,' Swift wrote, 'the views and interests of several powers and states in the alliance have taken a new turn.' He explained that 'To have a prince of the Austrian family on the throne of Spain is undoubtedly more desirable than one of the House of Bourbon, but to have the [German] Empire and Spanish monarchy united in the same person is a dreadful consideration,' and contrary not merely to the spirit but the letter of the Grand Alliance. As St John observed in 1711, 'If the Empire and the dominions of Spain are to unite in the person of this prince [Charles], the system of the war is essentially altered.'[25]

Conveniently for the Tories, it was now plausible to leave Philip in Spain and bring the war to a speedy conclusion. Something had indeed turned up: this was the 'shower from heaven', the 'favourable accident', to which Swift had referred. The arch-Whig Daniel Defoe, for one, was persuaded. In a pamphlet of May 1711 he warned 'of the injury a too great accumulation of power to the House of Austria may bring upon us in ages to come'. He now brought his organ, the *Review*, which had been founded in 1704 with the express purpose of scourging Louis XIV, over to the cause of peace. Defoe also tried to rally moderate Whigs and religious dissenters behind Harley on the new danger of a Habsburg preponderance. He did this not because he was an opportunist who set his sails according to the prevailing winds, but because the changes in European politics warranted a rethink in grand strategy. But many other Whigs disagreed. To them, French power was so enormous that it required an equally powerful Habsburg bloc to balance it. For this reason, they had accepted in 1703 that the Austrian candidate to the Spanish throne should succeed to the entire inheritance; this bullet had already been bitten. Hare argued in November 1711 'that the Emperor, with all his hereditary countries, and the entire Spanish monarchy, would not yet be equal, much less superior to France alone'. One way or the other, the divide between Tories and Whigs in 1711–13 was not simply one between navalists and Continentalists. It was also about differing conceptions of the European balance and how it should be upheld. In the end, the argument for peace became irresistible because it appeared to satisfy those who believed that the original aim of upholding the balance had been achieved; it appealed to the large number of Tories who wanted to humiliate the Whigs, and those who were simply weary of war. Britain began to bail out of the war, and abandon her allies, not because she had been militarily defeated, but because the strategic paradigm with which she had begun the conflict was believed to have failed.[26]

Harley had begun secret talks with the French as early as the autumn of 1710. In April 1711, the Tory negotiators agreed the outlines of a peace, according to which Philip would remain King of Spain, Charles and the Austrians would be compensated with territory in Italy, the 'barrier' would be maintained, but the Dutch excluded from all South American trade. In order to strengthen his negotiating position, Harley stepped up the tempo of military operations. Ironically his pet project, the Quebec Expedition, was a complete fiasco, whereas the despised Marlborough secured some notable successes in his remaining months as supreme commander in Flanders. By September 1711 the 'preliminary articles' of peace were public. It now became clear that Britain would secure the *Asiento* for the slave trade to the Spanish colonies, vital to Harley's own economic and fiscal vision. She would also retain her colonial gains in North America. From the colonial or 'blue water' perspective, therefore, it looked as if there would be much to celebrate.

Among those concerned with the European balance, and Britain's Continental 'counterscarp', however, there was profound alarm. It was only with some difficulty that Harley managed to secure the vital Barrier in the Low Countries. Louis had wanted the Elector of Bavaria to exchange his territory for the Spanish Netherlands. This would have paid off a luckless ally and given Louis a clear run against the Dutch. The barrier eventually secured was less satisfactory than the treaty of 1709, but better than Ryswick. In general, the Tories showed themselves much less concerned about the security of the Low Countries, and St John, or Viscount Bolingbroke as he had now become, even showed himself willing to let Louis have the bitterly contested fortress of Tournai in Flanders. Moreover, the Whigs complained that the guarantees concerning the separation of the French and Spanish crowns were far from watertight. They were not reassured by the rapid demise in 1711–12 of the French princes in the line of succession; with each of Louis's bereavements, Philip of Spain seemed to edge closer to the French succession. The Whigs would have been even more aghast had they known for certain what they then only suspected: that Britain was in the process of a unilateral withdrawal from the war. Right at the end of December 1711 Marlborough was sacked as allied supreme commander. His replacement, the Duke of Ormonde, effectively wound down the war against France from January of the following year. He did not, however, deign to inform the Austrians and Dutch, who were thus left to twist precariously in the wind. In May 1712 Ormonde was issued with the subsequently notorious 'restraining orders', by which he was instructed to desist from combat operations against the French. As a result, the Austrians and Dutch were beaten two months later at the Battle of Denain. Harley would have preferred to act in tandem with the allies, but his fellow Tory Bolingbroke positively revelled in Britain's new unilateral course. When the French asked him what they should do if they encountered the imperial commander – Prince Eugene, a hero second only to Marlborough for many Britons – Bolingbroke replied brutally: 'Fall on him and cut him to pieces.'[27]

Not surprisingly, the Dutch and Austrians were aghast at these negotiations when they learned of them. So too was the Elector of Hanover, who was only one heartbeat away from the English throne. He protested vigorously that the preliminaries of peace were a breach of the Grand Alliance which would allow Louis to impose the Pretender on Britain. He wrote in November 1711 that 'The most solid foundation, upon which the present and future posterity of Great Britain, and indeed of all Europe, can be established, is to humble France.' It was, of course, in George's interest to oppose a separate peace, in order to maintain the diplomatic isolation of the Jacobites and the upkeep of an army which could be used to enforce the Hanoverian succession. Moreover George himself had been present at the Battle of Denain – where he had nearly lost his life to Bolingbroke's treachery. It gave him a personal object lesson in the dangers of British disengagement from Europe. The Hanoverians therefore began to take a very keen interest in British politics. George repeatedly floated the idea of sending his son, the future Prince of Wales (and George II) ahead in order to secure the succession. Perhaps understandably, Queen Anne baulked at this blunt anticipation of her own mortality. Undeterred, the Hanoverian envoy to London, Baron Bothmer, tirelessly reminded the ministry of Hanoverian concerns, so much so that Harley complained to George about unwarranted meddling. The main concern of the future King of England was not just to safeguard his inheritance, but also to ensure that Britain could continue to play a positive role in the maintenance of the European balance of power. It was for that reason that the Whigs had invited William of Orange to take the throne, and for that same reason that he had accepted. In short, the Hanoverians would ascend the throne in 1714 not just to secure English freedoms, but to defend the 'liberties of Europe' against France.[28]

The final Treaty of Utrecht, which was concluded in April 1713, reflected Tory concerns. Philip was left in Spain, but the two royal houses were never to be united; many doubted, however, whether Philip could be made to renounce a fundamental right to the French throne. Britain's Catalan allies were not only left to their fate, but the Royal Navy was sent to bludgeon Barcelona into submitting to Philip. Charles was compelled to surrender his claims to the Spanish throne, and was confined to his Austrian possessions. In compensation, he was awarded the former Spanish Netherlands, which would serve as a renewed barrier against French expansion; Dutch troops would man the border fortresses. Britain won monopoly rights to trade with the Spanish Empire, especially the coveted *Asiento*. These commercial benefits were exclusive to Britain, unlike the treaty of 1709, when Townshend had granted the Dutch a half share in order to keep them in the war. Britain's naval position in the Mediterranean was buttressed by the retention of Gibraltar and Minorca, which had been captured during the war. For the first time since the reign of Charles II, Britain now had a foothold in southern Europe. Yet the Treaty was to come under ferocious attack, not just for partisan reasons.

The Whigs condemned what they regarded as the high-handed betrayal of Britain's allies in the negotiations that had led up to the Treaty. As Hare wrote to the Duchess of Marlborough in October 1713, ' 'Tis the cause of Europe you have made your own ... The [Tory newspaper] *Examiner* would not have us look abroad or trouble ourselves with foreign affairs.' 'Some of us,' he continued, 'can't help pitying the Catalans & the poor emperor, & ... the Dutch.' He finished by remarking that 'Heaven can only clear up this dark scene, or knows what it will end in. Nothing human can deliver people from the dangers that threaten, who seem to think of nothing less than delivering themselves.' Hare and most Whigs believed that the Tories had put the European balance, the crucial Dutch Barrier, and thus the security of Britain in mortal danger. Indeed, the determination not to repeat the mistakes of the Tory administration was to underlie much of British policy towards Europe after 1714. When the Whigs returned with George I, their first priority was not to demand more on the nation's behalf, but to try to rebuild her battered alliances. Their critique was not that Britain had not secured enough for itself, but that the Treaty had not secured enough for her allies. 'Utrecht', indeed, was to have a long afterlife in British political polemic well into the eighteenth century.[29]

During the strange strategic interregnum between the signing of Utrecht in early 1713 and the death of Queen Anne a little over a year later, the Tory ministry discovered how difficult it was to manage Europe without effective allies. For example, Bolingbroke was much concerned to shore up Sweden against Russia in the Baltic in order to maintain the balance of power there, and safeguard the supply of vital naval stores from the area. Here the help of the Austrians and Dutch, in the Holy Roman Empire and in naval matters respectively, was crucial, and withheld. Bolingbroke also ran into difficulty in Italy, where he was determined to contain Austrian power. In order to do so, he promoted the Duchy of Savoy as a counterweight, and even sought to join them with the French into a triple alliance against Vienna. As a true Tory, Bolingbroke put his faith in the Royal Navy, 'instead of running into the extravagant ruinous schemes of maintaining armies on the Continent'. This was all well and good, as far as the defence of the new Savoyard territory of Sicily was concerned, but it was of no use at all with regard to Savoy itself, which was where the main Austrian blow could be expected to fall. In spite of these problems, Tory diplomats remained relatively unconcerned about Britain's isolation. In March 1714 Matthew Prior, the envoy to the French court, rejoiced that 'England is once more free from foreign entanglements, and in a possibility of being a happy nation.'[30]

It was only as Queen Anne's health progressively declined, and the prospect of the Hanoverian succession moved ever closer, that some Tories began to realize that their grand strategy was leaving them dangerously exposed politically. Harley made a last ditch attempt to rebuild relations with the Emperor. The veteran diplomat Charles Whitworth was sent to Germany in July 1714 with the instruction to seek connections with 'those princes and states who were confederated in the last war'. This transparent attempt to escape nemesis at the hands of the reversionary interest – the expectation of compensating for disfavour under the reigning monarch by a privileged position under his son and heir – got nowhere. The worsening decrepitude of Anne now paralysed the Tory ministry. By the summer of 1714 Harley had lapsed from opportunism into apathy. In late July his envoy to France had been left uninstructed for so long that he wrote to Harley, asking him to clarify whether he was still 'the minister of Great Britain'. He pleaded that 'Matthew should be writ to, his conduct ... directed, and his actions justified before he leaves this court by the person who sent him to it.' For it did not require much imagination to see that the resurgent Whigs accompanying George would initiate a spate of impeachments. In the meantime, Bolingbroke ploughed on with the quest for a grand alliance between France, Savoy, Spain and Britain against Austria, and seemed on the verge of concluding it that summer. He knew that only a rapprochement with Louis or a return of the Pretender could preserve him from the terrible wrath of the Whigs. In the end the clock simply ran out.[31]

For the Dutch and the Austrians were not the only aggrieved parties at Utrecht. Another was the Elector of Hanover, Georg Ludwig, who had been one of Louis XIV's most determined adversaries. He never forgave the Tories for abandoning the common cause, and was further repelled by Bolingbroke's support for Savoy, whose prince still entertained a claim to the throne of England. George also fell out with them in 1713–14 over the future of Sweden, a French ally, which the Tories wanted to preserve as a Protestant bastion in the north, but which he planned to despoil first. The winding down of the war and the unravelling of the Tory administration thus moved in tandem throughout 1714. The Dutch had folded at Utrecht itself; the Emperor fought on until March, when he concluded the Treaty of Rastadt with France. The Empire itself, and thus the Elector of Hanover, finally buried the hatchet at the Treaty of Baden shortly after, in September of that year. By then Queen Anne and the dowager Electress of Hanover were both dead a month, and George had been proclaimed King of England.

Queen Anne's ministries had achieved much. They had seen off the challenge of French universal monarchy, pushed through the union with Scotland and secured the Hanoverian succession. All the same, the issues which confronted their successors after 1714 were very similar to those which had dogged them. The Stuart pretender to the throne, 'James III', and later his heir Charles Edward, the 'Bonnie Prince', remained a constant presence for the first sixty years of the century. It was already obvious that French power was still formidable, and France remained, with the exception of a lengthy interlude between 1716 and 1731, Britain's main enemy throughout the century. There were also emerging threats to the east and south in the shape of Russia, a resurgent Spain, and in the 1720s even Austria. The forces available to repel these threats were stretched to the limit. The Whig executive and the monarchy had difficulties in persuading the political nation to pay for any sort of standing army, at least in peacetime. Whereas Parliament had agreed to pay for nearly 150,000 soldiers at the end of the War of the Spanish Succession in 1712, this was down to some 16,000 in 1714. Only half of these had been British; the rest were mercenaries or subsidized allies. The numbers mobilized in Britain itself – some 75,000 – compared poorly to the wartime performance of France, with some 350,000 men under arms; the Habsburg monarchy with 100,000; Russia with 220,000; and Holland with 130,000. Moreover, even if all the stops were pulled out, Britain simply did not command even the potential manpower to match France: it had some 6 million inhabitants in 1715 (excluding Ireland) against some 20 million in France. In an age which still measured state power largely in terms of population, as well as financial muscle, this was a sobering fact.[32]

On the other hand, the men who ran British foreign policy inherited the most advanced national security apparatus of the time. In the course of the late seventeenth century England had developed the most powerful navy in Europe. This was paid for through an unrivalled system of public credit. The Bank of England was the most visible sign of this; but the real strength of the structure lay in the efficient and largely consensual relationship between the political nation as represented in Parliament, the bureaucracy collecting the taxes voted, and the population as a whole. No other European state, certainly not her shambolic French rival, achieved such a degree of internal cohesion and financial rationality. It was a polity programmed for commerce and war.

More important still than this apparatus of credit was the strategic culture inherited by British statesmen after 1714. Most of them were profoundly convinced of the need to prevent the emergence of a single hegemon who might threaten their naval position, the integrity of the Low Countries and thus their own security. Britons referred not just to the 'balance of power', but to the 'Protestant interest' or 'the liberties of Europe', as well. The 'Protestant interest' came to mean less the fate of Protestants everywhere in Europe (a plausible interpretation for the sixteenth and early seventeenth century) than the containment of Roman Catholic designs on universal monarchy. The language of the 'Protestant interest' thus became a means of defending intervention in Europe. The 'liberties of Europe' referred not to the constitutional rights of all Europeans, but to the balance of power essential to English and later British liberties. At the same time, the liberties of Europe were believed to depend on those of England/Britain, because – paradoxically – the absolutist Stuarts were seen as weak tyrants, terrible to defenceless subjects but a laughing stock to the other European powers. The 'balance of power' was the secularized 'Protestant interest'; the two terms were used interchangeably at first, until the latter fell into disuse. It was a creed to which almost all strands of British political life subscribed, with Whigs believing that it could be maintained only by direct and sustained – often military – engagement in Europe, while Tories generally believed that naval measures would suffice and would countenance the dispatch of land forces only with the greatest reluctance.[33]

This grand strategy was not a charter for Protestantism and constitutional liberties across Europe. To be sure, British ministries and monarchs defended their co-believers where they could, and they often sympathized with the victims of absolutism. But the 'liberties of Europe' often required Catholic alliances and the suppression of individual liberties in other European states. Thus England's principal hope of containing universal monarchy before 1660 was France; thereafter it was Austria. At the same time, England and later Britain was quite prepared to ignore the plight of oppressed subjects or fellow Protestants. This was demonstrated by the short shrift given to Hungarian Protestant dissidents under the Habsburg monarchy in the decade after 1700, and by the attempts to persuade German Protestants to play down their religious grievances against the Emperor so as not to distract him from the war against Louis. Nor was the balance of power a self-righting mechanism; it needed constant maintenance. Sometimes, this had meant taking pre-emptive and even preventive action. Pre-emptive measures were standard practice and designed to forestall an imminent threat; preventive action involved anticipating possible dangers down the line and was considered legally much more dubious. Contemplating the growth of French power and the need for a European alliance to contain it around 1700, the *Observator* claimed that 'the head of such an alliance may be compared to a pilot of long experience at sea [who] knows how to discover the storm before its coming and to prepare whatever is necessary to resist its violence.' British statesmen, parliamentarians and the public respected the norms of interstate behaviour as much as they could, but they never fetishized legality at the expense of security.

Military action was not embarked on lightly. Wherever possible, British statesmen tried to avoid the expensive, domestically unpopular and risky deployment of British forces abroad. They were particularly cautious about committing themselves across the Atlantic. If it took about two weeks for instructions to reach central Europe, it took two months to contact commanders in America. Just how badly things could go wrong had been demonstrated by the Quebec Expedition of 1711. For this reason, British statesmen far preferred to use diplomatic leverage, subsidies and alliances with other powers. During the War of the Spanish Succession, for example, Britain concluded some 130 treaties with other powers. In the course of the eighteenth century many more agreements were entered into. These arrangements required not only deep pockets to finance coalitions or mercenaries, but also an informed engagement with European states and their ways of doing business. The British diplomatic service was still highly rudimentary, but already in the early eighteenth century it could command detailed knowledge of local rivalries and structures. The public looked to the government for guidance and information; it wanted governments to anticipate crises, not merely react to them. As one prime minister, Robert Walpole, was to lament later in the century, British statesmen were expected to be 'ministers of Europe'.

For this reason, those running British foreign policy were familiar with the outlines of western and central European politics. They followed the ups and downs of court intrigues at Versailles very closely, and as we shall see they despaired of the state of Dutch domestic politics. British statesmen, particularly the Secretary of State for the Northern Department, were also profoundly conscious of the constitution of the Holy Roman Empire. But the position in Germany was also very much the province of the Secretary of State for the Southern Department, responsible for France, Spain and the Mediterranean generally. This was because the main threat to the integrity of the Empire usually came from there, and because relations with both France and Austria could not be understood in isolation from Italy or the southern balance of power as a whole. The British elite therefore knew about Europe, and particularly about the German Empire. A considerable number had fought there during the war of Grand Alliance against Louis XIV, and more would do so in the 1740s and 1750s. British statesmen frequently accompanied the King to Hanover. Embarrassing gaffes or manifest geographical ignorance were rare in the parliamentary sphere, at least before 1760. The importance of Germany was also reflected in language. To our protagonists, the 'Empire' was not a place where the sun had yet to set, but the Holy Roman Empire, that is Germany. Likewise, to eighteenth-century British statesmen the 'Electorate' was not something whose votes they periodically sought, but the Electorate of Hanover, to which Britain was bound by dynastic union and to which their monarch regularly repaired. The world British statesmen inhabited – certainly before 1760 – was still a firmly Eurocentric one. And at the heart of that world lay Britain's relationship with the German Empire, the principal bulwark against French expansionism.[34]

The eighteenth-century public sphere was also dominated by concerns about Europe, though less with the German Empire specifically. The order in which the *National Journal* directed its printers to place news items was highly revealing. In the case of 'foreign news', articles from France should be placed first, those from Spain second, Portugal third, Italy fourth, Switzerland fifth, Austria and Hungary seventh, other parts of Germany eighth, and so on. Articles from Africa were last on the list, at number fifteen. 'London news' was to be presented with 'foreign articles' in first place, and 'Articles dated from the Plantations, Gibraltar or Port Mahon [Minorca]' last, at eighth place. This was as true for the provincial as for the London press, so much so that the *Grub Street Journal* jibbed at 'the great impropriety to begin with foreign news and end with domestic . . . like travelling into foreign countries before we have taken a survey of our own'. Moreover, colonial issues tended to be seen as part of a wider European framework: even as late as the American War of Independence, the yearly digest, the *Annual Register*, recorded transatlantic developments under the heading 'The history of Europe'.[35]

In part, the centrality of Europe in British debate reflected the balance of trade. In 1711–15, Britain exported £942,000 worth of goods to the East Indies, the British West Indies, North America and Africa; exports to Flanders, France, Germany, Holland, Denmark and Norway, Poland, Prussia, Sweden, Russia, Portugal, Spain, Constantinople, Italy, Turkey and Venice were worth £5,520,000 – more than five times as much. These proportions remained more or less unchanged for the first half of the century. Even in 1736–40, at the height of public enthusiasm for colonial war and expansion, exports to the colonies amounted to

£1,819,000; those to Europe, including re-exports from the colonies, were valued at £6,838,000, more than three times as much. At mid century, when the Whig orthodoxy was beginning to disintegrate, trade with Europe was still twice as important as that with the colonies: £8,557,000 as opposed to £3,086,000. This had not changed much by 1771–5, on the eve of the American War of Independence and at the height of Britain's disengagement from Europe, when trade with Europe at £7,725,000 was still double that with the colonies (£3,939,000). It was only after the loss of the American colonies, in 1786–90, that the colonial trade drew level with that of Europe. None of this meant that British policy was driven by commercial factors. Usually the two were conceived symbiotically rather than adversarially, but when in conflict, strategic considerations almost invariably prevailed.[36]

Maritime affairs were also important in eighteenth-century Britain, but in a European rather than a 'global' context. The main priority for the Royal Navy remained home defence, with most vessels stationed in the Narrow Seas to deter invasion. Beyond that, the Navy was used in the first instance to uphold the balance of power on the Continent. In the early eighteenth century, for example, the Baltic was a far more intense focus of British naval activity than the colonies. The same is true of the Mediterranean, where there were many more British ships and men stationed than in America or India, at least prior to 1750. Moreover, naval and colonial expansion was pursued not as an end in itself, but in order to secure the resources for European power projection or to deny them to rivals. Finally, until the mid eighteenth century at any rate, British statesmen were painfully aware that the Navy was not technically in a position to blockade enemy harbours on a permanent basis, or to guarantee that an invasion force would be intercepted in time. Naval power was still a very imprecise instrument. This meant that the enemy would have to be stopped before embarkation – in short, through an active policy of diplomatic and military intervention in Europe. Sometimes this could be done far from Britain's shores, as in the preventive campaigns against Russia in the Baltic and Spain in the Mediterranean. More often, as in the case of France in the 1740s and 1750s, and Austria in the 1720s, it meant confronting the enemy in the Empire, or even in Flanders. One way or the other, the first and most important lines of defence were still on the far side of the Channel.[37]

*

Before 1760 Tory heresies were – with difficulty – contained. During this period Britain built an empire in North America and India, not at the expense of her European commitments but in harmony with them. Thereafter, buoyed by the apparent success of the 'blue water' strategy in the Seven Years War, triumphant at the exponential growth in overseas trade, the British elite increasingly turned its back on Europe. The result – as we shall see – was isolation in Europe and disaster in America. The first British empire was built by Whigs; it was lost by Tories.

II

Imperial Opportunities

3

Imperial Restoration, 1714–1715

My lords, I am now to take my leave of your lordships, and of this honourable house, perhaps for ever! I shall lay down my life with pleasure, in a cause favoured by my late dear royal mistress [Queen Anne]. And when I consider that I am to be judged by the justice, honour, and virtue of my peers, I shall acquiesce, and retire with great content: And my lords, God's will be done.[1]

The Earl of Oxford, 1715, in response to charges of impeachment against his role in the abandonment of Britain's allies at the Treaty of Utrecht

The elevation of George Louis (formerly Georg Ludwig), Elector of Hanover, to the throne of Great Britain and Ireland in 1714 was both a strategic restoration and a geopolitical revolution. The commitment of the Whigs to European alliances was resumed, and the Holy Roman Empire – the Barrier and the Habsburg alliance – was soon restored to its former importance in British grand strategy. Dissenting Tories, especially Harley (now the Earl of Oxford) and Bolingbroke, were completely marginalized. The territorial context in which this took place, however, had been fundamentally transformed. The focus of British foreign policy shifted some 300 miles eastwards. Britain's horizons were now delineated by two German rivers, the Elbe and the Weser, as much as by the English Channel, the North American Ohio River, or any other more obvious natural boundary. The mental map of British statesmen and the British public had to be redrawn or at least enlarged. To the already extensive and far-flung British possessions in America and India, the Personal Union with Hanover added a substantial slice of Northern Germany. The Union flag – scarcely seven years old – remained unchanged, but the White Horse of Hanover was to become a distinctive feature of eighteenth-century political polemic and iconography. In short, by virtue of the Hanoverian succession Britain, or Britain-Hanover, as she might now be called, lay, whether she liked it or not, at the heart of Europe. For the next forty years or so, Britain became indisputably a German power, reigned over by Germans.[2]

Some of the Germans were already there. The most powerful man in London between the death of Queen Anne and the arrival of George was the Hanoverian envoy, Hans Caspar von Bothmer. He stood by the grate burning secret letters left by the late monarch; it was he who travelled in the second carriage at the procession to mark the proclamation of George as King, just behind the Lord Chancellor but in the company of Lord Buckingham, the President of the Privy Council. Bothmer advised on the knotty question of whether George's estranged wife, Sophie Dorothea, who was under house arrest in Hanover, should be remembered in prayers every Sunday; he thought not, and she wasn't. It was Bothmer who liaised with the Whig grandees and the minority of cooperative Tories on the Regency Council to prepare for any challenge to the succession. He considered mobilizing the Royal Navy to escort George to Britain, and calling upon the Dutch to enforce the succession in accordance with their treaty obligations. And it was Bothmer who was to advise George on the composition of his first administration, together with the Whigs who had rammed though the Hanoverian succession. With the new wind from Germany at their backs, they could now shrug aside domestic obstacles to a more interventionist policy in Europe, and they could make that strategy a loyalty test with which Tory opposition at home could be neutralized.[3]

George took his time about coming to Britain. This was not – as his detractors were quick to claim – because of any reluctance to claim his inheritance. Instead, the delay resulted from his desire to make adequate provision for the governance of Hanover in his absence. This was settled through the *Reglement* of 1714, which left the day-to-day running of the Electorate in the hands of a committee of councillors. The son of the Prince of Wales, young George Frederick, the darling of his grandfather, remained in Hanover, but the Prince himself came over to England, along with his wife, the formidable Caroline of Ansbach. George now made his way across the Channel, about a month after the news of Anne's death had reached him. His appearance was greeted with popular

4. Count Bothmer was George's ambassador in London before 1714, and a powerful figure in British politics after he became king

enthusiasm, though there was some momentary slapstick when the crowds, who had mistakenly hailed the Prince of Wales's boat, drifted away just as George himself was arriving.

Along with the new monarch came more Germans: family, advisors, soldiers, servants, pages, doctors, mistresses, cooks, confectioners and the court dwarf. They totalled no more than about seventy – far fewer than the aspirant Scottish retinue which had accompanied James I in 1603. Their number paled into insignificance beside the thousands of Dutchmen who invaded England in 1688 in order to put William III on the throne. Many of those arrivals were absorbed into the English establishment. The vast majority of George's Hanoverian entourage, on the other hand, left within two years, once he had settled in. Only about twenty-odd Germans remained; they were eclipsed in numerical terms by the King's English household, which was nearly a thousand strong. By contrast with the Dutch, none were to found enduring major landed or political dynasties like William's close crony Bentinck, who became Earl of Portland.[4]

All the same, the impact of the German connection on British politics was enormous, if often misunderstood. The sometime doyen of British popular historians A. L. Rowse wrote that 'George I and George II were

Germans: their contribution to English history was a negative one, but none the less useful.' This was because 'Since neither of them spoke English, and neither was a man of much ability, the business of the state was conducted by the cabinet without the advantage of their presence.' It is true that the new King was in many obvious ways a foreign body. The Earl of Clarendon, who as British envoy to Hanover was in a good position to judge, doubted whether George knew much about his new kingdom. He had not used the decade since the Act of Settlement to learn English, and it was only with difficulty that he managed to negotiate the coronation. Unable to make the speech from the throne, he had to call upon the Lord Chancellor to do so. His knowledge of the language did improve slightly towards the end of his reign, by which time he stopped demanding that reports from British diplomats be translated into French. It is also true that the new King – born a Lutheran – was an uneasy convert to the Church of England. Nor can it be denied that George's instincts were a great deal more monarchical than the Whig lords would have liked. He claimed to rule not by any form of contract but by a hereditary right which the Stuarts had forfeited only by virtue of their Catholicism, not their alleged despotism. This was a precarious argument, of course, since it suggested that all it would require from the Pretender, 'James III', to regain the throne was a renunciation of Rome.[5]

Yet in other ways George was well suited to his new role. He had never been, as his critics were to claim, a despotic ruler in Hanover, where he collaborated closely with the local nobility. Besides, as a Prince of the Holy Roman Empire, with its panoply of imperial courts, Imperial Diet, and (at the least notional) supremacy of the Emperor, George was quite used to irksome constraints on his power; he also proved a quick learner. He worked with and through Parliament. After all, the Civil List paid only for the rudimentary civil service, the royal household, the diplomatic service and the secret service. Most other important expenditure – especially on the army and Navy – had to be approved by Parliament. Remarkably, his rule – and that of his son George II – was not marked by the destructive confrontations with Parliament that had characterized the Stuart era, and indeed characterized the relationship between many eighteenth-century German princes and their representative assemblies. No bill that had passed both houses of Parliament was refused Royal assent after 1714.

In any case, George's freedom of action had been severely limited by the Act of Settlement in 1701, the same measure in which Parliament had stipulated that the succession after Queen Anne should fall to the Electress Sophia, and thereafter to her heirs, 'being Protestants'. Article three laid down that 'no person born out of the kingdoms of England, Scotland or Ireland', even if naturalized, 'shall be capable to be of the Privy Council, or a member of either house of Parliament, or to enjoy an office or place of trust, either civil or military.' This measure was specifically designed to prevent the favouritism which had made William III's entourage so hated. Other clauses compelled George to 'join in communion with the Church of England, as by law established'; and he was even forbidden to leave Britain 'without the consent of Parliament'. This was also designed to avoid a repetition of William's military and diplomatic peregrinations through Europe. In theory, at least, George and his Hanoverians had very little room to manoeuvre.[6]

The impact of the Germans on British politics was felt elsewhere. George broke with tradition by not appointing an English nobleman as new Groom of the Stole with direct access to the royal bedchamber. His two Muslim servants, Mehmet and Mustafa, captured by him during his spell fighting the Turks in the 1690s, were charged with protecting his privacy. Both men were unusually close to the King, although there does not seem to have been anything vicious in the connection. The seventeen English Gentlemen of the Bedchamber were not, in fact, admitted there. Courtiers and others were received in the Presence Chamber; diplomats and ministers were met in the Closet, at one remove from the inner sanctum. Moreover, George liked to spend his evenings with his German family and Hanoverian entourage where his feeble English was no handicap. They all resided at St James's Palace during the winter, moving to Kensington Palace in the spring, and to Hampton Court for the summer. Apart from George himself, the major figures in the royal household were the royal mistress Melusine von der Schulenburg and her three daughters, and – for the first few years – the Prince and Princess of Wales and their three daughters.

All this led to the formation of an antechamber of power around the King in which the Germans figured prominently. Many of them fitted into their new environment remarkably well. As the Hanoverian envoy who had mediated the succession, Baron Bothmer was already well established before 1714 and was on terms of intimacy with many leading English figures. He was a regular and welcome guest at dinners with such diverse individuals as the Duke of Newcastle, Lord Berkeley, the Bishop of Salisbury, the Duke of Roxburgh, the Marquis of Annandale, and many other aristocratic luminaries. Likewise, Count Friedrich Wilhelm von der Schulenburg, *Kammerherr* (chamberlain) to the King, was a popular figure in society: one dinner with Lord Halifax lasted eleven hours so that 'the pleasant evening and the good company induced me to go beyond my usual sobriety, and amused me for a long time'. His close friend and correspondent, Baron Friedrich Wilhelm von Görtz, who returned in 1716 to head the administration in Hanover, was respected by many Whigs and Tories alike.[7]

Some of the Germans, however, were quickly recognized for their influence and ambitions. Thus Andreas Gottlieb von Bernstorff, the most senior Hanoverian minister to accompany George in 1714, soon emerged as a key figure in the new dispensation. His English social circle – which largely consisted of staunch Whigs such as Lord Cadogan, the Earl of Sunderland and James Stanhope – was limited and soon shrank. Much of the time, Bernstorff worked in close collaboration with another 'German', the King's secretary, Jean de Robethon. Robethon was, in fact, a French Protestant – or Huguenot – by descent. His influence is still the object of some dispute, but was certainly considerable. He acted as a conduit in all major negotiations, and was generally regarded as a sinister power behind the throne until his fall from grace in 1719. Jonathan Swift, admittedly a biased observer, spoke of 'a little Frenchman, without any merit or consequence, called Robethon', who had tried to blacken the Tories with George. The 'Germans' drew their authority either from their proximity to George in the King's household, or their position in the German Chancellery, in London. This office was created to conduct the Hanoverian affairs of the King from a distance, but during the first decades of the Personal Union at least, the Chancellery took on a much broader function as an additional royal executive which was frequently mobilized in support of the King's European policy.[8]

The arrival of the Germans provoked an instantaneous xenophobic reaction among sections of the British public. They had already been irritated by the influx of destitute Palatines from south-western Germany fleeing overpopulation, bad harvests, religious discrimination and French oppression around the turn of the century. There were about 15,000 of them, but at least the vast majority moved on quickly to

Ireland and America. The Hanoverians were far fewer in number, but gave much greater offence. The anti-Dutch rhetoric of the Williamite period and the later stages of the War of the Spanish Succession was dusted off and adapted to George and his Hanoverians. A flood of popular pamphlets, ballads and broadsides now attacked the Personal Union as a threat to British political and religious freedoms. The sophistication varied but the same themes recurred over and over: the Germans were ungrateful, despotic and ubiquitous. Popular riots called 'Down with foreigners!', 'Down with the rump and the German!' and 'No foreign government!'. All this was garnished with xenophobic allusions to the obesity, gluttony, rapacity and impotence of the new King and his Germans. The image of George hoeing turnips in a field as he heard the news of Queen Anne's death proved particularly enduring and was clearly designed to ridicule the monarchy and undermine its legitimacy.[9]

One of the more effective attacks on the new monarch was launched by Francis Atterbury, the strongly Jacobite Bishop of Rochester. It appeared anonymously in 1714 under the title *English advice to the freeholders of England*. He argued that as a German and a Lutheran, George lacked all understanding of England, the constitution and Anglicanism. He even alleged, quite falsely, that the Prince and Princess of Wales had not taken Communion in the Church of England. In fact, the King and his family were careful to fulfil their obligations under the Act of Settlement, as well they might be, given that every church service they attended was conducted under close scrutiny. Perhaps in response to the Atterburys of his new home, the Prince made sure he was seen taking Communion 'publicly' in the parish church of St James. It was true, of course, that George was confessionally schizophrenic: he was an Anglican in England, a Presbyterian in Scotland, and became a Lutheran again on his return visits to Hanover. This was an unusual arrangement, to be sure, but one which – as far as Scotland and England were concerned – William, Anne and other monarchs had successfully negotiated. There was therefore some mileage in the religious argument against George, but not much.[10]

Many of Atterbury's other claims, such as a Hanoverian plot to expand the standing army in order to suppress English liberties, or to use British military assets for purely Hanoverian ends, were to become staples of anti-Hanoverian rhetoric for the next forty years or so. To many critics, the terms 'Hanoverian' and 'German' became synonymous with Continental European absolutism and even oriental despotism. Great play was made of Mehmet and Mustafa, whose exotic appearance and Mohammedanism suggested more than a whiff of the east. At one level, this was simply political opportunism: stressing the foreignness, despotism and religious heterodoxy of George was an effective antidote to Whig propaganda, which made very similar claims about the Pretender. Yet most of those playing the anti-Hanoverian card were not saying very much about George or even the Pretender. Instead, they were saying something more profound about the way in which they viewed themselves.

The Hanoverian succession was in fact a major step in the development of a British national identity. This identity was originally moulded by the sixteenth-century struggles against Spain, and reforged during the wars with Louis XIV. Fear of universal monarchy and anti-Catholicism were thus important factors in welding English and Scots together, as was – increasingly – imperial expansion. The German connection shaped this identity in two complex and contradictory ways after 1714. To what was still a significant minority, the Hanoverians replaced the Dutch as a rallying point for national feelings. The popular hostility towards the north German Protestants shows that the French and Catholics were not the only bogeys to trigger xenophobic exuberance. The Hanoverian connection thus also needs to be taken into account as a significant 'other', which served to define the nature of English and British identity. Moreover, Hanover provided a useful rallying point for these feelings in the period 1716–31, when Britain and France were actually in alliance. To many, probably the majority, the Hanoverian connection reaffirmed the sense of a common European project to defend their own freedoms and the 'liberties of Europe'. On this reading, George was a British warrior-king, the vindicator of European Protestantism and thus the defender of the balance of power. He and the Prince of Wales had, after all, served in the War of the Spanish Succession, and he was a direct descendant of the Elector Palatine of 1620. Indeed, many popular heroes were foreigners, for example William of Orange after 1690, and Louis of Baden during the War of the Spanish Succession. Some, such as the imperial commander Prince Eugene, were Catholic, though politically 'Protestant'. For many, perhaps for most, 'Britishness' was voluntary and open, not essential or inherited.[11]

To be on the safe side, some leading Whigs actively sought to generate loyalty. A few years before George had arrived in England, the Duke of Newcastle co-founded the Hanover Club. Its membership ranged across land and learning, and included such aristocratic figures as Lords Lincoln and Castlecomer, Whig cronies such as the younger James Craggs, MP and Cofferer (treasurer) to the Prince of Wales, distinguished diplomats such as Lord Methuen, major Commons orators such as William Pulteney, and the literary luminaries Joseph Addison and Richard Steele, who had founded the (shortlived) *Spectator* magazine. A Hanover Society was founded in the City of London in support of the succession. Pamphleteers spoke of the 'Hanover garland', and posited a choice between 'Hanover or Rome'. There were two Hanover coffee houses in London: one in Pall Mall and the other in Finch Lane in the City. Streets in the capital and across the country were named after German towns, provinces and figures throughout the eighteenth century. In the heart of Edinburgh's New Town, for example, lies Hanover Street, linking Princes, George's and Queen's Street, the three main avenues on the grid plan. To this day, London's Hanover Square, Mecklenburgh Square, Brunswick Place and many other addresses testify to the strength of the German connection long before Queen Victoria set her eye on Prince Albert.[12]

Across the Atlantic, the Hanoverian connection was also reflected in the naming of towns, counties and provinces, sometimes spontaneously, sometimes by state action. The Hanoverian succession was widely welcomed in British North America as a defence against popery, absolutism and French or Spanish aggression. By the mid eighteenth century, there were Hanover or New Hanover counties in Virginia and North Carolina, and Hanover townships in Pennsylvania and New Jersey. There were counties named after other Hanoverian links, such as Lüneburg and Brunswick – a whole province in Canada was named New Brunswick. All this was in addition to those counties and places named after the royal family more generally. So perhaps it is appropriate that the London base of the *New York Review of Books* should today be in Hanover Yard. George I, after all, ruled three kingdoms, twelve colonies and an Electorate.[13]

If the German presence furthered the process of English self-definition, the Hanoverians had their own views on the identity and character of their hosts. Friedrich Wilhelm von der Schulenburg, who served the King as *Kammerherr* for the first five years of his reign, was a particularly close and wry observer of the English scene. What stands out in his accounts is the perceived impulsiveness and emotionalism of his hosts. The John-Bull-like stolidity and reserve of later myth were not much in evidence. Schulenburg repeatedly refers to '*la chaleur angloise*'; he found James Stanhope, the chief minister, particularly hot-headed. He also considered the English congenitally fickle. He believed that the 'humour of the English' was such that 'one cannot count on them from one day to another'. On another occasion, when discussing the Earl of Sunderland, he refers once again to 'the inconstancy of the English, on whom one cannot count from one day to the next'. Later he attributed the English taste for masques to their '*changeante*' disposition. This picture of a garrulous and fickle English elite casts an interesting light on widespread contemporary English perceptions of English taciturnity and stolidity.[14]

Two other characteristics struck the German arrivals very forcibly. One was the deep and acrimonious rage of party. When describing parliamentary debates, Schulenburg was overwhelmed by 'the spirit of party in this country to which all else is sacrificed'. The prevailing spirit was so contrary, he noted, that 'one party has only to suggest something for the other to oppose it at first'. Indeed, he was to write a few years later, 'it is very difficult to keep three Englishmen united over a longer period'. The second characteristic was the related propensity for religious polarization, something which enlightened Germans were already putting behind them and which the consensual structures of the Holy Roman Empire were designed to contain. They were particularly shocked by some of the barbaric punishments directed against Roman Catholic priests under the Irish penal laws. Thus one Hanoverian report spoke of a 'remarkable clause' threatening all priests who fail to register with the authorities with 'castration'. A month later it applauded the 'repeal of the odious clause for the castration of priests'. The Hanoverians were also profoundly depressed by English cooking. The head of the Hanoverian administration back in Germany, Baron Görtz, was no doubt gratified to hear that at Hampton Court his rival Bernstorff 'feeds himself by an English *traiteur*, not having his household with him. The *traiteurs* are the *cuisiniers* of the King who sell dishes which one orders from their kitchen. I doubt if your excellency [Görtz] would be there at that price.'[15]

*

The most profound impact of the Hanoverian succession was on British foreign policy. To be sure, British statesmen had been intimately involved in the European balance of power ever since the Wars of Grand Alliance against Louis XIV. Moreover, Personal Unions were not uncommon at the time, particularly in Germany. Saxony and Poland had been joined since 1697; Hesse-Kassel and Sweden were similarly yoked for a while. Likewise, the emerging British state had long been a composite construction. Wales had been conquered by England, and therefore did not count, but Ireland was linked to England by a union of crowns. So was Scotland, which had also been welded closer through the Act of Union in 1707. Very recently, of course, England had been linked through William III in Personal Union with another European state, the United Provinces. Strange as the ramifications of the Personal Union might seem to modern eyes, they were not uncommon for early eighteenth-century Europeans, including Britons.[16]

All the same, the Hanoverian succession led to a fundamental change in Britain's role in Europe. She was now effectively a European power in territorial terms, and – unlike the relatively short interlude under William – remained so over a long period of time. If George continued to sign treaties as Elector of Hanover to which Britain was not a party, there was no such thing as a Hanoverian foreign policy separate from the will of the British monarch. There was no British diplomatic representation in the Electorate after 1714, and the few Hanoverian diplomats in foreign courts served the King in London rather than the caretaker government in Hanover. Whatever Parliament might say, British ministers knew that an attack on Hanover was usually intended and always perceived as an attack on the King of England. The two halves of the Personal Union were unequal in weight and ambition, but they were jointly and severally liable for the foreign policy of His Majesty's administration. This was nothing less than a geopolitical revolution for Great Britain.

As we have seen, British statesmen and diplomats had taken a keen interest in the affairs of the Holy Roman Empire for some time. Now the territorial and dynastic implications of the Hanoverian succession plunged them even deeper into the maelstrom of imperial politics, which often dominated British debate in the early eighteenth century. They knew that the Holy Roman Emperor was chosen by eight Electors – the the Electors of Bavaria, the Palatinate, Brandenburg (Prussia), Saxony,

(Habsburg) Bohemia, and the three Archbishop-Electors of Cologne, Trier and Mainz. His power rested in large part on his personal territorial holdings – for most of the eighteenth century, the Habsburg monarchy – but the Emperor could command some legal and even military instruments which were not to be despised. He dominated the imperial machinery – especially the Imperial Aulic Council (*Reichshofrat*) – that provided a sheen of legality to interventions in the affairs of smaller and middling principalities. Moreover, the Empire was divided into ten 'circles', the westernmost of which were still politically and militarily vibrant. Each circle had a director whose task it was to convene the representatives of the circle in time of war in order to vote men and funds to support the Emperor against external or internal violators of the imperial peace. In political and legal terms, for example, the defence of the Austrian Netherlands was an imperial matter, and thus a factor in British calculations.

All the major and many middling and minor princes sent representatives to the Imperial Diet at Regensburg, the *Reichstag*. This was in some ways merely a talking shop, but London knew that its endorsement was extremely useful in mobilizing public opinion against violators of German and European stability. British statesmen were keen partisans of the Protestant caucus in the Reichstag, the *Corpus Evangelicorum*, which was afforded equality with the more numerous *Corpus Catholicorum* in matters of religion. After 1714, the King-Electors of Britain-Hanover and their ministers sought effective if not formal leadership of the *Corpus Evangelicorum*, which rested somewhat uneasily with Saxony, whose Elector was in fact Catholic. If British statesmen sometimes claimed that their lives depended on these matters, that was because they did. If the Empire fell into the hands of a hostile power it would not only undermine the vital Barrier system, but also unhinge the whole European balance of power on which British security ultimately depended.

If the resulting picture of the mechanics of British diplomacy was complex, it was far from impenetrable. The question of whether or not Britain and Hanover were one or two states was not clear in the emerging system of international law; interestingly most informed legal and historical opinion now believes them to have been one state. The public symbolism of the monarchy reflected this ambiguity. Thus the personal flag of George I included not only the arms of England, Wales, Scotland

and Ireland, but also a distinctive white horse, the symbol of his Hanoverian lands. Some foreign diplomats and statesmen therefore professed an understandable bemusement about the King's two bodies – Frederick the Great of Prussia once famously asked whether he 'should consider the King of England as one or two persons' – but they were generally able to make the distinction when it suited them. For example, the minister of the middling German state of Saxony once asked for a Hanoverian envoy to be sent instead of a Briton, as he would not be '*purement anglois*'.[17]

Most of the time, British monarchs simply used whatever tool seemed

5. George I's flag, illustrating his dual role as King of Great Britain and Ireland, and also Elector of Hanover (the white horse).

most suitable for their purpose, employing Hanoverian avenues where these promised most success, or enabled them to bypass some ministerial or parliamentary constraint in London; but when these Hanoverians spoke for George, they generally did so in his royal and Electoral capacity combined. As we shall see, Hanoverian and British interests could clash, sometimes spectacularly so, but this happened less frequently than one might imagine. The generally symbiotic relationship between the two halves was epitomized by the figure of François Louis de Pesme, Seigneur de St Saphorin, the British envoy at Vienna. A Swiss Protestant by background, St Saphorin held the rank of Lt. Gen. in the British army; he had also served as military advisor to the most senior Hanoverian minister, Count Bernstorff. At various points he was to be instructed both privately and officially as a British envoy, and secretly by Bernstorff as a Hanoverian envoy. But the principal element of cohesion was supplied by the monarch himself. Much more than Queen Anne, the new monarch was right at the heart of the decision-making process in foreign policy: all the threads came together in his hands.[18]

The second change wrought by the Hanoverian succession was a restoration. Both George and his Whig backers were determined to revive the interventionist and Eurocentric orthodoxy abandoned by the Tories during the last years of Anne's reign. Their task – as they saw it – was to rescue what they could from the wreckage of the Treaty of Utrecht, the compromise peace by which Bolingbroke had brought the War of the Spanish Succession to an end. They also looked forward to a domestic settling of accounts with those Tories who had fled the fight in Europe and left Britain's allies to their fate in 1712–13. A wave of pamphlets and books now welcomed the Hanoverian succession, not only as a vindication of British liberties and Protestantism, but also as a blow against the prospect of French universal monarchy. Louis XIV, after all, still lived. As the terms of the Treaty of Utrecht demanded, he demolished the fortifications at Dunkirk, from whence French privateers had harassed British shipping in the last war, only to start construction of bigger and better facilities at nearby Mardyk. He recognized the Hanoverian succession but continued to maintain close links to the Jacobite court in exile under his protection in France. Relations between Philip V of Spain and his Austrian Habsburg rival, Charles VI of the German Empire and sometime 'Charles III' of Spain, also remained unresolved. Moreover Philip, despite his protestations, had clearly not given up hope of succeeding to the French throne on the death of Louis XIV, reviving the very Franco-Spanish power bloc which the war had been fought to frustrate.[19]

Nor was the situation much better in North America. Here, on the face of it, the Treaty of Utrecht was a triumph for Tory colonialism over Whig Eurocentricity. France was forced to cede Hudson Bay, Newfoundland and Acadia (present-day Nova Scotia and eastern New Brunswick). The population of her remaining North American territories was vastly outnumbered by the growing number of settlers in the twelve British colonies of Pennsylvania, Virginia, North and South Carolina, Delaware, Rhode Island, Connecticut, New York, New Hampshire, Vermont, Maryland and Massachusetts, which totalled about 360,000 by 1713. The Spanish promised not to surrender their empire to the French. In strategic terms, however, the outlook was rather different. The French had held on to Cape Breton, and thus control of the St Lawrence River. Thousands of well-armed and ill-disposed French settlers remained in Acadia. Many more were to the west in Quebec, the bone in the throat of British North America. The French also claimed all the lands between French Canada and their foothold on the Gulf of Mexico at Louisiana, which was growing since its foundation in 1698. By 1713, the French had founded Biloxi and Mobile. Four years later Louis XV gave the French Mississippi Company a monopoly of trade in the area, thus signalling his intention to mount at least a commercial challenge to Britain. Not long after that – in 1718 – the French founded New Orleans. If the threatened Franco-Spanish union in Europe came off, the ring of encirclement would be extended to include Florida, part of the Vice-Royalty of New Spain.[20]

Moreover, despite their growing numbers, the colonists themselves seemed incapable of providing much for their own defence. During the Tuscarora War against the Indians in 1711–13, for example, Virginia gave the worst-hit colony of South Carolina virtually no help. This earned them a stinging rebuke from the Carolinians, whose assembly pronounced themselves 'sorry and amazed that they to whom God has given great power and opportunities should be so deficient in giving that assistance'. Likewise, when some suggested the elimination of the Spanish fort at St Augustine in Florida, which would have eased the threat from the south, John Ash of the South Carolina Assembly condemned this as 'a project of freebooting under the specious name of war'. There was no overall strategic vision among the colonists themselves, and little common ground between the twelve assemblies beyond a determination to evade taxation for as long as possible.[21]

Some of the royal governors were men of vision, but their hands were tied. Thus in August 1718 the Lieutenant Governor of Virginia, Alex Spotswood warned of the French advances to the south and west, in tandem with their very active Indian policy. He spoke of the 'progress made by [the] French in surrounding us with their settlements'. The only solution, he argued, was to 'attempt to make some settlements on the lakes, and at the same time possess ourselves of those passes of the great mountains, which are necessary to preserve a communication with such settlements'. Spotswood was articulating a concept of security through expansion, which was to catch on much later. For the moment, his proposals echoed unheard. The colonies themselves were under the formal direction of the Secretary of State for the South, but the day-to-day running of them was left to the Board of Trade. Very little was done in the two decades after 1714 to defend them. It would be up to British policy in Europe to secure the safety of the overseas empire. For what was at stake in America was much more than a few homesteads and animal skins. Everything that happened there mattered because of its potential impact on the European balance. The colonies were an actual or potential source of revenue and recruits; Britain had great hopes that North America would in time serve as an alternative supplier of naval stores. For this reason, the Great Powers sought not merely to aggrandize themselves overseas, but to pre-empt others. Thus in 1716, a memorandum of the French Council of Regency described Louisiana as an 'advance guard' against Britain. It expressed the fear that Britain would seize first British Canada then Louisiana, the Spanish lands and ultimately the entire commerce of the Americas. 'But what would be for Europe,' it asked, 'the consequences and the shock of such a revolution?' It would be, the memorandum concluded, a body blow to the balance of power there.[22]

As far as the Whigs were concerned, the European balance of power was still in grave danger from France; it would not right itself without active British intervention. The Grand Alliance would have to be reconstructed. George agreed. As Elector of Hanover, he had not only been a staunch member of the coalition against Louis XIV; he had also been a loyal partisan of the German Emperor, both against France and within the Holy Roman Empire. On the journey over to England, he had conferred with the Dutch on how to repair the links broken by the Tories. Likewise, his Hanoverian advisors were almost to a man supporters of an interventionist policy in Europe. All this chimed perfectly with Whig strategic doctrine. The Earl of Sunderland told the King that 'the old Tory [notion] . . . that England can subsist by itself, whatever become of the rest of Europe . . . has been so justly exploded by the Whigs, ever since the Revolution [of 1688]'. The question of European policy, in fact, was to prove crucial to George's choice of his first ministry. This was decided not by the largest group in Parliament, which was still the Tories, but by the monarch himself. Indeed, some contemporaries still referred to the government as the 'court' not the 'ministry'.[23]

The composition of the Regency Council which governed in the interregnum between the death of Anne and George's arrival provided some straws in the wind. It included no supporters of the Treaty of Utrecht or opponents of an active British role in Europe. The King still kept an open mind on the question of party, however. To be sure, he took advice from Bothmer, who in turn was heavily influenced by the eminent Whig, Earl Cowper. All the same, George had originally intended to construct a mixed ministry, albeit one with a preponderantly Whig flavour; there had been, after all, four loyal Tories among the seventeen members of the Regency Council. This is not in the least surprising, for Tory opinion shaded into many different stripes. Jacobites and Jacobite sympathizers, of course, were beyond the pale. But there were plenty of anti-oligarchic, High Church 'Hanover Tories' who were not *per se* offensive to the new regime. Indeed, to some prominent Hanoverians, such as Görtz, the monarchical fervour of the Tories was positively attractive, and Schulenburg freely admitted that 'there are some extremely capable men among the Tories'. More than that, he thought that 'it is incontestable that . . . maintenance of the two-party [system]' was 'of great utility to the service of the King', because it enabled him to play one off against the other. In short, while faction, patronage, religion and party were all important factors, it was foreign policy which remained the constitutive force in British domestic politics after 1714.[24]

This was reflected in the composition of George's first ministry in 1714. It contained very few Tories, partly because they refused to serve on any basis other than parity with the Whigs, but primarily because they failed George's test on foreign policy. Bolingbroke was summarily dismissed as Secretary of State for the South. On the other hand, Tories who had distanced themselves from Utrecht could still find a berth. The most prominent example here was the Earl of Nottingham, but the young Lord Carteret, later one of Britain's most gifted and Eurocentric statesmen, also fell into this category; it is no accident that he was also close to the Hanoverian chief minister Görtz. In general, George favoured statesmen with a tried and trusted record in European politics.

Those Whigs who favoured Continental engagement – the Earl of Sunderland, Lord Somers (the former Lord Chancellor), the Duke of Wharton, Lord Cowper (the former Lord Keeper) and the Earl of Halifax – were rehabilitated. A younger generation, especially Robert Walpole (who had been Secretary at War at the height of the War of the Spanish Succession), James Stanhope (Earl Stanhope from 1717) and Charles, Viscount Townshend, who had come of age during the last war, gained high office. The King chose – with Bothmer's support – Townshend as Secretary of State for the Northern Department. Townshend was a friend to the Dutch and had been instrumental in negotiating the first Barrier Treaty in 1709. George's new Secretary of State for the South was Stanhope, an experienced general and diplomat with strong links to the Austrians, who had served on behalf of the Grand Alliance in Spain. Walpole was made Paymaster of the Forces, and from 1715 Chancellor of the Exchequer. His steady hand was critical in rallying the support of financiers to the Hanoverian succession. The equally staunch William Pulteney became Secretary at War. By contrast, George kept the more extremist Earl of Sunderland at arm's length, even though he was an ardent partisan of the Hanoverian succession, had served as ambassador to Vienna, and could converse in German. He had pointedly excluded Sunderland from the Regency Council which governed during the interregnum, and did not relent after his accession to the throne. The King thought him too weak and excitable on foreign affairs. Instead, Sunderland was nominated as Lord Lieutenant of Ireland, the graveyard slot in British politics.[25]

The first task facing the new government was securing the Hanoverian succession domestically. It threw itself into the elections to a new Parliament in January–February 1715. George's Hanoverian entourage also took a close interest in the contest, which formed a staple part of the news being relayed back to the administration in Germany. They were particularly interested not only in the party affiliation of the candidates, but also in whether they were 'moderate' or not. The result was an overwhelming victory for the Whigs. The Tory majority, which had been increased at the last election in August–September 1713, was completely overturned. With this thumping endorsement, the ministry was well placed to move against the domestic enemy, that is against the Tory leadership of Oxford and Bolingbroke. The principal, indeed often the only, instrument which it deployed in Parliament was the alleged failure of Tory foreign policy in the period leading up to the Treaty of Utrecht. George set the tone in his opening speech to Parliament in late March 1715. 'It were to be wished,' he announced, 'that the unparalleled successes of a war, which was so wisely and cheerfully supported by this nation, in order to procure a good peace, had been attended with suitable concern.' The address of thanks in the House of Commons, drawn up by the arch-Whig Sir Robert Walpole, echoed this disappointment at the 'unsuitable conclusion of a war'. The peace treaty had, the critics claimed, neither protected trade, nor was 'care taken to form such alliances, as might have rendered that peace not precarious'. Walpole's address promised to 'enquire into these fatal miscarriages'.[26]

About a fortnight later, Stanhope brought forward a 'Motion for committee to inquire into the late peace, and the management of the late queen's ministry'. He presented 'all the powers, instructions, memorials, papers, etc., relating to the late negotiation of peace and commerce and to the late cessation of arms'. Nothing of importance, he told the House of Commons, had been excluded. A select committee of twenty was set up to examine the material, which would include such Whig stalwarts as Stanhope, Robert Walpole and the Secretary at War, William Pulteney. It would meet in secret. The intention was to pin the blame for the 'betrayal' of Utrecht on the outgoing ministry. Even the Hanoverian Tory John Ward, MP for Newton-le-Willows, agreed that 'though his principle was that kings can do no wrong [Queen Anne was in any case dead], yet he was of opinion, that ministers were accountable for their mal-administration'. The atmosphere became increasingly embittered and partisan. In early June Walpole expostulated in the Commons 'that he wanted words to express the villainy of the last Frenchified ministry'. Stanhope wondered aloud 'that men who were guilty of such enormous crimes had still the audaciousness to appear in the public streets'.[27]

Within a week the secret committee presented its report to Parliament and Walpole moved to impeach Bolingbroke for 'High Treason, and other high crimes and misdemeanours'. There was a stunned silence in the Commons when Walpole called upon dissenters to speak out, broken only by two feeble interjections in Bolingbroke's defence. Similar charges were laid against the Earl of Oxford (Harley) and the Duke of Ormonde, the former Commander-in-Chief. Every single one of the sixteen articles of impeachment against the Earl of Oxford, and the similar charges laid against Bolingbroke, concerned their alleged mismanagement or betrayal in foreign policy; almost all of them pertained specifically to the European balance rather than colonial or naval issues. Oxford was accused of having subverted the Treaty of Grand Alliance of 1701, the founding text of eighteenth-century Whig foreign policy, and thus exposed Europe to 'the heavy yoke of universal monarchy'. There then followed a repetitive catalogue of accusations that he and his cohorts had 'set on foot a private, separate, dishonourable, and destructive negotiation of peace' with France (Article I); that the Duke of Ormonde had been instructed not to press his military advantage in the field (Article VIII); that 'the good friends and ancient allies of Her Majesty and these kingdoms' were abandoned and that the 'Protestant Succession' was endangered (Article X); that he had conspired 'to dispose of the Kingdom of Sicily to the Duke of Savoy' at Austria's expense (Article XIV); that he had misrepresented 'the most essential parts of the negotiations' to the Queen and Parliament (Article XV). The punishment for these crimes, at least in theory, was death.[28]

As if all this were not bad enough, six further articles were laid against Oxford at the very end of July. Among other things he was now also accused of 'abandoning the Catalans to the fury and revenge' of the new Bourbon King of Spain, after Britain had incited them to revolt in the first place. A 'free and generous people, the faithful and useful allies of this kingdom, were betrayed, in the most unparalleled manner, into irrevocable slavery'. The most interesting additional article, however, was that concerning the mismanagement of colonial affairs. The original charge sheet had already accused him of sacrificing British commercial and colonial interests, in particular the Newfoundland fishery, 'the great support of the naval power and the chief nursery of the seamen of Great Britain' (Article XIII). Now the abortive expedition against Quebec of 1711 was alleged to have been a 'design' for 'weakening the confederate army in Flanders, and dissipating the naval force of the kingdom'. The diversion of forces from the Low Countries to America was said to have been undertaken on his advice. A similar train of thought underlay the Speaker's speech to the King on the money bills a few months later. He spoke of 'the trade of the kingdom given up by insidious and precarious treaties of commerce, whilst the people, amused with new worlds explored, were contented to see the most advantageous branches of their commerce in Europe lost or betrayed'. What was remarkable here was not so much the implausibility of these charges, but the powerfully

Eurocentric framework within which the Whig critique of Tory grand strategy was conceived and articulated.[29]

Oxford's rebuttal was simple. He denied any wrongdoing and pointed out that not only had 'the nation wanted a peace' but that his conduct had been 'approved by two successive parliaments' as well as by the Queen. Later Oxford mounted a more detailed defence of his actions in the formal answer to the impeachment charges, in which he justified the abandonment of Charles VI with reference to the changed balance of power after the death of the Emperor Joseph. He therefore invoked a 'rule by the law of nations, in references to leagues between princes. That if there happens a material change in what was the principal ground and cause of the treaty, the obligation thereof ceases'. It was no use. Oxford was brought before the bar of the House of Lords and voted to be sent to the Tower. Seeing the writing on the wall, Bolingbroke and the Duke of Ormonde fled to France in June–July and were duly attainted (that is, Parliament declared them outlaws, whose estates, titles and civil rights were forfeit). The new reign had opened with a settling of accounts on foreign policy. The Tories had been effectively decapitated.[30]

Jacobitism was a different matter. Here the problem was not so much English support for the Pretender, which was extensive enough, but the potential linkages between him, France, and the rebellious peripheries of the British Isles. According to the terms of the Utrecht agreement, the Pretender was expelled from St Germain-en-Laye near Paris, where the Stuart court had found refuge since 1689. He moved not very far down the road to Bar-le-Duc in Lorraine, just over the French border. He was still within striking distance of the Channel ports. In late March 1715, when the Hanoverian succession was not even a year old, Robert Walpole complained that 'the Pretender still resides in Lorraine, and he has the presumption, by declarations from thence, to stir up Your Majesty's subjects to rebellion.'[31] Moreover, the Pretender had a large reservoir of military and diplomatic talent at his disposal in the shape of the Jacobite diaspora. There were thousands of Irishmen, for example, serving as 'Wild Geese' in the service of France, Spain, Vienna, and even Baltic powers such as Sweden, Prussia and Russia. Many continued to slip away across the sea, escaping the brutal penal laws in search of education, military training and betterment in Continental Europe. British ministers lived in terror that one day the sky would darken with their return. No doubt the Whig oligarchy inflated the danger of a Stuart restoration after 1714 in order to marginalize the opposition, tar the Tories with the brush of sedition and justify a state of semi-permanent emergency. But the fear was real enough.[32]

The King's Hanoverian entourage also feared the Pretender. This was demonstrated by their panicked reaction to an assault on Caroline, Princess of Wales. Early one evening she was being borne on a sedan chair to see her daughters at St James's Palace when one of the bearers, an Irish Catholic by the name of Moore, suddenly spat in her face. To make matters worse, Moore claimed that 'neither she nor her husband [the Prince of Wales] had any business' being in England. Indeed, according to another German account, he justified his act by saying that he 'did not recognize any other legitimate king in these lands than James III, and that he regarded the reigning King and all his family as usurpers'. The horrified authorities initially thought her assailant to be either drunk or mentally disturbed; he denied this, saying that he 'had done only what it was his duty to do', whereupon he was sent to prison. Worryingly, Moore used his arraignment before a grand jury at Westminster to launch another tirade against the royal family as a whole.[33]

'James III', of course, made the most of the monarchy's German connections. His 'declarations' emphasized not only the corruption, unpopularity and cruelty of the Whig regime, but also the 'otherness' of the Hanoverians. 'We have beheld a foreign family,' he lamented, 'aliens to our country, distant in blood, and strangers even to our language, ascend the throne.' Moreover, he pointed to the implications that the acquisition of substantial areas on the north German coast might have for British liberties. 'By taking possession of the Duchy of Bremen,' he argued, 'in violation of the public faith, a door is opened by the usurper to let in an inundation of foreigners from abroad, and to reduce these nations to the state of a province, to one of the most inconsiderable provinces of the [German] Empire.' This was a direct appeal to people's primordial fear of being inundated by foreigners to the extent of losing their own liberty and identity. It was to form a staple of anti-Hanoverian critiques throughout the first part of the century. Throughout April and May 1715, in fact, Britain was rocked by severe anti-Hanoverian protests and riots following the coronation of George. A wave of anti-German propaganda targeted the dynasty. As one ballad of that year put it:

Now all true *British* Worthies
With Ormonde are discarded
Whilst Treacherous knaves, and *German* slaves
With places are rewarded

Only the introduction of the Riot Act in July 1715 – which greatly increased the powers of the civil authority – was able to quell the disturbances. But the threat of a joint action between Jacobites and other disaffected elements was by no means banished.[34]

If a Jacobite coup was to succeed it would need foreign support. It was for this reason that a close eye was kept on the exile court at St Germain, particularly after the arrival of Bolingbroke. His knowledge of European diplomacy was unrivalled: if he could moderate the Pretender's popish predilections and secure French support, an invasion on behalf of the Stuarts was a realistic possibility. It thus became imperative for George and the Whigs to ensure that James was exiled 'beyond the Alps', preferably to Rome. This would serve the double purpose of allowing early warning of any attack, and of reinforcing the Catholic associations of the Stuarts in the mind of the British public. These fears came to a head in the autumn and winter of 1715, when the highlands of Scotland rose in revolt under the Earl of Mar. The arrival of the Pretender himself, with foreign gold, arms and perhaps even troops was believed to be imminent; he was known to have left Lorraine. Bolingbroke had, as one Hanoverian put it, 'completely torn off the mask' and was said to be pressing Louis to support James. To make matters worse, the French attitude was ambiguous: Louis had abjured the Pretender at Utrecht, but this did not prevent him providing covert encouragement and even support to the cause. Loose tongues at the French court exulted in the expected triumph of Jacobitism. Thus in mid 1715 the French envoy to Sweden suggested to a then sceptical Charles XII of Sweden that he should support an invasion by the Pretender. The Hanoverian dynasty faced a massive domestic and possibly external challenge less than a year after its installation.[35]

Fortunately for George, the international context was a relatively benign one. Louis XIV died in September 1715. The Duke of Orleans, who stood in as Regent for Louis XV, who was still a minor of five, was hardly an Anglophile, but he wished to avoid confrontation with Britain, at least so long as the succession in France itself was fragile. The

Pretender was strongly discouraged from launching an attack on Britain. Spain was more encouraging – and Philip V was the largest contributor to Jacobite finances during this period – but he drew back temporarily when a commercial treaty with Britain seemed in the offing. George was also able to cash in the assets which an earlier generation of Whig statesmen had banked. Now the Dutch troops promised under the Barrier Treaty came into their own, at least in the south. In November 1715 the Jacobites were finally defeated at the Battle of Sheriffmuir, and the spectre of rebellion was banished. Having been held up by French obstruction, it took the Pretender until January 1716 to reach Scotland. By then, the rebellion had largely collapsed, and he returned to France a month later. The victory proved to be a mixed blessing, as it led to a further dispersal of Jacobites across Europe, where they continued to agitate against the Hanoverian succession.[36]

The Jacobite rebellion of 1715 was hardly a surprise, but it still came as a considerable shock. It showed just how weak the hold of the Whig establishment was on large parts of the country, how shallow the roots of the new dynasty were, and the extent to which foreign powers could take advantage of British domestic divisions. As the articles of impeachment against the seven rebel peers who had supported the rebellion made clear, it also reflected the failure of British diplomacy at Utrecht. 'The dissolution of the late glorious confederacy against France,' the argument ran, 'and the loss of the balance of power in Europe, were further steps necessary to complete the designs of the said conspirators.' 'The same being effected by the late ignominious peace with France,' it went on, 'the French King was rendered formidable, and the Protestant succession was thereby brought into the most imminent danger.'[37] Britain's first line of defence, in other words, was where it always had been: in Europe. Jacobitism and 'universal monarchy' were two sides of the same coin. They could only be dealt with through a series of interlocking diplomatic and domestic measures.

A twofold strategy was therefore adopted. First of all, the ministry strengthened its domestic grip. The Septennial Act of April–May 1716 increased the interval between elections from three to seven years. This was partly designed to reduce the expenditure and disruption repeated contests involved, but it was also intended to strengthen the royal prerogative and thus Britain's international position. The extent to which this argument was deployed by supporters of the Septennial Bill testifies to the importance which the primacy of foreign affairs also had for British domestic politics. Thus the Duke of Devonshire argued that frequent elections gave 'a handle to the cabals and intrigues of foreign princes'; longer intervals between them were therefore necessary to reduce outside interference and to channel the nation's energies into dealing with external threats. Moreover, as the Duke of Newcastle argued, the Septennial Bill would reduce domestic political controversy and thus make Britain a more dependable ally. 'The allies,' he told Parliament, 'having the sad experience of being left in the lurch [. . .] would certainly enter into alliances with us with more confidence, if they saw that our government was not precarious.' The memory of the past six years, when Parliament had first called for the abandonment of Britain's Continental allies, and then after the election of 1715 moved to impeach the architects of that policy, was still fresh in everybody's mind. If the ambitious programme of alliances with which the ministry sought to reorder European geopolitics was to take effect, then British domestic politics would have to be reordered in tandem.[38]

The primacy of foreign policy also underlay the question of the domestic military establishment. Every year, the debate on the 'Number of the Land Forces' and the 'Mutiny Bill' – the two measures which regulated the size of the army and the discipline to which it should be subject – generated the same exchanges in Parliament, and often in the public sphere as well. The arguments were not new – many had been in circulation since the late seventeenth century if not earlier – but they burst forth again with renewed vigour in the first years of the new reign. Britons differed fundamentally about what the best domestic response to the challenges of the international system was; and even where the integrity of the realm was not immediately in danger, the question of what measures should be taken at home in order to uphold British interest abroad was still a pressing one. To the King and his ministers, and to a large section of parliamentary and public opinion, it was clear that security through the maintenance of the European balance came first. As James Craggs, the Secretary at War, observed in early December 1717, 'in all wise governments, the security of the state is the rule chiefly to be regarded'.[39] To this end some sort of standing army would have to be maintained. Stanhope argued that 'it was now a matter of prudence, as well as necessity, to keep up a competent force, both to suppress any insurrection at home, or to repel any insult from abroad;

and to make good our engagements for maintaining the repose of Europe.'[40]

On the contrary, argued the Tories and many independent Members of Parliament. It was not just that they objected to the vast expense. Their main point was, as William Shippen put it, 'that the civil and military power cannot long subsist together; that a standing army in time of peace will necessarily impede the free execution of the laws of the land.' He rejected the argument of necessity. How many nations, he asked, 'had lost their liberties' because they listened to siren voices warning of 'the ambitious designs of their neighbour nations and the need to preserve the balance of power'. The Tories also attacked military mobilization as a form of 'German' politics, deriving from alien usurpers and not suited to British needs and traditions. Thus Shippen accused the ministry of having made demands 'which seem rather calculated for the meridian of Germany, than of Great Britain'. He went on to add that 'It is the only infelicity of His Majesty's reign, that he is unacquainted with our language and constitution.' He reminded ministers 'That our government does not stand on the same foundation with his German dominions, which, by reason of their situation, and the nature of their constitution, are obliged to keep up armies in time of peace.'[41]

This slight earned Shippen a four-month spell in the Tower of London for insulting the King, but he was making a much broader geopolitical point. A standing army might be suited to the 'meridian' of Hanover, which was in the middle of Europe and surrounded on all sides by hostile powers, but not to Britain, which had a very different meridian: it was an island. The army could therefore be safely reduced or even disbanded, without exposing the kingdom to immediate attack. As the Tory Thomas Hanmer put it in the same debates, 'our situation is our natural protection; our fleet is our protection.' It was an argument which was to resonate with many variations throughout the eighteenth century. Another Tory, Edward Jefferies, the MP for Droitwich, pointed out 'That this island has retained its freedom longer than the countries on the Continent, has been imputed to its situation, which not being so much exposed to the incursions of its neighbours, there was not the like pretence for keeping up regular troops.' He added that 'the preservation of our liberties to this time, is, in my opinion, rather to be ascribed to the due sense our forefathers had of the danger the public underwent from entrusting princes with a standing force in time of peace.' On this reading, geography was not enough; eternal vigilance was also required.[42]

Increasing British military striking-power and domestic cohesion was certainly necessary, but not enough. British diplomacy would have to be mobilized directly in defence of the succession. The first step was to improve relations with the United Provinces and revive the Grand Alliance. After all, the Dutch troops promised under the old Barrier Treaty had been one of the government's few disposable military assets in 1715, and the prevailing orthodoxy rated the United Provinces a major power well into the eighteenth century despite many indications to the contrary, in particular the progressive disintegration of the Dutch navy. As a result, the new British envoy to The Hague, Robert Walpole's brother Horatio, became a major figure in British foreign policy after 1714 and one of the most prominent exponents of a European orientation. This involvement with the Dutch went beyond the purely diplomatic sphere to interference in the long-running rivalry between the commercialist, neutralist and often pro-French oligarchs of Amsterdam, and the pro-British Stadholder party centred on the Prince of Orange; there had been no Stadholder since 1702 and there was to be none until 1747. Far from supporting their fellow oligarchs, the Whigs sought to strengthen the absolutist element as a bulwark against France: the preservation of 'European liberties' – the balance of power – was not necessarily synonymous with safeguarding the political rights of individual Europeans.[43]

The new ministry simultaneously began to repair relations with the Habsburgs, who had been so comprehensively abandoned by Bolingbroke's Tories. This was essential to restore the united front against France and to prevent any Austrian flirtation with Jacobitism, to which they were drawn by ties of family and affinity if not state interest. Besides, Britain would have to rebuild her battered position within the Holy Roman Empire in order to put the security of Flanders back on a viable footing. Britain would therefore have to mediate between Vienna and the United Provinces on the vexed question of the Barrier fortresses, for which the Austrians were supposed to pay out of local revenue in Flanders. The Dutch also wanted to keep the river Schelde and Antwerp closed to trade, and generally limit Austria's ability to develop the area economically, so as to maintain their commercial supremacy. The Austrians, on the other hand, fiercely resented these restrictions on their sovereignty and made no secret of the fact that they would rather have gained the smaller but geographically contiguous Electorate of Bavaria instead. In November 1715, a new Barrier Treaty was negotiated. This was commercially less favourable to Britain, but enabled the Dutch better to fulfil their strategic task of deterring a French attack. Moreover, from early 1716, Britain began to make a serious effort to iron out differences between Vienna and the Dutch in her search for an Austrian alliance. She also sought to reduce Austro-Turkish tension, which could only benefit France, by distracting the Emperor from the defence of Britain's European outworks in the west.[44]

By the beginning of 1716, therefore, much had been achieved. A Jacobite incursion had been seen off, albeit with some difficulty. Tory isolationism had been banished. The Whig strategic paradigm had been restored. Relations with the Dutch had been rebuilt, and with them the vital barrier to French expansion in Flanders had been strengthened. A rapprochement with the Austrians, vital to the reconstruction of Britain's buttresses in the Holy Roman Empire, was well under way. The ring of containment around France, which had come apart after 1710, was being reforged. All this had been achieved under the aegis of a monarch who shared Whig preoccupations with the European balance of power, and took up pretty much where William III had left off in 1702. The Hanoverian succession – like the Dutch connection before it – had been integrated into British grand strategy. So far, so familiar. But it would soon become clear that George had ideas of his own about Europe, which would take the Whig elite and Britain into new territory.

4

Britain's New European Empire, 1716–1717

We promise the King of Prussia that the said squadron shall in every way second operations in Pomerania against Sweden, and hope His Prussian Majesty will believe our word, that there will be no want in the fulfilling of this promise. But we could not give a written engagement, since the providing of the squadron pertains to us as King, and if we gave a written engagement we could not use our German ministers, but we should have to give it by the hands of our English ministers.[1]   George I, 1715

[A] strong representation [against the Russian occupation of Mecklenburg] will be presented to the Tsar by His Majesty's German ministers. The immediate interest of His Majesty as a Prince of the Empire makes it necessary that such a representation should be tendered by them ... but if contrary to the King's hopes and expectations the Tsar should push matters to extremity [and] bring troops into Zealand, or otherwise to molest the King of Denmark, His Majesty directs that you should in the best manner you can, be aiding and assisting to the King of Denmark.[2]

George I, instructions for Stanhope, Secretary of State, 1716

The Hanoverian succession made Britain not merely a German, but a North European power. British statesmen had long been accustomed to regard western Europe as part of their defensive system, and during the wars against Louis XIV they had become more and more aware of how developments in the Mediterranean and the Balkans might affect them. They were no strangers to the Baltic, where Elizabeth and Cromwell had sought alliances in their time, where London merchants did a brisk trade, and whence Britain's naval stores were supplied. Most recently, during the War of the Spanish Succession, they had dissuaded

Charles XII of Sweden from moving southwards in support of the French position in Germany. The accession of George I, however, forced British statesmen to broaden their horizons. They now had to regard not merely Flanders and western Germany as Britain's front line, but Mecklenburg on the Baltic, and the North Sea ports of Hamburg and Bremen as well. British forces were deployed against Sweden and then Russia. All this was not merely to stretch British grand strategy, sometimes to breaking point, but also to strain the relationship between some Whigs and their new King. Because the problems of the Baltic did not always fit neatly into the strategic frameworks of previous generations, they led to a realignment in party politics. The resulting row about British foreign policy, which erupted in 1716, thus mutated into a much broader political crisis in London, and was to rumble on until the early 1720s.

George had accepted the throne in 1714 not only to contain France, but also in order to parlay his new-found royal status into political advantage in Germany. It was an expectation widely shared in Hanover itself, where one cabinet memorandum in 1714 noted that the Elector had acquired a crown 'whose owner can decide the balance of the whole of Europe, and make himself respected'. For Hanover was a power on the make. It had been an Electorate only since 1692, and major gains such as Celle and Delmenhorst were added as recently as 1705 and 1711, respectively. Now, with the power of Britain behind him, the obvious theatre for George in which to invest his new capital was the Great Northern War. This had begun in 1700, shortly before the start of hostilities over the Spanish succession. It had been triggered by Charles XII of Sweden's attempt to achieve complete hegemony in the Baltic. After his massive defeat by Russia at the Battle of Poltava in 1709, however, it became essentially a war of the Swedish succession, fought to determine which of her rivals – Denmark, Hanover, Poland or Russia – should inherit which parts of the wreckage. This included not only present-day Sweden but also Finland, most of the Baltic states and a substantial foothold in northern Germany (Bremen, Verden and Vorpommern, the spoils of war at Westphalia in 1648). Of the Great Powers, only France supported Sweden, largely in order to support a counterweight to her Habsburg rivals in Germany, but also in order to contain Russia. The Habsburgs, on the other hand, resented the Swedish presence in the Holy Roman Empire, but were careful to avoid any action which might cause the Northern War to spill over into Germany; this would have caused the Danish, Saxon and Hanoverian contingents fighting with the allies against Louis XIV to be withdrawn. Marlborough, it will be remembered, had seen the danger at once, and his diplomacy at Altranstädt in 1707–8 had been as important as his military victories further west.[3]

Even before 1714, therefore, the Baltic was not an unimportant sphere in British foreign policy. During his short tenure as secretary of state, Bolingbroke had attempted to shore up Sweden against all comers, including the Hanoverians; it was not the least of George's grievances against him. After Utrecht, the conflict escalated sharply, as Sweden's military situation deteriorated. In June 1714, Prussia and Russia combined against Sweden; in April 1715, desperate to stave off a total collapse of her ally, France concluded a subsidy treaty with Charles XII. That same year, the Danes and Saxons occupied part of the Swedish duchies of Bremen and Verden. This was registered with alarm by George I in London. The prospect of a Danish annexation of Bremen, Verden and even Vorpommern was deeply worrying. In their hands, these territories would be a mortal military and commercial threat. As one Hanoverian memorandum put it, 'Since Denmark is already master of the Sound [between Denmark and Sweden], by acquiring the Duchy of Bremen it would also take complete control of the two great rivers of the Elbe and Weser, and would thus have the commerce not only of the entire Baltic but also of Germany in its hands.' For this reason George occupied Verden and the remainder of Bremen in 1713. It was an act of pre-emptive expansion.[4]

But if the Swedish collapse was a threat, it was also an opportunity. George's chief Hanoverian minister in London, Bernstorff, now saw his chance to effect a fundamental geopolitical reorganization of the north in Hanover's favour. Bremen and Verden should be permanently annexed by the King, if only to prevent them from falling into the hands of another power. In April 1715 Hanover signed a treaty with Prussia against Sweden, and by the end of the year agreements with Poland, Denmark and Russia followed. As Elector, George undertook to send Hanoverian troops to fight the Swedes and to deploy the Royal Navy to cut the Swedes off from Germany, and in particular from Stralsund in Vorpommern, where the garrison was under attack by the coalition. He also promised to guarantee the various cessions Sweden was to make to its assailants, including Ingria (a region to the south-west of St Petersburg), Karelia and Estonia to Russia. In return, Hanover was to buy Bremen and Verden from the Danes. In October, George took full possession of Bremen and Verden. At a stroke, the King had substantially enlarged his German possessions and thus his international standing. George's ambition found expression in the expansion of his princely gardens at Herrenhausen, outside Hanover. It was perhaps a portent that the statue bearing the figure of Europe bore a sword pointing north-west: towards Bremen and Verden. An impressive geyser – reaching up to 35 metres high – followed in 1721, and in 1727, the year of George's death, the Herrenhausen Allée, connecting the gardens with Hanover itself, was completed.[5]

George's ministers in Whitehall watched these northern developments with concern. Instability in the Baltic threatened their interests in two ways. They feared that it would give Louis XIV an opportunity to stir up trouble against Britain. Moreover, the measures taken by the Swedes against shipping in the Baltic profoundly affected British trading interests. There were important markets and suppliers at risk in the iron and grain trade, for example. Merchantmen trading with ports in the former Swedish territories on the Baltic now under Russian control were exposed to regular attack by Swedish privateers. In December 1714, British diplomats presented a stiff formal protest to Sweden and demanded compensation for the extensive losses to shipping. Far from heeding this request, the Swedes issued a new Privateering Edict in February 1715, which constituted a fresh threat to British commerce; in all some 136 British ships were lost. Mercantile pressure for some kind of naval intervention mounted and was to remain strong for the next four years. Karl Marx, in one of his less well known historical forays – the *Secret diplomatic history of the eighteenth century* – therefore saw the key to British policy in the Baltic, and the main reason for her toleration of the rise of Russian power, in commercial self-interest.[6]

In fact, protecting the Baltic trade was a strategic rather than a purely economic imperative; the monetary value alone gave no idea of its importance. The Secretary at War, James Craggs later pointed out that Anglo-Swedish trade had been much less extensive than outraged petitioners claimed. What mattered was that Britain was dependent on the Baltic for supplies of essential goods for the Royal Navy. It did not object to paying a market price for them, but it feared a rival power gaining a monopoly of the supply, or even being shut out altogether. This was also an argument which appealed to George's confidant Robethon, who spoke in July 1715 of the importance of naval stores 'of which we have an great need'; the King's Hanoverian servants were already thinking of their master's strategic needs in the broadest sense, not just in terms of Electoral interests. To be sure, alternative sources in North America were being pursued, but for the moment the colonies were unable to satisfy demand either quantitatively or qualitatively. For the foreseeable future, the sails, masts and ropes for the Royal Navy, the 'wooden walls' which protected Britain from Continental hegemons, would have to come from the Baltic. Whatever their views of Bremen and Verden, therefore, British ministers agreed that Sweden could not be allowed to keep her foot on Britain's naval windpipe.[7]

That said, the resulting measures to deter Sweden and intimidate her into making concessions to George I as Elector of Hanover were far from straightforward in British politics. Defending British shipping posed no difficulty, but the use of the Royal Navy to further purely Hanoverian aims was a clear breach of the Act of Settlement of 1701. This had specifically outlawed the use of British resources for 'foreign' purposes without the consent of Parliament. Ministers found in violation of the Act risked their careers, or worse. For this reason, the government sought to lock the Dutch – whose commercial interest in the Baltic was even greater and who stood to lose even more from Swedish depredations – into the naval demonstration against Charles XII. Here was the perfect alibi, and a joint task force under the reliable Whig partisan Admiral Sir John Norris was duly dispatched. The problem was that the Dutch commander, although friendly with Norris personally, was not only given clear instructions to avoid direct clashes and retaliatory action; he was also wary of being hijacked by a Hanoverian agenda. He was to deter attacks on Dutch ships, no more.[8]

By contrast, George and his Hanoverian advisors sought to use the squadron more openly against the Swedes. In order to do this, they opened up a secret, and constitutionally highly dubious, channel of communication with the British naval commander, Admiral Norris. The Admiral's written orders made it clear that the protection of British shipping was his principal task; this was the 'British' part. But his oral instructions, delivered in person by Bernstorff before his departure, briefed the commander on the need to attack the Swedes on whatever pretext necessary; that was the 'Hanoverian' part. Once in the Baltic, Norris was subjected to constant pressure from George, his Hanoverian entourage, and Hanoverian ministers in the region. Significantly, all correspondence from King Frederick William of Prussia relating to Norris's squadron was handled by George's Hanoverian envoy in Berlin, Baron Heusch. The British diplomats in the region were largely sidelined, or, like Lord Polwarth in Copenhagen, were Whig devotees determined to do the King's bidding.[9]

The choice of Norris to command the squadron was hardly an accident. His Whig affiliations were no secret. When the Secretary of State for the Northern Department, Lord Townshend, ordered him to return home and detach a 'discreet' officer to keep an eye on the Swedes, Norris knew exactly what he meant. His choice fell on one Captain Hopson, and again it was no coincidence that the eight vessels of his squadron were commanded by men who had been appointed since 1714 and were thought to be politically reliable. Moreover, Norris was eager to please the Hanoverians: he once asked for his compliments to be sent to Robethon 'that we might stand right with him'. He also seems to have been or become competent in the German language, a useful skill during his long stays in the Baltic. In short, Norris was a pillar of the Whig establishment and a staunch supporter of the Hanoverian succession. He could not very well refuse his monarch outright. At the same time, he was well aware of the precariousness of his position. As one Swedish observer put it, 'Norris did not want to obey his orders, saying that he had no desire to mount the scaffold for love of Mr Bernstorff.' Given the experiences of the past few years, particularly the impeachment of Harley, Norris's remark was only slightly hyperbolic. Getting foreign policy wrong, or obeying instructions which were later deemed contrary to British interests, could cost you your career and sometimes your liberty in early-eighteenth-century Britain. Norris knew that the presence of the Royal Navy in the Baltic had the potential to develop not only into war with Sweden but also into a full-blown constitutional crisis in Britain itself.[10]

Louis XIV died in 1715. The new ruler at Versailles, the Regent, was under pressure both from rivals inside France and the King of Spain, who had not given up his claim to the French throne. He was also worried about British intentions in North America. The idea of a Franco-British rapprochement suddenly began to make sense. In London the proposed geopolitical revolution, a complete reversal of some thirty years of European diplomatic alignments, quickly found favour with George. Initial scepticism on the part of Stanhope and Sunderland soon evaporated. They saw the force behind George's own support for a treaty with France. It provided both parties with some much-needed dynastic stability, and it would greatly increase British leverage in the Baltic. Townshend and Walpole remained doubtful. The principal reservation was that rapprochement with France should take place in step with, rather than at the expense of, the Dutch. Failure to keep the allies informed had after all been the nub of the Whig critique of Utrecht; and proceedings of impeachment against Oxford had been begun on that basis. All the same, Stanhope was dispatched to work out the details with the French chief minister, the Abbé Dubois. In order to speed up the negotiations the two men arranged to meet in Hanover, thus taking advantage of George's much-delayed first trip back to his native Electorate after ascending the throne. The venue, as Stanhope told Townshend, also served the purpose of secrecy. 'The less this matter is talked of . . . the better,' he stressed.[11]

Concluding an alliance with France was now a matter of some urgency. The situation in the Baltic was highly volatile. A breakdown of relations between the Russians and the other partners in the anti-Swedish coalition seemed to be looming. Stanhope feared that 'matters will soon come to extremities'. He added that 'This situation gives the King no small uneasiness when once the quarrel between these powers shall have broke out, it is to be feared France may blow the coals. His Majesty therefore wishes the treaty with France could be finished.' Were Britain to let the opportunity 'slip', Stanhope feared, 'we shall hereafter treat with France at a much greater disadvantage. The war with the Turk will in all probability last another campaign.' He was also worried that 'the Swedes may try to foment mischief in Britain'. Stanhope, who had served his diplomatic apprenticeship during the War of the Spanish Succession, thus demonstrated his ability to conceive the interconnections between the Turkish, Baltic and French parts of the European system.[12]

Before the King could commence his journey, however, several delicate constitutional issues had to be addressed. First of all, and most obviously, there was the clause in the Act of Settlement forbidding the monarch from travelling to Hanover without the permission of Parliament. Perhaps to everybody's surprise, this humiliating restriction was quickly lifted by a House of Commons which contained many opponents of the Personal Union. Secondly, a Regency Council would have to be established to govern Britain in the absence of the monarch. This body was nominated by George and its composition was largely determined by which of the major officers of state did not accompany the King. Controversially, George decided not to place the Prince of Wales at the head of the council as a viceroy while he was away. Interestingly, the regents could not assume their temporary powers until definite news had been received of the King's safe arrival on the Continent. This was because the monarch was deemed to be lord of the seas as well as Britain, so that he would only actually leave his dominion once he took the first step on dry land on the other side.[13]

Whenever George went to Hanover, the focus of British high politics and foreign policy moved with him. He was usually accompanied by a number of ministers, including one secretary of state for foreign affairs. Others simply went for reasons of prestige, to make their homage, or because they were fitting Hanover into their grand tour of Europe. In the space of a few months in 1719, for example, three peers – the Duke of Montrose, Lord Ryalton and Lord Peterborough – visited the King at Hanover. In some cases, there seems to have been no more than whimsy at play. As Schulenburg remarked of one visitor in 1718: 'I cannot understand the reason . . . He is not young enough to make it out of curiosity nor well enough versed in foreign affairs to be employed on a commission.' Foreign diplomats in London also scrambled to join the Hanover circuit. Thus on the occasion of the 1716 visit, the French envoy to London, d'Iberville, travelled to Hanover via Paris, leaving only a secretary behind. Likewise the imperial [Austrian] envoy, Count Volkra, made ready to follow George to the Electorate. Some, such as the Danish envoy, even accompanied the King's party in one of the yachts; perhaps he was eager to press his country's demands for support from the Royal Navy squadron in the Baltic. Some of these men, no doubt, were also taking a holiday or visiting their families; but their determination to follow George does reflect the extent to which foreign policy was made, or was perceived to be made, by the monarch to whom they were accredited, rather than in the capital of the state whose policy they were supposed to be observing.[14]

The Anglo-French alliance negotiated at Hanover in the autumn of 1716 brought the long rivalry to a temporary close. Both sides gained what mattered most to them: strategic and dynastic security. The French agreed to expel the Pretender 'beyond the Alps', from Avignon to the Papal States. They not only reaffirmed their acceptance of the Protestant Succession in Britain but also guaranteed George's German possessions. The controversial port facilities at Mardyk were to be dismantled. In return, the British guaranteed the French succession against the pretensions of Philip of Spain. This was an important step beyond Utrecht, where it had been agreed to separate the two thrones, but Philip was still left the option of abdicating in Spain and claiming his French throne; for obvious reasons, this was of greater concern to Versailles than London. Efforts to bring the Dutch into this alliance were now redoubled and they were finally brought into the fold in January 1717, making it a Triple Alliance.

There remained the question of Austria. Ever since the Hanoverian succession, Whig statesmen had been trying to mend fences with Vienna. So too had the Hanoverian entourage around the King. A British proposal for an Anglo-Dutch compact with the Austrians had been on the table for some time. But there were several obstacles to be surmounted. First of all, as the British noted with alarm, the Austrians were seriously distracted by the Turkish threat. Secondly, British diplomats overloaded the wagon with specifically Hanoverian requests. Thus Sir Luke Schaub, the British and Hanoverian envoy in Vienna, listed along with the usual concerns about the Pretender the hope that 'the Emperor will enter with [George] into the agreements necessary to maintain and conserve the lands which he possesses in Germany, and particularly the Duchies of Bremen and Verden'. The Austrian response was instructive. Schaub was told that the Emperor would gladly enter into an alliance, '[b]ut [that] the two points of the [Protestant] Succession and the gains made at Sweden's expense' were proving a hindrance 'even if the difficulty was more in the formality than the substance of affairs'. Some compromise formula on the succession would have to be found, which did not embarrass the Emperor as a Catholic. As for George's German possessions, the Austrians argued that 'the treaty in question [which was between Britain and Austria, not Britain and the Empire] was not the right place to deal with them': a separate conference would be needed, at which the Emperor would judge this issue from the imperial point of view.[15]

In other words, one would have to proceed in accordance with the German imperial constitution. This message was reinforced a few days later, when Schaub reported that the Austrians welcomed an alliance, 'and that in order to conclude it with all dispatch [they] wished that it not be complicated by the German affairs of His Majesty [George]'. The Austrian position was not merely politically important, it was also crucial in legal terms: George would not be in full legal possession of his gains in Bremen and Verden without having been formally invested by the Emperor. These investitures were to be a long time in coming, and for the moment Vienna refused to budge either on this issue, or on the question of an explicit guarantee of the Protestant Succession. British ministers were even more aghast at Vienna's demand for naval support in vindication of Habsburg claims to the Spanish Mediterranean empire. Britain was quite prepared to guarantee the Emperor's position in Italy, a cornerstone of the Utrecht Settlement and a vital bulwark against Spanish Bourbon expansionism. She was even willing to mute her support for the Dutch in the delicate negotiations on the Barrier Treaty. But using the Royal Navy to support an Austrian Habsburg *reconquista* of Charles VI's lost Spanish inheritance was not within the realms of the possible or desirable. There would have to be another way to an alliance with Vienna.[16]

It was the burgeoning Franco-British rapprochement which unlocked relations with Austria, which feared being sidelined. At the Treaty of Westminster in April 1716, Britain guaranteed the Austrian position in Italy, while the Emperor agreed to the annexation of Bremen and Verden by Hanover, though he still held back with the formal investiture of the titles. Four months later, the Austrians were unsettled to hear of the successful conclusion of the negotiations between Britain and France. Schaub reported that the Imperial Vice Chancellor Sinzendorf 'was more agitated than ever about the alliance between His Majesty and the Regent of France'. According to opinion in Vienna, he continued, Britain had concluded the alliance 'in order to guarantee the King's new acquisitions in Germany'. It only made them more determined, for the time being, to repair relations with Britain. Charles VI waited until August 1718 before joining the Triple Alliance, but the alliance system jettisoned in 1713 had now largely been restored.[17]

As the negotiations with France, Austria and the Dutch drew to a close, Britain was drawn ever more deeply into the Baltic vortex. In 1715 the

Swedes were successfully deterred from molesting British merchantmen; Norris thus had no pretext to attack them, even if he had wanted to. Instead, he limited himself to a demonstration in support of the hard-pressed Danish fleet. This caused considerable concern and puzzlement to George's Danish, Prussian and Russian allies, all of whom thought that the King of England had promised the deployment of the Royal Navy against the Swedes. Matters came to a head in late 1715 and early 1716, when the coalition planned to invade Sweden itself and knock Charles XII out of the war for good. In March 1716 the Danes sent a mission to Britain to ask for British assistance in the operation; a Russian envoy was dispatched to London with the same aim in mind. The Swedes gave every impression of being prepared to fight to the death, and to throw their enemies off balance, they invaded the Danish province of Norway. George's bluff was about to be called.[18]

All this coincided with the emergence of a new threat to George's interests in the Baltic. In late 1715, a Russian army had occupied Mecklenburg, partly in order to put further pressure on the Swedes, and partly to support Tsar Peter's ally, the reigning Duke Charles Leopold against his refractory nobility, or 'estates'. The King's chief Hanoverian minister, Bernstorff, himself a Mecklenburger with properties there, viewed this with some distaste, but the main cause for concern was strategic. The Russians gave the distinct impression of being in for the long haul. A glance at the map reveals why George, and particularly his Hanoverian ministers, viewed this as a mortal threat to the adjacent Electorate, and the integrity of Germany in general. Mecklenburg lay just across the Elbe on Hanover's northern border. The rising power of the Baltic – Peter the Great's Russia – was now established right on George's doorstep. Russian power seemed on the verge of erupting into Germany. A crisis in the Empire was imminent.[19]

Hanoverian troops were mobilized along the border. At the same time, George moved to create a political front against Peter, using British diplomats. The British ambassador in Vienna was given the task of setting up a league between Austria, Hanover and Saxony-Poland, with the aim of expelling Russian forces from Germany. Representations against the Tsar of Mecklenburg were best made by George's Hanoverian servants, on the strength of his 'immediate interest . . . as a Prince of the Empire'. The broader task of deterring the Russians from moving further south and west devolved to British ambassadors, such as the ambassador to Vienna, the veteran German expert, Charles Whitworth, who was the envoy to Berlin, and the envoy to Copenhagen. The ministry in London agreed that the containment of Russia was now the first priority, partly in order to pre-empt the rise of a naval rival in the Baltic, but also because continued tension would give the French an excuse to meddle in the affairs of northern Europe. Stanhope therefore stressed the need to 'divert the Tsar from attempts which would immediately throw all Germany into a flame; and give France the best opportunity she can ever expect of embroiling all Europe'. The Austrians were sympathetic, but because they were still preoccupied with their Turkish War, George could not count on their military help. The Russians would have to be ejected from Germany with British and Hanoverian muscle, and in particular the use of the only military asset which George held in the Baltic Sea itself: the Royal Navy. Direct British military intervention in the affairs of the Holy Roman Empire was about to begin.[20]

Norris was given fresh and more belligerent unofficial instructions to confront the Swedes, preferably having first sloughed off the responsibility of protecting the merchantmen to the Dutch. As one Hanoverian observer noted, 'The orders to Mr [sic] Norris to attack the Swedes will be very clear and he will be the better able to put them into effect because he will no longer be escorting any merchant vessels.' A Hanoverian observer in London noted with approval that Norris had once again chosen as captains only those known to be '*bien intentionez*', which was Hanoverian code for Whigs sympathetic to the court and the Personal Union. Unfortunately, the Dutch commander, Captain Grave, still stubbornly refused to be complicit in such a stratagem; moreover, without the merchantmen, Norris lacked an adequate alibi for his presence. All the while, George's allies grew more impatient. In the late autumn of 1716 the King of Prussia asked Norris whether his orders were from George as King or Elector; the uncomfortable Norris replied that they were from the King. But in October 1716, the Danes published a declaration from which it was clear that George had promised British resources in pursuit of Hanoverian ends. The issue could no longer be finessed.[21]

To Townshend, Secretary of State for the Northern Department back in London, taking on the Swedes and annexing Bremen and Verden was problematic, but defensible. He also supported the containment of Russia. If the Tsar actually planned 'to make himself master of the whole coast of the Baltic,' he wrote in September 1716, then 'strong [and]

vigorous' measures should be taken to stop him. The question of Mecklenburg, on the other hand, seemed to him a complete sideshow. He
suspected Bernstorff's concern to be motivated not by grand strategy,
but by his own stake in his native Mecklenburg. To make matters worse,
Bernstorff was pursuing a private vendetta with Frederick William of
Prussia over some disputed manors, thus seriously complicating relations
with Berlin. Likewise, James Craggs described Bernstorff as 'a mischiev-
ous old man', whose 'views . . . so confined his ideas to Mecklenburg
and his three villages, that the credit and security of all Europe are not
able to rouse him'. Robert Walpole's brother Horatio, envoy to the
United Provinces, complained from The Hague that 'I can't for my life
see . . . why the whole system of affairs in Europe, especially in relation

6. Bernstorff was the most senior Hanoverian statesman and a force to be
reckoned with in British politics.

to the interest of England, must be entirely subverted on account of
Mecklenburg.' There was in fact widespread unease among British
statesmen about the perceived subordination of British to Hanoverian
interests. A gulf now opened up between those who believed that George
was exceeding his constitutional authority in foreign policy, and those
who were prepared, for whatever reason, to indulge him. The First Lord
of the Admiralty expressed himself strongly against using the Royal
Navy to attack the Swedes. Townshend occupied a similar position.

The impeachment of Queen Anne's secretaries of state was a terrible reminder of the fate of those who got British foreign policy and high politics wrong.[22]

Dissent on foreign policy rarely went down well with George. Townshend compounded the offence by seeming to delay the conclusion of the Anglo-French alliance, in order to move in step with the Dutch. Stanhope and Sunderland now saw their chance. By supporting George's northern policy, Stanhope could consolidate his already formidable position with the King at the expense of his co-foreign secretary, Townshend. Likewise, the Earl of Sunderland grasped an opportunity to gain the preferment he had failed to secure in 1714. So while Townshend was fretting in London, Stanhope was integrating himself still further into George's Hanoverian entourage. At one particularly intense session with sixteen Germans in Hanover, seventy bottles of claret and six of brandy were polished off, according to one observer, 'as if it had been syrup'.[23] More importantly, Stanhope now began to monopolize policy areas which were within Townshend's field of competence as Northern Secretary. As George grew more and more irritated over Mecklenburg and Townshend's apparent reluctance to speed up the negotiations with France, orders were increasingly sent directly from Hanover to Norris and British diplomats in the Baltic, rather than via London. Townshend was out of the loop.[24]

Townshend and his allies were caught unawares. 'The surprise of these gentlemen,' one Hanoverian observer wrote at the very end of December 1716, 'is the greater because they do not know where the blow which has hit them has come from.' Townshend resigned before he could be sacked, and Walpole followed him in sympathy. Pulteney, the Secretary at War, also resigned in protest, perhaps less in outrage over the policy than at the treatment of his political allies. He was succeeded by James Craggs the Younger. Stanhope took over the Treasury. He also switched from the Southern Department to the Secretaryship of the Northern Department, a sure sign of the importance of Britain's new strategic orientation. He thus became the King's acknowledged chief minister. Stanhope passed on formal control of the Northern Department to his co-conspirator Sunderland in April 1717. Their triumph was now complete. Joseph Addison briefly succeeded him as Secretary of State for the South. After a long resistance, Townshend was finally sent under protest as Viceroy to Ireland. As Schulenburg remarked cruelly,

'Lord Townshend has in the end married the whore (*putain*) which he had so decried.' This was an irony which Sunderland, himself banished to that political wilderness only two years earlier, must have relished.[25]

7. Charles Townshend got on the wrong side of George I on German politics during the Baltic crisis, and learned a lesson he never forgot.

British politics were now in profound crisis. The marginalized Whigs did not take their humiliation lying down. George had lost not only one of his greatest experts on European affairs, Townshend, and a reliable secretary at war, William Pulteney, but perhaps most damagingly of all, Walpole at the Treasury. These were all men of impeccable Whig standing, well known supporters of the Hanoverian succession, friends to the Dutch alliance, and prominent scourges of Jacobitism. All this was bad news for British public credit, and the City of London was convulsed by anxiety after the loss of a respected chancellor of the exchequer. Walpole himself was widely believed to be stoking the rumour mill in order to make the point that only he could guarantee financial stability. Under these circumstances the management of Parliament and public finance was going to be very difficult.[26]

The result of this intra-Whig spat was the first major domestic controversy over the Personal Union and Britain's role in Europe. Hatred of George and his Germans had, of course, been a feature of popular xenophobic discourse since 1714. It now resonated not only in pubs and coffee houses, but also in high political circles. The flames were fed, as one might have expected, by the Tories, Jacobite polemicists, and the aggrieved Swedes, who sponsored some damaging pamphlets attacking the ministry. It therefore suited Sunderland, and particularly Stanhope – both of whom wanted to avoid a total breach with Walpole if they could avoid it, not least in order to reassure the money markets in the City – to suggest that the root of their fall lay in George's Hanoverian entourage. As the historian J. H. Plumb wrote in his celebrated biography of Walpole, 'The trouble was the Germans. They had always been the trouble.'[27]

Some of the rivalry boiled down to money and preferment. In spite of the King's general policy of not granting English titles to Germans, it was rumoured that Bernstorff wanted a seat in the House of Lords, and others were believed to be after baronetcies; the naturalization of the King's mistress Melusina von der Schulenburg in 1716 and her later elevation as Duchess of Kendal in 1719 did not help matters, of course. Certainly large bribes were paid to the Germans, men and women, around George, in order that they might intercede with him for places. As one Hanoverian observer noted, it was public knowledge that 'Robethon had demanded of Lord Townshend at the beginning of this reign that one should make a present of £40,000 to the Germans who had served the King so well. Of this twenty thousand should go to Bernstorff, six to Bothmer, [and] five thousand to himself [Robethon].' Particular venom was reserved for Robethon, who was 'decried as the most nasty and most infamous of all men'. Walpole attacked him more or less directly in Parliament. He had 'no objections against the German ministers, whom His Majesty brought with him from Hanover, and who as far as he had observed, had all along behaved themselves like men of honour; but that there was a mean fellow, of what nation he could not tell [a coded reference to the ambiguity of Robethon's position as a Huguenot exile in Hanoverian service], who took upon himself to dispose of employments'. By drawing attention to the Huguenot Robethon's religious and national difference – Nonconformists were, after all, banned from full participation in politics, Oxbridge and other walks of national life – Walpole had thus neatly combined the themes of virtue, patriotism and religion. Ironically, he had thus appropriated the very rhetoric which was to be used against him during the twenty years of his political ascendancy after 1721.[28]

The perceived political and religious 'otherness' of the Hanoverians also gave offence. Their Lutheranism, long a matter of suspicion, was once again magnified, particularly by Jacobites keen to turn High Church Tories against the Personal Union. The Lutheranism of Charles XII of Sweden, on the other hand, was extolled as part of his identity as an implausible Protestant hero, assailed by the Russian Orthodox Peter the Great. George's expansionism in northern Germany also resonated alarmingly with those predisposed to see the Hanoverian succession as a step towards Continental absolutism. It was feared that the newly annexed ports in the Duchy of Bremen would be used as an embarkation point for George to ship troops to Britain to suppress British liberties. But the centrepiece of the opposition Whig and Tory attack inside and outside Parliament was the use of British military power for Hanoverian ends. Daniel Finch, the MP for Rutland – a Whig with a Tory background – announced 'it was a shame that one was governed by a gentleman from Mecklenburg [a clear dig at Bernstorff] and that because of his love for his country Great Britain was embroiled in a war to save it.' Pulteney, the former secretary for war, likewise loosed off a barrage against the new ministry, 'the Germans', and even came close to criticizing George himself. He ended by doubting 'that any Englishman advised His Majesty to send such a message [for money to pay for the Baltic policy]', but that he was sure 'the resolutions of a British parliament would make a German ministry tremble'. When the question of voting money for measures against Sweden came to Parliament in early April 1717, William Shippen launched into another philippic against the ministry and the dynasty. It was 'a great misfortune,' he announced, 'that so wise and so excellent a prince as His Majesty was as little acquainted with the usage and forms of parliamentary proceedings, as with the language of our country'. 'If he had known either,' Shippen continued, 'he would not have sent such a message . . . and therefore it [is my] opinion, that it was penned by some foreign minister, and then translated into English.'[29]

The German connection was now used to attack ministerial foreign policy across the board. Thus in March 1717 complaints were voiced about the employment of troops supplied by the Duke of Saxe-Gotha and the Bishop of Münster. These had been used to replace Dutch garrisons in the Barrier withdrawn in 1715 in order to support the Protestant Succession against the Jacobite rebellion. They were thus very much part of the architecture of Britain's European and domestic security. As Stanhope pointed out, the demands for papers relating to the treaty with Münster and Saxe-Gotha to be laid before Parliament were made 'with a design to find fault with them, and to bring a censure upon some German ministers who had been employed in those transactions'. The request was in any case heavily defeated. Disaffected Whigs and the Tories – now by some reckonings a majority in the House of Commons – also lambasted the hiring of 6,000 Dutchmen during the suppression of the rebellion. According to Pulteney, 'there had been great sums of money embezzled in this expedition'. Walpole supported Pulteney so violently and at such length that, as the parliamentary history records, he 'strained his voice to that degree, that he was taken with a violent bleeding at the nose, which obliged him to go out of the House [Commons chamber]'. Some of this was pure theatre. Thus after his philippic in Parliament against the Germans, Pulteney was reported to have 'repented of his foolishness [sottise], [and] wrote a letter of submission to the King, asking his pardon for having being too heated during his speech'.[30]

Against this onslaught, Stanhope set out the British national interest with clarity. There was an explicitly geopolitical argument for the annexation of Bremen and Verden, even if 'it was never in His Majesty's thoughts to engage Great Britain in a war to support that acquisition.' 'If gentlemen would give themselves the trouble to cast their eyes upon the map, to see where Bremen and Verden lie,' Stanhope argued, 'they would not be indifferent as to the possessor of these two duchies, but would agree with him, that their being in the King's hands suits far better with the interest of Great Britain.' The alternative, he argued, was that they might fall into 'the hands either of the Tsar, who gives already but too much jealousy to the Empire; or of the King of Sweden, who endeavoured to raise a new rebellion in Great Britain, and harbours our fugitive rebels.' In this context, the issue of Mecklenburg, of which critics had made such play, was irrelevant. As far as the Russians in Mecklenburg were concerned, Stanhope claimed, the King had 'acted in all this as Elector and Prince of the Empire', and had not as King 'tied up his hands with respect to his interest in Germany and a Prince of the [German] Empire'. All the same, Stanhope could not help reminding Parliament that 'long before His Majesty's accession to the crown, Great Britain was in strict union with the Emperor and Empire'. For this reason, he continued, 'if, by virtue of ancient alliances, the Emperor should require Great Britain to use those instances with the Tsar, which the King has made only as Elector of Hanover, Great Britain could not avoid complying with his request.' To be sure, Stanhope was attempting to have it both ways, but he was also drawing attention to the essentially symbiotic nature of British and Hanoverian interests in Germany. Indeed, in May 1717 Stanhope told the Austrians that Britain regarded Hanover as one of its own provinces.[31]

Contrary to what many believed at the time and since, George's Hanoverian ministers were by no means out to destroy Townshend and Walpole. Rather, the key to the deepening Whig split was to be found in the escalating feud between the King and the Prince of Wales. Relations between them had never been particularly warm – unsurprisingly perhaps, when one considers that the Prince had seen his mother torn from him at a young age and exiled to the castle of Ahlden in Hanover. The Prince was also offended by the care which the King had taken to prevent him from taking over the Regency during his absences in Hanover. Matters came to a head over the baptism of the Prince's second son. George felt that the choice of godparents was a royal prerogative; the Prince and Princess were adamant that this was their exclusive right. There was also disagreement over whether George or the Prince should decide the marriage partners for the Prince's three daughters, a question with profound implications for British foreign policy. In December 1717, after a particularly fierce row, the Prince of Wales was banned from the royal palaces. For the next three years, until the royal reconciliation in 1720, the two Georges found ever more inventive ways of tormenting and isolating each other. For a time, the Prince refused to attend meetings of the Privy Council and turned his back on Parliament; the King took temporary control of the upbringing of his grandchildren and tried to restrict membership of the Prince's court. The reverberations of the dispute were to be felt well beyond the court in the spheres of high politics and foreign policy.[32]

Townshend's rivals quickly took advantage of the split to improve their position with the King. Stanhope's attempts to 'mediate' soon degenerated into straightforward brow-beating. At one meeting with the Princess of Wales, 'he discoursed long and hard about the present conduct of the Prince towards his father', according to Schulenburg's account, and told Caroline that the Prince's failure to cooperate with the King had brought the royal split to public attention. As so often, Stanhope's temper got the better of him in the course of the meeting. 'The anger of that man,' the Hanoverian observed, 'grew during the discussion [and] very harsh things were said about the Prince should he not change his manners towards his father.' Most of Stanhope's attempts to arbitrate, in fact, ended in full-scale rows. But by far the most extreme voice during the royal split was that of Charles Spencer, Earl of Sunderland, whose hatred for the Prince of Wales and determination to regain the King's favour were mutually reinforcing. As Schulenburg noted, 'Sunderland is of the opinion that [the King] should impose his will on the Prince by force without entering into any compromise with him.' At one point, Sunderland even suggested that the Prince should be transplanted to the colonies if he refused to bow to the King's will. It is therefore not surprising that the Prince drew a distinction between Stanhope, to whom he was prepared to speak, and Sunderland, who would not be admitted to his presence unless carrying a communication from the King. Sunderland, in turn, ended up avoiding the formidable Princess of Wales; 'There is no way,' she told her lady-in-waiting Mrs Clayton, 'of my seeing Lord Sunderland. He is so afraid of me that he puts it off from one day to the next.'[33]

The divide between the Prince and the court Whigs (that is, those in government) went deeper than just Stanhope and Sunderland. Thanks to clumsiness and misunderstanding on both sides, it soon extended to the Court Chamberlain, the Duke of Newcastle. Early relations between the two had been cordial: the gregarious Newcastle had entertained the Prince sumptuously at his seat of Claremont in 1716. He was a man who Horatio Walpole said was 'like the children in the wood ... not knowing what's proper to be said or omitted according to whom he talks to'. But there was calculation as well as artlessness. Just as Newcastle shifted his loyalties from the Walpole–Townshend connection to the Stanhope–Sunderland axis, so did his relations with the Prince deteriorate. Matters came to a head when Newcastle was imposed by the King as a godfather to the Prince of Wales's second son. An angry exchange between the two, in which Newcastle mistook the Prince's accented English for a challenge to a duel, descended into farce. For some time thereafter, the Prince bore a grudge against Newcastle. During a debate in the House of Lords, for example, he ostentatiously left the chamber as Newcastle rose to speak. Later the Prince was to say that

Newcastle was not fit to be chamberlain at a minor German court. It was a bad start to a relationship which was to last for more than thirty years after the Prince came to the throne as George II in 1727.[34]

All this facilitated the emergence of a counter-court, or 'reversionary interest', centred on the Prince of Wales. He enjoyed one crucial advantage over his father: contrary to legend, the Prince spoke good English, albeit with a marked German accent. His intelligent and articulate wife, Caroline, made efforts to reach out to English opinion, in contrast to the lack of an obvious consort for the King. Inevitably, the Prince became a rallying point for discontent with the ministry and the monarch. When he attended service at St James's, he was accompanied by an approving crowd shouting 'High Church'. Perhaps even more worryingly, the Prince began to embrace popular anti-Hanoverian rhetoric in order to embarrass his father and the hated ministry. He publicly approved parliamentary attacks on the Personal Union, including Pulteney's hurtful remarks about German 'foreigners'. His most provocative gesture, however, was to send a groom of the bedchamber, General Churchill, to visit the openly Jacobite MP William Shippen in the Tower, bearing an offer of £1,000. Shippen had been sent there to cool off after describing George I as a foreigner, unacquainted with the English language and constitution, whose main aim was to aggrandize his German homeland. Probably for this reason, he therefore declined this offer from the Prince, who was when all was said and done, a Hanoverian.[35]

The burgeoning alliance between the Prince and disaffected Whigs copper-fastened the ascendancy of Stanhope and Sunderland, at least for the time being. But for the King's German ministers the royal split and the secession of the Townshend–Walpole interest was an unmitigated disaster. It put them in the invidious position of choosing between members of the royal family; it was obviously damaging to the image and stability of the dynasty; and it also posed severe practical problems for the German ministers. How was one to organize a Regency to govern while George was in Hanover with a disaffected Prince left behind to fester? Moreover, the Whig split created a series of domestic and diplomatic headaches for George. As Schulenburg noted, Townshend's successor as Secretary of State, Joseph Addison, might be a fluent pamphleteer, but he was 'too little versed in matters of state and especially foreign affairs to occupy the post of the second Secretary of State'. He considered Stanhope 'very much unable to manage the lower chamber'.

It was to be expected that Walpole would attack the ministry and the court via the money supply for the Baltic fleet, and perhaps even force the return of the squadron. Furthermore, there was the effect of these domestic squabbles on Britain's standing among the other European powers to be considered. 'The signs of their disagreements,' Schulenburg wrote, 'are striking and will be regarded abroad as well as in this country as the seed of a public divide and a future rupture.' As if all this were not bad enough, the Hanoverians were also acutely conscious of the fact that the Whig split also damaged the standing of the ministry among financiers in the City of London, which was closely linked to, and to a certain extent manipulated by, Walpole. The heavy parliamentary clobbering duly took its toll: a crucial supply vote passed the Commons by only four votes while Walpole, usually the guiding spirit of the House, looked on in Sphinx-like silence.[36]

Senior Hanoverian figures such as Bernstorff and Bothmer therefore had every reason to heal the rifts among the Whigs and within the royal family, not to deepen them. They did their best to save Townshend, not least because George wanted to avoid a fuss. They tried to persuade him to accept the Irish posting, and to reconcile himself to Stanhope and Sunderland. The Hanoverians also tried to mediate the split in the royal family. Bernstorff and Bothmer held long meetings with the Prince and Princess of Wales to try to resolve their dispute with the King. They even involved sympathetic Members of Parliament, such as the Speaker of the House of Commons, in their arbitration efforts. In short, it was the Germans who kept the royal lines of communication open at this trying time for the dynasty. For the moment all attempts to bring father and son together failed due to obstinacy and pride on both sides. If in the end it was all to no avail, the reason does not lie either in the northern policy or in the machinations of 'the Germans'.[37]

A major beneficiary of the Whig split was the Earl of Oxford, the most prominent surviving victim of the war on Jacobitism and foreign policy dissent, imprisoned since early July 1715. He had essentially been forgotten about, and in late May 1717 the political nation was reminded of him when he petitioned the House of Lords for an immediate trial. The fear, as the Duke of Buckingham put it, was that unless the House of Lords 'interposed, his imprisonment might become perpetual'. All this found the men of the Commons Secret Committee, who had originally made the case against Oxford, in disarray. Some had themselves become peers in the meantime, some were away and, as the parliamentary history puts it, 'others grown remiss and indifferent in the matter'. Over the next few weeks, the Lower House vainly tried to hold up the trial, for which it was not ready. The committee which had been appointed to consider the state of the case against Oxford reported on 12 June 1717, blamed the lack of progress on the recent Jacobite revolt, and begged for more time.[38]

The response of the Commons to this suggestion was hardly a ringing endorsement. Some suggested that for the sake of speed and simplicity the absurdly long list of charges be reduced to two articles of impeachment, both of them capital offences. William Shippen remarked snidely 'that after all, those who had first begun the impeachments, ought to be satisfied with having got the places of those that were impeached which, indeed, seemed to be what they had principally in view'. To this Walpole responded rather feebly that 'he had of late looked over some of the most material papers relating to this impeachment, and he was still convinced in his conscience that the late ministry had given themselves up entirely, and were ready to deliver up the nation to France'. Walpole clearly now had other things on his mind, especially the feud with Stanhope. The venom against Oxford had largely dissipated; what remained was embarrassment about a legal proceeding brought but not completed. The peers would have none of this. They were open to a genuine case of national security, but unwilling to detain a man indefinitely simply because the authorities had not got around to mounting a trial or – worse still – refused to admit that they had insufficient evidence to proceed. In the end, after a short trial, Oxford was acquitted by the House of Lords.[39]

Significantly, none of this drove the Whigs or the royal family to reunite in the face of a common threat. The criminalization of the Utrecht policy, which had so characterized British politics in the first few years of the Personal Union, was over. The debate had moved on and so had the context. The rapprochement with France, which had seemed so culpable in 1714–15, appeared less so in the light of the 1716 alliance.

The King's Hanoverian entourage noted the rise of anti-German sentiment, particularly in Parliament, with concern. Schulenburg observed over a period of six months that 'in the debates one has heavily attacked the German ministers'; that 'one had never spoken against the Germans as much as today'; that MPs were demanding 'a petition to the King to banish all the Germans'; and that 'one still threatens to attack the Germans'. Parliamentary accusations that the dispatch of the Baltic squadron was a violation of the Act of Settlement seem to have sent a particular shiver down Hanoverian spines. Outside Parliament, a great deal of energy was expended trying to combat the wave of critical pamphlets which accused the King of not wanting to take up the English crown, of being under the thumb of his mistress, of having a dim view of his new subjects, and of dragging Britain into foreign wars in pursuit of his narrow interests. George's Hanoverian ministers also worried about the effect which royal absences in Hanover might have on public opinion. One report lamented that 'The messengers of the ill-disposed continue to print and spread clandestinely among the public satires and vaudevilles against the Whigs and against the present government.'[40]

Censorship and rebuttal was one way of dealing with these difficulties, but George tried to find other ways of countering the threatening rise of popular and political xenophobia. One method was a conscious attempt to anglicize the dynasty. The King was too old to reinvent himself, but his grandchildren were another matter. He had left the eldest, a boy, behind in Hanover to be brought up as a German; this had been adversely remarked upon. He now seems to have decided to give the remaining grandchildren, three girls, both of whose parents were German, an English education. George signalled to their existing governess, Miss Gemmingen, 'that he had taken the resolution of introducing an English lady into the company of the princesses'. The Dowager Duchess of Portland was appointed in her place, and a chaplain was appointed to teach them English; French and German were not neglected, of course, and two sub-governesses were selected to take care of instruction in those languages. Another sign of George's new 'British' sensibility was his rejection of a Dutch invitation to 'reanimate' the Republic by becoming a candidate for the Stadholdership in 1716. This was attractive to George in diplomatic terms, but it would almost certainly have intensified unflattering comparisons between him and William III.[41]

The most radical solution, of course, was to break the Personal Union itself. Even before the Baltic crisis, George had begun to think about how this might be effected. This not because he had lost interest in the Electorate, but because he feared that Hanover might be neglected, and had become anxious about domestic criticisms. In early 1716 George therefore began to explore the possibilities of separating Crown and Electorate. The Chief Justice, Thomas Parker – later the Earl of Macclesfield – was asked to deliver an opinion on whether, in the event of there being a younger brother, or a suitable male in a collateral branch of the family, an Act of Parliament could ensure the succession of the eldest son to the crown of England and that of the younger or some other figure to the Hanoverian Electorate. Parker's response did not pronounce on whether or not such a separation would be desirable. Instead, his opinion set out with remorseless logic why the planned rupture would open a whole can of legal, dynastic and diplomatic worms.[42]

Parker began by reminding George that 'by law there is never the least interregnum but the moment the king or queen dies the successor is the same moment completely king or queen.' If this were not the case, disaffected figures might somehow insert themselves into the interregnum. There was thus no way that the separation could be effected between the death of the king and the succession of his heir. Moreover, and here Parker was making a crucial constitutional point, Parliament could not overrule the laws of succession of the German Empire, to which the Electorate was subject. Unhelpfully, imperial law was quite clear that the succession should be strictly by primogeniture. This was certainly the Emperor's view, who held that the eldest son could not be forced to give up the Electorate. Of course, Parliament might make the renunciation of Hanover a condition of succeeding to the crown of England.

The problem was that what Parliament had done, it could undo. It had – as Parker pointedly reminded George – repealed 'several articles in the Act of Settlement ... particularly that which restrained His Majesty from going abroad'. It was quite possible, Parker continued, that once in possession of the throne, the eldest son would then proceed to inveigle his ministers and Parliament into supporting a war to recover the Electorate. The position of the younger son, with a distinctly shaky title to Hanover in terms of German imperial law, would then be particularly precarious: 'He would have neither the laws of the Empire, nor the laws of England, nor forces, nor money suitable to such an undertaking to support his pretensions.' Neighbouring powers might well be dragged in. The only way of effecting the separation and avoiding such a war of the Hanoverian succession in Germany was by persuading the Empire to pass a law making the second son Elector in preference to his elder brother. Otherwise, the two territories were irrefragably joined, for better or for worse. Britain was, whether she liked it or not, effectively part of the Holy Roman Empire.

This was not quite the end of royal schemes to separate the two territories. In 1719, George approached the Emperor with a request to waive the primogeniture rule, but nothing came of it. After the birth of the Prince of Wales's second son, William Augustus, the Duke of Cumberland, in 1721, the subject came up again. The Prince suggested that the Duke succeed to the English throne while his elder son, George Frederick, should become Elector. This had the advantage of getting around the imperial primogeniture rule and it made some sort of sense for George Frederick, who was already in Hanover and whose horizon, at this point, was firmly German. Whether the Prince also sought hereby to discriminate against his eldest son, whom he hated as cordially as he had his father and his father him, is not clear. George agreed to the scheme, providing that George Frederick gave his assent; but nothing came of this when the Prince of Wales acceded to the throne in 1727.

Anglicizing the monarchy and thinking about separating Crown and Electorate were long-term solutions. In the meantime, Stanhope and Sunderland were confronted with some very immediate challenges. Thanks to their support for George's Baltic policy and their intrigues against Walpole and Townshend, they found themselves mired in constitutional controversy and parliamentary uproar by late 1716. Over the next three years, the secessionist Whigs were to become an increasingly threatening presence. In March 1717, Parliament voted the army estimates through comfortably, but the money to pay for the Baltic squadron passed by only eight votes. Walpole agitated against the Mutiny Bill and against the repeal of the Occasional Conformity and Schism Acts. He blocked taxation to pay for military preparations against foreign attack. He opposed the Peerage Bill. At the beginning of 1717 most of this still lay in the future, but the dimensions and implications of the Whig split were clear to all. As one Erasmus Lewis triumphantly remarked to his fellow Tory Jonathan Swift: 'Morally speaking, nothing but another rebellion can ever unite them.' It was time to play the Jacobite card.[43]

The government had for some time monitored the development of a Swedish plot in support of the Pretender. This hare-brained scheme was the brainchild of the Swedish chief minister Görtz and the Swedish ambassador to Britain, Count Gyllenborg. Both were convinced that the only way of saving Sweden's German provinces was by reversing the Hanoverian succession and placing 'James III' on the throne; it was hoped that Charles's Protestant credentials would make the Pretender more acceptable to British opinion. Görtz, whose chief preoccupation was the parlous state of the Swedish finances, also seems to have regarded his involvement with the cash-rich Jacobites as an elaborate form of low-interest loan. In January 1717 the government moved in to arrest Gyllenborg and confiscate his papers, extracts from which were presented to Parliament in February and published with tremendous fanfare. Persuading some sections of opinion to see this dossier as evidence of a real threat was not difficult: in 1717, the Swedish King overran Norway, giving him a plausible base from which to descend on Scotland. The diplomatic cost, however, was considerable. Treating an officially accredited envoy in this manner was – as even a Hanoverian observer sympathetic to the administration conceded – problematic under international law. At the very least, the British government breached convention by publishing the correspondence; but then there was no established legal procedure to deal with diplomats who were abusing their privileged status to conduct subversion in the country to which they were accredited.[44]

In the medium term, the move against Gyllenborg also backfired domestically. It did not drive the opposition Whigs back into Stanhope's arms, not least because they were anxious to claim the credit for themselves. Townshend, as one Hanoverian observer noted, 'makes a great virtue of having managed for such a long time and so well the unmasking of the intrigue of the Swedish minister'. None of this convinced Tory and popular critics of the administration. They protested that Charles XII had only turned to the Jacobites after Admiral Norris had been ordered to attack his ships in the Baltic. There was something in this: after all, the Swedish King had rebuffed French overtures in support of the Pretender as recently as 1715. It would not be the last time that government policy was to create a constituency for Jacobitism where none had previously existed.[45]

The period immediately following the Hanoverian succession had been a turbulent one. Tory grand strategy had been discredited, its protagonists banished, marginalized and in some cases even imprisoned. A Jacobite rising had been seen off. Britain's Continental alliances were rebuilt. But by the end of 1717, the domestic and diplomatic kaleidoscope had been shaken once more. At the King's insistence, Britain had hurled herself into the vortex of Baltic power politics, triggering a domestic explosion. Parliament was in turmoil and the royal family divided. The Jacobite threat returned on the back of the Baltic controversy. Above all, the old hatchet with France was buried. This was a momentous and quite unexpected diplomatic revolution. Nothing would now be quite the same. And there were new threats brewing in the north and south, which would put the alliance to severe test.

5

Preventive War in the Mediterranean and the Baltic, 1718–1719

For various reasons His Majesty could not join the alliance [between Hanover, the Emperor and Poland] as King, but that would not prevent the British fleet in the Baltic from operating in support of that alliance, and applying the right to self-defence as it has done against Sweden in the past and still does, even though His Majesty has not declared war on the King of Sweden.[1]

George I's Hanoverian chief minister, Count Bernstorff, in 1718, on why George could not provide an official guarantee to use the Royal Navy against the Russians

Very shortly after the Utrecht Settlement, it became clear that the new geopolitical architecture of Europe was designed to contain the old threat – from France – and not the emerging challenges in northern and southern Europe. By the end of the decade, it became clear that the biggest danger to Britain's security came from the rising power of Tsar Peter the Great in the Baltic, and the resurgence of Spanish ambitions in the Mediterranean. In both cases, the threat was as much to the overall balance of power as to the position of the Royal Navy; indeed, because neither Madrid nor St Petersburg hesitated to play the Jacobite card, the Protestant Succession in Britain itself was also in peril. The two theatres were separated by huge distances, and yet the problems were interconnected, not least because two of the most important European powers, France and Austria, had interests in both spheres. In each case, the use of naval power provided a tempting but as it turned out insufficient solution. In the end, the balance in the Mediterranean and – less successfully – the Baltic, and with them Britain's naval supremacy, could only be safeguarded through skilful diplomacy. Stanhope's grand design for

Europe provided for the time being, at least, a collaborative framework within which British interests were secured. He responded to the unfamiliar challenges not by drawing in his horns, but by broadening Britain's strategic perspective.

Britain's policy in the Mediterranean after 1714 aimed at 'double containment'. Stanhope preached the need to guard against the revival of French power, especially an attempt to reunite the Spanish and the French crowns. But he was also profoundly concerned about Spanish ambitions to rebuild her Mediterranean empire at Austrian expense, especially in Italy. At the same time, Britain sought to restrain the Austrians: the Holy Roman Emperor, Charles VI, the sometime 'Charles III' of Spain, was still smarting from the loss of his own claim to the Spanish throne; and he still had a substantial following among Catalans opposed to Castilian domination. Finally, Britain had her own, narrower agenda in the region: holding on to Gibraltar and Minorca (two key naval bases retained at Utrecht); to exploit the *Asiento*, or the right to trade in slaves with the Spanish colonies; and to consolidate her trade with Spain. The instruments available to pursue these interests were limited: a Royal Naval squadron and the bases at Minorca and Gibraltar, but no ground forces worth speaking of. What Britain lacked in brute coercive power would have to be made up through diplomatic manoeuvre, bribery, persuasion and bluff. Moreover, she would not just react to threats, but seek to forestall them.

While Louis XIV still lived, a fresh struggle with France for control of the Mediterranean could not be ruled out. After his death in 1715, Spain soon emerged as the principal threat. For Elizabeth Farnese, the second wife of the King of Spain, was concerned to find suitable inheritances for her children; Philip's family by his first wife would succeed in Madrid. This could only be achieved in Italy, at Austria's expense. But first Philip's chief minister and a close confidant of Elizabeth, Cardinal Alberoni, needed to neutralize the Royal Navy; only then could a combined naval and ground assault on the Austrians take place. To that end, Alberoni granted Britain favourable terms in a new commercial treaty in December 1715. He hoped thereby to win over merchant and colonial interests in London, and give them an incentive to oppose a military confrontation with Spain. This was a clever strategy: not only was there a large overseas trade at stake, but British manufacturing exports to Spain and Portugal were steadily expanding, almost the only European market where that was still the case.[2]

Confrontation with Spain thus made no commercial sense at this point. Indeed, the Tory MP for Scarborough later complained, after the outbreak of hostilities, that he had 'carefully looked over all the treaties before them but found not one article in them for security of the English commerce and desired that in this address they would mention it to His Majesty'. If Stanhope refused to turn a blind eye to Spanish ambitions in the western and central Mediterranean, it was because strategic concerns mattered more to him. He responded to Alberoni's advances with his own vision for a geopolitical reordering of the Mediterranean. Stanhope envisaged a set of interlocking exchanges and guarantees. The Emperor, Charles VI, should forgo his claim to the Spanish crown; in return he would be confirmed in possession of his territories in Italy and the Netherlands. At the same time, Charles should offer the Savoyards Sardinia in exchange for Sicily. This would create greater contiguity for both states, and thus strengthen them in their respective barrier functions. Spain would have to renounce her more extensive claims in Italy, but Elizabeth Farnese's son, Don Carlos, would secure the reversionary interest on Parma, Tuscany and Piacenza: they would fall to him after the reigning Duke died. Britain, for her part, was willing to surrender Gibraltar if that would lead to a stable settlement; after all, bases were a means to an end, not the end itself.[3]

Stanhope was therefore prepared to make sacrifices for a lasting settlement in the Mediterranean. Elizabeth Farnese, however, would not accept anything less than the return of all or at least a major part of the former Spanish European empire. In 1717 the Spaniards seized Habsburg Sardinia in a coup de main. It was clear that Spain would have to be coerced, and in order to do so Stanhope had to embed his Mediterranean strategy within a broader European vision. French cooperation was clearly essential, another argument in favour of the alliance which Stanhope pursued with such success in 1716. Equally important were the Austrians, with whom relations were also restored in 1716–17. But Stanhope had to take into account not only Britain's bilateral relations but also the relations of her allies with third parties. Of particular worry was the distraction caused by the resumption of hostilities between the Austrians and Turks in 1716. It was for this reason that British and Hanoverian observers looked to a rapid Austrian victory.

As Schulenburg remarked to Görtz, news of Habsburg successes 'had revived the low spirits here' and would have 'a very positive effect for His Majesty's interest in all areas' – that is, in the Baltic and the Mediterranean. Britain therefore also helped to mediate the Peace of Passarowitz in July 1718, between the Emperor and the Turkish Sultan.[4]

All this involved a widening of British diplomatic horizons. Of course, the connection between the northern and western balances had already been grasped by Marlborough; and the need to relieve the Emperor of the Turkish threat had been a consideration in London since the Nine Years War. Still, Britain had hitherto never really had a holistic eastern policy, designed to see issues in the round rather than in isolation. This was a function not so much of ignorance as of institutional blinkers, resulting from the division of foreign affairs into a Northern and a Southern department. This was bad enough in the case of relations with France, where British statesmen were well aware of the ways in which Mediterranean and northern affairs could interconnect. But it was critical in the case of Austria, Russia and Turkey, which were peripheral to both departments. A modern observer would have noted that there was a distinct lack of 'joined-up government' in British foreign policy. Coherence had to be supplied by an individual, either the monarch or a dynamic chief minister, as Stanhope was.

The Spanish problem, however, remained. Taking advantage of Britain's preoccupation in the Baltic, and hopeful that her commercial diplomacy had made the cost of war unacceptably high to London, Spain continued her Mediterranean advance. There was little the Austrians, who had no navy worth speaking of, could do about this beyond appealing to Britain and France for help. Counter-measures were hampered by the paralysing effect of the Whig split, which the Spanish ambassador to London exacerbated wherever he could. In Parliament, Walpole not only opposed the Baltic policy, but also tried to block approval of the money supply for the Mediterranean fleet, on the grounds that it would lead to war with Spain. Stanhope was acutely conscious of these constraints. In mid February 1718, he wrote of his determination 'to hide from foreign nations if possible our nakedness'.[5]

But it was the Spanish invasion of Sicily, and the expulsion of the Austrian garrison, in July 1718, which finally forced Britain's hand. Shortly afterwards, Daniel Defoe summed up the resulting strategic threat to the British position in the Mediterranean. 'If the present Spanish

King sets up a superiority of his naval power,' he wrote, 'Sicily, in such a hand, would be like a chain drawn across the mouth of the Levant Sea.' 'Great Britain,' he went on, 'cannot acquiesce in letting Spain possess Sicily without giving up her trade to Turkey and the Gulph of Venice . . . to Gallipoli for oil, to Messina and Naples for silk; and in a word her whole commerce of the Mediterranean.' Defoe concluded by asking, 'How long shall we be able to carry on our navigation and commerce with our people in Jamaica, Barbados etc., if the naval strength of Spain shall be suffered to grow to such an immoderate and monstrous pitch?' As if all this was not bad enough, there were also fears of an attack from New Spain on the British in the Carolinas. In George's mind, the looming Spanish hegemony in the Mediterranean and the confrontations with Sweden, Prussia and increasingly Russia in the Baltic seemed to blend into one continuous encircling front against him. He was enveloped not only in Britain and America but in Hanover as well. Something drastic needed to be done.[6]

Within a month, the Mediterranean squadron of the Royal Navy under Admiral Byng attacked and annihilated the Spanish fleet off Cape Passaro. Since Britain and Spain were not yet at war, this action, as the naval historian Alfred Thayer Mahan noted, was the 'destruction not of an actual but of a possible rival'. It was a preventive strike designed to eliminate a potential threat to British interests at an early stage. As Sunderland remarked to the Duke of Newcastle on hearing the news, 'there is now a thorough end put to the Cardinal's great projects and to the rising power of Spain at sea.' Likewise, the Hanoverians around the King welcomed the news of the Spanish defeat as a relief not only in the Mediterranean. 'Clipping Spain's wings in Italy,' Schulenburg hoped, would ease Britain's situation in the Baltic: 'it would be very convenient for us to be secure from that side while we are being threatened by some terrible catastrophe from the opposite corner [of Europe]' – that is, the Baltic. Military action was accompanied by active diplomacy. The Hanoverians, especially Bernstorff and Bothmer, were very active in helping to bring about the Quadruple Alliance of August 1718, by which Charles VI joined the Triple Alliance of Britain, France and the United Provinces with a view to containing Spain. Through a combination of coercive and collaborative instruments, the Spanish advance in the Mediterranean had been contained, and the rise of a naval rival forestalled.[7]

All the same, many in the political nation and in the public sphere at

8. The destruction of the Spanish fleet at Cape Passaro was an example of pre-emptive action, not only to forestall a Spanish invasion of Sicily, but also to prevent the emergence of a rival naval power in the Mediterranean.

large were profoundly ambivalent about the triumph at Cape Passaro. Rather than retrospectively sanction the operation, one critic, Lord Strafford, announced that 'before they approved the sea fight, they ought to be satisfied whether the same happened before or after the signing of the Quadruple Alliance.' He therefore moved that Byng's instructions should be laid before Parliament. Likewise, Walpole – still determined to make mischief for his rivals in the ministry – argued that 'the giving sanction . . . to the late measures, could have no other view, than to screen ministers, who were conscious of having done something amiss, and, who having begun a war against Spain, would now make it the Parliament's war.' Instead of applauding, he continued, Parliament 'ought to show their entire dissatisfaction with a conduct that was contrary to the laws of nations, and a breach of solemn treaties'. Stanhope responded to these charges robustly. He made clear that Cape Passaro had been an act not merely of tactical but also strategic pre-emption. It was aimed, first of all, at stopping Spain from breaking out of the constraints of the Utrecht Settlement, rebuilding their Mediterranean empire and perhaps even reuniting the French and Spanish thrones. Secondly, Stanhope argued, 'it was high time for Great Britain to check the naval power of Spain'. Better to confront it now than later. Indeed, rather than disavowing Byng, Stanhope stressed that the Admiral was following royal instructions. The King, in turn, had 'acted by the advice of his Privy Council; that he was one of that number; and he thought it an honour to have advised His Majesty to these measures', which he believed to be necessary in the national interest. All the procedures, in short, had been followed. The ministry were all in this together. Stanhope spoke with such passion and eloquence that most were persuaded.[8]

War was formally declared between Britain and Spain in December 1718, followed by a French declaration of war on Spain in January 1719. Three months later, the French launched a successful invasion of northern Spain, supported by a diversionary British operation in Galicia. Meanwhile, the Royal Navy drove the Spaniards from the western Mediterranean. Despite the fact that all three combatants had extensive colonial holdings, this was essentially a European war, fought in Europe for European ends. Spain tried to unseat George by sponsoring a Jacobite invasion of Scotland in April 1719. James III, however, was unable to make a landfall, and the rebellion under the Earl of Mar soon fizzled out. The unequal contest lasted less than a year. In December 1719 Alberoni was dismissed and in early 1720 Spain made her peace with the Quadruple Alliance. All Spanish–Austrian differences were referred to a future Congress at Cambrai, which would meet early in the new decade. Perhaps fortunately for those who had begun the war in such legally dubious circumstances, it had ended well.[9]

Exultant Whigs saw in this outcome not only a vindication of their policies but also a guarantee of their domestic political ascendancy. As Newcastle wrote to Stanhope in October 1719, he could not 'apprehend that we have anything to fear' in new elections. He believed that their 'merit of having settled a universal peace in Europe' would ensure the King's 'hearty adherence to the Whig interest'. Likewise Stanhope saw 'the prospect of seeing a peace both in the south and the north before next spring'. 'This good situation,' he added, 'will probably put our friends in good humour at our opening the Parliament.' Indeed, it would be advisable 'to make the best use and advantage possible of this good humour' by pushing through contentious domestic measures such as the Peerage Bill. Not everybody shared this optimism. It was true, as Schulenburg noted in August 1718, that 'once re-established, the tranquility of the south will add great lustre to the King our master, I wish I could say the same for the north, and in order to render the happiness of the King complete, the submission of the P[rince of Wales] must round off these grand projects. I hope it without believing.'[10]

For in the Baltic, Britain-Hanover faced a massive new threat to her interests: Russia. Ever since the turn of the century, when Peter the Great's ambition erupted on to the European scene, British statesmen and publicists had watched the growth of Russian power with apprehension. By promoting Russia through the provision of naval expertise, England and later Britain seemed to have nurtured a potential rival. As the Whig pamphleteer Daniel Defoe wrote in 1705, the example of Russia 'may serve to remind us, how we once taught the French to build ships, till they are grown able to teach us how to use them'. By 1718, the British representative in Russia, James Jefferys, was warning that 'The improvements he [Peter] has made, by the help of English builders, are such as a seaman would think almost impossible for a nation so lately used to the sea.' The Russians, he lamented, had now 'built three sixty-gun ships, which are in every way equal to the best of that rank in our country'. Some time later, in April 1719, Jefferys asked Stanhope 'whether it will be for the interest of Great Britain to be a spectator of so growing a power as this, especially at sea, and brought about by her own subjects'. As the Swedish empire in the Baltic disintegrated and the Russians advanced into Estonia, Latvia, Finland and Mecklenburg, unease turned to alarm.[11]

British policy was driven by strategic, not economic considerations. Indeed, there was a strong commercial lobby which wished to avoid war with Russia at all costs. As one Hanoverian reported in the autumn of 1719, there were many 'English merchants who trade with Russia [who] have made representations to the Regents that they have more than two million pounds sterling worth of assets which they would risk losing if one hastily [*brusquement*] declared war on the Muscovites'. There were also merchants who complained of Swedish depredations against British commerce, and so these economic considerations had a way of cancelling each other out, in that a breach with either country would be economically costly. Moreover, Britain had an existential reason to fear Peter. Ever since the failed rebellion of 1715, Jacobites had swarmed across Europe armed with letters of introduction from James III, many of them to Russia. Their expertise was welcomed there with open arms. Supporters of the Pretender trained Peter's army, built and led his navy, and one even served as his personal physician. As relations with Britain deteriorated, these men gained ever greater prominence. Throughout 1716, they tried to mediate a peace between Sweden and Russia, so that either or both sides would be free to attack George. In 1718, they tried again, this time with a view to bringing Spain into the alliance as well. Of course, whether Britain was compelled to oppose Peter because of his support for Jacobites, or whether he felt obliged to support them because of British hostility, is a moot point. Ministerial measures had partly helped to create the threat they sought to contain.[12]

The main instrument of British policy in the Baltic would have to be the Royal Navy, if possible with Dutch support. 'By all I can learn here of the state of affairs in the north,' Stanhope wrote in late May 1719, 'I think it would be of the utmost consequence if we could appear with a joint force in that sea sufficient to give weight to our mediation.' One method considered by Stanhope was a surprise attack on the Russians by sea, if necessary without formal declaration of war. He wanted to inflict a 'Cape Passaro' on them, a phrase which in those days had something of the quality that 'Copenhagen' had for the nineteenth- and early-twentieth-century navy. Clearly, the strategy of pre-emption, which had served so well against Spain in 1718–19, was infectious. But Stanhope knew that – as in the Mediterranean – military instruments alone would not suffice. If Russia was to be contained, a fundamental rethink of policy in the Baltic was required. Fortuitously, an opportunity was now at hand.[13]

In December 1718, Charles XII was killed in action in Norway, to almost universal relief; his more moderate sister Ulrica Eleonora succeeded to the throne. This was the moment for a rapprochement with Sweden, in order to restore it as a bulwark against Peter the Great. The choice of envoy to Sweden fell upon Lord Carteret. This was significant, because it shows the extent to which the King was swayed by foreign political considerations rather than just party ones. Carteret's family background was Tory, albeit loyal; he himself had a voting record in Parliament as a Hanover Tory. But what really recommended him to George was his firm European orientation and his linguistic skills. Schulenburg described Carteret thus: 'He is a young nobleman who has very good qualities, and much more politeness and obligingness towards foreigners than is usual among islanders and free peoples [les peuples libres]. He speaks French, which has enabled him to get to know the King, who values him for his merits.' He finished by saying that 'if so far he has not, properly speaking, belonged to any party, he was far from being odious to the Whigs and Tories', both of whom were now assiduously courting him. Of course, it did Carteret no harm that he was on good terms with some of the King's Hanoverian ministers, particularly Görtz, and seems to have been regarded with a good deal of suspicion by the Prince of Wales; Caroline confessed to her lady-in-waiting Mrs Clayton that 'I am afraid of him'. He even got on with the famously cantankerous and suspicious Admiral Norris.[14]

Carteret finally set off for Sweden in May 1719, accompanied by 'three secretaries, two chaplains, three chefs, a pastry-chef [confiseur] and several other servants'. By the time he arrived, Sweden was in dire straits and on the verge of invasion by the Tsar. Only Britain, Carteret argued, now stood between Russia and the total domination of the Baltic. If nothing was done, he warned Robethon in late July 1719, 'the Tsar will be absolute master of Sweden and of the Baltic, which would not be in Britain's interest nor that of the whole of Europe'. For this reason Carteret repeated over and over that 'we ought for the sake of our own interests as English [sic] men not to stand by as unconcerned spectators but prevent their ruin if possible.' Moreover, Carteret warned that failure to prop up Sweden might well lead to a Russo-Swedish rapprochement at Britain's expense. Given the determination of the Swedish parliament – the Senate – to come to terms with Russia, this was perfectly possible. 'If they had made peace with the Tsar, or even should be upon good terms with him while he remains in the Baltic,' he wrote, 'they may in conjunction not only affront in these seas, but also give us trouble at home.' In other words, they might support a Jacobite invasion. This was not just about state interests, he argued, but also about the preservation of the 'Protestant cause', something which he knew to be dear to George's heart.[15]

Predictably, the chief stumbling block was Bremen and Verden. George would have been happy to trade the duchies for an 'equivalent'. His Hanoverian diplomats, however, soon realized that the Swedes were insisting 'on the restitution of the duchies of Bremen and Verden without an equivalent'. Despite their parlous situation, the Swedes were determined to maintain their footing in Germany. Indeed, the presentation of Carteret's credentials in Stockholm led to an immediate row. The President of the Swedish Chancery, Count Cronhielm, quickly spotted that the list of his monarch's titles therein was incomplete because it did not include the two duchies. All this put Carteret in the very difficult situation of appearing to press George's Electoral ambitions at the expense of the British interests he was sent to represent. He did not doubt that the duchies could be secured if George 'would give more and engage himself to do more for them than they are worth'. This price would be an alliance, subsidies, military and naval assistance 'to reduce the Tsar to his ancient limits'.[16]

In spite of these tensions, Carteret worked closely with the King's Hanoverian servants. The Electoral minister in Stockholm, Count Bassewitz, proved a useful source of information at the Swedish court, and Carteret was careful to coordinate most of his moves – particularly the delicate matter of bribing Swedish politicians – with him. He summed up the extent of his cooperation with the Hanoverian when he reported to Stanhope that 'I have obeyed your lordship in giving Mr Bassewitz all the assistance and support I can, & I believe he will say that I have not been unuseful to his negotiation. I shall take care in forming the defensive alliance to follow your lordship's instructions in relation to the guaranty of the Provinces in Germany and of the Duchy of Sleswick.' What is further remarkable here is that this is not a dispatch to the King, but between two British ministers, indicating the extent to which Hanoverian concerns were part of their remit. But then as Carteret remarked, he believed 'the Electoral interests are inseparable from the royal ones' in Sweden. Both shared the overriding aim of containing Russia. In the end, the Swedes conceded the loss of Bremen and Verden, essentially because they had no choice. 'Our success,' Carteret reported, 'is owing chiefly to the Tsar. He at the gates of Stockholm has reasoned the best for us.' Wisely, he did not crow about his victory in Stockholm, but rather sought to conciliate the browbeaten Swedes and motivate them for the coming showdown with Russia. 'I am never for pushing a victory too far,' Carteret remarked sagely.[17]

If George's British and Hanoverian ministers agreed on Sweden, they were bitterly divided over how to proceed in the southern Baltic. Here too the Hanoverians feared Russian power, which still threatened the Electorate from Mecklenburg in the north-east and, more remotely, from Poland in the east, where Russian troops were stationed. One Hanoverian described the Tsar's forces, sent to Mecklenburg to support its Duke against his nobility, as 'as much Vandals as Russians'. Bernstorff turned to the Austrians for help. The treaty he proposed in July 1718 was intended to block passage through Poland, and thereby 'prevent the

Tsar and Sweden from intimidating the King [George] or the Polish Republic into joining them and thus opening the door for them to return to the [German] Empire whenever it pleased them'. Before entering into any such alliance, however, the Austrians wanted to know whether George would 'join the alliance as King as well and [whether] he would support it with an adequate fleet'. It was exactly the same issue which had complicated the coalition against Sweden and contributed to the Whig split in England. But Bernstorff had in the meantime fallen out with Stanhope and Sunderland and was in no position to make any such commitment on Britain's behalf. In the end he had to go behind Stanhope's back and provide a written undertaking that George would protect Danzig and Elbing with the naval resources at his disposal.[18]

The resulting Austro-Hanoverian treaty of January 1719 was designed to stabilize the situation in Poland and Mecklenburg. It was concluded by George in his capacity as Elector only, not as King of England. Both parties undertook to maintain the territorial integrity of Poland; external powers should not be permitted to meddle in Poland's internal affairs or to undermine the domestic cohesion necessary for it to act as a buffer state. The parties to the contract also undertook to enforce a resolution of the Reichstag – which Charles had blessed two years earlier – calling upon the Duke of Mecklenburg to come to terms with his nobility. In reality, of course, the intention was not so much to uphold imperial law as to contain the Tsar: after all, what was the point of slamming the front door shut in Poland if the Russians could arrive by sea through the back entrance in Mecklenburg? This intervention – known as a *Reichsexekution* – went ahead successfully in late February and early March 1719. The Russians abandoned Karl Leopold, Duke of Mecklenburg, and withdrew from Poland. To everybody's relief, George was never called upon to fulfil his commitment to use the Royal Navy to defend the Polish ports of Danzig and Elbing against the Russians.[19]

Stanhope watched these developments with alarm. He had been deliberately sidelined over the Austrian treaty, which was directed at least as much against Prussia as against Peter the Great. Bernstorff's worries about Russia in 1716–18 had been genuine, but they were largely limited to Mecklenburg; even the ejection from Poland was secondary. In fact, most Hanoverians were relatively relaxed about the Russian threat once the situation in Mecklenburg was resolved and the Royal Navy was on its way. Prussia, by contrast, was a much more immediate threat in geopolitical terms. Bernstorff's view was also heavily coloured by the fact that he owned three villages which the King of Prussia had promised to cede to Hanover by the Treaty of 1715, but which he had so far stubbornly refused to evacuate. Stanhope, on the other hand, saw Berlin as crucial to the ring of containment around Russia in the Baltic. He was horrified by Bernstorff's unconstitutional and – as he saw it – impolitic promise to use the Royal Navy to defend Polish ports against the Prussians and Russians. As Schulenburg reported at the height of Bernstorff's discussions with the Austrians, 'the English ministers are very unsettled by the fact that one does not keep them at all informed on the plans and views one has on the affairs of the north. They would be seriously embarrassed if called to account by the House of Commons, or to explain the cost of the squadron that has been sent there.'[20]

Instead, Stanhope was determined to conclude an alliance with Berlin in 1719, so that the Prussian army and the Royal Navy might combine to rein in Peter the Great. In this spirit, the British ambassador in Berlin approached the Prussian king and 'represented the advantage and necessity of establishing such a friendship on a solid foundation in respect to the ties of blood, the situation of their states, their common interests in the Empire and the Protestant religion'. As far as Stanhope was concerned, Bernstorff's policy was bad for both British and Hanoverian interests. The resources necessary to take on both Frederick William and Peter were simply not available. 'We should not be able at the same time to break with the Tsar and the King of Prussia,' Stanhope told Carteret. 'The King's territories would thereby be exposed to too evident dangers to which we should not be in a condition to resist.' This in turn would expose him to another round of parliamentary clobbering at a time when his northern policy was already under pamphlet attack. The ministry, in fact, could ill afford the continuing divisions between Whig and Tory, and among Whigs. Re-establishing domestic unity was central to a strong foreign policy, and yet the direction of policy was a matter of intense political controversy. Thus when George and Stanhope tried to conciliate the Tories over domestic issues, even offering to drop measures in favour of Dissenters in return for parliamentary support on foreign policy, they found that continuing differences over that policy proved insuperable.[21]

These concerns interacted with a developing high-political confrontation between the Hanoverians, particularly Bernstorff, and the court

Whigs over the Peerage Bill of 1718–19. This measure was the brainchild of Sunderland and was enthusiastically adopted by Stanhope. It severely limited the number of new peerages which George's successor would be able to confer. Ostensibly this was intended to prevent a repeat of the massive surge of Tory peerages in the years before 1714, and to make Britain a more reliable partner on the international scene by reducing instability. The real motive, however, was the determination of the court Whigs to secure themselves against the reversionary interest after George's death. The King himself was persuaded of its merits, if only in order to torment the Prince. Predictably, the Bill was rejected by the Tories, by Townshend and by Walpole, in his case on the not altogether plausible grounds that it precluded the upward corporate mobility which made the English system go around. It was also, of course, furiously opposed by the Prince of Wales, who saw in it a means not only of 'attacking' him but perhaps a first step towards excluding him from the throne altogether. As Caroline reported to Mrs Clayton, she and the Prince were 'working like dogs' to prevent it; she recounted with some pride and clear Germanic intonation her success in mobilizing 'Torries' and 'Vecks' (Whigs) against the Bill.[22]

What Stanhope and Sunderland had perhaps not reckoned with was the resistance or at best ambivalence of the Hanoverian ministers. To be sure, Germans were keen to do the King's bidding; but they were not prepared to be a party to depriving the Prince of his birthright. For this reason, they not only persisted with their attempts to bring about a reconciliation between father and son, they also opposed anything which tended to deepen the rift or force them to take sides. Besides, Bernstorff was unhappy with any measure that tended to curb the royal prerogative. The result was a rapid breakdown in relations between him and the court Whigs. Moreover, the German ministers seemed to be on the verge of successfully mediating the royal split. From the point of view of Stanhope and Sunderland, the reconciliation threatened to endanger their relationship with George, which had been at least partly based on their staunch partisanship during the estrangement. Unbolting the 'German' ministers now became a priority.[23]

Against this background, the gulf that was opening up between Stanhope and Bernstorff on the Prussian issue was a threat, but it was also an opportunity. Crucially, George himself came around to the Prussian alliance, and had always differed with Bernstorff about the magnitude of the Russian threat. Just as Stanhope had used Baltic policy in 1716–17 to supplant Townshend, he now exploited the question of a Prussian alliance to consolidate his position yet further with the King and to wrap himself in the patriotic rhetoric of British interests over Hanoverian sectionalism. Bernstorff's concern with Mecklenburg and his three villages, which had formed such an important part of the opposition Whig critique in 1716–17, now made Stanhope's breeze to blow. The fact that an alliance with Lutheran and Calvinist Prussia could be spun in favour of the 'Protestant interest' in Germany – whereas Bernstorff had just concluded a pact with the Empire's foremost Catholic prince – did Stanhope no harm at all with British public opinion. This was because a row had erupted in the Empire which was to set the tone for British foreign policy in the coming decade.[24]

In September 1719, the Catholic Elector Palatine Charles Philip banned the Protestant catechism in his territories, and evicted the reformed congregation from the Heiliggeistkirche in his capital of Heidelberg. This was a direct violation of the Treaty of Westphalia, which had laid down that Catholics and Protestants should enjoy the *Simultaneum*, that is share the church in question. Even if they had wanted to, George and the ministry could not have ignored this challenge to the religious status quo in central Europe. A cry went up not only in Germany itself, but also in Britain. Almost immediately, the September 1719 edition of the *Political state of Great Britain* warned that the Elector's coup was regarded as part of a pan-European attack on Protestantism. Two months later, the House of Lords passed an address in support of the Palatine Protestants. Their cause and that of European Protestants was thought by many to be one and the same. The Palatinate, after all, was where the fatal critique of the Stuarts had begun exactly one hundred years earlier. The Protestant outworks of Britain were once again under threat.[25]

As in the seventeenth century, this was not so much a religious as a strategic judgement. Austria had exhausted its potential usefulness to George: the Spanish threat in the Mediterranean had been seen off, and Vienna was of limited use in the Baltic. Moreover, the Austrians were dragging their heels on the investitures for Bremen and Verden. Taking on Vienna over the Palatine also enabled George to bid for control of the *Corpus Evangelicorum*, still nominally presided over by the Catholic King of Poland, and to pre-empt Prussian ambitions there. But the really decisive factor was the growing sense that the ambitions of Emperor

Charles VI in Germany and the Mediterranean represented a threat to European stability, and thus to the security of Britain itself. It was in this context that the spectre of another Catholic League in Germany revived memories of the bitter defeat of the Elector Palatine and European Protestantism in the 1620s. Only by shoring up the Empire, therefore, could Britain's security be guaranteed. Indeed, in October 1719 and again in May 1720, Stanhope went so far as to suggest that Britain should join France and Sweden as a guarantor power of the 1648 Treaty of Westphalia. So when George took up the cause of the Palatine Protestants he was motivated by more than just religious solidarity, however genuine, or the desire to improve Hanover's standing in the Empire. He was positioning himself within a Protestant English discourse about grand strategy.[26]

In these circumstances, Bernstorff's strongly pro-imperial leanings

9. *An allegory of the power of Great Britain by land*, painted when Britain's diplomatic reputation was at its zenith thanks to Stanhope's skill in settling the affairs of the south and, with less success, those of the north.

were a liability. The showdown took place in Hanover, in the course of George's visit in the summer of 1719. He was accompanied, once again, not only by his retinue, his German ministers, some favoured English aristocrats and various foreign diplomats, but also by Stanhope as Secretary of State. If at first sight Stanhope appeared outnumbered and on foreign turf, he had taken the precaution of loosening some of Bernstorff's teeth in advance by conspiring with his rivals in Hanover, particularly George's Hanoverian secretary, Johann Philip von Hattorf and Görtz. In late June / early July, they struck: Hattorf presented a memorandum of complaint against Bernstorff's management of business, while Stanhope used the question of a Prussian alliance to undermine his position with the King. Their victim does not seem to have put up very much resistance, perhaps because he was no longer in the best of health. Even before his departure for Hanover, Schulenburg had noted with a certain *schadenfreude* that Bernstorff was 'extremely weak and dispirited' from gout, and that he was 'declining strongly and losing his memory'. Bernstorff received no help from Robethon, with whom he had also fallen out. The movements of the various parties in late June 1719 say it all: Bernstorff repaired to his estates to lick his wounds, Robethon stayed in Hanover, while the triumphant Hattorf and Stanhope joined George for the waters at Bad Pyrmont. On the first day of August, Admiral Norris was told henceforth to take instruction only from Stanhope.[27]

Court Whigs were quick to claim this as a victory of English over 'German' interests, and later generations of historians were inclined to agree. As Sunderland reported to Newcastle from George's hunting lodge in Hanover, 'The world will be convinced by what the King will both say and do that neither Bernstorff nor Cadogan [William, Earl of Cadogan, a Privy Councillor and a highly influential Whig] have any credit & that he will not suffer any foreigner to meddle in our affairs, this you may depend upon.' Stanhope echoed this view a week later: 'I cannot promise that the old man [Bernstorff] will be left behind,' he wrote, 'but I may safely assure your grace that though he should come the King will do whatever shall be proposed to him to make everybody sensible that he is not to meddle in English business.' Back in London, Newcastle faithfully spread the word. What the King had done, he wrote, 'must please all those that pretend to be Englishmen and Whigs. He has told Mr Bernstorff & all the rest of the Germans that if ever they pretend in any manner whatsoever to meddle in English affairs, he will turn them out of his service & have nothing more to do with them.' It now appeared that, as Sunderland claimed, 'our affairs in all parts go as well as can be wished'. Newcastle also exulted that 'Everything goes as well abroad as possible. As to the south, the Catalans will all take up arms for the recovery of their liberties. The courts of Sweden and Prussia do just what we would have them.' He added that with the 'figure our King makes abroad, the few enemies he has must be forced to submit'. Stanhope could now press ahead with his plans for a Prussian alliance directed against Russia, which was concluded in September 1719. A pact to support the Protestant cause in the Empire was agreed in May 1720. These negotiations were carried out with the full support and involvement of George, as Elector, and with the cooperation of his Hanoverian diplomats. The sidelining of Bernstorff and the conclusion of the Prussian alliance was therefore hardly the reassertion of British over 'German' interests, though it suited Stanhope to give that impression. Rather, it was the triumph of one form of 'German' policy over another.[28]

The time seemed right to make a last effort to push through the Peerage Bill, which had been withdrawn after a first attempt in 1718. As Stanhope argued in late October 1719, now was the time to parlay diplomatic success into domestic political gain. The good news from Europe, he wrote, 'prepares us to expect speedily the submission of Spain to our terms. Even the Tsar . . . is said to put water in his wine.' He hailed 'the prospect of seeing a peace both in the south and the north before next spring. This good situation will probably put our friends in good humour at our opening the parliament and it seems to us very advisable to make the best use and advantage possible of this good humour by getting the Peerage Bill.' It was now or never for the Peerage Bill. Stanhope and Sunderland pulled out all the stops, even appealing to the Tories. 'You are mad,' one of the supporters of the Peerage Bill told a Jacobite: 'if this Bill fails, there may be reconciliation in the royal family & then where is your hope?' 'Are these not honest people,' Caroline commented bitterly, fearing the Bill would be the signal for a general assault on the Prince. 'The prince,' she wrote, 'has reliable information that if the bill passes the House of Commons, one will attack him even to the point of excluding him [from the succession].' But the combined forces of Walpole and the Prince and the Princess of

Wales proved too strong. The Peerage Bill was finally defeated in the Commons in December 1719. This damaged the ministry, though as yet not fatally.[29]

Despite a promising start, things also began to go badly in the Baltic. It was not the diplomacy that was at fault. As we have seen, Carteret had executed the difficult manoeuvre of allying with Sweden against Russia while despoiling her of Bremen and Verden on behalf of his monarch. At the same time, the British mediated a settlement between the Prussians and the Swedes, at some territorial cost to the latter; this was designed to enable a common front against the Tsar. The rhetoric of the Protestant cause was now deployed to rally Lutheran Sweden and Prussia against Russia. The Danes returned most of what they had grabbed, but were permitted to retain Schleswig, which they seized from the Swedish ally, the Duke of Holstein-Gottorp. Hostilities between Sweden and Poland were brought to an end in 1720, again with significant British involvement. Stanhope's grand plan for the reorganization of the North was taking shape. Peter the Great was now on his own.

The problem lay in the fraught and unpredictable application of military power. As soon as agreement with Sweden had been reached, Carteret began to implore Admiral Norris to move against the Russians. Norris, however, was a Baltic veteran, and he had been badly burned by the controversy over Bremen and Verden. He insisted on more explicit instructions from London before he would move. In the meantime, Carteret frantically urged him on. 'The scales of the north are in your hand,' he wrote in late August 1719. 'You can cast the balance as you please. The cause of Liberty and the Protestant religion will be served by rescuing this brave nation [Sweden] and I know by experience how true a friend you are to those sentiments both at home and abroad.' When Norris finally did take on the Russians, all he could do was to deter the Tsar from launching a landing on Sweden or from establishing an effective blockade. What he could not deliver was a decisive blow against the Russian navy. This was because the Tsar's main fleet sheltered under the cover of shore batteries along the Baltic coast. Moreover, the Russians possessed numerous galleys and shallow draught vessels which could operate off islands and inlets where they could not be engaged by Norris's force. There was thus no way of preventing the devastation of the Swedish coast, the consequent growth of war-weariness in Stockholm, and the progressive disintegration of the anti-Russian coalition.[30]

To make matters worse, Stanhope failed to mobilize Prussian, Polish and Austrian ground forces to attack Peter the Great across his western border. The principal reason for this lay in Berlin: Frederick William of Prussia could just about grasp that a residue of Swedish power should be preserved to counterbalance Russia, but he was too terrified of Peter and too mistrustful of Britain to move to open conflict. In short, by late 1720 the policy of containment of Russia was in ruins. Sir Josiah Burchett, Secretary of the Admiralty, summed up the British predicament in the Baltic in a pamphlet published that year. 'What will be the event of the accession of so great a power by Sea and Land,' he wrote, 'in the hands of a Prince, Master of so wide a Dominion, peopled with such infinite multitudes, and what alterations in the affairs and interests of Europe it may occasion, I leave to the politicians to discuss.' Six years into the Hanoverian succession, therefore, there was still no cause for complacency.[31]

All the same, a great deal had been achieved. Britain's traditional European alliances with the Emperor and the Dutch had been restored. France had been first contained, and then – from 1716 – co-opted into a collaborative management of the European balance. As the Undersecretary of State, George Tilson, put it in October 1721 after Stanhope's death, 'I think he made ... use of France both in the North and the South, for things which were necessary to us.' The sense of isolation and disengagement which had characterized British policy immediately before and after the Treaty of Utrecht had been overcome. Britain was now a German power, and the better for it. The new King had brought with him a wealth of expertise in himself and his Hanoverian ministers, which was to stand Britain in good stead in central and northern Europe. A sustained popular and parliamentary critique of the German connection had been weathered, though by no means suppressed. Jacobite challenges, particularly in 1715 and 1719, had been seen off; no effective collaboration between the Pretender and a foreign power had been established. The threat of Spanish expansionism in the Mediterranean had been contained, at least for the time being, and British naval ascendancy there was copper-fastened by the French destruction of Spanish dockyards during the invasion of 1719. Above all, the interventionist orthodoxy in foreign policy, which had been eclipsed under the Tories, was re-established. Overseas interests were not neglected, but kept in proportion to Britain's primary concern of maintaining the European balance of power. The Royal Navy had been used extensively, but generally as an instrument in European politics: in 1715–17 against the Swedes in the Baltic, in 1718 against the Spaniards in the Mediterranean, and in 1719–20 in the Baltic again, this time to intimidate Russia. At the beginning of 1720, therefore, the Whig ministers had some grounds for satisfaction. They could not have foreseen that British politics were about to be thrown into turmoil by a bolt, if not quite out of the blue, then at least from the deep blue sea. The first of many eighteenth-century colonial bubbles was about to burst in their faces.[32]

III

Imperial Challenges

6

A Protestant Empire, 1721–1724

*I cannot help being a little surprised, that those gentlemen who are so
well acquainted with the circumstances of our affairs abroad, did not
consider . . . [that] our Protestant brethren abroad should be more severely
dealt with, [and] we should in vain complain of the breach of treaties and
of the laws of the [German] Empire, when we have broke through the
common ties of humanity.*[1]

Thomas Lutwyche, Tory MP for Callington, May 1723,
opposing further repressive legislation against Roman Catholics

British politics and foreign policy in the new decade were dominated by
events in the Holy Roman Empire. The situation there loomed more
largely in the consciousness of Crown, ministry and Parliament than the
inflation and collapse of the 'South Sea Bubble', with which the early
1720s are more normally associated. These years saw both the final
relegation of the 'Germans' in the King's entourage, and the re-
emergence of a distinctly 'German' focus in British grand strategy. As a
result, the crucial relationship in British politics was not so much that
between George and his parliamentary 'manager' Robert Walpole, but
between the monarch and his Secretary of State for the North, Charles
Townshend. Both men knew that Russian ambitions in the Baltic, and
especially towards northern Germany, were still uncontained. Above all,
George and Townshend were becoming increasingly concerned with the
ambitions of the Holy Roman Emperor, Charles VI. His aggressive
stance in Germany threatened traditional bulwarks of the European
balance in central Europe and signalled the presence of a hostile power
in the Low Countries, which had fallen to Charles at Utrecht. Those
Britons who had come of age in the late seventeenth century knew

well the commercial, ideological and strategic challenge the Emperor presented. It was for this reason that British foreign policy became preoccupied with the Holy Roman Empire; and in this context the connection with Hanover, which had been so controversial during the Baltic crisis, became both an asset and a potential Achilles heel. This period, in short, was dominated not by colonial rivalries between Britain, France and Spain – though these continued to rumble on in the background – but by the old 'imperial' problem of how to prevent the Holy Roman Empire from being used as a base from which to outflank the Barrier, and to overturn the European balance of power upon which British security depended.

In 1711, the Tory ministry of Robert Harley conceived the idea of a South Sea Company as a counterweight to the Whig-dominated Bank of England and East India Company. Over the next few years the Company prospered, thanks to the trading privileges, especially the *Asiento*, the right to supply slaves to the Spanish American colonies, which had been secured for thirty years at the Treaty of Utrecht in 1713. There was much in the South Sea scheme which appealed to a public predisposed to believe in the prospect of fabulous colonial wealth. This fuelled massive investment in the South Sea Company, which far exceeded realistic returns on capital. Indeed by 1720 the South Sea Company had drawn in not only Tories, but a broad cross-section of the political nation and the royal family itself. Even the Hanoverians scrambled to get aboard the great gravy train. The head of George's Electoral administration in Hanover, Baron Görtz, explained to Sunderland in July 1720 that 'All our people, who have been in England with the King, have become very rich by the profits they have made through the South Sea Company.' He therefore expressed the 'hope that we here could also take our share ... That is why I am taking the liberty of asking your lordship to obtain for me by your authority some subscriptions.' Indeed, he wanted to know not only whether one could have more than two subscriptions per person, but whether he might also take out one in his wife's name.[2]

When the South Sea Bubble finally collapsed in December 1720, the reverberations were felt throughout the British political class. A wave of suicides and bankruptcies followed. Accusations of bribery shot back and forth; many of these swirled around the Hanoverians still in London,

CAROLVS VI. D. G. ROM. IMP. SEMPER AVGVSTVS

10. Emperor Charles VI, whose suspected alarming plans for 'universal monarchy' in Europe determined British politics and grand strategy for much of the 1720s.

some of whom were accused of accepting favours to lobby on behalf of the Company. The South Sea crisis shook the political class to its foundations, but it was not in itself enough to force a change of ministry. In fact, British public finance and investor confidence recovered very quickly in 1721. Rather the triumph of Robert Walpole was the result of a botched intrigue by Bernstorff, spun from his banishment in Hanover. In 1720, rumours began to reach Stanhope and Sunderland that Bernstorff was conspiring with Robert Walpole to supplant them. It was in order to pre-empt the 'Germans', as much as to strengthen his sagging ministry, that Stanhope brought Walpole and Townshend back into government in the spring of 1720. The symmetry was now complete: if Stanhope had used the Germans against Walpole in 1717, and had sidelined the Germans in 1719, he now used Walpole against the Germans. When Stanhope died in February 1721, he was succeeded by Townshend as Secretary of the Northern Department – where he was careful not to repeat his mistake of the Baltic Crisis and show solicitude for Hanover. The way was now clear for his crony and brother-in-law Walpole, who began his twenty-year ascendancy as First Lord of the Treasury and chief minister with the promise to re-establish political stability, keep the 'Germans' in their place, and restore the battered financial credibility of the British state – and the tacit agreement to support the King's interests in the Empire. It was events in Germany, not colonial matters, which ultimately brought Walpole to power.[3]

Walpole has come to be known as Britain's 'first prime minister', who continued the erosion of royal power. But although his influence in domestic matters – especially those relating to finance and patronage – was paramount, it was much more limited in the sphere which really mattered to the monarch, that of foreign policy. Ministers were after all summoned by the Crown, not Parliament; and the man who mattered most to George I was the man with whom he had to do business in order to promote Anglo-Hanoverian interests in Europe. The dominant figure here was the senior of the two Secretaries of State, which was Townshend for most of the 1720s. German politics, which had driven Walpole and Townshend from power in 1717, and brought them back again in 1720, continued to be at the heart of things throughout the following decade. Walpole recognized this by taking more of a back seat in this vital sphere, at least for the moment; Townshend by positioning himself ever more closely to the King's own strategic vision for central Europe.

For the most pressing business facing the ministry in the early 1720s was the multiple strategic challenges facing Britain–Hanover. The six years since 1714 had shown that Britain could no longer be conceived of in purely insular terms. British foreign policy was conducted in tandem with that of a medium-sized German state. For example the British envoy to Prussia in the early 1720s, Lord Whitworth, was instructed by Stanhope as Secretary of State; by the King through his Hanoverian Chancellery; and by the Hanoverian administration in the Electorate itself. The King himself seems to have made no particular distinction between his royal and Electoral roles in foreign policy. Letters relating to British business were routinely sent to the Hanoverian Chancellery for translation. British ministers, even and especially Townshend, worked closely with the King's Hanoverian servants. They often accompanied George on his trips to Hanover. In part, of course, this was driven by the hope of royal favour, and the fear of political marginalization which Walpole and Townshend had experienced in 1717.[4]

Yet the German connection was also an important force multiplier for Britain. The Hanoverian diplomatic service, with its German expertise and its presence in many of Europe's capitals, was at the disposal of the King of England. Moreover, Hanover became the hub of the British intelligence operation in Europe. Letters from foreign powers were routinely intercepted at the north German town of Celle before being sent on to the Secret Office of the Post Office in London. Here a team of four, including a German translator (a knowledge of French as the principal language of diplomatic discourse was taken as read), worked under the direction of the Reverend Edward Willes. As a result British ministers were often extremely well informed about the intentions of other powers; Willes was later rewarded with a bishopric. So if the relationship between British and Hanoverian concerns might often have been conflictual, it was essentially symbiotic. Britain was now very much a north German state, deeply implicated in the complex balances of the Baltic and the Holy Roman Empire, just as the Hanoverian Electorate was now woven into the many commercial and colonial threads which linked London with the wider world.[5]

This was just as well, because George and his ministers were going to need all the help they could get. In the course of the early 1720s, Britain-Hanover was to come under sustained assault from three corners of the compass. To the south, the situation in the Mediterranean remained precarious. To be sure, the Quadruple Alliance of January 1720 had temporarily coerced Spain into good behaviour, and weakened links between Madrid and the Jacobites. It was also true that the French alliance gave London reassurance there; the Franco-Spanish marriage plans of 1721 were therefore welcomed. But beneath the surface, the anxieties which had wracked British statesmen only a few years before persisted. Philip V of Spain was suspected, with justice, of continuing to harbour designs on the French crown. Elizabeth Farnese was believed, with equal justice, to be obsessed with recovering the Spanish empire in

Italy, and thus providing patrimonies for her sons. Relations with Spain in the colonies and on the high seas, particularly in the Caribbean and around Florida, were abysmal. To make matters worse, decision-making in Philip and Elizabeth's Madrid took place in a matrix of neurosis, hyperactivity and despair which made any kind of rational accommodation impossible.

One straw in the wind was the renewed demand for the return of Gibraltar. The British presence on the Rock, right on the doorstep of a great colonial power, was perceived in Madrid as a bitter humiliation. In fact, both Stanhope and George I were prepared in principle to exchange Gibraltar for Cuba or Florida. As the King's letter to Philip made clear, this could only be done with the 'consent of my parliament'. Parliamentary opposition could probably have been overcome if the ministry had been persuaded that the gesture would not simply have whetted Spanish appetites. The flexibility on Gibraltar was not driven by an abject desire to appease Spain, or any sense of colonial priority. Rather, it reflected the sober strategic truth that the mainstay of Britain's position in the western Mediterranean was not the Rock, but Minorca. It therefore made considerable sense to trade Gibraltar as part of an overall reconciliation with Spain in Europe, if one was on offer.[6]

The situation in the Baltic was far worse. Here relations with Peter the Great's Russia remained poisonous. By late May 1721, Townshend had given up all hope of containing Russia in the Baltic and was concentrating on keeping Peter out of Germany. He argued that it was not enough just to make peace in the north. Rather, Townshend claimed, 'it is necessary to turn our attention to that which remains to be done to prevent him from expanding beyond that area and disturbing the peace of the [German] Empire, after having made his accommodation with the King of Sweden.' When the Great Northern War was finally brought to an end by the Treaty of Nystad in August 1721, its terms were little short of catastrophic for Anglo-Hanoverian interests in the Baltic. Russia walked off with the lion's share of the Swedish empire, including much of present-day Latvia, Estonia and Karelia. The local balance had been fundamentally and irrevocably altered.[7]

No wonder that George's Hanoverian councillors dubbed the treaty 'the most pernicious work and the ultimate evil', which left Russia in charge of the Baltic provinces and thus left the 'German coasts completely open [to him] to do what he wants', especially with regard to

Rügen, Rostock, Wismar and Lübeck. The head of the Hanoverian administration, Görtz, saw this as evidence that 'the Tsar is once more creating a great disturbance in the north; this is the result of allowing him to gain a foothold on the Baltic.' But London was equally alarmed. If Peter had dropped Karl Leopold of Mecklenburg, he now embraced the cause of the Duke of Holstein-Gottorp, to whom he married off his favourite daughter, Anna. This opened up the prospect of another Russian-backed drive to upset the status quo in the Baltic, especially with regard to Denmark, at whose expense the Holsteiner's dynastic claims would be met. Some four months after Nystad, Townshend spoke of 'the manifest dangers and irritations which a neighbour so formidable, so restless and so enterprising must inevitably give rise to'. So concerned was Walpole about the turn of events in the Baltic that he announced his intention to find an alternative source of naval stores in the twelve colonies of North America.[8]

One of the reasons for the failure of Britain's Baltic policy lay in the attitude of Austria. Vienna, Townshend complained, 'does not want to see the danger to which she and the [German] Empire are exposed by the neighbourhood of the Tsar'. There was nothing George wanted more, he reported, than to continue with the 'old system' of a 'firm and indissoluble link between the House of Austria and the two maritime powers, whose natural and common interests cause them invariably to oppose France and the Tsar'. The failure to bring such an understanding about reflected not so much differing views of the Russian threat, but the progressive bilateral collapse of relations between Britain–Hanover and Emperor Charles VI, which exploded into open hostility in the 1720s. For the next decade or so, in fact, British foreign policy was to become obsessed, sometimes exclusively so, with events in the Holy Roman Empire.[9]

This became clear over the increasingly vexed issue of the investitures. If George had enjoyed vacant possession of Bremen and Verden – the fruits of his northern policy – for some time, the legal title to them had to be 'invested' by the German Emperor. By the early 1720s, it was obvious that Charles VI was stalling. In August 1721, Townshend complained of Austrian 'chicanes' in delaying the investitures. In vain did Townshend protest towards the end of the year that George was not only a loyal ally of Austria, but also 'the Prince of all Germany who has always shown the most regard for imperial authority as well as for the

law and constitutions of the [German] Empire'. Austrian foot-dragging
on the investitures continued throughout 1722, with all kinds of conditions and objections from Vienna. In March of that year there was
further imperial 'chicanery' to report. Nor had things progressed by the
late summer of 1723, when the Saxons attempted to mediate. Yet the
investitures were only a symptom. Relations between Britain–Hanover
and Charles VI in the Empire were deteriorating across the board.[10]

As was often the case, this found expression in prolonged religious
wrangling between the Catholic Austrians and the Protestant Hanoverians. George had already begun to burnish his credentials as Protestant
hero in foreign policy over the Palatinate. Now he vigorously asserted
'the liberty of the Protestants' and 'the cause of the Protestant part (*la
cause du corps Protestant*)' of the Empire. His diplomats were quick to
unmask Austrian attempts to 'divide the Protestant princes of the
Empire' at the Reichstag. The fact that the British-Hanoverian representative in Vienna, Louis St Saphorin, was a rebarbatively long-winded
sectarian Swiss Protestant did not help; lengthy dispatches were called
'St Saphorins' in London as late as the 1740s. Indeed, St Saphorin's
delegation, including the envoy himself, sometimes literally came to
blows with the local Catholic population whenever they felt slighted on
religious matters. One of these incidents, which took place in late May
1721, shows how seriously some British diplomats took their role as
defenders of Continental Protestantism. Returning to town one day, the
British ambassador to Vienna ran into a procession bearing the Blessed
Sacrament. He and his lackeys were called upon by the participants to
kneel down before it. St Saphorin instructed his servants to remove their
hats and to descend from the carriage, and told the priest and his
parishioners who he was, so that they would let him pass without further
ado. At this point, one of the crowd grabbed his cane with the stated
intention of thrashing St Saphorin's servants, if neither they nor their
master would kneel down before the Sacrament. They refused to comply,
and one of the servants was struck on the head with a 'large stick',
apparently on the order of the priest.[11]

Many critics saw the hidden hand of Hanover behind Britain's intense
involvement in German affairs. Thus the Jacobite paper *True Briton*
claimed in 1723 that 'The obtaining and securing those additions to the
Electorate of Hanover, have been the secret springs that have governed
and directed our behaviour in all foreign affairs.' In this case, however,

the Hanoverian tail was not wagging the British dog. George pointedly rejected the suggestion that he delay the opening of a congress to discuss European affairs until he had received the investitures. 'The King,' Townshend explained, 'wishes that things should be put in order, but he would never hold up public business for his own particular concerns.' In other words, George was looking beyond narrowly Hanoverian concerns to the broader picture. Besides, much of British public opinion accepted that the defence of European and especially German Protestantism was also their cause; it had been conditioned to think so since the seventeenth century. If anything, the ferociously anti-Catholic public sphere felt that the ministry was not doing enough to defend their co-religionists abroad.[12]

It was not just German issues which were poisoning Anglo-Austrian relations in the early 1720s. Ever since Charles VI had taken possession of the former Spanish Netherlands – present-day Belgium – after the Treaties of Utrecht and Rastadt, the commercial development of the Flemish Channel port of Ostend had been a sore point between London and Vienna. The Emperor was expected to maintain the province as a barrier to France, yet at Dutch insistence various economic restrictions, in particular the continued closure of the Schelde to commerce, were placed on the kind of development which would provide the necessary resources. In December 1722 Charles founded the Ostend Company with a view to building up a Habsburg commercial empire overseas. This was a direct threat to the joint Anglo-Dutch economic hegemony in the Channel, the North Sea and the colonies. As George I had told Parliament in his opening speech of 1721, it was 'commerce, upon which the riches and grandeur of this nation chiefly depend'. By February 1723, Townshend was complaining that the Ostend Company was doing serious damage to British traders; the competition, he claimed, was costing Britain £60,000 per annum. Not least among ministerial concerns at this time was the threat of parliamentary criticism on the Ostend issue. Yet what was primarily at stake over the Ostend Company was not commerce, but the strategic implications of the venture, and the broader European context in which it had been launched.[13]

The root cause of Anglo-Austrian estrangement lay in the growing British belief that the Habsburg monarchy – not France, Russia or Spain – was now the greatest threat to the European balance. Of all the European powers, it was Austria which had grown the most spectacularly since the last quarter of the seventeenth century, encouraged of course by England as a counterweight to Louis XIV's France. Transylvania and Hungary proper had been recovered from the Turks by 1699; the Austrian Netherlands, Milan and Naples were added in 1714; and four years later, the Habsburg commander Prince Eugene lopped off another large slice of the Ottoman Empire, adding North Serbia and western (or 'little') Wallachia, in what is now Romania. Moreover, Charles was suspected, not without justice, of ambitions to recover the Habsburg inheritance in Spain, part of which he had ruled as the candidate of the Grand Alliance during the War of the Spanish Succession. Here Charles's retention of Spanish titles and the elaborate Spanish court ritual was not reassuring. If the growth of Austrian power in Europe was unwelcome, the prospect of a reconstituted empire of Charles V was an anathema. After all, Britain had bailed out of the War of the Spanish Succession to prevent such a thing.[14]

For this reason, London was profoundly ambivalent about the 'Pragmatic Sanction', which Charles VI had devised in 1713 in order to ensure the undivided inheritance of his children to the Austrian Habsburg lands. This was necessary, because the daughters of his elder brother Joseph, who had reigned as emperor until his death in 1711, might otherwise be able to stake a powerful claim to at least a part of their father's lands. One married the Elector of Bavaria in 1719, the other the King of Saxony-Poland in 1724; both were compelled to make a renunciation. As time went on, the Pragmatic Sanction began to look increasingly unsafe, not least because the Emperor's only son died young and Joseph's daughters produced strapping male offspring. By the early 1720s, it was becoming clear that Charles would have to expect one of his daughters to succeed him. The Pragmatic Sanction therefore acquired a double purpose: to keep the Habsburg lands together and to guarantee the female succession. If before 1711, British and English policy had been to uphold the Austrian Habsburgs as a bulwark against France, after the accession of Charles VI, this was overtaken by fear of a reconstituted Austro-Spanish conglomerate. Moreover, from 1716 the French alliance rendered Charles VI's barrier functions obsolete, at least for the moment. So when Charles set about securing the approval of the various representative assemblies to the changed order of succession, which he finally settled on his eldest daughter, Maria Theresa, in 1723, the British response was distinctly lukewarm. It was not hard, in the climate of the early and mid 1720s, to argue that some form of partition, or at least reduction, of Austrian lands to satisfy the claims of Bavaria and Saxony-Poland, might be in the national interest.

In this context, Austrian policy in other areas took on a threatening aspect. The Ostend Company seemed to portend a Habsburg commercial challenge in the New World and a steady flow of subsidies to fund an expansionist programme in Europe, just as Charles V had done; as the mid 1720s were to show, this fear was far from fanciful. The same went for the Byzantine and often petty bickering in the Holy Roman Empire, where Vienna was suspected of harbouring hegemonic ambitions. Thus in June 1721 Townshend remarked that 'one had had grounds to hope that Vienna was beginning to descend from its high horse and that they were not far from believing that they were not so far above the rest of the human race.' They seemed, he continued, to accept that they could not 'direct the affairs of this world according to their own wishes and without the assistance of any other power'. Two years later, Townshend accused Austria of 'attempting under the pretext of asserting imperial authority to its highest, to subject the Princes of the [German] Empire to humiliating conditions'.[15]

Not all British statesmen approved of the new anti-Austrian policy. Sunderland, Stanhope, Cadogan and Carteret, who became Secretary of State for the South in 1721 and enjoyed an excellent rapport with the King, were strong supporters of the 'old system'. But natural wastage and high-political intrigue thinned the ranks of the Austrophiles. Stanhope died in 1721, Sunderland not long after in 1722. The loss of these powerful patrons left Cadogan and Carteret exposed to the intrigues of Newcastle, who made what was probably an opportunistic choice against Austria at this time,[16] and Townshend. From the vantage point of Hanover, Townshend was well placed to ensure – as he put it – Cadogan's 'mortification'. Carteret was to a considerable extent the author of his own misfortunes, when an elaborate scheme to marry the Countess of Darlington's daughter by George into the French nobility came unstuck. He was quickly dumped in Ireland, the purgatory for British politicians.[17]

The Austrians, of course, had their own grievances against Britain. Not least among these was the belief in a British tendency to desert the common cause. As far as Vienna was concerned, England had abandoned her at the Treaty of Ryswick in 1697 and again – most spectacularly – in the two years leading up to the Treaty of Utrecht in 1713. This last instance of diplomatic slash and burn was a Tory legacy, but the Whigs were saddled with the consequences. In 1716 Vienna once again felt sidelined by the Anglo-French-Dutch entente, and although Austria soon came around, the spirit of the Grand Alliance had long since dissipated. More specifically, Vienna felt that George was trying to undermine imperial authority in the Holy Roman Empire in pursuit of his own ambitions, was insensitive to Austrian commercial and strategic differences with the Dutch over the Barrier, and hostile to Austrian ambitions in Italy and the Mediterranean as a whole.[18]

Even Britain's French alliance seemed unsafe. When in 1723 the Regent of France died, there was considerable anxiety that his successor, the Duke of Bourbon, would be more pro-Jacobite. Rumours abounded of an imminent rupture with Versailles, and of a Franco-Russian rapprochement which would have aggravated the situation in the Baltic. A change of regime also threatened the relationship with the Dutch. The Stadholderate had lapsed in 1702, and the lack of a strong executive meant that Dutch politics had become increasingly divisive and sclerotic. After the latest bout of domestic unrest in The Hague, Townshend remarked that 'He hoped that no matter what great change one makes in the government of the Netherlands, that one will religiously observe all the stipulations of the Barrier Treaty.' He went on to hope that the Dutch would not fail to provide punctually the troops, the subsidies or anything else they had agreed to. In short, British statesmen were in a state of near-permanent anxiety throughout the early 1720s. They had more or less given up the Baltic as lost, and sought to shore up the defences of northern Germany against the Russian surge; they feared Spanish and Austrian irredentism in the Mediterranean; they feared the prospect of a Franco-Spanish Bourbon condominium as much as they did that of an Austro-Spanish condominium under Habsburg auspices. And they feared the consequences of a breach between France, Spain and Austria, which might unravel the elaborate diplomatic architecture of Stanhope. He wanted the Great Powers neither to get on too well – and thus gang up on Britain – nor to fall out too badly – thus dragging Britain into the resulting hostilities.[19]

The system of barriers constructed at Utrecht now seemed almost completely irrelevant to the principal challenges facing Britain. It was true that British-held Gibraltar and Minorca hemmed in Spanish ambitions, even if they also served to inflame them. But there was nothing to stem the rising Russian and especially Austrian threat. The Barrier, designed to intimidate Versailles, now separated Britain's French ally from her Dutch ally. It was useless against Austrian ambitions in Germany. To the modern eye, the Barrier resembled nothing more than the Maginot Line of 1939 or the fortress of Singapore in 1942, whose guns famously faced the wrong way. Nor was reliance on military power the answer. At some 20,000 men, the army hardly even enjoyed the striking power of a middling German state such as Bavaria; and while British naval superiority was assured, and could help to stabilize the situation in the Mediterranean and Baltic, it was of little use on mainland Europe.

Throughout the early 1720s, therefore, the British government attempted to remedy the weakness of their armed forces, appealing to the unsettled domestic situation and particularly that of the European state system. Thus Townshend reminded Parliament that the disbanding of the army at the close of the previous century had not only encouraged Louis XIV to disregard the Spanish Partition Treaties, but also to revive his military support for the Pretender. Likewise, Carteret warned that there were enemies all around just waiting to 'throw off the mask'. In that event, he concluded, the Navy would not be adequate protection, because 'whatever force we may be supposed to have at sea, it is hardly possible to prevent a sudden invasion'. All this, of course, was an argument for a perpetual state of emergency, which would have profound implications for politics at home. Year in and year out, therefore, critics rejected increased military expenditure as a stalking horse for royal or ministerial despotism. Thus the 'Protest against the number of Land Forces' by the House of Lords in 1723 warned of 'the most dangerous consequence to the constitution of this kingdom', which might 'bring on a total alteration of our government from a legal and limited monarchy to a despotic' one. Taken together with recent allegedly unprecedented increases in the Crown's power of detention, designed to deal with Jacobitism, the idea of enlarging the standing army took on a distinctly sinister character. Instead, they believed the way forward was to recognize that 'the greatest and only lasting security to His Majesty and his government, is in the hearts and affections of his subjects'. The realm would thus, they concluded, be best protected by 'curing [domestic] discontents, by removing or lessening the occasions of them'.

Clearly, the security of Britain could not be guaranteed from its own military and naval resources, not least because the political structure of the state made large-scale mobilization domestically highly controversial.[20]

The British response would therefore have to be diplomatic, especially as far as Austria was concerned. Fortunately, the King of England, as an Elector of the Holy Roman Empire, was well placed to mobilize the formidable political and moral resources of that body to contain Charles VI. For the next decade or so, British diplomacy in central Europe, and British foreign policy in general, revolved around the German courts and the Reichstag at Regensburg, at which all the constituent parts of the Empire were represented. Here George sought, as Townshend put it in September 1722, to effect 'harmonious and cordial union between the Protestant princes [of the Empire]'. George now placed himself at the forefront of the religious struggle of the Protestant states in an Empire in which the principal institutions – the imperial crown, the council of imperial electors, and the imperial courts of arbitration – were dominated by Catholics. He took a keen interest in appointments to the *Reichskammergericht* – the imperial chamber court – at Wetzlar, which had a Protestant and Catholic co-presidency, and was designed to arbitrate disputes between component parts of the Empire. As luck and dynastic paradox would have it, the directorate of the Protestant caucus at the Reichstag – the *Corpus Evangelicorum* – lay with the Elector of Saxony, who as King of Poland was perforce a Catholic. The British ambassador to Vienna observed in despair that 'it is . . . a great drawback that the leadership (*directoire*) of the Protestants should be, in these circumstances, in the hands of a court of which the prince is not only a Catholic, but of which the ministry seems for some time to be entirely devoted to that of this court here [Vienna]'.[21]

Yet there was also an opportunity here. So long as rival Prussian aspirations could be kept at bay, Saxon weakness enabled George to stake a claim to the leadership of the *Corpus Evangelicorum*. The *Corpus* was potentially a vital tool for British-Hanoverian policy, as controversial issues could by convention be declared religious. These would then no longer be resolved by majority vote – which would allow the Emperor to play on Catholic solidarity – but by '*itio in partes*'. This process interpreted the Reichstag as being made up of two equal Protestant and Catholic halves, the differences between which would have to be resolved by *relation*, or compromise. Used creatively, the mechanism could help to frustrate Charles VI's project to dominate the Empire. It was to come in handy, at least as an option, in the years ahead. Moreover, championing the Protestant cause in the Empire was popular domestically. The language of religion there mirrored that of contemporary Britain, in which royal, parliamentary and popular references to 'popery', the 'popish Pretender' and 'the spirit of popery which breathes nothing but confusion', were routine. It also chimed with the religious prejudices of many ministers such as Townshend, an ardent Anglican, and the Duke of Newcastle, who was a member of the 'Society for the Propagation of the Gospel in Foreign Parts'. Yet the enemy was never, as the rhetoric sometimes suggested, Catholicism as such. George was not a 'Protestant crusader', but the advocate of 'estate rights' – the privileges of the smaller and middling principalities – against an overweening Emperor, who happened to be Catholic. In this context it is no accident that Britons were accustomed to refer to the 'defence of the Protestant cause, and the liberties of Europe in general', in the same breath. In short, George's entry into the religious struggle in Germany, with all its accompanying rhetoric, was not primarily about theology but represented a central part of the British response to the threat of Austrian universal monarchy.[22]

This strategy of forward engagement in Germany – a British imperial policy or *Reichspolitik* – involved close cooperation between British and Hanoverians at Vienna (where St Saphorin effectively combined the Electoral and royal functions), Berlin, Regensburg and other German courts. During this period both Carteret and Townshend accompanied the King on his visits to Hanover, from where they were able to pursue the anti-Austrian policy more effectively. None of this amounted, as critics in Britain claimed, to a 'Hanoverian' policy. Indeed, there was widespread unease among the King's Hanoverian ministers at the increasingly anti-Austrian drift of British policy. They felt that George should concentrate on securing the investitures and avoid rocking the boat in other areas. Traditionally the Hanoverians had been good imperialists, and hostility to Vienna did not come naturally to them. By contrast, British ministers threw themselves into the task with gusto. No doubt, this was partly due to a desire to curry favour with George; and the biennial pilgrimages to Hanover can be explained by the imperative not to make the mistake of remaining in London again. As Townshend wrote, 'we all serve one master, and both the English and the German ministries must follow his orders.' No doubt, a religious animus against the Catholic Habsburgs, to which many British ministers – especially Townshend – were prone, also played a role. But the main reason for Britain's engagement in Germany was a genuine realization that the Holy Roman Empire was a key front in the European struggle against Austrian hegemony.[23]

On this reading, as Townshend argued in August 1721,

the honour of the [English or British] nation demands that one should not impose any further conditions on the King than those which have been given to the King of Sweden. It is true that the lands in question pertain to the King's German domains, and might therefore be considered separately from his Kingdom of Great Britain ... But all the loyal subjects of His Majesty of both nations must have the same regard and zeal for everything that touches on his honour and his interest ... There is not a man in the kingdom, however slight his acquaintance of the present situation, or of the interest of his country, who cannot see that the interest of His Majesty both as King and Elector are inseparable and that his German affairs cannot suffer without weakening his government here.

One should never forget, he stressed, that although the King had both a royal and an Electoral personality (*caractères*), there was only one person, and 'consequently' one interest. The idea that Britain-Hanover was a single composite state in foreign policy terms could not have been more clearly put.[24]

One solution was a rapprochement with Prussia. An alliance with Berlin would strengthen the balance in the Baltic, act as a bulwark against Russian penetration of northern Germany, and help to deter Charles VI. As a largely Lutheran territory with a Calvinist monarchy, Prussia certainly shared the Anglo-Hanoverian concern about Charles's aggressively Catholic imperial policy. Relations steadily improved throughout the early 1720s, smoothed by the Prussian queen, George's daughter Sophie Dorothea. In August 1720, the Hanoverian chief minister, Görtz, hailed 'the good understanding' between George and the King of Prussia; indeed, 'the two houses had never been in such a perfect harmony as they are today'. Three years later, George went to Berlin in person, where he received a 'cordial reception'. This resulted in the Treaty of Charlottenburg (1723), in which Frederick William agreed to support George in the Empire, in return for British support for Prussian claims to the western German duchies of Jülich and Berg. In order to consolidate the relationship, a double marriage between the Prussian Princess Wilhelmina and George's grandson, and between Crown Prince Frederick (later Frederick the Great) and a granddaughter of George, was mooted. For the moment, George was able to contain his dislike of the Prussian King.[25]

British attempts to contain Austria and Russia were not confined to Europe. A broader view of the strategic chessboard opened up another option: using the Ottoman Empire to distract Russia on her southern flank. As St Saphorin pointed out, the Tsar was 'always at risk of being attacked from that side'. On the other hand, there was also the danger that the Russians would expand more or less unopposed in that direction and thus gain yet further territory and European weight on the cheap. Thus in late June 1722, Townshend wrote that whereas Russian initiatives in the Baltic were unlikely that year, he expected that Peter would 'turn his attention to his weak neighbours in the Orient, where he can reckon on making progress without risking too much', as well as deploying his naval forces and army 'at less expense and at less hazard than against Germany and Poland'. The origins of the Eastern Question, which was to dominate early-nineteenth-century British European diplomacy, were thus already clearly visible.[26]

The main prop of British diplomacy, however, was the French alliance. This partnership was domestically unpopular, religiously incongruous – though no more than the Grand Alliance with Austria had been – and historically counter-intuitive. All the same, the Franco-British alliance of 1716 continued to furnish vital leverage in three areas of British interest. First of all, it provided depth to British-Hanoverian *Reichspolitik*, particularly among those German states with long-standing ties to Versailles; of this more later. Secondly, Versailles exercised a powerful calming influence on Spain through the Quadruple Alliance. Britain therefore welcomed news of a forthcoming match between Philip V's three-year-old daughter and the future Louis XV, which the French Council of Regency had accepted. Carteret remarked in September 1721 that 'we begin to be very easy about the late matches in France and Spain. The Regent has sustained himself by them and will still stand in need of the King if he thinks of preserving his succession to the crown of France.' It is no surprise, therefore, that the need to cooperate with Versailles was repeatedly dinned into diplomats by Newcastle.[27]

Perhaps most importantly of all, the French alliance was a very effective antidote to Jacobitism and the threat of an externally sponsored invasion. It not only denied the Pretender his base of first choice, but focused the formidable diplomatic and intelligence-gathering resources of France against him. Jacobite agents were known to be active in Russia and in contact with Russian diplomats across Europe; London was well aware of this, although not of the sheer extent of their activities. In 1721–2 Jacobite representatives met with the Russian ambassador to France, Prince Dolgorouky, and again on his visit to Madrid in December 1721. In 1723 the Jacobite emissary Daniel O'Brien visited St Petersburg at Peter's request, unknown to London. Here the French alliance was particularly valuable, because after the final rupture with Russia in 1719, British intelligence in St Petersburg was effectively 'blind'. London was utterly dependent on cooperation with Versailles for whatever crumbs of information it did get.[28]

This mattered, because the Jacobite card was very much still in play. In 1717 the Pretender had settled in the papal fief of Urbino, far enough away to allow London plenty of warning of a dash across the Channel, if British intelligence was up to the mark, but well placed to intrigue with the Austrians, who were now the main enemy, and the Spaniards, who had not gone away. Moreover in 1720, Charles Edward – the future 'Bonnie Prince Charlie' – was born, so that a viable male heir to James III was available; a spare in the shape of Henry Benedikt, later the Cardinal Duke of York, followed in 1725. This put a renewed premium on the value of the French alliance in the struggle against Jacobitism. It was resoundingly vindicated by the events of the Atterbury plot of May 1722, named after the same Jacobite Bishop of Rochester who had lampooned George in 1714. This was a serious attempt to capitalize on the political disruption caused by the South Sea Bubble to overthrow the Hanoverian succession in Britain. The Pretender drew up quite detailed plans for Russian-sponsored descents on Scotland and Ireland in conjunction with local risings. These would be accompanied by Russian diversions against the King's German dominions, and would take advantage of the King's absence there. The scheme came unstuck, not only because it was betrayed to London by the French, but also because of Britain's success in isolating the Jacobites diplomatically. The King's Speech to Parliament in October 1722 noted with some satisfaction that 'the conspirators have, by their emissaries, made the strongest instances for assistance from foreign powers; but were disappointed in their expectations.' Indeed, the commission of inquiry into the plot reported that one prominent Jacobite – Lord Orrery – was 'constantly of opinion, that nothing could be done to any purpose in the Pretender's favour without foreign forces'.[29]

The threat of internal subversion and external invasion led to a severe government crackdown in 1722–3. It was driven by the need, as George put it, 'to let the world see, that the general disposition of the nation is no invitation to foreign powers to invade us, nor encouragement to domestic enemies to kindle a civil war in the bowels of the kingdom'. The Black Acts of 1722–3, famously interpreted by E. P. Thompson as an act of class warfare, were primarily intended to curb political sedition rather than social unrest. They were, in other words, not about property, but about popery, or rather Jacobitism. Even more extreme measures were mooted, including the idea of a special punitive tax on Catholics. The trouble was that although strategic imperatives drove domestic repression, they also constrained it. Thus Earl Cowper warned in late May 1720 'that the King of Spain and the regent of France had used their good offices in behalf of those of their own religion amongst us'. He went on to remark that given 'those two powerful princes had given undoubted proofs of their friendship to His Majesty, in discovering and quashing of the late conspiracy, so they could not but think themselves indifferently requited for it, if this Bill should pass into law'. For one thing, it would expose European Protestants to reprisals. Paradoxically, George's position as defender of the Protestant cause in Germany would be damaged by excessive harshness against Catholics at home, and by measures which subverted the French alliance from which his diplomacy in the Empire drew such strength.[30]

There were also many other good arguments against anti-Catholic discrimination, which the Tory MP Thomas Lutwyche summarized in an eloquent speech in early May 1723. It would be manifestly unjust unless it was supported by good intelligence, without which 'we may involve innocent persons in a punishment only due to the guilty'. Targeting Catholics as a group, he argued, made no sense; 'it would be the highest injustice to make one man suffer for the crime of another.' Indeed, Lutwyche announced that he 'look[ed] upon persecution to be a doctrine odious in itself, highly reflecting upon the honour of Parliament, and greatly infringing upon the freedom of the subject'. It would create Jacobitism rather than suppress it. 'I do imagine,' he went on, 'that as the Pretender's scheme is unjust in itself, it can be formed upon no better hopes than the discontents of the people; and the more room there is for complaint, the better prospects he has of success.' In any case, Lutwyche did not see the world in terms of a grand contest pitting Protestantism against Popery. 'The contest,' he said, 'does not lie betwixt the Protestant and Roman Catholic religion,' rather he believed that 'it is obvious . . . how the leaders of each party promote their own mercenary ends by possessing their followers with unnecessary fears and groundless jealousies.'[31]

There were strains within the Anglo-French entente. A marriage project between George's eldest daughter Anne and Louis XV foundered on insurmountable religious differences. Moreover, it was clear that the French Minister of the Navy, Maurepas, had ambitious plans for French maritime expansion likely to lead to conflict with Britain in the long run. Throughout the 1720s, British traders of the Royal Africa Company sometimes came to blows with French and other rivals. Relations were tense in India, where both sides were in competition for trading privileges and alliances with local princes. But the biggest area of contention was North America, where Britain remained encircled by the French to the north and New Spain to the south. This sense of geopolitical exposure began to form part of an initially subdued transatlantic chorus on British grand strategy. Pamphleteers on both sides of the ocean intoned that there could never be stability in North America until the French had been ejected. Quebec was bad enough, but the founding of Louisiana was the last straw. As one London pamphlet – penned by an American in 1720 – warned, in the event of war it would be easy for the French 'with the assistance of the Indians, to invade [from Louisiana] and Canada all the English plantations at once, and drive the inhabitants into the sea'. Moreover, he continued, putting his finger on the issue which was to plague strategic thinking about British North America until the outbreak of revolution in 1775, the colonies were incapable of providing for their own defence. 'His Majesty's Dominion on this continent,' he lamented, 'is canton'd into so many petty independent states or commonwealths, whereof there is scarce one that can expect relief or assistance from another, in the most imminent danger.'[32]

In particular, the French population in British-annexed Acadia – present-day Nova Scotia and New Brunswick – was a running sore.

Here religion and grand strategy were inseparable, for the French openly used the Catholic Church, particularly the Jesuit order, as an instrument of foreign policy. As the *Intendant* of New France – in charge of finance, economic development and the administration of justice – François Bigot remarked in 1715, 'religion is the most powerful motive to hold those savages for us.' A missionary struggle now erupted for the souls of the Indians, when London pitched the evangelical Society for the Propagation of the Gospel into the area in 1717. In 1724 this low-level cold war had resulted in many deaths, including that of the legendary Jesuit soldier-priest Sebastien Role at the hands of a Massachusetts raiding party. Given that in early-eighteenth-century Acadia French-speakers outnumbered English-speakers by a factor of about thirty, the problem could only get worse. One much discussed solution was to provide foreign Catholic priests, but where would they come from? France and Spain were out of the question, and the British were not yet imaginative enough to think of Ireland. The obvious source was Austria, but here relations were deteriorating at the very moment that Acadia came on the agenda. An extreme option was expulsion, which the Board of Trade openly considered in 1721. 'We are apprehensive,' they wrote, that the Acadians 'will not become good subjects to His Majesty whilst the French governors and their priests retain so great an influence over them.' For this reason, the Board continued, 'they ought to be removed as soon as the forces which we have proposed to be sent to you shall arrive in Nova Scotia.'[33]

Britons were not just in North America because they were there. If the overseas empire, and the twelve colonies in particular, were worth contesting, it was for European reasons. Colonial trade was still much smaller in volume than that with Europe, but it was by far the more dynamic sector, with immense potential for the future, or so it was thought. Moreover, the settlements were seen as a religious and strategic extension of the home country. On this reading, America could serve as the source of religious revitalization and supply the fiscal muscle which Britain needed to secure her position within the state system. As in the seventeenth century, many still interpreted Britain's role in terms of the 'Protestant interest'. Thus the Irish churchman and philosopher George Berkeley argued in 1724 that America was the best place for Protestants to 'make up' ground lost to Catholicism in Europe, to forestall 'Spanish missionaries in the south [Florida] and the French in the north [Canada]', and thus safeguard Britain's overseas sources of wealth. Many Britons in the 1720s thus saw themselves as locked into an ideological and strategic struggle spanning the Atlantic, which led into the wastes of Canada and down the rabbit-holes of the Holy Roman Empire.[34]

British statesmen, for their part, were conscious of colonial factors, but not yet preoccupied by them. Nobody of any stature had actually been to the colonies, least of all those who were in charge of overseas policy. Thus Carteret carried the title of 'Palatine of the Carolinas', but all of his travel was in other directions; in any case, it was the German Palatinate which most exercised British ministers in the 1720s. Likewise, Newcastle, who as Secretary of State for the South from 1724 was increasingly involved in colonial affairs, made sure to exploit the opportunities for patronage, but when he later overcame his aversion to travel it was to go to Hanover, not America. Besides for the moment, at any rate, none of this interfered with the primacy of good relations with France in Europe. The same report of the Board of Trade which lamented the Franco-Spanish encirclement of the twelve colonies, suggested that France was not a more serious threat in North America solely because of her European distractions. If relations with France were to deteriorate, of course, all this would change.[35]

By the beginning of 1725, in any case, some sort of equilibrium seemed to have been reached in Europe. Louis XV had reached his majority in 1723, reducing some of the dynastic instability in Britain's French ally. That same year the former Jacobite and high priest of Tory foreign policy, Bolingbroke, was suspected of trying 'to creep to Hanover' and make his peace with George; the ministry now felt strong enough to allow him to return to Britain, although he was barred from sitting in the House of Lords. Relations with Russia were improving in late 1724. As Newcastle observed in September of that year, 'This great work of the reconciliation with the Tsar being now almost finished, in which you have had so great a share, we now have little reason to apprehend what our enemies either at home or abroad can do against us.' The death of Peter the Great in February 1725 was further good news in that, unlike the Tsar's own assurances, it seemed to guarantee a period of decreased turbulence in the Baltic due to increased Russian domestic turmoil. One month later, Newcastle summed up the growing if tentative mood of complacency with the remark, 'there never was . . . so universal a satisfaction and tranquillity throughout the nation as there is at present; so it is hardly to be imagined that the Jacobites can be mad enough to think of making any disturbance at this time.'[36]

There were, however, mounting signs of trouble ahead. Relations with Austria continued to deteriorate. In March 1724 Townshend had all but given up. 'Making representations at Vienna,' he wrote, 'is a lost cause, because all gestures of moderation are interpreted there as a sign of weakness.'[37] At the end of the year came news of the '*Blutgericht*' – 'blood justice' – of Thorn (now Toruń) in Poland, where local Protestants were judicially murdered for their faith. The outrage of their co-religionists throughout Europe, and in Britain in particular, was much magnified by the belief that Austria was shielding the perpetrators. George and the British ministry noisily championed their cause, partly because they saw the event as part of a European-wide assault on Protestantism and partly in order to embarrass King Augustus of Poland, who was also Elector of Saxony and an important ally of Charles VI in the Empire. Here they could depend on a favourable response from the public sphere, even in obscure provincial periodicals. Thus the *Northampton Mercury* devoted a whole page of each issue for three months to the events in Thorn. A Yorkshire paper printed nine pages of the Jesuit advocate-general's summing up for the prosecution. The interest here was driven not by sensationalism or pure bigotry but by the widespread sense that British freedoms ultimately depended on the fate of Continental liberties.[38]

Moreover, Spain remained utterly disaffected: the congress called to discuss compensation for their Italian losses finally met in Cambrai in April 1724, but broke up in acrimony six months later. The sticking point had been British unwillingness to cede either Minorca or Gibraltar, and the failure to recognize the dynastic claims of Elizabeth Farnese's sons to Tuscany and Parma. Dark rumours – which Newcastle discounted – were circulating about an imminent Austro-Spanish rapprochement. Finally, the Jacobite threat could not be written off, especially in a hostile diplomatic environment. In April 1724 Townshend wrote to the King that 'the Jacobite party is still very strong . . . the foreign ministers who are best acquainted with this country . . . constantly represent the present tranquillity of this nation, as owing more to the despair of giving Your Majesty any disturbances from abroad, than to any real change of submission wrought in the minds of the Pretender's adherents.' In short, if France or Spain were minded to help the Jacobites, 'the sparks and resentments, which now lye smother'd, would break out into as fierce a flame as ever.' And in early February, Newcastle fretted about the attitude of Spanish diplomats, particularly the Irishman Sir Patrick Lawless, who 'is so attracted to the interest of the Pretender, & so declared an enemy to the King and his government that it ... give[s] the greatest handle to our enemy to brag of the assistance of the court of Spain'. All this contributed to a growing sense of anxiety in London. Nothing, however, prepared British statesmen for the impending diplomatic revolution in Europe, which was to shake British grand strategy to its very foundations.[39]

7

The Return of Charles V, 1725–1726

You know how weak in health King Philip is and not likely to be long-lived, and the Prince of Asturias is in a hectical and consumptive way, so that in all probability Don Carlos will come to be the King of Spain by the time the intended marriage takes place, and being sent to Vienna to be bred up there and having the Austrian dominions joined to the vast territories of Spain may become more formidable to the rest of Europe than ever Charles V was.[1]

> Charles Townshend, Secretary of State for the Northern Department, 1725

If we are to be engaged in a war, 'tis to be wished that this nation may think an invasion, the support of the Pretender, and the cause of the Protestant Succession are the chief and principal motives that obliged us to part with that peace . . . which we now enjoy.[2]

> Robert Walpole, October 1725

[A]s to the secret article of that alliance in favour of the Pretender, His Majesty had received from several parts such positive informations, that if the safety of the state permitted to lay those advices before the House, they would no more question the certainty of such an article, than if they had been present at the signing of it. But His Lordship hoped that an illustrious assembly would not think any of His Majesty's servants, who had the honour to sit amongst them, so audacious as to tell them down-right untruths, or to presume to impose upon their Lordships by alleging facts of so great importance, without sufficient vouchers.[3]

> Charles Townshend, January 1727

In early May 1725 Britain was stunned to hear of the conclusion of an Austro-Spanish alliance, and possible marriage compact, at the Treaty of Vienna. The recreation of a vast Habsburg–Spanish Bourbon bloc – in effect, the old empire of Charles V – was now a possibility. More immediately, Britain was under attack at Gibraltar, and in the Mediterranean generally. The biggest threat was in the Holy Roman Empire. Hanover was directly menaced by Austrian troops, while Charles was also present in strength in Flanders, only a short hop away across the Channel. Both Madrid and Vienna openly flirted with the Jacobites. Worse still, both Prussia and Russia were sucked into the orbit of the Austro-Spanish alliance; the Baltic, German and Mediterranean balances were thus all inextricably linked. The naval and colonial measures to relieve Gibraltar and intimidate Spain were what made the headlines and what has lodged in the popular memory of this crisis, but the root of the problem was believed to lie in Germany. Britain's response, therefore, was to embark on her most active imperial policy yet, designed to mobilize the Holy Roman Empire against this latest threat to the European balance, and thus to the barriers which underpinned her security. It was to this end that all British initiatives – from the interception of Spanish-American bullion being sent to support Charles VI in Germany, through the attempted remodelling of Italian geopolitics, to the promotion of an Ottoman diversion against Austria's south-eastern flank – were directed.

The shattering news from Vienna was the direct result of unforeseen shifts in the dynastic geopolitics of Europe. Louis XV announced his intention not to marry the Spanish Infanta who was, on account of her extreme youth, unable to provide him with the desperately needed heir quickly. When nothing came of plans for a British bride, Louis turned to Poland, marrying Maria Leszczyńska, daughter of Stanislas, former King of Poland. In Spain, Elizabeth and Philip took the rejection very badly, and on the rebound sought an accommodation with Austria at the Treaty of Vienna in 1725. The resulting public, private and commercial treaties committed Charles VI not to obstruct Spanish demands for the restitution of Minorca and Gibraltar. The Emperor also agreed to the installation of Don Carlos, Philip's son by Elizabeth Farnese, in the Italian duchies she had coveted so long. In return he secured Madrid's endorsement of the Pragmatic Sanction and commercial privileges for his growing Ostend Company.

In London this news came as a terrible blow. At one level the threat was economic: an Austro-Spanish commercial cartel would exclude Britain from the lucrative trade with the Indies. This was of considerable concern to commercial lobbies. As Townshend remarked a few months later, during negotiations with the Prussians: 'I see by the letters from England that the question of Ostend is so close to the heart of our merchants' that 'the City of London would be most irritated to find that its particular concerns were not being taken into account'. But the principal threat from the Ostend Company was strategic. Its success would lead to a corresponding increase in the financial strength, and thus the European leverage, of the two powers. The ability of the perennially broke Charles VI to subsidize and bribe German princes, or the delegates to the Reichstag, would be greatly enhanced. Moreover, the growth of Ostend would turn it into a Habsburg naval base on the very doorstep of Britain. As one government report on the Treaty of Vienna warned, 'The Emperor has long been desirous to have a naval force, and ... should the Ostend Company go on with success, by the natural course of things the Emperor will in time have a naval force on the coast of Flanders.' Indeed, the report continued, 'The command of the seas has frequently passed from one nation to another, and tho' Great Britain has continued longer in possession of this superiority than perhaps any nation ever did, yet all human affairs are subject to great vicissitudes. We have seen one considerable maritime power established in the north in our memory.' The link between the containment of Charles VI and the maintenance of British naval superiority was here made very directly.[4]

But the principal cause of British anxiety at this time was the fact that the Treaty of Vienna threatened to turn Charles VI into the hegemonic power in Europe. His previous posture in Germany and over Ostend was bad enough, but British paranoia was further fed by speculation about what Spain had been granted in return. It was feared that a secret clause in the treaty envisaged a Habsburg–Bourbon marriage project between Charles's daughter Maria Theresa and one of the Spanish princes. These anxieties were fed by the British envoy in Madrid, William Stanhope, who reported that both powers 'have their heads filled with such ambitions and presumptious notions as make them look upon themselves as the arbiters and masters of the rest of Europe'. All this raised the possibility of an Austro-Spanish conglomerate which would in effect resurrect the empire of Charles V. Such a bloc would stretch from the English Channel to the heel of the Italian boot, and from Silesia to the very walls of Gibraltar. It was that same prospect which had finally led Britain to bail out of the War of Grand Alliance some ten years before. For this reason, as Townshend explained in August 1725, Britain must act 'for disappointing the vast projects the Imperial and Spanish courts seemed to have formed together to awe and confound the rest of Europe'. Horatio Walpole told the House of Commons that 'there were just grounds to believe, that the unforeseen reconciliation of the Emperor and the King of Spain was owing to the constant view of the House of Austria, of rendering the imperial dignity hereditary in their family.' Moreover, it was believed that the treaty would be 'cemented' by a 'match between the Emperor's eldest daughter and the Infante Don Carlos'. The consequences of such a marriage, he continued, were clear. 'The issue male that might come from it, might in time, be possessed not only of all the hereditary dominions belonging to the House of Austria and of the imperial dignity, but also of all the dominions of the Spanish monarchy; which would entirely overthrow the balance of power' and jeopardize 'the liberties of all the rest of Europe'.[5]

In this context, even the Spanish agreement to the Pragmatic Sanction was suspect. If at one point this would have been welcome as a sign of Madrid's acceptance of the Mediterranean status quo, it now reinforced fears of a union between Spain and the undivided Habsburg inheritance. As Townshend put it in August 1726, 'the court of Vienna knows that the maintenance of the general system of Europe, as well as the interest of the King, requires above all things that the succession of his imperial majesty should fall on the eldest of the archduchesses, provided she is given in marriage to a suitable prince, such as the Prince of Lorraine.' In other words, not a Spanish prince. Failing that, British ministers wanted to keep open the option of breaking up the Austrian bloc in due course. The question of the 'Spanish match', and its strategic implications for the 'Protestant interest' and the balance of power, which had so roiled English politics in the early seventeenth century, was now back on the agenda with a vengeance.[6]

As if all this were not bad enough, Austrian diplomacy succeeded in drawing Russia into the Treaty of Vienna, largely by the support they had given Russia in the Baltic. In July 1725, news arrived that Peter's successor, Catherine I was putting Sweden under pressure to provide a harbour for the use of the Russian fleet, whether to threaten Denmark or to install Russia's satellite Karl Frederick of Holstein-Gottorp on the Swedish throne was not quite clear. Townshend realized that, as he put it, this would be potentially a 'fatal . . . blow . . . to the interest of His Majesty's dominions in particular, and to the balance of Europe in general'. At stake in all of this was nothing less than the whole balance of power in the north. As Townshend remarked in October 1725, 'we shall see next spring who will be master in the Baltic'. And in the following month Newcastle put his finger on the nightmare scenario of an anti-British coalition spanning the length, and most of the breadth, of Europe, when he saw 'an alliance on foot between Muscovy, the Emperor and Spain, to which Sweden will be invited'.[7]

In short, British statesmen were in no doubt about the acute danger presented by the Treaty of Vienna. The problem was that these threats were less evident to the British public, and more particularly to Parliament, which would have to fund the necessary countermeasures. In this context, it made sense for the administration to play the Jacobite card, which could always be counted on to galvanize opinion in support of a controversial foreign policy. The King's Speech at the opening of the parliamentary session in January 1726 therefore claimed that his enemies were 'soliciting and promoting the cause of the Pretender'. That is not to say that the government acted in bad faith or that the Jacobite threat did not exist. The dangers and the fears were real. Townshend's remarks of October 1725, for example, were made in confidential correspondence, not for public consumption: 'You will see,' he told the British envoy to Sweden, 'what a game the Tsarina and the Duke of Holstein are playing with the Jacobites and the King of Spain, in which the Emperor in all likelihood will have his share.' Likewise, Townshend suspected the Spaniards of trying to 'perplex our affairs at home, in order to prevent our meddling or interfering with them abroad'. And with the Austrians only a short sail away across the Channel, the development of Ostend as a naval hub seemed to portend another avenue of Jacobite infiltration. Government paranoia was heightened by the sense of an unnatural calm in the Scottish Highlands, where two revolts in support of the Pretender had taken place within the past ten years. Townshend, for one, was 'apt to believe that the present submission of the Highland clans is no more than a blind', and Ireland was also believed to be vulnerable to a combined invasion and Jacobite rising. The threat from the Pretender, in short, was strategic rather than domestic in origin; it waxed and waned in relation to Britain's position within the state system.[8]

Britain's military resources were quite inadequate to cope with these escalating threats. To be sure, the Royal Navy could be used as a deterrent. For example, Robert Walpole suggested in October 1725 that 'a sufficient fleet, sent early enough to the Baltic, and another to be employed in our own seas, as occurrences shall direct, may possibly defeat the project [of a Russian invasion].' In June of the following year, the ambassador to Vienna, St Saphorin, argued rather ambitiously 'that sending a small number of ships with a bomb vessel or two to lie off Naples would most effectually frighten the imperialists & prevent their giving any disturbance in Germany or in any other place'. But there were limits to naval power, and these could not be made good by the British army, whose every expense was scrutinized annually in the debate on the Mutiny Bill. Everybody knew that any expeditionary force would not exceed a few tens of thousands of men, not enough to right the threatened balance in Italy and Germany, or to shield the King's German dominions from attack. George freely admitted to his son-in-law Frederick William I that the constitution of Great Britain did not enable him to field an army strong enough to deliver on his European obligations.[9]

The system of barriers and alliances devised at Utrecht had partly been designed to compensate for Britain's conventional military weakness. But these continued to crumble at an alarming rate. Even though this was not immediately obvious at the time, the Dutch oligarchy – which was after all treaty-bound to support the Protestant Succession – was determined not to be dragged into European quarrels on London's behalf. Moreover, decision-making in the United Provinces was painfully slow. The Grand Pensionary would make proposals to the States (assemblies) of Holland and the States-General of the entire Union. On crucial matters something like unanimity was needed, and the resulting differences led to interminable local consultations, not unlike those that paralysed the Holy Roman Empire. Besides, if the Dutch feared the commercial potential of the Ostend Company, they feared the military might of Austria even more, especially in the southern and eastern provinces of the United Provinces. The mainstay of the old Grand Alliance was disintegrating. Worse still, the Austrian Netherlands had now mutated from a bulwark against France to a potential springboard for the ambitions of Charles VI against Britain. The future of the Barrier was uncertain. The Austrian ambassador warned nonchalantly that 'the Emperor was indifferent as to who controlled the Netherlands, and that he would happily renounce them in order to preserve the friendship of the King of France.'[10]

All this forced British statesmen to reconceive the European balance and Britain's role in it. A radical rethink on the Barrier was floated by Townshend in August 1725: he suggested that Flanders might be partitioned between the British, Dutch and French. According to this scheme, Britain would get Bruges, Nieuport and Ostend, with territories 'sufficient to maintain the garrisons in those places'. Britain, Townshend argued, should take on the protection of the Barrier itself, rather than subcontracting it to another power; it would have to defend Flanders in an emergency anyway. Had this plan been implemented, the tradition of a Continental outpost, the legacy of Calais and Dunkirk, would have been given a new lease of life, and British history might have taken a completely different path. There was also some reflection on the future of the German Empire, once Charles VI, who was not in the best of health, had died. Might it not be better, it was asked in London, if the imperial dignity passed to the Bavarian Wittelsbachs? The very fact that this question – which would have been heretical in the time of the Grand Alliance – was even being asked, was a reflection of the depths to which Anglo-Austrian relations had plunged.[11]

Fear of Austrian expansionism also drove Britain to a new geopolitical vision for Italy. Savoy, which had been primarily thought of as a barrier against France, was now reconceived as a bulwark against Austro-Spanish hegemony in the peninsula. In late 1725 Horatio Walpole ruminated that it would be best to give Sicily to Savoy in order to make her 'more dependent upon England and France . . . preserve the balance of Italy, and keep the Emperor in awe on that side'. There was only one problem: Savoy had no interest in Sicily, and when approached for a defensive treaty by Britain in early 1726 demanded Milan instead. This was rejected in London: Milan would be the last province Austria would cede and the first she would recapture. Sicily, on the other hand, was easily protected by Anglo-French naval power, and unlike Milan was not an imperial fief, and thus would not create complications with the Reichstag. Horatio Walpole observed to the British envoy to Turin in mid November 1726 that George 'as Elector of Hanover, a Prince of the [German] Empire . . . could not come into a treaty for the alienation of a fief of the Empire, having in no other respect any difficulty about augmenting the King of Sardinia's dominions on the side of the Milanese'. Although the negotiations with Savoy dragged on for nearly two years, they produced no satisfactory result. In terms of the new British geopolitics of Italy, however, they had achieved their purpose by keeping Charles VI guessing. As Newcastle observed in February 1727, discussion should be spun out, 'for should it be entirely at an end, the Emperor by that means might in a great measure be freed from any apprehension of being attacked in Italy', which would enable him to deploy troops elsewhere, particularly in Germany.[12]

What these discussions and initiatives make clear is that British statesmen had an integrated view of Europe. All sides of the balance were seen as interconnected. In January 1725 Townshend pointed out 'how fatal any disturbance in the north must be to our affairs in the south at this juncture'. Likewise, Newcastle wrote a month later that 'the affairs of the north and south are so interwoven together, that any stand or rub that happens in one place must in consequence affect the other.' After the thunderbolt of the Treaty of Vienna, this was even more true. In October 1725 Townshend set out the need to contain Russia in the Baltic, in order to concentrate on Germany and southern Europe. If Russia were 'able to gain Sweden . . . there would rise in that quarter of the world so formidable a strength against us, which would give us so great a diversion, that the court of Vienna . . . would think they had it in their power to make us submit to whatever they should think fit to impose on us'. A year later, the Russian accession to the Treaty of Vienna emboldened Madrid to such an extent that the British ambassador, William Stanhope, described the Spanish court in September 1726 as 'too much elevated and even intoxicated with their fancied irresistible power, upon their new additional strength from the Tsarina's accession'. And three months later, as war with Spain loomed, Townshend put his finger on the integrated nature of the balance with his warning that 'though the fire begins so far off as Gibraltar, yet the train is so laid that the flame would soon reach to the north.'[13]

The best way to respond to the Austro-Spanish challenge was to renew and expand Britain's own system of alliances. Here the Hanoverian connection came into its own once more, for the Electorate now served as a forward base and pivot on which a European counter-alliance could be mobilized. It was with this purpose in mind that British, French and Prussian representatives convened at Hanover in September 1725. The resulting Treaty of Hanover pitted London, Versailles and Berlin against Vienna and Madrid. All Spanish and Austrian attempts to drive a wedge between Britain and France failed. Now French power would be applied on behalf of British-Hanoverian ends in central Europe. Britain formally recognized the French right to guarantee the imperial constitution as set down in the Treaty of Westphalia (1648). Indeed, that month Newcastle wrote warmly of France as the 'Kingdom it is now so necessary to support in order to preserve the balance of Europe'. At a stroke, it seemed, Austro-Spanish pretensions had been contained, and Hanover secured into the bargain. On the face of it, British diplomacy had scored a great success.[14]

All the same, if Parliament was to throw its wholehearted support behind the treaty – and pay for the necessary subsidies – the administration's arguments would have to be clearer than the truth. Conjuring up the prospect of Austro-Spanish European hegemony, the commercial challenge of the Ostend Company, the loss of Gibraltar and Minorca and even the spectre of 'fatal combinations . . . extend[ing] themselves into Russia', to quote the King's Speech to Parliament, was easy enough. The Lords, in their address of thanks, accepted that 'The world must now be convinced, that the courts of Vienna and Madrid have laid the foundations of such an exorbitant and formidable power, as may, in time, overturn the balance and destroy the liberties of Europe.' But in order to ram home the message, the government once again resorted to the Jacobite bogey. The King claimed to have 'received information from different parts, on which I can entirely depend, that the placing the Pretender upon the throne of this kingdom is one of the articles of the secret engagements' between Austria and Spain. Many in Parliament remained unpersuaded. Some dismissed the threat of Jacobitism outright. John Hungerford, the MP for Scarborough, derided 'fears of the Pretender [as] groundless and chimerical, and he could not see how [the Russians and Spaniards] could bring him over, unless they borrowed one of Gulliver's floating islands'. Similarly, the protest of the House of Lords against the government's handling of foreign policy noted pointedly that 'any such engagement . . . is absolutely denied on the part of the crown of Spain'. For this reason, they continued, 'we cannot agree to the resolution, because time may evince, that the informations His

Majesty has received concerning that engagement were not justly grounded.' Faced with this scepticism, the government resorted to special pleading and spoke of 'positive informations', which 'the safety of the state' did not allow them to lay before Parliament. In fact, there seems to have been no such article in the treaty. But the claim had been made in good faith, and Walpole appears to have gone to his death convinced that some sort of formal Austro-Spanish accord in favour of the Pretender existed.[15]

The main thrust of the opposition critique, however, concerned the handling of the balance itself. This took two forms. On the one hand, it was argued that the defence of the balance of power threatened to send Britain off in pursuit of imaginary dragons. William Shippen argued that 'the matter of peace and war is of the greatest weight that can fall under the consideration' of Parliament, and that no consent should be given to measures 'which seemed preposterous, before they knew either what those measures were, or whether those dangers were real'. At the same time, the lurch from an Austrian to a French alliance allowed critics to question the very coherence of government policy. Tories such as Sir William Wyndham observed 'That of late years our measures had been in perpetual fluctuation; that Penelope-like, we were continually weaving and unravelling the same web.' He derided ministers for 'at one time raising up the Emperor to depress France, and now ... [being in favour of] depressing the Emperor, which could not be done without aggrandizing France, which in the end, may make the latter too powerful: so that at this rate, under pretence of holding the balance of Europe, we should be engaged in continual wars'. That indeed was the problem: as Lord Bingley complained, the notion 'that it is the prerogative, as well as the interest of Great Britain to hold the balance of power in Europe', could 'serve to justify any rupture ... for if this prerogative were wantonly exerted, it might engage us in perpetual wars' to the detriment of British commerce.[16]

But the principal charge was that the treaty represented yet another breach with Austria, and thus with the principles of the Grand Alliance. This line was taken by opposition Whigs such as the Earls of Stair and Chesterfield, whose demands for a rapprochement with Vienna now became a staple of strategic debate, and of the attacks on Walpole, for the next twenty years or so. They argued that the turn away from Austria was so contrary to Britain's natural interests that it could only be explained by the King's partiality for his German dominions. Thus William Pulteney ventured 'that the imperial court's backwardness in granting the investiture for Bremen and Verden, might have been the motive to some late measures'. It did not help, of course, that the alliance was called the 'Treaty of Hanover'. In fact, Hanoverian considerations had played little role in the formation of the alliance. The question of the investitures, which had loomed large in the early 1720s, now slipped down the list of priorities. Besides, most of George's Electoral ministers – traditionally pro-imperial – were appalled by the progressive deterioration in relations with Vienna. Moreover, when the Prussians offered to guarantee the neutrality of Hanover in February 1727 against the forces of Charles VI, this was turned down by Britain because it would release Austrian troops to do greater mischief elsewhere. In short, it was not that the Treaty of Hanover was designed to protect Hanover, but that Hanover had to be protected because of the Treaty of Hanover.[17]

For the next two years British diplomats worked to expand the alliance of Hanover by winning over previously uncommitted powers, and by isolating Spain and Austria. In the south, approaches were made to Portugal to dissuade her from joining the Treaty of Vienna. In the north, negotiations were begun with Sweden and Denmark, never an easy task given the hostility between the two powers. At the same time, Britain stepped up her active diplomacy in Germany. The aim here was twofold. First of all, to mobilize the middling and smaller states against Charles VI, in support of the Treaty of Hanover and in defence of the King's German dominions. In October 1725 Horatio Walpole spoke of the imperative of 'engaging as many princes of the [German] Empire, as we can, whether little or great', to protect Hanover and Prussia against a joint Austro-Russian attack. An agreement with the Danes and Hesse-Kassel, Townshend believed, would serve 'to cover the King's territories in Germany'. The second and related aim was to deny Charles the political and military support of the Empire. Britain had to stop him from mustering a large enough constituency to have the Treaty of Hanover condemned by the Reichstag. In particular, Austria must be prevented from declaring the defence of Ostend (which Townshend feared might 'be reckoned a part of the [imperial] circle [Reichskreis] of Burgundy', which formed the western border of Germany) an affair of the Empire. If Charles succeeded in this, any move against the Ostend Company would in theory put George beyond the pale in Germany, because the Emperor could then argue that the integrity of one of the 'circles' of the Holy Roman Empire had been violated. For the next two years, therefore, British diplomacy was at pains to uncouple the two issues. For example, in late April 1727 Newcastle argued that war with Austria was likely to arise out of an unprovoked attack on Gibraltar, so that the princes of the Empire would have 'no sort of pretence to concern themselves in it'. The links between the northern and southern balances could not have been more clearly demonstrated. As a German state, ruled by a German prince, Hanover-Britain was highly sensitive to the norms and conventions according to which the political commonwealth of the Empire functioned, and which placed effective restraints on the unilateral exercise of power.[18]

All this involved close collaboration between George's British and Hanoverian ministers. When Isaac Leheup was sent as new British envoy to Regensburg in the autumn of 1726, he was furnished with funds to bribe the various envoys on the advice of George's Electoral representative, Baron Gerlach Adolf von Münchhausen; he was also told to work closely with the French envoy. 'The more regard is paid to the other German princes,' Newcastle wrote in late September 1726, 'the more it raises them, and inclines them, to withstand any unjust authority that the Emperor may pretend over them, which, in the present posture of affairs, is what we ought to desire.' The first port of call was the Protestant territories: Britain needed to mobilize the *Corpus Evangelicorum* against the Emperor. And although that would not necessarily be enough to outvote the imperial faction in the Reichstag, Münchhausen ingeniously suggested that a unified Protestant front against Austria would enable George to call for an *itio in partes*, which had been designed to protect Protestants from Catholic majoritarianism on religious issues, not as a lever in the European balance of power.[19]

If religion was important to British strategy, it was far from decisive. True, George had agreed at the Treaty of Hanover to concert measures with Prussia for the defence of the treaty rights of Polish Protestants. Yet by then British ministers were already beginning to have second thoughts about mounting this particular charger. Thus in March 1725 Horatio Walpole had expressed the hope that the King of Prussia would not go to war over the issue and thus 'make the Polanders desperate and oblige them to fling themselves into the hands of the Emperor'. Soon

British diplomats were being instructed to tone down their religious rhetoric over the Protestants of Thorn. Here, the primacy of foreign policy trumped religious solidarity. This, as Newcastle noted with satisfaction in March 1726, was also the case for France. Welcoming the rise of the staunchly Catholic Cardinal Fleury in Paris, he wrote that although the chief minister 'has always had the reputation of being bigoted to his own religion, yet he has constantly given the most public and convincing proofs of his desire to cultivate the good understanding between England and France, and has forwarded, as much as in him lay, the union with Prussia, Sweden, Holland, and all those other Protestant powers, which it is thought necessary to bring into our alliance'. In particular, he might have added, Catholic France was helping to rally German states against the Catholic Emperor.[20]

The same flexibility was shown within the Empire. Townshend wrote that British and French envoys were being sent to Regensburg not merely to 'encourage the Protestant states', but also to 'inspire even those Catholic states who love the fundamental laws and constitutions of the [German] Empire [with] the desire to maintain the liberties and privileges of Germany against the despotism of the court of Vienna'. The key thing was to mobilize not so much Protestant states, as anti-Austrian, and especially strong states. As Townshend put it: 'it is very useful to cultivate the friendship of all Protestant states, and to try to attract them to our interests, but in the first instance His Majesty seeks to strengthen his hand through the most powerful princes and states.' He went on to say that once George had formed an alliance with the greater princes, Hanover would be safe and the lesser princes in the Empire would respect him for it all the more. Likewise St Saphorin, who was something of an anti-popish fire-breather in Vienna, included Catholic Bavaria in any alliance along with the usual Protestant suspects. Indeed, he suggested that the *Corpus Evangelicorum* should mute its hostility towards Munich, despite the ill-treatment of Protestants in the Upper Palatinate, for that very reason. By the end of 1726, British policy in the Empire was beginning to bear fruit. In March of that year a subsidy treaty with the Hessians was signed, not only to secure troops for the alliance of Hanover but also to deny them to the Emperor. In August Townshend was bullish about the military situation. Even without the Dutch and the Swedes, he reckoned the French, Hessian, Danish and Hanoverian troops to field about 80,000 men in the Empire.[21]

Yet if there were some successes to report, there were also significant reverses. Relations with Russia had been deteriorating. Rumours of a large invasion force intended for Sweden multiplied in February 1726, and prompted Swedish requests for the dispatch of a British squadron. This was duly sent under the command of Vice-Admiral Sir Charles Wager in March. In early August 1726 Catherine of Russia finally joined the Treaty of Vienna, and committed herself to supply 30,000 men for the purpose of mutual defence. Moreover, Prussia was beginning to wobble. For no sooner had Frederick William I committed to the Treaty of Hanover than he began to distance himself from it. In part this was motivated by dynastic pique. The Prussian King had expected the announcement of a marriage between the Prince of Wales's son, Frederick, and his daughter Wilhelmina, but it rapidly became clear that nothing would come of this. He then began to explore the idea of an Austrian marriage. Frederick William was, in any case, a difficult and paranoid man – Newcastle described him as 'an unaccountable creature, neither interest nor reason will prevail upon him to do right' – who suspected his father-in-law of planning a secret Austro-British rapprochement at his expense, and of much else besides. The Russo-Prussian defensive treaty of August 1726 was also a bad sign. In October of that year, Prussia finally joined the Austrian camp by the Treaty of Königswusterhausen. This was a major blow. It had a sobering effect in Sweden and slowed alliance negotiations there. More importantly, it blew the British position in north Germany wide open. Hanover and Britain's whole imperial policy were now in mortal peril.[22]

Putting pressure on Austria in Germany had just failed; so had the attempt to contain Russia in northern and eastern Europe. But British statesmen still had one card to play: the Ottoman Turks. They noted that after the successful conclusion of their war against the Persians, which secured the eastern flank of the Ottoman Empire, the Turks were now free to turn their attention to the north. In November 1725 Townshend told the British envoy in Constantinople, Abraham Stanyan, that he should 'see how reasonable it is and even necessary it is that His Majesty should seek to divert the Tsarina in any possible way and to stir up trouble within her territories in order to frustrate her Jacobite plans, and to prevent her from troubling His Majesty in his own lands'. For this reason Stanyan must do everything he could to sabotage a Russo-Turkish treaty, 'and make every effort to stir them up against the Muscovites'. In this spirit, the Turks were encouraged to occupy Astrakhan, on the Caspian Sea, and so, as Townshend put it, 'by pre-occupying the Tsarina so much on the side of Asia that she may be less attentive and less enterprising to create trouble and uneasiness to the King on this side'.[23]

11. British diplomats had to think of Europe in the round. As representative in Constantinople, Abraham Stanyan was often charged with encouraging the Turks to attack Britain's enemies in the 1720s, Austria and Russia.

In theory, the Ottoman card could also be played against Austria, whose long and exposed border made an inviting target. The problem here was that any suspicion that the King of England had encouraged the Turks – the old oriental bogey – to attack the Emperor would immediately put George beyond the pale in Germany itself, and wreck his entire *Reichspolitik*. For this reason, the British envoy to Constanti-nople was specifically instructed 'not to say or do anything which would appear to stir the Ottomans up against the Emperor'. For the next eighteen months or so, Britain ritually denied any attempts to incite a Turkish attack, and dismissed these accusations as the product of a '*conscience mauvaise*' in Vienna over their contacts with the Pretender. This did not, of course, prevent Britain from playing an elaborate and deniable form of psychological warfare with the Emperor, by which the Turks were discouraged from withdrawing troops from the border with

Hungary so as to prevent the Austrians from redeploying their own forces to Germany. In short, the Ottoman card as played in 1725–7 showed how British statesmen's strategic conceptions of Europe were wide-ranging but also constrained. They did not want to gain on the swings of Constantinople only to lose on the roundabouts of the Empire.[24]

Britain also put pressure on what was believed to be the weakest link in the Treaty of Vienna: Spain. Relations with Madrid were not viewed through the largely commercial and colonial prism of later years, but rather within the framework of the European balance. The main enemy was Austria, and the hand of Vienna was seen behind every Spanish move. Thus Britain's ambassador to Madrid, William Stanhope, reported in late February 1726 'that peace or war depends entirely upon the designs and views of the imperial court and that this is and will be solely and absolutely governed by the inspirations it shall receive from thence'. In this context, attacking the Spanish monkey rather than the Austrian organ-grinder may seem perverse, but it made perfect sense. For it was through Spanish subsidies that Austria hoped to fund her active policy in Germany. British diplomats feared that gold from the New World would be used to bribe German princes. As the ambassador to Paris, Thomas Robinson, reported in January 1727, these funds would be 'lavish[ed] ... away upon the Emperor'. It was therefore imperative to cut off the flow of Spanish bullion from the New World: the *Flota*, embarking from Veracruz in the Carribbean, which served Mexico and its environs, and the *Galleones*, embarking from Porto Bello on the Isthmus of Panama, which served Chile and Peru. So when Admiral Hosier was dispatched with his squadron to intercept the Spanish treasure fleet in April 1726, and another squadron under Jennings later made a show of force off Santander, neither man was engaged in the kind of maritime smash-and-grab raid which so delighted the British public. Rather they were using naval instruments to contain Charles VI in Germany.[25]

There were other advantages in confronting Spain first. As we have seen, a direct attack on Austria or Ostend itself would bring Britain into conflict with the Empire. On the other hand, an Anglo-Spanish war arising out of an unprovoked attack on Gibraltar would put Charles VI on the spot. He would then be compelled to side with his ally, and turn himself into the aggressor against George within the Empire. If Charles failed to deliver on his obligations, Spain would probably turn away from Vienna in disgust. Once again, British statesmen showed themselves adept both at thinking of the European balance in the round, and tailoring their policy to take the realities of an international organization like the Holy Roman Empire into account. In the course of late 1726 and early 1727, rumours and counter-rumours of Spanish-backed Jacobite invasions and surprise attacks in the western Mediterranean swirled back and forth. The Spanish finally commenced a fitful siege of Gibraltar, and were in turn attacked on the high seas. In short, by a direct chain of causation and logic, the Austro-British struggle in central Europe led inexorably to a naval war with Spain.[26]

In the meantime, relations with Vienna seemed to have broken down irretrievably. Matters came to a head at the end of the year, when the Austrian envoy to London, Baron Palm, submitted a sulphurous memorandum to the government attacking British policy, and was promptly expelled. St Saphorin was booted out of Vienna in retaliation. Ignoring the Austrian demand that he leave the Empire altogether, St Saphorin repaired to Munich, where he took up the threads of his anti-Austrian policy. Meanwhile, the British envoy to the Reichstag lived in constant terror of expulsion at the hands of Charles VI.[27] As the confrontation with Austria escalated, British anxieties for the security of Hanover increased. Large Austrian deployments were reported in Silesia, ultimately threatening the Electorate from the east; Saxon and other German contingents were said to be joining them. Newcastle pointed out that 'the whole bent and study of the court of Vienna is to be revenged upon the King, by falling upon his dominions in Germany'. All that Britain had available to meet this threat in the summer of 1726 was 12,000 British troops, 9,000 Hanoverians and the 6,000 hired Hessians.[28]

The last line of defence, and certainly the greatest deterrent, was the French alliance. For this reason, as Newcastle wrote in April 1727, it was essential to secure firm commitments from the French about 'how they will come to the King's assistance in case any attempt be made upon him in Germany'. The problem was that although some German states could be mobilized to contain Charles, sensitivities about the integrity of the Empire also cut across any sort of rational military planning. Versailles was extremely reluctant to send troops across the imperial border without a waterproof mandate, which could only be supplied through an invitation of the Reichstag. Newcastle conceded that the deployment of French or British troops might well be counter-productive, by giving 'the Emperor a handle to infuse fears and jealousies into the princes of the Empire, as well as to reproach us with being the aggressors'. All the same, London felt that the French were making rather a meal of the niceties of imperial law. Throughout 1726–7, therefore, Europe was treated to the unusual spectacle of British ministers trying to persuade France to intervene more forcefully in Germany; indeed, they were prepared to let French troops into the Austrian Netherlands, thus compromising the Barrier. In June 1726, Newcastle argued that France was legally entitled, as a guarantor of the imperial constitution, to move into the Reich to repel an invasion by Russia or any other power. He wanted the French to keep 'a body of troops upon the Rhine in a readiness' to allow them to enter 'into the Empire in case of need'. If necessary, they could use the threat of the 'Muscovites being in motion in order to disturb the peace of the Empire'. In all these matters, the French were thinking legally, the British geopolitically. London was aware of, and prepared to make use of, the German imperial constitution, but it did not fetishize it.[29]

Military action was also taken against Russia. At the end of April a Baltic squadron sailed from the Nore, at the mouth of the Thames Estuary, under the command of Vice-Admiral Sir Charles Wager. He was to pre-empt any outbreak of hostilities in the north 'which might easily spread to other countries and set the rest of Christendom [a seventeenth-century archaism for "Europe"] in a flame in the present critical situation of affairs'. More specifically, Wager was to intimidate Russia, partly to protect British trading interests, but principally because of the 'undoubted intelligence of the court of St Petersburg having entered into measures in favour of the Pretender and his adherents'. British ships returned to the Baltic the following year under Admiral Norris, with orders not to confront the Russians head on but to 'repel force by force' in the event of a Russian attack on Denmark. In any case, experience had shown that the fleet was not able to enter the shallow waters of the eastern Baltic, and was thus incapable of delivering a knockout blow; but it could and did provide a protective shield against Russian attempts to impose their candidate, the Duke of Holstein-Gottorp (who was married to Peter's daughter Anna), on Sweden and Denmark. The strategy paid off: in March 1727 the Swedes acceded to the Treaty of Hanover, and in April 1727 Denmark acceded if not to the Treaty of Hanover, then at least to a compact for the defence of lower Saxony, and thus of Hanover. Once again, naval power had been used not as an instrument in its own right, but as part of an integrated grand strategy.[30]

12. Vice-Admiral Sir Charles Wager, who commanded the Navy squadron sent to protect British interests in the Baltic.

The whole of Europe now seemed on the verge of a conflagration spanning almost the entire continent: from the eastern Baltic to the Rock of Gibraltar and from the Channel ports of the Austrian Netherlands to the Crimea two armed blocs faced off. On the one side there was Britain-Hanover, France, Denmark, Sweden, the Ottoman Turks and a host of smaller German states; on the other side stood Austria, Spain, Russia and possibly Prussia. The first shots had already been exchanged before Gibraltar and on the high seas. But Europe was not plunged into war; instead, the Austrians began to pull back from the brink. Already in late December 1726 there were signs of a change of heart in Vienna; overtures were made to London and Paris. At first these led nowhere. As 1727 wore on, however, the reality of the situation began to sink in at the imperial court. The Ostend Company would not survive open conflict with the Royal Navy; the Spanish treasure fleet could not be depended upon to clear the British blockade on every occasion; and without guaranteed financial support Austria simply lacked the resources to go to war. Without increasing the tax burden at home, British diplomacy had mobilized more than 300,000 men against 380,000 loyal to the Alliance of Vienna; and Austria needed to watch her back against the Ottomans. Charles backed down. London rejoiced: a great victory had been won, most of it with mirrors.[31]

The immediate result of the crisis over the Treaty of Vienna was that France and Britain were driven closer together. Ministers now routinely expressed their complete confidence in the alliance. As Newcastle observed in May 1727, 'the preserving and cementing the union betwixt England and France which has proved so useful and advantageous to both kingdoms is what His Majesty looks upon as a principle not be departed from'; this he attributed to 'the constancy, firmness and upright behaviour of France'. Most importantly, the alliance had not only survived but been strengthened by a change of personnel at Versailles. The new chief minister, Fleury, the Bishop of Fréjus, now became synonymous with the Anglo-French entente. When Philip V had sought to drive a wedge between the partners by offering to transfer the *Asiento* to France, Fleury turned him down. If the French were reluctant to move into Germany as quickly as London wanted, they did warn the Prussians in early 1727 that they would defend Hanover if it was attacked. British ministers reciprocated in the autumn of that year, when they refused to countenance any marriage with Prussia unless agreed by France, with reference to 'the rule H. M. has laid down, to go hand in hand with the most Christian King in all things that concern the public affairs of Europe'.[32]

In late April 1727, Newcastle even suggested joint operations in the Mediterranean. His plan was to detach some of Vice-Admiral Wager's squadron at Gibraltar to cruise with the French in a demonstration against Naples and Sicily. Another idea was to put some French infantry on British galleys to occupy Portolongone on the Mediterranean island of Elba, which would have been the first Anglo-French amphibious operation. As an aside, he added that there should be no trouble over saluting the colours, as 'we do not pretend to any superiority beyond Cape Finisterre'. In a bizarre moment of harmony, Horatio Walpole suggested in May 1727 that George should meet with the French Marshal, the Duke of Berwick, James II's natural son, in Holland to confer on military measures in defence of north Germany. Britain's position in Europe, and with it the Protestant succession and English liberties, had never seemed more secure.

8

The Resurgence of France, 1727–1732

*We have been like a man in a room, who wants to get out, and though
the door be open, and a clear way to it, yet he stalks around the room,
breaks his shins over a stool, tumbles over a chair, and at last, rumbling
over every thing in his way, by chance finds the door and gets out, after
an abundance of needless trouble and unnecessary danger.*[1]

William Wyndham, January 1732, in the House of Commons

*The preserving the imperial dominions entire is necessary for preserving
the balance of power in Europe: if we had delayed entering into that
guaranty [the Pragmatic Sanction] until his Imperial Majesty's death, it
would have been too late.*[2]

Horatio Walpole, January 1732, in the House of Commons, on why
Britain had decided to support the succession of Maria Theresa in Austria

No sooner had Britain mastered the Austro-Spanish threat, than the
European state system was thrown back into flux. Relations with Spain
were patched up, but only at the price of damaging the French alliance,
inflicting serious damage on Austria's position in Italy, and disappointing an increasingly assertive public sphere, which hoped for rich pickings
in the Spanish-American empire. At the same time, France was beginning
to plan the dismantlement of Austrian power in Germany. Fleury was
hoping at the very least to claim the Duchy of Lorraine; if all went well,
the Habsburgs might even be unbolted from the imperial title after the
death of Charles VI. All this led to yet another characteristic lurch in
British policy and politics in response to the shifting European kaleidoscope. Charles Townshend, who had been rehabilitated on the back of
his support for George I's 'German' policies, was now once more

banished, because he would not do the bidding of the new King in Germany. Henceforth Britain's imperial preoccupation would no longer be the containment of Austrian ambitions, but how to bolster the Habsburg position in the Holy Roman Empire against the resurgence of French power.

In July 1727 news arrived of the death of George I, appropriately enough on his way to Hanover. All eyes now turned to contemplate his son and successor George II, who was crowned in October. Some opposition papers saw this as an opportunity for a less German and Hanover-centric policy. One opposition peer claimed expectantly in November 1727 that 'The popular topics of a *new family* and a *foreign reign* are in a great measure removed, our present most gracious sovereign being the *second British* monarch of that illustrious House having constantly resided among us for above these thirteen years.' George, he believed, had 'made our *language* and constitution familiar to him, which is more than can be said of the Pretender'. Some hoped the new king would look with greater favour on the emerging support for a colonial and naval 'blue water' policy in the public sphere. The disillusionment caused by the South Sea Bubble had completely dissipated: once more, many Britons saw a colonial crock of gold over the horizon. They also increasingly believed that Britain's true destiny was not European, but naval. For this reason, the severe countermeasures which Spanish customs officers took against British merchantmen attempting to muscle in on Spain's South American trade gave particular offence. It seemed intolerable that the greatest maritime and commercial power on earth should subject itself to the humiliation of searches on the high seas, confiscation of alleged contraband, and even the arrest of her sailors. Had the Royal Navy not laid down the law to Spain during the Armada, the Commonwealth, in 1718–19, and most recently in the standoff over the Treaty of Vienna in 1725–7? Even such a protagonist of Britain's European destiny as Daniel Defoe now succumbed to the navalist temptation. ' 'Tis my stated opinion (speaking without national prejudice),' he wrote in 1727, 'that England is so far from being in danger by a war with Spain, that it would be no loss to us if we never had any peace with them.'[3]

Moreover, the popular view was that the successful naval mobilization of 1725–6 had been directed against Spanish commerce *per se*, rather than being a strategy designed to deny her Austrian ally the subsidies to

13. George II was very much a German prince, who had spent most of his life before the age of thirty in the Holy Roman Empire.

pursue central European aims, as was in fact the case. These sentiments were summed up in 1727 by James Thomson's famous poem 'Britannia':

> And is a Briton seizd! And seiz'd beneath
> The slumbering terrors of a British fleet?
> Then ardent rise! Oh great in vengeance rise;
> O'erturn the proud, teach rapine to restore:
> And as you ride sublimely round the world,
> Make every vessel stoop, make every state
> At once their welfare and their duty know.

This is your glory; this is your wisdom; this
The native power for which you were design'd
By fate, when fate designed the firmest state,
That e'er was seated on the subject sea

Navalist sentiment, even arrogance, could also be found in the political elite, though far less than later in the century. Thus Lord Tyrawly, the extraordinary envoy to Lisbon, told George in July 1729 that Britain should use the 'roughest means' to coerce Portugal, which had no allies to stop her, if the King 'had a mind to lay this country to ashes' from the sea. European powers noted Britain's naval power, and deeply resented it. Elizabeth Farnese, for example, complained in 1727 that Britain had burned 'their fleet and pretended to lord it over everybody'.[4]

It soon became clear that there would be no radical change of course in grand strategy. In his first statement to the Privy Council, George stressed that 'As the alliances entered into by the late king, my father, with foreign powers, have contributed to the restoring the tranquillity, and preserving the balance of Europe, I shall endeavour to cultivate those alliances, and to improve and perfect this great work, for the honour, interest, and security of my people.' His speech to both Houses on his accession to the throne at the end of the month reaffirmed this commitment to continuity in foreign policy. How could it be otherwise? The second George was certainly more 'British' or 'English' than his father, but he was still fundamentally a German. He spoke English fluently, but with a marked accent. He had only moved to England at the age of twenty-seven, having served in German campaigns for most of his adult life so far. His wife, Caroline of Ansbach, was a German. George was to spend a substantial part of his reign in, or travelling back and forth from, Hanover; he maintained a separate Hanoverian diplomatic establishment in Germany and even in France; and he continued his father's custom of employing Hanoverian envoys for British purposes and vice versa. The split personality of the King and thus of British foreign policy did not change after 1727.[5]

This was strikingly demonstrated a few years after George II's coronation, when the new Hanoverian representative, who bore the very un-German name of Saladin, was being accredited at Versailles. He was instructed by the King to 'have care for the letters which will be addressed to you from [both] our German ministers [in Hanover] and by our

German court here [the Hanoverian chancellery]'. In his turn, Saladin was to inform both the London and Hanover Germans of events at the French court. No mention in this case was made of the King's British ministers, so that George was in effect maintaining a parallel diplomatic service. This certainly confused the French, who were unclear in which capacity, royal or Electoral, Saladin was serving George. His master's letter of accreditation asked Louis simply 'to give complete credence to everything which [Saladin] will have the honour to tell you on my behalf from time to time'. Saladin had coordinated the presentation of these credentials with the British ambassador, Lord Waldegrave, only to be told by the *Garde des Sceaux* (Privy Seal) that having 'only the rank of resident [he] could not request an audience with the King'. Indeed, Saladin reported, 'he raised several objections to the Electorate of Hanover, and [suggested] that since my predecessors had been content to present their accreditation to an audience of ministers, one wished him to take the same path.' London instructed Saladin to hold his ground. It was only after a lot of toing and froing, and some effort on Waldegrave's part, that the matter was cleared up to Saladin's, and George II's, satisfaction.[6]

Like his father, George II conceived of his German and his British interests not separately, but symbiotically. British ministers continued to coordinate their moves with the Hanoverian ministers, both in London and in the Empire. It therefore comes as no surprise to find the King asking his British Secretary of State for the North – still Townshend – for advice and help on German politics. 'I believe it to be high time,' he wrote of a measure linking Hanover to Saxe-Gotha and perhaps Hesse-Kassel, Bavaria and the Bishop of Würzburg as well, 'to accede as Elector to this treaty and I wish you would draw some sketch of those articles that should be added, leaving those out which I cannot come into'. At around the same time, Townshend was sending George 'a draft of a dispatch to Mr Walpole, which I humbly submit to Your Majesty's consideration together with a paper I received from Monsieur Hattorf [the King's Hanoverian minister in London]. If Your Majesty approves of the enclosed, I will dispatch them immediately to Mr Walpole.' Here the King's British minister was coordinating both the royal and the Electoral dimensions.[7]

All this had important consequences for British high politics. Attention to the King's German interest remained a potential ticket to royal favour.

Townshend, against whom the Hanoverian card had been played with such devastating effect under George I ten years earlier, understood this better than anybody. As George II's Secretary of State for the North, he was best placed to take advantage of the situation. Royal marginalia on his dispatches in the late 1720s testify to the high regard in which he was then held by George: 'I have read this paper with great satisfaction'; 'this letter is very well drawn'; 'These instructions are very proper and I see nothing to be added to them'; 'I like the draft very well'; 'I approve entirely of this draft'; and 'I believe this letter may have a very good effect'. Newcastle certainly looked on all this with great suspicion. 'Hanover is Lord Townshend's great merit,' he complained, 'and we have all been represented as wanting zeal.' On another occasion he feared that 'His Lordship has represented us, as giving up Hanover quite.' Horatio Walpole likewise lamented that Townshend 'endeavours to make all measures Electoral, preferable to all other considerations, which is entirely agreeable to the King' sentiments'.[8]

There were very good reasons for the preoccupation with Hanover. The Electorate was under constant threat from Frederick William of Prussia, with whom relations had been tense ever since Prussia's defection from the Treaty of Hanover in 1726. In November 1727, Prussia – at the behest of its queen, George's sister – made overtures suggesting a marriage between the Prince of Wales and Frederick William's daughter Wilhelmina; his son, the future Frederick the Great, was to marry George's daughter Anne. Frederick William, however, was stand-offish; and the putative happy couples were not too keen either. In the end, the plans fizzled out, but not before causing renewed suspicion and resentment. Moreover, relations with Berlin were greatly aggravated by Frederick William's peculiar taste for large, well-formed young men to serve in his personal guard regiment of *lange Kerls*. Prussian recruitment squads regularly infiltrated across the Hanoverian border to kidnap likely lads, much to George's fury. In July 1729 a full-scale war over this issue seemed possible, and Frederick William mobilized. One British observer in Berlin remarked that 'the King of Prussia waits with impatience for an opportunity to do some action, which to use his own expressions, may make some affronting stroke on the side of Hanover.' The crisis proved to be a victory for George's imperial policy, because his British and Hanoverian ministers succeeded in mobilizing allies in his support: Hesse-Kassel, the Dutch, the Swedes, the Danes and especially the French all made commitments. Townshend, never to be outdone, even promised to send British troops. Isolated in Germany and Europe, Frederick William backed off.[9]

To George, and even more so to British statesmen, Hanover was only part of the much broader issue at stake in Germany and Europe as a whole. This was the containment of Austrian power. Here too the initial continuity to the previous reign was striking. The Emperor would have to be stopped in Germany, and all other issues – instability in neighbouring territories or the threat of Prussian invasion – were seen in this context. Thus in early 1728 George looked to 'a considerable number of princes in the Empire to defend and support the rights and immunities of the whole Germanic body against any usurpations or encroachments on the part of His Imperial Majesty'. So when the King and his ministers became obsessed with events in some smaller German principality – such as Mecklenburg, which bordered on Hanover – this was driven by much more than narrow-minded or opportunistic concerns with George's German homeland. As Townshend argued in June 1728, 'If the Emperor should establish such a despotism over Germany, as he plainly aims at by way of disposing of the Duchy of Mecklenburg, all his neighbours will soon feel the effects of his overgrown power.' They would then see 'how boundless imperial ambition is, when backed with the might and force of an arbitrary force in the Empire'. The conflicts in Germany thus directly affected the European balance. It was there that Austria might secure the resources with which to bid for universal monarchy. Moreover, failure to pin Charles VI down in central Europe would enable him to pursue a vigorous Mediterranean policy, challenge Britain commercially and colonially through the Ostend Company, sponsor Jacobitism, and generally unravel Britain's naval dominance. British security, therefore, was being defended on the Elbe, however odd that seemed to popular and parliamentary critics.[10]

George was not much interested in Anglo-Spanish relations, but he believed strongly that the northern and southern balances were intimately linked. Like his father, he wanted to make sure that the Queen of Spain's son, Don Carlos, did not marry Charles VI's daughter and thus open the path to an Austro-Spanish condominium which would wreck the European balance of power. Since the principal enemy throughout the 1720s had always been Austria, it made sense to repair relations with Spain and thus split the axis between Vienna and Madrid.

At the Convention of the Pardo in March 1728, therefore, Britain came to terms with Spain. The Royal Navy was withdrawn from Spanish waters in Europe and North America; in return Spain lifted the siege of Gibraltar. The contraband issue was referred to a future congress at which all outstanding matters would be resolved. This congress met at the French town of Soissons in June 1728 and sat until July of the following year. It was designed to wrap up all the loose ends left over from the Treaties of Vienna and Hanover, especially with regard to Spain. Here Britain was determined to avoid both an Austro-Spanish union of crowns resurrecting the empire of Charles V, and excessive Austrian or Spanish gains at the expense of the other. Britain was also concerned to prevent, if possible, the outbreak of open hostilities between the two powers, which would disturb the stability of the Mediterranean. Above all, the French alliance must be maintained, and any unfavourable dynastic permutations nipped in the bud. As the British envoy at Soissons, Stephen Poyntz, remarked, 'I had nothing before my eyes for two or three days together, but the Emperor, France and Spain united for the present; Princes of the House of Bourbon fixed on the three most powerful thrones of Europe for ages to come.'[11]

For this reason, Britain remained profoundly ambivalent about the Pragmatic Sanction, Charles VI's device for leaving the entire Habsburg lands to his eldest daughter, Maria Theresa. Maintaining a strong Austria had long been a commonplace of British strategy, but what if the Emperor was hostile, and worse still, what if he would pass on not only an undivided inheritance but also that of Spain as well? As Townshend remarked in November 1729, 'however the maritime powers may be engaged . . . to prevent any division of the Austrian territories, this is by no means a proper time to propose a guarantee of the Pragmatic Sanction.' This question could be resolved to Britain's strategic satisfaction only when it became clear who Maria Theresa's husband was going to be, and whether there was any prospect of the fatal Spanish match rumoured at the time of the Treaty of Vienna. British policy towards Spain and Austria should therefore be seen in the round, even if the principal focus was Vienna. Neither problem could be solved in isolation. Failure to settle with one would embolden the other. Moreover, as in the mid 1720s, the Austrians were dependent on Spanish subsidies. Townshend noted in March 1729 that Austria would need Spanish gold to pay for treaties in the (German) Empire. So long as there was hope of help from Madrid, in short, Vienna would remain intractable. The colonial, naval and central European spheres were thus all closely linked. In the mid 1720s London had sent Admiral Hosier to interrupt the supply of New World bullion; now it would try to uncouple Spain from Austria by diplomatic means.[12]

Coordinating British policy in these circumstances was not easy. The chief minister, Walpole, usually took a back seat in the day-to-day running of foreign affairs, and the interlocking issues concerning Spain and Austria were dealt with by two separate departments: that of the Secretary of State for the South, headed by the Duke of Newcastle, and that of the Secretary of State for the North, headed by Townshend. Only the King had a complete overview. Matters were further complicated by the temptation not only to indulge the monarch, but also to sideline political rivals. Thus at the very moment when Townshend should have been working together with Newcastle, he was writing to the King, 'This is a private letter I intend to write to Mr Walpole if Your Majesty approves of it and as it is a secret correspondence which only Your Majesty knows of, I beg no mention may be made of it before the Duke of Newcastle.' To this George responded simply, 'This letter is very well drawn & you may depend upon the secret.' For the moment, this structure worked, but it was to come under increasing strain as the century wore on.[13]

Newcastle and Townshend did, however, manage to settle the differences with Spain. In the resulting Treaty of Seville in 1729, Britain regained the *Asiento*, and her right to send an annual ship to trade with the Spanish colonies, which had lapsed during the cold war of 1727–9, was resumed. Spain revoked the privileges she had granted to the Ostend Company. But the core of the treaty concerned European affairs. Spain ended the siege of Gibraltar; Britain agreed to convoy Spanish troops to Italy to secure the succession of Don Carlos to the contested Duchies of Tuscany, Parma and Piacenza. She also guaranteed the Pragmatic Sanction, much to the annoyance of France. In this way, the Austro-Spanish alliance was ruptured, while – it was thought – the future of Austria as a bulwark in the European balance of power was assured. To be on the safe side, several thousand Hessians were hired to defend Hanover from attack by Charles VI. The ministry also pointedly refused to rule out attacking the Emperor in Flanders and the Rhineland, in the event of Austrian aggression elsewhere. Here the principle of what has since come to be known as 'horizontal escalation' was being applied: Charles was being put on notice that bad behaviour in one part of Europe might lead to reprisals in another.[14]

The treaty was immediately attacked, partly because of its supposed failure to reflect Britain's commercial, colonial and insular destiny. Grievances against Spain concerning trade had been keenly felt, and many felt that these had not been adequately addressed; in the course of the following decades these voices were to increase in volume. There were also some who objected to Britain's increased involvement in Europe. Besides, the commitment of British naval resources to effect Don Carlos's succession meant that, as the dissenting peers put it, 'we are much farther obliged than we were before, and than we think we ever ought to be, to meddle in disputes about territories at a great distance from us, and in which our national interest seems no way concerned.' The Treaty of Seville, and the resulting expenditure on Continental subsidies, was even seen as a betrayal of Britain's insular identity and destiny. One pamphlet asked 'what advantage we may expect to reap from the situation of our country, as an island'. Finally, there were the usual parliamentary critics, who felt that British interests were being sacrificed to the Electorate. Thus George Heathcote, a West India merchant, attacked the government with what another MP called 'a flaming speech against the court, which he had collected from a commonplace book on tyranny and arbitrary power and extracts of treatises on a free government'. In the spring of 1730, frustrated parliamentarians and pamphleteers were able to vent their fury over the hiring of 12,000 Hessians, who were needed to protect the Electorate against the Emperor lest he retaliate against the Treaty of Seville by attacking Hanover. These men were, as the protesters claimed, 'intended for purposes that do not concern Great Britain'.[15]

But the principal point at issue was the treaty's impact on the European balance of power. Critics such as the Tory peer Lord Bathurst argued that the article which allowed Don Carlos and his men into the Italian duchies was 'a manifest violation of . . . the Quadruple Alliance', which had been designed to prop up the Habsburg position in the peninsula, and would 'tend to involve this nation in a dangerous and expensive war; and to destroy the balance of power'. Indeed, of the ten objections entered in the protest of twenty-odd peers against the treaty, only one specifically related to trade. Most concerned the new geopolitics of Italy and their implications for Austria and thus the European balance of power. Undermining the Emperor in this way, it was argued, might lead to the loss of 'such an ancient, powerful and faithful ally'. On this reckoning, the Austrian losses in Italy upset the overall balance rather than restored it. Moreover, inserting Spain into Italy at Austria's expense could only benefit France in the long run. Much of parliamentary and most popular opinion had never shown much enthusiasm for the French alliance. Those opposed to the treaty recalled 'the great expense of blood and treasure, which it had cost this nation to reduce the exorbitant power of France' and argued 'our joining with France, and attacking the Emperor in Flanders or upon the Rhine, would naturally throw Flanders and perhaps a part of Germany, into the hands of the French; by which that monarchy would again become terrible to Europe'. They argued further 'that French alliances, through the unfaithfulness of that people and their inveterate malice to us, had always proved destructive to the interest and trade of this nation'. In short, helping to install Spain in Italy 'could tend to nothing but the ruin of that balance of power in Europe . . . [and] in the present conjuncture of the affairs of Europe, the balance of power by our being beaten might suffer; by our being victorious, it would be entirely be destroyed and lost perhaps for ever'.[16]

Having solved, as they saw it, the Mediterranean, British diplomats made a fresh attempt to shore up their position in the Holy Roman Empire. Townshend's plan was nothing if not ambitious: he envisaged the geopolitical reordering of north Germany in accordance with British interests. If Prussia could not be unbolted from Austria, she must be punished. In that event, Townshend wrote, it would be necessary 'to strip her [Prussia] of two or three places which give him [Frederick William] opportunities of being a very uneasy neighbour to the Dutch; and to reduce him to the necessity of living upon better terms with all the Princes of Lower Saxony than he has hitherto done'. Beforehand, Britain would make one last attempt to win over Frederick William. In 1730, therefore, Britain once again made overtures to Prussia. The marriage plan, buried only a year before, was disinterred in a last triumph of hope over experience. A diplomat, Sir John Hotham, was dispatched to Berlin to resolve the outstanding issues, including the recruitment of George's subjects, and a host of relatively minor German matters, but especially to promote the marriage plan which would support British policy against Austria.[17]

The mission was another complete failure. Hotham was instructed to push for the marriage of the Prince of Wales to Princess Wilhelmina, by now a very old chestnut, and that of Crown Prince Frederick to George's daughter, this time Amelia. Frederick William, however, was keen only on the marriage of Frederick and Amelia, installing his son as Stadholder – effectively the viceroy – of Hanover. Here George overplayed his hand, by insisting that Amelia should be Stadholder, and that the couple should come to live in England at least part of the time. Had that happened, of course, history would have been very different, but Frederick William, who nursed a pathological suspicion of his brother-in-law, refused. Hotham remarked that 'It is very plain he will sell his son, but not give him.' In the end, the British envoy left empty-handed and in bad odour. Not long afterwards, Frederick famously attempted to escape his father's clutches, was caught and forced to witness the execution of his accomplice and best friend. There is no evidence of any British involvement, but Frederick William was convinced that George was somehow to blame.[18]

The only other hope was a system of alliances with the middling and smaller German princes, pivoting on the Bavarian Wittelsbachs, both as a long-term check on Vienna and as an immediate military stop-gap. As always, this was something of a psychological minefield for British diplomats, who had to deal with princely sensibilities. Rulers were highly offended if Britain offered them too little, and sometimes if it offered anything at all. The Bavarian envoy to Paris, for example, complained in the summer of 1729 that British envoys were trying to hire his master the Elector of Bavaria like a hackney cab. In the end, Parliament refused to pay for the necessary subsidies, and the plan foundered in 1730. It was simply not possible to sustain an active policy in Germany without gaining Prussia, spending large sums of money on subsidizing allies, or conciliating Austria, either at Spanish or French expense, possibly both. Something would have to give.[19]

Meanwhile, Britain was becoming increasingly alarmed at the resurgence of French power and ambitions. Fleury had acted essentially as an arbiter at Soissons, much to the chagrin of the opposition press. Versailles had become more assertive after the birth of the Dauphin in 1729 had settled the question of the French succession, and thus negated the prospect of a personal union between the Spanish and French Bourbons which had underlain so much of the tensions of the previous decade. It was also true that Anglo-French relations overseas were threatened by the extensive French programme of naval construction and colonial rivalries, particularly in Canada, but also in the Caribbean. But the principal cause of the estrangement was differing perceptions of the balance of power. France was offended by the looming British guarantee of the Pragmatic Sanction, which closed off the opportunity to partition the Habsburg lands on the death of Charles VI; London was on her guard for the very same reason. By the late 1720s, in fact, there were signs that a large-scale parliamentary revolt over foreign policy and the French alliance was approaching. Pamphlet critiques and parliamentary rumblings continued throughout 1728, mostly concerning the inability of the French alliance to prevent attacks on British commerce; to restrain France in North America and the West Indies; and to deliver the dismantling of the fortifications and harbour facilities at Dunkirk. In February 1729, Admirals Norris and Vernon launched an attack on these fronts in the House of Commons. All the same, the ministry was not prepared for the massive parliamentary controversy which exploded in early 1730 over the question of Dunkirk.[20]

In February 1730, the Tory and crypto-Jacobite William Wyndham launched a blistering attack on the government for its failure to neutralize Dunkirk, which could be used not only to harass British shipping in the Channel, but also as a launching pad for an invasion of the south coast. Nor was this simply paranoia: informed French opinion at the time was becoming increasingly robust about the likely political efficacy of a privateering war against British trade. The Duc de Broglie, the French ambassador to Britain, wrote that he had 'seen with my own eyes during the several years that I have been at London, that a captured vessel belonging to a merchant or to one of the English companies makes the nation cry out more than does the loss of ten battles'. At the end of February the Commons resolved to request that 'proper application be made to the court of France, not only for putting a stop to the works carrying on, but for demolishing such as had been made by the inhabitants of Dunkirk, for repairing the port and channel there'. In this context, the critique of the alliance of Hanover, which had rumbled on since 1725, gained greater traction. For to stress the danger from France, was to make the case for an alliance with Austria. In 1726, two prominent opponents of Walpole – the Whig William Pulteney and the Tory

Lord Bolingbroke – had come together to found the *Craftsman*. This journal was to be a thorn in Walpole's side, partly for its excoriating attacks on domestic affairs – the Prime Minister's legendary corruption and oligarchical tendencies – but especially for its broadsides against the abandonment of the Austrian alliance. Nor was it a coincidence that Bolingbroke – of all people – should have written such a fulsome tribute to Marlborough's efforts in defence of 'the Empire' for the Column of Victory at Blenheim erected in 1731. The opposition critique of British foreign policy now focused on the failure to maintain the House of Habsburg as a pillar of the European balance.[21]

Increasingly, the ministry had to concede that the critics had a point. They too were irritated by colonial differences, but their main worry was Europe. The parliamentary pummelling over Dunkirk reflected an unease which British ministers themselves felt about Fleury's failure to deliver even the most basic stipulations of the Treaty of Utrecht nearly twenty years on. Newcastle observed in March 1730 that 'if the works there be not forthwith destroyed, and everything put upon the foot of the treaties of Utrecht and the Triple Alliance, it will . . . greatly tend to set people against [the French] and their alliance.' Moreover, doubts now began to emerge about French intentions in general. It was one thing to cooperate with Fleury in order to introduce the Spanish garrisons into Italy, as a bridle on Charles VI. It was quite another to fight any resulting war not in Italy itself, or in the Mediterranean, but in the Austrian Netherlands, as the French preferred. That would have subverted the Barrier overnight, and with British approval. It was for this reason that Frederick William predicted to the British envoy that 'he did not doubt but in a year or two, we should return to the old system as he [Frederick William] termed it, and join hands against France'.[22]

Ministers now began to suspect that the French planned not merely to clip the Emperor's wings – to which they had no objection – but to dismember the Austrian lands themselves. The French foreign minister, Germain-Louis de Chauvelin, was reported as saying in August 1730 that France intended 'to divest the Emperor of all the dominions he had in Italy'. In this context, the apparent French attempt to sabotage the Pragmatic Sanction – which Britain itself had regarded with very mixed feelings throughout the 1720s – was very sinister. Fleury was now busy building up not just an anti-Austrian but an anti-Pragmatic Sanction constituency in northern Europe and Germany. At the very least, France was believed, correctly, to have its eye on Lorraine, a territory on the western border of Germany which would greatly increase the security of France, and give her an ideal staging post for further expansion eastwards. In February 1730 Poyntz remarked 'how hard it is on one side to keep the Cardinal [Fleury] up to the firmness necessary in the present situation of affairs, and how impossible on the other to bring him even to think of giving an absolute guaranty to the Emperor's succession'. The French alliance, in short, was now increasingly defunct. As Newcastle put it with uncharacteristic succinctness, 'the Cardinal is not dead, but dead to us'.[23]

Some ministers were moving to a realization that the anti-Austrian and pro-French course of British policy during the previous decade needed to be rethought; in this respect, they were years behind their parliamentary and pamphleteering critics. France was clearly the major threat, and the relative danger posed by Madrid and Vienna was no longer obvious. Newcastle, however, now believed that the principal danger came from Spain, and not Austria. The appeasement of Spain in 1729 had merely whetted her appetite. After all, from late 1730 new Spanish forts and gun emplacements were trained on Gibraltar. In this context, it became imperative to secure the Pragmatic Sanction as quickly and comprehensively as possible, 'it not being our interest,' to quote one British diplomat, 'to see the Austrian dominions pulled to pieces.' Indeed, by the summer of 1729, Britain had indicated clearly – over Townshend's protests – that it would support the Pragmatic Sanction, in return for a guarantee that Maria Theresa's marriage would not threaten the European balance. A formal offer to that effect was made in June 1730, with a secret clause excluding a Bourbon – that is a Spanish or French – match. In August 1730 an unconditional guarantee was made. The hatchet had been buried.[24]

From guaranteeing the Pragmatic Sanction it was only a short step to a full-scale alliance with Austria. Ever since Britain and Austria had retreated from the brink in 1727, there had been intermittent attempts at reconciliation. At that time, the contacts had petered out, not least because of continuing disagreements over German issues such as Mecklenburg, and the perennial investitures. They were resumed a year later, when the imperial ambassador, Count Kinsky, met Walpole and expressed hopes of a 'return to the old system of politics in Europe'. Yet the rapprochement with Austria was by no means plain sailing. Many

British politicians and diplomats, particularly the Secretary of State for the North, Townshend, had invested too much in the Protestant cause in Germany and his inveterate opposition to the Pragmatic Sanction. This made some sort of collision inevitable. But it placed Newcastle in an excellent position to profit from the deepening rift between Townshend and his former ally Walpole. The death of Townshend's wife in 1727 – who was Walpole's sister – weakened the family bond between the two men; but more damaging was the disagreement over the cost of an active policy in Germany, of which Townshend was a long-standing advocate, but which Walpole was finding increasingly difficult to defend in Parliament. Finally, in May 1730, disenchanted with the softening attitude towards Austria, Townshend resigned. He was forced out not because he had lost the confidence of the King, but because his staunchly anti-imperial stance was incompatible with a ministry now bent on restoring the 'old system' with Austria.[25]

Even with Townshend out of the way, there remained serious Austro-Hanoverian differences – the 'Electoral points' – to be cleared out of the way before George could countenance an alliance. At issue were not only the investitures of Bremen and Verden, but also the fate of East Friesland, which was disputed with Prussia, and particularly Mecklenburg. As Thomas Pelham, the MP who was secretary to the embassy in France, remarked with some exasperation, 'The German affairs have been the chief clog to this negotiation.' The Austrians skilfully tried to drive a wedge between the two sides by appealing to British ministers over the head of the King. Thus Horatio Walpole observed that the Austrian negotiator Prince Eugene 'makes the distinction between the King and the Elector and appeals to Robinson [the British ambassador in Vienna] as an English minister'. Eventually, the Treaty of Vienna was signed in January 1731. Austria finally agreed to wind up the Ostend Company, and accepted the dispatch of 6,000 men to Spanish garrisons in Parma, Piacenza and Tuscany to secure the future succession of Don Carlos. The Elector of Hanover received no satisfaction with regard to Mecklenburg, but finally secured the coveted investitures for Bremen and Verden. Britain in turn guaranteed the Pragmatic Sanction. Britain, Austria and the Dutch Republic gave each other a reciprocal territorial guarantee against aggression. The 'old system' had been restored, just as Frederick William of Prussia had predicted.[26]

The impact in Germany was immediate. It now no longer suited

14. Robert Walpole's brother Horatio was one of the most experienced British diplomats and an ardent supporter of engagement on the continent.

George to play the avatar of Protestantism quite so stridently. In the 1720s British ministries had championed the cause of the Palatine and the Thorn Protestants. When the Archbishop of Salzburg, a close ally of the Emperor, turned on the Protestant enclaves in the Alpine valleys of Austria in 1731–2, the reaction was rather more muted. There was considerable popular sympathy in Britain, but the issue lacked the resonance of the Palatine agitations of the 1620s and 1720s, which had taken place in the context of fears of Habsburg universal monarchy. Now the backdrop was British recognition of the Pragmatic Sanction in order to contain France. Concern for the maintenance of Austrian power was not just an elite preoccupation: when the *Newcastle Courant* started printing general essays at the start of each issue, one reader protested that this should 'by no means . . . jostle the Emperor and his dominions out of your paper'. Nor did parliamentary critics make it much of an issue: they had spent most of the past ten years criticizing the abandonment of the Austrian alliance, and they were to spend the next decade attacking the ministry for failing to do more in fulfilment of it after 1731. Significantly, while the failure to support the Palatine cause had ranked high in Parliament's grievances against Charles I, the Salzburg Protestants were completely ignored in the subsequent attempts to impeach Walpole; the failure to support Austria against the machinations of Cardinal Fleury, on the other hand, was to be the principal charge against him.[27]

At first, British ministers hoped that France and Spain could be co-opted to the Treaty of Vienna. The Royal Navy now immediately escorted the Spanish garrisons to Italy. France was invited to join the treaty on condition that it guaranteed the Pragmatic Sanction. But Fleury would have none of this: he saw the Austro-British rapprochement as a betrayal. He turned to Spain, with whom there was now common ground both against Britain overseas, and against the Anglo-Habsburg position in Italy. The first Bourbon 'Family Compact' uniting Versailles and Madrid duly followed in 1733. The Anglo-French alliance of 1716 was now over; so was the shortlived rapprochement between Britain and Spain. The European kaleidoscope had been shaken once again. A new geopolitics of Europe was in the offing.

In this context, Britain's recent Italian policy, which benefited Spain at Austria's expense, seemed like a colossal own goal. It was not so much relations with Madrid that were the problem. Admittedly, these were fraught, partly because of the continuing commercial differences in the colonies. The resulting grievances were ventilated in various pamphlets and raised on a number of occasions in Parliament. But the principal difficulty was the fact that the introduction of the Spanish garrisons had weakened Austria's hold on Italy, and thus her capacity to resist French encroachments there. As one of the British envoys in Paris, who had seen this coming, remarked sheepishly in August 1730, 'it never was His Majesty's intention to new model the possession of Europe, and to make a new distribution of dominions and territorys for pleasing the Queen of Spain'.[28]

The geopolitical realignments of the early 1730s – which pitted Britain and Austria against France and Spain – suddenly brought the exposed condition of the Austrian Netherlands back into focus. Originally designed at Utrecht in 1713 as a check on France, the 'Barrier' had fallen into desuetude during the decade of antagonism against Austria; indeed, the French had been encouraged to transgress it in order to put pressure on Charles VI in Germany. Compounding the problem was the fact that Austria – which was constrained by treaty from exploiting the full economic potential of this territory – very much wished to exchange it for a less remote province. Already in 1714–15, Austria had signalled that she would rather have Bavaria than the Spanish Netherlands; now there was a distinct possibility that she might barter them for a French territory. This posed a double threat: at best such an exchange would leave the Barrier in the hands of a weaker third power less able to contain France; at worst it would actually bring the French into the

Low Countries, to threaten the United Provinces and north Germany directly. British statesmen had no answer to this headache, which was to grow in urgency as the question of the Austrian succession loomed larger.[29]

If the international environment was now far more threatening than it had been after the triumphs of the mid 1720s, there was no commensurate increase in British military capabilities. Underlying the annual discussions over the Mutiny Bill and the 'Augmentation of the Land forces' was not mere parsimony, but a fundamental divergence about what Britain's role was or should be in Europe. Those opposed to a standing army insisted on a British exceptionalism, which would spare their island the fate of Continental despotism which had overtaken the previously free states of Spain, France and Germany in their turn. Instead, opponents of a large standing army, Continental subsidies and indeed an active role in Europe in general, put their trust in the power of the Royal Navy. They responded, in other words, to the new challenges of the 1730s by reaffirming Britain's maritime and insular identity. 'The country party,' as one observer of the debates on the Hessian troops noted, 'were against continuing those troops in our pay, because they apprehended that they could not be of any service to Great Britain, for as we were surrounded by the sea, our fleet was our only real and proper security . . . [and] that many wars might happen on the Continent with which we had nothing to do.' Two years later, the Earl of Strafford argued that 'this new sort of defence [a land army] has been but lately thought on, and never can be a proper defence for the nation.' Instead, Britons should 'put our whole trust in our natural strength, which consists in our fleet'. A large standing army was not only a huge expense, and a possible threat to civil liberties, but also a temptation to meddle in European affairs. Thus the Earl of Winchelsea argued that large armed forces in peacetime 'made ministers of state more daring than otherwise they durst venture to be, both in contriving and executing schemes and projects that were grievous and burthensome to the people, schemes that never could enter into the heads of any but those who were drunk with an excess of power'.[30]

British Continentalists rejected these arguments. They saw the evolution of Britain within the general European mainstream. The case against a standing army, they claimed, took no account of changes in warfare and military organization. Robert Walpole pointed out that

'Nations, as well as private men, must accommodate their measures to the times they live in. The circumstances of Europe are now much altered from what they were in former days.' Now standing armies were the norm, and all of Britain's neighbours had much larger ones than she. So long as this was done with the consent of Parliament, he averred, there could be no question of constitutional impropriety. A respectable standing army would serve as an important deterrent and increase Britain's room for manoeuvre within the European state system. Thus Robert Walpole argued that 'if we reduce the number of our forces, our influence abroad will decrease.' Here the experience of the disbandment of the army in 1697, under parliamentary pressure, which sapped British ability to contain Louis XIV over the Spanish succession, weighed heavily. 'It is well known,' Sir William Yonge (one of the lords of the Treasury and a staunch Whig) observed in late January 1732, 'how fatal [. . .] the disbanding of our army after the peace of Ryswick' had been. Likewise Horatio Walpole argued that 'A parliamentary army never yet did any harm to this nation, but reductions of that army have often been fatal.'[31] British liberties and a strong military were thus seen as inextricably linked.

There were also many parliamentarians who simply rejected the whole idea of Britain's special maritime identity. 'As to our trusting altogether to our fleet,' the Whig peer and soldier, the Duke of Argyll, remarked, 'the experience of all ages shows us the precariousness of such a dependence.' What if the Armada had made landfall, he asked? What about the French-sponsored Jacobite invasion attempt of 1708? What if the Spanish-backed descent of 1719 had been more effective? 'Even the happy Revolution [of 1688],' Argyll argued, 'is an instance how little a fleet is to be depended on.' It was only because of adverse winds, he noted, that the English fleet had not been able to sail and scatter the Dutch. 'By this accident we discovered our liberties, but if we should ever resolve to trust entirely to our fleet, the same accident may hereafter be the cause of our losing them.' Salvation, in short, should not be sought from the sea alone. Britain's security would depend first and foremost on her European bulwarks.[32]

IV

Imperial Visions

9

Imperial Retreat, 1733–1736

[T]*he success of either side may elate the minds of victors, and make them resolve to carry their conquests much farther than they at the beginning really intended, and farther than is consistent with the balance of power, or the liberties of Europe; and therefore, though this nation was, at first, no way concerned with the motives or causes of the war, yet it may at last come to be very deeply concerned in the event.*[1]

Lord Hinton on the War of the Polish Succession,
House of Lords, January 1735

It is not however possible for them [Britain and Holland] in the present situation of things, and by the nature of their respective governments, ever to think of engaging their people in the expense and hazards of a war, till they shall have been enabled to show the world, that all possible means have been tried in vain to avoid it.[2]

Lord Harrington, Secretary of State for the North, May 1734

One Mrs Mopp, a famous she bone-setter and mountebank, coming to town on a coach with six horses on the Kentish Road, was met by a rabble of people, who seeing her very oddly and tawdrily dressed, took her for a foreigner, and concluded she must be a certain great person's mistress. Upon this they followed the coach, bawling out, No Hanover whore, no Hanover whore. The lady within the coach was much offended, let down the glass, and screamed louder than any of them, she was no Hanover whore, she was an English one, upon which they all cry'd out, God bless your ladyship, quitted the pursuit, and wished her a good journey.[3]

Pulteney to Swift, December 1736

By the mid 1730s British foreign policy was once again in profound crisis: Walpole's ministry was now under sustained attack for its strategic mismanagement. Part of the popular and parliamentary critique concerned the perceived neglect of Britain's overseas interests, particularly in relation to the illegal trade with Spanish colonies. The principal complaint, however, concerned the progressive collapse of the British position in the German Empire. To many critics, the War of the Polish Succession was no obscure eastern European spat, but the beginning of a French-inspired assault on the integrity of the Habsburg monarchy. The Austrian position in southern Italy and the Mediterranean was smashed, and Lorraine was about to fall to France. One by one, it seemed, the pillars of the European balance were falling to the French advance, with all the implications that had for the Barrier and ultimately for the security of the island itself. As Britons searched around for scapegoats, many resorted to the tried and trusted device of blaming the Hanoverian Electorate for their domestic and diplomatic problems. One way or the other, Britain remained a central European power firmly locked into the Holy Roman Empire.

In London, the extent of Britain's growing isolation in Europe was at first not fully grasped. Indeed by 1733 a certain complacency was beginning to creep in. The King's Speech of January of that year announced that 'It is a great satisfaction to me, that the present situation of affairs, both at home and abroad, makes it unnecessary for me to lay before you any other reason for my calling you together at this time; but the ordinary dispatch of the public business.' This was the first time in many years that Parliament was not being asked to consider some far-reaching, controversial and expensive British scheme to maintain the European balance of power. It was almost as if London had cut itself off from Europe. This mood worried some MPs. Sir Thomas Aston, the MP for Liverpool, responded that he did 'not really think that our affairs are in the best situation either abroad or at home. Are not our neighbours the French still going on in fortifying and restoring the harbour of Dunkirk under our very nose, and contrary to the faith of the most solemn treaties? We can no longer say the French are our good allies.'[4]

This crisis was not just a product of shifts within the European balance beyond the control of ministries. It also reflected a much deeper conceptual failure. There was no longer a Stanhope or even a Townshend at the helm, capable of looking at Europe in the round. This accentuated the existing tendency to view foreign policy through the lens of the two departments for the North and South. Newcastle, who was Secretary of State for the South, remarked on this in a private letter to Horatio Walpole concerning the distribution of Austrian dispatches. 'I don't know,' he wrote, 'whether they have been sent to you or no, for you know we know nothing of what goes from the other office, except on the material points, and they are not always considered so much as they should be; but this *entre nous*.' British policy was now made not by visionaries or innovators, but by technicians. Admittedly, many of these men, such as Horatio Walpole, were very able technicians indeed. Some of them, such as the Duke of Newcastle, were more able than they were given credit for, and were still ascending a learning curve in grand strategy. The gifted if somewhat unpredictable Carteret, on the other hand, now languished in opposition, waiting for an issue and opportunity which would return him to power.[5]

British diplomacy now made a determined attempt to reforge the ring of containment around France. The marriage of Princess Anne to the Stadholder of the Netherlands in March 1734 was designed to buttress the sagging Dutch Barrier. The marriage contract explicitly spoke of the desire to renew 'that happy alliance which has existed in the past' between the two Houses and for 'the maintenance of the Protestant religion'; it was domestically popular. Further east, Britain continued to pursue a *Reichspolitik* designed to strengthen the Empire against French encroachments. This meant throwing nearly a decade of anti-Austrian diplomacy and propaganda into reverse. For the moment, however, Britain proved unable to mobilize a substantial party in the Empire; made no headway at all towards a Prussian alliance; and risked being dragged into the disputes over Mecklenburg, which flared up again in the first years of the decade. For in 1730 Duke Charles Leopold of Mecklenburg returned from exile, reviving British anxieties that the Russians and Prussians, and prior to 1731 the Austrians, might use him to put pressure on Hanover. Nor could any instability necessarily be contained. Thomas Robinson, the British ambassador to Austria, warned that there was a danger 'of drawing on a universal war from the least disturbance in Lower Saxony'.[6]

A sustained effort was also made to shore up bulwarks in the Baltic and the Mediterranean. Thus British diplomats tried to repair the

15. Three of George II's daughters – Anne, Amelia and Caroline. Marriages were sought for them and their sisters in support of British diplomatic aims. Princess Anne married the Dutch Stadholder; Princess Louisa the King of Denmark; and Princess Mary the Hereditary Prince of Hesse. Amelia and Caroline never married.

self-inflicted wounds in Italy by pursuing an alliance with Savoy. A sustained push was undertaken to bolster Britain's position in the Baltic. Relations with Sweden were poor, however; here, the founding of a Swedish East India Company in 1731 was a worrying sign. The Danes did the same at Altona, just outside Hamburg, although Danish designs on the Swedish crown were a much greater concern. The principal aim in Scandinavia now was no longer to block Russia, but to contain the increasing French naval presence, and to prevent Versailles from gaining ground at Copenhagen or Stockholm. The strategic aim in both instances was to safeguard the supply of naval stores, and to stop the French from gaining naval allies and thus overturning Britain's dominance on the high seas. The European balance and Britain's maritime security were thus closely linked.[7]

None of this sufficed to cushion the shock which the outbreak of

European war in 1733 was about to administer to Britain. The conflict has gone down in history as the 'War of the Polish Succession', but it was really about France, and most of the fighting took place in Italy. At issue in the first instance was the question of the Polish crown, which became vacant in February 1733 on the death of Augustus of Poland and Saxony. A French-backed candidate, Stanislas Leszczyński – who was also Louis XV's father-in-law – was officially proclaimed his successor in September by the Polish parliament – making him King of Poland for the second time in his life. The Russian- and Austrian-sponsored Augustus III of Saxony was proclaimed in opposition to Leszczyński a month later by a rival group of nobles. France and Sardinia concluded an alliance at Turin in September. By now the Russians had invaded Poland to support their candidate, and very soon French, Sardinian and Spanish troops were heavily engaged against the Austrians in Italy. In Poland, the Russians quickly defeated Leszczyński, who was chased into Prussia by July of the following year. Danzig was besieged, and finally taken. But in Germany, things went badly for Austria, with the siege of Kehl on the Rhine in 1733, and that of Phillipsburg a year later; the outer buttresses of the Barrier system were under threat. And in Italy, Austrian forces were worsted by the French at Parma in June 1734, and Philip's son Don Carlos, whom the British had so controversially ensconced in the northern Duchies, took control of Naples and southern Italy, which had been in Austrian hands since the Treaty of Utrecht. Soon after, Spanish troops began to besiege Mantua in the north. Charles VI appealed to Britain for help, particularly in the Mediterranean, under the terms of the Treaty of Vienna.

All this was viewed with increasing alarm in Whitehall. To see Poland turned into a French ally was bad enough: it would effectively constitute a ring of encirclement around the Habsburg monarchy. But the threat was far greater than that: a major Austrian defeat might spark off the dismemberment of the Habsburg bloc and thus transform the war effectively into a War of the Austrian Succession. Poland and Danzig themselves were not the issue; the problem of French power very much was. 'What relates singly to Poland is a very remote consideration for His Majesty,' Newcastle argued, what mattered were the 'liberties of Europe'. Horatio Walpole echoed him in late March 1734: 'the balance of power in Europe entirely depends on the event of that war'. Likewise, the new Northern Secretary, Lord Harrington, saw the 'Liberties of

Europe . . . in the greatest danger from the rapid successes of France and her allies'. By May 1734, as the military position of Austria deteriorated, British diplomats were anxiously wondering 'how far they [the French] were prepared to push their conquests'. In particular, they were worried about French negotiations with 'several of the [German] Electors'. These, Harrington continued, 'gave just reason to apprehend, that they intended the destruction of the House of Austria; for it could not be thought, that those Electors would enter into engagements against the Emperor, and the Empire, with any other prospect than an absolute annihilation of that House'. Worse still, the Barrier was in danger. One parliamentarian lamented the 'weak and defenceless condition [the] Barrier in Flanders is [in] at present'. The Dutch were in a complete funk. An observer in Whitehall remarked that 'Their Barrier is naked; no secret is kept among them, and they fear that if they talk like men in a conference . . . the French will attack them.' The only sensible first step, he continued, 'should be the sending our quota [of troops] to their assistance to secure the Barrier,' but he doubted that the Dutch would have the courage to admit them. Fears for the steadfastness of the Dutch were openly voiced in Parliament. For all these reasons, the King's Speech at the opening of Parliament in 1734 recognized that the war 'is become the object of the care and attention of all Europe; and though I am no ways engaged in it . . . I cannot sit regardless of the present events, or be unconcerned for the future consequences of a war, undertaken and supported by so powerful an alliance'. The insouciance of early 1733 had evaporated.[8]

Inevitably, the increased international tension led to a revival of anxiety about Jacobitism. At first, London had been concerned that the Pretender would seek the Polish throne for himself, on the strength of his marriage to the Polish princess Clementina Sobieska. Later, British ministers worried that he might take advantage of international instability to conclude new alliances with European powers. Jacobite correspondence was therefore closely monitored. News that Charles Edward – the 'Bonnie Prince' – had been in contact with Don Carlos fed anxieties. Newcastle remarked to Walpole in early September 1734, that 'His being received by Don Carlos was certainly abominable'. In fact, London need not have worried. Shifts in the international scene had left the Jacobites even more exposed. Many of their best men were now locked into the militaries of powers which had now reconciled to Britain, or were at least enemies of Britain's enemies. By a strange twist of irony the French fleet was defeated off Danzig in June 1734 by Admiral Thomas Gordon, a Jacobite in Russian service, while the Russian army which deposed the French candidate in Poland was commanded by the Jacobite Peter Lacy.[9]

16. The Pretender had succeeded in marrying a wealthy Polish princess, despite George I's attempts to prevent it.

Britain would now have to decide whether to enter the War of the Polish Succession. There were many good grounds for honouring the spirit of the Treaty of Vienna and weighing in on the Austrian side, at least in the Mediterranean theatre of war. Newcastle, for one, tended in that direction. Already in 1732 he was describing himself as '*bon-Impérialiste*'. As the Habsburg cause plummeted in 1734, he fretted that 'I own I cannot but have a concern for them, as thinking their power not dangerous and the support of their interests to a certain degree very material for the common cause.' And yet Britain remained neutral. There were many reasons for this. Popular opinion would probably not have accepted the costs of intervention, and Britain did not want to provoke France into supporting a Jacobite invasion. But the principal reason was that the ministry itself – and in particular Walpole – was unpersuaded of the need for a military commitment to Austria at this point. He was genuinely averse to the blood-letting which would inevitably have followed. 'Madam,' Walpole famously told the Queen, 'there are fifty thousand men slain this year in Europe, and not one Englishman.'[10]

The result was a policy of passivity. Significantly, the King's Speech of January 1734, despite its robust warnings about the dangers to the balance of power, committed itself only to 'take time to examine the facts alleged on both sides'. Instead of supporting Austria, Britain launched a joint mediation effort with the Dutch, aimed at, as Newcastle put it in May 1734, the 'preservation of the balance of power in Europe'. The Austrians were bluntly told that there was no prospect of Britain entering the war until Parliament and public opinion had been convinced 'that all possible means have been tried in vain to avoid it'. In other words, British public opinion and Britain's representative system placed a larger burden of proof on those who sought to take the country into conflict. For this reason, it was vital to establish French intentions clearly. 'If their demands and views shall appear exorbitant,' the Secretary of State for the North, Lord Harrington continued, 'and tend to endanger the balance of power in Europe, it will not only justify His Majesty . . . to [his] own people, but even put [him] under a necessity of taking such vigorous measures in conjunction with the Emperor as will then be found expedient for their common safety and for the preservation of the Liberties of Europe.'[11]

The shock of the War of the Polish Succession gave a new impulse to the domestic debate on the armed forces. The feeble performance of the Polish militia was noted. In the debate on the Mutiny Bill in the House of Lords in March 1735, one speaker remarked that 'considering the difference between regular forces and militia, which the late troubles in Poland have made sufficiently manifest . . . the number of regular forces kept up in this nation, ought always to bear some sort of proportion to the number of regular forces kept up by neighbouring states.' These, he noted, had recently massively increased, 'especially our neighbouring kingdom of France, the nation from which we have the most to fear'. Indeed, the perceived threat to the European balance was regularly advanced in support of an increase in the land forces. After all, another parliamentarian asked in February 1734, 'when such a general war is broke forth in Europe, when the united forces of France, Spain and Sardinia are tearing the Emperor's dominions in Italy asunder, are we to be altogether inattentive? Are we to sit entirely regardless of a war which may end in the total overthrow of the balance of power in

Europe?' Likewise, the MP George Heathcote argued that 'we are perhaps amongst the most remote from danger, but it may reach us at last.'
Britain, after all, could not cut itself off from developments in Europe.
'Our house is not yet on fire,' the argument ran, 'but our neighbour's is
all in a flame; and then certainly it is time for us to prepare the engines
necessary for preserving our own: these are a powerful fleet and a
sufficient body of regular well-disciplined troops, ready to march at the
first word of command.' In short, the link between Britain's exposed
international position in Europe and increased militarization at home
was widely accepted in parliamentary discourse.[12]

Opponents of standing forces continued to stress Britain's insular
identity and rejected the 'very extraordinary', and 'new maxims in politics', by which Britain should keep up regular armies in competition
with its neighbours. 'If we were so unlucky as to be situated on the
Continent,' one peer argued, 'or to have any neighbours that could come
at us by land,' that would be one thing, 'but as we have the happiness
to be surrounded by the sea; as we have the happiness to have a fleet,
superior to any that can probably be sent against us; we have no occasion
to be worried.' It was conceded, however, that other European countries
might be compelled to keep up a standing army in a threatening international environment. Even the Dutch, or at least their exposed eastern
provinces, were believed to be subject to a different geopolitical imperative. 'As the situation of that country is very different from the situation
of this,' one speaker argued, 'it is at all times necessary for them to keep
up a numerous army. They have the misfortune to be situated upon the
Continent, and may consequently be suddenly invaded by great armies;
they have an extensive frontier to defend.' What was striking here was
the extent to which even those who defended 'English liberties' against
standing armies argued from Britain's strategic position in Europe.[13]

The challenge of the Polish succession contributed to an acute sense
of domestic crisis, from which Britain's strategic failures were believed
to stem. It came in the midst of a bruising controversy over the Excise
in 1733-4, when Walpole attempted to shift some of the tax burden
from the landed proprietors by converting customs duties on tobacco
and wine into inland duties. This provoked a flood of petitions and
widespread unrest. Walpole – by now also facing a parliamentary revolt
– backed down. It was the first time his domestic authority had been
seriously questioned. Thus the Whig grandee Pulteney argued in mid

January 1734 that 'there are many, many grievances both foreign and domestic, under which the nation groans at present, and which call loudly for redress.' 'Therefore,' he concluded, 'the state of the nation must be called for'. In other words, there should be a searching formal examination of Britain's declining domestic, international and fiscal situation, which Pulteney believed to be 'owing to the mismanagement of those at home'. The only way of identifying the evil, and remedying it, was through greater openness. The perceived decline in Britain's European position thus galvanized a long-running debate on the relationship between secrecy, security and consultation in Britain. This came across most clearly in the question of whether Parliament should be kept abreast of diplomatic negotiations, a demand which was pushed with greater vigour whenever external danger loomed. After all, Pulteney pointed out, 'If the question itself should come before us, whether or no we ought to take any part in the present war? Can we pass any judgement upon such a question, without first knowing how we stand engaged to the several powers abroad?' Pulteney therefore called for the creation of a 'secret and select committee to inspect such papers, and to report what they find in them relating to the affair under our consideration'.[14]

Ministers argued forcefully that Parliament should enjoy no such right. Thus Sir William Yonge, then a lord of the Treasury, but soon to become the secretary at war, did not deny that Parliament had the right 'of calling whatever papers they may think ... yet we ought in no case to call for those papers which may contain secrets, the publishing whereof might be of signal disadvantage to the commonwealth'. The danger, he continued, was that publication of secret documents 'might perhaps open new sores and give offence to some powers with whom we have at present a good understanding'. Hence he was prepared to countenance the release of 'any particular paper, which ... may be necessary for the information of the House', but not a comprehensive publication. Walpole also rejected the opposition demands, adding for good measure that they seemed 'calculated rather for giving gentlemen an opportunity of declaiming against those who have the honour to serve the Crown, than for procuring any proper information to the House or any advantage to the country'. That said, even those supportive of Britain's active role on the Continent were anxious to get the balance between constitutional and strategic imperatives, between military effectiveness and political freedoms, right. 'Is there no way of preserving the liberties of Europe,' the Earl of Winchelsea and Nottingham asked in March 1734, 'without making a sacrifice of the liberties of Great Britain?' He was not the first or the last man to ask that question.[15]

Critics dismissed the arguments for secrecy as a smoke-screen for arbitrary rule. After all, Sir William Wyndham asked, was there any 'prince [or] state whom we have not disobliged and fallen out with by turns'? The demand for diplomatic sensitivity was thus effectively a plea for perpetual secrecy, with the clear aim of shutting Parliament out of the deliberative process altogether. Yet the demand for accountability ran up against a paradox. Nearly all the measures, including controversial treaties and subsidy payments, had been approved by the very Parliament that critics were mobilizing to censure them. It was hard to argue, therefore, that Walpole's foreign policy had been entirely hatched in secret, behind Parliament's back. What critics could and did claim was that the approval of a House of Commons so comprehensively controlled by Robert Walpole's patronage machine was no defence against the charge of treason, still less of incompetence. William Pulteney announced in full view of his quarry, Walpole, in late 1734 that 'I have known, in former parliaments, most scandalous things done by a corrupt majority; any things being done or resolved on by a majority, even of this House, will not make it right, nor convince the nation that it is so.' He was not saying, though he came close to doing so, that the majority had no right to be wrong. Pulteney was claiming that a corrupt Parliament was not fit to decide the nation's destinies. It was a short but momentous step from that to argue that the defence of Britain's European position required a more representative House of Commons.[16]

The policy of mediation and non-intervention proved highly controversial in the political nation and the public sphere. To be sure, the ministry won all the votes in Parliament. Thus in January 1735, the Commons congratulated the King on 'steadily pursuing such measures as have tended towards peace and accommodation, rather than to involve too precipitately this kingdom, and all Europe, in a general and bloody war'. Parliament also resolved that 'the crown of Great Britain could never appear with greater honour and lustre, than by Your Majesty's interposing your good offices between the contending parties.' There was widespread support for reserving judgement on French intentions until the policy of mediation had run its course; only once all reasonable offers had been refused should intent to subvert the European balance be inferred. All the same, some saw in even the limited mediation effort a betrayal of Britain's colonial and maritime destiny, which was still being challenged by Spain overseas. Thus Sir William Wyndham accused the ministry of 'backwardness' in making use of British power 'when repeated insults have been offered to the nation, when our merchants have been pillaged, and our sailors murdered, and that for years together'. By contrast, he complained, ministers were 'unseasonably forward in engaging in disputes where the interest of the nation may call upon them to be at least neutral'.[17]

There was also scepticism about the nature of the European threat. It was 'ridiculous', they claimed, 'to put the nation to a great expense, to provide against a danger which may never happen'. In any case, Sir Thomas Lumley Sanderson argued, Britain would not be attacked if it remained neutral. He therefore objected to paying for an increase in the army 'whenever any little quarrel happens between any two of our neighbours, and that whether we are to have any share in the quarrel or not'. Likewise, William Pulteney accused ministers of 'raising *fantômes* in the air, in order to find pretences for loading the people of England with taxes'. Underlying opposition to intervention, or even mediation, on the Continent was the fear of creating a dependency culture within Europe. Thus one parliamentarian dismissed concerns about the weakness of the Dutch Barrier with the words,

For God's sake, are we thus to be eternally the dupes of Europe? If the Emperor, or any other power, neglects to keep their fortified places in a proper posture of defence, must we answer for that neglect? Are we, for the sake of preserving the balance of power to undertake, at our own charges, to defend every power in Europe, and to prevent their being invaded or conquered by any of their neighbours?

In the same spirit another critic warned that 'this nation should [not] set itself up as the Don Quixote of Europe', or else 'most of the powers of Europe, who are not immediately attacked, will leave the whole burden upon us'.[18]

The colonialist and neutralist critics of the ministry were vocal, but relatively few. Most members of the political nation accepted the notion that it was Britain's calling to think on behalf of the whole of Europe regarding the maintenance of the balance. As one speaker observed in January 1735, 'though all the nations of Europe are equally concerned with us in preserving the balance of power, yet some of them may be blind to their own interest.' He went on to ask whether '[we] are . . . to neglect what is necessary for our own security, or to refuse contributing any thing towards preserving or restoring the balance of power, because every one of the other parties concerned will not contribute their proportionable share?' If some powers, such as the Dutch, refused to recognize the growing danger and act upon it, that was to be deplored not imitated. It was up to Britain to make them see. She would have to act as a persuader for the balance of power.[19]

By far the strongest case against British policy on the Polish succession, therefore, was made by those who felt that the government had not been sufficiently concerned with Continental affairs. At the very least, they believed that Walpole had mismanaged the European balance of power. The Treaty of Hanover – which had completed the estrangement from Vienna and driven Britain closer to France – received another pounding. So did the Treaty of Seville, by which Britain had allowed Spain to prise loose the Austrian hold on Italy. William Pulteney argued that 'the moment you separated the courts of Vienna and Spain, every thing that has since happened might have been foretold.' 'By that treaty,' it was argued, 'the ancient union between France and Spain [was] restored; and by the introduction of Spanish troops into Italy, we not only opened the way for the Spaniards, but by that very step, we lost the King of Sardinia, by which we opened a way likewise for the French into the same country, and thereby united those three powers in that close confederacy, which occasions the present disturbance in Europe.' Walpole, in short, had lost Italy.[20]

Critics were quick to see Hanoverian considerations at work in all this. The Jacobite Sir John Hynde Cotton announced 'an objection to the passage where we promise to provide for the security of His Majesty's kingdoms, "rights" and "possessions" '. He saw these words as a code to 'include His Majesty's German dominions' in the guarantee. Cotton believed that the phrase would certainly be 'understood in this sense by all without doors'. The ministry furiously denied any such intent, but the claim had the effect of putting them on the back foot. Behind these manoeuvres lay the fear that Britain would be sucked into the war in the wake of George's German ambitions. If, as William Wyndham noted in March 1734, the King of England had not yet taken part in the war, 'yet he certainly has as Elector of Hanover: and as this nation has by some fatality or another, been generally engaged in the same quarrel which our King, as Elector of Hanover, espoused, if the same thing should again happen, this nation may then indeed come to be threatened with some danger or insult.' It was widely believed then and since that only popular opinion, Walpole's wiles, and the cooperation of Queen Caroline prevented George from dragging Britain into the war in support of Hanover and the Emperor.[21]

In fact, the charge was unfair. George did vote at Regensburg for an imperial war against France, and his Hanoverian minister in London, Hattorf, tried to persuade British ministers to intervene. But George did not seem much concerned by French incursions along the Rhine; his Hanoverian troops only joined Prince Eugene in June 1734, well after the start of hostilities. In truth, the King was heavily distracted throughout by developments in Mecklenburg, which had erupted once again in 1733–4. Duke Karl Leopold had attempted a coup with the help of the bourgeoisie, clergy and peasants. This was almost immediately suppressed by a joint Prussian–Hanoverian operation that same year. Two years later both powers occupied the Duchy as collateral for the repayment of the costs of the intervention. Indeed, George seems to have toyed with the idea of annexation. Because many European powers regarded Hanover as a weathervane for British policy, George's restraint in his Electoral capacity was widely interpreted as a confirmation of the neutrality policy. As the Spanish chief minister Patino remarked to the British ambassador in 1734, 'proceedings in his Electorate . . . are looked upon as prognostics of the part England will take in favour of the Emperor', or not, as the case might be.[22]

Rather than be beholden to the King's German interests, the opposition argued, Britain could and should be responsible for the whole of the Continental balance of power. As Robert Walpole remarked with some exasperation, 'really by some gentlemen's way of talking, one would imagine that the ministers of England were the ministers of Europe; or that madness and folly reigned at this court, and that the most profound wisdom prevailed at all others.' His brother Horatio elaborated on this theme. 'There are some gentlemen,' he complained, 'who seem to have laid it down as a principle, that every thing that's wrong, happen in what corner of Europe it will, must be owing to the mismanagement of the ministers of Great Britain.' Even as he fended off opposition attacks, Horatio Walpole's anguish was clear. 'I would gladly ask them,' he exclaimed, 'where or when any of them have prophesied, what potentate, or in what manner any potentate, would interfere in the election of a king of Poland? Have any of them prophesied that the King of Sardinia would grant a passage to the French troops through his territories to Italy; or did they prophesy, that he would join with France in declaring war against the Emperor?' Like many political practitioners then and since, he would not allow the judgement of hindsight. In short, the greatest threat to the ministry came not from those who wished to turn their backs on Europe, but those who demanded greater involvement.[23]

In the end, the Polish succession was decided without Britain. Although the war did not officially wind up until 1738, hostilities in the west came to a close in October 1735. There was a palpable sense of unease in London, as Britain awaited the outcome of negotiations in which Britain was, for the first time in decades, entirely on the sidelines. France accepted the Saxon Elector Augustus as King of Poland, but Austria was forced to pay a heavy price for her defeats in Italy. Sicily and Naples were surrendered to Don Carlos, and thus effectively to the Bourbon family compact. This was a catastrophe for the Italian balance. Vienna had been comprehensively humbled, and a major blow dealt to the basis of British policy since 1731. In a long dispatch from Vienna, lamenting the decline of Austria, the British ambassador, Thomas Robinson, claimed that the 'Emperor cannot live for a moment in security without a guarantee from the maritime powers of what shall be left to his family'. A few months later he warned that Austria had been lost to 'the general balance of Europe against the House of Bourbon'. Robinson feared that 'this family cannot without a miracle be retrieved at all, or even with one, be entirely recovered', for many years. It seemed as if the partition of the Habsburg monarchy had begun while Charles VI was still alive.[24]

To make matters much worse, France had secured the reversion of Lorraine. In return for renouncing the Polish throne, Stanislas Leszczyński had been installed as Duke of Lorraine, with the understanding that it would pass directly to France on his death; Francis Stephen of Lorraine, Maria Theresa's husband, had to make way. British statesmen and diplomats contemplated this with dismay. Thomas Robinson feared that 'When the French are once nested in Lorraine, that signal acquisition will give them strength . . . to take Luxembourg upon the first trouble, of which they themselves will be the authors.' There was thus every likelihood that the French tide would surge ever further eastward, as in Louis XIV's day. This was certainly in Robinson's mind when he referred in March 1736 to the 'danger of France's erecting, one time or other, a chamber of reunion, like the famous one of Metz', in the later seventeenth century, when Louis XIV had cobbled together various spurious claims to reunite lands on France's eastern border with the monarchy. In this context, the fact that the cession of Lorraine had originally been suggested by Britain in order to detach France from the anti-Austrian coalition was a recognition of how desperate London had been to salvage what it could from the Habsburg wreckage.[25]

The implications of the loss of Lorraine also shook the political nation at large. As one parliamentarian pointed out in mid January 1736, France had ended hostilities not because of any British military demonstration, as the ministry weakly argued, but because of the 'annexing to the crown of France for ever the whole dominions of the duke of Lorraine . . . a cession which this nation, as well as the rest of Europe, may soon have reason to repent of'. Another rejected any peace which would lead to Britain being 'slaves to France'. Indeed, he thought that 'the balance of power is brought into more danger by the peace, than it was by the war, because if the war had continued, it was in our power whenever we have a mind to take Lorraine from France or to get the Emperor, Poland and Muscovy to join to retrieve it.' If, the argument continued, 'France was before an over-match for any power in Europe, the addition of anything, even the smallest village, to that crown, is a step towards overturning the balance of power; but the addition of such a populous and fertile province as the dukedom of Lorraine, is certainly a most wonderful stride.' The geopolitical implications of the loss of Lorraine were immense. It was 'a part of the Empire, it was a barrier for all that part of the Empire situated between it and the Rhine'. It had been an outer rampart and an early warning post. Now 'France will be enabled to surprise and take possession, whenever she pleases, of all that part of the Empire between Lorraine and the Rhine.' That was to say: Zweibrücken, much of Trier, the Electoral Palatinate, the Bishoprics of Speyer, Worms, and so on. In short, Walpole, having lost Italy, was on the verge of losing Germany as well.[26]

In Europe, the initiative now passed wholly to France. The Austrians, as the ambassador to Vienna complained, were now 'entirely in the power' of France; they relied 'upon the King [George II] singly for their future safety once out of their present troubles'. Yet British credit in Vienna was at its lowest point. The Austrians were outraged at Walpole's refusal to countenance anything more than a mediation on their behalf. Indeed, Newcastle wished that 'we could have been so happy as to have persuaded the Emperor that we, viz. England and Holland, really wished him well (which perhaps, he may doubt)'. 'Our affairs abroad,' as Horatio Walpole put it bleakly in October 1736, 'are in a most loose and shattered situation.' They were to get worse still. Britain looked on helplessly as Austria was dragged into a war against the Ottoman Empire in 1737. What happened there mattered intensely to Britain. If Austria did not join Russia in the attack, the Tsarina might overrun the Turks quickly, cross the river Bug, and make unilateral gains at their expense. As the British ambassador to Constantinople pointed out, Russia and Austria 'would then become borderers, and a weak declining [Ottoman] empire is a less dangerous neighbour than one that is in full strength and vigour'. Given that the local populations were Orthodox – and 'look upon the Tsarina as their natural protectress' – there was nothing to stop the Russian tide from extending still further. 'Moldavia and Walachia,' he warned, 'are open as well as rich provinces, and he who is master of the first, may possess them both as soon as he can march over them'. The resulting weakening of the Habsburg monarchy would be bad for Britain's overall strategy of using Austria to contain France.[27]

On the other hand, the decline of the Ottoman Empire was also to be discouraged, partly because it had often been a useful lever to put pressure on either Russia and Austria, and partly for commercial reasons. As one British diplomat remarked in late August 1736, public opinion was 'arguing how dangerous it would be to trade, to the Protestant religion and to our civil interest to have the Turk driven out of Europe'. The eighteenth-century British definition of Europe and the Protestant interest was elastic enough to include the preservation of the Ottoman Empire, which was, of course, to become a shibboleth of the next century. Yet when the Turks appealed to Britain for mediation in early May 1736, she was too isolated and distracted to help. In the event, the Austrian offensive quickly foundered: there was to be no repeat of Prince Eugene's short, sharp victorious campaigns of 1716–18. Significantly, the Austrians looked to Paris not London for mediation to get them out of this mess. The resulting Treaty of Vienna in November 1738 brought Austria closer into the French orbit.[28]

All these European developments had profound implications for Britain's maritime position. Thus one parliamentarian observed in mid January 1736 that 'as by the situation of Lorraine the frontiers of France will be contracted, rather than enlarged, which will prevent her being obliged to keep up any greater land force than formerly, we may presume, that this whole sum will be employed yearly towards increasing and keeping up her naval armaments . . . which may so probably increase the naval power of our greatest and most dangerous rival.' More generally, the decline of British standing in Europe made it less likely that she could pin down French resources there through Continental coalitions, as in the wars against Louis XIV. The long-standing link between Britain's European position and her maritime security was thus reprised in the light of the War of the Polish Succession.[29]

French naval preparations did indeed take off in the 1730s. Squadrons were dispatched to the Baltic in 1734 and 1738. Moreover, Fleury entered into a secret agreement with Spain to challenge Britain's maritime and colonial dominance. The Bourbon family compact of 1733 now effectively encircled Britain from the St Lawrence to the Gulf of Mexico. The French pushed further and further into the Mississippi Valley and the west, which they tended to regard as a strategic unity. Spanish depredations against British merchants continued, and became the subject of increasing parliamentary protests. French encroachments in Canada also gave rise to concern. Newcastle complained of unauthorized settlement in Newfoundland. Even more worryingly, French missionaries continued to subvert British authority in Acadia. 'How to prevent the ill consequences,' the Lieutenant Governor of Massachusetts, Lawrence Armstrong, wrote, 'I know not, without we could have missionaries from a place independent of that crown, but this will prove a considerable expense, which the French King bears at present with alacrity for very political reasons.' 'It is most certain,' he continued, 'that there is not a missionary neither among the French nor Indians who has not a pension from that crown.' Thanks to Walpole's cheese-paring, the Royal Navy was in a state of some disrepair. In short, the failure to contain France in Europe was directly injurious to Britain globally.[30]

In the colonies themselves, the deteriorating strategic position was noted with some concern. The underlying geopolitics had long been masked by the French alliance of 1716; with the collapse of that entente and the emerging Franco-Spanish axis these realities reasserted themselves. Thus the Pennsylvanian grandee, James Logan, wrote in 1732 that 'Tho' Canada as an encroachment has always given uneasiness to the English colonies, yet as it is generally a very cold and not very fruitful country, there never appeared any great probability of its being very considerable, 'till the Sieur la Salle about the year 1680 discovered the great river Mississippi, to which the English notwithstanding had a prior pretence.' In this the French had made no progress, he continued, until after the peace of Utrecht, 'but now they surround all the British dominions on the Main. They have a valley in the interior a thousand miles wide, accessible only from the St Lawrence and the Mississippi, while the British have merely a coastal strip 300 miles in width.' Moreover, the French were well organized and had co-opted the Indians to their cause. The twelve colonies would either have to expand or risk stagnating – or even being driven back into the sea by the surrounding Bourbons.[31]

There was not much point in relying on the Americans themselves to remedy the situation. The colonial assemblies were characterized by disunity and mutual suspicion in the face of the common enemy. James Logan was a highly unusual Pennsylvanian – a rare Quaker geopolitician. Most of his co-religionists were strongly of the view that security should be established through accommodation with the French and Indians, not by military means. Even Benjamin Franklin, who was later to do so much to create a common American strategic consciousness, spoke around this time of the need 'more fully to bend our minds to the study of the true interest of Pennsylvania', rather than of the twelve colonies as a whole. Most other Americans had similarly limited horizons. Until the late 1740s, Virginia was such a strategic backwater that the colonist William Byrd could write in 1735, 'we live here in health and plenty in innocence and security fearing no enemy from abroad or robbers at home.' In short, as James Logan lamented, while the French were 'under one general command' in North America, the situation 'in the British colonies is too much the reverse. Each of them is a distinct government wholly independent of each other, pursuing its own interest and subject to no general command.'[32]

It would therefore be up to London to keep the Bourbons at bay. In 1733, action was finally taken against the threat of Spanish infiltration from Florida and New Spain by setting up the new colony of Georgia.

This would provide a much-needed buffer zone to shield the Carolinas. In time, of course, Georgia would need its own buffer in Florida; such is ever the argument of complete security. To a certain extent, such measures were self-financing – with colonists driven by hopes of betterment – but it was clear that the broader task of shoring up British defences in Canada, building forts to the west and so on, would be a massive drain on the exchequer. For this reason, London began to reflect on ways in which the thirteen colonies could be persuaded to share the cost. Thus in 1739 the former colonial governor and pamphleteer Sir William Keith suggested the introduction of a Stamp Duty in order to pay for the dispatch of British soldiers necessary to deter France. This plan was rejected by Walpole, who had been badly burned by the Excise protests in 1733. He is said to have replied that 'I have old England set against me, and do you think I will have new England likewise?' Instead, Walpole preferred to generate revenue indirectly through trade. 'This,' he argued, 'is taxing them more agreeably both to their own constitution and to ours.'[33]

Despite all these difficulties, most Britons regarded the colonization of North America as an investment in their own security. As Logan wrote, 'It is manifest that if France could possess itself of those [British] dominions [in North America] and thereby become masters of all their trade, their sugars, tobacco, rice, timber and naval stores, they would soon be an overmatch in naval strength to the rest of Europe, and then be in a position to prescribe laws to the whole.' His memorandum is known to have reached Walpole himself, and these ideas, which became commonplace in the 1750s, were already gaining wide currency among the political elite and decision-makers. British dominance overseas was believed to be the key to defending the European balance of power. So as settlers and colonial governors limbered up for war with France and Spain in the 1730s, they did so only in part to resolve the struggle for mastery in America itself. What was ultimately at stake, in their minds and those of the British ministries, was the future of Europe itself.[34]

10

The Colonial Mirage, 1737–1739

I believe the people of Great Britain are governed by a power that was never heard of as a supreme authority in any age or country before. This power, sir, does not consist in the absolute will of the Prince, in the direction of Parliament, in the strength of an army, in the influence of the clergy; neither, sir, is it a petticoat government: but, sir, it is the government of the press. The stuff which our weekly newspapers are filled with is received with greater reverence than Acts of Parliament; and the sentiments of one of these scribblers have more weight with the multitude than the opinion of the best politician in the kingdom.[1]

John Danvers, House of Commons, February 1738

No man can prudently give his advice for declaring war [on Spain], without knowing the whole system of the affairs of Europe as they stand at present, and how the several potentates of Europe now stand affected towards one another.[2]

Sir Robert Walpole, House of Commons, March 1738

Nothing fired the imagination of the British public more than the gruesome fate of Captain Robert Jenkins of the merchantman *Rebecca*. In April 1731, Spanish coastguards, fed up with the growing illegal contraband trade with their American colonies, intercepted his vessel off Cuba, confiscated the cargo, and tortured Captain Jenkins. He was being made an example of. As a final indignity, one ear was lopped off. Jenkins did not – as one account had it – appear himself at the House of Commons with his ear preserved in a box or bottle, but his case formed a staple of a subsequent press campaign for war with Spain, and was mentioned in parliamentary debates. The amputation of an ear was still a legal punishment in Britain for certain offences, so there was nothing intrinsically cruel and unusual about his treatment; but in the perfervid context of the time it was perceived as a national slight. Jenkins was certainly luckier than one Dutch captain, who had his hand amputated, cooked in front of him, and was forced to eat it. One way or the other, by the late 1730s Spanish colonial governors – some of them acting on their own intitiative – were clearly upping the ante on the contraband trade, adding a flood of new complaints to those of the 1720s and early 1730s, with which popular opinion was already obsessed.[3]

1. Spanish Guarda Costa boarding Capt. Jenkins's Ship and Cutting off his Ear

17. A popular print illustrating the incident that outraged Britain and sparked the War of Jenkins's Ear.

The maritime war with Spain, which followed at the end of 1739, is therefore known as the 'War of Jenkins's Ear', and has become a byword for popular chauvinism, and for the increased importance of commercial and overseas concerns in British politics and policy. It followed a prolonged debate about British strategic priorities in which Tories and radical Whigs contrasted the naval and insular virtue of 'true Englishmen' with the Continental 'entanglements' and apparent timidity of Walpole's ministry. The late 1730s thus saw the revival of the navalist discourse in British politics which had flourished in the late seventeenth century, triumphed briefly towards the end of the War of the Spanish Succession, but had deflated in the 1720s. For throughout this period, British statesmen were very reluctant belligerents. To them, the economic case for war with Spain was far from proven, and their primary concern was not with overseas expansion *per se*, but the impact which colonial resources would have on the European balance of power. Ministers thus had their eye primarily on developments within Europe. The rise of Spanish power in Italy after the War of the Polish Succession – and the consequent collapse of Austrian power there – was a greater concern than the activities of the Spanish coastguard. Even more worrying was the French advance in Germany. As ever, the main concern of Crown and ministry in London was not the looming conflict over the Spanish American Empire, but the deepening crisis within the Holy Roman Empire.

In late July 1735 Horatio Walpole rebuked Newcastle, who as Secretary of State for the South was responsible for colonial affairs, for neglecting the Caribbean. 'Believe me,' he warned, 'you do not know what may be the consequence in all respects of your great indolence and neglect on this point; if you heard half what I hear from all quarters, friends and foes, on this head, I think it would affect you.' The British South Sea Company, which had in the meantime recovered from the burst 'bubble', had been making vigorous representations against the Spanish 'depredations' at Whitehall, and at Madrid through its agent there, who was none other than the British ambassador, Sir Benjamin Keene. After the end of the War of the Spanish Succession, the Company had been awarded the *Asiento*, the coveted right to ship slaves to the New World, for thirty years. The Company's principal demand was that this privilege be extended beyond its original expiry date of 1744, to take into account those years of warfare in the 1720s when it was not in operation. Meanwhile British merchants and sailors engaged in a very profitable illegal trade with the Spanish colonies. Spain, however, was determined to regain full control of her colonial trade, primarily in order to generate the resources necessary to support her great-power pretensions in Europe. This created tension between London and Madrid, not least because the Royal Navy openly colluded with the smugglers. There were also tensions in Central America, over the British settlement on the Mosquito Shore (now the east coast of Nicaragua). To make matters worse, Britain and Spain now faced off over Georgia, which had been founded in 1733 as a buffer against incursions from New Spain: by 1736–7 a full-scale Spanish attack on the colony was believed to be imminent.[4]

All the same, the storm which hit the administration from late 1737 took ministers by surprise. In October, merchants launched a concerted campaign of petitioning and parliamentary agitation to force the government into confronting Spain on the high seas. Their immediate objective was to secure the right to trade directly and unmolested with the Spanish colonies, but there was a more ambitious and sometimes overt intention to supplant Spain there altogether. In both cases, the argument was framed within a navalist rhetoric which rejected any right of search on the high seas. Thus the great petition of 11 October demanded 'that no British vessels be detained or searched on the high seas by any nation, under any pretence whatsoever'. It added, more delphically, 'that the trade to America may be rendered secure for the future by such means, as Your Majesty in your great wisdom shall think fit'. The merchants rejected any Spanish right to search British ships on the high seas as the 'claiming and exercising the sole sovereignty of the seas'. Heavy lobbying by West Indian merchants and other pressure groups ensued. A wave of depositions, petitions, declarations and proofs now piled up on ministers' desks and reverberated around the halls of Westminster.[5]

The protests in the City of London were led by Sir John Barnard, a High Church Tory who was Lord Mayor in 1737–8. His successor, Micajah Perry, was also a long-standing Hispanophobe. By the following year the 'Spanish depredations' had become a truly popular patriotic cause. Government policy was routinely lambasted in the provincial and London press, in pamphlets, ballads and even stage performances; ministerial censors scrambled to suppress the worst offenders. Tremulous society ladies attended the relevant parliamentary debates in March 1738, no doubt in the hope of catching a glimpse of one of Jenkins's severed extremities. The Prince of Wales spearheaded a boycott of French wines and Italian songs. Opera and claret were, for the moment, deeply unfashionable. British products were exalted in their stead. In mid 1738, the *London Evening Post* announced that 'If such resolutions as these prevail, we may hope to find that OPERAS, CLARET and CAMBRICKS, will become as distasteful to the POLITE as PENSIONS, EXCISES and STANDING ARMIES are to the honest part of the BRITISH NATION.'

Britain, in short, was experiencing the cultural retrenchment which often accompanies national crisis.[6]

Many contemporaries remarked on the rising importance of the press and the growth of a public sphere in foreign policy. Those who welcomed the discomfiture of the government rejoiced in it, others deplored it. In what was neither the first nor the last outburst of its kind, the MP John Danvers lamented that 'the people of Great Britain are governed by a power that was never heard of as a supreme authority in any age or country before . . . the government of the press.' The opinions of these 'scribblers', Danvers went on, 'is received with greater reverence than Acts of Parliament'. It was the old notion of power without responsibility, with which the press has been charged down the ages. The ministerial supporter, Bishop Hoadly of Salisbury, condemned the popular on-slaught in similar terms. 'They in the opposition,' he lamented in early March 1739, 'have many advantages, without doors, over those in the ministry. They have the happiness of being looked upon by the people as advocates for their rights. This gives great weight to all they say or print. They likewise never fail to cover all their designs with a word that is clear to every free-born people, Liberty. This, my lords, gives them a fine field for declamation.' It was one of many references, approving and disapproving, to the new importance of opinion 'out of doors'. Lord Bathurst had referred to it in February; so did Lord Carteret. The Earl of Cholmondeley even warned that 'if . . . we make those without doors not only partners but judges of our councils, we are then in a deplorable situation'.[7]

Those who called for a greater parliamentary role in foreign policy were quick to turn the popular fervour to their advantage. Ironically, it was the Tories who were the supporters of parliamentary, as opposed to executive supremacy in this context. In 1738 their leader Sir William Wyndham claimed the right to demand and scrutinize diplomatic correspondence. In particular, he requested that treaties should be placed before Parliament for ratification. How else, the opposition MP Pulteney asked, could Parliament discharge its obligation as 'His Majesty's great and chief council'? If there were any papers 'which ought not, for the sake of public good, to be exposed to public view, it [was] the business of the Crown to tell us so', not that of the ministry. Indeed, Pulteney announced that 'no gentleman can take upon him to dictate what papers are proper, and what are improper for our inspection'. The arguments which had been hurled at Walpole over the War of the Polish Succession were now dusted off and applied to the Spanish 'depredations'. Further petitions were presented in mid March 1738. In late March, a packed House of Commons met to discuss them. There were calls for relevant papers to be presented and translated. There was no let-up in the attacks, and Carteret launched a long diatribe in early May. In the end, the ministry was embarrassed into approving additional naval spending and promising to back up diplomacy with force.[8]

The campaign against the Spanish depredations was ostensibly about trade, but it was also about much more than that. It provides a fascinating snapshot of British identity and strategic conceptions on the eve of the War of the Austrian Succession. To be sure, straightforward xenophobia was an important part of the picture. The late 1730s saw a renewed surge of anti-French and anti-Spanish sentiment. The classic themes of Continental absolutism and popery were reprised and contrasted with British roast beefery. The Spaniard, by contrast, was dismissed as a self-basting foreigner. But there were also more subtle arguments about honour. It was widely felt that Britain had lost face in Europe, and that her predicament on the high seas was an indication of a universal contempt which could only be dispelled by war. 'A dishonourable peace,' the independent Whig Sir John Barnard argued in March 1738, 'is worse than a destructive war . . . All nations are apt to play the bully with respect to one another; and if the government or administration of a nation has taken but one insult tamely, their neighbours will from thence judge of the character of that nation . . . and will accordingly treat them as bullies do noted poltroons; they will kick and cuff them upon every occasion.' At times, the appeal to national honour became histrionic. Alderman Willimot, for example, condemned the mistreatment of captured British sailors in particularly heated terms: 'Our countrymen in chains! and slaves to Spaniards! Is not this enough . . . to fire the coldest? And shall we . . . sit here debating about words and forms, while the sufferings of our countrymen call out loudly for redress?' Another parliamentarian announced that 'in this affair we have already made use of so much ink and paper without any effect, that I am afraid it will appear necessary for us to begin to make use of another sort of ammunition . . . I mean . . . the weight of our metal, and the sharpness of our swords.'[9]

*

This strategic discourse was not just driven by popular and parliamentary machismo. It was part of a much more subtle intellectual project led by the principal Tory thinker on foreign policy, Bolingbroke, who had been in semi-voluntary exile in France since 1735, partly in order to escape his creditors, and partly because of increasing government attempts to silence him. There British diplomats were keeping a close eye on him. The ambassador William Waldegrave reported in mid November 1737 that Bolingbroke 'was quite retired, and meddled no more with politics'. He could not have been more wrong. It was around this time that Bolingbroke was working on his famous tract, *The patriot king*, which soon circulated in manuscript form, although it was not published until a decade later. Its author argued that 'the true interest of several states' depended on the 'situation of countries'. On this reasoning, Bolingbroke continued, 'The situation of Great Britain ... the character of her people, and the nature of her government, fit her for trade and commerce.' This was because 'The sea is our barrier, ships are our fortresses, and the mariners, that trade and commerce alone can furnish, are the garrisons to defend them.' For this reason, he continued, 'the government of a PATRIOT KING, will be directed constantly to make the most of every advantage that nature has given, or art can procure towards the improvement of trade and commerce.' The implicit contrast with the current failure of monarchy and ministry is obvious, the appeal to the reversionary interest of the Prince of Wales – the expectation that the death of George II would bring better times under his son and heir – only slightly less so. 'For eighteen years,' Bolingbroke thundered, 'we have tamely suffered continual depredations from the most contemptible maritime power in Europe, that of Spain.'[10]

On this reading, Britain was an island state, set apart from the rest of Europe. 'Great Britain,' Bolingbroke wrote, 'is an island: and whilst nations on the Continent are at immense charge in maintaining their barriers, and perpetually on their guard, and frequently embroiled, to extend or strengthen them, Great Britain may, if her governors please, accumulate wealth in maintaining hers.' For this reason, Britain might 'advise, and warn ... abet, and oppose; but it can never be our true interest easily and officiously to enter into action, much less into engagements that imply action and expense'. Britain should not 'dissipate [her] strength on occasions that touch us remotely or indirectly'. Instead, she

18. Bolingbroke, author of *The patriot king*, was the eighteenth-century father of the 'blue water' policy.

should devote 'a continual attention to improve her natural, that is her maritime strength'. In that way, Britain could be 'the arbitrator of differences, the guardian of liberty, and the preserver of that balance' of Europe. He concluded with a sentence which was to echo down history: 'Like other amphibious animals, we must come occasionally on shore: but the water is more properly our element, and in it like them, as we find our greatest security, so we exert our greatest force.'[11]

In this context, it was natural that patriots should look once again at the Hanoverian connection with a jaundiced eye. According to the diarist and courtier Lord Hervey, admittedly one of the King's detractors, George returned from the Electorate in 1735 with scarcely a good word to say about Britain. At a time when the nation was greatly exercised by maritime affairs, the King's prolonged absence with his mistress, Countess Walmoden, in the Electorate in 1736–7 appeared tactless. She was regularly abused in public as a 'Hanover whore'. The Hanoverian connection was also the target of pamphlet and literary attacks. Once again, the association between the Electorate and Oriental despotism, and the contrast with native British freedoms, was made. Thus in Lord Lyttelton's *Letters from a Persian in England to his friend at Ispahan*, the Persian dress of the narrator prompted the mob to assume that he 'was a German minister sent by the court to corrupt the electors'. And in 1738–9, Samuel Johnson's *Lilliput debates* were a thinly disguised attack on the King's German patrimony, which was dismissed as 'vast tracts of land ... too spacious to be constantly garrisoned and too remote to be occasionally and duly supplied'. He took another swipe at

Hanover – and Walpole – in his pamphlet *Marmor Norfolkiense* (1739). 'And, yet more strange! His veins a horse shall drain, / Nor shall the passive coward once complain'. Everybody knew what these lines meant: the Saxon horse was well known as the symbol of Hanover.[12]

Rumblings against the King's German preoccupations could also be heard behind the scenes. Every time George visited the Electorate, the focus of decision-making, at least in foreign policy, perforce had to follow him. As one British diplomat put it, 'business will naturally go to Hanover'. In 1736, for example, the King was accompanied by the senior undersecretaries of both the Northern and Southern departments. Sometimes he was joined by one or the other of the principal ministers, especially Lord Harrington, who was Secretary of State for the North. Moreover, British diplomats were now instructed to write to Hanover for the duration. Queen Caroline was left as 'guardian of the realm'. The King also attracted a steady stream of Englishmen on the grand tour. As George Tilson, an undersecretary of state who was with him in 1736, remarked, 'we are about to have a fresh cargo of English, who love to break in upon the King's retreat here. We have now two of Mr Vernon's sons, who are going to Geneva to pick up a brother and travel through Italy and France.' Some British statesmen and diplomats were not just worried that the King's presence in Hanover created a rival focus to London, they also fretted about consequent distortions in the content of policy. Even Horatio Walpole, who was no patriot harrumpher, privately complained in 1737–8 that 'those Electoral considerations in which we have not the least concern do often prove inconvenient to us'.[13]

There were good reasons for Walpole's irritation. Even as British policy sought to prop up the Catholic Emperor Charles VI in Germany as a counterweight to France, George championed the Protestant cause in the Empire every bit as much as his father had. He was an active presence in the *Corpus Evangelicorum*, and a doughty vindicator of Protestant grievances against the Emperor. But while George I's imperial policy had moved largely in tandem with a broader British concern to curb Habsburg pretensions to universal monarchy, that of his son cut across British plans to restrain Louis XV. Not only did the King use his Hanoverian servants to pursue this strategy, which was bad enough, but he also instructed British diplomats to cooperate with them. Thus in late March 1736 Thomas Robinson, the British ambassador to Vienna, was directed to defend Protestant rights against Charles VI. 'His Majesty's Electoral minister', the Secretary of State for the North, Lord Harrington, wrote, 'will have full directions for his conduct in this affair, and it is the King's pleasure that you should not only *second him therein*, but should likewise speak in the strongest manner in the King's name, *as King as well as Elector* [underlined in the original] for promoting what will be desired, His Majesty being concerned to do it in the former quality also.' A few months later Robinson was also told to 'concert with the other Protestant ministers', with regard to 'the address proposed to be obtained for the grievances of the Protestants in the Empire'. The imperial horizons of George II and his 'patriot' critics thus diverged. They inhabited quite separate strategic and geographical mental worlds.[14]

The unpopularity of the King was not just reflected in the upsurge in anti-Hanoverianism. The revulsion against the Spanish atrocities took place against a backdrop of, and contributed to, a much broader popular and political discontent. To be sure, there were social and economic grievances: a rash of poor harvests after a period of plenty led to shortages and hardship. But the principal bone of contention, as the opposition *Craftsman* pointed out, was political and strategic. It was, the argument ran, 'above all, the *Spanish depredations*, about which the people have so chafed themselves, that they have hardly patience to wait till our *vigilant* and *wise ministers* have made proper remonstrances'. The petitions for redress and action against Spain were directed at the monarch in person, and failure to react damaged his credibility. Even Horatio Walpole had to admit that the situation 'highly reflects upon the honour and dignity of the Crown, in not being able to protect her subjects'.[15]

As the gulf between monarchy and 'the people' grew, relations within the royal family took on a new significance. As in the late 1710s, a crisis in foreign policy went hand in hand with a royal split. Just as George II and his father had cordially hated each other, so did King and Prince of Wales in the 1730s. Tensions boiled over after Frederick married in 1736 and demanded a larger allowance. Queen Caroline also took strongly against her own son. She said of him that he was 'the greatest ass, and the greatest *canaille* [scoundrel], and the greatest beast, in the whole world, and that I most heartily wish he was out of it'. In September 1737 the Prince and his friends were banned from court; not even Caroline's death two months later helped to dispel the tension. Walpole, of course, backed George. Newcastle, his brother Henry Pelham and the Whig stalwart Lord Hardwicke tried to mediate, for the scene was a familiar one to them. They had seen twenty years earlier how divisions within the royal family had given enterprising politicians a handle with which to attack the ministry, quite apart from being a distraction from urgent matters of foreign policy.[16]

Now patriot opinion, and disaffected parliamentarians such as Pulteney, Lord Carteret, the Earl of Chesterfield and Lord Stair, looked to Frederick, Prince of Wales for leadership. The young William Pitt made his parliamentary debut in 1736 in defence of the Prince of Wales, thus earning the hatred of George, as well as a dismissal from the army. The issue moved from the courtly into the parliamentary sphere, as King and opposition tussled over royal allowances and much else. Only under the guidance of a 'patriot king', it was felt, could Britain find its way out of the European morass caused by Walpole's corruption and mismanagement. The Prince of Wales, in turn, attacked the failure to confront Spain and the general decline of British standing in Europe. In retaliation, George built up his own parliamentary following, telling Sandys, whom he otherwise detested but who had fallen out with the 'patriots', that 'Since they piss upon you, I will stand by you.' Moreover, the birth of a daughter to the Prince of Wales in 1737 was celebrated on the grounds that the differing succession laws in both territories might lead to a rupture of the Personal Union; that was indeed exactly what happened, but one hundred years later.[17]

One of those who came of age politically during this febrile period was the young William Pitt. Admittedly, Pitt's background was hardly that of a paragon of commercial virtue. His father, 'Diamond Pitt', had made his fortune in India, often in intense rivalry with the East India Company, and subsequently bought the rotten borough of Old Sarum and the parliamentary representation that went with it. Pitt himself sat for that borough until 1747, when he switched to a seat held by the Newcastle interest. In other words, unlike many of the anti-ministerial scourges, Pitt did not hold either a county or a metropolitan mercantile seat: he was dependent on patronage, not popular opinion. Nor was he a complete ignoramus on Europe, having gone on the grand tour in 1733 and even studied briefly at the University of Utrecht. During this period, Pitt was powerfully attracted to the anti-Walpolean 'boy patriots' led by Viscount Cobham, and cultivated the reversionary interest, being made a Groom of the Bedchamber to the Prince of Wales in 1737. He became known as one of 'Cobham's cubs'. They also shared the prevailing view that Walpole's Spanish policy had reached the end of the road, though, as we shall see, it was the parlous state of the European balance with which they were more deeply concerned.[18]

With the intellectual sponsorship of Bolingbroke, the political patronage of the Prince of Wales, and popular enthusiasm at their backs, the scene was set for a final parliamentary extravaganza. This agitation against the Spanish depredations was more than just inchoate maritime, insular and colonialist enthusiasm. It saw the revival of a classically naval strategic national vocation. On this reading, Britain's inferiority on land could be discounted. 'All we have occasion for,' the Opposition Whig MP George Lyttleton remarked in February 1738, 'is to send a superior fleet, with some land forces on board, to infest their coasts, till we have brought them to reasonable terms.' Another parliamentarian spoke of conflict with Spain as 'a war upon an element where we were sure to be masters'. A year later, Sir John Barnard – the independent Whig MP and Lord Mayor of London – said, 'I am not . . . much either of a soldier or a sailor . . . but I have read a little, and have heard a great deal with regard to the management of a war betwixt us and the Spaniards . . . [S]o far as I may be allowed to judge, there is but one way in which we can possibly attack them, and that is by sea.' Time was to show that a little reading on the management of war can be a dangerous thing.[19]

In March 1739, Lord Bathurst summarized the emerging consensus in a eulogy on amphibious warfare. He announced that

we might not only reap advantage by distressing them [Spain] at sea, but we might reap still greater advantages, and reduce them to greater difficulties by attacking them at land . . . by having a squadron with 5 or 6,000 land forces on board, continually roving around their coasts, and making inroads upon the country, as often as they found an opportunity, we might do infinite mischief to our enemies, and often get rich booties for our soldiers and seamen. Then with regard to their settlements in America . . . we might plunder them from one end to the other; or if we thought it more for our purpose, we might enable them to throw off the yoke of Spain.

This was, perhaps, the first time that the idea of regime change in the New World had been floated. The protagonists believed that it would be not only an easy, but a self-financing war of liberation. The *Craftsman* revelled in the prospect of capturing the silver fleet, taking Havana, and perhaps even Panama. Interestingly enough, some British intelligence sources concurred, stressing the weakness of Spanish defences and the restiveness of the local population. One British seaman predicted that 'Millions of miserable people would bless their deliverers; their hearts and their mines [sic] would be opened to us.' The reference to 'mines' for 'minds' was surely a Freudian slip, revealing as it did the synergy between liberation and resource extraction.[20]

It should come as no surprise that all this was accompanied by a surge of interest in Britain's past naval heroes. Tellingly, Lord Cobham's new Temple of British Worthies at Stowe contained busts of Queen Elizabeth and Sir Francis Drake, as well as that contemporary metropolitan hammer of the Spaniards, Sir John Barnard. The idols of the past decades, generals such as Marlborough, were no longer in fashion. Inevitably this naval fervour and a sense of insular identity translated into even greater opposition to a standing army during the annual Mutiny Debates. The patriot George Lyttleton argued that there was no point in fetishizing 'that in which the King may be rivalled by every petty prince of any little state in Germany'. He went on to say, with calculated offensiveness, that 'If the greatness of a state is to be measured by the number of its troops, the Elector of Hanover is as great as the King of England.' Others believed that constitutional liberties should be qualified by considerations of national security. There was clearly no point in turning Britain into an absolutist state in order to defend against French or Jacobite absolutism. At the same time, it would be perverse to cling to every peacetime right, if that endangered the security of the realm upon which all British liberties ultimately depended. Henry Fox, the pro-government MP for Hindon, argued that 'there is no country in the world, nor I believe was there ever any people, who were so scrupulously attached to their original forms of government, as not to dispense with them when a too strict adherence to these forms might endanger their liberties.' To him, the maintenance of a standing army was 'evidently agreeable to the first maxims of all constitutions, which is the safety of the people'.[21]

If the opposition attack was driven by their view of Britain's role in the European state system, so was the government response. The ministry was entirely unpersuaded by the economic case for war with Spain.

Despite all the mercantile bleating, Henry Pelham argued that trade and colonies might 'have suffered a little by the late behaviour of Spain toward us, but their sufferings are not, I believe, near so considerable as some people seem fond of representing'. Indeed, the government believed that the commercial consequences would be disastrous. For all the colonial froth generated over the past decade, trade with 'Old Spain', regulated by a treaty of 1667, was far more valuable than the illegal contraband trade with Spanish America. In any case, seizures by the Spanish coastguard affected only about 2 per cent of that trade. Salted fish and woollens were exported to Spain; oil, dye-stuffs, wine and wool were imported. This trade was carried in British ships and managed by British merchants. The balance of trade was largely favourable. All this, Walpole warned Parliament in March 1738, would be hazarded by war with Spain. The weakness of the commercial lobby against war reflected not economic but politico-cultural realities. Most of the trade with Old Spain was in the hands of marginal men: Jews, Irish and English Catholics (none of them represented in Parliament; many of them Jacobites). They were not able to compete with the colonial crock of gold so many saw over the horizon.[22]

Moreover, as ministerial voices were quick to point out, taking on Spain over this issue effectively meant condoning smuggling, and thus violating international law. 'Such a war,' Lord Hervey pointed out in February 1739, 'would certainly be unjust upon our part; because it would be, and by all Europe would be considered, as war for supporting the smuggling trade, that may be carried by our subjects in the Spanish West Indies.' The aggression, self-confidence and chauvinism of the war lobby also grated with many. The Prime Minister pointed out that 'in contests between nations, it is the same as in contests between private men: each party thinks himself right.' Ministers were therefore unimpressed with the demand for a more robust British diplomacy. Henry Pelham reminded the House of Commons in late March 1738 that 'I believe we never made a treaty, where we could obtain all that was convenient for us; I believe, no nation ever did; for a *carte blanche* is not properly a treaty; it is the law which the conqueror prescribes to those he has conquered.' As for the constant allegations of cowardice, Walpole responded that in a private matter, a man might respond instinctively, because 'he has nothing but his own life to lose'. A statesmen, on the other hand, had to act more responsibly, because 'the lives of many thousands were concerned; and those who are to deliberate and determine in what manner, or how soon, an injury ought to be resented, are generally those whose lives, in case of a rupture, will be the last of being brought into danger'.[23]

Moreover, at this point war was militarily just too risky. The fleet and the army were unprepared, even for the easy war that many seemed to expect against Spain; and those in the know thought her no pushover. Sir Charles Wager, an MP with many years of naval experience, warned the House of Commons that 'no nation in the world, I believe ever declared war, till they were ready to enter upon action; and as we at present have neither a fleet nor an army ready sufficient for attacking such a powerful nation as Spain, I think we ought not to yet do anything, that may look like a declaration of war, or even like a resolution to declare war.' No wonder then that Horatio Walpole argued that 'It was a maxim with Julius Caesar, never to venture even a battle, if the disadvantages that might ensue from a defeat appeared to be greater than any advantages he could expect from a victory.' In these circumstances, he continued, bearing 'many insults and indignities' might be the statesmanlike thing to do, if 'only because by a little patience' one might 'obtain a victory with less bloodshed'.[24]

But the main reason why British statesmen opposed war with Spain, was the alarming condition of the European state system. The War of the Polish Succession had dealt a severe blow to the balance. First of all, it had seen the ejection of the Austrians from Naples and Sicily, and their replacement by a French-leaning Spanish Bourbon dynasty. Secondly, France had secured the reversion of the Duchy of Lorraine, which further exposed the western flank of the Holy Roman Empire. Meanwhile, the Dutch were hopelessly ill-equipped, and in any case disinclined to man the fortresses in the Austrian Netherlands. More generally, as the British ambassador to Spain, Benjamin Keene, remarked in April 1738, 'the Dutch will abandon us in the conflict, and get private advantages by our fighting for a cause in common to both nations.' The Emperor, Charles VI, was getting on, and no definitive solution to the Habsburg succession was in sight. And if all this was not bad enough, Charles had embarked on a disastrous war with Turkey in 1736, which tied down the bulk of his forces. In other words, the barriers to the advance of French power in central Europe were weakening at the very moment when the power of the House of Habsburg was on the wane, and distracted to boot. Nor did the end of the Austro-Turkish war in 1738 bring relief: quite the opposite. It was brought about by French mediation, which greatly increased French prestige in Vienna at Britain's expense. Indeed, there were now fears in London that Austria was becoming a French satellite and that a Habsburg–Bourbon alliance might even be in the offing. British diplomats referred apprehensively to 'the union which subsists between the Houses of Austria and Bourbon'. Elsewhere, the picture was one of almost unrelieved gloom. In the Baltic, rumours of a Franco-Danish treaty 'for subsidies on account of a body of Danish troops designed to be at the disposition of France'. A coup in Stockholm displaced the pro-Russian and generally pro-British 'Cap' party, and brought the pro-French 'Hats' to power once more. In December 1738 news of a proposed Franco-Spanish double marriage hit London. It seemed as if bastions were falling north, south and across Europe.[25]

To cap it all, after a relatively calm period, relations with Prussia were once again on a knife-edge from early 1738. Frederick William had been inflamed by the disputed succession in Jülich-Berg, a small but strategically important principality on the western border of the Holy Roman Empire. This pitted Frederick William against the French, the Austrians and the Elector-King, who supported the rival claims of Pfalz-Sulzbach. George opposed a Prussian presence there on the grounds that it would have increased the encirclement of Hanover (the Prussians were already in nearby Cleves-Mark), and strengthened her standing within the Empire, where the leadership of the *Corpus Evangelicorum* was in dispute. Prussian military preparations were watched with anxiety from London. The Northern Secretary thought that although Frederick William might be bluffing, 'all his neighbours would certainly do well to be on their guard against any surprise'. In the broader scheme of things, George's anti-Prussian stance both supported and subverted British strategy in central Europe. It provided some much-needed support for Austria in the Empire, and thus bolstered the ailing Charles VI; on the other hand, it threatened to drive Frederick William into the arms of France.[26]

More immediately, the looming clash with Berlin meant that the ministry would have to consider the safety of Hanover. At a bad-tempered and alcohol-fuelled dinner in the Prussian capital in late June 1738, the Prussian chief minister, Grumbkow, appealed to Protestant solidarity against Vienna and Versailles, failing which Prussia 'would invade Silesia and Hanover'. He threatened not only to support the Pretender, but that the Prussians 'would overrun Hanover, and that would only be a breakfast'. Grumbkow also threatened to invade Holland into the bargain. The British ambassador was left to bluster that 'they would not find His Majesty's dominions so defenceless as they seemed to imagine, and that ... if they came and breakfasted there without being invited, they could rest assured His Majesty would take the liberty of dining and supping with them longer than perhaps they should care for his company.' All this was a further reminder, if one was needed, that even relatively minor German disputes could suck Britain-Hanover back into the vortex of central Europe.[27]

This was therefore not the moment, Newcastle argued, to launch a naval war with Spain. 'So many changes,' he warned in March 1738, 'may happen at the several courts of Europe, that nothing but omniscience can foresee them ... so many schemes may be formed, for disturbing the present tranquillity, that no omnipotent power can, with authority, say, none of them shall take effect.' And because it was 'our business to preserve the peace of Europe,' Newcastle went on, Britain needed to be on the lookout for further French encroachments. So long as Fleury prevailed, all might be well, but after his death all bets would be off. 'The new ministry,' he feared, 'might fall in with the views of Spain and ... instead of guaranteeing the Emperor's dominions in Italy, they would join with Spain in endeavouring to drive him entirely out of the country.' Besides, Britain would have to hold back land and naval forces to deter an assault by the Spaniards on her ally Portugal. 'I do not know,' Newcastle remarked, 'how soon a war may be kindled up in Europe, by their ambitious projects against Portugal or Italy.' What is striking here is the extent to which he feared Spanish ambitions in Europe far more than overseas.[28]

Moreover, Newcastle saw the colonial and the European balances were closely linked within a Eurocentric framework. He pointed out that if 'any of our European neighbours ... suspect[ed] that we had formed a design to dismember any part of the Spanish monarchy from that crown, there is not the least doubt but they would look upon us with a very jealous eye'. It would be a clear violation of the Treaty of Utrecht, which forbade any further Spanish territorial losses. Besides, it was by the same treaty that France 'was obliged to give up all claim to

... any commerce to the Spanish settlements ... This ... has always been looked upon as a necessary step towards preventing any nation in Europe from becoming too powerful for the rest'. For this reason, he continued, 'preserving the sole right of navigation and commerce to and from the Spanish settlements in America to the Spaniards themselves, was not the effect so much of Spanish policy, as of the jealousy which the powers of Europe entertained ... themselves, lest any other should acquire too great a property in that valuable trade of commerce'. Because, he continued, 'should too large a share of [these profits] come into the hands of another nation in Europe, whose situation, power or trade, render them perhaps already formidable to their neighbours, they might be employed to purposes inconsistent with the peace of Europe, and which might one day prove fatal to the balance of power.' In other words, control of the Spanish American Empire was primarily to be feared for its implications for the general European balance.[29]

The deterioration of relations with Spain brought with it an increased fear of Jacobite machinations on the Continent. For much of the 1730s the opposition had dismissed the Pretender as a Walpolean fiction designed to keep them in their place at home, and to justify an inflated military establishment. 'All the dangers [alleged] either abroad or at home,' the Earl of Chesterfield protested in March 1738, 'depend on maybe's which must always subsist. A minister may die, a prince may have ambitious views, a prince's success may raise the jealousy of others, his misfortunes may revive their hopes, there may be a design to invade us, though we have not, at present, the least item of it.' He therefore accused ministries of 'terrifying us with imaginary plots and invasions, and making the tour of Europe in search of possible dangers, in order to show us the necessity of keeping up a mercenary standing army'. In the same vein, the Tory leader Sir William Wyndham said that Walpole's preoccupation with Jacobitism was a 'phantom of his own brain. This phantom haunted him about from place to place, and nothing could drive it out of his head.' In fact, the Pretender was indeed rallying diplomatic and military support in Europe in expectation of a rupture with Spain, and a close eye was kept on his movements. Diplomatic relations were broken with those states, such as Venice in 1737, which were deemed to be too close to the Jacobites. In March 1738 the Pretender welcomed news of deteriorating relations between London and Madrid as 'great progress towards a rupture'. Moreover, Elizabeth Farnese regularly played the Jacobite card herself: she reportedly announced in May 1738 'that if we force her to a war, she can raise such troubles in England as will make us sick of it'.[30]

British ministers were acutely conscious of their limitations in the face of these mounting threats. 'I wish,' Walpole remarked with some exasperation, 'that it were in our power to give laws to every potentate in Europe, and to prescribe to them how they should behave, in every case, not only to us, but to one another. But this is at present impossible.' It might, with difficulty, be possible to master Spain, but only if France did not intervene. It was for this reason that Walpole rejected opposition demands for the seizure of Spanish vessels in reprisal. 'I am far from thinking,' he remarked in May 1738, 'that we are not a sufficient match for the Spaniards . . . But give me leave to say that I think we are not a match for the Spaniards and French too.' At the beginning of the following year, he returned to this theme. 'I know that gentlemen . . . are apt to imagine, from the military glory of this nation, that our arms are invincible, and I own . . . that this is a most prevailing argument, especially in a popular assembly. There is somewhat in it, that flatters the ambition.'[31]

For all these reasons it was essential that Britain should not appear as the aggressor in any war with Spain. Patient negotiation in good faith, Newcastle argued, 'will convince the other powers of Europe that we have right as well as power on our side. But should we precipitately enter into a war with Spain . . . without giving them an opportunity of making us reparation in an amicable way, the other powers of Europe would immediately take alarm.' They would suspect a British design to partition the Spanish colonial empire. Likewise, Walpole did not 'think it would be prudent in us to attempt making use of our power in a manner too positive and haughty lest by so doing we should provoke the other powers of Europe to unite together, in order to reduce the power of this nation'. Indeed, precipitate war 'might stir up some of the other powers of Europe to join with Spain, who would otherwise have remained neutral'. Above all, it was vital that Britain maintain good relations with France and especially with her chief minister, Fleury. He was now well into his eighties and his health became something of an obsession for British statesmen and diplomats. So long as Fleury held the line on Jacobitism; so long as he kept demands for a closer naval relationship with Spain at arm's length; and so long as the Habsburg humpty-dumpty kept together; for so long, Britain would be relatively safe.[32]

All this, of course, was grist to the opposition mill. If Britain was constrained by the deteriorating situation on the Continent, then surely this suggested some mismanagement of the European balance. Pulteney argued that 'if the political affairs of Europe have been negotiated into such a system [that] . . . this nation [is] not provided with any one ally, whose assistance we can depend on', then one might have to appease Spain; but then one would also need to 'deliver [Britain] from the councillors who have brought it into those difficulties'. Another parliamentarian argued that if Britain was isolated in Europe, 'would it not be our duty, to enquire into the state of the nation, and deliver our country from such polluted hands'. After all, he continued, 'if any powerful alliance be formed against us, and we cannot form a sufficient counter alliance, it must be owing to some late weakness or mistake in our conduct'. The MP, diplomat and entrepreneur Edward Wortley Montagu supported the call for an inquiry, 'for the affairs of Europe can never be brought into a bad situation for us, without some mismanagement of our own'. Very soon, as Britain's isolation in Europe deepened still further, the opposition critique of Walpole's management of the Continental balance of power was to gain much greater traction than its attack on the neglect of the maritime rivalry with Spain.[33]

The ministry was now visibly under pressure. Behind the scenes it was beginning to panic. Thus at the very end of October 1737 Horatio Walpole complained to the British ambassador at Madrid that 'If the outrageous depredations lately committed by the Spaniards upon our commerce in the West Indies . . . are true, I cannot see how we can avoid interrupting a little the variety of diversions which Their Catholic Majesties seem to enjoy with so much tranquillity.' He doubted whether 'the English nation will bear as quietly their taking our ships, as they do their taking away Farinelli [a celebrated Italian castrato who had been lured away from his contract in London to sing at the Spanish court]. I must own but that you seem silent on that subject.' This, it must be remembered, from one of the most ardent British Eurocentrics. By the spring of 1738, it was clear that some concession to popular fury would have to be made. The ministry introduced a measure authorizing retaliatory action by authorized private contractors – bearing 'letters of marque and reprisal' – against Spanish shipping. This had the advantage of subcontracting the job to local agents; intrinsically a half-measure any-way, it was also weakened by the fact that no private investor was likely to sink money into such vessels while a deal with Spain remained imminent. It could be no more than a stopgap solution, to allow more time for diplomacy.[34]

By the beginning of 1739, popular agitation was increasingly setting the ministerial agenda. In the King's Speech at the opening of Parliament, mention was made of 'how sensibly I have been affected with the many hardships and injuries sustained by my trading subjects in America'.[35] One last effort was made to settle differences without war. The increasingly bizarre condition of the Spanish royal family made this all the more difficult. The Spanish King himself was a virtual prisoner in the Escorial Palace, where he was serenaded every day by Farinelli. Elizabeth Farnese was in total control. All the same, in mid January, British and Spanish negotiators agreed the Convention of the Pardo. By its terms, all the various obligations and claims were totalled and it was determined that Spain would pay the difference of £27,000, a fraction of the British claims, to be sure, but not a trivial sum. Six weeks later, commissioners were appointed to resolve the boundary disputes between Georgia and New Spain, which had been left open.

On 8 February the Convention was laid before Parliament. It was followed by a flood of condemnatory petitions from West India merchants and figures within the City of London. The MP Sir Thomas Sanderson said that 'The Convention now before us ... is the most dishonourable, the most deceitful, the most ruinous treaty this nation ever made; I will be bold to say that ninety-nine out of a hundred of the people are of the same opinion.' What is striking is the extent to which the critique of the Convention of the Pardo hinged not on any points of detail, even once this was known, but on the rather nebulous concept of national 'honour'. 'If we do not vindicate our honour,' Lord Bathurst urged, 'and assert the rights and privileges of our people, in all parts of the world where they may have occasion to go, we must give up our foreign trade.' In the House of Commons one speaker claimed that 'the heart of every Englishman should be inflamed ... I look upon this Convention as disadvantageous to the King, and ignominious to the nation.' Even the young William Pitt weighed in, stating that 'This Convention ... I think from my soul is nothing but a stipulation for national ignominy.' Indeed, the government was widely suspected not only to have caved in to Spanish maritime demands, but also of having agreed to the surrender of Georgia. The ministry rejected this hawkish fervour and the overt contempt for the very notion of negotiations. Lord Hervey responded that 'People may call the Convention a paper-peace, or by what other name they please, but if ever we make peace, we must trust to paper, or we can trust to nothing. Negotiations may be supported or enforced by military preparations, but they must be carried on in paper.' After all, he concluded, 'since paper was invented, I never heard of a peace that was concluded without paper . . . there can be no other sort of peace.'[36]

As always, it was the primacy of Europe which underpinned ministerial thinking and rhetoric on the Convention of the Pardo. As the Duke of Portland pointed out, the quarrel with Spain 'relat[ed] entirely to trade: [it was] not founded on her aspiring to universal monarchy'. There was therefore no pressing reason for war. Lord Hervey argued that 'at a time when the affairs of Europe are in such a situation, that we can form no confederacy against them [France and Spain], at a time when, if we engage in war, we must stand single and alone against these two powerful nations . . . at such a time it would be prudent to suspend our vengeance . . . till a more proper opportunity should offer.' Moreover, the Dutch remained completely useless. Trevor, the British ambassador to the United Provinces, complained that 'the present inaction of this court is so great' that it was hardly worth bothering with a dispatch. In vain he pressed the Grand Pensionary – in effect the Dutch prime minister – about 'France's growing ascendant in the North'; in vain he stressed the need for a *contrepoids* [counterweight] to the formidable monarchy'. Like the ministry in London, Trevor was worried by the 'far-fetched and expensive alliances which France was now negotiating in the north', which were intended 'to indispose and divert the several Protestant powers in Lower Saxony [the Principality of Lippe, the Duchy of Brunswick and the Electorate of Hanover itself] from contributing their forces towards opposing any enterprise that France may come to make on the Rhine or on the side of Flanders; and that the least I could estimate such a diversion at, was the difference of 50,000 men in the common cause'. All the spheres of Europe, in other words, were interconnected in this conception of Britain's security interests.[37]

The basic problem was the domestic weakness of the Dutch Republic. Trevor's venomous reports on Dutch internal politics, he suggested, 'may serve to give one a pretty just idea of the Republic's interior economy, or rather its want of it'. He inveighed against the 'ingenuous and pathetic lectures' of Dutch politicians, and the 'pucrility and confusion of their proceedings' in 'this decrepit state'. 'I do not know,' he concluded crushingly, 'the danger they would not dissemble, nor the affront they would not put up [with] rather than bestir themselves effectually.' All this, he remarked, was due to the Dutch sense of their 'domestic liberty', which would endanger the 'natural' liberties of Europe. Besides, the Dutch lived in terror of France: Trevor spoke of 'the very conviction of the superiority of France'. Even one of Trevor's interlocutors admitted the weakness of the United Provinces, which he described as 'a trunk without feet, without arms and without a head . . . her weakness appeared to him incurable'. The only remedy, he believed, was 'some standard erected in the cause of public liberty', to which the healthy forces in the United Provinces could rally. But that was a long way off. For the moment, no help could be expected from this quarter. Things were no better in Vienna. 'The House of Austria,' Walpole noted in March 1739, 'is now in so weak a condition' on account of the Turkish war, that it was unable to provide any assistance to Britain; Trevor also remarked on the Emperor being 'drained so low by his late and disastrous war'. Moreover with the increase of French influence in Vienna, some sort of attempt to subvert the Barrier itself was daily expected. The German princes were preoccupied with the Palatine succession, Sweden was hostile, Russia was 'at too great a distance to afford us any relief'. Britain was, in short, 'at present without any one ally upon the Continent'. Indeed, it was perfectly possible that 'the greatest part of Europe would unite against us'.[38]

In any case, there was no guarantee that military action would be successful. 'I am not sanguine,' Lord Hervey remarked, 'as to think that we have victory chained to our chariot-wheel, or that we must be successful in every war we engage in.' The Earl of Isla, a staunch Scottish Whig like his elder brother the Duke of Argyll, reminded peers that 'Wars and victories . . . make a fine figure in history, or even in a newspaper . . . but upon balancing accounts we should have found, I believe, that the profit would not answer the charge.' Horatio Walpole warned, 'The event is doubtful, let the hopes of either party at the beginning be never so well founded. It is not the first time we have heard of the event of war's turning out contrary to all human appearances.'

Indeed, the recent example of Charles VI's disastrous attack on the Turks was a sobering one. In a pamphlet widely distributed by his brother Robert, Horatio Walpole punctured the idea of a lucrative risk-free naval bonanza. In a privateering war Spain would give as good as it got. But as the pro-government cleric, the Reverend Henry Etough later noted, 'This very instructive and prophetic pamphlet, as it had no influence on a mad and vain nation, is a memorable proof of the tenacious force of nonsense.'[39]

Meanwhile, British ministers made strenuous efforts to escape isolation on the Continent. Negotiations for the renewal of the treaty of 1734 with Denmark were set in train. This was vital if Sweden was to be contained in the Baltic. Talks were begun in 1738, but almost immediately stalled when the Danes attempted to annex the territory of Steinhorst, and were ejected by the Hanoverians after a short battle. Once again, the King's German preoccupations threatened to cut across British grand strategy. By May 1739, however, a subsidy treaty with Denmark was on the table. Even the sceptic Carteret, who had been bitterly critical of government passivity, accepted that this was a move in the right direction. Unless Britain could escape her isolation and 'form a confederacy' in Europe, she would have no hope of containing France and Spain. The Danish treaty, therefore, was 'but a preparatory step towards accomplishing so great and necessary a design'. He supported the paying of what was literally Danegeld, in order to deny France an alliance with Denmark. This was essential not just to secure the 'tranquillity of the north' but also because 'if the French should join with the Spaniards against us, it would be of the most dangerous consequence, to have the navy of France increased and supported by the ships and seamen of Denmark as well as Sweden.' The link between Britain's European isolation and the danger of naval inferiority was once again made explicit.[40]

This connection between Britain's Continental alliances and her naval security was central to British strategic discourse. As the Lord Chancellor, the Earl of Hardwicke, put it in March 1739, 'I know . . . it may be said, that as we have the good luck to be environed by the sea, and have a fleet superior to any that France and Spain, joined together, can bring against us, we may protect our own trade and dominions, and so much infest the trade and dominions of our enemies, as to make them, at last, glad to agree reasonable terms.' The snag, he pointed out, was that 'if our enemies are, by their great land armies, absolute masters upon the Continent, they may not only prevent our receiving assistance from any of the princes or states upon the Continent, but they may induce or oblige them all to join against us,' and close their ports to British trade. Britain's commercial prosperity, in short, was dependent on the European balance of power. So was her naval predominance. As Lord Hervey argued, 'We are at present superior to both [France and Spain] at sea; but as France has great numbers of seamen, they would soon get ships of war, if they were to be at no expense in defending themselves at land; so that they might soon rig out a powerful squadron.'[41]

None of this could deflect a last great burst of naval chauvinism. Patriot speeches now challenged Britain's enemies to bring on the three corners of the world in arms so that Britain could shock them. The Duke of Argyll announced that 'We . . . are masters of that element whereon the cause must be decided, and let all our enemies, either professed or secret, nay, let all the neutral powers in Europe unite their naval force, we have a fleet now at sea that is able to beat them all.' As the year wore on, the demand for war grew ever shriller. In early May, Argyll announced that 'We must beat them [the Spaniards] into a better, I hope a righter opinion of us,' for they were a 'contemptible, though insolent nation'. 'For God's sake,' he cried, 'what are we afraid of? . . . Must we do nothing but what France gives us leave to do?' 'Let France take whatever part she will,' Chesterfield remarked in early June, 'She cannot look us in the face at sea; she cannot prevent our seizing the Spanish plate fleet.' Patriot scribblers, such as Sir William Keith, dismissed all European entanglements and called instead for a 'powerful armament by sea' and praised the 'British admiral, at the head of his fleet [as] by far the best ambassador and plenipotentiary, that can be made use of in a conjuncture such as the present'. Press critics of the pacific policy towards Spain, such as the *Gentleman's Magazine*, also refused to acknowledge any serious European constraints.[42]

A general sense of crisis now gripped the country, as the frustration over the maritime disputes with Spain mutated into a much broader critique of Walpole's foreign policy. Pulteney remarked that 'considering the unfortunate situation the affairs not only of this nation but of Europe, are in at present, it is a subject of as serious a nature, as ever came before a British parliament.' Everybody knew what that meant: it was code for impeachment. 'We have got no security,' Carteret thundered around the same time, 'and, I am afraid, little or no reparation.' 'The state of affairs in Europe is . . . formidable' and was 'growing every year more and more so'. All this, he claimed, was the result not of 'the nature of things, but [of] the late measures pursued by France and us'. There followed a long diatribe against the Treaty of Hanover, the alienation of the Emperor over the Ostend Company, the uselessness of the Dutch, the Spanish advances in the Mediterranean, and so on. Britain was now 'insulted and plundered by impotent neighbours abroad'. All this, he concluded, was the result, not of 'a vigorous but a pusillanimous conduct'.[43]

The ministry wilted under the pressure. Boxed in by Hanoverian concerns, the deteriorating European balance, domestic distractions and the patriot din, they began to turn on each other. Thus Horatio Walpole complained to his brother that 'nobody has credit or courage enough to speak plainly . . . in their respective departments; and if you venture to do it sometimes, 'tis in a cursory manner. You receive short answer; domestic affairs employ your time and your thoughts; and the foreign mischief continues.' At the same time, perhaps sensing the inevitable, ministerial figures now began to adopt naval and insular rhetoric themselves. Hardwicke, for example, conceded in March 1739 that 'it is the peculiar happiness of this island, that no one nation in the world can attack us.' Newcastle in particular made a rapid – and temporary – conversion to maritime measures. After all, he remarked in late September,

if we go on despising what people think & say, we shall not have it long in our power, to direct what measures shall be taken . . . A little yielding to times, a plain dispassionate stat[ing] of our case, with proper assurances to the Public, that right Measures & vigorous ones, shall be undertaken against Spain, might have a good effect before the parliament meets, but if we are to go on in extolling the Convention, I say it with great concern, it will not do, & we shall feel the consequences of it.

Newcastle now set out to re-educate himself as a navalist, starting with Swift's famous pamphlet of 1711, *The conduct of the allies*. He became a prisoner of the public mood and his own demands for additional resources to intimidate Spain. 'I dread the consequences,' he wrote at the very end of September, 'of an expensive but necessary preparation, without having done any thing, or seeming to have any real solid plan for that purpose. It can only be done in the West Indies, & there the author of *The conduct of the allies* says we should have carried our arms [in] the last war.' Newcastle added that although he was 'always answered, that it is improper to say we will undertake some thing, or some expedition in the West Indies, till we know what. Let us determine to do something; we shall soon find out what may be undertaken.' In effect, the Duke was succumbing to the view that 'something' – anything – was better than doing nothing. Newcastle was reinforced in this stance by intelligence reports which showed the French to be bluffing.[44]

In the late summer and early autumn of 1739 the situation quickly worsened. As a final feeble gesture towards public opinion, yielding to the spirit of the time and in order to put pressure on Spain to make rapid restitution under the Convention, Newcastle refused to withdraw Admiral Haddock's squadron from the Mediterranean as promised at the Pardo. Spain refused to pay up their £27,000 until he did so. Thus was the Convention ruptured and war with Spain duly followed in September. In mid November, the King's Speech at the opening of Parliament cited 'the repeated injuries and violences committed by that nation upon the commerce of these kingdoms, and their obstinacy, and notorious violation of the most solemn engagements [which] have rendered [war] unavoidable'. For the first and last time in the eighteenth century, Britain had entered into a major war primarily for colonial and commercial reasons.[45]

II

Imperial Isolation, 1740–1742

If there is no diversion by a land war upon the Continent and we have no security against invasion from France besides our own strength ... I am afraid that by next spring or summer, the seat of the war will be in this island.[1]

Horatio Walpole, late 1740

By this accident, the princes of Germany are left without a head ... the Germanic Body is thereby rendered lifeless and inactive, and the House of Austria is on every side environed with enemies, ready to tear from it the whole or a great part of its dominions.[2]

Lord Hyndford, future ambassador to Prussia, on the death of Charles VI, 1740

The [German] Empire may be considered as the bulwark of Great Britain, which, if it be thrown down, leaves us naked and defenceless.[3]

Henry Pelham, April 1741

I fear that now America must be fought for in Europe. It looked last year, as if the old world was to be fought for in the new; but the tables are turned ... Whatever success we have in the former [America] I doubt it will always finally follow the fate of the latter [Europe].[4]

Earl of Hardwicke, August 1741

At the beginning of the new decade, Britain was forced to grapple with two overlapping imperial crises. In the colonies and on the high seas there was a hot war with Spain, which went well initially but soon stagnated. Meantime, France was limbering up to a naval intervention in support of Spain; there was widespread fear that without some form of Continental diversion, Britain would face the combined might of the Bourbon fleets alone. The resulting domestic controversy was soon overshadowed, however, by events in Europe. The death of Emperor Charles VI, and French sponsorship of rival claimants to the imperial crown, weakened Britain's position within the Holy Roman Empire. Worse still, Frederick the Great's surprise invasion of Silesia threatened to trigger a partition of the Habsburg monarchy. The French advance also reopened the question of the security of Hanover. All this triggered a searching strategic debate in London about the need to shore up Britain's bulwarks in the Empire, and which politicians should be blamed for their neglect. Britain had begun a war of choice with Spain in the colonies; it now faced a struggle against France in central Europe which could not be avoided.

The war with Spain was the most popular and sought-after conflict in British history. 'No war,' Carteret remarked, 'was ever entered into with greater unanimity amongst all ranks and degrees of men.' Only the old Jacobite MP Sir John Hynde Cotton refused to support it. Parliament saw a last great explosion of exuberant chauvinism. 'War,' Carteret claimed in mid November 1739, 'is a sort of storm, and like other storms, the more violent it is, the sooner it will be over. If we push it vigorously, and in the right place, it cannot be of long continuance.' A fortnight later, Pulteney gave the Commons an impromptu lecture on naval strategy. He rubbed his hands at the prospect of 'annoy[ing the Spanish] as much as possible, by making incursions, and plundering the coasts of their dominions, even in Europe. Can they prevent this as long as we are masters at sea? No, sir.' Henry Archer, the MP for Warwick and a major supporter of the new colony of Georgia, announced that 'it is with pleasure . . . that we must now behold the naval strength and power of our country sent forth to avenge our wrongs, spreading terror round the coasts of our enemy, and assuming the sovereignty of the sea without a rival.' Not even the diplomatic isolation of Britain could puncture this navalist reverie. 'If we have now . . . the misfortune of having no allies,' Carteret argued, 'we have, at least, this advantage resulting from it' – which was that the war against Spain could be prosecuted unilaterally, 'without asking the advice of any power in Europe'. Walpole himself was unmoved by the jingoistic spectacle. 'They are ringing the bells now,' he famously remarked, 'very soon they will be wringing their hands.'[5]

The war fever was not confined to Parliament. A huge wave of popular enthusiasm also swept the country as a whole, particularly the capital and the seaports. The Royal Navy set off in pursuit of colonial glory in the Atlantic, the Caribbean and the Pacific Ocean. There were high hopes that the commanding Admiral, Edward Vernon, would deliver a mortal blow to the Spanish position in Central and Southern America. He had been a navalist thorn in the side of the ministry throughout the late 1730s. In 1729, after a failed attempt by another admiral to take the Spanish stronghold of Porto Bello on the Isthmus of Panama – where most of the dreaded Spanish coastguard was based – Vernon had promised to take the place with six ships. Now one would see. The European market, which was worth vastly more than the entire British colonial trade, was left to the mercy of Spanish, and soon French, privateers. A quick look at the convoys organized by the Royal Navy in 1739–40, after the outbreak of war, confirms these priorities. There were twenty-five outward convoys from Britain to Portugal and the Mediterranean, and only ten to the West Indies and North America; thirty-one homeward from Portugal and the Mediterranean and fourteen from the West Indies and North America. The trade with 'Old Spain' alone was worth more than what Britain could hope to gain from her in the colonies.[6]

At first, all went well. In November Admiral Vernon captured the notorious Spanish coastguard base of Porto Bello, with six ships. The effect of this news was electric. The Admiral became an instant popular hero: ballads were composed, maps and prints produced, and trees planted in his honour. More medals were struck for Vernon than for any other eighteenth-century British figure. To this day, many Portobellos across the British Isles, including the Portobello Road in London, the Portobello area of Edinburgh, and the Portobello barracks (now officially known as Cathal Brugha barracks) in Dublin bear testimony to the celebratory mood of the time. Vernon was the ideal popular and anti-governmental hero. As one might expect, enthusiasm for Vernon also ran high in the North American colonies. Benjamin Franklin was an enthusiastic supporter of the Admiral, and of the whole idea of commercial expansion at Spain's expense. Over the next two years, some 3,600 Americans, most of them Franklin's fellow Pennsylvanians, volunteered to serve with Vernon as he carried the war further southwards. One American who did so was Lawrence Washington, who named his estate in Virginia 'Mount Vernon' in honour of his former commander. In 1761, the estate was inherited by his younger half-brother and later first President of the United States, George Washington. The public acclaim for Admiral Vernon was about more than Porto Bello, the Spanish war, colonial commerce as a whole, anti-Catholicism, popular patriotism, and even attacking the despised ministry of Robert Walpole. It was nothing less than a celebration of British patriotic, naval and insular virtue. Every ballad, every pewter mug, every statue devoted to Vernon and Porto Bello underlined the claim that the key to British identity, security and prosperity lay not in Europe, as the old Whig orthodoxy had it, but overseas.[7]

19. The most unlikely objects were used to celebrate national events. This fan shows the familiar image of Admiral Vernon's six ships blasting the seaport of Porto Bello in 1739. The poem on the reverse of the fan reads:

> *Hark the British Cannon Thunders,*
> *See my lads six ships appear;*
> *Every Briton acting wonders,*
> *Strikes the Southern World with fear.*
> *Porto Bello fam'd in story*
> *Now at last submits to fate;*
> *Vernon's Courage gains us glory,*
> *And his mercy proves us great.*

Members of the government tried hard to claim the victory as their own, but their minds were elsewhere. Popular opinion and opposition rhetoric at this point largely ignored Europe; the ministry could not afford to. For in 1739–40, Britain was more isolated than at any previous point in her history. Things were potentially much worse than in 1711–13, when Britain had ditched her Dutch and Austrian allies towards the end of the War of the Spanish Succession. That had been in the course of disengaging from a long conflict during which all sides had exhausted themselves. Now Britain would *begin* the struggle alone. No help could be expected from the Habsburgs, who had been comprehensively alienated by Britain's failure to support them during the War of the Polish Succession; it had been the French not the British who conducted the prestigious mediation which allowed the Austrians to disengage from their disastrous war with Turkey in 1738–9. Nor was there much point in looking to Frederick William of Prussia, with whom relations had been poor ever since the 1720s. It was probably not the government's fault that the Dutch were refusing to cooperate, but that was little comfort. It seemed as if Britain had turned its back on the Continent; now the Continent had turned its back on Britain.

Dominating everything was the question of French intentions. Here British intelligence sources indicated that a rapid Spanish collapse, perhaps precipitated by the fall of the key fortress of Cartagena on the north coast of South America, would bring France into the war. This was one of the reasons, apart from natural inertia, why the administration did not follow up Vernon's victories with greater vigour. The intelligence reports were accurate. For the moment, it suited Fleury to see Britain sink deeper into a colonial morass. This kept the Royal Navy occupied, and tied Madrid closer to Versailles. He did not mind some opportunist British 'piracy', but refused to countenance any gains which would tilt the European balance in Britain's direction. As Fleury told the British ambassador in April 1740: 'Pillage and plunder as much as you can, but don't possess yourselves of any places belonging to the Spaniards.' Fleury, it is clear, had his eye firmly not so much on the colonial sphere *per se*, but on the relationship between the overseas and European theatres.[8]

Walpole put his faith in the restraint of Fleury: this was the prize for which the government had surrendered so much. But how long would that last? More to the point, how long would *he* last, and how long would he be able to keep more radical voices in Versailles on a leash? British ministers knew that the pressure for naval action in support of Spain and the Bourbon family compact was growing by the day. 'We take for granted,' the Duke of Newcastle, Secretary of State for the

South, remarked in August 1739, before the commencement of hostilities, 'that France will join Spain, and that we shall be attacked at home'.[9] Three months later he warned the House of Lords that 'notwithstanding the great age of [Fleury], notwithstanding his present peaceable disposition, we cannot entirely trust to it: we know that he can alter that disposition, when he finds it proper or necessary so to do.' Moreover, the French navy had expanded considerably in the late 1730s; together with the Spanish fleet it was a serious threat, as Newcastle and others never tired of repeating, just across the English Channel. To make matters worse, the Pretender, who had been a useful parliamentary and popular bogeyman throughout the 1730s, now became once again a major strategic factor in British calculations. In 1739–40 the Spaniards, unsurprisingly, made approaches to Charles Edward, and if in Versailles, Fleury was still refusing overt support for the Pretender, what would happen after he died or was sidelined was anybody's guess. From early 1740 onwards, in short, Jacobitism had to be reckoned a real threat if supported by Franco-Spanish naval power. Worst fears were confirmed in September 1740 with news of a French squadron setting sail for the West Indies in order to deter British attacks on Spanish forces there.[10]

There was one ray of hope on the horizon. Frederick William of Prussia – George II's old *bête noire* – died in May 1740, to be succeeded by his son, Frederick II. The time seemed ripe for an overture to Berlin. Frederick's mother, Sophie Dorothea, was the sister of George II of England; in late June 1740 she floated yet another plan for a double marriage. The Hanoverian government was enthusiastic. Nobody was expecting any trouble from the young King, who was known to have suffered terribly under his brutish father, and who had been covertly financed by George II in the 1730s. In terms of foreign policy Frederick, the author of *Anti-Machiavell* (1739), a tract critical of bad faith and rapacity in politics, was thought to be a moderate figure. But there were worrying signs. One of the first things Frederick had done on coming to the throne was to repay the money George had sent him as crown prince, as if to demonstrate his independence. At the same time, he was stubborn on the question of the western German principalities of Jülich-Berg which George – fearing to provoke France – was unwilling to let him have. In the end, the Prusso-British alliance negotiations were to founder on this very issue in the summer of 1740. Britain remained isolated.[11]

George tended to see all these problems not only from London, but also from Hanover, where he spent the summer of 1740 in the company of his Secretary of State for the Northern Department, Lord Harrington. Some British observers had worried that Hanoverian concerns would interfere with a Prussian alliance: Horatio Walpole spoke in September 1739 of the 'little, low, partial, Electoral notions', which might drive Berlin into the arms of the French. In fact, George was open to the idea of an agreement with Prussia, and sent his Hanoverian chief minister, Gerlach Adolf, Baron Münchhausen, to Berlin for negotiations in 1740. At this time his Hanoverian servants generally regarded their fellow Protestant Prussian neighbours with benevolence. In August 1740 a Hanoverian memorandum actually called for a Prussian succession in Jülich and Berg, on the grounds that it would strengthen the barrier against France. Indeed, it was seen as desirable that Prussia should expand further in that direction, since the larger the gain, the stronger the barrier would be. This paper seems to have been intended primarily for the consideration of British ministers, as part of the debate on grand strategy. It was a gambit to which Castlereagh would return more than sixty years later.[12]

If anything, the reluctance to engage Frederick came from London. The problem was that concessions to Frederick would always be at the expense of France or Austria. There was no way of squaring this circle: Britain would have to choose between winning Berlin and offending either Vienna or Versailles, perhaps both. Newcastle, for example, complained that 'the advantages to be gained to the King by this alliance were purely Electoral; so that this country is to go into a war with France to procure great acquisitions for the King of Prussia and as great ones for the Elector of Hanover.' In part, this grumbling reflected Newcastle's steady alienation from Walpole's crumbling administration, in part also his fear of being supplanted in the King's affections by Harrington in Hanover; and in part the reflex that 'low Electoral [Hanoverian] notions' were always to blame. But most of all, it showed how the need to prevent France from being driven into the arms of Spain trumped all other concerns. When George refused Frederick's demand to annex Jülich and Berg, therefore, he was speaking as King and not as Elector.[13]

Towards the second half of 1740, things suddenly took a turn for the worse. In October, the Emperor, Charles VI, died. Europe had been preparing for his death for nearly fifteen years, and yet when it happened it took nearly everybody by surprise. British ministers saw the danger at once. If France was going to unpick the Pragmatic Sanction – the arrangement by which Charles's eldest daughter Maria Theresa was to come into the undivided Habsburg inheritance – this was the time to do so. If France managed to unbolt the House of Austria from the imperial crown of Germany by pushing through her own candidate at the forthcoming election, the resulting loss of Austrian power could be fatal to Britain. The Scottish peer and diplomat Lord Hyndford, soon to be ambassador to Prussia, warned that the death of Charles had left 'the princes of Germany ... without a head'. This in turn, Hyndford continued, rendered 'the Germanic Body ... lifeless and inactive', exposing the Habsburgs to invasion and partition. At the very least, as Newcastle fretted, the election of a new Emperor would 'furnish a loophole' to those who wished to unpick the Pragmatic Sanction. All this mattered to Britain, Hyndford stressed, because it threatened 'the liberties of Europe', and thus 'the trade [and] the navigation of this kingdom'. He warned of the 'dangerous state this nation will be reduced to, if the northern powers should be engaged in a war against one another, and the flames of a civil war kindled among the princes of Germany'. The result he feared was that 'The several branches of the House of Bourbon will then be left at full liberty to turn their whole united force against this nation, and against this united force we must stand single and alone.' As ever, British statesmen worried that the fall of bastions in Europe would be followed by the erosion of British naval supremacy and a cross-Channel invasion. Exactly the same arguments were being made in the privacy of the cabinet. It was, in short, events in the Holy Roman Empire, not in Spanish America, that most concerned them in 1740.[14]

By now, the government and the public were nursing a massive postcolonial hangover. Throughout 1740 Admiral Vernon's campaign stagnated, partly because the ministry feared that too vigorous a prosecution of the war would bring in the French, and partly because of factors beyond London's immediate control, such as the weather, disease and the fortunes of war. Spain proved to be no pushover. In June 1740 an attack on the Spanish fort of St Augustine in Florida miscarried. A few months later, Vernon was unsettled by the arrival of a Franco-Spanish squadron in the western hemisphere. This was the first tangible manifestation in the colonial and naval theatre of Britain's European isolation. In late 1740 Captain Anson was dispatched around Cape Horn with much fanfare to attack Spanish shipping on the west coast of South America, but his ships were heavily battered by storms; all of the small landing force died on the voyage. The Spanish War, which started with such high hopes, was fast becoming a 'tar baby', with which nobody wanted to be associated. In late October 1740, as the Duke of Newcastle tried to justify himself, Walpole replied tersely: 'What do you mean? This war is yours, you have had the conduct of it, I wish you joy of it.'[15]

The opposition exploited these disasters to attack the government from two sides. First, it demanded greater openness through the release of 'Papers relating to the war with Spain', so that the conduct of the war could be subjected to parliamentary and public scrutiny. The intent here, of course, was to embarrass Walpole, but the call also reflected the sense that the nation's security was the legitimate concern of its parliamentary representatives. As Sir John Barnard argued, 'a parliamentary inquiry into a minister's conduct is not a trial: it is a sort of debt which every minister owes to the public. A minister is a sort of agent or steward for the public; and is not every steward obliged to give an account for his stewardship?' The people, he claimed, thus had a right to know how war with Spain had come about. 'Is it not natural,' he continued, 'for the people to inquire, how we came to allow the Spaniards quietly, on our part at least, to wrest from our ancient ally the Emperor the rich and beautiful kingdom of the two Sicilies?' Was it not reasonable to ask why the Royal Navy had been used to install the Spanish claimant, Don Carlos, there? And as for the argument that inquiries were improper during hostilities, William Pulteney argued that parliamentary scrutiny was more necessary in wartime than in peace, 'because weak measures may then do much more mischief ... A time of war is, therefore, so far from being an improper time for a parliamentary inquiry, that such inquiries are more necessary, and ought to be more frequent in time of war, than in time of peace.'[16]

By going back to the late 1720s, Barnard indicated just how wide-ranging the proposed inquiry was intended to be. It would not just cover the countdown to war with Spain, but the whole fiasco of Britain's European isolation: the betrayal of Austria during the War of the Polish Succession in the 1730s; selling the pass to Spain over Italy after 1729; and perhaps even as far back as the Treaty of Hanover in 1725. And as for it not being a 'trial', Walpole knew that a parliamentary inquiry, with attendant popular frenzy, would be more of a lynch mob. There were hundreds in Parliament, and tens of thousands without, who would like nothing better than to impeach Walpole and possibly even send him to the scaffold. For this reason he and his allies were determined to prevent an investigation at all costs. 'All such inquiries,' his brother Horatio argued, must 'be of dangerous consequence to the tranquillity of the nation', because they were 'generally set on foot by the personal enemies of those in the administration, and are usually carried on with a zeal for condemning, which stifles every sentiment of compassion, and makes human frailties appear to be monstrous crimes.' In any case, he remarked, an inquiry would reveal British intentions towards Spain and thus compromise military operations.[17]

Vernon's early victories towards the end of 1739 briefly eased the public pressure on Walpole, but prompted his political opponents to redouble their efforts. In late February 1740, Pulteney proposed a motion 'For an inquiry into the conduct of the authors and advisors of the Convention with Spain'. In the course of introducing it, he rather let the cat out of the bag by announcing that the 'discontents at present lie smouldering under the hopes of a successful war, but they are far from being removed or extinguished'. It was becoming clear that nothing would deflect the opposition from its intent to pin the crisis of British grand strategy on the personal corruption and unconstitutionality of the 'Robinocracy', as Walpole's vice-like grip on national politics was dubbed. The underlying opposition strategy, which was to use the failure of British foreign policy as a lever to demonstrate the unconstitutionality of Walpole's administration, had not changed. But the critique had now shifted from the demand for war to a critique of its execution.[18]

The opposition now alleged the government was failing to prosecute the war with sufficient vigour and with the right strategy. Thus in April 1740 it put forward a motion to censure the ministry 'for not sending land forces with Admiral Vernon to America'. The Duke of Argyll claimed that 'had such a number been embarked ... I make no doubt but by this time we might have been in the possession of a place in the West Indies, which might have paid us for all the expense of this war, had we kept it.' Critics suspected that the campaign was bogged down not just because the ministry had denied Vernon the reinforcements he needed, but because it had failed to grasp the whole concept of a naval strategy. Many parliamentarians and pamphleteers now turned themselves into amateur naval strategists. A judicious combination of blockade, major fleet actions and amphibious operations, they argued, would suffice to win the war on their own. However large the Spanish army, Pulteney argued in late November 1739, it could not prevent a landing force from putting ashore to 'ransack a great part of the adjacent country, and to retire with safety on board their ships'. In this way, he enthused, 'we might harass their troops, and keep their whole seacoast [American and European] in a perpetual alarm'. Porto Bello had whetted, not satisfied, appetites; and if the idea of a self-financing war had not worked out, then the answer seemed to be more war, more competently executed.[19]

As opportunities were missed overseas, the sense of vulnerability grew at home. The ministry knew that isolation in Europe would very quickly translate into naval inferiority. The trouble was, as Horatio Walpole remarked in late December 1740, that whereas in previous years the bulk of the Navy had been in home or European waters, 'at present the Royal Navy may be said to be employed in America, a thing unknown until now'. This would be very dangerous if there was an open rupture with another European power. And worse was to come. In his anticipatory enthusiasm, one pamphleteer had described Vernon as the 'Conqueror of Cartagena'. This fortress lay on the north coast of Spanish South America, in present-day Colombia, and was the next target. But the assault on Cartagena in March–April 1741 was repulsed with heavy loss of life; an attack on Santiago de Cuba in July–August also ended in fiasco. Of 10,000 men sent to the Caribbean, more than 7,000 died, mainly of disease. Vernon had dealt with the shore batteries at Cartagena quickly enough, but the army proved unable to take the forts, which were commanded by an elderly Spaniard with only one eye, one leg and one arm. Vernon commented that 'Our gentlemen of parade [the army], who having been long trained in nothing but reviews, can't so readily shake off the rust of idleness as our active scene seems to require of them.' Following the Admiral's lead, contemporary critics blamed failure on the lack of a unified command structure, the incompetence of the army, or political constraints on the Navy. The hand-wringing and finger-pointing predicted by Walpole was in full swing.[20]

For the moment, however, navalist enthusiasm remained unabated. Unlike subsidy payments, and land forces in Europe, naval operations, particularly combined ventures in the colonies, were popular. They had been ever since Drake famously singed the Spanish King's beard at Cadiz

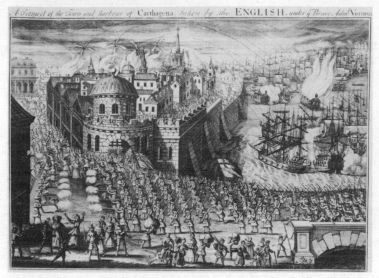

A Prospect of the Town and harbour of Carthagena *taken by the* ENGLISH *under ye Brave Adml* Vernon

20. Despite the optimistic title of this print, Cartagena proved to be a port too far. The failure plunged the British political nation into deep despair.

in Queen Elizabeth's time, and they have remained so in the British popular historical imagination ever since. But in reality, combined operations were messy and expensive; one was as likely to burn one's own fingers as any Spanish beards. For a start, the word 'combined operations' is not only a modern anachronism, but misleading. These were really 'consecutive', not combined, operations. Getting to the objective, which was often thousands of miles away, and putting the army ashore required considerable navigational skill on the part of the Navy. But that was still, relatively speaking, the easy part. Most landings were uncontested and, unlike in the twentieth century, the Navy could generally suppress the shore batteries. Once on dry land, however, and out of range of the ships' guns, the lightly equipped assault force was on its own, often with very poor intelligence and vulnerable to disease, particularly in exotic climes. It therefore made sense to divide the command between two equals, one naval and one military, as neither could command the necessary expertise on their own, and there was generally enough time to discuss options at some length. In short, the Caribbean campaign against Spain ran into difficulties because of Vernon's determination to run a land war for which he was not qualified. One way or the other, amphibious expeditions were not the universal panacea for Britain's strategic and political ills which the 'patriots' of the late 1730s had made them out to be.[21]

As true believers, the advocates of maritime and colonial expansionism were not sobered by the failures at Cartagena and Santiago. On the contrary, they argued that their hero had not been enough supported, that weak and perhaps treasonable ministers had betrayed the project. Already in late 1739 the constituents of one Nottingham MP had warned that 'It is not a little low piratical war . . . but a vigorous prosecution of the war . . . that will . . . maintain and defend our ancient trade, commerce and navigation.' Now, as the euphoria of Porto Bello ebbed without further victories, the government's critics unleashed a torrent of strategic and tactical second-guessing in and out of Parliament. Why, it was demanded, had Vernon not been instructed to pursue his advantage? Why were no naval and land reinforcements sent to enable him to do so? Why had there been no amphibious descents on Spain itself? Why had Admiral Haddock not been ordered to attack Spain more vigorously in the Mediterranean? All this was garnished with unfavourable comparisons with bygone Elizabethan and Cromwellian exploits across the globe. In that respect it closely resembled elements of the patriot critique of James I in the early 1620s. The problem, as far as the critics were concerned, was not that British policy had been too navalist and too isolationist, but that it had not been sufficiently so.[22]

Like the celebrations of Vernon the year before, the parliamentary and extra-parliamentary debates of late 1740 were not just about policy towards Spain and attacking the government of the day. They were also about the British constitution and Britain's wider role in the world. It was through a foreign policy critique that the opposition, the political nation and the 'people' could articulate their demands if not for broader participation, then at least for constraints on executive power. Ministers, by contrast, pointed to the limitations and vagaries of military power. 'People in all countries,' the Duke of Newcastle complained, 'and in this more than any other, are fond to hear of sieges, battles and bloodshed, and apt to imagine that there is nothing too difficult for their fleets and armies to undertake; and therefore they are very apt to complain, when their warmest expectations are not answered.' To this Lord Bathurst

21. The most important theatre of naval operations during the War of the Austrian Succession was the Mediterranean. Admiral Haddock was accused of letting the Spanish army land in Italy unopposed so that the French would spare Hanover the rigours of military occupation.

responded that 'the people when they are engaged in war, expect to hear of battles and bloodshed: as they pay heavy taxes for supporting the war, and suffer many inconveniences on account of it.' Indeed, he concluded, the nation 'have a right to that expectation: because the more hotly it is pursued, the sooner it will be at an end'.[23]

Central to all this was the demand for greater openness on foreign policy, at least in Parliament. This had been a staple of the opposition critique in the late 1730s, and it was raised again in early 1740 as the

British war effort lost momentum, but by late 1740, and especially after the fiasco at Cartagena at the beginning of 1741, these voices swelled to a mighty chorus. Ministerial arguments for the need for secrecy to protect national interests were rejected. The Earl of Chesterfield argued that 'it is a very new doctrine, to say, that nothing can be communicated to this House without making it public.' Members of Parliament, he continued, 'not only may, but sometimes ought to offer ... advice to the Crown, even with respect to foreign affairs, or the affairs of peace and war'; and to do so they had to be properly informed. Similarly, William Pitt observed that 'our time cannot be more usefully employed during a war than examining how it has been conducted, and settling the degree of confidence that may be reposed in those to whose care are entrusted our reputations, our fortunes and our lives.' It was for this reason that the thinly veiled charges of treason took on so much importance. 'Have we prosecuted the war in the most proper places? Have we prosecuted it in any place?' one peer asked rhetorically in November 1740. The reason it had not been, he suggested, was that 'there seems to have been something more than neglect: there really seems to have been a formed design, to prevent his [Vernon] being able to prosecute the war' in the West Indies.[24]

Moreover, the opposition recognized and welcomed the force of popular opinion. 'I am sorry to observe,' the Earl of Halifax, a confirmed navalist, told Parliament, 'that it is now a common topic in our debates here, as well as in our conversation without doors, that public praise ought to be despised, and the opinion of the giddy multitude altogether disregarded.' Instead, one should engage with the popular 'clamour' and put the public right where necessary. The opposition Whig Sir John Barnard explained the 'unpopularity of our minister' not with the bellicosity of the mob but 'from their having judged better, and more disinterestedly, of the circumstances of our foreign affairs'. Indeed, Barnard expanded this argument into a more general critique of the political system and its failure truly to represent the opinion of 'the people'. 'It is well known,' he claimed, 'how unequally the nation is represented in this House,' particularly London. This meant that 'we ought not to judge of the sentiments of the better sort of people from what appears to be the sentiments of this House'. Barnard then went on to argue that a foreign policy, either pacific or bellicose, which was not in tune with this political nation was doomed to failure. The case for parliamentary reform, though not spelt out in this instance, was at least very strongly implied.[25]

Then, right at the end of December 1740, came the thunderbolt after which nothing would ever be the same again. Frederick II invaded Silesia, making clear his determination to annex the province, even at the price of a total partition of the Habsburg lands. Prussian armies swept south and defeated the Austrians at a hard-fought battle at Mollwitz on 10 April 1741. To make matters worse, Frederick embarked on negotiations with the French, concluding a defensive alliance in June of that year. In it he was promised Lower Silesia and Breslau in return for his vote in support of the French candidate for the German imperial crown. By then it was abundantly clear that the French were planning a bid for supremacy in Germany, probably by putting forward their ally the Bavarian Elector, Charles Albert, for election as Emperor. If that happened, Newcastle warned, it 'must end in flinging the whole Empire into the hands of France'. The Dutch refused to budge. Hanover was in danger from French forces. All eyes in London now turned to central Europe. If Austria collapsed, and with it the European balance upon which Britain's security rested, any colonial triumph would be transitory at best.[26]

This was immediately grasped by the opposition. Their hatred of Walpole and his 'Robinocracy' may have had its roots in the corruption, oligarchy and manipulation of the past twenty years, but it was foreign policy which dominated the parliamentary 'Motion for the Removal of Sir Robert Walpole' in mid February 1741. Five of the seven accusations related in one way or another to diplomacy, strategy or the armed forces. Moreover, the foreign-policy charges were also qualitatively the most serious. This was, as Carteret explained, because 'errors in foreign affairs are worse than in domestic, for you cannot correct them.' And there could be no more fatal or culpable dereliction of duty than that alleged in article five of the motion, which stated that 'we apprehend that, by the conduct of Sir Robert Walpole, in relation to foreign affairs during the course of this administration, the balance of power in Europe has been destroyed; the House of Bourbon has been aggrandized . . . [and] the House of Austria has been depressed.' Moreover, the article continued, 'if such a change in the system of Europe, occasioned by the misconduct of any minister whatsoever, would be criminal, we cannot think it the less so in one who joined in the prosecution of the authors of the Treaty of Utrecht upon the particular charge of having reduced the House of Austria too low, and left the House of Bourbon too powerful.' The purpose of the motion was thus not merely to depose Walpole but to clear the way for his impeachment.[27]

Many thought – and the ministry feared – that it would not end there. The young William Pitt, who was already beginning to make a name for himself as a firebrand critic of Walpole and particularly his foreign policy, announced in February 1741 that 'The minister who neglects any just opportunity of promoting the power, or increasing the wealth of his country, is to be considered as an enemy to his fellow subjects.' Walpole, he charged, had betrayed the very instrument – the Navy – 'by which victory might be obtained'; he had 'impoverished the nation', rather than enriched it; and raised armies 'only to be exposed to pestilence' and 'compel[ed] them to perish in sight of their enemies without molesting them'. This was a very wide definition of malfeasance, but there was more. A mere censure, which was all the initial motion suggested, could not be enough. Surely, Pitt thundered, he 'who has doomed thousands to the grave, who has cooperated with foreign powers against his country, who has protected its enemies and dishonoured its arms' should be 'stripped' not only of office and honours, but also 'of his life'. At the very least, he should be deprived of his ill-gotten gains.[28]

All the foreign policy debates of the previous two decades now burst into new life: the old arguments about the Treaty of Hanover, the Treaty of Seville, the French reversion on Lorraine, the Austrian losses in Italy, and the recent colonial grievances with Spain were now given another thorough airing. But the centrepiece was undoubtedly the imminent collapse of Austrian power in central Europe; the critique was couched in terms of the European balance of power, not of navalist virtue. It was not too much but too little commitment to the Continent of which the government was accused. Thus Pulteney devoted virtually his entire speech in support of the motion to the balance of power, and dealt with Spain largely in the European context. He was particularly critical of the Treaty of Hanover against the Emperor, which, he claimed with old-style Continentalism, was contrary to 'our ancient plan of politics'. The opposition MP Sir John Barnard claimed that by 'neglecting to perform our guaranty to the Emperor in the year 1733 [the start of the War of the Polish Succession], the balance of power, and the liberties of Europe, have been brought into their present danger'. Scarcely one paragraph of Barnard's speech dealt with Spain and commercial grievances; the other five were devoted to Europe and the balance of power. The enthusiasms and controversies of 1739–40 – Vernon and Porto Bello – suddenly seemed very remote. 'Who lost Austria?' was now the call.[29]

In the meantime, the government had to address the new threat in Europe as best they could. Britain, after all, was not yet a belligerent. One solution was to resume the stalled alliance negotiations with Prussia of the previous year. These were designed to keep Frederick out of the French orbit. In mid March 1741, therefore, Lord Hyndford was dispatched on a mission to Berlin with powers to bribe Frederick with Jülich-Berg, if necessary. At the same time, in view of Dutch weakness and the Habsburg vacuum, London began to think seriously about the future of the Barrier against France. One proposal, which surfaced for the first time during the summer of 1741, was that of ceding the Austrian Netherlands to Prussia. 'If what is proposed with regard to the King of Prussia's having what the late Emperor possessed in the Low Countries, can be brought about and the Dutch be induced to agree to it,' Newcastle wrote, 'we do not see, in the present circumstances, and considering the great danger of those countries falling into the hands of France, any reason for His Majesty's not acquiescing in it.' This gambit was soon overtaken by events, but the problem it sought to address was not going to go away.[30]

The overtures to Prussia led nowhere, partly because Frederick felt that the French could offer him more, for the time being at least, but also because George II and his Hanoverian administration were profoundly ambivalent. As far as they were concerned, Frederick had put himself beyond the pale of civilized behaviour in the Empire: they would never trust him again. In fact, their immediate instinct after the invasion was to close ranks with Vienna and engage in some punitive territorial despoliation of the offender. But this mood did not long survive the reality of the Prussian advance in Silesia, and Frederick's ability to occupy Hanover more or less at will. He could, as Horatio Walpole observed in January 1741, 'ruin us there in one morning'. By early 1741 the Hanoverian administration had entered into negotiations with Frederick at which George II demanded Hildesheim, Osnabrück, and even parts of Mecklenburg, East Friesland and Paderborn. Hyndford was instructed 'to cooperate with [the Hanoverian envoys] to the utmost of his power . . . wherein the interests of [George II's] German dominions are concerned'. In the end, the negotiations failed. The King and Elector continued to blow hot and cold on Prussia. Indeed, throughout 1741 and much of the following years, George could never quite make up his mind whether he should jump on the Prussian bandwagon or join in plans for her partition.[31]

Another solution was to arbitrate between Frederick and Maria Theresa. Given the current military realities, this meant persuading Austria to shed a few territorial feathers for what was regarded as the common good of Europe. This was not desirable, but it was to be preferred to further warfare, which would only be to the benefit of France. Maria Theresa's steadfast refusal to countenance any such compromise caused irritation and alarm in London. 'It is with the greatest of concern,' Newcastle wrote in mid July 1741, 'that we observe, the Court of Vienna has given so little attention to His Majesty's most salutary advice for accommodating their differences with the King of Prussia.' After all, he continued, 'the King's advice to the Queen of Hungary [Maria Theresa] to yield a small part of her dominions, was only with a view to preserve the rest, now in imminent and certain danger, and to continue, in the House of Austria, the imperial dignity, which could hardly be procured any other way, but by the concurrence of the King of Prussia.' By giving way on Silesia, he argued, Austria could prevent further losses, secure the imperial crown for Maria Theresa's consort Francis Stephen, 'and by preserving the weight and interest of the House of Austria, have greatly contributed to the maintenance of the balance of power in Europe'. It was of course easy for Newcastle to sleep on a Habsburg wound.[32]

If all attempts to co-opt Prussia, or mediate, failed, Britain would have no choice but to intervene on behalf of Austria. It was not so much the contractual obligations of the 1731 alliance which weighed in the balance – these had been evaded during the War of the Polish Succession – as the broader imperative of propping up the Habsburgs. British statesmen now began to think about increasing the armed forces, and providing Maria Theresa with enough subsidies to keep her afloat. Approaches were to be made to the Dutch in order, as Newcastle put it, to 'lay before them the imminent danger which threatens the liberties of Europe', and 'to animate and rouse the Republic from the fatal lethargy and inaction which they have been in for some time'. Likewise, the

Russians should be urged 'not to suffer France to overrun all Europe, as is at present to be apprehended, if proper measures are not forthwith taken to oppose it'. Some provision also needed to be made for the defence of Hanover. Britain, in short, would have to re-engage in Europe or face war with the combined Bourbon powers alone. So in early April 1741 the Prime Minister, Sir Robert Walpole, approached the House of Commons for a subsidy for Maria Theresa. Walpole embarked on this course in the knowledge that any expenditure on Continental Europe, especially while the conflict with Spain raged unsuccessfully overseas, would expose him to attack. In an overt challenge to the isolationist rhetoric of the opposition, Walpole elaborated the importance of alliances to the balance of power and thus to British security. 'The use of alliances,' he explained, 'has in the last age been too much experienced to be contested; it is by leagues well concerted . . . that bounds are set to the turbulence of ambition, that the torrent of power is restrained.'[33]

The enemy was now clearer in view than at any point since Louis XIV. The threat, as more than one government speaker elaborated, came from the boundless ambition of a revived France bent, as Thomas Clutterbuck, the MP for Plympton, put it, on 'the attainment of universal dominion, the destruction of the rights of nature and the subjection of all the rest of mankind'. As in the days of the Grand Alliance, the only viable antidote was to keep the French out of Germany and shore up the Habsburgs as much as possible. The King's Speech had already announced the government's intention to prevent 'by all reasonable means, the subversion of the House of Austria' and to maintain 'the liberties and balance of power in Europe'. Central to this endeavour, the government reminded the House, was not only keeping the Habsburg inheritance intact, but also forestalling any French attempt to seize control of the imperial crown through their Bavarian proxy. The Empire, Henry Pelham remarked, was nothing less than the 'bulwark of Great Britain', which if breached would leave the country 'naked and defenceless'. For this reason, Pelham argued, subsidizing Maria Theresa was no act of 'romantic generosity' but a vital British national interest. The defence of Britain, in short, began in Germany. It had ever been thus since the late sixteenth century.[34]

Foreign policy did not play much of a direct role in the general election of May 1741. It rarely did: elections were decided largely by patronage in the boroughs, and many other factors were in play in the counties.

All the same, the relentless battering which Walpole's foreign policy had received since the last election in 1734 took its toll. Once all the results were in, it was clear that Walpole had suffered a heavy defeat. Two hundred and eighty-six supporters in the Commons now faced 131 opposition Whigs and 136 Tories. Walpole's majority had been halved from 40 to just under 20, primarily because he had lost the backing of the Duke of Argyll. He was also opposed by the Prince of Wales. The outcome of the contest certainly reduced the ministry's chances of pursuing a vigorous grand strategy, and thus its value to the King, with whom the power of summoning a chief minister rested. With its increased parliamentary strength, the opposition now had every incentive to pursue the impeachment of Walpole, and his alleged mismanagement of foreign policy was the central plank of this campaign.[35]

The French armies which entered Germany in the early summer of 1741 to support Charles Albert of Bavaria in his claim to the imperial throne were a direct challenge to the British position in Europe; they were also an immediate threat to the security of the King's homeland of Hanover. Equally worrying were the Prussian forces assembling at Magdeburg, just beyond the eastern border of the Electorate. The Franco-Prussian defensive treaty of June 1741 was therefore a nasty shock. 'This unexpected event,' wrote Newcastle's confidant – effectively his private secretary – Andrew Stone, 'has given, as your Lordship will imagine, some alarm at Hanover, the Hessians and Danish troops are to be drawn towards the King's Electoral Dominions as soon as possible, and His Majesty's own troops to be disposed in such a manner, as to enable them to act as occasion may require.' George, in fact, had been preparing for this eventuality since the spring. He canvassed various options, including pre-emptive occupations of nearby neutral imperial cities in order to deny them to the enemy. But it was clear that with a population of little more than one million and an army of about 20,000, it was simply not feasible for Hanover, even with the help of British-funded Danish and Hessian mercenaries, to hold off the French unaided. Even in faraway Ireland, George's distress was registered and relished. The Cork poet Séan Clarach McDomhnaill observed that 'Louis is a guiding light, striking and audacious, vengeful, invincible, firm in optimism, his men are at the gates of Hanover and Bremen, Holland is hobbled and they won't dare to move.'[36]

During the summer of 1741, the centre of British high politics shifted not merely mentally but physically to Germany. In June George travelled to Hanover to oversee measures for its defence in person; the Secretary of State for the Northern Department, Lord Harrington, went with him. Throughout July George bombarded the ministry in London with requests for increased military assistance. Without it, he warned, he would be forced 'to enter as Elector into a neutrality with the enemies of the throne of Austria'. The government, however, refused to countenance such a neutrality because it would undermine the new front they were opening up against France in central Europe. Mindful of his ambiguous constitutional position, British ministers stressed that their advice 'can only relate to what it may be advisable for His Majesty to do, in this respect, as King of Great Britain'; this left them – and him – with a loophole. The Duke of Newcastle rammed this message home again at the very end of the month. After offering subsidies for some 12,000 men, he added that 'if the King should think, that either this number of troops will not be sufficient, or the time of their coming not early enough, we cannot presume to interfere in any other measures that his Majesty as Elector, may think proper to take for the security of His Electoral dominions.'[37]

George and Harrington could be forgiven for taking this as a green light for a neutrality agreement. The most they had got out of London was a general acknowledgement of an obligation to defend Hanover or at least to redeem it at a subsequent peace conference; any specifics were evaded. Once it became clear that London would send no further assistance for the time being, George had to explore other options. Indeed, if he did not, he might find his escape route back to Britain blocked by the French advance. So in August, George dispatched Count Hardenberg, a Hanoverian diplomat, to Versailles with a view to averting a French invasion. Secrecy was vital to the mission, and for this reason London, which was likely to disapprove, was kept in the dark. The British government would certainly have been furious to learn that article four of Hardenberg's instructions read: 'If the Cardinal [Fleury] mentions the war between us and Spain, the reply should be: indeed this matter applies to our English affairs and concerns our English ministry.' Then came the give-away line: 'However, the Cardinal and all the world will have noticed Our dislike of, and tardiness in, going into war. Hence it should be easy to deduce that We incline towards making a reasonable peace.' As for whether Hardenberg was speaking for George as King or Elector, he was instructed to leave that open. It was a letter which smacked of desperation, and insofar as it related to the prosecution of the war with Spain it could potentially have been construed as treasonable. If it had become public, it would have formed the basis of a further opposition onslaught on the ministry and perhaps the Crown itself.[38]

The British minister with the King, Lord Harrington, who had been Secretary of State for the Northern Department since 1730, was kept fully abreast of developments, and now became complicit in the deception. In a letter to Trevor, the British envoy in The Hague, Harrington insisted that the sole purpose of the Hardenberg mission was to enquire about French intentions towards Hanover. 'Neither that gentleman, nor any other person,' he averred, 'have any intention or powers for conducting a treaty of neutrality with France for His Majesty's Electorate, or any treaty whatsoever.' Newcastle, who had seen all this many times before, was correspondingly suspicious. 'I stated and lamented,' he wrote to his confidant the Earl of Hardwicke, 'the Hanover influence which had brought many of these misfortunes upon us.' A month later he complained of 'the great inconveniences that arise from suffering these Electoral considerations to prevail so much in the King's councils'. For this, he earned a sharp rebuke from the Prime Minister. It was Stanhope and George I all over again: a British minister had gone behind the backs of his colleagues in London in order to make himself more amenable to the King.[39]

George and Harrington pressed ahead regardless and concluded the Neutrality Convention of September 1741. The French refrained from occupying Hanover, and agreed to defend it against a third party (effectively, Prussia) in return for complete military neutrality in the war with Austria and George's vote, as Elector, for the French candidate at the forthcoming imperial election. This agreement was concluded by George strictly in his capacity as Elector. The first article specifically committed him 'en qualité d'Électeur'. If that was not clear enough, the separate and secret annexe stressed that the agreement had 'no connection whatsoever with the affairs of Great Britain'. Shortly afterwards, the Hanoverian chief minister, Baron Münchhausen, signed the 'Neustadt Protocol' with the French envoy François de Bussy, by which it was agreed that neither British nor French troops were to be quartered in Hanover.[40]

Given the popular and parliamentary controversy surrounding the defence of Hanover, one might have expected British ministers to be relieved at this turn of events: the projected subsidies could be saved, the troops deployed elsewhere. Instead, they were furious and for good reason. Newcastle called it the 'capitulation of the Electorate'. He sniffed untruthfully that 'our opinions were never so much as asked'. Even if George had not, as was at first feared, signed as King of England, the distinction between George as Elector and King would puzzle European opinion. How could the King – as British monarch – claim to lead a broad coalition with a sword in one hand, and sign himself out of the conflict with the other? Newcastle certainly felt that news of the Neutrality 'must so greatly have discouraged other powers that might have assisted the Queen of Hungary'. 'It cannot be expected,' he elaborated three weeks later, 'that other powers will enter into any measures, in opposition to France, till they know that His Majesty is determined to put himself at the head of a party for the defence of the liberties of Europe'.[41]

In Holland, for example, rumours of the agreement had exposed the British envoy, Trevor, to the 'reproaches of my friends and the taunts of my enemies'. Indeed, Trevor continued, 'this piece of news has raised as great a consternation here, as the separation of our troops in 1712'. Given that the Dutch were not keen on coalition action against France in any case, the indignation, as Trevor noted, was somewhat synthetic. 'To hear people lament it,' he continued, 'you would swear, they had set their hearts upon pushing the war to the gates of Paris. At the same time, should this alarm blow off . . . I don't expect that things will go a whit better here than heretofore.' Likewise Harrington remarked, 'I cannot well see how people in Holland could justly complain of it, after the States having . . . refused to acknowledge that the engagements of their defensive treaties extended to His Majesty's Electoral dominions.' All the same, by recalling the closing stages of the War of the Spanish Succession, a neuralgic point for any orthodox Whig Continentalist, the critics had hit a raw nerve. The original hope of a new front in Germany to draw off some of the heat from Maria Theresa had been completely undermined.[42]

Moreover, George had not simply left Austria's western flank wide open, he had actually committed himself to supporting the French – and therefore the anti-British – candidate for the imperial crown. Newcastle noted with horror that George had sent 'Electoral ministers to all the courts of the enemies of the Queen of Hungary with offers to engage himself, as Elector, not to oppose any measures they may be carrying on against the House of Austria'. This ran a coach and horses through Britain's traditional *Reichspolitik*, which was to ensure that the Habsburgs should be able to mobilize the resources of Germany against French encroachments. It brought the Duke of Newcastle to the very edge of despair: his correspondence of this period is laced with references to the 'melancholy situation', the 'fatal' neutrality of Hanover, the French 'giving law to all Europe', 'What are we to do? For I am at a loss', and so on.[43]

But there was a greater threat still. The Hanover Neutrality not only endangered British security, it also put the ministry into the line of fire, and individual ministers within the shadow of the Tower. Newcastle, who could remember the foreign-policy impeachment controversies of his youth, feared the wrath of Parliament and the pent-up anger of his political rivals. The reality, he wrote, was that little had been done to help Maria Theresa: they might deceive themselves, 'but the truth will undoubtedly come out; and I think it will be impossible to prevent a parliamentary inquiry into this conduct'. Newcastle elaborated the resulting constitutional implications ten days later. 'A very sensible person said to me,' he wrote, 'if it should appear that [the King] had given up the interest of the country, in order to secure the Electorate, no one could tell what might be the consequence.' For this reason, British ministers should stress that the 'Neutrality by no means relates to the King, as King; or to the Dominions of Great Britain; that His Majesty, on the contrary, is determined to perform, as King, his engagements to the Queen of Hungary, taken by the treaty of 1731, and to support the liberties of Europe.' Newcastle concluded that 'If something of this kind is not immediately done, the Electoral Neutrality will be, to all intents and purposes, a regal neutrality: and the English ministers who acquiesce in the one will make themselves the author of the other. And then the Lord have mercy upon them!' He was not exaggerating. This was not some sordid subsidy scuffle; the whole balance of Europe, and with it the security of Britain, was at stake. The opposition would not hesitate to impeach him, and any other member of the government, if they were in any way associated with exposing vital British interests on behalf of narrowly Hanoverian considerations.[44]

Newcastle's response to the Hanover Neutrality was a classic example of the extent to which so much of eighteenth-century British security and political life was bound up with the integrity of the Empire and the balance of power. A Hanoverian Neutrality would force 'the lesser princes of Germany' and 'the more considerable powers of Europe' to make the best deal they could with France. It would deprive them of the 'example, weight and authority of England' and leave London 'exposed to the whole resentment of France'. Newcastle therefore wanted to place on record 'the consequences that might arise from these measures', and that he had supported the dispatch of the 'Hessians and the Danes, [and] the English contingent' to Maria Theresa. He concluded by warning of 'the fatal consequences, that may happen, if it should be surmised' that Hanoverian constraints had prevented George from 'acting as King in support of the Pragmatic Sanction, and thereby suffered France to over-run all Europe'. The implications of that, he added, 'must be, sooner or later, felt by this country'. Clearly, the 'fatal consequences' to which Newcastle referred was not just the imminent French triumph but the 'surmise' that he might be to blame for it.[45]

For this reason, the ministry spent the autumn of 1741 'clarifying' the Neutrality Convention. An official declaration was sent to all British ambassadors and foreign courts which stressed that 'This is purely an Electoral affair and does not in the least tie up His Majesty's hands as King or engage him to anything relating to his future conduct, as such, or to the affairs of England.' Whether or not such a circular should be sent had been the subject of some debate, with Robert Walpole – who was now more than ever dependent on royal support – arguing that a strong wording might be 'thought to be proposing to the King to eat his own words'. But the fear that the French would try to use the Hanover Neutrality to keep Britain out of the war, and lever her out of the diplomatic front against France, was perfectly justified. In early January 1742, Count Hardenberg was reporting from Paris that the French had difficulties in distinguishing between King and Elector, or affected to. They were furious at continued British subsidies for Maria Theresa and refused to accept that these were the responsibility of Parliament and the ministry rather than George personally. 'One knows,' they warned, 'that Your Majesty is the master of his parliament, in the sense that all the measures he takes against France cannot but be imputed to him.' At their next meeting, the French chief minister stressed that it was 'difficult to separate Hanover from England'. 'I told him,' Hardenberg wrote, 'that I understood well that the King and the Elector were physically the same person, but with respect to their territories they were motivated by quite different considerations.' A better summary of the schizophrenia which the Personal Union caused in British foreign policy would be hard to find.[46]

If the previous year had ended in anxiety, 1741 ended in despair. Pitt thought 'the scene abroad a most gloomy one'. He wondered 'whether day is ever to break forth again, or destruction and darkness is finally to cover all'. 'As matters stood,' he believed, there was 'no hope that an *Aurora Borealis* will light us to salvation'; 'France by her influence and her arms means, to be sure, to undo England and Europe.' The war with Spain overseas had completely fizzled out; British trade in Europe was under steady attack from French and Spanish privateers. A Spanish army was ferried across the Mediterranean undisturbed to attack the Austrians in Italy. Maria Theresa was now assailed on all sides. True, in October 1741 the British envoy Lord Hyndford had succeeded in mediating a ceasefire between the Austrians and the Prussians at Klein-Schnellendorf. This had – for the time being – taken the pressure off Maria Theresa from the north, but it came at the price of ceding Lower Silesia. Britain had thus connived at the weakening of Austria without winning Prussia; and there was no telling how long Frederick would honour the truce. In any case, the Austrians would still have to face the Spanish to the south, and the French and their German allies in the west. Most of what the anti-isolationists had predicted in 1738–9 had come to pass.[47]

All of this, of course, further stimulated the opposition onslaught on the ministry. The Neutrality Convention, in particular, provided parliamentary critics with an open goal. Lord Bathurst pointed to the discrepancy between the acute threat to the European balance and the special treatment accorded to Hanover. Whereas 'the whole Continent,' he noted, was 'now in confusion, laid waste by the ravages of armies . . . One happy corner of the world indeed is to be found secured from rapine and massacre, for one year at least, by a well-timed neutrality.' He therefore wanted to know 'on what terms it was obtained . . . and whether it was purchased at the expense of the honour of Great Britain, though the advantages of it are confined to Hanover'. There was some justice in the charge. George had been preoccupied with the Electorate, and it was no secret that he had received the news of Cartagena there in July 1741 with something approaching indifference. More specifically, it was claimed that the Royal Navy had been instructed not to intercept the Spanish armada on the way to Italy, for fear that the French would retaliate by occupying Hanover. 'The invasion of Italy,' Carteret told the House of Lords, 'is permitted to preserve Hanover from the like calamity.' This notion was to resurface at regular intervals over the next two years. Thus the Tory MP Sir John St Aubyn argued in December 1742 that bolstering the Austrians in Italy should 'properly ... be considered as the support of the balance of Europe, if timid neutralities had not intervened, and our naval strength had properly interposed to her assistance'. Interestingly, the critique of the administration here was couched very much in terms of the European balance, rather than narrow naval issues, or even the control of the Mediterranean.[48]

But the real issue was the general collapse of Britain's position in Europe. Over the past two years, the opposition had already made failures in foreign policy the centrepiece of their demand for a parliamentary inquiry into Walpole. In the meantime there had been further fiascos overseas and in Germany. 'If we extend our view over the whole world,' Chesterfield told the House of Lords, 'and enquire into the state of all our affairs, we shall find nothing but defeats, miscarriages and impotence, with their usual consequences, contempt and distrust.' 'The present discontent of the British nation,' the Duke of Argyll claimed, 'is almost universal, that suspicion has infused itself into every rank and denomination of men, that complaints of the neglect of our commerce, the misapplication of our treasure, and the unsuccessfulness of our arms, are to be heard from every mouth.' In its hatred of Walpole, the opposition accused him not merely of incompetence and corruption but of deception and treason as well. William Pitt even went so far as to repeat rumours that Walpole had been in treasonable communications with the French, adding hypocritically, 'what truth there is in these assertions, I shall not pretend to answer'. Pulteney spoke of Britain's diplomatic and military failures as 'crimes' for which Walpole should be held accountable.[49]

The climax came in late 1741 and early 1742. The opposition Whig mainstream – Chesterfield, Pulteney and Carteret – had already signalled in early 1741 that Walpole's failure to manage Britain's European alliances would be a central plank in their critique. Now, at the end of the year, they mercilessly pressed home their advantage. To be sure, the failures at Cartagena and Santiago formed part of the charge sheet, yet even those such as Pulteney who emphasized the Spanish war did so at least as much in the Mediterranean context – particularly the threat to the Austrians in Italy – as the colonial context. But the main thrust concerned the collapse of Austria and the seemingly inexorable advance of France. Once again, the old debate on the Treaty of Hanover in 1725, to which the opposition traced present woes, was reignited. Chesterfield traced the abandonment of Austria back to 1721. 'If our administration had been a French one,' he remarked, 'they would have been the ablest in the world.'[50]

In early December Carteret launched his most devastating attack yet. 'The liberties of Europe,' he argued, 'are now in the utmost danger . . . [and] the House of Bourbon has arrived almost at that exalted pinnacle of authority, from whence it will look down with contempt upon all other powers.' Nor, he continued, could Britain be sure to 'long remain exempted from the general servitude'. Instead, Carteret enunciated a domino theory: 'when the [German] Empire is subdued, the Dutch will quickly fall under the same dominion, and . . . all their ports and all their commerce will then be in the hands of the French . . . [and] our commerce will be quickly at an end. We shall lose the dominion of the sea, and all our distant colonies and settlements, and be shut up in our own island.' Carteret repeated his message a few days later: 'The liberty of and repose of Europe is almost lost; after which we shall not keep ours long.' These were the same charges that Englishmen had hurled at Charles and the two Jameses in the seventeenth century. The bastions and outworks of the nation had fallen; soon the enemy would overrun the inner line of defence in the Low Countries, and it would not be long before he attacked Britain itself.[51]

Walpole hobbled on through January 1742. There was more bad news that month, albeit not unexpected: George went ahead and voted for the French candidate Charles Albert of Bavaria in the contest for the imperial title. The Empire had effectively fallen to France. With a much reduced majority in the House of Commons since the election, Walpole's grip on Parliament weakened. He was dogged by defections, such as that of his own Secretary of State for the South, the Duke of Newcastle, who remained in office despite manifest disloyalty. Towards the end of January a motion for a secret inquiry into Walpole's ministries was frustrated with some difficulty. It was only royal support which sustained him now. In early February Walpole finally conceded defeat and resigned the seals of office. But the opposition continued to hound him. In the debate on the motion for an immediate inquiry into the alleged misdeeds of the outgoing administration, which took place in early March 1742, Pitt accused his quarry of having brought 'not only this nation, but all our friends on the Continent . . . into the most immediate danger'. To be sure, colonial grievances featured in the charge sheet, but European concerns figured much more prominently. Here Pitt went back to 1725, long before his own political career had even started, on the grounds that 'The Treaty of Hanover deserves indeed to be first mentioned, because from thence springs the danger, which Europe is now exposed to; and it is impossible to assign a reason for our entering into that treaty, without supposing that we then resolved to be revenged on the Emperor for refusing to grant us some favour in Germany.' He then moved on to the Treaty of Seville in 1729, which Pitt claimed had laid the basis for 'uniting the courts of France and Spain'. He accused Walpole of having 'had a spite against the House of Austria', by endorsing the Pragmatic Sanction without intent to enforce it, and abandoning Austria to her fate in the War of the Polish Succession.[52]

As a result, Pitt thundered, 'we are become the ridicule of every court in Europe, and have lost the confidence of all our ancient allies; by these we have encouraged France to extend her ambitious views.' It was not, he piously claimed, a desire for 'revenge . . . but a desire to prevent future' disasters, 'that makes me so sanguine for this inquiry'. However severe the punishment, he argued, it would be 'but small atonement to his country for what is past; but his impunity will be the source of many future miseries in Europe, as well as to his native country'. Mercy might be shown, as appropriate, 'but sentence we must pronounce, and for this purpose we must inquire, unless we are resolved to sacrifice our own liberties, and the liberties of Europe, to the preservation of the guilty man'. By a tiny majority, 244 votes to 242, Parliament rejected the motion. The House of Commons came within two votes of launching an inquiry, which would surely have ended with impeachment proceedings against the former chief minister. It was only by the narrowest of margins that Walpole escaped prosecution for the most serious charge in eighteenth-century British politics, that of betraying the European balance of power.[53]

In the end, Walpole was toppled because of his failures in Germany. He had been unable to shore up the Habsburg monarchy against Prussia, Spain and especially France. Walpole had thus jeopardized the barriers upon which British security rested. He had tolerated a neutrality agreement for Hanover which cut right across British policy in the Holy Roman Empire. In short, Walpole fell not because he had failed to vindicate the 'patriot' vision against Spain, but because he had abandoned Britain's imperial mission in Germany.

V

Imperial Recovery

12

The Empires Strike Back, 1742–1745

The only basis upon which the balance of power can now be established, is to restore a firmer union and good correspondence among the several princes of Germany . . . to restore activity or force to the Germanic body.[1]
Edmund Waller, House of Commons, December 1742

We may talk of our being an island: we may now boast of the superiority of our naval power: we may now in a great measure depend upon it as a security against our being invaded; but in this state of things, which Europe may probably be reduced to, if we do not powerfully interfere, I am afraid we shall not long have reason to boast of the superiority of our navy. If France were again in possession of the Netherlands, and freed from all apprehensions of an attack by land, she would certainly apply herself with the utmost diligence and application to the increase of her navy, and might in a very few years be able to fit out a most formidable squadron.[2]
Sir William Yonge, Secretary at War, 1742

All that we have to do, in my opinion, is to prepare for battle, to procure an early and universal attendance of all our people, and to blow the Hanover flame to height.[3]
Earl of Chesterfield, Whig rival of Carteret, 1743

Walpole left the security of Britain in the most parlous situation it had been in since the War of the Spanish Succession. Everywhere in Europe, French power or that of her allies was on the advance; British power, or that of her principal ally, Austria, was in full retreat. In Italy, Maria Theresa seemed about to lose the remaining Habsburg possessions to local Bourbon or Bourbon-backed forces. In Germany, the imperial crown had been alienated from the Habsburgs, while Frederick of Prussia and an opportunistic alliance of German princes threatened to partition the Habsburg conglomerate there and then. The continuing colonial war with Spain, so controversial in 1739–40, was increasingly lost to view as the Spanish resurgence in the Mediterranean took centre stage. Within two years, the new ministry under Lord Carteret had restored the situation. The financial resources of the British Empire were harnessed to the political and military potential of Germany; an army composed of Hanoverian and other German contingents, the 'Pragmatic Army', was sent to uphold the integrity of the Habsburg lands. This strategy was designed not only to restore the European balance of power, but also to divert French energies from a naval assault on Britain. It triggered the most searching domestic debate yet on the question of the Hanoverian connection in particular, and Britain's place in Europe more generally. By the end of 1743, however, the strategy had been resoundingly successful, as the victories at Dettingen and elsewhere showed. In this way, the combined resources of two Empires – the British and the German – were deployed to contain the French threat, and to ensure the maritime security of Great Britain.

Unlike Walpole, who had led from the Treasury, the new chief minister, Carteret, chose the Secretaryship of State for the North. It was a portent both of his determination to work closely with the King on foreign policy, and of the future centre of gravity of British policy, which would be Germany. Carteret was a known quantity. True, he had been a powerful advocate of the war against Spain, and remarkably insouciant about the French threat to the Pragmatic Sanction. His eloquent navalism of the past three years was a matter of record. Yet anybody who had observed Carteret's career since the 1720s knew him as a committed Continentalist. He had cut his teeth as a young diplomat in Stockholm, trying to secure a Swedish alliance in order to contain Russia. He had been a firm opponent of the Hanover Treaty, which he regarded as a deviation from Britain's traditional pro-Habsburg policy, and a supporter of Austria in the 1730s. He had travelled widely in Europe, had many friends there, including Hanoverians, took a keen interest in European literature, and spoke several languages: French, of course, but also Spanish and German. He was able to give the House of Lords an impromptu tutorial on the constitution of the Holy Roman Empire.

Europe and particularly Germany became Carteret's obsession for the next two years.[4]

His priority now was to rescue the House of Austria. This he considered to be the 'cause of the [German] Empire and of Europe, as well as that of the faith and public security'. According to his mother, the new chief minister even sent one claimant for preferment packing with the assertion that he 'was never interested in anybody's business, his whole mind being taken up with DOING GOOD TO THE NATION, and till the French was drove out of Germany and Prague was taken he could not think of such a bagatelle'. The first thing that Carteret did, therefore, was to try to persuade smaller German princes to provide mercenaries in support of Maria Theresa. In early March 1742 he told Prince William of Hesse of his alarm at seeing 'France disposing in a sovereign manner of the [German] Empire and its provinces, and thus by consequence of the future of Europe'. This was because the new Bavarian Emperor would not have enough independent weight to maintain the balance of power in the Empire and thus in Europe as a whole. 'Who knows,' he argued, what would happen to 'a House which, for more than a century, has been its principal instrument for defending and maintaining the liberties of the Empire and of Europe?' The new Emperor, he feared, would be 'eternally dependent' on French support.[5]

The next step was a concerted diplomatic and military offensive to take the pressure off Austria and contain France. William Pulteney, who had taken a peerage as the Earl of Bath and become a supporter of the new ministry, now spoke the language of classic Whig strategy. He 'laid it down as a maxim that this nation was to hold the balance in Europe. There was no supporting it but by a power on the Continent able to oppose France: that power was the Queen of Hungary.' It was therefore necessary to 'show France we were prepared: that Flanders was barrier to us, as well as to Holland. Therefore that we should send forces thither . . . [which] if it had no other effect, would occasion a powerful diversion in favour of the Queen of Hungary.' From the spring of 1742 onwards, therefore, British forces under the command of Lord Stair began to deploy to the Austrian Netherlands in preparation for opening up a new front against the French and easing the pressure on Maria Theresa. Officially, these men were fighting for Maria Theresa and not against France, as war with that power was not yet declared.[6]

Carteret was at first successful in Germany: Lord Hyndford mediated a preliminary peace agreement between Prussia and Austria at Breslau in June 1742. He also succeeded in concluding a defensive alliance with Frederick the Great at Westminster in November 1742. The problem with these gambits was that they involved unilateral concessions by Austria, which weakened the Barrier and made Britain complicit in Maria Theresa's distress. As she herself pointed out, there would have to be some sort of compensation for the loss of Silesia. 'Since England has insisted with great vehemence on accommodation with Prussia,' Maria Theresa wrote in mid June 1742, 'and has not seen fit to provide [me] with any help . . . the loss will have to be made good somewhere else.' Carteret's solution was nothing if not audacious: it was to construct a whole new geopolitics of central and southern Europe in order to keep the Austrians up, and the Bourbons out. Maria Theresa would be reconciled to the loss of Silesia and the imperial crown through compensating her with 'equivalents', perhaps Lorraine and parts of Alsace. In Italy, Carteret hoped to restore Naples to Austria. Taken together, both moves would reverse the consequences of the War of the Polish Succession at a stroke.[7]

At the same time, Carteret sought to detach the new Emperor Charles VII from France. This was attempted in the negotiations at Hanau in July 1743, when generous subsidies were offered to Charles Albert through his appointed mediator, Prince William of Hesse. Carteret and George also considered proposals to offer Bavaria the prospect of territorial gains in Germany at the expense of some of the smaller German bishoprics and imperial cities; the ethical and legal implications do not seem to have bothered them. This was of a piece with the traditional 'Protestant' *Reichspolitik* of the first two Georges. In return, Charles Albert was to break with France, and ensure France's withdrawal from Germany. Shortly afterwards, the Treaty of Worms created a generously funded alliance between Britain, Austria and Piedmont-Savoy in September 1743. The two gambits had separate geographical foci but the same aim, which was to strengthen the Habsburgs and thus restore the European balance of power.[8]

Both schemes hit two more or less immovable objects. First of all, there was the unwillingness of other powers to be shunted around in accordance with British conceptions of the European balance. Maria Theresa, in particular, was loath to give up Silesia or to forego the chance of venting her wrath on the Bavarians. If pressed, she preferred neighbouring Bavaria as an equivalent for Silesia, to the return of distant Lorraine. Emperor Charles Albert disliked the idea of 'secularization' – that is the despoliation of ecclesiastical principalities – because it would have damaged his standing in the Catholic half of the Empire. Secondly, there was the anticipated scepticism of the British parliament, which was reluctant to pay more than absolutely necessary to Maria Theresa and even more so to enter into an open-ended commitment to the Savoyard territory of Sardinia. The 'treaty' of Hanau was therefore never completed: it was rejected by Carteret's fellow ministers in London, the Earl of Hardwicke, the Duke of Newcastle and his brother Henry Pelham, as well as by Maria Theresa herself.

Their reasons were in part personal. The Regency Council in London, to which the government had been entrusted after George left for Hanover in May 1743, was terrified that Carteret would exploit his proximity to the monarch to sideline them. They had seen it happen only two years earlier with Harrington; now they feared that Carteret would press the claims of his candidate, Pulteney – Lord Bath – over those of Henry Pelham to succeed Lord Wilmington at the Treasury. But there was a more fundamental strategic disagreement – aggravated by a measure of misunderstanding – which had sprung up between London and Carteret in Germany. Newcastle was quick to see in the negotiations an attempt by Carteret to indulge the King's Hanoverian ambitions at the expense of Austria. Indeed, it was at this point that the commander of the British forces, Lord Stair, resigned because he thought that Britain was about to leave Maria Theresa in the lurch. They feared that Carteret was about to 'lose' Austria all over again. Underlying this was a crucial ambiguity in British *Reichspolitik*. It had been axiomatic until about 1720 and again since the early 1730s that the containment of France required a strong Emperor and a strong Habsburg monarchy; before 1740, the two were identical. But what if the Emperor were not a Habsburg? In that case, Newcastle felt, there was no point in supporting him. Far better, he thought, to distract the French in Europe by distressing his German ally. 'I dread,' Newcastle wrote in late May 1743, 'having France and Spain singly on our hands ... The Emperor is the weak point of their question; he is more than half conquered already; there we must press France, and there we shall get the better of them.'[9]

Diplomacy was only one part of Carteret's strategy; military coercion was another. In the Mediterranean, the Royal Navy now engaged the

Spanish fleet, and occasionally the French – with whom they were not yet formally at war – with much greater vigour. French ships were driven into St Tropez in 1742 and burned. That same year, Commodore Martin sailed into the Bay of Naples, trained his guns on the royal palace and threatened to level it unless King Charles of the Kingdom of the Two Sicilies withdrew from the anti-Habsburg coalition. This he promptly did, an event which was much celebrated as an advertisement for British naval diplomacy. By the following year, Spain was forced to send reinforcements to Italy via France, as the route by sea had become too insecure. She concluded a family compact with France in October 1743, but this did nothing to change the fact that the naval balance had swung back towards Britain. And this was felt not so much in the colonies but in the crucial European theatre, the Mediterranean. This is borne out by the disposition of British naval forces in 1742–3. In 1742 there were 16,000 seamen in the colonies, nearly 13,000 in the Mediterranean, and about 16,000 in home waters; in 1743 the figures were respectively 11,000, 19,000 and 15,000. Even the great naval innovation of the 1740s, the permanent western squadron cruising between England and Cape Finisterre – the brainchild of Admiral Vernon – pertained to home waters. The colonial war against Spain – the War of Jenkins's Ear – in fact stagnated in 1742–4. There were so many more important things happening in Europe.[10]

Here the crucial front lay in the west: in Flanders, the Rhineland and the Palatinate. It was here that the French would have to be checked and pinned down. One option was to seek an auxiliary corps from Russia, where some measure of stability had returned with the accession of the Tsarina Elizabeth in November 1741. As Russia was still at war with Sweden, Carteret sought to mediate in order as he put it 'that they may have their hands free to act in a greater, more useful and more salutary manner'. The auguries for Britain were good, as the French had disgraced themselves in St Petersburg not only by their overt partisanship for their traditional ally Sweden, but also because they were suspected of trying to incite the Ottoman Turks to attack from the south. Paradoxically, the large Jacobite contingent in the Russian army does not seem to have been much of an obstacle. On the contrary, their fighting skills were so highly prized that British policy hinged on keeping them in Russia, if only to deny them to France. In the end, the problem in Russia was that everything moved very slowly. A defensive treaty was secured in 1742, and the pro-British Count Alexis Bestuzhev triumphed as Chancellor in 1744 and became Tsarina Elizabeth's chief minister, but a treaty between Maria Theresa and the Tsarina Elizabeth – the Treaty of the Two Empresses – did not come about until 1746, and it was only in 1748 that Russian troops actually arrived in central Europe, much too late to make any difference to the outcome.[11]

There was thus no alternative to the deployment of a British, or at least British-sponsored, army in Germany. Carteret quickly realized that the key to that enterprise was bringing Hanover into the war. The Electorate had a substantial population – about 700,000 inhabitants – and the armed forces were, at 20,000 men, not insubstantial by mid-eighteenth-century standards. Moreover, while Elector George was constrained somewhat by the laws of the Holy Roman Empire, he had a reasonably free hand in foreign policy; there was no Hanoverian equivalent to the Westminster parliament. The Neutrality Convention was therefore revoked, and Hanover became the mainstay of an army fighting in Germany and Flanders. This force, which came to be known as the 'Pragmatic Army', numbered about 14,000 British troops, 14,000 Austrians and some 22,000 British-paid Hanoverians. It was commanded initially by the British general Lord Stair and then by George II in person. The French rose to the bait: Fleury had been attacked for letting George off the hook with the Neutrality Convention in 1741, and the reopening of hostilities seemed to give the French a second chance to attack Britain's perceived Achilles heel.[12]

Hanover, in other words, was co-opted for the British war effort. As Carteret remarked, he could not 'discover any clause by which we are forbidden to make use in our own cause of the Alliance of Hanover, or by which Hanoverians are forbidden to assist us'. As one undersecretary of state reported him as saying in March 1742, Carteret 'staked his whole on keeping the Elector an Englishman'. 'England,' Carteret argued, 'was subservient to Hanover. But Hanover is now subservient to England.' This was, he explained, because 'The Electorate is regulated by our measures and is, not without the utmost danger, engaged in a war which might easily have been declined.' The Hanoverian envoy was told that the 'distinction between His Majesty as King and as Elector must cease'. On the other hand, Carteret was brutally clear that Britain could no longer be blackmailed through Hanover. Frederick the Great was wasting his time when he warned George II in December 1742 that he 'would have him remember that Hanover is at a very little distance from me, and that I can enter there when I please'. He had already been told, as Carteret instructed Lord Hyndford, the British minister in Berlin, that 'His Prussian Majesty will much deceive himself, if he thinks the King will be frightened from pursuing the system of England, and be brought to abandon the liberties of Europe by the danger with which his German dominions may be menaced.' On the contrary, Carteret warned that George II could 'firmly rely on all the weight and power of these Kingdoms being exerted in defence of them, whenever they shall be involved with England in the great and general cause'. British and Hanoverian security, in short, were not in contradiction, but symbiotically linked.[13]

This co-option of Hanover was reflected in the coordination between British and Hanoverian diplomats. In October 1742 the British minister at the Saxon court at Dresden was not only instructed to search for allies in Germany to help Maria Theresa against the French, but also to go via 'Hanover to receive there such lights [instructions] as will be given you by the King's Electoral ministers'. In April of the following year, the Hanoverian ministers not only kept Lord Hyndford briefed on the situation in Germany, but also supplied copies of documents which were to be 'sent to the German ministers of the King at foreign courts so that they can modify their language accordingly'. In other words, British and Hanoverian policy was being synchronized. And in May 1743 Carteret, accompanied by his German-language tutor Caspar Wetstein, set off to join George in Hanover. The Hanoverians themselves were certainly under no illusion that it was a British and not a Hanoverian war that was being waged after 1742. Thus the instructions sent by the Hanoverian ministers to their representative at the Reichstag stated that the Elector, 'in order to please the English nation, wished to continue the war in Germany out of rancour against France'.[14]

In military terms, Carteret's strategy was at first quite successful. From the spring of 1742, France – as yet still formally at peace with Britain – was forced to engage the Pragmatic Army. Rather than concentrating on attacking Britain overseas, she found herself bogged down in Germany. The Marquess of Tweedale told Parliament in 1742 that French ambitions in the (German) Empire and throughout Europe had been contained, and that 'the power of the House of Bourbon has been diminished on every side, its alliance has been rejected, and its influence disregarded.' Even such a staunch independent Whig critic as Sir John

Barnard, who excoriated 'the extreme complaisance' that Carteret's ministry had 'shown to the Crown with regard to domestic affairs', was moved to grant that 'with regard to foreign affairs, our conduct seems to be a little altered: our new ministers seem to act with more vigour, and to show a little more regard to the preservation of the liberties of Europe, than their predecessor ever did.' In late June 1743, George II, spurring his troops on in broken English, led the Pragmatic Army to victory at Dettingen, the last British monarch to do so. The King had been, as Carteret proudly related, 'all the time in the heat of the fire'. This was the sort of leadership which Britons appreciated, and the initial enthusiasm for George was not far behind that for Vernon over Porto Bello. One of Newcastle's stewards put the success down 'to His Majesty's being there', and remarked that the people were now happier to pay up for the war and drink to the royal family 'and the rest of the brave fellows abroad'. Moreover, the Electoral contingent had made a major contribution to the victory; 'no artillery was better served,' one account of the battle related, 'or did more execution, than the Hanover.' Against this background Newcastle, who harboured a profound mistrust for Carteret, was forced to concede that keeping Hanover in the war was 'the best thing he ever did'. The German Empire had been effectively mobilized against France.[15]

In political terms, however, the decision to co-opt Hanover and pay for the Hanoverian contingent in the Pragmatic Army was to prove highly controversial. The issue of the 'Hanover troops' now became a sounding board for a much broader discussion about British foreign policy, Britain's place in Europe, and British identity more generally. It was a debate which was conducted both in Parliament and 'out of doors': the distinction is a fine one, because the themes and the protagonists were often the same whether they were to be found in popular pamphlets or on the floor of the Houses of Parliament. None of the arguments advanced was new, but never before had they been advanced by so many and with such vigour or clarity. Some 45 pamphlets were published on the conduct of the war in 1743, and in 1744 it was 50; by 1747, it was only 7. As the Lord Chancellor and Whig stalwart Hardwicke complained in 1744, 'In the last winter before this time, there were volumes of virulent pamphlets published, which did infinite mischief.' There was never again to be quite such a sustained discussion of British foreign policy, until perhaps the closing stages of the Seven Years War.

22. King George II leading his troops at the Battle of Dettingen.

But then, there did not need to be: it had all been said, many times over.[16]

The resulting debates were ferocious, particularly in the House of Lords. In mid December 1743, for example, the Earl of Litchfield lamented that the idea that the liberties of Britain and Europe 'should be sacrificed to a mere Hanover job ['job' was eighteenth-century parlance for the corrupt provision of employment to a crony at public expense], raises my indignation, I must confess, above that coolness with which every lord ought to express himself in this House. I say, my lords, a Hanover job, it is not only a Hanover job, but a job of the most sordid kind: a low trick to draw the nation in, to give a large sum of money to Hanover yearly.' A month later it was the turn of the Earl of Westmorland to condemn the hire of Hanoverian troops as a 'job, a mean, despicable job; a job invented only to enrich Hanover and by enriching Hanover, to recommend the minister to a job to plunder the nation, and to advance the fortunes of sycophants and prostitutes.' He went on to say, 'I hope, my lords, I shall be forgiven if my indignation has transported me to the use of some expressions which, upon any other occasion, might justly be censured. For, my lords, my natural hatred of a job leaves me not sufficiently master of my temper.' This was strong language even by the standards of the time. Thus the Earl of Cholmondeley deplored 'the licentious language and unusual virulence, which have appeared in the discussion of this question', which had seemed to 'authorize every man to offer his sentiments with very little premeditation, and to set himself free from the anxious observation of forms of decency'. In this perfervid atmosphere, it was perhaps no surprise that Carteret and Arthur Onslow, the Speaker of the House of Commons, both received death threats during the Hanover debates.[17]

On the face of it, the response to the hiring of the Hanoverians was simply another attack on Hanover and the Personal Union itself. It was led in the House of Commons by Edmund Waller, the Opposition Whig stalwart, and in the Lords by the Earl of Chesterfield. Together, they wrote *The case of the Hanover forces in the pay of Great Britain, impartially and freely examined* (1742/3). The weekly *Old England, or the Constitutional Journal* also kept up a steady barrage of anti-Hanoverian rhetoric. Many of the pamphlets were written by peers or MPs, so that Parliament and the press formed an echo chamber in which the arguments resonated to devastating effect. It was alleged that the war was being waged solely to enlarge 'insignificant' Hanover, that the hiring of the Hanoverians was simply a device for fleecing British taxpayers, and that all this was highly unconstitutional. 'It is Hanover, and Hanover only,' one MP lamented, 'that seems to be our care: that is to be guaranteed by all our treaties . . . Is this not contrary to the Act of Settlement? Is this not unhinging the very frame of our constitution?' In the House of Lords, the naval enthusiast the Earl of Sandwich lamented 'that England has no longer the honour of being the arbitress of the Continent; that she is considered only as the ally of an Electorate'. And all this, as the Earl of Chesterfield claimed, in order to pay for a militarily worthless force. 'I have been told by all the German officers I have ever conversed with,' he claimed, 'that they are among the worst troops in Germany.' But the most ferocious attack was launched by William Pitt, for whom these debates represented a political and oratorical breakthrough. 'It is now too apparent', he thundered, 'that this great, this powerful, this formidable kingdom, is considered only as a province to a despicable Electorate.' Pitt, according to one observer, 'spoke like ten thousand angels'.[18]

Some attacks did not stop short of the throne itself. Chesterfield's suggestion that the 'partiality shown to the Hanoverians', stemmed from the fact that George was 'born and bred a Hanoverian', left him on the right side of the law if not of convention. But in December 1742, Pitt suggested to uproar that George had submitted to 'temptations of greater profit' in hiring the Hanoverians. The implication that the King had sold out the national interest for pecuniary gain could certainly be construed as lese-majesty. So could the speeches of the MP John Hynde Cotton who, oddly for a Jacobite, hinted that exile, the fate of James II, beckoned. Likewise Lord Lonsdale warned that admirable though George's affection for Hanover was in itself, 'Our own late history has furnished us with an example of a king, that was drove from his throne for extending too far a quality that was in itself highly commendable: zeal for religion.' The sense of menace was unmistakable. Clearly, it was not just ministers who could fall if the affairs of the nation were mismanaged, but even kings.[19]

Much of the argument was crude, but some of it did not lack sophistication. The Hanover treaties, the opposition claimed, violated not just the British constitution, but that of the German Empire as well. For this purpose Sandwich turned himself into something of a barrack-room imperial lawyer. 'It is necessary,' he announced, 'to take a view of the constitution of the Germanic body, which consists of a great number of separate governments . . . subject in some degree to the Emperor as the general head.' Now that Charles VII had received the endorsement of the Reichstag at Regensburg, Sandwich claimed, 'none of the troops of Germany can . . . be employed against him, without subjecting the prince to whom they belong to the censure of the ban, a kind of civil excommunication.' This argument was – as Carteret soon demonstrated – quite specious, but it was not straightforwardly ignorant. It found its way into the protest of the twenty-five dissentient lords, who objected to the Hanover payments 'because we apprehend that the troops of the Elector of Hanover cannot be employed to act in Germany against the head of the Empire'. Likewise, the accompanying pamphlet literature argued that Hanover was barred by imperial law from sending troops against Charles.[20]

Far from allaying these concerns, the victory at Dettingen actually inflamed them in some quarters. The fact that George had charged into battle wearing not British colours, but the yellow sash of Hanover, gave particular offence. Some of the attacks, such as the ballad entitled 'The Yellow Sash, or Hanover Beshit', were openly scatological. It was alleged that the Hanoverian contingent, despite shirking battle, had been given special marks of royal favour and that the British commander Lord Stair had been deliberately slighted and subordinated to the Hanoverians. 'The omniscient Hanoverians,' Sandwich alleged in the House of Lords, 'had the unrivalled direction of every movement', thanks to 'fawning ministers'. 'Thus,' he lamented, 'was the honour of our country, and the success of our undertakings, sacrificed to Hanover.' Most of these criticisms were ill-founded. It was true that George had worn Hanoverian yellow at Dettingen, but there was no reason for him not to do so, as Britain was not yet formally at war with France. In any case, he had worn the same dress at the Battle of Oudenaarde back in 1708, during the War of the Spanish Succession, when a Hanoverian contingent had served under Marlborough. The message for those who were disposed to recognize it was the continuity of Francophobe Continentalism. All the same, John Wootton's painting of the battle, which hangs in the National Army Museum in Chelsea, tactfully renders the sash in blue. Nor was there much in the accusations of favouritism. Indeed, George had specifically instructed his Hanoverian generals to take orders from Stair. Thus the cavalry commander, General du Pontpietin, was to keep Stair informed of his movements and 'to await instructions from the same in which way he is to join him with the corps entrusted to him and where the rendezvous is to take place'. Once in Germany, of course, George took over direct personal command from Stair.[21]

Unsurprisingly, the Jacobites and Tories sought to take advantage of the controversy. Hynde Cotton accused British ministers of being 'biased and blinded by their fondness for the project of adding a part of the Prussian dominions to the Electorate of Hanover'; he criticized the 'great flow of riches into the Electorate of Hanover' and deplored that 'the views of Hanover have been the pole-star of our political compass ever since the death of the late Emperor, as they had been for many years before'. At the same time, John Campbell of Cawdor claimed to be 'well informed that the government know the Pretender's instructions are to run down Hanover as much as possible'. Ministers hoped, he argued, thereby to distract from the unpopularity of the Pretender himself. Indeed, as Horatio Walpole observed wearily in December 1742, 'if we have a mind effectually to prevent the Pretender from ever obtaining this crown, we should make him Elector of Hanover, for the people of England will never fetch another King from there.'[22]

But it was really the non-governmental Whigs and disaffected grandees who made the running. So much so, that the government made strenuous efforts to suppress public discussion by harassing printers and confiscating their stock. For if the outrage directed at Hanover was genuine and popular, it was also tactical. It is clear from the large and potentially risky print runs that the principal motivation was political, not commercial. Indeed, the whole campaign in and out of Parliament was directed by the opposition Whig leader, the Earl of Chesterfield, with the express purpose of bringing down the ministry. To do this, he believed, it was necessary 'to blow the Hanover flame to height'. The balance between spontaneous popular feeling and party-political manipulation is illustrated by some remarks of the Earl of Sandwich. 'The clamour and general discontent of all ranks of people on account of our late Hanoverian measures,' he told the Duke of Bedford, 'is greater than I could have imagined it could possibly have been; and, if rightly pursued by a vigorous attack at the beginning of the session, may be productive of very good ends.'[23]

Most of the fire was concentrated on Carteret, who was accused of having used the Hanoverian issue to ingratiate himself with the King. One sixpenny ballad ran thus:

> Abroad our gallant army fights
> In Austria's cause for G—rm—n Rights
> By English Treasure fed
> Hessians and Hano—— too
> The gainful trade of war pursue,
> With C——T at their head[24]

This theme was echoed in Parliament. 'If we are thus to go on,' the extremist Tory MP for Cornwall, Sir John St Aubyn thundered, 'and, if to procure the grace and favour of the Crown, this is to become the flattering measure of every successive administration – this country is undone!' Only a 'thorough-paced courtier,' George Lyttleton argued, 'may perhaps think that the cause of Hanover is the cause of Europe'. Lord Barrington argued that 'an unpopular and detested minister must think of courting the favour of his prince, and . . . [f]or this purpose he must humour and flatter his favourite passions and prejudices, let them

be never so inconsistent with the interest or happiness of the nation.'
George Dodington attacked the 'Hanoverianized' ministers. Pitt even
went so far as to describe Carteret as 'an English minister without
an English heart, a Hanover troop minister'. The opposition Whigs
were joined by former supporters of Walpole in their quest to supplant
Carteret. In a letter to his brother, Henry Pelham, Newcastle wrote that
'that which particularly at this time makes it, in my opinion, impracticable to go on with him [Carteret] is that his chief view in all he does or
proposes to do is the making court to the King by mixing Hanover
considerations to all others. By this method he secures the closet [i.e. the
King's favour] whether his schemes succeed or not.' Twenty-five years
on from the Baltic crisis of 1717 not much had changed.[25]

The Hanover controversy of 1742-4 was about much more than just
the Personal Union and political infighting. It was also a far-reaching
discussion of Britain's role in Europe and the wider world. Many of
Carteret's critics were themselves supporters of the European balance
of power, the Austrian alliance and the Protestant Succession. Lord
Stair, the military scourge of the Hanoverians, was certainly one. He had
a long pedigree of Francophobia and staunch support for the 'balance of
power'. He had even supported vain attempts in 1734 to bring Britain
into the War of the Polish Succession on the Austrian side. Nor – as a
strong anti-Jacobite – could he be accused of deliberately making the
Pretender's breeze to blow. Much the same could be said of many other
Whig critics of the Hanover troops, including Chesterfield and Pulteney.
Thus when Stair launched his diatribe against the Hanover troops in
early December 1742, it was not the neglect of colonial expansion he
attacked, but the abandonment of Austria in the War of the Polish
Succession – 'deserting her in the year 1733' – the alleged partiality
towards France, and the general mismanagement of the European balance of power. Likewise, when Lord Quarendon went into massive
historical detail to demonstrate the mistakes of the Walpole administration, most of it pertained to European grievances. After fifteen col-
umns, he was just over halfway into his speech, and was still not past
1720. Opposition to the Hanover troops, therefore, did not as such
signal hostility to engagement on the Continent.[26]

Indeed, much of the opposition critique was devoted to outlining an
alternative European policy. The *Old England* journal accepted in June
1744 that 'true Britons' should remain engaged in Europe, but 'only' in

the 'necessary defence of that part of the Continent . . . in which England has any concern, I mean the Barrier'. Later that year it criticized the ministry for failing to come to grips with the depth of Austro-Prussian rivalry. The same point was made by Edmund Waller in the House of Commons, when he argued that relying on a revitalized Austria was not enough to contain France: the Prussians, Bavarians and a whole range of other German princes would have to be co-opted as well in order 'to restore activity or force to the Germanic body'. The Opposition also professed faith in Britain's traditional Dutch ally. Here the thinking was somewhat contradictory: intervention should wait for the Dutch, but British troops should not be sent to Flanders for fear of provoking the French to attack the Dutch. Even the Earl of Chesterfield, scourge of the Hanover troops, agreed that Britain should intervene actively in support of the balance. 'We might lay it down as an invariable maxim,' he argued, 'never to enter into a land war, never, but when the Dutch Barrier was in danger.' The problem was that upholding the Dutch Barrier was not possible without maintaining the House of Habsburg, which in turn involved a major commitment to the European balance of power.[27]

But for many, Hanover was just a pretext to ventilate navalist and even isolationist tendencies. Thus Lord Sandwich saw Britain 'entangled in a labyrinth in which no end is to be seen . . . that we are involved in a foreign quarrel only to waste that blood and that treasure, which might be employed in recovering the rights of commerce, and regaining the dominion of the sea'. Spain should therefore be 'subdued' first. In the meantime, he concluded, Britain should not 'engage in a distant war, in a dispute about the dominion of princes in the bowels of the Continent; of princes of whom it is not certain, that we shall receive either advantage or security from their greatness, or that we should suffer any loss or injury by their fall'. This isolationist trend found a loud echo in the public sphere. The author of *The political maxims* (1744), for example, announced that 'A prince or state ought to avoid all treaties, except such as tend towards promoting Commerce or Manufactures . . . All other alliances may be looked upon as encumbrances.' Among Britain's allies, of course, all this produced horror and incomprehension. The Dutch statesman Count Bentinck asked in 1745 what seventeenth-century Englishmen would think, 'if they had heard an English nobleman say that it signifies as little who is Emperor, as who is Lord Mayor of London'. It was, after all, the failure of James II to react to events in the Empire which had broken the back of the Stuarts in 1688.[28]

If Continental alliances were suspect *per se*, then so was the old Whig orthodoxy by which France was to be tied down in Europe, in order to secure Britain's naval superiority. 'The maxim,' Edmund Waller argued, 'of our keeping France and Spain involved in a land war, in order to prevent their attacking us with their joint force, by sea, ought not to be received without some qualification.' If 'the land war must be chiefly supported at our expense, we ought rather to take our chances of supporting a naval war by ourselves alone, than engage in any such war by land, because it would divert us from prosecuting the war by sea . . . by which alone we can expect to reap any benefit to ourselves'. Likewise the pamphlet *The interest of Hanover steadily pursued* (1743) wondered 'Whether it might be conducive to the true interest of this nation to rely wholly upon that situation which disjoins it from the rest of the world, to increase its naval force, and to give its great application to the marine without concerning itself with the intrigues of the neighbouring states.' This struck the author as preferable to limbering up 'once more to cover Flanders with our troops, to negotiate, to fight, and to expend our treasure, in restraining the overgrown power of France, and in preserving the balance of Europe'. Of a piece with this navalist thinking were the demands for coastal raids on France, which first surfaced in Opposition rhetoric in 1743-4.[29]

Underlying this thinking was a disenchantment with the whole idea of the balance of power, or at least of its viability. Thus another prominent navalist, Lord Halifax, saw no British interest in paying for the Hanover troops, only a rather woolly desire for 'the general happiness and liberty of all the nations of Europe'. Indeed, he claimed that 'We are now . . . about to fight, not for our lives or our estates, or for the safety of our families, or the continuance of our privileges; we are contending only to support what has been so often shaken that it is not easy to find how it can be fixed; we are only attempting to settle the balance of Europe.' Halifax dismissed the balance of power as a catch-all of the politics of fear, designed to fleece the nation, curtail their liberties, and deter them from asking searching questions about how their money had been spent. Similar points were made by Edmund Waller in the House of Commons. 'We have of late,' he remarked in January 1744, 'got into a ridiculous custom of making ourselves the Don Quixotes of Europe.' This was because Britain 'sometimes under the pretence of preserving a balance of power in Europe, at other times under the pretence of preserving a balance of power in the north', had 'engaged . . . in the quarrel of almost every state in Europe, that has, by its imprudence or ambition, brought itself into any distress'. The result, Halifax complained, was that 'whilst we take upon ourselves the burden of defending our allies, they give themselves very little trouble about defending themselves.' Too much British intervention on the Continent, in other words, had created a dependency culture among the other powers.[30]

These parliamentary and popular debates were ostensibly about foreign policy, but they were also very much about the nature of British, or English, identity. It is well known that eighteenth-century 'Britons' constructed their identity in opposition to a Catholic and French 'other'. What is less well known is that the most sustained popular and elite engagement with the 'other' concerned Protestant and German Hanover. Antagonism to the Personal Union became a way of accentuating one's own patriotism. Thus the opposition Whig John Tucker, MP for Weymouth and Melcombe Regis, claimed that 'all true Englishmen' were against the Hanover troops, and that 'Whig and Tory has been laid aside a good while and the distinction of Court and Country is now sunk into that of Englishmen and Hanoverians.' Looking forward to the 1742 debates, the opposition Whig Richard Grenville wrote that 'We shall then see . . . who are Hanoverians, and who Englishmen.' A year later, the Duke of Bedford described the Hanoverians as guilty of 'partiality, insolence and disobedience' and also as 'strangers to England'. The Earl of Chesterfield pronounced that 'The people of this kingdom have already conceived a sort of aversion to Hanover . . . I am resolved that let this question go how it will, it shall appear upon your journals [i.e. the parliamentary record], that I acted upon this occasion like an Englishman.' The twenty-six peers who voted against the Hanover payments registered their dissent so that 'our names in the books may transmit us to posterity Englishmen'. To underline the point, one version of the division list printed the names of the ayes in Hanoverian yellow and the nays in glorious British red.[31]

The sense of British identity which emerged from the Hanover debates was not so much ethnic but political. Critics repeatedly stressed their 'freedom' and 'liberty' against the Continental despotism of Hanover and the King: they were, in the words of one peer, 'stubborn freeborn

Englishmen, who had from their infancy conceived a notion of rights and privileges inherent and unalienable'. Lord Lonsdale stated it as axiomatic 'that any freeborn Englishman ought to precede a hireling of Hanover'. Sometimes, this rhetoric took on an orientalizing streak, when one peer spoke about the 'Electoral divan [having] regulated the operations'. On this reading the Hanoverian connection had the taint not merely of central European but eastern – Ottoman – despotism.[32]

For this reason, the suspected aggrandizement of Hanover was not just a violation of the Act of Settlement but a mortal threat to the constitution itself. The *Old England* journal argued in December 1743 that 'He that govern'd by will and pleasure in one country would be apt to think himself extremely unlucky that he could not do the same in another; other than continue thus unhappy he would endeavour to introduce and establish, if not exactly his own arbitrary system, something that might answer his ends almost as well. And this might be easily and safely done by his dodging between the two capacities of K[ing] and E[lector].' Moreover, the employment of Hanoverian troops fuelled fears that they might be employed by the monarchy and corrupt ministers to threaten British liberties. Thus St Aubyn argued that the Hanoverians 'lived under a prince who being used to arbitrary power in his dominions abroad, was minded to establish it here; and that all his measures were calculated for that end and this of Hanover troops in particular'. Likewise, Sandwich fretted that 'These troops may support the minister, which may ruin the nation; nor is this the first body of auxiliaries which courtiers have called in to their assistance.' In this context, of course, the acquisition of Bremen and Verden took on a particularly sinister aspect. As one pamphleteer pointed out, a future monarch with absolutist pretensions could enslave Britons by embarking troops in 'these outlets from Germany', as many men 'as he should think necessary for fitting us with manacles'. Once again, therefore, the Hanoverian connection became a focal point for fears of Continental contamination.[33]

Central to all this was an insular conception of British identity, which the Hanoverian connection and its resulting European entanglements seemed to threaten. Chesterfield, who held rather different views in private, showed no hesitation in playing to the gallery on this issue, in his famous pamphlet *The case of the Hanover forces*. 'Hanover,' he argued, 'robbed us of the benefit of being an island and was actually a pledge for our good behaviour on the Continent.' If England were to take on the defence of Hanover, the *Old England* journal argued in April 1744, it 'would lose the very benefit of being an island, and become a most wretched part, of a most contemptible particle of the Continent'. This theme was elaborated in the September issue, when the writer James Ralph argued that 'as an island and an independent people, we have no more to do with the present war, than we could have in a war betwixt Kublai Khan and Prester John.' Lord Barrington plaintively hoped that 'an Angel could come and tell us, I will separate you from Hanover, I will make you an island again.' On this reading, Britain's proper element was the sea, not the European continent. Thus the Tory MP John Phillips told Parliament that the navy was 'our natural strength'; exactly the same phrase was used by Edmund Waller exactly one year later.[34]

The xenophobia of the parliamentary onslaught was taken to new heights in the popular debate. The *Old England* journal dismissed the Electorate as a 'province scarce known to the world, scarce to be found on the map'. A ballad described Hanover as a 'tatter'd Nurse of aspect glum', Britain as 'an Island-Nymph most fair'. Hanoverian 'slaves' were contrasted with 'free-born' Englishmen. The *Westminster Journal* dismissed Hanover as 'a spot of German furze and heath'. The 1743 ballad entitled 'Beef and butt beer against . . . Pumpernickle' speaks for itself. Prints routinely depicted the Electorate as a desolate and impoverished principality, producing only kings, linen and mercenaries for export. Attacking Hanover, therefore, became a way of defining what it meant to be British. By implication Britons were not fat, slow-witted, morose, gluttonous, flatulent, drink-sodden, humourless, venal, ruled by a despotic prince, or inhabitants of a small territory in the middle of an unpleasant and intractable European continent. Instead, they were free-born, virtuous, prosperous men who lived on a temperate island; and of course they had a special sense of humour.[35]

In the main, however, the ministry and its supporters responded to the Hanover attacks with a robust restatement of their policies and beliefs. The growing isolationist and navalist trend came in for a particularly serious battering. Lord Perceval, a Whig critic of Walpole's grand strategy, lamented to Parliament that 'a doctrine has been taught and inculcated for some months past, that it is of no importance to this nation what may happen on the Continent; that this country being an island entrenched within its own natural boundaries, it may stand secure and unconcerned in all the storms of the rest of the world.' He pro-

An Actual Survey of the Electorate, or Face of the Country whereon Hanover Stands, with a View of Herenhausern and the Seats of Manufactures.

23. A satirical 'view' of Hanover which, with its sarcastic caption, is typical of the Hanover-bashing of early eighteenth-century British debate.

nounced 'this doctrine' – which was being articulated 'without these walls' – to be 'contrary . . . to the universal principles of policy by which this nation hath been governed from the Conquest to this hour'. In the same vein, Carteret argued that engagement in European alliances and wars was not just some 'sort of superfluous heroism'; Britons were not simply wasting lives and treasure on 'romantic expeditions'. On the contrary, failure to intervene on the Continent would simply allow the French to realize their plans for universal monarchy. To disband the Hanoverians would be to 'leave the French to ravage provinces without resistance . . . and make half the princes of Europe the slaves of their pride'. Naval power alone would not suffice. 'Armies,' as Carteret stressed, 'were only to be repelled by armies.' To this end, Samuel Sandys, the Whig MP for Worcester and a confirmed opponent of a large standing army in peacetime, was prepared not only to swallow his constitutional objections to standing armies, but also to dig deeply into his pocket. He therefore condemned the fact that 'The bulk of mankind can see no danger but what is directly before their eyes, and consequently are unwilling to contribute to the charge of guarding against a danger which they cannot see.' 'The people,' the Paymaster-General Thomas Winnington lamented, 'expect to be protected by their government, they expect to be secured even from the approach of danger, and yet they grudge every expense which becomes necessary for that purpose.'[36]

Of course, Britain could not contain France alone. Keeping Austria intact, Horatio Walpole argued in December 1742, was therefore crucial to the 'harmony and unanimity of the Germanic body', upon which in turn 'the balance of power must now depend'. 'The preservation of the House of Austria,' Thomas Winnington argued in late 1743, 'and in that the balance of power, is a measure which has, ever since the Revolution, been judged necessary for this nation to pursue.' Indeed, as Sandys remarked, 'the House of Austria is the Ucalegon [a neighbour whose house is on fire] of Great Britain; for if ever that house should be destroyed by the flames of a war lighted up by France and Spain, Great Britain will certainly be next, because we are next in power.' A direct link between the Austrian alliance, the stability of the Holy Roman Empire, British security and the political achievements of the Glorious Revolution of 1688 was thus established. It was in fact the same argument which had driven the critique of Stuart foreign policy from the early seventeenth century. As each Continental bastion was washed away by the French tide, Britons saw the threat of universal monarchy inch closer and closer to them.[37]

Moreover, these men made the same ritualized and instinctive connection between British naval power and the European balance which had characterized British grand strategy since the time of William of Orange. For Carteret, Horatio Walpole, Newcastle and other advocates did not see engagement in Europe as preferable to naval expansion; they saw it as essential in the long term to the maintenance of British maritime supremacy. Europe and America, on this reading, were not opposites but linked in a vital and virtuous circle. If France were ever to gain control of Flanders, the Secretary at War William Yonge warned, then she would be freed of all European distractions and able to challenge Britain more effectively at sea. The same point was made by Horatio Walpole, who insisted British intervention on behalf of Maria Theresa was essential for the maintenance of British naval superiority. If Britain had remained inactive, he argued, 'and allowed France to parcel out the Austrian dominions as she pleased, what fatal consequences might we not have expected? France would then have had no occasion for keeping up a very great land army ... and applied all that saving towards repairing and augmenting her naval force'. For this reason Walpole argued that 'by land we beat them out of the sea. We obtained so great and so many victories at land, that they were forced to neglect their sea affairs.' On the other hand, he concluded, if both France and Spain were to unite against Britain, 'and we should have no one to assist us, nor they any enemy to fear at land, I would not have gentlemen vainly imagine that we should be in no danger of losing our superiority even upon our own element'. He elaborated these arguments the following year and again in January 1744.[38]

The model for a successful European intervention was generally taken to be the early and middle stages of the War of the Spanish Succession, when Britain, Austria and the Dutch had grappled with the French on the Continent, while the allied navies eventually prevailed overseas. As Horatio Walpole observed in late 1742, 'If we had then had no assistance from the Dutch, we should not perhaps have found ourselves such an overmatch for the French at sea, as some people imagine we now are; and yet, during all that time, she kept up most numerous armies at land.' That being so, he continued, 'what then have we to expect, should the whole treasure and strength of France, or the greatest part of both, be turned towards gaining a superiority or at least an equality at sea?'[39] By contrast, the final stages of the conflict, when a Tory government was believed to have abandoned Britain's allies and the common cause against France, was a traumatic memory for Whig Continentalists. Thus one MP warned in early 1744 that to withdraw from the European war 'will be a more unjustifiable measure than the desertion of the Grand Alliance in 1712: the Queen then declared by the mouth of the Bishop of Bristol, her plenipotentiary at Utrecht, that she looked upon herself as free from all her engagements to her allies'. He added that to abandon Maria Theresa was to 'repeat the perfidy without giving the warning'. The immediate result, he added, would be an Austrian accommodation with France in which she would 'surrender her part of the Barrier to France or to a prince who may be a dependant on France'.[40]

In this context, Hanover was not merely a source of useful mercenaries, or a forward base to mobilize the Holy Roman Empire, but the keystone of the Continental diversion. Thus the anonymous author of the *Plain reasoner* argued that:

If it be true, as our minor politicians say, that our business [in Germany] is only to defend Hanover, I hope there will always be a Hanover there . . . so the French may always be kept in Germany at the hazard of the ruin of France. And I conceive that if there was neither a Hanover nor a House of Austria in Germany, yet one would contrive to find something else, to keep them employed on that side to keep them in a perpetual waste of wealth and strength rather than they should come with their force and vigour to our own doors.

If Hanover did not exist, in other words, Britain would have had to invent it. It would be hard to find a more succinct defence of the classic Whig Continental strategy, and Hanover's developing role in it. [41]

It is therefore unsurprising that in early 1744, as the Hanoverian troop debates reached their climax, British ministers paid a backhanded compliment to the Personal Union. The King, shaken by the anti-Hanoverian rhetoric of the past two years, had begun with his German servants to explore the viability of breaking the connection between the two countries. On the first occasion the issue had arisen, around 1720, British ministers had counselled George I against the move. This time both London and the Hanoverian ministers were opposed. The King's German advisors foresaw a legal headache: though George could renounce his own rights, he had no authority to do so on behalf of his son. Moreover, they saw value in the link: it helped to maintain Protestant solidarity in the Empire, while providing a support to Austria against France. On this reading, Hanover was a British asset in Germany, through which coalitions and subsidies could be organized. George backed off for the moment, though he was to return to the subject thirteen years later when another Hanoverian neutrality treaty raised very similar issues. [42]

The employment of Hanoverian troops and the protection of the Personal Union was thus a necessary part of the containment of France, the maintenance of the European balance, and the preservation of British naval security. In late January 1744, as the debates on the Hanoverian troops reached their climax, Carteret thus drew together all the elements of the Whig orthodoxy in a compelling peroration. French universal monarchy, he argued, could only be stopped by supporting the House of Austria as a counterweight:

For if the French monarch once saw himself freed from a rival on that continent, he would then sit secure in the possession of his conquests, he might then reduce his garrisons, abandon his fortresses, and discharge his troops; but that treasure which now fills the plains with soldiers, would soon be employed in designs more dangerous to our country: we should see the project of forming a rival force renewed, the ocean would soon be covered with the fleets of France, and it would contribute very little to our security that we are surrounded with waters and by rocks.

In this context, Sir William Yonge argued in Parliament, 'it was right in us to take the first troops we could get, which happened to be those of the Electorate of Hanover.' Besides, the Hanoverians were hired more or less at cost and not – as with other troops – at a premium. Pro-government voices were not slow to point this out. In the end, all of the votes on the Hanover troops in 1742–4 were carried by the government with comfortable margins.[43]

Moreover, some enthusiasts saw Hanover as a potential British out-post on the Continent. Not only could it be, as Carteret had argued, co-opted into the common anti-French front: the Electorate, and especially the Hanoverian ports of Bremen and Verden, were nothing less than a British foothold in Germany. Thus Horatio Walpole claimed that the question of whether 'those countries which command the navigation of the Elbe and the Weser, the only inlets from the British seas in Germany', should be allowed to fall into the potentially hostile hands of Sweden or Denmark, or should be 'annexed for ever to the King's Electoral dominions', was one 'which can easily be decided by a bare inspection into the map of Europe'. Lord Bathurst argued in his *Letter to a friend concerning the electorate of Hanover* in 1744 that 'it is known to everybody of what consequence maritime forts and harbours are to the trade of this nation . . . I do not see why the same arguments may not in some degree hold good with respect to our having a naturalized tenure among the Germanic body on the Continent.'[44]

But there were also some who openly deplored the xenophobic groundswell which characterized so much of the Hanover debates. The Duke of Marlborough regretted that 'It is not possible to mention Hanover or its inhabitants, in any public place, without putting the whole house into a flame, and hearing on every hand expressions of resentment, threats of revenge, or clamours of detestation.' Indeed, he continued, 'Hanover is now become a name which cannot be mentioned without provoking rage and malignity and interrupting the discourse by a digression of abhorrence.' Lord Raymond spoke of a 'vehemence' which was 'inclined to intimidate enquiry, and intimidate opposition'.

He went on to remark 'That the people of England are by nature or habit enemies to foreigners, is generally believed; but surely, my lords, this is not one of our native qualities of which we ought to boast.' He added that 'in the eye of reason, my lords, it is more laudable to make an estimate of a man by his merit, than by his country, and to enquire rather how he has passed his life than whence he received it?' Instead, Raymond lamented, 'the people have been taught to hate the Hanoverians'; and this, one might add, at a time when Britain needed all the help it could get.[45]

Within two years of the fall of Walpole, therefore, the strategic position of Britain was greatly improved. The Austrian collapse had been halted at least for the time being. France was mired in an unsuccessful war in Germany which sapped her naval and colonial efforts. British strategic doctrine about the need for a Continental engagement was further refined. Hanover had been turned from a military and constitutional liability into a strategic asset, albeit one that was still domestically controversial.

13

The American Empire Restores the Balance in the German Empire, 1745–1748

> At length she comes, the goddess fair
> Victoria! Whom we late implor'd;
> Advancing with majestic air,
> At once both dreaded and ador'd
>
> But not on Flandria's hostile plain
> As we, mistaken, then besought,
> The British blood is spilt in vain,
> For not the British cause is fought.
>
> Beyond the wide Atlantic sea
> She rises first to crown our toils,
> Thither to wealth she points the way,
> And bids us thrive on Gallic spoils
>
> When solid measures we pursue,
> Our arms she ever will uphold:
> And while of these we lost the view,
> New England's sons have taught the Old.
>
> Gentleman's Magazine, 1745[1]

British fortunes in the final years of the War of the Austrian Succession were mixed. After the triumph of Dettingen, and the recovery of Maria Theresa in 1742–4, the situation in the Empire began to deteriorate once more. Prussia re-entered the war, wreaking havoc with British policy in Germany. The only ray of hope there was the death of the Emperor Charles VII in 1745, which allowed the election of Maria

Theresa's husband Francis of Lorraine as his successor. One pillar of Britain's imperial security structure had therefore been restored. The other pillar, however, was now crumbling at an alarming rate. Austria, preoccupied with Frederick the Great, made only feeble efforts to defend the Barrier in Flanders against the French advance. From 1745, the fortresses there began to fall with depressing regularity; this worried the Crown and ministry even more than the arrival of Bonnie Prince Charlie in Scotland in 1745 and his advance into England. In this context, the spectacular victory over the French at Louisburg in Canada was not just a 'good news' story for the ministry. It moved the New World from the margins of strategic debate closer to the centre of attention. British statesmen became more conscious of the value of colonial resources to their standing and effectiveness in Europe. Even more importantly, the victory at Louisburg provided London with a vital bargaining chip to restore the fallen bastions in Flanders. From now on, British statesmen would begin to integrate the New World more systematically into their conception of the European balance of power.

By early 1744 Carteret's European policy, which had been quite successful in 1742–3, was in trouble. In March 1744 France finally declared war on Britain and Hanover. In some ways, this simply legitimized the existing state of affairs. The French continued to be heavily engaged in Germany and Flanders; their operations overseas ground to an almost complete halt. This was all to the good. But Carteret was unable to uncouple the Emperor from Versailles. He also failed to contain the Franco-Spanish advance in Italy. Above all, he inadvertently provoked Prussia into rejoining the war against Austria. He had already irritated Frederick with the Treaty of Worms in September 1743, and in December of that year he compounded the offence by helping to mediate a treaty between the Austrians and the Saxons, which appeared to have a secret article implying the creation of a land link between Saxony and Poland at the expense of Prussia. In May 1744 Frederick set up the Union of Frankfurt in conjunction with the Emperor, William of Hesse and the Elector Palatine; he also occupied the north German principality of East Friesland. In August 1744 he launched his second attack on Maria Theresa. Carteret's German policy had therefore collapsed and with it the credibility of a ministry already heavily battered by the Hanover controversy.

The final straw had been not just European developments, but the accompanying press campaign which Frederick the Great and Carteret's domestic enemies had carefully manipulated. For in August and September 1744, the 'treaty' of Hanau, by which Carteret had sought to uncouple the Bavarian Emperor from the anti-Habsburg alliance, and which many had believed buried the previous year, was exhumed and its failure laid at Carteret's door. These months saw the publication of two Prussian-inspired pamphlets and the appearance of a 'narrative' by the slighted Prince William of Hesse, who had acted as Charles Albert's intermediary at Hanau. It was not the highways and byways of German imperial politics which mesmerized British audiences, but the allegation – which Carteret proved unable satisfactorily to refute – that the King's chief minister, not the cabinet as a whole, had sabotaged the negotiations, and thus set in motion the train of events which brought Prussia back into the war. This blunder was blamed on Carteret' s desire to pander to the King's Hanoverian prejudices. In particular, the Prussian envoy to London proved adept at fuelling the press campaign to undermine Carteret. He made a valuable convert in the Earl of Chesterfield, whose pamphlet *Natural reflexions on the present conduct of His Prussian Majesty*, did additional damage. 'Who lost Prussia?' was now the cry.[2]

In November 1744, Carteret's Whig rivals pounced. He was reproached with failing to explore potential links to the Russians and Saxons with sufficient vigour; with neglecting to bring the Dutch into play; and with making no effort to court Prussia. Within a very short time, Carteret had resigned, yet another British statesman to fall due the perceived failure of his German policy. He was replaced by a ministry dominated by Newcastle as Secretary of State and his younger brother, Henry Pelham, at the Treasury. Yet the Continentalist orthodoxy, which had been reasserted from the fall of Walpole in 1742, continued to prevail. The deployments after 1744 bear this out. In that year, there were 37 Royal Navy ships in colonial waters, with crews of about 11,000 men. There were 48 in the Mediterranean, with crews of more than 20,000 men, as well as 24 ships in home waters with more than 10,000 sailors on board. Twelve months later, the relative proportions had not much changed. In both years, there was a preponderance of larger, heavy-gunned ships on the near side of the Atlantic. Moreover, the bulk of the colonial deployments, particularly of battleships, were to the Caribbean, not to North America. Their purpose was in accordance with traditional British grand strategy: to safeguard the revenue flows and deny France the colonial resources to fund European expansion. The picture was even clearer with regard to troop dispositions: there were scarcely 2,000 men in North America, and a few more in the Caribbean. The bulk were to be found in Europe: 19,000 in Britain itself, 8,000 in the Mediterranean and a whopping 21,000 in Flanders. In short, the main effort by the Royal Navy and the British army throughout the War of the Austrian Succession was made in Europe.[3]

Newcastle elaborated his thinking in the course of the coming years. In late 1745, he justified his support for a land war against France by 'the danger and hazard of being alone at war with France and Spain, which two powers, by being absolutely disengaged from all expense on the Continent, would soon be able to be superior to us at sea'. Against Pitt, who wanted to wind down the European operations, he argued 'that a defensive war upon the Continent and an offensive war at sea was better than only an offensive war at sea, which was what they proposed'. This was because 'if France and Spain had nothing to deal with but England, they might . . . soon have a marine superior to ours, and then what a condition should we be in?' In the War of the Spanish Succcession, he continued, 'we destroyed their marine by creating them business on the Continent . . . by delivering them from expenses on the Continent, we should force them to re-establish their marine, of which we should hereafter feel the bad effects.' He was thus very much against, as he put it, 'reducing ourselves to our wooden walls'. A couple of months later he returned to this theme when he argued for the need to 'employ France on the Continent, that the whole weight of their power may not fall upon us'. The main outlines of Carteret's German policy and his broader strategic framework thus remained in place.[4]

The new ministry sought to persuade Maria Theresa to accommodate Frederick and concentrate on fighting the French. Chesterfield, who had now become the envoy to The Hague, thus lamented Maria Theresa's failure to 'make up with' Prussia: 'the immediate effect of that obstinacy and greediness,' he predicted, would be another Franco-Prussian rapprochement. Like Carteret, the ministry also pursued an active imperial policy. In January 1745 Britain, Holland, Austria and Saxony concluded a defensive treaty at Warsaw by which all contractants agreed to uphold the Pragmatic Sanction and the balance in the Empire. The chance of prising open the French position in Germany came unexpectedly in January 1745 with the sudden death of Charles Albert of Bavaria and thus another imperial vacancy. Thus Chesterfield was particularly keen to secure the Elector of Saxony, to 'snatch him up', as he put it, before the French did so, if necessary by supporting his candidacy as Emperor. Newcastle, on the other hand, stuck to the traditional line; he thought that the Saxon Elector was not sufficiently strong in his own right to maintain the Barrier function of the German Empire. 'It is for the general interest of Europe,' Newcastle pronounced in February 1745, 'that the imperial crown should be fixed in the House of Austria ... A weak Emperor will be (and sooner or later must be) a French Emperor.' The centrality of the Empire to British grand strategy thus remained unchanged. In the end, British policy in Germany was successful more through luck than judgement: Charles Albert's successor as Elector, Max Joseph, took Bavaria out of the war at the Treaty of Füssen and cast his vote for the Austrian imperial candidate, Maria Theresa's husband, Francis Stephen of Lorraine.[5]

At the same time, a sustained attempt was made to win over Prussia. Here the Hanoverian ministers and the King proved once more a major obstacle. George had reacted to the second Prussian attack on Maria Theresa by putting punitive action against Frederick, and the aggrandizement of the Electorate at his expense, back on the agenda. Carteret had rather indulged these plans, perhaps to humour George. Their logic was clear enough: Frederick had now broken imperial law for the second time. He was not to be trusted and had to be eliminated, for France could only be beaten if Austria were able to deploy all of her might against her. Moreover, Frederick had infuriated George in late 1744 by his threat to invade Hanover if George moved against Charles Albert. The ministry certainly considered the partition of Prussia. 'I don't know,' Chesterfield mused in 1745, 'whether the dismembering of him [Frederick] is not the shortest way of getting out of our difficulties.' The problem with the proposed policy of freeing Maria Theresa from Prussian distractions by military force was not its desirability but its impracticality. So by the Convention of Hanover in August 1745 with Prussia, Britain agreed to mediate with Austria, while Frederick agreed to make peace with Austria and to vote for the Austrian candidate as Emperor. Maria Theresa soldiered on for a few months, but after the Saxons were crushed by Frederick at the Battle of Hohenfriedberg in

November–December 1745, she threw in the towel at the Treaty of Dresden in late December 1745 and made her peace with Frederick for the time being. Francis Stephen was duly elected Emperor. The Empire was back in Habsburg hands, and Austria was now free to turn all her attention against France in the west.[6]

There was still the public relations problem of what to do about the Hanoverians. Here an elegant solution was found. The existing subsidies were loudly discontinued. Henceforth, some 6,000 troops would be paid for by the King himself out of his Hanoverian revenues. As for the rest, the government would simply record the sum as a subsidy to Maria Theresa, but pay the money directly to the Hanoverian minister in London. This required a certain amount of financial juggling. Hanoverian troops in British service were paid more than their counterparts in Electoral service. When the two fought alongside each other, George refused to pay the difference, so the British exchequer footed the bill. It was still a good deal. As Newcastle noted with some satisfaction in January 1746, because the King was paying for many of the men 'upon his own Electoral account' this enabled the ministry to 'avoid the objections arising from an estimate for taking those troops into the British pay, and the King, as Elector, will contribute considerably towards the war in Flanders'. The bottom line was that Britain was getting some of her Hanoverian troops on the cheap. Moreover, the Hanoverians were an important part of the allied war effort, even after Britain became a belligerent. The Whig George Grenville – a bitter critic of Hanoverian troops – contrasted their performance with those of the British and their Dutch auxiliaries during the lost Battle of Fontenoy in May 1745. 'The Dutch horse behaved scandalously,' he wrote, 'their foot but indifferently; the Hanovers very well.' He blamed the defeat in part on the (British) Brigadier General Ingoldsby 'who several times refused to attack' despite being ordered to do so. In the end, the assault was launched by 'two Hanover battalions, which were cut to pieces, whilst Ingoldsby looked on with four choice English battalions; for which neglect, or not to mince the word, *poltronnerie*, he is to be tried as soon as he recovers [from] his wounds'. Throughout the war, in fact, the King's German soldiers remained an important asset for Britain. Opposition to the Hanover troops petered out, with only a small row over those subsidies in early 1745.[7]

The continued reliance of the new ministry on 'Continental measures' did not go unremarked. Horatio Walpole later claimed that 'the Duke of Newcastle . . . grew as fond of the war abroad as Lord Granville [Carteret]'. In Parliament Lord Strange condemned the manoeuvres over the subsidies as 'a piece of low legerdemain' and lamented the 'use of the Queen of Hungary as the cat's paw for drawing that sum out of the pockets of the people of England'. Edward Turner complained that his 'patience is worn out, in seeing patriots swallow down ministerial puddings piping hot without so much as blistering their tongues'. There was also a fresh surge of press derision. In spring 1745 the *Westminster Journal* renewed the demand for a separation of Kingdom and Elector-ate, before the latter siphoned off more British resources 'which ought to act only in defence of our own trade and honour'. The opposition paper *Old England* predicted a few months later that the country would soon be 'the wretched appendix of a despicable corner of Germany', in which Hanoverian sergeants would 'beat up' for 'recruits on the streets of London'. Far from putting the Germans in their place, it complained, the new ministry had indulged them still more.[8]

But by then, the government had much more important things to worry about. For on 23 July 1745 Charles Edward Stuart, the son and heir to the pretender to the throne, went ashore on the Isle of Eriskay in Scotland with a small band of followers. The goblin which Pulteney had dismissed in the early 1740s had landed. Britain would have been glad of a few more Hanoverians on those street corners.

To the clansmen who trickled to the Stuart standard at Moidart, Charles Edward represented a chance to turn the tables on the British and the lowland Scots establishment. But his appeal to the nation as a whole was couched in more patriotic terms, in which criticism of the Hanoverian connection and European entanglements played an import-ant part. Thus the 'Declaration of James III', drafted in late December 1743 in preparation for a planned landing, claimed that Englishmen had 'seen the treasures of the nation applied to satiate private avarice, and lavished for the support of German dominions'. Moreover, the Pretender argued, following classic anti-Hanoverian propaganda, the past twenty years had found 'the nation involved in wars, which have been . . . carried on without any advantage to Britain, and even to the manifest detriment and discouragement of its trade, and a great body of Hanoverians taken into the English pay and service' to whom 'preference and partiality' had been shown. Likewise, the Jacobite pamphleteer

William Harper argued that it was preferable to be ruled by Charles Edward's backers, the French, than by Germans. 'The first,' he claimed, 'has a frankness and generosity to temper, qualify and soften it: but a German despoticism, being grafted on a stock of sullen, sour, morose, bitter nature congenial to the nation, is by far the more dangerous and dreadful of the two.' Britain, so the Jacobite argument ran, was being fleeced by Hanover; George II was really a German with absolutist pretensions, while Charles Edward represented a local dynasty.[9]

For the next nine months or so, Charles Edward proceeded to run riot, defeating the government forces in Scotland and marching south as far as Derby. It was the failure of French support to materialize, and the hesitation of English Jacobites, rather than the immediate military resistance which eventually persuaded the majority of Charles's council, though not the Young Pretender himself, that the time had come to retreat. Charles – as he had always stressed – was no absolutist, and to his great mortification he was outvoted. This was certainly a missed opportunity. The only loyal troops between the Jacobites and London were a detachment of militia cowering at Finchley. They would have been shrugged aside if Charles's council had decided to press on.

While the capital lay open to a force of rebels who had marched almost the length of the island pretty much unopposed, large contingents of British troops were deployed elsewhere. There were 28,000 men in Flanders; but just 16,000 regulars in the whole of Britain. In fact, what is striking about the governmental response to the Forty-five is the relative nonchalance with which the Jacobite threat, *per se*, was regarded. True, Newcastle wrote in November 1745 that 'Every day shows that this rebellion is by no means a trifle.' On the other hand, Chesterfield, admittedly from the distance of Dublin Castle, saw 'nothing more ridiculous than that rascally Highland army, with which His Royal Highness Prince Charles intends to conquer us, except it be our army that runs away from such a pack of scoundrels'. Two months later he declared that 'the number and condition of the rebels is contemptible, and should they be joined by any insurrection in England, they would only be joined by people still more contemptible than themselves.' What worried the British far more was the prospect of a French invasion in support of the Pretender. 'If they have no foreign assistance,' Chesterfield argued, 'there must be an end of them one way or another.'[10]

Outside intervention seemed in the offing at the very end of 1745, when a French army of about 10,000 men assembled at Boulogne. The spectre of French invasion explains the ferocity with which the government pursued the 'pacification' of the Highlands after the defeat of the Bonnie Prince at Culloden in April 1746. They were determined to put an end to Scottish Jacobitism once and for all. Newcastle wrote that 'The rebellion must be got the better of in such a manner that we must not have another next year. And, if this power of the Highlands is not absolutely reduced, France may play the Pretender upon us whenever she pleases, when perhaps, we shall not be so well prepared to resist it as we were even this time.' Fears of an invasion remained acute, even after the army at Boulogne was stood down. Likewise, fear of a renewed Jacobite rebellion, this time with substantial French help, continued to plague the government for some time. Thus Charles Edward was quoted in messages intercepted by the British in October 1746, as saying that 'If the English force us to lay aside all sort of management with them we do not want the means to raise new disturbances in their islands.' In short, the Jacobite rebellion of 1745 was seen – as the threat of the Pretender had always been – through the prism of the European balance and the French threat.[11]

For most of the period of the rebellion, in fact, Britain remained far more concerned with developments in Flanders. It was there, and not in Scotland, that London felt most threatened; and it was in Flanders that the military tide began to turn in France's favour. As Horatio Walpole later remarked, 'the war was not better managed on the Continent after [Carteret] was turned out.' Instead, the French heavily defeated the British army at Fontenoy and advanced northwards with alarming pace. George Grenville wrote that 'people hang their heads about this battle'. In July 1745, only a fortnight before the landing of the Pretender, the Earl of Sandwich wrote that 'we are all greatly alarmed with the melancholy posture of our affairs in Flanders.' The fall of Ostend – with 'dreadful consequences' – seemed imminent. The Duke of Newcastle was no more sanguine: 'our foreign affairs go ill indeed,' he wrote in October 1745. The general gloom was summed up by Sir Benjamin Keene, a long-serving ambassador then between postings. 'I have not the heart to touch upon any political affair,' he wrote. 'They seem to be in so very bad a way that I neither see the light or conceive hopes of our bringing them to a good conclusion. The French do what they please in Flanders . . . what can a handful of men do against a country which now every body feels the power of?' The Barrier was in danger. In August 1745, scarcely four weeks into the Rebellion, Newcastle stressed that 'the recovery of Flanders is so capital a point for this country that we cannot but humbly hope that it will take place of all other considerations.' Shortly afterwards he repeated 'that it was essentially our interest . . . to keep them [the Dutch] an independent state'. Britain's security, in other words, was more dependent on the European balance, particularly on keeping the French out of the Low Countries, than it was on keeping the Pretender out of Britain itself.[12]

Popular opinion in 1745–6 became profoundly exercised by British weakness. Most agreed that the kingdom should be protected by a system of European alliances, but they were also of the view that Britons ought better to be able to provide for themselves. As always in a time of national crisis, the nation was beset by a series of moral panics in the early 1740s. Ideas of 'public virtue' were closely linked to perceptions of military vibrancy: defeats or apparent lack of leadership were explained through corruption. The demand for inquiries and 'answers', which had so dogged the final years of the Walpole administration, now spilled over into scrutiny of the armed services. Even the otherwise popular Navy came under increasing scrutiny, particularly during the controversy between Matthews and Lestocq, which followed the Toulon engagement in 1744. Unlike in earlier years, however, the critique now centred more on society as a whole, rather than the ministry and the court, though these did not escape censure. These anxieties peaked in 1745, when the nation looked on in horror as a band of despised Highlanders marched as far south as Derby, scattering all before them. The indignity of having to hire 6,000 Hessians to deal with them was keenly felt, even if the Rebellion was ultimately suppressed by a British force under the Duke of Cumberland.[13]

The King, for his part, remained far more preoccupied with the Prussian threat to Hanover than what was happening in Scotland or even Derby. Frederick the Great's re-entry into the war had not only increased the pressure on Britain's ally Maria Theresa, but also opened up a potential new front to the east. It was with some difficulty that Newcastle and his brother Henry Pelham dissuaded George from withdrawing the Hanoverian contingents from Flanders – where they were a highly valued fighting force – to cover the Electorate. Yet the King remained anxious for his German homeland: as Chesterfield observed in December 1745,

George would not want to see Hanover 'expose itself to another visit from Maillebois', the French general who had nearly occupied the Electorate in 1741. All this was clear evidence, if any more were needed, that the war was being continued for British and not Hanoverian purposes. The problem was that the security of the King's German lands and the integrity of the Dutch Barrier were closely linked: if the Dutch made a separate peace, the western flank of Hanover was open to renewed French attack. And in Flanders things looked very bleak.[14]

The problem facing Britain in the Low Countries was fundamentally structural in nature. Ever since the Treaty of Utrecht in 1713, London had looked to the Austrian presence in Flanders and the stiffening of the Dutch Barrier fortresses to keep the French out. In this way the politics of the Grand Alliance were to be perpetuated. At the height of the French alliance in the 1720s, this had been of little relevance, but by the late 1730s, the revival of Anglo-French antagonism had made the Low Countries once again an area of extreme geopolitical sensitivity for Britain. Throughout the early 1740s, as we have seen, great hopes were still being placed in the Dutch. After France had joined the war in 1744, the Dutchmen manning the Barrier were directly engaged, though the United Provinces itself was not yet formally at war. Their lacklustre defence of the fortresses – and the blatant sabotage of the Dutch war effort by the Francophile 'patriot' party within Holland – punctured any expectations of help from that quarter. By September 1744, Newcastle was complaining that the Dutch 'absolutely renounce the precedents of former wars'. In March 1745, the British envoy to The Hague judged that the notion of a 'Grand Alliance and universal plan of operations' with the Dutch was 'impracticable'. At the same time, the other pillar of the Grand Alliance was beginning to wobble. Maria Theresa was too preoccupied by her losses in Germany, and intimidated by the French advance, to carry out the role allotted to her by Britain. 'You will find,' Chesterfield predicted to Newcastle, 'that, when Silesia is out of the question, the Queen of Hungary will be very indifferent about everything else and even impatient to make her peace with France.' Indeed, he continued, 'She will then tell you that Flanders has been only a burthen and not an advantage to her, and that it is the business of the maritime powers alone to defend it.'[15]

These developments prompted a rethink of Britain's traditional European policy. If the Dutch and the Austrians would not defend the Barrier, who would? In May 1746 the idea of a perpetual neutrality of the Low Countries, that is the Dutch Republic and the Austrian Netherlands, was briefly floated. This found little favour with Newcastle, who feared that it would take the United Provinces out of the European balance of power and remove a constraint on French power in Germany. More generally, British statesmen had to confront the fact that Prussia and not France was now the principal enemy of Austria. The ramifications of this for Britain's European policy took some time to sink in. Those who, like Chesterfield, thought that France could only be contained if Britain proceeded to 'whisper and agree with *Antimac* [Frederick – a reference to his *Antimachiavell* tract of 1740, in which he challenged Machiavelli's ideas on statecraft]' were still a minority. A Prussian alliance had been canvassed before, but since December 1740 it always came at the price of alienating Austria; the time was not far off when that price would be worth paying. For the moment there was nothing for it but to try to bring the war to a rapid close before the French overran the rest of the Low Countries. As Chesterfield wrote in late November 1745, 'I would make peace with 'em [the Dutch] and through 'em. Oh! But then it will be a bad peace, and we won't have a bad peace. I can't help that, but when you are beaten and can't carry on the war any longer unless to be beaten still more (which is our present case), all I know is that you must make the best peace you can, and that will be a bad one, which is always the case of the vanquished.' To this end, peace negotiations were eventually commenced at Breda in October 1746.[16]

It was into this scene of unrelieved gloom that news of a great victory in North America burst towards the end of 1745; ironically, like that of Cartagena, it reached George in Hanover. For in mid June, a naval expedition under Admiral Peter Warren, supported by colonial militia, captured the key French fortress of Louisburg at Cape Breton. This base was believed to control the mouth of the St Lawrence and thus access to Quebec, Montreal and most of Canada. It was the first British success of any note overseas since Porto Bello some five years before. There were now many who hoped to make it a stepping stone for further and decisive action in North America, starting with an expedition to capture Quebec in the summer of 1746. It was planned to send some 5,000 regulars and twenty ships in order 'to effect the entire reduction of Canada'. The purpose of this move, as Governor Shirley wrote to the

Duke of Newcastle, was to enlarge the British Empire, not as an end in itself, but in order to 'lay a foundation for a superiority of British power upon the continent of Europe'. He was thus articulating a grand strategy for Britain which had long existed in outline but was to become the new orthodoxy. Not only would Britain secure her maritime dominance through European alliances, but she would also use the Royal Navy to support these alliances and promote overseas expansion. Now colonial expansion would underpin naval superiority and the European balance in a virtuous circle.[17]

24. The capture of Louisburg on Cape Breton was the most spectacular British colonial victory of the war. It was exchanged for a French withdrawal from the Low Countries.

The capture of Louisburg and the prospect of further gains reinvigorated popular colonialist and navalist discourse. Once again maritime virtue was contrasted with European vice. This was epitomized by the 'Hymn to Victory on the taking of Cape Breton', published in the July 1745 edition of the *Gentleman's magazine*. It celebrated a success 'not on Flandria's hostile plain', but 'beyond the wide Atlantic sea', where the sons of 'New England' were instructing the 'old'. In the same vein, the *Universal Spectator* announced that 'It is presumed our success at Cape Breton, which the French have so much interest in defending, will encourage us to some farther attempts upon their settlements in America: By which we might more effectively distress them, and serve ourselves, than by showing them our B[ac]k s[i]des in Flanders. The Leeward Islands seem on this occasion the most inviting object.' Likewise, the *Newcastle Courant*, following leads in London newspapers, wondered 'whether Quebec, St Augustine, the Havannah, St Domingo, or the fortress of Martinico, be not of more importance to us than Tournay, Mons, Namur, Brussels, Antwerp, or Bergen-op-Zoom.' All of these latter towns and fortresses lay not in a far-off corner of eastern Europe, but in the strategically crucial Low Countries.[18]

Victory at Louisburg was particularly celebrated, of course, in the thirteen colonies. Americans regarded it as very much their own triumph. Because of the priority given to Europe, the expedition had been mounted largely by the colonists themselves, with the Royal Navy in a supporting role. The fact that the Massachusetts Assembly had endorsed the attack by only one vote in January 1745 was quickly forgotten. A wave of sermons and pamphlets celebrated both the campaign and its mastermind, Governor Shirley. At the very least, they were determined to hold on to Louisburg. Thus the Boston cleric, the Reverend Thomas Prince, attacked the Tories for having handed back Cape Breton at the Treaty of Utrecht in 1713, a clear shot across the ministry's bows. In 1746 sermons given to mark the first anniversary of the victory helped to keep the issue on the boil, as did newspapers such as the *Boston Weekly Newsletter* and the *Boston Evening Post*. These American papers borrowed material from the *Westminster Journal* and other London publications. Taken together, they constituted an emerging single trans-atlantic public sphere, whose principal preoccupation was the direction of British grand strategy.[19]

Henceforth colonial politics would be dominated by one thing: whether or not the security of British North America was best served through a policy of pre-emptive expansion, designed to drive the French from Canada and ultimately from the western lands as well. The geopol-itical rhetoric of barriers, so familiar to audiences in London and West-minster, was imported from Europe and applied to the new continent. In Massachusetts and other colonies, expansionists now rallied to Gov-ernor Shirley's imperial vision. One Pennsylvanian wrote in 1746 that 'Nothing but a wide river, or inaccessible mountain, are sufficient to separate us from such monsters in nature' as the French. The Massachusetts writer William Bollan, who was the agent for the colony in London, pointed out that Louisburg was 'so situated, as to be either of inestimable value, or inconceivable detriment to the English nation . . . It shuts up as it were, the entrance into the Gulf, and consequently the river of St Lawrence.' Depending on who held it, Louisburg either cut communications between France itself and New France in Quebec, or cut off Newfoundland from the rest of British North America. It was, in short, the 'key to all the British territories in the vicinity'.

Moreover, Louisburg would serve as a springboard for the complete expulsion of the French from the St Lawrence. 'I look upon the reduction of Canada,' Bollan wrote, 'as the natural (I had almost said necessary) effect of reducing Cape Breton.' This would be 'by far the greatest advantage we have hitherto gained by the war'. The strategic value of Louisburg was not just geopolitical, Bollan believed. It was also – and here he followed Shirley's thinking – a potentially decisive contributor to Britain's naval strength and thus to her European standing. The region was not only a source of naval stores, such as pine for masts, but also a centre of the fur trade and the hub of the highly lucrative cod-fishing industry. Above all, Louisburg could be 'a chief nursery for seamen', perhaps up to 30,000 sailors. 'Taken out of the hands of our enemies,' he argued, 'and added to our own trade,' these advantages 'ought . . . to be accounted in a duplicate proportion to the real sum'. In short, 'having that fund of seamen to supply our fleets upon any emergency', and denying these to the enemy, made possession of Louisburg a 'main sinew of war'. All this, he claimed, would soon make George II 'the greatest prince in Europe'.[20]

The euphoria of Cape Breton wore off quickly. It was followed by the fall of Madras to the French in October 1746, a major blow to the British position in India. The planned follow-up expedition against Quebec was caught in a thicket of competing agendas in London, and ultimately cancelled. Besides, the European balance commanded a far higher priority. Here the situation had gone from bad to worse after the defeat at Fontenoy. In February 1746, the French entered Brussels, in July, Mons. Two months later, they marched into Namur and in October, the French worsted the allied army at the Battle of Rocoux. All this showed that the Austrians and Dutch were no longer able or willing to defend the Barrier. A subsidy treaty concluded between the Dutch, British and Austrians at The Hague in August 1746 sought to pin down Maria Theresa to further commitments, but the impact on the ground was negligible. 'The United Provinces,' Chesterfield wrote in late October 1745, 'are impotent by their form of government, which does not seem likely to be altered; they are beggared by their long mismanagement, and soured by their late misfortunes, and I will venture to prophecy that you will soon see 'em in a state of quiet subserviency to France. So that, as an ally, they are really not worth a sacrifice.' The problem was that simply abandoning the Dutch was not an option: as Chesterfield had put it, 'if we break with them, we have not an ally left in the world.' Regime change at The Hague seemed to be the only answer.[21]

The Orangist coup in April–May 1747, which restored the Stadholder to power at The Hague, was probably not sponsored directly by Britain. But a Royal Navy squadron was sent to the Schelde to support the putschists, and the enthusiasm which the news of the change of government in Holland produced among British statesmen was unmistakable. Newcastle hailed it as 'a great event . . . for this country and all Europe; for by it, in all probability, the Republic of Holland will recover its ancient weight and strength, and England have a useful friend and ally instead of a jealous, timid and burthensome neighbour.' There was good reason to expect that this would be the case: on a number of occasions over the past one hundred years, an ailing Dutch government had been toppled to make way for a more robust prosecution of the war against France. On this occasion, however, history was a poor guide to future events.[22]

That summer, the Duke of Cumberland was defeated at Lauffeldt in the Low Countries, despite – as Pitt put it – the bravery of his 'British and Electoral troops [who] did all that can be expected from men overpowered by numbers'. One key fortress after another fell to the French advance, including the crucial Bergen-op-Zoom in September; its 86-year-old Dutch commander lacked the vim of the octogenarian who had defended Cartagena against Vernon. 'Holland seems gone,' the younger Horace Walpole (Robert's son) remarked. 'How long England will remain after it, Providence and the French must determine.' Maastricht fell in May of the following year. If peace were not made soon, the French would overrun the whole of the Dutch Republic as well and thus completely overturn the European balance of power as London understood it. Not since the days of Parma and Louis XIV had the outworks of England been in such danger.[23]

25. A French depiction of their victorious attack on Bergen-op-Zoom, which had formed a key part of the Barrier.

In this situation, Louisburg was virtually the only card British ministers could play. It could be traded for a French withdrawal from the Low Countries, and perhaps also for Madras. This was certainly the view of Lord Harrington, who briefly returned as Secretary of State for the Northern Department in 1746. British ministers were also aware, however, that to do so would unleash a storm of public indignation. Key ministers, such as Bedford and Sandwich, argued for its retention; but the Dutch were adamant that they should not be subjected to continued French attack for the sake of Louisburg. Bedford and Sandwich's insistence on Cape Breton was part of a much broader strategic conception. They believed that Britain's destiny lay in the colonial and maritime sphere, rather than supervising the European balance through presences in the Barrier or the Mediterranean. Indeed, Bedford argued that it would be better to exchange Gibraltar, if that were necessary to hold on to Louisburg. While he knew restitution of Gibraltar to be 'a rock all ministers will fear to split on', he thought 'there are advantages Spain could and I believe would, give us in the West Indies that it might be worth parting with it for, especially as peace founded upon that basis might be reasonably supposed to be a lasting one.' What was heretical here, from the traditional Whig perspective, was not the willingness to exchange Gibraltar for a lasting peace with Spain – that had been countenanced by George I and Stanhope twenty years earlier – but the suggestion that a major European asset should be bartered for colonial or commercial gains.[24]

The result was a prolonged period of buck-passing during which ministers tried to delay the inevitable, or at least to pin the blame for it on someone else. 'The affair of Cape Breton,' Chesterfield argued in late November 1745, before negotiations had even got under way, 'is the great and insurmountable difficulty, and I think you should buy it, if you can, with almost anything else; for I really don't know who will venture to sign it away.' Newcastle agreed. 'Cape Breton is a difficulty,' he wrote in March 1746, 'which I do not see how it can be got over at present. France will not make peace without it, and that you may depend upon; and who will dare to give it up, I know not.' Indeed, Louisburg had become a millstone as much as a trump card. Henry Pelham described it as 'a stumbling block to all negotiation'. 'You may remember,' Chesterfield had told Newcastle, 'I was aware at first of the difficulties it would create; and, when I heard people bawling and huzzaing for its being taken, I wished it in their throats. But now I think you have no option left, and you might much easier give up Gibraltar and Minorca.'[25]

In the end, as the peace negotiations dragged on at Breda from 1746 to 1748, and the relentless French advance continued, Britain was forced to bite the bullet. At the peace of Aix-la-Chapelle in October 1748, she exchanged Louisburg for a French withdrawal from the Low Countries; border questions in North America were referred to joint commissions. The crucial Barrier was thus restored. The return of Louisburg also placated the Dutch, ever jealous of British colonial gains, and resentful of London's unwillingness to surrender a 'loose and precarious acquisition in America' in order to safeguard their security. The sense of relief in London was palpable. Henry Pelham looked 'upon it as almost a miraculous deliverance for this country and the Republic, considering the great and successful army of France, and the weak and unfortunate one of the allies'. He defended the treaty in Parliament by asking whether 'any gentleman will say that it was not more for the interest of this nation to restore to France the possession of Cape Breton than to leave her in possession of Hainault, Flanders, Brabant and Namur, and consequently of the whole coast . . . from Zealand to the westernmost part of Bretagne'. For this reason, he argued, 'our restoring Cape Breton upon this consideration was for the interest of England, without any regard to our allies, or to the balance of power in Europe'. Madras, by contrast, 'was of . . . little moment', and Cape Breton 'of no manner of consequence'.[26]

When Sandwich protested against the return of Louisburg, Newcastle conceded that 'the cession of Cape Breton is infinitely more material than any that is proposed to be made by his [George II's] allies'. But, he continued, desirable though its retention was, the course of the war had made it too burdensome. For this reason, Britain would have to surrender the fortress not only to secure peace but also to ensure

a restitution of the Low Counries, and immediate relief to the Republic of Holland, and a tolerable settlement of Europe, which by a most perfect and well-concerted union between the present allies and such other powers who may also dread the growing power of France, and by proper measures after the conclusion of the peace, may still secure the liberties of Europe and preserve them from being overturned by that power, which will always have it in view, though, from the great success of His Majesty's naval operations, their trade, commerce and marine have suffered so greatly that it is to be hoped that they will not have it so soon in their power to affect it.

Of course, this was a short-term solution only. What was the point of restoring the Barrier if the Dutch and Austrians were not prepared to defend it? As Chesterfield warned,

to restore it [Louisburg] for a town or two more in Flanders, which neither the Dutch nor the Queen of Hungary will defend, and which France can most certainly take again whenever it pleases, will be giving up a very real advantage from England for a precarious and shortlived one for the Dutch . . . the peace, whenever it is made, will not leave us what used to be called the Balance of Europe . . . We may keep Cape Breton by our fleets, but I fear we and the Dutch together shall never be able to keep Flanders by our armies.

It was a problem with which Britain would have to grapple further over the next decade.[27]

The return of Louisburg provoked an outraged response from popular advocates of a 'blue water' policy. As the *Newcastle Courant* remarked sourly, Britain agreed not only to 'restore Cape Breton to the Crown of France . . . but also [to] expend, in a firework [to celebrate the peace], a sum little inferior to the original demand upon Spain [i.e. for compensation for the 'depredations' of the Spanish coastguard]'. The notion that

Britain should make any sacrifices on behalf of the European balance was likewise dismissed. As Viscount Tyrconnel, a Whig MP, remarked in 1748, 'if a nation can ever learn wisdom by past sufferings, we shall never more enter into a consuming land war, we shall leave the balance of power upon the Continent, and the liberties of Europe, a couple of cant words'; he also famously attacked 'this execrable, detestable, ruinous, ill-advised, ill-concerted, romantic, Quixotic, senseless, all-consuming land war'. In America the return of Louisburg also distressed the emerging public sphere, though perhaps less than might have been expected. The howls of protest generally originated in London and were reprinted there. There was not a peep out of either Shirley or the Massachusetts assembly. The military cooperation between the metropolis and colony had in any case not been an entirely happy one. The individual colonies sank back into apathy and introspection. In any case, many Americans accepted the primacy of European concerns, and saw the role of the colonies as supporting Britain's position within the state system. The development of a strategic debate in the thirteen colonies faltered until revived soon after by the French penetration of the Ohio Valley.[28]

The colonial successes of the 1740s and the disappointments of the peace of Aix-la-Chapelle gave new impetus to insular and navalist arguments in Parliament. 'As we are by nature disjointed from the Continent,' Venters Cornwall, the Tory MP for Herefordshire, told the House of Commons in 1748, 'and surrounded with the sea, it ought always to be a maxim with us, to have as little to do as possible with the disputes among the princes of Europe, and never to engage as principals in a land war.' He rejected the conduct of the War of the Spanish Succession as a strategic template. Instead, he argued that British policy had taken a wrong turning 'soon after the Revolution. We then began to interfere in disputes upon the Continent, more than we ought to have done.' All this, he claimed, had turned Britain into the 'Don Quixote of Europe'. For this reason, he argued against the return of colonies to France: 'no success of the French upon the Continent can force Great Britain, if directed by British counsels only, into an ignominious peace; for experience has shown, that we can support a naval war with success both against France and Spain.' All this was accompanied, in the usual way, with swipes against the 'extravagant zeal' with which ministers had tried to protect 'that German dominion [Hanover]'.[29]

The late 1740s also saw the greatest surge of popular navalism since the clamour for war with Spain in 1738-9. A ballad of early 1748, which warned against the betrayal of colonial interests in the peace negotiations, was not untypical:

> If Britain's sons all Gallic Arts despise.
> Why listen we at Aix to Gallic lies?
> If on our navy Heaven confers success.
> Why this long quibbling, and this fine address?
>
> Why not our wooden world in motion keep?
> Say, is not Britain regent of the deep?
> Superior force invincible is ours.
>
> If the Grand Monarch [Louis XV] will insist on things
> Beneath the dignity of generous kings;
> Let him insist – and if he's e'er so stiff
> Man well the fleet.

Here it was again, the same blend of popular enthusiasm, jingoistic exuberance and divinely inspired naval destiny. It was perhaps no coincidence that the authorized account of Anson's celebrated and gruelling Pacific voyage of 1740–44 was published in 1748 and reprinted no fewer than five times.[30]

If the true interest of British foreign policy was colonial expansion, the war had been fought in vain. If, on the other hand, Britain's chief concern was the restoration of the European balance of power, then it had all been worth it. Austria had not been partitioned. The threat of French hegemony on the Continent, and the resulting loss of naval security overseas and in home waters, which had loomed so large in 1739–41, had been averted. For this reason, as Henry Fox, the Secretary at War, told the House of Commons in 1748, all pressure for a purely maritime war had been rejected: 'because our conquests at sea, or in America, would in the end signify nothing if, while we were busied about them, the French should make themselves masters of the continent of Europe'. For if they were to achieve that, Fox continued, and 'have it in their power to command the Dutch, and all the other maritime powers of Europe, to join with them against us, no one can suppose that we could be able to carry on even a naval war against all the powers of Europe united against us.' The result would be not only the swift loss of whatever had been gained overseas, but the bringing of 'this island into the same thraldom with the rest of Europe'. 'This consideration,' he concluded, 'will justify the conduct of our ministers in the wars of King William and Queen Anne: this will justify every treaty, and every alliance, we have made ever since the Revolution.' In short, the Europeanist orthodoxy, which had dominated British foreign policy since the Glorious Revolution, and had been briefly eclipsed in 1739–40, had reasserted itself. It had emerged from the debates on war with Spain, the temporary collapse of Austrian power, the Hanover debates, the Barrier discussions, and the Louisburg controversies, in a refined but essentially unchanged form.[31]

And yet, within this Eurocentric framework, America had been decisive. In seeking to solve their geopolitical predicament, English and British statesmen had always widened their perspective as appropriate. For centuries, this impulse had sucked them ever eastward in the quest to uphold the Barrier in Flanders. Now, they looked west across the Atlantic as well. It was there that Britain could make good the leverage she had lost in Europe. The need to safeguard these assets led to the development of a whole new language of barriers and geopolitics in America which formed such an important part of strategic discourse in decades to come. British statesmen had thus – to borrow a phrase coined for the nineteenth century – called a new world into being in order to redress the balance of the old.

14
Imperial Pre-emptions, 1748–1752

How will it sound in our annals that an Elector of Cologne, [a] Bishop of Munster, [and the bishops of] Paderborn and Osnabrück [were] lost . . . for a pension of £20,000 sterling per annum for four years? . . . A naval force . . . unsupported with even the appearance of a force upon the Continent will be of little use . . . France will outdo us at sea, when they have nothing to fear by land . . . I have always maintained that our marine should protect our alliances upon the Continent; and they, by diverting the expense of France, enable us to maintain our superiority at sea.[1]

Duke of Newcastle, September 1749

It is evident . . . that it is our interest, to have the peace of Europe preserved, and as we cannot do this by ourselves alone, we must unite with . . . the Dutch and the Empire of Germany, both . . . our most proper our most natural allies . . . For this reason . . . I must lay it down as a maxim, that it may be often necessary for us to give subsidies in time of peace, in order to form and keep united a proper confederacy for preventing a war; and for this purpose nothing can at present be so effectual as that of getting the Archduke Joseph chosen King of the Romans. This . . . will establish the peace and restore the vigour of the Germanic Body.[2]

William Pitt, Paymaster General, to the House of Commons,
February 1751

I am no enemy to the former grand alliances; I am sensible they saved Europe and this country . . . Neither would I desert or disoblige those powers who joined so zealously and usefully with us in these grand alliances for the common cause. But the misfortune is, that the powers who composed those alliances are so reduced and exhausted as to be incapable of making the same vigorous efforts against France, now as formidable as ever.[3]   Horatio Walpole, 1751

The government and trade of these our colonies [are crucial to] maintaining the independency of the sovereignty of this nation, amidst contests in Europe, for universal dominion; for wherever, and whenever, such contests happen it will be found that the auxiliary power of American colonies (as the source of maritime power) in some shape or other, will contribute, to the support, or overthrow, of European nations ... It is now, from experience evident, that a very great accessory power may be derived from thence, to the principal states. No European nation can be so blind, but to see with envy the particular benefit arising to this nation, from these our American colonies.[4]

James Abercromby, London agent for North Carolina and Virginia,
writing in 1752

British strategic thinking leading up to the outbreak of the Seven Years War in 1756, a contest which Winston Churchill famously referred to as 'the First World War', was dominated by the Empire. The leading figure in British foreign policy, the Secretary of State for the North, the Duke of Newcastle, thought of little else. The principal preoccupation of the King, George II, was also the Empire. Even British maritime dominance and the security of the island itself depended on getting imperial policy right, or so it was thought. The 'empire' in question, of course, was not what we have since come to know as the 'British Empire', in India, Africa, the Caribbean and particularly North America. Rather, what concerned British statesmen between the peace of Aix-la-Chapelle in 1748 and the Diplomatic Revolution of 1756, was the future of the Holy Roman Empire – Germany – and its outworks. The most mortal threat to British interests, they believed, was to be found not in the Pennsylvania and Virginia backcountry, Canada, or the Ohio Valley, but in northern and north-western Europe, where the geopolitical system erected by an earlier generation was in a state of terminal disrepair.

Ever since the 1730s, the twin interlocking bulwarks of the Barrier and the Holy Roman Empire had been tottering. Austrian power was not only generally in retreat, it was also in the throes of a fundamental reorientation. Over the past twenty years or so, the Habsburgs had shed several significant territorial feathers. First, after Austria's defeat in the War of the Polish Succession, Naples and Sicily were lost. Then, in 1740, Silesia had been wrested from her by Frederick the Great. This loss not only greatly undermined the Habsburg position in Germany, and reduced resistance to French encroachments, but it also led to a reorientation of Austrian concerns away from containing France, towards fighting the new enemy, Prussia. The result was a weakened Austrian desire and capacity to defend the Barrier, which in turn was increasingly exposed by the retreat of Austrian power on its eastern flank. As if all this were not bad enough, the Dutch – to whom the task of garrisoning the Barrier fortresses fell – were also indisposed or incapable of discharging the task which the Treaty of Utrecht had envisaged for them. No surprise, then, that British attention between 1748 and 1754 was primarily fixed on the project to revive Habsburg power within Germany. The Holy Roman Empire was not only the strategic hinterland of the Low Countries, it also provided the politico-legal context within which the integrity of the Barrier could be defended.

By contrast, few people at the highest level in London were much interested in America, as such. They would have been startled to hear

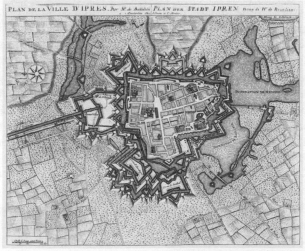

26. The progressive decline of Dutch military power made Barrier fortifications such as this one at Ypres increasingly vulnerable.

that they were about to embark on a 'great war for [American] empire'. To be sure, whole swathes of British public opinion continued to be mesmerized by the prospect of colonial wealth. It is also true that there were some statesmen, such as the Duke of Halifax, President of the Board of Trade, the Earl of Sandwich during his first and brief tenure at the Admiralty, and the Duke of Bedford, as Secretary of State for the Southern Department, who were enthusiasts for colonial expansion. They were both attracted by the possibilities for expansion in North America, and fearful of French encroachments; some of these concerns were already beginning to resonate in cabinet. But for most of the principal decision-makers, especially the Duke of Newcastle, First Secretary of the Treasury, his brother Henry Pelham, and of course the King, European concerns came first. They always had. Indeed, very few Britons of substance, even those who championed colonial causes, actually went to America; the European grand tour, by contrast, was part of the formation of most upper-class Englishmen. The roots of Britain's foreign policy before 1756, therefore, are to be found in Europe, not America.[5]

All the same, the naval, colonial and continental European spheres were believed to be closely linked, not least because Britain faced the same adversaries in all three: France, and to a lesser degree Spain. The key here was not the fact that British sea-power could be deployed in support of diplomatic aims in Europe, though that was true. Nor was it just that colonial resources were seen as crucial to the support of the European balance of power: by deploying them in subsidy form, or in the shape of direct military intervention; or by denying them to the Bourbons, though all this was also true. Rather, the pursuit of a vigorous European policy was believed to be central to the security of Britain itself, and the maintenance of the naval superiority on which her colonial dominance rested. First of all, because the defence of the Dutch Barrier would deny France the use of the Channel ports and thus the best staging ground for an invasion. Secondly, because a continental European distraction – in Germany and the Low Countries – would divert French resources from their navy to the army. Without it, so the prevailing orthodoxy maintained, France would soon outbuild Britain on the maritime front. It is against this background that Britain's policy leading up to the Seven Years War should primarily be viewed.

For the Treaty of Aix-la-Chapelle, which brought the War of the Austrian Succession to an end in 1748, turned out to be an eight-year armistice, at most. The Habsburgs held on to the imperial crown they had briefly and disastrously lost in the early 1740s. Prussia was confirmed in possession of Silesia; but Vienna remained utterly unreconciled to its loss. France evacuated the territory she had captured in the Netherlands in return for the restitution of Louisburg; but the question mark over the long-term viability of the old Barrier was not lifted. In North America, the thorny question of boundary demarcations was left to Anglo-French commissions to resolve. Only in the Mediterranean did the prospects for a lasting settlement look good: here the obsessive Habsburg focus on Prussia paved the way for an Austro-Spanish rapprochement. Yet, as we shall see, even this development was to have destabilizing implications for London and the balance as British statesmen saw it.

Britain was certainly better off in 1748 than she had been at the height of her isolation in 1739–40. But the threat from France had been merely contained, not banished. Her commerce, in particular, was quick to recover. Between 1720 and 1780, French transatlantic trade grew tenfold, and there was no appreciable slowing mid century: quite the reverse. The great French sugar islands of Haiti, Martinique and Guadeloupe were booming; the import of slaves – a sure sign of prosperity – continued apace. Within six years of the peace, as one worried correspondent of the Duke of Newcastle wrote, France 'seem[ed] to be pushing for Universal Commerce, as Lewis the 14th [did] for what we call Universal Monarchy. I own myself to be more afraid at this hour of French credit and French commerce than of French fleets and French armies.' Very soon, it was feared, credit and commerce would translate into fleets and armies.[6]

Moreover, the French were growing increasingly restive in North America. In Canada, from about 1750, a full-scale guerrilla war was in progress between British forces and the Francophone settlers in Acadia, ably supported by the French governor of Quebec. Further south, the French began to construct a chain of forts designed to pin the British against the coast, or at the very least to prevent them from expanding into the Ohio Valley. Here they clashed with the Ohio Company of Virginia, established in 1747 with the aim of westward expansion, and with colonists pressing in from Pennsylvania. The French dominated the fur trade, which they pursued primarily in order to achieve informal influence among the Indian tribes. Not only were they more economically competitive than the British traders, they were much more culturally adept at winning over the local Shawnees and Iroquois. Thus every beaver shot and every local agreement between the French and the chiefs undercut Britain's position in this strategically important wilderness. To the Earl of Halifax, the dynamic new President of the Board of Trade since 1748, these were all matters which needed urgent attention. Halifax was an enthusiast for colonial expansion, and a keen backer of the Ohio Company. His tenure at the Board of Trade marked the emergence of strategic synergies between colonial governors, London lobbyists and sections of the press about the direction which British strategy should now take.[7]

For the moment, however, Halifax's colonial concerns were 'spinning in neutral'; they had not yet meshed with the broader thrust of British grand strategy. He was unsuccessful in obtaining a cabinet place for himself on the strength of American matters over the objections of the King; and he did not get very far with the idea of a separate colonial secretariat either. Overseas affairs, in short, were by no means ignored, but definitely of secondary importance. After the experience of the 1730s, moreover, London was wary of being stampeded into war by popular opinion. It was particularly anxious not be sucked into conflict by overzealous governors on the ground, or to be swept up by synthetic press outrage at the latest French atrocity or encroachment. Thus Carteret confided to a foreign diplomat in December 1751 his fear that Nova Scotia might become another 'Jenkins's Ear'. He had clearly learned his lesson.[8]

British statesmen were much more worried about the fact that the French were once again devoting increased resources to their navy. Ministers were under no illusions about the dangers this posed. The French, Hardwicke observed in August 1749, clearly had the 'design of restoring and raising their marine'. Indeed, he added that he was 'persuaded that one principal view of France in making the peace . . . was to give time to restore and raise' their naval power. Admiral Vernon, the hero of Porto Bello, warned of aggressive French intentions against Britain in 1749. Each of the parliamentary debates on the naval estimates in 1750, 1751 and 1752 cited fear of France. Press opinion was equally concerned. The *Newcastle Courant*, for example, expressed alarm that France seemed 'resolved to maintain a balance of power at sea'. A sense of national paranoia about French naval intentions now gripped the nation. It was heightened by the fact that the Royal Navy, much to the disgust of the Earl of Sandwich at the Admiralty, was weakened by cost-cutting measures insisted on by the thrifty First Lord of the Treasury, Henry Pelham. He in turn was grappling with a national debt which had jumped from £49,000,000 at the outbreak of the War of the Austrian Succession, to £76,100,000 at its close.[9]

Pelham was not the only one who was concerned at Britain's mounting debt. In 1752 the Scottish philosopher David Hume published his famous treatise 'Of public credit' as part of his *Political discourses*. The author attacked not so much the corrupting effects of debt on the body politic, as its potential to threaten Britain's position within the European state system. Rejecting isolationism, Hume stressed the need to uphold the balance of power which, experience had shown, was 'too unequal to be preserved without our attention and assistance'. The tract needs to be seen in conjunction with 'Of the Protestant Succession' and 'Of the balance of power', which were also published in the *Political discourses*. Tory in so many other ways, in foreign policy terms David Hume was at this point very much a Whig within the mainstream Continentalist tradition; moreover, as a diplomat with experience of Vienna and Savoy, he was familiar with the issues facing Britain at the time. His political thought was always powerfully influenced by the question of Britain's position in Europe. He feared that a financially constrained government would retreat behind its island ramparts, abandon European allies, and cede the Continent to French universal monarchy. Instead, Hume argued, Britain should not hesitate to spend funds ear-marked for debt service on foreign policy, and devil take the money-markets. This is what Hume meant by his famous dictum that 'either the nation must destroy public credit, or public credit will destroy the nation'. Far from being a call to fiscal prudence *per se*, it was a clear articulation of the primacy of national defence over economic doctrine.[10]

Britain's position in Europe was in any case under serious threat, especially from deteriorating relations with Prussia. These had already been strained throughout the 1740s, due to Frederick's attack on Britain's principal European ally, Austria. In 1744 there was fresh tension when the Prussians occupied the North Sea port of Emden on the death of the reigning prince, expelling the Dutch garrison. George II had protested bitterly if ineffectively, as this step meant that Prussia now threatened the Electorate not only from the east but also the north-west.

Moreover, the acquisition of Emden brought with it commercial ambitions which caused deep disquiet in London. For in 1752, Frederick the Great announced the creation of the 'Prussian Asiatic Company in Emden to Canton in China', or 'Emden Company', for short. Rather like the Ostend Company some twenty-five years before, the Prussian venture seemed to suggest another challenge; however embryonic, to Britain's commercial position. In retaliation, Parliament contemplated measures to deny new foreign companies British insurance policies, and the government came under increasing pressure to take action against the Company. The Emden Company did not in the end amount to very much: there were never more than about four ships in operation at any one time, and the outbreak of the Seven Years War put it out of business for good. Just to complicate things further on the economic front, Frederick was refusing to honour the 'Silesian Loan', that is to keep up repayments on money borrowed against Silesian collateral by Emperor Charles VI during the War of the Polish Succession, which the British argued should now be the responsibility of the new Prussian masters of Silesia. His pretext for defaulting was London's refusal to compensate Prussia for shipping losses at the hands of British privateers – a good example of the diplomatic costs of unilateral naval measures during the War of the Austrian Succession.[11]

The escalating tension with Prussia produced two security headaches for Britain. In order to torment London, Frederick ostentatiously courted the Pretender from the late 1740s. For the crushing defeat at Culloden had by no means eradicated Jacobitism. To be sure, the metropolitan variety was weakened by the death of Sir John Hynde Cotton in 1752, which deprived them of a significant voice in the House of Commons. There were still enough supporters in England, however, to mount the conspiracies which rocked Westminster in the early 1750s. In 1750, Charles Edward even paid a secret visit to Britain. At the same time, Scottish Jacobitism, despite or perhaps because of the depredations of the Duke of Cumberland after Culloden, remained vibrant. All this seemed the more ominous, of course, in the light of foreign sponsors. In August 1749, Newcastle expressed his fear that France would 'attempt, a second time, the overturning our happy constitution, and that with more prospect of success than the last; when we shall have fewer friends on the Continent than we had then'. Likewise, in October 1752 the Lord Justice of Scotland was ebullient about the state's ability to deal with local Jacobites 'unless we were to be overpowered from the Continent'.[12]

London therefore learned of Frederick's overtures to Charles Edward with some alarm. In this context, it did not help that British policy in Russia had involved the expulsion of local exiles there. When the Tsarina sent her gifted general James Keith packing, he promptly joined the Prussian service. In a calculatedly provocative move, his brother George was made ambassador to Versailles. This Jacobite presence in Prussia was the more worrying as it coincided with a major war scare in Hanover in 1752–3. British and Hanoverian statesmen were painfully aware that Frederick might vent his anger on the Electorate. Indeed, Hanoverian memoranda had been stressing since the mid 1740s that the containment of Prussia rather than France was the highest priority. Newcastle, for one, was highly receptive to these warnings, which resonated in his mind with fears of Jacobitism. For much of the early 1750s, in short, Britain's principal immediate Continental enemy was Prussia, not France.[13]

Greater still than any direct danger from Frederick, was his impact on the Barrier system. His assault on the Habsburgs led to a fundamental strategic reorientation in Vienna, the implications of which began to work themselves out in the years after Aix-la-Chapelle. Prussia not France was now the main enemy, and although the Habsburgs wished to retain the British alliance if they could, not least for financial reasons, the two powers were now moving along diverging axes. London was enthusiastic only about helping Maria Theresa against France and in the Low Countries – far from the Prussian armies which Vienna feared most. There were also a number of smaller irritations, such as British involvement in the Italian peace process, where Austria felt that London had tilted too much towards Savoy; the unpredictability, 'lethargy' and 'indolence' of British ministries; the British obsession with trade, colonial expansion and commerce, as they saw it; the commercial privileges accorded the Dutch under the Barrier treaties, which continued to rankle (there were even some who advocated reviving the Ostend Company in order to restore Habsburg finances). In general, the Austrians were fed up with being shunted about in accordance with some grand British geopolitical scheme. The instructions for their ambassador to London, Count Richecourt, in mid November 1751 spoke of the British tendency 'to want to be at the head of everything and to direct everything according to its wishes (diriger tout à sa fantaisie)'.[14]

All this posed a huge threat to the traditional architecture of British security in Europe, which had always hinged on keeping as much as possible of the western European coastline, and especially the Channel ports, out of enemy hands. The Dutch Barrier, the Holy Roman Empire, Hanover and the Habsburg monarchy were conceived as part of a mutually supportive, interlocking system; as Hume had noted in 'Of the Protestant Succession', the Electorate served 'to connect us more closely with the House of Austria, our natural ally'. Austria's increasing obsession with Frederick now left the eastern flank of the Barrier hanging in the air, reduced imperial enthusiasm for the defence of the Low Countries, led to the neglect of the vital Barrier fortresses, and thus opened up a gap on Hanover's western side. As if this were not bad enough, the other buttress, the Dutch Republic itself, was looking distinctly shaky. Much to Britain's disappointment, the restoration of the Stadholderate in 1747 had done little to promote either internal stability or a common front against France, or to bolster the crumbling Barrier. Here the dynastic link to the Stadholder through George's daughter Princess Anne, in which London had invested such high hopes in the 1730s and 1740s, proved to be a rather limited asset.[15]

Accompanying the strategic unease was a mounting sense of cultural and moral malaise. British public discourse in the 1750s was characterized by fears of degeneracy and emasculation within the body politic. No doubt shifting gender, literary, behavioural and economic factors played a role, or were perceived to, but this national performance anxiety was mainly about foreign policy and Britain's place in the world. These fears were nothing new – similar moral panics had spread at times of acute emergency in the 1690s, 1730s, and most recently in the 1740s. Thus in 1750, the independent Whig Sir James Lowther announced that Britain was 'undone as a nation, or shall be in a few years under the heels of France thanks to the excess of gaming and diversions of all kinds'. On this reading, the root cause of Britain's declining international stock was society's taste for 'luxury' and thus for 'corruption'.[16]

The debate threw up various interrelated remedies. Many called for a new politics of virtue to be presided over by a Bolingbrokian Patriot King, or at least a patriot leader. The Prince of Wales and his court at Leicester House remained a focal point for this sentiment until his sudden death in 1751; thereafter this role was taken up by his son, the future George III. Others demanded more '[overseas] empire', which came to represent an 'antidote' to the virus of aristocratic cultural treason, effeminacy and abdication of national responsibility. Empire became, in the words of one historian, an 'imaginative imperative', which was driven by a providential sense of Britain's maritime destiny as much as any prudential concern for profit. Admiral Vernon's speeches on the need for greater naval service were disseminated by the *Penny London Post*, one of the less expensive London papers. Others still sought to combat national degeneracy through cultural mobilization. At the lower end of the spectrum, the 'Anti-Gallican Society', formed in 1745, called on tradesmen and artisans to buy British rather than French products. The 'Society for the Encouragement of Arts, Manufactures and Commerce' was more exalted in terms of membership, but it had largely the same agenda. In both cases patriotic sentiment and economic self-interest combined.[17]

All this, of course, was garnished with a hefty dose of popular xenophobia and national chauvinism, which went hand in hand with the development of a British national identity forged in war and adversity. Yet these effusions provided an unstable basis for the generation and projection of British military power. Patriotic discourses exalted martial valour, to be sure, but they were also intensely suspicious of anything that smacked of Continental militarism or its twin, absolutism. When the Duke of Cumberland attempted to introduce European-style discipline into the army – essential to national efficiency – he was accused of Germanic despotic tendencies. In 1751, Lord Egmont – an associate of the Prince of Wales, with whom the King was still in bitter feud – even wrote a pamphlet alleging that Cumberland was planning a *coup d'état*. It did not help, of course, that Cumberland was figured indelibly in the public mind as the 'butcher of Culloden', and the scourge of the Highlands, a deliverer who had become an embarrassment. Further north, in fact, the British state was engaged in a transformative process of a rather different sort. It too was driven by a sense of strategic vulnerability, for the ministry was determined that the events of 1745–6 should never be repeated. The system of fortifications and roads begun after 1715 was further expanded. In July 1747, ward-holding was abolished, and with it the form of land-tenure by which tenants could be called out for military service. The use of English was encouraged; Highland dress was banned. Dragging the Highlands into the eighteenth century was thus designed to secure the northern flank against another hostile eruption.[18]

That said, if Britain was to get off the back foot with France, the principal effort would have to be made in the sphere of strategy and foreign policy itself. It was only through a successful European policy that Britain could keep the Pretender at arm's length, disrupt French domination of the Continent and secure her position overseas. For although the retrospectively most obvious threat to British interests after 1748 was in North America, the British response was by no means – as has often been asserted – a turn away from Europe. On the contrary, mainstream British – and for that matter French – strategic thought interpreted developments overseas in terms of the European balance of power. It was true that by 1750 colonial trade made up a slightly larger share of Britain's commerce than it had fifty years earlier: just over 20 per cent rather than 15 per cent. It was also true that the thirteen North American colonies were now more valuable than the West Indies, and that the re-export of colonial goods to Europe through Britain tended to mask the true extent of trade. Moreover, the trajectory was upwards. All the same, more than three-quarters of British commerce was still with Europe. The preoccupation with colonial trade therefore reflected not economic but strategic concerns. Colonial expansion was not an end in itself, but designed to secure the resources necessary to pursue European interests, or to deny those resources to the enemy. Britain asserted herself overseas in order to secure her position within the Continental Great Power system; and she engaged in Europe in order secure her maritime dominance.[19]

This is what Newcastle meant by his famous pronouncement of September 1749. He argued that 'a naval force', however large, would be useless without 'a force upon the Continent'. This was because France would 'outdo' Britain 'at sea' if it was not threatened 'by land'. For this reason, Newcastle continued, he had always argued the Royal Navy should protect Britain's 'allies upon the Continent', while 'they by diverting the expense of France', enabled Britain to maintain its 'superiority at sea'. This was the crispest enunciation of a doctrine which went back to the Nine Years War. All this drove Newcastle's attempts to rebuild and extend Britain's European alliances. Thus in August 1749, he lamented that 'the principle of supporting the Continent, at any expense, in time of peace, has been so decried'. Newcastle argued that 'if this principle is not a little corrected, the Continent is forever abandoned', and then 'France by her subsidies, in time of peace, will more effectually subdue, and reduce, all the powers in Europe, than by her numerous and victorious armies.' This would allow her to 'establish a marine . . . to restore their trade and encroach upon ours . . . [and] to extend their limits in America'. For this reason, Newcastle believed that 'this is the time to form such an alliance and party in Europe . . . [to] discourage France . . . from . . . giving us disturbance without running the risk of a general war. If they go on in buying up all the powers upon the Continent . . . [they] run no risk of engaging themselves in a new war. Whereas, if we had a tolerable system, and force upon the Continent, though by no means equal to France and Prussia, the experience of the last war shows us, that France would not wantonly engage in a new war.' In other words, France was to be deterred from aggression in America by the threat of war in Europe. With this in mind, he concluded, Britain should approach the Austrians, the Russians, the smaller German princes, and even the Dutch. Only through such a combined naval and diplomatic demonstration could France be contained. It was therefore not enough, as Newcastle famously put it in January 1752 during one of the Continental subsidy negotiations, to rely only on the 'wooden walls' of the Royal Navy.[70]

Colonial expansion, in turn, would provide Britain with the resources to maintain her naval supremacy and her position within the European state system. 'If we lose our American possessions or the influence and weight of them in time of peace,' Newcastle observed in 1750, 'France will, with great ease, make war with us whenever they please hereafter.' This was the overarching framework within which British colonial policy was conceived and executed. Thus William Shirley, the Governor of Massachusetts, never tired of stressing the potential of North America, especially for naval stores and seamen. The Americans themselves agreed with this analysis. They too increasingly saw the links between the European state system and their own safety; but they were also confident that they could contribute to the security of the mother country. James Abercromby, who served as London agent for North Carolina and Virginia from 1748, wrote in 1752 of the importance of the colonies for 'maintaining the independency, of the sovereignty of this nation, amidst contests in Europe, for universal dominion'. This was because 'the Auxiliary power' of the colonies would 'contribute . . . to the support, or overthrow, of European nations'. He therefore concluded that it was now clear that America provided a 'very great accessory power . . . to the principal states'. Joseph Robson, who had six years as surveyor to the Hudson's Bay Company to his credit, wrote in 1752 that Britain should not only protect but enlarge her colonies. 'This and this alone,' he claimed, 'will enable her to maintain the balance of Europe, and to preserve herself from becoming one day a tributary dependent upon some more active and vigilant power'.[21]

In the colonial mind, the American and the European theatres were thus inextricably interlinked. This emerges in the works of the Bostonian William Douglass in his *A summary, historical and political, of the British settlements on North America*, which was published in Boston between 1749 and 1752. 'The French,' he wrote, 'are the common nuisance and disturbers of Europe, and will in a short time become the same in America, if not mutilated at home, and in America fenced off from us by ditches and walls, that is; by great rivers and impracticable mountains.' Some form of geopolitical system of barriers, in other words, would be needed in America, while French power would have to be checked in Europe itself. But at the same time, Douglass warned, the French were 'more capable of swarming into their colonies than we are; in order to preserve a balance in Europe, they [the French] ought to be curtailed or dismembered there [in America], which will effectually at the same time prevent their too great growth in America'. The two theatres, America and Europe, were thus symbiotically connected in the minds of British strategists and the emerging transatlantic public sphere.[22]

These themes were echoed, from a different perspective, in strategic thinking among the French. They saw naval and colonial expansion as a device to knock Britain off her European pedestal. In 1748 one French memorandum spoken of the threat of a British '*monarchie universelle de la mer*'. 'The English,' it went, 'regard navigation and commerce as the soul and life of the state. It is not by land that they achieve universal monarchy; it is only by sea.' Because Britain could amass power through trade, 'commerce is the true source of the power of state', with which she could intervene in Europe and 'kindle dangerous wars'. Likewise, the Marquis de la Galissonière, the Governor-General of Canada, wrote in December 1750 that 'If anything can . . . destroy the superiority of France in Europe, it is the English naval forces; it was these alone . . . which caused France to lose the fruit of the entire conquest of the Austrian Low Countries at the close of the last war.' If not stopped, he continued, Britain would become totally dominant overseas and the resources she 'would draw from thence, to the exclusion of other nations, would most certainly give them superiority in Europe'. Canada, therefore, would have to be defended at all costs, 'inasmuch as that is the only way to wrest America from the ambition of the English, and as the progress of their empire in that quarter of the globe is what is most capable of contributing to their superiority in Europe'.[23]

A year later, the French Minister of Foreign Affairs, the Comte de Saint-Contest, argued that Britain could only be cut down to size in Europe by curbing her naval power. 'The diminution of the navy of England occasioning that of her commerce,' he wrote, 'she would no longer be in a position to bear the expenses of all the quarrels that she or her allies are always disposed to pick with France.' For this reason, he recommended naval alliances with Sweden, Denmark and Spain. In short, the French attack on British naval and colonial power was part of a wider European strategy. They poured money into Canada for strategic, not economic motives. Their frenetic programme of fort construction in and around the Ohio Valley – Fort Presque Isle, Fort Machault, Fort Le Boeuf and Fort Duquesne, was driven by European concerns. if they lost the American interior to Britain, it was believed, they would in time cede dominance on the other side of the Atlantic as well. The French planned to conquer Europe in America, and so Britain would have to defend her European position there.[24]

The dichotomy between 'Europe' and 'America' which has mesmerized so many historians is thus a false one. If maintaining the European balance was the key to America, then American resources were believed to be the key to the European balance. It was therefore unsurprising that Britain sought to head off the French threat, not by a spoiling attack in America, as the restless colonial governors demanded, but with a pre-emptive diplomatic coup in the Empire.

For Newcastle, the 'only solid system in Europe' after 1748 remained the alliance with Austria and the Dutch against France. Unlike some Whigs, Newcastle's greatest trauma was not so much the Treaty of Utrecht, painful though the memory of it was to him, but the period of estrangement from Austria between the Treaty of Hanover in 1725 and the Treaty of Vienna in 1731. When confronted with the obvious collapse of the system in the late 1740s and early 1750s, therefore,

Newcastle's instinct was not to replace the 'old system' but to reinvigor-ate it. He persuaded Pelham, who had wanted to default for cost-cutting reasons, to disgorge the final subsidy payment to Austria in 1749, and set about developing a comprehensive British strategy for Europe. In a memorandum in the early summer of 1750, he set out his priorities: strengthening the Habsburg claim to the German imperial crown; joining the Austro-Russian treaty of 1746; sorting out the Austro-Dutch disputes over the Barrier and 'the putting of that in some way of being restored'; reconciling the Protestant German princes with the Habsburgs; and 'making up our differences with Spain'.[25]

Britain began with Flanders. 'Till what is called the Barrier is restored to some condition of defence,' Hardwicke observed in August 1749, 'it is really no barrier. If they [the forts] remain in this state, this will be one of the greatest temptations to that power [France] to begin a new war, when she is ripe for it; for she may immediately, with little trouble or expense, march two armies into Holland.' To British statesmen, indeed, this area had long been regarded as almost a part of the British archipelago itself. Newcastle described it as 'a kind of common country in which we, the Dutch, and the Empress-Queen [Maria Theresa] are all interested'. The Barrier Treaty of 1715, which regulated the respective roles in the containment of France, was – in the words of Sir Charles Hanbury Williams – nothing less than 'the cement which unites the Maritime Powers to the House of Austria and which makes the basis of the defence of the liberties of Europe'. For this reason, Hanbury Wil-liams, echoing Newcastle, told Maria Theresa that 'she was far from being the independent sovereign of the Low Countries, that she was limited by her treaties with the maritime powers'. A sustained attempt was made to enforce, or at least renegotiate, the terms of the old Barrier treaties.[26]

At the same time, British statesmen wrestled with the problem of how to restore Austrian power more generally. The key here was Germany. It was potentially strong enough to contain France. As David Hume remarked when he travelled there in 1748, 'Germany is undoubtedly a very fine country, full of industrious, honest people, and were it united it would be the greatest power that ever was in the world.' A crucial strategic lesson of the War of the Austrian Succession had been the fatal results of allowing the alienation of the imperial crown from the Habsburgs. Austria alone did not have the weight to sustain the role assigned to her in the European balance. 'This substantial work for the House of Austria,' Newcastle wrote in June 1750, 'cannot be done without those inferior princes. Neither is the House of Austria, alone, of that weight and use for preventing a war, that it is when supported and joined with the princes of the Empire.' This was not a pressing issue: the current Emperor, Francis Stephen, and the Empress, Maria Theresa, were both young and in good health. British Continentalists were looking not only ahead, but also felt that settling the succession issue in advance would strengthen Austrian power in the immediate future. Besides, the ministry had been unsettled in June 1748 by reports that Frederick the Great was discussing a conversion to Catholicism in order to pursue the next imperial vacancy. However implausible this story, it fitted with what London had heard of Prusso-Jacobite contacts.[27]

Newcastle therefore proposed that the Electors of the Holy Roman Empire should elect the Habsburg heir-presumptive, Maria Theresa's son, the Archduke Joseph, as 'King of the Romans' (the title traditionally given to the emperor-in-waiting), and thus as the automatic successor of his father. He hoped thereby to eliminate any potential interregnum and forestall a repeat of 1740–41, when a French-backed candidate successfully contended for the title. The move would also strengthen Austria against the rising power of Prussia, which was now Vienna's principal worry. The overall effect would be to strengthen the Habsburg position in Germany, and thus their ability to act as a counterweight to France, not least by defending the Barrier. In short, Newcastle argued, this would construct a 'system, which . . . will greatly tend to secure the future peace and tranquillity of Europe, in which we are so essentially concerned'. Moreover, it was very much part of the overall strategy of diverting France in Europe: the famous statement of September 1749 about making France 'fear by land', was preceded by the question, 'How will it sound in our annals that an Elector of Cologne, Bishop of Munster, Paderborn and Osnabrück was lost . . . for a pension of £20,000 per annum for four years?' The impetus here – it should be noted – was entirely British, not Hanoverian; and it was not a reaction to an unforeseen or imminent event. The plan was conceived from a standing start, in order to address a contingency which most agreed was far down the line. It was an attempt, in fact, to anticipate events. Thus was born the 'Imperial Election Scheme', which was to dominate British foreign policy throughout the early 1750s. It was an exercise in strategic pre-emption, designed not to decapitate an enemy but to bolster an ally.[28]

Carteret, now the Earl of Granville and out of office, was temperamentally attracted to such a wide-ranging plan. He waxed so lyrical that one observer accused him of talking 'more like a madman than a grave counsellor of the King's . . . with such a heap of wild stuff and nonsense'. Another remarked that 'wine had heightened his zeal and eloquence; and he was so fond of showing his ardour for the conclusion of the Election . . . that he would fight out the point, when everybody were of the same mind.' There was, of course, more to Carteret's enthusiasm. Henry Pelham remarked that 'He hurries forward all these German affairs, because he thinks he shows his parts and pleases the King . . . He has as much vanity and ambition as he ever had; and he hopes, therefore, in these contradictory circumstances, something may fall out, and then, he imagines, he is sure to succeed.' Memories of Stanhope and the Baltic crisis were obviously still strong.[29]

A more surprising enthusiast was Pitt, who described the plan as 'a most wise and salutary measure . . . provided the election of the Archduke be accomplished'. 'The object all must applaud,' he added, 'and the greatest economists not complain.' Pitt did not simply take this line because he was the Paymaster General, through whose office the resulting bribes would have to flow. He subscribed to the broader strategic framework within which Newcastle had conceived the scheme. In a speech to Parliament in mid January 1751, Pitt stressed the need for 'tranquillity' in Europe, in order to achieve 'a firm alliance between His Majesty and such a confederacy upon the Continent, as will be an overmatch for the House of Bourbon'. The greatest threat to this tranquillity, as 'recent experience' had shown, was the possibility of 'the death of the Emperor of Germany before the election of a King of the Romans'. This, Pitt claimed, would 'rekindle the flames of war all over Europe'. Moreover, he pointed out shortly afterwards, apart from the United Provinces, 'the Empire of Germany' was Britain's 'most natural' ally. It could not act with the necessary 'vigour' when the imperial throne was vacant. The only way of remedying this was by organizing an election in advance, and paying the requisite subsidies to persuade the Electors.[30]

The Imperial Election Scheme proved to be extremely controversial in Britain. As an exercise in pre-emption and bribery, the plan was vulnerable in both philosophical and practical terms. It addressed a remote, not an immediate, contingency; it forced Britain and others to declare their hands before they needed to; it rested on an increasingly questionable assessment of German politics; it whetted appetites for British gold where none had previously existed; and it laid the administration open to charges of partiality towards Hanover. Newcastle's own brother was prominent among the sceptics. 'To buy a prince of the Empire,' he wrote, was 'to do that which England, at best, is but collaterally concerned in. And how do we know we should have the vote at last?' In other words, there was a considerable question mark over the reliability of the Electors: once bought, would they stay bought? He also feared accusations of pandering to the King's Hanoverian concerns. The Lord Chancellor, Hardwicke, likewise had his doubts. In time, he warned, the payments would 'become perpetual and as much expected as the grant of the Civil List at home'. Moreover Hardwicke felt that the whole scheme attached too much weight to the German Empire as a potential bulwark of the balance of power. 'The Empire,' he argued, 'must be allowed to be a very great and respectable body, but is so disjointed and divided, from want of real authority and influence in their head, and by reason of territorial and family disputes among themselves, that the experience of above half a century has shown little strength can be expected from them.'[31]

But the greatest hurdle to the Imperial Election Scheme on the British side was the instinctive reluctance to pay out subsidies in peacetime, whatever the circumstances. One of those who openly opposed the scheme was the colonial and naval enthusiast, the Duke of Bedford, the Secretary of State for the South since 1748, and his young protégé at the Admiralty, the Earl of Sandwich. Bedford attacked the subsidy treaties as they went through the Lords; old Horatio Walpole and another of Bedford's protégés, Richard Rigby, took aim in the Commons. Here personal animosities were as important as disagreements over policy. Bedford and Sandwich were strong opponents of Continental engagements, but they were also Newcastle's bitter rivals for control of British foreign policy. Newcastle outmanoeuvred them both by playing the Hanoverian card. In 1748 he made his first trip to the Electorate, and another followed in 1750. Newcastle took advantage of his proximity to the King: in June 1751, Bedford and Sandwich were duly replaced by Anson at the Admiralty and the Earl of Holdernesse as Secretary of

State for the South. Both were close political allies and committed Continentalists; once again the rise and fall of political careers had been determined by the European balance and especially German politics.[32]

Now the Imperial Election Scheme could go ahead. Pelham and Hardwicke reluctantly agreed to fund the venture. They would not, as Newcastle had implored them, allow 'this great system to fail for twenty or thirty thousand pounds . . . [and thus] fling the whole Empire into France for the sake of perhaps ten thousand pounds'. Pelham conceded that 'whatever objection' he had to subsidiary treaties, if Joseph could 'actually be elected King of the Romans for £20,000 for six years', then nobody could deny that it was 'a purchase cheaply made, and that the great end, when obtained, is national'. The aim was to secure a majority of the nine Electors. The Elector of Hanover, of course, was already in the bag. Likewise, the Bohemian vote was controlled by the Austrians and posed no difficulty. Nor did the preferences of two of the ecclesiastical Electors, Mainz and Trier, which were strongly pro-imperial. There was not much point in pursuing the Elector of Brandenburg, also known as Frederick II of Prussia. That left the Electors of Saxony, Bavaria, the Palatinate and Cologne. Newcastle had switched from the Southern to the Northern Department in 1748 and was thus in direct charge of German negotiations. In early 1750 he secured the Elector of Cologne; this was quite a coup, given that Cologne, although an ecclesiastical principality, and thus presumptively pro-Austrian, had long been in the French orbit. Later that year, a treaty was concluded with Bavaria, another former French ally. Unfortunately, the terms offered to Bavaria were so favourable that the Elector of Cologne immediately threatened to welsh unless he was granted more. If Britain's first purchase refused to stay bought so quickly, this was not a good omen for the whole project.[33]

Newcastle, however, ploughed on. In September 1751 he signed up the Saxons, at considerable expense. Their negotiator, Count Brühl, had played off Britain against France so effectively that he had shown himself capable, as Hardwicke observed, of 'knocking at two opposite doors at the same time', and of 'tak[ing] with both hands' as well. Ratifications were exchanged in November, and the treaty sailed through the Commons with a large majority – 236 to 54 – and without a division in the Lords; but the rejoicing in London was premature. It transpired that Brühl had signed 'selon les lois et constitutions de l'Empire' ('in accordance with the laws and constitution of the Empire'), which was code for the notion that a simple majority of Electors was not enough; the College of Princes – in which those territories whose rulers did not enjoy the privilege of electing the Emperor were represented – would have to agree as well. Incredibly, the British negotiator, Hanbury Williams, seems to have ignored, misunderstood or simply overlooked this caveat, which was soon to unravel the whole project. Nor did Newcastle grasp it at first. In the meantime, Britain set about securing the remaining Electoral vote, that of the Palatinate.[34]

All this was achieved through the large-scale deployment of not only British financial but also diplomatic resources. For the first time in more than twenty years – and the only occasion during the reign of George II – a British envoy, Onslow Burrish, was dispatched to the Reichstag at Regensburg. Here he was to reinforce Hanoverian efforts to win over German princes to the Imperial Election Scheme; and was to play an important role in courting the Bavarians. Critics mistook Newcastle's strategy as subservience towards the King's Electoral interests. He 'Hanoverizes more and more every day,' Horatio Walpole observed in 1749. In fact, it was the other way around. Britain deployed Hanoverian assets in support of its own German policy. After all, Cologne had been signed up to the Imperial Election Scheme by a subsidy treaty signed by George in his Electoral capacity only; the negotiations had been conducted by the Hanoverian minister there. Likewise, the Dutch were persuaded to lend their financial and diplomatic muscle to the subsidy treaties. Only half of the Bavarian subsidy treaty of 1750, for example, came out of Britain's pocket; the balance was split evenly between the Hanoverians and the Dutch. So enthusiastic did the Dutch statesman Count William Bentinck and the Prince of Orange become about the whole project, that they claimed the idea as their own. So did George himself, prompting Hardwicke to comment that 'A prince cannot make a minister a greater compliment than by making his measures his own.' Here European engagement was by no means a capitulation to foreign interests. Rather it was conceived of as a device to marshal European energies towards British ends.[35]

The linchpin of this policy was the burgeoning relationship between Newcastle and George's chief Hanoverian minister, Gerlach Adolf von Münchhausen. They met during Newcastle's visits to Hanover, and their ties were strengthened by the fact that in 1749 Philip von Münchhausen,

Gerlach's younger brother, was the head of the German Chancellery and thus the most senior Hanoverian official in London, where he remained until 1762. Newcastle conducted many of the alliance negotiations of the early 1750s from Hanover, in collaboration with the King and Elector. Policy was closely coordinated; information was shared freely, even from London. Newcastle told the older Münchhausen that 'I strongly desire that Your Excellency and His Excellency Mr de Steinberg should be informed of all that passed . . . You will see from the attached papers the various measures which they have undertaken.' So confident was Newcastle of Hanoverian cooperation that in the subsidy negotiations of 1751 he wanted to persuade the Saxons to follow Hanover's lead in the Empire. Hanover thus became the forward base for Britain's alliance policy in Europe.[36]

27. The relationship which the Hanoverian chief minister Münchhausen struck up with the Duke of Newcastle was central to British foreign policy in the 1750s.

By early 1752 Newcastle was ready. He had assembled a majority of Electors – those of Saxony, Bavaria, Mainz, Trier, Hanover and Bohemia – in favour of Joseph as King of the Romans; there were hopes of securing the Palatinate too, and even of winning back Cologne. Newcastle therefore hoped to proceed to a formal election in the summer. Lord Hyndford was dispatched on a special mission to Vienna to sort

out the modalities. To Britain's surprise, the Austrians were unco-
operative. They refused to share the burden of a subsidy treaty with the
Palatinate. Even more worryingly, Vienna insisted that no election could
take place on the basis of a simple majority in the College of Electors
alone. Britain would have to produce not only a majority in the College
of Princes as well, difficult enough, but also Prussian and French assent
into the bargain. The reasons for this Austrian volte-face were many.
They worried that the extensive bribery of German princes was lining
the pockets of their enemies in the Empire, and thus threatening to
weaken the very power it was intended to bolster. In general, they felt
that British gold would be better invested in the containment of Prussia.
Furthermore, Prussian and French agitation within Germany against the
scheme had been so intense that Vienna feared provoking their active
intervention and thus the very war it was trying to forestall. Moreover,
the controversy also promoted Franco-Prussian understanding, always
a bad thing from the Austrian point of view. Finally, after the experience
of the Pragmatic Sanction in the 1730s, when Charles VI had bought
and re-bought the German princes and the European powers, there was
widespread scepticism in Vienna about the efficacy of such arrangements. By 1752–3 it had become clear that British enthusiasm for
electing Joseph King of the Romans far exceeded that of Austria. Newcastle, in short, was being more imperialist than the Empress herself.[37]

As the whole scheme unravelled, Newcastle vented his fury to Münchhausen. It was bad enough 'that the more we advance and the affair of
the election nears its conclusion', the more France and Prussia should
seek to frustrate it. 'But,' he continued, 'the worst thing is . . . that we
do not [even] expect a favourable response from the court of Vienna.'
If this was as negative as expected, Newcastle said that he 'could not
but regret, that all the generous efforts of the King for the establishment
of a stable system for the tranquillity of the Empire and Europe should
be once again exposed to great peril, solely by the fault of the power
which was most interested in having prevented it'. Likewise Hardwicke,
who expressed himself 'never more shocked in my life' at Austrian
'monstrous ingratitude and impertinence'. He believed that 'The consequences hereof will be fatal to this administration and to the present
system of foreign affairs. The nation will be said to have been duped
and deluded; and the ministers will have no other way to defend themselves, but by openly throwing the blame upon the Court of Vienna.'

This, Hardwicke continued, would be a gift to those 'who dislike the present system, and . . . [y]ou will be told you have nothing to do but to break your connection with this ungrateful impracticable court of Vienna, and be well with France. Thus you will run into the politics of 1725.' The Treaty of Hanover, the old trauma of alienation from the House of Habsburg, was rearing its head again. Several attempts were made to revive it after 1752, but the Imperial Election Scheme was effectively dead. It provided plenty of material for satire, testament in the eyes of its critics to the folly of grandiose Continental engagements. Richard Rigby, the Bedfordite MP for Sudbury, observed that 'unless the Germanic body will give themselves the trouble to adjourn to the House of Lords, and hear the necessity of their own welfare explained to them there, I do not see that we are likely to succeed in that truly British measure.' As Horace Walpole remarked, a 'King of the Jews' was now more likely than a King of the Romans.[38]

The waning of the Austrian alliance strengthened the hand of the Prussophiles. Horatio Walpole had been arguing for a rapprochement with Berlin for some time; in the late 1740s and early 1750s he was joined by Henry Pelham. The strategy here was not to supplant Habsburg power, but to supplement it: Prussia would thus bolster rather than subvert the 'old system', by neutralizing or co-opting Austria's most formidable German enemy. 'The generality of mankind,' Pelham wrote in November 1748, 'will say the only way to preserve the old system, or to recover it, in case it is now so broke to pieces that one can scarce give it a name, is to renew our alliances with the House of Brandenburg.' At the very least, Berlin could be kept out of the French orbit and dissuaded from supporting the Pretender. Newcastle was half convinced by these arguments, and promised to use his 'best endeavours towards promoting a perfect union and good correspondence with Prussia'. A British envoy, Henry Legge, was dispatched to Berlin in 1748, followed by Charles Hanbury Williams in 1750–51 in order to explore the possibility of an alliance. Both missions were complete failures, especially the latter, which ended in a breakdown of relations between a caustic Frederick and the scarcely less outspoken Hanbury Williams. After one of their bruising exchanges, the latter remarked that he would 'rather be a monkey in the island of Borneo than a subject of His Prussian Majesty'.[39]

Personality clashes did not help, but the real problems were structural. Frederick was anxious not to be drawn into a Continental conflict as a result of Anglo-French colonial rivalries. 'If there is another war,' he remarked, 'it will probably be between France and England; there is no point at all in allying with them or involving ourselves. What do cod and Cape Breton signify to us?' The only use Frederick had for a British alliance was as a lever against Austria. This was the one thing Britain was determined to avoid. 'To be sure,' Newcastle wrote in July 1748, 'it is to be wished to gain the King of Prussia; but we must not gain him and lose all our other allies, and that is what I am afraid the King of Prussia means to drive us to do.' Likewise Hardwicke agreed that a rapprochement with Prussia 'would be right, if it were practicable'. Behind it all still loomed the memory of the fatal split with Austria of the 1720s. This, Hardwicke was quick to remember, had been supported by Horatio Walpole and had led to 'the weakening of the House of Austria' and the Treaty of Hanover, 'the fundamental source of all the mischief'. 'I am convinced,' Hardwicke continued, 'nothing would satisfy him [Horatio Walpole] but reducing and depressing the House of Austria, partly for the sake of his exorbitant views in the Empire and partly from the principle that he, who does the injury, never forgives.'[40]

If Prussia could not be won over to the old system, she would have to be contained. It was with this in view that British statesmen began to look at a Russian alliance with renewed interest after 1748. Newcastle was at best ambivalent about approaching St Petersburg – the Russians had arrived too late in the previous war to make any difference and he dismissed their army as made up of 'troupes des comédiens, des danseurs, et des gens du néant' – but he had little choice. Here the key was Poland: if it could be kept free of Franco-Prussian subversion, then Russia could act as a powerful constraint on Frederick's supposed naval pretensions and Jacobite propensities. Charles Hanbury Williams was therefore authorized to think of ways of securing the Saxon succession to the Polish throne, not least in order to avoid a repeat of the 1730s, when the War of the Polish Succession did so much to weaken Britain's Continental ally, Austria. The purpose, as Newcastle wrote in February 1753, was to encourage 'a spirit among the nobility of Poland to take such steps as may best secure the liberties of their own country and prevent them from flinging themselves into the hands of France and Prussia'.[41]

The parallels to the Imperial Election Scheme are obvious. And rather like that scheme, plans to regulate the Polish Succession were given a lukewarm reception by their putative beneficiaries, the Russians. They too wanted to keep out the French and any local candidate who might be bribed by the French, or refuse to be bullied by St Petersburg. But there was no rush from the Russian point of view: the reigning King of Poland was in good health; his eldest son, and presumptive successor under the British scheme, was not. Moreover, the Austrians and Russians rejected British ideas of linkage, by which London's help in eastern Europe would be rewarded by Vienna and St Petersburg with support for Hanover and the Barrier in western and central Europe. Newcastle had supported the Saxon subsidy in August 1751, on the grounds that 'I think all thoughts of a system [of alliances] upon the Continent must be laid aside . . . for Russia alone when the Empire and Poland are lost would signify little and therefore this measure is necessary, even with a future view to Russia.' Newcastle, in other words, conceived of central and eastern Europe as a whole: each player was allotted its part in the broader scheme. But by the mid 1750s it was clear that the scheme was going nowhere. The British preoccupation with the Polish succession in the early 1750s was a good example of the dangers of Continental overstretch.[42]

In the meantime, Britain was having more success in Spain. Here there were two principal concerns. One was to keep Madrid and Versailles apart for as long as possible. As the experience of the past decade had shown, the colonial and naval implications of a renewed Bourbon family compact would be devastating. The prospects for an Anglo-Spanish rapprochement were good. Ferdinand VI, who had succeeded to the throne in 1746, was well disposed, as was his chief minister Don Joseph Carvajal. As Newcastle put it in July 1753, 'We hear the Spanish navy is growing very considerable. As long as Mr Carvajal has the direction, the more powerful the better for the common cause and the liberties of Europe: but it increases my desire to keep to the most perfect and intimate union with them.' Fortunately, Madrid was determined to avoid war for the time being, in order to concentrate on domestic reforms which would make her more effective on the international scene in the long run. In order to secure Spanish goodwill, or at least neutrality, the British government was prepared to make substantial commercial concessions. Newcastle instructed Sir Benjamin Keene, who was sent back to Madrid in 1748, to regard trade negotiations 'not as a commercial, mercantile affair only; but as the first opportunity that has offered of really separating the two branches of the House of Bourbon'.[43]

It was for this reason, too, that British statesmen sought to play down Anglo-Spanish colonial rivalries. The publication in 1748 of Anson's stirring account of his voyage around Cape Horn and attacks on Spanish possessions in the Pacific was therefore deeply inopportune. Even worse was talk in 1749 of Anson's plans for another expedition. 'We are talking in England of making new discoveries in consequence of Mr Anson's voyage,' Keene lamented to one correspondent. 'Wall [Don Riccardo Wall, the Spanish ambassador to London and later foreign minister] has made representations against it. You who can judge of the tenderness of this subject can judge it does not forward my affairs here at all.' He added, 'One coup of this nature sets aside, or retards at least, all my endeavours to make us as one people, to do good to ourselves reciprocally, and to do good to the rest of the world by preserving peace and being of terror at the same time to those who would break it.' A renewed confrontation with Spain in the early 1750s would have skewed the naval balance, and stretched Britain's forces overseas to the limit. It was bad enough having to deal with the French in Canada and the Mississippi, without having to contend with Spain in Florida and the Caribbean as well.[44]

The upshot was the Anglo-Spanish trade treaty of October 1750. In purely commercial terms, this represented a retreat from earlier British positions. The claims of the South Sea Company were abandoned, and the prized *Asiento* relinquished in return for a one-off compensation payment of £100,000. The Company itself ceased to trade. Commerce with Old Spain, however, was put on a better footing, with British merchants regaining the privileges of Charles II's reign. To anybody who remembered the controversies of the late 1730s, this was an astonishing reversal. Yet it was defended even by such old scourges of Walpole as Pitt, who was honest enough to retract his belligerent statements against Spain before Parliament in January 1751. As one observer reported, 'Pitt declared for a peace on any terms . . . recanted his having seconded the famous question for the "no search" [the parliamentary demand that Spanish coastguards should not be allowed to search British vessels] . . . said it was a mad and foolish notion, and that he was since grown ten years older and wiser.' In short, the primacy of foreign policy had persuaded Pitt to set his commercial enthusiasm for confrontation with Spain to one side.[45]

But rapprochement with Madrid was not just about maintaining British naval superiority over France in general. It was also part of Britain's overall European policy of bolstering Habsburg power. If the old Austro-Spanish rivalry in the Mediterranean could be defused, so the argument ran, this would enable Vienna to fulfil her role as bulwark against France in the west more effectively. For this reason, Britain threw her weight behind the Italian peace process in 1751–2, particularly the negotiations between Austria and Sardinia, but also those between Spain and Austria. These came to fruition in June 1752 with the Treaty of Aranjuez, which brought to an end nearly forty years of Austro-Spanish antagonism in the Mediterranean. It was negotiated with the help of Keene at Madrid, but the representative at Turin, Lord Rochford, played a not unimportant role in bringing a sceptical Victor Amadeus of Savoy on board. The agreement came as a shock to France, the more so as Newcastle offered a British squadron in the Mediterranean to guarantee it. In London this diplomatic revolution could be regarded as a triumph comparable to, or perhaps even exceeding, that of the Quadruple Alliance of 1718, which had merely contained rather than reconciled Spain. The fact that the arrangement appeared to strengthen Savoy as a barrier against French designs on Italy was an additional and intended bonus. Within a few years it also became clear that in supporting the treaty, Britain had scored a spectacular own goal. For what London had not grasped was that Austria had signed at Aranjuez, not in order to concentrate on France, but the better to fight Frederick the Great.[46]

By the end of 1752, Britain's strategy of imperial pre-emption had failed its first test. Newcastle had been unable to reorder the German Empire in support of the Barrier System against France, or to put in place the European alliances which would divert France from expanding her navy. It was also becoming increasingly evident that Maria Theresa had no intention of playing the role in the European balance assigned to her by London. The principal struggle in Germany was now no longer between Habsburg and Bourbon, but between Austria and Prussia; the implications of this for British strategy in the Holy Roman Empire were still sinking in. Only in the Mediterranean were things looking up: skilful diplomacy helped to keep Spain pacific, which eased the naval and colonial burden and spared Britain yet another European front, for the time being at least. Overseas, the situation was deteriorating, but not critical. Although skirmishing between French and British outposts had been routine for some years, neither side had yet initiated full-scale hostilities. There British statesmen sought to contain offensive French action by an active diplomacy in Europe, while looking to the colonies for the additional resources which would give them the edge in Europe. Over the next three years, however, this strategy was to be placed under almost unbearable strain, as the French onslaught in America gathered pace and British statesmen began to fear the repercussions this would have for the balance on the near side of the Atlantic. The impending struggle in America was indeed to be a 'great war for empire', but not in the way that generations of British and American colonial historians have seen it.

VI

Imperial Triumph

15
Transferring the Seat of Empire?
1753–1756

All that is part of Creation that lies within our observation is liable to change. Even mighty states and kingdoms are not exempted. Soon after the Reformation, a few people came over into this new world, for conscience sake. Perhaps this apparently trivial incident may transfer the great seat of empire into America. It looks likely to me. For if we remove the turbulent Gallicks, our people according to the exactest computations, will in another century become more numerous than England itself. Should this be the case, since we have I may say all the naval stores of the nation in our hands, it will be easy to obtain the mastery of the seas, and then the united force of Europe will not be able to subdue us.[1]*

John Adams, future American patriot, October 1755*

In the three years before 1756, Britain's twin imperial crises worsened. French penetration of the Ohio Valley proceeded apace, threatening British hopes of redressing their European weakness through colonial expansion. Moreover, London was faced with a colonial and naval struggle against an enemy who – for the first time – would not have to reckon with a Continental distraction. Worse still, the system of alliances designed to hold French attention in Europe, and defend the Barrier, disintegrated completely. By 1755–6, it was clear not only that Austria had been 'lost' for good, but that an unprecedented Habsburg–Bourbon rapprochement was in the offing. At the same time, relations with Frederick the Great remained tense. This meant that Britain's Continental Achilles heel – Hanover – would need to be secured against possible French and Prussian attack. The resulting measures provoked a final round of intense but futile anti-Hanoverian rhetoric. So although the colonists thought about 'transferring the seat of empire' to North

America, British statesmen remained convinced that their fate remained inextricably linked with that of the German Empire.

The policy of engagement in Europe after 1748 had been designed to deter France overseas, but by the 1750s this strategy was clearly failing. As the Imperial Election Scheme collapsed and the Barrier fell further into disrepair, the centre of British attention shifted in 1754, for the first time, to the overseas empire. For in the previous year the French had seized the Caribbean islands of St Lucia, St Vincent, Dominica and Tobago, which both London and Versailles had previously agreed should stay neutral. French penetration of the Ohio Valley continued; the situation in Acadia was no better. In both cases, the French made skilful use not only of their own settlers but also of the Indian tribes they cultivated so assiduously. All this led to mounting alarm on both sides of the Atlantic, where the old spectre of 'encirclement' now dominated strategic discourse. 'If they go on in the project they have in view,' Horatio Walpole predicted in July 1754, 'they will encompass all our northern colonies in the back by a chain of communication between the rivers [of] Canada and [the] Mississippi, and [be]come masters of all the Indians, and the trade on that continent.' 'They are building forts,' Newcastle warned, 'taking possession of uninhabited countries, and endeavouring, à la sourdine [on the quiet], to confine our great valuable and extensive dominions in north America to a bare lizière [narrow strip] of country towards the sea.' British North America, in short, was being pinned against the sea. 'There is no repose for our thirteen colonies,' the American Benjamin Franklin remarked, 'so long as the French are masters of Canada.'[2]

Local attempts to dislodge the French in the Ohio Valley proved unsuccessful. In 1754, some Virginian militia under George Washington were defeated and he himself taken prisoner. In 1755, a large force of regulars under General Braddock was routed with huge loss of life on the Monongahela River. Massive French-sponsored Indian raids on frontier settlements followed. The resulting unpleasantness seemed to many observers as so much pointless savagery – much amplified, of course, in the telling. Unfortunately, it was not: the French and Indians were pursuing a calculated strategy of psychological warfare designed to drive away the British colonists. Moreover, the Indians were now so militarily sophisticated that they could take on larger formations of militia, and even regulars, and defeat them. The Seven Years War – what came to be known as the 'French and Indian War' in America – had begun, and Britain was losing it.[3]

In 1754-5 the limitations of the existing American military establishment, which had performed well in earlier conflicts, became clear. At the purely technical level, this reflected poor training and equipment. But it was primarily a political problem: the colonists seemed to lack any sense of cohesion and wider vision. Some years later, Washington recalled that in 1753, after he had 'brought undoubted testimony even from themselves [the French] of their avowed design, it was yet thought a fiction and a scheme to promote the interest of a private company, even by some who had a share in the government. These unfavourable surmises caused great delay in raising the first men and money.' It was thus a ferocious struggle in 1754 to get the Virginia House of Burgesses to approve monies for self-defence. The Virginia grandee Landon Carter wrote in his diary that 'When the £10,000 was granted, it was so disagreeable a subject that much art was used to get one penny raised for the defence of the country.' Moreover, he continued, 'although we had then certain intelligence our enemy had taken our lands, no steps were taken to endeavour to stop them.' Even in the 1755 campaign, when the French and Indian threat was plain for all to see, the commander of the Frederick County militia in Virginia declined point-blank to deploy his men beyond the county boundaries.[4]

Pennsylvania, which was dominated by the pacifist Quakers, had no military to speak of. Already in 1748, the Quaker preacher John Churchman had helpfully warned the assembly that 'If those in authority do suffer their own fears and the persuasion of others to prevail with them to ... enact laws in order to [effect] their own protection and defence by carnal weapons and fortifications, styled human prudence, he who is Superintendent, by withdrawing the arm of his power, may permit those evils they feared to come suddenly upon them, and that in his heavy displeasure.' And when the Pennsylvania assembly met in December 1755 to discuss the crisis, the eastern representatives, who were furthest from the fighting, seemed more interested in sniffing out unconstitutional plots by the proprietors – the descendants of the founder William Penn and still the dominant voice in the colony – than mobilizing against the Indians. 'They did not know their liberties were invaded,' so the argument ran, 'but they were sure their lives and estates were.' The Quakers, for their part, were strongly opposed to conscription, tended to take the Indian side in any dispute, and believed that the problem would go away if the Indians' grievances were met. They seemed completely oblivious to the broader strategic context, and the French threat. The upshot was that the assembly would not even grant militia commanders sufficient powers to discipline their men. Things were not much better in many other colonies, especially the southern ones. When the governor of Maryland appealed to his assembly to help the embattled Virginians in March 1754, he was told that 'we humbly conceive that the situation ... of our neighbours of Virginia, with regard to any violence or outrage, threatened or perpetrated against them, by the French, does not require our immediate aid or assistance, by the raising of an armed force here ... and therefore we do not think it is necessary to do anything in that matter at present.'[5]

All this plunged London into despair. Surely, Horatio Walpole argued in July 1754, the French threat was 'a common cause to all our northern colonies', who he thought 'considering their connection and the number of their inhabitants, [could] soon disperse the French and their Indians'. The trouble was, as Newcastle pointed out shortly afterwards, that while 'The situation of our northern colonies, and the encroachment and insult of the French, require our most serious consideration,' the 'remedy does not seem to me so easy'. 'For,' he continued, 'tho' we may have ten times the number of people in our colonies, they don't seem to be able to defend themselves even with the assistance of our money.' For this reason, the British government began to think of ways of organizing a more effective imperial defence. The Earl of Halifax at the Board of Trade, which was responsible for the colonies in London, spoke of the need for a 'design of uniting the colonies under one general direction ... for defraying the expense of the ordinary annual service', and 'in cases of attack or invasion where an extraordinary expense may become necessary'. Certainly, he believed, more men would be needed to suppress the French in Nova Scotia and to create a 'barrier' to shield New England.[6]

Yet the colonists were not oblivious to their situation, far from it. The early 1750s, in fact, marked a new phase in the development of an American interest in foreign affairs and grand strategy. Colonial newspapers, for example, contained much more foreign news than their nineteenth- and twentieth-century successors did. This was as true for the highbrow *Newsletter* and the *Evening Post* in Boston, as it was for the light-hearted *Pennsylvania Gazette*; for the *Virginia Gazette* as for its South Carolina counterpart. These journals covered central, southern and eastern Europe as well as British news. Just like the British government, they saw the colonial contest within the broader framework of the European struggle, but naturally they took a keener interest in their own theatre of war. They agreed that the thirteen colonies were in severe danger of encirclement. The Bostonian William Clarke wrote in 1751 that the French were engaged in 'surrounding the English colonies, and building forts upon the lakes, and most convenient rivers on the back of the English settlements from St Lawrence River to Mississippi, and claiming an exclusive navigation in those lakes and rivers, and the property of all that part of the continent'. Three years later, Archibald Kennedy, who worked for the customs and excise of New York, warned that 'the French are now drawing a line along the borders of our settlements in every province, from the mouth of the St Lawrence to the mouth of the Mississippi, and building forts to secure the most convenient passes on the lakes that form the communication; by which they will effectually cut off all intercourse and traffic between us and the Indians inhabiting the inland countries.' He concluded that 'one great step, if not the greatest, to this grand monarch's [Louis XV] universal system, is that of being possessed of this northern continent.'[7]

Some colonists also realized that a much greater degree of inter-colonial coordination was necessary to repel this threat. As Benjamin Franklin wrote in some exasperation in his tract *Plain Truth*, 'Perhaps some in city, towns and plantations near the river, may say to themselves, An Indian War on the frontiers will never come near our habitations; let those concerned take care of themselves.' He went on to lament that 'others who live in the country, when they are told of the danger the city is in from attempts by the sea, may say, What is that to us? The enemy will be satisfied with the plunder of the town, and never think it worth his while to visit our plantations: let the town take care of itself.' Benjamin Franklin had already written in 1747–8 that 'At present we are like the separate filaments of flax before the thread is formed, without strength, because without connection; but union would make us strong, and even formidable.' 'The confidence of the French,' he argued in 1754, 'seems well grounded in the present disunited state of the British colonies, and the extreme difficulty of bringing so many different governments and assemblies to agree to any speedy and effectual measures for our common defence and security.' The answer, he stated soon after, was 'That a union of the colonies is absolutely necessary for their preservation'.[8]

These Americans were already thinking much further ahead than the administration in London. They called not only for effective measures of self-defence, but also demanded that Britain go on the offensive to eliminate the Bourbon threat once and for all. This agenda had two planks. First, the colonists took aim at the French presence in Quebec to the north. 'I have a great desire,' the Massachusetts grandee Ephraim Williams remarked in 1755, 'that Canada should be demolished.' A year later the New York magnate William Livingston echoed this view. 'Canada must be demolished,' he announced, '*Delenda est Carthago*, or we are undone.' Secondly, and even more ambitiously, some colonists sought to break out of the Bourbon encirclement through westward expansion. Thus Benjamin Franklin called for the 'breaking off the French communication between Canada and Louisiana'. In his 1751 *Observations concerning the increase of mankind* Franklin claimed that 'two strong colonies . . . between the Ohio and Lake Erie' would not only 'be a great security to the frontiers of our other colonies, by preventing the incursions of the French and French Indians of Canada, on the back parts of Pennsylvania, Maryland, Virginia, and the Carolinas'; the new colonies would also serve as a springboard for offensive action: 'In case of war, it would be easy, from those new colonies, to annoy Louisiana, by going down the Ohio and Mississippi; and the southern part of Canada, by sailing over the lakes, and thereby confine the French within narrow limits.'[9]

Moreover, some Americans were beginning to argue that westward expansion would also pre-empt a French settlement of the area and thus a tightening of the ring of encirclement. The Virginia planter Lewis Burwell argued in 1751 that it would be 'highly for the interest of the Crown to encourage the settling the lands westward as soon as possible to prevent the French'. 'The dreaded junction of the French settlements in Canada with those in Louisiana would be prevented,' Franklin argued in much the same vein. He wrote in his *Plan for settling two western colonies*, penned around 1755, that it was easier to colonize the west now 'and thereby prevent the French from settling there, as they seem now to intend, than to remove them when strongly settled'. Finally, new

28. Throughout the first half of the eighteenth century, as this French map shows, British North America was surrounded on all sides by hostile Bourbon Spanish and French colonies.

colonies would save the existing settlements from being bottled up along the coast and provide the *Lebensraum* they so desperately needed. Thus Franklin praised 'the prince that acquires new territory, if he finds it vacant, or removes the natives to give his own people room'. As yet, the expansionist voice was still a minority one in colonial councils, but it was getting louder. In this way, both the American expansionists and the Duke of Newcastle were engaged in similar projects throughout the early and mid 1750s: reordering the German and the American empires, in order to bring them into line with British interests.[10]

All the while, Americans stressed not only what Britain should do for them, but what they could do for Britain. The Bostonian William Clarke warned in 1755 that without the colonies, the French navy 'would increase to such a degree of superiority over that of Great Britain, as must entirely destroy her commerce, reduce her from her present state of independency to be at last nothing more than a province of France.'

The American resident John Payne took up this theme a year later. Stripped of America, he wrote, 'we would become a French province, and see that proud perfidious nation stand without a rival, distributing laws to all the maritime powers of Europe. We would . . . behold them universal lords of the sea, and bidding fair for the monarchy of Europe.' Finally, Franklin argued that securing living space for the Americans was a vital British interest. 'What an accession of power to the British empire by sea as well as land!' he enthused, 'What increase of trade and navigation! What numbers of ships and seamen! We have been here but little more than 100 years, and yet the force of our privateers in the late war, united, was greater, both in men and guns, than that of the whole British navy in Queen Elizabeth's time.' He concluded by stressing 'How important an affair then to Britain is the present treaty for settling the bounds between her colonies and the French, and how careful should she be to secure room enough, since on the room depends so much the increase of her people.'[11]

These visions were all very well, but they did not solve the immediate problem. On the contrary, in 1754 London was confronted with the fiasco of the Albany Congress, which met in the colony of New York to discuss inter-colonial defence cooperation against the French and Indians. It was summoned at the suggestion of Governor Shirley of Massachusetts, who drew up a 'Draft of a plan or project for a general concert to be entered into by His Majesty's several colonies upon the continent of North America for their mutual and common defence and to prevent or remove any encroachment upon His Majesty's dominions'. Under this scheme, individual colonies would no longer deal ad hoc and autonomously with the Indians, but would pool resources and coordinate efforts. All Indian affairs, treaties and land issues would be dealt with by this 'Union', including those of the Ohio Valley and Great Lakes area. The proposed executive, the 'General Government', would be headed by a Crown appointee, the President-General, in effect a viceroy, but he would work with a Grand Council chosen by the colonial assemblies. Its purpose, as the Auditor-General of Plantations put it in June 1754, was to provide a 'plan of union' against the French 'that are so strong and border upon' the settlers.[12]

All of the colonies rejected the plan, even those, such as Pennsylvania, who had the most to lose from continued disunity. Governor Shirley observed that the assemblies 'don't like the plan concerted by the

Commissioners at Albany which all of 'em conceive to infringe upon their colony-liberties and privileges'. The problem, as Franklin recognized at the time, was that 'the colonies were seldom all in equal danger at the same time, or equally near the danger, or equally sensible of it; that some had particular interests to manage, with which a union might interfere; and that they were extremely jealous of each other'. The Governor of Virginia, Robert Dinwiddie, later remarked that although 'From the number of our inhabitants it may be suggested that we may easily raise a pretty little army,' in fact 'the case is otherwise; for most of the people are freeholders and ... have votes for choosing assembly men'. American liberties, in short, had become a barrier to the necessary security measures. In these circumstances Franklin thought the best way forward was to establish an Act of Union through an Act of Parliament. This came to nothing, but it was clear that the issue which had given rise to the Albany Congress would not go away. As Franklin remarked at the end of that year, 'It is, I suppose, agreed to be the general interest of any state, that its people be numerous and rich; men enough to fight in its defence, and enough to pay sufficient taxes to defray the charge; for these circumstances tend to the security of the state, and its protection from foreign power.' For the moment, however, this American interest in grand strategy did not translate into greater cohesion between the colonies. Franklin's was literally a voice crying in the wilderness.[13]

Faced with this lack of cooperation, London began to lose patience with the colonists. The Lord Chancellor, Hardwicke, complained that ' 'Tis monstrous that people will not help themselves', and the supreme commander in America, the Earl of Loudoun, complained that 'the universal plan in this country is, to throw all expenses off themselves and lay it on the mother country'. Desperate measures were now taken. The French-speaking and Catholic Acadian population of Nova Scotia had long been a thorn in the side of the British government. In part, the issue was religious, but the principal concern was that the Acadians constituted a fifth column in thinly defended British Canada. It was the French loyalties of the Catholics rather than the Catholicism of the French which was at issue. In 1755, this nettle was grasped. Much of the troublesome Acadian population – about 7,000 of them – were deported to the thirteen colonies and dispersed, principally in Massachusetts, Virginia and Maryland, and ultimately to Louisiana. They now no longer posed a serious threat. As in the Highlands of Scotland, the British state had solved a pressing strategic problem through what would today be described as 'ethnic cleansing'. In the early to mid 1750s, therefore, London was faced with a choice of three imperial pre-emptions. The election scheme in Germany had been tried and failed. The removal of some of the 'turbulent Gallicks', had been achieved. The third option – western expansion in order to head off the threat of Franco-Spanish encirclement – was not even contemplated. Little did London know that it was this issue that would ultimately cost them the thirteen colonies.[14]

Meanwhile, Britain's position in Europe deteriorated still further. The all-important Barrier was still unsecured. This worried Newcastle more than the naval threat. He remarked in late October 1753 that 'His Majesty's fleet (tho' at a very great expense) is in a better condition than it was ever known to be, in time of peace', but the best constraint on France would still be a resolution of the Barrier question. Hopes of animating the Dutch to greater efforts were fading. By early 1754, Newcastle's exasperation was palpable. 'I am really quite tired out with your unintelligible proceedings,' he told the British envoy to The Hague, Joseph Yorke. 'Is it not a shame that instead of having any assistance from Holland . . . we have more opposition and plague from them, than from all the courts of Europe besides. Ask Bentinck what they will contribute to save Europe and *themselves* [underlined in original]'. Things stood no better with Austria. Hanbury Williams was dispatched on a special mission to Vienna in 1753 and found Maria Theresa very 'animated upon the affair of the Barrier', but not disposed to cooperate. Once again, Britain's record of unilateralism came back to haunt her. 'Her jealousy of being governed,' Hanbury Williams wrote, 'broke out very often and particularly in the whole story of the maritime powers having signed the preliminaries at Aix without her.' The Austrian chief minister, Wenzel Anton Kaunitz, maintained that the treaty of 1731 guaranteed only George's lands in Europe and only if Britain was not the aggressor overseas, something which Britain could not promise, and in any case could not prove to Vienna's satisfaction when push came to shove. The real problem, of course, was that Austria now saw Prussia rather than France as the main enemy. In spite of this, the trauma of the Treaty of Hanover and sheer strategic inertia drove Newcastle to hug

Vienna as close as possible. For this reason, he announced that he would 'overlook . . . any little immaterial incidents in the behaviour of the court of Vienna, which I may have wished otherwise but do not affect the system'.[15]

By late 1754, however, London was beginning to grasp that a revived Austrian alliance and Old System was not feasible; the Barrier had collapsed beyond repair. Kaunitz dismissed it in November as 'an indefensible country, open on all sides, and designed moreover to defend the frontiers of the [Dutch] Republic and England'. The Dutch and Austrian defections not only exposed the Barrier itself, but also the German hinterland which provided defence in depth. 'What then,' Secretary for the South Holdernesse asked, 'becomes of the union between England and the House of Austria, when cut off from any communication with the Empire?' 'I see the great system upon the point of being dissolved,' Newcastle wrote in mid December 1754. 'The court of Vienna is driving the [Dutch] Republic, and with her this country, from them as fast as they can. The moment the Barrier Treaty is out of the question, Holland will and must seek for protection from France or Prussia.' 'The great point is,' he asked Bentinck, 'what will the Republic do? Can you, will you keep your troops in the Barrier towns? If you withdraw them, the system founded upon the Grand Alliance is at an end.' The brutal answer was that the Dutch would – and probably could – provide little backbone to the Barrier. Newcastle had done his best. He had thrown money and time at the problem. The geopolitical ground had simply shifted under his feet.[16]

All this prompted an abrupt and radical rethink in London. Hitherto, British policy had followed the old Continental orthodoxy, according to which Britain's colonial and maritime supremacy was defended in Europe. French forces were diverted from naval to Continental purposes, and France was denied alliances with other naval powers wherever possible. British naval and colonial dominance in turn secured the overseas resources necessary to sustain her European position, and denied these to France. This policy had achieved some notable successes: the French and Spanish were kept apart, and in 1753 Madrid pointedly declined to renew the Family Compact. But more generally, it had failed. One way or the other, the threats in America, the subversion of the Barrier, the hostility of the Prussians and the defection of the Austrians appeared to show that this tried and trusted policy was no longer working. Newcastle was reluctantly forced to concede that Europe should be neutralized while Britain concentrated on the naval and colonial struggle with France. He now became, if only by default and temporarily, a navalist to safeguard his primary objective, which was to defend the European balance against France. In August 1755, British privateers were given permission to attack French shipping, and more and more vessels were deployed across the Atlantic.[17]

At the same time, navalist sentiment in the public sphere, which had been strong for some time, peaked. In August 1755, a Tory weekly essay paper, the *Monitor*, was founded by Richard Beckford, the brother and political associate of the planter-MP William Beckford, an ardent Pittite. It had a print run of 500 and a decidedly patriot bent, and was conceived very much as a beacon for 'blue water' sentiment of the Tory or Whig radical stripe. A spate of pamphlets now appeared, elaborating familiar colonial and insularist themes. A typical example would be *The important question concerning invasions, a sea war, raising the militia and paying subsidies for foreign troops*. 'Great Britain,' the author announced as his first proposition, 'being an island, is secure from an invasion, and having no designs of making conquests, and no interest of her own to pursue on the Continent, has no need of foreign assistance.' Besides, he stated as his second proposition, 'The strength of Great Britain lies in her fleets: these should be her principal, her only care. And if we carry on the war wholly by sea, and have nothing to do with the Continent, we shall have everything to hope and nothing to fear.' Part of this discourse, as usual, was a revival of anti-Hanoverian sentiment, including a spate of prints. One lowly balladeer from Taunton, for example, versified against the 'bondage' of the nation: 'from whelps [Guelphs: Hanoverians] to Stewarts let ye crown return,' he wrote. At the other end of the social spectrum, Lord Poulett, a disaffected Lord of the Bedchamber, launched an abortive attempt in April 1755 at a petition against George's forthcoming visit to the Electorate. All the same, even such a resolute navalist as the MP Richard Rigby wrote in late August that there was 'not the least tittle of public news from America, or more important, Germany'.[18]

The determination to concentrate on the colonial struggle was subject to three powerful constraints. Key figures such as the Secretary at War, Henry Fox, the Duke of Cumberland (the King's brother and Britain's most senior military figure) and George II himself remained committed to a forward European policy. There was also the need to maintain naval superiority in home waters. 'I think it would be a dangerous measure,' Anson observed in December 1755, 'to part with your naval strength from this country, which cannot be recalled if wanted, when I am strongly of the opinion that whenever the French intend anything in earnest, their attack will be against this country.' Finally, there was the desire to avoid a breach in Europe as long as possible. Newcastle even sent pineapples from the renowned glasshouses at Claremont to Madame de Pompadour, the mistress of Louis XV, in order to encourage her pacific tendencies. If the Royal Navy and British privateers were authorized to conduct unrestricted war on French commerce from August 1755, London remained anxious not to provoke open hostilities through major fleet actions. To do otherwise, given Britain's isolation in Europe, was too risky. In June 1755, Newcastle registered his 'unease'

29. George II in the House of Lords. The King was a major player in the politics of the 1750s.

at the robust instructions for Admiral Hawke, which must lead to 'general hostilities [with] France in Europe . . . I own I tremble, when I reflect that we shall begin a war in Europe without one single ally . . .' Six weeks later, Hardwicke wrote that 'The oldest man living never saw such a scene, wherein Great Britain is alone . . . to cope with France. 'Tis a time of great thoughtfulness.'[19]

Moreover, the escalating naval and colonial war with France put a premium on avoiding a breach with Spain. For this reason, Newcastle stressed in January 1754 the need to find out more about the 'naval strength of Spain, their finances and their army'. 'All we do is but patchwork,' Newcastle remarked a few days later, 'till we get Spain into an alliance with us and the House of Austria' – preferably through Britain's accession to the Treaty of Aranjuez. Britain therefore lobbied hard in 1754 that Carvajal should be succeeded as chief minister by Count Riccardo Wall, who was positively Anglophile, despite his Irish Jacobite background. Britain's maritime position, in short, still needed Continental diplomacy to defend it. Besides, the security of the Electorate still had to be guaranteed, now more than ever. In this respect, whatever the prevailing strategic orthodoxy in London, Britain always remained a continental European power. The shift to a narrowly colonial policy in 1754–5 had simply transformed Hanover from the linchpin of British policy in Europe in the late 1740s and early 1750s, into its Achilles heel. Now that the 'old system' was collapsing, the Electorate would have to be protected by a new ring of alliances and subsidy treaties. Paradoxically, therefore, Britain was forced into a particularly intensive bout of European diplomacy as a result of withdrawing from the Continent. It was significant, however, that when the King set off for what turned out to be his last voyage to Hanover in 1755, Newcastle did not accompany him as he had in previous years, although he remained in close contact with Münchhausen. For once, the American empire had a greater hold over him than the German one.[20]

The most direct threat to Hanover in 1755 still came from Prussia, but that from France was not negligible either. In April of that year, the French ambassador to Berlin was treated to a spontaneous outburst from Frederick the Great. The French, he suggested, should occupy Hanover at the outbreak of war, 'this is the surest way to teach that [expletive deleted; meaning George II] a lesson'. The Hanoverian ministers themselves were profoundly concerned and protested to London; they strongly favoured some form of Hanoverian neutrality, as they had in 1741. Münchhausen feared that the King's German lands would be 'caught up in the struggles of his kingdom [Britain], and exposed to obvious danger'. Hence he stressed the need to make sure that Hanover would not be 'abandoned to the vengeance of the enemies of England'. Newcastle freely acknowledged a moral obligation to defend Hanover.

'We believe ourselves obliged,' he wrote, 'in justice, by law and in gratitude, to propose a scheme which will produce a real and efficacious security for the possessions of His Majesty in Germany.' But at this time, the diversion of French resources on the Continent formed no part of his strategy, quite the reverse. For this reason, Newcastle rejected what he called 'general and extended plans' for securing Hanover in favour of 'confin[ing] our views and efforts for the present to the sole defence of the King's German dominions'. Britain, he explained, was simply too preoccupied with America, and with naval expenditure, to consider 'the additional burden of a war on the Continent'. No second front against France was planned at this stage.[21]

A last attempt was now made to mobilize the Austrians in defence if not of the Barrier, then at least of Hanover. The Electorate became, as in years past, the 'advance headquarters' for Britain's Continental policy, as the King sought to rebuild the system of alliances. But the negotiations of June–July 1755 at George's summer residence of Herrenhausen, just outside Hanover, came to nothing. Newcastle was left to fulminate against the 'obstinacy and extravagance' of Vienna. It became clear that Vienna saw a British alliance as useful only against Prussia, not France. Mere diplomacy could not bridge the geopolitical divides opened up by Frederick's attack on Silesia. More generally, the Austrians were wary of being sucked into a Continental war on behalf of British aims overseas, remote though any such intention was from Newcastle's mind. Kaunitz complained that England was focused almost completely on naval power, 'at the expense of the Continent'. He continued that Britain wished 'against all proportionality, against precedent and in violation of clear agreements, to burden us [Austria] with the largest part of the load [of a Continental war], without holding out any hope that we might profit from this in the slightest way'. Moreover, the Austrians were now wise to Newcastle's diversionary strategy. As Kaunitz remarked in late November 1755, 'until now England has drawn its greatest advantage from the fact that France has exhausted most of her forces on a land war and has therefore been less able to concentrate on naval affairs. Should, however, the opposite be the case, then the fatal consequences for England are not hard to foresee.'[22]

At around the same time, the British position in Germany suffered another blow. The hereditary prince of Hesse-Kassel, who was married to George's fourth daughter, Mary, converted to Catholicism. Fearful that this might signify a departure from the British-Hanoverian orbit after the death of his staunchly Protestant father, anxious for the well-being of Princess Mary, and conscious that such conversions violated the spirit and sometimes the letter of the Treaty of Westphalia, Newcastle sounded the alarm in London, Vienna and The Hague. 'The infamous part of the Prince of Hesse,' he wrote, 'calls for our immediate attention. I hope in God all the Protestant powers will unite in that.' The urgency was dictated by the fact that Britain traditionally hired Hessian troops. Any dynastic instability or change of policy in Hesse-Kassel would threaten those arrangements at a time when even modest military assistance was better than none. The strongest card in his pack was the Prince of Wales, the future George III, whom it was proposed to marry off to the Princess of Wolfenbüttel. This may not seem a great coup, but Protestant marriage partners were limited, and Wolfenbüttel was strategically placed to support Britain's imperial policy. Newcastle thought it would be 'in every respect a very convenient and desirable match', for strategic reasons. 'I am,' he continued, 'more than ever confirmed in my opinion that in the present situation' it made sense, as far as the King and his family were concerned, 'to make friends of the neighbouring princes.' So even as he immersed himself in the affairs of America, Newcastle found himself being sucked back into the German Empire.[23]

Subsidy treaties to defend Hanover were duly concluded with Hesse-Kassel and the Margrave of Ansbach in the late summer of 1755, but everybody knew that would not be enough. A network of German alliances might be a useful tripwire, but it would not deter a French or Prussian attack. Only a major Continental power could do that. So in April 1755, Charles Hanbury Williams was appointed special envoy to St Petersburg with the task of concluding a subsidy treaty to protect Hanover, and to contain Prussia more broadly. 'The King of Prussia,' Newcastle explained, 'fears above all things Russia, and the conclusion of our treaty with her.' A Russian treaty would make clear to Prussia that she must stay out of a Franco-British war and that Britain 'will not permit that the German lands are attacked in consequence of these troubles'. Something more extensive than the treaty of 1742, by which Russia had committed 12,000 men, was envisaged. But the Russians were in a strong position and knew it. They were also ill-disposed. As the Tsarina complained to Williams on his arrival, Britain had treated the Russians like mercenaries throughout the 1740s. Moreover, London had not even permitted them to be represented at the peace negotiations at Aix-la-Chapelle. Once again, Britain's unilateralism had come back to haunt her. The Russians drove a hard bargain. They insisted on excluding an attack on the Barrier and developments in Italy and in America from the agreement. The upshot, in September 1755, was a very expensive treaty which committed the Russians to mobilize a large force on Frederick's eastern border and thus deter him from attacking the Electorate.[24]

All this was executed within a broader European vision. For one thing, there was the danger that St Petersburg might be distracted by events elsewhere from fulfilling her obligations towards Hanover. Here British statesmen were particularly anxious about the fortress of Ingul, which was hotly disputed between Russia and the Turks. A war over this outpost, which would not only tie down Russia but might also drag in Austria as well, was regarded as a major threat to British policy. Already in June 1755, Holdernesse had observed that the row over Ingul 'would bring about what France and Prussia have hitherto in vain attempted, and destroy at once the possibility of forming such a system as might enable us to make head against those powers in Europe'. Britain therefore did its best to mediate between the Russian and Ottoman empires on the issue. Moreover, the Russian alliance was seen as part of an interlocking system. British statesmen saw St Petersburg as the key to Vienna and thus to the whole 'old system'. 'We can do nothing,' Thomas Robinson observed in late July 1755, 'without the Dutch, the Dutch nothing without the Austrians, nor the Austrians anything without the Russians. When we are masters of the latter we may take the part we please.' A Russian alliance to check Prussia would give the Austrians sufficient strategic depth – by protecting their rear – to defend the Barrier. In short, even to secure relatively limited aims in central Europe – the safety of the Hanoverian Electorate – Britain had to take a Europe-wide view of developments.[25]

The impact of the Anglo-Russian subsidy treaty – which Parliament never ratified – on Prussia was spectacular. To this extent, British calculations of Frederick's fear of Russia were vindicated. Threatened on his eastern flank by British-subsidized troops, he hastened to guarantee Hanover himself, in return for a British subsidy of his own. The result was the Convention of Westminster between Britain and Prussia in January 1756, by which both parties contracted to uphold the peace of the Holy Roman Empire. Unlike earlier British imperial initiatives, which sought to mobilize Germany for the 'common cause', the Convention was narrowly designed to protect Hanover, for which Frederick was to be paid a thinly disguised Danegeld. The Austrian Netherlands – and thus the Barrier – were expressly exempted at Prussian behest, even though they were part of the Holy Roman Empire. Despite long-standing suspicions of Prussia, the move was popular in Hanover, where Münch-hausen viewed the alliance largely in terms of Protestant solidarity. By contrast, he saw Maria Theresa's determination to regain Silesia at all costs as a dereliction of her duty to defend the Empire against France. Indeed, Münchhausen argued that now was the time to cement relations with Prussia in dynastic terms. George II was more ambivalent about the Prussians, but in the circumstances of early 1756, he had little choice. From Britain's perspective, the Convention was intended to be comple-mentary to the Russian treaty and even a new accord with Austria; there was no sense that they had chosen Frederick over Maria Theresa.[26]

In Parliament and the public sphere, and among certain members of the ministry, on the other hand, the Hessian, Russian and Prussian treaties encountered furious opposition. If the administration had ex-pected some popularity bonus from putting America first, it was to be disappointed. Halifax complained that the money would have been better spent bribing Indian tribes attacking Virginia, Maryland, Pennsyl-vania and New York. Critics saw these measures not as part of a temporary holding operation on the Continent, but as yet another example of entangling alliances. They would merely inflame the threat they were supposed to contain. As the treaties passed through Parlia-ment, they were subjected to sustained attack. In November 1755 one critic described the Hessian subsidies as 'a measure to kindle – invite – a general war upon the Continent'. Likewise the Duke of Bedford privately argued that 'these late subsidiary treaties . . . seem to me to be calculated more to bring on a war on the continent of Europe than for the sole defence of His Majesty's Electoral dominions.' Navalist enthusiasm, in and out of Parliament, reached heights not seen since the late 1740s. 'Sea war, no Continent, no subsidy,' Newcastle remarked, 'is almost the universal language.'[27]

Moreover, these treaties were avowedly for the defence of Hanover and not, as in the 1740s, part of an overall European strategy against France. As such, they presented an inviting target along familiar lines.

The years 1755–6, therefore, saw a renewed flowering of anti-Hanoverian and anti-German feeling across the public sphere and political nation. In December 1755 the Opposition Whig Lord Temple lamented that the subsidy treaties had turned Britain into nothing more than 'an insurance office to Hanover'. In 1756 a collection of addresses from Yorkshire to the King proclaimed that 'if a continent must be supplied [and] our spoils be shared, let AMERICA partake rather than ungrateful Germany, the sepulchre of British interest.' And around the same time, Samuel Johnson, the editor of the *Literary Magazine*, published his 'Observations on the foregoing treaties' in June–July 1756. He dismissed Hanover as 'a territory on the Continent, of which the natives of this island scarcely knew the name till the present family was called to the throne, and yet know a little more than that our King visits from time to time'.[28]

As in the 1740s, critiques of Continental entanglements and Hanoverian measures were laced with insular and xenophobic rhetoric. Johnson argued that the subsidies were a waste of money at best, a 'foreign [i.e. Hanoverian] interest' at worst, since 'nature has stationed us in an island inaccessible but by sea, and we are now at war with an enemy, whose naval power is inferior to our own, and from whom therefore we are in no danger of invasion.' For good measure, literary and pamphlet attacks also accused the ministry of having diverted resources from America to Hanover, thus exposing Braddock to disaster on the Monongahela. In Parliament the charge was led by William Pitt. He dismissed the subsidy treaties as a 'chain and a connection, [which] would end in a general plan for the Continent which this country would not support'. Some three weeks later Pitt reiterated his view that 'both Russian and Hessian treaties [were] singly entered into on account of Hanover'. That same month, Horace Walpole observed that Pitt was 'scouring his old Hanoverian trumpet', to refresh his patriot credentials and embarrass Newcastle. In mid November, Pitt launched a ninety-minute assault on the Hessian and Russian treaties on the grounds of their partiality to Hanover, and predicted that that measure would hang like a millstone about the neck of the minister who supported it and sink him into disrepute amongst the people'. A week later, Newcastle finally dismissed Pitt as Paymaster General for his attacks on the government's Continental policy.[29]

Out of office, Pitt intensified his attacks. In December, he claimed that the treaties were 'advised, framed, and executed, not with a view to the defence of Great Britain . . . but purely and entirely for the preservation of Hanover'. The tail, in other words, was wagging the dog. Britain, as Pitt lamented in what was surely not a coincidental allusion to military compulsion, was being 'pressed into the service of an Electorate'. In May 1756, he condemned the Convention of Westminster with Prussia, designed to defend Hanover, as another example of Electoral manipulation, and 'ardently wished to break these fetters which chained us, like Prometheus, to that barren rock', that is Hanover. In the same speech, Pitt told the House of Commons that Hanover was 'a place of such inconsiderable note that its name was not to be found in the map'. Instead of wasting resources on 'incoherent un-British measures' in Germany, Pitt argued, Britain should concentrate on naval expansion and the American war.[30]

The parallels to the anti-Hanoverian agitation of the 1740s were obvious. James, Earl Waldegrave, wrote that 'His Majesty's very natural affection for his German Electorate was brought as an undoubted proof of his settled aversion to his British subjects. All these calumnies . . . had been formerly very successfully employed by some of the same persons, when Lord Carteret was minister.' The aim of the ring-leaders then and now, he argued, was 'to create as much confusion as might be necessary to bring themselves into power; which being once obtained they were ready to talk a different language'. In some respects, Waldegrave was not far off the mark. Pitt's rediscovery of anti-Hanoverianism in the mid 1750s was closely related to his sponsorship by the Prince of Wales's entourage in Leicester House, and the need to find a stick to beat the ministry with. But Pitt's dispute with the ministry in 1755–6 was only superficially about Hanover, supposed royal partiality to it, and his own quest for 'popularity'.[31]

For Pitt, the real issue was the whole conception behind the new Continental policy of 1754–6, and the role assigned to Hanover therein. In private, he freely acknowledged the 'obligation of honour and justice' to the Electorate; it was 'the practicability' of the proposed measures which he doubted. Not only, he told Hardwicke, would subsidy treaties be domestically unpopular, they 'would end in a general plan for the Continent which this country could not possibly support'. Instead of pre-empting a European war, as envisaged, they would precipitate one. Pitt 'ridiculed extremely the notion of supporting Hanover with 8,000 men, which was too little, if Hanover was attacked, and a most unnecessary expense without it'. Britain would pay twice over, once to defend Hanover unsuccessfully, and then to recapture or buy it back. A more viable course of action was to allow a temporary French occupation and redeem the Electorate at a peace settlement; Pitt suggested setting aside £5 million for the purpose. This was also the Duke of Bedford's view: although he believed that Britain should 'pursu[e] the war in [her] own way', she 'would be bound . . . to insist on full reparation' at the peace settlement. Many MPs agreed with this. In short, few were suggesting that Hanover should simply be abandoned. To risk a broader European war simply to defend Hanover, or to send ground forces to the Electorate solely for that purpose, however, was getting British strategic priorities back to front.[32]

In any case, Pitt's attempts to revive the anti-Hanoverian fervour of the mid 1740s and turn it to his immediate advantage failed. He proved unable to reignite public opinion; on this occasion pamphleteers and poetasters did not respond well to his bombast, and the parliamentary speeches fell flat. His dramatic reversal on the issue of Hanoverian troops had not been forgotten. In 1754, one satirist reminded Pitt of his earlier rhetoric and had him say, 'Must I not expect to have the *name of Hanover* resounded in my ears, as I once wished it might be branded on my forehead if ever I voted for the hire of the troops of the Electorate?' Pitt's appeal was also blunted by the fact that the strategic case for the subsidy treaties and the deployment of the Hanoverians was compelling. Mainstream opinion – as in the 1740s – remained firmly Continentalist. As Hardwicke remarked in November 1755, 'No man of sense or integrity will say that you can quite separate yourselves from the Continent. A commercial kingdom must have connections there.' Moreover the European and American spheres were believed closely connected. One pamphleteer observed in 1755 that 'It would be to no purpose to be constantly sending fresh reinforcements to the New World if we did not first appoint proper checks upon the power of France in Europe.' Even though the administration had justified the treaties in narrowly Hanoverian terms, they were sometimes interpreted within the framework of traditional Continental strategy. Thus one peer welcomed the subsidies by announcing that although he was 'not a deep politician', it seemed clear to him that 'if you will in a war with France absolutely disconnect yourselves from all the powers upon the Continent, France may disband one hundred men.' Then, he warned, 'she may throw all her men and money into the marine, and if she does will soon make superior to yours, and what army she has she may use it to subdue you in America or invade you in Britain.' In the end, the treaties passed with large majorities in December 1755, by 85 to 12 votes in the Lords and 318 to 126 in the Commons.[33]

Both parties believed that the Convention of Westminster in January 1756 allowed them to square the circle. Frederick felt that he had had a narrow escape. He knew that France intended to fight a largely naval war against Britain, to avoid Continental entanglements and to forego attacking Hanover. Frederick had also expressly excluded the Austrian Netherlands from his guarantee, so the option of pressurizing London through the Barrier – which had worked so well in the mid to late 1740s – was still open to the French. For this reason he did not expect Versailles to be much offended by a treaty to defend Hanover against a phantom threat. At the same time, he had secured British funding and, as he thought, banished the Russian spectre on his eastern border. British statesmen, likewise, saw no contradiction between engagements to St Petersburg and Berlin, and their continuing efforts to woo Austria. Indeed, in their solipsistic world, they saw the Prussian treaty as a fresh opportunity for Austria to defend the Barrier. There was no sense in London that Britain had opted for Berlin, and thus finally given up on Vienna. Rather, British statesmen believed that they had simply coopted Prussia for the 'old system' in order, as Newcastle wrote in March 1756, 'to strengthen and maintain it in opposition to its natural enemy, France'. The Secretary of State for the North, Holdernesse, told the Austrians with even greater solipsism '[that] the present treaty with the King of Prussia puts them in a possibility of repairing that breach in the system of Europe which the union between France and Prussia had so fatally made; and they may now without running any risk of being attacked in Germany detach some considerable reinforcements into the Low Countries'.[34]

In fact, the Anglo-Prussian rapprochement gave massive offence in Vienna, Versailles and St Petersburg. Throughout the spring and early summer of 1756 the Tsarina – who believed that the Convention made an attack by Frederick upon her more likely – expressed her displeasure by ostentatious mobilizations on Frederick's eastern border. The Austrian reaction was even more drastic. They were not consulted on the Convention of Westminster, and – rather paradoxically in view of past discussions – took umbrage at the exclusion of the Barrier from the Prussian guarantee, which they took to be an invitation to attack the Austrian Netherlands rather than Hanover. There was clearly no pleasing Kaunitz or Maria Theresa. Anglo-Austrian relations, which had been in serious decline since the mid 1740s, completely and suddenly collapsed. Meanwhile, the French felt betrayed by Frederick. In the space of a few months both powers – united in their loathing of Prussia – drew together. On 1 May 1756, they signed the Treaty of Versailles. A diplomatic revolution had taken place. It came not only as a blow but also as a complete surprise to London. In part, this was a failure of imagination. Britons could agree on few things, but they assumed that the Habsburg–Bourbon divide was a constant of the European state system. They should not have done so – after all, Britain had been allied to France between 1716 and 1731 – but they did. To them, the Treaty of Versailles was an alliance of opposites: it should not have happened. But there was also a failure of intelligence. Britain was well informed of thinking in Versailles, in the technical sense, but it completely misread French intentions.[35]

What happened was this. Like Britain, France was determined to concentrate on a sea war because it believed – in tacit tribute to the success of some fifty years of British strategy – that Britain wished to draw off French resources through a Continental war. The Swedish ambassador to Versailles set out this thinking with exemplary clarity. Louis, he claimed, wanted 'a sea war only', for four reasons. First of all, because 'however successful diversions in the Netherlands have been they have not hindered England from pursuing her plans'. Secondly, waging a land and sea war simultaneously was 'impracticable without exhausting the kingdom of men and money, and sea war is already inevitable'. In any case, thirdly, 'France required her whole strength by sea to thwart the aggressive views of England in the colonies'. Fourthly, 'once a land war was begun it would by degrees spread further and further', sucking in ever greater resources. There was, moreover, no intent to put pressure on Hanover. This news – which reached Newcastle through his network of informants – came as a great relief to London in late 1755 and early 1756. He too, as we have seen, planned to neutralize the Continent, in order to protect Hanover, and to devote

British resources entirely to the struggle in America and on the high seas, where it had already begun.[36]

Welcoming the neutralization of Europe was one thing, a Franco-Austrian alliance was quite another. That was a major shock to the system, and British intelligence was slow to see the warning signs. Towards the end of May 1756, one of Newcastle's agents still saw no great cause for alarm. 'It is whispered,' he wrote, 'that something hath been concluded between this court [Versailles], and that of Vienna; if it is true, which I doubt, it must only tend to maintain the Catholic religion in the [German] Empire according to the Treaty of Westphalia'; it might also, he speculated, have something to do with the succession in Hesse. As for a French attack on Britain itself, he was 'persuaded all thoughts of an invasion have been laid aside since the Hessians and Hanoverians were taken into the English pay'. This he continued, 'will allow your court to finish the contest in North America by sending a large body of regular troops there'. So far, so good, but a few days later more details of the treaty began to filter out. Now the informant wrote somewhat less optimistically that 'I assured you long ago that France would use every art to light up a war in the Empire and I am daily more confirmed in that.' He was very wide of the mark, as far as French intentions were concerned, but what other explanation could there be for such an extraordinary reversal of the natural diplomatic order?[37]

By the Treaty of Versailles, both sides agreed to come to the aid of the other with 24,000 men if attacked, unless the adversary was Britain. The worrying bit for London was Maria Theresa's commitment not only to stay neutral in such a conflict, but to come to France's aid if attacked by any of Britain's allies; this could only mean Prussia. At a stroke, the basis of British European policy had collapsed. France would now be free to concentrate all her efforts on the maritime war; the increased exposure to attack was merely a minor problem in this context, albeit the most pressing one. A shocked Newcastle wrote of 'the great, and surprising change of affairs, made by the treaty concluded between the court of Vienna and France whereby the ancient system is totally dissolved'. He believed that the treaty 'tho' nominally *defensive*', was 'to all intents and purposes ... offensive'. And although Newcastle regarded the pact as an 'unnatural union', he now saw it as part of the long development of Austrian policy: 'they were glad to declare the old system dissolved and to take new arrangements'. Newcastle also suspected them of 'blind bigoted designs against the Protestants in the [German] Empire and the Protestant cause'.[38]

The most sinister spectre, however, was not actually mentioned in the treaty – in which France promised to respect the integrity of the Low Countries – but had been in the air throughout the final stages of the negotiations. As the summer wore on, British nightmares were fed by alarmist intelligence reports of Kaunitz's agreement in principle to give up the Austrian Netherlands, in return for French help in the recovery of Silesia. 'I am told,' one informant wrote to Newcastle, 'that an overture hath been made for furnishing the Empress Queen a much larger and more effectual succour than what's stipulated in the Treaty, if she will consent to the cession of the Pays Bas to France.' He added that 'it's certain that this court has the acquisition of the Pays Bas at heart' – perhaps to give it to Elizabeth Farnese's second surviving son, Don Philip of Parma, who had caused London so many headaches in the 1720s and 30s as a result of his mother's determination to restore the Spanish position there at Austria's expense. This was the last straw. Whether Flanders was handed to Don Philip, one of Britain's perennial diplomatic bad pennies, or to France directly, the Barrier was now in mortal danger. In mid June the Dutch undertook to stay neutral so long as the French stayed out of the Netherlands, but the experience of the 1740s had shown that there was not very much they could do about it if Versailles changed its mind.[39]

Newcastle responded to this looming catastrophe in the only way he knew. 'We must either endeavour (I admit at an immense expense) to form a counter alliance to this formidable one,' he argued, 'or all Europe will be given up to France.' In short, Newcastle was once more finding himself being drawn back into an active Continental policy.[40]

Yet the isolation of Britain was now nearly complete. Her one ally on the European mainland was surrounded on all sides by hostile major powers, at least two of which – Austria and Russia – made no secret of their intent to attack in the near future. The integrity of the Dutch Barrier had been fatally compromised by the Austro-French rapprochement. Nor did the picture look any better in North America, where the French continued to encroach; or at sea, where French squadrons repeatedly gave the Royal Navy the slip as they deployed overseas. The situation would have been far worse had not skilful British diplomacy and a pacific agenda at Madrid kept Spain neutral. 'What havoc would a junction of two powerful crowns on ticklish American disputes have made upon poor Great Britain!' Keene mused in early May 1756. Britain declared war on France formally in May. Then came the hammer blow, which took London by surprise despite the fact that French preparations had been taking place in slow motion since the beginning of the year. The French landed in Minorca, shrugging aside ineffectual attacks from Admiral Byng's squadron which had been sent to intercept them. By the end of June they were in complete control of the island. The whole British position in the western Mediterranean was now in doubt, and Gibraltar looked distinctly vulnerable. Its governor, Lord Tyrawly, warned in August 1756 that 'I am not so thoroughly satisfied that Gibraltar is so formidable a place as the common cry thinks it.' He was sceptical of British boasts. 'That Gibraltar is the strongest town in the world, that one Englishman can beat one Frenchman, and that London Bridge is one of the seven wonders of the world, are the natural prejudices of an English coffee-house politician.'[41]

To the parliamentary opposition and the public sphere, the fall of Minorca was further proof of a deep strategic and moral crisis of the nation. It provoked a much larger wave of pamphlets and ballads than Braddock's disaster the previous year. About forty addresses from more than thirty constituencies were sent to Parliament on the subject; many were reprinted in the press. Some now feared a domino effect, which would spill over to America. One broadside lamented that 'Minorca is lost; and America too / Soon my good Folks, will be taken from you: / And when to the French you've lost all your Trade / Soon to French Slaves vile slaves you'll be made.' Typically, the Tory satirist and staunch opponent of European engagements John Shebbeare blamed Hanover for the disaster in his *Fourth letter to the people of England*, on the grounds that the resources needed to defend Minorca had been wasted on Hanover. But the principal strategic reason why Minorca rankled more than the massacre on the Monongahela, was that it was a major reverse in European waters, rather than a lurid skirmish in the wilderness. The American contest was ultimately linked to the European balance; the Mediterranean was central to it. Moreover, the defeat was of a piece with other signs of a British retreat in Europe, such as the continued French refusal to demolish the fortifications at Dunkirk. In this sense, the patriot effusions over Minorca were a tribute to the ingrained Eurocentricity even of most 'patriots'.[42]

A steady chorus now demanded an inquiry into this painful reverse and the punishment of the guilty. Much of this focused on Byng himself, but many believed that he was simply a scapegoat and that the blame went much higher, to Anson at the Admiralty and, indeed, to the head of the administration itself. There were dark rumours that Newcastle had been bought with French gold, or so corrupted with Gallic ways that he did not need to be. Likewise, the Earl of Hardwicke received a poison pen letter asking him, 'Pray how much did you sell Port Mahon for?' In September 1756, one observer remarked that 'This morning I heard the whole city of Westminster disturbed by the song of a hundred ballad-singers, the burthen of which was "to the block with Newcastle, and the yard-arm with Byng".' The periodic fears of British ministers throughout the eighteenth century that failure to manage the European balance of power might bring them to the scaffold was thus by no means fanciful. The autumn and winter of 1756 was a moment when that very political form of death loomed before them. One way or the other, somebody was going to have to be held accountable for this major strategic disaster.[43]

The shock of Minorca exposed anxieties of national power which went much deeper than the debate over individual engagements or even grand strategy. A profound sense of paranoia and unease now gripped not only popular opinion but much of the political nation. Britain had been defeated not just on land, but in her own element: at sea. Joseph Reed the poetaster wrote despairingly, 'Ask the proud battlements in Dunkirk rais'd / In undemolish'd Dunkirk, they will tell / In what contempt our dreadless fleets are held / While luxury and avarice unman / The native spirit of our little isle.' Byng was a coward because he was believed to be a fop, and – worse – a court favourite. He was unfavourably compared with traditional maritime heroes such as Drake and Raleigh. There was also a revival of interest in Admiral Vernon, whose manliness, potency and contempt for effeminacy and court life was emphasized. He had been MP for Ipswich since 1741, and lately a Director of the British Herring Company; his attacks on the government had become so colourful that some suggested he take a job at the fish market at Billingsgate. Byng thus became a lightning conductor for a much more widespread cultural crisis and angst about the decline of British maritime virtue. Even the unemployed tin miners of Cornwall blamed Byng for their misery: he was dragged in effigy through Falmouth with a caption cursing him as 'The Friend of Monsieur Ragout and the Tinners' scourge'. *Mutatis mutandis*, the presence of a French chef in the Prime Minister's household took on a distinctly sinister aspect. In this perfervid atmosphere it comes as no surprise to find a relatively serious figure such as Lord Tyrawly demanding the expulsion of French servants, dancing masters and hairdressers from London on the grounds that they constituted a potential fifth column. What he meant, probably, was not so much that they would spy on Britain, or physically sabotage the war effort, but that their foreign ways would subvert the manly qualities of true Englishmen when they were most needed.[44]

According to the patriot critique, the solution to Britain's predicament in late 1756 could not just be a change of men and measures, though that was urgently necessary, but a complete programme of national revitalization through political change. It therefore took aim at the fiscal-military complex, which had developed to finance and profit from Britain's wars against France. As merchants, shopkeepers and tradesmen of the middling sort, patriots looked on the behemoths of the Bank of England and the whole architecture of what has become known as the 'Financial Revolution', with the greatest suspicion. Tear it all down, they called, and set free the natural energy of the nation. At the same time, patriots demanded the creation of an effective militia, which would take the defence of the country out of the hands of the corrupt, sly, homosexual and cross-dressing elite, and return it to the people, where it belonged. In early December 1755 Pitt and his crony George Townshend (MP for Norfolk and a former soldier) had already put a motion to the Commons for a revival of the militia; Temple (the Opposition Whig peer and associate of Pitt), Bedford and Halifax revived the issue in May 1756 in the House of Lords; and there was another spate of militia enthusiasm after the fall of Minorca. This surge of patriotism and martial ardour, however, came with a substantial dose of scepticism about the militarization of British society and politics. In practice, military service was a bore and wasteful. The Militia Act soon ran into difficulties. Many feared that they would not be paid, or would be drafted to serve abroad with the regular army. The local gentry were often hostile. Moreover, even as they enthused about the parliamentarian and naval hero Vernon, patriots fretted at the danger which the 20 per cent of MPs with military backgrounds posed to their political liberties. The line between turning Britain into an absolute state in order to defeat absolutist France, and laying oneself open to Franco-Jacobite invasion through military weakness, was clearly a fine one.[45]

The militia was also furiously opposed by the Whig establishment. This was partly because they feared the uses to which the arms might be put by the middling and lower orders. Ministers were particularly adamant that there should be no militia in Scotland, believed to be still a hotbed of Jacobite activity. But the principal objection was a genuine belief among Newcastle, Hardwicke, Carteret and the King himself that only a professional army would do. Moreover, a large militia would damage the economy, and deprive Britain of its undoubted comparative advantage within the European state system, which was its commercial vibrancy and its unique capacity to draw on this strength in the domestic and international money markets. Hardwicke put it thus: 'I never was more convinced of any proposition in my life than of this, that a nation of merchants, manufacturers, artisans and husbandmen, defended by an army, is vastly preferable to a nation of soldiers.' It was from trade, manufacture and arts, he reminded people, that 'have flowed your commerce, your colonies, your riches, your real strength; which has enabled you . . . to balance the power of your neighbours; some of whom have far outgone you in national military force'. By late 1756, however, all this looked much less convincing than it once had. To enraged patriots, Britain now resembled nothing so much as ancient Carthage just before it succumbed to the military discipline and agrarian virtue of Rome. All its commerce, they warned, had been unable to save that city. The poet John Free wrote, 'Our Tyrian colonies were Traders all / In war they purchas'd aids; then purchas'd peace / And thought the world would follow money's call / No native troops, the while, their wealth secur'd / Nor longer than they paid, their sovereign strength endur'd.' There were some things that money could not buy, the argument went, and one of these was security.[46]

Newcastle's parliamentary position began to buckle under the failure of his foreign policy. His voting strength remained robust, but there was a steady haemorrhaging of confidence in his ministry. It could still win the vote, but the argument was being lost. Newcastle told the King that 'Tho' we did not want numbers, we wanted hands and tongues in the House of Commons'. The government was forced, with some misgivings, to establish an inquiry into the loss of Minorca and to prosecute Byng.

Its most senior legal figure, Lord Chancellor Hardwicke, was sceptical. 'The affairs of the Admiralty,' he wrote in October 1756, 'consist of so many branches, and admit of such a variety of opinions, that nobody knows how far inquiries may be carried.' Hardwicke predicted that 'Ill success will be worked up into mistakes, mistakes into neglects, and neglects into crimes, where, in conscience, there is no crime at all.' The Opposition were determined to make any inquiry into the loss of Minorca as wide-ranging as possible, in order to implicate the ministry as a whole, not just the unfortunate Byng. This failed. Byng was charged, not with cowardice, but with want of zeal, of 'failing to do his utmost to take or destroy the enemy's ships'. Under the articles of war, the punishment for this was death. His defence was inept, to say the least, and he was slaughtered by the press. Byng was duly found guilty, and shot on his own quarterdeck in March of the following year. Voltaire famously observed that he had been shot '*pour encourager les autres*', that is to inspire the rest of the Navy to heroism. It was a timely reminder that in eighteenth-century Britain strategic misjudgements were punishable by death.[47]

The domestic disturbances surrounding the fall of Minorca and the court-martial of Byng distracted the ministry and divided Britons when national unity was needed. They also damaged the international standing of Britain. Throughout the eighteenth century, European governments tended to confuse debate with weakness. They never understood the unique discursive dynamic of British politics, which they mistook for anarchy. In 1753 the British ambassador to The Hague, Joseph Yorke, remarked that he was 'convinced that the constitution of no country is so little known as that of England'. 'Half the world,' he continued, 'imagine that all government is confusion with us; and the other half that our kings are as arbitrary as any other, and that all they do in a view to satisfy the nation is pure grimace'. Europe was more ignorant of Britain than Britain was ignorant of Europe, but for this very reason Newcastle was anxious to avoid the impression that he had lost control of the domestic debate. There were two options. One was to try to stifle criticism through legal means. Newcastle was so infuriated by Shebbeare's accusation that he neglected America in favour of Hanover, that he wanted to take him to court. Hardwicke counselled against this, arguing that even if he was successful, Shebbeare would merely be given additional publicity. The later attempts to bring John Wilkes to heel showed that this was good advice. Indeed, the *Grub Street Journal* remarked that a sojourn in prison or in the stocks 'is so universally esteemed, that he, who has had the honour to mount that rostrum, is always looked upon amongst them, as a graduate of his profession'. The alternative to censorship and prosecution was promoting an aggressive press campaign in defence of ministerial policies. Thus in November 1756 David Mallet, once a patriot scribbler, was hired under the Secret Service budget to write pamphlets supporting Newcastle's foreign policy.[48]

As if all this were not bad enough, the country was rocked by an invasion scare in the summer and autumn of 1756. Now that France had secured her back on the Continent, she was free to organize a naval assault on the island of Britain itself. The government requested Dutch assistance; they had supplied around 16,000 men in 1715 and 1745. But this time the Dutch, who were themselves in terror of a French attack, refused, and declared their neutrality in late May 1756. So there was nothing else for it but to bring over Hessian and Hanoverian troops. Ironically, Hanover – so recently derided as an albatross around Britain's neck – had now become a net exporter of troops in defence of Britain. This fact rather than silencing the critics, only served to inflame them. They saw the deployment of foreign mercenaries as a national humiliation. 'What an inglorious picture for this country,' Pitt lamented in May 1756, 'to figure gentlemen driven by an invasion like a flock of sheep.' It was a slap in the face for those who favoured a militia and savoured of some sort of sinister unconstitutional agenda. Indeed, the *Monitor* put it about in July 1756 that the ministry 'have formed a design to render Their Majesty [George II] absolute to change the government into an oligarchy by the aid of a powerful standing army of natives, Hessians and Hanoverians'. Pitt was thus able to borrow from a venerable anti-absolutist rhetoric in which the Hanoverian connection figured as a Trojan horse for Continental militarism and absolutism. Responding to Pitt's transparent bid for popularity, his great rival Henry Fox, Secretary of State for the Southern Department, accused him of trying to make 'the fatal distinction . . . of Englishman and Hanoverian'. Still, despite being much chewed over in ballads and prints, the Hanoverian issue fizzed and sputtered; it never really ignited.[49]

In late 1756, Pitt made a last attempt to blow on the embers. One of the Hanoverian soldiers deployed in southern England was accused of the theft of a handkerchief and thrown into prison. He was released on the intercession of his Hanoverian commanding officer and that of the Secretary of State for the North, Holdernesse. This incident, which seemed to imply some sort of legal extraterritoriality for the Hanoverians, caused public outrage. Some believed that the administration refused to prosecute the soldier for the most sinister of reasons. They accused Newcastle of wishing to use the Hanoverians as a 'Germanic Praetorian Guard', to shield the ministry from the wrath of the people, or even for the purposes of conducting a coup. Pitt condemned the decision as 'the most atrocious act of power and the grossest attempt to dispense with the laws of England since the days of Lord Strafford'. In this way, he was once again able to appeal to the enduring contemporary stereotype of the pilfering and absolutist Hanoverian. Indeed, one of Pitt's stated conditions for joining the administration in October 1756 was that Hessian and Hanoverian troops be placed under English law for civil offences. When the Hanoverians were finally sent home at the close of the year, Pitt was quick to claim the credit. All the same, Pitt's attempt in the summer and autumn of 1756 to generate an unstoppable surge of anti-Hanoverian sentiment failed as miserably as it had over the subsidy treaties in the previous year. There was a widespread political and public consensus in favour of the Hanoverians and Hessians, even if it was publicly muted. British opinion could be bloody-minded, but it was not completely obtuse. Most accepted the strategic arguments for the deployment: the Germans were all that were available and one could not afford to be choosy. As one Pittite observed in June 1756, 'Hanover treaties and Hanover troops are popular throughout every country [sic]. The almost universal language is, Opposition must be wrong, when we are ready to be eat up by the French.'[50]

What eventually made Pitt's breeze to blow was not the Hanover card, but the cascade of diplomatic and military disasters which befell the ministry in 1755–6. It started with Braddock's fiasco on the Monongahela, continued with the Austro-French rapprochement and the fall of Minorca; and culminated with the undignified thrashing about in the face of invasion at the end of the year. Throughout the past twenty months the bells had been tolling throughout Europe, and now the alarm had been sounded in Britain itself, just as Whig doctrine had always predicted it would be. Pitt was now a vindicated prophet: he became a Churchillian figure who had foreseen the rise of French power, and the inadequacy of governmental countermeasures. He was compared to Cicero and Demosthenes; he was Cato, who had warned that Carthage must be destroyed. The change of ministry which loomed at the very end of 1756 did not take place because Newcastle had actually lost his parliamentary majority – though he would have in time – but because he had been worsted in the public debate, and he had lost that debate because he had lost Minorca. The Whig establishment now turned to Pitt, as Waldegrave remarked, 'not because [they] liked him better, but because he had the nation on his side and consequently had the means of doing most service, to his King and Country'. He was to be a rhetorical reinforcement to a ministry which was losing the war and needed to find a new narrative.[51]

As in 1740, Britain was rescued by Frederick. His position was incomparably worse. The Convention of Westminster, far from breaking the ring around him, had drawn it tighter by pushing France and Austria further together. To the east, the Russians continued to menace his borders, and to the south Saxony looked as if it would be complicit in the general conspiracy. An Austrian war of revanche for Silesia appeared imminent; the only question was whether it would not also be a much more extensive dismemberment of Prussia. The phrase '*destruction totale de la Prusse*', which was rattling around in the cabinets of eastern and central Europe, might mean just that, or perhaps simply cutting the Hohenzollerns down to size. Frederick decided not to wait: in August 1756 he invaded Saxony. Unlike the totally unprovoked assault on Silesia in 1740, this was very much conceived as a pre-emptive strike, to catch his enemies off balance. Frederick was confident that an aggressive intent on the part of Saxony could be proved, and spent some time ransacking the archives of Dresden for evidence. The Austrian and Russian response was swift. Perhaps more importantly, the French now threw their overseas commitment into reverse and turned east to confront Prussia. The Continental war that Britain had so much wanted to avoid had erupted with a vengeance. 'Here is a fire lighted up in Germany,' the Earl of Chesterfield remarked, 'which, I am persuaded, I shall not live to see extinguished, but of which the effects must, in the meantime, be dreadful to England.' It is an image which puts later readers in mind of Sir Edward Grey's famous prediction in 1914 that the lights were going out all over Europe.[52]

If British pamphleteers thought Frederick's action a violation of customary international law – which it undoubtedly was – they kept such reservations to themselves. Most saw it as a legitimate pre-emptive strike against a gathering coalition, and many were already exhilarated by the emergence of an authentic 'Protestant hero'. Ministers, on the other hand, were aghast. At first sight, the move seemed to sink them deeper into the morass, not show them a way out. Britain was now committed to subsidize Prussia; Hanover was, willy-nilly, back in the front line. Neutrality – abjuring the engagements to Frederick – was a plausible option, as Prussia had violated the terms of the Convention of Westminster by starting a war in Germany. The King was strongly in favour of doing so in order to spare Hanover, a sure sign that the Prussian alliance very quickly lost its original purpose of protecting the Electorate. But Newcastle refused to do so, primarily because he was reluctant to lose Britain's only ally; his old Continentalist instincts were reviving. In any case, Newcastle was unable to give the unfolding crisis in central Europe his full attention. His ministry had been holed below the waterline and by the end of the year it was clear that he would have to stand down, at least temporarily.[53]

Pitt was sent for. Ostensibly, he demanded not only the removal of Newcastle, but a Militia Bill, an inquiry 'into the past measures' [i.e., Minorca] and an investigation of the affair of the Hanoverian soldier. But in private, he was concerned not to burn all his boats with the ministry and the Crown. The Duke of Newcastle reported that Pitt 'talked with the greatest respect of Hanover; said he would take care, whatever he might do, not to let drop an unguarded expression with regard to Hanover', though he remained adamant that defending Hanover militarily was not practical. He seems to have hinted that, as young Horace Walpole recalled, 'Hanover might not lose all its friends' after he came to power. Moreover, Pitt was a confidant of the Countess of Yarmouth, a naturalized Hanoverian who was the King's mistress. The Pittite press now began to prepare the ground for a reversal on Hanover. As the *Con-Test* wrote in November 1756, 'An *accidental* and *immediate* exigency may render a regard for a *foreign* interest a probable security for the preservation of our own . . . So that an alteration of principles, is so far from being a conclusive argument of inconsistency, that, on the contrary, it may be evidence of a steady attention to national benefit. A member of the legislative, therefore, ought not to be condemned for standing in opposition to the same measures, which he once earnestly patronized.'[54]

So when the King objected that 'Mr Pitt won't do my German business', Newcastle replied, 'If he comes into your service, sir, he must be told he must do Your Majesty's business.' The King repeated, 'But I don't like Pitt: he won't do my business.' Newcastle responded again: 'But unfortunately, sir, he is the only one who has ability to do the business.' In short it was the primacy of foreign policy, the pressure of global and European events, which drove Newcastle and the King to opt for Pitt, however personally distasteful this course of action might be. 'I think Pitt must come,' Newcastle concluded. 'He will come as a *conqueror* [underlined]. I always dreaded it. But I had rather be conquered by an enemy who can do our business.' Just how well Pitt would do the business, even Newcastle cannot have known. He had stumbled into the winning combination, an Anglo-Prussian alliance, which was to facilitate the British triumph in the Seven Years War, by accident, not by design. In the next few years it was Pitt who turned that expedient into a system.[55]

16

The Imperial Missions of William Pitt, 1757–1759

I overheard a West-Country gentleman whispering to a baronet that a Right Honourable personage is shortly to move for a subsidy of two hundred thousand pounds to be paid to the Elector of Hanover: 'Zookers,' says the baronet, 'that won't look well from one who proposed last year that a single shilling of money should never be sent to Germany, but if France offered any insult to Hanover on account of the part His Majesty acted in the present war, it would be time enough before the sword should be sheathed, to insist that atonement should be made.'[1]

The Test, 19 February 1757, on an imaginary conversation at the Cocoa-Tree Club

Mr Pitt moved for two hundred thousand pounds to be granted to the King for the support of an Army of Observation in Germany to protect His Majesty's Electoral Dominions against any invasion from France. Mr Pitt upon this made a long speech, said among many things that if any gentleman had a mind to attack his consistency that he hoped ... he did not insist on being literally and nominally consistent as long as he thought he was substantially so.[2]   Henry Digby MP, former Undersecretary of State for Foreign Affairs, in a letter of 1 March 1757

See Godlike Prussia shines in arms complete,
Like Marlborough glorious, and as Eugene great,
Of soul ambitious, and in thoughts refined;
Religion's friend, his country's and mankind,
Hail glorious prince, Britannia's thanks are due,
Whose real safety rests comprised in you[3]
        Gazetteer and London Daily Advertiser,
                3 December 1757

I am told it was said in full circle that there are not better troops in the world than the Hanoverians when they have a good general at their head: that the greatest obligations are due to the King of Prussia for giving Prince Ferdinand to that army: that Prince Ferdinand loves that army, and the troops adore Prince Ferdinand, etc.[4]

James Grenville to George Grenville, 29 June 1758,
on hearing news of the defeat of the French at Krefeld

Britain was now once more at war. To many Britons at the time and since, the Seven Years War marked the apogee of the British Empire, with victories in America, India and on the oceans of the world. British strategists, however, remained preoccupied with the German Empire, where the future of the European balance would be decided, and where the Continental war necessary to distract France from the naval struggle would have to be fought. It was the peculiar genius of Britain's leading minister, the Secretary of State for the Southern Department, William Pitt, that he managed to make these imperatives complementary rather than contradictory, and to build a diverse domestic political coalition around an extremely controversial and expensive policy. Paradoxically, Britain was never to be more involved in the German Empire and in the defence of Hanover than at the moment when she was laying the foundations for the greatest expansion of her overseas empire yet. The first half of the Seven Years War, in short, was to see the apotheosis of Britain's twin imperial missions in America and Europe.

The man who was now to guide Britain's destinies, with a brief interruption, for the next five years, did not lack self-confidence. 'I am sure I can save this country,' Pitt proclaimed in late 1756, 'and nobody else can.' To later generations of English historians and schoolboys, he came to epitomize commercial virtue, naval triumph, and a colonial destiny. Before him, it seemed, Britain had never enjoyed a victory, under him it never experienced a defeat. In 1759, the 'bells of victory' – as Horace Walpole put it – were famously worn out from ringing to mark the capture of Niagara, Ticonderoga, Crown Point and, of course, Quebec in North America; the heroic defence of Madras in India; the triumphs of Quiberon and Lagos at sea; and the Battle of Minden in Germany. Yet Pitt was only one of many cooks stirring the British broth during the Seven Years War. He perfected a policy that had long existed, and had only temporarily been abandoned. Pitt was thus no maritime or amphibious deus ex machina; he did not suddenly loom out of the azure main. Rather, he emerged from the old Whig Continentalist tradition. In short, the ascension of Pitt was a restoration not a revolution in British strategy.[5]

In the winter of 1756-7 all eyes turned with a mixture of *schaden-freude*, envy and curiosity to see what the new Secretary of State for the South would do. He was a man who enjoyed neither diplomatic experience, nor the confidence of the King; the former was desirable, the latter usually essential to the conduct of an effective foreign policy. Moreover, Pitt had inherited a poisoned chalice. Controversial decisions about the war, particularly concerning Europe and Hanover, would have to be made. Yet Pitt could not risk his greatest asset: his popularity and reputation for 'patriotic' probity. As Robert Walpole's son Horace remarked with some glee in November 1756, 'If he Hanoverizes, or checks any inquiries, he loses popularity, and falls that way: if he humours the present rage of the people, he provokes two powerful factions.' Likewise, Earl Waldegrave predicted that once in office, Pitt would deny his former opinions 'with an unembarrassed countenance'. For some, even the acceptance of office was a betrayal. *The Test* lampooned 'that ever-memorable Patriot, who after the mountain had groaned for a considerable time, was at length delivered of his mouse . . . His mighty promises and all his patriot cares, which in the morning dazzled the reader's eye, perished, like summer insects, with the setting sun, and have ever since been chilled and inanimate.' It too reminded readers of Pitt's 'unembarrassed countenance' in the 1740s, when he had violently opposed the Hanoverian troops 'in one session of Parliament' only to reverse himself 'the very next year'.[6]

The problems facing Britain in early 1757 were more pressing than they had been at any time since 1739-41, but they revolved around the same set of debates and choices that had structured British politics and debate since the Revolution. Contemporary observers, such as the *Annual Register*, identified two schools of thought. There were those who saw France as the main threat. It could be contained through 'a constant attention to the balance of power', while Britons should seek their 'particular safety and liberty in the general safety and liberty of Europe'. This would be achieved by subsidies and alliances. According to this strategy, the Navy 'ought by no means to be neglected', but should 'only be cultivated and employed subserviently to the more comprehensive Continental system'. The 'popular party', on the other hand, agreed only that France should be contained. They argued that Britain's (geographical) 'situation' dictated a 'safer and a less expensive plan of politics'. Britain 'ought never to forget', moreover, 'that we are an island' and that '[our] natural strength is a maritime strength'. They therefore concluded that Britain should not 'enter that inextricable labyrinth of Continental politics' and 'waste the blood of our peoples in all the quarrels that may arise on the Continent'. Indeed, Britons could have 'nothing to fear from the superiority of France on the Continent' while they 'preserved [their] superiority at sea'.[7]

In this debate Pitt – the erstwhile scourge of the subsidy treaties – came down firmly in favour of a 'Continental' strategy. He had already told the House of Commons in December 1756 that it 'must go as far as if the interest of this country were combined with those of the powers of the Continent, for combined they were'. His very first speech as Secretary of State in the Commons was in support of £200,000 towards the defence of Hanover. This paid for the Army of Observation, a Hanoverian force under the command of the Duke of Cumberland tasked with the defence of the Electorate. At the same time, Pitt became a vocal champion of the Prussian connection – it was never a formal alliance, although George referred to Frederick as 'his good ally' in his message to the House of Commons. This support did not go unrecognized at Potsdam and stiffened Frederick in his resolve, as it was meant to do. The plan was not, in the first instance, to 'conquer America in Germany', although colonial success was an intended by-product of the strategy. Rather, Pitt's endorsement of Continental alliances, subsidies, and ultimately of troop deployments was embedded within a broader and highly traditional strategic framework.[8]

The purpose behind British strategy, the Commons was told during the debate on the deployment and payment of the Army of Observation, was to keep Britain 'a Protestant, free, and an independent people'. This could only be effected if Britons understood that 'the interest of England ... comprehends the whole system of public liberty in Europe'. If that was 'shocked' or 'endangered', then 'the interest of England is endangered'. It was the same argument which had informed English foreign policy since the late sixteenth century. Moreover, if Britain had remained 'an unconcerned spectator of the troubles of Europe', France would have been in a better position to dispute 'the empire of the seas' with Britain. Everybody agreed, the argument continued, that the French fleet was formidable, not least because Versailles would 'never be at a loss for materials to build a navy, while they preserve their superiority on the Continent'. That being so, it followed that nothing could 'prevent France from having a marine superior to ours, whenever she is at freedom to bend her power and employ her subjects on that, and that alone'. In short, support for the Army of Observation and for Frederick – in whom the 'public liberty' of Europe now had 'a champion' – was central to the maintenance of British liberties and the maritime security on which they depended.

Expansion in America was part of this broader strategy. Its purpose was to secure the resources to sustain Britain's position in Europe, and to deny these to the French. This was, as the Commons was informed, a zero-sum game: 'The French . . . know that the source of power lies in riches, and that the source of the English riches lies in America. They know that in proportion we are weakened there, in the same proportion they are strengthened.' The best way of countering this threat, the argument went, was 'by supporting His Prussian Majesty, divert[ing] the French from pursuing those schemes that must infallibly give them a superiority by sea'; thereby 'we provide the most effectual manner for our settlements in America'. In short, 'the distinction between Germany and America', was too narrow, 'for when they have nothing to fear from Germany, we shall have everything to fear for America'. Of course, defending British security through the European balance of power, and diverting French resources away from their navy, were seventeenth- and early eighteenth-century strategic commonplaces. The idea that the overseas colonies, and particularly America, buttressed Britain's European position had gained ground by 1750, and underlay Newcastle's concern about French encroachments. Where Pitt broke strategic new ground was in fusing these two strands of British thinking.

All this, of course, produced a further barrage of criticism in and out of Parliament against 'Continental connections'. *The Test* accused Pitt of allowing his 'love of popularity' to 'be swallowed up by an eagerness for preferment'. It reminded readers once again of his record as a man who had 'in the year 1745, publicly declare[d] that Hanover troops should never appear again upon a British estimate', and then paid them through the back door via the Austrians. As far as patriots were concerned, it was at least the third time they had been let down: first by Pulteney in 1742, then by Paymaster Pitt in 1746, and then by Pitt again. Yet the Earl of Holdernesse, who stayed on in the new ministry as Northern Secretary, was wrong to suggest that Pitt's 'opinions upon foreign affairs now he is in office [were] exactly the same with mine, however different they were some time ago'. He had not 'Hanoverized' in the narrow sense that Walpole and his domestic critics claimed.[9]

For in reality, Pitt had never been the navalist know-nothing he so often acted in Parliament. His correspondence shows him to have been well informed about the imperial constitution. He was familiar, for example, with the classic texts of Samuel von Pufendorf on the Holy Roman Empire, and with a relatively obscure work on imperial public law, which he recommended to his nephew at Cambridge in January 1756 as 'an admirable book in his kind, and esteemed of the best authority in matters much controverted'. These are perhaps not the sort of tomes one associates with the creator of the first British empire, but they formed very much part of the mental world of the eighteenth-century British statesman. Moreover, Pitt had a capacity to learn and develop; he was not simply an opportunist. If he had famously attacked the Hanover troops in the early 1740s, he had quietly paid the same subsidies as Paymaster General later that decade. If he had fulminated against the Hessian, Russian and Prussian treaties, he had supported the grand sweep of the Imperial Election Scheme only a few years before. To be sure, Pitt was a politician and played to the domestic gallery as best he could. But beneath all the rhetoric was a set of firm intuitions about Britain's place in Europe and the wider world, which placed him firmly within the orthodox Whig mainstream.[10]

Moreover, Pitt had opposed the subsidy treaties of 1755–6 not only because it was popular to do so, but because he believed them to invert Britain's European priorities. Britain should not shell out vast sums for purposes which were, in his view, narrowly Hanoverian in focus; unlike the preceding Imperial Election Scheme, these measures would not suffice to defend the Electorate anyway. Pitt now proposed not to withdraw from Germany, but to engage there more deeply. His initial demand during the coalition negotiations of late 1756 had been for the Northern Secretaryship, hardly a sign of a man determined to concentrate on colonial issues, which tended to fall more within the remit of the

Southern Department, covering France and Spain. Only George's stubborn opposition had denied him that office, and forced him to settle for the Southern Secretaryship. All the same, Pitt now became the guiding spirit of Britain's commitment to Germany and remained so for most of the war. In this sense, his focus became resolutely 'imperial': his principal strategic interest was fixed on the Holy Roman Empire.[11]

There is little evidence, by contrast, of any colonial 'mission' on Pitt's part: he saw the American contest very much within a European framework, and not as an end in itself. True, he had been a supporter of war with Spain in the 1730s, and an episodic advocate of a more maritime strategy in the early 1740s. But in most other respects, Pitt was an implausible colonial and commercial hero. He knew very few of the major City financiers, and like virtually all other members of the British elite – including those with pronounced imperial sympathies – he never went to the colonies himself. Pitt's metropolitan connections were less exalted and more sectional. Thanks to his 'patriotic' postures, he was the hero of Tory and Opposition Whig City tradesmen and the 'middling sort', who revelled in attacks on the Crown, corruption, the Hanoverian connection in general and Continental entanglements in particular. In political and commercial terms, Pitt was directly linked only to the violently Francophobe and anti-Spanish West India interest, which commanded some twenty MPs. It was an important lobby, but it was not 'the colonial interest', still less 'the City'. Here his greatest ally was the flamboyant London MP William Beckford. By early November 1756, Beckford had become so alarmed at the 'melancholy prospect of public affairs' – by which he meant the loss of Minorca and the retreat overseas – that he turned directly to Pitt as 'the instrument of our deliverance'. 'A new system is now absolutely necessary,' he added, and 'in our present political warfare, I intend to act as one of your private soldiers without commission.' This endorsement came with the support of the *Monitor*. In the short term, however, 'patriot' support meant that the press would now hold Pitt's feet to the fire on grand strategy.[12]

In this context, the open hostility of the King, damaging in other respects, was a boon to Pitt's public profile. Throughout the first half of 1757, the monarch continued to regard Pitt as an intolerable imposition, and dismissed his commitment to the defence of Hanover. So in April 1757, Pitt was unceremoniously sacked, at the behest of Cumberland, who wished to cover his back before setting off for Germany. There was then a popular clamour for his return, which was less widespread than Pitt claimed, but sufficient to shake the Crown and the establishment. In addition, all attempts to construct an alternative ministry failed, and George was forced to back down and reinstate Pitt. The whole episode had strengthened Pitt at a crucial moment. It confronted the King with the fact that there could be no viable government without him. At the same time, it had revived Pitt's patriotic reputation at the very moment when it looked as if it was being irreparably tarnished by office and the demands of the German war. By the end of the month, the *Monitor* summed up Pitt's tenure to date, with some ambivalence: 'Foreign connections were not disregarded: neither were they admitted to the chief attention of the British policy. Our allies were not to be deserted: neither were we to enter as principals into their quarrels.' The patriot press continued to blow hot and cold on Pitt's strategy throughout 1757, but the immediate danger had passed. For the next three years or so, his direction of British grand strategy would not be seriously challenged by either the Crown, his political rivals, or public opinion.[13]

Pitt brought two things to the British effort. The first was dynamism and cohesion. This was by no means just a subsequent construct, but a clearly expressed view at the time. The Austrian chancellor, Kaunitz, at this point allied to Britain's enemy France, described in May 1758 how 'Pitt has his hand on the tiller. His former conduct has furnished convincing proof that he does not live from day to day, but goes to work in a systematic fashion, and knows how to direct the decisions in his part of the world towards a single aim.' The Duke of Newcastle, no uncritical admirer, was to remark later on in the war that 'I know nobody who can plan or push the execution of any plan agreed on in the manner Mr Pitt did.' The other contribution – as we have seen – was a restoration of Britain's Continental policy. Military and financial engagement in Europe, tentatively embarked upon in the first phase of his ministry, deepened. This was a progressive development, which was qualified and even denied at every stage with public obfuscations; but each step committed further British resources to the German war against France. Even in June–July 1757, before the dispatch of ground troops to Hanover, only a minority of the army was deployed overseas: 21 battalions in North America, 1 each in Antigua, the East Indies and Jamaica. No fewer than 58 battalions were deployed for home defence or in the Mediterranean. The naval contrast was less stark but still remarkable: 43 ships of the line overseas, as opposed to 54 in home waters and the Mediterranean. By the end of the war, more than 70,000 British soldiers had served in Germany.[14]

Over the coming years, Pitt was to elaborate his broader strategic vision on many occasions. He sought to safeguard the old Whig concerns with the 'liberties of Europe' and the Protestant cause – with the European balance of power, in short. He spoke of the need 'to prevent the final overthrow of all Europe, and [of] independency amongst the powers of the Continent', and of 'the formidable progress of the arms of France, and the danger to Great Britain and her allies resulting from a total subversion of the system of Europe'. There is no sign here of a Tory or Opposition Whig preoccupation with America: Europe came first. The means were equally Whig: an alliance with a Continental Great Power, now Prussia rather than Austria, which shared these preoccupations. Thus in late March 1757, Pitt expressed his 'sentiments of veneration and zeal for a prince [Frederick], who stands the unshaken bulwark of Europe, against the most powerful and malignant confederacy, that ever yet has threatened the independence of mankind'. Rather than inaugurating a new imperial era at the expense of Europe, therefore, Pitt actually reversed the disengagement reluctantly attempted by Newcastle in the mid 1750s.[15]

Moreover, Pitt's ministry strongly believed that confronting France in Europe was not just an end in itself, but also essential to the maintenance of Britain's colonial and naval superiority. The British envoy in The Hague, Joseph Yorke, argued in July 1757 that this was worth doing in all circumstances:

Our point should be to keep alive the diversion against France, for whether *beat* or *beaten*, it is a very important affair for us to make France spend upwards of 20 millions sterling in a year, an expense she must soon grow weary of, and which, without the King of Prussia's assistance, she would not make, at least it would all be employed directly against us. I hope therefore, we shall not be too much cast down, for we had better lose ten battles in Bohemia than one province in America.[16]

The connection between the American and European theatres was thus explicit from the start. A week later, Yorke noted the 'part the French take in the affairs of Germany, which turns their attention, as well as their money, from their marine, and . . . making expeditions to our colonies'. He estimated the 'diversion given to France' as 'obliging her to keep 100,000 or 150,000 men in Germany'. This made it all the more imperative, he concluded, to stop the French from knocking the Prussians out of the war, which would allow them to concentrate all their resources against Britain. As Newcastle remarked in late January 1757, Britain must cling to Frederick, or else risk 'falling between two stools', and wind up completely isolated in Europe.[17]

In this context, the dynastic link to Hanover was a potential asset, if it could be subordinated to a broader Continental strategy. George II was at first distinctly doubtful about the Prussian alliance, which he feared might compromise his German lands. Thus in October 1756, after Frederick's victory at Lobositz, George expressed his 'great apprehension of the future increase of the King of Prussia's power, expecting advantages for himself, as the King of Prussia would certainly have new acquisitions from this war'. Indeed, he hinted that he might want to call in the French to deal with Frederick's ambitions in the Empire. Fortunately for Britain, the chief minister in Hanover, Baron Münchhausen, had been a close confidant of Newcastle since the late 1740s, and regarded the Prussian alliance as a bulwark of German Protestant solidarity against the ambitions of the Franco-Austrian Catholic threat. He saw the resolutions of the Reichstag against Frederick as 'clear proof that that its plans are driven by Catholic concerns'. For this reason, Münchhausen agreed that to abandon the King of Prussia was 'to lose the sole ally remaining to us'. In short, the developing British–Hanoverian strategic partnership during the Seven Years War was by no means a sop to the King, or even suggested by him, but transcended purely dynastic considerations.[18]

Meanwhile, Pitt sought to inject new energy on the colonial front. The King's Speech at the opening of Parliament in early December 1756, which Pitt had drafted, announced that 'the succour and preservation of America cannot but constitute a main object of my attention and solicitude.' For the first time a British supreme commander for North America, the Earl of Loudoun, was appointed; in the past, colonial warfare had been conducted very much on an ad hoc basis, with various coalitions of American militias supporting British regulars and the Royal Navy. Pitt threw money at the colonial front, and eventually persuaded Parliament to pay for local levies. Even so, Loudoun had his work cut out. He lacked the authority to enforce his demands, and much of his time was spent wheedling and cajoling the individual colonial assemblies. The northern colonies contributed the most – far more than ever before – but those in the south, with the exception of Virginia, did very little. Indeed, the war exposed the inadequacy of the colonial militia system. Most refused to serve outside of their areas, or to accept proper military discipline. To cap it all, most Americans, far from being the crack shots and scouts of legend, were military novices and incompetents, many of whom did not possess arms, or even know how to fire a gun. General James Wolfe, the future victor of Quebec, declared that 'The Americans are in general the dirtiest, most contemptible cowardly dogs that you can conceive. There is no depending on them in action. They fall down dead in their own dirt and desert by battalions, officers and all.' These 'rascals', in short, were 'rather an encumbrance than any real strength to any army'. British officers complained that Americans were incapable of creeping through the woods like the Indians, but instead crashed through the undergrowth 'hooping' and 'hallooing', perhaps to keep their spirits up, thus surrendering the element of surprise. If British critics of the militia system wanted to, they had only to point to this monumental fiasco in vindication of their scepticism.[19]

In the end, it was left to London and the regular army to sort out the problem. Diplomacy was an important part of the solution. For the colonial balance involved not merely the French, but the Indians. As Samuel Johnson pointed out, 'The English and the French may have relative right', in North America, 'and do injustice to each other, while both are injuring the Indians. And such, indeed, is the present contest; they have parted the northern continent of *America* between them, and are now disputing about their boundaries, and each is endeavouring the destruction of the other by the help of the Indians, whose interest it is that both be destroyed.' Many Indians could only agree: 'Damn you,' the Delaware chief Shamokin Daniel exclaimed, 'why do not you and the French fight on the sea? You come here only to cheat the poor Indians and take their land from them.' They were forever destined to be buffeted by storms brewed in other men's worlds. For whether they liked it or not, the Indian tribes had become an integral part of the European state system. They could not choose to opt out of the Anglo-Bourbon antagonism; they could only take sides. Most supported the French, whose settler footprint was distinctly lighter, and who were much more adept at massaging native egos. By late 1756 and 1757, however, British Indian diplomacy was improving, as more and more funds were made available for it. Unlike the unfortunate Braddock, the new commander, Brigadier John Forbes, understood the need for local accommodations with the tribes. This was a controversial strategy, since the stream of presents and weapons had to be paid for, and the resulting debate was in many ways a microcosm of the equivalent discourse across the Atlantic on the effectiveness of European subsidies. This policy enjoyed at least moderate success: thanks to careful cultivation of the Cherokee and Catawba there was a marked decline in backcountry raids in late 1756 and early 1757. A smallpox epidemic also helped.[20]

The successful prosecution of the war in America depended not only on increasing British resources there, and diverting French efforts towards Europe, but also on ensuring that no further enemy entered the lists on either side of the Atlantic. So in the Mediterranean, Pitt carried on the policy of conciliation with Spain. Madrid had to be hugged close for as long as possible. A coalition between the two Bourbon naval powers, with all its implications for the maritime balance in the colonies and home waters, was to be avoided at all costs. In order to ensure this, Pitt was willing to think as radically as his Whig forebear Stanhope. He offered to surrender Gibraltar to Spain in return for help in winning back Minorca, which had been occupied by France since mid 1756. To a later generation of navalists, this was tantamount to treason. An astonished Alfred Thayer Mahan – the renowned naval historian – was to comment that 'It seems incredible that even the stern and confident William Pitt should, as late as 1757, have offered to surrender to Spain the watchtower from which England overlooks the road between the Mediterranean and the Atlantic, as the price of her help to recover Minorca.' Yet Mahan should not have been surprised. Minorca was, after all, regarded as the more important of the two bases throughout the eighteenth century. In short, for Pitt the question of Gibraltar was interpreted in the context of a wider British western Mediterranean strategy and global situation. If Gibraltar was the price for securing naval superiority overseas and at home, so be it.[21]

Besides, Pitt saw Spain very much as a *European* threat as well as a colonial one. He knew that the current fair wind from Madrid would cease as soon as the presumptive heir to the throne, the rabidly Anglophobe Charles of Naples, succeeded. Already at this point, Pitt was looking ahead to the implications this would have for the balance of power in the Mediterranean. He feared that Charles – who had refused to sign the Treaty of Aranjuez in 1752 – would try to secure 'to his second son the eventual succession to the kingdom His Sicilian Majesty now enjoys, in case he shall hereafter come to mount the throne of Spain', rather than handing it on to his brother, Don Philip. This raised the spectre of an eventual reunion of the crowns of Spain and Naples and thus the resurrection of the Spanish empire in the Mediterranean. All this shows that even as Pitt was immersing himself in the colonial struggle and the German war, he remained sensible to the geopolitical complexities of the Mediterranean balance.[22]

Throughout early 1757, public pressure for greater efforts in the colonies and at sea – and withdrawal from Hanover – continued unabated. At the same time, Frederick the Great, under sustained attack from all sides, sent out repeated pleas for a British diversion against his enemies, perhaps the dispatch of a squadron to the Baltic to intimidate the Russians, or British ground troops to Germany to shore up the Army of Observation against the French, or whipping up the Ottoman Turks against Russia in order to take the pressure off Frederick's eastern flank. None of these proposals appealed to Pitt: the Continental subsidies were controversial enough; sending the army was, for the moment, a step he would not defend politically. A Baltic squadron was ruled out partly for lack of spare naval capacity and partly in order to avoid provoking St Petersburg, with which Britain was not formally at war. By mid 1757, however, British excuses were beginning to wear thin: Frederick's situation became ever more precarious, and the navalist clamour increasingly insistent.[23]

Pitt's solution had more to do with politics and diplomacy than with strategy. For the next three years or so, he was to launch a series of coastal raids on the French Atlantic seaboard, including Rochefort, St Malo, and Belle Île. They were intended to divert French forces from Germany, thus taking the pressure off Frederick's western flank. They would, as the *Monitor* noted in August 1757, 'presently cure [France] of marching the strength of their country ... beyond the Rhine'. The method might have been naval, but it was employed in pursuit of a double Continental policy: France was to be distracted not only in Germany but on her coasts. These amphibious operations were to meet with decidedly mixed success, but they allowed Pitt to have it every way. They went some distance towards meeting Frederick's demands, they reduced pressure from local enthusiasts for the German war to send troops to Germany, they employed forces that were not currently deployed anywhere else. Best of all, the attacks could not be dismissed as a Hanoverian measure – they made the German subsidies more palatable, and appealed to all those who saw Britain's calling as a fundamentally maritime one.[24]

By the autumn of 1757, however, British arms remained no more successful in America and on the high seas than they had been in 1756. An attempt to recapture the French Canadian fortress of Louisburg miscarried with heavy loss. French ships repeatedly squeezed past the western squadron off Brest in January and March 1757 to concentrate in Canada or the West Indies. In Germany, the Duke of Cumberland's British-financed Army of Observation was hanging on by a thread. The only victories for Britain to savour – vicariously – were those of her Prussian ally. But Frederick, too, was in great difficulties. In January 1757, the Russians, Austrians and Swedes concluded the Treaty of St Petersburg, directed against Prussia. On 1 May 1757, France committed itself to recover Silesia for Austria at the second Treaty of Versailles. In July 1757 the French occupied the Prussian port of Emden, cutting off the Army of Observation's line of communication with Britain. These defeats aggravated the sense of national malaise which had always afflicted Britain in times of crisis and had been building since the late 1740s. In a sweeping diatribe against contemporary decadence, published in 1757, the Reverend John Brown spoke of 'How far this dastardly spirit of effeminacy hath crept upon us, and destroyed the national spirit of defence'. In Brown's view, the French were militarily stronger because the absolute monarchy ensured national unity and their aristocracy was not corrupted by trade. For good measure, he condemned Italian opera, but exalted Handel, who had now become an honorary Englishman. All this reflected the widespread feeling in 1756–7 that Britain was on the verge of being eclipsed by France. The national emergency did not produce an unquestioning loyalty to the military: quite the contrary. Never before had so many demands for inquiries flown back and forth; never had the nation seen so many moral panics about the cowardice of its leaders and soldiers.[25]

The gloom deepened in the summer and autumn of 1757, when the French advanced on Hanover. The Duke of Cumberland's Army of Observation proved unable to hold them back. In mid June 1757 the two sides met at Hastenbeck. After a short skirmish, the Duke retreated and soon capitulated at the Convention of Kloster-Zeven and agreed to the neutralization of the Electorate. He had done so with the permission of the King himself, who was now openly thinking of ways in which Hanover could be taken out of the war. In Hanover itself Münchhausen lamented that George was now 'without a country, without an army, without subjects and without money, and we are with the country at the power and mercy of the enemy'. In August 1757, George – through his Electoral ministers – sought Austrian mediation; he also let it be known at the Reichstag at Regensburg that he was open to the idea of neutrality for his German dominions. Vienna agreed to guarantee such a neutrality, provided French armies might traverse Hanover in order to attack Frederick. One might have thought that the British government would welcome such an arrangement. If securing Hanover while pursuing the colonial war in America was their only aim, this was their chance. After all, the Prussian alliance had only been contracted in order to protect Hanover. Yet when Newcastle, Pitt and other ministers were consulted before the neutrality was agreed, their response was distinctly lukewarm. Because the whole issue was a Hanoverian matter, they believed themselves constitutionally debarred from expressing a view; and there was no practical help they could offer either.[26]

Indeed, the prospect of a Hanoverian Neutrality Convention filled London with horror. As in 1741, the damage to British credibility would be massive and immediate, and no amount of rhetoric about the continued value of the Prussian connection and the commitment to the war against France could compensate for it. The distinction between George's behaviour as Elector of Hanover and as King of England would be entirely lost on Britain's ally Prussia and her friends in Holland. Joseph Yorke pointed out that 'People will not believe that the great person can have taken such a step without the knowledge and approbation of the British ministers and therefore don't understand what we mean by saying we will support the King of Prussia to the utmost of our power.' He feared 'a total dissolution of the little remains of a system we had on the Continent'. Likewise, Hardwicke lamented that 'nothing is more clear than that France and Austria will insist that the King should in some way or other engage not to give any succour or aid to His Prussian Majesty either in troops, or money, as King. How will the King then be able to perform his absolute promise to the King of Prussia to give him a subsidy? The case of Great Britain and Hanover is so mixed and entangled in this instance, that neither the court of Vienna nor that of Versailles will suffer them to be separated.' Newcastle took the same view. All this was aggravated by the contacts between the King's Electoral ministers and the Austrians. Pitt argued that 'the application to the court of Vienna was worse than to France, for that implied a *change of system* [underlined], by flinging off the King of Prussia and returning to the Queen of Hungary'.[27]

The neutralization of Hanover would also create two strategic headaches. It threatened to leave the western flank of Frederick the Great exposed. Pitt, as one observer reported, 'was much alarmed at the effect this would have upon the King of Prussia', and recommended continued subsidies to keep him 'in his present system, and not to make peace'. However, Newcastle went on, 'when the King has made his peace as Elector . . . it will be impossible for the King of Prussia, attacked on all sides, to stand out alone', not least because George had included Britain's allies, the Landgrave of Hesse and the Duke of Wolfenbüttel, in the neutrality. 'The Army of Observation,' Pitt predicted, 'which will now be dissolved, was the only barrier for the King of Prussia's country on that side.' These fears were entirely justified: the British representative in Prussia, Andrew Mitchell, described how the neutrality provoked Frederick into rages against the *canaille* of Hanover, and hinted that he might make a separate peace. Moreover, if Hanover was neutralized it would also leave the Dutch Barrier itself hanging in the air. In August 1757, news arrived that the Austrians had allowed the French to occupy Ostend and Nieuport in the Netherlands for the duration of the war. No wonder Pitt spoke of a 'total subversion of the system of Europe . . . especially from the fatal admission of French garrisons'. The Barrier had been breached; and if Hanover and North Germany went, the French tide might lap at the eastern borders of the United Provinces, just as it had done in the 1680s. 'The [German!] Empire', Pitt lamented, 'is no more, the ports of the Netherlands betrayed, the Dutch Barrier Treaty an empty sound, Minorca and with it, the Mediterranean lost, and America itself precarious.' This was a call straight out of the dictionary of seventeenth-century interventionism.[28]

For British statesmen, the Hanover Neutrality was therefore fraught with domestic perils. The parallels with 1741 were all too obvious. Ministers risked the accusation that they had acted treasonably in allowing the monarch to compromise British national interests in favour of narrowly Hanoverian concerns. For this reason, Pitt announced to his colleagues 'that the English ministers must, for the sake of their honour, disculpate [sic] themselves', from the Convention. Moreover, the whole business would, as Hardwicke observed, confirm the 'notion, which the disaffected have always propagated, of the inconsistency of the interests of the two countries, and of the fatal influence of Hanover councils on English alliances and measures'. Sure enough, patriot opinion was quick to make a direct – and entirely spurious – connection between the Convention and the failure of the expedition to Rochefort. As Horace Walpole observed, 'The City of London talk very treason, and . . . cry out that the General had positive orders to do nothing, in order to obtain gentler treatment of Hanover.' Once again, the parallels to 1741, when Opposition opinion linked the Neutrality Convention with the unchallenged movement of a Spanish army across the Mediterranean, are obvious. Moreover, the predicament of the Landgrave of Hesse, potentially left high and dry by the Neutrality, set nerves jangling. He was, after all, father-in-law to George's fourth daughter Anne, and protected her from his wayward son who had converted to Catholicism in 1754. Her 'distresses', George Grenville remarked to Pitt, 'must put everybody in mind of the unhappy Queen of Bohemia in the last century' (James I's daughter Elizabeth, wife of the Elector Palatine). In this narrative, nobody wanted to be accused of neglecting Britain's Protestant bulwarks in Europe, as James, Charles and their ministers had been.[29]

The ministry was therefore determined to break the Convention and to bring Hanover back into the war against France. On 18 September Holdernesse sent an official circular distancing Britain from its terms. A few weeks later, the administration promised to pay for the upkeep of the Army of Observation as soon as it had 'recommence[d] the operations of war, against the forces of France, in concert with the King of Prussia'. On 8 October 1757, George finally agreed to repudiate the Convention, and appointed a Prussian general, Prince Ferdinand, Duke of Brunswick, who was also his cousin, as commander to replace the hapless Cumberland. The remit of this force was much broader than simply the defence of the Electorate. Newcastle therefore immediately warned Münchhausen that payments would not be forthcoming so long as the army remained inactive. 'Once the army has commenced operations,' he wrote, 'it can be paid and supplied from here, but if it remains inactive, we cannot grant it any support'; Münchhausen seems to have marked this passage in the margin for emphasis. Newcastle concluded by 'recommending IN THE STRONGEST POSSIBLE MANNER, a REAL and UNRESERVED agreement between His Prussian Majesty, who is the only power from which we can gain any advantage who is disposed towards acting in alliance with us'. He was to repeat this injunction many times in the months and years ahead. The fate of Prussia and that of the Electorate were henceforth inextricably intertwined in the minds of British ministers. By the beginning of December, Ferdinand's army was back in action against the French. There was a perceptible sigh of relief in London, especially from Pitt, who wrote to his wife that 'The Army of Observation was before Hamburg, on the Elbe, and operations actually begun.'[30]

From now on the Army of Observation was clearly not about reluctantly honouring an obligation to defend the Electorate; the Convention of Kloster-Zeven would have guaranteed that. Hanover, in fact, was a crucial plank in the wider Continental strategy, rather than an albatross around the neck of a maritime one. It was the keystone in the twin pillars of British geopolitics in western and central Europe: the Barrier system and the Holy Roman Empire of which it formed a part. Hanover provided a base for operations designed to divert French resources from overseas; and it was a useful source of recruits for Ferdinand's army, which Pitt did his best to maximize over the next years. The Army of Observation also covered Frederick's western flank, and gave him the strategic depth to manoeuvre against the Austrians and Russians. The Duke of Brunswick's force was clearly conceived of as a British army: unlike Cumberland's force, which reported to the Hanoverian Council, and George as Elector, the line of command ran directly to the King and the British cabinet. As the Bavarian representative in London, Baron Haslang, remarked in early December 1757, 'the system has now completely changed. It has now become that of England', rather than being driven by Hanoverian concerns. All this was reflected in the fact that the rather low-key appellation of 'Army of Observation' increasingly gave way to the more forthright 'His Britannic Majesty's Army in Germany'. The withdrawal from Europe had lasted scarcely more than three years. Once again, Britain's front line ran along the Weser and the great North German plain.[31]

The ministry's determination to carry on the war in Germany caused considerable resentment with the King. He complained bitterly that his ministers 'did as we pleased: he was *nothing* here; that he wished he had stayed at Hanover in 1755'. When Newcastle asked him, somewhat disrespectfully, 'if he thought he should have been so quiet at Hanover, when there was, or would have been, a war in Germany', George responded, 'But you don't know which side I would have taken.' The exchange should not be taken too seriously, but it does give a sense of the ambivalence George felt about his dual role and his loyalties. The Hanoverian ministers were also strongly in favour of neutrality. In the immediate context of the defeat of Hastenbeck, they felt they had no choice. Kloster-Zeven, as Münchhausen put it, was 'a desperate remedy'. Indeed, many Hanoverian ministers favoured taking the Electorate out of a war they believed was being waged for purely British ends. They also suspected – quite reasonably – that Hanover had been allotted the task of dividing French resources. They recognized Pitt's strategy as a variant of the old Continental orthodoxy, and they did not like it.[32]

So much ill-feeling was generated by the Convention of Kloster-Zeven, and its repudiation, that George once again began to consider an end to the Personal Union. In the autumn of 1757 he canvassed his Hanoverian ministers on the subject. Some sort of decision was now pressing, as his heir and grandson, the future George III, had never been to Hanover, and was known to view the connection with the utmost suspicion. The Electorate could expect no help from him in the future. On balance, the ministers felt that a separation was impracticable and undesirable. It would have to be agreed to by all of the royal princes in order to prevent future claims. Münchhausen, who argued for the status quo, feared that any change in status would allow the Emperor and other ill-intentioned forces to unravel the whole Hanoverian conglomerate in North Germany. But there were also signs of a fundamental disenchantment with the way in which Britain was perceived to have turned its back on Europe for overseas expansion. If, as the Hanoverian minister August Wilhelm von Swicheldt argued, 'England decides not to bother itself further with the land powers of Europe but to focus solely on the assertion of the dominion of the seas', this would be a good argument for separating the Crown and the Electorate. For in those circumstances, he continued, Hanover would be 'abandoned to its fate in emergencies such as an attack by a more powerful, restless neighbour or a religious war'. Moreover, Hanover might be exposed to such attack simply on account of the British connection. Another Hanoverian minister observed in his memorandum of October 1757 that the interests of the two halves might 'conflict'. 'Since England's interest is directed at maintaining maritime superiority and above all at weakening France's power, the latter may seek to revenge itself upon the German states during every war if it does not consider itself a match for England.' After all, as one Hanoverian pamphleteer, David Georg Strube, remarked in the following year, what was Acadia to the Hanoverians?[33]

In the end, the Hanoverians accepted the inevitable: they had to do as they were told. By March 1758 Münchhausen was fully signed up to support the 'balance of Europe and of German liberty and [that] of religion'. He also agreed that 'a perfect understanding with the King of Prussia', must 'form the basis of current policy'. The prospect of future territorial gain, or 'compensations', helped to reconcile the Hanoverians to the risks of continuing the struggle. Here they had their eyes on the bishoprics of Osnabrück, Hildesheim and Paderborn, as well as the territory of the Eichsfeld. These ambitions, which seriously affected the balance of North Germany, infuriated Frederick, who complained bitterly to the British. He fulminated against the scheme 'to aggrandize Hanover . . . like usurers, to lend money on mortgages'. Münchhausen saw it as more of an investment. After all, he observed, the monies voted by Parliament were not enough to pay for the Hanoverian forces or the campaign more generally – more evidence that Hanover was a net contributor to the war effort. The King, he continued, would be quite happy to contribute even more to the security of his kingdoms, 'in his capacity as Elector', but he did so 'in the hope that this would be a further reason to seek at the right time and place to secure for him as Elector some sort of compensation'. One way or the other, the Hanoverians now swung behind the war. There would be periodic grumbles from Hanover, particularly about the lack of consultation by London, but there would be no further serious threat to Britain's Continental policy, through a neutrality or any other unilateral action. They were in for the duration.[34]

The continuation of the European war in late 1757 was vindicated and made possible by the revival of Prussian military fortunes. As Pitt wrote in late October 1757, once the decision to fight on had been taken, 'The King of Prussia keeps the field and his cause is still alive. An event or two may yet change the gloomy prospect.' In November 1757,

Frederick bested the French and imperial forces at Rossbach; 'Heaven be praised for this great event,' Pitt rejoiced. The following month saw a resounding victory over the Austrians at Leuthen. Pitt now intensified his commitment to Germany. A subsidy treaty with Prussia in April 1758 promised £670,000 in subsidies over four years; these were to defray all but one-fifth of Frederick's military expenditure throughout the war. The relationship with Berlin was formalized: no separate peace was to be concluded except with the explicit approval of the other contracting party. At the same time, Britain agreed to undertake 'a useful diversion' on the French coast, and to relieve the Prussian garrison at Emden. Most importantly of all, London contracted to maintain a force of 50,000 men in Germany itself. George, as Elector, agreed to increase the number of Hanoverian levies to 5,000. Two months later, the subsidy to Hesse-Kassel was renewed. These were variations on the themes of the last two years. But in June 1758, Pitt took advantage of the parliamentary recess to propose the dispatch of 6,000 infantry and four cavalry brigades to Germany. This was a major new departure, rendered even more controversial by the inclusion of infantry, which could other- wise be deployed in North America or on coastal operations. From then on nearly a third of Ferdinand's army – about 20,000 out of 70,000 men – was to be made up of British troops.[35]

Pitt now placed increasing reliance on Frederick and the Duke of Brunswick – the 'German war' as it was now generally called. By late March 1758, the Duke had more or less cleared the Electorate of all French troops; this helped to reassure the Hanoverian administration. In June 1758, Pitt received news of the Duke's victory at Krefeld with enormous satisfaction. 'We are sending twelve squadrons of cavalry to this glorious school of war . . . and I hope to share a sprig of Germanic laurel very soon.' Newcastle welcomed the dispatch of troops 'where they could be of most use', that is in Germany. 'We are here full of rejoicings,' the flinty Charles Jenkinson, Undersecretary of State for the Northern Department, wrote, 'I write this amid the sound of cannon bells, and marrow-bones, which are loudly expressing their joy, and I suppose as soon as it is dark we shall have illuminations.' More import- antly, Jenkinson continued, England 'now seems to be gaining the ascendant', because the French finances were nearly 'exhausted'. With the French thus distracted, it was now possible to launch major offen- sives in America. General Abercromby thrust with 25,000 men towards

Quebec and Montreal. Amherst and Wolfe were sent with 14,000 troops and strong naval support against Louisburg. Further south General Forbes was dispatched to attack Fort Duquesne, and take some of the pressure off Virginia and Pennsylvania. The pressure was also kept up on the French coast, with a major raid against the Breton port of St Malo in May–June 1758.[36]

Holding these disparate measures together was a strong sense of Britain's European destiny. Newcastle, for one, exulted in the triumph of 'Continent measures'. 'It is with pleasure I see them now coming into fashion,' he wrote to Hardwicke in July 1758, 'they are the only true solid ones, fresh from whence any great and real advantage can come. It is a great point for Continent politicians (as you and I are) that 9,000 men are sent into Germany. We must play a little with expeditions, to make that go down.' The area 'from the Elbe to the Meuse', in other words the Empire, he argued, was 'the place where our joint enemy is most to be affected'. But Pitt was no less conscious of the centrality of Europe. His instructions for the attack on St Malo defined the general aim as the maintenance of the 'liberties of the (German) Empire' and the 'independancy of Europe'. The American war was part of this broader concern. William Beckford, not a man to minimize the importance of colonial concerns in their own right, illustrated this in a letter to Pitt in September 1758. 'France is our object, perfidious France,' he wrote. 'Reduce her power, and Europe will be at rest. This cannot be done in any other way than by destroying those resources from whence she draws money to bribe Germany and the northern powers against their own interest.' The parallels with French thinking about the centrality of colonial resources to Britain's European leverage is striking. Even such a commercial champion as Beckford, therefore, framed colonial issues in primarily European terms.[37]

There was, of course, a domestic price to be paid for these policies. When British forces were sent to Germany, the Secretary at War, Lord Barrington, welcomed 'this new beginning of right measures at the risk (and certainly there is some risk) of popularity'. Pitt, in particular, was attacked for being too attached to the Continent and a slave to Hanover. A widely discussed article in the *Gazetteer* in the summer of 1758 did not object to subsidizing Prussia but claimed that most would 'repine at the sending of forces to Germany, because they imagine it is done for the sake of Hanover, and fancy they perceive something unconstitutional in it'. Even the friendly *Monitor*, shaken by the dispatch of British troops, fired a broadside against their hero in July 1758. Perhaps the most surprising thing, however, was that there was not more criticism. Pitt's Tory allies were inclined to give him the benefit of the doubt. In July 1758, for example, Beckford credited him whatever success British arms had gained to date. Noting victories in 'Africa, on the Rhine, and [somewhat prematurely] at St Malo', he claimed that 'all this good news was ascribed to you and you only; this was the general voice of the people'. The *Monitor* oscillated between censure and apologia: a favourite strategy was simply to deny that Pitt was responsible for the offending decisions. Even the Prince of Wales's circle at Leicester House (under the King's grandson George after the death of Frederick, Prince of Wales in 1751), which now regarded Pitt with considerable ambivalence, due to differences over coastal expeditions and Hanover, went along with the German deployment, so long as it was limited. In this context, the successes of the Duke of Brunswick took on a particular significance. After Krefeld in June 1758, even such a Leicester House sceptic as the Marquis of Bute, a Scottish peer of Tory and anti-interventionist inclinations, and the Prince of Wales's favourite, was moved to 'congratulate' Pitt, and admit that now 'the most peevish person will be brought to assent to the assistance of Prince Ferdinand's army'. In a remarkable testimony, penned in August 1758, well after the Continental drift of Pitt's policy had become obvious, Bute eulogized Pitt for reviving Britain's courage at a time when 'valour was despised, America neglected, and you left single-handed to plead the cause of both'.[38]

Here Pitt's own mastery of public opinion and rhetoric helped immensely. Despite the fact that the dispatch of troops to the Continent had been his initiative, Pitt put on a great show of reluctance. As a speechless Newcastle wrote in mid July 1758, 'If you hear that Mr Pitt was against sending these troops abroad, it is entirely false. Nobody was more forward than himself; and three regiments were added . . . without my knowledge tho' greatly with my approbation.' There was ostentatious sucking of teeth and head-shaking at the costs, but these, as with the number of troops, continued to rise. Throughout 1757–8, therefore, Pitt used a number of devices to make the German war more palatable, or to obscure his central role in it, but the principal instrument was the Prussian alliance, which enabled him to disguise measures in support of Hanover. As one of Pitt's correspondents observed, 'The bitter part of the pill is Hanover troops, the sugar plum, the K[in]g of Prussia.' That said, the German war was undoubtedly a domestic minefield for Pitt, particularly after the dispatch of British troops. This raised the thorny issue of command and reopened a whole Pandora's box of constitutional and national controversy reminiscent of the Pragmatic Army in the early 1740s. Sure enough, within fewer than two months of the deployment, the Duke of Marlborough, who commanded the British contingent in the Duke of Brunswick's army, was complaining that a Hanoverian 'had been made a general of foot over my head'. This prompted him to demand an equivalent: 'I hope,' he told Pitt with asperity, 'if I am thought unworthy of that rank personally, I may be excused, as an Englishman, for not quite tamely submitting to so strong a mark of the English being thought fit for nothing, but to be hewers of wood and drawers of water to the Hanoverians.' All this was a timely reminder for Pitt that the passions which he had helped to stir fifteen years before still beat furiously in the chests of Englishmen.[39]

The political nation and the public sphere persevered with the German strategy in 1758 for three reasons. In part, they had no choice, because at this stage the Continent was the only theatre where British, or at least British-funded, armies had anything to show for some two years of war. The American campaigns of 1757 had been a disaster and there were few signs of improvement in early 1758. An assault on Ticonderoga miscarried. On the French coast, the attack on Cherbourg effected the demolition of the harbour and could be reckoned a success. However, although the much-trumpeted raid on St Malo did considerable damage to French commerce and privateers, the port itself was not taken. Furthermore, Pitt's expectation that coastal raids would prove a domestic rallying point was only partly fulfilled. Indeed, the botched execution of most operations led to subsequent recrimination as the various protagonists sought to score strategic debating points or shield their protégés from censure. Leicester House – the focal point of the reversionary interest which had gathered around the Prince of Wales and his favourites – made itself the vigorous champion of the commander of St Malo in order to deprive the government of a scapegoat. Much of the Tory and patriot Opposition thought resources would be better deployed in America. Others stressed the execution rather than the conception of the raids. A particularly sore point was the question of combined command. 'I have often lamented,' William Beckford wrote in October 1757, 'the fatality attending conjunct commands.' In order to avoid being let down by the army, he argued that Britain should adopt the French system where command was decided simply by seniority. Finally, there was also considerable scepticism within the administration about the military utility of the raids, which was to persist throughout the war. The Paymaster General Henry Fox, who had to find the money, dismissed the attacks as 'like breaking windows with guineas'.[40]

Moreover, the German war was popular in the army. To the contemporary British military mind, service in Germany was considered far more glamorous than messy amphibious raids on the French coast. After the decision to send troops to Germany was taken in the summer of 1758, there was a general rush to seek commissions there and a distinct lack of enthusiasm for combined operations. Both the Duke of Marlborough and Lord George Sackville, for example, wanted to be sent to Germany in 1758 rather than St Malo. Ambitious soldiers wanted to go to Germany – classic original Marlborough country – not get their feet wet off Brittany. Newcastle observed with satisfaction that 'Our generals have found that it is better fighting upon land than beating about at sea.' In this hierarchy, the shortest straw was drawn by those sent to the colonies. Colonial warfare was despised as a form of social and professional oblivion. For most British military men the choice was simple. Either they could serve with a renowned commander – the Duke of Brunswick – in a prestigious and relatively proximate theatre of war. Or they could take themselves off to a remote backwater where there was no society; women were few, unattractive or opinionated; and there was a fair chance of being captured, eviscerated and even, as they believed, eaten by savages. At best one could hope to be marinated in brine for months on end, or to be racked by exotic fevers. Most preferred more temperate and traditional forms of death. This was certainly the view of Major-General James Wolfe, who was to immortalize himself at Quebec in 1759. Unaware of his future iconic colonial status, he had originally volunteered to join the Duke of Brunswick in Germany but was sent to Canada instead. In December 1758 he wrote to a friend in Germany, 'It is my fortune to be cursed with American services, yours to serve in an army commanded by a great and able prince [Ferdinand].' Like so many figures from the eighteenth-century 'imperial' firmament, Wolfe was a European by choice and an American by default.[41]

Besides, there were already signs by early 1758 that the Continental strategy was paying dividends and turning North Germany into a quagmire for the French. In January Charles Hanbury Williams reported from Hamburg that they were 'at a moderate computation bury[ing] two hundred men a day in the Electorate of Hanover', albeit because of disease and the cold, not as a result of enemy action. More to the point, by March 1758 Münchhausen calculated that the French effort in Hanover was costing them well in excess of what they could extract from the country itself. He noted that France 'sees itself cheated of the only advantage it sought to draw from its invasion, since it has realized that the idea of extorting from the King through the devastation of his German lands a peace prejudicial to his Kingdoms was as chimerical as it was outrageous'. Indeed, he continued, 'the resulting dispatch of the very large sums which it has been obliged to provide has made this war ruinous [to them] in any case'. As one MP remarked, 'the French outwitted themselves by their marching to Hanover, and their spoils of the Electorate . . . did not compensate for the immense sums of money and numbers of men which the conquest of it cost them'. And this – it should be added – was before one reckoned the substantial subsidies which France was paying not only to Austria but also to middling powers such as Sweden; the latter alone swallowed 30 million livres between 1750 and 1762. The crude naval figures spoke volumes: Britain had 117 battleships and 74 cruisers in 1755; the French had 57 and 31 respectively. By 1760, the British totals had jumped to 135 battleships and 115 cruisers; France had 54 and 27, fewer than she had started the war with. In both contemporary perception and in fact, Pitt had created a morass into which Versailles was sinking the resources which might secure them victory in America.[42]

Finally, Pitt's German strategy was redeemed in the popular mind by the successes of Frederick the Great. Throughout 1757, when British arms were in retreat in America and the high seas, and before Prince Ferdinand of Brunswick had made his mark in Hanover, British opinion became every bit as fixated with the triumphs of the Prussian monarch as the ministry was. At times, press and public interest in his campaigns far exceeded that in the American war. The King of Prussia was now adopted by the British public as a Protestant hero: his face was to be found not merely in popular prints and frontispieces but also on crockery, beer mugs and fine vases; young Horace Walpole reported in 1758 that 'the people, I believe, think that Prussia is part of Old England', and so, in strategic terms, it was. There are still public houses in Britain bearing the name of 'The King of Prussia'. This burgeoning cult was comparable to the sanctification of Admiral Vernon after Porto Bello, and greater than the enthusiasm generated by the Duke of Cumberland after his victory at Culloden in 1746. On the occasion of Frederick's birthday in late February 1758, the *Gentleman's Magazine* announced that 'All England has kept his birthday; it has taken its place in our calendar next to Admiral Vernon's . . . We had bonfires and processions, illuminations and French horns playing out of windows all night.' All this was remarkable in that it celebrated neither a popular naval victory, nor a crucial blow against Jacobitism, but a foreign prince and a British-funded war in Germany.[43]

30. Staffordshire teapot depicting Frederick the Great, a popular hero thanks to his victories in the Seven Years War.

The Prussian alliance provided a rhetorical bridge across which former navalists could join the Continentalist consensus without much loss of face. For the truth was that after Rossbach, Frederick hardly saw a Frenchman. The brunt of the fighting thereafter fell to the Duke of Brunswick. That did not stop patriot opinion from emphasizing Frederick's victories over those of the Duke's Anglo-Hanoverian army. Pitt thus found in Frederick the Great the domestic rallying point which had eluded him with coastal operations. Those who questioned the subsidies were now few and far between. As Chesterfield observed in January 1758, 'Everything goes smoothly in Parliament; the King of Prussia has united all our parties in his support; and the Tories have declared that they will give Mr Pitt unlimited credit for this session.' All this before British arms in America were to register any significant success.[44]

The maintenance of the European balance of power, rather than global expansion as such, remained the primary objective throughout. British naval power remained focused first and foremost on dominance of home and European waters: the Channel, the Baltic and the Mediterranean. Few ships were permanently stationed in colonial waters and these tended to be smaller vessels, which were easier to maintain at great distances from naval dockyards. Throughout the Seven Years War, even at the height of the colonial campaigns, about two-thirds of ships' days were spent in European, that is either home or Mediterranean, waters. Moreover, the colonies were primarily valued not as an end in themselves, or as a means of lining private pockets, but as the source of wealth, raw materials and manpower to support Britain's European interests. Thus in 1757 John Mitchell's *The contest in America between Great Britain and France* noted the 'incredible number of seamen and mariners' to be found there. It was not just a matter of securing these resources to the war effort, but of denying them to the Bourbons. Likewise, the American William Livingston wrote in that same year that the colonies were so rich, or potentially so, that 'if suffered to fall into the hands of the French, such will be the accession to their already extended commerce and marine strength, that Great Britain must not only lose her former lustre, but dreadful even in thought! Cease to be any longer an independent power.' This would facilitate 'the long-projected design for that aspiring nation, for setting up an universal monarchy: for, if France rule the ocean, her resources will enable her to subject all Europe to her sway.'[45]

Perhaps the best example of the Eurocentric framework within which the commercial struggle was understood was Malachy Postlethwayt's mercantilist tract of 1757, *Great Britain's true system*. He warned readers right at the beginning that the experience of past wars had shown that it was difficult enough to 'restrain' France in league with 'the strongest confederacies'. It was chimerical, therefore, to trust 'to the single strength of England'. Security could only be ensured in alliance with Continental powers, and by 'find[ing] him [Louis XV] so much work at home as may oblige him rather to think of defending his own dominions, than invading those of his neighbours'. In order to allow Britain to increase her navy, send troops to the Continent, and to subsidize allied powers, Postlethwayt continued, she would have to increase her fiscal power. This could only be done, he went on 'if our domestic affairs also, shall be conducted as to coincide with the system of our foreign concerns, and particularly, in regard to the Public Revenue'. To that end, Postlethwayt proposed a number of initiatives, including a national 'mercantile College', designed to increase the economic productivity of the nation. In this context, he saw Hanover as a potential economic asset. More importantly, he saw the Electorate as a strategic bulwark, which buttressed Britain's Continental ramparts. Together with Prussia, he argued, Hanover provided the Dutch with a secure 'barrier' to the east; if only, he lamented, 'the Dutch had another Hanover to protect their present defenceless Barrier [to the south] against the common enemy'. All this, he concluded, made the King's German dominions 'an ally of great importance to our interests'. On this reading, the Hanoverian connection, the Barrier, and British commercial expansion were all part of one virtuous strategic circle, by which the security of the realm was guaranteed.[46]

By midsummer 1758, Pitt was conscious that time was running out for his strategy. He could not continue to throw resources at America and Germany indefinitely. His Tory allies were clamouring for results. Sooner or later there might well be a French invasion of Britain itself. A major colonial or naval victory was needed, and fast. As Pitt wrote to his wife at the beginning of July, as he waited for news from America and the Continent, 'Expectation grows every hour into more anxiety – the fate of Louisburg and of Olmütz [in Moravia] probably decided, though the result unknown.' 'I trust my life,' he continued, in 'the same favouring Providence that all will be well, and that this almost degenerate England may learn from the disgrace and ruin it shall have escaped, and the consideration and security it may enjoy, to be more deserving of the blessing.' Very shortly afterwards came word of the capture of Louisburg by British forces. This success, which reversed the controversial cession of ten years before, gave Pitt's public standing an immense boost. No fewer than fifty addresses of congratulations followed, in addition to a wave of triumphant poems and ballads. Pitt immediately claimed this as a vindication of his strategy. The King's Speech of November 1758, which reflected a consensus of his views and those of the Whig traditionalists Newcastle and Hardwicke, specifically cited the War of the Spanish Succession as a paradigm of how France could be contained through both European and maritime measures. In the same way, the argument went, Frederick the Great and Duke Ferdinand had tied down France, so that Britain's 'operations both by sea and in America have derived the most evident advantage'. It was a good moment to confess, as one observer recalled, that 'he had formerly notions that this country could stand by itself and ought not to meddle with the Continent'. Now, however, 'he saw his error, it was a narrow and erroneous way of thinking'.[47]

The growing commitment to Europe was reflected in the distribution of British forces by 1759. The bulk of the army continued to be deployed in Great Britain and Ireland: 55,000 men, including 20,000 militia. There were 45,000 troops in America, of whom 25,000 were local colonial levies; 7,500 men in the West Indies; and 7,000 in Gibraltar. In Germany there were now 10,000 men plus 50,000 British-funded German troops. It was the largest army which Britain had ever had to supply, and it involved a major logistical operation. The grand total of British regulars in Europe, excluding the British Isles, was thus 17,000 as against 27,500 overseas. But if one looks at the number of British-funded troops, the ratio is almost reversed: 67,000 for Europe (some 60,000 of them in Germany) against 52,000 in North America and the West Indies. Whichever way one finessed these figures, it was clear that the European theatre had taken on an importance which nobody, navalist or Continentalist, could have foreseen just before the outbreak of war. Moreover, the trend in Europe was upwards. The army in Germany was reinforced three times in the course of 1759, and by 1760 the number of British troops in Germany stood at 22,000 men. This was about as many regulars as there were in North America.[48]

The synergies between the colonial and European theatres were long in coming, but when they finally did, they surpassed all expectations. In June 1759 the second most important French sugar island of Guadeloupe was taken; the even greater prize of Martinique still held out. In August the Anglo-Hanoverian force under the Duke of Brunswick scored a notable victory over the French at Minden in Westphalia. That same month, a French squadron was worsted in the Bay of Lagos off Portugal. A month later, news arrived of the capture of Ticonderoga, Niagara and Crown Point in North America. Not long afterwards came the ultimate triumph: James Wolfe's capture of Quebec; his gallant death in battle only added to the heroic narrative. And in November, Admiral Hawke's patient patrolling off Brittany paid off, when he smashed the French fleet in the Bay of Quiberon. Amid this cornucopia, the most significant European victory – that of the Duke of Brunswick over the French at Minden – was now merely one of many. It gave Pitt much joy all the same. He wrote to his wife that 'favouring Providence blessed our immortal Ferdinand. May heaven send success on the Oder.'[49] The news from the battlefield contained a significant and politically explosive sting in the tail, however. In his triumphant dispatch, Duke Ferdinand had made slighting reference to the role of the British cavalry, under Lord George Sackville, which had failed or refused to engage until the battle was practically over. Much huffing and puffing between Sackville – who played heavily to the gallery on his outraged English honour – and the Duke ensued.

This duel had been long in coming: Sackville had succeeded the late Duke of Marlborough as commander of the British troops in Germany in October 1758. Marlborough – as we have seen – had always been on the lookout for slights, and his successor promised to be more accommodating. Sackville assured Pitt in November that 'as far as relates to Prince Ferdinand, I shall meet with no difficulty whatever'. But already in late 1758, scarcely a month after his appointment, Hanoverian officers were complaining, that – as the Prince of Wales reported – 'his lordship is so imperious, and satirical, that none of the foreign troops can bear him, and that if he is to remain at the head of the British troops, they expect some fracas between the different corps that compose the Allied Army.' Sackville's position was bolstered by support from Leicester House, with whom relations had previously been cool, but which now saw a splendid opportunity for point-scoring. 'I think it is pretty pert,' the Prince of Wales – the future George III – wrote, 'for a little German prince to make public any fault he finds with the English commander, without first waiting for instructions from the King on so delicate a matter.' The Minden controversy thus resembled that of Dettingen and General Stair in 1743, the last time a British commander had fallen

31. The 'dog' in this cartoon is Lord George Sackville, whose alleged cowardice at the Battle of Minden in 1759 became a matter of national controversy in Britain and dogged his later career.

out with the King and the Hanoverians over the conduct of military operations. It could potentially provide a rallying point for navalists and Germanophobes attacking the monarchy and the administration, and unravel the Continentalist consensus which had developed between 1757 and 1759.[50]

In this context, Pitt's response was an indication of the value which he attached to the European theatre of war, even when it was domestically controversial. He had been a shrill partisan of Stair in 1743, and his relations with Sackville hitherto had been very cordial. Now he unhesitatingly took the Duke's side. Sackville was court-martialled, and some thought him lucky to escape with his life. In ministerial circles Sackville was ostracized. He was cut by Pitt. Crucially, a key patriot paper, the *Monitor*, took an anti-Sackville line, though not vigorously. The Minden controversy fizzled, but it never ignited in the way that it would have done in the early 1740s. The Prince of Wales complained that he thought 'the whole proceeding against Ld. George the most extraordinary and contrary to our constitution affair [sic] I have ever before met with'; and defiantly signalled his intention to continue to receive Sackville. George's championship of Sackville was to bear unforeseen and disastrous fruit nearly twenty years later when he, as Lord George Germain, emerged from obscurity to take charge of the American colonies.[51]

In the course of 1759, therefore, Pitt had won over most of the sceptics to his integrated European and colonial strategy. The Prussian subsidies encountered no Tory opposition in December 1758, and in January 1759 Beckford averred that the Prussian subsidy 'was giving money to America by this diversion on the continent of Europe and that if Hanover were lost, he would vote one hundred millions sooner than not recover it'. Truly, as he was later to boast, Pitt had brought the Tories to support his war coalition on 'Whig principles', by which he meant, of course, foreign policy principles. In broad sections of the public sphere, too, the conversion was complete. Here again, the *Monitor* led the way. Support for Hanover and Prussia, it argued repeatedly throughout the year, was not ministerial toadying, but part of a broader British project for the 'preservation of a bulwark to arbitrary power and universal monarchy on the Continent'. 1759 also saw the creation of the London 'Troop Society' which was dedicated to help the widows and orphans of men killed in Germany. Loyal addresses to congratulate the King were already making fewer attempts to highlight colonial over Continental victories. The two theatres were increasingly seen, even by former navalists, as part of a single war effort. Even more to the point, popular opinion had accepted the central role of Hanover. Thus one print showed the British lion in collaboration with the Hanoverian horse against the French cock. 'O pretty! O pretty!' the lion exclaims, 'Thus hast save[d] me a great deal of labour and trouble, I have crush'd the Cock & secured America.' In effect, Pitt had created a new basis of legitimacy for himself. His standing in the country and particularly the City of London now rested on his conduct of the war rather than the patriot postures of previous years.[52]

Not only did these European successes contribute to victory in America, but triumph in the colonies was widely perceived as underpinning Britain's effort in Europe. The French certainly thought so. Already in October 1758, François de Bernis, the French foreign minister, had blamed the German campaigns for the loss of Louisburg, and in March of the following year, his successor, the Duc de Choiseul, observed that 'The true balance of power now resides in commerce and in America. The war in Germany will not prevent the evils that are to be feared from the great superiority of the English at sea.' The penny was beginning to drop in Versailles that if they wished to deny the British crucial colonial resources it made sense to reduce the scale of their own operations on the Continent. As Choiseul explained to the sceptical Austrians in June 1759, a French withdrawal from Europe was to their benefit too. 'The true interest of [the King of France's] allies,' he argued, 'is connected with the preservation and extension of his power at sea; it is that which furnishes the means of maintaining large armies for the defence of his allies, as it is the maritime power of the English which today arms so many enemies against them and against France.' It was, however, too late. Moreover, French hopes of a decisive blow across the Channel were also dashed in 1759. In late 1758 Choiseul had been preparing for an invasion force of about 50,000 men. Unlike earlier ventures, this was designed not to restore the Stuarts *per se* but to capture London, disrupt commerce and the conduct of the American war, and thus knock Britain out of the war; a diversionary attack on Ireland would also be launched. A descent was planned in the Clyde, at Portsmouth, and perhaps later in Essex. The naval battle of Quiberon, however, scattered the planned escorting force. Later Mahan was to describe this triumph as the 'Trafalgar' of the Seven Years War, because it had put an end to any hopes of an invasion of Britain. The only landfall made by French forces at this point was briefly at Carrickfergus in Ulster.[53]

The successes in Europe and overseas also meant that the controversial coastal expeditions could now gradually be wound down. So long as they employed troops not needed elsewhere; so long as they went at least some way towards appeasing Frederick's demand for a diversion; and so long as they helped to divert domestic attention from expensive Continental measures; for so long such raids were sustainable. But they had now become redundant, and the resources were already earmarked for attacks on the French in Africa and the Caribbean. One of those for whom an end to the raids was overdue was the Duke of Newcastle. In April 1759, he had warned against 'not wasting our force by sea and land with useless and expensive expeditions ... We are engaged in expenses infinitely above our strength ... expedition after expedition, campaign after campaign'. The following year, as another attack was in the offing, he wrote, 'My Claremont road [i.e. to his country seat] is filled with wagons, heavy ordnance stores, etc. . . . Where they go, God knows . . . Would to God they were all now at Wesel [in Germany].'[54]

Pitt's mastery of the House of Commons on foreign policy was now complete. In December 1758, Horace Walpole observed that 'The parliament is all harmony': Pitt had 'provoked' and 'defied' objections, promising only 'enormous expense'. To general wonderment, Walpole continued, 'Universal silence left [Pitt] arbiter of his own terms. In short, at present he is the absolute master, and if he can coin twenty millions, may command them.' By late November 1759 Pitt had even won over the King, who was grudgingly reconciled on the basis of his support for 'German measures'. A month later, when the Prussian and Hessian subsidies were approved in Parliament, the Earl of Chesterfield noted with amazement: 'No less [fewer] than twelve millions; a most incredible sum, and yet already all subscribed, and even more offered!' Moreover, he continued, 'The unanimity of the House of Commons, in voting such a sum, and such forces, both by sea and land, is not less astonishing. This is Mr Pitt's doing, and it is marvellous in our eyes. He declares only what he would have them do, and they do it.' At around the same time, an Undersecretary of State, Richard Potenger, remarked that thanks to the recent victories 'everything passes in the quietest manner in the House of Commons; there is scarce more than one voice there upon affairs of the most national consequence.' It was a good moment for Pitt to press the case of his crony Earl Temple for the Order of the Garter, in return, as the would-be beneficiary remarked, 'for all the great and eminent service to the King, and to the Electorate [of Hanover].'[55]

The victories of 1759 were a huge relief to the administration, but they did not induce megalomania. Instead, British statesmen now sought for ways to end the war on favourable terms. After Minden, Pitt had hoped that 'happy peace [may] wind up the glorious work, and heal a bleeding world'. Two months later, he told Hardwicke of his hope for a 'solid and general pacification of Europe'. Newcastle and Hardwicke were of a like mind; if anything, they were even more anxious to bring hostilities to a close. So in late 1759 the King, on Hardwicke's instructions, duly told Parliament of his desire to 'see a stop put to the effusion of Christian blood'. Britain's war aims were defined – rather generally –

as an acceptable resolution of her North American gains, the return of Minorca and the security of Hanover. The war, though successful and affordable, had been extremely expensive. This was not something which much bothered Pitt, who took a very optimistic view of these things; but it increasingly kept Newcastle and Hardwicke awake at night. Secondly, France had been largely contained both in Europe and overseas: the original – essentially defensive – objectives had thus been reached. Thirdly, continuing the war might jeopardize these gains, and expose Britain to possible reverses. At the same time, further victories would tilt the colonial scales even more in Britain's favour and might precipitate a Spanish entry into the war. The resulting Franco-Spanish naval union was something Britain wished to avoid at all costs. Moreover, with the death of Ferdinand VI and the accession of Charles III as King of Spain in August 1759, relations with Spain were already on the decline. This was the same Charles, after all, who had been King of Naples and whose palace Commodore Martin had famously threatened to flatten in 1742. It was not the last time that a piece of naval bravado was to come back to haunt Britain.[56]

The Spanish were indeed horrified by the wave of British colonial successes, and the French sought to persuade them that the only way of upholding the European balance was to intervene forthwith, either militarily or through mediation. 'The King [of France] believes,' Choiseul had told the Spaniards in 1758, 'that it is possessions in America that will in the future form the balance of power in Europe, and that if the English invade that part of the world, as it appears they have the intention of doing, it will result therefrom that England will usurp the commerce of the nations, and that she alone will remain rich in Europe.' For this reason Charles III instructed his ambassador in London to tell Pitt 'that His Catholic Majesty could not regard with indifference the disturbances by the English conquests of the balance of power in America, as established after the Peace of Utrecht'. He consequently wanted 'to see the naval war concluded by a peace in which England would show generosity and moderation, and was himself ready to act as an intermediary'. The Spanish offer of 'mediation' was an opportunity for Britain, but also a shot across her bows. Newcastle remarked in October 1759 on the Spaniards speaking of the '*équilibre* in America'; 'the term,' he thought, 'is certainly of new coinage.' Relations overseas were already beginning to break down. This was a particular problem in the southern colonies abutting Florida, part of New Spain, where a Spanish naval build-up in Havana was under way, and where the outbreak of war with the Cherokees that same year heightened fears of a joint Hispano-Indian invasion similar to those launched by the French further north.[57]

The main threat from Spain lay where it always had: in Europe. For contrary to the provisions of the Treaty of Aix-la-Chapelle, and as Pitt had feared, Charles did not leave Naples and Sicily to his brother Philip – thus ensuring the separation of those territories from Spain – but to his younger son, Ferdinand. This maintained the status of Naples and Sicily as a subsidiary line of the Spanish Bourbons, but the separation was less final than if Don Philip had succeeded. It was perceived as keeping open the possibility of Ferdinand succeeding in Spain when Charles died, thus resurrecting the Spanish Mediterranean empire, which had been broken up at Utrecht, and which Elizabeth Farnese had so desperately tried to revive after 1713. Pitt had been anxious about this for some time, and in mid September 1759 he repeated his concern that 'the King of Naples might find himself at the head of the Spanish monarchy, and consequently possessed of all that due weight inseparable from that crown, which cannot but greatly affect the system of Europe'. In the medium term, therefore, the impending conflict with Madrid was not just colonial in nature but took on the character of another war for the Spanish succession.[58]

Spain was the most important of the neutral powers, but it was not the only one which viewed the growth of British colonial and naval power with alarm. Relations with the Dutch, it will be remembered, had been cool since the early 1750s for reasons to do with the steady collapse of the Barrier. They deteriorated further on the outbreak of war in 1756, as Dutch traders sought to take advantage of the commercial opportunities. For the next seven years, the Republic was forced to tread carefully between the British on the one hand, who could completely devastate their commerce, and the French, who could invade at will. In its 'Rules of the War of 1756', the High Court of the Admiralty determined that neutrals should not carry in war what they could not carry in peace because of the restrictions of the Navigation Acts. This was a direct blow to the Dutch, who were now scourged by British privateers and the Royal Navy. In 1757 the Dutch fell still lower in London's estimation when they stood by as the Austrians invited French troops

into the Barrier fortresses, while their garrisons went off to fight Frederick in the east. By late 1758 and early 1759, war between the two
countries seemed possible; matters were not helped by a huge popular
surge of anti-Dutch feeling, fuelled by the *Monitor* and other Tory
media, based on a traditional religious (Anglican v. Calvinist) and commercial rivalry dating back to the seventeenth century.[59]

There was no prospect now of the Dutch entering the lists on Britain's
side, but naval cack-handedness might still drive them and other neutrals
into the arms of France. At a time when Britain was in the midst of a
new French invasion scare, the last thing she needed was another enemy,
especially Holland, whose naval strength and geographical situation
accentuated the threat to the British Isles. So in May 1759 Pitt and
Newcastle pushed through an Act of Parliament to regulate British
privateers, much to the disgust of Beckford and the Tories. They saw
such activity as a particularly English form of virtue dating back to
Elizabethan times; the administration saw primarily the mounting diplomatic costs on the Continent. Forgotten was the fact that Elizabeth I's
strategy had depended heavily on a Dutch alliance, or at least on keeping
as much of the coast of the Low Countries out of enemy hands as
possible. With the Austrian Netherlands now in the French camp and
the Barrier breached, war with Holland was to be avoided at all costs.
Newcastle worried about the emergence of some sort of Dutch and
Danish northern league to vindicate their maritime rights. He was right
to do so: this was exactly what happened twenty years later in the
League of Armed Neutrality, when British policy was in the hands of
men less conscious of the dangers of British isolation than he.[60]

For all these reasons, British statesmen were prepared to show
restraint in the peace negotiations with France, and resist pressure from
a public sphere whose appetite had been whetted by the victories of
1759. The *Monitor*, the *Evening Post* and many pamphleteers expected
the complete ejection of the French from Canada, at the very least. In
contrast, the government was even prepared to be flexible on the future
of Canada; they did not think in terms of total annexation. To do so
seemed to them a recipe for perpetual war. As Newcastle observed in
1759, 'To think of being able to extirpate the French from North
America, or if we could, that our business was done by doing so, or that
such a nation as France would sit down tamely under it, is to me the idlest
of all imaginings.' Hardwicke agreed. 'The nonsense of the populace and

of the printed papers about holding and keeping everything and reducing France to nothing,' he wrote, 'should be battered down and discountenanced . . . What did we get after all the Duke of Marlborough's amazing successes by rejecting the terms offered at the Treaty of Gertruydenberg and The Hague?' He added, 'If you keep Quebec, you must keep all Canada and Louisburg as the key to it, and is that possible without fighting on for ever?'[61]

All this – coming as it does from the same Whig Continentalists who had exchanged Louisburg for the Barrier in 1748 – is no surprise. More remarkable is Pitt's pragmatic attitude to colonial gains at the peace settlement, which contrasted not only with that of the public sphere but also of the King. 'Mr Pitt,' Newcastle reported in October 1759, 'had much ridiculed the King's way of talking about the conditions of peace and the retaining "all our conquests"'. True, Pitt wanted to keep Niagara, the lakes, Crown Point and security for British colonies, but – the account continues – 'Quebec, Montreal and even Louisburg, they were points to be treated upon – not be given up for nothing, but what might deserve consideration and be a proper matter of negotiation.' Pitt returned to this theme a few months later. 'He sees,' as Hardwicke reported, 'that in order to obtain peace, so much of our acquisitions must be given up', though he expected 'the populace, who have been blown up to such an extravagant degree, and of whom [Pitt] is unwilling to quit his hold, will be so much disappointed, that [Pitt] is ready to start at the approaches to it.' But Hardwicke's scepticism was unjustified: Pitt remained committed to an exchange of territory for peace throughout the negotiations. He was prepared to make difficult choices.[62]

Moreover, British statesmen were determined to make peace in conjunction with their European ally, Frederick, and not over his head. The question of colonial gains would therefore be resolved in a European context. When in December 1758, the Tory MPs Beckford and Phillips had demanded a guarantee that Louisburg would not be returned to the French in order to bail out Britain's Continental friends, as it had been in 1748, Pitt refused to give any firm commitment: 'he would not give up an iota of our allies for any British consideration'. Instead, the Prussians were kept fully abreast of British intentions in meetings in September 1759 and again in March 1760. Frederick was happy to agree to a separate peace between Britain and France, so long as French troops were withdrawn from Germany altogether. Some pamphleteers – even colonialist ones – took the view that the Prussian alliance was so vital to British interests, that overseas gains should be forgone, if necessary, in order to keep Frederick in play. Underlying the determination not to abandon the Prussians was a long-standing trauma in eighteenth-century British foreign policy: Utrecht. Pitt himself referred to the 'Treaty of Utrecht, the indelible reproach of the last generation'. This was a theme to which Pitt, and many other British statesmen who favoured continued engagement in Europe, would return on numerous occasions. In short, the primacy of Europe in British foreign policy was maintained, even at the moment of greatest colonial triumph. The victories of 1759 produced not ministerial hubris but restraint.[63]

If Pitt was prepared to hazard his popularity in this way, he was also determined to face down the King. By late 1759, George had emerged as one of the most ardent annexationists, partly because he was genuinely swept up by the general imperial enthusiasm, but primarily because he hoped to float his Hanoverian boats on this tide as well. George now expected to be compensated for the devastation the Electorate had suffered in pursuit of the Continental policy, if not financially then at least with territory. 'My Lord,' he told Newcastle, 'you won't give me money, and therefore you must increase my dominions by acquisitions from my enemies.' He demanded Hildesheim, Paderborn and full control of Osnabrück, in which an interest had been signalled back in 1758. These were modest requests in the overall scheme of things, but Pitt firmly put his foot down. Any such move would be domestic dynamite, particularly if it could be linked to colonial concessions to the French, and he knew that it would reduce Frederick to apoplexy, as it had in 1758. Hazarding his popularity through vast Continental subsidies 'for the sake of the whole', Pitt pointed out, was one thing; but 'to aggrandize or promote any acquisition for Hanover' was quite out of the question. Various royal tantrums followed, during which George threatened to 'leave them' and 'go to Hanover', but the ministers stood their ground.[64]

These exchanges led to a final and brief discussion about breaking the Personal Union. Once again, the initiative came from the King, this time offended by the refusal of his British ministers to consider territorial gains for Hanover. 'Since you will do nothing for me,' he told Newcastle, 'I hope you will agree to separate my Electorate from this country.' When the minister challenged him on how that was to be done, George responded, 'very easily – pass a short Act of Parliament, that whoever possesses this crown, shall not have the Electorate, and that they should have the choice'. Newcastle retorted, 'that can't be done, without the consent of the Princes'. 'No!' the King came back at him, 'George [Prince of Wales] will be King and his brother Elector.' Then Newcastle asked whether this could 'be done consistently with the laws of the [German] Empire?' The King insisted it could be and abruptly terminated the conversation. This was, of course, familiar ground, which ministers had first traversed with the King's father some thirty years earlier. As the government's chief legal and constitutional officer, the Lord Chancellor the Earl of Hardwicke pointed out, the question had 'been seriously talked of before, but nobody could see their way through it either here or in Germany'. It might lead to a whole new generation of Hanoverian 'Pretenders'. The exchange underlined once again the extent to which Britain was dynastically, legally and politically joined at the hip with the Holy Roman Empire.[65]

The year 1759 marked the high-water mark of the British commitment to Europe and thus the impetus behind her recent unprecedented imperial expansion. Further overseas gains would follow, but the Continental tide which had floated the naval and colonial boats was about to recede. Pitt had co-opted and refined a strategic tradition which went back to the Glorious Revolution. He created – for the time being at least – the prefect strategic virtuous circle, in which Germany was defended in America, and America was won in Germany. He turned Hanover from a liability back into a geopolitical asset. He created a Protestant hero to replace the 'old system'. He rallied a motley army of radicals, planters, Tories and orthodox Whigs. He made lions lie down with lambs. He ate his own words and persuaded many to bite their lips. It was too good to be true, and it did not last. The unstable intellectual, political and strategic coalition which had sustained this policy was about to come apart. Britons now felt they had to choose between Europe and America. Never again would the two empires work in such synergy for the security of Great Britain.

17

An Island Once Again, 1760–1763

I really did work them ... I persuaded republicans to give money to the King of Prussia. I convinced the House of Commons that the troops sent to Emden were not designed for Germany. I made anti-Hanoverians and the enemies of Germany send men we could ill spare, and money we could ill raise to the aid of Prince Ferdinand ... I gained honour every day by disgrace being thrown upon measures to which I assented, in which I assisted. The oftener I altered my opinion the more I was esteemed for my consistency.[1]

Elizabeth Montagu, in an unpublished satire against Pitt, 1760

No one can rejoice more sincerely than I do, on the reduction of Canada; and this not merely as I am a colonist, but as I am a Briton. I have long been of opinion, that the foundations of the future grandeur and stability of the British Empire lie in America; and though like other foundations, they are low and little seen, they are nevertheless broad and strong enough to support the greatest political structure human wisdom ever erected ... All the country from the St Lawrence to the Mississippi will in another century be filled with British people. Britain itself will become vastly more populous, by the immense increase of its commerce; the Atlantic sea will be covered with your trading ships; and your naval power, thence continually increasing, will extend your influence around the whole globe, and awe the world.[2]

Benjamin Franklin, 1760

If 1759 had been a good year for Britain, it nearly proved disastrous for Frederick. Assailed by Austrian and especially Russian armies, the Prussians barely held their own. In August, the same month as Brunswick triumphed at Minden, Frederick was worsted by the Russians at

Kunersdorf. By early 1760, it seemed possible that Prussia would be knocked out of the war. This would not only expose Hanover, but also permit the French to concentrate their efforts entirely on the colonial and naval struggle; in the meantime, the wisdom of continuing to throw hundreds of pounds in subsidies after a lost cause could be questioned. From Hanover, Münchhausen warned that a Prussian collapse was imminent, and that a Russo-Austrian partition, tolerated by France, could not be ruled out. For this reason, he urged the King to put out peace feelers and convene a congress immediately. All this caused alarm in London. Already in February, Newcastle had feared that Vienna and St Petersburg might persuade France that 'the means of regaining their conquests in America is to seize the territories of His Majesty and his allies in Germany'. Three months later Newcastle celebrated the final victory over France in Canada, with the fall of Montreal, but he remained haunted by the thought of a decisive blow against Frederick. Britain, Newcastle argued, would soon be unable to continue the war, for financial reasons if for no other. In a highly significant phrase, Newcastle rejected the suggestion that bailing out of the war would necessarily revive the spectre of Utrecht and the betrayal of Marlborough. This was the surest sign yet that a separate peace was under active consideration.[3]

It soon became clear that the French were willing to come to terms. As Joseph Yorke, to whom the exploratory talks at The Hague were entrusted, reported, the French were happy to treat through Spain and 'in any other manner'. They had 'offer[ed] to include Lower Saxony in their peace with England, [that is,] the Electorate, Hesse and Brunswick, and will do their best to contribute to help the King of Prussia out of his scrape'. The general French strategy, as Holdernesse told the Duke of Brunswick, was to 'distinguish between the war between England and France and the war in Germany, and to treat them separately'. The resulting public discussion forced the King to 'declare publicly and formally that his resolution was to listen to no peace proposal except in accord with the King of Prussia and his other allies'. At the same time, Holdernesse stressed that a blanket precondition of no peace without Prussia would cripple negotiations from the start. There was no talk, however, of a unilateral disengagement from the German war. In a meeting in mid March, the Prussian envoys had made their position clear: they were happy for the negotiation to proceed 'on the supposition, however, that the King, their master, shall be included in the separate peace to be made with France; but if His Prussian Majesty shall not be so comprehended, they shall then think any such separate treaty a contravention of the treaty between His Majesty and the King of Prussia'. Pitt himself insisted that Prussian interests be taken into account; and he repeated this point over the next two months. The Prussian representative in London was kept abreast of developments throughout March–April 1760. In any case, by May 1760 the talks in The Hague were getting nowhere and were broken off.[4]

That said, fears for Frederick's future were mixed with irritation at his failure to land a knockout blow against his enemies. Pitt, for one, warned in September 1760 that unless Prussia scored a major victory soon, Britain would have to review its policy. Frederick might well be an obstacle to peace, but one who would have to be won around or strong-armed, rather than simply abandoned or ignored. 'Our difficulty,' Newcastle observed, 'is with the King of Prussia. We must know his thoughts, and both Mr Pitt and myself have talked strongly to the Prussian ministers.' Still, Pitt's enthusiasm for Frederick remained undimmed: as late as November 1760 he compared him favourably to Alexander the Great, 'who had only one empire to fight'. Indeed, in 1760, for the first time in more than a year, Pitt began to press for another coastal attack on France, partly in order to gain another bargaining counter for the peace negotiations, partly to appease navalist opinion, but primarily to draw off some of the pressure on Frederick. Pitt also argued that the maintenance of the Prussian alliance was worth the sacrifice of colonial gains. When Newcastle told him that fiscal constraints meant that the war would have to be brought to a close within the year, Pitt responded 'that *we* did not want a peace, but that for the sake of the King of Prussia, we were willing to forego the great advantages which we had reason to promise ourselves from this campaign in every part of the world'. Here Pitt seemed to be following a direct request from Frederick that Britain give up some of its colonial gains in order to get the French off his back.[5]

Pitt's nervousness about the German war was accentuated by a revival of colonialist and anti-Continental public rhetoric from mid 1760. His great supporter William Beckford was challenged in the City of London during the election of March–April on account of their connection; there were rumblings in early 1760 against the 'German war and the

German minister, Mr Pitt'. These were old themes, but the changed strategic situation gave them a new urgency. Inevitably, the scale and completeness of the victory overseas, particularly in North America, seemed to make the European strategy redundant. A straw in the wind was the way in which Pitt now, much more than in 1759, sought to distance himself in the popular mind from the German war and particularly from the commitment to Hanover. 'It is amazing to me,' Hardwicke remarked, 'that considering how much depends upon the events of this campaign in Germany, he [Pitt] should not even propose the sending of some British infantry to that country. Perhaps he wants to be ravished to it.' This was a very astute observation: so much of Pitt's public persona and personal popularity depended on the impression of being forced into controversial but necessary measures in Europe.[6]

The administration was able to hold the line on the German war without too much difficulty until late 1760. Then Britain's Continental strategy and the culture of intervention was dealt a double blow from which it was not to recover fully until after the American War of Independence. The first shock came with the death of George II in October. With him expired a wealth of European military and diplomatic experience dating back to the early eighteenth century. His grandson and successor, George III, was in his early twenties, stubborn and opinionated. George later came to cherish his German roots, but at this point his attitude towards the Continent and the Hanoverian connection was one of almost contrived truculence. He was particularly fond of striking 'English' poses. In 1749, when George was a boy, his father the Prince of Wales had organized some amateur theatricals at Leicester House at which Addison's *Cato* was performed. In the Prologue, which was probably composed by his father, George was given the following lines to recite:

> Should this superior to my years be thought
> Know, – 'tis the first great lesson I was taught,
> What, tho' a boy! It may with truth be said
> A boy in *England* born, in England bred,
> Where freedom best becomes the earliest sate,
> For there the love of liberty's innate.

Addison's words had been put in George's mouth, but he was to embrace them with enthusiasm. While there is no evidence that George was directly influenced by Bolingbroke's 'Patriot King', the fact that he was the first heir presumptive to be born in England for many decades was considered significant, not least by George himself. In late 1757, when George II had pondered breaking the Personal Union after Kloster-Zeven, his Electoral ministers were quick to point out that after his death 'A prince will succeed to the Kingdom of Great Britain and the Electoral lands who has been raised in the former and has never seen the latter.' This would make him less suited to governing Hanover and more reliant on ministers whose competence he would be less able to judge. Perhaps some of George's barbed comments about Hanover had already crossed the English Channel. Nearly two years later, George was famously to remark that difficulties in Germany were 'entirely owing to the partiality [the King] has for that horrid Electorate which has always lived upon the very vitals of this poor country'. He added, somewhat bathetically, 'I should say more and perhaps with more anger did not my clock show 'tis time to dress for Court.' These words were written just before news of the Battle of Minden, the greatest victory for Anglo-Hanoverian arms in Europe in the Seven Years War.[7]

Contempt for Hanover did not automatically translate into opposition to the German war, of course. Even as late as November 1757, the Prince of Wales had seemed to subscribe to the Continentalist orthodoxy. Responding to rumours that Frederick the Great had made a separate peace with France, he told Bute that 'This will certainly bring the French back to their native air, and enable them by putting soldiers into their ships to man a great fleet.' George had rather got hold of the wrong end of the stick here – the letter was penned at the time when Frederick was triumphing over his enemies at Rossbach and Leuthen. It does show, however, that the Prince of Wales seems to have made his mind up about grand strategy relatively late in the day. Perhaps George's hatred of his former ally Pitt, whom he regarded as an arrogant apostate, drove the Prince towards a more 'patriot' foreign policy. He certainly complained to Bute about Pitt's lack of consultation: 'he treats both you and me with no more regard than he would a parcel of children, he seems to forget that the day will come, when he must expect to be treated according to his deserts.' In any case, by early 1758 the Prince of Wales's circle at Leicester House – the 'reversionary interest' – had become a focus of navalist and colonial aspirations. It was also the last refuge of failed military men, such as Lord George Sackville, and other disaffected elements. George allowed his brother, Prince Edward, to sail with the St Malo expedition as a gesture of support for maritime operations; he was outspoken in his support for Lieutenant-General Thomas Bligh, the commander scapegoated for the reverse there.[8]

Unlike most of the British public, including navalist opinion, George's response to Prussian victories was sometimes distinctly tepid. Here he was of one mind with Bute, who professed admiration for the 'great abilities, and amazing resources of the great King of Prussia', but stressed that he preferred to rely on 'the true palladium of this country, our naval power . . . that, properly managed under a prince that knows its consequence, will ever keep Britain formidable without impoverishing it, and prove a surer means of humbling France, than any other whatever.' As the war progressed, the Prince's hostility to German measures became more pronounced. In October 1760, just before his accession to the throne, George responded to plans for another expedition to France by observing, 'I myself imagine 'tis intended sooner or later for Germany; if that should be the case I hope this nation will open her eyes and see who are her true friends, and that her popular man [Pitt] is a true snake in the grass.' Clearly, hatred of Pitt and of the Continental commitment had become more or less one and the same in his mind. If this was any indication of what the new dispensation would be like, the German war looked like being the first casualty of the new reign.[9]

A foretaste of what could be expected was George's sabotage of plans to marry him off to Princess Caroline, the eldest daughter of the Duke of Brunswick-Wolfenbüttel. This project went back to an initiative of George II in 1755, who saw it as a shrewd piece of dynastic consolidation which might also secure Hanover at a time of acute British international isolation. By 1759, the scheme was expanded to include a match between the Prince of Wales's eldest sister, Augusta, and a son of the Duke. George refused point-blank to cooperate. As the Duke's councillor reported in January 1759, the Prince believed that he would be 'betraying the obligations of dignity and independence in accepting a wife chosen without his agreement'. The King was furious and sent the jilted Caroline a ring as a mark of esteem, but the Prince remained unmoved. 'The more I think of the D. of Br[unswick's] letter,' George wrote a month later, 'the more I am incensed against him; it manifestly shows a mind greatly embitter'd against our part of the family and a certain pride that generally attends those petty princes.' No doubt emerging sentimental notions about marrying for love, and escaping (grand-) parental jurisdiction played a role in all this. What was striking here was not just the venom with which George reacted to this specific proposal, but the obvious hauteur with which he regarded 'petty princes' of the Holy Roman Empire; it did not bode well for British Continentalism.[10]

As if all this were not bad enough, the Continental policy was dealt another blow in November 1760, when the dissenting minister and woollen merchant Israel Mauduit published his devastating pamphlet, *Considerations on the present German war*. The author provided no new information or interpretation, but he was the first to marshal the arguments against engagement in Europe so effectively and, it seemed to many, so irresistibly. As one jaundiced observer put it to the British representative to Prussia, Andrew Mitchell, 'There is nothing new in the arguments but they are handled in a manner not unlikely to raise a flame among the vulgar and abet the prejudices of the many.' In fact, although the *Considerations* was clearly a polemic, it was not a rant. There were relatively few gratuitous swipes at Hanover, the monarchy and personalities. Instead, Mauduit rehearsed and polished a range of existing themes and arguments with compelling vigour: Britain was in her element at sea, hence land warfare should be avoided; only a united Germany was any use as a barrier against France, hence interference in what was essentially an Austro-Prussian 'German civil war' was redundant; there was no religious obligation to help the Protestant Prussians; and let the German constitution protect Hanover, as defending it would only subject it to devastation. Eventually, Mauduit suggested, British withdrawal would allow Germany to unify and repel the invader. Most importantly of all, however, the author sought to show that the Continental 'diversion' was no such thing, partly because it was not undertaken by choice, but primarily because it was more costly to Britain than France.[11]

The impact of the *Considerations* was massive and instantaneous, comparable only to Swift's famous *Conduct of the Allies* during the War of the Spanish Succession. Horace Walpole claimed that Mauduit 'had more operation in working a change in the minds of men than ever perhaps fell to the lot of a pamphlet'. It appeared at a moment when the Continental policy had just passed its peak and was, in the eyes of many, beginning to outlive its usefulness. Some 5,000 copies were printed in five editions, which were read and reviewed not only in taverns, inns, newspapers and journals throughout London but also – somewhat unusually – in such towns as Coventry, Newcastle and Birmingham as well. They provided a ready-made quarry which critics of government policy could mine in support of their own pamphlets or parliamentary speeches. Mauduit himself claimed that it had been cited on twenty occasions in the Commons and twice in the Lords. When, in December 1760, Pitt proposed the usual Prussian subsidy for the following year, Sir Francis Dashwood quoted Mauduit in opposition to the measure. Pitt responded that 'A certain little book, that was found somewhere or other, has made a great many orators in this House.' Mauduit's message resonated among Americans on both sides of the Atlantic and found a home in Benjamin Franklin's library.[12]

By the beginning of 1761, therefore, the contours of a new high-political and discursive dynamic were visible. Bute assumed ever more influence from the shadows. In March 1761 the Northern Secretary, Holdernesse, was forced out, and Bute took his place. From now on that key department would be run by a man fundamentally sceptical of the 'German war'. Moreover, the rhetorical hegemony of the Continental policy had been punctured at the very moment when it had come adrift from its monarchic moorings. In his first speech from the throne the new King spoke of an 'expensive but just and necessary war'; he had with some difficulty been dissuaded from calling it 'bloody and expensive', which was a sentiment much closer to his heart. He also proclaimed that 'born and educated in this country, I glory in the name of Britain'. The phrase was clearly intended as an echo of Queen Anne's speech from the throne nearly sixty years earlier. She had announced that 'I know my heart to be entirely English', unlike her sister, whose husband William of Orange was perceived by many to have mired England in alien European conflicts. By the same token, George was consciously trying to draw a line beneath the German connections and policies of his two predecessors and signal a new patriotic and British reign. The Whig oligarchs were to be sidelined. In both cases, the result was to be a Tory ascendancy, a turn away from Europe which ended in near-fatal isolation.[13]

The signal George sent out on his accession was quickly picked up. For the first time since 1714, attacks on Continental connections and the Personal Union were now calculated to win royal favour rather than provoke ostracism. Moreover, there was no prospect of any immediate or medium-term change. As Hardwicke remarked in April 1761, 'There is now no reversionary resource. Instead of an old King and a young successor, a young King and no successor in view.' George was well aware of the factional implications of his new course. He suspected the Whig grandee George Grenville, for example, of criticizing the German war in order to please him and sideline Newcastle. The gulf between the monarchy and the patriot end of the public sphere narrowed perceptibly. On the other hand, the ministry remained in place for the time being. For the next two years or so, therefore, the political nation was treated to the unusual spectacle of an elite which was far more 'German' and solicitous of the welfare of Hanover than the Elector of Hanover himself.[14]

Supporters of the German war were now under constant assault. A wave of pamphlets attacking the war and Hanover, and demanding the end to Union followed. Israel Mauduit now enjoyed public royal favour; Bute later paid him a pension. Not even the Duke of Brunswick was spared: he was accused of corruption and collusion with his kinsman Frederick the Great. Prussia's stock also fell with Frederick's declining fortunes, and it did not help that he reclaimed the last Prussian from Brunswick's army in the spring of 1760. In the face of all this, Pitt's advocacy seemed increasingly threadbare. 'I convinced the House of Commons that the troops sent to Emden were not designed for Germany,' one anti-Pittite satire ran, 'I made anti-Hanoverians and the enemies of Germany send men we could ill spare, and money we could ill raise to the aid of Prince Ferdinand ... The oftener I altered my opinion the more I was esteemed for my consistency.' In 1761 one pamphleteer rejected Pitt's diversionary strategy on the grounds that 'the supplying a French army in Germany did not take one hand from one of the ports of France, their navy was not impaired by it, their marines and seamen were not lessened'. An old scourge, the translator and writer Philip Francis, popped up again in 1761, to accuse Pitt of toadying over Hanover, an odd charge after the death of George II. All this showed that the public and many parliamentarians had tired of Pitt's wizardry.[15]

In the face of this barrage, the Continentalists stuck to their guns. One pamphleteer responded to Mauduit in short order by pointing out that 'Before the Electors of Hanover were Kings of Great Britain, Great Britain had armies in Germany' to maintain. This was because it was essential to fight the French wherever possible, be it upon a 'dung-hill'. In early 1761 further reinforcements were sent to deal with an expected

32. As the German war stagnated, the British public lost faith in Pitt.

major effort by the French to improve their bargaining position at the peace talks. Pitt himself continued to reject any separate peace at Prussia's expense, just as he had throughout 1760. After the accession of George III, he announced 'that if the system of the war was to undergo the least . . . shadow of a change he could no longer be of any service'. Following a request from Frederick some six months earlier, Britain – at Pitt's behest – undertook in December 1760 to leave at least part of the Duke of Brunswick's army to the Prussians after an agreement with France – and to pay for it. At the same time, Frederick was asked to set out what his financial needs would be *after* an Anglo-French settlement. The Secretary of State for the North, Holdernesse, remarked in amazement that same month that he 'little thought [he] should have seen an English minister have courage and credit enough to support a war upon the Continent, as auxiliary, when our English quarrel with France is at an end; that miracle now appears in favour of the King of Prussia'. Frederick himself – not a man otherwise much moved to praise – conceded around the same time that 'He was truly touched and affected' by the goodwill of British ministers at this point.[16]

Pitt's policy towards Prussia in 1760–61 was striking in two respects. First of all, it showed the lengths to which he was prepared to go to retain his Prussian ally, even after Britain's quarrel with France had been settled. Far from being an out-and-out navalist who had simply appropriated the Continental war for short-term profit, Pitt was taking the long view of Britain's European alliances. Secondly, it showed the use to which the Hanoverian connection could be put in order to promote British interests on the Continent. Pitt was looking well beyond the immediate prosecution of the war to the balance of power within Europe, and especially within the Holy Roman Empire, after a peace settlement. Newcastle likewise feared that short-term economies would isolate Britain for the future, leaving her 'without one single friend in Europe'. Never before had the Whig interventionist doctrine found such pure expression.[17]

In the public sphere and in government, however, the battle was already being lost. The attitude of the *Monitor* showed the direction in which popular opinion was moving. In late November 1760, it welcomed the prospect of a British-born monarch in terms which echoed George's own rhetoric. 'The sovereign who glories in the name of Briton,' it argued, 'will glory in every measure that is conducive to the glory of his country, and in discouraging and rejecting every connection that shall tend to diminish that glory or to oppress his people for the advantage of a foreign state.' What was remarkable here was not the argument, which was familiar and derivative, but the fact that it was being advanced in an organ which had converted to the German war in 1757 and had for three years consciously eschewed such divisive rhetoric. By 1761, in fact, the *Monitor* had come out against the German war, which it proceeded to ignore thereafter. This was a sure sign that the Continental war was now a declining stock in the City of London. It was also rapidly depreciating at court. To be sure, the new King did not completely disavow Hanoverian interests. In June 1761, for example, he demanded the cession of Hildesheim and Osnabrück as 'satisfaction and indemnification appertaining to us as Elector'. Three months later, in a lengthy dispatch to his Hanoverian ministers, he engaged with the security of the Electorate in some detail. He expressed his concern that movements of enemy forces in the area presaged some sort of assault on the city of Hanover itself, and he pressed Ferdinand to do all he could to guard against this threat.[18]

By comparison with the late King, however, Hanoverian concerns were relegated; there were now fewer attempts to deploy Britain in support of Electoral interests in the Holy Roman Empire. George's failure to address the question of the succession to the Electorate of Cologne, and the Bishoprics of Hildesheim, Münster, Osnabrück and Paderborn, were indications of new priorities. Neither his grandfather nor his great-grandfather would have hesitated. Indeed, part of the new more 'insular' conception of Britain which prevailed under Bute and George III was casting off the albatross of a Continental connection. 'Let the French once perceive,' Bute remarked in July 1761, 'that you lower your terms in proportion to the danger threatening the Electorate, they will not fail to superadd new conditions. Thus they have ever acted.' The palpable retreat from an active *Reichspolitik* in Germany was also evident in the reduced importance attached to marriage policy. George, as we have seen, had refused a match with the daughter of the Duke of Brunswick-Wolfenbüttel. The criteria by which he chose his bride, Charlotte of Mecklenburg-Strelitz are not clear, but they seem to have had nothing to do with strategic considerations. His decision certainly gave massive offence to the other small princely houses of North Germany to which Britain had been traditionally linked. Prince Louis of Brunswick responded to the news of the match in the summer of 1761 by complaining that 'our family have four princes fighting for them [the British] every day without any other reward than the opportunity of being knocked on the head'. The prospect of a match between George's eldest sister, Princess Augusta, and the Hereditary Prince of Brunswick was held out as a consolation prize, but the negotiations moved so slowly as to compound the offence. By late September 1762 this shift had registered with the French. One diplomat noted that George was not much interested in the Empire, was loath to spend on it, and tended towards a 'policy of indifference' [*système d'indifférence*] there.[19]

The disrespect shown towards old friends in the Empire was of a piece with the contempt heaped by George upon Britain's most important European ally. Frederick was condemned as a 'cavalier', 'impertinent' and 'subsidized monarch'. When Lord Halifax was made Secretary of State for the North in mid October 1762, George 'instantly ordered him to treat the Prussians ... with that contempt which they deserve'. A barbed Prussian memorandum complaining about alleged British misdeeds was dismissed by the King as 'by far the most impertinent, and illusory paper, that was ever sent to any court'. On another occasion he spoke of Frederick as that 'TOO AMBITIOUS MONARCH' and 'PROUD OVERBEARING PRINCE'. He also suspected the Prussians of being about to leave him in the lurch. 'What measures have we to keep,' he complained in late April 1762, 'with one who is ready to leave us at the first opportunity, yet thinks he has reason to complain if we don't even show him the papers that pass between us and any court; I own the getting rid of him is what I most ardently wish.' Throughout 1761 and 1762, in short, it was becoming clear that monarch and favourite would ditch the Continental commitment as soon as they decently could, perhaps sooner.[20]

At the same time, rhetorically at least, the new administration played to the patriotic and navalist gallery. In mid October 1761, Newcastle accused Bute of trying to cherry-pick the war. 'Lord Bute,' he reported, 'wants to have the popularity of carrying on the war in popular places, and the merit of easing the nation of the exorbitant expense upon the Continent. I am afraid this will not do, and it will be found that the only way to ease the nation will be by . . . bringing about a reasonable peace.' A fortnight later, he returned to the same theme, in the context of George's coronation speech, which was being drafted by Hardwicke. 'My Lord Bute,' Newcastle remarked, wanted 'a paragraph to get popularity, by conveying to the people that the King would not give up the least interest of this country on any consideration whatever (which his lordship himself explained to be for the sake of Hanover).' As far as Continentalists were concerned, the navalists failed to see that the strategy that had emerged in 1757 was a seamless whole.[21]

While George and Bute were eager for peace in Europe, their patriot sympathies made them more determined to secure victory overseas. Here choices loomed which went to the heart of what British grand strategy in the new reign should be. Spain would have to be dealt with, but should it be by simply increasing British efforts across the board, as Pitt demanded, or by diverting resources from the German war, which was what Bute favoured? France would have to shed some substantial feathers from her American empire, but should these be Canada or the Caribbean sugar island of Guadeloupe? The debate had already begun under George II, at the very end of 1759, after the whole of North America began to drop into Britain's lap. The first sally, *A letter addressed to two great men, on the prospect of peace; and on the terms necessary to be insisted upon in the negotiation*, was published in December of that year. The author saw the retention of Canada as not only vital to British commerce, but also to the maintenance of British naval power. 'The whole navy of England,' he claimed, 'may be equipped with the products of English America.' Moreover, annexing Canada was the only guarantee of lasting security for the thirteen colonies: it would smash the Bourbon ring of encirclement. As one pamphleteer was later to put it: 'They hold our colonies between the two ends of a net, which if they tighten by degrees, they may get all of them into the body of it, and then drown them in the sea.' Of course Americans, who regarded themselves as co-sponsors of the British imperial project, enthusiastically supported the retention of Canada. In mid 1760 Benjamin Franklin weighed in with an anonymously published pamphlet on *The interest of Great Britain considered with regard to her colonies and the acquisitions of Canada and Guadeloupe*. He too argued that only annexation would bring a final resolution of the long struggle with France for supremacy in North America; it would also cut the Indians off from Great Power sponsorship.[22]

Others pointed out that Guadeloupe was economically far more valuable to Britain. Not only was it the centre of the incredibly lucrative French sugar trade – whose revenues would then flow to Britain – but unlike North America its produce did not duplicate that of England itself. William Beckford, Pitt's great backer and a sugar trader himself, pushed strongly for Guadeloupe, even though its annexation would create competition for the Jamaica lobby. The motivations here were not primarily financial. The *Remarks on the letter address'd to two great men* – probably penned by Edmund Burke's kinsman William – argued that the Caribbean would automatically translate into an increase of British power globally. '*There is no situation*,' he wrote, '*in which wealth is not strength, and in which commerce is not wealth* [italics in original].' For this reason, the advocates of a Caribbean strategy condemned, as one anonymous pamphleteer put it, 'the false and destructive ambition of extent of territory'. 'The having all North America to ourselves, by acquiring Canada, dazzles the eyes,' he argued, 'and blinds the understanding of giddy and unthinking people, as it is natural for the human mind to grasp at every appearance of wealth and grandeur.' Besides, a complete ejection of the French from Canada would offend other European powers, by which the author certainly meant Spain. After all, the

Remarks argued, 'There is a balance of power in America as well as in Europe . . . To desire the enemy's whole country upon no other principle but that otherwise you cannot secure your own, is turning the idea of mere defence into the most dangerous of all principles. It is leaving no medium between safety and conquest. It is to suppose yourself never safe, whilst your neighbour enjoys any security.' This was the classic security dilemma: the absolute safety of one state could only be bought at the expense of the absolute insecurity of its rival.[23]

The driving force here was not so much colonial expansion *per se* as the preservation and increase of British power within the international state system – in other words, within Europe. Thus the author of *Remarks on the letter address'd to two great men* argued that 'the utmost rational aim of our ambition, ought to be to possess a just weight, and consideration in *Europe*'. Even Bute's sour comments on Canada reveal the essentially Eurocentric framework. Contemplating the chilly wastes he was about to acquire, he asked in July 1761 how he could 'advise the King to sit down satisfied with a barren country, not equal in value to the duchies of Lorraine and Bar'. This was a particularly barbed comment, given the fact that those two provinces were France's booty in the War of the Polish Succession, and were soon expected to fall to her formally after the death of the elderly Stanislas Leszczyński. And so for the best part of three years the debate raged back and forth. 'Some are for keeping Canada, some Guadeloupe,' Pitt remarked in despair. 'Who will tell me which I shall be hanged for not keeping?' In the end, the arguments for resolving the situation in North America once and for all proved decisive. As Alderman Sir William Baker, who was close to Newcastle, argued in mid October 1760, 'keeping Canada [was] the most necessary for preserving the peace; which cannot be done whilst Canada and those parts are divided between two rival powers, England and France, as the Indians will always be stirred up one against the other.' And if keeping Guadeloupe 'might be more beneficial in point of trade', retaining 'the other [would be] for the preservation of the peace'. To say that in opting for Canada, Britain favoured strategic over commercial considerations is only half true. When in doubt strategic imperatives *invariably* prevailed: the choice here was not between commerce and security, but between two distinct conceptions of security, the one fiscal and insular, the other territorial and Continental.[24]

But the French were determined to retain at least one toehold in, or to be more precise, off Canada. They proved intractable on the Newfoundland fisheries. Although France was prepared to surrender Cape Breton, it insisted on the continued right to land catches and dry fish. Newcastle reported in August 1761 that 'The point of the fisheries is and has been almost the sole obstacle to our peace.' This was an important commercial issue, but the main question was strategic. Bute feared that any French enclave might grow into 'another Louisburg'. Most importantly, the Newfoundland fisheries were a crucial source of manpower for the French navy. Establishing total control over them would not only consolidate British control of Canada, but perpetuate the naval imbalance between the two powers for the foreseeable future. For this reason, Bute adopted a robust – almost arrogant – attitude towards France. He told the British negotiator, the Duke of Bedford, that 'an ultimatum from a beaten enemy is most unusual in the beginning of a treaty.' He added, 'We know the French are exhausted,' and reminded Bedford that 'they in the most humiliating manner sued for peace.'[25]

If there was more than a touch of hubris in the rhetoric of the new ministry, the public sphere, intoxicated by the victories of 1759–60, was rampant. In late December 1760, the *Public Ledger* announced without conscious irony that 'a long series of victories had so raised [the population's] self-esteem that they regarded the permanent maintenance of their conquests as an indispensable condition.' There was exuberance among Americans too. 'All the country from the St Lawrence to the Mississippi,' Benjamin Franklin wrote in 1760, 'will in another century be filled with British people. Britain itself will become vastly more populous, by the immense increase of its commerce; the Atlantic sea will be covered with your trading ships; and your naval power, thence continually increasing, will extend your influence around the whole globe, and awe the world.'[26]

All this made the task of negotiating a peace doubly difficult. The MP Richard Rigby reported in August 1761:

I have conversed with some of my neighbours about peace, which they all wish for, and will tell you they shall be undone if the war continues; but . . . they will tell you in the same breath, that you must keep everything which you have taken from the French, and have everything returned to you which you have lost by the war. Depend on it, my Lord, this is the madness of the times, and there is but one cure for it, and that is a defeat of some one of our projects. Whilst we succeed and make conquest and bonfires, the value of the capture is no part of the consideration – fresh fuel is added to the delirium, and the fire is kept constantly fanned. For my own part, I am so convinced of the destruction which must follow the continuance of war, that I am not sorry to hear that Martinico or the next windmill which you attack should get the better of you.

Rigby had put his finger on the central paradox: by now British victories were a barrier, not an incentive, to a negotiated peace.[27]

At the time, many doubted that total victory was possible; few thought that it might be counterproductive. One of them was the chief British negotiator, the Duke of Bedford, who argued that the choice lay between a lasting peace and a truce which would eventually lead to a French revanche. In a remarkable letter to Bute he counselled against further operations to improve Britain's bargaining position. It was pointless to regard Belle Île – an island off the west coast of France captured by a British expeditionary force – as 'a good thing to carry to market . . . we have too much already – more than we know what to do with; and I very much fear that if we retain the greatest part of our conquests out of Europe, we shall be in danger of over-colonizing and undoing ourselves by them, as the Spaniards have done.' He was, in other words, warning of imperial overstretch. Bedford also felt that the retention of Belle Île – which was 'as much a part of France as the Isle of Wight is of England' – would be a humiliation too far for France. Britain would not put up with it if the boot were on the other foot. 'If this is the case,' he concluded, 'let us do as we would be done by, the most golden rule, as well as in what relates to the public and the private life, which exists, and I believe ought always to be observed, as well in good policy as in good conscience.'[28]

Bedford returned to these themes three weeks later. It was in Britain's long-term interest, he argued, to show moderation, particularly in the naval sphere. 'The endeavouring to drive France entirely out of any naval power is fighting against nature,' he wrote, 'and can tend to no one good to this country.' Instead, it would serve only to 'excite all the naval powers of Europe to enter into a confederacy against us, as adopting a system, viz. that of a monopoly of all naval power, which would be at least as dangerous to the liberties of Europe as that of Louis XIV was, which drew almost all Europe upon his back'. For this reason, Bedford thought that the French should be allowed their place to dry fish, which would pose no commercial threat to Britain; this was a tacit acceptance that France would be permitted to maintain naval ambitions. An immediate and wise peace was therefore necessary: what was the point of 'taking another island, or burning a few miserable villages upon the Continent'? Much better, Bedford concluded, for George to secure a 'glorious and reasonable peace (which is the only one that can be lasting), and the rest of Europe an instance of his moderation'. Likewise, George Grenville warned the House of Commons 'against intoxicating the nation with our successes'. In short, these men were warning against the very things which would lay British policy low in the two decades to come: naval hubris and imperial overstretch.[29]

This policy was strongly opposed – and with good reason – by Pitt. He became increasingly belligerent, telling George III in mid April 1761 that Britain could fight on until the 'total destruction of the French' overseas. Pitt was perfectly prepared to ride the navalist wave when it suited him, but what drove him here was not crude jingoism or the arrogance of power. Rather, he saw a unique opportunity to break the back of the French navy once and for all. Ejecting the French from Canada settled control of North America but it left the global task half done. Pitt, in short, was seeking to prevent the emergence, or re-emergence, of a strategic threat many years down the line. In 1760 he demanded the cession of 'all Canada, Cape Breton, the islands, the harbours, the fisheries, and particularly the exclusive fishery of New-foundland'. After all, he argued, France was 'chiefly, if not solely, to be dreaded ... in the light of a maritime power'. For this reason it was necessary 'to break beyond hope of resuscitation the naval power of France'. Moreover, he was right to fear a French revanche. Already in early April 1762, even before peace had been concluded, Choiseul was writing that 'If I were in charge ... England would be reduced and destroyed by us within thirty years ... our navy is in bad shape, but it will recover; not everything is done in a day.' In short, Pitt's policy was not hubris, but foresight. It was of a piece with his determination to retain the Prussian alliance and thus a check on French power in Europe itself, which would divert resources from the French navy. His clash with Bedford reflected not the confrontation between arrogance and wisdom, but the incompatibility between two fundamentally different geopolitical visions.[30]

Both Bedford and Pitt were taking the long view, but there was a much more proximate reason to show either moderation or audacity. The collapse of the French American empire was received with mounting concern in Madrid, which had been grumbling about the threat to the colonial balance for some time. Newcastle warned that too hard a line in the peace negotiations would precipitate a Spanish entry into the war. What was the greater danger to Britain, he asked: conceding on the Newfoundland fisheries, or risking further war, and war with Spain, too? Choiseul, for his part, spun out the exchanges with Britain in the hope of securing Spanish help. But throughout 1760–61 Britain refused to relax its terms for France, to countenance any Spanish territorial demands, or even to accommodate Spain's various complaints about British naval and colonial infractions, such as the seizure of contraband or the illegal cutting of logwood in Honduras. Pitt, who had seriously considered ceding Gibraltar in 1757 in order to buy Spanish support for the recapture of Minorca, was now opposed to any concessions; he saw no need for them. In mid August 1761, goaded beyond endurance by further British victories such as that at Belle Île in June 1761, the Spaniards concluded a Secret Convention and thus a third 'Family Compact' with the French. They had waited so long largely in order to secure the safe return of their annual treasure fleet from the Americas. Now Choiseul could let the Franco-British discussions, which had been resumed five months earlier, peter out in September.[31]

Pitt's response to the impending breach with Spain was to call for a pre-emptive strike. This was, as he well knew, a popular demand, calculated to revive his standing in patriot circles. One critic remarked that Pitt 'governs not only in the cabinet council but in the opinions of the people too'. They had long had Spain in their sights. By early 1762, the – putative – partition of the Spanish American empire was well advanced. 'Iberius', writing in the *London Chronicle* in January 1762, demanded the annexation of Florida and French Louisiana so as 'to fix our colony's security beyond the reach of rival states in future times to endanger'. The colonial mirage, which had dominated the British debate in the late 1730s, now once more shimmered before the public. In late January 1762 the *London Evening Post* salivated that 'As the Spanish colonies on the South Sea are extremely ill fortified and badly garrisoned, depending for their preservation more upon their situation than strength', they could easily be taken by British privateers, and either fleeced or settled. British victories were seen as a sign of Providence, and a spur to further action.[32]

Pitt did nothing to puncture these reveries, but his principal goal was pre-emption, not acquisition. Spain had to be neutralized quickly, before it could unite with France. The 'total union of councils and interests between the two monarchies of the House of Bourbon,' he wrote in his famous memorandum to King and cabinet, 'are matters of so high and urgent a nature as to call indispensably on His Majesty to take forthwith [the] necessary and timely measures.' He planned, as George Lyttleton remarked a month later, to act 'à la Prussienne and strike first, while the enemy was unguarded'. But Pitt's strategy was not merely tactically pre-emptive but also strategically preventive in conception. He was already looking well beyond the colonies towards the European balance of power itself, which would be upset if Spanish demands for Gibraltar and Minorca were realized, and perhaps even more so if the reunion of the Spanish Mediterranean empire came to pass through dynastic convergence.[33]

Contemporaries were not much concerned with the legality or moral propriety of what Pitt was proposing, but they had grave doubts about its wisdom. The King was flatly opposed and saw the chance of getting rid of Pitt at the right moment. 'Were any of the other ministers as spirited as you are, my dearest friend,' he wrote to Bute on the same day as he received the demand for a pre-emptive strike against Spain, 'I would say let that mad Pitt be dismissed, but as matters are very different from that we must get rid of him in a happier minute than the present one.' Pitt's plan was also rejected by fellow ministers, including navalists such as Bute, as too radical and impracticable. Newcastle felt that opening a new front against Spain would add to the already prohibitive expense of the war. Moreover, it would extend the list of Britain's enemies at the very moment when her forces were fully stretched. At the Admiralty, Anson warned that there were simply not enough ships to spare for war against Spain. Moreover, as in 1739, the commercial case was far from clear-cut. The huge British trade with old Spain was at risk; British ships in Spanish harbours would certainly be lost. In October 1761, Joseph Yorke warned against 'an immediate and unnoticed rupture with Spain. Had this happened, besides all the cries of Europe, we should soon have had the curses of the United Kingdoms, for what a property would have been sacrificed unwarrantably and passionately.'

British ministers thus chose the worst of both worlds. They would not snuff out the Spanish threat while there was still time, but neither would they defuse that threat through moderating their territorial demands against France, or showing some flexibility on maritime or colonial issues of concern to Madrid. It was a lethal blend of hubris and indecision.[34]

In the face of all this and the growing controversy over the German war, Pitt resigned in October 1761. His ostensible reason for doing so was Spain, which after all fell within the remit of his own Southern Department. It was certainly the justification offered to cabinet, and publicly in a famous letter to his ally Beckford, which reverberated in the City at the end of the year, and cited 'A difference of opinion with regard to measures to be taken against Spain'. The real reason, however, may have been a determination to exit on a high popular note, before the German war, which he believed essential but which was now politically unsustainable, exploded in his face. The court chaplain, Dr Pyle, may have had a point when he condemned Pitt as 'a very inconsistent and shameless man ... [who] went out in a huff; in order to continue a popular IDOL'. The popular and literary reaction to Pitt's departure was muted and in places even hostile, certainly by comparison with the outcry which greeted his sacking in 1757. He was now seen as too committed to Continental measures and the old Whig establishment; George III, by contrast, still basked in popular approval. Newcastle was relieved to see the back of a feared rival, but in truth his position was much weakened by the resignation. The German war had lost its most eloquent defender within the ministry. That same month Bute, who had taken over from Holdernesse as Secretary for the Northern Department, now ruled out the idea of a British auxiliary force to help Frederick, as Pitt had demanded.[35]

After his resignation, Pitt continued to defend the German war on numerous occasions, warned of 'very bad consequences if we deserted it', and made no secret of his suspicion of royal sniping. The most remarkable (re-) statement of his strategic concept was made in early December in a long speech to the House of Commons. He began by reminding his listeners of the 'original cause of our present connections in Germany' in 1755-6. At that time Newcastle, fearing a French attempt to indemnify themselves in Hanover for losses in America, had sought to protect Hanover through subsidy treaties. The problem with ministerial thinking, Pitt argued, was that 'their whole thoughts seemed to be turned to the preservation of the Electorate'. In other words, the strategy was back to front: it put Hanoverian interests – narrowly conceived – before British ones, and was counter-productive to boot. For good measure, he added that 'whoever preferred Hanover to England, he would pursue that gentleman to the last'. He then immediately proceeded to have it both ways. From being the unwilling executor of an inherited policy, he portrayed himself as the advocate of a Continental diversion against France. It was then that he elaborated his famous claim of the previous month that 'Had the armies of France not been employed in Germany, they would have been transported to America ... America had been conquered in Germany.'[36]

This Continental strategy was not primarily designed to underpin overseas expansion, though this may have been a welcome by-product. Rather it was part of the traditional Whig concern to preserve British maritime security. 'However inconvenient and expensive the German war is for England,' Pitt argued, 'it is more inconvenient and more expensive for France.' Pitt, in fact, portrayed himself very much in the traditional mould of Whig Continentalism. 'I always thought and shall always think, that England is not a match for France single-handed in Europe.' He went on to say, 'Whenever you leave France to do whatever she pleases upon the Continent, you will leave her hands at liberty and then an invasion of this country may be no chimerical project. All the world knows how soon France established a very formidable marine in the time of Louis XIV. She may as readily re-establish that which she has now lost when she shall be at liberty to employ all her measures and men for that purpose.' This was, of course, merely a variant on Newcastle's dictum of 1749 that France would overawe Britain at sea if she were not distracted by Britain's allies on the Continent.

Crucial here is the central role played by Hanover in the Continental strategy. It functioned as a bait to draw off French power on the Continent, and a breakwater for Britain's principal ally, Prussia. Pitt noted that 'France has beat herself in vain against the rock of Germany; she has found a resistance there that has exhausted her strength, and she has been more shocked at the patience and magnanimity of His late Majesty than by the victories of his fleets and armies in the Asiatic and American world.' Indeed, he continued, 'too much cannot be said of that greatness of soul and generosity towards this country which induced His late Majesty to expose his native land and patrimony and his

33. The House of Commons in the mid to late eighteenth century. Parliament was the principal arena in which the great debate about Britain's role in Europe took place, and foreign policy was usually the most important item of business

unhappy Hanoverian subjects to the fury of a vengeful enemy for this country. How natural would be thought the desire to preserve them were any of us to put ourselves in the same situation.' The truth, of course, is that George tried twice – in 1741 and 1757 – to do just that, but British ministers would not let him. They were determined that, as Pitt put it in November 1761, if Hanover had once been 'a millstone round our necks' it should henceforth be 'round that of the French'. In short, Pitt concluded, it was not in 'the real and lasting interests of Great

Britain to cease to have any power in the [German] Empire, any influence upon the Continent'. Pitt was thus affirming the importance of Hanover as a British outpost on the Continent, and a strategic asset. The Empire which loomed largest in Pitt's strategic framework was the German Empire.[37]

For the moment, Pitt's rhetoric, which reflected mainstream Whig thinking, swayed the House. There were few openly dissenting voices. One, Richard Rigby – taking his cue from George II perhaps – referred to Frederick as 'a little subsidized Prince'. There was a broadside from the radical patriot Colonel Isaac Barré, 'who abused the late King and his whole reign, as having been entirely governed by German measures', and accused Pitt of behaving like a 'chameleon'. Most lined up behind Pitt. Charles Townshend pronounced that to abandon the German war would be 'the most disgraceful, and reproachful measure, as well as the most pernicious one, imaginable'. The colonial enthusiast Beckford also voiced his support, as he had since 1757. Even the flinty Henry Legge, who 'never spoke for the Continent war in his life, till now' joined the chorus. Following Pitt, he spoke of the need 'to indemnify our allies in Germany, for having abandoned them'. The Whig grandee George Grenville expressed scepticism about the Continental strategy overall, but urged that Britain should not 'abandon' her allies. This, he explained, would be to do to Frederick what James I had done to the Elector Palatine. Nobody wanted to be accused, as the Stuarts had been, of losing the Empire and with it the European balance on which British security rested.[38]

Within three months, Pitt was to be vindicated on the Spanish front. Alarmed at the speed with which the colonial and naval balance was being overturned by Britain, Spain continued its preparations to intervene. War was finally declared in January 1762. At sea and in the Americas, the result was a new wave of British victories in the Caribbean and Pacific. Havana was taken in August, Manila in October. War with Spain was costly – about one-third of the attacking force at Havana succumbed to malaria and other diseases – but it was as popular and successful as Pitt had predicted it would be. Unlike in the early 1740s, British forces did not disappear into a tropical morass. In Europe, the situation developed rather differently; here Pitt was never to receive the resounding vindication he demanded – quite the reverse. Two developments now interacted. The first was the Franco-Spanish threat to Portugal, Britain's oldest ally on the Continent. British troops were sent to Portugal at the very moment when the costs of naval war soared with the belligerency of Spain. All this increased the pressure to retrench in Germany or perhaps to bail out of central Europe altogether. George certainly felt so. He asked Bute in early April 1762, 'cannot we refuse him [Frederick] his subsidy and make use of it in Portugal'?[39]

Meanwhile, the German war was under further attack from within the ministry and in Parliament. In January 1762, Bute raised the idea of withdrawing the troops from Germany and baling out of the German war. A month later, the Duke of Bedford introduced a motion in the House of Lords calling for the withdrawal of British troops from Germany; his associate Richard Rigby proposed the same in the Commons. Bedford announced that he 'always thought the German war, as it has been hitherto carried on, a most destructive measure'. It was driven, he claimed, not by treaty obligations, rather the 'real motive . . . for this measure was fondness for Hanover'. Bedford then launched into an attack on the Continental orthodoxy. 'Those who pretend,' he complained, 'that we entered into a German war to employ the French, did not consider' that it diverted Britain more than France. 'We might have been employed elsewhere to much greater advantage,' he continued. In short, 'we should consider ourselves as insulars, and rest upon our separate and independent support, a commercial interest'. Bedford might have been the principal advocate of restraint towards France, but there was arrogance in his modesty.[40]

These themes were echoed by the ardent Pittite, the Earl of Shelburne. 'The happy situation and peculiar advantages of Britain,' he proclaimed, 'render it wholly independent upon the Continent, and consequently render Continental connections unnecessary.' He then went on to condemn 'partiality' to European states since William III, particularly that of George II towards Hanover. 'Hanover,' he claimed, 'in the beginning of this war was our first object on the Continent, and Hanover drew us again into the ruinous measure of burying our men and money on the Continent.' His speech was significant, because it underlined the extent to which the colonial and maritime element of Pitt's strategy had always commanded much greater loyalty than the Prusso-Hanoverian plank. The debate was also remarkable in that the voices raised against the Continental commitments were now no longer on the margins of English politics, as they had been before 1760, but on the verge of becoming a new orthodoxy.

Bute himself certainly shared a fundamental scepticism about Continental measures, which he believed distracted Britain from the struggle overseas. His mouthpiece, the *Briton*, accused the *Monitor* of using the 'old hackneyed expressions of the balance of power, the Protestant religion, and the liberties of Europe'. During the debate on the Bedford motion, Bute likewise poured scorn on the idea that 'the totality of the war was supported by German measures, and that our conquests in Asia, Africa, and America were gained by Hessians and Hanoverians in the plains of Westphalia'. All the same, he warned against too 'hasty' assumptions of British 'independence' from the Continent. 'Notwithstanding we are insulars,' he observed, 'we are either by our political or commercial interest connected with every power in Europe.' He therefore warned against the 'effects of the universal contempt and indignation, which we must incur by at once deserting a cause which we have so strenuously supported'. This would be, he added with an emphasis that would come back to haunt him, a 'breach of contract', unprecedented 'even among the most uncivilized and barbarous nations'. He therefore still shrank from taking the final step. Instead, Bute tried to use the Prussian subsidies as a lever to force Frederick into a compromise peace. The King of Prussia reacted extremely badly to this. At the end of January, Frederick suggested to his London envoy that Bute should be packed off to a lunatic asylum [*aux petites maisons*]; the letter was intercepted and soon found its way to Bute. In March 1762 Bute suspended payments on the grounds that there were no signs that Prussia was seriously seeking an accommodation with Austria. From Berlin, Mitchell warned against treating Frederick as a simple mercenary. 'The knowledge I have of the King of Prussia's temper,' he wrote that same month, 'and of his caprices, [induces] me to write with this freedom; and I believe nothing will more disgust that monarch than if he should imagine himself to be treated as a pecuniary dependent.'[41]

Of course, as far as public rhetoric was concerned, Bute was happy to stoke anti-Hanoverianism, partly to please the King but also in order to emphasize his own British identity. Ever since his rise to power, and particularly after the resignation of Pitt, the patriot and Whig press had mercilessly lampooned Bute's Scottishness, which was deemed to set him apart from the English elite and suggested a propensity towards absolutism, if not Jacobite connections. It did not help that his family name was 'Stewart'. In this context, anti-Hanoverianism, the attacks on the 'German' war, and the loud championship of naval and colonial projects all served to integrate the insecure Bute into the establishment. This could backfire: the word 'Britain' in the King's Speech was seen as code for 'Scottish'. Besides, as we shall see, abandoning the German war would expose Bute to the gravest charge in the eighteenth-century British lexicon, that of endangering the European balance of power on which the independence and liberties of Englishmen rested.[42]

Faced with this onslaught, supporters of engagement in Europe were reduced to familiar mantras. Newcastle was prepared to countenance a change in allies – he sent out some abortive feelers to Vienna in early 1762 with a view to reviving the Habsburg link – but he was unyielding on the Continental commitment itself. For Newcastle and many others, the shadow of Utrecht, and the abandonment of valuable allies, loomed large. Joseph Yorke called upon Bute in mid January 1762 not to abandon the 'cause of liberty upon the Continent'. In late February, Hardwicke proclaimed that the Prussian subsidies could not 'finally be refused consistently with the King's honour'. These had long been agreed in principle and only the modalities were in dispute. There were some press voices who agreed. To be sure, the days when the *Monitor* and other patriot organs enthused about the German war were over. But the first pamphlets attacking Bute had appeared in October–November 1761 in the aftermath of Pitt's resignation. At first, these sallies were not so much concerned with constitutional issues, or even attacks on Bute personally, as with a defence of Pitt's patriotism and his war strategy. Given that Bute was a sponsor, and certainly a beneficiary, of Israel Mauduit's *Considerations*, it was not surprising that anti-Buteite propaganda should fasten on the Prussian alliance as a rallying point. This burst into the open for the first time in May 1762 with the *North Briton*, whose editor, the MP John Wilkes, had been a frequent contributor to the *Monitor*. The developing attack on Bute soon morphed into a much broader critique of ministerial despotism, the 'Scotch' lobby, royal favouritism and so on, but it had its origins in a debate about British grand strategy.[43]

The showdown finally came in the late spring and early summer of 1762. In mid April Grenville demanded an end to the Prussian subsidy, and the redeployment of resources towards Portugal. He argued that the

German war cost as much as the naval struggles against France and Spain taken together, and was crippling the entire war effort. At around the same time, George was outlining his 'thoughts on the German war' to Bute. 'The more I consider the Prussian subsidy,' he wrote, 'the more objections arise in my mind against it, and as to the German war I am clear that if France is not willing for peace, we must instantly knock it on the head, and if men [Newcastle] will leave my service because I love my country preferably to any other; it will be they that will be run at and not me.' Once again, George couched his foreign policy in terms of patriotism, and he showed a keen sense of how this would 'play' with the public. A final push came in early May. Bedford, who supported a peace with France on all fronts, supported an end to Continental measures only, on tactical grounds. In effect, he was recommending what would today be called 'salami' tactics – slicing off parts of the war individually. The conflict, he argued, could be carried on 'provided we confine ourselves entirely to our own war, and keep out as much as possible of Continental wars in Europe'.[44]

The fact that British government was fractured by two radically different strategic conceptions could now no longer be finessed. Ever since Bedford's motion of February 1762, Newcastle had 'always feared that sooner or later, that fatal measure would be taken', of breaking with Prussia. He told Bute to his face that 'I like your peace tho' I don't like your war', that is 'his silly maritime war'. He reflected, 'My Lord Bute's schemes for foreign affairs are very different from ours. Popular maritime expeditions in war and a total dislike of all Continental measures, are the basis of his politics.' Newcastle went on to say that 'these differences of opinion in essentials make it impossible for us to draw together, even less than with Mr Pitt; for though he had all that popular nonsense about him, he mixed it with real system and backed it with a Continental support which had sense in it.' The situation had now become intolerable. 'In business, that is foreign business upon which everything depends,' Newcastle complained, he was simply being overruled.[45]

So Newcastle decided to bring things to a head at a meeting at which all the issues were thrashed out for a last time. The Continentalists pleaded with Bute not to make 'two more great and considerable enemies, the Tsar and the King of Prussia'. They argued for a Pittite strategy of fighting on all fronts, whatever the cost, and using the war in Germany to keep up pressure on Choiseul during the peace negotiations. Pitt himself spoke to this effect in the Commons. 'The Continental plan,' he argued, 'is the only plan', without which all Europe would be intimidated from relations with Britain by the 'haughty oppressions of the House of Bourbon', and the country would be reduced to the status of 'an overgrown pirate'. He went on to say that 'Increase of power must be continued with increase of commerce or both will dwindle.' So far from being a betrayal of Britain's heritage, he claimed that 'Continental measures had been practised by all our great princes, by Queen Elizabeth, by King William, and were the reverse of those which dishonoured this country for four reigns [under the Stuarts].' More expense, he continued, was 'to be preferred to the perpetual dishonour of the nation, the aggrandizement of the enemy, the desertion of your allies, all which tend to an inglorious and precarious peace . . . Think of your greatness in every part of the world.' Besides, in Pitt's view, Britain could easily raise 'Twelve, thirteen, fourteen or even fifteen million the next year. I know it without seeking information from bundles of papers and accounts.' Truly, as one observer remarked, Pitt was the Inigo Jones of British politics: brilliant at grand designs, but less fertile in providing the means to realize them.[46]

To outraged ministers, the breach with Prussia and the withdrawal from Europe was a short-sighted pitch for popularity. At the critical meeting, Newcastle 'found [that] a popular (as it was thought) preference was to be given to the Portugal war'. 'My only crime,' Newcastle continued, 'was my resolution not to abandon the war in Germany . . . They think, but in that they may be mistaken, that the abandoning Germany, the King's Electoral dominions and our allies in this scandalous manner, will make them popular, and those that are on the contrary side of the question the reverse.' The resulting debate in Parliament, he believed, suggested 'far otherwise': 'Mr Pitt, without knowing anything of me, spoke upon my plan with regard to the war in Germany and the necessity of a further sum being now given. And I am told by good hands, if my friends had put a question either for that purpose or with regard to the German war, we should have carried it by near two to one.' There had been no need for a rehearsal: both men were playing from a familiar score sheet, to which Pitt could tune in, even if he was no longer the conductor.[47]

All this was in vain. Bute and George were determined on a change of course. The subsidies to Prussia were abruptly terminated; Frederick – much to his fury – was unceremoniously dumped. The German war and with it more than four years of successful engagement in Europe came to an end. Instead, Portugal would be supported against Spain; Pitt's injunction to subsidize both Prussia and Portugal was ignored. Newcastle resigned in June 1762. He was succeeded at the Treasury by Bute, who became the acknowledged first minister. Grenville became Secretary for the Northern Department. Those hostile to European alliances, and to Frederick in particular, now dominated the administration. Once again, a British minister had fallen over foreign affairs. Once again, Britain was baling out of a European war at the expense of her allies. Britain was, in strategic terms – or at least in terms of strategic self-perception – an island once again.

After the breach with Prussia, British Continentalists continued to plead for engagement in Europe. At the time of his resignation, Newcastle reaffirmed that he 'ever was, and ever will be, for supporting as powerful an interest as I could procure, upon the Continent, to be composed of such powers, as would best ... defend us against the views and power of the House of Bourbon.' As with Pitt, this commitment was not negotiable. In late July, when Bute put out feelers that he might want 'to *raccommode*', in other words arrange a return to the ministry, Newcastle and Hardwicke gave him a dusty answer. Bute was told that Newcastle 'and his friends adhered to the two grand points upon which the great difference had broke out, viz. the support of the German war and the preserving of the connection with the King of Prussia'. After all, as Newcastle stressed a little later, his 'difference of opinion with my Lord Bute did not singly depend on the peace'; he was 'equally zealous after the peace, for establishing some plan of connection with, and support of the Continent; that that was contrary to my Lord Bute's opinion, and that of those he consulted, and was directed by'. For good measure, Hardwicke also reminded Bute that he could not 'cherry pick' the war: 'a contracted war, whether by striking off the German part, or by making peace with France only and continuing the war with Spain, would leave the nation still in hot water, create a strong jealousy and persuasion that France collusively assisted Spain, and continue nearly the same burden.'[48]

The problem, as Continentalists saw it, was that British credibility in

Europe had now been fatally compromised. Joseph Yorke reported from The Hague with some understatement that 'The late change in England has occasioned much speculation abroad, and I should tell an untruth if I pretended to say that it has raised our reputation or increased our credit.' Once again, the historical analogy which immediately suggested itself to distraught Whigs was the closing stages of the War of the Spanish Succession. Hardwicke remarked in October 1762 that 'by giving out such strong positive declarations of a PEACE MADE OR SURE, they have laid themselves under the greater necessity of concluding a peace, and consequently given France an advantage over them in the negotiation, as Queen Anne's ministers did in the Treaty of Utrecht.' Newcastle observed simply that 'they copy the Treaty of Utrecht throughout'. There could be no greater criticism in the Whig lexicon, and ministers could be impeached for less.[49]

None of this cut much ice with the new dispensation in London. The Secretary of State for the Northern Department, the Duke of Halifax, who had succeeded Grenville in October 1762, showed little interest in the activities of the British army in Germany. He was an enthusiastic colonialist, who had moved from a very active twelve-year stint at the Board of Trade and Colonies. In view of the low priority given to Hanoverian affairs and Europe generally under the new ministry, this comes as no surprise. George, after all, had privately referred to the Duke of Brunswick as a 'petty prince'. The weekly newspaper sponsored by Bute called the *Briton* – a reflection of Bute's own assimilationist ambitions – rejected all obligations to defend Hanover. In July 1762 it argued that 'it is the duty, the interest of the Germanic Body to see justice done to any of its constituent members that shall be oppressed', but hoped that 'the Elector of H——r will never again have influence enough with the K——g of G——t B——n, to engage him in a war for retrieving it.'[50]

With the German war and its advocates out of the way, the new ministry could resume the task of negotiating a peace. This was certainly the King's wish: he told Bute in early June that he was not 'mad for peace, no quite otherwise if it can't be honourable I am against it, but if it can, the sooner the better'. A neutrality agreement for north Germany – which British ministries had previously opposed so violently for the Electorate – was to be the first step. To this the French negotiator, François de Bussy, at first objected, arguing that the French ought to be compensated for the land they held in Hanover, since capturing it had diverted their resources and led to colonial losses. If Bute recognized de Bussy's remarks as a resounding vindication of the despised 'Continental' measures, he kept this to himself. In any case, the French soon realized that their Hanoverian hostages no longer counted for anything in London, if indeed they ever had. When Bute floated the 'idea of comprehending Hanover in the neutrality', towards the end of the year, the French expressed 'no objection to it' and suggested they 'would do it with pleasure'.[51]

At the Reichstag at Regensburg, the British envoy, George Cressener, now worked to implement the 'Neutrality proposed to the Diet by the King [of England] in concert with His Most Christian Majesty [the King of France]'. Here George's Hanoverian servants came in handy. There was nothing paradoxical about this: after all, many of them had long desired peace and saw the war as a conflict waged for British not Hanoverian ends. Thus Cressener praised the Hanoverian envoy to the Reichstag, Baron Gemmingen, 'who has been pleased to assist me in the most friendly manner, his acquaintance with the several ministers of the Diet, his knowledge of the laws, customs and ceremonies to be observed here ... have guided me'. Indeed, Gemmingen had looked after the papers of the previous British envoy, reinforcing the sense of institutionalized cooperation between Briton and Hanoverian. George's 'anti-Hanoverian' phase had not lasted for long. Henceforward, British and Hanoverian diplomats would work together once more; but their activities would reflect George III's personal agenda and not any long-standing 'Continental' policy.[52]

In the colonial sphere, Bute now sought disengagement rather than maximalist positions. His aim was not so much to reduce French power in the colonies – as his robust rhetoric of 1761 had suggested – but to lay the foundations for a lasting peace. To this extent, he had taken Bedford's strictures to heart. Thus he demanded the island of St Lucia 'not only with a view to cut off all other present matters in dispute between us ... but chiefly to render the peace stable and permanent: to remove everything likely to produce animosities thereafter'. Likewise in late June 1762 the new Secretary of State for the South, the Earl of Egremont, announced that Britain's plan was 'not to extend our possessions into a country a great part of which is useless ... [but] chiefly to establish peace on solid and lasting foundations and to forestall all disputes regarding the boundaries of the two nations'. The idea was that 'with each nation keeping to its side of the river [Mississippi] they would have in future nothing to adjust with each other.' Clear borders, in other words, would make for good neighbours.[53]

If this sounded like a cloak for further annexations, Bute had in fact bitten the bullet. Under the 'preliminaries', which emerged in late 1762, Martinique and Guadeloupe would be returned to France. Britain also failed to secure the exclusive right to the Newfoundland fisheries, or to take control of St-Pierre and Miquelon islands (off the Newfoundland coast), thus virtually guaranteeing the survival of French naval power. Instead, Bute had to settle for complete control of the rest of Canada, the 'barren wastes' he had so recently dismissed. Britain also annexed Florida, again not for economic reasons, but in order to create a buffer zone against possible Spanish attacks from the south. Havana, on the other hand, was to be returned to Spain; this so offended the two Secretaries of State, Grenville and Lord Egremont, that they resigned in October 1762. This was the first instance of high-political change over colonial as opposed to European issues, and thus a sign of the new times. Perhaps surprisingly for a war allegedly fought for economic reasons, there is no evidence that any commercial lobbies influenced the final outcome of the negotiations. As the dividing line along the Mississippi – which cut across a natural economic unit – made clear, boundaries were drawn with strategic considerations in mind, rather than commercial ones. British policy throughout the period leading up to the Treaty of Paris was driven by what has been called 'the primacy of geopolitics'.[54]

The enemies of the ministry now lined up to attack the proposed peace. Once again, it was foreign policy which drove domestic political polarization, or at least reflected it. Some of the criticism centred on colonial settlement, but few could work up much enthusiasm on that account alone. Thus if George III apparently confused the Ganges and the Mississippi, Newcastle confessed that as he was 'far from knowing exactly the state and limits of those countries, I said nothing further upon that head'. Europe and naval affairs were quite another matter, however: the issues here were very familiar. The main objection was to the abandonment of Britain's vital Continental connections, and especially her Prussian ally, and to allowing the French navy the means for a future revanche. This meant – so the accusation ran – that the job

495

of containing France had been left unfinished. Both the *Monitor* and the *London Evening Post* pummelled the preliminaries mercilessly. The *North Briton* warned that if Bute made a bad peace, he should be dragged 'even from behind the throne should he take shelter there, to receive the just punishment of so great a treachery to his injured country'. Everybody knew what that meant: impeachment. Indeed, the French minister Choiseul noted that both Bute and Bedford seemed obsessed by the threat of the scaffold. And with good reason: neglecting the European balance of power was a capital offence in eighteenth-century British politics.[55]

In the face of these attacks, Bute vainly sought to broaden his parliamentary base. As Hardwicke had predicted: 'if they get a peace, it will be such a one as will want all hands to support it.' Pitt and Newcastle, however, refused to compromise on their support of the German war; their close ally, the Duke of Devonshire, resigned as Lord Chamberlain in November, further increasing the pressure on Bute. Battle was therefore joined in the final climactic parliamentary showdown of the war: the debate on the peace preliminaries in early December 1762. Critics accused Bute of having sought a separate peace at Frederick's expense. William Beckford, reaching for the heaviest weapon in the Whig arsenal, condemned the peace as 'more infamous than that of Utrecht'. To be sure, Beckford and other colonialists would have liked to see more gains in the Caribbean, but the reference to Utrecht shows that it was the abandonment of the Continental ally which gave the greatest offence. Likewise, Pitt objected to the failure to retain the exclusive rights to the Newfoundland fisheries. This, he lamented, left France 'the means of recovering her prodigious losses and of becoming once more formidable to us at sea'. His principal complaint, however, was the loss of the Prussian alliance and the resulting British isolation in Europe. Pitt now became something of a Cato figure, warning of Britain's isolation and reminding Parliament that his successors had left the job half done. France was still a threat, and should be humbled for good. As one observer remarked, Pitt saw in the treaty 'the seeds of a future war. The peace was insecure, because it restored the enemy to her former greatness. The peace was inadequate, because the places gained were no equivalent for the places surrendered.'[56]

The aim here was not just to frustrate the peace, but to destroy Bute.

It was to this end that the Duke of Newcastle launched his remaining cohorts, in order, as he subsequently put it, 'to deliver this country from the sole and arbitrary power of my Lord Bute'. Newcastle did this more in hope than expectation. 'I have long doubted,' he confided shortly before the debate, 'both from observation and reflection, whether it would be advisable for us to give any opposition to the peace.' Apart from a few hotheads in the House of Commons, he lamented, there was no appetite for rejecting the preliminaries. He was almost resigned to the fact that there was 'little disposition anywhere . . . to attack the present power [of Bute] in any shape'. As Newcastle had feared, the bid failed, not because Britain had become a dictatorship, or because Members of Parliament were stupid, or even because they had been bribed, though undoubtedly some were. Rather, Bute prevailed because he spoke well – perhaps better than ever before or since – and because he was able to marshal a formidable case in favour of the preliminaries. The country was exhausted, the original war aims had largely been achieved, and there was nothing better on offer. Nor were the colonial gains to be despised. In his contribution to the debate, the Earl of Shelburne pointed out that 'the security of the British colonies was the first cause of the war'. For this reason, the expulsion of the French and Spanish was of 'millions more consequence than all our other conquests . . . [and] ensures to Great Britain the pleasing hopes of a solid and lasting peace'. The preliminaries passed both Houses comfortably and the Treaty of Paris was finally signed in February 1763. Bute had weathered the storm. Newcastle's adherents were to pay the price, and they were now systematically unbolted from all patronage. Moreover, the public was largely with Bute. The *Critical Review* remarked that 'the popular tide seems to have taken a turn favourable to the pacific measures of the present administration'.[57]

Newcastle and Pitt had lost the vote, they had lost the high-political high ground, they lost many trusted lieutenants in the clearing-out that followed their defeat over the preliminaries, they were losing public support, and they were exhausted, but they were not convinced that they had lost the argument. They believed, as Newcastle had put it, that they would have achieved a better peace 'for ourselves, for our allies, and for the support of our connection with the Continent'. In early March 1763 Pitt predicted that the peace 'was hollow and insecure, and *that it would not last ten years* [emphasis in the original]'. At around the same time, Newcastle wrote his swansong to his old friend the Dutch statesman Bentinck, like himself a relic of a bygone age:

My principle is, ever was, and ever shall be, an invaluable, an invariable Union with the Republic, the Stadholder at the head; a solid connection with such considerable powers upon the Continent, in conjunction with Holland, as are not, either in interest, or inclination, connected with France. This is the principle I always acted by when I was in power, and I shall always wish well to, now that I am out of it.

This, of course, had been the classic Whig credo since the 'Revolution' of 1688. As at the beginning, so at the end. Newcastle still had a few more years to live, and there was still ambition enough in him, but his time had passed.[58]

VII

Imperial Hubris

18

Imperial Retrenchments, 1763–1765

It suffices to read the treaty [of Paris in 1763] . . . to show how this arrogant power relished the pleasure of having humiliated us, to gain new proofs of the injustice of the cabinet of St James . . . It contains the harshest and the most unjust stipulations . . . You ought to overcome it when you find occasion. If you neglect it . . . you become the object of the contempt of your century as well as of future races.[1]

Charles Gravier, Comte de Vergennes, French chief minister,
in a memorandum to Louis XVI, *c.*1784

Mr Pitt thinks that we ought, by well chosen alliances, to prevent the approach of danger, weaken the connections of France, and maintain the balance of power in our own hands. Mr Grenville disclaims all knowledge of foreign affairs; and thinks no alliance worth the money paid.[2]

St James's Chronicle, 1765

Even before the triumphant end of the Seven Years War, a sense of hubris began to grip the British public. The rough handling of neutral shipping throughout the war was one sign of the new unilateralism; the celebrations of British arms another. Writing in 1759, the year of victories, the Venetian traveller Giacomo Casanova observed that 'The island . . . appears to be completely different from the Continent . . . all the inhabitants have a peculiar character, and they feel themselves superior to any other people.' Two years later, the Nonconformist minister Andrew Kippis told his flock that George III was 'governor of a nation . . . large, powerful and prosperous; a nation which abounds in wealth, agriculture, manufactures and commerce'. The King, he continued, ruled a country which was 'distinguished for science, literature, taste and politeness; which possesses ample territories in the remotest parts of the globe; which is the unrivalled mistress of the seas, holds the chief place among the seats of Europe, and is the most illustrious seat of civil and religious liberty that ever existed'.[3]

The Peace of Paris, which was finally signed on 10 February 1763, seemed to vindicate this exuberance fully. Benjamin Franklin congratulated a friend in London 'on the glorious peace you have made, the most advantageous for all the British nation, in my opinion, of any your annals have recorded'. British power remained supreme on the Indian subcontinent, where the French presence was still confined to a number of port towns and their environs. In Africa, Britain had wrested control of Senegal and various other important trading posts; in the Caribbean, she gained Grenada, St Vincent, Dominica and Tobago. But it was in North America that the British triumph was most striking. More than a hundred years of French control of the St Lawrence had come to an abrupt end. Only a toehold in the Atlantic remained: the islands of St-Pierre and Miquelon. The Earl of Shelburne, soon to be President of the Board of Trade, exulted that 'The total exclusion of the French from Canada and the Spaniards from Florida gives Great Britain the universal empire of that extended coast.' In compensation for Florida, Madrid was awarded the formerly French Louisiana Territory in 1764. It was with some difficulty that Britain was compelled to disgorge Manila and remove herself from the Pacific, which was still a Spanish lake. Truly, as the Irish-born traveller Sir George Macartney was famously to observe ten years later, Britain now commanded 'a vast empire, on which the sun never sets, and whose bounds nature has not yet ascertained'.[4]

Across Europe, the extent of the British victory was keenly felt. The experienced French diplomat the Comte de Vergennes lamented 'the ascendancy which England has acquired over France', and the extent to which that 'arrogant power relished the pleasure of having humiliated us'. He later spoke of the Treaty of Paris as being 'engraved on my heart'. Voltaire – as Horace Walpole noted with satisfaction – entitled a new chapter of his *Universal history*, 'Les Anglais vainqueurs dans les quatre parties du monde'. In Ireland, and perhaps especially there, the implications of the French defeat for the Jacobite cause were quickly realized. As the West Cork priest Father Liam o'hIrlarhaithe lamented around 1760, 'There'll be a great mass of clouds over Ireland some time, chasing and voyaging over the sea for a while, the violence of armed warriors growing, until possession is taken for the rightful King', by which he meant the Stuart claimant, Charles Edward Stuart, the 'Bonnie Prince'. Even among the Indians of North America there was a growing sense that a once fine balance between Britain and the Bourbons had now tilted irrevocably in favour of the former. As news of the negotiations trickled through to them in early 1763, aghast Shawnee tribesmen complained that the French had signed over 'their country'. Now, they fretted, 'the English would soon be too great a people in this country'.[5]

Despite this, many Britons felt that the Treaty was not good enough, or that their negotiators had set the wrong priorities. Some would have preferred greater gains in the lucrative sugar islands, rather than the wastes of Canada (Guadeloupe, Martinique and St Lucia were returned to France). Others again thought that Britain should simply have grabbed the lot. And – it must have seemed to them – why not? Britain enjoyed undisputed mastery of the seas. Over a period of three or four years the French fleets had been repeatedly sunk, captured and dispersed; the remnants cowered in Brest, penned in by a close blockade. The unfortunate Spaniards had been worsted in a much shorter period. Bourbon strongpoints across the globe such as Quebec, Havana and Manila had been forced to lower the flag. Surely this was the moment for Britain to push home her advantage. At the very least, she should have rammed a stake through the heart of French naval power, by depriving her of St-Pierre and Miquelon in Newfoundland, and thus of the nursery of future seamen. One of Newcastle's correspondents grumbled that Britain had returned 'territories that had been very many years annexed to the crown of Great Britain and are now severed from it without consent of Parliament'. Many contemporaries felt that a better peace could have been had.[6]

This was the paradox of victory. The absolute security of Great Britain could only be bought at the price of the absolute insecurity of her rivals. As one pamphleteer had warned in 1761, 'To desire the enemy's whole country, upon no other principle, but that otherwise you cannot secure your own, is turning the idea of mere defence into the most dangerous of all principles. It is leaving no medium between safety and conquest.' A few British observers warned against the mounting hubris. One of these, as we have seen, was the Duke of Bedford, who feared the growth of a European naval confederacy against an over-mighty Britain. Another who feared that victory would be more fatal to Britain than

France was the diplomat and philosopher David Hume. His tract *Of public credit* appeared in a new edition in 1764. Its original point of departure in 1752 had been the danger that the collapse of public credit might prevent Britain from playing her role within the European state system. Now Hume worried that Britain's mobilization during the Seven Years War had 'much exceeded not only our natural strength, but even the greatest empires'. Rather than being laid low by poor financial management, Britain risked being tempted by the Roman 'spirit of conquest' and the 'ancient Greek spirit of emulation'. It was a very prescient addition: Hume foresaw that the greatest danger would come not from fiscal overstretch *per se*, but the political hubris which apparently unlimited credit – on a shaky basis – provided.[7]

Here Hume was simply reflecting a broader national performance anxiety about the state of Britain's finances and its implications for her Great Power position. He was not turning back to a nostalgic agrarian Toryism, but facing into a bleak future within the international state system. Like so many others, Hume was convinced that Britain was now in a race with time: if her own credit gave out and France's recovered, she would simply be overwhelmed.[8]

For it rapidly became apparent that the triumphs of the Seven Years War had not banished the Bourbon spectre for good: quite the reverse. Instead of a largely commercial agglomeration of trading posts and colonies, Britain was now responsible for a sprawling territorial empire, with a new and even more vulnerable perimeter line. Paradoxically, the 'blue water' triumphs of the war had left Britain with an extended line to hold on the ground. The string of forts established in North America at the end of the Seven Years War and shortly after – Fort Michilimackinac (1764), Fort Chartres (1765), Fort Panmure (1765), Fort Mobile (1763), Fort Pensacola (1763) and Fort Bute (1765) – were in total at least 1,000 miles apart. If the old encirclement of the thirteen colonies had been banished, there still lay to the west a miasmic border with the Spaniards and the increasingly unruly Indian tribes along the Mississippi Valley. In India and the Caribbean, French power recovered much more quickly than had seemed possible; so did the Bourbon navies. Far from sleeping more easily in their beds after 1763, therefore, British statesmen lived in even greater fear that thieves would break in and steal the new treasure they had laid up for themselves.[9]

The scale of the British victory, and especially the growth of British outposts, unnerved the Indians, and drove them to try to re-establish the American balance of power. In April 1763, hardly two months after the peace, an Ottawa chief named Pontiac convened an assembly of tribes and showed them his wampum belt (on which treaties and agreements were recorded in beadwork), as one report put it, 'from his Great Father, the King of France, to induce him to attack the English'. Soon large parts of the thirteen colonies were ablaze, including the troubled Pennsylvania and Virginia backcountry. Now the abject failure of British Indian diplomacy became manifest: in some ways the unilateralist trend in Europe was mirrored, indeed had been prefigured, across the Atlantic. Many officials were unable to conceive of relations with the natives on any other terms than those of condescension and intimidation. Thus in August 1761 General Amherst had threatened the Indians that if they ever revolted again, he was able 'not only to frustrate them, but to punish the delinquents with entire destruction'. By contrast, commerce and Indian alliances had, as we have seen, acted as a force multiplier for the French. As the Commissioner for Indian Affairs, Sir William Johnson, remarked in May 1762, the French 'spared no labour, or expense, to gain their friendship and esteem . . . whilst we . . . not only fell infinitely short in our presents . . . to the Indians, but have of late . . . been rather premature in our sudden retrenchment of some necessary expenses'. The combination of imperial hubris and fiscal retrenchment which followed victory in the Seven Years War made the British disinclined to humour the tribes through bribes and gifts. This was a case of being penny wise and pound foolish. Instead, their idea of a force multiplier was biological warfare, when General Amherst made his famous suggestion in July 1763 – apparently never acted upon – to send the Indians contaminated blankets.[10]

The main reason for the renewed panic in London and especially among administrators on the other side of the Atlantic was that the colonial defence structures had collapsed as quickly as they had in the mid 1750s in the face of the enemy. For example, the Pennsylvania Assembly, rather than voting new levies to serve with the regulars, only agreed to raise a few hundred men for local service, and that with difficulty. The settlers appeared to have learned nothing; they were if anything even more dependent on the regular army than during the Seven Years War. Nor did it help that the internal cohesion of many frontier areas, with their babel of Irish, Scottish and German sentiment, tended to disintegrate under pressure, while the influential Quaker community tended to take the Indian side of the argument when in doubt. The problems of colonial defence that existed at the start of the Seven Years War remained unresolved at its end. What eventually brought Pontiac's rebels to reason was not any military mobilization by the colonists, or even the dispatch of British regulars, but the failure of French help to materialize after the Treaty of Paris. Indeed, Versailles prevailed upon the chief to call off the campaign in order to deprive the British of any pretext to oppress or even deport the remaining French settlers. Once again, America had been secured in Europe. But it had all been an unsettling reminder of just how precarious Britain's hold on North America was. Clearly, the decisive factor in continued security there was going to be the containment of France globally, but especially in Europe.[11]

Further north, in Canada, Britain now had a well-established and potentially belligerent French Québecois community to deal with. At some 70,000 souls it was too large to be summarily expelled; it would have to be appeased, or at the very least contained. Here the question of religion proved particularly vexed. The Earl of Egremont, who was briefly Secretary of State for the Southern Department, expressed concern in August 1763 'that the French may be disposed to avail themselves of the liberty of the Catholic religion . . . in order to keep up their [the Canadian settlers'] connection with France, and, by means of the priests, to preserve such an influence over the Canadians as may induce them to join, whenever opportunity should offer, in any attempts to recover that country'. Likewise, the threat of renewed Franco-Indian cooperation, under cover of pastoral pretexts, remained acute. It is no accident that the largest concentration of British troops in North America for the next decade or so was to be in the valley of the St Lawrence. Even in Acadia, where the French population had just been brutally deported, the security situation was hardly encouraging. In the summers of 1765–6, the Governor of Nova Scotia was warning London that local Indians, neglected by Britain, were going to rendezvous with French priests from the island of St-Pierre 'As they passed on their way,' he reported, '[the Indians] declared that they were to meet French forces and threatened to destroy the . . . settlements on their return.'[12]

Nor were things much better in the West Indies. Britain's most valuable asset in the entire western hemisphere, the sugar island of Jamaica, remained as it had been before 1756, hemmed in by Bourbon possessions: Spanish Cuba, which cut it off from the British Bahamas, immediately to the north; French Haiti and Spanish Santo Domingo to the east and, of course, the entire Spanish American Empire to the south and west. After the humiliations of the Seven Years War most of them had vengeful governors with something to prove. And almost immediately, the coasts erupted with exotic demarcation disputes which were to drag on for the next two decades. On the other side of the globe, the future of the Indian subcontinent was by no means clear. The French presence after 1763 looked minuscule on the map, but it was not innocuous. Thus in February 1764, hardly a year after the peace was signed, two East India Company representatives warned the cabinet that while they could deal with local enemies, they would need 'protection from the attacks which they were likely to meet from the European states of France and Holland'. The French had hung on in at Chandernagore in Bengal, and at Pondicherry in the Carnatic. In 1767, the former was to acquire a dynamic new governor in the shape of Jean-Baptiste Chevalier, whose programme of fortifications turned the outpost into a kind of Indian Dunkirk. At the same time, the challenge from local Indian rulers intensified: in 1767–9 Hyder Ali and the Mysore War unsettled the hinterland opposite Pondicherry. Moreover, the French were also present on the islands of Mauritius and Réunion off Madagascar, and thus posed a standing threat throughout the whole Indian Ocean.[13]

There was also a lot to worry about much closer to home. To be sure, the threat of Scottish Jacobitism had somewhat receded, partly because of the death of the Old Pretender in 1766, and partly because of the severity of government security measures after the Forty-five, which had effectively led to large-scale deportation of Highlanders to North America. But Ireland was another matter. The bulk of the Catholic population was by no means politically apathetic, or merely an impoverished rabble of hobbledehoys. Instead, it was made up of artisans, publicans, traders and substantial tenant farmers. These were no petty people, but petit bourgeois. Some of them were in regular contact with the 'Wild Geese', Irish aristocratic and military exiles in France and Spain, who continued to plot the resurrection of what they believed to be the legitimate (Jacobite) order. Contrary to expectation, Ireland had remained largely quiet in 1745, and during the Seven Years War. In truth, Irish Catholic opinion was in flux. Much of it was now edging

towards accommodation with the Hanoverian establishment; but a substantial proportion remained firmly wedded to the idea of a Stuart
restoration. Nobody could be sure which way the argument would
go. For this reason, the authorities were unsettled by a series of rural
disturbances – led by the mysterious 'Whiteboys' – which roiled east
Munster and south Leinster in 1761–5 and again from 1769 to 1776,
during which the dreaded Jacobite white cockades were sighted.[14]

It was not the riots themselves which caused anxiety, but the possible
links to Irish 'Wild Geese' in French or Spanish service, who might
facilitate a Franco-Spanish invasion. Thus one Irish ascendancy pamphleteer spoke in 1767 of a camp in the Galty Mountains in the south
of Ireland where the disaffected were 'regularly paid, [and] carefully
trained by one Bourke, their adjutant general, an experienced foreign
officer'. Indeed Jacobites were well aware that their plans were entirely
dependent on the state of the European system. Gaelic opinion – far
from sunk in introspection and sentimental reverie – was therefore highly
sensitive to the broader diplomatic environment. In dozens of poems
and folk songs the ebb and flow of Anglo-French and Anglo-Spanish
relations and their implications for Ireland were noted; there was even
a serious engagement with the Hanoverian link and the strategic opportunity it offered to Britain's enemies.[15]

What made all of these threats – colonial, Jacobite, and archipelagic
– so acute was the fact that the Bourbon powers were busy rebuilding
their navies, and rethinking their strategy. This had begun well before
the end of the war, in fact in 1758, when Britain's Continental policy
began to prove a serious distraction. The French chief minister Choiseul
was later to observe of the diplomatic revolution of 1756, which had
embroiled him with Prussia in Germany, that 'This new alliance neglected the sea war and the struggle in America, which was the decisive
theatre of operations [qui était la véritable guerre]. All resources were
enthusiastically and unthinkingly deployed in support of a land war, the
aim of which was to benefit the House of Austria.' In recognition of
this, Choiseul wrote in November 1760 that 'Colonies, commerce, and
the maritime power which accrues from them . . . will decide the balance
of power upon the Continent.' Unlike traditional French strategy, which
had concentrated on besting the Habsburgs in Italy, Germany and the
Low Countries, the emphasis would now be on the maritime, commercial and colonial struggle with Great Britain. For much of the period

after 1763, therefore, French diplomacy concentrated not on cultivating central or eastern European alliances, but rather on Madrid, whose cooperation was vital if the naval balance was to be restored. In the meantime, the alliance of 1756 with Austria survived the end of the war in 1763 and was used to neutralize Europe, especially Germany, and prevent Britain from creating a diversion there. French interests in Europe would be pursued by extensive subsidies but no longer by direct military intervention. The aim of this volte-face was not the despoliation of Britain's overseas empire as such, but rather the re-establishment of the *European* balance of power.[16]

This, of course, was easier said than done. France desperately needed new shore facilities, access to seasoned timber for masts, as well as trained seamen, crews and officers. These could not be provided overnight, by a simple flick of a fiscal switch. But Choiseul could and did set in motion a shift in priorities which eventually, after many interruptions and delays, increased the paper strength of the French navy from 60 ships of the line to 67 by the end of the decade, a growth of some 10 per cent. The increase in the number of battle-ready vessels was even more respectable: from 50 to 60 ships of the line. Spain was slow to follow suit, but by 1770 she too could boast 55 battleships, at least on paper. Thanks to a highly effective intelligence system, news of all this reached London swiftly, sometimes in distorted and magnified terms, where it caused considerable alarm. But British ministers were right to be worried: in the same month as the Peace of Paris was signed, they learned of French plans to station 23,000 men on fleets and the West Indian islands; two months later Louis XV was already demanding secret surveys of the English coast in preparation for a future invasion. Moreover, while French naval assets were increasing, albeit from a low base, those of Great Britain declined from a high point of 139 battleships shortly after the Peace of Paris to 126 at the end of the decade. The point at which the combined Bourbon fleet – nearly at level-pegging – would surge ahead could now be measured in years rather than decades.[17]

Just across the Channel, the controversy surrounding the port of Dunkirk showed how seriously the French were preparing for the next round. Here and across the globe Versailles played a game of 'grandmother's footsteps' with the British which eventually rendered all the treaty restrictions redundant. By November 1763, hardly six months after the conclusion of the peace, Alderman Beckford warned Parliament that the French were numbering each stone as they dismantled the fortifications so as to reassemble them rapidly at a later date. In New-foundland, the British Governor noted despairingly that the French were not even sticking to the fishing limits allotted to them; and by the end of 1764, cabinet minutes were still lamenting 'the encroachments made by the French at Gorée [an island which is part of present-day Senegal] upon the English possessions on the [west] coast of Africa'. In short, the world into which Britain's new empire was born after 1763 was a dangerous place, and that was before you looked at the rest of Europe.[18]

At first sight, the answer was obvious: complete naval dominance. In concrete terms, this meant that Britain would have to maintain a two-power naval standard by which the Royal Navy would be larger than the Spanish and French fleets combined. As William Pitt put it in 1770, 'The first great and acknowledged object of national defence in this country, is to maintain such a superior naval force at home, that even the united fleets of France and Spain may never be masters of the Channel.'[19] The problem was that the requirement for continued naval spending came at a time of a severe post-war fiscal pressure across all government departments in Britain. During the Seven Years War the national debt had more or less doubled to £133 million. The public looked forward to a peace dividend; they baulked at shouldering new burdens. They were not ready to absorb the truth that their many conquests had made them less not more secure. Unsurprisingly, the chief minister, Grenville, foresaw 'great and universal uneasiness' if yet more was to be spent on the navy.[20]

The defence of British naval superiority was not simply a matter of greater naval mobilization, skilful deployment or superior seamanship. Traditionally, Britain had defended her colonial and naval position by playing an active role within the European state system. She had always sought to prevent a union between the fleets of her two largest rivals, usually France and Spain, and to stop the navies of smaller powers, such as Sweden and Denmark, from falling into Bourbon hands. This could be effected, as a last resort, by pre-emptive military action, but diplomatic measures were generally more effective. At the same time, Britain had tried to draw off French resources from the maritime sphere by promot-ing a second front in Europe. As we have repeatedly noted, the guiding axiom of British strategic culture throughout the first sixty years of the century had been that France would be more than a match for the Royal Navy if she had nothing to fear on land.

It would therefore have made sense to reconstruct Britain's battered alliance system, which had collapsed under the strain of the final stages of the Seven Years War. There were several barriers to doing so. Some were beyond the control of British statesmen. For a start, the whole European balance had shifted eastwards from the western centres of gravity in the first half of the century. From being aspirant powers, both Prussia and Russia, especially the latter, had moved up to a position of equality and some thought dominance, certainly in the east. This mattered, because now Prussia and Austria were competing for a Russian alliance against each other, rather than a British alliance against France. At the same time, the progressive erosion of France's diplomatic position in the east, together with her increased focus on the maritime sphere, made her less threatening there, and thus the task of British diplomats more difficult. The western and southern balance had also shifted decisively. By the 1760s British statesmen were no longer surprised by the ineffectiveness of the Barrier, originally designed to keep the French out of the Low Countries, but Dutch neutrality in the late war had still come as something of a shock. Moreover, the Habsburg–Bourbon alliance of 1756 remained in place, with the result that the Austrian Netherlands were no longer in friendly hands. London also found itself in uncharted waters further south. The Treaty of Aranjuez had brought decades of Franco-Spanish-Austrian rivalry to an end and thus effectively neutralized Italy and the western Mediterranean; here Britain found herself diplomatically shut out. In short, British statesmen cannot be blamed for finding many features of the European state system after 1763 unfamiliar and baffling. Their dispatches sometimes reflected this puzzlement: one diplomat spoke of a 'state of no system in Europe'; another despaired that 'there is no real system anywhere . . . and therefore not knowing who and who is together, every court . . . lives from hand to mouth without any great principle of policy or carrying his views beyond the present hour.' Gaining traction in this new configuration would not be easy.[21]

To make matters worse, the post-war years saw intense domestic unrest and high-political instability in Britain. Disagreements about grand strategy were central to these controversies, at least initially. The King made serious efforts to tempt Pitt back into the ministry in mid

1763, but on each occasion the stumbling block proved to be European policy. George had sent for him in order to effect a 'general strengthening to his government at the close of the peace'. He was prepared to offer him the Secretaryship of State vacated by the death of Lord Egremont. Pitt declined because his demands for a rapprochement with Prussia were rejected. George – as one observer put it – 'shrunk at the unreasonableness of the terms he demanded'. Pitt announced that he could never serve in a government 'which was not founded on true Revolution principles; that it was a Tory administration'. What Pitt was referring to here was the great issue of Britain's role in Europe, which had divided Whigs and Tories since 1688. The great debates which had racked and destroyed ministries throughout the first part of the eighteenth century thus rumbled on in the early 1760s.[22]

Moreover, the honeymoon between George III – the King who 'gloried in the name of Britain' – and the public was over. In early April 1763 Bute was physically attacked by a mob opposed to the terms agreed with France, as he was returning home after steering the peace treaty through Parliament. A shaken Bute resigned, to be succeeded by Grenville at the Treasury as new chief minister. Yet again, a British minister had fallen over foreign policy. That was by no means the end of it, for in late April of that year, the radical Whig MP and pamphleteer John Wilkes published his celebrated issue no. 45 of the *North Briton*. His critique advanced on many fronts. Some of them related to domestic politics, which were alleged to have taken a turn for the despotic under a Tory-leaning monarch and his favourite Lord Bute. Wilkes framed his case in the familiar language of xenophobic patriotism, in which Bute's Caledonian origins marked him out as a foreigner; at that time Scots faced even greater prejudice in England than the Welsh do today. There was also a distinct undercurrent of homophobia and suggestions of sexual impropriety. In some ways, therefore, Bute was subject to the same charges as the Duke of Buckingham had been in the 1620s. Yet as with Buckingham, the core – and the bulk – of the Wilkite assault related to foreign policy: he was himself an ardent Pittite who believed in the Prussian alliance, an ardent supporter of the German war and by extension of the Continental commitment. The *North Briton* was therefore simply carrying forward a debate which had begun with Pitt's resignation in late 1761 and erupted with a new ferocity once the peace preliminaries became public knowledge a year later. Now Bute was once again accused of betraying British interests by 'deserting' Prussia and her 'magnanimous' King Frederick, insulting the 'eminent' Duke of Brunswick, 'who has had so great a share in rescuing Europe from the yoke of France', by receiving the disgraced Lord George Sackville at court, and concluding an 'ignominious' peace.[23]

Wilkes was not acting alone but in concert with Whig cronies of Pitt. For them the attack on the peace, and the restoration of the Prussian alliance, was a potential ticket back to power. They welcomed Wilkes's demand that 'the ministers who had signed it [the peace] [sh]ould be impeached'. Frederick the Great cheered them on and stirred the pot through his former envoy Michell, who remained in touch with the Opposition from Berlin. All this was also part of a familiar attack on the executive and the royal prerogative. Even after Bute's resignation the attacks continued. The *Gentleman's Magazine* argued in 1764 that the King could do 'nothing of himself, but everything by the advice of his Council and ministers'. It reminded readers that 'The speeches from the throne; treaties of peace and war; the application of public revenue ... in a word, every other [action] of government must be always debated, questioned and blamed as the act of the minister.' For this reason, Bute should not be allowed to hide behind the authority of the monarch. It was the peace policy itself, and what it said about the new King's relations with his ministers, which so outraged critics. The charges made in issue 45 of the *North Briton* were thus not necessarily Bute-specific. As the blunt reference to the fate of Harley in 1715 (impeached for his role in bringing about the Peace of Utrecht) showed, any minister who was seen to betray Britain's strategic interests could reckon with prosecution. So when traditional Whigs and radicals referred to 'Utrecht', this was no mere mantra, but code for the judicial settling of scores that would follow the strategic restoration of the European commitment in due course.[24]

Faced with such an overt threat to its authority, and indeed the safety of its members, who were being threatened with trial, imprisonment, and possibly worse, the ministry responded with a writ of seditious libel and issued a warrant for Wilkes's arrest. This turned him instantly into a popular martyr and changed the contest between Wilkes and the establishment from a traditional and potentially deadly spat over foreign policy into a new and disruptive, but less fraught, legal and consti-tutional argument about civil liberties. The resulting disturbances rumbled on throughout the decade and constituted both a distraction from foreign affairs and a liability for British diplomacy. An exasperated Russian ambassador to London complained during the Polish crisis of 1763–4 that British ministers seemed more concerned with the elections in Essex than those for the Polish crown at Warsaw. As the Secretary of State for the North Lord Sandwich remarked in May 1765, 'every one of these convulsions weakens the government, and whoever gets the better, the state always suffers in some degree, and our credit diminishes among foreign nations'. Popular unrest was aggravated by ministerial instability. Thus in August 1767 another Secretary of State for the North, Harry Seymour Conway, explained sheepishly that 'the situation of things here and my own particularly, were [for] some time, in such a state of uncertainty, that except where the public service seemed to require it, I had in some measure suspended the functions of my office.' It was to be a common complaint from both foreign and British ministers alike. Frederick the Great sarcastically remarked that George changed his ministers as frequently as his shirts.[25]

Yet – historically – British statesmen and diplomats were no strangers to either geopolitical shifts or domestic disturbances. An earlier generation had responded to the shifting balance with considerable success. To the rise of Russia and the Spanish threat after 1714, they replied with the French alliance of 1716; to the emerging Diplomatic Revolution of 1755–6 with the Prussian alliance. It was in the nature of the state system that the kaleidoscope would be shaken every few decades. Previous practitioners were expected to cope with this, and they had often done so in circumstances of extreme domestic instability, for example in 1715, 1723 and 1745. In that sense, the 1760s and 1770s were very similar to the decade after 1714, when the focus had shifted from central Europe to the Baltic and Mediterranean peripheries; although against these earlier upheavals, post-1763 Britain looked positively stable. After all, the Jacobite threat had more or less evaporated with the death of Charles Edward Stuart in 1766, by which time the French had long since given up all serious plans of overturning the Revolution Settlement.

The roots of Britain's problematic engagement with the European state system after 1763 lay elsewhere. They were to be found in a profound shift in British strategic culture and debate in the early 1760s. The dominating discourse to emerge from the triumphs of the Seven Years War was not merely, as we have seen, hubristic, it was also deeply naval, colonial and isolationist. 'Great Britain,' the playwright Oliver Goldsmith proclaimed in 1763, 'is stronger, fighting by herself and for herself, than if half Europe were her allies.' The very idea of military intervention in Europe had been widely discredited by the force of Israel Mauduit's *Considerations on the present German war*. Indeed, as far as foreign policy was concerned, the Tory Bolingbroke and the radical Whig Mauduit were interchangeable. This was reflected in the much reduced number of pamphlets on European matters from the mid 1760s. These had dominated the public sphere, with a steady stream of polemics becoming a veritable tsunami on occasion in 1742-4 and 1755-62. Now the flow was reduced to a trickle, with disquisitions on the public debt, the colonies and especially America moving centre stage. Britons were simply less interested in Europe. And all this was happening at a time when the British press and public debate was expanding as never before.[26]

In part, this shift in focus reflected the increased importance of American and colonial trade by the 1760s. But at heart the shift was a political and a cultural one. 1763 was seen as the triumph of a middle-class, libertarian and virtuous imperial project over traditional European links. Hitherto, Lord Cobham's classic Whig pantheon in his Temple of Fame at Stowe, which dated from 1735, had included such heroes as King Alfred and Milton. After 1763, themes were added which reflected commerce and empire. Moreover, the Seven Years War had considerably broadened the horizons of MPs and those with military experience. Most of the experience was in Canada and the West Indies, but the political nation was also becoming increasingly conscious of the thirteen North American colonies. Only one Member of Parliament had had military experience there in the early eighteenth century; this figure rose to eleven after 1754. Of course, one should not exaggerate: the absolute numbers of those with first-hand knowledge of the world outside Europe was still very small, and nobody of any political consequence ever visited the colonies in person. Even if those who had 'interests' overseas – such as the West Indies and East India lobbies – are taken into account, there were never more than a few dozen MPs for whom this was a relevant consideration. The surge of colonial and navalist sentiment after 1763 was thus largely a superstructural phenomenon with shallow roots in Britain's material concerns.[27]

A good example of the new buccaneering mood abroad was Robert

Clive's letter to Grenville of October 1764. The conqueror of India wrote from Rio de Janeiro of the 'deplorable condition of this capital and rich settlement of the Portuguese'. He went on to say that he should think himself 'deserving of everlasting infamy' if he were unable 'with one battalion of infantry' to make himself 'master of Rio de Janeiro in 24 hours', and indeed of the whole of Brazil. He represented this as an exercise in pre-emption, a 'means of preventing these valuable possessions from falling into the hands of the French or Spaniards'. If that was the way Clive proposed to treat one of Britain's oldest allies, Portugal, it boded ill for future coalitions in Europe. David Hume's fears of 'spirit of conquest' and 'jealous emulation' were by no means exaggerated. Grenville did not take up the suggestion, perhaps because it would have involved additional expense.[28]

There was nothing remarkable about popular hubris, navalism, colonialism and anti-Continentalism, of course. What was new was the way in which they were now seeping into elite discourse. Nobody epitomized this trend more than Lord Sandwich, who was briefly Secretary of State for the North, and later went on to lead the Admiralty. To be sure, Sandwich knew Europe reasonably well. He went on the grand tour in 1737, though he seems to have skipped central Europe. In 1744 he founded the short-lived Turkish Society or Divan Club, for those who had visited the Ottoman Empire. He headed the peace negotiations at Breda in 1746–7 and served as British representative in the discussions leading up to the Treaty of Aix-la-Chapelle. In March 1747 he was prepared to surrender Gibraltar in order to detach Spain from the French alliance. Throughout the 1740s he was close to Anson, a committed Continentalist who was linked to the Whig establishment through his marriage to the daughter of the Earl of Hardwicke. By affinity, therefore, Sandwich was certainly a Whig. All this time, however, he was also something of a cuckoo in the Continentalist nest, who made rousingly navalist speeches in Parliament against the Hanover troops and European alliances. Moreover, he emerged from the War of the Austrian Succession with a low view of Austrian trustworthiness and a bleak assessment of Dutch power, which he had hitherto greatly overestimated.[29]

After 1763, in any case, Sandwich adopted the fashionable insular rhetoric of the time. In November 1764 he wrote that Britain did not intend to 'throw away the advantages of its situation by making it part of the Continent, but will never lose sight of the great weight and

influence which it must always have there, and which it can only maintain by making a proper use of its power as an island'. Alliance with
Britain would thus not result from negotiation between equals, but
should be the object of supplication by other powers. In August 1764,
for example, Sandwich told the Undersecretary of the Northern Department, Richard Phelps, that 'there was no occasion for us to be very
precipitate in forming new alliances, though this consideration would
not make us unwilling to renew our old ones when proper attention was
paid to us by those whose interest it is to be united with us.' The tone
of his dispatches towards smaller powers, such as Denmark, whose
policies were described as 'trifling', 'inconsequent' and 'despicable', was
usually peremptory. Even such an important court as Vienna did not
escape condescension. When the Austrian ambassador Count Seilern
prevaricated on renewing the 'old system', Sandwich commented
grandly that

it is agreeable to the interests of this country, as well as to the dignity of this
crown, that by cultivating a fair and friendly correspondence with our neighbours,
we may avail ourselves of our happy situation, and be considered as the power
whose alliance is most worthy to be courted, and whose influence will be most
effectual, whenever the affairs of Europe shall fall into such a system, as may
make it an object to us to throw our weight into the scale.

In earlier years, this blend of insouciance and confidence would not have
raised an eyebrow as a backbench parliamentary rhodomontade, or as
part of a pamphlet broadside, but it would have been unusual in a
formal dispatch from a Secretary of State.[30]

Nor was Sandwich an isolated case. One British observer warned the
British representative at the Reichstag in Regensburg in 1763 that 'your
post is full of ceremony. You cannot spit out the window without
offending the head or paraphernalia of an Excellence.' The same sense
of *hauteur* comes across in the letters of another lowly envoy, William
Gordon. He wrote en route to his posting at Regensburg in 1764 that
'The war we carried on with such success and reputation to our arms,
the support we gave to those powers with whom we were connected
and the finishing the war [with] so glorious and honourable a peace
has struck such an awe upon all foreigners, that they look upon us as a
race of people superior to the rest of mankind.' Even Grenville, the
chief minister, though conscious of the need not to drive France to

'extremities', announced his determination 'never to suffer France, after having been conquered, to speak to England in the terms of conquerors, and that he was persuaded that the way to avoid mischief was to hold a firm language to her'. Against this background, it is hardly surprising that the new generation of British statesmen and diplomats lost the keen sense of reciprocality, which had traditionally underpinned engagement in Europe. Nowhere was this more manifest than in their steadfast refusal to countenance the 'Turkish clause', that is promising British assistance in the event of an Ottoman attack on the Tsarist empire, as part of a Russian alliance. This insistence and the mentality underlying it, killed not only the Russian overtures, but all other Continental gambits stone dead in the 1760s. At times it seemed as if British statesmen would have to relearn the idea that they might have to do for others something that they did not want to do, in order to persuade somebody else to do something for Britain that they in turn did not want to do.[31]

A similar dynamic was at work in the new and much more restrictive attitude to Continental subsidies. These had always been highly controversial, especially in peacetime; and the huge costs of the Seven Years War made retrenchment imperative after 1763. But it was a distinctive blend of parsimony and indifference which now prevailed. Thus Sandwich reported in September 1764 that 'I find His Majesty much averse to any of these pecuniary arrangements with the Powers on the Continent.' Not long afterwards, Sandwich stated bluntly that 'Great Britain will not advance [£]40,000 nor engage in any subsidy treaty on the Continent.' And when the Russians pleaded that Britain should make up for the absence of the 'Turkish clause' with a generous subsidy payment, Sandwich responded that 'an alliance with Great Britain is too considerable in itself to want the assistance of money to render it valuable'. The diplomatic costs of this attitude did not go unremarked. In 1765 one British writer accused Grenville of believing 'that the saving of half a crown to the Sinking Fund is a more important subject, than the credit [meaning European standing] of the nation and the affection of our allies'.[32]

Instead of Continental alliances, Britain demonstrated a penchant for unilateral naval intervention and display, which was well suited to the new colonial focus. Thus in 1763 ships were sent to intimidate the French over Turks Island in the Caicos Islands, and the Spaniards in the Gulf of Honduras. In 1765, the French presence in the Gambia was

roughly handled by British vessels. Spain was routinely and unsuccessfully threatened with naval punishment for failing to pay the 'Manila
ransom', the money which the Royal Navy had extorted in 1762 for not
sacking that city. On one occasion British ministers even showed the
French ambassador the fleet and the Royal Dockyards in order to ram
home British superiority, much in the same way that the Inquisition had
shown Galileo their torture implements. In the Channel foreign vessels,
especially French, were required to make a much-resented salute to the
British navy. For example in 1770 when a French frigate refused that
'act of obedience to the British flag', the British vessel going alongside
fired a shot into her and compelled her to strike her colours, an exchange
which was described in Parliament with much satisfaction. All this was
of a piece with the prevailing navalist mood after 1763, and satisfying
and effective enough in its own way. It came, however, at a diplomatic
cost to relations with European powers which would later become clear.
It was only with some difficulty that George and the Secretary of State
for the South, Lord Rochford, intervened in 1771 to stop Sandwich
from naming two vessels after Raleigh and Drake, for fear of giving
'great offence to the Spaniards'. All this tended to antagonize rather
than deter Britain's enemies in the long run.[33]

The most striking evidence of official Britain's naval and colonial
preoccupations, and the relative decline of European concerns, was the
creation of the third secretaryship of state in 1768. The new Secretary
for the Colonies took over part of the former responsibilities of the
Southern Department. For the moment, he did not enjoy equal standing
with his colleagues. All the same, the net result was to devalue the two
European departments, and to deepen the bifurcation – now trifurcation
– of vision at the heart of British decision-making. There were now
three rather than two secretaries of state at the very moment when the
monarch himself was becoming less engaged with Europe. Truly, as the
ambassador to The Hague, Joseph Yorke, observed a few years later,
Britain had become quite 'uncontinental'.[34]

These processes were hastened by a generational changing of the
guard in British foreign policy, which was reaching completion in
the early 1760s. Those years saw the reintegration of the Tories into
the political mainstream under the aegis of George III. They also, not
coincidentally, saw the death, retirement or marginalization of a whole
generation of British interventionists: Carteret had died in 1752 and

Horatio Walpole in 1757, while Newcastle and Hardwicke fell from power in 1762, never to return. Many of their younger lieutenants were swept out in the 'massacre of the Pelhamite innocents', the Buteite purge which followed Newcastle's unsuccessful attempt to sabotage the peace preliminaries in 1762–3. Some of those who were to loom large in British politics throughout the 1760s and 1770s, such as the Whig Lord Rockingham, were largely ignorant of, and completely indifferent to, foreign affairs. At the same time, the old Pittite consensus, which had supported a controversial European commitment, fractured beyond repair. Significantly, once the turbulence over the ruptured Prussian alliance had passed, it was Pitt's colonial legacy which endured, not the German war which had made it possible. His following had always been held together by personal charisma and the war policy, not by any overarching ideology. With the exception of a short period in 1766–7, therefore, the former advocates of a Prussian alliance either reverted to navalism, were dispersed, or at the very least in opposition.[35]

A telling sign of the reduced importance of Europe was the increasing difficulty in filling even the more prestigious diplomatic posts. To be sure, David Hume agreed to go to Paris as secretary to the embassy in 1765–6; it provided him a good vantage point from which to observe the dangers he had predicted. Yet at around the same time the ministry could not find anybody to take charge in Madrid. Joseph Yorke turned it down and so did several others. Eventually, somebody was found. Horace Walpole remarked: 'Sir James Gray goes to Madrid. The embassy has been sadly hawked about; not a peer would take it.' This was embarrassing because it suggested that Britain was not taking Spain seriously enough, and might expose her to the humiliation of seeing the Spanish envoy recalled 'in order to send a man of inferior rank', as Shelburne feared. It did not help that Grenville was still pressing enthusiastically for cuts in governmental expenditure, especially on wasteful diplomatic representation. The constant changes of ministry, and especially of secretaries of state for foreign affairs, was extremely disruptive. It contrasted sharply with the stability of the early eighteenth century, when many survived the fall of Walpole. Thus the Duke of Newcastle ran the Southern Department for more than twenty years between the mid 1720s and the mid 1740s; there were seven Southern Secretaries in the 1760s, four of them in 1765–6 alone.[36]

But perhaps the most decisive factor in the shift in strategic culture in

1760–63 lay in the figure of the new King, George III. With his calculated embrace of 'Britain' over the Hanoverian Electorate in his coronation speech, George seemed to embody the triumph of Bolingbroke's 'Patriot King'. Because the new King never went to Hanover, his ministers did not either, leading to a narrowing of British vision in Europe. The traditional, almost biennial immersion in Continental politics lapsed. Levels of British representation at the smaller German courts declined perceptibly over the next two decades. Moreover, unlike under the first two Georges, there was no longer any high-political advantage to be gained from promoting Hanoverian concerns or Continental entanglements. The whole framework in which British strategy was formulated had changed fundamentally. All this left British polemicists temporarily at a loss: they no longer had Hanover to kick around. Indeed, it is likely that Bute's Caledonian origins served as a form of surrogate Hanover-bashing in their eyes. First it had been the Dutch, then the Germans, and now it was the Scots: the old patriot saw of foreign despotism behind the throne had lost none of its potency.[37]

As Britain turned its back on Europe, so Europe gave up on Britain. Thus Frederick the Great complained in August 1764 that 'England does not need any foreign help' and that 'she is not interested in anything but naval dominance and her possessions in America ... [and] guided by these sentiments, she ... [will] not pay any attention to Continental European affairs.' Moreover, the rough handling of neutral powers during the Seven Years War had further damaged British standing.[38]

The transformation of British strategic culture after 1760 was not immediate, nor was it complete. There were many loose ends and incongruities: even as the head became progressively more colonial in orientation, many of the limbs in the body politic remained reflexively European. Not all statesmen were John Bulls or Jack Tars, and some could call on military or diplomatic experience on the Continent which was every bit as extensive as that available under the first two Georges. The Earl of Rochford, for example, who served successively as both Northern and Southern Secretary in the late 1760s and early 1770s, had many years of diplomatic service to his credit and extensive personal links to Europe. Likewise, the Duke of Richmond, who served briefly as Southern Secretary in 1766, may not have been Britain's finest diplomatic brain, but neither was he a country bumpkin, having served at

34. George III as a military leader. Although he grew ever more attached to Hanover, he never went to Germany, and the beginning of his reign marked the end of a long period of intense British engagement in Europe.

Minden and as ambassador to France in the mid 1760s. British intelligence continued to rely heavily on Hanover as an intercept station at which European diplomatic traffic was monitored. The chief source of naval intelligence – other than agents in France and Spain itself – was Holland. Britain continued to engage in Europe, albeit uncomfortably and unprofitably. The old Continental orthodoxies were not so much completely superseded as diluted by the navalist surge. Many of those in key positions after 1763, such as the long-serving representative at The Hague, Joseph Yorke, remained ardent proponents of an active balance of power policy; and British diplomatic rhetoric was still shot through with appeals to defend the 'liberties of Europe' which would not have looked out of place in the age of William III or Queen Anne.[39]

The underlying reason for this, as always, was the need to maintain pressure on France in Europe in order to prevent her from concentrating entirely on naval expansion. As one retired British diplomat, James Porter, wrote in 1763, the Austrian alliance would allow the French to divert resources from the army to the navy. On the other hand, if relations with Vienna could be restored, then the Bourbons would 'not be secure under such a reduction but be obliged to keep up their land army, and they cannot supply for both'. According to this model, naval power was still seen first and foremost as an instrument in support of the Continental balance and thus of home defence. Even Sandwich believed that the navy's primary role after 1763 remained dominance in European waters, and especially control of the Channel. His robust naval responses to French colonial challenges were conducted with one eye on the Continental balance. Thus in August 1764 he urged a firm line over the Turks Islands because 'all Europe has its eyes fixed upon us to observe how we bear that insult. The curiosity of France itself is I am persuaded raised as high as that of the indifferent spectators, and they will shape their future conduct according to the spirit or weakness that we shall show upon this occasion.'[40]

Naval deterrence in support of European credibility was seductive, because it offered gratification without commitment. Time would show that its power to coerce was far more limited than its advocates conceded. What was immediately clear was that a chauvinistic popular culture of intimidation put government at the mercy of public opinion, and risked dragging ministries into confrontations they could have avoided. As Bedford argued in the autumn of 1764, the controversy over the dismantling of Dunkirk was a case in point. His claim that the port could serve as an outlet for 'an infinity of our manufactures' was perhaps stretching it a bit. But his subsequent warning must have struck home. 'It is really contrary to Christianity and humanity,' he continued, 'to destroy a flourishing city and country to please hackney writers and a populace who can never be contented. Let us act as faithful servants of the Crown and of the public, with a consciousness of doing uprightly, and never heed what the newspapers say of us.' 'For God's sake,' he concluded, 'let us take heed not to hurry ourselves precipitately into a war in order to gain a popularity.'[41]

One way or the other, Europe still mattered to British statesmen, and they still wanted European support if they could get it on the cheap. A renewed alliance with Prussia was, for the moment, out of the question. This was partly because Frederick, who had taken the breach towards the end of the Seven Years War very badly, would not countenance a reconciliation. He was, moreover, increasingly convinced that Prussian security lay in a Russian alliance, rather than a British one, which could only suck him into the next round of the Anglo-French slugging match. But there was not much enthusiasm in London either. The British establishment from George III downwards was deeply Prussophobic: they had let down the Prussians in 1762 and they had never forgiven them for it. A small minority of statesmen and diplomats such as the representative in Prussia, Andrew Mitchell, and Pitt himself continued to swear by Frederick, but they were on the sidelines for most of the 1760s. Moreover, pursuing the Prussian option was likely to complicate relations with Austria and the revival of the fabled 'old system'. Thus in January 1765, Sandwich assured the Austrian minister in London, Count Seilern, of his 'absolute resolution to keep clear of any such engagement', and towards the end of that month Lord Stormont assured the Austrians that Britain 'stood quite clear' of Frederick.[42]

A return to the status quo ante with Austria thus seemed desirable from several points of view. First of all, it would break up the threatened Franco-Spanish-Austrian axis. This had existed de facto since Spain's entry into the war in 1761, but in 1763–5 there were persistent rumours – to which London gave exaggerated credence – that the Bourbon family compact was to be formally extended so as to include the Habsburgs. Here Britain was particularly concerned to prevent any Austrian guarantee of Spain's overseas possessions, but any connection, even if it were confined to Europe, especially Italy, was to be regretted. This was because 'it would still carry the appearance of an addition of strength to the House of Bourbon, and might lessen their inclination for peace.' Moreover, given the fraught state of relations between Spain and Portugal at the time – they were on the verge of war – London was anxious to deny Madrid Habsburg help in case Britain was called upon to defend Portugal, her 'oldest ally'. Secondly, and more generally, the renewal of the old system would allow Britain to break out of her European isolation. The two powers had never been formally at war, but diplomatic relations had been ruptured, at Austria's initiative, in 1757. They were restored in 1763 at Britain's urging, with the dispatch of Lord Stormont, a stalwart of Continental engagement. His instructions spoke of London's 'sincere desire to return to the ancient system of union, intimacy and communication of counsels'. Meanwhile, in London, Lord Sandwich was telling the Austrian ambassador 'how much it was to be wished, that [the] union which formerly subsisted with the House of

Austria might be re-established; [and] that we were the natural allies of each other'.[43]

The pretext or instrument for this rapprochement was to be the security of Hanover. For the deteriorating relations with Frederick the Great, and the public belligerence of his ambassador in London, made Sandwich fear that he could 'not conceive how he can effect what he [Frederick] calls doing himself justice, but by offering some insult upon His Majesty's dominions in Germany'. This was a threat, but it was also an opportunity. As Sandwich remarked, there was now 'an opening for the most friendly communications with the court of Vienna, and a prospect, by that means, of recovering an ancient, natural, [and] in my opinion, most useful alliance'. For this reason, Stormont was 'particularly' instructed to use his 'best endeavours to engage the Emperor to promise to assist His Majesty in the most efficacious manner, in case any insult should be offered to his German dominions, on account of the difference which may hereafter arise with the King of Prussia'. Indeed the British ambassador, when pressing for Austrian guarantees for Hanover, explicitly 'said that [he] hoped this would be a step towards restoring our ancient union'.[44]

In the resulting discussions the British diplomat proved himself as able an interpreter of the German imperial constitution as any of his predecessors. He expressed his hope that if it came to a breach, the Emperor 'would strongly resent so unjust an attack upon one of the principal members of the Great Body of which he was the head, and would be ready to assist the King as Elector in the most efficacious manner'. After all, he explained, if Frederick

insulted Hanover for a dispute with the crown of Great Britain, it was manifest that such an insult would be as direct a violation of the constitution of the Empire and as flagrant an act of injustice as one member of the Germanic Body could commit against another; and that my court was persuaded the Emperor would consider it as such and would be ready de prêter au Roi comme Électeur un secours réel et efficace [to afford the King as Elector real and effective assistance].

This exchange could have taken place in the mid 1750s, or indeed at any point since 1714. At one level, therefore, very little seemed to have changed: Britain was still geopolitically part of Europe. British statesmen remained committed to the defence of Hanover, and they continued to use the Electorate as a vehicle for the establishment of a broader alliance network, or 'system', on the Continent. Yet the goal of a renewed Austrian alliance eluded them. Stormont proved unable to extract more than a vague promise to defend the stability of the Empire, and eventually he 'saw that [he] should never draw from [them] a formal promise of effectual succour', and left it at that. More seriously, he proved unable to resurrect the old system in any shape whatever.[45]

Ironically, one reason was Austrian irritation towards Hanover. For although George had famously 'gloried in the name of Britain', he proved a much more active Elector than anybody had expected on his accession. The Hanoverian minister in London, Philip Adolf von Münchhausen, remarked in late October 1760 that the new monarch had given ample evidence of his goodwill 'particularly with regard to his attachment to his German dominions'. The King stoutly defended Hanoverian interests during the Anglo-French negotiations of 1761–2: article 25 of the Peace of Paris guaranteed to George and his successors all his German lands held in his capacity as Elector. Indeed, one critic complained to Newcastle that 'by this article Great Britain guarantees Hanover, which I cannot find was ever done before, and seems directly contrary to the second limitation of the Act of Settlement.' He added a swipe against 'those who have dared to lay this new burden on the nation, after having declaimed against Germany and extolled the reigning indifference for dominions in that part of the world'.[46]

The new King took his Hanoverian duties more and more seriously. When the Elector of Cologne failed to list 'the King's German titles' in correspondence, the local British envoy was tartly requested to 'prevent anything of this sort happening in the future'. George could write and read German and took a keen interest not merely in the external security but also the internal welfare of his German dominions. His command of the language was good enough to converse with envoys from the Empire. Indeed, the King's grip on the internal governance of the Electorate was in some ways stronger than that of his predecessors: the Hanoverian minister in London after 1760 was generally more dominant than the chief minister in the Electorate. All of his sons except the Prince of Wales were sent to Hanover to learn German. Admittedly, George never went to visit the Electorate, although in the early 1760s rumours were rife that he would do so. But we should not read too much into this: he appears not to have visited Scotland, Ireland, Wales or even the north of England either. Moreover, in his testament of 1765, the King gave up the idea – which the first two Georges had seriously entertained – of dividing the succession. The future George IV would reign over both territories. 1760 therefore marked a break in British grand strategy and a rhetorical shift on the German connection, but by the mid 1760s the link to Hanover was much more important to George than anybody would have predicted shortly after his accession.[47]

In short, Britain remained dynastically and, to a limited extent, strategically joined at the hip with the Continent. George III was a German prince like his predecessors, and the Holy Roman Empire was George III's other empire. It provided him with a peacetime army of about 15,000 men, not a trivial number in the 1760s, especially by comparison with Britain, on which he could later draw to release British forces for the war in America. Besides, George showed himself from the beginning a doughty defender of imperial liberties and a keen champion of the Protestant cause in Germany. The British envoys to the Empire were instructed not only 'to preserve the peace of the Empire, upon the principles of the laws and constitutions thereof', but also 'on all occasion, to countenance and support . . . the just demands of the Protestants and to cultivate a particular good understanding with the members of the Evangelic Body [*Corpus Evangelicorum*].' Here George was pushing an open door with many German princes, who feared a revival of Charles VI's imperial ambitions: the Palatine minister at Regensburg told the British envoy in February 1763 of the need 'to prevent [the court of] Vienna from ever more forming a project of enslaving the Empire'. The latent tension between George and the Austrians burst into the open over the question of the Bishopric of Osnabrück which, according to the compromise negotiated in the Treaty of Westphalia at the end of the Thirty Years War, rotated between a Catholic bishop and a Protestant candidate from the House of Hanover. In February 1764 George ensured the election to the bishopric of his second son, Frederick Duke of York, who was only one year old at the time. Then George, in complete defiance of tradition, insisted that the cathedral chapter in Osnabrück hand over control of government to the King's representative. The matter soon ended up before the Reichstag, which resolved against George. A Rip van Winkle who had fallen asleep during George I's German battles in the 1720s and awoken forty years later would have found himself in at least superficially familiar territory.[48]

Hanoverian complications did not help, but they were not the main obstacle to an Austrian alliance. This was Austrian chief minister Kaunitz's manifest determination to persevere with the French connection. Stormont reported in January 1764 that 'The warm friends to the old system here, and there are many such here, seem to think that Count Kaunitz is so hampered and entangled by his connections with France that it will be very difficult for him to extricate himself so as to attempt bringing things back to their old and natural channel.' Indeed, he soon gave up on Kaunitz and turned to his arch-rival Count Colloredo, who was believed to have opposed the French alliance in 1756 and to be a 'constantly declared . . . friend to the old system,' and to whom Stormont 'talked much more fully and strongly . . . of our desire to bring things back to their old and natural channels'. But the British ambassador made very little headway there either. It very soon became clear, in short, that Austria was going to be weaned off the French alliance only 'by degrees'. There was no hope at all of winning over Kaunitz: 'the evil,' Stormont remarked, 'seems to me, to be without remedy.' Those in the know predicted 'that this court will abide by their present unnatural system, till the behaviour of their new friend [France] awakens them out of their dream'. Not even the death of Kaunitz's great advocate Madame de Pompadour made much difference. Stormont had to admit defeat for the time being: 'As the best friends to the old system are clearly of opinion that it cannot be revived at present, and that any attempt towards it would do more harm than good, and that therefore the only thing to be done at present is to lie by and wait events.'[49]

The vain quest to resurrect the old system epitomized much of what was wrong with British European policy after 1763. It proved to be more of a mantra, or a straitjacket, than a guide; and London was unwilling to offer anything substantial in return. British statesmen and diplomats were reduced to bewailing the 'unnaturalness' of the Franco-Austrian alliance; Vienna would in time, it was believed, revert to its old affiliations. In the meantime, all Britain could do was to wait for Kaunitz to die or to be toppled.[50]

A Russian alliance was now the only option. Here Britain's aim was, as Austrian ministers were assured, not to supplant the old system, but to enlarge it into an Anglo-Russian-Austrian axis. As early as March 1762 the Earl of Buckinghamshire was dispatched to St Petersburg in search of an alliance. He was relieved shortly afterwards by Sir George

Macartney. Neither made much headway, even though the Russians were keen to incorporate Britain into their emerging 'Northern System', or at the very least to explore a subsidy agreement and naval support. Partly, this was a problem of attitude. The 1742 alliance had been an almost mercenary affair, in which Russian troops were hired for the job. Nobody thought of them as an equal partner. Throughout the 1760s British statesmen and diplomats never missed an opportunity to suggest that the Russians should really be courting them, rather than the other way around. The instinctive sense of superiority which British diplomats felt, and their failure to grasp how much Russia's belief in her own self-importance had grown, was reflected in some rather cack-handed attempts to bribe Tsarist officials. Whereas in earlier times Britain had routinely suborned senior figures at St Petersburg – including the Chancellor during the Seven Years War, Count Bestuzhev – this new gambit wounded Russian *amour propre*, perhaps because the sums involved were not large enough, and proved counter-productive.[51]

The two main obstacles to an alliance went deeper. First of all, British administrations of the 1760s were much more parsimonious than their predecessors. The cabinet meeting of September 1763, called to consider the project of a Russian treaty, rejected this 'unanimously' not least because it required Britain 'even *to furnish money*' – here the very italics reveal a sense of outrage. Looking back on his failed negotiations, Buckinghamshire wrote that 'the economy of the English Treasury during the year 1764' had 'rendered ineffectual a negotiation which ... would have proved materially useful to my country'. Indeed, he plausibly claimed that it would 'have given a different cast to every political transaction in which England since that time has been engaged'. Grenville's cheese-paring had cost the country dear. It did not help, of course, that the Northern Secretary, Sandwich, was also charged with the time-consuming prosecution of John Wilkes. The link between Britain's domestic and foreign troubles could not have been better illustrated. France, by contrast, continued to subsidize her European allies heavily: to the tune of 16 million livres in subsidies in the period 1762–73.[52]

Secondly, London was profoundly suspicious of anything that might tend to embroil Britain in 'fresh disturbances', for example 'by engaging to take part in the Polish disputes' about the election of a new king there. This reluctance emerged most strongly in Britain's insistence on excluding the Ottoman Empire from any mutual security guarantee, precisely the power from whom the Russians had most to fear. Catherine the Great, who came to the throne right at the end of the Seven Years War, was, on a point of principle, unwilling to countenance such an unequal bargain, and the 'Turkish clause' was to become a sticking point between London and St Petersburg for more than a decade. To make matters worse, Frederick the Great had queered the pitch on this issue by instantly agreeing to the Turkish clause in his negotiations with Russia, on condition that St Petersburg make the same demand of every other power. The resulting Russo-Prussian treaty was a nasty shock to Britain, but also set an unfortunate precedent, which was followed by the Danes a year later. A commercial treaty with Russia was signed in 1766, but no broader strategic cooperation ensued.[53]

Only in the Baltic did British diplomacy concert with that of Russia. Here ministers saw a direct maritime interest in securing the traditional supply of naval stores and in ensuring that local navies were not thrown into the global balance against them. Thus Sandwich instructed the British ambassador to Sweden, Sir John Goodricke, to coordinate measures to 'preserve a true balance of power in the north, and from thence extend itself to the rest of Europe'. In practice this meant containing French influence by supporting the anti-French camps in Stockholm and Copenhagen. Britain was particularly determined to deny France access to the fleets of Denmark and Sweden. Thus in late June 1764 Goodricke was asked to find out 'whether it is true . . . that [the French party] have engaged to carry through the next Diet [parliament] a treaty for delivering the marine of Sweden to the disposal of France'. Likewise, the British envoy in Copenhagen was told that it was 'very essential . . . that this government should have the most authentic intelligence of the state of the marine of the north of Europe'. To this end he was requested to procure 'the earliest accounts . . . of the Danish navy, both with respect to the number as well as the condition of their ships'. Once again, the link between British naval security and the European balance was clearly made.[54]

The British ambassador was therefore instructed to throw himself into the bear-pit of Swedish politics. Together with the Russian envoy Count Ivan Ostermann, Goodricke now sought to persuade, cajole, suborn and often simply bribe support at court and in the Swedish parliament, the Rikstag. There were ideological divides between the Swedish camps; the Hats were mostly aristocrats while the Caps sought the abolition of noble privilege and enjoyed the support of the burghers, peasants and clergy. But the diplomatic contest in Stockholm was largely a matter of realpolitik. Britain backed the Caps not because of her anti-absolutist sympathies, but because their rivals in the Hat camp were perceived to be proxies for Versailles. In 1765 these efforts bore fruit in the triumph of the Cap party at Stockholm, which seriously damaged French prestige there and throughout the Baltic. A British–Swedish friendship treaty followed a year later.[55]

Where there was no obvious naval gain to be made, British diplomacy took much more of a back seat. In 1763–4, for example, the principal issue in European diplomacy was the future of the Commonwealth of Poland, where the death of King Augustus III left a vacuum which a French-backed Saxon successor and a Russian candidate both sought to fill; Frederick the Great, on the other hand, simply sought to keep Poland anarchic in order to maximize his influence there. This time St Petersburg was particularly anxious to ensure that the crown did not go to a Saxon, and thus create the impression of hereditary status in that line. Britain was pressed to support the Russian position, but responded firmly that she 'did not choose to interfere in the affairs of that country'. This was not from ignorance – London was well informed – but from indifference Sandwich allowed no fewer than thirteen dispatches from Thomas Wroughton, his envoy to Warsaw, to go unanswered in the period April–May 1764, nor did he pay much attention to the reports of his ambassador to Vienna on this subject. In the end the Russian candidate, Stanislas August Poniatowski, was elected without British help. None of this would have mattered much were it not for two things. First, cooperation over Poland had been a possible path to a Russian alliance. The affairs of the Commonwealth were repeatedly raised by Russian negotiators as an issue in 1763–4. Secondly and conversely, given the radical shifts in the European balance, it was precisely over such issues as Poland that some sort of rapprochement might have been fashioned with France, as an innovative path out of isolation. Simply staying on the sidelines, in any case, deprived Britain of any influence.[56]

19

Imperial Pre-emptions, 1765–1767

Only the revolution which will occur some day in America, though we shall probably not see it, will put England back to that state of weakness in which Europe will have no more fear of her.[1]

Duke of Choiseul, French chief minister, 1765

The King of Prussia, tired of soliciting England for the arrears due to him, informed the Hanoverian ministers that unless he was paid for (or indemnified), and immediately, that he would seize upon the [Hanoverian] duchy of Lauenburg and immediately. This so alarmed [the Hanoverian minister] Münchhausen that he sent an express to the King with his alarms, and saying at the same time that no man could deal with the King of Prussia ... but Mr Pitt ... This determined the King so suddenly and so unexpectedly to send for Mr Pitt.[2]   Earl of Albemarle, 1766

One may indeed be surprised to find that any minister, in any part of the world, even the most remote, needs at this period, to be told of the importance, nay of the grandeur and glory of this nation. The unparalleled successes of the last war, the natural result of such exertions of force and vigour as were equally unparalleled, have set England in so high a point of light, that the envy of our neighbours is more to be dreaded than a contrary sentiment; and the great object of our ministers is rather to abate the jealousy of the European powers, than to increase their reverence towards us.[3]   Henry Seymour Conway, Secretary of State for the Northern

Department, 7 October 1767

British ministers were unable to devote more time to Europe, even if they had wanted to, because of the onset of crisis in America from 1764.

Of course, the two spheres were closely linked: it was precisely fear of her European rivals, France and Spain, which provided the dynamic behind Britain's policy across the Atlantic. For, as we have seen, the acute sense of strategic vulnerability there had not decreased in the first years of peace. It had got worse. The ministry was loath to leave security – or at least anything beyond Indian-fighting – to the locals. The fiasco of the Albany Congress of 1754, when the colonists had spectacularly failed to coordinate their defence efforts, and pool resources, as the Seven Years War loomed, was still fresh in their minds. Moreover, the disastrous impression which the colonial militia had made throughout the war itself on British observers persisted well beyond 1763. Even after the peace, the commanding officer in Detroit, Major Henry Bassett, described the settlers there as 'the outcasts of all nations, and the refuse of mankind'. The Indian rising of 1763–4 reminded everybody that the problems had not gone away.[4]

There was no good reason why Americans should not defend themselves: they were numerous and wealthy. The problem lay in the lack of imperial defence coordination. As Benjamin Franklin remarked despairingly after Pontiac's revolt, if united the colonists would be able to defeat the Indians 'in one summer', yet he also recognized 'that such a union is impracticable'. He therefore concluded that 'tho' strong, we are in effect weak; and shall remain so, till [Britain] take some measures at home to unite us'. Franklin was thus calling upon London to supply the coherence which the colonists were unable or unwilling to create themselves. As matters stood, the Americans were hard put to contain the Indians, let alone a Franco-Spanish revanche. Nor was there much point in relying on the French Canadian force suggested by General Amherst in 1764. As one district governor in Canada pointed out in 1764, Britain could not expect to levy large numbers of Canadian forces 'especially as we have still amongst us so many priests and French officers, whom we cannot help suspecting would be apt to poison the minds of Canadians going to war'. Finally, the strategic vulnerability of the thirteen colonies was aggravated by the inexorable westward advance of settlers in search of new land. These provoked the Indians into raids which British regulars were expected to contain.[5]

London was fully seized of the problem. Already in September 1762 Bute's mouthpiece, the *Briton*, spoke of the need for 'considerable supplies of men ... to maintain all the countries and islands which we have wrested from the enemy'. It stressed particularly 'the extent of our conquests in North America', which were 'peopled by new subjects, indisposed to our dominion from national as well as religious aversion, and surrounded by innumerable nations of fierce Indians, whom it will be absolutely necessary to overawe and restrain by a chain of strong forts and garrisons'. Thus the King's Speech of 25 November called on Parliament to 'consider of such methods in the settlement of our new acquisitions as shall effectually tend to the security of those countries'. The problem with settlement was that it caused as many problems with the Indians as it purported to solve, and in any case experience had shown that the colonists were unreliable. In short, nothing less than a substantial force of British regulars would do.[6]

The ministry now moved swiftly to grasp the nettle, and launched a spate of initiatives designed to put imperial defence on a stable footing. First, in October 1763, it issued a proclamation that there should be no settlement west of the Appalachians, which came to be known as the 'proclamation line'. This measure was designed to conciliate the Indians living there; to allay Franco-Spanish fears of untrammelled British colonial expansion; and to reduce the perimeter line to be defended by the already overstretched Crown forces. Together with other measures of 'Indian diplomacy', this exercise did help to reduce pressure on the western border. Secondly, plans were drawn up to increase the military establishment in America from under 4,000 men to just over 10,000 men. About two-thirds of these were to be deployed in North America, mostly along the western frontier; the rest were destined for the Caribbean. Not only did this scheme involve doubling the existing garrisons on the other side of the Atlantic, but it should be seen in the context of an overall peacetime establishment which had traditionally numbered around 20,000 men. The plan was controversial in London primarily because of the vast expense involved. When Welbore Ellis, the Under-secretary for the Army, presented the overall military estimates to a parliamentary committee in late March 1763, Alderman Beckford 'opposed it as to number and manner as dangerous to liberty and as increasing the influence of the Crown'.[7]

There was in fact no suggestion whatever that the increased force should be used to coerce recalcitrant colonists: it was intended purely for external defence. Those who supported the estimates, such as Pitt, argued that the continued threat from the Bourbons meant that vigilance and capabilities would have to be maintained. Pitt warned that the Treaty of Paris was just an 'armed truce'. 'Mr Pitt,' one observer reported, argued 'that in so early a peace the nation ought to show itself on a respectable footing, that the peace was inadequate, precarious and hollow, that it would soon be broke, that he looked on the union of the House of Bourbon now in a more formidable light than the old union of the House of Austria was, that whenever France broke with you, she would do it without giving notice.' For this reason, Pitt supported the enlarged American garrisons, and in addition no fewer than 18,000 men for home defence alone, as well as a revived militia. What Pitt did not reveal was how all this was to be paid for. In 1764–5 Britain confronted the fact that the Seven Years War had cost some £70 million, leaving a staggering total national debt of about £140 million, once the interest and new charges since the peace had been added. But it was not just a question of debt and yearly interest payments, but also of the increasing running expenditure in the colonies: this had quintupled since 1748. Moreover Britain had foregone – with the enthusiastic support of North American opinion – the financially lucrative sugar islands of the Caribbean in order to hold on to strategically significant Canada. In these circumstances, it made sense to demand that the colonies should make a significant contribution to their own defence. Indeed, as we have seen, the idea that the overseas empire should support Britain's Great Power position had been a staple of British strategic thinking for some time. Thus Thomas Whately, Secretary to the Treasury, argued in 1765 that 'the trade from whence [Britain's] greatest wealth is derived, and upon which its maritime power is principally founded, depends upon a wise and proper use of the colonies.'[8]

Moreover, the colonies were seen as a source not only of current but of great potential wealth. If the bulk of British trade in the 1760s was still with mainland Europe, the spectacular growth of imperial commerce seemed to suggest where the future lay. Besides, in the contemporary calculus, population was also widely regarded as an index of commercial and especially military strength. Here the statistics seemed to tell an unambiguous story. The population of Britain was believed to have slightly declined between 1720 and 1750, not least due to emigration. From 1750 to 1770 it had increased from 6.5. to 7.5 million, but that of the North American colonies had jumped from 1.2 to 2.3 million, a much greater surge of nearly 100 per cent during the same period.

Various projections doing the rounds in Britain and the American colonies suggested that by 1786 the thirteen colonies would have 4 million inhabitants, with corresponding commercial benefits for Britain, and would outstrip the mother country in due course. For the first time, North America now began to loom larger in British conceptions of the colonies than the sugar islands.[9]

Opinions differed as to how the great fiscal potential of empire should be harnessed. The ad hoc arrangements which had hitherto existed, and which Pitt had maximized with great skill, were no longer viable. Britain was, or ought to be, as the colonial expert Thomas Pownall argued in 1768, 'a grand marine dominion consisting of our possessions in the Atlantic and America united into one empire, [with] one centre, where the seat of government is'. Pownall himself believed that this system could only work if Americans were brought into it on some basis of equality, rather than subjected to administrative fiat from London. Others, such as George Macartney, stressed that the 'one great superintending and controlling dominion' should be the British parliament. Others still, including Edmund Burke, the political thinker and MP for Bristol, emphasized the insurmountable problem of distance. One way or the other, it was clear that a new form of imperial architecture, or at least of fiscal extraction, would have to be found in order to solve the problems of common defence.[10]

It was in this context that the British government took its first step towards confrontation with the Americans, as they came to be known. Grenville felt strongly that although the colonists should not be expected to 'raise the whole' sum involved, they should at least 'contribute towards it'. 'Protection and obedience,' he later remarked, 'are reciprocal. Great Britain protects America; America is bound to yield obedience.' He added, 'When they want the protection of this kingdom, they are always very ready to ask it. That protection has always been afforded them in the most full and ample manner. The nation has run itself into an immense debt to give them their protection; and now they are called upon to contribute a small share towards the public expense, an expense arising from themselves.' To that end, he brought forward first a Sugar Act, and then a Stamp Duty on property, 'equally spread over North America and the West Indies'. It was designed to support the upkeep of a substantial regular force in the Ohio and Mississippi valleys. The colonists should no longer be, as we would say today, 'free-riders' in security matters.[11]

America was by no means the only target of this programme of fiscal reform and strategic retrenchment. Similar measures were conceived for Ireland, and especially for India, where the East India Company was effectively an arm of the state. Here too British ministers believed there was a potential fiscal gold mine. Bengal, for example, had a population of some 20 million and it was optimistically reckoned to enjoy a public revenue about a quarter that of the British Isles. By contrast with America, the impulse towards greater revenue extraction and security drove a process of territorial expansion which was ultimately to envelop the whole of the subcontinent. In India, the British state and its servants succumbed to the very imperial dynamic which it had eschewed in the thirteen colonies. The problems which the British state confronted in India and the thirteen colonies between 1750 and 1783 were very similar, though the policies and the outcome were to be very different.[12]

All this was part of a Europe-wide quest for fiscal and societal efficiency driven by the dictates of the state system. The Habsburg monarchy, particularly after the accession of Maria Theresa's son Joseph as co-regent in 1765, was engaged in a flurry of fiscal, social and other reforms designed to prepare Austria for the next round of conflict in Germany. The same was true of Spain, which embarked on a sustained round of colonial and domestic reforms in the 1760s and 1770s. Catherine the Great of Russia and Frederick the Great of Prussia were also always on the lookout for ways to strengthen internal cohesion. Imperial relations were also being redefined in New Spain as part of a strategy to make the home country a more viable actor in the European state system. Only France seemed to stand out through its administrative and developmental languor: here the executive sought to compensate for the lack of domestic vigour by setting different strategic priorities. London thus risked her position within the state system if she lagged behind her rivals in imperial governance and resource extraction. The British government was therefore proposing a perfectly routine, coherent and defensible strategy; but it soon became clear that ministers had committed the cardinal political error of making a decision before they had to, and by so doing bringing on a strategic crisis much greater than the one they were trying to anticipate.[13]

Neither the Sugar Act, which would have paid for one-seventh of the projected new American Army, nor the Stamp Act, which would have defrayed another third or so, were in any sense what we today call 'stealth' taxes. They were not designed to fleece unsuspecting colonists for the benefit of the metropolis, nor were they intended to support an army which would deprive Americans of their liberties. All the same, the Sugar Act, the Stamp Act, and all other subsequent measures, met with intense resistance in America. The principal sticking point for the colonists, and the one which has resonated with subsequent generations, lay in the British parliament's claim to legislate for and to tax the colonists without their consent. 'No taxation without representation' has become a common slogan. The Americans, in contrast to the Scots after 1707, saw themselves as linked to Great Britain not by Parliament, in which they were not represented, but like the Irish – who had their own parliament until 1800 – through allegiance to a common monarch. Some colonies, such as Massachusetts, even drew an analogy with Hanover, where again the link was through the sovereign. Indeed, Benjamin Franklin visited the Electorate in 1766, and took up the comparison three years later. But the controversy over the Stamp Act and subsequent British measures was not just about taxation and representation. It was also very much part of the transatlantic debate on British grand strategy and the imperial architecture best suited to implement it.[14]

For a start, the colonists did not see themselves as passive beneficiaries of British protection, but as joint stakeholders in a common imperial project. Indeed, the author of *A brief state of the services and expences of the province of the Massachusetts Bay in the common cause* pointed in 1765 to their contribution in past conflicts with some pride. During the War of the Spanish Succession, the colony had helped to subdue Nova Scotia and attack Quebec. Moreover, 'It ought not to be forgotten, that, in this period, notwithstanding their hands were so full at home, they gave assistance even to distant parts of the British Dominions.' Two companies of foot had been sent to Jamaica, of whom few had returned. In the War of the Austrian Succession, he continued, Massachusetts had 'raised more than was required'. And all this before the effort during the Seven Years War, during which, the author computed, 'several colonies raised a larger proportion of men than any other part of His Majesty's dominions'. Moreover, the colonists claimed that they were contributing to the fiscal health of the mother country if not through direct taxation then through commerce and the Navigation Acts, which restricted the carriage of goods to British ships and did not allow the Americans to trade directly with other European states. The value of the colonies, the

American pamphleteer William Bollan argued, lay in trade, not revenue: American manufacturing was restricted by parliamentary laws, to the benefit of British producers, who enjoyed a captive market there. The early and mid eighteenth century thus saw the emergence of a colonial compromise in the mind of the Americans, by which they accepted curbs on their manufactured goods – which were bought from Britain – in return for exemption from direct taxation, security against French and Indian attacks, and unlimited agrarian expansion to the west, which would allow the colonies to escape the corrupting influences of luxury, commerce, industry and urbanization.[15]

All that said, many Americans accepted that there was a problem with imperial finance and defence. John Dickinson, later a prominent American patriot, admitted in his speech to the Pennsylvania Assembly that by refusing to vote monies the colony had left itself open to the charge of neglecting its own defence. 'The conduct of this province during the late war,' he noted in late May 1764, 'hath been almost continually condemned at home [sic]. We have been covered with the reproaches of men, whose stations give us just cause to regard their reproaches,' including the Secretary of State for the South in London. Nor was the broader question of helping to defray the costs of imperial defence universally disputed. Around the same time, Benjamin Franklin, the agent of Pennsylvania in London, accepted that the Crown might need 'to keep troops in America henceforward, to maintain its conquests, and defend the colonies; and that the Parliament may establish some revenue arising out of the American trade, to be applied towards supporting those troops'. Thoughtful Americans also realized that some new form of imperial governance was required to coordinate the defence effort, and to deal with matters which concerned the colonies as a whole. Thus William Bollan, a vigorous opponent of the Stamp Act, conceded that it was necessary to reconcile 'the nature of the British empire, divided by the situation of its several parts, with the necessary unity of the supreme power over the whole'. The real issue in this great debate, therefore, was not whether Americans would have to dig deeper into their pockets to pay for their security; that was not seriously in dispute among the more far-sighted. What was furiously contested, and constituted the fundamental bone of contention between the colonies and the executive in London, was the use to which these resources should be put. It was competing strategic visions – the maintenance of an imperial defence perimeter line as opposed to pre-emptive expansion – not consti-tutional principles, which was to drive the two sides further apart.[16]

Like their ministerial counterparts in London, many Americans saw in the frontiers of 1763 a source of further threats; unlike them, they also saw opportunities. On their reading, security could only be guaranteed through expansion. Benjamin Franklin had long been an advocate of this view, and in the mid 1760s he took up the theme with renewed vigour. 'A well-conducted western colony,' he argued in September 1766, 'would be of great national advantage with respect to the trade, and particularly useful to the old colonies as a security to their frontiers.' Not long afterwards he tried to persuade Lord Shelburne, who was charged with the management of the colonies from London, of the 'various advantages' of expanding into the Illinois country, in particular, 'raising a strength there which on occasion of a future war, might easily be poured down the Mississippi upon the lower country, and into the Bay of Mexico, to be used against [the Spanish colonies of] Cuba or Mexico itself.'[17]

The imperialist vision, which later generations have sometimes seen as a corruption of the founding ideals, was thus part of the American project well before independence. It was in fact an outgrowth from the home country. An 'expansionist' lobby now began to make its presence felt in the colonial assemblies of North America: in many ways the issue was to structure American politics for the next twenty years at least. The expansionists articulated a vision not just of territorial growth but of greatness. To this end, they were prepared to accept a greater role for the (British) state. 'Would to God we had a little more government here,' the expansionist William Smith exclaimed in the mid 1760s. For the moment, moreover, this project was to be pursued in tandem with the metropolis, not in opposition to it. The expansionist vision was of a single unified British geopolitical space on the continent, from sea to shining sea – from the Atlantic Ocean to the Gulf of Mexico. It was anachronistic in that it was based on an agrarian framework which would survive into the nineteenth century, but not much longer than that. It was Utopian, in that it allotted to the British government a role which it would not fulfil. In due course, Britain's successors in Washington were to realize this vision, and more.[18]

The Proclamation Line of 1763 was thus a serious blow to the colon-ists. Having seen off the French and their Indian allies, as they saw it,

Americans expected to be awarded the Ohio Valley as the fruit of their struggles. No man or ministry, they felt, should set limits to the march of an empire. As the *The grievances of the American colonies* complained, 'these colonies whose bounds were fixed . . . reaped no sort of advantage by these conquests; they are not enlarged, have not gained a single acre of land, have no part in the Indian or interior trade; the immense tracts of land subdued, and no less immense and profitable commerce acquired, all belong to Great Britain.' The colonists had got nothing: if they were then to be rewarded by 'the loss of their freedom; better for them. Canada still remained French, yea far more eligible that it ever should remain so, than that the price of its reduction should be their slavery.' Failure to expand, moreover, would create negative synergies for the colonies and the empire as a whole. If they were cooped up to the east of the Proclamation Line, Franklin predicted, the settlers would be forced to abjure agriculture and turn to commerce to survive. Moreover, there was always the danger that the French and Spanish would move into the vacuum. Western expansion was therefore conceived as a preventive strike to secure the British Empire in the long run.[19]

For the moment, the line was little more than an administrative fiction in London. Colonists continued to pour across it – to the fury of the Indians, the despair of British governors and the anger of the anti-expansionist lobby. Thus John Blair, the Council President of Virginia, condemned the settlers who went beyond the line as 'banditti' who would enrage the Indians and 'open afresh those sluices of blood'. Apart from the natives, the principal victims were the Québecois, who found themselves cut off from their natural hinterland. George Washington referred to the line as 'a temporary expedient to quiet the minds of the Indians and [which] must fall of course in a few years'. It was only when the British government moved later to enforce the Proclamation Line that conflict became inevitable. All the same, the measure was a sign of the increasing bifurcation of American and metropolitan strategic visions.[20]

To many Americans, colonial expansion was not an alternative to Europe, but served to reinforce Britain's standing there. 'Without the colonies,' James Otis asked from Boston in 1764, 'would Britain, as a commercial state, make any great figure this day in Europe?' Not only, one pamphleteer argued a year later, did the colonies 'bring an increase of revenue by their traffic, consume vast quantities of our manufactures, produce, and still increase in producing many raw materials', but they were 'so situated, their numbers so increased, their martial abilities so well known, as to give vast addition to the consequence of Great Britain'. Indeed, Daniel Dulany went so far as to suggest that the maintenance of the colonies was 'even necessary to the defence of Great Britain herself, because ... Great Britain could not long subsist as an independent kingdom after the loss of her colonies'. In short, Americans considered the colonies, as William Bollan claimed in 1766, to be 'one of the chief sources of our commercial and naval empire'. For the colonists had always seen themselves in a Eurocentric context. To them the Nine Years War was 'King William's War'; the War of the Spanish Succession was 'Queen Anne's War'; the War of the Austrian Succession was 'King George's War'; and the Seven Years War was 'the French and Indian War'. The names they gave to past conflicts reflected no sleight of hand or incipient anti-British agenda, but rather a strategic framework which was still firmly British and European. As Franklin assured the House of Commons in 1766, the Americans would always help Britain in case of European war. 'For any thing that concerned the general interest,' he explained, 'they consider themselves a part of the whole.' Looking back after his break with the mother country, the patriot John Adams recalled that he 'had been educated from the cradle' to believe that Britain 'was the bulwark of the Protestant religion and the most important weight in the balance of power in Europe against France'.[21]

That said, the Americans were as divided as metropolitan Britain was on the wisdom of Continental commitments. For many in their rapidly emerging public sphere, the Eurocentric preoccupations of earlier British ministries took on a new relevance. The return of Louisburg at the Treaty of Aix-la-Chapelle in 1748 now loomed large as evidence of metropolitan perfidy and mistaken priorities. Daniel Dulany, a prominent American partisan, noted that 'it was a notable service done by *New England*. When the militia of that colony reduced *Cape Breton*, since it enabled the *British ministers* to make a peace less disadvantageous and inglorious than they otherwise must have been constrained to submit to, in the humble state to which they were then reduced.' Likewise, the New England cleric Amos Adams reminded Britons that Louisburg had been 'the *single* equivalent for all the conquests of France', and 'the price that purchased the peace of Europe', by getting France out of the Low Countries. In short, the colonists had a very shrewd sense of how they fitted into the European state system. Indeed, as future events were to show, their grasp of that system was to be more acute than that of their supposedly more experienced antagonists in London.[22]

Taken together, the Proclamation Line and the Stamp Act seemed to Americans to violate the tacit governing compromise which had so far regulated relations between the colonies and the metropolis. It propelled them to join the great debate on British grand strategy in force. They did not primarily complain that they were neglected in favour of European issues which no longer concerned them. Some did, but most demanded rather the prosecution of a more active anti-French and anti-Indian policy, which would extend the borders of the empire ever westwards, make the eastern seaboard more secure, and enrich the mother country through increased commerce. And by expanding in America, the colonists argued, echoing a familiar theme in British strategic discourse, they were making the home country more powerful in Europe. London was thus being punished not for its imperial hubris but for its imperial restraint; not for being too preoccupied with Europe, but for not making Britain powerful enough there.

Colonial discontent, which had been brewing throughout 1763–4, culminated in the 'Stamp Act Congress', which convened in New York for two weeks in October 1765. Twenty-seven delegates appeared, representing most of the thirteen colonies, including New York, South Carolina, Massachusetts and Pennsylvania. The main thrust of their remonstrances concerned taxation: the Sugar Act, the duty on molasses, and of course the new stamp duties. But the Proclamation Line of 1763 also came in for heavy criticism. A colonial public sphere, which had been emerging over time, was now consolidated. Metropolitan action was creating Americans. Thus the Rhode Island Assembly called upon all the colonies 'to enter with spirit into the defence of their liberties; if some method could be hit upon for collecting the sentiments of each colony, and for uniting and forming the substance of them into one common defence of the whole'. The very sense of colonial coordination which British strategists had been for so long trying to generate was now coming to pass – directed against Britain. As the Philadelphia patriot John Dickinson predicted in 1765, 'we can never be made an independent people, except by Great Britain herself; and the only way for her to do it, is to make us frugal, ingenious, united and discontented.' What is more, western expansionists now began to gain ground within the individual assemblies, especially in Massachusetts and South Carolina, and even in Quaker-dominated Pennsylvania, not least because of the influence of their agent, Benjamin Franklin, the ur-expansionist. Critics of imperial policy would continue to argue for a change of direction in London, but henceforth the real debate was to be between those Americans who believed that the colonies could only survive through territorial enlargement in the west, with or without British blessing, and those who held that an independent America would not be viable in the predatory world of Great Power politics, or might fall victim to internal dissension.[23]

Given the administration's problems at home, it was hardly surprising that the Americans found vocal champions on the other side of the Atlantic. But resistance to the Stamp Act, and to coercion of the colonists in general, was not simply an opportunistic political wrecking tactic. It reflected a genuine sense that conflict would only benefit Britain's European rivals. 'Should any ambitious neighbouring power embrace the present juncture to revenge their past disgraces,' one pamphleteer asked in 1765, 'can we be sure that the Americans will immediately forget their animosities against us, and join with their former zeal in our assistance?' Likewise, in January 1766 William Pitt urged the repeal of the Stamp Act because of the looming threat of Franco-Spanish unity. A month later, the Opposition MP General Henry Seymour Conway predicted that 'civil war in America' would soon lead to war with France and Spain as well, and thus to 'absolute ruin to this country'. Nor were these fears in the slightest fanciful. At that very moment – 1765 – the French chief minister Choiseul was telling Louis XV that 'England is the declared enemy of your power and of your state, and she will be so always.' He foresaw that 'Many ages must elapse before a durable peace can be established with this state, which looks forward to supremacy in the four quarters of the globe.' For this reason Choiseul predicted that only 'revolution' in America would put 'England back to that state of weakness in which Europe will have no more fear of her'.[24]

Moreover, the colonists themselves were conscious of the European implications to their cause, and played on it ruthlessly. Thus in 1766 William Bollan warned that if division between the mother country and the colonies persisted, this would make the latter 'the object of the enemy's policy and force'. Another author threatened that same year that British legislation would throw colonists 'into the hands of the French'. And the New Yorker Nicholas Ray – writing from London – argued, 'The ruling policy of every state is unquestionably self-interest; the policy therefore of every state of Europe, and particularly our inveterate enemies, must induce them to wish a revolt of our colonies on the continent of North America.' Not all these warnings were just for the record: even in private, prominent Americans thought that disunion with the colonies would damage Britain's position within the European state system. Thus the New York grandee Robert Livingston wrote in late December 1765 that the question was whether Britain's 'empire and trade shall be so extended as to make her the envy of the world', or whether 'being debilitated by the universal disaffection of her colonies she shall fall into decay and be finally ruined by the superior power of her European enemies'.[25]

In the end, Britain was forced to withdraw the stamp duties, but not before issuing a Declaratory Act, reiterating Westminster's right to tax the thirteen colonies. Clearly, the question had been shelved not resolved.

The preoccupation with America which began in the mid 1760s was to last almost two decades. It began at a time of continued ministerial instability in London. Grenville fell and was replaced by Rockingham as chief minister. The Duke of Grafton, an amiable nonentity, became Northern Secretary; Henry Seymour Conway, a Pittite, was made Secretary of State for the Southern Department. Meanwhile, as Britain's back was turned, the situation in Europe shifted dramatically to her disadvantage. In 1766, upon the death of Louis XV's father-in-law, Stanislas Lesczyński, Lorraine was finally annexed by France. This had been expected since the close of the War of the Polish Succession in the 1730s, but it was still most unwelcome. What had not been foreseen was the sudden increase of French activity in Sweden in 1766, which British intelligence picked up from dispatches intercepted at Hanover. Choiseul, in fact, now temporarily backed off from his commitment to naval revanche with Britain in order to concentrate on France's European interests, especially the use of her Swedish, Polish and Ottoman allies against Russian expansion. Versailles, it soon transpired, had abandoned its traditional support for the 'Hats' in favour of a restoration of royal absolutism in Sweden. Nothing else, Choiseul believed, would suffice to contain Russia. Of course, the forward strategy in Stockholm was also designed to secure Swedish naval support and the supply of Baltic naval stores, and thus to further an anti-British agenda in the long run. Choiseul was waging war against Britain in Europe.[26]

This news could not have come at a worse time. Relations with Prussia were still very poor and the danger to Hanover remained acute. In the autumn of 1766, in fact, Frederick the Great threatened to occupy a part of the Electorate in retaliation for the non-payment of sums which he believed were owed to him by Britain. In the resulting discussions, Newcastle went back over the question of the discontinued Prussian subsidies, like a tongue seeking out a sore tooth. 'I never exerted myself more upon any question in my life than upon that,' he remembered, so 'that His Majesty might have one ally in Europe'. Well might Newcastle emphasize this, as the current isolation of Britain in Europe spoke for itself, and it was on the demand for a rapprochement with Frederick that all royal attempts to inveigle Pitt back into the ministry since 1762 had impaled themselves. The wounds were still raw. It was therefore by no means fanciful for contemporaries to suspect that the Earl of Chatham (as Pitt had now become), the Prussians, and perhaps even the Hanoverian minister, were acting in collusion. One way or the other, the King decided on a change of ministry. Unpopular at home, stymied in America, and now facing a crumbling balance in Europe, which jeopardized the Electorate, George turned to the man who had once before turned defeat into victory. William Pitt, as the Earl of Albemarle wrote in the autumn of 1766, was recalled to office not least 'by advice' of the King's 'German ministers', as one well-placed observer put it. The Pittite and Wilkite strategy of 1762–3, by which foreign policy and especially the Prussian alliance would be used to recapture the executive, appeared to have worked.[27]

The new, and as it turned out final, administration of William Pitt was to be a last brief roll of the dice for traditional Whig big government and interventionist grand strategy before the onset of war in America. Pitt had stayed true to his interventionist convictions throughout the five wilderness years from 1761, even at the risk of irritating the King. Thus he greeted news of the marriage of Princess Augusta of England to the nephew of the Duke of Brunswick as good news for 'the Protestant interest and the independence of the [German] Empire' and together with a Russian alliance, a step towards 'the maintenance of a stable system in Europe'. His new Secretary of State for the North, Conway, was not completely free of navalist flourishes, but was generally more conciliatory than Sandwich had been. He observed in October 1767 that 'The unparalleled successes of the last war . . . have set England in so high a point of light, that the envy of our neighbours is more to be dreaded than a contrary sentiment; and the great object of our ministers is rather to abate the jealousy of the European powers, than to increase their reverence towards us.' In 1766–7, therefore, overtures were made to Russia and especially Prussia to construct a northern system of alliances. There was, as Pitt put it in late October 1766, *a great cloud of power in the north*, [which] should not be neglected'. Its purpose, as Conway elaborated, was to 'form a firm and solid system in the north, as may prove a counter balance to the great and formidable alliance framed by the House of Bourbon on the basis of the Family Compact'. He looked upon 'connections of Great Britain with the two great crowns of Russia and Prussia as the natural foundation of such a system'. Andrew Mitchell was sent back to Berlin; Pitt's crony Hans Stanley was put on notice to leave for St Petersburg, though in the end he never went. The Danes, Russians, Swedes, Dutch and a number of smaller German states were also approached. One observer spoke of 'the great northern constellation of alliances, which is to be the polar star of the European hemisphere, and it is supposed that this new discovery in astronomy is to be the object of Mr Stanley's mission'.[28]

The quest for a Russian alliance focused British attention once more on Poland, a classic eighteenth-century 'failed state', whose instability perpetually threatened to suck in outside powers. Here, as Conway put it in August 1767, the main aim was to 'prevent the effect of those unhappy commotions from spreading wider, or endangering the public tranquillity'. In fact, Poland returned to the European agenda with a vengeance in 1767–8, with the unveiling of King Stanislas August's reform plans. These might potentially turn Poland from a basket case into an eastern European power centre, threatening both Russia and Prussia. As the situation in Poland escalated in late 1767, London became anxious. In mid December 1766 Conway had grandly announced that as far as Britain was concerned, Poland was the least important country in Europe. Now he conceded that 'The continuance of the confusions in Poland is far from being an indifferent object and may be attended with events which cannot, at present, be exactly foreseen.' Intermittent concern for 'the toleration of the [religious] dissidents' was expressed. However, any sense of religious solidarity retreated before the strategic imperative to maintain European stability. Thus Conway feared that Catherine 'has touched two delicate points, the liberty and religion of the Poles, and the last, especially, if too hard pressed on, may occasion the most violent resistance'. In other words, London hoped that St Petersburg would not precipitate war through too hard a line against Polish Catholic chauvinism. But Britain's main concern was, as Conway put it in early January 1768, 'the cultivation of a perfect harmony' with Russia, which was 'the most central part of our northern politics'. No Russian alliance resulted, however.[29]

The approaches to Frederick the Great also came to nothing. He remained profoundly suspicious of Britain, repeatedly citing the 'betrayal' of 1762. Conway referred to 'the extreme backwardness His Prussian Majesty has shown towards any ideas of a more intimate connection with this court'. Frederick complained to Mitchell of 'the treatment he had met with from us when the late peace was made'. He also thought that British domestic instability made her an unreliable alliance partner. He 'talked of the instability of our measures and sudden changes in our administrations, which made it almost impossible to transact business with us with any sort of security'. Moreover, he feared being dragged into a Franco-British war, whereas his main quarrel was with Austria. There was still no joy in Vienna, where the British ambassador lamented in January 1767 that Austria's continuing attachment to the French alliance risked to 'see the liberties of Europe left, as it were, at the mercies of the House of Bourbon, having by the new connections of Austria lost one of their chief supports against the encroachments of that ambitious and powerful family'. The British envoy to St Petersburg likewise despaired. 'A treaty of alliance' with Russia, he ventured in February 1767, was 'as distant and unlikely to be brought about, as a league with Prester John [the mythical African King], or the King of Bantam [a sultanate on the island of Java]'. The Pitt of 1766–7 thus proved to be a very much reduced figure from the dynamo of a decade earlier. He was often unwell and his administration, which had begun with much fanfare and expectation, soon fizzled out.[30]

All this had serious implications for Britain's maritime position. As Charles Jenkinson, the Undersecretary at War, remarked in 1767, the question of the size of the Royal Navy was driven by the general European context. 'You must know what is the naval force of those who may become the enemies of this country,' he argued; what was decisive were the '[c]onsiderations arising from our own political state compared with that of the other nations of Europe'.

We were formerly considered as one only of the naval powers, and in conjunction with Holland and alliance with Spain were to resist the naval force of France alone ... After this, you [Britain] and Holland came to resist France and Spain [and] you after that began a war with Spain alone [1739], and just as France declared war with you Holland came to your assistance. She brought some good will but very little force in the last war [1756–63]: you stood against France and Spain singly but this was not all; every other power of Europe resisted you upon a great question of naval and commercial right to which if you had yielded it would have rendered your naval force half useless ... without a spirit of prophesying I will venture to say that you will begin a new war much in the same situation. France and Spain will be your direct enemies, and every other state of Europe will endeavour to draw commercial profit from the state of the war.

The upshot of all this, Jenkinson warned, was that 'We shall begin the next war with two enemies at a time.'[31]

British naval supremacy, in other words, had always been relative, and would not survive European isolation, at least not without massive additional expenditure. What is remarkable here is that Jenkinson had already lost sight of the Continental diversion; he failed to grasp that the lack of European allies not only deprived Britain of naval auxiliaries, but also enabled France to concentrate on ship construction. One way or the other, the resulting financial burden was considerable. As Jenkinson went on to observe, Britain's position was difficult, but it was 'at the same time great'. He warned MPs that 'your requisite establishments are enormous if you intend to maintain your position'.[32] All the same, Jenkinson did not flinch from the consequences:

The two great ends of security and economy, may seem at first view to combat each other, but it is our duty to reconcile them. Security must have the first place. Without this the whole may be lost, the whole is at least in danger. Economy can save a part only. The first therefore must be obtained, but in obtaining we should apply every principle of economy to render the burden as light as possible, and when once obtained we should stop.

He was thus articulating a broader primacy of foreign policy, by which strategic considerations took precedence over all others.[33]

In this context, it was unsurprising that ministers and public opinion should revisit the idea that the resources of Britain's imperial possessions could be further tapped, not merely to pay for their own defence, but to underpin British power more generally. In some parts of the Empire, London was reasonably successful, at least for the time being. Pressure was brought to bear on the East India Company to make a substantial contribution to imperial defence. In early February 1767 the Company agreed to pay the government £400,000 a year in return for a guarantee of its territories and various trading concessions on tea. The parliamentary regulation of that year – not least the measures designed to prevent the creation of 'faggot votes', the splitting of large stock holdings to maximize the vote of great shareholders – marked the beginning of increased government interference in the affairs of India. In 1771 the India Recruitment Bill increased the supply of soldiers. The reform of imperial defence and the architecture of government also moved ahead in Ireland, which was not strictly speaking part of the Empire. In 1767 Chatham stipulated that the Lord Lieutenant was henceforth to reside in Ireland full-time, not just while the Irish parliament was in biannual session. The intention here was to curb faction, exert greater control over the legislature, and thus ease the way for greater taxation. Moreover, in 1768–9 the Dublin parliament was eventually persuaded to agree to an increase of the Irish military establishment from the 12,000 men fixed under William of Orange to 15,000. For most of the century – in theory – no Irishmen were to be recruited into the British army. Catholics were believed to be unreliable, and Protestants were required to keep an eye on them at home. In 1771, however, this doctrine was formally dropped, and three years later an oath of allegiance for Irish soldiers was brought in to replace the more offensive religious test. Rebuffed in America, British strategists began to look to the great reservoir of Irish Catholic manpower as a 'weapon of war untried', which might yet serve to square the circles of imperial defence.[34]

But the most obvious source of additional financial muscle was America. Picking up earlier themes, the imperial propagandist and pamphleteer John Mitchell argued in 1767 that the thirteen colonies could make up for the relatively small population of the mother country. 'The increase of the colonies,' he wrote, 'would be a constant addition to the power and wealth of this nation,' and would thus ensure 'a balance of power more in favour of Great Britain'. Indeed, he concluded, America was 'the only equivalent [Britain] has, or can expect, for that great superiority, in numbers, which our enemies have over us in *Europe*'. So in 1767 the administration, under the direction of Charles Townshend, the Chancellor of the Exchequer, attempted to impose commercial duties on America. Like the Stamp Act this was a modest measure, designed solely to finance imperial defence, rather than the British military effort in general. According to its architects, the proposed duties on paper, tea, paints, glass and lead would have covered about 10 per cent of the cost of the American garrisons, hardly an extravagant sum. But to the colonists it was the thin end of the wedge, and they responded with another barrage of protests. Once again, they saw the taxes as a breach of the colonial compromise, because they were designed not to regulate trade but to generate revenue. The northern colonies and Virginia, in particular, were roiled by disturbances, but there was trouble in Boston and even Rhode Island. Two regiments were sent from Canada and another two from Ireland to deal with them, provoking cries against 'standing armies'. After 1768, Boston was effectively under military occupation. From this point onwards, violence in the thirteen colonies began to spiral out of control. The first fatalities were recorded at the 'Boston massacre' of March 1770, which left five civilians dead.[35]

As over the Stamp Act, the radical opposition in Britain was quick to side with the Americans. Not only did they emphasize the general link between domestic and colonial oppression, but they continued to argue that coercion in America would encourage European powers to take advantage of Britain while her back was turned. This came across very powerfully in a two-part print of 1768 entitled *The colonies reduced*, 'designed and engraved for the *Political Register*'. It foresaw a truncated and bankrupted Britannia beside a globe, her navy beached and easy prey for French and Dutch predators. Louis XV makes off with an Indian – clearly representing America – and proclaims, 'Now me vil be de grande monarque indeed! Me vill be King of de whole World.' Rounding out this picture of misery was a figure of the unfortunate Bute, long since fallen from power, helping Spain to sodomize Britain with a sword. In this way, Opposition discourse brought together popular xenophobia, homophobia and fear of relegation to the rank of second-class power. It was much the same association between effeminacy and national enfeeblement which had powered critiques of the court in the seventeenth century and of the ministry in the 1750s.[36]

35. Critics of the British government's confrontational policy towards the colonies stressed that only France and Spain would benefit. This satirical engraving shows the unmentionable fate in store for the nation.

Once again, London was forced to retreat. The Townshend duties were shelved; American affairs were hived off to the new Colonial Secretaryship created in 1768; and the inevitable confrontation was put off for another day. The net result of the continued tension between London and the colonists was to strengthen the hand of the annexationists in America, who now went from strength to strength in the colonial assemblies. As their influence grew, so did their ambitions. Benjamin Franklin, once a stalwart of *British* imperial expansion, now began to articulate a specifically American vision of grandeur. 'America,' he wrote in April 1767, 'an immense territory, favoured by nature with all the advantages of climate, soil, great navigable rivers, and lakes, etc., must become a great country, populous and mighty; and will, in less time than is generally conceived, be able to shake off any shackles that may be imposed on her, and perhaps place them on the imposers.' At the end of the decade the elections to the Massachusetts Assembly led to further gains for the 'expansionists'.[37]

Moreover, just as they had been during the Stamp Act crisis, the

Americans were aware of the European dimension, and increasingly used it as leverage against the ministry in London. A series of pamphlets in 1768 warned that only France and Spain could benefit from dissension between the colonies and the mother country. As Benjamin Franklin remarked in the following year, 'all Europe (except Britain) appears to be on our side of the question. But Europe has its reasons. It fancies itself in some danger from the growth of British power, and would be glad to see it divided against itself.' Not long after that – in April 1770 – he remarked that 'All Europe is attentive to the dispute ... At the same time the malignant pleasure which other powers take in British divisions may convince us on both sides of the necessity of our uniting.' At around the same time, a Boston pamphlet warned that it was only thanks to the colonies that Great Britain enjoyed 'her present opulence and greatness, which so much distinguish her among the powers of Europe', and that this position would only be maintained by cooperation with the Americans. Two years later again, a writer in the *Essex Gazette* of Salem wrote that 'It is evident, to every discerning eye, that perilous times are coming on in Europe, and that Britain is in imminent danger.' Hence, he continued, 'Nothing in the nature of things, can preserve Great Britain, but the affection and union of the Americans with her; and nothing can preserve this union, but a firm and speedy establishment of American liberty.'[38]

The ministry's second retreat over American duties in two years was not only a colonial and domestic humiliation; contemporaries believed that it undermined Britain's standing in Europe. Thus Franklin recognized that even those who were uneasy about the measure could not stomach the denial of parliamentary supremacy and the implications of American defiance. 'They fear,' he wrote in 1769, 'being despised by all the nations round if they repeal them; and they say it is of great importance to the nation that the world should see it is master of its colonies, otherwise its enemies on a conceit of weakness, might be encouraged to insult it.' In early October of that same year, a writer in the *Boston Gazette* traced the evil back to the Stamp Act. 'For tho' it was soon repealed,' he wrote, 'it yet created such a jealousy between the mother country and the colonies, as it is to be feared will never wholly subside.' All this, the author predicted, might well 'end in the ruin of the most glorious Empire the sun ever shone upon, or at least may accelerate consequences, arising from American independence, which, whenever they happen, will be fatal to Britain herself'. The thirteen colonies, so long a force-multiplier for Britain in Europe, were fast becoming a new front in the struggle between Britain and her Great Power rivals.[39]

20

Empire Adrift, 1768–1772

*I confess my political creed is formed on the system of King William,
England in conjunction with the House of Austria and the [Dutch] Republic seems the most secure barrier against the [Bourbon] Family Compact,
and if Russia could be added to this, I think that the court of Versailles
would not be in a hurry to commence hostilities.*[1]   George III, 1771

Just how far Britain had fallen from the pinnacle of 1763 was to become
apparent in a series of reversals from 1768. Within five years, a number
of bastions across Europe – Corsica, Sweden and Poland – had fallen.
These were not just diplomatic defeats affecting the overall European
balance; they had, and were widely perceived to have had, profound
implications also for Britain's naval security. In part, the responsibility
rests with the King, whose feel for the European situation was far weaker
than that of his grandfather. But George was a constitutional monarch,
and so the principal responsibility must rest with his ministries. European policy was in the hands of a succession of young and inexperienced
secretaries of state. Only the Earl of Rochford, who served for two years
as Northern Secretary from October 1768, was an old hand in the classic
Europeanist tradition. He provided some coherence after taking over as
Southern Secretary in 1770, by effectively acting as the senior Foreign
Secretary, but by then the damage had been done. Besides, he too was
prone to the general post-1763 arrogance, and mercilessly bullied the
Spaniards, not least over the Manila Ransom, the indemnity which the
Spaniards had promised in return for the sparing of Manila during
the Seven Years War, but which had not yet been paid. Otherwise the
ministries which took office after January 1768 were largely inexperienced in foreign affairs. The Prime Minister, the Duke of Grafton, was

a man of little understanding of European politics, despite his brief tenure as Northern Secretary. His successor, Lord North, was a more formidable figure generally, but not much better on European affairs. The principal courts of the Continent, convinced that Britain was entirely focused on the colonies, as well as domestically unstable, no longer thought her alliance worth having.

The first blow fell in the Mediterranean, and it was almost entirely unexpected. Ever since the Treaty of Aranjuez in 1752, which had brought centuries of Habsburg–Bourbon rivalry in Italy to a temporary end, the region had hardly featured in British concerns. Nobody, therefore, paid very much attention to the long Corsican rebellion against their Genoese occupiers. It was only in late April, when definite news of some form of phased and conditional transfer of the island from Genoa to France was in the offing, that London reacted. Shelburne responded that 'The fate of that island may undoubtedly become an object of the most serious nature to Great Britain . . . in case it should come . . . into the actual possession of France.' This was because 'it must be a great accession to that kingdom, not only of commerce, but of strength, by affording the goodness of some of its ports, the greatest advantages for annoying our Italian and Levant trade in time of war.' Some in London, such as Grafton and Shelburne himself, wanted a naval mobilization to head off the occupation. It was too late: France completed the purchase of the island from Genoa in May 1768. There was, in fact, nothing that could be done at this stage. Tentative overtures were made to the Sardinian ambassador, some belated support was given to the Corsican rebels as a delaying action. But it was a fait accompli. By mid 1769 France was in full effective control of the island. Neither Britain, nor France's own ally Spain – who was also opposed to the annexation – could do anything about it.[2]

There were many reasons for the Corsican fiasco. It came at a time when Britain was just emerging from the row over Townshend's American duties, and in the process of being convulsed by another round of Wilkite agitation. But the principal cause was the failure of British grand strategy, from which all these problems flowed. Since 1763, it had relied heavily on the naval deterrent. But this could not be brought to bear in the relatively favourable circumstances of the Corsican crisis, because of the priority accorded to America in British thinking. The prevailing view within the ministry was that France should be appeased over Corsica in order to concentrate on the thirteen colonies. Moreover, unlike in the earlier part of the century, British statesmen simply had no coherent view of the Mediterranean beyond Gibraltar, no system of alliances in Europe in general, and hence no room for manoeuvre as the crisis loomed. Yet the French acquisition of Corsica was not just – as Shelburne seemed to think – a limited threat to British commerce. It was a serious blow to Britain's position in the western Mediterranean, and reduced the security of her bases in Gibraltar, and particularly Minorca. It both symbolized and hastened Britain's general European decline. Nor was Corsica – after Lorraine – just France's second straight territorial gain in two years: it also came at a time of renewed French diplomacy across Europe, especially in Sweden. But perhaps the greatest damage was done to Britain's status as a Great Power. Her failure to curb this unilateral change to the Mediterranean balance, and thus to that of Europe as a whole, confirmed the already widespread view that Britain had turned her back on the Continent and was interested only in America. Britain, as the Russian chief minister Count Nikita Panin remarked in late October 1768, was no longer a 'land power'.[3]

The decline of British power was also manifest in the continued disintegration of the Dutch Barrier. In mid December 1769 news of Austro-French negotiations on 'settling the limits' of the Low Countries reached London. It was rumoured that in return for some concessions, such as the cession of Furnes or Ypres in Flanders, the French would support the opening of the Schelde, which would be – as the British ambassador to The Hague pointed out – the 'ruin' of the United Provinces. This was a double threat to British interests: not only did it weaken an old, though now very decrepit, ally but it would also loosen the system of constraints on French expansion. For this reason, British diplomats were instructed to remind the Austrians of treaties 'which expressly stipulate that no part of the Austrian Netherlands should pass into the hands of France or those of any other power by cession, exchange or in any shape whatever'.[4]

Unfortunately for London, the perception of British weakness was gaining ground at the very moment when she might have been poised to profit from new instability in the European state system. The outbreak of war between Russia and Turkey in 1768 seemed to provide an opportunity for a fresh approach to Catherine, not least because Choiseul was believed to be inciting the Ottomans. On the face of it, therefore, Russia and Great Britain had common ground against France, and in that year Lord Cathcart was sent on a mission to St Petersburg. Almost immediately, these negotiations impaled themselves on Britain's continuing refusal to countenance a subsidy payment in peacetime – Britain was after all not at war – or the 'Turkish clause'. Catherine was not prepared to accept the implied lack of reciprocality. She was also dubious about the value of alliance with a power in such obvious domestic distress, which had only just taken a massive French insult over Corsica lying down. This feeling was shared by many foreign diplomats in London who, as one observer remarked, 'wonder at our inattention to the proceedings of France'.[5]

Undeterred, Britain pursued a more active Mediterranean policy, partly to intimidate France but principally in the hope of getting closer to Catherine. The Russian fleet was afforded considerable logistical support – which in practice amounted to its reconstruction – while in transit from the Baltic to the Mediterranean. In the summer of 1770, as rumours of a French attack on the passing Russian ships mounted, British squadrons interposed themselves in the western Mediterranean, leading to a tense stand-off. The crushing victory of the Russian over the Ottoman fleet at Chesme on the Aegean coast of Turkey in July 1770 was thus very much down to the Royal Navy. On the strength of this, Rochford sanctioned a new approach to Russia in the autumn of 1770. The aim throughout was not to intervene in the Russo-Turkish conflict *per se*, but to release Russian forces for deployment in central, eastern and northern Europe, where British interests were more closely involved. Britain even offered to guarantee Russia's gains against Turkey in return for a Russian guarantee of British overseas possessions, a clear example of the relative priority awarded colonial and European concerns at the time, and of the prevailing strategic myopia in London. It also marked the beginning of Russia's geopolitical penetration of the Mediterranean, a process which Britain initially assisted but which later came back to haunt her.[6]

Nor was Britain any more successful in central Europe. Clearly, there was much that the two German great powers could do for Britain; it was less clear what London could do for them. As Joseph II, co-ruler of Austria with Maria Theresa, observed in the late 1760s, the value of a British alliance was very doubtful. Ministries in London were 'on a very weak and changeable footing', making Britain an unreliable ally. 'The frequent changes of ministry, the lack of unity between the various parties', and other domestic weaknesses were all noted in Vienna. Given this, the problems in America, and London's unwillingness to pay subsidies in peacetime, Joseph argued that 'Britain is no longer as formidable a power', nor would she be able to come to the aid of her allies as she had used to do. Moreover, Britain was currently 'isolated and almost without allies'. At the same time Austria and Prussia feared being dragged into a new Anglo-French colonial conflict via Hanover. They believed Britain to be pursuing the strategy of Continental diversion. As Joseph II put it, Britain would try to 'tie down [the French] through a land war, and thus give Britain the opportunity to concentrate all its resources on the Navy'. In August 1769, therefore, at their meeting at Neisse in Silesia, Frederick and Joseph II agreed to neutralize Germany in the event of hostilities between Britain and France, or indeed any similar European conflagration. Moreover, both princes were aware that they could retaliate against Britain in Germany itself. Thus Frederick the Great argued in the late 1760s that 'If we have serious disagreements with England, we can revenge ourselves on her by seizing the Electorate of Hanover, a territory ill-prepared to defend herself.'[7]

For the dynastic link to Hanover meant that Britain was still effectively a central European power. George III was still a German prince, who was taking an increasing interest in his Electoral lands. He greatly encouraged agricultural innovations there, and – significantly – in the early 1770s began once more to speak of plans to visit Hanover. Perhaps it was in anticipation of the voyage that in the summer of 1772 George commissioned a new Hanoverian silver service, by the French royal goldsmith, Robert-Joseph Auguste. This was delivered to his German palaces over the next decade, and the neo-classical swank of the design spoke volumes for George's desire to cut a figure within the Holy Roman Empire. Not for him the obsolete rococo centrepieces common at the smaller German courts, such as that of the neighbouring prince-bishop of Hildesheim. Interestingly, for all his bluff affectations, George's eating habits were conventionally cosmopolitan, with dishes from both of his empires; some of them had a distinctly German flavour. Thus the King and Queen Charlotte might dine on Italian 'Chicken Vermicelly' and French 'Pâté Perriguex', but also on Indian 'Rice Pillaw' and the ominously Teutonic 'Metworst of Sweetbreads' and 'Brounmole'. The latter was a stew brewed from pig's ears and feet. All this was garnished by turnips and ham shipped from the Electoral lands.[8]

More importantly, George was deeply involved in the politics of the Holy Roman Empire, both as King and Elector. His British envoy to the Reichstag at Regensburg remained essentially under the direction of his Hanoverian minister there. The instructions of January 1770 unambiguously told him 'in an especial manner [to] communicate with and take the advice of our [Hanoverian] minister, who by his capacity and experience in those matters will be able to give you the most exact informations and best advices'. In this way, George kept a close eye on the German balance of power. For example, Saxon ambitions were causing some concern in the early 1770s, and the British envoy to Electoral Saxony was instructed to investigate Saxon plans to infiltrate the major imperial ecclesiastical offices 'and thereby form a considerable power on the Lower Rhine'. The principal focus of George's German policy, however, was Catholic Austria. Here George's British aim of restoring 'the system of King William' through an alliance with Austria was completely at odds with his role as Elector; indeed, he was already planning to form a league of German princes against the Emperor. George had long been concerned about the threat which imperial ambitions posed to the integrity of the Empire and the security of the Protestant princes, particularly after the accession of the dynamic reformer Joseph II as co-regent in Vienna in 1765. Joseph in turn was highly suspicious of George, whom he regarded as in thrall to his Hanoverian ministers. He accused the King of allowing them 'a complete liberty to cabal as much as they wish with other Protestants and constantly block imperial authority'. As far as Joseph was concerned, the Hanoverian ministry was 'directed by Protestant zealots' who threatened the peace of the Empire. Charles VI could not have put it better. In short, the King of England was no less exposed in central Europe around 1770 than his predecessors had been in the forty-odd years after the Hanoverian succession.[9]

On the other side of the world, meanwhile, Britain continued to throw its naval weight around. The 1760s had been punctuated by a series of colonial stand-offs with Spain, usually caused by overzealous colonial subordinates. In 1770–71 these culminated in the Falkland Islands crisis. For in June 1770, the tiny British garrison at Port Egmont was ejected by a Spanish force. Thanks to the prevailing Francophobic paradigm, London was convinced – quite erroneously – that the directing mind of

Choiseul lay behind the Spanish action. In September, London mounted a substantial naval demonstration in response, particularly in the Mediterranean, indicating the Royal Navy's ability to escalate the conflict into areas closer to Spain itself. Such was the speed and power of British preparations that they quickly outstripped those of the Spaniards, and in consequence encouraged the ministry to take a harder line with them than was absolutely necessary. Parliament and public opinion erupted in a belligerent frenzy – Chatham made no fewer than eight speeches on Spain and the Falklands in 1770–71, voted 40,000 seamen, and generally limited the room for compromise. Throughout the controversy North was driven by the fear that Chatham would use the issue to lever him out of the ministry.[10]

At stake here, of course, were not the islands themselves. The lieutenant of marines stationed there wrote that the Falklands were 'the most detestable place I ever was at in my life', barren of everything 'except sea lions and seals', and swarms of 'fishy geese'. Edmund Burke described them as 'a barren, desolate rock'. What was at issue was nothing less than the question of hemispheric dominance: the Falklands were a staging post for a British drive into the Pacific Ocean around Cape Horn. Hitherto the Pacific had been an entirely Spanish lake, whose tranquillity had only been briefly interrupted by Anson's expedition around Cape Horn in the 1740s, and the attack on Manila in 1762. Now, or so it seemed to Madrid, the British tide seemed to lap at both ends, from both the Indian Ocean and the South Atlantic. The British, on the other hand, were determined not to allow another slap in the face on Corsican lines. The ministry would not survive one. Fortunately for London, Spain had pressed ahead in expectation, but without assurances, of full French backing. Choiseul, however, was not yet ready for a revanche. Even combined, the Bourbon fleets were still unable to match the Royal Navy; in purely numerical terms, they might be slightly larger, yet the disparities in experience and seamanship were such that Choiseul preferred not to risk it. Moreover, he remained firmly concentrated on Europe: he feared that war with Britain would prevent him from containing Russia in the east. Louis XV also got cold feet. In the end, with the rug pulled from under its feet, Spain had to back down, and settled for a secret promise that Britain would evacuate the islands in due course. Choiseul was sacked. On the face of it, Britain's triumph was complete.[11]

It proved to be a pyrrhic victory. Naval intimidation came at a considerable diplomatic cost. The repeated humiliations of the Bourbon powers stored up resentment for the future and destroyed any hopes of reconciliation. Nor did the crushing of Spain somehow expunge the shame of Corsica, or make Britain a more attractive alliance partner in Europe, least of all to Russia. On the contrary, none was to be more critical of British naval arrogance than Catherine. A sense that Britain had become a law unto itself on the high seas – a maritime 'universal monarch' – was now commonplace in Europe. But the greatest damage was to the intellectual fabric of British policy. Once again, naval measures had won out; all the prevailing unilateralist instincts were confirmed. The Southern Secretary, Lord Weymouth, had been prevented with difficulty from launching a pre-emptive naval attack on Spain. These tendencies were confirmed by the return of Sandwich to the Admiralty in 1771. In a purely technical sense, he was superb, and his activities generated an enthusiasm for the Royal Navy in the royal family not known since the Stuarts. The problem was that in the absence of any European allies, Sandwich was fashioning an efficient policy instrument on which London increasingly relied, and this made British statesmen lazy. Not everybody thought this preoccupation with sea power a good thing. Even such an ardent colonialist as Lord Hillsborough, Secretary of State for the Colonies, lamented the widespread notion that British 'naval power is able to give the whole universe laws . . . A language of this nature may be very fine in romance, but men of business experimentally know, and laugh at the absurdity.'[12]

The decline of Britain's international position stoked the domestic critique of Crown and ministry. In particular, the letters of 'Junius', which burst on the scene in January 1769, attacked the weakness of British foreign policy. In May of that year, it was argued that Corsica 'would never have been invaded', if Britain had shown firmness, a theme to which he returned again and again. The nation, the author claimed, was being treated with 'contempt' by foreign powers. He also lambasted the 'economy' which had led to 'disgrace . . . in the eyes of Europe'. Britain, this radical polemicist argued, should spend more on Continental subsidies. After the Falklands crisis, 'Junius' lamented that the chance for a preventive war on Spain, while France was still weak, had been lost. This, he claimed, would have 'dissolved the Family Compact' and allowed Britain to dictate 'the law to Spain'. 'Junius' concluded by warning that the nation would come to regret this timidity 'when the collected strength of the House of Bourbon attacks us at once'.[13]

In Parliament, Chatham called for a parliamentary inquiry into the circumstances surrounding the French annexation of Corsica. 'By suffering our natural enemies to oppress the powers less able than we are to make a resistance,' he argued, 'we have permitted them to increase their strength.' With Corsica, he lamented, 'France has obtained a more useful and important acquisition in one pacific campaign, than in any of her belligerent campaigns: at least while I had the honour of administering the war against her.' He compared this 'pacific conquest' to the case of Lorraine, which had fallen under the effective control of France in the 1730s, and was formally annexed in 1766. Likewise, the West Indian merchant William Beckford lamented that 'no notice . . . is taken of an impending war', because 'the desertion of Corsica, and the addition of that island to the power of France, has made a war with that powerful and insidious neighbour' more likely. Moreover, he pointed out, both France and Spain were not only engaged in extensive naval armaments, but also had forces deployed overseas threatening British colonies. 'These are objects,' he concluded, 'that require attention, and yet no attention is paid to them.' The loss of Corsica was also seen as a further nail in Britain's naval coffin: the Marquis of Rockingham predicted that 'this island would prove a great addition to the strength of France, with respect to her marine; both from its harbours, and the timber it produced'.[14]

Beckford's prescription, however, was straight out of the lexicon of British navalism. Rejecting 'servile, slavish, tame, temporizing measures', he was 'for striking the first blow', that is a pre-emptive naval smash-and-grab raid on the Spanish overseas empire to remedy Britain's 'scarcity of silver'. Nearly forty years on from the Spanish agitation of the 1730s, the colonial mirage – the idea of rich pickings at the expense of New Spain – was still potent. Perhaps realizing the absurdity of his demand, Beckford concluded by admitting that 'My zeal . . . may perhaps have carried me away from the particular point in view.' Even Chatham, who knew full well the limitations of naval power, resorted to the unilateralist maritime rhetoric of his youth, when he unfavourably contrasted British policy during the Falklands crisis – which was drastic enough – with the 'peremptory demand[s]' of the Grenville ministry during the row with France over Turks Island. What was needed now, he argued, was 'peremptory, decisive language' against the 'mean and crafty' Spaniards. This was, of course, a return to his demand for a pre-emptive strike in 1761, only this time the strategy was no longer embedded in a Continental alliance, but conceived within a framework of deepening European isolation.[15]

Britain was thus ill-equipped to deal with the triple crisis which erupted in northern and eastern Europe. In September 1770 Britain's Baltic position, so robust in the 1760s, suddenly began to unravel when the well-disposed Danish chief minister was deposed in a palace revolution. His successor, the court physician Count Struensee, was seen as pro-French and anti-Russian. He exerted a strange supremacy over the feeble Danish King, and – worse still – had become the lover of the Queen, George III's sister, Caroline Mathilda. Not only had Denmark been 'lost', but the dignity of the British royal family had been compromised. The overthrow of Struensee in January 1772 by a court cabal only created new problems. Caroline Mathilda was now threatened with execution on the grounds of treason and adultery. Britain chose to interpret this as a slight on George, who was outraged by his sister's behaviour but feared for her life. Once again, London resorted to a naval demonstration, which was paradoxically designed to protect the lover of the pro-French minister from the wrath of Britain's natural allies. Thanks to this intervention, Mathilda was released, and in a final gesture of naval hubris the Danes were forced to salute the British ship sent to pick her up. This was a victory of sorts, but it had been bought at the price of humiliating a friend.[16]

Even as Britain flexed its naval muscles at Copenhagen, the ground was beginning to shift in Stockholm. For in August 1772 King Gustavus of Sweden launched his long-awaited royal *coup d'état*, with French support, utterly outflanking British and Russian countermeasures. If British statesmen or pamphleteers were revolted by this reassertion of European absolutism, they concealed it well. As Horace Walpole remarked in autumn 1772, since 'whichever gets the better, the people will still remain slaves, I am pretty indifferent to which side the power of tyranny falls'. It was purely strategic considerations which drove the Secretary of State for the South, Lord Suffolk, to try to restore the Swedish constitution of 1720 with Russian help. A French triumph – which threatened to throw the Swedish navy into the scales on their side – was bad enough, but the violent Russian response was even more worrying. Throughout late 1772 and 1773 an invasion of Finland, and even an amphibious assault on the Swedish heartland of Scania itself, in the south of the country, seemed likely. France threatened to attack the Russian Mediterranean squadron. Britain risked being caught in the middle. As Rochford put it, if Russia invaded Sweden, perhaps in concert with Prussia, 'and if a French fleet in consequence of it sails to the Baltic, we cannot be idle spectators, and a general war must of course ensue'. The usual naval demonstrations followed, but while these could help to contain the problem, there was nothing Britain could do about the loss of Sweden. As the veteran British diplomat Joseph Yorke noted with alarm, 'a new scene is opened in Europe which may break through many schemes and arrangements, and which French money has brought about.'[17]

Nothing illustrated the diplomatic irrelevance of Britain – and the indifference of the political nation towards the European balance of power – better than the partition of Poland. For in August 1772, the three eastern powers announced that the old Polish Commonwealth would be divided between them. Russia lopped off a substantial slice of eastern Poland, the Austrians grabbed the prosperous province of Galicia, while Frederick the Great contented himself with a smaller but strategically vital strip of West Prussia which rounded off his territories. The still substantial rump of the Polish state remained nominally independent. This crisis had been brewing for some time, yet in the midst of it, Lord North, who had taken over as Prime Minister in 1770, was telling Sandwich at the Admiralty that he did 'not recollect to have seen a more pacific appearance of affairs than there is at the moment: France, neither from the disposition of her prince or her minister or from her own situation, seems likely to engage in a war for some years.' He concluded, 'This is the time, if ever there was a time, for a reasonable and judicious economy.' Even allowing for North's concern to cut naval expenditure and reduce the national debt, the disconnect between the British Prime Minister's perception and the conflicted reality of the European state system at the height of the Swedish and Polish crises was remarkable. Even more surprisingly, the division of Poland, a major European state, caused barely a ripple in London, and in the public sphere. Once upon a time, British statesmen and opinion had been profoundly preoccupied by events there: whether or not Britain should enter the lists on the Austrian side in the War of the Polish Succession had dominated politics in the 1730s. Forty years later, several million square miles of land and millions of souls changed hands almost noiselessly. There can be no better illustration of the extent to which Britain had turned her back on Europe as a whole, and had become mesmerized by developments across the Atlantic.[18]

There was some unease in diplomatic circles about the shameless collusion of three great powers at the expense of a weak state. 'As to all the iniquitous transactions in Poland and the tyrannical treaties which confirm them,' Joseph Yorke remarked from Holland, 'they make me quite sick.' The British ambassador to Vienna, Lord Stormont, also vented his outrage. Thus Maria Theresa noted in early September that 'Stormont, who was hitherto well-disposed, is at present hostile, outraged as he is by the partition of Poland.' Others welcomed the partition as a well-deserved comeuppance for the bigoted Polish nobility. The sufferings of Poland, one newspaper correspondent wrote, 'have been greatly her own fault. Her intolerancy in religion, her tyrannical oligarchy, her senseless *liberum veto* [by which a single magnate could block progress in the Polish diet], her systematic corruptness, could not well afford a prospect of a less deplorable catastrophe than what they are now undergoing.' Now that the eastern empires had finally decided to foreclose on this failed state, the argument ran, this could only be for the greater good.[19]

Moreover, the ministry was divided on which eastern empire to back. Most continued to support the resurrection of the old system with Vienna, so in theory any gain in Austrian power was a bonus. As one newspaper correspondent observed, the despoliation of a state could not be condoned, but in principle 'for every foot of land which Austria gets it were devoutly to be wished that she should get twenty, if but to raise her to a most necessary and desirable pitch of greatness, relative to France and Spain.' But the crucial thing was to secure a Continental ally. As Suffolk argued in September 1772, the King 'therefore will be cautious how he takes any step that may hereafter embarrass and throw impediments in the way of this capital object'. Certainly, he continued, the Polish partition was 'not of sufficient present importance ... to induce His Majesty to risk that invaluable consideration' of a European alliance. Besides, taking on the Prussians or Austrians would endanger Hanover. From Holland Joseph Yorke warned that 'Hanover [was] ready to be swallowed; which is a dead weight.' 'Atticus' asked who would 'protect Hanover (the only thing we can be stripped of by Prussia) against the invasion of these three united powers?' Likewise, a correspondent in the *Morning Chronicle* feared for Britain's 'Hanover possessions on the Continent', which would provide 'convenient' pickings for her enemies. The *Bristol Gazette and Public Advertiser* remarked, 'It is generally imagined by those who seem best acquainted with the secret springs of government, that the dread of a Prussian army in the Electorate of Hanover has altered the intentions of our court relative to the propriety of sending a squadron up the Baltic.'[20]

For all these reasons, the King's Speech of late November 1772 expressed no view beyond hoping for peace in eastern Europe. In the House of Commons the MP who moved the address of thanks argued that the conflict between the Russians and the Turks, which had prompted the partition, 'was but a matter of little or no consequence to Great Britain'. He added that, 'thank God, the ideas that formerly governed the British councils in matters of this nature no longer exist' – in other words, that the interventionist consensus of the years before 1760 was no longer in the ascendant. There was no Opposition assault on the passivity of the ministry. A public sphere which had long been extraordinarily sensitive to and well informed about European developments, now had very little to say about a major shift in the general balance of power. Neither the ministry nor popular opinion proved able to grasp the real lesson of the crisis: that the Austro-Prussian-Russian constellation over Poland effectively destroyed any chance of exploiting differences between them to achieve an alliance. America crowded everything else out. George III admitted as much in early August 1772, at the height of the crisis, when he told Lord North that 'We must get the colonies into order before we engage with our neighbour.'[21]

There was not much else to be done. The partition of Poland, and Britain's obvious irrelevance to the emerging eastern European order, starkly exposed the limitations of naval power. As Horace Walpole famously remarked in the context of Polish partition, the fleet 'being so formidable will, I suppose, be towed overland to Warsaw and restore the Polish constitution and their King to his full rights – how frightened the King of Prussia must be'. He was satirizing the conceptual impoverishment of British foreign policy, which had degenerated into a series of ad hoc naval demonstrations against vastly inferior powers. Because the British could so easily compel, they had forgotten how to persuade. It was a Palmerstonian 'gunboat diplomacy', *avant la lettre*. Most had no quarrel with this. All the familiar isolationist themes, which now constituted the hegemonic discourse in Britain, were rehearsed once again. In July 1772 the *Gazetteer and New Daily Advertiser* pronounced against 'involving the nation in a Continental war . . . in which we have as little concern as we should have in a war between China and Japan'. 'By whom hath Great Britain been injured?' 'Pacificus' asked in September. 'Let us no longer play the Quixote,' he demanded, 'by meddling with matters, and entering into quarrels, wherein neither our honour nor our interest are at all concerned.' All this was garnished with classic navalist and insular rhetoric. Rather than taking on the eastern empires, one correspondent argued, 'France and Spain are the powers we ought always to view with a jealous eye, because they are great maritime powers; and it is on the sea alone we can ever be hurt by a defeat . . . The sea is our only bulwark.'[22]

The debate over Poland, and indeed the conduct of British policy as a whole, pointed to another mental constraint in London: the reflexive anti-Bourbon, and particularly anti-French framework within which all strategic thinking took place. A graphic illustration of the popular failure to comprehend diplomatic developments beyond the Franco-centric paradigm was the engraving *The Polish plum cake*, by J. Lodge, which was published two years after the Partition. Not unreasonably, it depicted the three eastern powers settling down to carve up the Polish cake; quite gratuitously and misleadingly, France, which had vigorously defended Poland's integrity, was also shown taking its slice. There were two problems with this tunnel-vision. First of all, it distorted strategic thinking: many Britons were unable to see the broader picture for hatred of France. 'What do you say to the affronts offered to France,' one British observer exulted in early July 1772, 'where this partition treaty was not even notified . . . How that formidable monarchy is fallen, debased.' The idea that the partition of Poland might have damaged British interests in ways unrelated to France occurred to only a few. Secondly, the ingrained Francophobia of the British elite and public sphere frustrated the chance of a rapprochement with Versailles which opened up in the early 1770s. The new French chief minister, the Duke of Aiguillon, who took over from Choiseul in 1771, was anxious to continue the containment of Russia in the east, and thus open to a British alliance. For a brief moment, France trod softly in the colonies and on the high seas, so as not to provoke her potential ally. Rochford and one or two other British statesmen were prepared to consider his overtures, and the shock of the Polish partition also made George III see the merits of cooperation between London and Versailles.[23]

But the prevailing Francophobia, which they had done so much to encourage, deprived ministers of all room for manoeuvre. Thus Chatham attacked any attempt to support the Ottoman Empire, or to mediate a peace between it and the Russians, as a service to France. He also opposed any succour for France's traditional allies, Sweden and Poland. Even Rochford himself, in many ways the most sophisticated British practitioner of the time, remarked in April 1771 that 'the national policy as well as the dignity of this country can never admit us to be quiet spectators whilst France is glorying in the work of her own hands, in the elevation of her determined ally the King of Sweden.' Pamphleteers poured further scorn on the idea of a French alliance. Aiguillon's overtures were thrown back in his face. 'Conscious of their own weakness,' 'Atticus' crowed, '[the French] sue for our friendship. If they are now too weak to be dreaded, that is no reason why we are to make them our bosom friends.' One correspondent demanded that 'neither Hanover nor Poland [should] serve for a cover to so false a measure as that of any connection or concert with the courts of Versailles and Madrid'. The very idea, another objected, 'is a Tory measure entirely conformable to Tory politics. Tories have ever been friends to France.' All this blocked the possibility that Britain might, as after 1716, break out of her isolation through a French alliance based on common interests in the Baltic and the Mediterranean.[24]

Only a small minority of observers believed that the Partition of Poland heralded a massive shift in the European balance of power, and indeed in the customary law of nations. One of these was the Irishman Edmund Burke, a loyal Rockinghamite Whig. More to the point, he was a staunch Whig in foreign policy, who believed that British power should be deployed in support of the liberties of Europe. To Burke the Partition was, as he claimed in his celebrated article in the *Annual Register* for 1772 (which appeared in July 1773), 'the first very great breach in the modern political system of Europe'. The unprovoked dismemberment of a large European state by a coalition of predators seemed to create an ominous precedent. This – it was argued – was not just of general concern, but a direct threat to British interests. After all, as one observer remarked, 'It is impossible for Great Britain to remain an unconcerned spectator of the troubles on the Continent.' Likewise the pamphleteer John Lind noted, 'You in England are very apt to say, "We are an island and what have we to do with the affairs of the Continent?"' Yet, he continued, 'you must maintain your commerce to which you owe the value of your lands, your wealth and your importance in Europe: and therefore whenever the transactions on the Continent affect your commerce so materially, as the present designs do, you are as much concerned in them as the powers of the Continent themselves.' Likewise, Burke doubted that 'the insular situation of Great Britain weaken[ed] the application' of the principles of the balance of power as much as some claimed. He ventured, not without irony, 'that a single man, cast out from the laws, the protection and the commerce of his whole species, might in that solitary situation, with as rational and well-grounded a probability, propose to himself convenience and security, as any single state, in the present political and physical state of Europe could expect independence and safety, unconnected with all the others.' Britain might physically be an island, but no state was actually completely cut off from other countries. The echoes of John Donne were unmistakable.[25]

Far from being a remote Eastern European spat, some felt that the Partition of Poland had weakened the Holy Roman Empire and its barrier function. According to John Lind, the dynamic unleashed by the 'final loss of Poland will be the signal for the ruin of the whole Germanic body'. Indeed, he continued, 'What security have Denmark and Sweden, the states of Germany and Holland, the cantons of Switzerland and princes of Italy, that this alliance will not be as fatal to them as to Poland?' Likewise, Burke noted that 'Poland was the natural barrier of Germany, as well as of the northern crowns, against the overwhelming power and ambition of Russia'. The partition now threatened 'totally to unhinge the ancient system of Germany and the north'. Poland might now be 'the road by which the Russians will enter Germany'. In the *Annual Register*, Burke spoke of Poland as a 'barrier . . . to prevent the clashing of the German and Muscovite empires'. All this also greatly increased the exposure of Hanover to attack at the hands of the eastern powers. In short, on this reading, the Partition of Poland was a devastating blow to the European balance of power, which Burke described as the 'system [thanks to which] this small part of the western world [Britain] has acquired so astonishing (and otherwise unaccountable) a superiority over the rest of the globe'. Military action to reverse it, he implied, would be fully justified. 'Wars may be deferred,' he wrote, 'but they cannot be wholly avoided; and to purchase present quiet, at the price of future security, is undoubtedly a cowardice of the most degrading and basest nature.'[26]

The fates of Corsica and Poland made a considerable impression in the thirteen colonies. Enthusiasm for the Corsican patriot Paoli and his resistance to French occupation peaked in late 1768–9. In part, this was generic sympathy with fellow victims of despotism, as Americans saw it, but there was also outrage, to quote a toast of the 'Sons of Liberty of Boston' at the 'infamous attack from France, while shamefully neglected by every power in Europe'. Some feared that because Britain was now so weak, America would go the same way and be partitioned at the hands of a Bourbon coalition. The progressive military retreat from areas beyond the Appalachians was symbolized by the abandonment of Forts Bute and Panmure on the Mississippi in 1768, and Fort Chartres in 1772, for reasons of cost. This was not encouraging for those colonists who saw their future within a dynamic and growing empire, and who wished to forestall French and Spanish claims to these regions. To them, the British Empire was already collapsing, long before the Revolution; indeed, it was this sense of imperial collapse which prompted them to rebel, not the other way around. Others, particularly those who opposed western expansion, thought that the Polish experience was an argument against independence from Britain, which would simply deliver them into the maw of her European rivals. All were sobered by events in Poland. Indeed, the Partition would have an important afterlife in America, resurfacing during the constitutional debates of 1787, when it was advanced as an argument against a weak central government in an age of predatory great powers. James Madison, for example, claimed that 'Germany and Poland are witness to the danger' of a weak executive influenced by outside powers. Americans had seen the Polish Commonwealth all but destroyed; a weak state had been dismembered in full view of Europe, and without the British ministry lifting a finger. What neither London nor the colonists yet knew, was that the bell would soon toll for the British Empire as well.[27]

By the early 1770s, British isolation in Europe was an established fact. Rochford wrote in November 1772 that 'The situation of Europe at this

36. Like many American patriots, John Adams started out as an ardent
British imperialist and remained preoccupied with the European state system
throughout his career.

very instant of time is become . . . critical.' This was largely because, in
his view, British restraint had allowed 'our natural great rival [France]
an opportunity of forming such connections in the north which may
make them as formidable there as they have for some time been by their
alliance in the south, whilst we have not a single friendly power or ally
to boast of'. Surveying the European scene, Rochford noted the total
Bourbon stranglehold in the Mediterranean, and Vienna's acquiescence
in it. He lamented the 'arbitrary and tyrannical' dismemberment of
Poland, and argued that the French-sponsored 'revolution in Sweden'
prevented Britain 'from forming any system there to counterbalance
her southern alliances'. Meanwhile, the search for an Austrian alliance
continued: the triumph of hope over experience. The ambassador in
Vienna was instructed to seek a 'renewal of our ancient and reciprocal
friendship'.[28]

All this mattered intensely because Britain, contrary to contemporary
navalist rhetoric, was by no means completely separate from the Continent. To be sure, England itself was still largely invulnerable to attack,
but the same was certainly not true for Ireland. In mid October 1770,
at the height of the Falklands crisis with Spain, the Lord Lieutenant

Viscount Townshend (elder brother of the unfortunate Charles Townshend who had attempted to impose duties on America in 1767), was
asked to 'suggest what [was] necessary for the defence and security' of
Ireland 'should things with the united powers of France and Spain
proceed to extremity'. He took the opportunity to remind London that
there was 'not one good and permanent fortress' on the island and
of the 'disproportion of numbers between the Protestants and Catholics,
the oppressed and wretched condition of the latter, devoted to their
priests'. He went on to point out that in 'three out of four' provinces –
Ulster was the exception – security was guaranteed only by the 'protection of the British fleet and the submission of the wealthy Roman
Catholics to His Majesty's government'. As if all this were not bad
enough, Jacobite sympathies persisted not only among the Irish abroad,
but also in key southern regions. France and Spain, Townshend warned,
were 'a restless enemy in constant correspondence with the disinherited
and bigoted inhabitants of their own religion'. Worse still, England itself
seemed to be in danger. George was receiving reports of a possible enemy
surprise attack against Portsmouth. The naval situation was critical, he
was told, because with 'our Austrian alliance dissolved, and the armies
and arsenals of that, and of every other great power removed to a
considerable distance from her frontiers', France was now free 'to establish the seat of war in England'. The Duke of Newcastle and generations
of Whig strategists could not have put it any better.[29]

Britain's isolation was thus also a naval disaster. For the past decade
the Admiralty had been following the progress of French naval preparations with concern. Sandwich felt Britain's relative naval weakness
keenly, the more so as British isolation led to greater reliance on the
naval deterrent. With regard to the Falklands crisis, he observed, 'Had
we broke with Spain the other day, I am convinced that we should have
lost the East Indies and possibly Gibraltar, and suffered by the capture
of an immense number of our merchantmen, before we could have had
a fleet in readiness.' He drew from this the lesson, however, that Britain
should hold back from Continental entanglements, rather than press
ahead with them in order to divide the naval strength of her enemies, as
an earlier orthodoxy had had it. Thus in the autumn of 1772 he
expressed his anxiety about 'the late event in Sweden, which if it
occasions an alliance with Russia, as it very probably may, will most
likely draw us into a war in the course of the next year'. Moreover, time

was very soon to show that European isolation would matter to Britain's position overseas as well. By late 1772 the news from intelligence sources was truly alarming. 'Since the peace,' Rochford was told, 'the greatest attention has been paid to their [France's] navy.' The result was that France now possessed a fleet 'far superior to that at the beginning of the last war from the goodness of the ships, which are mostly built since the peace'. Moreover, although numerically still much weaker – about one-third the size of the Royal Navy – the French fleet had a 'great advantage . . . in manning their fleets, which . . . will always give them a superiority at the beginning of war'. In short, the report concluded, 'the French with their present force are a very formidable maritime power, and which force will be considerably increased in a very few years as they are building very fast in all their ports.' He might have added that Britain was now failing to divide its potential naval adversaries, or to divert their resources from shipbuilding into the army through an active balance of power policy. The worst-case scenario, which Jenkinson had been warning about in 1767, was moving closer.[30]

A glance at the figures shows how British naval power was beginning to lose ground to France in the late 1760s. In 1765 the total British tonnage was still greater than that of the two Bourbon fleets combined. Five years later that was no longer the case, and by 1775 France and Spain had drawn still further ahead. In 1766–70, Franco-Spanish new construction of ships was more than double that of Britain. Indeed Britain only began to increase its naval construction substantially in the early 1770s, but not in time to make up the lost ground before the outbreak of the American War.[31]

At the same time, Britons remained profoundly divided at home. To those who complained that domestic disunity damaged Britain's European standing, which was certainly true, critics responded equally plausibly that a divided Britain could not be an effective actor on the international scene. Thus the MP Sir William Meredith was not proposing 'that we should tamely suffer the insult of Spain'. Rather, he claimed that 'till our rulers have the confidence of the people, it is impossible' for Great Britain 'to do herself justice'. 'As the first requisite therefore to obtain justice abroad,' he concluded, 'let the people be satisfied at home.' Edmund Burke warned in 1772 that 'he who shall advise hostilities against the Bourbon Compact, till a compact shall take place between Great Britain and her colonies, is a foe or a driveller.' It was only 'by mutual confidence and attachment,' he elaborated, that 'we may look our enemies in the face'. Pitt charged the ministry 'with having destroyed all content and unanimity at home, by a series of oppressive, unconstitutional measures; and with having betrayed and delivered up the nation defenceless to a foreign enemy'. On this view, the successive failures of the British state in Europe and overseas, and its increasing despotism at home, were all part of a broader malaise. From the late 1760s, only a few years after the triumphs of the Seven Years War, Britons had seen first the loss of Lorraine, then the unexpected fall of Corsica, and finally the dismemberment of Poland. Yet each of these pillars of the balance fell not with a crash, as in previous crises, but with a barely audible whimper in Britain. The rapid disintegration of Britain's architecture of European security was not enough to trigger a change of ministry in London. It would take a crisis across the Atlantic to do that.[32]

VIII

Imperial Nemesis

21

Fighting for Europe in America, 1773–1777

[W]hat can France desire more, than to see her rival sinking every year, from being mistress of the world, land and sea, into the bubble of her enemies, and the scorn of nations. She will therefore leave us to pursue, unmolested . . . our own plans of self-destruction, and let peace ruin us, without risking a war.[1]

Earl of Chatham to Baron Bridport (Admiral Hood),
6 June 1773, Burton Pynsent

No one doubts the advantage of strict union between the mother country and the colonies, if it may be obtained and preserved on equitable terms. In every fair connection, each party should find its own interest. Britain will find hers in our joining with her in every war she makes, to the greater annoyance and terror of her enemies; in our employment of her manufactures, and enriching of her merchants by our commerce; and her government will feel some additional strengthening of its hands by the disposition of our profitable posts and places. On our side, we have to expect the protection she can afford us, and the advantage of a common umpire in our disputes, thereby preventing wars we might otherwise have with each other; so that we can without interruption go on with our improvements, and increase our numbers. We ask no more from her and she should not think of forcing more from us.[2]

Benjamin Franklin, 1773

[T]he page of future history will tell how Britain planted, nourished, and for two centuries preserved a second British empire; how strengthened by her sons, she rose to such a pitch of power, that this little island proved too mighty for the greatest efforts of the greatest nations. Within the space of twenty years, the world beheld her arms triumphant in every quarter *of the globe, her fleets displayed victorious banners, her sails were spread, and conquest graced the canvas. Historic truth must likewise relate, within the same little space of time, how Britain fell to half her greatness; how strangely lost, by misjudging ministers, by rash-advised councils, our gracious sovereign, George III, saw more than half his empire crumble beneath his sceptre.*[3]

Duke of Manchester, House of Lords, November 1775

Was it for us, who had exclaimed so loudly against universal monarchy, to raise such a combination against us, which might one day prove our ruin, whether we conquer or we are conquered?[4]

Alexander Carlyle, Scottish clergyman, sermon of 1776

By the early 1770s, Britain's project of imperial reconstruction was in some disarray. The East India Company – which had promised to be such a milch-cow in the late 1760s – was effectively bankrupt by 1772. It would now be hard put to sustain the defence of British interests on the Indian subcontinent, let alone cross-subsidize the security of the Empire as a whole. All this had very serious implications for Britain's strategic situation. As the MP William Burwell remarked in November, during the discussion on the future of the Company, 'let no gentleman think this is a trivial question of ministry or opposition. No, sir, it is [the] state of Empire' which was at issue. He added that 'perhaps upon it depends whether Great Britain shall be the first country in the world, or ruined and undone'. Chatham hoped that 'Hindostan, under the present plan, may not bury Old England in its incurable disorders and inextricable confusions'. The ministry reacted by effectively taking over the East India Company: the Regulating Act of 1773 ensured that the Company would be responsible to London. Meanwhile the colonial and naval cold war with the Bourbon powers escalated. As Edmund Burke put it, 'we are not engaged in open hostilities, but we maintain an armed peace. We have peace and no peace, war and no war. We are in a state, to which the ingenuity of our ministry has yet found no apt name.' A solution to Britain's fiscal crisis would therefore have to be found, and quickly, if she was not to put her global security in jeopardy.[5]

This made Lord North all the more determined to press ahead with fiscal and governmental reform in America. The overarching question, as it had been throughout the eighteenth century, was what form of imperial organization could best deploy and multiply British power within the global – especially the European – state system. Some argued that Britain's strength lay in its commercial vibrancy, which would be lost to civil strife. As Josiah Tucker warned in 1775, 'a shopkeeper will never get the more custom by beating his customers: and what is true of a shopkeeper is true of a shopkeeping nation.' So should one try to work with the grain of existing, ad hoc and organically developed structures, as Edmund Burke advocated, or should a thoroughgoing programme of reform and standardization be forced through? This, proponents believed, might lead to short-term disruption, but was the only way of guaranteeing fiscal solvency and military security over time. Almost exactly the same problems were confronted at the same time in Joseph II's Habsburg monarchy, so the British experience was not unique, though it was to be particularly painful.[6]

In May 1773, Lord North introduced his famous Tea Act. It was designed not to coerce the Americans, but to help the flagging East India Company stamp out smuggling and to maximize colonial revenue. The move was driven by London's need to secure its position in the international system, not by any constitutional and fiscal vendetta with the thirteen colonies. Confrontation with the Americans, however, was to be the inescapable consequence. Ever since the late 1760s a low-level conflict between customs officials and smugglers had poisoned relations, and discussions about the establishment of an Anglican episcopacy in the thirteen colonies – which horrified Nonconformist opinion there – only added to the tension. In this context, North's Tea Act was seen as yet another threat to the liberties of colonists. More importantly, while the Americans supported a hard line with the Bourbons, they had no intention of paying for it, at least not under a ministry in which they had lost all confidence. As far as the colonists could see, Britain was in full-scale hemispheric retreat. The last of Britain's mouldering forts in the interior were abandoned before they crumbled into the Mississippi. More seriously, the plan for a new western colony – to be named 'Vandalia' in honour of Queen Charlotte's Germanic ancestors – finally collapsed in the summer of 1773. In May 1774 the Falkland Islands were evacuated, partly to save money and partly to appease Spain. The Americas were being given over to the Bourbons, or so it seemed, and there was much worse to come.[7]

American radicals responded to the Tea Act with the famous 'Boston Tea Party' of December 1773, during which thousands of pounds' worth of East India tea was seized and hurled into the water. An impasse had been reached in North America. Troops had been billeted there since 1768; the first blood had been split in Boston in 1770. On each previous occasion, in 1764–5, in 1767–8 and now in 1773, the colonists had seen off the metropolis. This time London was determined not to back down. British retaliation was swift. Parliament passed a series of coercive measures, starting with the Boston Port Act, designed to punish the immediate perpetrators, or at least to force the local authorities to do so. Various other steps followed, culminating in the Massachusetts Government Act of March 1774, which was designed to eliminate the unruly 'democratic' element in the colony. News of this reached America a month later. British troops now began to assert themselves by searching for arms, and intimidating patriot leaders. The Americans did not dispute London's right to levy lucrative indirect duties on colonial commerce, all of which was carried in British vessels. But they would not yield on the question of direct taxation which, in the absence of representation at Westminster, they regarded as a violation of their rights as free-born Englishmen. At this stage, only a tiny minority of the colonists thought of independence. They saw themselves as subjects of George III, but not as subjects of his subjects, that is the Westminster Parliament. Instead, they wanted a personal union with Britain under the Crown which was not entirely unlike that with Hanover, although the comparison with Ireland was more common.[8]

To many contemporaries, and to later generations, the quarrel seemed to be about taxation and representation; liberty and authority; ideology and religion; and even identity. The war certainly was, or came to be, about all of those things as well. But in its origin and essence, the struggle in America was a particularly drastic form of debate between two visions of British grand strategy. For what finally precipitated the breach was North's move to settle the problem of Quebec. As war with the Bourbons loomed in the early 1770s, it became imperative to neutralize any potential French Canadian fifth column. Moreover, as the Anglican Bishop of Nova Scotia warned in 1771, the Indians – many of whom were believed to be under the sway of French Jesuits – could not currently be relied upon in the event of a war of revanche either. The solution was the conciliation of Catholics under the Quebec Act of June–July 1774. This was modelled on the arrangements for Minorca after 1713, where a modus vivendi with local Catholics had quickly been reached, in order to secure Britain's position in the western Mediterranean. The Act was driven by strategic considerations – to cut the Catholic population loose from France – rather than any more general late-eighteenth-century intellectual shift towards toleration. It was of a piece with other security-inspired relief measures of the 1770s, particularly in Ireland. Here a rapprochement between the government and the Catholic elites was on the cards, as the threat of elite Jacobitism receded after the death of the Old Pretender in 1766, and the British state looked longingly at the untapped reserves of Irish Catholic manpower. The problem was that religious toleration was a political threat to colonists on both sides of the Atlantic, as it tended to undermine the very basis of their supremacy. For this reason, the Quebec Act produced immediate controversy in both Britain and North America. The colonists and their metropolitan sympathizers objected strongly to the acceptance of French law and the absence of representative assemblies; the toleration of papists was regarded as an additional affront.[9]

Yet when all was said and done, the principal reason why the Quebec Act gave such mortal offence to the thirteen colonies had nothing to do with religion, or liberty *per se*, and everything to do with strategy. For the Act not only regulated the *internal* governance of Quebec, it also laid down the *external* borders of the province. All land between the Ohio and the Mississippi – subject of furious debate between London and the expansionist settler lobby since 1763 – was now incorporated into Quebec. In the eyes of many North Americans this threatened an encirclement of the thirteen colonies by an absolutist government – a resurrected New France; it restored the pre-1763 threat. Benjamin Franklin lamented that 'the establishing an arbitrary government on the back of our settlement might be dangerous to us all'. The Act awarded to Quebec the very western territories into which the colonists hoped to expand, partly to line their own pockets, partly to create a buffer zone, and in some visionary cases – such as Franklin himself – in order to place British imperial power on an even more secure footing. If the Act were allowed to stand, the thirteen colonies would be penned into a geopolitical reservation from which they could not hope to escape.[10]

Moreover, unlike with the Proclamation Line of 1763, the British government now had the troops to enforce the Act. Throughout June

1774 the Bill was subjected to savage parliamentary attacks by Chatham, who worked closely with American representatives, especially Benjamin Franklin, but to no avail. In September the patriot Arthur Lee announced that 'every tie of allegiance is broke by the Quebec Act, which is absolutely a dissolution of this government; the compact between the King and the people is done away with.' To be sure, much of this was outrage at the Act's religious provisions, but Lee was also reflecting the sense that London had abandoned the security of the colonies and the 'Protestant cause' in America. The religious and the strategic critiques here were two sides of the same coin, just as they had been in seventeenth-century England. In his 1774 *Summary of the rights of British America*, Thomas Jefferson attacked the Proclamation Line on the grounds that the King had 'no rights to grant lands of himself'. After some discussion among the colonists at the Continental Congress, the Quebec Act also formed part of the petition of grievance sent to the King at the end of the year.[11]

It is therefore no coincidence that the irrevocable slide to revolution in America took place at the very moment, 1774, that the government had finally foreclosed all the options thrown up by the transatlantic debate on British grand strategy. Only a year before, Franklin had responded to whispers of renewed war with France by announcing that 'as the House of Bourbon is most vulnerable in its American possessions, our hearty assistance in a war there must be of the greatest importance'. On the narrowly economic issues, some Americans still had an open mind. Thus in 1774 Franklin still argued that the Navigation Acts, or at least 'those parts of [them] which were of most importance to Britain, *as tending to increase its naval strength*, viz. those restraining the trade . . . were as acceptable to us as they could be to Britain'. In other words, the path to a reconciliation with the colonists would be through a mutually agreed strategy of expansion. Even as late as August 1774, Franklin claimed that with the right policies 'we might have gone on extending our western empire, adding province to province as far as the South Sea [Pacific Ocean]'. The strategic choice for the colonists now was to break out or to abandon their grand imperial vision for good. The American Revolution, in short, had its origins in a long argument about the direction of British foreign policy, and the increasingly pressing but essentially subordinate question of who should pay for it. It was exactly the same issue which had driven Englishmen to fight each other during the two seventeenth-century civil wars.[12]

Moreover, the American crisis was not taking place within a European vacuum, quite the contrary. Britain was as isolated as ever. Relations with Frederick the Great were particularly frosty, not least because the London government was opposed to Prussian plans to acquire the vital Baltic port city of Danzig. British public opinion, on the other hand, could not work up much passion about this – nobody wanted to die for Danzig – but it mattered to Frederick and deepened his suspicion of Britain. In November 1772 – twenty years after the ill-fated Emden Company – Frederick the Great founded the Prussian *Seehandlung*, ('Oceanic Trading company') a modest but clear claim to a share of the maritime cake and a calculated poke in the eye for Britain. Elsewhere things were no better. In June 1773 Anglo-Russian negotiations, which had dragged on since the late 1760s, finally collapsed after a dismissive audience between Catherine and the British ambassador. As for the United Provinces, Yorke wrote in December 1773 that these were 'not worth talking about . . . whilst the Republic persists in its absurd and feeble system'. One way or another, London had ceased to be of much account; so when in January 1774, after the death of Sultan Mustapha III, the Chief Black Eunuch at Constantinople (the Master of the Harem and effectively the second most important man in the empire after the sultan) asked London to mediate with Russia, this was surely a sign of desperation on his part rather than a recognition of British power.[13]

Nobody saw the dangers more clearly than Burke. In May 1774, the month of the Quebec Act, he upbraided the ministry 'for that conduct which saw Corsica seized in one part of Europe, and Poland dismembered in another, with the most torpid indifference'. He put the aggression of the other Great Powers – all of whom had made substantial territorial gains since the mid 1760s – down to the low regard in which Britain was held. He predicted that 'the time will come when the new system will be seen in all its impotence and folly; and when the balance of power is destroyed, it will be found of what infinite consequence its preservation would have been.' Burke repeated his lament for Poland. 'Pray dear sir, what is next?' he asked. 'These powers [Austria, Russia and Prussia] will continue armed. Their armies must have employment. Poland was but a breakfast, and there are not many Polands to be found. Where will they dine?' Yet not even Burke foresaw that the partitioning powers were to the south, and that they would next dine in America.[14]

As if all this were not bad enough, the showdown with the colonists in 1773–4 loomed at the very moment when George III's cold war with the Austrians in central Europe was reaching its climax. Here the King was not just pursuing a narrowly Hanoverian agenda; there were many German princes who were worried about the ambitions of Joseph II. George also saw the Holy Roman Empire as part of a much broader European arena. He sought to deny the French any German subsidy treaty, perhaps with Bavaria, 'in case of a war arising in Germany'. Likewise, his concern with Saxon ambitions was firmly in the context of fears about French interference in Germany. At the same time, George sought to raise the cost of the French alliance for Vienna, through a vigorous and religiously sectarian *Reichspolitik,* and thus ease the way for a resumption of the old system. As the new decade dawned, therefore, George was becoming increasingly embroiled in a stand-off with the Emperor. His British envoy to Regensburg was instructed to warn the Austrians that Joseph would not be allowed to attack the rights of the 'estates', the princes and entities who made up the Holy Roman Empire. Insults, religious polemics and straightforward Hanoverian obstruction-ism became routine and threatened to bring the public business of the Empire to a complete halt. George was thus not only facing a possible Bourbon coalition on the high seas, but also remained completely friend-less in Germany. No wonder Joseph Yorke complained in mid December 1773 that Britain was 'so hampered with the situation of all the Great Powers of Europe, that we hardly know which way to turn ourselves'.[15]

It was to get worse. The British minister at the Reichstag was instructed 'in an especial manner [to] communicate with, and take the advice of our [Hanoverian] minister, who by his capacity and experience . . . will be able to give you the most exact information, and best advices for your behaviour and acting at Ratisbon'. No sign here of the strict separation between British and Hanoverian concerns often associated with George III. The main target of this cooperation remained Austria. In July 1774, on the eve of the American War of Independence, George and Hanover blocked the reform of the imperial courts, one of Joseph's pet projects, and he in turn made a declaration blaming the King and his Electorate for the delays. All this certainly wore down the Austrians, as intended, but it also ate into precious reserves of German goodwill at the very moment when George and Britain were going to need them. Moreover, as under the first two Georges, ministers were shy of taking on the King over Hanover. The Austrian envoy to London, Count Belgioso, reported that when he complained about George's latest intervention in German politics, it became clear that 'no British minister will dare to make unwelcome representations to the King, and expose himself to falling into disfavour as a result, over a matter so far from his own concerns'. Vienna was furious and instructed Belgioso to make 'verbal representations of our dissatisfaction'. If the King of England continued to behave like a German power, the Austrians were tempted to treat him as one, particularly in order to retaliate against Britain. Goaded by George's provocations, the Austrian envoy to London was reported as saying that 'If the King of Great Britain avowed the language lately held by his Electoral minister, he must expect the Emperor to oppose him in every step he took in the Empire.' By mid December of that year the British ambassador to Vienna was observing all this with increasing despair. 'If you ever should be singular enough to wish to see daylight [brought] into the obscure arcana [secrets] of the Holy Roman Empire,' he wrote to Anthony Chamier, the Secretary to the Commander-in-Chief of the Army in London, 'I will carefully anatomize the whole of that *rotten carcase* for your inspection.'[16]

The serious escalation of violence in the thirteen colonies continued throughout 1774, and culminated in the inaugural meeting of the Continental Congress in Philadelphia in September. For the first time since the fiasco at Albany twenty years before, Americans met and deliberated as one body. The dozens of mini-debates on westward settlement which had been played out in the various assemblies now fused into one great discussion. It was the final triumph of the expansionists: the west would be won, if necessary without Britain. As Henry Laurens predicted in February 1775, 'a mighty empire . . . will arise on this continent where she [Britain] cannot hinder its progress.' Fighting between Crown forces and rebels broke out in Massachusetts in late April of the following year, and by mid June 1775 British troops were engaged in full-scale warfare with the Americans. The first major battle at Bunker Hill went badly for the rebels, but in political terms it was a heavy defeat for London. In August 1775 George issued a Royal Declaration of a state of rebellion in the colonies. America, a hard-won strategic asset, had now become a major liability.[17]

And yet most in America still shrank from independence. Many of those striking extremist positions in 1774-5 did so in the hope of undermining the North ministry and compelling George to recall Chatham. They hoped that he would reconcile all domestic factions and the colonists in a common strategic enterprise founded on westward expansion and war with the Bourbons. It was to be 1756 all over again. That was certainly Franklin's strategy, but it did not work. Even so, in its resolution of October 1774, the First Continental Congress still explicitly referred to 'our connection with Great Britain [which] we shall always carefully and zealously endeavour to support and maintain'. The following year, the Second Congress announced that 'we mean not to dissolve that Union which has so long and so happily subsisted between us . . . we have not raised armies with ambitious designs of separating from Great Britain and establishing independent states.' Apart from sentiment, what held Americans back was the fear that an independent state would not long survive in the predatory world of the Great Powers. As the Virginian Robert Beverley remarked in 1775, 'We may rise, grow rich, and be happy under the fostering protection of Great Britain, but without her parental aid, must become victims to the first foreign invader.' Europe, in other words, was still keeping Americans and Britons together; soon it would help to drive them apart.[18]

For it was not only competing strategic visions for the west which now divided the two sides, but also the question of European connections. The Tory emphasis on Britain's imperial, insular and maritime destiny, which made so many in London determined to hold on to America, played very differently in the thirteen colonies. Transplanted there, it suggested that Americans should hold themselves aloof from Europe and reject attempts by the home country to involve them in the affairs of the Continent. Israel Mauduit's *Considerations on the present American war* had been widely read, as was Bolingbroke's *Letters on the spirit of patriotism*, of which the New England patriot John Adams was a particular fan. The themes of both men were reprised by James Burgh in his *Political disquisitions*, which appeared in Philadelphia in 1775. In it Burgh attacked 'Continent schemes' and 'Continent connections'. The Americans, he argued, should best 'keep clear of quarrels among other states'; they should not 'entangle [themselves] with the disputes between the powers of the Continent'. Even Franklin, who had long hoped for an Anglo-American strategic partnership against the Bourbons, came to believe this. In 1770 he wrote that 'the enormous load of debt, which sinks us almost to perdition' had been run up in support of 'our romantic European continental connections', not as a result of colonial defence. By early 1775 he had convinced himself that – as one of his fictional characters put it – 'I have no natural cause of difference with Spain, France or Holland, and yet by turns I have joined with you in wars against them all. You would not suffer me to make or keep a separate peace with any of them, though I might easily have done it to great advantage.' Those who supported the Crown in America were known as 'Tories', and yet the 'patriots' who demanded independence have a much better claim to be regarded as heirs to the 'Tory' and 'patriot' tradition in British foreign policy. They were heirs of Boling-broke, and they were to be no less partial to France than he had been.[19]

If London rejected accommodation with the colonists, this was primarily because of European imperatives. First of all, America was seen as a vital test of British credibility: backing down would involve a fatal loss of face. As Joseph Yorke, the long-serving ambassador to Holland, remarked shortly before the outbreak of the rebellion, 'I don't see how the government can give way, without losing the colonies and becoming the scorn of Europe.' 'We must set America aside,' he wrote in mid December 1774, 'before we can negotiate in Europe with ease of heart.' George III expressed himself very similarly. Secondly, America was not just a question of Britain's reputation, but also of vital resources necessary to sustain her European position. The belief that the colonies were an essential pool of some 50,000 seamen may have been absurdly exaggerated – there were hardly one-tenth of that number actually available – but it was no less genuine and ubiquitous for that. Thus nineteen dissident peers pointed out in 1775 that it was the 'valuable resources' of America 'which enabled us to face the united efforts of the House of Bourbon' in the last war.[20]

This was not a straightforward question of money: the sugar islands of the West Indies were much more valuable in that sense, and these remained loyal throughout. Indeed, some ministerial voices in London were beginning to ask whether the thirteen colonies were all worth fighting for. The Undersecretary at War, Charles Jenkinson, no friend to the Americans, believed the northern colonies to be a millstone around Britain's neck. Not only did they contribute little economically, but they were expensive to defend. 'In a political light,' he wrote in 1775, 'it is my opinion that the four New England provinces are not only no advantage but a considerable detriment to Great Britain unless they are made to bear their proportion of the common defence.' For this reason, he recommended that the 'wisest measure that can be pursued will be to endeavour to conquer the southern provinces only and to make Hudson's River the barrier of our Empire'. One way or the other, he did not think it was 'worth [Britain's] while at any time to reduce to a complete state of subjection the northern provinces, which are not in a commercial light of any advantage to her'. The 'credit' at stake in America was both strategic and moral – in terms of 'reputation' – but it was not financial in any meaningful sense of the word.[21]

But whereas ministerial opinion was firmly of the view that America had to be coerced into pulling its weight in support of Britain's Great Power role, the Opposition came to a completely different conclusion from the same starting point. Thus the London pamphleteer Egerton Leigh argued that 'America is a hen that lays her *golden eggs* for Britain'; Britain should not 'kill' America if she wanted to sustain her European position. Another argued a year later that 'It is by the American continent only that the balance of power can be any longer in [Britain's] hands.' By controlling the thirteen colonies, he argued, 'you command both the Americas, command Spain and Portugal, influence France and other powers of Europe and . . . therefore instead of checking her increase by a jealous and hostile policy, you ought to encourage it by every just and generous institution'. Only through cooperation with the colonists, the argument ran, could Britain uphold her Great Power status; the ministry maintained that this could only be achieved through force. Either way, what Britain was really defending in America was not the British Empire as such, or an abstract constitutional principle, but her European position.[22]

The patriots, of course, were well aware of Britain's strategic anxieties, and traded on them. In October 1773 the Boston Committee of Correspondence – which had been established by the assembly of Massachusetts in 1764 to coordinate opposition to the stream of legislation coming from London – noted that 'Great Britain was expected to find itself in a [European] war in the near future,' which would give the colonists leverage to overturn repressive measures. The Virginian Arthur Lee remarked that 'There is not a part of the world upon which France looks with a more attentive eye than upon America. There is not the smallest event, relative to our proceedings towards the colonies, of which they are not minutely informed.' Likewise in the summer of 1775 Thomas

Jefferson noted that 'the component parts of the [British] Empire have ... been falling asunder, and a total annihilation of its weight in the political scale of the world seems justly to be apprehended.' Moreover, he continued, 'if indeed Great Britain, disjoined from her colonies, be a match of the most potent nations of Europe with the colonies thrown into their scale, they may go on securely. But if they are not assured of this, it would be certainly unwise.' Clearly, Jefferson had read the European situation better than his adversaries in London. So too had the Second Continental Congress. Its Declaration of July 1775, most of which Jefferson had drafted, claimed that 'Our cause is just. Our union is perfect. Our internal resources are great, and, if necessary, foreign assistance is undoubtedly attainable.' The patriots, in short, would not hesitate to widen the conflict into a European war if need be.[23]

Despite this, many in the British elite slithered into war with the colonists in a cloud of hubris and bluster. From his posting in Vienna, Sir Robert Murray Keith wrote that: 'I am out of all patience with the six hundred congresses of as many ragged American villages ... I would not hurt a hair of their crazy heads if I could help it, but I would enforce the laws with temper and moderation in order to impress upon their memories the first salutary lesson of filial obedience.' He added that 'John Bull can quarrel and box with his own brother, and give or take a black eye with every exertion of his hot headedness, but to shake hands and be friends again, without the smallest remnant of rancour, is a species of benevolence which, as far as I know, belongs to John exclusively.' To those who stressed the 'impracticability of conquering America', the head of the Admiralty, the Earl of Sandwich, responded, 'Suppose the colonies do abound in men, what does that signify? They are raw, undisciplined, cowardly men. I wish instead of 40 or 50,000 of these brave fellows, they would produce in the field at least 200,000, the more the better, the easier would be the conquest.' The MP George Lyttleton dismissed fears that war in America would precipitate Bourbon intervention. He called on the ministry 'to exert yourselves, even as a means of keeping your natural enemies and ambitious neighbours in that state of awe and reverence towards you'. Others – perhaps the most far-sighted among them – believed they had no choice but to throttle a potential rival at birth. Thus Lord Mansfield warned that 'If we do not ... get the better of America, America will get the better of us.'[24]

For the first time ever, Britain was fighting a colonial war without the distraction of a European campaign or the threat of one. It proved to be a much less straightforward matter than many expected. The prosecution of the war raised some immediate problems. True, Britain enjoyed command of the sea, and could thus deploy forces at will along the coasts of the thirteen colonies. Further inland, however, it was quite another matter. Unlike previous conflicts, the Americans were now on the other side; British regulars were few and far between. Short of a mass mobilization in Britain, which would take time and was politically undesirable, London had only two options. One was to raise men locally, which in practice meant bribing Indians or arming runaway slaves; this was done with some misgivings. The other possibility was to revert to the tried and trusted German mercenary. Here the Hanoverians proved extremely useful once again. In 1775, troops were sent from the Electorate to Gibraltar and Minorca in order to release British forces for service in America. Later, in 1781, two more battalions were sent to India. In total, George as Elector was to 'lend' himself as King five Hanoverian battalions. This helped, but more troops would be needed. To that end, Britain sought to hire men from German princes. This proved difficult, not least because of the failure of Britain's European policy. Frederick the Great disrupted the process at every turn. Undeterred, British agents and diplomats pursued an assiduous *Reichspolitik* – or rather *Soldatenpolitik* – among the smaller German courts, which was closely coordinated with the authorities in Hanover. In the end, some 18,000 trained and equipped Germans from Hesse-Kassel, Waldeck, Hesse-Hanau, Brunswick and one or two other principalities were ready for battle in 1776, a huge number without which the British campaign would surely have collapsed in the early stages. It was in recognition of this contribution that Joseph Yorke wrote in March 1776 that he planned to meet the hired Hanau Regiment on its journey to British service: 'I wish to show these honest Germans who are to fight our battles, some attention when they fall in my way.'[25]

These troops came not only at a financial but also at a strategic price. Some of the German princes – feeling exposed by the departure of their forces – insisted on British security guarantees. Thus the Landgrave of Hesse-Kassel was assured by treaty that in case he 'should be attacked or disturbed in the possession of his dominions, His Britannic Majesty promises and engages to give him all the succour that it shall be in his power to afford'. All being well, this was a purely hypothetical commitment, but in the context of increasing Austrian encroachments in Germany nobody could be sure. As one peer, the Earl of Effingham, observed, the guarantee was only supposed to cover self-defence, but took no account of the imperial constitution. 'A case may happen,' he speculated, 'in which by a decree of the imperial chamber [the courts of the Holy Roman Empire], the directors of the circle [the sub-unit of the Empire to which Hesse-Kassel belonged] are ordered to march into the country, to compel the Landgrave to some act of justice or restitution.' In that case, Effingham concluded, 'we must either excuse our breach of the treaty by our ministers' ignorance of the imperial constitutions, or else enter into a war, to subvert the liberties of the Germanic body'. Even as she tried to prosecute an entirely colonial war, therefore, Britain found herself being sucked willy-nilly back into the European state system.[26]

All of Britain's eighteenth-century conflicts were domestically controversial, but the American War divided the country as never before. Most now refer to the conflict which led to the creation of the United States as the 'American Revolution' or the 'American War of Independence'. But it was also the first American civil war, which pitted loyal colonists and Indians against rebel colonists as much as it did redcoats against Yankees. The rebels did not for the most part begin their struggle with independence in mind, but sought rather the vindication of their rights as Englishmen. In March 1775, for example, the patriot Arthur Lee accused ministers of 'violently blowing the coals into a flame that will lay waste the whole British Empire . . . In short a civil war is inevitable.' Their cause found a corresponding echo across the Atlantic, where it became the perfect stick with which Whig critics, 'country' Tories and radical agitators could beat the government and the monarchy. Depending on how one computes them, the American Revolution was the 'third or fourth civil war' on this side of the Atlantic, or, to be more precise, the 'first *British* civil war'. Thus in 1775 Lord Camden lamented a 'civil and unnatural war'. Nineteen dissident peers of 1775 – protesting against the coercion of the Americans – spoke of an 'unnatural war'. In short, from the outbreak of war in 1775 to its conclusion in 1783, controversy over America racked British popular and parliamentary politics. British defeats were received with ill-concealed *schadenfreude* by the Opposition; toasts were drunk to the rebel commander, George

Washington; insults were exchanged in and out of Parliament on a regular basis; and challenges to duels were carried back and forth. The Secretary of State for America, Lord George Germain, was hounded at every turn by an Opposition determined to resurrect his alleged coward-ice at the Battle of Minden during the Seven Years War, some twenty years earlier.[27]

At its most basic, critics believed that Britain was simply in the wrong. 'We are the aggressors,' Chatham argued. 'We have invaded them. We have invaded them as much as the Spanish Armada invaded England.' 'If I were an American,' he added, 'I would never lay down my arms – never – never – never.' Opposition was also driven by a political agenda. Its purpose was to isolate the King and the Tory ministers who had encouraged him in what Whig critics regarded as the unconstitutional use of his prerogative. On this reading, the attack on American freedom was of a piece with the attack on their own rights. The Earl of Rocking-ham, a Whig grandee, feared in June 1775 that 'If an arbitrary military force is to govern one part of this large Empire . . . it will not be long before the whole of this Empire will be brought under a similar thraldom.' As the Whig leader Charles James Fox put it towards the end of the conflict: 'if the ministry had succeeded in their first scheme on the liberties of America, the liberties of this country would have been at an end.' He was therefore 'pleased with the resistance which had met their attempt'. In a nutshell, the survival of British liberty at home required the survival of American liberty, and in consequence the military defeat of Britain. Those who wished to bring this about were not traitors; they simply had a different way of expressing their patriotism.[28]

Because the American cause was believed to be about English liberties, the ministry's use of unfree men and supposed savages to suppress it gave particular offence. Edmund Burke remarked in 1775, when there was talk of hiring men from Catherine the Great to send to Poland, 'I cannot with ease see Russian barbarism let loose to waste the most beautiful object that ever appeared upon this globe.' The Duke of Rich-mond condemned the emancipation of blacks to fight the colonists. 'To arm negro slaves against their masters,' he argued, 'to arm savages, who we know will put their prisoners to death in the most cruel tortures, and literally eat them, is not, in my opinion, a fair war against fellow sub-jects'. 'Merciful heaven!' John Wilkes exclaimed. 'Thousands of Indian savages let loose, by the command of a British general, against our

The Parricide.
A Sketch of Modern Patriotism.

37. The American Revolution was not merely a civil war in the thirteen
colonies, but also, as this print suggests, a British civil war.

brethren in America! Human nature shrinks from such a scene.' The
Indian, he claimed, 'drinks the blood of his enemy, and his favourite
repast is human flesh'. Such a policy, he concluded with a xenophobic
flourish common to progressives at the time, was 'only becoming a
Jewish priest to a Jewish King, in the most bloody and barbarous of all
histories, the history of the Jewish nation.'[29]

In this context, the hire of Hanoverians – if only to free up British
forces – and the dispatch of German mercenaries for service in America
took on the appearance of a sinister absolutist plot. This was, of course,
an old trope in British discourse, except that it was now deployed by
Whig critics against the Tories. Thus a Commons protest of 1775 stated
that the deployment to Gibraltar and Minorca of 'Electoral troops,
without any previous consent, recommendation or authority of Parliament, is unconstitutional'. It went on to complain: 'That Hanoverian
troops should, at the mere pleasure of the ministers, be considered as a
part of the British military establishment, and take a rotation of garrison
duties through these dominions, is, in practice and precedent, of the
highest danger to the safety and liberties of this kingdom.' The move, in
short, was a violation of the Act of Settlement. Highlighting the issue of

Hanoverians and the Hessian mercenaries thus enabled the Opposition to revive the old narrative of British liberty versus German despotism. John Wilkes, now Lord Mayor of London, condemned this use of 'Hanoverians and Hessians, who are now called to interfere in our domestic quarrels'. Governor Johnstone asked 'whether there is any step that can reduce the reputation of this country so low, as that of depending on the Electorate of Hanover for the interior government of its own subjects? . . . How are the mighty fallen since the peace of 1763? What a spectacle for Europe.' 'Can German officers,' he enquired, 'without knowing our language, swear they will administer justice according to a law they do not understand?' All this showed that the question of the King's German identity, which many had thought settled by the accession of George III in 1760, remained very much a live issue in British politics.[30]

But opposition to the American War was not just an extension of the ideological splits and high-political wrangling of the 1760s and early 1770s. It was first and foremost part of a continuing critique of British foreign policy since 1763. Whatever one felt about America, many thought that the ministry was waging the wrong war. They considered Britain's principal enemy to be France and Spain, not the colonists, and they expected the Bourbon powers to take advantage of Britain's predicament to further their agenda in Europe, or even worse, to unite with the colonists against Britain. Thus in 1774, the Opposition MP George Johnstone, naval officer and former governor of British West Florida, argued that 'every wise man must foresee, that our rivals in Europe cannot be idle spectators'. These voices swelled after the outbreak of hostilities in 1775, as the eyes of Europe turned to America. 'There is not a man of sense in Europe,' Keith observed from Vienna, 'who does not think that the question now in agitation between Great Britain and her colonies, is one of the most important, as well as most singular that have been canvassed for centuries.' The Opposition MP David Hartley argued in early May 1775, 'It is next to infatuation and madness, for one moment to suppose that we can have an American without a French and Spanish war . . . Nothing but the most infantine credulity can believe the contrary.' For as the nineteen dissident peers opposed to coercing the thirteen colonies pointed out, 'while we are making these fruitless efforts' to suppress the Americans, 'we are preparing an easy prey for those who prudently sit quiet' for the time being.

Likewise, Edmund Burke was reported warning in mid November 1775 that 'The longer our distractions continued, the greater chance there was for the interference of the Bourbon powers, which in a long protracted war, he considered not only as probable but in a manner certain. That he was very sure this country was utterly incapable of carrying on a war with America and their powers acting in conjunction.' On this reading, the war was a form of British self-laceration. The *London Evening Post* lamented that 'The death of every soldier, and every American in this war, and every destruction of property in America is an irreparable loss to Great Britain and matter of joy to France, who will always be on the watch to destroy us.'[31]

These critics, in short, viewed the American War primarily through the framework of European Great Power politics. They agreed with the ministry and George III that the loss of America would be a body blow to Britain's European position. Thus the Whig Sergeant (his first name, not his rank) Adair warned the House of Commons that the commerce of America 'will not only be totally lost to [Britain], but, at least as to the benefits of their commerce, thrown into the hands of other powers, most probably her natural enemies'. He foresaw that Britain would be 'Reduced to her insular dominions; curtailed in her commerce', while 'the principal source of her wealth and naval power' would be 'transferred into the hands of her enemies'. Britain's 'blood and treasures' would be 'exhausted ... her revenues lessened' and she would be 'oppressed with an enormous debt'. In short, he predicted, 'debilitated with unsuccessful exertions', Britain would 'lose her power and consequence in the system of Europe, and be exposed almost a defenceless prey to the first neighbour who shall choose to invade her'. In the same vein, the *London Evening Post* predicted in July 1775 that Franco-Spanish support for American rebels endangered Britain's position in Europe and 'threatened to reduce her to a province of France'. Even at this early stage of the war, therefore, there were some who had apocalyptic visions of Britain's nemesis.[32]

For this reason, critics demanded that the colonists be conciliated rather than coerced. Thus Chatham introduced a bill in January 1775 demanding the recall of the troops from Boston, the withdrawal of taxes, and the recognition of the right of the Continental Congress to meet; in return it asserted parliamentary sovereignty over America and demanded that the colonists voluntarily vote the Crown a perpetual revenue to the King for the common defence. In order to reinforce his message, Chatham warned on 20 January 1775 of 'Foreign war hanging over your heads by a slight and brittle thread: France and Spain watching your conduct, and waiting for the maturity of your errors; with a vigilant eye to America, and the temper of your colonies, be they what they may'. Edmund Burke's resolutions on America in March called for the repeal of the coercive acts. The aim behind these manoeuvres, and the enthusiastic press campaign of the *London Evening Post* which accompanied it, was not so much to force a change of policy as to hail Chatham once again as the potential saviour of Britain in crisis.[33]

All the same, the American War was a popular one, at least at the beginning. Men as diverse as Samuel Johnson and John Wesley came out strongly against the Americans. One contemporary observer later recalled that 'There does not perhaps occur in the annals of Britain a single instance of a war more popular at its commencement than that which fatally took place between Great Britain and her colonies.' This sentiment found expression in a surge of patriotic and loyalist addresses, even though most of the petitioners preferred that American concerns be addressed peacefully. 'Who would have imagined,' the Opposition peer Lord Camden complained in early January 1776, 'that the ministry would have become popular by forcing the country into a destructive war and advancing the power of the Crown to a state of despotism?' Unlike in previous conflicts, many of those committed to Britain's maritime destiny backed the ministry. As was to be expected, many of those who now lined up to attack the colonists were the anti-Hanoverian and navalist scourges of an earlier age: Israel Mauduit, Samuel Johnson and John Shebbeare. This was, after all, their war. A sea war, without a Continental war: a Tory war.[34]

If the protagonists of colonial and sea war thought that the campaign against the Americans could be prosecuted without any reference to Europe, or the European powers, they were mistaken. The need to keep the French and Spaniards at arm's length seriously constrained operations against the colonists. In particular, the Royal Navy was instructed not to intercept French ships carrying munitions and other supplies to the rebels with too much vigour. It was permitted to engage these vessels in American waters at will, but not in European waters, where they were much easier to catch. In such circumstances no meaningful blockade of the rebels was possible. Looking back from the perspective of December 1777, Sandwich admitted that for the first two years of the war, 'The fleet has not been employed in the purposes in which it can be most useful towards distressing the enemy.' Instead, 'the enemy got the supplies from Europe by which they have been enabled to resist us.' That same year one outraged naval pamphleteer remarked that 'Our navy . . . would not have observed much delicacy with them, if the commanders of our ships had not been privately instructed to be extremely cautious in their conduct towards the French.' Paradoxically, a Britain which had become increasingly navalist since 1763 found itself fighting a major land war on another continent. In short, a purely maritime war was not possible; Britain always had to take European considerations into account even when deploying the Royal Navy.[35]

The naval blockade of the thirteen colonies was pursued with more vigour against the smaller European powers. But here too there were diplomatic costs and constraints. For the time being, the Danes, Portuguese and Swedes could be intimidated without difficulty. The Dutch, however, were another matter. Notions of Dutch benevolence and support had already been shaken by the experience of the Seven Years War and Dutch neutrality, but London was still hopeful enough to make a formal approach for a loan of the Scots Brigade in Dutch service in October 1775. This was originally recruited from Scotland and had first been set up during the Dutch revolt of the sixteenth century. By the late eighteenth century it was largely made up of mercenaries but it would still have been a valuable contribution to the British war effort. In that context, it did not help that at least half of the contraband captures made by the Royal Navy in 1775–8 were of Dutch vessels, many of them trading with the rebels via their West Indian entrepôt of St Eustatius, off St Kitts. Nor of course did the foghorn diplomacy of the envoy to The Hague, Sir Joseph Yorke, who sought to browbeat the Dutch into seeing their true interests of alliance with Britain. Thus in late May 1775, after being instructed to interdict the supply of Dutch munitions to the rebels, Yorke remarked, 'I found myself under a necessity of cutting the matter short, and declaring roundly that if they would not comply, we should visit all ships we suspected bound for the West Indies. This declamation seconded by some frigates placed under my orders from the coast soon decided the affair.' The long and short of all this was that the Dutch, who regarded the British as bitter commercial rivals, refused to lend the

Scots, either for service in America or for deployment at home (to release British troops to fight against the colonists).[36]

Even with the continued Franco-Spanish neutrality and the transfusion of German mercenary blood, Britain proved unable to crush the colonists in 1776. In mid March Crown troops were forced to evacuate Boston, and General George Washington prevailed at the Battle of Trenton in New Jersey. Britain was more successful in the second half of the year with an amphibious descent on New York, and the repulse of an American assault on Canada in June. Hearteningly, the French Canadian population did not rally, as the Americans had hoped, to their 'liberators'; to this extent the Quebec Act had paid off. The naval strategy was a tactical success, in that colonial shipping and the maritime economy were devastated, but it was a strategic failure in that it did not break the capacity or will of the rebels to resist. The Americans hung on: the year closed with no end to the war in sight. As the Duke of Richmond observed, 'all the efforts of our arms, exerted to the utmost, supplied with most extravagant loans of money, unencumbered by any foreign war, have for two years proved ineffectual' to subdue any of the thirteen colonies, even 'with addition of German mercenaries and savages'. By the end of that year, London was close to despair. The Russians were approached with a view to the loan of troops, but gave a dusty answer; indeed, they were much offended to be classed as mercenaries.[37]

Worse still, the contest was now no longer just a police action against rebels, but an international conflict. In September 1775 a declaration by the Continental Congress had pronounced 'foreign assistance [to be] undoubtedly attainable'. Two months later the Secret Committee was formed in Philadelphia. Its task, in the first instance, was the establishment of foreign links to provide military supplies. In March 1776 Silas Deane was sent to France. By the end of the year he was beginning to reflect on the value not only of French logistical assistance but also of a full-blown alliance. 'If France will but join us in time,' he wrote to the Secret Committee in early October, 'there is no danger but America will soon be established an independent empire, and France drawing from her the principal part of those sources of wealth and power that formerly flowed into Great Britain will immediately become the greatest power in Europe.' The potential gain to France was clear. As Vergennes observed in late 1775, victory for the colonists would mean that 'The power of England will diminish and our power will increase to the same degree.' The same would be true of commerce; and there was every likelihood that some of the lands lost in 1763 could be recovered. His memorandum to King Louis of March 1776 looked forward to the 'humiliation of England'. So in early May 1776 Vergennes agreed to supply covert aid to the rebels even at the risk of a rupture with Britain, and he allowed American privateers to operate out of French ports; but he wanted to avoid open hostilities for the time being. This was partly because he needed time to complete his naval preparations, even though the combined Franco-Spanish tonnage was now 25 per cent greater than that of Britain. The navy minister, Antoine de Sartine, was instructed to step up the increase of the navy; the comptroller-general of finances, Robert-Jacques Turgot, was told to swallow his fiscal objections to another war.[38]

Vergennes's initial restraint also reflected a certain unease at being associated with the rebellious subjects of a lawful monarch, and a percipient sense that an independent America would pose a hemispheric threat to all the European colonial powers in the long run. Spain too was circumspect. Of course it welcomed the prospect of humbling Britain, of recovering Florida and banishing the bandits illegally cutting logwood in the Gulf of Honduras. Many American privateers who were moved on from France were allowed to slip into Spanish ports. These, however, were still pinpricks. For the moment Spain preferred to try to leverage its neutrality for territorial gain, Gibraltar if possible. Madrid was far from ready in naval terms, and after the fiasco of the Falkland Islands it was reluctant to move before the French did. Moreover, with their vast and unstable colonial holdings in America, anything that smacked of rebellion made the Spaniards distinctly nervous. Indeed, Charles III refused to recognize US independence until the very end of the war. Finally, Spain was at this point much more concerned with Portugal.

In June 1776, the patriot Richard Henry Lee submitted a resolution to the Continental Congress 'that these United Colonies are, and of right ought to be, free and independent states, that they are absolved from all allegiance to the British crown, and that all political connection between them and the state of Great Britain is, and ought to be, totally dissolved.' This, he explained, would pave the way for 'alliance with proper and willing powers in Europe'. The trouble was that 'no state in Europe will either treat or trade with us so long as we consider ourselves subjects of G.B.' It was therefore, 'not choice ... but necessity that calls for independence, as the only means by which foreign alliances can be obtained and a proper confederation by which peace and union may be secured'. His reasoning was echoed by the elective American, Tom Paine. Paine's vigorous tract in support of independence, *Common sense*, appeared in 1776. All four reasons he advanced in favour of independence related to foreign policy. First, he claimed that it was essential to secure outside mediation. Secondly, France and Spain would be unlikely to support the colonists militarily so long as they feared that the breach might be repaired, thus making Britain stronger than ever. Thirdly, no power could openly support rebels, which was what the Americans were so long as they remained subjects of the King. Fourthly and finally, it would enable Congress to send diplomatic representatives to foreign courts. The colonists had always seen themselves as part of the European balance of power: now a declaration of independence would turn them from objects into subjects of the state system.[39]

America's entry into the international community was also designed to pre-empt possible partition at the hands of the Great Powers. The colonists had observed the fate of Poland with alarm, and many felt that their security could no longer be guaranteed by a declining power. Thus the American Daniel Leonard had remarked in 1775 that the major powers might gang up and that then 'the whole continent would become their easy prey, and would be parcelled out, Poland-like'. Likewise, Richard Lee remarked in April that 'A slight attention to the late proceedings of many European courts will sufficiently evince the spirit of partition, and the assumed right of disposing of men and countries like livestock on a farm ... Corsica and Poland indisputably prove this.' Only by establishing themselves as a strong sovereign state, could the thirteen colonies guard against such an outcome. Ultimately, therefore, the perception of British *weakness* proved to be far more damaging to the royal cause in America than allegations of despotism. Just as Britain after 1707 was a constitutional construct designed for the better containment of France, and the expansion of empire, so did the failure of containment, and the restraints which London imposed on expansion, necessitate the dissolution of the union between the colonies and the mother country. It was, in short, the primacy of foreign policy which drove the rebels towards separation.[40]

On 4 July 1776, the thirteen colonies duly issued a formal Declaration of Independence. It closed down the last chance of a reconciliation. The radical MP Isaac Barré lamented that ministers had 'lost America'. Looking ahead, some British critics foresaw that the Declaration of Independence had conjured up the spectre of a new and powerful rival. Thus Robert, Earl Nugent, MP for St Mawes and Vice Treasurer for Ireland, warned Parliament that 'the contest now was, not whether America should be dependent on the British parliament, but whether Great Britain or America should be independent?' He predicted that 'Both could not be so, for such would be the power of that vast continent across the Atlantic, that was her independence established, this island must expect to be made a dependent province.' Lord Lyttleton asserted that 'We were contending for the very existence of the [British] Empire; should America prevail, instead of submitting to Acts of Navigation from hence, she would prescribe them to us.' 'In the course of twenty years,' he predicted, 'America, when she had established her marine, would be a superior empire.' This was an exaggeration, of course. It would take longer than that.[41]

One way or the other, the Declaration of Independence marked the end of a fractious but extraordinarily successful Anglo-American strategic partnership that had begun in the late seventeenth century. There was genuine regret on Franklin's part when he heard the news. 'Long did I endeavour,' he wrote in July 1776, 'with unfeigned and unwearied zeal to preserve from breaking that fine and noble china vase, the British Empire, for I knew that, being once broken, the separate parts could not retain even their share of the strength or value that existed in the whole.' There was rather more relish in Thomas Jefferson's reaction, but the sentiment was the same. 'We might have been a free and great people together,' he wrote, 'but a communication of grandeur and of freedom it seems is below their dignity. Be it so, since they will have it; the road to glory and happiness is open to us too, we will climb it in a separate state, and acquiesce in the necessity which pronounces our everlasting adieu.'[42]

To many Americans, then and since, the Declaration of Independence opened up a vista of insular splendour, at one remove from what their commander-in-chief and first president George Washington was later to call 'entangling alliances' in Europe. Paine argued that the connection with the mother country only served to drag America into European quarrels. 'Let Britain waive her pretensions to the Continent [of

38. A satirical print depicting Benjamin Franklin attempting to bestride the world. American patriots finally realized that their strategic interests could no longer be reconciled with their loyalty to Great Britain.

America],' he argued, 'or the Continent throw off the dependence, and we should be at peace with France and Spain, were they at war with Britain.' He added that the 'miseries of Hanover during the last war [1756–63] ought to warn us against connections'. For this reason, he argued, America should 'steer clear of European contentions, which she never can do, while, by her dependence on Britain, she is made the makeweight in the scale of British politics'. The words here were carefully chosen. What Paine meant was that in contemporary British strategy, the thirteen colonies were an important part of the defence of the European balance. As such, America was vulnerable to attack by Britain's rivals. Moreover, the role thus thrust upon Americans was alien to their natural insular and continental vocation. He went on to say that 'there is something absurd, in supposing a continent to be perpetually governed by an island. In no instance hath nature made the satellite larger than its primary planet; and as England and America, with respect to each other, reverse the common order of nature, it is evident that they belong to different systems. England to Europe; America to itself.' It was a fascinating transplantation of the old Tory strategic critique, only in this case it was not Britain which was being dragged into Europe by Hanover, but America and Hanover which were being caught in the Great Power crossfire.[43]

Others stressed the 'insular' destiny of the new state. The patriot William Henry Drayton, who served as Chief Justice of South Carolina, argued that 'If America is to be secure at home and respected abroad, it must be by a naval force. Nature and experience instruct us that a maritime strength is the best defence to an insular situation.' Indeed, he continued, 'is not the situation of the United States insular with respect to the power of the Old World: the quarter from which alone we are to apprehend danger? Have not the maritime states the greatest influence upon the affairs of the universe?' This proto-Mahanian eulogy would not have been out of place in a Tory pamphlet from about 1690 onwards, or a 'patriot' broadside of the 1730s. Paine and Drayton had put their finger on the duality of America and its foreign policy: it was both island and continent. It would therefore be both Tory and Whig in strategic terms. For if Americans were instinctive 'Tories' in some ways, they now had to become 'Whigs': to seek European connections in order to secure their new-found independence. The revolutionaries of 1642 and 1688 had had to depose the king in order to pursue the grand strategy they wanted; they then devised a foreign policy to defend their revolutions. So it was in 1774–6: the Americans made a revolution to conduct an expansionist grand strategy; and they then crafted a foreign policy to defend the revolution.[44]

The colonists now pressed ahead with Continental overtures. Later that year a delegation was sent to Paris; envoys were also sent to the Habsburg court, Spain and Prussia. At first there was some American pressure for a French attack on Hanover. Silas Deane, the American representative in France, called for a great European alliance against Britain 'after which, Great Britain having her whole force employed in America, there could be nothing on the one hand to prevent Spain and France from reducing Portugal . . . nor from Prussia and France subduing . . . Hanover and the other little mercenary Electorates.' This policy had a triple object in mind: to win Franco-Spanish naval support, to tie down British forces on the Continent, and to cut Britain off from her valuable source of German mercenaries. The Americans knew, of course, that this could be achieved only at the risk of a European conflagration, but that was a price they were prepared to pay. Thus the patriot Robert

Morris wrote in September 1776 that 'It appears clear to me that we may very soon involve all Europe in a war by managing properly the apparent forwardness of the court of France; it's a horrid consideration that our own safety should call on us to involve other nations in the calamities of war.' He wondered whether 'this be morally right or have morality and policy nothing to do with each other? Perhaps it may not be good policy to investigate the question at this time.' The colonists were quick to lose their diplomatic innocence, if they had ever had any.[45]

Even during the early stages of the war, therefore, the Americans pursued a European policy of considerable sophistication. They always had one eye on the broader picture, especially when the military tide in America itself appeared to turn against them during early 1777. Thus one patriot greeted the loss of Fort Ticonderoga with the remark, 'What vexes me most is the disgrace which the evacuation of such a strong-post will fix upon our arms, in Europe.' Moreover, the Americans were capable of leveraging not only their strength but their weakness. When the prospect of humiliating Britain through a patriot victory failed to persuade the Bourbons, they tried another tack. A rebel defeat, it was argued, would so enhance the power of Britain as to upset the European balance. Thus in February 1777, the Americans warned Vergennes that 'if Britain is now suffered to recover the colonies and annex again their great flowering strength and commerce to her own, she will become in a few years the most formidable power by sea and land that Europe has yet seen.' A month later Arthur Lee told the Spanish court, 'If Great Britain should again be united to America by conquest or conciliation it would be vain to menace her with war.' He also warned that 'Great Britain knit again to such growing strength would reign the irresistible though hated arbiter of Europe. This, then, is the moment in which Spain and France may clip her wings and pinion her for ever'. American independence, in other words, had become a European necessity.[46]

As the threat of Bourbon intervention loomed, Britain began to look around for European allies. Yet she never developed a really coherent strategy towards the Bourbon powers. While the Earl of Suffolk, the Secretary of State for the North, wanted to appease the Spaniards and concentrate on America, Weymouth, the Southern Secretary, who had breathed fire over the Falklands, favoured a much stiffer line against Madrid. Once again, the structure of British foreign policy making – the divisions between the Northern, Southern and Colonial Secretaries –

militated against an integrated approach. In March 1777 Stormont was warning that peace in Europe would last no longer than a year unless a decisive victory could be won in America. For this reason one of the rising stars of the British diplomatic service, James Harris, was dispatched to Russia in pursuit of an alliance. Joseph Yorke described this overture as 'the most important mission we have, and heartily wish you may bring about a permanent alliance with that country, the only one I care twopence about.' For this reason, he added, Britain 'should not weigh grains and scruples', nor should she – and this was the key point – 'either formerly or now stick at a Turkish article'. The bullet of reciprocity, in short, should be bitten. It had taken some fifteen years to grasp that British security depended on the exchange of favours, and the realization came too late to make up the diplomatic ground lost in the meantime.[47]

It is no coincidence that the old Whig paradigm, so decisively rejected after 1760, now began to experience a restoration. Thus the old Pittite Thomas Townshend, MP for Whitchurch, told Parliament that the naval crisis facing Britain was due to two factors. First of all, because the Americans who had served during the Seven Years War were now on the other side. Secondly, and more importantly, because 'in the last war, the French had other objects to think of, besides an invasion of these islands.' He reminded MPs, 'You had an army in Germany that held at bay, and found ample work for 150,000 of the best troops in France. What chance have we now of such a diversion of their force?' It was a good question, and one that would be asked with ever-increasing frequency as the war dragged on. Furthermore, American resources would be central to war with France. Thus Lord Cardiff argued in late October 1776 that 'The wealth and additional strength which we have hitherto derived from our colonies, have enabled us to retain our consequence and superiority in the grand European system.' Without it, he continued, Britain would lose her 'importance in that system and in the end ... become a province of the first ambitious power, who might think proper to attack us.' Another parliamentarian noted in the following year, that the thirteen colonies were 'the fountain of our wealth, the nerve of our strength, the nursery and basis of our naval power'. Likewise, the Duke of Richmond argued that 'to support [the] Navy, we must have commerce; and possessions in distant parts of the globe are the soul of that commerce. America of itself answered every purpose we could wish as to trade; and besides, produces those naval stores, without which we can have no fleet.'[48]

For the most part, however, the British establishment regarded the prospect of a confrontation with the Bourbons with ebullience. The Earl of Rochford suggested in 1775 that France and Spain would hardly 'set so dangerous an example to their subjects in the New World, by assisting the British colonies to shake off the dominion of the mother country'. In any case, the Admiralty was confident that Britain had maintained a two-power standard against her nearest rivals (the Royal Navy was larger than the next two largest navies together). Sandwich claimed in 1775 'that we had a fleet superior to any that the combined force of France and Spain could fit out'. And in mid March 1777 Lord George Germain, the Colonial Secretary, sought to deter French intervention by victory in America, and isolating the continent navally from Europe. To this end, Britain should take control of American ports and station a line of cruisers between St Augustine and Halifax. Once again, naval solutions were being suggested to a political problem. Underlying this confidence was a profound sense of Britain's fiscal strength. 'The nation never was so strong since it existed by land and sea as at present,' Joseph Yorke observed in June 1778, 'and I am convinced as much as I am that two and two makes four that we shall have a million sterling left when France has not a farthing, so even that way we shall beat them.' It was certainly true that Britain's fiscal-military complex was still unrivalled in the world, and fully capable of rising to the financial challenges of the conflict. The problem was that fiscal strength too readily became a substitute for diplomatic manoeuvre rather than a supplement to it. The government thus still clung to the prevailing post-1763 assumption that security could be guaranteed through sea power alone.[49]

The Opposition, by contrast, continued to lament the diplomatic isolation of Britain and the threat of French intervention. The Opposition MP, ardent Pittite and former Secretary of State for the North General Conway pointed out in early 1777 that Britain was 'no nearer making a conquest of America' than it had been a year ago, and claimed that French intervention would follow once she was sufficiently exhausted. The result would be 'a war with the united powers of France, Spain, Naples, Sardinia [Piedmont-Savoy] and the Emperor, without a single ally strong enough to counterbalance such a junction of all the Great Powers of the southern part of Europe'. Not even the Dutch, who were, as the Earl of Coventry reminded Parliament, 'our ancient, and, in some respects, our natural allies', were cooperative. In short, he concluded, Britain 'had been for some years insulted and condemned by almost every power in Europe, with whom we had anything to do'. Even the diplomat Joseph Yorke had to admit to another ambassador that the situation 'Grows every day worse and worse for an English minister, but such is our fate that in my short career of thirty years, I have seen the blessed effects of British generosity producing the blackest ingratitude towards us in the House of Austria, the House of Branden-burg, and our unnatural children, the Americans; what your children are to see, I don't pretend to guess.'[50]

Britain's only friends, Thomas Townshend scornfully remarked, were 'the powerful states of Anspach, Waldeck, and those several formidable allies who have furnished us with troops; who have sold us blood in return for our money'. Likewise, Edmund Burke asked 'what alliances we had formed to support us in case of a rupture with the Bourbons', and 'reprobated the contact with the princelings of Germany as mean and humiliating'. He accused ministers of 'courting the alliance of a few traders in human flesh'. Not only did the German links aggravate opinion in America, they also gave the Opposition the chance to play the Hanoverian card in a way that had not been possible since the accession of George III. Thus in late May 1777 Chatham accused the government of 'ransack[ing] every corner of Lower Saxony; but 40,000 German boors never can conquer ten times that number of British freemen'. He then went on to ridicule the government for being 'at the mercy of every little German chancery'. Chatham returned to this theme when he spoke of 'traffic and barter with every little pitiful German prince', adding that 'Our ministers have made alliances at the German shambles'. The immediate target was the Hessians, but the Hanoverians did not escape. 'Gibraltar is garrisoned by Hanoverians,' Chatham observed, 'I am told, if any accident should happen to the present commanding officer there, that the care of the fortress, and the command of the troops would devolve on a foreigner', whose name he affected to forget. A few months later, he returned to these themes with even greater vigour. 'We had,' he said, 'swept every corner of Germany for men: we had searched the darkest wilds of America for the scalping knife. [But] peace . . . would never be effected, as long as the German bayonet and Indian scalping-knife were threatened to be buried in the bowels of our

American brethren.' So desperate and unprincipled was the ministry, Chatham argued, that we 'should not be surprised if their next league was with the king of the gypsies'.[51]

The increasing sense of panic in late 1777 and early 1778 reflected not only the looming French threat, but the catastrophic news from America itself. For in mid October 1777 a substantial British force under General Burgoyne was crushed at Saratoga; most of the American guns had been supplied by France. News of this disaster reached London in early December 1777. The sinking feeling of losing a war of attrition now gave way to the possibility of straightforward military defeat. Moreover, the victorious American commander, General Horatio Gates, had craftily sent back a message of conciliation with the vanquished Burgoyne which was calculated to inflame domestic divisions in Britain. 'The United States,' he wrote, 'are willing to be the friends, but will never submit to be the slaves of the parent country: they are by consanguinity, by commerce, by language, and by the affection which naturally spring from these, more attached to England than to any country under the sun.' For this reason, Gates continued, Britain should not 'spurn the blessing which yet remains' and 'cultivate the friendship and commerce of America'. His missive was read to the House of Lords in mid February 1778.[52]

All this duly did galvanize the Opposition to renewed attacks on government strategy. 'America,' Sir Charles Bunbury told Parliament, was 'invincible'. In these circumstances, he argued, 'perseverance' was mere 'obstinacy'. In the House of Commons the Opposition MP David Hartley introduced a motion 'relative to the enormous expenses of the American War' with a call to end 'this fatal war, and all the ruinous consequences which await the landed and commercial interest of this country'. In the Lords Chatham was moved to another jeremiad: he saw 'prospects full of awe, terror, and impending danger'. In each case, critics continued to see the conciliation of the colonists as essential to the maintenance of Britain's European position and naval supremacy. Chatham saw in this civil war nothing less than the strategic suicide of Britain. 'Be the victory to whichever host it pleases the Almighty to give it,' he lamented in late September 1777, 'poor England will have fallen upon her own sword.' In May 1778 he introduced a motion to 'put a stop to hostilities in America', by urging peace with the colonists before it was too late. 'The gathering storm,' he warned, 'may break; it has already opened, and in part burst . . . if an end is not put to this war, there is an end to this country.' Later that same year, he warned again that France and Spain would 'most inevitably profit of our want of wisdom, if we do not immediately prevent it'. By contrast, supporters of coercion continued to argue throughout 1777 that European imperatives made the suppression of the revolt essential. 'We humble ourselves to our rebellious subjects,' Lyttleton complained. 'What would in that event all Europe think of us?' He predicted that '[t]hey would despise as well as detest us. It would operate to afford them the highest encouragement to attack us. They would immediately conclude, that we were weak, defenceless, pusillanimous.'[53]

Saratoga did indeed move Versailles further towards war. Throughout 1777 maritime relations between Britain and France went from bad to worse. The number of intercepted ships increased; naval stand-offs on the high seas became commonplace; rumours of French expeditions to the West Indies swirled about London; and the French barely bothered to conceal their covert support for the rebels. In February 1778, the French concluded treaties of commerce and alliance with the American Congress. But Vergennes still moved cautiously. He preferred to make Britain appear the aggressor, so as to invoke the mutual defence clauses of the Bourbon Family Compact. This meant foreswearing all attempts to recover Canada. As he told the ambassador to Madrid, the Comte de Montmorin, that summer, 'We must work resolutely to weaken this enemy of ours, but we must not display intentions which would only do us harm because the jealousy that they would arouse against the House of Bourbon would give England friends and allies.' Moreover, Vergennes was shy of any initiative which might precipitate the return of Pitt.[54]

What finally tipped the balance was the first British steps towards conciliation. In February–March 1778, three conciliatory Bills went through both Houses without too much difficulty. The Massachusetts Government Act of 1774 was repealed. Three Commissioners – William Eden, a young Undersecretary, the colonial veteran George Johnstone and the Earl of Carlisle were sent to negotiate with the Americans; this overture became known as the Carlisle Commission. Most importantly the Renunciation Act gave up Parliament's claim to tax Britain's overseas possessions. It was not only all too little too late, but the prospect of a rapprochement between Britain and the colonists actually served to precipitate French intervention. Vergennes now feared that an Anglo-

American rapprochement would free Britain to concentrate on containing France and thus wreck his plans to avenge 1763. He immediately concluded secret treaties of commerce and alliance with the colonists, which made the French entry into the war inevitable. London was to discover that belated moderation can be as dangerous as initial obstinacy.[55]

It was at this critical moment that Chatham finally succumbed to illness in May 1778, collapsing in the middle of a speech in the House of Lords. His monument in Westminster Abbey announced that he had 'Exalted Great Britain, to an Height of Prosperity and Glory, unknown to any former Age'. He was shown as 'extending the sway of Britannia by means of Prudence and Fortitude over Earth and Ocean'. The cenotaph in London's Guildhall was even more poignant and pointed: it depicted a figure in imperial Roman garb whose career had been marked by 'unity at home – by confidence and reputation abroad – by alliance wisely chosen and faithfully observed – by colonies united and protected – by decisive victories by sea and land – by conquest made by arms and generosity in every part of the globe – and by commerce, for the first time, united with and made to flourish by war'. Every word here was a barb as well as eulogy. When these phrases were being inscribed, it seemed that the home front had never been more disunited; Britain's reputation abroad had never been lower; her colonial possessions never more fractious and exposed; British arms never less successful, except perhaps at the outset of the Seven Years War; conquests never more conspicuously absent; commerce never less synchronized with the war effort; and – above all – Britain's alliance system never before in such a state of complete and terminal disrepair. The world which Pitt had done so much to create was on the verge of the collapse he had predicted. America was about to be lost in Europe.[56]

The ministry still responded to the French threat with a restatement of navalist verities. Its ambassador to Holland pronounced that 'we never were so strong by land and sea since we were a nation, and therefore may laugh at their *pistoles* [swaggering]'. More pragmatically, the ministry fell back on what has become known as the 'two-power standard'. Sandwich reiterated that 'our navy is more than a match for that of the whole House of Bourbon'. Indeed, he added with a flourish that was to leave a large hostage to fortune, that 'if I permitted at any time the French and Spanish navy united, to be superior to the navy of this country, I should, indeed, be wanting in the discharge of my duty.' Likewise Lord Mulgrave, MP for Huntingdon and one of the Lords of the Admiralty, dismissed the 'rottenness' of the French ships, and claimed that the Royal Navy was 'much superior to the whole naval force the House of Bourbon were able to send forth'. The Earl of Suffolk repeated in early 1778 that 'Our fleets were hitherto irresistible; our navy was at present in the most respectable condition.' At the same time, the ministry continued to resist Continental commitments through alliances. These, Lord North sought to remind Parliament in May 1778, 'cost Great Britain a vast deal, and the return they made was not adequate to the expense'.[57]

But this was now navalism with a difference. For the Admiralty, the focus shifted from naval dominance off America and in the Caribbean, to control of home waters around the United Kingdom itself. The two-power standard, Sandwich pointed out, related 'only to the home defence'. As ever, it was in the Western Approaches off Devon and Cornwall, and the Channel, especially between Dover and Dungeness, that the future of Great Britain would be decided. And here the picture was increasingly bleak. Already in May 1778, while he was still putting a brave face on things in Parliament, Sandwich privately warned the prime minister that sending a substantial naval force to America 'if the whole fleet of France and Spain remains in Europe, will leave us absolutely at the mercy of the House of Bourbon'. Two days later, Admiral Augustus Keppel wrote that 'the determination of taking eleven of the finest ships from under my command for foreign service . . . leaves me in a situation I must think alarming for the safety of the King's home dominions.' He then proceeded to sketch a doomsday scenario involving a French foray 'up the Channel', a demonstration off the Isle of Wight, and even a *coup de main* against Portsmouth itself. Shortly after that, Keppel feared that the Brest fleet was 'so formidable' that he could not guarantee the outcome of any engagement, with potentially disastrous results for 'the fate of England'. After all, as Admiral Sir Hugh Palliser pointed out in early July, 'The stake France has depending on the event is not to be compared with that of this country, whose very existence depends upon her fleet.'[58]

The symptoms were maritime and colonial, but the roots of Britain's malaise lay in her failed European policy, and the exuberant navalism which had followed the triumphs of 1763. Britain was threatened at sea because her diplomacy had failed to keep her enemies at peace, or at least divided. This had never happened before. As Suffolk pointed out in early 1778, Britain was now strategically in uncharted waters. 'The situation of France,' he remarked, '[is] much changed from what it was, at any time since the commencement of the present century. She [has] changed her system: and, instead of keeping on foot great standing armies, [has] turned her attention entirely on her marine; and now dispute[s] the empire of the sea with us.' He concluded that 'This uniting with the circumstance of the revolt of our colonies, form[s] a period, totally unknown in the annals of this country.' One of the ministry's most vociferous critics, the Duke of Richmond, agreed that 'the present formed a new era in politics as far as France and England were concerned; that the finances of France were in the train of being put on a respectable footing; that her attention was called from her armies to her marine; that she now disputed the empire of the ocean with us.' Yet even now, Sandwich did not grasp the link between the two spheres, and showed himself quick to sacrifice political capital for short-term naval advantage. In early July 1778 he instructed Keppel that while 'we should be strong in argument that we are not the aggressors . . . it will not be discreet to give up any material point to that political question'. Indeed, he volunteered that 'we have no objection to a war, or to being called the aggressors, if we can strike a material stroke at first.' The old predisposition towards pre-emption was still strong, but here it was deployed in place of diplomacy rather than in support of it.[59]

Even without a British spoiling attack, war came soon enough. In June 1778 Vergennes stated that the rationale for open conflict with Britain was 'the significant weakening of England caused by taking away a third of her empire'. The Americans also felt that British maritime arrogance required a restoration of the European balance. The following month France finally declared war using Britain's continuing naval infractions as a pretext. London began to receive reliable reports of French troops assembling in Normandy for an invasion. The American War had become a European and thus truly a global war for Britain.[60]

22

Losing America in Europe, 1778–1779

I do not love war but, in the present moment, I should not be sorry to see one in Germany on account of the Bavarian succession, provided it would completely occupy the French.[1]

Lord North, Prime Minister, late January 1778

However expensive a Flanders or a German War may be, yet as directing to a distance the army and treasures of France – it removes danger – affords security to these kingdoms, and allows of the effectual exertion of our naval force . . . No such situation yet exists, and probably from the expense and disappointment of former wars they will avoid being drawn into it.[2]

Anonymous memorandum to the British administration in London about the defence of Ireland, March 1778

We hear that a divorce of a very extraordinary nature, *between* John Bull *and his wife* Americana, *is shortly to take place, which will astonish all Europe. The cause of the quarrel originated one morning over their tea, which would have been instantly made up, but for the roguery of Mr Bull's servants, who had an* interest in keeping them at variance. *Now it* has spread so wide, that a reconciliation is thought impracticable; *as every meeting, instead of mediating, ends in hostilities. The consequences of this divorce will be, that* John Bull *will have nothing to live upon but the* little farm *he had before* marriage; *whilst his wife will be in the sole possession of the great estate* she brought him; *and if she marries Nick Frog (as there is a great probability she will) God knows whether they may not strip* John Bull *of his paternal inheritance, and turn him out onto the street.*[3]

Connecticut Courant, 2 June 1778

Nobody was in any doubt that Britain now faced a mortal threat. Viscount Stormont, soon to be Secretary of State for the North, feared that 'France and America . . . [are] indissolubly linked for our destruction.' At the very least, Britain's enemies were determined to render her 'a petty state of the second class, of no importance, and disgraced in the eyes of all surrounding nations'. He claimed that the French and Americans had concluded a secret treaty demanding 'that the wings of Great Britain must be clipped, lest she should soar too high', indeed 'that some articles of this secret treaty went not only to the independence of the colonies in arms, but to the dismemberment of the British Empire and the parcelling out and partitioning of its insular and other American possessions among the contracting parties, part to France, and part to America.'[4]

But the main threat now lay in Europe. For a start, France's entry into the war fundamentally transformed the strategic situation in Ireland. In the early stages of the conflict, there was considerable Protestant sympathy for the colonists: the rebel blend of liberty, anti-popery and expropriation appealed to them. For the same reason, the Gaelic response to the early stages of the American Revolution was muted. They saw it essentially as an Anglo-Saxon civil war,[5] a position they shared with many colonists and their British sympathizers. There was a certain reflexive *schadenfreude* at Britain's difficulties, but no more. As the possibility of French and Spanish intervention in favour of the Americans increased, however, Gaelic interest quickened. War in Europe, not American liberty, was what excited them. England's difficulty, as the cliché would later have it, would be Ireland's opportunity. The Irish Protestant minority and the Dublin administration were right to be paranoid; they knew that the Jacobites had not gone away. The faces pressed to the Anglo-Irish window-pane were unbeguiled by the Augustan splendour of the Protestant ascendancy. The fleeting figures among the haystacks, maiming cattle and harassing the authorities, were much magnified by the imagination, no doubt, but they were there. They and their poets constituted a 'low Jacobitism', which had long paralleled the now defunct 'high' Jacobitism of the diplomatic circuit. This 'hidden Ireland' was not just a cultural space but a political movement, a Jacobite underground with links to the Continental Great Powers. The measures that the London government took to contain it were much aggravated by local Protestant bigotry, but they were principally driven by considerations of national security.[6]

Henceforth Irish Jacobites observed the course of the war with rapt attention until Britain threw in the towel in 1783. In particular, they hoped for a French or Spanish invasion. The poet Seamus O'Dalaigh wrote, admittedly with more enthusiasm than accuracy, that 'The King of Sardinia, and Louis heroically, / Philip and the Emperor, the ruler of Bohemia, / With ships and hosts are fiercely and furiously, / Coming over the sea with a Stuart to claim me.' A ballad composed by Eoghan Rua O'Suilleabhain in the summer of 1778 rejoiced that 'George is in distress, though great is his strength at sea . . . the [Holy Roman] Empire is forcefully coming for him . . . and will leave him enfeebled and their parliament exhausted.' Moreover, he continued, 'the French and Spaniards are powerful and have no sympathy, affection or pity for him, they are ones who'll put the evil rogue to flight from the Crown with armed combat.' The reference to confrontation between Britain and Austria reflects not so much confusion on the part of the author, as awareness of the poor relations between George III as Elector and the Holy Roman Emperor.[7]

As if all this were not bad enough, the French declaration of war caused an additional headache in central Europe. First of all, it threatened the supply of German mercenaries so central to the American War effort; secondly, it exposed the King's German territories to direct attack. After all, thanks to the Hanoverian connection, Britain was still very much a central European power, in reality if not in self-perception. Thus in March 1778 one British survey of the strategic situation remarked that the French entry into the war would not only lead to the withdrawal of the German contingents serving in America, but would also expose Hanover. Britain, the memorandum warned, was 'in no position to assemble a great army' to protect the German princes 'or to pay the immense damages, that would accrue from the French taking possession of their country. Besides, it would be a fair pretence for entering Germany, and seizing the Electorate [of Hanover], if such a pretence can be wanted.' Rumours of a French attack on Hanover, perhaps in alliance with the Austrians – plausible enough in view of the poisonous relations between George and Joseph – began to reach London in early 1778. The link between the American and the European spheres, so familiar from the Seven Years War, was also central to this war. The net result of all this was to destroy any hope of rapid victory in America. 'It seems probable,' the memorandum concluded, 'that the beginning of a French war, will be the end of an offensive American one.' Without the German mercenaries, which would be withdrawn at France's insistence, Britain would lack the striking force to carry the war to the Americans. Indeed, what remained was 'barely sufficient for the preservation of New York and its dependencies'. Hence, the memorandum concluded, even if it were 'disagreeable and humiliating ... There seems no alternative to abandoning the thirteen American Provinces', while continuing to defend the sugar islands, harassing those of the French 'and bringing the remainder [of the mercenaries] home for our own defence'.[8]

In the face of these new naval, military and subversive challenges, the British state embarked on its most intense programme of mobilization so far. During the first two or three years of the war – when America was the only theatre of operations – the level of British military mobilization was low. The war itself was popular domestically, at least further down the social spectrum, where pro-American feeling was less strong, but the resulting burdens were not, and so the government was concerned to minimize the financial outlay and disruption to the civilian economy as much as possible. The resulting drive to mobilize the nation more intensively in support of the war profoundly affected British society. The reach of the state was extended. In the case of the army, the 1778 and 1779 Recruitment Acts permitted the conscription of healthy unemployed men and criminals. A 1779 Act increased forcible impressments into the Navy. It brought into the armed forces not merely the usual aristocratic and deadbeat suspects at both ends of the social spectrum but also many from middling and artisan backgrounds. The achievements of this unprecedented mobilization drive were impressive: if the Royal Navy boasted 66 ships of the line in 1778, it had 90 in 1779 and 95 in 1780; the number of seamen had jumped from 60,000 to 100,000 in the same period. In Ireland, the British government continued to be mesmerized by the prospect of tapping into the vast manpower potential of Catholic Ireland. There had already been important moves in this direction before the war, but it was only in 1778, as conflict with France loomed, that the first substantial relaxation of anti-Catholic legislation was effected. This was the Catholic Relief Act, which excused Catholics from taking an oath of allegiance to Anglicanism on joining the armed forces; repealed laws relating to the prosecution of Catholic clergy and the suppression of Catholic schools; and allowed Catholics to buy and inherit land without restriction. These measures were particu-

larly significant in Ireland. Perhaps more surprisingly, the onset of war
with France and Spain did not reverse the slow movement of middle-class
and aristocratic Catholics towards cooperation with the Hanoverian
state. And the British government, in turn, responded by lifting some of
the Penal Laws in order to mobilize the Catholic population for the war
effort.[9]

39. In this cartoon America is sawing the horns off the cow of British
commerce, which is being milked by a Dutchman for the benefit of France and
Spain. A distraught Englishman stands next to the unconscious British lion.

But the main effort would have to be political and diplomatic. Britain
needed to gain friends, and to divert her enemies, or at least try to avoid
adding to them. Keeping Spain neutral was therefore the immediate task.
The primary danger here was a union between the two Bourbon fleets.
One possibility was pre-emption – the tactic which Pitt had advocated
in 1761. Thus in May 1778 Admiral Palliser mused on the possibility
of diverting 'the French and Spaniards with an alarm of expeditions
intended – suppose to Buenos Aires, to assist the Portuguese in that
quarter and to favour insurrection in the Spanish settlements in the
South Sea'. Indeed, he believed 'that such measures would be justifiable
after the part France and Spain have acted respecting our colonies'.
Palliser concluded by predicting that 'Independent states and a free trade
in the South Sea would affect the Spaniards as much as the loss of

America will affect Britain.' Likewise, Joseph Yorke hinted darkly at Spanish vulnerability in Peru and Mexico: 'in common sense, Spain has an even deeper stake in this American contest than we have'. Moreover, the containment of Spain might be achieved without firing a shot. For example, the British representative at Constantinople hoped that 'the amazing havoc made by our cruisers amongst the French traders [may] begin visibly to influence the negotiations of their minister here, as it lowers their assumed importance. I am in hopes we shall continue to receive such news as will operate the same effects all over Europe, and secure the Neutrality of Spain.' The idea of intimidating the Spanish on the high seas and raising their colonies against the motherland was not just a response to the American rebellion, but went back to the clamour for war with Spain in the late 1730s.[10]

Others sought to head off, or at least to delay, a Spanish entry into the war through conciliation. In Parliament, Governor Johnstone pleaded that Britain should not respond to Spain's colonial provocations. In February 1777 he had warned that 'our revolted colonies, aided by a foreign force, must prove an over-match for us . . . I therefore think it would be madness to irritate any other power.' He concluded that 'our situation is such at present, that I think it better to suffer any insult, than provoke a foreign power openly to assist the Americans, or to form any alliance with them, which must make their return to the allegiance of this country more difficult, if not impossible.' Interestingly, Sandwich — otherwise very much an advocate of naval intimidation — pointed to the vulnerability of Britain, especially in the Mediterranean, and argued that 'In this situation, with regard to Spain it seems obvious that we should not offend them on any account.'[11]

Keeping Versailles and Madrid apart was a difficult, but by no means an impossible task. After all, the two powers had clashed severely over French prevarication in the Falkland Islands dispute and over various other issues. Moreover, Spain more than any other power was wary of creating a precedent for rebellion, and viewed the colonists with pronounced disdain. Even in purely strategic terms, Spanish and American interests were already beginning to diverge over such areas as the West and the Gulf of Mexico. There was thus some chance that skilful diplomacy would appease Madrid. One much-discussed possibility was the cession of Gibraltar, which British strategists had always regarded as dispensable if the broader interests of the state demanded it. After all, not only George I and Stanhope but even the elder Pitt had seriously considered its return to Spain; in any case, Minorca would suffice to defend Britain's interest in the Mediterranean. But popular and parliamentary opinion would not hear of it. Thus the Duke of Richmond argued that whereas the latter might be lost and regained, as in the Seven Years War, 'if ever we lose Gibraltar, which is . . . a British fortress in the heart of Spain, we shall never get it back again. Our possession of it is particularly galling to the pride of Spain, and no consideration will ever tempt her to restore it.'[12]

Britain's obvious distress drove a revival of the old Whig strategic paradigm, by which France should be deflected from her naval and colonial ambitions to the European mainland. Thus one strategic survey argued in March 1778 that although a war in Flanders or Germany might be expensive, it would serve to 'direct to a distance the army and treasures of France', and thus help to preserve the security of Britain and her naval superiority. In mid April, with a sea war imminent, Britain's long-serving ambassador to the United Provinces remarked that 'As Englishmen we have only to wish for either way that may engage France in more trouble and expense, and that on the land side.' Sending the army to America, Charles James Fox argued, was a waste of time. Instead, it should be sent to the 'continent of Europe' where it could 'contend with France in a manner that would make her feel her own consequence was at stake'. Unfortunately, he continued, 'the old Whig system of alliances on the Continent had been given up, and we were left to fight all our battles by ourselves. If these alliances were renewed, France might then be taught, that rashness, not prudence, had made her enter into the American confederacy.' He concluded with a flourish which consciously echoed Pitt: 'America . . . might be won in Europe, while England might be ruined in America.'[13]

Throughout 1778, therefore, British diplomats scoured the Continent in pursuit of an alliance to contain and divert France. They recognized that the new geopolitical configuration of Europe, especially in the east, made their task doubly difficult. As the Undersecretary of State for War, Charles Jenkinson, remarked in mid March 1778, the future belonged to 'The great military powers in the interior parts of Europe,' whereas 'France and Great Britain, which have been the first- and second-rate powers of the European world, will perhaps for the future be but of the third and fourth rate.' Russia, in particular, turned out to be a lost cause. She was at this time completing the shift from her Baltic-centred 'Northern System', in which the cooperation of London was deemed desirable, to a southern strategy against the Ottoman Empire, to which Britain was largely irrelevant. London's overtures were rebuffed. By mid December the British ambassador to St Petersburg was forced to admit not only that the Northern System was completely defunct, but that 'I see no friendly countenances on the Continent, and much fear that the number of our enemies will be increased.' Britain had higher hopes of an Austrian alliance: Vienna had, after all, expressed public disdain for the rebels and refused diplomatic relations with them. But the overtures made in early 1778 led nowhere. Austria refused either to foreswear the French alliance or to become embroiled in Britain's colonial affairs.[14]

Moreover, London's approaches were seriously complicated by the dire state of Austro-Hanoverian relations within the Empire. These had been bad enough at the start of the American War, but they deteriorated sharply in late 1777 and early 1778, when Joseph II persuaded Elector Karl Theodor of Bavaria – who had no legitimate heir – to trade his Electorate for Habsburg territories in the west and places in the imperial bureaucracies for his brood of illegitimate children. Almost immediately, Austrian troops moved to create a fait accompli by occupying most of lower Bavaria. This provoked Frederick the Great of Prussia into a violent response, and the War of the Bavarian Succession soon followed. George III, as Elector, was equally horrified by the potential increase in Joseph's power. For Britain, too, the Austrian action was potentially disastrous. It raised the prospect that Joseph would allow the French to occupy the Austrian Netherlands in return for the absorption of the whole of Bavaria. The Barrier was thus in deadly danger, which was averted only when Vergennes declined the offer. Joseph's gambit also made it more likely that London would be called on its security guarantee to the smaller German states from which it had hired troops in 1776. Finally and most pressingly, there was Hanover. As Elliot reported from Berlin in early April, 'it is to be feared a rupture between the courts of Berlin and Vienna will sooner or later involve His Majesty's Electoral Dominions in the general calamity'. Indeed, Kaunitz suggested to the French some months later that 'We could concert on several things relative to the Electorate of Hanover.' The resulting tension between British and Hanoverian concerns was summed up by the British envoy to the Hague, Sir Joseph Yorke, as follows: 'In this American quarrel the former [Austria] has undoubtedly been more friendly than the latter [Prussia]. To be sure Hanover is in the right; is England so too, that is the question?' For a brief moment Britain was faced with the nightmarish possibility of having to defend Hanover against one or the other German Great Power. This promised all of the expense of a European war with France, with none of the benefit of diverting French resources from America.[15]

Yet the Electorate could also be turned into an asset, just as early generations of British strategists had done. Throughout the next two years, the security of Hanover became a useful pretext in the search for a Continental alliance; Hanoverian assistance could also be traded for Prussian cooperation with Britain more generally. Thus in late February 1778, Elliot suggested 'giving the King of Prussia to understand that if the King, in his Electoral capacity, seconds his views in the Empire, an equally cordial cooperation will be expected from the court of Berlin in all those concerns which nearly affect the interests of Great Britain'; in other words, Hanover was being used for British purposes. Similarly in early April, Elliot was asked to 'endeavour to learn what measures the King of Prussia is disposed to suggest or concert for their [Hanover's] safety'. In what was surely an intentional echo of the events of 1755-6, Suffolk added that if the overtures were successful 'we should look forward to an alliance as a very agreeable consequence and in that case would not hesitate to grant a subsidy to the King of Prussia for the defence of Hanover, and the possessions of the several princes from whom we have been supplied with auxiliary troops'. As so often before, British diplomacy made full use of Hanoverian diplomats, with whom Elliot maintained 'a regular correspondence' in order to keep abreast of developments within the Empire; he even offered to transmit Hanoverian messages, if necessary. The schizophrenia implicit in the entire Anglo-Hanoverian relationship was vividly illustrated three months later when Elliot acted as a conduit for a Hanoverian message. 'It is by no means proper,' Suffolk reproved him, 'for you to interfere in any matter which relates to His Majesty's Electorate or to depart from the line of your duty as His Majesty's minister'.[16]

In short, as Sir Robert Ainslie wrote from Constantinople, 'The eyes of all Europe' were 'now turned on Germany'. For a brief moment in 1778-9 it seemed as if the scenario of 1739-41 and 1755-6 was about to be repeated. Once again, it seemed, two quite separate wars – in

Europe and overseas – were about to merge, and release Britain from
her perilous isolation. Thus, at the beginning of 1778, Lord North
looked forward to a war in Germany 'provided it would completely
occupy the French'. Joseph Yorke remarked of the Bavarian succession
that he 'hope[d] somewhere it will create a diversion in our favour'. A
few days later he elaborated that 'There seems to be no doubt of a war
in Germany and as little that Prussia acts in concert with France, [so] I
will flatter myself that order will arise out of this confusion and that old
England will be the better for it.' Suffolk bragged to the House of Lords
that 'one German soldier was worth four French'. Press opinion was
quick to spot, and to welcome, the analogy to the Seven Years War.
Even regional newspapers such as the *Cumberland Pacquet*, the *York
Courant* and *Farley's Bristol Journal* could see it.[17]

Unsurprisingly, therefore, the American rebels feared the outbreak of
war in Europe for exactly that reason. They had always had a very clear
sense of the importance of the state system to their struggle. It will be
remembered that in 1776 the patriot envoy Silas Deane had looked to
France to tie Britain down in Europe. But they soon realized that a
European war – a *general* European war – would be a very mixed
blessing. The last thing the Americans wanted was to see the French
sucked into a Continental war, and thus distracted from fighting Britain
overseas. The danger of this was already beginning to dawn on John
Adams in May 1777, when he wrote that 'I must confess that I am at a
loss to determine whether it is good policy in us to wish for a War
between France and Britain, unless we could be sure that no other
powers would engage in it.' He predicted that 'if France engages Spain
will, and then all Europe will arrange themselves on one side and the
other and what consequences to us might be involved in it I don't
know.'[18]

By 1778, therefore, there had been a marked shift in patriot geopolitics. In 1776 the Americans had wanted a European war to distract
Britain; now they realized that it would distract France. 'I am sorry to
inform you,' the patriot William Lee wrote from Paris to the President
of Congress in late February 1778, 'that there is now appearances of an
approaching rupture between the Emperor and King of Prussia, relative
to the possession of the late Elector of Bavaria's estates.' His brother
Arthur noted that 'Great Britain, whose expiring hope sustains itself on
every straw, finds comfort in the expectation that this will involve

France, and divert her from engaging in our war.' The sense of relief of the American agent in Paris, Ralph Izzard, was palpable. 'The death of the Elector of Bavaria,' he wrote in July 1778, 'was a circumstance that occasioned some alarm here, as it was feared that France might be forced into a Continental war in support of the succession of the Elector Palatine. This, however, in some degree has passed over and I hope the German princes will be left to settle their differences by themselves.'[19]

More specifically, the Americans were quick to spot the strategic value of Hanover in Britain's negotiations with the German powers. Thus Arthur Lee predicted in June 1778 that Frederick the Great would not ally with the United States because he valued Hanoverian cooperation against Joseph. A month later John Adams observed that 'The unforeseen dispute in Bavaria has made the Empress Queen [Maria Theresa] and [the] King of Prussia cautious of quarrelling with Great Britain, because her connection with a number of the German princes, whose aid each of those potentates is soliciting, makes her friendship or at least her neutrality, in the German war of importance to each.' The rebel belief that Hanover, or at least a Continental war arising out of it, was a British asset surfaced again in the following year. Thus William Lee, the American representative in Frankfurt, welcomed offers of Prussian mediation and diplomatic recognition in September 1779 with the observation that this 'might render us much more effectual service than by sending an army of fifty thousand men into Hanover, which step he could not take without arming the Emperor and the whole German Empire against him'. Here again we have the recognition that any attempt against Hanover, far from being a soft option, actually threatened Britain's enemies with incalculable consequences. The rebels too seemed aware that Britain had won America in Germany, by distracting France, and might regain her there.[20]

In the end, history did not repeat itself. Britain won no Continental allies, and Hanover was not invaded. On the other hand, she did secure assurances concerning the neutralization of Hanover: the Electorate would not become the target of French, Prussian or any other attack. Thus in late April 1778 Elliot reported from Berlin that Frederick 'had positive assurances from France of her intention not to send any troops into the [German] Empire'; in return Frederick expected Hanoverian support against Austria. In October 1778 the British ambassador to

Russia, Sir James Harris, reported the following remarks of Count Panin, the Russian chief minister, from St Petersburg: 'If they [France and Austria] declare openly in favour of their pretensions on the Bavarian succession, you may depend on having powerful and useful allies on the Continent.' If on the other hand they did not, Panin continued, 'you need have no apprehensions for the Electorate of Hanover, but be able to direct your whole force towards the defence of that part of the British dominions, which the court of Versailles seems to be the most desirous to wrest from you.' If Austria and France allied over Bavaria, Panin continued, then Russia would join a British and Prussian coalition against them. If Austria and France did not combine, he concluded, then Britain would be in the happy position of dealing with France overseas 'on an element alone, where you hitherto have always had, and are still so likely to maintain a superiority'. Here Panin was almost taunting the British diplomat with phrases drawn from Tory and 'blue water' rhetoric.[21]

There were two reasons why 1778 was not 1756. First of all, no Continental power was prepared to ally with Britain. Prussia, in particular, was determined to avoid a repetition of the events which followed the Convention of Westminster, when Britain and Prussia had agreed to neutralize Germany, thus driving France and Austria closer together, and ultimately triggering the Prussian invasion of Saxony and a general war. Maintaining peace with France, so as to avoid activating the Habsburg–Bourbon alliance, was an absolute priority for Frederick. He remained, moreover, extremely bitter about what he regarded as British perfidy towards the close of the Seven Years War; Suffolk could only lament these 'prejudices'. By the beginning of May, the British ambassador had to admit defeat. There was no Prussian alliance in the offing for the foreseeable future. Britain had no European card to play.[22]

Secondly, French strategy had changed fundamentally since the two wars in mid-century. This time, Vergennes was determined not to be dragged into a European war but to concentrate on the colonial struggle against England; he saw the Austrian alliance as a device to deny Britain succour in Europe, not as a platform for offensive operations in Germany. He was heedful of the warnings of the French diplomat Jean-Louis Favier, whose critique of Louis XVI's foreign policy, *Doutes et questions*, was first published in 1778: stay out of Hanover. In early January 1778 Favier repeated his warning in a private letter to Vergennes. 'We have today but one great aim. This matter [the Bavarian succession] is not a minor affair and it is to be feared that a German war would be as unhappy a diversion of our means and efforts for the *great national cause* as that of 1757. One must never forget the words of M. Pitt that America was conquered in Germany.' Few Frenchmen knew Germany as well as Vergennes: he had been in Hanover during the Imperial Election Scheme of the early 1750s. Military intervention in German politics was something he was determined to avoid. In short, the Hanoverian option in French policy was 'fool's gold'. It might promise easy leverage over Britain but invariably sucked France into fatal European commitments. Moreover, by the Treaty of Teschen which ended the War of the Bavarian Succession in 1779, Catherine the Great became a guarantor of the German Empire, thus complicating any attack on the Electorate still further. Hanover was spared not because of British efforts on her behalf, but because it was in nobody's interest to attack her.[23]

It took until the end of 1778 for this to sink in on the other side of the Channel. Reporting from the Reichstag in early December, the British envoy Ralph Heathcote noted that 'the sentiments of the French King are nearly the same as those of His Majesty' on the subject of Germany itself. The French agreed that the rights of both claimants to the Bavarian succession should be respected. If George III as Elector of Hanover agreed with Louis XVI, there was no chance of embroiling France in Germany. The ministry was also slowly coming to this realization. In late November 1778 Suffolk predicted that France would 'rather give up the interest of her ally than be drawn into a German war under her present circumstances'. The reason for French restraint in Germany was only too obvious. As the British envoy to the Archbishop of Cologne, diplomat and veteran German expert George Cressener pointed out, intervention in the Holy Roman Empire would be at the expense of France's naval effort, the very thing that Britain wanted and Vergennes was determined to avoid. 'I find it the general opinion,' he wrote in early November 1778, that the French 'are resolved to carry on the war by sea and build a formidable [navy] to dispute the dominion of the sea with us, and they hope by the assistance of Spain to succeed.' For this reason, he continued, 'I wish we may form an alliance with the court of Petersburg and thereby maintain our superiority on the ocean.' The link between Britain's European alliances and her naval predominance, once so central to strategic discourse in London, was here resoundingly restated. It was a particular irony that the recipient of this letter was none other than the Undersecretary at War, Charles Jenkinson, who had so signally failed to take all this into account in his assessments of the Royal Navy's needs in the 1760s.[24]

All the same, the hope of a Continental diversion died hard. Even as the prospect of a German war receded, the ambassador to Vienna enthused in June 1779 about the 'noble and spanking [Austrian] regiments' which passed him on the way back from the war against Prussia. 'May I live to see these fine fellows once more joined to a handsome corps of John Bulls,' he observed sadly, 'and hastening to pay the French for all their double-dealing ... But these are only political dreams, which, alas! Have no appearance of being realized in *our* days.'[25]

The failure to promote a Continental diversion against France on the back of the Bavarian succession made the maintenance of peace with Spain even more imperative. She had been showing signs of increasing restlessness throughout 1778, and while she refused to enter the war on France's side immediately, as Vergennes had hoped, her offer to 'mediate' in April 1778 was an ominous sign. Spain's principal aims were European: to secure the return of Gibraltar and Minorca, if possible peacefully. Instead, Britain offered West Florida, a pale colonial substitute for a large European asset, which the Spaniards promptly rejected. By the beginning of 1779, it was clear that Spain would enter the war. In April of that year, she concluded the Treaty of Aranjuez with France, and hostilities followed that same month. The joint justificatory manifesto issued by both powers underlined the extent to which they were driven by resentment of past British arrogance and humiliations. It spoke of France and Spain's intent 'To avenge their respective injuries, and to put an end to that tyrannical empire which England has usurped, and claims to maintain upon the ocean.' Vergennes's aim was to cut Britain down to size, not to eliminate her as a Great Power. More specifically, the French agreed that Gibraltar and Minorca should be returned to Spain, along with Mobile and Fort Pensacola in Florida; the British logwood cutters were to be ejected from the Gulf of Honduras.[26]

The implications of the Spanish entry into the war were disastrous. Britain's position in the western Mediterranean, already precarious, was now under immediate threat. More generally, the naval balance now shifted even further against Britain. Already in 1775, the combined

Franco-Spanish fleet exceeded that of Britain by some 25 per cent; thanks to the intense Bourbon programme of naval construction, this figure had jumped to 44 per cent by 1780. To be sure, the Royal Navy was better trained and led, but at some point quantity was bound to translate into quality. The French captured Dominica as early as June 1778. A year later, they captured first St Vincent and then Grenada, which was, after Jamaica, the second most important of Britain's sugar islands. In September 1779 a battered Admiral Barrington returned from the West Indies with a tale of woe. Britain, he reported, had forfeited her naval superiority, at least locally, and with it probably the rest of her sugar islands. At the same time, Britain lost control of the Mediterranean. For this reason, the Earl of Bristol lambasted Sandwich for 'the disgraceful and ignominious figure you have made to all the different powers and states on each side of the Mediterranean Sea, from the Straits of Gibraltar up to the coast of Syria'.[27]

Most worrying of all, the British archipelago itself was now in danger of a Franco-Spanish invasion. Ireland was in ferment. 'It [is] no secret,' the Duke of Manchester warned Parliament in 1779, 'that France intend[s] . . . to make an attempt on either, perhaps both kingdoms' of England and Ireland. But now even the south coast of England was vulnerable. Much against his better judgement, Vergennes allowed himself to be browbeaten by Spain into approving a joint invasion of the British Isles. In the summer and autumn of 1779 a large Franco-Spanish armada stood poised to strike across the Channel. Thirty thousand men were assembled in the ports of northern France. It was for good reason that the Undersecretary at War, Charles Jenkinson remarked in early September 1779, 'I believe this country was never in so perilous a situation as it is at present, and the events of the next fortnight will probably be as important, as ever were known in history.' And for the first time ever, Britain faced invasion without a single Continental ally. It was only through a combination of good luck, favourable winds, and Bourbon timidity that the projected invasion was called off.[28]

The question of how to respond to the new threat divided Britons. George III showed his customary robustness. To him, the war was now a matter not only of principle but of credibility. 'Whether the laying a tax was deserving of all the evils that have come from it,' was one thing, the King argued in June 1779, but independence was quite another. This was something 'which this country can never submit to'. If America were to 'succeed in that, the West Indies must follow them', and 'Ireland would soon follow the same plan'. In the end, he warned, 'this island would be reduced to itself, and soon would be a poor island indeed'. Britain, on this reading, would be merely the last domino to fall. As the bad news came flooding in from the West Indies, the King rebuked his commanders for their 'despondency'. 'No one,' he announced in September of that year, 'is more convinced than myself of the unexpected magnitude of the naval force now collected by the united House of Bourbon, but dejection is not the means of lessening it.' Instead, he demanded 'resolution' and 'boldness'. But this was a pose, not a policy. Moreover, the triumphs of the Seven Years War now proved to be a millstone around British policy, as they set the bar of expectation so high as to make territorial compromises impossible. Such a peace, George warned, was one that 'he that gave one to Europe in 1763 never can subscribe to'. Britain, in his view, should stay the course.[29]

Much of Parliament and the public sphere expressed itself with similar ebullience. Far from being depressed by Britain's isolation, Earl Nugent told Parliament without obvious irony 'that though we ha[ve] no foreign ally, we ha[ve] the best of all allies, unanimity at home. We [a]re allied among ourselves.' At the very end of August the *Morning Post and Daily Advertiser* suggested that

> Tho' *Monsieur* and *Don* should combine
> What have true *British* Heroes to fear?
> What are Frogs, and soup-meagre, and wine,
> To beef, and plumb-pudding, and beer?

In the same spirit, army recruiters highlighted the chance to 'pillage the Don'. Rather than tearing his hair out at the prospect of another enemy entering the lists, one naval officer claimed in June 1779 that a Spanish war 'is always agreeable to the Jack Tars of Britain'. To these men, the colonialist mirage, which had so mesmerized earlier generations of hackney writers and mariners, now shimmered once more invitingly before them. On this reading, the answer to the Bourbon threat after 1778–9 was more not less navalism; a greater engagement in the colonies, not a return to traditional European priorities. Indeed, as Earl Nugent suggested, the weapon which France and Spain had used against Britain might be turned on *them* with devastating effect. 'Spain,' he argued, 'might be conquered by her own doctrines. She might be deeply wounded in South America. Let us go and preach up independence there; not only preach it up, but assist South America in the obtaining of it.'[30]

For others, the outbreak of hostilities with Spain was yet more evidence of Britain's international isolation. In a petition of protest, more than twenty peers remarked pointedly that 'with the whole force of Great Britain and Ireland, aided by the most lavish grants, assisted by 30,000 Germans, unobstructed for a long time by any foreign power', the government had 'failed in three campaigns against the unprepared provinces of North America'. Therefore, they argued, 'we should hold ourselves unworthy of all trust, if we were willing to confide in those abilities which have totally failed in the single contest with the colonies, for rescuing us from the united and fresh efforts of France and Spain in addition to the successful resistance of North America.' Now, they lamented, 'the British Empire [is] rent asunder; a combination of the most powerful nations formed against us, with a naval superiority both in number of ships and alacrity of preparation. And this country now, for the first time, [is] left entirely exposed, without the aid of a single ally.' The remedy, they insisted, had to be 'a change of system in the principles and conduct of the war', starting with the restoration of Britain's 'credit and reputation abroad' in order to 'induce foreign nations to court that alliance from which they now fly'. Britain's colonial problems, in other words, required a European solution.[31]

The ministry itself was beginning to reach a similar conclusion. It was not enough, Sandwich privately conceded, to increase British naval construction, because the contest with the Bourbons would be decided by *relative* not absolute naval strength. And the mathematics were clear enough: together, undistracted by European conflicts, France and Spain could outbuild the Royal Navy. British Continentalists had been arguing this for nearly a century, but the penny finally dropped for Sandwich in mid September 1779. 'It will be asked why,' he told the cabinet, 'when we have as great if not a greater force than ever we had, the enemy are superior to us. To this it is to be answered that England till this time was never engaged in a sea war with the House of Bourbon thoroughly united, their naval force unbroken, and having no other war or object to draw off their attention and resources.' Moreover, Sandwich added, 'We unfortunately have an additional war upon our hands . . . [and] we have no one friend or ally to assist us.' The Prime Minister, Lord North, defended his own role in Britain's progressive isolation in very similar terms. He remarked in 1779 that 'The great glorious victories of the late war, and our decided superiority on the ocean, created us many enemies, and an alarm in the other powers of Europe.' These, he argued, no longer feared the French, but sought to cut Britain down to size. Under these circumstances, he claimed, 'the system of Europe . . . admitted of no Continental alliances, for to what end would they have been directed?' A little later, he pleaded that 'if we had not as yet any allies, it was not to be attributed to [my] dislike of Continental connections', but to the absence of any overt French threat to the European balance; 'it was not [my] fault'. The result, however, was the same: North conceded that 'when the whole House of Bourbon was suffered to collect this force unmolested, and to bring it to bear upon this country, it was impossible for Great Britain to prevent them from outnumbering us in ships.' In other words, North was publicly admitting that Britain's naval troubles were primarily the result of her European isolation. He did not seem to realize that this was no defence but part of the indictment.[32]

At the same time, British naval superiority was not an end in itself, nor simply the guarantee of defence and of her colonial ambitions; it formed the basis of Britain's position within the European state system. As Sir Horace Mann, a diplomat of considerable experience, warned in 1779, 'Strip us of our marine pre-eminence, and where must we find ourselves? Not among the first powers of Europe, far from it. Many countries exceed us indefinitely in extent of dominion, others in native produce and perhaps manufactures.' If Britain should ever suffer the loss of superiority 'upon our proper element . . . our importance must go'. For this reason, he added, news of British naval reverses that summer were having a catastrophic effect in Europe. He had been on the Continent during the summer naval campaign and in Vienna when the news of the defeats in the West Indies on 27 July arrived. 'The court of Vienna,' he said, 'heard it with astonishment . . . They imagined Great Britain lords paramount of the ocean, and invincible at sea . . . and did not hesitate to declare, that if once the empire of the ocean came to be seriously disputed by France, or any other nation, Britain would shortly be disrobed of her power and greatness.'[33]

In the light of all this, some Britons took a new long hard look at their strategic commitments. Thus in December 1779, seven months into the war with Spain, Commodore Johnstone argued that 'Gibraltar is the key upon which alone any true Spaniard can be brought to vindicate this war.' If, however, 'Gibraltar could be ceded,' he was persuaded that 'Spain might be brought to assist in reducing the American colonies, guaranteeing each other's dominions, and commanding France to desist.' Of course, public opinion would oppose this. But, Johnstone concluded, 'We had a cry at the loss of Calais; we had a cry at giving up Tangier; we had a cry at ceding Louisburg; but England flourished after all those cessions, and perhaps more than if she had retained them . . . I apprehend this would be the same with Gibraltar.' No single asset, in other words, should be privileged at the expense of Britain's long-term strategic interests.[34]

All this came at a time of continued domestic unrest, not just in Ireland, but in England itself. 1779 saw the emergence of the Yorkshire Association and other popular patriotic unions determined to agitate for parliamentary reform. As was so often the case, progressive sentiment was indistinguishable from xenophobia and obscurantism, particularly at the popular end of the spectrum. Fears of 'popish' subversion – fuelled by talk of Catholic emancipation – erupted in the Gordon Riots in May of the following year. These were led by the unstable but charismatic bigot Lord George Gordon. Mobs rampaged through London attacking Catholic chapels, harassing Members of Parliament and vandalizing foreign embassies. Arrogance had given way to paranoia in the search for scapegoats on whom the defeats in America could be blamed. Clearly, domestic calm would have to be restored if foreign war was to be prosecuted with any chance of success. Much of the domestic unrest, however, was actually driven by international failure. Nothing damaged the standing of the ministry and the Crown more than the morass into which the British army had slithered in America; Britain's diplomatic isolation; and the crisis the Royal Navy was facing on the high seas as a result of a misjudged European policy. The protagonists of the Yorkshire Association, especially Christopher Wyvill, blamed the disintegration of Britain's position and reputation within the European state system on the 'Toryism' of ministry and court. Only a thoroughgoing programme of domestic reform, it was argued, could restore Britain to her rightful place among the powers.[35]

It is therefore not surprising that the Duke of Richmond defended his motion for 'Economical Reform of the Civil List Establishment' primarily with reference to the strategic situation. Britain, he argued, was now faced with 'dishonour, if not national ruin', because it was 'now engaged in a contest with the two chief branches of the House of Bourbon', which it could not win. 'Britain,' he elaborated, '[stands] alone, with one-third of her subjects confederated with this formidable alliance, without a single ally, either in Europe or elsewhere.' In this context, Richmond claimed, it was essential 'to enquire, what internal resources she ha[s] to bear her out in so unequal a struggle?' For this reason he demanded a reduction of 'lavish and wasteful' public expenditure, especially on the Civil List. In this discourse, domestic virtue neatly dovetailed with strategic imperatives. A few months later, Edmund Burke picked up this theme in his famous plan for 'economic reform'. 'We must recollect,' he told Parliament, 'that with but half our natural strength, we are at war against confederated powers, who have singly threatened us with ruin.' He added that 'we must recollect that whilst we are left naked on one side, our other flank is uncovered by any alliance.' At the same time, he spoke with a new respect of French public finance. 'When I look . . . into the proceedings of the French King,' he continued, 'I am sorry to say it, I see nothing of the character and genius of arbitrary finance . . . On the contrary, I behold with astonishment, rising before me, by the very hands of arbitrary power, and in the very midst of war and confusion, a regular, methodical system of public credit.' It was this, he concluded, which provided 'the resources with which France makes war on Great Britain'. He therefore rebuked the government for the complacent 'contempt' with which it had dismissed French potential. Instead, Burke argued, Britain should 'imitate' the French, or at least recover its former 'public frugality', which was the basis of all 'national strength'.[36]

One important plank of economic reform was the abolition of the third secretaryship of state. Even ministerial figures agreed that the traditional system of northern and southern secretaryships, which had been further complicated by the creation of a colonial secretaryship in 1768, was in need of an overhaul. 'War,' the Secretary to the Treasury, John Robinson observed in mid August 1777, 'can't be carried on in departments; there must be consultation, union, and a friendly and hearty concurrence in all the several parts which set the springs at work and give efficacy and energy to the movements, without which the machine must fail.' Interestingly enough, however, the Opposition demand was justified not so much in terms of efficiency, as of monetary saving, and 'lessening the influence of the Crown'. Targeting the third secretaryship – in effect that for the colonies – not only reduced expenditure, it also had the advantage of annoying the incumbent, Lord George Germain, as well as his royal sponsor, George III. Virtue and economy, and political point-scoring, not integrated governance, was the Opposition's primary concern.[37]

Some important steps were taken in the direction of reform. A Bill to Relieve Dissenters was introduced in March 1779, which released ministers and schoolmasters from the obligation to subscribe to most of the Thirty-nine Articles. Not everybody accepted the strategic imperative for reform. Indeed, some cleaved to an alternative reading of the primacy of foreign policy, and argued that a period of severe international instability was no time to be rocking the boat at home. Thus Lewis Bagot, Dean of Christ Church, Oxford opposed increased toleration for Nonconformists on the grounds that 'It cannot be prudent to make essential alterations in your constitution at a time of public calamity.' Likewise at a tempestuous gathering of the Yorkshire Association in late December 1779, one grandee with close links to the Prince of Wales argued, with explicit reference to the international situation, that it was hardly the moment to raise demands for electoral reform. On the contrary, what the nation now needed was an increase in royal power to steady the ship.[38]

It was indeed a moot point whether Britain's national effectiveness would be heightened – crudely speaking – by more or by less freedom. To anybody looking at continental Europe – which was for many informed British observers a more obvious frame of reference than America – it was clear that the 'free' polities of Poland, Sweden and the United Provinces were in terminal decline. The future seemed to lie with the central and eastern European autocracies, which had streamlined their societies for military mobilization and expansion. As the Undersecretary of State for War had pointed out in mid March 1778, 'the great military powers in the interior parts of Europe, who have amassed together their great treasures, and have modelled their subjects into great armies, will, in the next and succeeding period of time, become the predominant powers.'[39] The question now was: how much domestic freedom should Britain surrender in order to defend its national liberty and its position within the European state system upon which this depended? For the situation was to get worse still. The old decade had ended in crisis and recrimination; the new decade would open with catastrophe and despair.

23

The Partition of Britain, 1780–1783

The revival of the Old System becomes utterly impossible if England loses her weight in the general scale, and she must lose it if this war ends in such a manner as to deprive her of those resources that feed and maintain her strength and which if preserved, may be advantageously employed, as they often have been, in the support of the general interest of Europe.[1]

Lord Stormont, Secretary of State for the North, December 1780

If Russia declares against us, we shall then literally speaking be in actual war with the whole world . . . The powers united will dismember our state and make such partition among them as they see fit.[2]

Lord Sandwich, Chief of the Admiralty, January 1781

She [France] could devote all her finances to her navy; because she had no land war; because we have no Continental ally, and because the frontier of France was secure and peaceable. There was the deep evil, the source, and the only source of danger to this country! While the frontier of France was undisturbed, and the Rhine flowed quietly within its banks, we had every reason to be alarmed, because while matters remained in that state, France could support her navy, she could recruit it rapidly, and could add daily to its number, its strength and its service.[3]

Nathaniel Wraxall MP, House of Commons, February 1781

After the Spanish declaration of war, renewed efforts were made to secure both Russia and Austria. In late 1779 Lord Stormont, a committed supporter of Continental alliances, became Secretary of State for the North. He argued that an Anglo-Russian-Austrian alliance would force France to break off the war in America. Throughout early 1780, therefore, the British ambassador importuned the Russian government in search of an alliance. By late June he had to admit defeat. 'I have the strongest confirmation,' Harris wrote, 'of the opinionative systematic hatred of Count Panin, whose inveteracy against England, after brooding ten or twelve years, now breaks forth with all the acrimony of an enemy.' Since there was now nothing more to be done, Harris earnestly requested his own recall. For the rest of the year, he was tormented by visions of Franco-Prussian collaboration, and taunted by Russian courtiers and ministers. 'These all,' Harris remarked in late November 1780, 'hold out the necessity of humbling us; that we are too great, too enterprising; that we are sea-tyrants, etc.' 'The absurdity of our being all this,' he added, 'when we are with difficulty defending ourselves against *half Europe and America*, is self-evident.'[4]

Austria seemed a better bet, especially with the waning of Maria Theresa, who finally died in late November 1780. She had never forgiven Britain for her lukewarm support during the War of the Austrian Succession. The accession of Joseph II as sole ruler, and the expectation of a decline in Kaunitz's role, gave British diplomats grounds for hope. They had been for some time of the opinion that, as the ambassador to Vienna put it, Joseph had a 'a good opinion of John Bull and his children'. Thus the Paymaster to the Forces, Richard Rigby, hoped in late January 1781 that 'this courier from you brings good tidings from the Emperor, of a friendly disposition to this country, which at this hour is in a state it never found itself before'. The first omens were indeed positive. Keith reported that same month that 'Our Emperor has behaved like an angel ever since his accession.' As ever, the aim was to revive the 'old system' with Vienna. Stormont called on Austria 'to pave the way for the return of that system which I hope and trust it will be the pride and joy of the Emperor's life to restore'.

Four months later he spoke of the need to 'restore the ancient system, as far as in the present circumstances of Europe it can be restored'. There was much talk of 'bring[ing] things back to their natural course'. To this end, Britain was prepared to make substantial concessions. Keith, the representative in Vienna, was told by Lord Stormont, Secretary of State for the North, that if he could 'discover any object of ambition to which the Emperor's views are pointed, any project of his, the execution of which could be promoted by Great Britain, upon your mentioning it to me, it will be taken immediately into the most serious consideration'.

The concept of 'linkage' and reciprocality, which British statesmen had jettisoned in the hubris of 1763, was now firmly re-established in British diplomatic thinking, but it was too late.[5]

It rapidly became clear that Joseph had no intention of becoming embroiled in the American War on Britain's side, or even of abandoning the French alliance. Keith's approaches were met with polite stonewalling. 'I am mortified,' he reported in early August 1780, 'to find myself deprived of the means of giving your lordship satisfactory intelligence relative to the Emperor's stay at Petersburg.' Kaunitz, he continued, 'has avoided the slightest mention of politics in the several visits I have paid him in the country'. Keith was therefore dependent on 'second-hand' information; he was completely out of the loop. Ten days later, he lamented that 'the whole of the Bourbon party are in much greater favour at this court than they were six weeks ago'. One stumbling block was Joseph's plans for the Low Countries, the traditional neuralgic point for British foreign policy. 'I often heard,' Stormont remarked in early August 1780, 'that one of the favourite projects of the Emperor was the restoring the commerce of Flanders to its former prosperity by opening the navigation of the Schelde through Antwerp. The project is every way worthy of the greatness of his views; and surely the present situation of Europe affords a very favourable opportunity for attempting the execution of such a design.' By early September there were rumours of a forthcoming visit by Joseph to Flanders to assess whether such a move would be viable. None of this unduly worried London: indeed it was welcomed as an irritation to the Dutch (who feared trading competition from Antwerp), with whom war was inevitable in any case over their commerce with the rebel colonists, especially if Joseph extended toleration to Protestants and thus attracted 'respectable inhabitants' from further north. But it soon emerged that there was more to it than that. For at the same time, Kaunitz was floating – to considerable British alarm – the idea of an Austrian East India Company. In other words, at the very moment that Britain was bogged down in the colonies and isolated in Europe, her potential Austrian ally was proposing a revival of the Ostend Company of the 1720s.[6]

Another problem was Hanover. The one sphere in which Austria could use British help – the Holy Roman Empire – was the one area where George as Elector was at daggers drawn with Vienna. In early December 1779 Hanoverian sabotage produced an outburst from Sir

Robert Murray Keith in Vienna against 'that spirit of chicanery which is but too often remarked in the dealings of the Hanoverian ministry towards this court'. It was not, he continued, that he wished 'to see a style of subserviency adopted by any man who has the honour to serve the King (in England or Germany) in his correspondence with the ministers of any foreign prince whatever. But at least . . . whilst the King is seeking to cultivate the friendship of their imperial majesties let us not find his language *contradicted* by the harsh punctiliousness of His Hanoverian Chancery.' Nor was Keith imagining it all: 'the Empress herself has complained to me of this contradiction'. It was perhaps for this reason that British ministers now sought to distance themselves from the Hanoverian connection as much as possible. Thus Suffolk told the envoy to Prussia once again that it was 'by no means proper for [him] to interfere in any matter which relates to His Majesty's Electorate, or to depart from the line of your duty as His Majesty's Minister'. Surprisingly, British critics of the ministry did not pick up on the problem, which earlier generations would have used to embarrass the monarch and his servants.[7]

In the following year, as Anglo-Austrian negotiations dragged on, rivalry between George III and Joseph II in the Holy Roman Empire continued to complicate British attempts to resurrect the 'old system'. The two sides clashed over the question of the election of a coadjutor – deputy and successor – to the Archbishop of Cologne. Joseph was determined to push his younger brother, the Archduke Max Franz, into this position. Thus in early August the ambassador in Vienna reported that 'Kaunitz believes that the Hanoverian ministry are active in their opposition to the Archduke's election at Münster; and while that belief lasts, your lordship will not be surprised at the suspension of that confidence with which he had so constantly honoured me.' Stormont responded by assuring him that 'I would not lose a moment in contradicting an opinion which is certainly groundless and . . . I am confident that the Hanoverian ministers took no active step whatever in opposition to the Archduke.' Indeed, he went on, 'His Majesty's resolution, from the beginning, was not to interfere in that business either as King or Elector.' The difficulty here was not so much the German connection as such, as the failure to parlay the King's Hanoverian assets into Continental allies for Great Britain. In the context of the time, these were not minor irritations, but potentially fatal to Britain's position in Europe and thus globally.[8]

In the autumn of 1780 George's Hanoverian ministry did make some attempt to conciliate Vienna. Britain offered to support Joseph II in the Empire, if he would give up the French alliance. Thus Britain and Hanover rejected Frederick's attempts to sabotage the election of Joseph's brother Max Franz as coadjutor to the archbishopric of Cologne. In September 1780 there were even hopes in Vienna of a Habsburg–Hanoverian rapprochement, which would split the *Corpus Evangelicorum*, and isolate Prussia. This was picked up by the ambassador in Vienna, who announced in mid September, perhaps as much in hope as expectation, that henceforth 'the language and conduct of Great Britain and of the Electorate of Hanover will be entirely consonant with each other'. The King's interest in matters German was increased still further in the following year when his favourite son, the Duke of York, moved there to reside as the Prince-Bishop of Osnabrück. One way or the other, sixty years after the accession of George I, twenty years into the reign of George III, who had gloried in the name of Britain, and five years into a global conflict for control of America, Britain remained a central European power ruled by a German prince.[9]

This slight warming of relations between Britain-Hanover and Vienna in the Empire was not enough to secure an Austrian alliance. A Prussian or Russian alliance seemed even more remote. To European powers a British alliance was simply not worth having. Not only was she mired in a colonial morass, Britain was also wracked by domestic instability. Frederick the Great, Joseph and Catherine the Great routinely cited these disturbances as evidence of British weakness. This impression was confirmed by the increasingly frantic tone in which London suggested that such a 'system' was not only in Europe's but also their own best interests. In particular, the Gordon Riots of 1780 – which saw the spectacular collapse of public order, the mistreatment of foreign envoys and an explosion of anti-Catholic rhetoric – did not help British diplomats seduce Austria, the foremost Catholic power of central Europe. By contrast, the Americans had successfully muted their ingrained hatred of popery in order to secure French and Spanish support.

As 1780 wore on, many despaired that the country would ever break out of her isolation. In early May, General Conway told Parliament that Britain was now 'at war with America, with France, and Spain, without a single ally, without a single power our friend'. '[O]n the contrary,' he continued, 'every one of the foreign powers, great as well as small, [is] acting either directly or indirectly in a manner inimical to our interests: even the little Lübeckers, the Danzigers, and the town of Hamburg [are] against us.' To cap it all, 'Holland, our natural ally, [is] adverse to our interest, and refusing the least assistance.' Britain was therefore, he concluded mournfully, 'turned out for the hunt, like the stricken deer, deserted and abandoned by all the herd'. A few months later he wrote that 'we are now evidently struggling [with] a superior force, after contriving to shake off everything we could ever call our ally'. The Whig MP William Eden (who later went on to a distinguished diplomatic career) spoke simply of 'a moment of universal gloom overspreading our political hemisphere'.[10]

40. England (as a sailor) fighting the 'four confederates' – the Dutch, the French, the Americans and the Spanish. Many in Britain considered it a badge of honour to be at war with practically the whole world.

But no wail of sorrow compared with that of the British ambassador to Vienna, who exclaimed in mid October 1780,

What is the matter with Old England ... that she has lost every grain of her ancient spirit and perseverance? The absurdities with which every paper has been filled ... and the mean-spirited despondency which one half of our fellow citizens display upon the least untoward accident, are to me constant sources of shame, as well as sorrow. I find it a hard matter to hold my head high as I shall ever wish to hold it, amidst a score of foreign ministers who (upon the faith of our representation of the situation of our own affairs) look upon the faithless Bourbons as the very lords of the ascendant.

Surely, Keith protested, this despondency was premature. Things would still have to get a great deal worse 'ere it can be possible for such a nation as ours to lose its weight and consideration in Europe'. For this reason he asked his correspondent 'to ransack all London for such good news, or at least well-founded expectations, as may enable me to stem with honour, the torrent of falsehood and presumption with which the Bourbons are preparing to overflow all Europe', and indeed to keep his own morale up.[11] Clearly, it was Britain's role in Europe rather than the position in America *per se* which exercised Keith.

Moreover, Stormont observed, European isolation endangered Britain's maritime dominance, upon which in turn her standing within the state system rested. Thus in early September he saw 'designs of France [and] the court of Berlin' to use 'every endeavour to overturn the whole system of Europe, by destroying the maritime power of Great Britain and striking her weight out of the general scale'. Later that year, he made the link between the naval, colonial and European spheres more explicit, when he claimed that if Britain lost her 'weight in the general scale', which she would do 'if this war ends in such a manner as to deprive her of those resources that feed and maintain her strength . . . in the support of the general interest of Europe', then any chance of resurrecting the 'old system' to contain France in Europe would be forfeit. On the other hand, Stormont argued that the French 'must relinquish their expectation of crushing the maritime power of this country, unless they can create new enemies of Great Britain'. In short, even as a desperate battle was being fought in America, a diplomatic struggle was raging in Europe, in which the stakes were higher still.[12]

The damaging effect of Britain's maritime preoccupation on her European position was heightened by the manner in which she conducted herself on the high seas. Stopping neutral ships, checking them for contraband and if necessary confiscating it, made sense as a device to blockade the American colonies; but the diplomatic cost of such high-handedness was about to become clear. London brushed all neutral protests aside as self-interested or, worse, manipulated by France. The smaller powers, such as the Danes and Swedes – no friends to the American colonists – could be bullied more or less with impunity. Count Creutz, the Swedish ambassador at Paris, objected to Britain's 'despotism at sea'. By mid 1780, however, after years of what they regarded as British provocation, it became clear that the Russians, Prussians and Dutch were no longer going to take their maritime subordination lying down. Catherine the Great, in particular, felt buoyed up by her triumph in mediating the Treaty of Teschen, which concluded the War of the Bavarian Succession, and was disposed to put Britain in her place. In March 1780, the Russians sponsored a declaration of neutral rights, the original idea for which had come from Denmark. The Swedes and Danes signed up openly in July. Eventually, the Armed Neutrality was to include Russia, Austria, Prussia, the Kingdom of the Two Sicilies, Holland, Denmark and Sweden. If one bears in mind that Britain was already fighting France, Spain and the American colonists, this meant that she was now in a state of war or cold war with virtually the entire occidental world.[13]

News of the Armed Neutrality hit British diplomats like a thunderbolt. Thus the ambassador to Vienna spoke of 'this wicked league', which came at a time 'when Great Britain, though fighting under a wise and virtuous monarch, in the fairest and most just cause that ever unsheathed the national sword has, from a fatal combination of circumstances, not one single friend in the wide extent of Europe, or at least one friend who can lend her the smallest assistance'. Moreover, London now feared that the Prussians would attempt to develop the league into an offensive alliance. Stormont believed that Frederick the Great was now so totally in thrall to France that he would use 'his utmost endeavours to turn the Northern Union into a powerful and formidable league against this country'. In Parliament, the Earl of Shelburne saw the Armed Neutrality as the result of 'the total neglect on the part of ministers, to procure alliances on the continent of Europe, and the disobliging the few friends we had'. Even the Austrians, whose maritime trade was hardly extensive, sympathized with the Armed Neutrality and eventually joined it. They were particularly offended by the activities of British privateers in the Mediterranean and the Admiralty Court at Minorca, at which Austrian ships were regularly condemned (i.e. confiscated as prizes). The Austrian envoy to London, Count Belgioso, regularly complained about British attacks on their shipping in the Mediterranean. 'It does not seem possible,' he expostulated, 'that the court of London would wish to approve such brigandage.' In mid December 1780 the British ambassador in Vienna reported that Kaunitz had 'c[o]me up to me with a very serious air, and said "Can it be possible, sir, that Great Britain has determined to quarrel with the whole world? It would seem to, by her treatment of the subjects of a neutral power." Indeed, he claimed that "The Barbary Corsairs are less rapacious than you are, and their courts of justice less partial than your Court of Admiralty in Minorca." '[14]

If the Armed Neutrality epitomized Britain's deepening isolation, it was also a mortal threat to her naval dominance. As the Earl of Shelburne observed, the consequences of a new maritime code, which gave France and Spain unrestricted access to naval stores, would be disastrous. 'Being thus deprived,' he warned, 'of the advantages which had given us the superiority, during the three last wars, over the House of Bourbon, the foundation taken away, the superstructure erected upon that basis must fall to pieces, and then farewell for ever to the naval power and glory of Great Britain.'[15]

The Armed Neutrality showed how far Britain's relations with neutral Europe had deteriorated, particularly with the Dutch. Ever since the late 1730s, of course, Britain had felt that the United Provinces had not been pulling their weight in the containment of France. After all, the performance of the Dutch Republic in the War of the Austrian Succession had been so dismal that Britain had had to trade colonial gains to get the French out of the Low Countries. Dutch neutrality during the Seven Years War had also gone down very badly. But it was only in the late 1770s that irritation began to harden into hostility. For the Dutch had been the most flagrant covert traders with the American colonists, and they gave sanctuary to American cruisers preying on British shipping. Britain's response was consistently high-handed and contemptuous, to the delight of Tory opinion which had been violently anti-Dutch since the Glorious Revolution. Thus the Earl of Shelburne complained that 'We treated them more like the wretched dependants, or the subjects of petty Italian Republics, than a state which filled so respectable a niche in the grand European system.' Since November 1779 the Dutch had armed their convoys, which had led to tense stand-offs with the Royal Navy on the high seas. Moreover, the Stadholderate, which was traditionally friendly to Britain, was in sharp decline. French influence was strong, and believed by London to be rampant. In the face of this, the long-serving British ambassador, Joseph Yorke proposed to step up the pressure on Holland. It was hoped thereby to force the Dutch to come off the fence, and at the same time to precipitate a crisis which would strengthen the Stadholderate and thus benefit Britain. The aim was to secure Dutch maritime collaboration, but not active belligerence on Britain's side, because that might provoke a French invasion, as in 1747, and thus create further liabilities. It was a strategy of startling eccentricity and originality.[16]

It was also completely misjudged. Dutch public opinion was by now rabidly anti-British, and the increased naval harassment was the last straw. Holland would have been happy to remain neutral, but British policy was consciously designed to push her over the brink, in order to free the hands of the Royal Navy to take on Dutch commerce openly. War with the Dutch followed in December 1780. Now Britain was directly threatened with invasion not only in Ireland, the Western Approaches and the Channel, but from the Low Countries and in East Anglia. Bearing in mind that Austria had joined the Armed Neutrality, the entire coast of Western Europe from northern Spain to Emden in north Germany, and beyond, was now in hostile hands. The nightmare of Elizabethan foreign policy, and English grand strategy ever since, had come to pass. All the counterscarps, outworks, and forward bastions of the nation had been lost. Only the wooden walls now stood between it and the enemy.[17]

For many, the outbreak of hostilities with the Dutch, Britain's 'natural allies' for the past century, was the final straw. As conflict approached, the Earl of Shelburne had lamented that Britain had now 'become the contempt and standing jest of all Europe; and from a great, glorious and happy people, who had borne our arms triumphant to every quarter of the globe', they 'were fallen to a degree of insignificance and humiliation'. Later he exclaimed, 'A Dutch war! A war with Holland! As soon as it reached [my] ears, [it] filled [me] with amazement. What, a war with Holland! With our ancient allies and natural friends! Whose efforts and connections, for more than a century, have proved the chief security of both states! . . . It benumb[s] all the faculties of [my] mind, and in its first effects, left no impression there but wonder and amazement.' This was a colonial threat – the French were now permitted to use Dutch bases at the Cape, Sumatra and Ceylon – but the main danger lay in

Europe, just across the Channel. An alarm had been sounded. The last war with the Dutch in the 1670s had been followed not long after by invasion and revolution. Both once again seemed possible, under a Tory administration, which like its seventeenth-century predecessors privileged a maritime quarrel with the Dutch over broader strategic considerations of the European balance of power.[18]

Even Sandwich at the Admiralty had to admit that the outlook had never been worse. Keeping Russia out of the hostile coalition was now more imperative than ever, if necessary through the cession of Minorca. 'If Russia declares against us,' he told the cabinet in January 1781, 'we shall then literally speaking be in actual war with the whole world.' There was now an acute danger of the partition of the British Empire. 'The powers united will dismember our state,' he feared, 'and make such partition among them as they see fit.' 'We shall,' he wailed, 'never again figure as a leading power in Europe, but think ourselves happy if we can drag on for some years a contemptible existence as a commercial state.'[19]

Yet a substantial section of British popular, parliamentary and political opinion saw Holland simply as yet another foreigner to be vanquished. Far from despairing at the appearance of yet another enemy, it responded with an almost suicidal exuberance. They believed the Dutch to be contemptible and thus easy pickings. The ambassador to Russia, James Harris, dismissed the Dutch as 'ungrateful, dirty, senseless boors'. To a hostile Europe, he spat defiance. 'Let us . . . go on boldly,' he wrote to a friend. 'England, when united in itself, is a match for all Europe; and an English minister, active, upright, and sincere, has nothing to hope or fear from either the intrigues of his foreign colleagues or those of the court where he resides.' In Belfast enthusiastic preparations were made for attacking Dutch commerce. The capture of the Dutch island of St Eustatius in March 1781 was greeted with bonfires. The MP Sir Horace Mann, who had extensive diplomatic experience, consoled Parliament – perhaps ironically – that 'though we were without an ally, we had obvious advantages, if we would agree among ourselves, and act with vigour and firmness'. Richard Rigby, a voice of moderation towards the end of the Seven Years War, announced that 'I wish for a sea fight, even at a disadvantage of numbers; for nothing puts the people of this country so much (nor in my opinion so justly) out of humour as these inactive naval campaigns.' A popular caricature made the same point even more bluntly. In it Jack England – symbolizing the Royal

Navy – contemplates France, Spain, Holland and the Americans – and announces 'Sink me but I could beat them all if our landlubbers would but pull together.' This was both a jibe at the failures of the army in America, and a restatement of the classic navalist myth. But they didn't and he couldn't.[20]

Others, by contrast, saw the Dutch entry into the war as yet more proof of the need for a European alliance. Thus Thomas Townshend lamented 'our want of alliances, and [can] not rejoice at the compact state which others [seem] so much pleased with'. After all, he remarked brutally, he did not 'believe that what was done against Lewis XIV would have been more easily achieved by attacking him without any allies at all.' He noted that 'year after year', North 'ha[s] told the House of a new enemy; but since the commencement of the American War, he ha[s] never brought down the welcome news of our having gained an ally'. Likewise, Charles James Fox, responding to the suggestion that Britain was better off on her own, remarked 'that if that doctrine were true, Great Britain [i]s the most flourishing nation in the world'. All this, the argument ran, had been at considerable cost to Britain's naval position. Britain, Fox continued, was 'at a hundred times more expense in our American operations' than the French. He therefore recommended that 'we might carry on the war with greater success, by [re]calling all our forces from America', and attacking the French. He concluded that 'As it was said in the last war, that France was conquered in Germany, so if ever America [i]s to be conquered, it must be in France.' Here it was in a nutshell: the old Continentalist doctrine that Britain's colonial position depended on the management of the European balance of power, garnished with the ritual invocation of the Pittite strategic legacy. This was, as Townshend made clear, a call for the return to a Whig foreign policy. Invoking the glories of William III, Marlborough, and the 'first years' of Queen Anne, he claimed that 'In those reigns, in the time of all Whig ministries, great alliances were sought and obtained. This country had not then the madness to hazard a war with all the world, without a single ally.'[21]

All these themes were pulled together by Nathaniel Wraxall, MP for Hindon, and a man with extensive European experience. In a devastating parliamentary critique, he called upon the House 'to consider a little what had been our practice in former wars, and whence we had chiefly derived our success'. He attributed the 'present misfortunes' to 'a new policy, which this country had lately adopted' and was based on 'blind bigotry' to a false 'tenet', to wit that 'Continental connections [are] incompatible with the true interests of Great Britain'. Rather, he urged, 'Let the House advert to the wars of King William, the wars of Queen Anne, and the still more recent wars of 1741 and 1756, and they [will] see, from the incontestable evidence of established facts, that this country, in all those wars, ha[s] deduced most essential advantages from our having Continental connections'. From this 'doctrine' Wraxall 'demonstrated the necessity of our procuring an immediate ally on the Continent'.[22]

Against this analysis, Sandwich – who had already privately conceded the disastrous naval effects of Britain's European isolation – fought a desperate parliamentary rearguard action. 'Continental connections,' he argued, 'had always, and ever would be productive of Continental wars; and after the experience of the four great wars since the Revolution,' he believed, 'no real friend to his country would wish to behold a fifth.' He concluded by observing that since the current war was not about Europe at all but 'a maritime struggle, and that we possess . . . the advantages' he had 'so often alluded to,' he thought 'we should be infatuated to the last degree not to improve them'. In short, the administration was publicly defending a paradigm in which they had themselves privately lost faith. This was a sign of impending defeat, and it could do no more than prolong the agony.[23]

Across Europe, Britain now enjoyed an unenviable reputation for weakness and arrogance. 'The most notorious falsehoods,' the ambassador to Russia complained, 'have been made use of to describe us as being cold, reserved, haughty, and supercilious.' The Earl of Shelburne, returning from Continental travels, reported on the 'increasing jealousy . . . and general odium which . . . prevailed all over Europe'. Indeed, he continued, 'All Europe was hurt and alarmed; we were called a nation of pirates and public plunderers.' This, he went on, 'created . . . the seeds of that jealousy, the unhappy fruits of which have been the principal cause that one half of Europe are in arms against us, and the other half remain inactive, and express a kind of silent pleasure at our approaching downfall'. Likewise, one Alderman Sawbridge 'insisted that the haughtiness of Great Britain had combined the world against her; and that the war with Holland was unjust and impolitic'. He went on to say that 'While France was the first power in Europe, the nations around were confederated against her.' Yet, 'when Britain rose to an envied pitch of greatness, a just apprehension of a similar hostile confederacy should have taught her justice, wisdom, and moderation.' Finally, Edmund Burke attributed Britain's isolation to 'a spirit of arrogance in our councils'.[24]

Despite all these disasters, Britain was not, or did not believe herself to be, entirely without options in Europe. Even if a Continental ally could not be secured, perhaps diplomacy might serve to split the hostile coalition. An opportunity to do this with regard to France arose in the summer and winter of 1780, when the French Director-General of Finances, Jacques Necker, tormented by the crippling expense of the war, approached North. The moment passed, not least because British statesmen saw the overture as a sign of weakness, rather than as an opportunity. Thus the King remarked that 'France is certainly in greater difficulties than we imagined or she would [not] by such various channels seem to court peace.' The prospect of a separate arrangement with Spain was explored in much greater detail. Father Thomas Hussey – an Irish Jacobite priest based in Spain, and former chaplain of the London embassy – was sent in late 1779 as an emissary after rumours of a possible British cession of Gibraltar. London responded to the overture by sending Richard Cumberland, a Secretary of the Board of Trade and a confidant of the Colonial Secretary Lord George Germain, back to Spain with Hussey. The Spanish demand was for the return of Gibraltar, in exchange for a territorial 'equivalent'. 'The importance of Gibraltar,' Cumberland later reported, 'is above computation' for Spain. For some in the British cabinet, however, Gibraltar was also a sticking point. Thus the Northern Secretary declaimed 'with great vehemence and emphasis, that if the map of the Spanish Empire was spread before him, he could not lay his finger upon that portion of it, which he as minister would treat for in exchange for Gibraltar'. He would not, in other words, trade a European asset for a colonial bauble. British inflexibility on this point effectively cut the ground from beneath Cumberland's feet. 'I entered Spain under instructions,' he later complained, 'which left me nothing to grant but Pensacola [in Florida], and that upon equivalent.' Madrid argued that the retention of Gibraltar was 'proof that we choose to keep up this motive of constant enmity and distrust between the two nations'. In February 1781 Cumberland was finally recalled. The war with Spain would continue.[25]

The other gambit was to persuade one of the Great Powers to mediate on Britain's behalf. At first, Britain sought to effect this by leveraging her weakness. Rather than overselling the merits of a British alliance – which had got them nowhere since 1763 – diplomats now sought to convince the eastern powers that the collapse of British power would have disastrous consequences for the European balance more generally. The British ambassador to Vienna was therefore instructed to impress upon the Austrians 'how much every great power in Europe, France alone excepted, would be affected by Great Britain losing the weight she has hitherto had in the general scale'. The same argument was tried with the Russians. Thus Harris told Catherine's favourite, Prince Potemkin in late December 1780 that Britain would certainly suffer 'some diminution, either of power or of our possessions', and that 'our natural friends would then see their error, and when it was too late, lament their having been the cause of giving additional weight to courts [i.e. France] in interests opposite to theirs'. This was not a completely abstruse argument: it was possible that a French triumph would make her more inclined to defend Poland, Sweden and Turkey against further Russian encroachments. But Potemkin's reply was crushing: 'He asked why I was repeating what I had so often said, and whether I thought any doubts remained in his mind of the crisis in which we were, and of the erroneous conduct of this and of several other courts who ought to be our friends.'[26]

In the end, British statesmen realized that Russia was not going to do anything for nothing. It would have to be bought. As Britain's position deteriorated still further in 1780–81, the idea emerged of purchasing a Russian mediation through territorial concessions to the Tsarina in the Mediterranean; or, at least, to ensure that any concessions that Britain had to make to extricate herself from the American War would not benefit France. The British ambassador hinted that 'if we were ever reduced to the disagreeable necessity of making cessions, it would . . . be wiser for us, as well for our own good, as for the sake of the balance of Europe in general, to make them to our natural *friends*, rather than to our natural *enemies*.' Harris hoped that 'such an act might rouse' Britain's friends 'to activity'. Potemkin took the bait. Rejecting all colonial offers of sugar islands, he immediately demanded Minorca. His imagination now ran away with him as he spoke of 'a Russian fleet stationed at Mahón, of its peopling the island with Greeks; that such an acquisition would be a column of the Empress's glory erected in the middle of the sea, and that he would be responsible; he could lead her to any lengths under the promise of such a cession'. Harris could not have known this, but what Potemkin was articulating was the dream of a Russian Mediterranean mission which was to haunt British policy-makers throughout the nineteenth century. On the contrary, Harris saw the surrender of Minorca, which was on the verge of falling to Spain anyway, as an exit strategy from complete isolation. He hinted to Stormont, the Secretary of State for the North, that there were 'greater advantages in changing the present system of Europe' and in 'making . . . a great and powerful ally', than holding on to that island.[27]

The problem with such a bold stroke was that it would run foul of public opinion. As Stormont remarked, 'Minorca, besides its many real advantages, stands very high in the esteem of the nation at large, a circumstance that must be attended to in a constitution like ours.' All the same, if the price were right the sacrifice could be made, but only 'for great and essential service actually performed'. This meant nothing less than the 'restoration of peace between Great Britain, France, and Spain' on the basis of the Treaty of Paris in 1763. On these conditions, Britain would hand Minorca over to Catherine. But in the end, even that was not enough to tempt the Russians off the fence. The eastern plates were at this moment in the process of shifting as Catherine sought an understanding with Joseph II – culminating in the secret Austro-Russian treaty of 1781 – which would pave the way for further assaults on the Ottoman Empire. In these circumstances, it made no sense at all for St Petersburg to take any risks in order to help Britain.[28]

If Britain was prepared to reconsider her position in the western Mediterranean to secure a Russian alliance, war with Holland, the first in more than one hundred years, forced British statesmen to rethink their traditional conception of the Barrier as a joint Anglo-Dutch project. Thus Stormont noted that the southern Dutch province of Zealand was so alienated from the anti-British 'Amsterdam faction' that there was 'very good reason to believe that they would desert the federative union, if they could find sure and permanent support elsewhere'. Moreover, he 'had intelligence . . . that if the Austrians attempt to open the Schelde, grant liberty of conscience . . . and join with England, Zealand will be disposed to withdraw itself from the union, and join with the lords of the Schelde.' This 'project', he claimed, was being 'publically talked of in the streets of Middelburg [the capital of Zealand]'. He concluded that 'There appears to me something very captivating in this idea.' It is easy to see why: the scheme promised to strengthen the Austrian Netherlands, and thus the Barrier against France; to facilitate a Habsburg alliance; and to punish the Dutch. Within a few months, however, the plan had been humiliatingly overtaken by events. In 1781 the Austrians expelled the Barrier garrisons without consulting Britain – a signatory to the original Barrier Treaty. With the departing Dutch troops went the last vestiges of the Utrecht Settlement. It was yet another reminder of how low Britain's position in Europe had fallen. The traditional counter-scarps and outworks of England were now in mortal danger. Over the past one hundred years, ministers had been impeached for much less, yet there was no public outcry.[29]

British ministers were now rapidly running out of options. Another possible solution was to bail out of the American War and concentrate on fighting France and Spain. This was the thrust of General Conway's Bill of early May 1780 'For quieting the troubles in America'. He called for 'an end to the war with America, the better to enable us to carry our arms successfully against the House of Bourbon'. Charles James Fox, Burke and the Duke of Richmond all argued in a similar vein. The administration steadfastly refused to countenance any such withdrawal for fear that it would trigger an unstoppable chain reaction. The Colonial Secretary, Lord George Germain, predicted that what 'would follow' was that, 'France and America united would in a very short time send a powerful force against Newfoundland: they would seize upon our fisheries, and destroy that great nursery of our navy. Canada would fall next, and the possessions we yet had in the West Indies would be wrested from us.' It would all end, he concluded, with Britain being 'vigorously attacked in every quarter of the globe'. Besides, withdrawal from America would come at the price of royal favour. The King himself played on these fears in his demands for more offensive action overseas, even at the risk of exposing Britain itself to attack. 'If nothing but measures of caution are pursued,' he warned in September 1779, and ministers failed to show that 'boldness which alone can preserve a state when hard pressed, I shall certainly not think myself obliged, after a conduct should have been held so contrary to my opinion, to screen them from the violence of an enraged nation'. This would leave the administration completely exposed to Opposition inquiries into the causes of the disaster. Memories of ministers left twisting in the wind from Buckingham, through Strafford, Danby and Oxford, were still fresh. Until the situation became absolutely unbearable, it made more political sense to humour the King in his determination to die in the last ditch, than to confront him with the brutal truth and to cut Britain's losses.[30]

Finally, there was the option of making good the lack of European allies through internal reform. In St Petersburg James Harris told the Russian chief minister Potemkin despairingly that Britain had been 'abandoned by all our friends' and could thus 'only rely on the justice of our cause, and on such resources as our own internal strength supplied us with'; these were, he conceded, 'not inexhaustible'. 'We want,' Edmund Burke told Parliament, a 'great minister, who, like [the French minister] Necker, would strike out bold and new paths suitable to the pressure of affairs.' But as Wraxall pointed out, domestic reform was not the real source of France's current strength or Britain's new weakness. Instead, Wraxall 'feared her because she could devote all her finances to her navy; because she had no land war; because we have no Continental ally ... There was the deep evil, the source, and the only source of danger to this country!' In short, no matter how they looked at the problem, British observers always came back to the realization that isolation in Europe was the root of their troubles in America and on the high seas.[31]

At the end of 1780, British military prospects in America were at last beginning to look up. It had been a relatively good year: true, the Spaniards had taken Mobile in Florida in mid March, but in May British forces had captured Charleston and appeared set to take control of much of the South. Here they were helped by their emancipationist message to the black plantation slaves. The jubilee was brought by the British army advancing from the sea; the royal banner was the flag that set them free. Politically, of course, these moves had the effect of smashing the remaining porcelain among southern whites, and drove them ever more firmly towards the 'patriot' cause. Once again, American patriots looked to Europe, and sought to parlay their distress into an argument for increased Bourbon intervention. Thus in February 1781 Benjamin Franklin warned Vergennes that 'If the English are suffered ... to recover that country, such an opportunity of effectual separation as the present may not occur again in the course of ages.' He predicted that 'the possession of those fertile and extensive regions and that vast sea coast will afford them so broad a basis for future greatness, by the rapid growth of their commerce and breed of seamen and soldiers, as will enable them to become the *terror of Europe*, and to exercise with impunity that insolence which is so natural to their nation, and which will increase enormously with the increase of their power.' In effect, the French were being told that they would have to fight on behalf of the Americans in order to prevent the European balance from being overturned.[32]

Franklin need not have worried. America was strategically already lost. For the entry of the three most significant European naval powers into the war between 1778 and 1780 turned the balance on the high seas temporarily but fatally against Britain. To be sure, the Dutch had been made to pay a high price for their belligerency, but the naval and colonial war against the Bourbons was going badly. The classic roll call of victories familiar to Britons from other wars was reversed. The Royal Navy was overstretched and outnumbered. The Mediterranean was completely abandoned. French privateers – including those captained by Irish Jacobites – harassed British shipping: Dominica had fallen to the French as early as 1778; in 1779 they took St Vincent and Grenada. Tobago followed in 1781, as did most of western Florida, and Pensacola, which was overrun by Spain. Even Jamaica, the centrepiece of Britain's sugar economy in the Caribbean, was under threat. But the shift was felt most keenly in America itself. In 1780–81 the French succeeded in landing a force on Rhode Island, and French troops deployed in support of George Washington's army besieging Lord Cornwallis at Yorktown. Because Britain had lost command of the sea, all attempts to relieve him failed; a British attempt to break through the French blockade in September 1781 and lift the siege was repulsed. In October 1781 Cornwallis and all his army surrendered to Washington, a direct result of Britain's European isolation during the past decade. 'Oh God,' North was reported as saying on receipt of the news. 'It is all over.'[33]

The news of Yorktown had a shattering effect on British domestic politics. Belief in the importance of America remained unchanged. Even after the defeat, Lord George Germain told the Commons that 'He thought that this country depended upon its connection with America for its very existence. Take away America, and we should sink into perfect insignificance; preserve it, and he would venture to say, it was yet the brightest jewel in the crown.' Likewise in January 1782, the King was still arguing the loss of America 'would annihilate the rank in which this British Empire stands among the European states'. In other words, the ministry was still fighting for Europe in America. For this reason North called for a continuation of the struggle. 'Must we give up the conflict,' he asked, 'because we ha[ve] failed in this particular instance, or because we ha[ve] failed in other instances? No: it ought to rouse us into action; it ought to impel, and urge, and animate us: for by bold and united exertions, every thing [may] be saved; by dejection and despair, every thing [may] be lost.' But North had no new policy, and his ministry was increasingly discredited. The Lord Advocate, Henry Dundas, openly demanded a 'human sacrifice', of Sandwich and the Colonial Secretary, Lord George Germain. An attempt to stave off the inevitable by throwing Germain to the wolves in early February 1782 only underlined the problem. Welbore Ellis, who succeeded to the Colonial Secretaryship for a month before it was abolished, was a name to conjure with. As a long-standing navalist scourge of Continental commitments, he was a man who had learned and forgotten nothing. Moreover, the defeat reminded Britons once more of their dismal isolation. In the Yorktown debate, Lord Camden lamented that 'ministers seemed to be totally ignorant . . . that almost every power in Europe which had not declared against us were nevertheless in a state nearly approaching to actual hostility.'[34]

As Britain's fortunes in America were extinguished, the Opposition now began a sustained assault on the ministry, and in particular on the performance of the Admiralty. The resulting parliamentary debate soon showed that the real problem lay not in Sandwich's management of technical detail and accounts, which had been superb, but with the broader strategic and diplomatic framework within which naval policy had been conceived. He put up a spirited defence. Surveying the scene since his arrival in 1771, he claimed to have remedied a decade of neglect, to have improved the timber supply, to have copper-bottomed 'the whole fleet of England', reformed the dockyards, and much else. The net result, he claimed, was that 'our present naval force is greater than in the preceding war'. The problem was – and here Sandwich picked up a verity he had first acknowledged in 1779 – that 'we are now engaged in a war with the House of Bourbon, closely united and their

THE STATE TINKERS.

The National Kettle, which once was a good one,   *The Master he thinks, they are wonderful Clever,*
For boiling of Mutton, of Beef, & of Pudding,   *And cries out in raptures, 'tis done! now or never!*
By the fault of the Cook, was quite out of repair,   *Yet meeting the Tinkers their old Trade pursue,*
When the Tinkers were sent for, ___ Behold them &Stare.   *In stopping of one Hole ___ they're sure to make Two.*

Publish'd Feb[y] as Pacts by W.Humphrey, N[o] 227 Strand.

41. As the American War entered its final phase, critics became convinced
that British policy was being directed by incompetents.

naval force unbroken'. Moreover, 'these powers have no Continental
struggles to draw their attention and to exhaust their finances, so that
they are enabled to point their whole efforts to their naval departments'.
To cap it all, he added, 'we are also at war with Holland and America,
and ... our peace with all the Northern Powers hangs upon a very
slender thread.' But these 'unnatural combinations against us', he was
at pains to stress, were 'not the fault of the Admiralty'. All things
considered, Sandwich concluded, he had done rather well.[35]

All this might have been an eloquent apologia for Sandwich's stewardship of the Admiralty, but it was also a formidable indictment of British
foreign policy as a whole. His argument was promptly demolished by

Fox, who observed scornfully that 'the noble lord ha[s] told the committee, in the language of exultation and triumph, that the navy of England now [i]s greater and more numerous than the navy of England in the last war'. 'Good God!' he expostulated. '[I]s the navy of England of this day to fight the navy of England of that day? If it [is], the argument would be a good one.' 'The fact [i]s,' Fox concluded, 'the navy of the House of Bourbon [i]s greater than ever it ha[s] been known; the navy of England [i]s to fight that navy, and the sole question, [i]s it greater and stronger than the navy of the House of Bourbon? That [i]s the only comparative point of view in which the matter [can] be regarded.' In short, both sides of the argument agreed that Yorktown was a naval defeat originating in European developments.[36]

North's ministry hung on throughout the winter of 1781–2. In late February it was heavily defeated over General Conway's motion against continuing an 'offensive war' in America. His political back broken, North stepped down on 20 March 1782. Yet another eighteenth-century British ministry had fallen over its mismanagement of the European balance of power.

The new government was a coalition of Whigs led by Rockingham, Charles James Fox and the Earl of Shelburne, an Irishman who admired Oliver Cromwell. Their first priority was to restore Britain's position within the European balance of power. The situation was now dire. Relations with the powers of the Armed Neutrality were still very fraught: it was, as the Austrians warned their ambassador in London, 'only a few steps away from [becoming] a formal hostile alliance against Britain'. Minorca had fallen to a Spanish invasion in August 1781; Gibraltar had been relieved again in April 1781, but remained exposed. It had been relieved for the first time in 1780 by Admiral Rodney, and was to be on a third occasion in October 1782. Each was regarded as a naval triumph, and have come to be seen as harbingers of a British revival in the last years of the war. In a sense, this was true. Yet these victories were hardly reassuring: relieving Gibraltar was so easy that it had to be done over and over again. The entire British position in the western Mediterranean was still very much in the balance, and the fact that the Royal Navy was repeatedly required to prove its mettle showed that the underlying problem of Britain's European isolation remained to be addressed.[37]

As if this were not bad enough, in the spring of 1782 the Barrier fortresses were demolished, with the exception of Antwerp and Luxembourg. To be sure, the Utrecht system was long defunct, and the Franco-Dutch cooperation during the American War merely confirmed this, but the news was still a profound geopolitical shock. The British ambassador to Russia, James Harris, remarked that 'I confess nothing amongst the numberless singular incidents I have been witness to during my political life, struck me more forcibly than the perfect indifference with which all Europe saw this measure resolved on, and carried into execution.' It was the final catastrophe of Britain's grand strategy in Europe, and especially her policy towards the Empire of which the Barrier formed a part. Meanwhile, British standing across the Continent was at rock bottom, with Harris now demanding his recall from St Petersburg on a regular basis. Faced with these calamities, the new ministry did not despair, or simply attempt to manage the decline. Its leading diplomatic brain, Lord Shelburne, told Parliament in July 1782 that 'if the sun of England would set with the loss of America', as so many claimed, 'it [is my] resolution to improve the twilight, and to prepare for the rising of England's sun again'.[38]

Our story ends here. The strategic paradigm prevailing since 1763 had been utterly discredited. Over the next eighteen months, British ministries tried to rescue what they could from the wreckage in America. More importantly, they sought to restore British power, and contain that of France, where it mattered most: in Europe. To that end, they launched a stream of initiatives, both domestic and diplomatic. The machinery of foreign policy was comprehensively overhauled. The division of the Foreign Secretaryship into departments for the North and South was abandoned; a single minister was installed at the new Foreign Office. For various reasons, this did not immediately provide 'joined-up thinking' at the heart of government, but a start had been made. Efforts were made to restore domestic cohesion, the lack of which had so damaged military mobilization and Britain's European standing. Ireland was conciliated with the granting of legislative independence. The land war in the thirteen colonies was wound down; the loyalists were left to their fate. Naval supremacy was gradually restored. Admiral Rodney won a famous victory over the French at the Battle of the Saints. This was too late to affect the outcome in America, but it strengthened Britain's hand in Europe.[39]

In the end, salvation came, as it had so often come in the past, from the east. As Russian ambitions towards the Crimea – which was under the suzerainty of France's Ottoman ally – became clearer, Vergennes became increasingly nervous. He was now anxious to liquidate his maritime and western European commitments in order to turn his attention more fully to the collapse of the French position in eastern and south-eastern Europe. It still took until early 1783 to hammer out a comprehensive preliminary peace agreement. Right at the end of November 1782, the British negotiators finally agreed the formula by which the thirteen colonies were recognized as independent. Almost all the American demands were conceded. In late January of the following year, Vergennes, the Spanish negotiator and the British plenipotentiary Alleyne Fitzherbert came to an agreement. Minorca and Florida were ceded to Spain, various islands were surrendered or restored to France. Some British possessions, such as the Bahamas, were to be returned, but the terms were still onerous. As Vergennes had cruelly remarked during the negotiations in late 1782, 'the English are buying peace rather than making it. Indeed their concessions with respect to boundaries, fisheries and the loyalists exceed anything I would have believed possible.' The preliminaries were certainly a blow to Britain's standing in the world. In January 1783, Joseph II observed that Britain 'could no longer be considered one of the first rank powers of Europe'.[40]

All this was savaged by the press and in Parliament, on the grounds that it conceded too much to the Bourbons, and did not take sufficient account of British debts, or the interests of American loyalists; there were also complaints that Shelburne had conceded too much on the western frontier and the demarcation line between the United States and Canada. Predictably, members of North's former administration took particular pleasure in pointing out these deficiencies. In February 1783 Parliament formally rejected the preliminaries, partly because it believed better terms could be got, partly in order to vent its frustration at Shelburne, who played his cards very close to his chest, and partly in order to curb the executive. It was the best attended debate since the accession of George III twenty years earlier: a testament to the importance of foreign affairs. Shelburne's administration had been holed below the waterline. He limped on to resign in April, yet another prime minister to fall victim to the acrimonious debate on grand strategy which had structured British politics throughout the eighteenth century.[41]

The bitter debates over the preliminaries may seem futile in retrospect, but they were of great significance to the protagonists. Both government and Opposition knew that ministers could be punished for a bad peace. Thus Sir Andrew St John, the MP for Bedfordshire, soon to become an undersecretary of state in the new Foreign Office, 'called to the recollection of gentlemen the conduct of the House on the Treaty of Utrecht, to prove that there was no mode of getting rid of a peace that had once been concluded by the royal prerogative; that the only redress that could be acquired for the most dishonourable peace, was the punishment of the ministers who had made it'. He went on to remind Parliament further that 'The nation, enraged at the Treaty of Utrecht, had, by the House, proceeded to the punishment of the ministers who had fabricated that treaty; one was sent to the Tower, the other went into voluntary banishment.' Nor would Members of Parliament have forgotten the threat of impeachment which had hung over Walpole in his last years; and ministers knew that it was a fate which even veterans such as the Duke of Newcastle had feared at least at one point in their lives. British foreign policy was not a risk-free environment, even in the apparent safety of Westminster and Whitehall. The price for failure could be imprisonment and theoretically even death.[42]

All this limited the ministry's room for manoeuvre – Shelburne complained bitterly about press coverage – but it did not much improve the terms on offer. Fox, having sniped from the sidelines for nine months, got no further himself after April 1783. All attempts to divide the Americans from the Bourbon powers, or France and Spain from each other, failed. By any standards, the final peace settlement of the Treaty of Versailles in September 1783 was a terrible blow. The thirteen colonies were irrevocably lost; Minorca and Florida were surrendered to Spain, and the American loyalists were left twisting in the wind. Once again Parliament erupted in rage and unfavourable comparisons with the Treaty of Paris twenty years earlier. Chatham's son, the young William Pitt, by now Chancellor of the Exchequer, spelt out the brutal truth. These 'scenes of ruin', meant that Britain could not hope 'to dictate the terms of peace'. The treaty, he continued, was not 'seriously [to be] compared with the Peace of Paris'. All the same, Pitt recalled nostalgically how Britain had 'at the close of a war, far different indeed from this . . . dictated the terms of peace to submissive nations. This, in which I place something more than a common interest, was the memorable aera of England's glory. But that era is past: she is under the awful and mortifying necessity of employing a language that corresponds with her true condition: the visions of her power and pre-eminence are passed away.'[43]

Britain did not accept the terms solely because she had no choice, but because the principal aim of post-North ministries – halting the collapse of Britain's position within the overall balance of power – had been achieved with the end of hostilities with America. After all, as the Marquess of Carmarthen rejoiced, 'The confederacy that had been formed against England was dissolved' by the peace, ensuring that 'Great Britain, pursuing the plans of wisdom, moderation and peace, would still be one of the first powers of Europe.' If an alliance with the United States had not been achieved, then at least France had not been able to secure a lasting one either, for the two powers went their separate ways at the conclusion of the peace. Likewise, the MP Thomas Powys thanked the administration 'for having broken the confederacy in arms against this country, and which threatened her absolute ruin'. In other words, there might be many small reasons to oppose the preliminaries, but there was one big reason not to do so: the beginning of the end of Britain's European isolation. The Peace of Versailles thus echoed that of Aix-la-Chapelle in 1748, with the difference that this time Britain surrendered not merely a fortress – Louisburg – to maintain the European balance, but a whole continent.[44]

American independence was still a catastrophic defeat for Britain, which paved the way for the emergence of the United States as a world power. Horace Walpole looked further ahead than he could have imagined when he responded to the Declaration of Independence in 1776 with the prediction that 'This little island will be ridiculously proud some ages hence of its former brave days, and swear its capital was once as big as Paris, or – what is to be the name of the city that will then give laws to Europe – perhaps New York or Philadelphia.' The French, of course, rejoiced at the humbling of Britain. The French King, as Vergennes exulted, had 'erased the stain of 1763'. All the same, the last laugh was on them. When one Frenchman predicted that the thirteen states would become 'the greatest empire in the world', a member of the American delegation in Paris shot back 'Yes, sir, and they will all speak English, every one of 'em.'[45]

Conclusion

The Honourable Gentleman exhibited two pictures of this country; the one representing her at the end of the last glorious war, the other at the present moment. At the end of the last war this country was raised to a most dazzling height of splendour and respect. The French marine was in a manner annihilated, the Spanish rendered contemptible; the French were driven from America; new sources of commerce were opened, the old enlarged; our influence extended to a predominance in Europe, our empire of the ocean established and acknowledged, and our trade filling the ports and harbours of the wondering and admiring world. Now mark the degradation and the change! We have lost thirteen provinces of America, we have lost several of our islands, and the rest are in danger; we have lost the empire of the sea, we have lost our respect abroad and our unanimity at home; the nations have forsaken us, they see us distracted and obstinate, and they leave us to our fate. Country! ... This was your situation, when you were governed by Whig ministers and by Whig measures, when you were warmed and instigated by a just and a laudable cause, when you were united and impelled by the confidence which you had in your ministers, and when they again were emboldened by your ardour and your enthusiasm. This is your situation, when you are under the conduct of Tory ministers and a Tory system, when you are disheartened, and you have neither confidence in your ministers nor union among yourselves.[1]

An account of a speech by Charles James Fox during the debate in the Commons on the Address of Thanks, 1781

The price of strategic failure in eighteenth-century Europe was partition and sometimes extinction. Spain lost not only Flanders but also her central Mediterranean lands in 1713. Most of Sweden's Baltic empire was divided up between Hanover, Prussia and Russia in 1715–21. In 1733–38 and 1740–48, the Habsburg monarchy was partitioned at the hands of Spain, France and Prussia, but remained largely intact as a Great Power. Several attempts were made to despoil the Ottoman Empire throughout the century: successfully in 1716–18; largely unsuccessfully in 1736–8; and again successfully in 1768–74. Spain and France were stripped of large parts of their colonial empires in 1763. Poland suffered the indignity of partition in 1772, and complete extinction, after this book ends, in 1795.

In 1778–83, Britain was in turn partitioned. Some three million vexed and troubled Englishmen took their leave of the Empire; Florida was surrendered to Spain. Like France twenty years before, Britain had lost a continent, or most of it. Ireland very nearly went the same way. Minorca was lost to Spain: this was part of the progressive dismantling of Britain's strategic position in the western Mediterranean. Corsica had already been 'lost' in 1768; Gibraltar was only retained with great difficulty. After seventy years and three victories, Britain had now suffered an unmistakable, unprecedented and quite unexpected defeat. Or, to put it another way, in 1713 and afterwards, Britain had called upon others to make sacrifices for the sake of the European balance. Spain was told to accept the loss of her Mediterranean empire; Sweden her Baltic pre-eminence; and in the 1740s and 1750s, London had urged Austria to get over the loss of Silesia. From 1778, Britain was asked to make such sacrifices herself. She did not like it.

The collapse of Britain's international position after 1763 was shocking to contemporaries. In July 1782 the Earl of Shelburne remarked that 'It had ever been his opinion, that the independence of America would be a dreadful blow to the greatness of this country; and that when it should be established, the sun of England might be said to have set.' 'There is not a ray of light left,' wailed Lord Stormont, Britain's former foreign secretary and a distinguished diplomat. 'All is darkness.' He went on to complain that whereas the Spanish negotiators at Westphalia in 1648 had managed to hold on to ten of the seventeen provinces in the Netherlands, the British negotiators had failed to retain a single one of the thirteen rebel colonies. The Earl of Buckinghamshire, an experienced former diplomat, wrote in July 1783 that he saw 'this unhappy disgraced country surrounded by every species of embarrassment,

42. Defeat in America led to the partition or, as this print graphically portrays it, the dismemberment of Britain.

and . . . now circumstanced as a human body in the last stage of decline'.[2]

George III had come to the throne amid great hopes in 1760; twenty-three years later he had presided over the greatest and most irrevocable strategic disaster in British history. As the Duke of Grafton subsequently remarked, 'Few princes have ever ascended the throne under more advantageous and auspicious circumstances . . . Few kings, however, have lived to see . . . the condition of their subjects so wholly changed as no longer to afford to the enquiring eye the view of that once happy nation, enjoying every blessing that could be desired under a well-principled government at home, and one which was admired, courted and respected abroad.' Not only had George enjoyed unprecedented popularity in the first years of his reign, but the dynasty had been in tune with the naval side of the nation in ways not seen since the Stuarts. This contrasted with his grandfather and great-grandfather, both of whom had been enthusiastic commanders of ground forces; the same had been true of George II's son the Duke of Cumberland. Despite this, the King had suffered defeat on the element most congenial to him: the sea. As we shall see, it is no accident that the most 'naval' monarchs in British history were also the least successful.[3]

A similarly pessimistic mood pervaded the public sphere. Three years after the loss of America, the *Newcastle Chronicle* wrote that Britain had made huge strides in the century since the Revolution of 1688: 'Since that period,' it argued, 'Britain has acquired a new political existence, and held a bolder career in arts and arms. From the accession of Queen Anne to the commencement of the American War, she was the first power, and the prime mover in the political system. Seated on a small island, hardly to be distinguished in the map of the world, she spread over the four continents, held the balance among the nations, and gave law to the globe.' Unfortunately, the *Chronicle* continued, 'Everything human . . . has its period: nations, like mortal men, advance only to decline; dismembered empire and diminished glory mark a crisis in the constitution; and, if the volume of our frame [national story] be not closed, we have read the most brilliant pages of our history.'[4]

The post-mortem on this colossal defeat, which began well before the formal end of the war in 1783, ranged widely. To some contemporaries, the loss of America was divine punishment for the spirit of hubris which had pervaded the country after 1763. Already in 1776, shortly after the beginning of the war, Gibbon had warned in his *Decline and Fall of the Roman Empire* that even the most mighty power could be brought down through a combination of moral decadence and external assault. Halfway through the conflict, Bishop Porteous announced to the House of Lords in February 1779 that the triumph of 1763 had been 'too great for our feeble virtue to bear' and that the wealth acquired had 'produced a scene of wanton extravagance and wild excess, which called loudly for some signal check; and that check it has now received'. The Earl of Shelburne told Parliament in 1781 that 'when the brilliancy and rapid succession raised the name of Briton to the highest pinnacle of fame and military glory, they dazzled the eyes of the multitude, and in some means sanctified the means by the end; but, even then, when men reasoned, he could perceive either in the words or actions of those he mixed with, a secret, or public disapprobation, indeed, of detestation'.[5]

Others blamed defeat on moral corruption, the machinations of the Crown, ministerial corruption or the lack of proper parliamentary representation; all these charges were linked, of course. In 1782 William Cowper's poem 'Table Talk' suggested that national effeminacy would 'enervate and enfeeble' Britain and embolden its enemies. Here critics were picking up a theme which had been well rehearsed during the catastrophic start to the Seven Years War. Thus Charles James Fox told the House of Commons in 1781 that

There was one grand domestic evil, from which all our other evils, foreign and domestic, had sprung. To the influence of the Crown we must attribute the loss of the army in Virginia; to the influence of the Crown we must attribute the loss of the thirteen provinces of America; for it was the influence of the Crown in the two Houses of Parliament, that enabled His Majesty's ministers to persevere against the voice of reason, the voice of truth, the voice of the people. This was the grandparent spring from which all our misfortunes flowed.

During a parliamentary debate in late November 1781, the Marquis of Rockingham traced the root of the mismanagement since the accession of George III to the rise of 'a proscriptive system, a system of favouritism and secret government'.[6]

Outside Parliament, the sense that the humiliation in America stemmed from the weaknesses of the constitution was even stronger. Thus one of the London livery companies resolved in late January 1782 'that the unequal representation of the people, the corrupt state of Parliament, and the perversion thereof from its primitive institution, have been the principal causes of the unjust war with America, of the consequent dismemberment of the British Empire, and of every grievance of which we complain'. All these voices were part of the language of moral panic which had always peaked at times of national crisis. Consequently they believed that the national regeneration necessary to enable Britain to regain its rightful place in the state system was dependent on recovering her masculinity, on purging corrupt politicians or reforming the franchise, or a combination of these measures.[7]

Yet Britain was not defeated for want of effort or enthusiasm. The American War, in fact, saw the greatest British military mobilization hitherto. For example, the army, which numbered 72 battalions in 1774, could boast 118 in 1783. If Britain had 16,000 seamen on the books at the outbreak of war, this figure jumped to 60,000 in 1778 and 100,000 in 1780. Somewhere between one in seven and one in eight British men of fighting age served in the armed forces. This is lower than the figures for the Napoleonic Wars and the First World War, but higher than those for the Seven Years War (about one in nine or ten) and the War of the Austrian Succession (one in sixteen). It was also a truly national effort: if German mercenaries had played a substantial role in the early years of the war, by 1781 only 9 per cent of expenditure was on them, as compared to about 25 per cent in the War of the Spanish Succession and even the Seven Years War. In the American War, Britain relied on its own resources and energies: it was the least 'European' of its many conflicts. The military effort was accompanied by a huge psychological and cultural mobilization of patriotism and civic virtue, some of it directed but most of it spontaneous.[8]

Nor was Britain primarily laid low by the lack of a proper naval grand strategy, 'imperial overstretch' or the 'imperial attention deficit', which periodically afflicts empires, especially those with opinionated and easily distracted publics. It was true, of course, that the imperial defence perimeter had expanded massively in 1763, at the very moment when the debts of past wars were peaking and domestic issues were resurfacing. To cap it all, Britain was now fighting the colonists who had been on their side in earlier wars. It was also undeniable that Britain had been bested on its own element: the sea. This was certainly the view of the naval historian Alfred Thayer Mahan, who had no doubt where the blame lay. 'Europe, North America and the West Indies,' he wrote in his magisterial *The influence of sea power upon history*, 'should have been looked upon as one large theatre of war, throughout which events were mutually dependent.' All these factors played a very important part, but it is remarkable that Britain should have been defeated at sea and in the colonies at the very moment when her interest in naval and colonial matters was greater than ever before. Moreover, the financial overstretch imposed by the burdens of empire and war never became terminal in itself.[9]

On the contrary, the British fiscal-political system had never been more effective. Even in the dark days of 1780–81, the British state was able to raise more money, more cheaply, than its many enemies. It was not enough. As Sir Robert Murray Keith, the ambassador to Vienna, complained in November 1781, 'it is not *money* we want . . . but *blood* for our money (as John Bull used to say); for how the devil do you think we can make a *peace* for you till you have shown that you can make war in the *old British style*?' Thomas Pitt, MP for Okehampton, complained in February 1783 that the papers before Parliament proved 'that the interest of the public debt was increased from less than four and a half millions at the beginning of Lord North's war, to near nine and a half at present. That this six years war had cost us therefore considerably more than all the successes of the Duke of Marlborough and Lord Chatham put together, from the time of the Revolution.' In September

1780, George III had warned that the struggle would be a 'war of credit': he won that contest, but lost the war itself. As Montesquieu had warned, money did not save Carthage, nor was it enough to rescue another maritime and commercial hegemon from its fate. Britain's naval and fiscal strength cushioned her fall – and insulated her against the worst – but it could not prevent it.[10]

Victory is rarely conducive to reflection. The triumph of 1763 produced, as we have seen, no shortage of popular and parliamentary hubris. Yet those charged with the security of the British Empire were by no means complacent. They were well aware of the threat to their new empire, both from settler aspirations and, more importantly, from rival Great Powers. The fiscal policies adopted after 1763 were rational measures designed to put imperial defence on a sounder footing. The Proclamation Line limiting settlement to the west was a sensible attempt to live in peace with the Indian tribes and thus reduce troop levels. Although British administrations in the two decades before the loss of America were more 'colonial' than ever before, they were accused by the settlers of not being aggressively colonial enough. London, as Franklin's biographer Gerald Stourzh put it, was holding back 'manifest destiny'. American independence was thus the result of a particularly drastic form of British foreign policy debate. Those who called for expansion in the western hemisphere – such as Benjamin Franklin – lost the argument in London, but later won the war in America.[11]

All this points to the central paradoxes of British grand strategy after 1763. The result of an active 'blue water' policy of colonial expansion was the acquisition of borders which had to be defended on the ground. The policies developed to pre-empt and contain the Franco-Spanish war of revanche actually helped to bring it about. To foresee a problem was not to forestall it, while attempts to pre-empt the danger actually precipitated it.

Others have seen the decline of Britain's European position as the result of shifts in the state system beyond London's control. It is certainly true that the rise of the eastern powers had created a new dynamic in which the containment of France was no longer at the heart of European politics. It is also true that the move to a more naval and colonial strategy among the Bourbon powers put Britain under greater pressure overseas at the very moment when the rest of Europe ceased to worry much about French or Spanish revanchism. Yet the state system before

1763 was not static. It had been convulsed in 1711, when the death of Emperor Joseph I threatened to reconstitute the empire of Charles V; it was roiled again by Spanish and Russian expansionism after 1713; and in 1740, by the dramatic arrival of Frederick the Great on the international scene. In each case, Britain's response had been radical and highly controversial, but effective: bailing out of the War of the Spanish Succession; concluding an entente with France in 1716; and effecting a rapprochement with Prussia in 1756.

Moreover, France had mounted serious challenges to Britain at sea before, especially when Maurepas was minister for the navy. The loss of naval supremacy had loomed in the 1730s, when the Bourbon Family Compact with Madrid underpinned a surge in naval construction and colonial assertiveness. Coupled with some clever European diplomacy – and ministerial ineptitude in London – this left Britain isolated by the late 1730s. Disaster threatened once again in 1755–6, when Britain stood friendless in Europe, and under siege overseas. In each case, Britain was saved not only by good luck, and the mistakes of her enemies, but also by the capacity of the executive and the political nation to rally around a policy of engagement in Europe. In short, there was nothing within the state system itself, or the policies of other powers, which made Britain's defeat, or at least the extent of it, inevitable.

Besides, late-eighteenth-century British administrations enjoyed certain advantages over those of the pre-1763 period. They no longer needed to fear Jacobitism, except perhaps in Ireland, where that creed had mutated back into generic hostility. The Hanoverians were now an established dynasty; the monarchy was genuinely popular for the first decade or so after 1760, and was to become so again. Relations within the royal family were always fraught, but the 1760s and 1770s saw none of the damaging splits between King and Prince of Wales which had characterized the first two Georges. Britain commanded a larger and wealthier empire than at any time previously in her history. The fiscal-military state which had developed from the late eighteenth century was, as we have seen, more formidable and resilient than ever. The reasons for Britain's defeat, therefore must lie elsewhere.

We must start with an explanation for Britain's three quite extraordinary victories in the early to mid eighteenth century; it is only in this context that her single defeat can be understood. All of these wars – the Spanish

Succession, the Austrian Succession, and the Seven Years War – were successes, although only the last is customarily described as a triumph. In each case, Britain led an international coalition against France. In part, Britain prevailed because of her internal strength: the fiscal-military state and the navy. The domestic structure of the nation was largely brought into line with the external needs of the state: it was reflected in extensive military and naval expenditure, emergency powers and if necessary deportation of security risks. Moreover after the union between England and Scotland in 1707, Britain proved able to develop a durable constitutional architecture suited to the waging of prolonged conflict. The problems of Ireland remained unsolved – and she never became a net contributor to British security – but she was at least kept out of hostile hands. America was not yet an issue.

The greatest asset which Britain could bring to bear before 1763, however, was an effective strategic framework. Since the sixteenth century, Englishmen and then Britons had developed a coherent view of the European state system and Britain's place in it. They had an integrated sense of the whole and the individual regional balances. They were able to think sophisticatedly in terms of international law, custom and precedent where it was appropriate, for example in the politics of the Holy Roman Empire. They cultivated Britain's European alliances as if their lives depended on them, because they did. The importance of the 'balance', the 'Protestant interest' and the 'liberties of Europe' was drummed into the political nation from the start; it was reflected in public and parliamentary debate, not least in the annual Mutiny Bill, which was specifically justified with reference to the 'balance of power'. At the same time, Britons were capable of the utmost ruthlessness and radical political manoeuvring: for most of the century they cleaved to the 'old system' of alliance with Austria, but they were prepared to abandon it in the 1720s and 1750s, when it was no longer of service. They were convinced, in short, that only a close and sustained commitment to the European balance would guarantee the security of Britain from invasion and thus their own liberties.

All this would have been true even if the King of England had not been Elector of Hanover. What the German connection did was to accentuate the sense that Britain was a European power. Britain now had, whether she liked it or not, a Continental land border to defend. To be sure, Hanover was used as an instrument in British high politics:

showing solicitude for the Electorate was a reliable path to royal favour before 1760; attacking it was a sure method of courting 'popularity'. Newcastle and Pitt tried both at various stages in their career. But Hanover was more than that: it was part of Britain's Continental strategy. The King's German servants served as a diplomatic force-multiplier; Hanoverian troops served in every major British war from 1714; and the territory itself provided both a useful base for Continental diplomacy and a jumping-off point for military operations in northern and central Europe. Whenever the separation of Britain and Hanover was proposed, therefore, as under George I around 1720, and again in the 1740s and 1750s, British ministers strongly opposed the idea. This was not just because disentangling the two territories would cause insoluble legal and dynastic complications, though it would. Even when the neutralization of Hanover was proposed in 1727, 1741 and 1757, British ministers thrice opposed it. They were in no doubt that Hanover was a British strategic asset.

British ministers had a clear sense of what Europe was and should be, but they were also sensitive to how it might develop. Throughout the early and mid eighteenth century, they kept a close eye on possible dynastic permutations and potential shifts in the balance of power. They were always prepared to act pre-emptively and even preventively to squash or even forestall emerging threats. This could manifest itself tactically, for example in the destruction of the Spanish fleet in 1718, before war had been formally declared. But it could also be more strategically driven: in this case the need to stop the emergence of a naval rival in the western Mediterranean in good time. Not all pre-emptive and preventive action was military: much of it was dynastic, commercial and political. Thus in the 1720s, Britain took severe action against the Ostend Company to prevent the emergence of a commercial rival, likewise in the 1750s against the Emden Company.

Many of the grand alliance schemes cooked up in London were designed to anticipate future threats as well as current ones. The perennial fear of the recreation of the empire of Charles V in the 1720s was one example; the attempt to weld the House of Habsburg more firmly to the German imperial title in the 1750s was another. These schemes were deeply controversial at the time because they involved ruinous expenditure, or because critics saw them as addressing remote contingencies, or because they feared to precipitate the very problems they wished to forestall. Ministers were rarely given credit for successful preventive action, though historians have been kind to Stanhope's Baltic and Mediterranean schemes, and they were invariably crucified for their failures, such as the Imperial Election Scheme.

In the prevailing strategic framework before 1760, European concerns outweighed commercial, colonial and maritime interests. Not long after its capture, British statesmen were willing to trade Gibraltar for lasting stability in the Mediterranean. At the end of the War of the Austrian Succession they exchanged Louisburg for a withdrawal from the Low Countries. Most commercial lobbies, even the mighty East India and South Sea Companies were weak when strategic matters were at stake. When in doubt, British statesmen chose security over profit. The retention of Canada rather than Guadeloupe in 1763 showed that. Moreover, the economic value of a trade was no necessary index of its political importance: the supply of naval stores from the Baltic, for instance, was a vital interest in a way that trade with the Spanish colonies was not. The strategic importance of maritime trade lay elsewhere. It lay in its role as a 'nursery' for seamen to the Royal Navy; in the provision of economic muscle to sustain an active foreign policy; and in denying these to the enemy.

But if British statesmen recognized the primacy of Europe, they also had a very clear sense of the link between the Continental and the colonial or maritime spheres. They held a set of assumptions about the interplay between the European balance of power, naval supremacy and colonial expansion, which was expressed with remarkable regularity and consistency in the decades before 1760. First of all, as we have seen, most British statesmen believed that the Continental commitment, far from being a betrayal of Britain's insular destiny, was crucial to the maintenance of her naval superiority, and thus her commercial and colonial dominance. The collapse of the European balance of power, and its inevitable corollary, 'universal monarchy', was seen as a twofold threat to the Royal Navy and thus to the integrity of Britain. It would enable the European hegemon, usually France, to concentrate all its resources on naval construction and the subjugation of Britain. Secondly, it was widely believed that engagement in Europe would enable Britain to secure its position overseas. By the 1750s, this consideration, rather than the balance or naval superiority *per se,* was looming larger. In the mid 1750s, for example, Newcastle mistakenly hoped that a ring of alliances in Europe would deter the French from sending more troops to North America. If he hoped that America would be defended in Germany, Pitt was soon famously to suggest that 'America had been conquered in Germany', by drawing off French troops and treasure from the colonial and maritime theatre of war.[12]

Thirdly, it was widely believed that Britain's control of overseas resources, or denying those resources to the enemy, was crucial to maintenance of the European balance of power. This was an extension of the principle which had led to the return of Louisburg: the colonies could be used not only as bargaining counters to extort European concessions, but also to make up for whatever weight Britain lacked in Europe. Likewise, the colonial triumphs of the Seven Years War were welcomed because they gave Britain additional standing *in Europe*. Even the American colonists recognized this imperative, though they sometimes resented it, and therefore based their demands for greater colonial expansion on the need for Britain to achieve an enhanced European profile. Conversely, sea power was used to cut off the enemy from resources which could be used against British interests in Europe. When the Royal Navy was dispatched to disrupt the Spanish treasure fleet in the mid and late 1720s, it was with the express purpose of denying Madrid's Austrian ally the subsidies to attack British interests in Germany; it was sent in pursuit of a European not a global agenda. Even those who advocated a more navalist policy, therefore, were often doing so within a framework which was ultimately Eurocentric. One might thus say more accurately that Germany was conquered in America.[13]

In short, by mid-century a coherent British strategic culture had emerged. It was firmly Eurocentric: it gave absolute priority to preventing the growth of a hegemon on the Continent. It was mainly, though not exclusively, Whig: after all, the arch-Whig in domestic matters, Robert Walpole, was something of a Tory in foreign policy. In this strategy political, diplomatic and fiscal instruments counted as much as military or naval ones; sometimes more so. It was restrained and conscious of the limits of British power. The colonial and naval spheres were subordinated to the Continental theatre; at the same time, the Continental strategy ensured continued naval superiority. Underpinning everything was a powerful sense of structure: Europe was conceived as an overall balance with a combination of regional balances. British statesmen thought and spoke of Europe in terms of 'systems', 'barriers' and 'natural allies'. Rather than being fixated on the 'moat' of the surrounding 'silver sea', they conceived of the European mainland itself as an integral part of Britain's defences – a 'rampart', just as their sixteenth- and seventeenth-century ancestors had before them. They were expected to be, and often perforce were, to use Walpole's phrase, 'ministers for Europe'.

Of course, the Continental commitment was not a foolproof template. There may well have been times when Britain's resources might have been better spent on the Navy. Perhaps British statesmen, and therefore this book, spent more time down German rabbit-holes than was strictly necessary. The Duke of Newcastle certainly threw British taxpayers' money into a bottomless pit in the 1750s during the Imperial Election Scheme. Continental interventionism was also an ambiguous template. The Whig interventionists after 1713 oscillated between the Scylla of the failed peace negotiations with Louis XIV at Gertruydenberg, where they realized that they had set their demands too high, and the Charybdis of Utrecht, when Britain's allies and the cause of the balance had supposedly been 'betrayed'. But how to know which was which in the very different contexts of the 1720s through to the 1750s? Similarly, the whole concept of pre-emption and prevention was wrapped in an eternal paradox: you would be blamed for the costs of a successful pre-emption, and you would certainly be blamed for precipitating conflict, but you would rarely get any credit for getting it right. The Continental commitment, in short, was not a policy in itself. It was a framework, a state of mind, almost a temperament. It required judgement in the application.

Nor was the European commitment simply an elite phenomenon. It was 'owned' not only by much of parliamentary opinion, but also by many in the public sphere as well. There it was subjected to constant scrutiny and debate. What was at issue for most before 1763, was not whether Britain was or should be part of Europe, but how that role should be interpreted. The arguments used were often clearer than the truth. Ministries resorted routinely to distortion and shock tactics about threats of Jacobitism, universal monarchy, or – increasingly – to the 'balance of power'. Conversely, critics rarely failed to warn of 'betrayal', incompetence and insouciance at the highest levels. Yet for all that, the eighteenth-century British public debate on grand strategy was a relatively informed one, given the constraints of time and place. In the short to medium term, Parliament and popular opinion could have a distorting effect on policy, especially when it insisted on maximalist positions. But there was also no better forum than Parliament and the bar of public opinion for showing up a discredited policy and calling time on a failed paradigm. This was done at least twice: first in the early 1740s, when Walpole seemed unable to get a grip on the rise of French power, and in 1782, when it became clear to most that North had dug himself into an American and European morass from which he would never extricate himself unaided.

It would be wrong to speak of the rise of parliamentary accountability in foreign policy before 1763. From Buckingham, through Strafford and Danby to the three peers accused of betraying national interests with the Spanish Partition Treaty of 1698, ministers had always been accountable. British politics routinely punished, even criminalized, strategic failure. The impeachment of the Earl of Oxford in 1715, hardly a year into the new reign, set the tone. He was accused of betraying Britain's allies at Utrecht. The British admiral in the Baltic, Admiral Norris, throughout the 1710s and the 1720s feared for his head if he made the wrong move. When the attack on Cartagena miscarried in 1740, critics ominously accused the ministry of a 'formed design' to sabotage the prosecution of the colonial and maritime war. The campaign to impeach Walpole was driven, at least on the surface, very much by foreign policy. Newcastle feared for his head over the neutralization of Hanover in 1741; and there were popular calls for his execution over the loss of Minorca in 1756.

All this had implications for how Britons viewed themselves. It is true, of course, that the Act of Union with Scotland, the common Protestant and political heritage, and the project of empire-building helped to weld the peoples of the Atlantic archipelago together. It is also true, as Linda Colley's celebrated account has shown, that the British identity was 'forged', both shaped and counterfeited, by the struggle against the European, usually French 'other'. Yet one must not forget the extent to which Britons defined themselves within Europe, and with Europeans, not just against them. Also, if John Bull had been invented in 1712 as part of the Tory reaction against the War of Grand Alliance, then for the first sixty years or so of the century this was an identity, and a sense of strategic community of fate, to which the American colonists subscribed. They too saw their destiny as lying within the broader European state system.

After 1763, the Eurocentric strategic paradigm fragmented. It had long been under attack from those who believed in a more colonial and naval destiny for Britain. Insular rhetoric now became the prevailing tone in public, even as thousands of Britons visited Europe between 1763 and 1783, more than ever before; tourism as such contributes little to strategic understanding. After all, William Pitt and the Duke of Newcastle had little direct experience of Europe; the latter had been making policy on Germany for twenty years before he ever set foot there in the company of George II. The accession of George III was another reason for the blurring of Britain's European vision. For fifty-odd years after 1714, the kings of England had often made Hanover the strategic and even physical focus of their diplomacy. This ceased abruptly in 1760. Further fragmentation set in with the creation of a third foreign secretaryship, for the colonies, in 1768. At the same time, the debate on grand strategy across the Atlantic began to diverge from that of the mother country. Americans became increasingly insistent that the British Empire should expand ever westwards, partly in order to make Britain more formidable in Europe, but increasingly as an end in itself.

All this was accompanied by an over-reliance on naval deterrence. The navy had been a useful weapon, but there were limits to what it could achieve. France and Spain did not remain intimidated for long. Naval power was unable to prevent the occupation of Corsica in 1768 just as it was powerless to end covert and later open Bourbon assistance to the Americans. Commodore Martin's squadron had over-awed Naples in 1742, for sure, but that piece of unilateralism came home to haunt Britain after 1759, when the King of Naples became the King of Spain. The application of gunboat diplomacy required calibration and judgement. A pre-emptive attack on Spain, which Pitt had advised in 1761, would probably have been vindicated, especially if the Prussian alliance had been upheld. A precipitate breach with Spain to forestall intervention in America, which Sandwich demanded from 1778, was little short of lunacy given Britain's European isolation. Naval power, in short, now tended to replace rather than supplement diplomacy.

Of course, British strategic culture did not change overnight. British statesmen continued to see Europe as their primary focus, but they were now working within a context which was more stridently colonial and maritime than anything they had previously known. Unlike the first forty-odd years after 1714, they now found themselves working with a monarch – George III – who was firmly opposed to the 'German war'. The same was broadly true of Parliament. Contrast the sophisticated debates on Europe of the first part of the century with the parliamentary ignorance and indifference of the 1760s and 1770s. Moreover, British statesmen were themselves not immune from the naval exuberance which had accompanied victory in the Seven Years War; and they were less willing than an earlier generation to make concessions in support of a Continental alliance. Contrast for example, Newcastle's heroic efforts to implement the Imperial Election Scheme in the early 1750s, with the steadfast refusal of British statesmen, twenty years later, to agree to the 'Turkish clause' with Russia. The new men seemed unable to grasp that if they wanted European powers to act on Britain's behalf, they would need to offer them something in return. They were also less able to adapt to shifting balances. Contrast the speed with which Stanhope adjusted to the Russo-Spanish threat after 1716, with the helplessness with which British statesmen watched the balance of power shift eastwards after 1763. In short, the American War was first lost where all wars are initially decided: in the mind.[14]

For the consequences of the changing strategic paradigm after 1760 soon became clear. As Britain limbered up to fight the colonists in 1775, she had been isolated in Europe for more than ten years. None of the many gambits in Berlin, Vienna and St Petersburg had come off. The chance for a 1716-style rapprochement with France, which genuinely seems to have existed in the early 1770s, was not taken. So Britain went to war in America, and later in Europe, more isolated than she has ever been in her history, before or after, 1940 not excepted (remember the Greeks). Of course, Britain had been isolated before, particularly in the late 1730s, but on each occasion she had found her way back. As Sellar and Yeatman famously said of the war of 1775–83, 'The War with the Americans is memorable as being the only war in which the English were ever defeated, and it was unfair because the Americans had *the Allies* on their side.' It remains the greatest diplomatic train wreck in British history so far.[15]

Worse, Britain went to war amidst a general popular sense that standing alone was a national badge of honour. Surveying the past twelve months on New Year's Day 1783, one rural vicar wrote in his church register that 'To the future it will appear to be an incredible thing, what however we know to be a fact, that these Kingdoms should maintain (as they have done) a glorious, but unequal conflict for several years, with the most formidable and unprovoked confederacy that could be formed against them; viz. France, Spain, the United Provinces of the Netherlands, and the thirteen revolted colonies of North America.' That was certainly one way of looking at it. The very mental structures which made Britain such a formidable enemy in the American War: cussedness, patriotism and resilience, were actually barriers to a path out of isolation.[16]

In part, the naval failure was due to poor tactics. Britain attempted to control the sea, and thus temporarily lost the command of it during the American War. Indeed, the moment of greatest peril in British history was probably not 1745, 1756, 1797, 1804–5 or even 1940, but 1779, when naval mastery was lost for a time. But the main reason Britain was defeated at sea in 1779–81 for long enough to tip the balance in America itself had nothing much to do with the Royal Navy. Rather it was the result of a series of decisions on European policy stretching back some twenty years, and the strategic culture underpinning them. Undistracted on land, France and Spain outdid Britain at sea, as generations of Whigs before 1760 feared they would. Britons thus paid a heavy naval price for the suicidal exuberance with which they acclaimed the appearance of each new enemy: the French, the Spanish, and most unnecessarily of all, the Dutch. In short, no amount of domestic mobilization, moral purity, insular virtue and naval prowess could replace the Continental system of alliances on which British security, prosperity and imperial expansion had rested. Persistence, courage, mobilization and domestic unity were all useful and admirable, but they were essentially second-order virtues. What was needed was the right policy, otherwise Britain was going to dig itself deeper and deeper into a hole. Doubling the resources would simply have squared the error.

This was not primarily an ethical or temperamental failure. Arrogance is of course a sin, but it was not hubris as such which led to the partition of 1783. The chauvinist exuberance which followed victory in the Seven Years War did not in itself constitute a bad policy. It aggravated but did not cause a wrong turning in grand strategy. After all, restraint is only a secondary virtue. It is hardly an end or good in itself, at least not in international politics. For example, hesitation would have been fatal in 1718, when Byng surprised and destroyed the Spanish fleet off Cape Passaro. Holding back in 1740–42 would have ruined the Habsburg monarchy, and thus the European balance of power. Some might also argue that restraint was misplaced in 1763, when Britain permitted France to retain the Newfoundland fisheries and thus the nursery of seamen which later went on to dispute command of the ocean briefly but fatally during the American War.

The fundamental problem here was judgement. Restraint in pursuit of durable solutions was deemed no virtue; robustness in pursuit of Britain's interests was considered no vice. But how was one to tell virtue from vice in foreign policy? The tragedy of British foreign policy and the debate on grand strategy after 1760 was that the public tended towards hubris when it ought to have been restrained; that the executive leant towards naval coercion, when diplomatic instruments would have been more appropriate; and that it showed restraint on the occasions when robustness would almost certainly have been more advisable. The European state system and the British political system punished restraint more often than it did robustness. Oxford narrowly escaped impeachment after he took Britain out of the War of the Spanish Succession. There was no more moderate Briton in foreign policy than Robert Walpole, and yet he too was lucky to weather national fury at his feeble defence of the European balance in the 1730s. And here his judgement was doubly at fault, because he allowed Parliament and public opinion to browbeat him into a disastrous conflict with Spain overseas, largely because he had refused to go to war in Europe on behalf of the Habsburgs.

It was the same combination of poor judgement and misplaced restraint which brought down Britain in America. For very good reasons, which later turned out to be ill-founded, London decided against further expansion westwards, partly because of financial exhaustion, but mainly because this would have given unbearable provocation to the Bourbons and the Indian tribes. It rejected American demands for ultimate security through unlimited settlement, and the complete expulsion of France and Spain from the western hemisphere, or at least its northern half. Instead, the British government boxed in the settlers east of the Proclamation Line and attempted to put imperial defence, finance and governance on a rational footing. They thought this sensible and far-sighted. The result was that the colonists revolted, not against the imperial hubris of London, but because they thought successive administrations insufficiently imperialist. In the end, Englishmen on both sides of the Atlantic went to war in 1775 – for similar reasons they had in the seventeenth century – because they had not done so against the French, Spanish and Indians after 1763.

For Britons contemplating defeat in 1783, this was only part of the story. They knew that it was not just individual decisions, or the personal weaknesses of their leaders, which were to blame. As they looked back on the fiasco of the American War and the decade of isolation leading up to it, they realized that the mistakes of 1763–5 in America, and the incompetence of subsequent ministers, both reflected and were aggravated by a deeper fault. In a nutshell, they had been defeated because they were friendless in a way never before experienced. There had been dangerous moments, and inept ministers, in the past, but the system had always righted itself. The American disaster was thus at root an intellectual and conceptual failure. British ministers had turned their backs on Europe, and the Continent in turn had left them to their fate. Britons resolved never to make the same error again. They did not quite put it this way themselves, but they knew that if they stuck henceforth to a European strategy they might lose their way, but they would at worst make the right mistakes. They would not, as North had done, make the wrong mistake.

The result of this debacle was the restoration of the primacy of European politics in Britain. Throughout the early and mid eighteenth century, most ministries rose and fell according to how well the King or the political nation felt they had performed in the strategic sphere; so did individual ministerial careers, that of George I and George II's Secrretary of State for the North, Charles Townshend being a classic example. The Tories triumphed in 1710, as the Spanish War stagnated. They were more or less proscribed after 1714, because of the Treaty of Utrecht. Thereafter, the fate of most Whig administrations was decided by foreign policy. As we have seen, Stanhope triumphed in 1716–17 because of his approach to Bremen and Verden. If Walpole came to power in 1721 as a safe pair of financial hands to sort out the South Sea mess, he lost it in 1742 primarily because of the imminent disintegration of the Habsburg monarchy. Carteret followed him two years later, again because of difficulties in central Europe. The loss of Minorca did for Newcastle in 1756; Spain for Pitt in 1761; the 'German war' for Newcastle in 1762; and the peace for Bute in 1763. To that extent, Walpole's ascendancy, based on control of the Treasury, gives a misleading view of the underlying political dynamic in the eighteenth century. From 1714 to 1721 and again from 1742 to 1763, all ministries were led from a Secretaryship of State; and it is a moot point whom George I and George II regarded as their most important minister, Walpole, or Townshend and Newcastle, the two secretaries with whom they spent most time.

The period 1763–75 was different, but less so than it might seem. Foreign policy played an important role in the return of Pitt in 1766 and the fall of Grafton in the late 1760s. Parliament became more intensely interested in grand strategy and the European balance from the mid 1770s onwards. North was held liable for the loss of America and the underlying disaster of European isolation. Yet, in important ways, ministers were less accountable in foreign policy towards the end of the century than they were at the beginning. Charles James Fox and others might mutter darkly about 'treacherous' ministers who had lost America, but the criminalization of strategic failure was a thing of the past. By 1782 ministers feared to lose their posts, but not their liberty or even their heads. Perhaps it would have concentrated their minds had they been so exposed. Be that as it may, there were no impeachment proceedings against North after 1782. British high politics were less deadly after 1763 than they had been for hundreds of years. Safer for statesmen but not, of course, for the soldiers and sailors who paid the price for a failed policy.

The long-term strategic consequences of the European war of 1778–83 were much more ambiguous. To be sure, Britain lost a continent, but the feared commercial decline did not take place. Indeed, British exports to and imports from America massively *increased* after Independence. A second empire was built in Africa, Asia and Australasia, most of which was to be much more expensive and strategically irrelevant than the first. By contrast, France, resurgent in 1783, soon fell into a terminal decline. In 1763 she had lost America, and recovered. In the 1780s she lost Europe. Across the Continent, French allies went down like ninepins: Poland to partition, the Ottoman Empire and Sweden to a milder form thereof. These blows, and the associated collapse of French state credit, ultimately brought down the monarchy.

Even the American War proved a pyrrhic victory: the expense made future interventions nearer home less feasible. The failure to defend the Dutch patriots in 1787 against Prussian invasion was the last straw. Louis now faced pamphlet attacks on his foreign policy that closely resembled the Opposition assault on Walpole in the early 1740s. Revolution followed in 1789, and in 1793, after treasonable correspondence with the Austrians, the King and Queen were executed.

The crisis facing Britain in the 1760s and 1770s was thus not unique in Europe. Many other states were trying to bring their domestic and fiscal structures into line with strategic imperatives. Most encountered severe resistance in so doing, especially Joseph II, whose reform programme in Austria almost ended in general revolution and European war. The British experience was to be uniquely painful, not because of anything inherent in the problems, but because of the diplomatic context in which they erupted. At least Joseph II had some allies, and he died before complete catastrophe struck. George III and Lord North stood quite alone in Europe, and Parliament only intervened in time to prevent European obliteration, not the loss of empire. Unlike Louis XVI and Charles I, however, George was not punished for the strategic failure of his ministers by revolution, deposition and decapitation. One way or the other, the 1780s showed that the European balance was not a zero-sum game for Britain and France: they could both lose.

Defeat in America did not end British attempts to bring fiscal and constitutional structures into line with security requirements, to wit the primacy of strategic over domestic affairs. On the contrary, these efforts were redoubled. At the purely technical level, there was the drive to strengthen the executive and make it more effective. The Northern and Southern Departments were amalgamated into a single Foreign Office designed to provide more coherent policy. Some even felt that a firmer monarchical touch was required. 'Whig as I am,' a despondent Earl of Buckinghamshire wrote in July 1783, 'and sufficiently vain of my descent from Maynard and Hampden [two enemies of Charles I], it sometimes occurs to me that something might be obtained by strengthening the hands of the Crown.' Many now began to think of some form of franchise reform to mobilize the hidden energies of 'the people'. Even if Pitt thought this premature, he was very much in favour of 'economical reform'. The context in which these changes were being brought forward was very much that of restoring Britain's European position.[17]

But the greatest lesson was in the mind. Here the post-mortem may not have been systematic, but it was clear. Few now suggested that the key to Britain's security lay in colonial expansion, or in exclusive reliance on the Navy. Instead, the strategic primacy of Europe in British strategic thinking was restored, at least until the end of the Napoleonic Wars. The Whig establishment – which had pleaded the cause of engagement in Europe throughout the eighteenth century with the king, in Parliament and in as many media as they could mobilize on their behalf – believed itself to have been resoundingly vindicated. The arch-Whig, the Marquis of Rockingham, located the origins of the defeat in the political shift immediately after the death of George II. Under that king, he reminisced, 'we triumphed over our enemies wherever we met them, and were successful in every quarter of the globe whither our arms were borne. We had a Pitt to direct our political machine. We had a Newcastle at the head of our finances. We had a Legge at the Exchequer, and an Anson at the head of our navy.' Europe and America were strategic alternatives only in the minds of popular and parliamentary critics. In the pre-1763 period, as Whigs liked to remind the Tory administration, Britain had gained both; after 1763, she had lost both. America was won in Europe, and lost there too.[18]

The first task of the Earl of Shelburne, who became Prime Minister in June 1782, was to extricate Britain from the war without further damage, and to deny America to the French. This was achieved at the Treaty of Paris in 1783. The next undertaking – which fell to the younger Pitt from 1784 – was to rebuild Britain's Continental alliances. This was effected more quickly than anybody had believed possible: a Triple Alliance was secured in 1788 with Holland and Prussia, only eight years after the Armed Neutrality. The old strategic paradigm had been restored. British statesmen once again believed that the key to national security and prosperity lay – not exclusively, but first and foremost – in Europe. They had come to realize this the hard way. It was a lesson which every generation of British statesmen has had to learn anew for itself.[19]

For this reason, Britain clung grimly to her Continental strategy during the Revolutionary Wars between 1793 and 1815. With the exception of some brief interludes, Britain resisted colonial sirens throughout this period. The tens of thousands of men lost to disease in expeditions to the West Indies in the 1780s were a shocking reminder of the costs of overseas expeditions, even those designed, as that one was, to secure to Britain the resources to continue the European struggle. After each failed attempt at a European coalition against Napoleon, British diplomats dusted themselves down and tried again. They kept sending troops to the Continent: the Grand Old Duke of York to Holland in the 1790s, expeditions to Stralsund in 1807, to Walcheren in 1809, and of course to the Peninsula for the last five years or so. Maintaining a land front against Napoleon was an article of faith. To many it seemed the triumph of hope over experience, but the British never despaired, or not for long. They knew that Britain's security depended on maintaining her ramparts in Europe. It was there, in Germany and in Flanders, in the 'counterscarp' of England, that Britain's fate would be decided, always had been and always would be.

Bibliography

Primary Sources

Archival sources

A wide range of manuscript material was used, concentrating particularly on the formulation of what later generations came to call 'grand strategy' rather than bilateral relations with individual European states. For this reason, particular attention was paid to the private papers of statesmen and diplomats, rather than the routine dispatches generated by various embassies; in those cases specific incisions were made. The author did not knowingly use an archival source when a satisfactory printed version of the document was available. A selection of the material used is listed below.

British Library Manuscripts Room (BL)

These were extensively used, particularly the Newcastle, Hardwicke and Carteret Papers: Add Mss 23798; Add Mss 22511 (Carteret mission to Sweden 1719); Add Mss 28851 (Cumberland mission to Spain, 1779); Add Mss 32783, 32791, 32794 (Polish Succession); Add Mss 32686, 32742–3, 32746, 32757 (Newcastle papers, mid 1720s); Add Mss 32697 (Hanover neutrality, 1741); Add Mss 32719 (Continental subsidies, 1749); Add Mss 32865 (1756 intelligence reports to Newcastle); Add Mss 32875, 32800, 32897, 32899 (Seven Years War, 1757–9); Add Mss 32977 (1766); Add Mss 33029 (re French encroachments in North America, mid 1750s); Add Mss 35514, 35515, 35517 (misc. British diplomatic correspondence 1778–9, mainly re Austria and Prussia); Add Mss 47562 (Fox Papers, British diplomacy in 1783); Egerton Mss 3455 (Barrier question, 1754–5).

National Archives, London (NA)

Selected files were used, especially the Chatham Papers 30/8/89–91 (Pitt and British relations with German powers); SP 43/1 Hanover (Stanhope correspondence from Hanover); SP 78/274 (re Corsican crisis of 1768); SP 80/32–3, 80, 120, 200, 204, 223 Germany/Empire (relations with Austria throughout the century); SP 81/143–4 (relations with smaller German courts); SP 84/378 Holland (re British perceptions of Dutch decline); SP 90/44, 102 Prussia; SP 104/240 (envoys to the Reichstag).

Niedersächsisches Staatsarchiv Hannover (NStAH)

These provided interesting insights into the influence of the Hanoverian connection on British policy, especially Cal. Br. 11 Nr. 2282 (Newcastle's correspondence with Münchhausen, the head of the administration in Hanover, 1752); Cal. Br. 11 Nr. 2534 (George III's response as Elector of Hanover to the partition of Poland 1772–4); Cal. Br. 11 Nr. 2558 (George III to Elector of Cologne 1780 concerning complaints re Austria); Cal. Br. 24 Nr. 1722–3 (reports of Hanoverians in London to the administration in Hanover 1718–21); Cal. Br. 24 Nr. 1736 (correspondence of George II's Hanoverian servants with the British envoy to

Berlin, Hyndford); Cal. Br. 24 Nr. 2004 (Harrington correspondence with Hanoverian ministers, 1741–2); Hann. 9e Nr. 324 (George III's concern for the Electorate in the 1760s); Hann. 91 du Pontpietin Nr. 1 (Hanoverian military preparations in 1741); Hann. 91 Münchhausen I Nr. 19, 22–4, 36 (Münchhausen correspondence with British secretaries of state Newcastle and Holdernesse, 1749, 1755); Hann. 91 St Saphorin Nr. 1/I–III; Nr. 3–4 (for British policy in the early 1720s); Hann. 91 St Saphorin Nr. 2–3 (Horatio Walpole–St Saphorin correspondence); Hann. 92 Nr. 91 (re failed marriage plan for the Prince of Wales, 1759); Hann. 92 Nr. 92 (re Princess Anne's marriage to Prince of Orange, 1733); Hann. 92 Nr. 2102 (George III's letters in German in his own hand); Hann. 92 Nr. 2109 (Norris, Cadogan and Bernstorff correspondence).

Hessisches Staatsarchiv Darmstadt (HStAD)

The papers of the head of the Hanoverian administration, Count Görtz, were crucial to understanding British policy in 1716–19, and the early stages of the Personal Union with Hanover more generally. Particularly useful were: F23A Nr. 124/1, 146/21, 156/28, 156/1–6 (Görtz correspondence with various British politicians, Carteret, Cadogan, Stanhope); and F23A Nr. 153/6 (Görtz and Schulenburg correspondence).

Haus, Hof und Staatsarchiv, Vienna (HHStA)

A small sample of papers was consulted here, largely for illustrative purposes: England Korrespondenz, Berichte Karton 100, 117, 128 (correspondence with the Austrian embassy in London, 1751–2, 1771–81); and Hausarchiv Sammelbände 88 (for Joseph II's thoughts on foreign policy in the late 1760s).

Royal Archives Windsor Castle (RA)

The documents consulted were crucial to understanding the importance of the Hanoverian connection during the early reign of George I, especially the Astle Papers (on the question of separating kingdom and Electorate); and the Georgian Additonal Mss (letters of Queen Caroline to her lady-in-waiting Mrs Charlotte Clayton)

Contemporary Printed Material

The advantages of the Hanover succession, and English ingratitude freely and impartially considered and examined (London, 1744)

Advice to Whigs and Tories: Or the interest of Great Britain considered; both in respect of domestick and foreign affairs (London, 1714)

The analysis of patriotism: Or, an inquiry weather [sic] opposition to government, in the present state of affairs, is consistent with the . . . (London, 1778)

Arguments against a Spanish war (London, 1762)

Atterbury, Francis, English advice to the freeholders of England (London, 1714)

[Bollan, William], The importance and advantage of Cape Breton: Truly stated, and impartially considered (London, 1746)

[Bollan, William], A succinct view of the origin of our colonies with their civil state: Being an extract from an essay lately published entitled the Freedom of speech and writing, etc. (London, 1766)

A brief state of the services and expences of the province of the Massachusetts bay in the common cause, sometimes attributed to Dennis de Berdt (London, 1765)

Britannia excisa: Britain excis'd. A new ballad to be sung in time, and to some tune (London, 1733)

Britannia in tears: An elegy occasioned by the dismission of the Right Honble. W. P—t, and H. L—ge, Esqrs; from the service of their king (London, 1757)

Britannia: Or the contrast between Robert W— and William P—. A pastoral dialogue, by way of allegory (London, 1741)

Britannia's loss: A poem on the death of England's Cæsar (London, 1702)

Britannia triumphant: Or, an account of the sea-fights and victories of the English nation, by the 'Society of Naval Gentlemen' (London, 1767)

British advice to the freeholders of Great Britain (London, 1715)

Britons awake, and look about you: Or, ruin the inevitable consequence of a land-war, whether successful, or not, by 'A Lover of His Country' (London, 1743)

Browne, Joseph, *Albion's naval glory, or, Britannia's triumphs: A poetical essay towards a description of a sea fight* (London, 1705)

Cappe, Newcome, *The voice of rejoicing in the tabernacles of the righteous: A sermon preached at York . . . on the 27th of November, 1757* (6th edn, Glasgow, 1758)

Chalmers, G., *An estimate of the comparative strength of Britain in the present and preceding reigns, and of the losses of her trade from every war since the revolution* (London, 1782)

Chesterfield, Philip Dormer Stanhope, Earl of, *Natural reflexions on the present conduct of His Prussian Majesty: The concern which England has* (London, 1744)

Chesterfield, Philip Dormer Stanhope, Earl of, *A vindication of a late pamphlet, intitled, The case of the Hanover troops considered: With some further observations upon those troops* (London, 1743)

Chesterfield, Philip Dormer Stanhope, Earl of, and Edmund Waller, *The case of the Hanover forces in the pay of Great Britain, impartially and freely examined* (London, 1742/3)

Clarke, William, *Observations on the late and present conduct of the French, with regard to their encroachments upon the British colonies in North America* (London, 1755)

Coade, George, *A letter to a noble lord: Wherein it is demonstrated, that all the great and mighty difficulties in obtaining an honourable and lasting peace . . .* (London, 1760)

A collection of letters publish'd in Old England: Or, the constitutional journal (London, 1743)

The conduct of the ministry compared with its consequences: Or an impartial view of the present state of affairs (London, 1733)

The conduct of the ministry impartially examined: And the pamphlet entitled Considerations on the present German war, refuted from its own . . . (London, 1760)

Conjectures on the present state of affairs in Germany: Containing, remarks on the conduct of His Prussian Majesty, by 'An Impartial Hand' (London, 1760)

Considerations on the expediency of a Spanish war: Containing reflections on the late demands of Spain; and on the negociations of Mons. Bussy (London, 1761)

Considerations on the present state of affairs in Europe, and particularly with regard to the number of forces in the pay of Great-Britain (London, 1730)

Considerations on the present state of affairs in Great-Britain (London, 1718)

Considerations relative to the North American colonies, attributed to John Fothergill (London, 1765)

The Con-Test, XXXIII (February–July 1757)

The convention vindicated from the misrepresentations of the enemies of our peace (London, 1739)

Dalrymple, Alexander, *A general view of the East-India Company, written in January, 1769: To which are added, some observations on the present state of their affairs* (London, 1772)

A defence of the rights of the House of Austria, against the unjust claims of the King of Prussia (London, 1741)

Defoe, Daniel, *A plan of the English commerce: Being a compleat prospect of the trade of this nation, as well the home trade as the foreign* (London, 1728)

Dickinson, John, *Speech delivered in the House of Assembly of the province of Pennsylvania, May 24 1764* (2nd edn, Philadelphia, 1764)

East India Company, *The present state of the English East-India Company's affairs, comprehending the accounts delivered in by the Court of Directors to the Treasury* (London, 1773)

English loyalty opposed to Hanoverian ingratitude: Being a vindication of the present and all former ministries since the accession (London, 1744)

An epistle to William Pitt Esq. (London, 1746)

An essay on the management of the present war with Spain, as far as it has been hitherto conducted on the part of Great Britain, by 'An Impartial Hand' (London, 1740)

The fable of the lion's share: Verified in the pretended partition of the Spanish monarchy. Done from the original printed in Vienna (London, 1701)

A fair and compleat answer to the author of the Occasional thoughts on the present German war, with a reply to the considerations on the same (2nd edn, London, 1761)

Forman, Charles, *A letter to the Right Honourable Sir Robert Walpole, concerning the election of a King of Poland* (London, 1733)

A full and candid answer to a pamphlet, entitled, Considerations on the present German war (London, 1760)

The great importance of Cape Breton, demonstrated and exemplified, by extracts from the best writers, French and English (London, 1746)

The grievances of the American colonies candidly examined, printed by authority at Providence in Rhode Island; reprinted for John Almon, attributed variously to Samuel Ward and Stephen Hopkins (London, 1766)

The happiness of the Hanover succession, illustrated from the conduct of the late administrators, wherein their designs are further exposed (London, 1715)

The importance of Cape Breton consider'd; in a letter to a member of Parliament, from an inhabitant of New-England, by 'Massachusettensis', sometimes attributed to Robert Auchmuty (London, 1746)

Keith, Sir William, *Some useful observations on the consequences of the present war with Spain* (London, 1740)

King, Charles, *The British merchant: Or, commerce preserv'd* (3 vols., London, 1721)

Lawson, John, *The history of Carolina: Containing the exact description and natural history of that country* (London, 1714)

A letter from a member of the last Parliament, to a new member of the present, concerning the conduct of the war with Spain (London, 1742)

A letter from Britannia to the King (London, 1781)

A letter to a Right Honourable Member of Parliament, demonstrating the absolute necessity of Great Britain's assisting the House of Austria, by 'An Impartial Hand' (London, 1742)

A letter to the people of England, upon the militia, continental connections, neutralities, and secret expeditions (London, 1757)

A letter to the Right Honourable the Earl of Bute, on the preliminaries of peace, by 'An Englishman' (London, 1762)

A letter to the Right Honourable William Pitt, Esq.: On the present negociations for a peace with France and Spain (London, 1762)

Little, Otis, *The state of trade in the northern colonies considered: With an account of their produce, and a particular description of Nova Scotia* (London, 1748)

Lyttelton, Baron George, *Considerations upon the present state of our affairs, at home and abroad, in a letter to a Member of Parliament from a friend in the country* (London, 1739)

Lyttelton, Baron George, *Farther considerations on the present state of affairs, at home and abroad, as affected by the late convention, in a letter to the minister* (2nd edn, London, 1739)

Lyttelton, Baron George, *Letters from a Persian in England to his friend at Ispahan* (London, 1735)

Mauduit, Israel, *Considerations on the present German war* (London, 1760)

Mauduit, Israel, *Occasional thoughts on the present German war: By the author of Considerations on the same subject* (London, 1761)

Mitchell, John, *The present state of Great Britain and North America, with regard to agriculture, population, trade, and manufactures, impartially considered* (London, 1767)

Molyneaux, T. M., *Conjunct expeditions or expeditions that have been carried on jointly by the fleet and army, with a commentary on a littoral war* (2 vols., London, 1750)

The necessity of forming a perpetual alliance, against the exorbitant power of the House of Bourbon, by 'L. D.' (London, 1738)

Oldmixon, John, *Remarks on a late libel privately dispersed by the Tories, entitled, English advice to the freeholders of England* (London, 1715)

Penhallow, Samuel, *The history of the wars of New England, with the eastern Indians: Or, a narrative of their continued perfidy and cruelty, from the 10th August* (Boston, 1726)

Postlethwayt, Malachy, *Britain's commercial interest explained and improved*, (2 vols., London, 1757)

Postlethwayt, Malachy, *Great Britain's true system* (London, 1757; reprinted New York, 1967)

The power and grandeur of Great Britain, founded on the liberty of the colonies, and the mischiefs attending taxing them by Act of Parliament (New York, 1768)

Pownall, Thomas, *A memorial, most humbly addressed to the sovereigns of Europe, on the present state of affairs, between the old and new world* (2nd edn, London, 1780)

The present state of affairs in Europe: Shewing, by authentick papers, what reason we have to expect peace or war (London, 1726)

The present state of the revenues and forces, by sea and land, of France and Spain: Compar'd with those of Great Britain (London, 1740)

Prince, Thomas, *Extraordinary events the doings of God, and marvellous in pious eyes: Illustrated in a sermon at the South Church in Boston, NE* (London and Boston, 1746)

Reasons for a war against Spain: In a letter from a merchant of London trading to America, to a Member of the House of Commons, by 'L. D.' (London, 1737)

Reasons for a war: From the imminent danger with which Europe is threatened, by the exorbitant power of the House of Bourbon (2nd edn, London, 1734)

Reasons for a war, in order to establish the tranquillity and commerce of Europe (London, 1729)

Sayre, Stephen, *The Englishman deceived: A political piece wherein some very important secrets of state are briefly recited* (London, 1768)

Shebbeare, John, *A fourth letter to the people of England, on the conduct of the m – rs* (6th edn, London, 1756)

Shirley, William, *A letter from William Shirley, Esq.; governor of Massachuset's Bay, to His Grace the Duke of Newcastle: With a journal of the siege of Louisbourg* (London, 1746)

Short verses in imitation of long verses in an epistle to W – m P – tt Esq. (London, 1746)

The Spanish merchant's address to all candid and impartial Englishmen: Being a short enquiry into the general conduct of the administration (London, 1739)

The Test (November–December 1756)

The true interest of the Hanover treaty consider'd: And how far France, and the rest of the allies, may be depended upon, by 'A Lover of His Country', attributed to Benjamin Good (London, 1727)

Truth develop'd, and innocence protected: Or, the merits and demerits of the late Commander in Chief of the British forces in Germany set forth, by 'A Free Citizen' (London, 1760)

A vindication of our present royal family principally with regard to Hanover, by 'A Friend to Hanover, tho' an Englishman' (London, 1744)

Walpole, Horace [Horatio], *The interest of Great Britain steadily pursued: In answer to a pamphlet, entitled, The case of the Hanover forces impartially and freely examined* (London, 1743)

Walpole, Robert, Earl of Orford, *Observations upon the treaty between the crowns of Great-Britain, France, and Spain, concluded at Seville on the ninth of November, 1729, N.S.* (London, 1729)

Printed Sources

Bedford, Duke of, *Correspondence of John, 4th Duke of Bedford*, ed. Lord John Russell (3 vols., London, 1842–6)

Bolingbroke, Lord, *Contributions to 'The Craftsman'*, ed. Simon Varey (Oxford, 1982)

Bolingbroke, Lord, *Letters on the spirit of patriotism and on the idea of a patriot king*, ed. Arthur Hassall (Oxford, 1926)

Bolingbroke, Lord, *The works of the late Right Honourable, Henry St John, Lord Viscount Bolingbroke*, ed. Dr Goldsmith (8 vols., London, 1809)

British diplomatic instructions 1689–1789, vol. 3, *Denmark*, ed. J. F. Chance (London, 1926)

British diplomatic instructions 1689–1789, vol. 5, *Sweden, 1727–1789*, ed. J. F. Chance (London, 1928)

British diplomatic instructions 1689–1789, vol. 6, *France, 1727–1744*, ed. L. G. Wickham Legg (London, 1930)

British diplomatic instructions 1689–1789, vol. 7, *France, 1745–1789*, ed. L. G. Wickham Legg (London, 1934)

Buckingham and Chandos, Duke of, *Memoirs of the court and cabinets of George III*, (2 vols.; rev. edn, London, 1853)

Buckinghamshire, Earl of, *The despatches and correspondence of John, second Earl of Buckinghamshire, ambassador to the court of Catherine II 1762–1765*, ed. A. d'A Collyer (2 vols., London, 1900–1902)

Burke, Edmund, *The correspondence of Edmund Burke*, ed. T. W. Copeland (9 vols., Cambridge, 1958–70)

Burke, Edmund, *The writings and speeches of Edmund Burke*, vol. 2, Party, Parliament and the American crisis, 1766–1774, ed. Paul Langford (Oxford, 1981)

Burnett, Edmund C. (ed.), *Letters of members of the Continental Congress* (8 vols., Washington, 1921–36)

Chance, J. F. (ed.), *List of diplomatic representatives and agents, England and North Germany, 1689–1727* (Oxford, 1907)

Chesterfield, Earl of, *The letters of Philip Dormer Stanhope, Earl of Chesterfield*, ed. J. Bradshaw (3 vols., London, 1893)

Chesterfield, Earl of, *The letters of Philip Dormer Stanhope, fourth Earl of Chesterfield*, ed. B. Dobree (6 vols., London, 1932)

Chesterfield, Earl of, *Private correspondence of Chesterfield and Newcastle, 1744–1746*, ed. R. Lodge (London, 1930)

Cobbett, William, *Parliamentary history of England* (36 vols., London, 1806–20)

Cowper, Countess Mary, *The diary of Mary, Countess Cowper, Lady of the Bedchamber to the Princess of Wales, 1714–20*, ed. Spencer Cowper (1865)

Defoe, Daniel, *The novels and miscellaneous works of Daniel de Foe* (London, 1854)

Devonshire, Duke of, *The Devonshire diary: William Cavendish, fourth Duke of Devonshire – Memoranda on State Affairs, 1759–1762*, ed. P. D. Brown and K. W. Schweizer (London, 1982)

Dodington, George Bubb, *George Bubb: The political journal of George Bubb Dodington*, ed. John Carswell and L. A. Dralle (Oxford, 1965)

Doniol, Henri (ed.), *Histoire de la participation de la France a l'établissement des États-Unis d'Amérique: Correspondance diplomatique et documents* (5 vols., Paris, 1886–9)

Drögereit, Richard, 'Das Testament Georgs I. und die Frage der Personalunion zwischen England und Hannover', *Niedersächsisches Jahrbuch für Landesgeschichte* 14 (1937), pp. 94–199

Drögereit, Richard, *Quellen zur Geschichte Kurhannovers im Zeitalter der Personalunion mit England 1714–1803* (Hildesheim, 1949)

Egmont, Earl of, *Diary of Viscount Percival, afterwards first Earl of Egmont*, ed. R. A. Roberts (3 vols., Historical Manuscripts Commission, 16th Report, 1920–23)

Egmont, Earl of, *Leicester House politics, 1750–1760: From the papers of John, second Earl of Egmont*, ed. A. Newman; Camden Society Miscellany Fourth Series, vii (London, 1969)

Elliot, Hugh, *A memoir of the Rt Hon. Hugh Elliot*, ed. Countess of Minto (Edinburgh, 1868)

Ellis, Henry (ed.), *Original letters illustrative of English history; including numerous royal letters, from autographs in the British Museum*, vol. IV (London, 1827; reprinted New York, 1970)

Fox, Charles James, *Memorials and correspondence of Charles James Fox*, ed. Lord John Russell (4 vols., London, 1853)

Franklin, Benjamin, *The papers of Benjamin Franklin*, vols. 16, 20, 21, ed. L. W. Labaree, W. B. Willcox *et al.* (27 vols. to date; New Haven, 1959–)

Frederick the Great, *Die Politische Korrespondenz Friedrichs des Großen*, ed. J. G. Droysen (46 vols., Berlin, 1879–1939)

Frederick the Great, *Die Politischen Testamente Friedrichs des Großen*, ed. G. B. Volz (Berlin, 1920)

Gardiner, Samuel Rawson (ed.), *The constitutional documents of the Puritan revolution, 1625–1660* (Oxford, 1889)

George III, *The correspondence of King George the Third from 1760 to December 1783*, ed. J. W. Fortescue (6 vols., London, 1927–8)

George III, *Letters from George III to Lord Bute, 1756–1766*, ed. R. Sedgwick (London, 1939)

Gerard, Conrad Alexandre, *Despatches and instructions of Conrad Alexandre Gerard, 1778–1780: Correspondence of the first French minister to the United States with the Comte de Vergennes*, ed. John J. Meng (Baltimore, 1939)

Grafton, Duke of, *The autobiography and political correspondence of Augustus Henry, third Duke of Grafton*, ed. Sir W. R. Anson (London, 1898)

Graham, G. S. (ed.), *The Walker Expedition to Quebec*, Navy Records Society Publications, xciv (London, 1953)

Grenville, George, *Additional Grenville papers, 1763–1765*, ed. J. R. G. Tomlinson (Manchester, 1961)

Grenville, George, *The Grenville papers, being the correspondence of Richard Grenville, Earl Temple, K. G., and the Right Honourable George Grenville, their friends and contemporaries*, ed. William James Smith (4 vols., London, 1852–3)

Hardwicke, Earl of, *The life and correspondence of Philip Yorke, Earl of Hardwicke, Lord High Chancellor of Great Britain*, ed. P. C. Yorke (3 vols., Cambridge, 1913)

Hervey, Lord, *Some materials towards memoirs of the reign of King George II*, ed. R. Sedgwick (3 vols., London, 1931)

Höfler, C., *Der Kongress von Soissons: Nach den Instruktionen des kaiserlichen Cabinets und den Berichten des kaiserl. Botschafters Stefan Grafen Kinsky* (2 vols., Vienna, 1871–6)

Horn, D. B. (ed.), *British diplomatic representatives 1689–1789* (London, 1932)

Horn, D. B., and Mary Ransome (eds.), *English historical documents, 1714–1783* (London, 1957)

Hume, David, *Essays: Moral, political and literary*, ed. Eugene F. Miller (Indianapolis, 1987)

Hume, David, *Political essays*, ed. Knud Haakonssen (Cambridge, 1994)

The Jenkinson papers, 1760–1766, ed. Ninetta S. Jucker (London, 1949)

Johnson, Samuel, *Political writings*, ed. Donald J. Greene (New Haven and London, 1977)

'Junius', *The letters of Junius*, ed. John Cannon (Oxford, 1978)

Keene, Sir Benjamin, *The private correspondence of Sir Benjamin Keene*, ed. Sir Richard Lodge (Cambridge, 1933)

Keith, Sir Robert Murray, *Memoirs and correspondence of Sir Robert Murray Keith*, ed. Mrs Gillespie Smyth (2 vols., London, 1849)

Knatchbull, Sir Edward, *The parliamentary diary of Sir Edward Knatchbull, 1722–1730*, ed. A. N. Newman, Camden Third Series, xciv (London, 1963)

Lenthe, Otto Christian von, *Briefe des Ministers Otto Christian von Lenthe an den Geheimen*

Kriegsrat August Wilhelm von Schwicheldt (1743–1759), ed. R. Grieser (Hildesheim, 1977)

Locke, John, *The second treatise of civil government and a letter concerning toleration*, ed. J. W. Gough (Oxford, 1948)

Lyttleton, Lord George, *Correspondence of George, Lord Lyttelton, 1734–1773*, ed. R. Phillimore (2 vols., London, 1845)

Madden, Frederick, and David Fieldhouse (eds.), *The classical period of the First British Empire, 1689–1783: The foundations of a colonial system of government* (Westport, 1985)

Malmesbury, Earl of (ed.), *Diaries and correspondence of James Harris, first Earl of Malmesbury* (4 vols., London, 1844)

Marchmont, Earls of, *A selection from the papers of the Earls of Marchmont*, ed. G. H. Rose (3 vols., London, 1831)

Mitchell, Sir Andrew, *Memoirs and papers of Sir Andrew Mitchell*, ed. A. Bisset (2 vols., London, 1850)

Münchhausen, Gerlach Adolf von, 'Eine Denkschrift Gerlach Adolf von Münchhausens über die hannoversche Außenpolitik der Jahre 1740–1742', ed. T. König, in *Niedersächsisches Jahrbuch für Landesgeschichte* 14 (1937), pp. 202–32.

Münchhausen, Gerlach Adolf von, 'Münchhausens Berichte über die Kaiserwahl des Jahres 1742', ed. F. Frensdorff, in *Nachrichten von der Königlichen Gesellschaft der Wissenschaften zu Göttingen, Philologisch-Historische Klasse* (Göttingen, 1899)

Münchhausen, Gerlach Adolf von, 'Münchhausens Berichte über seine Mission nach Berlin im Juni 1740', in *Abhandlungen der Akademie der Wissenschaften Göttingen, Philosophisch-Historische Klasse*, New Series 8:2 (Berlin, 1904)

Newcastle, Duke of, *A narrative of the changes in the ministry, 1765–1767, as told by the Duke of Newcastle in a series of letters to John White, MP*, ed. M. Bateson, (London, 1898)

Oberschelp, Reinhard (ed.), *Niedersächsische Texte, 1756–1820* (Hildesheim, 1983)

Paine, Tom, *Selected work*, ed. Howard Fast (London, 1948)

Pease, T. C. (ed.), *Anglo-French boundary disputes in the west, 1749–1763* (Springfield, 1936)

Pelham, Henry, *Memoirs of the administration of the Rt Hon. Henry Pelham*, ed. W. Coxe (2 vols., London, 1829)

Percival, M., *Political ballads illustrating the administration of Sir Robert Walpole* (Oxford, 1916)

Pitt, William, *Correspondence of William Pitt, Earl of Chatham*, ed. W. S. Taylor and J. H. Pringle (4 vols, London, 1838–40)

Pitt, William, *The correspondence of William Pitt, when Secretary of State, with the colonial governors and military and naval commissioners in North America*, ed. W. S. Kimball (2 vols., London, 1906)

Pribram. A. F. (ed.), *Österreichische Staatsverträge: England* (2 vols., Vienna, 1907–13)

Richmond, Sir Herbert (ed.), *Papers Relating to the Loss of Minorca in 1756*, Navy Records Society Publications, xlii (London, 1913)

Rockingham, Marquis of, *Memoirs of the Marquis of Rockingham and his contemporaries*, ed. Earl of Albemarle (2 vols., London, 1852)

Sandwich, Earl of, *The fourth Earl of Sandwich: Diplomatic correspondence 1763–1765*, ed. Frank Spencer (Manchester, 1961)

Sandwich, Earl of, *The Sandwich papers*, ed. G. R. Barnes and J. H. Owen (4 vols., London, 1932–8)

Stair, Earls of, *Annals and correspondence of the Viscount and the first and second Earls of Stair*, ed. J. M. Graham (2 vols., Edinburgh, London, 1875)

Stevens, B. F. (ed.), *Facsimiles of manuscripts in European archives relating to America, 1773–1783* (25 vols., London, 1889–98)

Swift, Jonathan, *The conduct of the allies and of the late ministry, in beginning and carrying on the war* (London, 1713), in Thomas Roscoe (ed.), *The works of Jonathan Swift containing interesting and valuable papers not hitherto published, in two volumes, with memoir of the author,* vol. I (London, 1841), pp. 410–28

Swift, Jonathan, *The correspondence of Jonathan Swift,* ed. F. E. Ball (6 vols., 1910–14)

Taylor, Stephen, and Clyve Jones (eds.), *Tory and Whig: The parliamentary papers of Edward Harley, third Earl of Oxford, and William Hay, MP for Seaford, 1716–1753* (Woodbridge, 1998)

Walpole, Horace, *Memoirs of the reign of King George II* (3 vols., London, 1846–7)

Walpole, Horace, *Memoirs of the reign of King George III* (4 vols., London, 1894)

Walpole, Lord Horatio, *Memoirs of Horatio, Lord Walpole,* ed. William Coxe (2nd edn, London, 1808)

Walpole, Sir Robert, *Memoirs of the life and administration of Sir Robert Walpole, Earl of Orford,* ed. William Coxe (4 vols., London, 1816)

Warren, Sir Peter, *The Royal Navy and North America: The Warren papers, 1736–1752,* ed. J. Gwyn, Navy Records Society Publications, cxviii (London, 1973)

Weber, Friedrich Christian, *Peter der Grosse und der Zarewitsch Alexei, vornehmlich nach und aus der Gesandschaftlichen Korrespondenz Friedrich Christian Webers* (Leipzig, 1880)

Wharton, Francis (ed.), *The revolutionary diplomatic correspondence of the United States,* vol. III (Washington, 1889)

Wiener, Joel H., and J. H. Plumb (eds.), *Great Britain: Foreign policy and the span of empire, 1689–1971* (4 vols., New York, 1972)

Williams, E. Neville, *The eighteenth-century constitution, 1688–1815* (Cambridge, 1965)

Wraxall, Sir Nathaniel, *Historical memoirs of my own time, 1771–1784* (2 vols., London, 1815)

Secondary Sources

Adams, Simon, 'Foreign policy and the parliaments of 1621 and 1624', in Kevin Sharpe (ed.), *Faction and parliament: Essays on early Stuart history* (Oxford, 1978), pp. 139–71

Adams, Simon, 'Spain or the Netherlands? The dilemmas of early Stuart foreign policy', in Howard Tomlinson (ed.), *Before the English Civil War: Essays on early Stuart politics and government* (London, 1983), pp. 79–101

Ahn, Doohwan, 'Europe or America: The economic dimension of the Whig split of 1717' (unpublished paper)

Ahn, Doohwan, 'The Tory free trade ideology versus the Whig jealous fear of France: The case of the Treaty of Utrecht of 1713' (unpublished paper)

Albion, Robert G., *Forests and sea power: The timber problem of the Royal Navy, 1652–1862* (Cambridge, Mass., 1926)

Aldridge, David D., 'English east coast trade with the Baltic in the closing years of the Great Northern War, 1714–1721', in Patrick Salmon and Tony Barron (eds.), *Britain and the Baltic: Studies in commercial, political and cultural relations, 1550–2000* (Sunderland, 2003), pp. 119–29

Aldridge, David D., 'Sir John Norris, 1660?–1749', in Peter Le Fevre and Richard Harding (eds.), *Precursors to Nelson. British Admirals of the eighteenth century* (London, 2000), pp. 129–49

Allen, Mitchell Dale, 'The Anglo-Hanoverian connection: 1727–1760' (PhD dissertation, Boston University, 2000)

Alstyne, Richard van, *Empire and independence: The international history of the American Revolution* (New York, London, Sydney, 1965; 2nd edn, 1967)

Alstyne, Richard van, 'Europe, the Rockingham Whigs and the War for American independence', *Huntington Library Quarterly* 25 (1961–2), pp. 1–28

Alstyne, Richard van, *Genesis of American nationalism* (Waltham, Toronto, London, 1970)

Alstyne, Richard van, 'Great Britain, the war for independence and the "gathering storm" in Europe, 1775–1778', *Huntington Library Quarterly* 27 (1963–4), pp. 311–46

Alstyne, Richard van, 'Parliamentary supremacy versus independence: Notes and documents', *Huntington Library Quarterly* 26:3 (1963), pp. 201–33

Alstyne, Richard van, *The rising American empire* (Oxford, 1960)

Alstyne, Richard van, 'The significance of the Mississippi Valley in American diplomatic history, 1686–1810', *Mississippi Valley Historical Review* 36 (1949), pp. 215–38

Althoff, Frank, *Untersuchungen zum Gleichgewicht der Mächte in der Außenpolitik Friedrichs des Großen nach dem Siebenjährigen Krieg (1763–1786)* (Berlin, 1995)

Anderson, Fred, *Crucible of war: The Seven Years War and the fate of empire in British North America, 1754–1766* (New York, 2000)

Anderson, George P., 'Pascal Paoli: An inspiration to the sons of liberty', in *Publications of the Colonial Society of Massachusetts* 26 (1924–6), pp. 180–210

Anderson, M. S., 'Great Britain and the growth of the Russian navy in the eighteenth century', *Mariner's Mirror* (1956), pp. 132–46

Anderson, M. S., 'Great Britain and the Russian fleet, 1769–70', *Slavonic and East European Review* 31 (1952–3), pp. 148–63

Anderson, M. S., 'Great Britain and the Russo-Turkish War of 1768–74', *English Historical Review* 69 (1954), pp. 39–58

Anderson, M. S., *The War of the Austrian Succession, 1740–1748* (London and New York, 1995)

Anderson, R. C., *Naval wars in the Baltic during the sailing ship epoch* (London, 1910)

Andrews, C. M., 'Anglo-French commercial rivalry, 1700–1750: The western phase', *American Historical Review* 20 (1914–15), pp. 539–56, 761–80

Anon., 'The Dukes of Marlborough and the Principality of Mindelheim', *Family History* 19 (1999), pp. 325–35

Aretin, Karl Otmar von, *Das alte Reich, 1648–1806*, vol. III (Stuttgart, 1997)

Aretin, Karl Otmar von, *Das Reich: Friedensgarantie und europäisches Gleichgewicht 1648–1806* (Stuttgart, 1986)

Aretin, Karl Otmar von, *Heiliges Römisches Reich 1776–1806: Reichsverfassung und Staatssouveränität* (2 vols., Wiesbaden, 1967)

Armitage, David, 'The British conception of empire in the eighteenth century', in Franz Bosbach and Hermann Hiery (eds.), *Imperium/Empire/Reich. Ein Konzept politischer Herrschaft im deutsch-britischen Vergleich: An Anglo-German comparison of a concept of rule* (Munich, 1999), pp. 91–107

Armitage, David, 'The Declaration of Independence and international law', *William and Mary Quarterly* 59:1 (Jan. 2002), pp. 39–64

Armitage, David, *The Declaration of Independence: A global history* (Cambridge, Mass., 2006)

Armitage, David, 'Greater Britain: A useful category of historical analysis?', *American Historical Review Forum* 104:2 (April 1999), pp. 427–45

Armitage, David, *The ideological origins of the British Empire* (Cambridge, 2000)

Armitage, David, 'A patriot for whom? The afterlives of Bolingbroke's Patriot King', *Journal of British Studies* 36 (1997), pp. 397–418

Armitage, David (ed.), *Theories of empire, 1450–1800* (Aldershot, 1998)

Armitage, David, 'Three concepts of Atlantic history', in Armitage and Braddick, *British Atlantic world*

Armitage, David, and Braddick, Mike, (eds.), *The British Atlantic world* (London, 2002)

Armstrong, E., *Elisabeth Farnese, 'the termagant of Spain'* (London, 1892)

Atherton, Herbert M., *Political prints in the age of Hogarth: A study of the ideographic representation of politics* (London, 1974)

Atkinson, C. T., 'British strategy and battles in the Westphalian campaigns of 1758–62', *Journal of the Royal United Service Institution* 79 (1934), pp. 733–40

Atwood, Rodney, *The Hessians: Mercenaries from Hessen-Kassel in the American Revolution* (Cambridge, 1980)

BIBLIOGRAPHY

Avery, Emmet L., and A. H. Scouten, 'The opposition to Sir Robert Walpole 1737–1739',
English Historical Review 83 (1969), pp. 331–6

Baack, Lawrence J., 'State service in the eighteenth century: The Bernstorffs in Hanover and
Denmark', International History Review 1 (1979), pp. 323–48
Bagis, A. I., Britain and the struggle for the integrity of the Ottoman Empire: Sir Robert
Ainslie's embassy to Istanbul, 1776–1794 (Istanbul, 1984)
Bailyn, Bernard, The ideological origins of the American Revolution (Cambridge, Mass.,
1967)
Ballschmieter, Hans Joachim, Andreas Gottlieb von Bernstorff und der mecklenburgische
Ständekampf 1680–1720 (Cologne, 1962)
Barker, Hannah, Newspapers, politics and English society, 1695–1855 (London, 2000)
Barker, Hannah, 'England, 1760–1815' in Hannah Barker and Simon Burrows (eds.), Press,
politics and the public sphere in Europe and North America, 1760–1820 (Cambridge,
2002), pp. 93–112
Barmeyer, Heide, 'Hof und Hofgesellschaft in Hannover im 18. und 19. Jahrhundert', in Karl
Möckl (ed.), Hof und Hofgesellschaft in den deutschen Staaten im 19. und beginnenden 20.
Jahrhundert (Boppard, 1990), pp. 239–73
Barnes, Donald G., 'Henry Pelham and the Duke of Newcastle', The Journal of British
Studies 2 (1962), pp. 62–77
Bartlett, Thomas, 'The augmentation of the army in Ireland, 1767–1769', English Historical
Review 96 (1981), pp. 540–59
Bartlett, Thomas, ' "A weapon of war yet untried": Irish Catholics and the armed forces of
the Crown, 1760–1830', in T. G. Fraser and Keith Jeffery (eds.), Men, women and war,
Historical Studies 18 (Dublin, 1993), pp. 66–85
Barton, H. A., 'Sweden and the War of American Independence', William and Mary
Quarterly 23 (1966), pp. 408–30
Basye, A. H., The Lords Commissioners of Trade and Plantations, commonly known as the
Board of Trade, 1748–1782 (New Haven, 1925)
Bauermeister, Christopher W., 'Hanover: Milde Regierung or Ancien Régime?', German
History 20 (2002), p. 308
Baugh, Daniel A., British naval administration in the age of Walpole (Princeton, 1965)
Baugh, Daniel A., 'British strategy during the First World War in the context of four
centuries: Blue water versus Continental commitment', in Daniel Masterson (ed.), The
sixth symposium of the US Naval Academy (Wilmington, 1987), pp. 85–110
Baugh, Daniel A., 'Great Britain's "blue water" policy, 1689–1815', International History
Review 10 (1988), pp. 33–58
Baugh, Daniel A., 'Maritime strength and Atlantic commerce: The uses of "a grand marine
empire" ', in Stone, Imperial state at war, pp. 185–223
Baugh, Daniel A., 'Why did Britain lose command of the sea during the war for America?',
in Black and Woodfine, British Navy, pp. 149–69
Baugh, Daniel A., 'Withdrawing from Europe: Anglo-French maritime geopolitics, 1750–
1800', International History Review 20:1 (March 1998), pp. 1–32
Baxter, Stephen B. (ed.), England's rise to greatness, 1660–1763 (Berkeley, 1983)
Baxter, Stephen B., 'The myth of the Grand Alliance in the eighteenth century', in Stephen
B. Baxter and P. Sellin (eds.), Anglo-Dutch cross currents in the seventeenth and eighteenth
centuries (Los Angeles, 1976), pp. 42–59
Baxter, Stephen B., William III and the defence of European liberty, 1650–1702 (London,
1966)
Bayly, C. A., 'The first age of global imperialism, c.1760–1830', Journal of Imperial and
Commonwealth History 26 (1998), pp. 28–48
Bayly, C. A., Imperial meridian: The British Empire and the world, 1780–1830 (London,
1989)
Beales, Derek, Joseph II: In the shadow of Maria Theresa, 1741–1780 (Cambridge, 1987)

695

Beattie, J. M., 'The court of George I and English politics 1717–1720', *English Historical Review* 81 (1966), pp. 26–37

Beattie, J. M., *The English court in the reign of George I* (Cambridge, 1967)

Beer, E. S. de, 'The English newspapers from 1695–1702', in Hatton and Bromley (eds.), *William III and Louis XIV*, pp. 117–29

Bemis, S. F., 'British secret service and the French–American alliance', *American Historical Review* 29 (1923–4), pp. 474–95

Bemis, S. F., *The diplomacy of the American Revolution* (New Haven, 1935; reprinted Bloomington, 1957)

Bennett, G. V., 'Jacobitism and the rise of Walpole', in N. McKendrick (ed.), *Historical perspectives: Studies in English thought and social history in honour of J. H. Plumb* (London, 1974)

Bennett, G. V., *The Tory crisis in church and state, 1688–1730: The career of Francis Atterbury, Bishop of Rochester* (Oxford, 1975)

Béranger, Jean, *Les Hommes de lettres et la politique en Angleterre de la Révolution de 1688 à la mort de George I* (Bordeaux, 1968)

Beresford, Marcus de la Poer, 'Ireland in French strategy during the American War of Independence, 1776–82', *Irish Sword* 12 (1975–6), pp. 285–97; 13 (1977–9), pp. 20–29

Bernstorff, Hartwig von, *Andreas Gottlieb von Bernstorff, 1649–1726: Staatsmann, Junker, Patriarch. Zwischen deutschem Partikularismus und europäischer Politik* (Bochum, 1999)

Bickham, Troy, *Savages within the Empire: Representations of American Indians in eighteenth-century Britain* (Oxford, 2005)

Bindoff, S. T., *The Scheldt question to 1839* (London, 1945)

Bingmann, Karl, *Das rechtliche Verhältnis zwischen Großbritannien und Hanover von 1714 bis 1837* (PhD dissertation, University of Würzburg, 1923; Celle, 1925)

Binney, J. E. D., *British public finance and administration, 1774–1792* (Oxford, 1958)

Bird, W. D., 'British land strategy in four great wars, 1702–1802', *Army Quarterly* 20 (1930), pp. 30–44, 307–18; 21 (1931), pp. 44–53

Birke, Adolf, and Kurt Kluxen (eds.), *England und Hannover: England and Hanover* (Munich and London, 1986)

Black, Jeremy, *America or Europe? British foreign policy, 1739–63* (London, 1997)

Black, Jeremy, 'Anglo-Wittelsbach relations, 1730–1742', *Zeitschrift für bayerische Landesgeschichte* 55 (1992), pp. 307–45

Black, Jeremy, 'An "ignoramus" in European affairs?', *British Journal for Eighteenth-Century Studies* 6 (1983)

Black, Jeremy, *Britain as a military power, 1688–1815* (London, 1998)

Black, Jeremy (ed.), *Britain in the age of Walpole: Problems in focus* (London, 1984)

Black, Jeremy, 'The British attempt to preserve the peace in Europe, 1748–1755', in Heinz Duchhardt (ed.), *Zwischenstaatliche Friedenswährung in Mittelalter und Früher Neuzeit* (Cologne, 1991), pp. 227–44

Black, Jeremy, *British diplomats and diplomacy, 1688–1800* (Exeter, 2001)

Black, Jeremy, *British foreign policy in an age of revolution 1783–1793* (Cambridge, 1994)

Black, Jeremy, *British foreign policy in the age of Walpole* (Edinburgh, 1985)

Black, Jeremy, 'British foreign policy in the eighteenth century: A survey', *Journal of British Studies* 26 (1987), pp. 26–53

Black, Jeremy, 'British intelligence and the mid-eighteenth century crisis', *Intelligence and National Security* 2:2 (1987), pp. 209–29

Black, Jeremy, 'British naval power and international commitments: Political and strategic problems, 1688–1770', in Michael Duffy (ed.), *Parameters of British naval power, 1650–1850* (Exeter, 1992), pp. 39–59

Black, Jeremy, 'British neutrality in the War of the Polish Succession, 1733–1735', *International History Review* 8:3 (1986), pp. 345–66

Black, Jeremy, *British politics and society from Walpole to Pitt, 1742–1789* (Basingstoke, 1990)

Black, Jeremy, 'The British state and foreign policy in the eighteenth century', *Trivium* 23 (1988), pp. 127–48

Black, Jeremy, 'The Catholic threat and British press in the 1720s and 1730s', *Journal of Religious History* 12 (1983), pp. 364–81

Black, Jeremy, *The collapse of the Anglo-French alliance, 1727–1732* (Gloucester and New York, 1987)

Black, Jeremy, *The Continental commitment: Britain, Hanover and interventionism, 1714–1793* (London and New York, 2005)

Black, Jeremy, 'The Crown, Hanover, and the shift in British foreign policy in the 1760s', in Black, *Knights errant*, pp. 113–32

Black, Jeremy, *The English press in the eighteenth century* (London, 1987)

Black, Jeremy, *The European question and the national interest* (London, 2006)

Black, Jeremy, 'Exceptionalism, structure and contingency: Britain as a European state, 1688–1818', *Diplomacy and Statecraft* 8 (November 1997), pp. 11–26

Black, Jeremy, *The foreign policy of Walpole* (Edinburgh, 1985)

Black, Jeremy, 'Fresh light on the fall of Townshend', *Historical Journal* 29:1 (1986), pp. 41–64

Black, Jeremy, 'George II reconsidered', *Mitteilungen des österreichischen Staatsarchivs* 35 (1982), pp. 35–56

Black, Jeremy, *George III: America's last king* (New Haven, 2006)

Black, Jeremy, *The grand tour in the eighteenth century* (Stroud, 1992)

Black, Jeremy, 'Hanover and British foreign policy, 1714–60', *English Historical Review* 120:486 (2005), pp. 303–39

Black, Jeremy, *The Hanoverians* (London, 2004)

Black, Jeremy, 'The House of Lords and British foreign policy, 1720–48', in Clyve Jones (ed.), *A pillar of the constitution: The House of Lords in British politics, 1640–1784* (London, 1989), pp. 113–36

Black, Jeremy, 'International relations in the eighteenth century: Britain and Poland compared', *Diplomacy and Statecraft* 13:1 (2002), pp. 83–112

Black, Jeremy, 'Interventionism, structuralism and contingency in British foreign policy in the 1720s', *International History Review* 26:4 (December 2004)

Black, Jeremy (ed.), *Knights errant and true Englishmen: British foreign policy, 1660–1800* (Edinburgh, 1989)

Black, Jeremy, *Natural and necessary enemies: Anglo-French relations in the eighteenth century* (London, 1986)

Black, Jeremy, 'Naval power and British foreign policy in the age of Pitt the Elder', in Black and Woodfine, *British Navy*, pp. 90–107

Black, Jeremy, 'Parliament and foreign policy in the Age of Walpole: The case of the Hessians', in Black, *Knights errant*, pp. 41–54

Black, Jeremy, *Parliament and foreign policy in the eighteenth century* (Cambridge, 2004)

Black, Jeremy, 'Parliament and the political and diplomatic crisis of 1717–1718', *Parliamentary History* 3 (1984), pp. 77–101

Black, Jeremy, *Pitt the Elder* (Cambridge, 1992)

Black, Jeremy, *The politics of Britain, 1688–1800* (Manchester, 1993)

Black, Jeremy, 'The problem of the small state: Bavaria and Britain in the second quarter of the eighteenth century', *European History Quarterly* 19 (1989), pp. 5–36

Black, Jeremy, 'Recovering lost years: British foreign policy after the War of the Polish Succession', *Diplomacy and Statecraft* 15 (2004), pp. 465–87

Black, Jeremy, 'The Revolution and the development of English foreign policy', in Cruickshanks, *By force or by default?*, pp. 135–58

Black, Jeremy, 'Swift and foreign policy revisited', in Richard H. Rodino and Herman Real (eds.), *Reading Swift: Papers from the second Münster symposium on Jonathan Swift* (Munich, 1993), pp. 61–70

Black, Jeremy, *A system of ambition? British foreign policy, 1660–1793* (2nd edn, Stroud, 2000)

Black, Jeremy, 'The Tory view of eighteenth-century British foreign policy', *Historical Journal* 31 (1988), pp. 469–77

Black, Jeremy, 'The Treaty of Rijswijk and the long-term development of Anglo-Continental relations', in Heinz Duchhardt (ed.), *Der Friede von Rijswijk 1697* (Mainz, 1998), pp. 115–26

Black, Jeremy, *Walpole in power* (Stroud, 2001)

Black, Jeremy, 'When "natural allies" fall out: Anglo-Austrian relations, 1725–40', *Mitteilungen des österreichischen Staatsarchivs* 36 (1983), pp. 120–49

Black, Jeremy, and Philip Woodfine (eds.), *The British Navy and the use of naval power in the eighteenth century* (Leicester, 1988)

Blanning, T. C. W., *The culture of power and the power of culture: Old regime Europe, 1660–1789* (Oxford, 2003)

Bloom, Edward A., *Samuel Johnson in Grub Street* (Providence, 1957)

Bordo, Michael D., and Roberteo Cortes-Conde (eds.), *Transferring wealth and power from the Old to the New World* (Cambridge, 2001)

Borgmann, K., *Der deutsche Religionsstreit der Jahre 1710–1720* (Berlin, 1937)

Bowen, H. V., 'British conceptions of global empire, 1756–1783', *Journal of Imperial and Commonwealth History* 26 (1998), pp. 1–27

Bowen, H. V., *Revenue and reform: The Indian problem in British politics, 1757–1773* (Cambridge, 1991)

Braddick, Michael J., *The nerves of state: Taxation and the financing of the English state, 1558–1714* (Manchester and New York, 1996)

Bradshaw, Brendan, and John Morrill (eds.), *The British problem c. 1534–1707: State formation in the Atlantic archipelago* (London, 1996)

Braubach, Max, *Die Bedeutung der Subsidien für die Politik im Spanischen Erbfolgekriege* (Bonn and Leipzig, 1923)

Braubach, Max, *Diplomatie und geistiges Leben im 17. und 18. Jahrhundert, Gesammelte Abhandlungen* (Bonn, 1969)

Braubach, Max, *Versailles und Wien von Ludwig XIV. bis Kaunitz. Die Vorstadien der diplomatischen Revolution im 18. Jahrhundert* (Bonn, 1952)

Brauer, Gert, *Die hannoversch-englischen Subsidienverträge 1702–1748* (Aachen, 1962)

Brecher, Frank W., *Losing a continent: France's North American policy, 1753–1763* (1998)

Brewer, John, *The common people and politics, 1750–1790s* (Cambridge, 1986)

Brewer, John, 'The misfortunes of Lord Bute: A case-study of eighteenth-century political argument and public opinion', *Historical Journal* 16 (1973), pp. 3–43

Brewer, John, *Party ideology and popular politics at the accession of George III* (Cambridge, 1976)

Brewer, John, *The sinews of power: War, money, and the English state, 1688–1783* (London, 1989)

Brewer, John, and Eckhart Hellmuth (eds.), *The eighteenth-century state in Britain and Germany* (Oxford, 1999)

Briggs, Robin, 'The great naval race, 1750–1815' (unpublished paper)

Bromley, J. S., 'Britain and Europe in the eighteenth century', *History* 66 (1981), pp. 394–412

Bromley, J. S., *Corsairs and navies, 1660–1760* (London and Roncevert, 1987)

Bromley, J. S., 'The second Hundred Years' War (1689–1815)', in D. Johnson *et al.* (eds.), *Britain and France: Ten centuries* (Folkestone, 1980)

Brooke, J., *The Chatham administration, 1766–1768* (London, 1956)

Brooke, J., *George III* (London, 1972)

Brooks, Colin, 'British political culture and the dismemberment of states: Britain and the first partition of Poland, 1762–1772', *Parliaments, Estates and Representation* 13 (1993), pp. 51–64

Brown, G. S., 'The Anglo-French Naval Crisis, 1778: A Study of Conflict in the North Cabinet', *William and Mary Quarterly* 3:13 (1956), pp. 3–25

Brown, Vera Lee, 'The South Sea Company and contraband trade', *American Historical Review* 31 (1925–6), pp. 662–78

Browning, Reed, 'The British orientation of Austrian foreign policy, 1749–1754', *Central European History* 4 (1968), pp. 299–323

Browning, Reed, *The Duke of Newcastle* (New Haven and London, 1975)

Browning, Reed, 'The Duke of Newcastle and the Financing of the Seven Years War', *Journal of Economic History* 31 (1971), pp. 344–77

Browning, Reed, 'The Duke of Newcastle and the imperial election plan, 1749–1754', *Journal of British Studies* 7 (1967–8), pp. 28–47

Brumwell, Stephen, *Paths of glory: The life and death of General James Wolfe* (London, 2006)

Brumwell, Stephen, *Redcoats: The British soldier and war in the Americas, 1755–1763* (Cambridge, 2002)

Bryant, Arthur, *Freedom's own island: The British oceanic expansion* (London, 1986)

Buddruss, Eckhard, *Die Französische Deutschlandpolitik, 1756–1789* (Mainz, 1995)

Buel, Richard, *In irons: Britain's naval supremacy and the American revolutionary economy* (New Haven and London, 1998)

Buffington, A. H., 'The Canada expedition of 1746: Its relation to British politics', *American Historical Review* 45 (1939–40), pp. 552–80

Bullion, J. L., 'Securing the peace: Lord Bute, the plan for the army, and the origins of the American Revoluton', in Schweizer, *Lord Bute*, pp. 17–39

Burtt, Shelley, *Virtue transformed: Political argument in England, 1688–1740* (Cambridge, 1992)

Butler, Rohan, 'The secret compact of 1753 between the kings of France and Naples', in Robert Oresko, G. C. Gibbs and Hamish M. Scott (eds.), *Royal and republican sovereignty in Early Modern Europe: Essays in memory of Ragnhild Hatton* (Cambridge, 1997), pp. 551–79

Butterfield, Herbert, 'British foreign policy, 1762–65', *Cambridge Historical Journal* 6 (1963), pp. 131–40

Butterfield, Herbert, *George III, Lord North and the People, 1779–80* (London, 1949)

Butterfield, Herbert, *The reconstruction of an historical episode: The history of the enquiry into the origins of the Seven Years War* (Glasgow, 1951)

Cain, P. A., and Anthony Hopkins, *British imperialism: Innovation and expansion, 1688–1914* (2 vols., London, 1993)

Calloway, Colin G., *The scratch of a pen: 1763 and the transformation of North America* (Oxford, 2006)

The Cambridge history of British foreign policy, 1783–1919, vol. I, *1783–1815*, ed. A. W. Ward and G. P. Gooch (Cambridge, 1922)

Campbell, I. B., 'From the "Personal Union" between England and Scotland in 1603 to the European Communities Act 1972 and beyond – enduring legal problems from a historical viewpoint', in B. S. Jackson and D. McGoldrick (eds.), *Legal Visions of the New Europe* (London, 1993), pp. 37–104

Campbell, I. B., 'The international and legal relations between Great Britain and Hanover', (PhD dissertation, Cambridge, 1965)

Cannon, John, 'George III and America', *Historian* 85 (2005), pp. 20–26

Cannon, John, *Parliamentary reform, 1640–1832* (Cambridge, 1973)

Cannon, John, *Samuel Johnson and the politics of Hanoverian Britain* (Oxford, 1994)

Cardwell, M. John, *Arts and arms: Literature, politics and patriotism during the Seven Years War* (Manchester, 2004)

Carlos, A. M., and Andrew S. Thompson, 'The micro-foundations of the early London capital market: Bank of England shareholders during and after the South Sea Bubble, 1720–25', *Economic History Review* 59:3 (August 2006), pp. 498–538

Carsten, F. L., 'Britain and Prussia', in *Essays in German History* (London, 1985), pp. 177–92

Carswell, John, *The descent on England: A study of the English Revolution of 1688 and its European background* (London, 1969)

Carswell, John, *The South Sea Bubble* (London, 1960)

Carter, Alice C., 'Britain as a European power, from her Glorious Revolution to the French Revolutionary War', in J. S. Bromley and E. H. Kossmann (eds.), *Britain and the Netherlands in Europe and Asia* (London, Melbourne, Toronto, 1968), pp. 110–37

Carter, Alice C., *The Dutch Republic in Europe in the Seven Years War* (London, 1971)

Carter, Alice C., *Neutrality or commitment: The evolution of Dutch foreign policy, 1667–1795* (London, 1975)

Cash, Arthur H., *John Wilkes: The scandalous father of civil liberty* (New Haven, 2006)

Cassels, Lavender, *The struggle for the Ottoman Empire, 1717–1740* (London, 1966)

Castries, René de la Croix, duc de, 'La Pacte de famille et la Guerre d'Indépendance Américaine', *Revue d'histoire diplomatique* 75 (1961), pp. 254–306

Ceadel, Martin, *The origins of war prevention: The British peace movement and international relations, 1730–1854* (Oxford, 1996)

Chance, J. F., *The alliance of Hanover: A study of British foreign policy in the last years of George I* (1923)

Chance, J. F., *George I and the Northern War: A study of British-Hanoverian Policy in the north of Europe in the years 1709 to 1721* (London, 1909)

Chance, J. F., 'John de Robethon and the Robethon papers', *English Historical Review* 12 (1898), pp. 55–70

Chandler, David, *The art of warfare in the age of Marlborough* (London, 1976)

Chandler, David, *Marlborough as a military commander* (London, 1973)

Charteris, Sir Evan, *William Augustus, Duke of Cumberland and the Seven Years War* (London, 1925)

Christelow, Allan, 'Economic background of the Anglo-Spanish War of 1762', *Journal of Modern History* 18 (1946), pp. 22–36

Christie, Ian R., *The end of North's ministry, 1780–1781* (London, 1958)

Christie, Ian R., 'George III and the historians – thirty years on', *History* 71 (1986), pp. 205–21

Ciencala, Anna M., 'The American founding fathers and Poland', in Jaroslav Pelenski (ed.), *The American and European revolutions, 1776–1848* (Iowa City, 1980), pp. 111–24

Clanchy, M. T., *England and its rulers, 1066–1272: Foreign lordship and national identity* (London, 1983)

Clark, J. C. D., 'The decline of party, 1740–1760', *English Historical Review* 93 (1978), pp. 499–527

Clark, J. C. D., *The dynamics of change: The crisis of the 1750s and English party systems* (Cambridge, 1982)

Clark, J. C. D., *English Society, 1688–1832: Ideology, social structure and political practice during the Ancien Régime* (Cambridge, 1985)

Clark, J. C. D., 'A general theory of party, opposition and government, 1688–1832', *Historical Journal* 23:2 (1980), pp. 295–325

Clark, J. C. D., *The language of liberty, 1660–1832: Political discourse and social dynamics in the Anglo-American world* (Cambridge, 1994)

Clark, J. C. D., 'Protestantism, nationalism and national identity, 1660–1832', *Historical Journal* 43:1 (2000), pp. 249–76

Clark, J. C. D., *Revolution and rebellion* (Cambridge, 1986)

Claydon, Tony, *William III and the Godly Revolution* (Cambridge, 1996)

Clayton, T., 'The Duke of Newcastle, the Earl of Halifax, and the American origins of the Seven Years War', *Historical Journal* 24 (1981), pp. 571–603

Clendenning, P. H., 'The background and negotiations for the Anglo-Russian Commercial Treaty of 1766', in A. G. Cross (ed.), *Great Britain and Russia in the eighteenth century: Contacts and comparisons* (Newtonville, 1979), pp. 145–63

Cogswell, Thomas, *The blessed revolution: English politics and the coming of war, 1621–1624* (Cambridge, 1989)

Colley, Linda, 'The apotheosis of George III: Loyalty, royalty and the British nation, 1760–1820', *Past and Present* 102 (1984), pp. 94–129

Colley, Linda, 'Britishness and otherness: An argument', *Journal of British Studies* 31 (1992), pp. 309–29

Colley, Linda, *Britons: Forging the nation, 1707–1837* (London, 1992)

Colley, Linda, *Captives: Britain, Europe and the world, 1600–1850* (London, 2002)

Colley, Linda, *In defiance of oligarchy: The Tory party, 1714–60* (Cambridge, 1982)

Colley, Linda, 'Size does matter: How a few islands won an empire', *Times Literary Supplement* (20 September 2002), pp. 12–13

Conde, A. de, 'Historians, the War of American Independence, and the persistence of the exceptionalist ideal', *International History Review* 5 (1983), pp. 399–430

Conlin, J., 'Wilkes, the Chevalier D'Eon and "the dregs of liberty": An Anglo-French perspective on ministerial despotism, 1762–1771, *English Historical Review* 120 (2005), pp. 1251–88

Conn, S., *Gibraltar in British diplomacy in the eighteenth century* (New Haven, 1941)

Conrady, Sigisbert, 'Die Wirksamkeit Königs Georgs III. für die hannoverschen Kurlande', *Niedersächsisches Jahrbuch für Landesgeschichte* 39 (1967), pp. 150–91

Conway, Stephen, *The British Isles and the War of American Independence* (Oxford, 2002)

Conway, Stephen, 'Continental connections: Britain and Europe in the eighteenth century', *History* 90:299 (July 2005), pp. 353–7

Conway, Stephen, 'From fellow-nationals to foreigners: British perceptions of the Americans circa 1739–1788', *William and Mary Quarterly* 59:1 (January 2002), pp. 65–100

Conway, Stephen, 'War and national identity in the mid-eighteenth-century British Isles', *English Historical Review* 116 (2001), pp. 863–93

Conway, Stephen, 'War, expansion and religious developments in mid-eighteenth-century Britain and Ireland', *War in History* (2004), pp. 136–9

Conway, Stephen, *The War of American Independence, 1776–1783* (London, 1995)

Conway, Stephen, *War, state and society in mid-eighteenth century Britain and Ireland* (Oxford, 2006)

Cook, R. I., *Jonathan Swift as a Tory pamphleteer* (Seattle, 1967)

Coombs, D., *The conduct of the Dutch: British opinion and the Dutch alliance during the War of the Spanish Succession* (The Hague, 1958)

Corbett, Julian S., *England in the Seven Years War: A study in combined strategy* (2 vols., London, 1907)

Corp, Edward T., *A court in exile: The Stuarts in France, 1689–1718* (Cambridge, 2004)

Corwin, E., *French policy and the American alliance of 1778* (Princeton, 1916)

Cotlar, Seth, 'The American Revolution in the Atlantic world', *Reviews in American History* 30 (2002), pp. 381–8

Cox, Richard H., *Locke on war and peace* (Oxford, 1960)

Cranfield, G. A., *The development of the provincial newspaper, 1700–1760* (Oxford, 1962)

Crout, R. R., 'In search of a "just and lasting peace": The treaty of 1783, Louis XVI, Vergennes, and the Regeneration of the Realm', *International History Review* 5 (1983), pp. 364–98

Cruickshanks, Eveline (ed.), *By force or by default? The revolution of 1688–1689* (Edinburgh, 1989)

Cruickshanks, Eveline (ed.), *Ideology and conspiracy: Aspects of English Jacobitism, 1689–1759* (Edinburgh, 1982)

Cruickshanks, Eveline, *Political untouchables: The Tories and the '45* (London and New York, 1979)

Cruickshanks, Eveline, and Howard Erskine-Hill, *Atterbury Plot* (Basingstoke, 2004)

Cruickshanks, Eveline, Stuart Handley and D. W. Hayton (eds.), *The House of Commons, 1640–1715* (5 vols., Cambridge, 2002)

Dann, Uriel, *Hanover and Great Britain, 1740–1760* (Leicester, 1991)

Darling, Arthur B., *Our rising empire, 1763–1803* (New Haven, 1940)

Davis, Ralph, 'English foreign trade, 1700–1774,' *Economic History Review* 2:15 (1962–3), pp. 285–303

Dawson, F. G., 'William Pitt's settlement at Black River on the Mosquito Shore: A challenge to Spain in Central America', *Hispanic American Historical Review* 63 (1983), pp. 677–706

Dawson, Jane, 'William Cecil and the British dimension of early Elizabethan foreign policy', *History* 74 (1989), pp. 196–216

Desbarats, Catherine M., 'France in North America: The net burden of empire during the first half of the eighteenth century', *French History* 11:1 (1997), pp. 1–28

Dickinson, H. T., *Bolingbroke* (London, 1970)

Dickinson, H. T. (ed.), *Britain and the American Revolution* (London and New York, 1998)

Dickinson, H. T., *Caricatures and the constitution, 1760–1832: The English satirical print, 1600–1832* (Cambridge, 1986)

Dickinson, H. T., *Liberty and property: Political ideology in eighteenth-century Britain* (London, 1977)

Dickinson, H. T., 'Party, principle and public opinion in eighteenth century politics', *History* 61 (1976), pp. 231–7

Dickson, P. G. M., 'English commercial negotiations with Austria, 1737–1752', in Anne Whiteman, J. S. Bromley and P. G. M. Dickson (eds.), *Statesmen, scholars and merchants: Essays in eighteenth-century history presented to Dame Lucy Sutherland* (Oxford, 1973), pp. 81–112

Dickson, P. G. M., *The financial revolution in England: A study in the development of public credit, 1688–1756* (London, 1967)

Dippel, Horst, *Germany and the American Revolution, 1770–1800: A socio-historical investigation of late-eighteenth-century political thinking* (Chapel Hill, 1977)

Dippel, Horst, 'Prussia's English policy after the Seven Years War', *Central European History* 4 (1971), pp. 195–214

Ditchfield, G. M., *George III: An essay in monarchy* (Basingstoke and New York, 2003)

Doll, Peter M., *Revolution, religion, and national identity: Imperial Anglicanism in British North America, 1745–1795* (Madison and Teaneck, 2000)

Dollot, R., 'La Garrison de la barrière dans les Pays-Bas autrichiens, 1715–82', *Revue d'histoire diplomatique* 17 (1904), pp. 421–37

Donoughue, B., *British politics and the American Revolution: The path to war, 1773–75* (London, 1964)

Donovan, R. Kent, 'The military origins of the Roman Catholic relief programme of 1778', *Historical Journal* 29 (1985), pp. 79–102

Doran, Patrick Francis, *Andrew Mitchell and Anglo-Prussian diplomatic relations during the Seven Years War* (New York and London, 1986)

Doran, Susan, *England and Europe, 1485–1603* (London and New York, 1986)

Doran, Susan, and Glenn Richardson (eds.), *Tudor England and its neighbours* (Basingstoke, 2005)

Dorn, W., 'Frederick the Great and Lord Bute', *Journal of Modern History* 1 (1929), pp. 529–60

Downey, Declan M., 'Irish–European integration: The legacy of Charles V', in Judith Devlin and Howard B. Clarke (eds.), *European encounters: Essays in memory of Albert Lovett* (Dublin, 2003), pp. 97–117

Downie, J. A., 'The development of the political press', in Clyve Jones, *Britain in the First Age of Party*, pp. 111–27

Draper, Theodore, *A struggle for power: The American Revolution* (London, 1996)

Duchhardt, Heinz (ed.), *Der Herrscher in der Doppelpflicht: Europäische Fürsten und ihre beiden Throne* (Mainz, 1996)

Duchhardt, Heinz, 'England-Hannover und der europäische Friede, 1714–1748', in Birke and Kluxen, *England und Hannover*, pp. 127–44

Duffy, Eamon, 'Correspondance fraternelle: The SPCK, the SPG and the Churches of Switzerland in the War of the Spanish Successsion', in D. Baker (ed.), *Reform and Reformation: England and the Continent, c.1500–c.1750* (Oxford, 1979), pp. 251–81

Duffy, Michael, *The Englishman and the foreigner: English satirical prints, 1600–1832* (Cambridge, 1986)

Duffy, Michael, 'Realism and tradition in eighteenth-century British foreign policy', *Historical Journal* 35 (1992), pp. 227–32

Dull, Jonathan R., 'Benjamin Franklin and the nature of American diplomacy', *International History Review* 5 (1983), pp. 346–63

Dull, Jonathan R., *A diplomatic history of the American Revolution* (New Haven, 1985)

Dull, Jonathan R., *The French navy and American Independence: A study of arms and diplomacy, 1774–1787* (Princeton, 1975)

Dull, Jonathan R., *The French navy and the Seven Years War* (Lincoln, Nebraska and London, 2005)

Dziembowski, *Un nouveau patriotisme français 1750–70: La France face à la puissance anglaise à l'époque de la guerre de sept ans* (Oxford, 1998)

Eagles, Robin, *Francophilia in English society, 1748–1815* (London, 2000)

Eccles, William, 'The fur trade and eighteenth-century imperialism', *William and Mary Quarterly* 3:40 (1983), pp. 341–62

Egnal, Marc, *A mighty empire: The origins of the American Revolution* (Ithaca and London, 1988)

Ehrman, J., *The Navy in the war of William III: Its state and direction, 1689–1697* (Cambridge, 1953)

Ehrman, J., *The Younger Pitt: The years of acclaim* (London, 1969)

Eldon, C. W., 'Document: The Hanoverian subsidy treaty with Ansbach (1755); a typical German subsidy treaty of the eighteenth century', *Journal of Modern History* 12 (1940), pp. 59–68

Eldon, C. W., *England's subsidy policy towards the Continent during the Seven Years War, 1756–1763* (Philadelphia, 1938)

Elliott, J. H., *Empires of the Atlantic world: Britain and Spain in America, 1492–1830* (New Haven, 2006)

Elliott, J. H., *The Old World and the New, 1492–1650* (Cambridge, 1970)

Ellis, Kenneth L., 'The administrative connections between Britain and Hanover', *Journal of the Society of Archivists* 3:10 (1969), pp. 546–66

Ellis, Kenneth L., 'British communications and diplomacy in the eighteenth century', *Bulletin of the Institute of Historical Research* 31 (1958), pp. 159–67

Ellis, Kenneth L., *The post office in the eighteenth century: A study in administrative history* (London, 1958)

Ericson, Lars, 'Economic warfare or piracy? Swedish privateering against British and Dutch trade in the Baltic during the Great Northern War, 1710–1721', in Patrick Salmon and Tony Barron (eds.), *Britain and the Baltic: Studies in commercial, political and cultural relations, 1550–2000* (Sunderland, 2003), pp. 111–18

Esteban, J. Cuenca, 'The British balance of payments, 1772–1820: India transfers and war finance', *Economic History Review* 54:1 (2001), pp. 58–86

Evans, Chris, Owen Jackson and Goeran Ryden, 'Baltic iron and the British iron industry in the eighteenth century', *Economic History Review* 55 (2002), pp. 642–65

Fayle, C. Ernest, 'The deflection of strategy by commerce in the eighteenth century', *Journal of the Royal United Service Institution* 68 (1923), pp. 281–90

Fayle, C. Ernest, 'Economic pressure in the war of 1739–48' *Journal of the Royal United Service Institution* 68 (1923), pp. 434–46

Ferguson, Niall, *Empire: How Britain made the modern world* (London, 2004)

Fichtner, Paula S., 'Viennese perspectives on the War of Independence', in Bela S. Kiraly and

George Barany (eds.), *East central European perception of early America* (Lisse, 1977), pp. 11–29

Finke, Hans-Joachim, 'The Hanoverian Junta, 1714–1719', (DPhil dissertation, University of Michigan, 1970)

Firth, Sir Charles, 'The study of British foreign policy', *Quarterly Review* 226 (1916), pp. 470–87

Foord, Archibald S., *His Majesty's Opposition, 1714–1830* (Oxford, 1964)

Forbes, Duncan, *Hume's philosophical politics* (Cambridge, 1975)

Fritz, Paul S., *The English ministers and Jacobitism between the Rebellions of 1715 and 1745* (Toronto, 1975)

Gauci, Perry, *The politics of trade: The overseas merchant in state and society, 1660–1720* (Oxford, 2001)

Gehling, T., *Ein europäischer Diplomat am Kaiserhof zu Wien, François Louis de Pesme, Seigneur de Saint-Saphorin, als englischer Resident am Wiener Hof, 1718–1727* (Bonn, 1964)

Geikie, Roderick, and Isabel A. Montgomery, *The Dutch Barrier, 1705–1719* (Cambridge, 1930)

Genzel, Fritz, 'Studien zur Geschichte des Nordischen Krieges 1714–1720 unter besonderer Berücksichtigung der Personalunion zwischen Grossbritannien und Hannover' (unpublished PhD dissertation, University of Bonn, 1951)

Gerhard, Dietrich, *England und der Aufstieg Rußlands: Zur Frage des Zusammenhanges der europäischen Staaten und ihres Ausgreifens in die außereuropäische Welt in Politik und Wirtschaft des 16. Jahrhunderts* (Munich and Berlin, 1933)

Gerhard, Dietrich, 'Kontinentalpolitik und Kolonialpolitik im Frankreich des ausgehenden ancien régime', *Historische Zeitschrift* 147 (1933), pp. 21–31

Gerrard, Christine, *The patriot opposition to Walpole: Politics, poetry and national myth, 1725–1742* (Oxford, 1994)

Geyken, Frauke, *Gentlemen auf Reisen: Das britische Deutschlandbild im 18. Jahrhundert* (Frankfurt and New York, 2002)

Geyken, Frauke, ' "The German language is spoken in Saxony with the greatest purity": Or English images and perceptions of Germany in the eighteenth century', in Joseph Canning and Hermann Wellenreuther (eds.), *Britain and Germany compared: Nationality and nobility in the eighteenth century* (Göttingen, 2001), pp. 37–70

Geyl, Pieter, 'Holland and England during the War of the Austrian Succession', *History* 10 (1925–6), pp. 46–51

Geyl, Pieter, 'William IV of Orange and his English marriage', *Transactions of the Royal Historical Society* 4:8 (1925), pp. 14–37

Gibbs, G. C., 'Britain and the Alliance of Hanover, April 1725 – February 1726', *English Historical Review* 73 (1958), pp. 404–30

Gibbs, G. C., 'English attitudes towards Hanover and the Hanoverian succession in the first half of the eighteenth century', in Birke and Kluxen, *England und Hannover*, pp. 33–51

Gibbs, G. C., 'Laying treaties before Parliament in the eighteenth century', in Hatton and Anderson, *Studies in diplomatic history*, pp. 116–37

Gibbs, G. C., 'Newspapers, parliament and foreign policy in the age of Stanhope and Walpole', *Mélanges offerts à G. Jacquemyns* (Brussels, 1968), pp. 293–315

Gibbs, G. C., 'Parliament and foreign policy in the age of Stanhope and Walpole', *English Historical Review* 77 (1962), pp. 18–37

Gibbs, G. C., 'Parliament and the Treaty of Quadruple Alliance', in Hatton and Bromley, *William III and Louis XIV*, pp. 287–305

Gibbs, G. C., 'The revolution in foreign policy', in Geoffrey Holmes (ed.), *Britain after the Glorious Revolution, 1689–1714* (London, 1969), pp. 59–79

Gilbert, Felix, 'The English background of American isolationism in the eighteenth century', *William and Mary Quarterly* 1:III (1944), pp. 138–60

Gilbert, Felix, 'The "New Diplomacy" of the Eighteenth Century', *World Politics* 4 (1951–2), pp. 1–38

Gilbert, Felix, *To the farewell address: Ideas of early American foreign policy* (Princeton, 1961)

Gipson, Lawrence H., 'British diplomacy in the light of Anglo-Spanish New World Issues, 1750–1757', *American Historical Review* 51 (1945–6), pp. 627–48

Gipson, Lawrence H., *The British Empire before the American Revolution* (15 vols., New York, 1936–70)

Gipson, Lawrence H., 'The imperial approach to early American history', in Ray A. Billington (ed.), *The reinterpretation of early American history: Essays in honor of John Edwin Pomfret* (San Marino, 1966), pp. 185–99

Glaisyer, Natasha, *The culture of commerce in England, 1660–1720* (Woodbridge, 2006)

Glaisyer, Natasha, 'Networking: Trade and exchange in the eighteenth-century British Empire', *Historical Journal* 47 (2004), pp. 451–76

Glendenning, Victoria, *Jonathan Swift* (London, 1998)

Glete, Jan, *Navies and nations: Warships, navies and state building in Europe and America, 1500–1860* (2 vols.; Stockholm, 1993)

Glickman, Gabriel, 'The career of Sir John Hynde Cotton, 1686–1752', *Historical Journal* 46 (2003), pp. 817–41

Goebel, J., *The struggle for the Falkland Islands* (New Haven, 1927; reprinted 1981)

Goldsmith, M. M., 'Faction detected: Ideological consequences of Robert Walpole's decline and fall', *History* 64 (1979), pp. 1–19

Gough, Barry Morton, *British mercantile interests in the making of the Peace of Paris, 1763: Trade, war and empire* (Lewiston, Queenston and Lampeter, 1992)

Gould, Eliga H., *The persistence of empire: British political culture in the age of the American Revolution* (Chapel Hill and London, 2000)

Gould, Eliga H., 'Zones of law, zones of violence: The legal geography of the British Atlantic, circa 1772', *William and Mary Quarterly* 60:3 (July 2003), pp. 471–510

Graham, G. S., 'The naval defence of British North America, 1739–1763', *Transactions of the Royal Historical Society* 4:30 (1948), pp. 95–110

Greene, Jack P., *Peripheries and centre: Constitutional development in the extended politics of the British Empire and the United States, 1607–1788* (New York, 1990)

Greene, Jack P., 'The Seven Years War and the American Revolution: The causal relationship reconsidered', *Journal of Imperial and Commonwealth History* 8 (1979–80), pp. 85–105

Gregg, E. G., 'Marlborough in exile, 1712–1714', *Historical Journal* 15 (1972), pp. 593–618

Gregg, E. G., *Queen Anne* (London, 1980)

Gregg, E. G., *The Protestant succession in international politics, 1710–1716* (London, 1972)

Gregg, E. G., 'Was Queen Anne a Jacobite?' *History* 57 (1972), pp. 358–75

Gregory, Jeremy, and John Stevenson, *The Longman companion to Britain in the eighteenth century, 1688–1820* (London, 1999)

Grieser, Rudolph, 'Die Deutsche Kanzlei in London, ihre Entstehung und Anfänge', *Blätter für deutsche Landesgeschichte* 89 (1952), pp. 153–68

Griffiths, D. M., 'Catherine the Great, the British Opposition and the American Revolution', in L. S. Kaplan, *American Revolution*, pp. 85–110

Griffiths, D. M., 'The rise and fall of the northern system: Court politics and foreign policy in the first half of Catherine II's reign', *Canadian-American Slavic Studies* 4 (1970), pp. 547–69

Groom, Nick, *The Union Jack: The story of the British flag* (London, 2006)

Gwyn, Julian, *The enterprising admiral: The personal fortune of Admiral Sir Peter Warren* (Montreal and London, 1974)

Gwynn, Robin, 'The Huguenots in Britain, the "Protestant International" and the defeat of Louis XIV', in Randolph Vigne and Charles Littleton (eds.), *From strangers to citizens* (Brighton, 2001), pp. 412–24

Habermas, Jürgen, *Strukturwandel der Öffentlichkeit: Untersuchungen zu einer Kategorie der bürgerlichen Gesellschaft* (2nd edn, Neuwied, 1965)

Haffenden, P., 'Colonial appointments and patronage under the Duke of Newcastle, 1724–1739', *English Historical Review* 78 (1963), pp. 417–35

Hahlweg, W., 'Barriere-Gleichgewicht-Sicherheit, 1646–1715', *Historische Zeitschrift* (1959), pp. 54–89

Hall, T. E., *France and the eighteenth-century Corsican question* (New York, 1971)

Halsband, Robert, *Lord Hervey: Eighteenth-century courtier* (Oxford, 1973)

Hanham, Andrew, 'Caroline of Brandenburg-Ansbach and the "Anglicization" of the House of Hanover', in Orr, *Queenship in Europe*, pp. 276–399

Hanham, Andrew, 'So few facts: Jacobites, Tories and the Pretender', *Parliamentary History* 19 (2000), pp. 233–57

Hanson, Laurence, *Government and the press, 1695–1763* (London, 1936)

Harding, Nicholas B., 'Dynastic union in British and Hanoverian ideology, 1701–1803', (unpublished PhD dissertation, Columbia University, 2001)

Harding, Nicholas B., 'Hanover and British republicanism', in Simms and Riotte, *Hanoverian dimension*, pp. 301–23

Harding, Nicholas B., 'Hanoverian rulership and dynastic union with Britain, 1700–1760', in Rexheuser, *Die Personalunionen*, pp. 389–416

Harding, Nicholas B., 'North African piracy, the Hanoverian carrying trade, and the British state, 1728–1828', *Historical Journal* 43:1 (2000), pp. 25–47

Harding, Nicholas B., 'Sir Robert Walpole and Hanover', *Historical Research* 76 (May 2003), pp. 165–88

Harding, Richard, *Amphibious warfare in the eighteenth century: The British expedition to the West Indies, 1740–1742* (Woodbridge, 1991)

Harding, Richard, 'British maritime strategy and Hanover, 1714–1763', in Simms and Riotte, *Hanoverian dimension*, pp. 252–74

Harding, Richard, 'Edward Vernon: Blue water advocate', in Le Fevre and Harding, *Precursors to Nelson*, pp. 151–75

Harding, Richard, 'Sailors and gentlemen of parade: Some professional and technical problems concerning the conduct of combined operations in the eighteenth century', *Historical Journal* 32 (1987), pp. 35–55

Harding, Richard, *Sea power and naval warfare, 1650–1830* (London, 1999)

Harlow, Vincent T., *The founding of the second British empire* (2 vols., London, 1952–64)

Harris, Bob, 'American idols: Empire, war and the middling ranks in mid-eighteenth-century Britain', *Past and Present* 150 (1996), pp. 111–41

Harris, Bob, 'Hanover and the public sphere', in Simms and Riotte, *Hanoverian dimension*, pp. 183–212

Harris, Bob, 'The London press, "popular power", and the fall of Sir Robert Walpole', in Schweizer and Black, *Politics and the press*, pp. 49–76

Harris, Bob, *A patriot press: National politics and the London press in the 1740s* (Oxford, 1993)

Harris, Bob, *Politics and the nation: Britain in the mid-eighteenth century* (Oxford, 2002)

Harris, Bob, *Politics and the rise of the press: Britain and France, 1620–1800* (London, 1996)

Harris, Tim, *Revolution: The great crisis of the British monarchy, 1685–1720* (London, 2006)

Hart, Jeffrey, *Viscount Bolingbroke, Tory humanist* (London, 1965)

Hartley, Janet, *Charles Whitworth: Diplomat in the age of Peter the Great* (London, 2002)

Hattendorf, John B., 'Alliance, encirclement and attrition: British grand strategy in the War of the Spanish Succession, 1702–1713', in Paul Kennedy (ed.), *Grand strategies in war and peace* (New Haven and London, 1991), pp. 11–30

Hattendorf, John B., *England in the War of the Spanish Succession: A study of the English view of and conduct of grand strategy, 1702–1712* (New York and London, 1987)

Hatton, Ragnhild, M., *The Anglo-Hanoverian connection, 1714–1760* (London, 1982)

Hatton, Ragnhild, M., *Diplomatic relations between Great Britain and the Dutch Republic, 1714–1721* (London, 1950)

Hatton, Ragnhild M., 'England and Hanover, 1714–1837', in Birke and Kluxen, *England und Hannover*, pp. 17–31

Hatton, Ragnhild, M., 'Frederick the Great and the House of Hanover', in Oswald Hauser (ed.), *Friedrich der Große in seiner Zeit* (Cologne and Vienna, 1987), pp. 151–64

Hatton, Ragnhild, M., *George I: Elector and king* (London, 1978)

Hatton, Ragnhild, M., 'In search of an elusive ruler: Source material for a biography of George I as Elector and King', in Friedrich Engel-Janosi, Grete Klingenstein and Heinrich Lutz (eds.), *Fürst, Bürger, Mensch: Untersuchungen zur politischen und soziokulturellen Wandlungsprozessen im vorrevolutionären Europa* (Vienna, 1975), pp. 11–41

Hatton, Ragnhild, M., 'New light on George I of Great Britain', in S. Baxter (ed.), *England's rise to greatness, 1660–1763* (Berkeley, 1983), pp. 213–55

Hatton, Ragnhild, M., and M. S. Anderson (eds.), *Studies in diplomatic history: Essays in memory of David Bayne Horn* (London, 1970)

Hatton, Ragnhild M., and J. S. Bromley (eds.), *William III and Louis XIV: Essays 1680–1720 by and for M. A. Thomson* (Liverpool, 1968)

Haydon, Colin, *Anti-Catholicism in eighteenth-century England, c.1714–1780: A political and social study* (Manchester, 1993)

Hayter, Tony, 'England, Hannover, Preußen: Gesellschaftliche und wirtschaftliche Grundlagen der britischen Beteiligung an Operationen auf dem Kontinent während des Siebenjährigen Krieges', in Kroener, *Europa im Zeitalter Friedrichs des Großen*, pp. 171–92

Hellmuth, Eckhart (ed.), *The transformation of political culture: England and Germany in the late eighteenth century* (Oxford, 1990)

Hellmuth, Eckhart, 'Why does corruption matter? Reforms and reform movements in Britain and Germany in the second half of the eighteenth century', in T. C. W. Blanning and Peter Wende, *Reform in Great Britain and Germany, 1750–1850* (Oxford, 1999), pp. 6–23

Henderson, Alfred J., *London and the national government, 1721–1742: A study of city politics and the Walpole administration* (Durham, NC, 1945)

Hendrickson, David C., *Peace pact: The rise and fall of America's federal monarchy* (Lawrence, 2003)

Hertz, G. B., 'England and the Ostend Company', *English Historical Review* 22 (1907), pp. 255–79

Higonnet, Patrice Louis-René, 'The origins of the Seven Years War', *Journal of Modern History* 40 (1968), pp. 57–90

Hildner, Ernest G., 'The role of the South Sea Company in the diplomacy leading to the War of Jenkins' Ear, 1729–1739', *Hispanic American Historical Review* 18 (1938), pp. 322–41

Hill, Brian W., 'Executive monarchy and the challenge of parties, 1689–1832: Two concepts of government and two historiographical interpretations', *Historical Journal* 13 (1970), pp. 379–401

Hill, Brian W., *The growth of parliamentary parties, 1689–1742* (London, 1976)

Hill, Brian W., 'Oxford, Bolingbroke, and the Peace of Utrecht', *Historical Journal* 16 (1973), pp. 241–63

Hoffman, R., and P. J. Albert (eds.), *Diplomacy and Revolution: The Franco-American Alliance of 1778* (Charlottesville, 1981)

Hoffmann, R., and P. J. Albert (eds.), *Peace and peacemakers: The Treaty of 1873* (Charlottesville, 1986)

Holmes, Geoffrey, *British politics in the age of Queen Anne* (London, 1967)

Holmes, Geoffrey, *The making of a great power: Late Stuart and early Georgian Britain, 1660–1722* (London, 1993)

Hont, Istvan, *Jealousy of trade: International competition and the nation-state in historical perspective* (Cambridge, Mass., 2005)

Hoover, Benjamin B., *Samuel Johnson's parliamentary reporting: Debates in the senate of Lilliput* (Berkeley, 1953)

Hoppit, Julian, 'The contents and contours of British economic literature, 1660–1760', *Historical Journal* 49 (2006), pp. 79–110

Hoppit, Julian, *A land of liberty? England, 1689–1727* (Oxford, 2000)

Hoppit, Julian (ed.), *Parliaments, nations and identities in Britain and Ireland, 1660–1860* (Manchester, 2003)

Horn, D. B., *The British diplomatic service 1689–1789* (Oxford, 1961)

Horn, D. B., *British public opinion and the first partition of Poland* (Edinburgh, 1945)

Horn, D. B., 'The cabinet controversy on subsidy treaties in time of peace 1749–50', *English Historical Review* 45 (1930), pp. 463–6

Horn, D. B., 'The diplomatic experience of secretaries of state, 1660–1852', *History* 41 (1956), pp. 88–99

Horn, D. B., 'The Duke of Newcastle and the origins of the diplomatic revolution', in J. H Elliott and H. G. Koenigsberger (eds.), *The diversity of history: Essays in honour of Sir Herbert Butterfield* (London, 1970), pp. 245–68

Horn, D. B., *Great Britain and Europe in the eighteenth century* (Oxford, 1967)

Horn, D. B., 'The origins of the proposed election of a King of the Romans, 1748–1750', *English Historical Review* 42 (1927), pp. 361–70

Horn, D. B., *Scottish diplomatists, 1689–1789* (London, 1944)

Horn, D. B., *Sir Charles Hanbury Williams and European diplomacy, 1747–58* (London, 1930)

Horti, *Der Herrenhausener Garten und Seine Statuen. Bedeutung. Symbolik* (Bad Münster, 1985)

Horwitz, Henry, *Parliament, policy and politics in the reign of William III* (Manchester, 1977)

Horwitz, Henry, *Revolution politicks: The career of Daniel Finch, second Earl of Nottingham, 1647–1730* (Cambridge, 1968)

Hotblack, Kate, *Chatham's colonial policy* (London, 1917)

Hotblack, Kate, 'The Peace of Paris, 1763', *Transactions of the Royal Historical Society* 3:2 (1908), pp. 235–69

Howard, Michael, *The Continental commitment: The dilemma of British defence policy in the era of the two world wars* (Harmondsworth, 1972)

Howat, G. M. D., *Stuart and Cromwellian foreign policy* (London, 1974)

Hughes, Michael, *Law and politics in eighteenth century Germany: The imperial Aulic Council in the reign of Charles VI* (Woodbridge, 1988)

Hutson, James H., 'Intellectual foundations of early American diplomacy', *Diplomatic History* 1:1 (1977), pp. 1–19

Hutson, James H., *John Adams and the diplomacy of the American Revolution* (Lexington, 1980)

Hutson, James H., 'The Partition Treaty and the Declaration of American Independence', *Journal of American History* 58 (1972), pp. 877–96

Hyam, Ronald, 'Imperial interests and the Peace of Paris, 1763', in R. Hyam and G. Martin (eds.), *Reappraisals in British imperial history* (London, 1975), pp. 21–43

Hyam, Ronald, 'The primacy of geopolitics: The dynamics of British imperial policy, 1763–1963', in Robert D. King and Robin W. Kilson (eds.), *The statecraft of British imperialism: Essays in honour of William Roger Louis* (London, 1999), pp. 27–52

Ingrao, Charles, *In quest and crisis: Emperor Joseph I and the Habsburg monarchy* (West Lafayette, 1979)

Ingrao, Charles, 'The Pragmatic Sanction and the Theresian succession: A re-evaluation', *Études Danubiennes* 9 (1998), pp. 71–87

Israel, Jonathan (ed.), *The Anglo-Dutch moment: Essays on the Glorious Revolution and its world impact* (Cambridge, 1991)

Israel, Jonathan, 'Garrisons and empire: Spain's strongholds in north-west Germany, 1589–1659', in *Conflicts of empires: Spain, the Low Countries and the struggle for world supremacy, 1585–1713* (London and Rio Grande, 1995), pp. 23–44

Jacob, Ilse, *Beziehungen Englands zu Russland und zur Türkei in den Jahren 1718–1727* (Basel, 1945)

Jacobs, Wilbur R., *Diplomacy and Indian gifts: Anglo-French rivalry along the Ohio and Northwest Frontiers, 1748–1783* (Stanford, 1950)

James, Lawrence, *The rise and fall of the British Empire* (London, 1994)

Jankovic, V., 'The politics of sky battles in early Hanoverian Britain', *Journal of British Studies* 41:4 (October, 2002), pp. 429–59

Jarnut-Derbolav, Elke, *Die Österreichische Gesandtschaft in London 1701–1711* (Bonn, 1972)

Jennings, Francis, 'The Seven Years War in Pennsylvania', in Shade, *Revisioning the British Empire*, pp. 55–74

Jones, Clyve (ed.), *Britain in the first age of party, 1689–1750: Essays presented to Geoffrey Holmes* (London, 1987)

Jones, Clyve, 'Further evidence of the splits in the anti-Walpole opposition in the House of Lords: A list of the division of 9 April 1741 on the subsidy for Austria', *Parliamentary History* 24:3 (2005), pp. 368–75

Jones, J. R., *Britain and Europe in the seventeenth century* (London, 1966)

Jones, J. R., *Britain and the world, 1649–1815* (London, 1980)

Jones, J. R., 'Limitations of British sea power in the French wars, 1689–1815', in Black and Woodfine, *British Navy*, pp. 33–50

Jones, J. R., *Marlborough* (Cambridge, 1993)

Jordan, G., and Nicholas Roger, 'Admirals as heroes: Patriotism and liberty in Hanoverian England, *Journal of British Studies* 38 (1988), pp. 201–44

Kagan, Robert, *Dangerous nation* (New York, 2006)

Kamen, Henry, *The War of Succession in Spain, 1700–1715* (London, 1969)

Kampmann, Christoph, 'Die englische Krone als "Arbiter of Christendom"? Die "balance of Europe" in der politischen Diskussion der späten Stuart-Ära, 1660–1714', *Historisches Jahrbuch* 118 (1998), pp. 312–66

Kaplan, Herbert H., *Russian overseas commerce with Great Britain during the reign of Catherine II* (Philadelphia, 1995)

Kaplan, L. S. (ed.), *The American Revolution and 'a candid world'* (Kent, Ohio, 1977)

Kaplan, L. S., *Colonies into nations: American diplomacy, 1763–1801* (New York, 1972)

Kearney, Hugh, *The British Isles: A history of four nations* (Cambridge, 1989)

Keen, M. H., *England and the later Middle Ages: A political history* (London and New York, 1973)

Kennedy, Paul M., *The rise and fall of British naval mastery* (London, 1976)

Kennedy, Paul M., *The rise and fall of the Great Powers: Economic change and military conflict from 1500 to 2000* (London, 1988)

Kennedy, Paul M., 'The influence and the limitations of sea power', *International History Review*, 10:1 (1988), pp. 2–17

Kennett, Lee, *The French forces in America, 1780–1783* (Westport, 1977)

Kenyon, J. P., *Stuart England* (London, 1978)

Kidd, Colin, *British identities before nationalism: Ethnicity and nationhood in the Atlantic world, 1600–1800* (Cambridge, 1999)

Kidd, Colin, 'North Britishness and the nature of eighteenth-century British patriotism', *Historical Journal* 39 (1996), pp. 361–82

Kissinger, Henry, *Diplomacy* (New York, 1994)

Klaus, Gustava-Alicia, *Friedrich Karl von Hardenberg (1696–1763)* (Hildesheim, 1990)

Knights, Mark, *Representation and misrepresentation in later Stuart Britain* (Oxford, 2005)

Koebner, Richard, *Empire* (Cambridge, 1966)

Koehn, Nancy, *The power of commerce: Economy and governance in the first British Empire* (Ithaca and London, 1994)

König, Theo, *Hannover und das Reich, 1740–1745* (Düsseldorf, 1938)

Konigs, Philip, *The Hanoverian kings and their homeland: A study of the personal union, 1714–1837* (Lewes, 1993)

Konopczynski, W., 'England and the first partition of Poland', *Journal of Central European Affairs* 8 (1948–9), pp. 1–23

Korr, Charles P., *Cromwell and the new model foreign policy: England's policy towards France, 1649–1658* (Berkeley, Los Angeles and London, 1975)

Kramnick, Isaac, *Bolingbroke and his circle: The politics of nostalgia in the age of Walpole* (Cambridge, Mass., 1968)

Kroener, Bernhard R., *Europa im Zeitalter Friedrichs des Großen. Wirtschaft. Gesellschaft. Kriege im Auftrag des Militärgeschichtlichen Forschungsamtes* (Munich, 1989)

LaFeber, Walter, 'Foreign policies of a new nation: Franklin, Madison, and the "Dream of a new land to fulfil with people in self-control", 1750–1804', in William A. Williams (ed.), *From colony to empire: Essays in the history of American foreign relations* (New York, 1972), pp. 10–37

Lampe, Joachim, *Aristokratie, Hofadel und Staatspatriziat in Kurhannover: Die Lebenskreise der höheren Beamten an den kurhannoverschen Zentral- und Hofbehörden, 1714–1760* (2 vols., Göttingen, 1963)

Langford, Paul, *Englishness identified: Manners and character, 1650–1850* (Oxford, 2000)

Langford, Paul, *The excise crisis: Society and politics in the age of Walpole* (Oxford, 1975)

Langford, Paul, *The first Rockingham administration, 1765–1766* (Oxford, 1973)

Langford, Paul, *Modern British foreign policy: The eighteenth century, 1688–1815* (1976)

Langford, Paul, *A polite and commercial people: England, 1727–1783* (Oxford, 1989)

Langford, Paul, 'William Pitt and public opinion', *English Historical Review* 88 (1973), pp. 54–79

Laprade, W. T., *Public opinion and politics in eighteenth-century England to the fall of Walpole* (New York, 1936)

Lawson, Philip, *The East India Company: A history* (London, 1993)

Lawson, Philip, *George Grenville: A political life* (Oxford, 1984)

Lawson, Philip, *A taste for empire and glory: Studies in British overseas expansion, 1600–1800,* (Aldershot, 1997)

Le Fevre, P., and R. Harding, *Precursors of Nelson: British admirals of the eighteenth century* (London, 2001)

Leach, Douglas Edward, 'Brothers in arms? Anglo-American friction at Louisburg, 1745–1746', *Massachusetts Historical Society Proceedings* 89 (1977), pp. 36–54

Lees, James, 'Retrenchment, reform and the practice of military-fiscalism in the early East India Company state' (unpublished paper presented to graduate workshop on the political economy of empire, 4.11.2006)

Legg, L. G., 'Wickham, Newcastle and the counter orders to Admiral Haddock, March 1739', *English Historical Review* 46 (1931), pp. 272–4

Leighton, Cadoc, *Catholicism in a Protestant kingdom: A study of the ancient Irish regime* (Dublin, 1994)

Levenson, Claire, 'Impact of gifts and trade: The Georgia colonists and the Yamacraw Indians in the colonial American southeast' (unpublished paper presented to graduate workshop on the political economy of empire, 4.11.2006)

Lillywhite, Bryant, *London coffee houses: A reference book of coffee houses of the seventeenth, eighteenth and nineteenth centuries* (London, 1963)

Lincoln, Margarette, *Representing the Royal Navy: British sea power, 1750–1815* (London, 2002)

Loades, David, *England's maritime empire: Sea power, commerce and policy, 1490–1690* (London, 2000)

Lodge, Sir Richard, 'English neutrality in the War of the Polish Succession', *Transactions of the Royal Historical Society* 4:14 (1931), pp. 141–74

Lodge, Sir Richard, 'An episode in Anglo-Russian relations during the War of the Austrian succession', *Transactions of the Royal Historical Society* 4:9 (1926), pp. 63–83

Lodge, Sir Richard, *Great Britain and Prussia in the eighteenth century* (Oxford, 1923)

Lodge, Sir Richard, 'The Hanau controversy in 1744 and the fall of Carteret', *English Historical Review* 38 (1923), pp. 509–31

Lodge, Sir Richard, 'Lord Hyndford's embassy to Russia, 1744–9', *English Historical Review* 46 (1931), pp. 48–76, 389–422

Lodge, Sir Richard, 'The mission of Henry Legge to Berlin, 1748', *Transactions of the Royal Historical Society* 4:14 (1931), pp. 1–38

Lodge, Sir Richard, 'The Polwarth papers', *Transactions of the Royal Historical Society* 4:15 (1932), pp. 243–69

Lodge, Sir Richard, 'Russia, Prussia and Great Britain, 1742–4'; *English Historical Review* 45 (1930), pp. 579–611

Lodge, Sir Richard, 'Sir Benjamin Keene: A study in Anglo-Spanish relations in the earlier part of the eighteenth century', *Transactions of the Royal Historical Society* 4:15 (1932), pp. 1–43

Lodge, Sir Richard, 'The so-called "Treaty of Hanau" of 1743', *English Historical Review* 38 (1923), pp. 384–407

Lodge, Sir Richard, *Studies in eighteenth-century diplomacy, 1740–1748* (London, 1930)

Lodge, Sir Richard, 'The Treaty of Seville, 1729', *Transactions of the Royal Historical Society* 4:16 (1933), pp. 1–45

Lodge, Sir Richard, 'The Treaty of Worms', *English Historical Review* 44 (1929), pp. 220–25

Lukowski, J. T., *The partitions of Poland, 1772, 1793, 1795* (London, 1999)

MacCaffrey, Wallace, *Elizabeth I: War and politics, 1588–1603* (Princeton, 1992)

McConnell, Michael N., *Army and Empire: British soldiers on the American frontier, 1758–1775* (Lincoln, Nebraska and London, 2004)

McDermott, James, *England and the Spanish Armada: The necessary quarrel* (New Haven and London, 2005)

MacInnes, Allan, 'Union failed, union accomplished: The Irish Union of 1703 and the Scottish Union of 1707', in Daire Keogh and Kevin Whelan (eds.), *Acts of union: The causes, contexts and consequences of the Act of Union* (Dublin, 2001), pp. 67–94

McJimsey, Robert , 'A country divided? English politics and the Nine Years War, 1689–1697', *Albion* 23:4 (1991), pp. 61–74

McJimsey, Robert, 'Shaping the revolution in foreign policy: Parliament and the press, 1680–1730', *Parliamentary History* 25:1 (2006), pp. 17–31

McKay, Derek, 'Bolingbroke, Oxford and the defence of the Utrecht Settlement in southern Europe', *English Historical Review* (1971), pp. 264–84

McKay, Derek, 'The struggle for control of George I's northern policy', *Journal of Modern History*, 45 (1973), pp. 367–86

McKay, Derek, and Hamish M. Scott, *The rise of the Great Powers, 1648–1815* (London, 1983)

McKelvey, James Lee, *George III and Lord Bute: The Leicester House years* (Durham, NC, 1973)

McKendrick, N., J. Brewer and J. H. Plumb, *The birth of a consumer society: The commercialisation of eighteenth-century England* (London, 1982; reprinted 1983)

Mackesy, P., *The coward of Minden: The affair of Lord George Sackville* (London, 1979)

Mackesy, P., *The war for America, 1775–1783* (London, 1964)

Mackinder, Halford, 'The geographical pivot of history', *Geographical Journal* 23 (1904), pp. 421–4

McLachlan, Jean O., 'The Seven Years Peace and the West Indian policy of Carvajal and Wall', *English Historical Review* 53 (1938), pp. 457–77

McLachlan, Jean O., *Trade and peace with old Spain, 1667–1750: A study of the influence of commerce on Anglo-Spanish diplomacy in the first half of the eighteenth century* (Cambridge, 1940)

McLachlan, Jean O., 'The uneasy neutrality: A study of Anglo-Spanish disputes over Spanish ships prized, 1756–59', *Historical Journal* 6 (1938–40), pp. 55–77

McLay, K. A. J., 'Combined operations and the European theatre during the Nine Years War, 1688–97', *Historical Research* 78:202 (2005), pp. 506–539

McLay, K. A. J., 'Wellsprings of a "world war": An early English attempt to conquer Canada during King William's War, 1688–97', *Journal of Imperial and Commonwealth History* 34 (2006), pp. 144–75

McLynn, Frank, *1759: The year Britain became master of the world* (London, 2004)

McLynn, Frank, *France and the Jacobite rising of 1745* (Edinburgh, 1981)

Madariaga, Isabel de, *Britain, Prussia, and the Armed Neutrality of 1780: Sir James Harris's mission to St Petersburg during the American Revolution* (London, 1962)

Madariaga, Isabel de, 'The use of British secret funds at St Petersburg, 1777–1782', *Slavonic and East European Review* 32 (1953–4), pp. 464–74

Mahan, A. T., *The influence of sea power upon history, 1660–1783* (Boston, 1890; reprinted London, 1965)

Malone, Joseph J., *Pine trees and politics: The naval stores and forest policy in colonial New England, 1691–1775* (London, 1964)

Mandler, Peter, *The English national character: The history of an idea from Edmund Burke to Tony Blair* (New Haven, 2006)

Mantoux, P., 'French reports of British parliamentary debates in the eighteenth century', *American Historical Review* 12:2 (1906–7), pp. 244–69

Marks, Frederick W., *Independence on trial: Foreign affairs and the making of the Constitution* (Baton Rouge, 1973)

Marshall, Dorothy, *Eighteenth-century England* (London, 1962)

Marshall, Peter J., 'Britain and the world in the eighteenth century. I: Reshaping the empire', *Transactions of the Royal Historical Society* 6:8 (1998), pp. 1–18

Marshall, Peter J., *The making and unmaking of empires: Britain, India and America c.1750–1783* (Oxford, 2005)

Marshall, Peter J., 'A nation defined by empire, 1755–1776', in Alexander Grant and Keith J. Stringer (eds.), *Uniting the kingdom? The making of British history* (London, 1995), pp. 208–21

Marshall, Peter J., 'Who cared about the thirteen colonies? Some evidence from philanthropy', in Robert D. King and Robin Kilson (eds.), *The statecraft of British imperialism: Essays in honour of William Roger Louis* (London and Portland, 1998), pp. 53–67

Marx, Karl, *Secret diplomatic history of the eighteenth century; and The story of the life of Lord Palmerston*, ed. Lester Hutchinson (London, 1969)

Massini, R., *Sir Luke Schaub, 1690–1758* (Basel, 1953)

Mearsheimer, John J., *The tragedy of great power politics* (New York and London, 2001)

Mediger, Walther, 'Great Britain, Hanover and the rise of Prussia', in Hatton and Anderson, *Studies in diplomatic history*, pp. 199–213

Mediger, Walther, *Mecklenburg, Russland und England-Hannover, 1706–21* (2 vols., Hildesheim, 1967)

Mediger, Walther, *Moskaus Weg nach Europa: Der Aufstieg Rußlands zum europäischen Machtstaat im Zeitalter Friedrichs des Großen* (Braunschweig, 1952)

Melkonian, Raffi, 'Franco-Spanish relations in the era of the American Revolution' (unpublished MPhil dissertation, University of Cambridge, 2002)

Meng, J. J., *The Comte de Vergennes: European phases of his American diplomacy, 1774–1780* (Washington, 1932)

Metcalf, M. F., *Russia, England and Swedish party politics, 1761–1766* (Stockholm and Totowa, 1977)

Metzdorf, Jens, *Politik–Propaganda–Patronage: Francis Hare und die englische Publizistik im spanischen Erbfolgekrieg* (Mainz, 2000)

Michael, Wolfgang, 'Ein schwieriger Fall aus dem Jahre 1719', *Historische Zeitschrift* 88 (1902), pp. 56–68

Michael, Wolfgang, *Englands Stellung zur Ersten Teilung Polens* (Hamburg and Leipzig, 1890)

Michael, Wolfgang, *Englische Geschichte im achtzehnten Jahrhundert* (5 vols., Leipzig, 1920–37) (Volumes I and II have been translated into English under the titles: *England under George I: The beginnings of the Hanoverian dynasty* (London, 1936); *England under George I: The Quadruple Alliance* (London, 1939))

Middleton, C. R., *The administration of British foreign policy, 1781–1846* (Durham, NC, 1977)

Middleton, Richard, *The bells of victory: The Pitt–Newcastle ministry and the conduct of the Seven Years War, 1757–1762* (Cambridge, 1985)

Middleton, Richard, *Colonial America: A history, 1565–1776* (Oxford, 2002)

Miller, D. A., *Sir Joseph Yorke and Anglo-Dutch Relations, 1774–1780* (The Hague, 1970)

Mimler, Manfred, *Der Einfluß Kolonialer Interessen in Nordamerika auf die Strategie und Diplomatie Großbritanniens während des Österreichischen Erbfolgekrieges 1744–1748: Ein Beitrag zur Identitätsbestimmung des britischen Empire um die Mitte des 18. Jahrhunderts* (Hildesheim, Zürich and New York, 1983)

Mitchell, Leslie, *Charles James Fox* (Oxford, 1992)

Morgan, William T., 'English fear of "encirclement" in the seventeenth century', *Canadian Historical Review* (1929), pp. 4–22

Morgan, William T., 'Some sidelights upon the general election of 1715', in Charles Seymour (ed.), *Essays in modern English history in honour of Wilbur Cortez Abbott* (Cambridge, Mass., 1941), pp. 133–76

Morgan, William T., 'Queen Anne's Canadian expedition of 1711', *Bulletin of the Departments of History and Political and Economic Science in Queen's University Ontario* 56 (1928), pp. 1–32

Morley, Vincent, *Irish opinion and the American Revolution, 1760–1783* (Cambridge, 2002)

Morris, R. B., *The peacemakers: The Great Powers and American Independence* (New York, 1965; 2nd edn, Boston, 1984)

Morris, R. B., 'The Treaty of Paris of 1783', in *Fundamental Testaments of the American Revolution* (Washington, DC, 1973), pp. 83–107

Mullan, John, 'Restless Daniel', *London Review of Books* (20 July 2006), p.26

Müllenbrock, Heinz-Joachim, *The culture of contention: A rhetorical analysis of the public controversy about the ending of the War of the Spanish Succession, 1710–1713* (Munich, 1997)

Murphy, O. T., *Charles Gravier, Comte de Vergennes: French diplomacy in the age of revolution, 1719–1787* (Albany, 1982)

Murray, John J., 'An eighteenth-century white book', *Huntington Library Quarterly* 13 (1950), pp. 371–82

Murray, John J., 'Baltic commerce and power politics in the early eighteenth century', *Huntington Library Quarterly* 6 (May 1943), pp. 293–312

Murray, John J., *George I, the Baltic and the Whig split of 1717: A study in diplomacy and propaganda* (Chicago and London, 1969)

Murray, John J., 'The Görtz–Gyllenborg arrests: A problem in diplomatic immunity', *Journal of Modern History* 28 (1956), pp. 325–37

Namier, Lewis B., *England in the age of the American Revolution* (2nd edn, London, 1963)

Namier, Lewis B., *The structure of politics at the accession of George III* (London 1928)

Namier, Lewis B., and John Brooke, *The House of Commons, 1754–1790* (3 vols., London, 1964)

Naumann, M., *Österreich, England und das Reich, 1719–1732* (Berlin, 1933)

Nelson, G. H., 'Contraband trade under the *Asiento*, 1730–1739' *American Historical Review* 51 (1945–6), pp. 55–67

Newman, Aubrey, 'Leicester House Politics, 1748–1751', *English Historical Review* 76 (1961), pp. 577–89

Newman, Aubrey, *The Stanhopes of Chevening: A family biography* (London, 1969)

Newman, Aubrey, 'Two countries, one monarch: The union England–Hanover as the ruler's personal problem', in Rexheuser, *Die Personsalunionen*, pp. 353–69

Newman, Aubrey, *The world turned inside out: New views on George II. An inaugural lecture delivered in the University of Leicester, 10 October 1987* (Leicester, 1988)

Newman, Gerald, *The rise of English nationalism: A cultural history 1740–1830* (London, 1987)

Nishikawa, S., 'The SPCK in defence of Protestant minorities in early eighteenth-century Europe', *Journal of Ecclesiastical History* 56:4 (October 2005), pp. 730–48

Nordmann, C., 'Choiseul and the last Jacobite attempt of 1759', in Cruickshanks, *Ideology and conspiracy*, pp. 201–17

Nulle, Stebelton H., *Thomas Pelham-Holles, Duke of Newcastle: His early political career, 1693–1724* (Philadelphia, 1931)

Oakley, S. P., 'The interception of posts in Celle, 1697–1700', in Hatton and Bromley, *William III and Louis XIV*, pp. 95–116

O'Brien, Conor Cruise, *The great melody: A thematic biography of Edmund Burke* (Chicago, 1992)

O'Brien, Patrick K., 'Inseparable connections: Trade, economy, fiscal state and the expansion of empire, 1688–1815', in *Oxford History of the British Empire*, II, pp. 53–77

O'Brien, Patrick K., 'The security of the realm and the growth of the economy, 1688–1914', in Peter Clark and Clive Trebilcock (eds.), *Understanding decline: Perceptions and realities of British economic performance* (Cambridge, 1997), pp. 49–72

Ó Ciardha, Éamonn, *Ireland and the Jacobite cause, 1685–1766: A fatal attachment* (Dublin, 2004)

Ogborn, Miles, and Charles W. J. Withers (eds.), *Georgian geographies: Essays on space, place and landscape in the eighteenth century* (Manchester, 2005)

O'Gorman, Frank, 'The myth of Lord Bute's secret influence', in Schweizer, *Lord Bute*, pp. 57–82

O'Gorman, Frank, 'The recent historiography of the Hanoverian regime' *Historical Journal* 29:4 (1986), pp. 1005–20

Ohlmeyer, Jane, 'Ireland independent: Confederate foreign policy and international relations during the mid-seventeenth century', in Jane Ohlmeyer (ed.), *Ireland from independence to occupation, 1641–1662* (Cambridge, 1995), pp. 89–111

Oliphant, John, *Peace and war on the Anglo-Cherokee frontier, 1756–1763* (London, 2000)

Olson, Alison G., 'The British government and colonial union 1754', *William and Mary Quarterly* 3:17 (1960), pp. 22–34

O'Reilly, William, 'The Naturalization Act of 1709 and the settlement of Germans in Britain, Ireland and the colonies', in Randolph Vigne and Charles Littleton (eds.), *From strangers to citizens* (Brighton, 2001), pp. 492–502

Ormrod, David, *Rise of commercial empires: England and the Netherlands in the age of mercantilism, 1650–1770,* (Cambridge, 2003)

Orr, Clarissa Campbell, 'Dynastic perspectives', in Simms and Riotte, *Hanoverian dimension*, pp. 213–51

Orr, Clarissa Campbell, *Queenship in Britain, 1660–1837: Royal patronage, court culture and dynastic politics* (Manchester, 2002)

Orr, Clarissa Campbell, *Queenship in Europe, 1660–1815: The role of the consort* (Cambridge, 2004)

O'Shaughnessy, Andrew J., *An empire divided: The American Revolution and the British Caribbean* (Philadelphia, 2000)

O'Shaughnessy, Andrew J., 'The formation of a commercial lobby: The West Indian interest, British colonial policy and the American Revolution', *Historical Journal* 40 (1997), pp. 71–95

Otruba G., 'Die Bedeutung englischen Subsidien und Antizipationen für die Financen Österreichs 1701 bis 1748', *Vierteljahrschrift für Sozial- und Wirtschaftsgeschichte* (1964)

Owen, John B., 'George II reconsidered', in Anne Whiteman, J. S. Bromley and P. G. M. Dickson (eds.), *Statesmen, scholars and merchants: Essays in eighteenth-century history presented to Dame Lucy Sutherland* (Oxford, 1973), pp. 113–34

Owen, John B., *The rise of the Pelhams* (London, 1957)

The Oxford History of the British Empire, vol. II, *The eighteenth century*, ed. P. J. Marshall (Oxford, 1998)

Oz-Salzberger, Fania, 'Exploring the Germanick body – eighteenth-century images of Germany', *Tel Aviver Jahrbuch für deutsche Geschichte* 26 (1997), pp. 7–23

Padfield, Peter, *Maritime supremacy and the opening of the western mind: Naval campaigns that shaped the modern world, 1588–1782* (London, 1999)

Palmer, William, *The problem of Ireland in Tudor foreign policy, 1485–1603* (Woodbridge, 1995)

Panayi, Panikos (ed.), *Germans in Britain since 1500* (London and Rio Grande, 1996)

Pares, Richard, 'American versus Continental warfare, 1739–1763', *English Historical Review* 51 (1936), pp. 429–65

Pares, Richard, *Colonial blockade and neutral rights, 1739–1763* (Oxford, 1938)

Pares, Richard, *King George III and the politicians* (Oxford, 1953; reprinted 1967)

Pares, Richard, *War and trade in the West Indies, 1739–1763* (London and Edinburgh, 1963)

Parker, Geoffrey, *The army of Flanders and the Spanish Road, 1567–1659: The logistics of Spanish victory and defeat in the Low Countries* (2nd edn, Cambridge, 2004)

Parkinson, Giles, 'War and peace in the early stock market' (unpublished paper delivered to graduate workshop on 'The Political Economy of Empire', 4 November 2006, King's College, Cambridge)

Parry, Glyn, 'John Dee and the Elizabethan British Empire in its European context', *Historical Journal* 49 (2006), pp. 643–76

Patterson, A. T., *The other armada: The Franco-Spanish Attempt to Invade Britain in 1779* (Manchester, 1960)

Patze, H., 'Zwischen London und Hannover, Bemerkungen zum Hofleben in Hannover während des 18. Jahrhunderts', in P. Berglar (ed.), *Staat und Gesellschaft im Zeitalter Goethes: Festschrift für H. Tümmler* (Cologne and Vienna, 1977), pp. 95–129

Pearce, Edward, *The great man: Sir Robert Walpole – scoundrel, genius and Britain's first prime minister* (London, 2007)

Penson, Lilian M., *The colonial agents of the British West Indies: A study in colonial administration, mainly in the eighteenth century* (London, 1924)

Penson, Lilian M., *Colonial background of British foreign policy* (London, 1930)

Penson, Lilian M., 'The London West India interest in the eighteenth century', *English Historical Review* 36 (1921), pp. 373–92

Peters, Marie, *The Elder Pitt* (London, 1998)

Peters, Marie, 'The *Monitor* on the constitution, 1755–1765: New light on the ideological origins of English radicalism', *English Historical Review* 86 (1971), pp. 706–27

Peters, Marie, 'The myth of William Pitt, Earl of Chatham, great imperialist: I. Pitt and imperial expansion, 1738–1763', *Journal of Imperial and Commonwealth History* 21 (2003), pp. 31–74

Peters, Marie, ' "Names and cant": Party labels in English political propaganda, *c.*1755–1765', *Parliamentary History* 3 (1984), pp. 103–27

Peters, Marie, *Pitt and popularity: The patriot minister and London opinion during the Seven Years War* (Oxford, 1980)

Peters, Marie, 'Pitt as a foil to Bute: The public debate over ministerial responsibility and the powers of the Crown', in Schweizer, *Lord Bute*, pp. 99–116

Phillips, Kevin, *The cousins' wars: Religion, politics, and the triumph of Anglo-America* (New York, 1999)

Pincus, Steven C. A., 'The English debate over universal monarchy', in Robertson, *A union for empire*

Pincus, Steven C. A., *Protestantism and patriotism: Ideologies and the making of English foreign policy, 1650–1668* (Cambridge, 1996)

Pincus, Steven C. A., 'To protect English liberties: The English nationalist revolution of 1688–1681', in Tony Claydon and I. McBride (eds.), *Protestantism and national identity* (Cambridge, 1998), pp. 75–104

Pittock, Murray G. H., *Inventing and resisting Britain: Cultural identities in Britain and Ireland, 1685–1789* (London, 1997)

Plumb, J. H., *England in the eighteenth century* (Aylesbury, 1963)

Plumb, J. H., *The growth of parliamentary stability in England, 1675–1725* (London, 1962)

Plumb, J. H., *Sir Robert Walpole*, vol. 1, *The making of a statesman* and vol. 2, *The King's minister* (London, 1958, 1960)

Pocock, J. G. A., *Politics, language and time: Essays on political thought and history* (New York, 1971), pp. 104–47

Porter, Bernard, *The absent-minded imperialists: Empire, society, and culture in Britain* (Oxford, 2004)

Prados de la Escosura, Leandro (ed.), *Exceptionalism and industrialism: Britain and its European rivals, 1688–1815* (Madrid, 2003)

Press, Volker, 'Kurhannover im System des alten Reiches, 1692–1803', in Birke and Kluxen, *England und Hannover*, pp. 53–79

Price, Jacob M., 'The imperial economy, 1700–1776', in *Oxford History of the British Empire*, II, pp. 78–104

Price, Jacob M., 'Who cared about the colonies? The impact of the thirteen colonies on British society c.1714–1775', in Bernard Bailyn and Philip D. Morgan (eds.), *Strangers within the realm: Cultural margins of the first British Empire* (Chapel Hill, 1991), pp. 395–436

Pritchard, James S., *Louis XV's navy, 1748–1762: A Study of Organization and Administration* (Kingston and Montreal, 1987)

Pyta, Wolfram, 'Von der Entente Cordiale zur Aufkündigung der Bundespartnerschaft. Die preußisch-britischen Allianzbeziehungen im Siebenjährigen Krieg, 1758–1762', *Forschungen zur brandenburgisch-preußischen Geschichte* 10 (2000), pp. 1–48

Quazza, Guido, 'Italy's role in the European problems of the first half of the eighteenth century', in Hatton and Anderson, *Studies in diplomatic history*, pp. 138–54

Rakove, Jack N., 'The decision for independence: A reconstruction', *Perspectives in American History* 10 (1976), pp. 217–75

Ranke, Leopold von, *Die Großen Mächte: Politisches Gespräch*, ed. T. Schieder (Göttingen, 1963)

Ransome, M., 'The reliability of contemporary reporting of the debates of the House of Commons, 1727–1741', *Bulletin of the Institute of Historical Research* 19 (1942–3), pp. 67–79

Rashed, Zenab Esmat, *The Peace of Paris, 1763* (Liverpool, 1951)

Reddaway, W. F., 'Great Britain and Poland, 1762–72', *Cambridge Historical Journal* 4 (1932–4), pp. 233–62

Reddaway, W. F., 'Macartney in Russia, 1765–67', *Cambridge Historical Journal* 3 (1929–31), pp. 260–94

Reese, Trevor, 'Georgia in Anglo-Spanish diplomacy, 1736–1739', *William and Mary Quarterly* 3:15 (1958), pp. 168–90

Reuner, Thomas, *Wirtschaft und Offentlichkeit Handelsinteressen und außenpolitischen Konzeptionen im Wirtschaftsdiskurs in England, 1739–1756* (Aachen, 1998)

Rexheuser, Rex (ed.), *Die Personalunionen von Sachsen-Polen, 1697–1763 und Hannover-England, 1714–1837: Ein Vergleich* (Wiesbaden, 2005)

Rice, G. W., 'Deceit and distraction: Britain, France and the Corsican crisis of 1768', *International History Review* 28 (2006), pp. 237–472

Rice, G. W., 'Great Britain, the Manila Ransom and the first Falkland Islands dispute with Spain, 1766', *International History Review* 2 (1980), pp. 386–409

Rice, G. W., 'Lord Rochford at Turin, 1749–1755: A pivotal phase in Anglo-Italian relations in the eighteenth century', in Black, *Knights errant*, pp. 92–112

Richmond, H. W., 'English strategy in the War of the Austrian Succession', *Journal of the Royal United Service Institution* 64 (1919), pp. 246–54

Richmond, H. W., *The Navy as an instrument of policy, 1558–1727* (Cambridge, 1953)

Richmond, H. W., *The Navy in the war of 1739–48* (3 vols., Cambridge, 1920)

Richmond, H. W., *Statesmen and sea power* (Oxford, 1947)

Richter-Uhlig, Uta, *Hof und Politik unter den Bedingungen der Personalunion zwischen Hannover und England: Die Aufenthalte Georgs II in Hannover zwischen 1729 und 1741* (Hanover, 1992)

Richter-Uhlig, Uta, 'Kommunikationsprobleme zwischen London und Hannover: Die Reisen Georgs II. von London nach Hannover, 1727–1740', *Blätter für deutsche Landesgeschichte* 121 (1985), pp. 207–27

Riotte, Torsten, 'George III and Hanover', in Simms and Riotte, *Hanoverian dimension*, pp. 58–85

Ritcheson, C. R., 'The Earl of Shelburne and peace with America, 1782–1783: Vision and reality', *International History Review* 5 (1983), pp. 322–45

Roberts, Michael, *British diplomacy and Swedish politics 1758–1773* (London, 1980)

Roberts, Michael, *Essays in Swedish History* (London, 1967), pp. 286–347

Roberts, Michael, 'Great Britain, Denmark and Russia, 1763–70', in Hatton and Anderson, *Studies in diplomatic history*, pp. 236–67

Roberts, Michael, *Splendid isolation, 1763–1780: The Stenton Lecture, 1969* (Reading, 1970)

Robertson, John (ed.), *A union for empire: Political thought and the union of 1707* (Cambridge, 1995)

Robertson, John, 'Union, state and empire: The Britain of 1707 in its European setting', in Stone, *Imperial state at war*, pp. 224–58

Robertson, John, 'Universal monarchy and the liberties of Europe: David Hume's critique of an English Whig doctrine', in Nicholas Phillipson and Quentin Skinner (eds.), *Political discourse in early modern Britain* (Cambridge, 1993), pp. 349–73

Rodger, N. A. M., *The command of the ocean: A naval history of Britain, 1649–1815* (London, 2004)

Rodger, N. A. M., 'The Continental commitment in the eighteenth century', in L. Friedman, Paul Hayes and Robert O'Neill (eds.), *War strategy and international politics* (Oxford, 1992), pp. 39–55

Rodger, N. A. M., *The insatiable earl: A life of John Montagu, fourth Earl of Sandwich, 1718–1792* (New York and London, 1993)

Rodger, N. A. M., 'Queen Elizabeth and the myth of sea-power in English history', *Transactions of the Royal Historical Society* 14 (2004), pp. 153–74

Rodger, N. A. M., 'Sea power and empire, 1688–1793', in *Oxford History of the British Empire*, II, pp. 169–83

Rodger, N. A. M., *The wooden world: An anatomy of the Georgian navy* (London, 1986)

Rogers, Nicholas, 'Brave Wolfe: The making of a hero', in Kathleen Wilson, *New imperial history*, pp. 239–59

Rogers, Nicholas, *Crowds, culture and politics in Georgian Britain* (Oxford, 1998)

Rogers, Nicholas, 'Popular protest in early Hanoverian London', *Past and Present* 79 (1978), pp. 70–100

Rohloff, Heide N. (ed.), *Großbritannien und Hannover: Die Zeit der Personalunion, 1714–1837* (Frankfurt, 1989)

Röhrbein, Waldemar, and Alheidis von Rohr, *Hannover im Glanz und Schatten des britischen Weltreiches: Die Auswirkungen der Personalunion auf Hannover von 1714 bis 1837* (Hanover, 1977)

Roider, Karl A., *Austria's eastern question, 1700–1790* (Princeton, 1982)

Roider, Karl A., 'The perils of eighteenth-century peacemaking: Austria and the Treaty of Belgrade, 1739', *Central European History* 5 (1972), pp. 195–207

Römer, Christof, 'Niedersachsen im 18. Jahrhundert (1714–1803)', in Christine van der Heuvel and Manfred von Boetticher (eds.), *Geschichte Niedersachsens: Dritter Band. Teil 1. Politik, Wirtschaft und Gesellschaft von den Reformation bis zum Beginn des 19. Jahrhunderts* (Hanover, 1998), pp. 221–346

Rosebury, Lord, *Chatham: His early life and connections* (London, 1910)

Rostow, Eugene V., *Breakfast for Bonaparte: US national security interests from the Heights of Abraham to the Nuclear Age* (Washington, 1993)

Rowen, H. H., *The princes of Orange: The stadholders in the Dutch Republic* (Cambridge, 1988)

Rowse, A. L., *The Elizabethans and America* (London, 1959)

Rowse, A. L., *The spirit of English history* (London, 1943)

Rudé, George, *The crowd in history: A study of popular disturbances in France and England, 1730–1848* (New York, London and Sydney, 1964)

Rudé, George, *Wilkes and liberty: A social study of 1763 to 1774* (Oxford, 1965)

Ruville, Albert von, 'Friedrich der Große und Lord Bute: Erwiderung', *Deutsche Zeitschrift für Geschichtswissenschaft* 12 (1894–5), pp. 160–71

Ruville, Albert von, *William Pitt, Earl of Chatham* (3 vols., London, 1907)

Sainty, J. C., *Officials of the secretaries of state, 1660–1782* (London, 1973)

Samuel, Raphael, *Theatres of memory*, vol. II, *Island stories: Unravelling Britain*, ed. Alison Light (London and New York, 1998)

Satow, Ernest M., *The Silesian loan and Frederick the Great* (Oxford, 1915)

Savelle, Max, 'The American balance of power and European diplomacy, 1713–1778', in Richard B. Morris (ed.), *The era of the American Revolution* (New York, 1939), pp. 140–69

Savelle, Max, 'The appearance of an American attitude toward external affairs, 1750–1775', *American Historical Review* 52 (1947), pp. 655–66

Savelle, Max, *Empires to nations: Expansion in America, 1713–1824* (Minneapolis, 1974)

Savelle, Max, 'The international approach to early Anglo-American history, 1492–1763', in Ray A. Billington (ed.), *The reinterpretation of early American history: Essays in honor of John Edwin Pomfret* (San Marino, 1966), pp. 201–31

Savelle, Max, *The origins of American diplomacy: The international history of Anglo-America, 1492–1763* (New York and London, 1967)

Scarisbrick, J. J., *Henry VIII* (London, 1968)

Schama, Simon, *Patriots and liberators: Revolution in the Netherlands, 1780–1813* (London, 1977)

Schiff, Stacy, *Benjamin Franklin and the birth of America: Franklin's French adventure, 1776–85* (London, 2006)

Schilling, Lothar, *Kaunitz und das Renversement des alliances: Studien zur außenpolitischen Konzeption Wenzel Antons von Kaunitz* (Berlin, 1994)

Schlenke, Manfred, *England und das friderizianische Preußen, 1740–1763: Ein Beitrag zum Verhältnis von Politik und öffentlicher Meinung im England des 18. Jahrhunderts* (Freiburg and Munich, 1963)

Schlote, Werner, *Entwicklung und Strukturwandlung des englischen Außenhandels von 1700 bis zur Gegenwart* (Jena, 1938)

Schmidt, H. D., 'The establishment of "Europe" as a political expression', *Historical Journal* (1966), pp. 172–8

Schmidt, H. D., 'The Hessian mercenaries: The career of a political cliché', *History* 43 (1958), pp. 207–12

Schmidt, H. D., 'The idea and slogan of "perfidious Albion" ', *Journal of the History of Ideas* 14 (1953), pp. 604–16

Schmitt, Carl, *Der Nomos der Erde im Völkerrecht des Jus Publicum Europaeum* (Berlin, 1988)

Schmitt, Carl, *Land und Meer: Eine weltgeschichtliche Betrachtung* (Cologne, 1981)

Schnath, G., *Geschichte Hannovers im Zeitalter der neunten Kur und der englischen Sukzession, 1674–1714* (4 vols., Hildesheim, 1938, 1976, 1978, 1982)

Schui, Florian, 'Prussia's "trans-oceanic moment": The creation of the Prussian Asiatic trade company in 1750', *Historical Journal* 49 (2006), pp. 143–60

Schumann, M. J., 'Mercantilism, communications and the early prehistory of the Seven Years War, 1749–54', *Nuova Rivista Storica* 89 (2005), pp. 83–103

Schumpeter, Elizabeth B., *English overseas trade statistics, 1697–1808* (Oxford, 1960)

Schweizer, Karl W., 'The Bedford motion and House of Lords debate, February 5, 1762', *Parliamentary History* (November, 1986), pp. 107–23

Schweizer, Karl W., *England, Prussia and the Seven Years War: Studies in alliance policies and diplomacy* (Lewiston, NY, 1989)

Schweizer, Karl W., *Frederick the Great, William Pitt and Lord Bute: Anglo-Prussian relations, 1756–1763* (New York, 1991)

Schweizer, Karl W., 'Lord Bute and the press: The origins of the press war of 1762 reconsidered', in Schweizer, *Lord Bute*, pp. 83–98

Schweizer, Karl W., 'Lord Bute and William Pitt's resignation in 1761', *Canadian Journal of History* 8 :2 (1973), pp. 111–22

Schweizer, Karl W., (ed.), *Lord Bute: Essays in re-interpretation* (Leicester, 1988)

Schweizer, Karl W., 'Newspapers, politics and public opinion in the later Hanoverian era', *Parliamentary History* 25 (2006), pp. 32–48

Schweizer, Karl W., 'The non-renewal of the Anglo-Prussian Subsidy Treaty, 1761–62: A historical revision' *Canadian Journal of History / Annales Canadiennes d'Histoire*, 13 (1978), pp. 383–98

Schweizer, Karl W., 'Pamphleteering and foreign policy in the age of the Elder Pitt,' in Taylor, Connors and Jones, *Hanoverian Britain and empire*, pp. 94–108

Schweizer, Karl W., 'A parliamentary speech by the Elder Pitt', *Historical Research* 4 (1991), pp. 92–105

Schweizer, Karl W., 'The Seven Years War: A system perspective', in J. Black (ed.), *The origins of war in early modern Europe* (Edinburgh, 1987), pp. 242–60

Schweizer, Karl W., *Statesmen, diplomats and the press: Essays on eighteenth-century Britain* (Lewiston, Queenston and Lampeter, 2002)

Schweizer, Karl W., and Jeremy Black, 'The challenge to autocracy: The British press and Europe in the 1730s', in Schweizer and Black, *Politics and the press*, pp. 33–47

Schweizer, Karl W., and Jeremy Black (eds.), *Politics and the press in Hanoverian Britain* (Lewiston, NY, 1989)

Schweizer, Karl W., and C. S. Leonard, 'Britain, Prussia, Russia and the Galitzin episode: A reassessment', *Historical Journal* 26 (1983), pp. 531–56

Scott, Hamish M., 'Britain as a European Great Power in the age of the American Revolution', in Dickinson, *Britain and the American Revolution*, pp. 180–204

Scott, Hamish M., 'Britain's emergence as a European power, 1688–1815' (unpublished paper)

Scott, Hamish M., *British foreign policy in the age of the American Revolution* (Oxford, 1990)

Scott, Hamish M., 'The decline of France and the transformation of the European states-system, 1756–1792', in Paul W. Schroeder and Peter Krüger, *The transformation of*

European politics, 1763–1848: Episode or model in modern history (Münster, 2002), pp. 105–28

Scott, Hamish M., 'Diplomatic culture in Old Regime Europe', in Scott and Simms, *Cultures of power*, pp. 58–85

Scott, Hamish M., 'Great Britain, Poland and the Russian Alliance, 1763–1767', *Historical Journal* 19 (1976), pp. 53–74

Scott, Hamish M., 'Hanover in mid-eighteenth-century Franco-British geopolitics', in Simms and Riotte, *Hanoverian dimension*, pp. 275–300

Scott, Hamish M., 'The importance of Bourbon naval reconstruction to the strategy of Choiseul after the Seven Years War', *International History Review* 1 (1979), pp. 17–35

Scott, Hamish M., 'Le Duc de Choiseul, la cour de France et la politique étrangère française, 1761–1770', *Revue d'histoire diplomatique* 118:3 (2004), pp. 281–300

Scott, Hamish M., 'Religion and realpolitik: The Duc de Choiseul, the Bourbon family compact and the attack on the Society of Jesus, 1758–1775', *International History Review* 25:1 (2003)

Scott, Hamish M., 'Review article: British foreign policy in the age of the American Revolution', *International History Review* 6 (1984), pp. 113–25

Scott, Hamish M., 'Sir Joseph Yorke and the waning of the Anglo-Dutch alliance, 1747–1788' (unpublished paper)

Scott, Hamish M., 'Sir Joseph Yorke, Dutch politics and the origins of the fourth Anglo-Dutch war', *Historical Journal* 31 (1988), pp. 571–89

Scott, Hamish M., ' "The true principles of the revolution": The Duke of Newcastle and the idea of the old system', in Black, *Knights errant*, pp. 55–91

Scott, Hamish M., John Elliott and Olwen Hufton (eds.), *The emergence of the eastern powers, 1756–1775* (Cambridge, 2001)

Scott, Hamish M., and Derek McKay, *The rise of the great powers, 1648–1815* (London, 1983)

Scott, Hamish M., and Brendan Simms (eds.), *Cultures of power in Europe during the long eighteenth century* (Cambridge, 2007)

Scott, Jonathan, *England's troubles: Seventeenth-century English political instability in European context* (Cambridge, 2000)

Sedgwick, Romney, *The House of Commons, 1715–1754* (2 vols., London, 1970)

Seeley, J. R., *The expansion of England: Two courses of lectures* (London, 1895; first published 1883)

Seeley, J. R., *The growth of British policy* (Cambridge, 1922; first published 1895)

Sellin, Paul R., *So doth, so is religion: John Donne and diplomatic contexts in the Reformed Netherlands, 1619–1620* (Columbia, Missouri, 1988)

Semmel, Bernard, *The rise of free trade imperialism: Classical political economy, the empire of free trade and imperialism, 1750–1850* (Cambridge, 1970)

Shade, William G. (ed.), *Revisioning the British Empire in the eighteenth century* (London, 1998)

Sheehan, Michael, 'Balance of power intervention: Britain's decisions for and against war, 1733–1756', *Diplomacy and Statecraft* 7 (1996), pp. 271–89

Sheehan, Michael, 'The development of British theory and practice of the balance of power before 1714', *History* 73 (1988), pp. 24–37

Sheehan, Michael, 'The sincerity of the British commitment to the maintenance of the balance of power, 1714–1763', *Diplomacy and Statecraft* 15 (2004), pp. 489–506

Sheridan, Richard B., 'The British credit crisis of 1772 and the American colonies', *Journal of Economic History* 20 (1960), pp. 161–86

Simms, Brendan, 'Hanover in British policy, 1714–1783: Interests and aims of the protagonists', in Rexheuser, *Die Personsalunionen*, pp. 311–34

Simms, Brendan, ' "Ministers of Europe": British strategic culture, 1714–1760', in Scott and Simms, *Cultures of power*, pp. 110–32

Simms, Brendan, 'Pitt and Hanover', in Simms and Riotte, *Hanoverian dimension*, pp. 28–57

Simms, Brendan, *The struggle for mastery in Germany, 1779–1850* (Basingstoke, 1998)

Simms, Brendan, and Torsten Riotte (eds.), *The Hanoverian dimension in British history, 1714–1837* (Cambridge, 2007)

Simms, J. G., 'The Irish on the Continent, 1691–1800', in T. W. Moody and W. E. Vaughan (eds.), *A new history of Ireland*, vol. IV, *Eighteenth-century Ireland, 1691–1800* (Oxford, 1986), pp. 629–56

Simms, J. G., *Jacobite Ireland, 1685–91* (London and Toronto, 1969)

Singh, R. J., *French diplomacy in the Caribbean and the American Revolution* (Hicksville, NY, 1977)

Skinner, Quentin, 'The principles and practice of opposition: The case of Bolingbroke versus Walpole', in N. McKendrick (ed.), *Historical perspectives: Studies in English thought and society in honour of J. H. Plumb* (London, 1974), pp. 93–128

Sloan, G. R., *The geopolitics of Anglo-Irish relations in the twentieth century* (London and Washington, 1997)

Smith, Hannah, *Georgian monarchy: Politics and culture, 1714–1760* (Cambridge, 2006)

Smith, Hannah, 'The idea of a Protestant monarchy in Britain, 1714–1760', *Past & Present* 185 (November 2004), pp. 91–118

Smith, L. B., *Spain and Britain: The Jacobite issue* (London, 1987)

Smith, L. B., 'Spain and the Jacobites, 1715–1716', in Cruickshanks, *Ideology and conspiracy*, pp. 159–78

Snyder, Jack L., *The Soviet strategic culture: Implications for limited nuclear operations* (Santa Monica, 1977)

Sofka, James, 'The eighteenth-century international system: Parity or primacy', *Review of International Studies* 27 (2001), pp. 147–63

Sosin, Jack M., 'Louisburg and the Peace of Aix-la-Chapelle, 1748', *William and Mary Quarterly* 14 (1957), pp. 516–35

Sosin, Jack M., *Whitehall and the wilderness: The Middle West in British colonial policy, 1760–1775* (Lincoln, Nebraska, 1961)

Speck, W. A., *The birth of Britain: A new nation, 1700–1710* (Oxford, 1994)

Speck, W. A., *The butcher* (Oxford, 1981)

Speck, W. A., *Tory and Whig: The struggle in the constituencies, 1701–1715* (London, 1970)

Spector, Robert D., *English literary periodicals and the climate of opinion during the Seven Years' War* (The Hague, 1966)

Spencer, Charles, *Blenheim: Battle for Europe. How two men stopped the French conquest of Europe* (London, 2004)

Spencer, F., 'The Anglo-Prussian breach of 1762: An historical revision', *History* 41 (1956), pp. 100–112

Starkey, David, 'Little Englanders have history on their side', *Sunday Times* (17 October 2004)

Statt, Daniel, *Foreigners and Englishmen: The controversy about immigration and population, 1660–1760* (Newark, Delaware, 1995)

Steele, I. K., *The politics of colonial policy: The Board of Trade and colonial administration, 1696–1720* (Oxford, 1968)

Stockley, Andrew, *Britain and France at the birth of America: The European powers and the peace negotiations of 1782–1783* (Exeter, 2001)

Stone, Lawrence (ed.), *An imperial state at war: Britain from 1689–1815* (London, 1994)

Storrs, Christopher, 'Ormea as foreign minister: The Savoyard state between England and Spain', in Andrea Merlotti (ed.), *Nobilta e stato in Piemonte: I ferrero d'ormea* (Turin, 2003), pp. 231–48

Storrs, Christopher, 'Savoyard diplomacy in the eighteenth century (1604–1798)', in Daniela Frigo (ed.), *Politics and diplomacy in early modern Italy* (Cambridge, 2000), pp. 210–53

Stourzh, G. S., *Benjamin Franklin and American foreign policy* (Chicago, 1954; 2nd edn, 1969)

Strong, R., 'A vision of an Anglican imperialism: The annual sermons of the Society for the

Propagation of the Gospel in Foreign Parts, 1701–1714', *Journal of Religious History* 30:2 (June 2006), pp. 175–98

Stuart, Reginald C., *United States expansionism and British North America, 1776–1871* (Chapel Hill and London, 1988)

Stuchtey, Benedikt, 'Neue historische Literatur: Das britische Empire in der neuesten Forschung', *Historische Zeitschrift* 274 (2002), pp. 87–118

Sutherland, L. S., 'The City of London in eighteenth-century politics', in Richard Pares and A. J. P. Taylor (eds.), *Essays presented to Sir Lewis Namier* (London, 1956), pp. 49–74

Sutherland, L. S., 'The East India Company and the Peace of Paris', *English Historical Review* 61 (1947), pp. 179–90

Sutherland, L. S., *The East India Company in eighteenth-century politics* (London, 1952)

Syrett, David, 'The failure of the British effort in America, 1777', in Black and Woodfine, *British Navy*

Syrett, David, *The Royal Navy in European waters during the American Revolutionary War* (1998)

Syrett, David, *Shipping and the American War* (London, 1970)

Szechi, Daniel, *1715: The great Jacobite Rebellion* (New Haven, 2006)

Szechi, Daniel, *The Jacobites: Britain and Europe, 1688–1788* (1994)

Taylor, Stephen, Richard Connors and Clyve Jones (eds.), *Hanoverian Britain and empire: Essays in memory of Philip Lawson* (Woodbridge, 1998)

Temperley, H. M. V., 'The causes of the War of Jenkins' Ear (1739)', *Transactions of the Royal Historical Society* 3:3 (1909), pp. 197–236

Thomas, Peter D. G., *British politics and the Stamp Act crisis: The first phase of the American Revolution, 1763–1767* (Oxford, 1975)

Thomas, Peter D. G., 'George III and the American Revolution', *History* 70 (1985), pp. 16–31

Thomas, Peter D. G., *George III: King and politicians, 1760–1770* (Manchester, 2002)

Thomas, Peter D. G., ' "The great commoner": The elder William Pitt as parliamentarian, *Parliamentary History* 22:2 (2003), pp. 145–63

Thomas, Peter D. G., *The House of Commons in the eighteenth century* (Oxford 1971)

Thomas, Peter D. G., *Lord North* (London, 1976)

Thomas, Peter D. G., 'Party politics in eighteenth-century Britain: Some myths and a touch of reality', *British Journal for Eighteenth Century Studies* 10 (1987), p. 204

Thomas, Peter D. G., *The Townshend duties crisis: The second phase of the American Revolution, 1767–73* (Oxford, 1987)

Thompson, Andrew C., *Britain, Hanover and the Protestant interest, 1688–1756* (Woodbridge, 2006)

Thompson, Andrew C., 'The confessional dimension', in Simms and Riotte, *Hanoverian dimension*, pp. 161–82

Thompson, Andrew C., 'Popery, politics and private judgment in early Hanoverian Britain', *Historical Journal* 45:2 (2002), pp. 333–56

Thompson, E. P., *Whigs and hunters: The origin of the Black Act* (London, 1975)

Thomson, Mark A., 'Louis XIV and the origins of the War of the Spanish Succession', in Hatton and Bromley, *William III and Louis XIV*, pp. 140–61

Thomson, Mark A., 'Parliament and foreign policy', *History* (1953), pp. 238–9

Thomson, Mark A., *The secretaries of state, 1681–1782* (Oxford, 1932)

Tombs, Robert and Isabelle, *The sweet enemy: The French and the British from the Sun King to the present* (London, 2006)

Tracy, N., 'British assessments of French and Spanish naval reconstruction, 1763–68', *Mariner's Mirror* 61 (1975), pp. 73–85

Tracy, N., 'The Falkland Islands crisis of 1770: Use of naval force', *English Historical Review* 90 (1975), pp. 40–75

Tracy, N., 'The gunboat diplomacy of the government of George Grenville, 1764–65:

The Honduras, Turks' Island and Gambian incidents', *Historical Journal* 17 (1974), pp. 711–31

Tracy, N., *Manila ransomed: The British assault on Manila in the Seven Years War* (Exeter, 1995)

Tracy, N., *Navies, deterrence and American Independence: Britain and sea power in the 1760s and 1770s* (Vancouver, 1988)

Trevelyan, G. M., *England under Queen Anne* (3 vols., London, 1930–34)

Trim, David J. B., 'Calvinist internationalism and the English officer corps, 1562–1642', *History Compass* 4 (2006), pp. 1024–48

Trim, David J. B., 'England and the Continental commitment: A Tudor and Stuart perspective' (unpublished paper given at 'The Continental commitment' conference, De Montfort University, July 1999)

Trim, David J. B., 'Oliver Cromwell and the intolerant inheritance of America's religious extreme', *Liberty* 101:6 (November–December 2006)

Trim, David J. B., 'Seeking a Protestant alliance and liberty of conscience on the Continent, 1558–85', in Doran and Richardson, *Tudor England*, pp. 139–77

Troost, Wout, *William III, the stadholder-king: A political biography* (Aldershot, 2005)

Tucker, R. W., and D. C. Hendrickson, *The fall of the first British Empire: Origins of the War of American Independence* (Baltimore, 1983)

Turner, E. R., 'Parliament and Foreign Affairs, 1603–1760', *English Historical Review* 34 (1919), pp. 172–97

Unger, W. S., 'Trade through the Sound in the seventeenth and eighteenth centuries', *Economic History Review* 2:12 (1959–60), pp. 206–21

Valentine, Alan, *Lord George Germain* (Oxford, 1962)

Varey, Simon, 'Hanover, Stuart and "the patriot king"', *British Journal for Eighteenth-Century Studies* 6 (1983), pp. 163–72

Varsori, Antonio, 'Is Britain part of Europe? The myth of British "difference"', in Cyril Buffet and Beatrice Heuser (eds.), *Haunted by history: Myths in international relations* (Providence and Oxford, 1998), pp. 135–56

Vaucher, Paul, *Robert Walpole et la politique de Fleury (1731–1742)* (Paris, 1924)

Ver Steeg, Clarence L., and Richard Hofstadter (eds.), *Great issues in American history: From settlement to revolution, 1584–1776* (New York, 1958, 1969)

Vincitorio, Gaetano L., 'Edmund Burke and the first partition of Poland', in Gaetano L. Vincitorio (ed.), *Crisis in the Great Republic: Essays presented to Ross J. S. Hoffman* (New York, 1969), pp. 14–46

Wakeman, Henry Offley, *The ascendancy of France, 1598–1715* (4th edn, London, 1947)

Walcott, Robert, *English politics in the early eighteenth century* (Oxford, 1956)

Walker, J. C., 'The Duke of Newcastle and the British envoys at the Congress of Cambrai', *English Historical Review* 50 (1935), pp. 113–19

Walters, John, *The royal griffin: Frederick, Prince of Wales, 1707–51* (London, 1972)

Wandycz, Piotr S., 'The American Revolution and the partitions of Poland', in Jaroslav Pelenski (ed.), *The American and European revolutions, 1776–1848: Sociopolitical and ideological aspects* (Iowa City, 1980), pp. 95–110

Ward, A. W., *The Electress Sophia and the Hanoverian succession* (2nd edn, London, 1909)

Ward, A. W., *Great Britain and Hanover: Some aspects of the personal union* (Oxford, 1899)

Ward, Matthew C., *Breaking the backcountry: The Seven Years War in Virginia and Pennsylvania, 1754–1765* (Pittsburgh, 2003)

Ward, Matthew C., ' "The European method of warring is not practised here": The failure of British military policy in the Ohio Valley, 1755–1759', *War in History* 4:3 (1997), pp. 247–63

Watkin, David, *The architect king: George III and the culture of the Enlightenment* (London, 2004)

Weintraub, Stanley, *Iron tears: Rebellion in America* (New York, 2005)

Wellenreuther, Hermann, 'Die Bedeutung des Siebenjährigen Krieges für die englisch-hannoveranischen Beziehungen', in Birke and Kluxen, *England und Hannover*, pp. 145–75

Wellenreuther, Hermann, 'Von der Interessenharmonie zur Dissoziation. Kurhannover und England in der Zeit der Personalunion', *Niedersächsische Jahrbücher für Landesgeschichte* 67 (1995), pp. 23–42

Wende, Peter (ed.), *Die englischen Königinnen und Könige der Neuzeit: Von Heinrich VIII bis Elizabeth II* (Munich, 1998)

Werner, Hans, 'The Hector of Germanie, or the palsgrave, Prime Elector and Anglo-German relations of early Stuart England: The view from the popular stage', in R. Malcolm Smuts (ed.), *The Stuart court and Europe: Essays in politics and political culture* (Cambridge, 1996), pp. 113–32

Wernham, R. B., *After the Armada: Elizabethan England and the struggle for western Europe, 1588–1595* (Oxford, 1984)

Wernham, R. B., *Before the Armada: The growth of English foreign policy, 1485–1588* (London, 1986)

Wernham, R. B., *The making of Elizabethan foreign policy, 1558–1603* (Berkeley and London, 1980)

Western, J. R., *The English militia in the eighteenth century: The story of a political issue, 1660–1802* (London, 1965)

Whiteley, Peter, *Lord North: The prime minister who lost America* (London and Rio Grande, 1996)

Wilkinson, Spencer, *The defence of Piedmont, 1742–1748* (Oxford, 1927)

Williams, Basil, *Carteret and Newcastle: A contrast in contemporaries* (Cambridge, 1943)

Williams, Basil, 'Carteret and the so-called treaty of Hanau', *English Historical Review* 49 (1934), pp. 684–7

Williams, Basil, 'The foreign policy of England under Walpole', *English Historical Review* 15 (1900), pp. 251–76, 479–94, 665–98; 16 (1901), pp. 67–83, 308–27, 439–51

Williams, Basil, *The life of William Pitt, Earl of Chatham* (2 vols., London, 1913)

Williams, Basil, *Stanhope: A study in eighteenth-century war and diplomacy* (Oxford, 1932)

Williams, Basil, *The Whig supremacy, 1714–1760* (Oxford, 1939; 2nd edn, Oxford, 1962)

Williams, Glyn, ' "The inexhaustible fountain of gold": English projects and ventures in the South Seas, 1670–1750', in J. E. Flint and G. Williams (eds.), *Perspectives of empire* (1973), pp. 27–53

Williams, Glyn, *The prize of all the oceans: The triumph and tragedy of Anson's voyage round the world* (London, 1999)

Williams, Judith Blow, *British commercial policy and trade expansion, 1750–1850* (Oxford, 1972)

Williams, William A., 'The age of mercantilism: An interpretation of American political economy, 1763–1782', *William and Mary Quarterly* 3:15 (1958), pp. 419–37

Willis, S. B. A., 'Fleet performance and capability in the eighteenth-century Royal Navy', *War in History* 11:4 (Nov. 2004), pp. 373–92

Wills, Rebecca, *The Jacobites and Russia, 1715–1750* (East Linton, 2002)

Wilson, Arthur McCandless, *French foreign policy during the administration of Cardinal Fleury, 1726–1743* (Cambridge, Mass., 1936)

Wilson, Kathleen, 'Empire, trade and popular politics in mid-Hanoverian Britain: The case of Admiral Vernon', *Past and Present* 121 (1988), pp. 74–109

Wilson, Kathleen, 'The good, the bad and the impotent: Imperialism and the politics of identity in Georgian England', in Ann Bermingham and John Brewer (eds.), *The consumption of culture, 1600–1800: Image, object, text* (1995), pp. 237–62

Wilson, Kathleen, *The island race: Englishness, empire and gender in the eighteenth century* (London, 2002)

Wilson, Kathleen (ed.), *New imperial history: Culture, identity, and modernity in Britain and the Empire, 1660–1840* (Cambridge, 2004)

Wilson, Kathleen, *The sense of the people: Politics, culture and imperialism in England, 1715–1785* (Cambridge, 1995)

Winkler, Karl Tilman, *Wörterkrieg: Politische Debattenkultur in England, 1689–1750* (Stuttgart, 1998)

Wood, A. C., 'The English embassy at Constantinople, 1660–1762', *English Historical Review* 40 (1925), pp. 533–61

Woodfine, Philip, 'The Anglo-Spanish War of 1739', in J. Black (ed.), *The origins of war in early modern Europe* (Edinburgh, 1987), pp. 185–209

Woodfine, Philip, *Britannia's glories: The Walpole ministry and the 1739 war with Spain* (London, 1998)

Woodfine, Philip, 'Ideas of naval power and the conflict with Spain, 1737–1742', in Black and Woodfine, *British Navy*, pp. 71–90

Young, Hugo, *This blessed plot: Britain and Europe from Churchill to Blair* (London, 1998)

Notes

Introduction

1. Seeley, *Expansion of England*, p. 9. On the dynastic link to Hanover and its implications, see Simms and Riotte (eds.), *Hanoverian dimension*. For the fiscal-military state, see John Brewer, *Sinews of power*; Dickson, *Financial revolution in England* and the discussion, with more emphasis on global than European aspects in Stone, *Imperial state at war*. The centrality of inter-state competition in eighteenth-century British political thought is demonstrated in Hont, *Jealousy of trade*, pp. 6, 11, 15–17, 53, 79, 81, 87, *et passim*. For the public sphere, see Bob Harris, *Politics and the nation*, pp. 7–9, 15–16, and *Politics and the rise of the press*, p. 37; Cardwell, *Arts and arms*, pp. 2, 13, 22, *et passim*. The figures in Schumpeter, *English overseas trade statistics*, esp. pp. 17–18, make the predominance of European trade very clear. For a useful recent statement about the importance of the often unglamorous European trade over more exotic overseas markets, see Evans, Jackson and Ryden, 'Baltic iron' (esp. pp. 642–4).
2. For the centrality of foreign policy in the early eighteenth-century parliament, see Gibbs, 'Parliament and foreign policy', esp. pp. 18–20, 26. On the other hand, Black, *Parliament and foreign policy in the eighteenth century*, p. 234, says that Parliament was 'dominated by local issues'. On the resulting 'strategic culture', see Brendan Simms, 'Ministers of Europe'. The centrality of Europe is stated in Black, 'Exceptionalism', p. 11, but questioned in Carter, 'Britain as a European power'. Despite its title, Penson, *Colonial background of British foreign policy*, pp. 17–18, also stresses the centrality of Europe. For a systematic working out of the implications of Britain's European commitments in British domestic history, see Bob Harris, *Politics and the nation*, p. 105, and Conway, *War, state and society*, pp. 4–5, *et passim*. See also Conway, 'Continental connections', pp. 353–5. Linda Colley has also expressed scepticism about the current vogue for 'imperial' and 'Atlantic' history, in her *Captives*, pp. 8–9, 160–61, 167, from the perspective of Britain's Mediterranean commitments. Historians of British foreign policy, of course, have always been conscious of the importance of Europe, especially Hamish Scott and Jeremy Black, although the latter is increasingly tending towards an 'imperial' and 'blue water' reading of eighteenth-century British history: Black, *Foreign policy of Walpole* and *System of ambition?*; Hamish Scott, *British foreign policy*.
3. Henrietta Marshall's book was republished in 2005 by the think-tank Civitas. Admittedly, the jacket cover of Bryant's book does also feature the celebrated charge of the Scots Greys at Waterloo, but the image of a Royal Navy warship looms much larger below.
4. Rodger, *Command of the ocean*, esp. pp. lxii–xv; Baugh, 'Maritime strength', esp. pp. 185–6; Baugh, 'Great Britain's "blue water" policy'; Baugh, 'British strategy'; Starkey, 'Little Englanders'; Armitage, 'Three concepts', p. 11; Kathleen Wilson, *Sense of the people* and *Island race*; Peter Marshall, 'Nation defined by empire.' See also Gould, *Persistence of empire*.
5. Jonathan Scott, *England's troubles*, p. 10. Colley, 'Size does matter'.

1 A Part of the Main: England in Europe, 1558–1697

1. Sackville's remarks are in Cobbett, *Parliamentary history*, I, col. 1305. For Donne's diplomatic activities on the Continent, see Sellin, *So doth*.

2. Medieval England's close involvement in Continental Europe is well known: see, for example, Clanchy, *England and its rulers*, esp. chapter 1, 'England's place in medieval Europe', pp. 13–35, and the section 'Henry's European strategy', pp. 230–34. See also Keen, *England and the later Middle Ages*, esp. pp. 380–408.

3. For Henry VIII's Continental ambitions, see Susan Doran, *England and Europe*, pp. 15, 23, 30–31, *et passim*. For Henry's candidature in the Holy Roman Empire, see Scarisbrick, *Henry VIII*, pp. 98–104. On the problems which 'Habsburgism' among the Irish magnates posed for England, see Downey, 'Irish–European integration'.

4. Wernham, *After the Armada*, pp. vi–vii, makes an effective critique of the navalist obsessions of nineteenth- and twentieth-century Tudor historiography. In the same vein: Wernham, *Making of Elizabethan foreign policy*, pp. 87–8. My view of the late sixteenth century has been much influenced by Trim, 'Seeking a Protestant alliance', esp. p. 142. For Scotland, see Jane Dawson, 'William Cecil'.

5. Trim, 'Seeking a Protestant alliance', pp. 150–53.

6. Cecil on 'counter-scarp' is quoted in Wernham, *Before the Armada*, p. 292. On 'counter-scarp', see Trim, 'England and the continental commitment', pp. 1–17, esp. pp. 7–8. I thank Dr Trim for discussing these issues with me and for supplying me with copies of his unpublished papers.

7. Wernham, *Before the Armada*, pp. 384–6.

8. The impact of the expansion of Europe on the state system is discussed in Elliott, *Old World and the New*, pp. 79–100 (Hakluyt quotation, pp. 90–91). On the importance of the New World to Spain's European position, see most recently Elliott, *Empires of the Atlantic*. On the perceived and actual role of New World wealth, see the ironically titled Bordo and Cortes-Conde (eds.), *Transferring wealth and power from the Old to the New World*, esp. pp. 10–12, 140–41, 155.

9. See Wernham, *Before the Armada*, p. 354. See also MacCaffrey, *Elizabeth I*, pp. 5–6; Adams, 'Spain or the Netherlands?', p. 81 (the term 'owned' is mine); Wernham, *Before the Armada*, p. 395. For the discussion in Parliament and the centrality of the Low Countries, see the speech by Sir Christopher Hatton of 22 February 1588, in Cobbett, *Parliamentary history*, I, cols. 847–50. On the Armada itself, see McDermott, *England and the Spanish Armada*, which stresses the importance of chance and the weather in England's deliverance.

10. On this, see Israel, 'Garrisons and empire', esp. the map on Spanish garrisons in North Germany, p. 25. See also Parker, *Army of Flanders*; 'Calvinist internationalism', esp. pp. 1032–6.

11. On the strategic context of the Anjou match, see Wernham, *Before the Armada*, pp. 358–9.

12. Palmer, *Problem of Ireland*, p. 79, *et passim*. See also the 'geopolitical moments' described in Sloan, *Geopolitics of Anglo-Irish relations*, pp. 75–88. For an example of the 'archipelagic' and 'three kingdoms' view, see Bradshaw and Morrill, *British problem*.

13. See Wernham, *Making of Elizabethan foreign policy*, p. 5.

14. My view of seventeenth-century English and 'British' politics has been heavily influenced by Jonathan Scott, *England's troubles*, *passim*. For seventeenth-century Irish history in its European context, see Ohlmeyer, 'Ireland independent'. See Adams, 'Spain or the Netherlands?', *passim* but esp. pp. 86–7 and 'Foreign policy', pp. 142–3.

15. See Werner, '*Hector of Germanie*', p. 113, *et passim*; and Adams, 'Spain or the Netherlands?', p. 81.

16. Quoted in Cogswell, *Blessed revolution*, p. 17.

17. See Cogswell, *Blessed revolution*, pp. 27, 44, 68 (St Albans quote), *et passim*, and Werner, '*Hector of Germanie*', pp. 113, 115, *et passim*. This is also the drift of Adams,

'Foreign policy', p. 160. Sir John Davies is quoted in Cobbett, *Parliamentary history*, I, col. 1186; Viscount St Albans in Cogswell, *Blessed revolution*, p. 68.

18. On this, see Cogswell, *Blessed revolution*, pp. 70–71, 177–8; and Adams, 'Foreign policy', pp. 164–5. On attacking Spain in the New World, see Cogswell, *Blessed revolution*, pp. 72–5; and Adams, 'Spain or the Netherlands?', p. 8. Rudyerd is quoted in Elliott, *Old World and the New*, pp. 90–91.

19. 'The Commons' declaration and impeachment against the Duke of Buckingham', 10 May 1626, in Gardiner, *Constitutional documents*, esp. article 8, p. 16.

20. 'Resolutions on religion drawn by a sub-committee of the House of Commons', 24 February 1629, in Gardiner, *Constitutional documents*, p. 78.

21. 'The King's declaration showing the causes of the late dissolution', 10 March 1628, in Gardiner, *Constitutional documents*, pp. 83–4.

22. See 'Specimen of the first writ of ship-money', 20 October 1634, in Gardiner, *Constitutional documents*, pp. 105–6. Cogswell, *Blessed revolution*, p. 97.

23. Adams, 'Spain or the Netherlands?', p. 84.

24. 'Extracts from the speech of Oliver St John in the Ship Money case', November 1637, in Gardiner, *Constitutional documents*, pp. 109–10.

25. See 'The Grand Remonstrance', 1 December 1641, in Gardiner, *Constitutional documents*, pp. 208–9; Adams, 'Spain or the Netherlands?', p. 101; Werner, '*Hector of Germanie*', p. 116; Cogswell, *Blessed revolution*, p. 76.

26. Ormrod, *Rise of commercial empires*, p. 31.

27. On this, see Korr, *Cromwell*, pp. 89–90, 183.

28. Trim, 'Oliver Cromwell', esp. p. 22.

29. See Pincus, *Protestantism and patriotism*, pp. 410–12, 416, 427.

30. Howat, *Stuart and Cromwellian foreign policy*, p. 102. Scott, *England's troubles*, p. 313.

31. On the Clarendon impeachment, see Pincus, *Protestantism and patriotism*, p. 427. Littleton is quoted Black, 'Revolution', p. 137.

32. Capel's remarks are in Cobbett, *Parliamentary history*, IV, col. 1280. See also Pincus, 'English debate', p. 53.

33. Hont, *Jealousy of trade*, p. 1. Howat, *Stuart and Cromwellian foreign policy*, p. 102. For England's experience with Tangier, see Colley, *Captives*, pp. 23–42. On the Stuart continuity in naval and commercial policy, see Loades, *England's maritime empire*, pp. 188–210. On economic rivalry with the Dutch, see Ormrod, *Rise of commercial empires*, pp. 31–59.

34. See Andrew C. Thompson, *Britain, Hanover*, pp. 43–4, and Gwynn, 'Huguenots'.

35. I have benefited here from conversations with Gabriel Glickman and from his abstract 'Policy, principle and partisanship: Foreign affairs in domestic debate, 1672–1697', for a forthcoming volume on the primacy of foreign policy in British history to be edited by Brendan Simms and William Mulligan (no publisher as yet). On this phenomenon, see most recently Knights, *Representation*.

36. On Stuart colonial geopolitics, see Morgan, 'English fear', esp. pp. 4, 9, 19.

37. See Baxter, *William III*, pp. 222–42, esp. pp. 222–3. The centrality of German resistance to Louis in the background to 1688 is also remarked on in Carswell, *Descent on England*, esp. chapter 6: 'William and the Germans', pp. 76–84.

38. On the centrality of England to the security of the United Provinces in William's thinking, see Troost, *William III*, pp. 173–94.

39. For an elegant account which tends to stress the 'British' and domestic context over the European, see Tim Harris, *Revolution*. On Ireland, see J. G. Simms, *Jacobite Ireland*.

40. See Israel, *Anglo-Dutch moment*; Locke, 'A letter concerning toleration', in *Second treatise*, p. 153. Richard H. Cox, in *Locke*, speaks (pp. 171–5) of 'the natural primacy of foreign policy' in Locke's thought (quotation p. 172).

41. The financial transformations after 1688 are discussed in Dickson, *Financial revolution in England*. On the stock market, see Parkinson, 'War and peace'. On the development of the 'fiscal-military state', see Brewer, *Sinews of power*. For the figures on loans and income,

see the table in Kennedy, *Rise and fall of the Great Powers*, p. 105; Scott, *England's troubles*, *passim*; and for a wider perspective, Braddick, *Nerves of state*.

42. On the 'culture of commerce' and the 'circulation of knowledge', see Glaisyer, *Culture of commerce*, esp. 143–83, which emphasizes the commercial over the political. On the nexus between Parliament, pressure groups and the dissemination of economic knowledge in the press, see Gauci, *Politics of trade*, esp. pp. 160–61 and 198–208.

43. Gibbs, 'Revolution in foreign policy'; Horn, *Great Britain and Europe*, p. 2, sees 1689 as the start of 'the continuous story of British intervention on the Continent'. The Williamite propagandist is quoted in Black, 'Treaty of Rijswijk', p. 121.

44. See Ehrman, *Navy in the war*, p. 609. On Parliament and the Navy, see Kenyon, *Stuart England*, p. 273.

45. On this, see Horwitz, *Parliament, policy and politics*, pp. 103–7, *et passim* and Jens Metzdorf, *Politik–Propaganda–Patronage*, pp. 43–4, *et passim*. For the parliamentary debates, see Cobbett, *Parliamentary history*, V, 'Debate on the state of the war', 2 November 1689, cols. 408–12; 'Debate on the King's Speech', 13 November 1693, cols. 776–94 (esp. Sir Thomas Clarges's swipes against the land war, cols. 783–9).

46. Horwitz, *Revolution politicks*, pp. 129–30. For the failure at Quebec, see McLay, 'Wellsprings of a "world war" ', pp. 155–75, esp. pp. 164–9.

47. See chapter 4, 'English xenophobia and anti-war sentiment', of Tony Claydon's *William III*, esp. pp. 122–34 and 145–6.

48. Defoe's satire is included in *Novels and miscellaneous works*, pp. 423–9 (quotation, p. 426). For the view that Britishness was essentially defined against the European 'other', see Colley, *Britons*, pp. 5–6, *et passim*. On the shift from 'Christendom' to 'Europe', see Schmidt, 'Establishment of "Europe" '. The unchauvinistic sense of much of English and British thinking on identity and Europe is stressed in Kidd, *British identities*, pp. 212–16. See also Mandler, *English national character*, pp. 14–15.

2 Marlborough Country: Britain and the Empire, 1697–1714

1. Marlborough's genius for war is demonstrated in Chandler, *Marlborough*; for his career in broader context, see J. R. Jones, *Marlborough*. For a parliamentary view of the Duke, see 'The Commons' address in favour of the Duke of Marlborough', 7 January 1707, in Cobbett, *Parliamentary history*, VI, col. 549.

2. See Thomson, 'Parliament and foreign policy'. The petitions are printed in Cobbett, *Parliamentary history*, V, cols. 1250–51 (Kentish petition, 8 May 1701) and cols. 1252–6 ('Legion memorial').

3. William is quoted in Wakeman, *Ascendancy of France*, pp. 333–4; the Tory is quoted in Metzdorf, *Politik–Propaganda–Patronage*, pp. 44–5. On the election and the importance of foreign policy concerns, see Speck, *Tory and Whig*, p. 114.

4. *Fable of the lion's share*, p. 3. Davenant is quoted in Metzdorf, *Politik–Propaganda–Patronage*, p. 103.

5. Commons quoted in Black, *System of ambition?*, p. 142. The fear of Louis was much exaggerated: incompetence and fear, rather than ambition, seems to have driven him into war over Spain; see Thomson, 'Louis XIV'. Terms of the Grand Alliance are quoted in Hattendorf, *England in the War of the Spanish Succession*, pp. 78–9.

6. See Gregg, 'Was Queen Anne a Jacobite?', esp. pp. 367–8, 370.

7. For the activities of British diplomats in Germany, see Hartley, *Charles Whitworth*, pp. 21–9, and Thompson, *Britain, Hanover*, pp. 54–6. For British diplomatic attempts at the Imperial Diet at Regensburg to bring the Empire into the war against France, see Charles Whitworth to James Vernon (Secretary of State for the Northern Department), 1 June 1702 OS, Ratisbonne (BL Add Mss 37348, fo. 18). The unusually high level of English/British representation in the German states during the War of the Spanish Succession is evident from Chance, *List of diplomatic representatives*, pp. 22–5, *et passim*. See Hattendorf, *England in the War of the Spanish Succession*, pp. 19–20, *et passim*,

on the strategy of encirclement. On the SPCK and similar bodies, see Eamon Duffy, 'Correspondance fraternelle'.

8. Admiralty instructions quoted in Richmond, *Navy as an instrument of policy*, pp. 358–9. On the importance of Blenheim, see Charles Spencer, *Blenheim*. For Marlborough's status as a prince of the Empire, see Anon., 'The Dukes of Marlborough'. The importance of British subsidies and diplomacy in the Holy Roman Empire is discussed in Braubach, *Die Bedeutung der Subsidien*, pp. 73–171, and *Diplomatie und geistiges Leben*, pp. 197–230, esp. pp. 204–5 re Marlborough and the Electorate of Trier after Blenheim. The increasingly dominant role of Britain in relation to Austria emerges very clearly from Jarnut-Derbolav, *Die Österreichische Gesandtschaft*, pp. 376–96.

9. See Black, *Parliament and foreign policy in the eighteenth century*, p. 38.

10. See Robertson, *A union for empire* and 'Union, state and empire', esp. pp. 239–42.

11. Speck, *Birth of Britain*, pp. 92–118.

12. MacInnes, 'Union failed, union accomplished'. On America, see Hattendorf, *England in the War of the Spanish Succession*, pp. 41–2.

13. Quoted in Metzdorf, *Politik–Propaganda–Patronage*, p. 64. The present author, who is an enthusiastic armchair strategist, readily sympathizes.

14. The emergence of a 'political culture of debate' is described in Winkler, *Wörterkrieg*, which perhaps tends to underestimate the importance of foreign affairs, at least for the period of the Spanish Succession, and more generally in Downie, 'Development of the political press', which virtually ignores foreign policy. On the centrality of war and foreign policy to the public sphere, see de Beer, 'English newspapers', esp. pp. 119, 122, 124–5, and Metzdorf, *Politik–Propaganda–Patronage*, pp. 58, 64, *et passim*. On foreign policy and party-political polarization, see Metzdorf, *Politik–Propaganda–Patronage*, pp. 45, 488, 495, *et passim*, and Coombs, *Conduct of the Dutch*, pp. 2–5, *et passim*.

15. Horwitz, *Revolution politicks*, p. 212.

16. On the Dutch barrier, see Geikie and Montgomery, *Dutch Barrier*, pp. 38–9 (1706) and pp. 156–60 (1709). On discussion concerning a possible German barrier, see Braubach, *Diplomatie und geistiges Leben*, pp. 231–67, esp. pp. 235–7, 245–7.

17. For Harley, see Hattendorf, *England in the War of the Spanish Succession*, p. 235. Tory attitudes to grand strategy in the early stages of the war are discussed in Horwitz, *Revolution politicks*, pp. 169, 172–7.

18. The change of ministry is described in Gregg, *Queen Anne*, pp. 297–392, esp. pp. 320–24. On the electoral popularity of Tory foreign policy, see Speck, *Tory and Whig*, p. 114.

19. Swift's comment about Parliament is quoted in Glendinning, *Jonathan Swift*, p. 103. See also Cook, *Jonathan Swift*, pp. 38–45; Müllenbrock, *Culture of contention*, pp. 173–6, which shows how Swift appealed to the strong anti-Austrian, insular and xenophobic strain in British opinion; and Black, 'Swift and foreign policy revisited'.

20. Hare is quoted in Metzdorf, *Politik–Propaganda–Patronage*, p. 392. Marlborough's flight is described in Gregg, 'Marlborough in exile', esp. pp. 593–6, 604.

21. Steele, *Politics of colonial policy*, pp. 134–42; Carswell, *South Sea Bubble*, pp. 40–59.

22. Veitch and Dummer are quoted in van Alstyne, *Empire and independence*, pp. 3–4; *Genesis of American nationalism*, p. 29; and *Rising American empire*, p. 12. On fear of the French in North America and the thinking behind the Quebec Expedition, see Hattendorf, *England in the War of the Spanish Succession*, pp. 191, 234. The phrase 'the American Carthage' is in Jeremiah Dummer to Lord Dartmouth, 3 January 1711, in Graham, *Walker Expedition*, p. 267.

23. 'Instructions for Robert Hunter, Captain General and Governor in Chief of New York', 6 February 1711, in Graham, *Walker Expedition*, pp. 269–70; 'St John to Governor Hunter', 6 February 1711, p. 277.

24. On the Mohawks, see Trevelyan, *England under Queen Anne*, vol. III, *The peace and the Protestant Succession*, p. 142.

25. Swift, *Conduct of the allies*, p. 424. St John is quoted in Black, *System of ambition?*, p. 146. On the 'barrier', see Geikie and Montgomery, *Dutch barrier*, pp. 241–83.

26. Metzdorf, *Politik–Propaganda–Patronage*, pp. 294 (Defoe), 300 (Hare); on the shifts in Defoe's thinking, see pp. 178, 285, 294, 376–7.

27. See Hill, 'Oxford, Bolingbroke', pp. 257–9.

28. Elector George is quoted in Metzdorf, *Politik–Propaganda–Patronage*, p. 361; See Hill, 'Oxford, Bolingbroke', pp. 257–8; Hattendorf, *England in the War of the Spanish Succession*, pp. 32, 253. Hanoverian interest in British politics and foreign policy is described in Schnath, *Geschichte Hannovers*, vol. IV, *Georg Ludwigs Weg auf den englischen Thron*, pp. 271–312.

29. Hare is quoted in Metzdorf, *Politik–Propaganda–Patronage*, p. 458. For Dutch fury at the neglect of the barrier, see Hatton, *Diplomatic relations*, pp. 30–39. For Austrian responses, see Ingrao, *In quest and crisis*, p. 219. For the depiction of Utrecht in political prints, see Atherton, *Political prints*, pp. 185–9.

30. McKay, 'Bolingbroke, Oxford', pp. 264, 268, 273.

31. McKay, 'Bolingbroke, Oxford', pp. 278, 281.

32. On the persistence of the Anglo-French antagonism, see most recently Tombs, *Sweet enemy*.

33. I differ here from Thompson's very stimulating *Britain, Hanover*, pp. 2–3, 16–17, 29, *et passim*, who stresses the causal power of religion more than I do, and am closer to Pincus, 'English debate', esp. p. 53. On 'strategic culture', see Snyder, *Soviet strategic culture*, p. 8, where the term was first coined. For the most recent discussion, see the issue of the *Oxford Journal of Good Governance* 2:1 (March 2006), edited by Asle Toje, which is entirely devoted to the concept of 'strategic culture', especially the article by Ken Booth, 'Strategic culture: Validity and validation', pp. 25–8. I have attempted to trace the contours of British strategic culture in the eighteenth century in Simms, 'Ministers of Europe'.

34. Military service in Europe is discussed in Black, *Natural and necessary enemies*, pp. 2–3. Travel is dealt with by Black, *Grand tour*; Richter-Uhlig, *Hof und Politik*, pp. 43–4; and Geyken, *Gentlemen auf Reisen*, pp. 54–100. On the centrality of foreign policy in Parliament, see Gibbs, 'Newspapers, parliament and foreign policy', esp. p. 295. For the traditional view of an 'ignorant' Parliament, see Firth, 'Study of British foreign policy', pp. 470–71. On the high quality of parliamentary speeches, see also Schweizer, 'Parliamentary speech', p. 92. The use of the word 'empire' is discussed in Black, *Parliament and foreign policy in the eighteenth century*, p. 86. Interestingly, the most recent study of the eighteenth-century British conception of empire makes only glancing reference to the fact that the term had connotations other than the colonial: Armitage, 'British conception of empire', p. 92. Koebner, *Empire*, deals with both the Holy Roman Empire and the British Empire, but does not discuss Britain's role in the former.

35. 'Directions for the printer of the *National Journal* on how to place or range the articles of news', 14 June 1746, in Hanson, *Government and the press*, p. 146. On the centrality of Europe in the press, see Cranfield, *Development of the provincial newspaper*, pp. 65–7 (*Grub Street Journal* quotation, p. 67); Black, *English press in the eighteenth century*, pp. 197–244: 'The press and Europe'. For the inclusion of colonial matters under the heading of 'History of Europe', see the *Annual Register* for 1774, chapters V to VII. Black, *Parliament and foreign policy*, pp. 146, 170, *et passim*.

36. The trade figures are taken from Schumpeter, *English overseas trade statistics*. The primacy of strategic over economic factors is clear from Neuner, *Wirtschaft und Öffentlichkeit*, esp. p. 58.

37. On the centrality of Europe and home defence over imperial commitments for the Royal Navy, see Rodger, 'Sea-power and empire'. The importance of home waters over the colonies is also stressed in Graham, 'Naval defence'. For the imprecision and limitations of naval power, see Black, 'British naval power', and Willis, 'Fleet performance and capability', esp. pp. 373–4, 387–92, which challenges myths about the omnipotence of the Royal Navy.

3 Imperial Restoration, 1714–1715

1. See Oxford's response to 'The articles of impeachment against the Earl of Oxford and Earl Mortimer', 9 July 1715, in Cobbett, *Parliamentary history*, VII, col. 106.

2. See Simms and Riotte, *Hanoverian dimension*. The jacket cover shows a 'Flag of George I, King of England', in which the White Horse of Hanover features prominently in the lower right-hand corner. The Hanoverian dimension from 1714 hardly figures in Groom, *Union Jack*.

3. Michael, *Englische Geschichte*, vol. I, *Die Anfänge des Hauses Hannover*, pp. 366, 369, 372, 376–7, *et passim*.

4. The definitive account is the superlative biography by Ragnhild Hatton, *George I: Elector and king*, pp. 111–46. For a very full account of the role of the Germans, see chapter 7, 'The court in politics', of Beattie, *English court*, pp. 217–48.

5. Rowse, *Spirit of English History*, p. 85; Michael, *Englische Geschichte*, I, p. 392; Hatton, *George I*, p. 130.

6. 'Act of Settlement, 1701', in Williams, *Eighteenth-century constitution*, p. 59.

7. On Sunderland and Stanhope's affection for Görtz, see Lampe, *Aristokratie, Hofadel und Staatspatriziat*, vol. 2, *Beamtenleben und Ahnentafeln*, p. 29.

8. For evidence of Robethon as a conduit in negotiations, see, among many examples, Schaub to Townshend, 28 August 1715, Vienna (NA SP 80/32, fo. 169). Swift is quoted in Chance, 'John de Robethon', p. 62.

9. See O'Reillly, 'Naturalization Act'; and Statt, *Foreigners and Englishmen*, pp. 121–65 re Palatine hostility, and p. 149 re Whig tolerance versus Tory prejudice.

10. Atterbury, *English advice*. For the religious observances of George and his family, see Robethon's reports to Hanover of 16 October 1714, St James's, and the report of 30 April 1715 (NStAH Cal. Br. 24 England Nr. 1713, fos. 5, 110). See the description in the report of Kreyenberg from the German Chancellery to the Hanoverian administration, 4 August 1716, London (NStAH, Cal. Br. 24 Nr. 1713, fo. 423). On Atterbury, see also Kathleen Wilson, *Sense of the people*, pp. 110–11.

11. On the role of the 'other' in moulding British identity, see Colley, *Britons*, pp. 5–6, *et passim*, and 'Britishness and otherness'. The work of Frauke Geyken, *Gentlemen auf Reisen*, pp. 51, 294–9, is a first step in the direction of recognizing this, although she neglects the period before 1740; it can best be accessed in English in 'German language'. The importance of George as a Protestant warrior-king who was 'naturalized' as a Briton is stressed by Hannah Smith in *Georgian monarchy*, pp. 15–16, 21, 23, 28–9, 41, 56–7.

12. See Basil Williams, *Carteret and Newcastle*, pp. 30–31; Kathleen Wilson, *Sense of the people*, pp. 87–9. On 'Hanover coffee houses', see Bryant Lillywhite, *London coffee houses*, p. 262.

13. On Hanoverian themes in America, see Phillips, *Cousins' wars*, p. 73.

14. Schulenburg to Görtz, 19 February 1717; 31 August 1717; 2 November 1717; 4 March 1718 (HStAD F23A 153/6, fos. 7–8, 118, 194–5). See also Langford, *Englishness identified*, pp. 176–98.

15. Schulenburg to Görtz, 2 April 1717; 6 April 1717; 7 February 1719 (HStAD F23A Nr. 153/6, fos. 24, 28–30, 255–6); reports of 24 October 1719 (London) and 26 September 1719 (London) (NStAH Cal. Br. 24 Nr. 1723, fo. 22); Schulenburg to Görtz, 23 July 1717 (HStAD F23A Nr. 153/6, fos. 65–7).

16. On the European phenomenon of Personal Union more generally, see Duchhardt, *Der Herrscher in der Doppelpflicht*. For a comparative view of the British and the Saxon–Polish experiences, see Rexheuser, *Die Personalunionen*.

17. See Campbell, 'International and legal relations', and Nicholas B. Harding, 'North African piracy'. I hesitate to disagree with the late Ragnhild Hatton, certainly the greatest expert on the Personal Union, who argues in *The Anglo-Hanoverian connection* that the two states 'were always two distinct international realities', p. 3. Re the dispatch of envoys, see Hatton, *George I*, p. 217.

18. Mediger, *Mecklenburg*, vol. I, p. 399; Hatton, *George I*, p. 216. On St Saphorin, see Gehling, *Ein europäischer Diplomat*.

19. Examples of Whig triumphalism are the anonymous pamphlets *Advice to Whigs and Tories* and *The happiness of the Hanover succession*. I am very grateful to my doctoral student Doohwan Ahn for drawing these to my attention. On the Pretender and France, see Corp, *Court in exile*, pp. 280–299. For the privateering threat in the Channel, see Bromley, *Corsairs and Navies*, pp. 73–102: 'The importance of Dunkirk reconsidered, 1688–1713'.

20. See Savelle, 'American balance', p. 144, *et passim*.

21. Egnal, *Mighty empire*, pp. 88, 105.

22. 'Governor Alexander Spotswood to the Board of Trade', 14 August 1718, in Ver Steeg and Hofstadter, *Great issues*, pp. 337–8. The French memorandum is quoted in Savelle, 'American balance', p. 147. For the colonies as a source of naval supplies, see Albion, *Forests and sea power*, pp. 230–80.

23. Schulenburg to Görtz, 8 March 1718 and 29 November 1718, London (NStAD F23A Nr. 153/6, fo. 247); and parliamentary exchanges in Cobbett, *Parliamentary history*, VII, col. 563.

24. Schulenburg to Görtz, 30 November 1717, London (HStAD F23A Nr. 153/6, fo. 132).

25. Hatton, *George I*, pp. 127, 210, 354. Colley, *In defiance of oligarchy*, pp. 13–14, tends to be sceptical of the importance of foreign policy for the party divide.

26. For Hanoverian views of the election, see reports of 5, 8, 19 and 26 February (St James's) (NStAH 1715, Cal. Br. 24 Nr. 1713, fos. 59–60, 61–2, 64–5, 66–7). Cobbett, *Parliamentary history*, VII, 21 March 1715, cols. 46–8. See also Speck, *Tory and Whig*, for figures.

27. Cobbett, *Parliamentary history*, VII, 1 June 1715, cols. 53–64.

28. See 'The articles of impeachment against the Earl of Oxford and Earl Mortimer', 9 July 1715, and 'Articles of impeachment of High treason and other high crimes and misdemeanours, against Henry Viscount Bolingbroke', 6 August 1715, in Cobbett, *Parliamentary history*, VII, cols. 74–104, 129–37.

29. 'Further articles of impeachment of High Crimes and Misdemeanours against Robert Earl of Oxford and Earl Mortimer', 30 July 1715, Cobbett, *Parliamentary history*, VII, cols. 126 and 219 (21 September 1715).

30. Ibid., col. 105; see also 'The answer of Robert Earl of Oxford and Earl Mortimer, to the articles exhibited by the knights, citizens, and burgesses, in parliament assembled, in the name of themselves and of all the Commons of Great Britain, etc.', 3 September 1715, cols. 157–211; and col. 160.

31. Ibid., 21 March 1715, col. 48.

32. See J. G. Simms, 'The Irish on the Continent', esp. pp. 630–44.

33. Report of 11 April 1718, London (NStAH Cal. Br. 24 Nr. 1722, fo. 158); Schulenburg to Görtz, 11 April 1714, London (HStAD F23A 153/6, fo. 268); report of 17/18 April 1718, London (NStAH Cal. Br. 24, Nr. 1722, fo. 165–6).

34. Printed in Cobbett, *Parliamentary history*, VII, col. 235. The ballad is quoted in Kathleen Wilson, *Sense of the people*, p. 84.

35. Reports of 30 November 1714, 18 December 1/14, 9 August 1715 (all St James's) (NStAH Cal. Br. 24 Nr. 1713, fos. 16, 21, 182). For Sweden and the Jacobites, see Murray, *George I*, pp. 144–5. On the 1715 rebellion in general, see Daniel Szechi, *1715*, who emphasizes the local nature of the confrontation.

36. See L. B. Smith, 'Spain and the Jacobites'.

37. 'Articles of impeachment of High treason exhibited against James Earl of Derwentwater etc.', Cobbett, *Parliamentary history*, VII, col. 240.

38. On this, see Walpole, *Memoirs of the life and administration of Sir Robert Walpole*, vol. I, pp. 136–8. 'Debate on the Septennial Bill', 10 April 1716, in Cobbett, *Parliamentary history*, VII, cols. 292–374.

39. 'Great debate in the Commons concerning the number of the land forces', 4 December 1717, in Cobbett, *Parliamentary history*, VII, col. 505.

40. 'Debate in the Lords on the Mutiny Bill', 18 February 1718, in Cobbett, *Parliamentary history*, VII, col. 538.

41. Cobbett, *Parliamentary history*, VII, cols. 508–9.

42. 'Mr Shippen committed to the Tower for reflecting upon the King's person and government', in Cobbett, *Parliamentary history*, VII, col. 511; see also 6 December 1717, cols. 519–20.

43. Horn, *Great Britain and Europe in the eighteenth century*, p. 97. Also see Hatton, *Diplomatic relations*.

44. The Barrier question is covered in Hatton, *Diplomatic relations*, pp. 61–73, and Geikie and Montgomery, *Dutch barrier*, 321–68. For the rapprochement with Austria, see Schaub to Townshend, 14 March 1716 (Vienna) and 11 March 1716 (NA SP 80/33 Germany/Empire, fos. 61–2, 59–60). On Austria's relations with the Ottomans in this period, see Roider, *Austria's Eastern Question*, pp. 58–70.

4 Britain's New European Empire, 1716–1717

1. Quoted in Hatton, *George I*, p. 187.

2. 26 September 1716 (NA SP 43/1, fos. 88–9).

3. Memorandum quoted in Wellenreuther, 'Von der Interessenharmonie', p. 28. See also Nicholas B. Harding, 'Hanoverian rulership', esp. pp. 393–403; Mediger, *Moskaus Weg*, p. 11 and Chance, *George I and the Northern War*, pp. 1–24.

4. Memorandum quoted in Mediger, *Moskaus Weg*, p. 12; Chance, *George I and the Northern War*, pp. 25–49.

5. On the statues, see Horti, *Der Herrenhausener Garten*.

6. Merchant lobbying reported 26 March 1715, St James's and 4 March 1718/19, London (NStAH Cal. Br. 24 Nr. 1713, fos. 119, 404). On the commercial importance of the Baltic, see Ormrod, *Rise of commercial empires*, pp. 66–76, 278–87, and Evans, Jackson and Ryden, 'Baltic iron', pp. 644–5. For the impact on British shipping, see Aldridge, 'English east coast trade', esp. pp. 120–22, and Ericson, 'Economic warfare', esp. p. 117.

7. 'Debate on the state of the trade to Sweden', 27 February 1717, in Cobbett, *Parliamentary history*, VII, col. 548; Robethon to Weber, 30 July 1715, St James's (NStAH Cal. Br. 24 Nr. 6580, I, fo. 257). On the strategic importance of the Baltic as source of naval supplies, see Albion, *Forests and seapower*, esp. chapter 4, 'Baltic timber and foreign policy', pp. 139–99. Chance, *George I and the Northern War*, pp. 9, 91 stresses strategic over commercial considerations. So does Ahn, 'Europe or America'.

8. Murray, *George I*, pp. 162, 169; Hatton, *Diplomatic relations*, p. 122. On Norris, see also the work of David Aldridge, most easily accessed in his 'Sir John Norris'.

9. Murray, *George I*, p. 178. On Polwarth, see Lodge, 'Polwarth papers', esp. pp. 243–61.

10. The quotations are from Murray, *George I*, pp. 239, 181, 187, 270. The letter in German is Admiral Norris to Bernstorff, 3 May 1720 os, Copenhagen (NStAH Hann. 92 Nr. 2109, fo. 11).

11. Stanhope to Townshend, 14 August 1716, Pyrmont (NA SP 43/1 Hanover, fo. 28).

12. Walpole, *Memoirs*, I, p. 163 and Basil Williams, *Stanhope*; Stanhope to Methuen, 25 September 1716 (NA SP 43/1 Hanover, fos. 82–3).

13. See report of 15/26 May 1719, London, for that visit; for the nominations that year, see report of 12 May 1719, London (NA Cal. Br. 24 Nr. 1722, fos. 376, 362).

14. See, e.g., reports of 6/17 February 1719, London ('*Il paroit que plusieurs ministres publics se proposent de suivre S.M. a Hannover*'); 6 June 1719, London; 9 June 1719, London; 9 June 1719, London (NStAH Cal. Br. 24 Nr. 1722, fos. 309, 390, 392, 394); Schulenburg to Görtz, 6 October 1718, Ems (HStAD F23A 153/6, fo. 235); Feuillet de Kreyenberg, 7 August 1716 (NStAH Cal. Br. 24 Nr. 1713, fo. 426).

15. See Schaub to Townshend, 5, 1 and 25 March 1716, Vienna (NA SP 80/33 Germany/Empire, fos. 53, 57–8, 69).

16. Schaub to Townshend, 28 March, 1 and 18 April 1716, Vienna (NA SP 80/33, fos. 71, 73, 83, *et passim*).

17. Austrian fears of being marginalized are described in Schaub to Townshend, 27 May 1716, Vienna, and 28 October 1716, Vienna (NA SP 80/33, fos. 107, 218).

18. Murray, *George I*, pp. 228–31.

19. See also Mediger, *Mecklenburg*, vol. I, p. 357. On Bernstorff and Mecklenburg, see Ballschmieter, *Andreas Gottlieb von Bernstorff*, esp. pp. 115–52. The Mecklenburg issue is discussed more generally in Hughes, *Law and politics*.

20. George I's instructions for Stanhope, 26 September 1716; Stanhope to Townshend, 29 September 1716, Hanover; Stanhope to Polwarth (NA SP 43/1, fos. 88–9, 87, 88). On Whitworth's fears of the Russian threat to the balance in the Baltic, see Hartley, *Charles Whitworth*, pp. 118–25. For naval issues, see M. S. Anderson, 'Great Britain and the growth of the Russian navy', pp. 132–5.

21. Report of 14 April 1716, St James's (NStAH Cal. Br. 24 Nr. 1713, fo. 367); Murray, *George I*, pp. 253, 278.

22. Townshend is quoted in Chance, *George I and the Northern War*, p. 186. Craggs is quoted in Baack, 'State service', p. 327; see also Basil Williams, *Stanhope*, p. 236. On the Admiralty, see Murray, *George I*, p. 115.

23. Quoted in Aubrey Newman, *Stanhopes*, p. 63.

24. On the Dutch dimension, see Hatton, *Diplomatic relations*, pp. 130–31, and *George I*, p. 182.

25. Report of 29 December 1716 (NStAH Cal. Br. 24 Nr. 1713, fo. 497); Schulenburg to Görtz, 12 February 1717, London (HStAD F23A Nr. 153/6, fo. 2).

26. See Black, 'Parliament and the political and diplomatic crisis'; Schulenburg to Görtz, 19 March 1717, London (HStAD F23A Nr. 153/6, fo. 19); Cobbett, *Parliamentary history*, VII, 12 April 1717, col. 443.

27. *Walpole*, I, p. 274. To be fair he goes on to note that the sources on the Germans tend to be biased.

28. Hatton, *George I*, p. 148; Schulenburg to Görtz, 12 February 1717, London (HStAD F23A Nr. 153/6, fo. 2); Cobbett, *Parliamentary history*, VII, col. 460.

29. Murray, *George I*, pp. 13, 97, 327; Cobbett, *Parliamentary history*, VII, col. 443, and 'Debate on the supply', 4 April 1717, cols. 435–6. On the public controversy about 'the Germans' more generally, see Laprade, *Public opinion*, pp. 205–28.

30. 'Motion relating to the Bishop of Munster's and the Duke of Saxe-Gotha's troops', 26 March 1717, Cobbett, *Parliamentary history*, VII, col. 435; and 4 June 1717, col. 467. See also reports on Parliament and background in Schulenburg to Görtz, 24 July 1717, London (HStAD F23A Nr. 153/6, fo. 37).

31. Cobbett, *Parliamentary history*, VII, 12 April 1717, col. 444. On Stanhope's remarks to the Austrians, see McKay, 'Struggle for Control', p. 372.

32. On George's attempts to limit the Prince's access to his children, see his instructions for the Dowager Countess of Portland (governess to the Princesses Anne, Amelia and Caroline) (RA Astle Papers, fo. 53038).

33. Schulenburg to Görtz, 6 April 1717, London, and 28 September 1717, Hampton Court (HStAD F23 A 153/6, fos. 28, 106v); Hatton, *George I*, p. 214. Caroline to Mrs Clayton, ?1718 (RA Georgian Additional Mss. 28, fo. 87).

34. Basil Williams, *Carteret and Newcastle*, p. 39.

35. For Hanoverian fears that the Prince was becoming the focus of opposition, see for example Schulenburg to Görtz, 11 May 1717, London, and 21 January 1718, London (HStAD F23A Nr. 153/6, fos. 41, 162). The incident in the Tower is described in Cobbett, *Parliamentary history*, XI, 14 February 1741, col. 1375. On Caroline, see Hanham, 'Caroline of Brandenburg-Ansbach', esp. pp. 286–7.

36. Schulenburg to Görtz, 4 February 1718, London; 6 and 23 April 1717, London 12 February 1717, London; 1 October 1717, Hampton Court; 16 November 1717;

19 March 1717, London (HStAD F23A Nr. 153/6, fos. 171, 29, 34–5, 3, 109–10, 124, 18–19). Cobbett, *Parliamentary history*, VII, col. 440.

37. See the very full description in Schulenburg to Görtz, 19 and 23 February 1717, London; 23 and 27 July 1717; 28 January 1718, London (HStAD F23A Nr. 153/6, fos. 8, 10v, 65–6, 67, 107).

38. See 'The Earl of Oxford's petition to be tried' and 'Debate on a motion for fixing a day for the trial of the Earl of Oxford', 22 May 1717, Cobbett, *Parliamentary history*, VII, cols. 461, 463, 465.

39. 'Debate on a motion for desiring the Lords to delay the trial of the Earl of Oxford', 12 June 1717; 'Proceedings at the trial of the Earl of Oxford', 24 June 1717, Cobbett, *Parliamentary history*, VII, cols. 478–9, 480ff.

40. Schulenburg to Görtz, 20 and 27 April, London; 1 June and 23 November 1717 (HStAD F23A Nr. 153/6 fos. 31, 37, 48, 128). Report of 12 September 1719, London (NStAH Cal. Br. 24 Nr. 1723).

41. As reported on 19 April 1718, St James's, and 31 May 1718, London (NStAH Cal. Br. 24 Nr. 1722, fos. 167, 195). See also Hatton, *George I*, p. 267.

42. See RA Astle Papers, 53039: 'An account of what passed in a conference concerning . . . the Succession to the Crown', and 'Draught of a report after a second conference . . . Concerning an Act of Settlement' (fos. 53043–69). See also Hatton, *George I*, pp. 166–8.

43. Murray, *George I*, p. 335.

44. See documents in Cobbett, *Parliamentary history*, VII, cols. 395–421; and Murray, 'An eighteenth-century white book'. For Hanoverian misgivings, see Schulenburg to Görtz, 12 February 1717, London (HStAD F23A Nr. 153/6, fo. 5). Murray, 'Görtz–Gyllenburg arrests'.

45. Schulenburg to Görtz, 12 February 1717 (HStAD F23A Nr. 153/6, fo. 5). Murray, *George I*, pp. 144–5, 343.

5 Pre-emptive War in the Mediterranean and the Baltic, 1718–1719

1. Quoted in Mediger, *Mecklenburg*, vol. I, p. 408.

2. See Armstrong, *Elizabeth Farnese*, pp. 61–5, for Elizabeth's Italian ambitions, and pp. 73–5, for commercial issues. See also Horn, *Great Britain and Europe*, p. 279.

3. Black, *Parliament and foreign policy in the eighteenth century*, p. 181.

4. Schulenburg to Görtz, 3 September 1717, Hampton Court (HStAD, F23A Nr. 153/6, fo. 93). See also in the same vein his letters of 7 September 1717, Hampton Court (fo. 94) and 22 February 1718, London (fo. 189).

5. Anxieties about Walpole are evident in Schulenburg to Görtz, 31 March 1718, London (HStAD F23A Nr. 153/6, fo. 205). Stanhope is quoted in Black, 'Parliament and the political and diplomatic crisis', p. 77.

6. Richmond, *Navy as an instrument of policy*, p. 385. George's fears of encirclement are in Mediger, *Mecklenburg*, vol. I, p. 400.

7. Mahan, *Influence of sea power*, p. 237; Sunderland to Newcastle, 29 August 1718 (BL Add Mss 32686, fo. 120); Schulenburg to Görtz, 15 September 1718, Ems (HStAD F23A Nr. 153/6, fo. 233); see A. W. Ward, *Great Britain and Hanover*, p. 113.

8. Cobbett, *Parliamentary history*, VII, col. 564; and 'Debate in the Lords on the address of thanks', col. 561.

9. See L. B. Smith, *Spain and Britain*, esp. pp. 163–240.

10. Newcastle to Stanhope, 14 October 1719, Claremont and Stanhope to Newcastle, 27 October 1719, Hanover (BL Add Mss 32686, fos. 152, 155); Schulenburg to Görtz, 11 August 1719, Emden (HStAD F23A Nr. 153/6, fo. 228).

11. Defoe is quoted in Murray, *George I*, p. 20. Jefferys is quoted in Wills, *Jacobites and Russia*, pp. 63, 30.

12. Reports of 8 September 1719, London, and 4 March 1718, London (NStAH Cal. Br. 24 Nr. 1723, fos. 7, 404). See Wills, *Jacobites and Russia*, pp. 41, 44–51, 60, 64, 85, 91.

13. Stanhope to Craggs, 26 May 1719 (NA SP 43/1 Hanover, fo. 182); Mediger, *Mecklenburg*, vol. I, p. 418.

14. Basil Williams, *Carteret and Newcastle*, p. 14; report of 31 January 1718, London (NStAH Cal. Br. 24 Nr. 1722, fo. 40). See the amicable correspondence in, e.g., Carteret to Görtz, 11 January 1719, London (HStAD F23A 124/1, unfoliated). Caroline to Mrs Clayton, 1719? (RA Georgian Additional Mss 28, fo. 48).

15. Details of Carteret's entourage are in the report of 29 May 1719, London (NStAH Cal. Br. 24 Nr. 1722, fos. 379v–80). His concerns about the possible collapse of Sweden are described in BL Add Mss 22511: Carteret to Robethon, 23 July 1719, Stockholm (fo. 27); Carteret to Stanhope, 12 July 1719, Stockholm (fo. 19); Carteret to Stanhope, 4 July 1719, Stockholm (fo. 16 *passim*); Carteret to Stanhope, 13 September 1719, Stockholm (fo. 52); and Carteret to Stanhope, 19 August 1719 (fo. 41). Chance, *George I and the Northern War*, pp. 333–59.

16. See the account in the report of 1719, London (NStAH Cal. Br. 24 Nr. 1720, fo. 453); Carteret to Stanhope, 3 July 1719, Stockholm (BL Add Mss 22511, fo. 12). For Swedish resentment on Bremen and Verden, see Carteret to Stanhope, 19 August 1719 (BL Add Mss 22511, fo. 37).

17. See Carteret to Robethon, 23 July 1719, Stockholm (BL Add Mss 22511, fo. 24), for the close coordination, telling him to refer to Stanhope for further information; Carteret to Stanhope, 14 August 1719, Stockholm (BL Add Mss 22511, fo. 34). Carteret's view on electoral and royal interests is quoted in Konigs, *Hanoverian Kings*, p. 47. Carteret to Stanhope, 12 July 1719, Stockholm (BL Add Mss 22511, fo. 15). Carteret's wise remark is quoted in Basil Williams, *Carteret and Newcastle*, pp. 28–9.

18. Schulenburg to Görtz, 11 April 1719, London. (HStAD F23A Nr. 153/6, fo. 267). Bernstorff is quoted in Mediger, *Mecklenburg*, vol. I, pp. 403, 407–8.

19. Mediger, *Mecklenburg*, vol. I, p. 409; Michael, 'Ein schwieriger Fall'.

20. Mediger, *Mecklenburg*, vol. I, pp. 419–21. Schulenburg to Görtz, 5 May 1719, London (HStAD F23A Nr. 153/6, fo. 274). On the showdown between Stanhope and Bernstorff, see also McKay, 'Struggle for control', p. 383 Schulenburg to Görtz, 19 November 1718, London (HStAD F23A Nr. 153/6, fo. 248).

21. Whitworth to Stanhope, 23 May 1719, Berlin (NA SP 43/1 Hanover, fo. 187); Stanhope to Carteret, 17 August 1719, quoted in Mediger, *Mecklenburg*, vol. II, pp. 163–4. On parliamentary and domestic dimensions, see McKay, 'Struggle for control', p. 378, and Black, 'Parliament and the political and diplomatic crisis', pp. 85–6, 90–92. See also Chance, *George I and the Northern War*, pp. 309–32, and Hartley, *Charles Whitworth*, pp. 152–8.

22. Walpole, *Memoirs*, I, p. 226; Black, *Parliament and foreign policy in the eighteenth century*, p. 212. See also the letters of Caroline to Mrs Clayton from 1719 (RA Georgian Additional Mss 28, fos. 37, 71, 94, *et passim*).

23. As described in detail in Schulenburg to Görtz, 5 May 1719, London (HStAD F23A Nr. 153/6, fo. 272).

24. See Mediger, *Mecklenburg*, vol. I, pp. 260–61.

25. The standard account of this is now Thompson, *Britain, Hanover*, pp. 62–87, etc.

26. Ibid., pp. 74, 84.

27. A list of those accompanying George is in the report of 12/23 May 1719, London (NStAH Cal. Br. 24 Nr. 1722, fo. 371). Schulenburg's gloating is in Schulenburg to Görtz, 12 May 1719, London (HStAD F23A Nr. 153/6, fo. 276). For the instructions to Admiral Norris, see Genzel, 'Studien zur Geschichte des Nordischen Krieges', pp. 171–3.

28. Sunderland to Newcastle, 20 October 1719, Göhrde; Stanhope to Newcastle, 27 October 1719, Hanover; Newcastle letter, late November 1719; Newcastle to ?, c.29 September 1719, Cockpitt (BL Add Mss 32686, fos. 149, 156, 88, 54). On British–Hanoverian diplomatic cooperation, see the report of the British ambassador to Berlin, Whitworth to Stanhope, 23 May 1719, Berlin (NA SP 43/1 Hanover, fo. 188): 'Yesterday, I had a long conference with his Privy Councillors, Monsr Ilgen and Mons Kniphausen at which

Monsr Heusch [the Hanoverian envoy] assisted.' See also Hartley, *Charles Whitworth*, pp. 159–63.

29. Stanhope to Newcastle, 27 October 1719, Hanover; Sunderland to Newcastle, 20 October 1719, Göhrde; Stanhope to Newcastle, 27 October 1719, Hanover (BL Add Mss 32686, fos. 155, 149, 156). Caroline's thoughts are in Caroline to Mrs Clayton, *c.*8 December 1719 (RA Georgian Additional Mss 28, fo. 56) as from the transcription and translation. Most of these have been checked against the originals, which are written in French (e.g. fo. 88). Not all the originals have survived.

30. Carteret to Norris, 27 July 1719 OS, Stockholm; Carteret to Norris, 20 August 1719 OS, Stockholm; and in the same vein Carteret to Norris, 21 August 1719 OS, Stockholm (BL Add Mss 22511, fos. 27, 44, 46–7).

31. Burchett is quoted in Murray, *George I*, p. 20. See also Chance, *George I and the Northern War*, pp. 423–4.

32. Quoted in McKay, 'Struggle for control', p. 386.

6 A Protestant Empire, 1721–1724

1. 'Debate in the Commons on the Bill for laying tax upon Papists', 6 May 1723, Cobbett, *Parliamentary history*, VIII, cols. 354–62.

2. On the huge profits of the Duchess of Kendall and others from the South Sea Company see Görtz to Schulenburg, 30 August 1720, Hanover; Görtz to Sunderland, 19 July 1720, Hanover, and Görtz to Schele, 26 July 1720, Hanover; Görtz's reminder to Sunderland on 20 August 1720 (HStAD F23A Nr. 153/5, unfoliated; 151/30, unfoliated; 156/28, unfoliated).

3. On the collapse of the Bubble, see Carswell, *South Sea Bubble*, pp. 174–206. For the rapid revival of investor confidence, see Carlos and Thompson, 'Micro-foundations'. On the role of Newcastle in this coup, see Nulle, *Thomas Pelham-Holles*, pp. 125–7, and Browning, *Duke of Newcastle*, p. 22. More generally, see Plumb, *Walpole* and *Growth of parliamentary stability*.

4. See Black, *Foreign policy of Walpole*, p. 32, who takes a dim view; and, e.g., Townshend to St Saphorin, 7 March (London), 23 June (Whitehall) and 29 August (Whitehall) 1721 (NStAH Hann. 91 St Saphorin Nr.1/I, fos. 9, 50–51, 116). Horatio Walpole used to stand in for Townshend during his absences in Hanover: 'Briefe Walpoles an den General St Saphorin betr. Die allgemeine Politik' (NStAH Hann. 91 St Saphorin Nr. 2, *passim*).

5. On Hanoverian diplomatic representation, see Horn, *Great Britain and Europe*, pp. 180–81. The role of Hanover in British intelligence is described in Black, 'British intelligence', esp. pp. 209–13; Ellis, 'British communications', pp. 162–3, and *Post office*, pp. 60–77. For intelligence prior to this period, see Oakley, 'Interception of posts'.

6. Hatton, *George I*, p. 225; George to Philip, 1 July 1721: the text of the letter is printed in Cobbett, *Parliamentary history*, VIII, col. 695, in a debate on Gibraltar of 18 March 1729. See also Conn, *Gibraltar*, pp. 28–71, and Horn, *Great Britain and Europe*, p. 48.

7. Townshend to St Saphorin, 23 May 1721, Whitehall (NStAH Hann. 91 St Saphorin Nr. 1/I, fo. 37).

8. Hanoverian councillors quoted in Mediger, *Mecklenburg*, vol. I, pp. 433–4. Görtz to Robethon, 17 March 1722, Hanover (HStAD F23A Nr. 150/12, unfoliated). Townshend to St Saphorin, 15 December 1721, Whitehall (NStAH Hann. 91 St Saphorin Nr. 1/I, fo. 211). See Wills, *Jacobites and Russia*, p. 104.

9. Townshend to St Saphorin, 23 May and 17 July 1721, Whitehall (NStAH Hann. 91 St Saphorin Nr. 1/I, fos. 37, 59–60).

10. Townshend to St Saphorin, 2, 30 January and 9 March 1722 (Whitehall); 5 August 1723 (Hanover); 4 August and 7 November 1721 (Whitehall) (NStAH Hann. 91 St Saphorin Nr. 1/I, fos. 1, 7, 17, 169, 97, 196).

11. See Andrew C. Thompson, 'Confessional dimension'; Townshend to St Saphorin, 8 March 1723, Whitehall, and 5 August 1723, Hanover (NStAH Hann. 91 St Saphorin

Nr. 1/II, fos. 142, 170); Necker to Bernstorff, 7 April 1723, Vienna (NStAH Cal. Br. 24 Nr. 4375, unfoliated). On 'St Saphorins', see Chesterfield, *Private correspondence*, p. 10. The fisticuffs are related in 'Copie de la lettre du General de St Saphorin au Comte de Sinzendorff, datée de Vienna', 22 May 1721 (NStAH Cal. Br. 24 Nr. 4913, fo. 7).

12. The *True Briton* is quoted in Black, 'British foreign policy in the eighteenth century: A survey', p. 42. Townshend to St Saphorin, 30 March 1722, Whitehall (NStAH Hann. 91 St Saphorin Nr. 1/II, fo. 38). See also Black, 'Catholic threat', esp. pp. 365, 367, 371–3; Nishikawa, 'SPCK'; and Haydon, *Anti-Catholicism*, pp. 23–8.

13. George I's speech is quoted in Black, *British foreign policy in the age of Walpole*, p. 93. Townshend to St Saphorin, 8 February and 8 March 1723 (Whitehall), 29 July and 4 September 1723 (Hanover) (NStAH Hann. 91 St Saphorin Nr. 1/I, fos. 134, 142 and Nr. 1/II, fos. 166, 178). For the Dutch position, see Hatton, *Diplomatic relations*, pp. 213–14. Hertz, 'England and the Ostend Company', concentrates on commercial aspects.

14. See Black, *Collapse of the Anglo-French alliance*, p. 4. On British objection to the use of Spanish titles, see Townshend to St Saphorin, 18 July 1721, Whitehall (NStAH Hann. 91 St Saphorin Nr. 1/I, fo. 90).

15. Townshend to St Saphorin, 23 June 1721, Whitehall, and 24 July 1723, Hanover (NStAH Hann. 91 St Saphorin Nr. 1/I, fo. 50 and Nr. 1/II, fo. 157).

16. See Browning, *Duke of Newcastle*, p. 26.

17. See Townshend to Newcastle, 12 July 1723, Pyrmont (BL Add Mss 32686, fo. 263).

18. On this, see Horn, *Great Britain and Europe*, p. 115.

19. See Wills, *Jacobites and Russia*, p. 87; Townshend to St Saphorin, 22 December 1724, Whitehall (NStAH Hann. 91 St Saphorin Nr. 1/II, fo. 266). On the decline of the Dutch, see 'The Stadholder problem' in Hatton, *Diplomatic relations*, pp. 215–18.

20. 'Debate in the Lords on the Mutiny Bill', 16 March 1724, Cobbett, *Parliamentary history*, VIII, cols. 385, 390; 'Protest against the number of land forces for the year 1723', 13 February 1723, cols. 60–63. In the same vein, see also the critics in 'Debate in the Lords on the Mutiny Bill', 16 March 1724, cols. 383 (Lord Trevor) and 387–8 (Duke of Wharton and Lord Bathurst).

21. Townshend to St Saphorin, 7 September 1722, London (NStAH Hann. 91 St Saphorin Nr. 1/II, fo. 91); 'Extrait de la lettre de Monsieur le Général de St Saphorin à Mylord Townshend de Vienne le 13 Fév. 1723'; St Saphorin to George I, 17 November 1723, Vienna (NStAH Cal. Br. 24 Nr. 4913, fo. 19; Nr. 4921, fo. 47).

22. The phrases on 'popery' are taken from the King's opening speech to Parliament on 11 October 1722, in Cobbett, *Parliamentary history*, VIII, cols. 25, 27. Browning, *Duke of Newcastle*, p. 82. For George as a Protestant crusader, see Black, *British foreign policy in the age of Walpole*, p. 119. For the liberties of Europe, see the Lords' response to the King's Speech to Parliament on 28 June 1727, in Cobbett, *Parliamentary history*, VIII, col. 596.

23. Görtz to Schulenburg, 12 July 1720, Hanover (HStAD F23A Nr. 153/5, unfoliated), re the need for religious solidarity among the Protestant powers. On the visits to Hanover, see Carteret to St Saphorin, 17 October 1723, Göhrde (NStAH Hann. 91 St Saphorin Nr. 1/II, fo. 202). On collaboration with the Hanoverians, see St Saphorin to Bernstorff 3 February and 26 March 1723, Vienna (NStAH Cal. Br. 24 Nr. 4921, fos. 17, 19); Necker to Bernstorff, 5 May 1723, Vienna (NStAH Cal. Br. 24 Nr. 4375, unfoliated); Cadogan to Bernstorff, 1 June 1720 (NStAH Hann. 92 Nr. 2109, fo. 14). On this, see also Hatton, *George I*, pp. 165, 243, 277. On frictions, see Townshend to St Saphorin, 21 February, 6 March 1724, Whitehall (NStAH Hann. 91 St Saphorin Nr. 1/II, fos. 216, 219, 220): 'Nous servons tous un maître, et le ministère tant Anglois qu'Allemand doit suivre ses ordres.'

24. Townshend to St Saphorin, 22 August 1721, Whitehall (NStAH Hann. 91 St Saphorin Nr. 1/I, fos. 102–3).

25. Görtz to Schulenburg, 30 August 1720, Hanover (HStAD F23A Nr. 153/5, unfoliated).

For George's reception in Prussia, see Townshend to St Saphorin, 27 October 1723, Göhrde (NStAH Hann. 91 St Saphorin Nr. 1/II, fo. 191).

26. St Saphorin to Bernstorff, 3 February 1723, Vienna (NStAH Cal. Br. 24 Nr. 4921, fo. 17); Townshend to St Saphorin, 26 June 1722, Whitehall (NStAH Hann. 91 St Saphorin Nr. 1/II, fo. 63). See also Jacob, *Beziehungen Englands*, pp. 67–76.

27. Carteret to Newcastle, 28 September 1721, Whitehall (BL Add Mss 32686, fo. 206). For the stress on collaboration with the French, see Walker, 'Duke of Newcastle'.

28. See Wills, *Jacobites and Russia*, pp. 74–5, 77–8, 86, 91, 93.

29. See the 'Report of the Committee of the House of Commons appointed to examine Christopher Layer and others touching the conspiracy', 1 March 1723, in Cobbett, *Parliamentary history*, VIII, cols. 97–8, 138, 141; King's Speech, 11 October 1722, col. 25. On Atterbury's role, see Bennett, *Tory crisis*, pp. 223–41. The seriousness of the threat is made clear in Fritz, *English ministers and Jacobitism*, pp. 137–40, and most recently in Cruickshanks and Erskine-Hill, *Atterbury Plot*, esp. pp. 238–9.

30. King's Speech, 11 October 1722, Cobbett, *Parliamentary history*, VIII, col. 27; 'Debate in the Commons on the Bill for laying a Tax upon papists', 26 April 1723, cols. 353–4; 29 January 1723, cols. 353–61; 20 May 1723, col. 363. Andrew C. Thompson, *Protestant interest*, p. 133. E. P. Thompson, *Whigs and hunters*, pp. 163–6.

31. Cobbett, *Parliamentary history*, VIII, 6 May 1723, col. 355.

32. Draper, *Struggle for power*, pp. 154–5. On Franco-British tensions in North America, see also Governor Burnet to the Marquis de Vaudreuil, 11 July 1721, in Ver Steeg and Hoftsadter, *Great issues*, pp. 340–47. On economic competition more generally, see C. M. Andrews, 'Anglo-French commercial rivalry', which concentrates on pamphlet debates.

33. Doll, *Revolution, religion*, pp. 40, 42–3, 39.

34. For the dynamism of colonial trade, see Davis, 'English foreign trade', esp. p. 290 and the figures on pp. 300–303. Berkeley is quoted in Doll, *Revolution, religion*, p. 201.

35. On the elite and the colonies, see Basil Williams, *Carteret and Newcastle*, pp. 12–13; Browning, *Duke of Newcastle*, p. 78; Black, *Walpole*, p. 106; Mimler, *Der Einfluß*, p. 28. Newcastle's solicitude for the colonies is discussed in Haffenden, 'Colonial appointments', esp. pp. 433–5.

36. Newcastle to Townshend, 5 July 1723, Claremont (BL Add Mss 32686, fo. 270); Newcastle to Horace Walpole, 26 September 1724, Windsor (BL Add Mss 32743, fo. 461); Wills, *Jacobites and Russia*, p. 99.

37. Townshend to St Saphorin, 6 March 1724, Whitehall (NStAH Hann. 91 St Saphorin Nr. 1/II, fo. 219).

38. Chance, *Alliance of Hanover*, pp. 35–6, and Andrew C. Thompson, *Britain, Hanover*, pp. 97–132. For the press, see Cranfield, *Development of the provincial newspaper*, p. 67.

39. On the Congress of Cambrai, see Basil Williams, 'Foreign policy', pp. 481–93, and most recently Hartley, *Charles Whitworth*, pp. 187–99. For rumours of an Austro-Spanish marriage project, see Newcastle to Horatio Walpole, 4 February 1725, Whitehall (BL Add Mss 32742, fos. 173–4). Townshend is quoted in Wills, *Jacobites and Russia*, p. 93. For Lawless, see Newcastle to Walpole, 4 February 1725, Whitehall (BL Add Mss 32742, fo. 172).

7 The Return of Charles V, 1725–1726

1. Quoted in Gibbs, 'Britain', p. 415.

2. Quoted in Wills, *Jacobites and Russia*, p. 110.

3. Cobbett, *Parliamentary history*, VIII, 24 January 1727, cols. 538–9.

4. Chance, *Alliance of Hanover*, pp. 114, 384, 7–8.

5. For fears about the Spanish quid pro quo, see Secretary to the Legation in Paris to Horatio Walpole, 29 May 1725, Paris, and William Stanhope to Newcastle, 22 June 1725, Segovia (BL Add Mss 32743, fos. 234–5, 294–306). Townshend is quoted in Chance, *Alliance of Hanover*, p. 124. Walpole's remarks are in Cobbett, *Parliamentary history*, VIII,

16 February 1726, col. 505. On the Treaty of Vienna, see Basil Williams, 'Foreign policy', pp. 665–98 (p. 666 re fears of Charles V), and Gibbs, 'Britain', pp. 413–16.

6. Townshend to St Saphorin, 25 August 1726 (NStAH Hann. 91 St Saphorin Nr. 1/III, fo. 119).

7. Chance, *Alliance of Hanover*, pp. 76–7, 79, 151, 107, 199, 146.

8. 'The King's Speech at the opening of the session', 20 January 1726, Cobbett, *Parliamentary history*, VIII, col. 493; Chance, *Alliance of Hanover*, pp. 141, 143, 147.

9. Walpole is quoted in Wills, *Jacobites and Russia* p. 109. St Saphorin's remarks are reported in Newcastle to Horatio Walpole, 8 June 1726, Whitehall (BL Add Mss 32746, fo. 256). For George's sense of his military limitations, see Chance, *Alliance of Hanover*, p. 58.

10. Reported in Thomas Robinson to St Saphorin, 20 March 1726 (NStAH Hann. 91 St Saphorin Nr. 3, fo. 3).

11. For discussion on the future of the Barrier, see Black, *Parliament and foreign policy in the eighteenth century*, p. 242; Chance, *Alliance of Hanover*, p. 174; and especially Black, 'Interventionism', pp. 735–7.

12. Chance, *Alliance of Hanover*, pp. 186, 570; Horatio Walpole to Hedges, 18 November 1726, Fontainebleau (BL Add Mss 32748, fo. 305).

13. Chance, *Alliance of Hanover*, pp. 14, 1, 13, 102, 492; Wills, *Jacobites and Russia*, p. 122.

14. Horn, *Great Britain and Europe*, p. 50. Black, *Foreign policy of Walpole*, p. 145.

15. 'The King's Speech on opening the session', 17 January 1727, Cobbett, *Parliamentary history*, VIII, cols. 524–5; 'The Lords' Address of Thanks', 18 January 1727, cols. 527, 532; 24 January 1727, cols. 538–9. For privately expressed fears of cooperation between the Pretender and outside powers, see Horatio Walpole to Newcastle, 5 and 18 May 1726, Paris (BL Add Ms 32686, fos. 15, 23).

16. Cobbett, *Parliamentary history*, VIII, cols. 530, 539.

17. See Black, *Foreign policy of Walpole*, p. 180. See also Black, *America or Europe?*, p. 53; Cobbett, *Parliamentary history*, VIII, 6 February 1726, col. 507. On the proposed neutralization of Hanover, see Chance, *Alliance of Hanover*, pp. 586–9.

18. Walpole is quoted in Chance, *Alliance of Hanover*, p. 169. Townshend to St Saphorin, 16 September 1726, Whitehall (NStAH Hann. 91 St Saphorin Nr. 1/III, fo. 129). British anxieties about Ostend and the Empire are discussed in Chance, *Alliance of Hanover*, pp. 396, 517, 519, 715.

19. Newcastle to Horatio Walpole, 22 September 1726, Whitehall (BL Add Mss 32747, fos. 424–6); see also re coordination with the French envoy.

20. Chance, *Alliance of Hanover*, pp. 35–6, 209–10, 230.

21. See Chance, *Alliance of Hanover*, pp. 57, 96, 173; Townshend to St Saphorin, 25 August 1726, Whitehall (NStAH Hann. 91 St Saphorin Nr. 1/III, fo. 115).

22. Chance, *Alliance of Hanover*, pp. 263, 574, 576; Townshend to St Saphorin, 25 August 1726 (NStAH Hann. 91 St Saphorin Nr. 1/III, fos. 113–14).

23. Townshend to Stanyan, 19 November 1725, Göhrde (NStAH Hann. 91 St Saphorin Nr. 1/III, fos. 36–8). See also Chance, *Alliance of Hanover*, p. 214. For British policy towards the Ottomans during this period, see Jacob, *Beziehungen Englands*, pp. 109–128.

24. See Townshend to Stanyan, 19 November 1725, Göhrde (NStAH Hann. 91 St Saphorin Nr. 1/III, fo. 38); Townshend to St Saphorin, 8 and 22 February 1726, Whitehall (NStAH Hann. 91 St Saphorin Nr. 1/III, fos. 17, 23–4). See also Chance, *Alliance of Hanover*, pp. 507, 627.

25. Chance, *Alliance of Hanover*, pp. 232, 471. Basil Williams, 'Foreign policy', stresses the extent to which war with Spain arose out of the principal conflict with Austria.

26. See Townshend to St Saphorin, 20 and 23 December 1726, Whitehall (NStAH Hann. 91 St Saphorin Nr. 1/III, fos. 172, 175). Also Black, *Collapse of the Anglo-French alliance*, p. 30.

27. Chance, *Alliance of Hanover*, p. 627.

28. Townshend to St Saphorin, 4 March 1727, Whitehall (NStAH Hann. 91 St Saphorin Nr. 1/III, fos. 213–14), which includes a copy of the letter declaring Palm to be 'no longer . . . a Public minister and requir[ing] him forthwith to depart from this kingdom' (fo. 220). On St Saphorin's experiences in Austria, see Townshend to St Saphorin, 28 April and 15 May 1727, Whitehall (fos. 224, 226). Newcastle is quoted in Chance, *Alliance of Hanover*, p. 629.

29. Ibid., pp. 282, 708. Newcastle to Horatio Walpole, 8 June 1726, Whitehall (BL Add Mss 32746, fos. 243–4). See also the separate letter of the same date from Newcastle to Horatio Walpole in BL Add Mss 32746, fos. 253–4.

30. Chance, *Alliance of Hanover*, pp. 339, 690.

31. Ibid., pp. 605, 651. For the troop figures, see Basil Williams, 'Foreign policy', pp. 696–7.

32. See 'Lettre particulière', Townshend to St Saphorin, 25 August 1726, Whitehall (NStAH Hann. 91 St Saphorin Nr. 1/III, fo. 120); also the letters of 15 November 1726 and 14 February 1727, Whitehall (fos. 147, 196). Chance, *Alliance of Hanover*, pp. 34, 583. Black, *Collapse of the Anglo-French alliance*, p. 39. See also Arthur McCandless Wilson, *French foreign policy*.

8 The Resurgence of France, 1727–1732

1. Cobbett, *Parliamentary history*, VIII, 13 January 1732, col. 875.

2. Ibid., cols. 877–8.

3. On George, see Aubrey Newman, *World turned inside out*. There is no satisfactory biography of George II, though Andrew Thompson is preparing one for Yale University Press. The peer is quoted in Nicholas B. Harding, 'Dynastic union', p. 140. Defoe is quoted in van Alstyne, *Genesis of American nationalism*, p. 23. The centrality of George to British foreign policy is demonstrated in Black, 'George II reconsidered'. For the growing tension with Spain, see Hildner, 'Role of the South Sea Company', pp. 322–8.

4. Thomson is quoted in Woodfine, *Britannia's glories*, p. 146. Tyrawly and Farnese are quoted in Black, *Collapse of the Anglo-French alliance*, p. 25 and p. 3.

5. Cobbett, *Parliamentary history*, VIII, col. 589; King's Speech to both houses, 27 June 1727, col. 595. On the use of Hanoverian envoys, see Black, *Collapse of the Anglo-French alliance*, p. 27. The continuity in foreign policy is stressed in Black, 'George II reconsidered', p. 40.

6. George II to Saladin, 30 October 1731, Hampton Court; George II to Louis XV, 26 October 1731, Hampton Court (NStAH Cal. Br. 24 Nr. 2002, fos. 2, 3).

7. George II to Townshend, no date, but probably 1728–9; Townshend to George II, 15 September 1728 (BL Add Mss 38507, fos. 231, 247).

8. The marginalia are in BL Add Mss 38507, fos. 228, 230, 234, 235, 236, 240. Newcastle and Walpole are quoted in Arthur McCandless Wilson, *French foreign policy*, p. 220, and Black, *Collapse of the Anglo-French alliance*, p. 153.

9. For an idea of the issues, see 'Chur-Braunschweigische Gravamina', in Höfler, *Der Kongress von Soissons*, pp. 152–60. The British observer is quoted in Black, *Collapse of the Anglo-French alliance*, pp. 139, 140.

10. Townshend is quoted in Black, 'When "natural allies" fall out', p. 122. See also Black, *Collapse of the Anglo-French alliance*, p. 62, and Hughes, *Law and politics*, pp. 206–58 (re Mecklenburg).

11. See Black, *Collapse of the Anglo-French alliance*, pp. 59–60, 71.

12. Black, *Collapse of the Anglo-French alliance*, p. 149; see also pp. 124–5, 101.

13. Townshend to George, no date but late 1720s, with royal marginalia (BL Add Mss 38507, fo. 230).

14. See the summary of the speeches by Sir Robert Walpole, Horatio Walpole, Lord Hervey and Sir William Yonge, 21 January 1731, Cobbett, *Parliamentary history*, VIII, col. 835. For the background to and consequences of the Treaty of Seville, see Basil Williams,

'Foreign policy', pp. 308–27, 439–51; and Lodge, 'Treaty of Seville', esp. pp. 37–9 re the centrality of anti-Austrian motivations.

15. On commercial issues, see 'Representation from the Board of Trade asserting the right of the subjects of Great Britain to cut Logwood in the Bay of Campeachy', March 1729, Cobbett, *Parliamentary history*, VIII, cols. 684–95; and 27 January 1730, cols. 776, 777. The attack on Heathcote is quoted in Black, *Parliament and foreign policy in the eighteenth century*, p. 66. On critiques of the Hanoverian connection, see 'Debate in the Lords, that the maintenance of 12,000 Hessian troops was burthensome and unnecessary', 17 April 1730, Cobbett, *Parliamentary history*, VIII, cols. 826–8.

16. Ibid., 27 January 1730, cols. 774, 776, 777; summary of speeches by Daniel Pulteney, William Pulteney and Sir William Wyndham, 21 March 1731, cols. 834–5.

17. Black, *Collapse of the Anglo-French alliance*, p. 155.

18. Ibid., p. 181.

19. See Black, 'Problem of the small state', pp. 11–13, and 'Anglo-Wittelsbach relations', esp. pp. 309–10. Black, *Collapse of the Anglo-French alliance*, p. 120; Black, *Parliament and foreign policy in the eighteenth century*, p. 209.

20. See Black, *Collapse of the Anglo-French alliance*, pp. 75, 83, 90.

21. Broglie is quoted in Arthur McCandless Wilson, *French foreign policy*, p. 86. For the parliamentary assault, see 'The Commons Address to the King respecting the harbour of Dunkirk', 11 February 1730, in Cobbett, *Parliamentary history*, VIII, col. 799. On the *Craftsman*, see Bolingbroke, *Contributions to 'The Craftsman'*, with entries on Austria and the balance of power: pp. 110, 120, 182–3, *et passim*. For the general framework of Bolingbroke's political thought and political activities, see Skinner, 'Principles and practice of opposition', which tends to place less emphasis on disputes about foreign policy. For Walpole's travails in foreign affairs, see Plumb, *Walpole*, II, pp. 200–32.

22. Black, *Collapse of the Anglo-French alliance*, pp. 173, 187, 183.

23. Ibid., pp. 163, 188. Browning, *Duke of Newcastle*, p. 61.

24. Ibid., p. 49. Black, *Collapse of the Anglo-French alliance*, p. 163.

25. Kinsky is quoted ibid., p. 130. My account here differs somewhat from Black, 'Fresh light', who tends to stress tensions between ministers (see esp. pp. 60–63).

26. Black, *Foreign policy of Walpole*, p. 40.

27. The *Newcastle Courant* is quoted in Cranfield, *Development of the provincial newspaper*, p. 69.

28. On commercial grievances, see 'The Commons consider of the petitions of the merchants of Bristol and Liverpool, relating to the Spanish depredations', 5 March 1731, Cobbett, *Parliamentary history*, VIII, cols. 859–60; and 'Debate in the Commons on the Spanish depredations', 13 February 1733, cols, 1191–4. For the pamphlet debate, see *Reasons for a war against Spain*; *The Spanish merchant's address*; and Lyttleton, *Considerations upon the present state*. Black, *Collapse of the Anglo-French alliance*, p. 188.

29. Horn, *Great Britain and Europe*, pp. 54, 95.

30. 'Debate in the Commons concerning the Hessian troops', 3 February 1731, summary of 'country party' speeches, Cobbett, *Parliamentary history*, XVIII, cols. 841–3. 'Debate in the Lords on the number of the Land Forces', 6 March 1733, col. 1236.

31. 'Debate in the Commons on the number of the land forces', 26 January 1732, ibid., cols. 902, 888, 896.

32. 'Debate in the Lords on the number of the Land Forces', 6 March 1733, ibid., cols. 895, 901, 1243–4, 1247.

9 Imperial Retreat, 1733–1736

1. Cobbett, *Parliamentary history*, VIII, 23 January 1735, col. 6.

2. Harrington to Robinson, 23 May 1734, Whitehall (BL Add Mss 32785, fos. 92–3).

3. Quoted in Woodfine, *Britannia's glories*, p. 128.

4. Cobbett, *Parliamentary history*, VIII, 16 January 1733, cols. 1168, 1175.

5. Newcastle to Horatio Walpole, 'private', 3 September 1734, Newcastle House (BL Add Mss 32785, fo. 409).

6. Copy of the marriage contract, 18 October 1733, Hampton Court (NStAH Hann. 92 Nr. 92, fo. 11). On the popularity of the match, see Hannah Smith, *Georgian monarchy*, p. 46. Robinson is quoted in Black, *Collapse of the Anglo-French alliance*, p. 184.

7. See Geyl, 'William IV', which contains a summary of the implications of Dutch decline for British perceptions of their own security, pp. 14–16.

8. Newcastle is quoted in Browning, *Duke of Newcastle*, pp. 66–7, Cobbett, *Parliamentary history*, IX, 28 March 1734, col. 589. Harrington to Robinson, 23 May 1734, Whitehall; Harrington to Waldegrave, 2 May 1734, Whitehall (BL Add Mss 32785, fos. 92, 16–20). Cobbett, *Parliamentary history*, IX, 17 January 1734, col. 182 (King's Speech). Concerns about the Barrier are to be found in ibid., 28 March 1734, col. 589 and Delafaye to Newcastle, 5 May 1734, Whitehall (BL Add Mss 32785, fos. 28–9).

9. Wills, *Jacobites and Russia*, pp. 145, 149. For monitoring of Jacobite correspondence, see e.g. the intercepted dispatch 'Copy of a letter from the Duke of Berwick [the Pretender's half-brother] to the Duke of Fitzjames [the Pretender]', 7 August 1734, Gaeta (BL Add Mss 32785, fos. 283–4). For Jacobite activity, see also Ó Ciardha, *Ireland and the Jacobite cause*. Newcastle to Walpole, 3 September 1734 (fo. 410).

10. Newcastle is quoted in Basil Williams, *Carteret and Newcastle*, p. 95. Newcastle to Horatio Walpole, 3 September 1734, Newcastle House (BL Add Mss 32785, fo. 409). Walpole's reported remarks are quoted in A. W. Ward, *Great Britain and Hanover*, p. 141. For a brutal critique of British policy during the War of the Polish Succession, see Lodge, 'English neutrality', esp. pp. 166–73. For a more positive view, see Black, 'British neutrality', esp. pp. 352, 356, 364–6.

11. Cobbett, *Parliamentary history*, IX, 17 January 1734, col. 182; Newcastle to Waldegrave, 23 May 1734, Whitehall; Harrington to Robinson, 23 May 1734, Whitehall (BL Add Mss 32785, fos. 86, 92–3).

12. 'Debate in the Lords on the Mutiny Bill', 13 March 1735, Cobbett, *Parliamentary history*, IX, cols. 870ff; 6 February 1734, col. 280; 'Debate in the Commons on the number of the land forces', 6 February 1734, col. 266.

13. 'Debate in the Lords on the Mutiny Bill', 13 March 1735, Cobbett, *Parliamentary history*, IX, cols. 876, 879–80.

14. 'Debate in the Commons on Sir John Rushout's motion for copies of the instructions sent to the British ministers in France and Spain, relating to the execution of the Treaty of Seville', Cobbett, *Parliamentary history*, IX, 23 January 1734, col. 210. See also 17 January, col. 198; 19 January, cols. 211, 212. On the Excise crisis, see Langford, *Excise crisis*.

15. 'Debate in the Commons on Sir John Rushout's motion for copies of the instructions sent to the British ministers in France and Spain, relating to the execution of the Treaty of Seville', 23 January 1734, Cobbett, *Parliamentary history*, IX, cols. 202, 206.

16. Ibid., col. 203; 'Debate in the Commons on Mr Sandys' motion for the instructions given to the British minister in Poland', 25 January 1734, col. 220.

17. Cobbett, *Parliamentary history*, IX, 23 January 1735, col. 690; various speakers on 7 February 1735 summarized in col. 693; 29 March 1734, col. 593. For other examples of commercial grievances against government, see 'Debate in the House of Lords on a motion relating to the Treaty of Seville', 6 March 1735, col. 868. See also Sir William Wyndham's remarks in the same vein in 'Debate in the Commons on Mr Sandys' motion for the instructions given to the British minister in Poland', 25 January 1734, col. 226.

18. 'Debate in the Commons on the subsidy to Denmark', 28 February 1735, in Cobbett, *Parliamentary history*, IX, col. 853, summarizing the speeches of Sir William Wyndham, Mr Pulteney, Sir John Barnard, Mr Sandys, Mr Shippen and Sir John Hynde Cotton; 6 February 1734, col. 277; 28 March 1734, col. 599.

19. Ibid., 23 January 1735, col. 682.

20. 'Debate in the Commons on Mr Sandys' motion for the instructions given to the British minister in Poland', 25 January 1734, cols. 218, 225; 'Debate in the House of Lords on a motion relating to the Treaty of Seville', 6 March 1735, col. 869.
21. 'Debate in the Commons on the address of thanks', 17 January 1734, Cobbett, *Parliamentary history*, IX, col. 190; 28 March 1734, col. 592. Basil Williams, *Carteret and Newcastle*, p. 94, takes the traditional view. For the latest account, see Andrew C. Thompson, *Britain, Hanover*, pp. 168–87.
22. Black, *Foreign policy of Walpole*, pp. 33, 41–3; Black, 'British neutrality', p. 260.
23. 'Debate in the Commons on Sir John Rushout's motion for copies of the instructions sent to the British ministers in France and Spain, relating to the execution of the Treaty of Seville', Cobbett, *Parliamentary history*, IX, 23 January 1734, cols. 216, 208; 'Debate in the Commons on Mr Sandys' motion for the instructions given to the British minister in Poland', 25 January 1734, col. 215.
24. See for example Horatio Walpole to Robinson, 19 May 1736, The Hague (BL Add Mss 23798, fos. 58–60); Robinson to Harrington, 5 February 1736, Vienna (NA 80/120 Germany/Empire, unfoliated). Robinson's fears about the remoteness of a Habsburg recovery are quoted in Black, 'When "natural allies" fall out', p. 120.
25. See (copy of) the secret letter from Robinson to Harrington, 7 March 1736, Vienna, and also 4 January 1736, Vienna (NA SP 80/120 Germany/Empire, unfoliated).
26. Cobbett, *Parliamentary history*, IX, 15 January 1736, cols. 981–2, 975.
27. Robinson to Weston, 5 February and 3 March 1736, Vienna (NA SP 80/120 Germany/Empire, unfoliated); Newcastle to H. Walpole, 3 September 1734, Newcastle House (BL Add Mss 32785, fo. 407). Horatio Walpole is quoted in Black, *Foreign policy of Walpole*, p. 15. The Ottoman Empire is addressed in Everard Fawkener to Newcastle, 16/27 May 1736 (BL Add Mss 23798, fo. 127). See also for French mediation, Cassels, *Struggle for the Ottoman Empire*, pp. 156–70.
28. Tilson to Robinson, 30 August 1736, Hanover; Sir Everard Fawkener to Newcastle, 8 May 1736, Constantinople (BL Add Mss 23798, fos. 541–3, 18). See Horn, *Great Britain and Europe*, p. 125.
29. Cobbett, *Parliamentary history*, IX, 15 January 1736, col. 982.
30. Van Alstyne, 'Significance of the Mississippi Valley', esp. p. 218. 'A petition from several Bristol merchants trading to America, complaining of the Spanish depredations', 6 February 1731, Cobbett, *Parliamentary history*, VIII, cols. 842–3. Newcastle to Waldegrave, 13 May 1734, Whitehall (BL Add Mss 32785, fo. 42). Armstrong is quoted in Doll, *Revolution, religion* p. 42.
31. Stourzh, *Benjamin Franklin*, p. 41, and van Alstyne, *Rising American empire*, p. 16.
32. Stourzh, *Benjamin Franklin*, pp. 50, 101. Egnal, *Mighty empire*, p. 88.
33. See Draper, *Struggle for power*, pp. 97–8 (remarks attributed to Walpole).
34. Van Alstyne, *Rising American empire*, pp. 15–16.

10 The Colonial Mirage, 1737–1739

1. Cobbett, *Parliamentary history*, X, 3 February 1738, col. 448.
2. Ibid., 3 March 1738, cols. 587–8.
3. See Woodfine, *Britannia's glories*, pp. 96, 88. This is the standard work.
4. Horace Walpole to Newcastle, 29 July 1735 (BL Add Mss 32791, fo. 353). See Woodfine, *Britannia's glories*, pp. 82, 119, 43; and Pares, *War and trade*, esp. pp. 1–52. On the collusion between the Royal Navy and smugglers, see Nelson, 'Contraband trade', p. 60. On Central America, see F. G. Dawson, 'William Pitt's settlement', pp. 682–4. On Georgia, see Reese, 'Georgia', and Levenson, 'Impact of gifts and trade'. I thank Miss Levenson and the organizers of the workshop for letting me have a copy of this paper.
5. 'The merchants' petition of 11 October 1737', in Woodfine, *Britannia's glories*, pp. 245, 133. For the depositions, see BL Add Mss 32796, fos. 77–110. See also the case of the *St James* of Bristol as discussed in Newcastle to Keene, 3 October 1737, Hampton Court

(ibid., fo. 1), together with the deposition of John Curtis, the commander of the *St James* (fos. 5–7). On the role of City merchants in the onslaught on Walpole, see Henderson, *London and the national government*, pp. 178–210. On the West Indian lobby generally, see Penson, 'London West India interest'.

6. The *London Evening Post* is quoted in Woodfine, *Britannia's glories*, p. 100. On theatrical indictments of the ministry's policy, see Avery and Scouten, 'Opposition to Sir Robert Walpole'. For attacks in the provincial press, see Cranfield, *Development of the provincial newspaper*, p. 132.

7. Cobbett, *Parliamentary history*, X, 3 February 1738, col. 448; 1 March 1739, col. 1131; Carteret on 1 February 1739, col. 877; Bathurst on 1 February 1739, col. 934; Carteret on 8 February 1739, col. 1014; Cholmondeley on 1 February 1739, col. 909.

8. Black, *Parliament and foreign policy in the eighteenth century*, p. 3; Cobbett, *Parliamentary history*, X, 3 March 1738, cols. 591, 594; Pulteney's marathon attack of 30 March 1738, cols. 643–62; 15–16 March 1738, cols. 636–8; 2 May 1738, cols. 745–54. On the additional naval spending, see Woodfine, *Britannia's glories*, p. 142.

9. Ibid., p. 183. On anti-Spanish stereotypes, see Michael Duffy, *The Englishman and the foreigner*, pp. 23–7, and especially the print depicted on p. 134. For prints on the Spanish 'depredations', see also Atherton, *Political prints*, pp. 169–71, with emphasis on 'honour' rather than trade or empire. Many of the images depict Britain in unnatural acts with the Bourbons. Barnard on 3 March 1738 in Cobbett, *Parliamentary history*, X, cols. 629–30; 'Proceedings in the Commons on the petitions relating to the Spanish Depredations', 3 March 1738, cols. 572, 622, *et passim*.

10. Waldegrave to Newcastle, 12 November 1737, Fontainebleau (BL Add Mss 32796, fo. 70), reporting a conversation which Lady Bolingbroke had had with Fleury. 'The idea of a Patriot King' in Bolingbroke, *Letters on the spirit of patriotism*, pp. 115–17. Hart, *Viscount Bolingbroke*, pp. 156–7, seems to underplay the importance of relations with Europe for his conception of a 'patriot king'. For the 'patriot king' as a critique of George II generally as well as his stance on the Spanish issue, see Varey, 'Hanover, Stuart'. For the idea as a protest against national corruption, see Burtt, *Virtue transformed*, pp. 103–9.

11. Bolingbroke, *Letters on the spirit of patriotism*, pp. 120–22. On the 'isolationist' and insular strain in Bolingbroke, see Kramnick, *Bolingbroke and his circle*, pp. 185–6.

12. Lyttelton, *Letters from a Persian*, p. 167. Nicholas B. Harding, 'Dynastic union', p. 169. See Cannon, *Samuel Johnson*, pp. 49–51. Original debates in Hoover, *Samuel Johnson's parliamentary reporting*, pp. 78–95. *Marmor Norfolkiense* is reprinted in Johnson, *Political Writings*, pp. 22–51 (quotation, p. 41).

13. Weston to Robinson, 22 May 1736, Whitehall (BL Add Mss 23798, fo. 73). Re communication, see Harrington to Robinson, 22 May 1736, Whitehall (fo. 71), which announces that the King has appointed Horatio Walpole 'to attend him during his residence in those parts'. Robinson was henceforth to correspond with Walpole there and receive royal instructions from him. Visitors to Hanover are remarked on in George Tilson to Robinson, 5 August 1736, Hanover (fo. 391). Walpole is quoted in Arthur McCandless Wilson, *French foreign policy*, p. 87.

14. Horatio Walpole to Robinson, 15 May 1736, The Hague, and 24 June 1736 (BL Add Mss 23798, fos. 50, 187); Harrington to Robinson, 23 March 1736, Whitehall (NA SP 80/120 Germany/Empire, unfoliated); Harrington to Robinson, 15 May 1736, Whitehall (BL Add Mss 23798, fo. 44). See also Horatio Walpole to Robinson, 15 May 1736, The Hague (ibid., fo. 50).

15. Woodfine, *Britannia's glories*, pp. 153 (from the *Craftsman*, 17 June 1738), 102.

16. Ibid., p. 121.

17. See 'Debate in both houses on the Prince of Wales' Allowance', 22 February 1737, Cobbett, *Parliamentary history* X, cols. 1352–60; Woodfine, *Britannia's glories*, p. 124; Nicholas B. Harding, 'Dynastic Union', p. 158. On Pitt's first speech, see Rosebery, *Chatham*, pp. 157–64.

18. Black, *Pitt the Elder*, p. 37.

19. Cobbett, *Parliamentary history*, X, 3 February 1738, col. 412; 2 May 1738, col. 760; 6 February 1739, col. 790. See also Woodfine, 'Ideas of naval power'.

20. Cobbett, *Parliamentary history*, X, 1 March 1739, col. 1213; Woodfine, *Britannia's glories* pp. 170, 176.

21. See Woodfine, *Britannia's glories*, p. 123; Cobbett, *Parliamentary history*, X, 6 March 1739, col. 1347; 3 February 1738, col. 421.

22. Ibid., 30 March 1738, cols. 705, 665. Black, *Foreign policy of Walpole*, p. 108.

23. Cobbett, *Parliamentary history*, X, 1 February 1739, col. 932; 3 March 1738, cols. 586–7, 689.

24. Ibid., 3 March 1738, cols. 636, 607.

25. Keene is quoted in Woodfine, *Britannia's glories*, pp. 36, 158. For fears of a Franco-Austrian rapprochement and French penetration of the Baltic see Dickens to Harrington, 22 February 1738, Berlin, and Harrington to Dickens, 6 January 1738, Whitehall (NA SP 90/44 Prussia, unfoliated).

26. Harrington to Dickens, 11 April 1738, Whitehall (ibid.).

27. Dickens to Harrington, 21 June 1738, Berlin (ibid.). See also the earlier dark hints in Dickens to Harrington, 8 April 1738, Berlin.

28. Cobbett, *Parliamentary history*, X, 9 March 1738, cols. 497–503.

29. Ibid., 2 May 1738, col. 767.

30. Ibid., 3 February 1738, cols. 512–13, 518, 445. Woodfine, *Britannia's glories*, pp. 32, 139. Wills, *Jacobites and Russia*, p. 154.

31. Cobbett, *Parliamentary history*, X, 30 March 1738, col. 688; 5 May 1738, col. 827; 1 February 1739, cols. 947, 591.

32. Ibid., 2 May 1738, col. 767; 30 March 1738, cols. 688–9. Woodfine, *Britannia's glories*, p. 22.

33. Cobbett, *Parliamentary history*, X, 30 March 1738, cols. 675–6, 697–9, 726.

34. Horace Walpole to Keene, 31 October 1737, The Hague (BL Add Mss 32/96, fo. 39). Woodfine, *Britannia's glories*, p. 138.

35. 'King's Speech', 1 February 1739, Cobbett, *Parliamentary history*, X, cols. 874–5.

36. Ibid., 23 February 1739, cols. 1039–40; 6 March 1739, col. 1260; 1 March 1739, col. 1212; 8 March 1739, cols. 1275, 1283. On parliamentary critcism re Georgia, see Reese, 'Georgia', pp. 184–7. For the question of 'honour', see Temperley, 'Causes', pp. 226–8.

37. Cobbett, *Parliamentary history*, X, 1 February 1739, col. 877; 1 March 1739, col. 1194. Trevor to Harrington, 16 January 1739, The Hague (NA SP 84/378 Holland, fos. 51–3). On Hervey's support for the ministry over Spain, see Halsband, *Lord Hervey*, pp. 240–41.

38. Trevor to Harrington, 6, 9 and 16 January 1739, The Hague (NA SP 84/378 Holland, fos. 1, 29, 55, 57, 58–9, 54). Cobbett, *Parliamentary history*, X, 8 March 1739, col. 1255. In the same vein, see also Hardwicke in ibid., 1 March 1739, cols. 1157–8. On the total failure of British overtures and Austria's growing dependence on France, see Black, 'When "natural allies" fall out', pp. 141–2.

39. Cobbett, *Parliamentary history*, X, 1 March 1739, cols. 947, 951, 1192, 1240. 'Debate in the Commons on the Convention with Spain', 8 March 1739, col. 1254. Woodfine, *Britannia's glories*, pp. 68–9. See also *Convention vindicated*.

40. Carteret's remarks are reported in Cobbett, *Parliamentary history*, X, 10 May 1739, col. 1378.

41. Ibid., 1 March 1739, cols. 1156–7, 1195.

42. Ibid., cols. 1214, 1136; 10 May 1739, col. 1393; 4 June 1739, col. 1416. Black, *America or Europe?*, p. 33. The lack of interest in Europe before 1740 is evident, e.g. in the *Gentleman's Magazine*, January to May 1739.

43. Cobbett, *Parliamentary history*, X, 6 February 1739, col. 1007; 1 February 1739, cols. 918, 922, 927.

44. All this is closely based on Woodfine, *Britannia's glories*, pp. 34–5, 59, 216, 224. Cobbett, *Parliamentary history*, X, 1 March 1739, col. 1157.

45. Ibid., 15 November 1739, cols. 1–2.

11 Imperial Isolation, 1740–1742

1. Quoted in Langford, *Modern British foreign policy*, p. 118.
2. Cobbett, *Parliamentary history*, XI, 18 November 1740, cols. 627–8.
3. Ibid., XII, 13 April 1741, col. 178.
4. Quoted in Black, *British foreign policy in the age of Walpole*, p. 21.
5. Cobbett, *Parliamentary history*, XI, 15 November 1739, cols. 19, 10, 20, 17; see also Pulteney in 'Debate in the Commons on raising a body of Marines', 27 November 1739, cols. 173, 175; 15 November 1739, cols. 12, 16, 84; 27 November 1739, col. 179.
6. On the importance of European trade, see Fayle, 'Economic pressure', p. 436. For Vernon, see Richard Harding, 'Edward Vernon', esp. pp. 163–4, 175.
7. Kathleen Wilson, *Sense of the people*, p. 146. On Americans and Vernon, see van Alstyne, *Rising American empire*, p. 147. On Vernon-mania, see Kathleen Wilson, 'Empire, trade and popular politics'.
8. Woodfine, *Britannia's glories*, p. 212.
9. Quoted in Black, *Foreign policy of Walpole*, p. 18.
10. Black, *America or Europe?*, note to p. 32. Black, *British foreign policy in the age of Walpole*, pp. 152–3. Wills, *Jacobites and Russia*, p. 202.
11. Richter-Uhlig, *Hof und Politik*, pp. 141, 145.
12. See Newcastle to Steinberg, 5 March 1740, Newcastle House (BL Add Mss 32802, fo. 103) and W. Blair to Robinson, 8 September 1740, Hanover (BL Add Mss 23806, fo. 75). On the Hanoverian memorandum, see Allen, 'Anglo-Hanoverian connection', pp. 103, 107. On Münchhausen's attempt to smooth the way for a Hanoverian–British–Prussian alliance, see his *Münchhausens Berichte*.
13. Newcastle to Hardwicke, 27 July 1740, Claremont, in Hardwicke, *Life and correspondence*, I, p. 243.
14. Cobbett, *Parliamentary history*, XI, 18 November 1740, cols. 627–8, 653. Newcastle's notes on the cabinet meeting of 7 October 1740 are quoted at length in Richmond, *Navy in the war*, I, p. 95.
15. Newcastle to Hardwicke, 25 October 1740, Newcastle House, in Hardwicke, *Life and correspondence*, I, p. 251. For Anson, see Glyn Williams, *Prize of all the oceans*.
16. Cobbett, *Parliamentary history*, XI, 29 November 1739, col. 303.
17. Ibid., 29 November 1739, cols. 291, 303, 271.
18. Ibid., 21 February 1740, col. 494.
19. See 'Debate in the Lords on a motion for a vote of censure, for not sending Land Forces with Admiral Vernon to America', 15 April 1740, ibid., cols. 582–98, 591; 27 November 1739, col. 179; see also Shippen, 28 November 1739, col. 252.
20. Ibid., 22 December 1740, cols. 930–31. See also Richard Harding, *Amphibious warfare*, pp. 83–122, who tends to blame Vernon rather than the blue water strategy itself, and Kathleen Wilson, *Sense of the people*, p. 149.
21. Richard Harding, 'Sailors and gentlemen of parade', esp. p. 41. See also Richard Harding, *Amphibious warfare*, passim.
22. Kathleen Wilson, *Sense of the people*, p. 149. Cobbett, *Parliamentary history*, XI, passim.
23. Ibid., 8 December 1740, cols. 781, 788.
24. Earl of Chesterfield, 1 December 1740, in Cobbett, *Parliamentary history*, XI, cols. 732–4; Pitt on 26 January 1741, col. 1009; see also 18 November 1740, cols. 620–21.
25. Sir John Barnard on 13 February 1741, ibid., cols. 1256–9. For popular and pamphlet attacks on Walpole, see Goldsmith, 'Faction detected'.
26. Newcastle to Harrington, 31 July 1741 (BL Add Mss 35407, fo. 61).
27. Cobbett, *Parliamentary history*, XI, 13 February 1741, cols. 1047, 1216–17; see also in the same vein, Carteret on 13 February 1741, col. 1047.
28. Ibid., 13 December 1741, col. 1363.
29. See debates in ibid., cols 1047–1106; 13 February 1741, cols. 1269–84, 1274. In the

same vein, see 'Substance of Sandys' speech . . . on moving to remove Sir Robert Walpole', 15 February 1741 (which leads with the Treaty of Hanover), cols. 1242–3; 13 February 1741, cols. 1262–5. For the importance of the strategic critique in press and popular attacks on Walpole, see Bob Harris, 'London press', esp. pp. 61–2.

30. Newcastle to Harrington, 31 July 1741, Whitehall (BL Add Mss 35407, fo. 62).

31. Allen, 'Anglo-Hanoverian connection', pp. 114–16. Richter-Uhlig, *Hof und Politik*, p. 150. Dann, *Hanover and Great Britain*, p. 31.

32. Newcastle to Harrington, 14 July 1741 (BL Add Mss 35407, fos. 46, 48, 50).

33. Newcastle to Harrington, 31 July 1741, Whitehall (BL Add Mss 35407, fo. 6). Cobbett, *Parliamentary history*, XII, 13 April 1741, col. 168; see also the 'King's Speech', 8 April 1741, cols. 147–8. See also Clyve Jones, 'Further evidence'.

34. Ibid., 8/9 April 1741, col. 155; Sir Robert Walpole on 13 April 1741, col. 169; also col. 178.

35. On this, see Black, *Walpole*, pp. 168–9.

36. Andrew Stone to Lord Hardwicke, 21 June 1741, Whitehall (BL Add Mss 35407, fo. 39). George's preparations are discussed in the memorandum 'Quelles mesures serrent à prendre pour mêtre à couvert les Pais Allemands de S. M. contre toute insulte et irruption ennemic?' April 1741 (NStAH Hann. 91 du Pontpietin Nr. 1, fos. 20–22). McDomhnaill is quoted in Morley, *Irish opinion*, pp. 7–8.

37. Dann, *Hanover and Great Britain* p. 34; Newcastle to Harrington, 14 and 31 July 1741, Whitehall (BL Add Mss 35407, fos. 47, 59).

38. For ministerial evasions, see Newcastle to Harrington, 20 August 1741, Whitehall (BL Add Mss 35407, fo. 81). Dann, *Hanover and Great Britain*, p. 35. Allen, 'Anglo-Hanoverian connection', p. 122.

39. Harrington to Hardenberg, 23 August 1741 (NStAH Cal. Br. 24 Nr. 2004, fo. 11): 'I have the honour of returning to your Excellency, the instructions of which you apprised me, and assure you that I find them perfectly well phrased.' Harrington to Trevor, 20 September 1741, Luitzburg (BL Add Mss 35407, fo. 104). Newcastle's angst is very manifest in Newcastle to Hardwicke, 19 June 1741, Claremont, in Hardwicke, *Life and correspondence*, I, p. 259. Newcastle's memorandum, 'Considerations upon Lord Harrington's letters', 24 August 1741 (BL Add Mss 32697, fo. 454).

40. Copy of Neutrality Convention (NStAH Cal. Br. 24 Nr. 2004, fo. 184; 'Article separe et secret', fo. 192). Allen, 'Anglo-Hanoverian connection', pp. 123–4.

41. Dann, *Hanover and Great Britain*, pp. 38–9. Newcastle to Hardwicke, 11 October 1741, Claremont; Duke of Newcastle, 'Considerations upon the present state of affairs', 1 November 1741, Claremont (BL Add Mss 35407, fos. 118, 132).

42. Trevor to Courand, 19 September 1741, The Hague; Harrington to Trevor, 20 September 1741, Luitzburg (BL Add Mss 35407, fos. 100, 104).

43. For Newcastle's fears, see his memorandum of 1 November 1741; Newcastle to Hardwicke, 9, 18 and 12 September 1741, Claremont (BL Add Mss. 35407, fos. 452, 89, 109, 98).

44. Ibid., 9 and 18 September 1741 (fos. 91, 110–12).

45. Newcastle's memorandum of 1 November 1741 (ibid., fos. 452–6).

46. The circular is quoted in Dann, *Hanover and Great Britain*, p. 39. Walpole is quoted in Newcastle to Hardwicke, 11 October 1741, Claremont (BL Add Mss 35407, fo. 117). Hardenberg to George II, 9 January 1742, Paris (NStAH Cal. Br. 24 Nr. 2004, fos. 193, 195).

47. Pitt to the Earl of Chesterfield, 6 August 1741, Clifden, in Pitt, *Correspondence of William Pitt, Earl of Chatham*, I, pp. 1–2.

48. Cobbett, *Parliamentary history*, XII, col. 286. Dann, *Hanover and Great Britain*, p. 34. Carteret is quoted in Nicholas B. Harding, 'Dynastic union', p. 170. Cobbett, *Parliamentary history*, XII, 10 December 1742, col. 951; see also George Lyttleton's comments a year later: 1 December 1743, col. 196.

49. Ibid., 1 December 1741, col. 234; 4 December 1741, col. 270; 9 March 1742, col. 556; Pulteney, 9 March 1742, col. 582.

50. See Chesterfield on 4 December 1741, ibid., cols. 232–42; see also Pulteney on 23 March 1742, col. 582; 4 December 1741, col. 224.
51. Ibid., 1 December 1741, cols. 254–5; 4 December 1741, col. 227.
52. Ibid., 9 March 1742, col. 484.
53. 'Debate in the Commons on Lord Limerick's Motion for an appointing a committee to enquire into the conduct of affairs at home and abroad during the last twenty years', 13 February 1742, ibid., cols. 492–6.

12 The Empires Strike Back, 1742–1745

1. Cobbett, *Parliamentary history*, XII, 10 December 1742, col. 961. See also cols. 964–5.
2. Ibid., 6 December 1742, col. 909.
3. Quoted in Bob Harris, *Patriot press*, p. 136.
4. On Carteret's German lessons, see Basil Williams, *Carteret and Newcastle*, pp. 83–7. On Carteret's interest in Cervantes, see Carteret to Keene, London, 26 March 1737 os, in Keene, *Private correspondence*, pp. 7–9. Cobbett, *Parliamentary history*, XIII, 9 December 1743, cols. 358–9, directed at the Earl of Chesterfield.
5. The quotations are from Basil Williams, *Carteret and Newcastle*, pp. 136, 82; and Carteret to Prince William of Hesse, 2 March 1742, London (NStAH, Cal Br. 24 Nr. 2004, fos. 258, 260).
6. Black, *Parliament and foreign policy in the eighteenth century*, p. 76.
7. Lodge, 'So-called "Treaty of Hanau" ', p. 387. On the need to keep Frederick neutral, see Lodge, 'Russia, Prussia and Great Britain', pp. 579–81.
8. See Lodge, 'So-called "Treaty of Hanau" '; pp. 390–91. On the negotiations with Charles Albert, see Black, 'Problem of the small state', pp. 17–22.
9. Lodge, 'So-called "Treaty of Hanau" ', pp. 399–401.
10. On this see Rodger, 'Sea power and empire', p. 175.
11. Black, *America or Europe?*, p. 83; Wills, *Jacobites and Russia*, p. 215.
12. See Dann, *Hanover and Great Britain*, p. 38.
13. Cobbett, *Parliamentary history*, XII, col. 847. Basil Williams, *Carteret and Newcastle*, p. 123. Cobbett, *Parliamentary history*, XIII, 27 January 1744, col. 583. Nicholas B. Harding, 'Dynastic union', p. 177. Dann, *Hanover and Great Britain*, p. 52. Basil Williams, *Carteret and Newcastle*, p. 127.
14. Dann, *Hanover and Great Britain*, p. 51. 'Korrespondenz der Geheimen Räte mit dem englischen [sic] Gesandten Lord Hyndfort [sic] zu Berlin betr. die Deutschen Angelegenheiten, 1743–1744', Hanoverian Privy Councillors (Geheime Räte) to Hyndford, 11 April 1743 (NStAH Cal. Br. 24 Nr. 1736, fo. 1).
15. For French preoccupation with the Continental war, see M. S. Anderson, *War of the Austrian Succession*, pp. 156–7, 187. Cobbett, *Parliamentary history*, XII, 16 November 1742, cols. 833 (Tweedale), 868–9 (Barnard). Newcastle is quoted in Lodge, 'So-called "Treaty of Hanau" ', p. 385. George's conduct during the battle is described in Carteret to Newcastle, 27 June 1743, Dettingen (BL Add Mss 35407, fo. 210); the Hanoverian contribution is praised in 'Account of the battle of Dettingen', 27 June 1743 (fo. 216). The popular response is described in Hannah Smith, *Georgian monarchy*, pp. 108–9, and in Bob Harris, 'American idols', p. 122 (quoting Newcastle's steward).
16. Bob Harris, *Patriot Press*, pp. 124–9; and Gibbs, 'English attitudes', pp. 33–5. I have based my account mainly on the printed versions of speeches in Cobbett, *Parliamentary history*. These largely match the record available in manuscript and in other printed sources such as the diary of the MP William Hay: see Taylor and Jones, *Tory and Whig*, pp. 184–93, for the entries for 16 November, 1, 3, 6, 10 December 1742, 1 December 1743, and 18 January 1744. Much of the pamphlet literature was based on parliamentary speeches. To save space and avoid repetition, I have kept reference to these to a minimum.
17. Cobbett, *Parliamentary history*, XIII, 9 December 1743, cols. 376–7; 31 January 1744, cols. 570–71; 27 January 1744, col. 598. In the same vein, see the Marquess of Tweedale

on 9 December 1743, col. 380, and Lord Perceval on 11 January 1744, col. 428. Dann, *Hanover and Great Britain*, p. 56.

18. Mr Philips on 10 December 1742, Cobbett, *Parliamentary history*, XII, col. 1015; 9 December 1743, XIII, cols. 276–7, 329; 10 December 1742, XII, col. 1035. Richard Grenville to George Grenville, 22 November 1742, in Grenville, *Grenville papers*, p.19. I have dealt with the broader question of Pitt and Hanover in my essay 'Pitt and Hanover'. For the Lords debate on Hanover troops, see Black, 'House of Lords' pp. 128–9.

19. Cobbett, *Parliamentary history*, XIII, 9 December 1743, col. 339. Dann, *Hanover and Great Britain*, p. 33. See Cobbett, *Parliamentary history*, XIII, 1 December 1743, col. 230; 9 December 1743, col. 367.

20. Ibid., XII, cols. 1081–2. See also Bob Harris, *Patriot press*, p. 149, and the account in Hay's diary entries for 6 and 10 December 1742, in Taylor and Jones, *Tory and Whig*, pp. 186–7.

21. Sandwich's remarks are in Cobbett, *Parliamentary history*, XIII, 9 December 1743, cols. 276–7. The Wootton portrait is discussed in Dann, *Hanover and Great Britain*, p. 63. For the Hanoverian instructions, see George to du Pontpietin, Kensington Palace, 24 August 1742 (NStAH Hann. 91 du Pontpietin Nr. 1, fo. 46).

22. See Cruickshanks, *Political untouchables*, pp. 34–5. Cobbett, *Parliamentary history*, XIII, 1 December 1743, cols. 221, 223, 227. Black, *America or Europe?*, p. 113. Nicholas B. Harding, 'Dynastic union', p. 182.

23. Bob Harris, *Patriot press*, pp. 131, 136. Sandwich to Bedford, London, 21 November 1743, in Bedford, *Correspondence*, vol. I, p. 16.

24. Quoted in Black, *America or Europe?*, p. 40.

25. Cobbett, *Parliamentary history*, XII, 10 December 1742, col. 953; 1 December 1743, XIII, col. 189; 6 December 1743, cols. 245, 269. Newcastle is quoted in Nicholas B. Harding, 'Dynastic union', p. 222.

26. Cobbett, *Parliamentary history*, XII, 10 December 1742, col. 960. Most of the debate was couched in those terms: cols. 953–68, 979–99; 18–19 January 1744, XIII, cols. 482–3. See also Waller and Chesterfield, *The case of the Hanover forces*, esp. pp. 1–23.

27. Bob Harris, *Patriot press*, pp. 169, 173, 143. Cobbett, *Parliamentary history*, XII, 10 December 1742, col. 961; see also cols. 964–5. Gilbert, 'English background', p. 145.

28. Sandwich's remarks are in Cobbett, *Parliamentary history*, XII, 1 February 1743, cols. 1071–2, 1080. *The political maxims* is quoted in Gilbert, 'English background', pp. 148–9.

29. Cobbett, *Parliamentary history*, XIII, 11 January 1744, cols. 425–6. Gilbert, 'English background', p. 145. See Bob Harris, *Patriot Press*, pp. 144–5.

30. Cobbett, *Parliamentary history*, XIII, 27 January 1744, col. 585; 11 January 1744, col. 425.

31. Colley, *Britons, passim*. Geyken, 'German language', pp. 68–9. See also Geyken, *Gentlemen auf Reisen*. Black, *Pitt the Elder*, p. 49. Cobbett, *Parliamentary history*, XIII, 9 December 1743, cols. 320–23, 342–3. Bob Harris, *Patriot press*, p. 128. Gerald Newman, *Rise of English nationalism*, emphasizes Gallophobia, but makes no reference to anti-Hanoverian agitation or the German connection.

32. Cobbett, *Parliamentary history*, XIII, 31 January 1744, col. 563.

33. Nicholas B. Harding, 'Dynastic union', pp. 194, 204. Gibbs, 'English attitudes', p. 46. Fourth Earl of Sandwich's speech on the Hanoverians, 27 January, 1744, in Wiener and Plumb, *Great Britain*, p. 84.

34. Nicholas B. Harding, 'Dynastic union', pp. 183, 117. Black, *Knights errant*, p. 115. Bob Harris, *Politics and the nation*, p. 117. John Phillips on 6 December 1742, Cobbett, *Parliamentary history*, XII, col. 913; Waller on 6 December 1743, XIII, col. 246. William Hay's diary entry for 18 January 1744, in Taylor and Jones, *Tory and Whig*, p. 190.

35. Bob Harris, *Patriot press*, pp. 157–9. For print depictions of Hanover, see Michael Duffy, *The Englishman and the foreigner*, p. 144, and Atherton, *Political prints*, pp. 181–3.

36. Lord Perceval on 10 December 1742, Cobbett, *Parliamentary history*, XII, col. 1044. Carteret speech of 27 January 1744, in Wiener and Plumb, *Great Britain*, pp. 85, 87. Carteret on 1 December 1743, Cobbett, *Parliamentary history*, XIII, cols. 123, 129; 27 January 1744 in Wiener and Plumb, *Great Britain*, p. 86; 1 December 1743, Cobbett, *Parliamentary history*, XIII, col. 121; 6 December 1742, XII, col. 916; Sandys on 6 December 1742, XII, col. 918; 29 April 1742, col. 613.

37. Ibid., XII, 10 December 1742, col. 971; XIII, 1 December 1743, col. 174; in the same vein also col. 178, and XII, 6 December 1742, col. 918.

38. Ibid., XII, 6 December 1742, col. 909; 10 December 1742, cols. 973–4. Walpole's speech of December 1742 quoted in *Memoirs of Horatio, Lord Walpole*, vol. II, pp. 48–9. Cobbett, *Parliamentary History*, XIII, 19 January 1744, col. 464; in the same vein, see 1 December 1743, cols. 218ff. See also Lord Berkeley on 1 December 1743, col. 107, and Thomas Winnington on 1 December 1743, cols. 178–9. Perceval on 10 December 1742, XII, col. 1044; and in same vein, on 11 January 1744, XII, cols. 428–9.

39. Cobbett, *Parliamentary history*, XII, 10 December 1742, col. 974. In the same vein, see also Sir William Yonge on 6 December 1742, cols. 909–10. See also the speech by Perceval (which was subsequently printed) on 11 January 1744, XIII, cols. 431–2, 447–9.

40. Mr Fane on 11 January 1744, ibid., col. 392. William Hay diary entry for 18 January 1744, in Taylor and Jones, *Tory and Whig*, p. 190.

41. Nicholas B. Harding, 'Dynastic union', p. 225.

42. See Allen, 'Anglo-Hanoverian connection', p. 162.

43. See Wiener and Plumb, *Great Britain*, p. 88; Cobbett, *Parliamentary history*, XII, 10 December 1742, col. 946, and again, col. 861. See also Hardwicke on 9 December 1743, XIII, cols. 343–50. 'A list of the members who voted for and against the Hanoverian troops being taken into British pay', 10 December 1742, XII, cols. 1053–7 (260 yes, 193 no), 1017; 9 December 1743, XIII, col. 381 (36 for vote to disband, 71 against); 11 January 1744, XIII, col. 393 (277 yes, 165 no, in debate on Flanders troops).

44. Walpole, *Interest of Great Britain*, pp. 12–13. Lord Bathurst is quoted in Nicholas B. Harding, 'Dynastic union', p. 212. Another defence of Hanover was *A vindication of our present royal family*.

45. Cobbett, *Parliamentary history*, XIII, 31 January 1744, cols. 564–5; 27 January 1744, cols. 574–5.

13 The American Empire Restores the Balance in the German Empire, 1745–1748

1. Quoted in Mimler, *Der Einfluß*, p. 90.

2. On this, see Lodge, 'Hanau controversy'. For a partial defence of Carteret, see Basil Williams, 'Carteret and the so-called Treaty of Hanau'.

3. For figures, see Mimler, *Der Einfluß*, pp. 43–6.

4. Newcastle to Chesterfield, 20 November 1745, Newcastle House; and 6 January 1746, in Chesterfield, *Private correspondence*, pp. 81–3, 97.

5. Chesterfield to Newcastle, 30 March 1745, The Hague; 23 February 1745, The Hague; 22 February 1745, Newcastle House, in Chesterfield, *Private correspondence*, pp. 34, 11, 16.

6. Dann, *Hanover and Great Britain*, pp. 59, 69. Frederick is quoted in Basil Williams, *Carteret and Newcastle*, p. 155. Chesterfield to Newcastle, 10 March 1745, The Hague, in Chesterfield, *Private correspondence*, p. 24.

7. The subterfuge over the payment of the Hanoverians is described in Peregrine Furze to Pitt, 31 July 1746, Paymaster-General's Office, in Pitt, *Correspondence of William Pitt, Earl of Chatham*, vol. I, p. 5. Furze was the secretary and accountant of the Paymaster's Office. Newcastle to Chesterfield, 6 January 1746, in Chesterfield, *Private correspondence*, p. 97. George Grenville to Thomas Grenville, 13 May 1745, Admiralty Office, in Grenville, *Grenville papers*, vol. I, pp. 37–8. For parliamentary discussion of the Hanoverians, see

Cobbett, *Parliamentary history*, XIII, 18 February 1745, col. 1198, and 22 February 1745, cols. 1201–2.

8. Walpole is quoted in Basil Williams, *Carteret and Newcastle*, p. 169. Strange and the *Westminster Journal* are quoted in Nicholas B. Harding, 'Dynastic union', pp. 227–8. Turner is quoted in Bob Harris, *Politics and the nation*, p. 6, referring to comments made in May 1746. *Old England* is quoted in Black, *America or Europe?*, p. 59.

9. The 'Declaration' is quoted in Cruickshanks, *Political untouchables*, pp. 47–8. [William Harper], *The advice of a friend to the army and people of Scotland* is quoted in Nicholas B. Harding, 'Dynastic union', pp. 229–30.

10. See Rodger, 'Continental commitment', p. 43 for the figures. Newcastle to Chesterfield, 20 November 1745, in Chesterfield, *Private correspondence*, p. 86. Chesterfield to the Duke of Bedford, 17 September 1745, in Bedford, *Correspondence*, vol. I, p. 50. Chesterfield to Newcastle, 25 November 1745, Dublin Castle, in Chesterfield, *Private correspondence*, p. 87. Chesterfield to Bedford, 17 September 1745, Dublin Castle, in Bedford, *Correspondence*, vol. I, p. 50.

11. Newcastle to Chesterfield, 5 March 1746, in Chesterfield, *Private correspondence*, p. 119. Wills, *Jacobites and Russia*, p. 226. F. J. McLynn, *France and the Jacobite rising of 1745*, argues that the rising would have succeeded if it had had effective French support.

12. Horatio Walpole is quoted in Basil Williams, *Carteret and Newcastle*, p. 169. George Grenville to Thomas Grenville, 13 May 1745, Admiralty Office, in Grenville, *Grenville papers*, p. 38. Sandwich to Bedford, 4 July 1745, London, in Bedford, *Correspondence*, vol. I, pp. 22–3. Newcastle to Chesterfield, 9 October 1745, in Chesterfield, *Private correspondence*, p. 74. Keene to Castries, 16 July 1745, New Park, ibid., p. 66. Newcastle on Flanders is quoted in Black, *America or Europe?*, p. 59. Newcastle to Chesterfield, 20 November 1745, Newcastle House, in Chesterfield, *Private correspondence*, p. 81.

13. See Bob Harris, *Politics and the nation*, pp. 123, 81.

14. Chesterfield to Newcastle, 6 December 1745, Dublin Castle, in Chesterfield, *Private correspondence*, p. 92.

15. Hamish M. Scott, 'True principles', p. 62. Chesterfield to Newcastle, 23 March 1745, and 6 December 1745, Dublin Castle, in Chesterfield, *Private correspondence*, pp. 30, 92.

16. Chesterfield to Newcastle, 25 November 1745, ibid., p. 89.

17. 'Joint representation of the Duke of Bedford and others to the Duke of Newcastle', 30 March 1746, London, in Bedford, *Correspondence*, vol. I, p. 65. Shirley is quoted in Draper, *Struggle for power*, p. 104. See Buffington, 'Canada expedition', pp. 556–9, 563, for the impetus given by the capture of Louisburg to 'blue water' thinking.

18. The *Gentleman's Magazine* is quoted in Mimler, *Der Einfluß*, p. 90. Newspaper quotations are from Black, *Natural and necessary enemies*, p. 50.

19. Prince, *Extraordinary events*, esp. pp. 18–19. See also Mimler, *Der Einfluß*, pp. 46–7; van Alstyne, *Genesis of American nationalism*, pp. 34–6; Egnal, *Mighty empire*, p. 39.

20. On expansionism in this period, see Egnal, *Mighty empire*, pp. 38–9. The Pennsylvanian is quoted in van Alstyne, *Genesis of American nationalism*, p. 36. Bollan, *Importance and advantage of Cape Breton*, pp. 76, 90–92, 101, 102–3, 154 (quoting with approval from a letter from a gentleman in New England to his friend in London).

21. On the importance of India, see Mimler, *Der Einfluß*, pp. 177–8. Chesterfield to Newcastle, 24 October 1745, Dublin Castle, and 25 November 1745, Dublin Castle, in Chesterfield, *Private correspondence*, pp. 78, 89.

22. Newcastle to Bedford, 21 April 1747, Newcastle House, in Bedford, *Correspondence*, vol. I, p. 210.

23. Pitt to Richard Grenville, 30 June 1747, London, in Grenville, *Grenville papers*, p. 66. M. S. Anderson, *War of the Austrian succession*, p. 174.

24. Bedford to Sandwich, 19 October 1747, London, and 28 January 1748, London, in Bedford, *Correspondence*, vol. I, pp. 273–4, 316.

25. Chesterfield to Newcastle, 25 November 1745, and Newcastle to Chesterfield, 15 March 1746, in Chesterfield, *Private correspondence*, pp. 89, 128. Draper, *Struggle for power*,

p. 133. Chesterfield to Newcastle, 24 October 1745, in Chesterfield, *Private correspondence*, p. 77.

26. On the Dutch, see Sosin, 'Louisburg', p. 521. Henry Pelham to George Grenville, 30 April 1748, in Grenville, *Grenville papers*, p. 74. Pelham is quoted in Richmond, *Navy in the war*, vol. III, p. 241. Cobbett, *Parliamentary history*, XIV, 5 February 1750, col. 684.

27. Newcastle to Sandwich, 29 March 1748, in Richmond, *Navy in the war*, vol. III, p. 240. Chesterfield to Newcastle, 24 October 1745, in Chesterfield, *Private correspondence*, p. 78.

28. The *Newcastle Courant* is quoted in Black, *Natural and necessary enemies*, p. 51. Rodger, 'Continental commitment', p. 39. American responses are discussed in van Alstyne, *Genesis of American nationalism*, pp. 40–41. For relations between Britain and the colonial militias, see Leach, 'Brothers in arms?', which surprisingly contains nothing on the return of Louisburg.

29. For Venters Cornwall, see Cobbett, *Parliamentary history*, XIV, 8 February 1748, cols. 157–64.

30. Black, *America or Europe?*, p. 60. See Glyn Williams, *Prize of all the oceans*, pp. 222–8.

31. Henry Fox, Cobbett, *Parliamentary history*, XIV, 8 February 1748, col. 167.

14 Imperial Pre-emptions, 1748–1752

1. Newcastle to Hardwicke, 2 September 1749, Claremont, in Hardwicke, *Life and correspondence*, vol. II, p. 23.

2. Cobbett, *Parliamentary history*, XIV, 22 February 1751, col. 965–6.

3. Quoted in Hamish M. Scott, 'True principles', p. 72.

4. Quoted in Draper, *Struggle for power*, p. 85.

5. Black in *America or Europe?*, p. 68, and 'British attempt' stresses the centrality of Europe at this point. For pericentric views, see Clayton, 'Duke of Newcastle', which stresses the impulses coming from London, and Higgonet, 'Origins of the Seven Years War', which emphasizes local initiatives.

6. Rodger, *Command of the ocean*, p. 261. See Baugh, 'Withdrawing from Europe', p. 12. Newcastle is quoted in Bob Harris, *Politics and the nation*, p. 5.

7. Documents on issues of demarcation are to be found in Pease, *Anglo-French boundary disputes*. On the worsening guerrilla warfare, see Matthew C. Ward, *Breaking the back-country*, p. 16. For Halifax and the Board of Trade, see Basye, *Lords Commissioners*, pp. 32–104. On differing policy on 'gifts', see Jacobs, *Diplomacy and Indian gifts*, esp. pp. 29–45: 'Presents: The British and the French systems compared'.

8. See Black, *America or Europe?*, p. 61. On the marginal importance of America, see Higgonet, 'Origins of the Seven Years War', pp. 60, 63; Clayton, 'Duke of Newcastle', pp. 572–3, agrees that Newcastle was not fully engaged until 1754.

9. Hardwicke to Newcastle, 30 August 1749, Wimpole, in Hardwicke, *Life and correspondence*, vol. II, pp. 17, 21. See Bob Harris, *Politics and the nation*, pp. 253 ,118–19. Black, *Natural and necessary enemies*, p. 57 (re *Newcastle Courant*). Rodger, *Command of the ocean*, p. 260.

10. David Hume, 'Of the balance of power' and 'Of the Protestant Succession', in *Essays*, pp. 332–41, 502–11. On Hume and Britain's position in Europe, see the very stimulating piece by John Robertson, 'Universal monarchy and the liberties of Europe', esp. pp. 350–54. 'Of public credit' is in *Political essays*, pp. 166–78. My reading of Hume has also benefited enormously from Istvan Hont's commanding and demanding *Jealousy of trade*, pp. 328–31, *et passim*.

11. This paragraph is largely based on Florian Schui, 'Prussia's "Trans-oceanic moment" ', and Ernest M. Satow, *Silesian loan*, pp. 24–35.

12. Newcastle to Hardwicke, 25 August 1749, Newcastle House (BL Add Mss 32719, fo. 71). Bob Harris, *Politics and the nation*, p. 167. Glickman, 'Career of Sir John Hynde Cotton'.

13. Wills, *Jacobites and Russia*, p. 231; Allen, 'Anglo-Hanoverian connection', pp. 176, 215.
14. 'Projet de mémoire instructif pour le Comte de Richecourt', 12 November 1751, Vienna (HHStA England Korrespondenz, Berichte Karton 100, fo. 23). On the decline of Anglo-Austrian relations more generally, see Schilling, *Kaunitz*, pp. 52–98, esp. pp. 53–4, 56, 62, 76. Browning, 'British orientation', takes a more positive view.
15. Hume, *Essays*, p. 510. Hardwicke to Newcastle, 30 August 1749, Wimpole, in Hardwicke, *Life and correspondence*, vol. II, p. 22.
16. See Kathleen Wilson, *Sense of the people*, pp. 186–7. Lowther is quoted in Bob Harris, *Politics and the nation*, p. 283.
17. Ibid., p. 18, on the call for a new Patriot King. Kathleen Wilson, *Sense of the people*, pp. 189, 191, *et passim*, on empire as an 'antidote' to national enervation; Black, *America or Europe?*, pp. 182–3, on the 'imaginative imperative' of empire.
18. For suspicions re Cumberland, see Romney Sedgwick's introduction to George III, *Letters to Lord Bute*, p. xx. On the continued threat in the Highlands, see Bob Harris, *Politics and the nation*, pp. 166–71.
19. For the figures, see Baugh, 'Withdrawing from Europe'; Schumpeter, *English overseas trade statistics*; and Richard Middleton, *Bells of victory*, p. 2.
20. Newcastle to Hardwicke, 2 September 1749, Claremont, in Hardwicke, *Life and correspondence*, vol. II, p. 23. Horn, *Sir Charles Hanbury Williams*, p. 50. Black, *America or Europe?*, p. 122. Horn, 'Cabinet controversy' pp. 463–4. See Black, *America or Europe?*, p. 69, for very similar remarks from September 1750.
21. Newcastle is quoted in Browning, *Duke of Newcastle*, p. 182. Abercromby and Robson are quoted in Draper, *Struggle for power*, p. 85, and Van Alstyne, *Genesis of American nationalism*, p. 47, from Joseph Robson, *An account of six years residence in Hudson's Bay from 1733 to 1736, and 1744 to 1747* (London, 1752).
22. Douglas is quoted in Savelle, 'Appearance of an American attitude', p. 660.
23. Quoted in Baugh, 'Withdrawing from Europe', pp. 14–16, and Stourzh, *Benjamin Franklin*, p. 113.
24. See Deobarate, 'France in North America'. On French strategy, see van Alstyne, *Empire and independence*, p. 19.
25. Newcastle to Keene, 8 December 1748, Newcastle House, in Keene, *Private correspondence*, p. 21. See also Newcastle's remarks of November 1748, quoted in Black, *America or Europe?*, p. 45; Browning, *Duke of Newcastle*, p. 163; Newcastle to Hardwicke, 3 June 1750, Hanover, in Hardwicke, *Life and correspondence*, vol. II, p. 25. My view of Newcastle and the Old System owes much to Hamish M. Scott, 'True principles', and Reed Browning's biography of Newcastle.
26. Hardwicke to Newcastle, 30 August 1749, in Hardwicke, *Life and correspondence*, vol. I, p. 21. Newcastle and Hanbury Williams are quoted in Horn, *Sir Charles Hanbury Williams*, pp. 147–9.
27. Hont, *Jealousy of trade*, p. 352. Allen, 'Anglo-Hanoverian connection', p. 209.
28. Newcastle to Pitt, 15 July 1750, Hanover, in Pitt, *Correspondence of William Pitt, Earl of Chatham*, vol. I, p. 39. On the imperial election scheme generally, see Browning, 'Duke of Newcastle and the imperial election plan' and 'British orientation', pp. 303–8; Horn, 'Duke of Newcastle', esp. pp. 253–4.
29. Pelham to Newcastle, 28 August and 29 September 1752; Holdernesse to Newcastle, 28 August 1752, in Hardwicke, *Life and correspondence*, vol. II, pp. 34, 35.
30. Pitt to Newcastle, 24 August 1750, Pay Office, in Pitt, *Correspondence of William Pitt, Earl of Chatham*, vol. I, p. 45. Cobbett, *Parliamentary history*, XIV, 17 January 1751, cols. 799–803; and 22 February 1751, cols. 965–6.
31. Pelham to Hardwicke, 6 October 1750 and 10 October 1752; Hardwicke to Newcastle, 30 August 1749, Wimpole, in Hardwicke, *Life and correspondence*, vol. II, pp. 26–7, 37, 18–21.
32. For an account of the parliamentary discussion, see Black, *Parliament and foreign policy in the eighteenth century*, pp. 89–90.

33. Newcastle to Hardwicke, 7 October 1750, in Hardwicke, *Life and correspondence*, vol. II, p. 26. Horn, 'Origins', p. 365. Browning, *Duke of Newcastle*, p. 166.
34. Horn, *Sir Charles Hanbury Williams*, p. 92.
35. For Burrish, see the listing in Horn, *British diplomatic representatives*, p. 41. Walpole is quoted in Black, *America or Europe?*, p. 92. The Hanoverian and Dutch contribution is discussed in Dann, *Hanover and Great Britain*, p. 82; Browning, *Duke of Newcastle*, p. 166; and Horn, 'Cabinet controversy', p. 465. The Austrian ambassador Richecourt noted the presence of Münchhausen at meetings with Newcastle on the imperial election scheme: Richecourt report, 9 July 1751, London (HHStA England Korrespondenz, Berichte Karton 100, fo. 14). On Bentinck and the King, see Horn, *Sir Charles Hanbury Williams*, p. 83, and Browning, *Duke of Newcastle*, p. 169.
36. See Dann, *Hanover and Great Britain*, pp. 80–81. Newcastle to Münchhausen, 15 August 1749, Newcastle House (NStaH Hann. 91 Münchhasuen I, Nr. 19, fo. 9). Further examples of cooperation are Holdernesse to Münchhausen, 29 August 1749, The Hague (fo. 8); Stone to Münchhausen, 12 September 1749, Whitehall (fo. 14); Münchhausen to Newcastle, 2 September 1749, [Hanover?] (fo. 3).
37. Horn, *Sir Charles Hanbury Williams*, p. 109; 'Mémoire instructif pour le Comte de Richecourt', January 1751 (HHStA England Korrespondenz, Berichte Karton 100, fos. 5, 8, 16; 13); 13 March 1751 (fos. 10–11, 27); and 21 May 1751 (fos. 9–12).
38. Newcastle to Münchhausen and Steinberg, 21 September 1752 (NStAH Cal. Br. 11 Nr. 2282, fos. 296–7); Hardwicke to Newcastle, 29 May 1752, in Hardwicke, *Life and correspondence*, vol. II, p. 33; Rigby to Bedford, 5 October 1752, in Bedford, *Correspondence*, vol. II, pp. 117–18.
39. Henry Pelham to Hardwicke, 14 November 1748, Esher Place, in Hardwicke, *Life and correspondence*, vol. II, p. 12; Newcastle to Pitt, 19 January 1748, Newcastle House, in Pitt, *Correspondence of William Pitt, Earl of Chatham*, vol. I, p. 27. Horn, *Great Britain and Europe*, p. 169. See also Horn, *Sir Charles Hanbury Williams*, pp. 61ff.
40. Langford, *Modern British foreign policy*, p. 156. Newcastle to Bedford, 17 July 1748, Hanover, in Bedford, *Correspondence*, vol. I, p. 401; Hardwicke to Philip Yorke, 12 October 1751, Powis House, in Hardwicke, *Life and correspondence*, vol. II, pp. 29–30.
41. See Dann, *Hanover and Great Britain*, pp. 73–4. Newcastle is quoted in Horn, *Sir Charles Hanbury Williams*, p. 143.
42. See ibid., pp. 91 (for Newcastle quotation), 157.
43. Browning, *Duke of Newcastle*, p. 162. On the fears of a Franco-Spanish alliance see Legge to Bedford, 14 July 1748, Berlin, in Bedford, *Correspondence*, vol. I, p. 398; Newcastle to Keene, 12 July 1753, London, in Keene, *Private correspondence*, pp. 33–4.
44. Keene to Abraham Castres, 29 May 1749, ibid., p. 128.
45. Black, *Pitt the Elder*, p. 84.
46. Rice, 'Lord Rochford', esp. pp. 106–7. See also Keene, *Private correspondence*, p. xviii. On the working out of the Italian settlement and the effective exclusion of Britain, see Butler, 'Secret compact'.

15 Transferring the Seat of Empire? 1753–1756

1. Quoted in van Alstyne, *Empire and independence*, p. 1.
2. Black, *America or Europe?*, p. 72. Newcastle to Keene, 24 January 1754, Newcastle House (BL Add Mss 32848, fo. 147). In the same vein: Newcastle to Colonel Yorke, 15 January 1754, Newcastle House (fo. 86). Mahan, *Influence of sea power*, p. 283. See also Higonnet, 'Origins of the Seven Years War', pp. 72–3; Clayton, 'Duke of Newcastle', pp. 572, 587.
3. French encroachments and the need to build a system of forts to stop them are discussed in 'Proceedings of the French in America – delivered by the Earl of Halifax to Sir Thomas Robinson, April 1754' (BL Add Mss 33029, fos. 109–18). See also Matthew C. Ward, *Breaking the backcountry*, pp. 7–8, and Fred Anderson, *Crucible of war*, esp. pp. 42–73.

4. Egnal, *Mighty empire*, p. 97.

5. Egnal, *Mighty empire*, p. 86. Matthew C. Ward, *Breaking the backcountry*, p. 66. Savelle, 'Appearance of an American attitude', p. 657.

6. Black, *America or Europe?*, pp. 72–3. Browning, *Duke of Newcastle*, p. 210; Halifax to Newcastle, 15 August 1754, Horton (BL Add Mss 32736, fos. 243–4).

7. Thus Max Savelle, 'Appearance of an American attitude', p. 656, *et passim*. Van Alstyne, *Genesis of American nationalism*, p. 46. Gilbert, 'English background', p. 150. Stourzh, *Benjamin Franklin*, p. 42. On the 'Englishness' of colonial discourse on grand strategy, see chapter 11 of Gilbert, *To the farewell address*, 'Insula fortunate: The English pattern for American foreign policy', pp. 19–43.

8. Stourzh, *Benjamin Franklin*, pp. 47, 44, 52–3. Stourzh points out that while the attribution of one of the quotations to Franklin is disputed, the words certainly express his sentiments.

9. Egnal, *Mighty empire*, pp. 42, 67. Stourzh, *Benjamin Franklin*, pp. 54, 63.

10. Van Alstyne, 'Significance of the Mississippi Valley', p. 219. Stourzh, *Benjamin Franklin*, pp. 63–4, 59. I use the word *Lebensraum* advisedly, following Stourzh, ibid., p. 62, who refers to 'living space'. On expansionism, see Egnal, *Mighty empire*, *passim*.

11. Draper, *Struggle for power*, p. 158. Van Alstyne, *Genesis of American nationalism*, p. 52, and *Rising American empire*, p. 20.

12. 'Draft of a plan or project for a general concert to be entered into by His Majesty's several colonies upon the continent of North America for their mutual and common defence and to prevent or remove any encroachment upon His Majesty's dominions', as an enclosure in Halifax to Newcastle, 15 August 1754, Horton (BL Add Mss 32736, fos. 247–52). See also Alison G. Olson, 'British government', pp. 24–6, who stresses the strategic thinking behind the plan.

13. Matthew C. Ward, *Breaking the backcountry*, p. 77. Draper, *Struggle for power*, p. 151. Stourzh, *Benjamin Franklin*, pp. 89, 83.

14. Draper, *Struggle for power*, pp. 165, 173. On the deportation of the Acadians as 'ethnic cleansing', see Fred Anderson, *Crucible of war*, pp. 113–14. See the review article by Peter Mancall, ' "The ones who hold up the world": Native American history since the Columbian quincentennial', *Historical Journal* 47 (2004), pp. 477–90, discussing Geoffrey Plank, *An unsettled conquest: The British campaign against the peoples of Acadia* (Philadelphia, 2001).

15. Newcastle to Keith, 22 October 1753, Whitehall, secret (BL Add Mss 32846, fo. 402); Newcastle to Colonel Yorke, 15 January 1754, Newcastle House (BL Add Mss 32848, fo. 86). Horn, *Sir Charles Hanbury Williams*, p. 146. Newcastle to Keene, 24 January 1754, Newcastle House (BL Add Mss 32848, fo. 146).

16. Schilling, *Kaunitz*, p. 94. Holdernesse to Keith, 26 April 1754, London (BL Egerton Mss 3455, fo. 8). Newcastle to Bentinck, 17 December 1754, Newcastle House (BL Add Mss 32851, fos. 327–8). For the Dutch perspective, see Carter, *Neutrality or commitment*, 'The death of the Barrier system', pp. 37–44, 81–2.

17. On Newcastle and Spain, see Newcastle to Keene, 24 January 1754, Newcastle House (BL Add Mss 32848, fo. 143). On Newcastle's shift to navalism, see Richard Middleton, *Bells of victory*, p. 2, and Browning, *Duke of Newcastle*, p. 218.

18. Peters, *Pitt and popularity*, pp. 13, 17. The pamphlet is quoted in Gilbert, 'English background', p. 146. Cardwell, *Arts and Arms*, pp. 31, 37, 106. Richard Rigby to the Duke of Bedford, 24 May 1755, Leicester Fields, in Bedford, *Correspondence*, vol. II, p. 163. On the increase of interest in the Royal Navy more generally, see Lincoln, *Representing the Royal Navy*.

19. Anson is quoted in Rodger, *Command of the ocean*, p. 265. Newcastle to Hardwicke, 30 June 1755, and Hardwicke to Royston, Powis House, 12 August 1755, in Hardwicke, *Life and correspondence*, vol. II, pp. 283, 284.

20. Newcastle to Colonel Yorke, 15 January 1754, Newcastle House, and Newcastle to Keene, 24 January 1754 (BL Add Mss 32848, fos. 85, 143). See also Keene, *Private correspondence*, pp. xix–xx. Holdernesse to Keith, 6 August 1754, Whitehall: 'I congratu-

late you on the great news from Madrid; I own I am sanguine in my hopes of good from that quarter; I know Wall' (BL Egerton Mss 3455, fo. 16).

21. Dann, *Hanover and Great Britain*, p. 93. Münchhausen to Newcastle, 4 July 1755, Hanover (NStAH Hann. 91 Münchhausen I, Nr. 22, fos. IV–3); Newcastle to Münchhausen and Steinberg, 18 July 1755, Newcastle House (fo. 11); Holdernesse to Münchhausen, 1 October 1755, London (Nr. 23, fos. 3–5). On Hanoverian thinking generally, see Wellenreuther, 'Die Bedeutung', pp. 164, 170–72.

22. The phrase 'advance headquarters' is Uriel Dann's in *Hanover and Great Britain*, p. 94. For British exasperation with Austria, see Holdernesse to Keith, 17 June 1755, Hanover (BL Egerton Mss 3455, fo. 42). Newcastle to Münchhausen and Steinberg, 18 July 1755, Newcastle House (NStAH Hann. 91 Münchhausen I, Nr. 22, fo. 10). Schilling, *Kaunitz*, p. 89. Braubach, *Versailles und Wien*, pp. 418–27.

23. Newcastle to Bentinck, 17 December 1754, Newcastle House (BL Add Mss 32851, fo. 328). Newcastle to Münchhausen, 25 July 1755, Claremont (NStAH Hann. 91 Münchhausen, I Nr. 22, fo. 16).

24. Horn, *Sir Charles Hanbury Williams*, p. 191. See also Eldon, 'Document'.

25. Horn, *Sir Charles Hanbury Williams*, pp. 192, 202; see also pp. 199, 201.

26. See Allen, 'Anglo-Hanoverian connection', pp. 252–3; Schweizer, *Frederick the Great*, pp. 13–25: and Münchhausen to Newcastle, 24 February 1756, Hanover (NStAH Hann. 91 Münchhausen I, Nr. 22, fo. 41).

27. Allen, 'Anglo-Hanoverian connection', p. 272; Bedford to Gower, 15 October 1755, Woburn Abbey, in Bedford, *Correspondence*, vol. II, p. 170. Browning, *Duke of Newcastle*, p. 220. On Halifax, see Draper, *Struggle for power*, p. 157.

28. The addresses from Yorkshire are quoted in Nicholas B. Harding, 'Dynastic union', p. 248. Samuel Johnson, 'Observations on the foregoing treaties', in *Political writings*, p. 181. See also Cannon, *Samuel Johnson*, p. 70; and Bloom, *Samuel Johnson*, pp. 106–8, for Johnson's views on foreign policy.

29. Johnson, 'Observations on the foregoing treaties' in *Political writings*, p. 180. See Cardwell, *Arts and arms*, pp. 96–7. Pitt's remarks are quoted in Hardwicke to Newcastle, 9 August 1755, Powis House, in Hardwicke, *Life and correspondence*, vol. II, p. 231; and in P.S. to Newcastle to Hardwicke, 3 September 1755, Powis House, in Hardwicke, *Life and correspondence*, vol. II, p. 243. Cardwell, *Arts and arms*, p. 23. Black, *Parliament and foreign policy in the eighteenth century*, p. 93.

30. Cobbett, *Parliamentary history*, XV, 15 December 1755, col. 664; *c*.11 May 1756, col. 704. See Peters, *Pitt and popularity*, p. 39.

31. Bob Harris, *Patriot press*, p. 177. See Peters, *Pitt and popularity*, p. 35. Pitt as quoted in Newcastle to Hardwicke, 3 September 1755, in Hardwicke, *Life and correspondence*, vol. II, p. 240.

32. Pitt as quoted in Hardwicke to Newcastle, 9 August 1755, Powis House, and Newcastle to Hardwicke, 3 September 1755, Newcastle House, ibid., pp. 231, 240. The views of the Duke of Bedford are described in Thomas Potter to Earl Temple, mid October 1755, in Grenville, *Grenville papers*, vol. I, p. 146.

33. Cardwell, *Arts and arms*, pp. 35, 19, 32. Dann, *Hanover and Great Britain*, p. 91. *The Orator's Political Meditation* (1754), quoted in Cardwell, *Arts and arms*, p. 20. Allen, 'Anglo-Hanoverian connection' p. 274. Black, *America or Europe?*, p. 142. Bob Harris, *Politics and the nation*, pp. 120–21.

34. Horn, *Sir Charles Hanbury Williams*, pp. 211–13.

35. See Braubach, *Versailles und Wien*, p. 453, on the importance of Austro-British estrangement.

36. This remarkable analysis is printed at length in Horn, *Sir Charles Hanbury Williams*, p. 210. It very much supports Baugh's analysis in 'Withdrawing from Europe'. Buddruss, *Die Französische Deutschlandpolitik*.

37. 'Intelligence' to Newcastle, 25 May 1756, Versailles, and 'Intelligence', 1 June 1756, Versailles (BL Add Mss 32865, fos. 110, 167–8).

38. Very private, Newcastle to Yorke, 11 June 1756, Newcastle House (ibid., fos. 257–61).
39. 'Intelligence' to Newcastle, 11 September 1756 (BL Add Mss 32867, fo. 168). Schilling, *Kaunitz*, pp. 207, 211. Baugh, 'Withdrawing from Europe', pp. 4–5.
40. Newcastle to Yorke, 11 June 1756, Newcastle House (BL Add Mss 32865, fos. 257–61).
41. Keene to the Bishop of Chester, 4 May 1756, Antigola, in Keene, *Private correspondence*, p. 474. Lord Tyrawly to Henry Fox, 27 August 1756, Gibraltar, in Pitt, *Correspondence of William Pitt, Earl of Chatham*, vol. I, p. 202. For Keene's warnings re Minorca, see Keene, *Private correspondence*, pp. 453–69.
42. See Peters, *Pitt and popularity*, p. 49. Cardwell, *Arts and arms*, pp. 93, 133. Nicholas B. Harding, 'Dynastic union', pp. 247–8.
43. Cardwell, *Arts and arms*, pp. 83–4.
44. Ibid., pp. 94, 65. See Bob Harris, *Politics and the nation*, p. 333.
45. On this, see the very pertinent remarks in Cardwell, *Arts and arms*, pp. 133, 120.
46. Ibid., pp. 114–16.
47. See Peters, *Pitt and popularity*, p. 62. Newcastle is quoted in Cardwell, *Arts and arms*, p. 144. Hardwicke to Joseph Yorke, 31 October 1756, in Hardwicke, *Life and correspondence*, vol. II, p. 334. On this whole episode, see Rodger, *Command of the ocean*, p. 267.
48. Black, *America or Europe?*, p. 103. Cardwell, *Arts and arms*, p. 130.
49. Hardwicke, *Life and correspondence*, vol. II, p. 261. *Monitor*, 31 July 1756, quoted in Nicholas B. Harding, 'Dynastic union', p. 252. Black, *America or Europe?*, p. 124. Cardwell, *Arts and arms*, pp. 109–10.
50. See ibid., p. 117. J. C. D. Clark, *Dynamics of change*, p. 271. For Pitt's preoccupation with the affair of the Hanoverian soldier, see Hardwicke's 'Relation of my conference with Mr Pitt', 24 October 1756, in his *Life and correspondence*, vol. II, p. 278. Hardwicke to Newcastle, 6 December 1756, Powis House, ibid., pp. 376–7. Peters, *Pitt and popularity*, pp. 61, 66. Cardwell, *Arts and arms*, pp. 167–8, 157. Thomas Potter to Mr Pitt, 4 June 1756, Bath, in Pitt, *Correspondence of William Pitt, Earl of Chatham*, p. 161.
51. See Cardwell, *Arts and arms*, pp. 161–2, 156.
52. See Baugh, 'Withdrawing from Europe', p. 17. Chesterfield is quoted in Cardwell, *Arts and arms*, p. 103. As Butterfield points out in *Reconstruction of an historical episode*, pp. 6–8, Frederick was right to be paranoid.
53. Schlenke, *England und das friderizianische Preußen*, pp. 227–34.
54. 'Relation of my conference with Mr Pitt, 24 October 1756; read to the King 26 October', in Hardwicke, *Life and correspondence*, vol. II, p. 278. Newcastle to Hardwicke, 3 September 1755, ibid., p. 240. See also the entry for 'September [1755]', in Dodington, *Political journal*, p. 322. Nicholas B. Harding, 'Dynastic union', p. 261. Black, *Pitt the Elder*, p. 124. Harding, 'Dynastic union', p. 262.
55. Newcastle to Hardwicke, 14 October 1756, in Hardwicke, *Life and correspondence*, vol. II, p. 323.

16 The Imperial Missions of William Pitt, 1757–1759

1. *The Test*, XV, 19 February 1757, p. 81. In the same vein, see also the issue of 26 March 1757, pp. 112–13.
2. Digby to Ilchester, 1 March 1757 (BL Add Mss 51341, fos. 42–3).
3. *Gazetteer and London Daily Advertiser*, 3 December 1757, in Schlenke, *England und das friderizianische Preußen*, p. 240.
4. Mr James Grenville to Mr Grenville, 29 June 1758, in *Grenville papers*, vol. I, p. 246.
5. Peters, *Pitt and popularity*, p. 63. For a sceptical view of Pitt's strategic prescience, see especially Middleton, *Bells of victory, passim* and Black, *Pitt the Elder*, p. 176. For a recent stirring account of the 'year of victories', see McLynn, *1759*. I have attempted to place Pitt in the continuity of British Continentalists in 'Pitt and Hanover'.
6. Peters, *Pitt and popularity*, p. 66. *The Test*, I, 6 November 1756, pp. 1, 4.

7. *The annual register: Or a view to the history, politics and literature for the year 1758* (9th edn, London, 1795), pp. 11–12.

8. Peters, *Pitt and popularity*, p. 69. On Frederick's gratitude, see the letter of the British envoy to Prussia: Andrew Mitchell to Pitt, 12 March 1757, Dresden, in Pitt, *Correspondence of William Pitt, Earl of Chatham*, vol. I, p. 225.

9. See 'The King's message concerning an Army of Observation and the Treaty with the King of Prussia', 17 February 1757, presented by William Pitt, in Cobbett, *Parliamentary history*, XV, cols. 782–8. This text must be approached with some caution, as there are – unusually for Cobbett – some anachronistic references to later events. None of the contributors to the debate are named, but the pro-interventionist arguments are clearly those of Pitt himself. See also *The Test*, XIII, 5 February 1757, pp. 68–9. Holdernesse, speaking in late November 1756, is quoted in Middleton, *Bells of victory*, p. 11.

10. Pitt to Thomas Pitt, 13 January 1756, Horse Guards, in Pitt, *Correspondence of William Pitt, Earl of Chatham*, vol. I, p. 152. See also Thomas Pitt to Pitt, 12 October 1756, Clare Hall, ibid. vol. I, pp. 176–7.

11. As noted by Uriel Dann, *Hanover and Great Britain*, p. 110.

12. On this generally, see Peters, 'Myth of William Pitt'. Middleton, *Bells of victory*, pp. 7–9. Peters, *Pitt and popularity*, p. 7. William Beckford to Pitt, 6 November 1756, Fonthill, in Pitt, *Correspondence of William Pitt, Earl of Chatham*, vol. I, pp. 185–6. Peters, *Pitt and popularity*, pp. 13, 17.

13. See Middleton, *Bells of victory*, p. 14 and Peters, *Pitt and popularity*, pp. 76–8. For a sceptical view of Pitt's popularity, see Langford, 'William Pitt'.

14. Black, *Pitt the Elder*, p. 181. Newcastle to Hardwicke, 15 October 1761, Claremont, in Hardwicke, *Life and Correspondence*, vol. III, pp. 338–9. Figures in Middleton, *Bells of victory*, p. 25.

15. Pitt to Keene, 23 August 1757, Whitehall, and Pitt to Mitchell, 31 March 1757, Whitehall, in Pitt, *Correspondence of William Pitt, Earl of Chatham*, vol. I, pp. 248, 251, 226.

16. Joseph Yorke to Hardwicke, 5 July 1757, The Hague, in Hardwicke, *Life and correspondence*, vol. II, p. 411.

17. Joseph Yorke to Newcastle, 15 July 1757, The Hague, in Hardwicke, *Life and correspondence*, vol. III, p. 158. Newcastle to Münchhausen, 25 January 1757, Newcastle House (NStAH Hann. 91 Münchhausen I, Nr. 24, fos. 6–7).

18. As reported in Newcastle to Hardwicke, 11 October 1756, in Hardwicke, *Life and correspodence*, vol. II, p. 318; Münchhausen to Newcastle, no date but from internal evidence probably early 1757 (NStAH Hann. 91 Münchhausen I, Nr. 24, fo. 11).

19. Black, *Pitt the Elder*, p. 132. See Matthew C. Ward, *Breaking the backcountry*, pp. 98, 159, on the central role of Pitt in this. Draper, *Struggle for power*, p. 178. See the comic descriptions in Matthew C. Ward, *Breaking the backcountry*, p. 93, *et passim*. On the centrality of British regulars to the war effort in America see Brumwell, *Redcoats*, pp. 11–53, esp. 39–41.

20. Rashed, *Peace of Paris*, p. 7. Jennings, 'Seven Years War', p. 55. On Indian diplomacy, see Matthew C. Ward, *Breaking the backcountry*, pp. 163, 238, 145. On improving Indian diplomacy, see Jacobs, *Diplomacy and Indian gifts*, pp. 161–7.

21. Pitt to Keene, 23 August 1757, Whitehall, in Pitt, *Correspondence of William Pitt, Earl of Chatham*, vol. I, pp. 249, 255. Mahan, *Influence of sea power*, p. 298. For Pitt's suggestion, see also Conn, *Gibraltar*, pp. 166–8.

22. Pitt to Sir Benjamin Keene, 23 August 1757, Whitehall, in Pitt, *Correspondence of William Pitt, Earl of Chatham*, vol. I, pp. 253–4.

23. Frederick's pleas are summarized in 'Moyens dont la Grande Bretagne pourroit se server pour ruiner les projets de ses ennemis, ou rendre la guerre difficile', enclosed with a dispatch of 9 December 1756 (NA Chatham Papers 30/8/89, fos. 41–3). See also Middleton, *Bells of victory*, pp. 23–8, and Black, 'Naval power', pp. 100–103.

24. Peters, *Pitt and popularity*, p. 92. Nicholas B. Harding, 'Dynastic union', p. 266.

25. Rodger, *Command of the ocean*, p. 268. Brown is quoted in Bob Harris, *Politics and the nation*, p. 87.

26. Münchhausen to Hardwicke, 20 September 1757, Hanover (NStAH Hann. 91 Münchhausen I Nr. 36, fos. 2–4). Allen, 'Anglo-Hanoverian connection', pp. 234, 251, 256. Newcastle to Hardwicke, 10 September 1757, and 3 August 1757, Newcastle House, in Hardwicke, *Life and correspondence*, vol. III, pp. 172, 161. On Cumberland and Kloster-Zeven, see Charteris, *William Augustus*, pp. 274–317.

27. Joseph Yorke to Hardwicke, 16 September 1757, in Hardwicke, *Life and correspondence*, vol. III, p. 177. In the same vein see also Joseph Yorke to Hardwicke, 19 July 1757, The Hague (p. 159); and Joseph Yorke to Royston, 12 August 1757 (p. 169); Hardwicke to Newcastle, 11 September 1757, Wimpole (p. 176); Newcastle to Hardwicke, 10 September 1757, Claremont (p. 172). Pitt as quoted in Newcastle to Hardwicke, 10 September 1757, Claremont (p. 174).

28. Newcastle to Hardwicke, 3 August 1757, Newcastle House, ibid., p. 161; Pitt to Keene, 23 August 1757, Whitehall, in Pitt, *Correspondence of William Pitt, Earl of Chatham*, vol. I, pp. 248, 251. On Frederick's reaction to Kloster-Zeven, see Mitchell, *Memoirs and papers*, journal entries for 19 September and 11 and 20 October 1757, pp. 371–2, 378.

29. As quoted in Newcastle to Hardwicke, 10 September 1757, Claremont, in Hardwicke, *Life and correspondence*, vol. III, p. 173; Hardwicke to Newcastle, 11 September 1757, Wimpole (p. 177). George Grenville to Pitt, 14 August 1757, in Pitt, *Correspondence of William Pitt, Earl of Chatham*, vol. I, p. 245.

30. Newcastle to Münchhausen, 10 October 1757, Newcastle House (NStAH Hann. 91 Münchhausen I Nr. 36, fo. 6). Newcastle to Münchhausen, 11 March 1758, Newcastle House (fo. 15); Horace Walpole, 13 October 1757, quoted in Pitt, *Correspondence of William Pitt, Earl of Chatham*, vol. I, p. 281. In the same vein, see also Thomas Potter to Pitt, 11 October 1757, Bath (p. 277). Middleton, *Bells of victory*, pp. 41–2. 'Minute of a meeting at Sir Conyers d'Arcy's lodgings', 7 October 1757 [at which Pitt, Newcastle and other important figures were present], (NA 30/8/89, fo. 52). Pitt to Lady Hester Pitt, 1 December 1757, in Pitt, *Correspondence of William Pitt, Earl of Chatham*, vol. II, p. 2.

31. See Allen, 'Anglo-Hanoverian connection', p. 231; Haslang to Comte Preysing, 2 December 1757, London (intercepted dispatch) (NA 30/8/89, fo. 58). For Hanover as a source of men for Duke Ferdinand, see Brunswick to Pitt, 26 November 1759, Krossdorf (NA 30/8/90, fo. 90).

32. As reported in Newcastle to Hardwicke, 27 September 1759, Claremont, in Hardwicke, *Life and correspondence*, vol. III, pp. 60–61. Dann, *Hanover and Great Britain*, p. 108; Münchhausen to Newcastle, draft, 6 November 1757 (NStAH Hann. 91 Münchhausen I Nr. 36, fo. 9).

33. Allen, 'Anglo-Hanoverian connection', pp. 261, 268; Nicholas B. Harding, 'Dynastic union', pp. 276, 279, 285.

34. Münchhausen to Newcastle, 28 March 1758, Hanover (NStAH Hann. 91 Münchhausen I Nr. 36, fos. 29–31); memorandum of Münchhausen, 21 November 1758, London (NA 30/8/89, fo. 325). Mitchell, *Memoirs and papers*, vol. II, journal entries for 25 June, 2 and 8 July 1758, pp. 31, 33, 35.

35. Pitt to Grenville, 29 October 1757, Hayes; and 15 November 1757, St James's Square, in Grenville, *Grenville papers*, vol. I, p. 227. See Hamish M. Scott, 'Britain's emergence', p. 41; Richard Middleton, *Bells of victory*, p. 63; Peters, *Pitt and popularity*, p. 115. The terms of the agreement are described in 'Declaration', 11 April 1758, London (NA 30/8/89, fos. 74–5). Dann, *Hanover and Great Britain*, p. 117. Pyta, 'Von der Entente Cordiale'.

36. Newcastle to the Marquis of Rockingham, 24 June 1758 (BL Add Mss 32881, fos. 37–8). Pitt to Grenville, 27 June 1758; and Mr Jenkinson to Mr Grenville, 27 June 1758, London, in Grenville, *Grenville papers*, pp. 244–5.

37. Rodger, *Command of the ocean*, p. 270. Middleton, *Bells of victory*, p. 69. Newcastle to Henry Campion, 15 July 1758, Claremont (BL Add Mss 32881, fo. 334). Beckford to

Pitt, 11 September 1758, Fonthill, in Pitt, *Correspondence of William Pitt, Earl of Chatham*, vol. I, p. 353.

38. Bute to Pitt, 28 June 1758, Kew, ibid., pp. 320–21. Lord Barrington to Newcastle, 24 June 1758, War Office (BL Add Mss 32881, fo. 35). Peters, *Pitt and popularity*, pp. 118–19. William Beckford to Pitt, 10 July 1758, Fonthill, in Pitt, *Correspondence of William Pitt, Earl of Chatham*, vol. I, p. 328. Peters, *Pitt and popularity*, p. 123. Bute to Pitt, 28 June 1758, Kew, and 20 August 1758, in Pitt, *Correspondence of William Pitt, Earl of Chatham*, vol. I, pp. 320–22, 335–6.

39. On this, see Patrick Francis Doran, *Andrew Mitchell, passim*, and Schweizer, *England, Prussia*, esp. pp. 62–3. Newcastle to Henry Campion, 15 July 1758 (BL Add Mss 32881, fo. 335). Peters, *Pitt and popularity*, p. 109. Duke of Marlborough, 18 August 1758, in Pitt, *Correspondence of William Pitt, Earl of Chatham*, vol. I, p. 338.

40. Peters, *Pitt and popularity*, p. 100. William Beckford to Pitt, 22 October 1757, Fonthill, in Pitt, *Correspondence of William Pitt, Earl of Chatham*, vol. I, pp. 279–80. Fox is quoted in Middleton, *Bells of victory*, p. 84.

41. Richard Harding, 'Sailors and gentlemen of parade', p. 43. Middleton, *Bells of victory*, pp. 75, 101. For the subsequent 'imperial' construction of Pitt, see Nicholas Rogers, 'Brave Wolfe'. Brumwell, *Paths of glory*.

42. Hanbury Williams to Duke of Bedford, 27 January 1758, Hamburg, in Bedford, *Correspondence*, vol. II, p. 322. Münchhausen to Newcastle, 16 March 1758 (NStAH Hann. 91 Münchhausen I Nr. 36, fos. 19v–20). Wilson, 'German armies. The King's message concerning an Army of Observation and the treaty with the King of Prussia', 17 February 1757, in Cobbett, *Parliamentary history*, XV, col. 759 (this speech is misdated in Cobbett and was probably given about a year later, but it reflects a strong view of the time). The naval figures are taken from Richard Harding, *Sea power*, table A2, p. 291. On the impact of the Continental war (even on a low flame) on French finances and naval spending, see Dull, *French navy and the Seven Years War*, pp. 122, 125, 158–60, 170–73. Likewise, Pritchard, *Louis XV's navy*, esp. pp. 184–208, argues that the French naval failure was due to financial shortcomings.

43. The classic account here is Schlenke, *England und das friderizianische Preußen*, esp. pp. 236–48; see also Cardwell, *Arts and arms*, pp. 170–72. Bob Harris, *Politics and the nation*, p. 136. For the comparison with Cumberland and the Walpole quotation, see Kathleen Wilson, *Sense of the people*, p. 197. Cardwell, *Arts and arms*, p. 171.

44. Chesterfield is quoted in Clark, *Dynamics of change*, p. 455.

45. Rodger, 'Sea power and empire', pp. 178–9. Mitchell is quoted in van Alstyne, *Empire and independence*, p. 10. Savelle, 'Appearance of an American attitude', p. 658.

46. Postlethwayt, *Great Britain's true system*, pp. ii–v, xii, xxviii, xci, cxxxvii, *et passim*.

47. Pitt to Lady Hester Pitt, 1 July 1758, Hayes, in Pitt, *Correspondence of William Pitt, Earl of Chatham*, vol. I, p. 322. The King's Speech is quoted in Middleton, *Bells of victory*, p. 97. Pitt's remarks are quoted in Devonshire, *Diary*, p. 29.

48. The figures are taken from: Pitt to Brunswick, October 1759 (NA 30/8/90, fo. 83); Peters, *Pitt and popularity*, p. 158; Pyta, 'Von der Entente Cordiale' p. 5; and Bird, 'British land strategy', issue 21, p. 50. On the logistical implications, see Hayter, 'England, Hannover, Preußen', pp. 178–80.

49. Pitt to Lady Hester Pitt, 6 August 1759, in Pitt, *Correspondence of William Pitt, Earl of Chatham*, vol. II, p. 9.

50. Lord George Sackville to Pitt, 11 November 1758, Münster, ibid., p. 367. Prince of Wales to Bute, November 1758, in George III, *Letters to Lord Bute*, p. 16. See Middleton, *Bells of victory*, p. 131, and Peters, *Pitt and popularity*, p. 149; on previous relations, see George III, *Letters to Lord Bute*, p. 16, note 2, and Prince of Wales to Bute, 11 August 1759, p. 29. See Mackesy, *Coward of Minden*, pp. 26–31, 39–41. See Valentine, *Lord George Germain*, pp. 46–8 re complaints before Minden, and pp. 49–70 re the battle and subsequent court-martial.

51. See for example Lord George Sackville to Pitt, 11 November 1758, Münster, in Pitt,

Correspondence of William Pitt, Earl of Chatham, vol. I, p. 367; Prince of Wales to Bute, 23 April 1760, in George III, *Letters to Lord Bute*, p. 43; Pitt to Lady Hester Pitt, 19 November 1759, in Pitt, *Correspondence of William Pitt, Earl of Chatham*, vol. I, p. 458.

52. Peters, *Pitt and popularity*, pp. 149, 132, 136-7, 157, 161, 169. The remarks about 'Whig principles' are quoted in Clark, *Dynamics of change*, p. 455. For the prints, see Cardwell, *Arts and arms*, pp. 246-7.

53. Baugh, 'Withdrawing from Europe', p. 18. See also Black, *Pitt the Elder*, pp. 187-8; Middleton, *Bells of victory*, p. 107; Mahan, *Influence of sea power*, p. 304; and Nordmann, 'Choiseul'.

54. The Newcastle quotations are from Middleton, *Bells of victory*, p. 116, and Browning, *Duke of Newcastle*, p. 268.

55. Pitt, *Correspondence of William Pitt, Earl of Chatham*, vol. I, p. 401. Potenger is quoted in Black, *Parliament and foreign policy*, p. 245. Earl Temple to Pitt, 13 October 1759, in Pitt, *Correspondence of William Pitt, Earl of Chatham*, vol. I, p. 438.

56. Pitt to Lady Hester Pitt, 6 August 1759, ibid., vol. II, p. 9. Pitt to Hardwicke, 20 October 1759, Hayes, in Hardwicke, *Life and correspondence*, vol. III, p. 241.

57. Savelle, 'Appearance of an American attitude', p. 658. Rashed, *Peace of Paris*, p. 47. Hardwicke to Newcastle, 24 October 1759, Wimpole, in Hardwicke, *Life and correspondence*, vol. III, p. 241. See Matthew C. Ward, *Breaking the backcountry*, p. 196 and esp. p. 147, and Oliphant, *Peace and war*, pp. 31-68, on the Anglo-Cherokee war. Reports of the Spanish naval build-up are described in the Duke of Devonshire's diary entry for 13 December 1759, in Devonshire, *Diary*, p. 34. For deteriorating relations more generally, see Pares, *War and trade*, pp. 556-67, and Christelow, 'Economic background'.

58. Pitt is quoted in Rashed, *Peace of Paris*, p. 46.

59. Rodger, *Command of the ocean*, p. 290, says that the vast majority of prizes were taken by the Royal Navy, not privateers.

60. See Carter, *Dutch Republic*, pp. 84-128, and Pares, *Colonial blockade*, pp. 242-79. For Newcastle's fears, see Browning, *Duke of Newcastle*, p. 267.

61. Newcastle is quoted in Browning, *Duke of Newcastle*, p. 268. Hardwicke to Newcastle, 16 October 1759, Wimpole, in Hardwicke, *Life and correspondence*, vol. III, p. 239.

62. Newcastle to Hardwicke, 31 October 1759, Claremont, ibid., p. 242. See also Hardwicke to Newcastle, 10 April 1760, Moor Park (p. 245); Newcastle to Hardwicke, 3 December 1760, Newcastle House (p. 314).

63. Pitt is quoted in Peters, *Pitt and popularity*, p. 133. Pitt to Keene, 23 August 1757, Whitehall, in Pitt, *Correspondence of William Pitt, Earl of Chatham*, vol. I, p. 251.

64. The accounts of conversations with the King are in Newcastle to Hardwicke, 5 October 1758, Kensington; 16 November 1759, Newcastle House; and 31 October 1759, Claremont, in Hardwicke, *Life and correspondence*, vol. III, pp. 230, 91, 241-2.

65. The conversation between George and Newcastle is described almost verbatim in Newcastle to Hardwicke, 21 November 1759, Newcastle House (BL Add Mss 32899, fos. 6-7). Hardwicke's response is in Hardwicke to Newcastle, 21 January 1759, Grosvenor Square (fos. 13-14).

17 An Island Once Again, 1760-1763

1. Quoted in Black, *Pitt the Elder*, p. 223.

2. Quoted in van Alstyne, *Rising American empire*, p. 26.

3. See Newcastle to Münchhausen, 20 May 1760, Newcastle House; and 26 February 1760, Newcastle House; and Münchhausen to Newcastle, 10 March 1760 (NStAH Hann. 91 Münchhausen I Nr. 69, fos. 10-11, 2, 4-6).

4. Joseph Yorke to Royston, 25 March 1760, in Hardwicke, *Life and correspondence*, vol. III, p. 243. Holdernesse to Duke of Brunswick, 25 April 1760, Whitehall (NStAH Hann. 9e 1085, Nr. 2, fo. 340). The insistence on coordinating with Frederick is repeated on

fos. 341, 344; and in 'Minute with the Prussian ministers', 13 March 1760, in Pitt, *Correspondence of William Pitt, Earl of Chatham*, vol. II, p. 29. See also Pyta, 'Von der Entente Cordiale', pp. 7–8 re January 1760.

5. Newcastle to Joseph Yorke, 28 November 1760, Newcastle House, in Hardwicke, *Life and correspondence*, vol. III, p. 313; Pitt to Frederick, November 1760, in Pitt, *Correspondence of William Pitt, Earl of Chatham*, vol. II, p. 84; and as reported in Newcastle to Hardwicke, 9 April 1760, Newcastle House, in Hardwicke, *Life and correspondence*, vol. III, p. 244.

6. See Middleton, *Bells of victory*, p. 165; Peters, *Pitt and popularity*, p. 191; Hardwicke to Newcastle, 10 April 1760, Moor Park, in Hardwicke, *Life and correspondence*, vol. III, p. 24.

7. Addison is quoted in George III, *Letters to Lord Bute*, pp. ix–x; see also pp. xix, lvi. Hanoverian views of George as Prince of Wales are expressed in the memorandum by Hake, 12 October 1757, Hanover, quoted in Nicholas B. Harding, 'Dynastic union', p. 281. George's 'horrid electorate' remarks are in Prince of Wales to Bute, 5 August 1759, in George III, *Letters to Lord Bute*, p. 28.

8. Prince of Wales to Bute, c.5 November 1757, ibid., p. 7. For George's complaints about Pitt's lack of consultation, see Prince of Wales to Bute, c.8 December 1758 (p. 18).

9. Prince of Wales to Bute, 17 January and 6 March 1758, ibid., pp. 15, 8, 9. Bute to Pitt, 8 September 1758, in Pitt, *Correspondence of William Pitt, Earl of Chatham*, vol. I, p. 349. Prince of Wales to Bute, 5 October 1760, in George III, *Letters to Lord Bute*, p. 47. On George's strategic thinking as Prince of Wales, see McKelvey, *George III and Lord Bute*, pp. 23–4, 68–70, *et passim*.

10. Councillor Schliestadt to unknown recipient, 19 January 1759, Brunswick (NStAH Hann. 92 Nr. 91, fo. 3). For the attitude of Princess Caroline, see 'Extrait d'une lettre de Mad. De Poigk, Gouvernante de la Princesse Caroline', 8 January 1759 (fo. 6); and Prince of Wales to Bute, c.22 February 1759, in George III, *Letters to Lord Bute*, p. 23.

11. See Mauduit, *Considerations* (I have used the second edition). The comments to Mitchell are quoted in Schweizer, 'Pamphleteering and foreign policy', p. 204.

12. See ibid., pp. 200, 205 (Walpole quotation), 207. Pitt is quoted in Peters, *Pitt and popularity*, p. 186. For America, see Franklin to Joseph Morris, 20 February 1761, London, in Franklin, *Papers*, vol. IX, pp. 276–7.

13. The speech is discussed with quotations in Nicholas B. Harding, 'Dynastic union', p. 300.

14. Hardwicke to Newcastle, 18 April 1761, Grosvenor Square, in Hardwicke, *Life and correspondence*, vol. III, p. 317. See George III to Bute, 6 May 1762, in George III, *Letters to Lord Bute*, p. 100. A point well made by Nicholas B. Harding in 'Dynastic union', p. 302.

15. The quotations are from Black, *Pitt the Elder*, p. 223 and Nicholas B. Harding, 'Dynastic union', p. 309. See also Peters, *Pitt and popularity*, pp. 216–17, 225, 223.

16. See *Full and candid answer*, pp. 39, 40. Pitt is quoted in Middleton, *Bells of victory*, p. 170. See also Pyta, 'Von der Entente Cordiale', pp. 15–16.

17. Newcastle is quoted in Schweizer, 'Vote of credit', pp. 31–2.

18. The *Monitor* is quoted in Nicholas B. Harding, 'Dynastic union', p. 30. George's interest in Hildesheim and Osnabrück is cited in Dann, *Hanover and Great Britain*, p. 14, and his concern for the defence of the Electorate is expressed in George III to Hanoverian Council, 8 September 1761, Hanover (NStAH Hann. 9e Nr. 324, fo. 1). On this, see the correspondence in George III, *Letters to Lord Bute*, pp. 52–62.

19. On this see Black, 'Crown, Hanover', p. 177, *et passim*; Bute to Bedford, 12 July 1761, in Bedford, *Correspondence*, vol. III, pp. 32–3. George III, *Letters to Lord Bute*, p. 192.

20. George III to Bute, 20 February 1762, 14 and 22 October 1762, 3 May 1762, in George III, *Letters to Lord Bute*, pp. 86, 147, 149, 96–7.

21. Newcastle to Hardwicke, 14 October 1761; Newcastle to Devonshire, 31 October 1761, Claremont, in Hardwicke, *Life and correspondence*, vol. III, pp. 333, 336.

22. Draper, *Struggle for power*, p. 7. Van Alstyne, *Empire and independence*, p. 14. Stourzh, *Benjamin Franklin*, p. 74.

23. Ibid., pp. 68–9. Draper, *Struggle for power*, p. 9.

24. Ibid., p. 7. Bullion, 'Securing the peace', p. 27. Pitt on Guadeloupe is quoted in Hyam, 'Imperial interests', p. 28. Namier, *England*, p. 274.

25. Newcastle to Bedford, 6 July and 9 August 1761; Bute to Bedford, 12 July 1761, in Bedford, *Correspondence*, vol. III, pp. 21, 35, 34.

26. Rashed, *Peace of Paris*, p. 69. Van Alstyne, *Rising American empire*, p. 26.

27. Rigby to Bedford, 27 August 1761, Mistley, in Bedford, *Correspondence*, vol. III, pp. 42–3.

28. Bedford to Bute, 13 June 1761, ibid., pp. 16–17.

29. Bedford to Bute, 9 July 1761, ibid. pp. 24–7. On this see also Rodger, *Command of the ocean*, p. 287. Grenville is quoted in Newcastle to Devonshire, 9 December 1761, Newcastle House (BL Add Mss 32932, fo. 79).

30. As reported in Newcastle to Hardwicke, 17 April 1761, Newcastle House, in Hardwicke, *Life and correspondence*, vol. III, p. 315. Rashed, *Peace of Paris*, pp. 67, 102, 134.

31. See ibid., pp. 59–60, 93, *et passim*.

32. Rigby to Bedford, 27 August 1761, in Bedford, *Correspondence*, vol. III, pp. 42–3. *London Chronicle*, 7 January 1762, *London Evening Post*, 30 January 1762; and also *Monitor*, 28 April 1762, quoted in Black, *America or Europe?*, pp. 157, 161, 163.

33. 'Advice in writing', 18 September 1761, in Grenville, *Grenville papers*, p. 387. Black, *Pitt the Elder*, p. 224.

34. George III to Bute, probably 19 September 1761, in George III, *Letters to Lord Bute*, p. 63. Middleton, *Bells of victory*, pp. 193–5. Joseph Yorke to Lord Royston, 16 October 1761, The Hague, in Hardwicke, *Life and correspondence*, vol. III, p. 333. Rashed, *Peace of Paris*, p. 40, *et passim*, thinks that diplomatic flexibility towards Spain might have averted war.

35. For his defiant final speech to the cabinet, see 'Minutes of the meeting of the council', according to Newcastle's account, in Hardwicke, *Life and correspondence*, vol. III, pp. 279–80. Pitt to Beckford, 15 October 1761, in Pitt, *Correspondence of William Pitt, Earl of Chatham*, vol. II, p. 158. Hyam, 'Imperial interests', p. 28. Cardwell, *Arts and arms*, p. 262.

36. Royston to Hardwicke, 13 November 1761, in Hardwicke, *Life and correspondence*, vol. III, p. 338. Schweizer, 'Parliamentary speech', pp. 98–105. There is also an account of the speech and the debate in Newcastle to Devonshire, 9 December 1761, Newcastle House (BL Add Mss 32932, fo. 81), which contains some details not in the Schweizer version. The following five paragraphs are based on my 'Pitt and Hanover'. Pitt's remarks are quoted in Newcastle to Devonshire, 9 December 1761, Newcastle House (BL Add Mss 32932, fo. 81) and Middleton, *Bells of victory*, p. 148.

37. Black, *Pitt the Elder*, p. 231.

38. See the account of the debate in Newcastle to Devonshire, 9 December 1761, Newcastle House (BL Add Mss 32932, fos. 79–91).

39. George III to Bute, 5 April 1762, in George III, *Letters to Lord Bute*, p. 89. On the pressure which the Spanish war put on the Prussian alliance, see F. Spencer, 'Anglo-Prussian breach', esp. pp. 105–6. For the capture of Manila, see Tracy, *Manila ransomed*, pp. 109–17 (re ransom).

40. Schweizer, 'Bedford motion', p. 112.

41. Black, *America or Europe?*, p. 177. Schweizer, 'Bedford motion', p. 115. Pyta, 'Von der Entente Cordiale', pp. 37, 40.

42. On this more generally, see Brewer, 'Misfortunes of Lord Bute'; and Riotte, 'George III'.

43. Joseph Yorke to Bute, 19 January 1762; Hardwicke to Newcastle, 25 February 1762, Grosvenor Square; Newcastle to Hardwicke, 17 April 1762, Claremont, in Hardwicke, *Life and correspondence*, vol. III, pp. 341, 345, 350. Peters, 'Pitt as a foil', esp. pp. 99, 100–101. Brewer, 'Misfortunes of Lord Bute', p. 12.

44. Hardwicke to Newcastle, 14 April 1762, Richmond, in Hardwicke, *Life and correspondence*, vol. III, p. 349. George III to Bute, 'mid-April', in George III, *Letters to Lord Bute*, pp. 92–3. See also Middleton, *Bells of victory*, pp. 208–9; Bedford to Bute, 4 May 1762, Bath, in Bedford, *Correspondence*, vol. III, p. 78.

45. Newcastle to Joseph Yorke, 14 May 1762, Newcastle House, in Hardwicke, *Life and correspondence*, vol. III, pp. 356–7. On Newcastle and the German War, see Namier, *England*, pp. 302–26.

46. For details of the meeting, see Newcastle to Joseph Yorke, 14 May 1762, Newcastle House, in Hardwicke, *Life and correspondence*, vol. III, pp. 356–7. Pitt is quoted by Black in *Parliament and foreign policy in the eighteenth century*, p. 100, and *Pitt the Elder*, p. 234.

47. Newcastle to Joseph Yorke, 14 May 1762, Newcastle House, in Hardwicke, *Life and correspondence*, vol. III, pp. 356–8.

48. Hamish M. Scott, 'True principles', p. 57. Hardwicke to Newcastle, 28 July 1762, Grosvenor Square, in Hardwicke, *Life and correspondence*, vol. III, pp. 402–3, 405. Black, *Europe or America?*, p. 179. Hardwicke to Newcastle, 28 July 1762, in Hardwicke, *Life and correspondence*, vol. III, p. 406.

49. Joseph Yorke to Hardwicke, 16 July 1762, The Hague; Hardwicke to Newcastle, 2 October 1762, Wimpole; Newcastle to Hardwicke, 7 October 1762, in Hardwicke, *Life and correspondence*, vol. III, pp. 400, 418, 419.

50. For Halifax's appointment, see Duke of Halifax to Duke of Brunswick, 15 October 1762, St James's (NStAH Hann. 9e Nr. 1079, fo. 18). There are many dispatches from Brunswick in this folder but few replies from Halifax; cited in Black, *America or Europe?*, p. 177.

51. George III to Bute, 8 June 1762, in George III, *Letters to Lord Bute*, p. 144. See Black, 'Crown, Hanover', p.121; George III to Bute, c.10 January 1763, in George III, *Letters to Lord Bute*, p. 183.

52. Cressener to Halifax, 10 February 1763, Regensburg (NA SP 81/143, unfoliated).

53. Bute is quoted in Bullion, 'Securing the peace', p. 31; Egremont is quoted in Hyam, 'Imperial interests', p. 34.

54. See, e.g., ibid., esp. pp. 32, 38, and more recently and trenchantly in Hyam, 'Primacy of geopolitics', esp. pp. 30–32. On the relative unimportance of the commercial lobby, see Sutherland, 'East India Company and the Peace of Paris', esp. pp. 183, 186. Gough, *British mercantile interests*, pp. 113–24, stresses the primacy of economic factors.

55. See the comic description of British ignorance of colonial affairs in Hyam, 'Imperial interests', p. 36; Newcastle is quoted on p. 25. See also Peters, *Pitt and popularity*, pp. 243–6; Schweizer, 'Lord Bute and the press', pp. 90–91. On the centrality of foreign policy to attacks on Bute, see Thomas, *George III: King and politicians*, pp. 73–84.

56. Hardwicke to Newcastle, 28 July 1762, Grosvenor Square, in Hardwicke, *Life and correspondence*, vol. III, pp. 402–3. Pitt is quoted in Rashed, *Peace of Paris*, pp. 104, 191.

57. O'Gorman, 'Myth', p. 60. Newcastle to Hardwicke, 29 November 1762, Claremont, in Hardwicke, *Life and correspondence*, vol. III, p. 438. Bullion, 'Securing the peace', p. 18. Schweizer, 'Lord Bute and the press', p. 91.

58. Newcastle to Hardwicke, 29 November 1762, Claremont, in Hardwicke, *Life and correspondence*, vol. III, p. 438. Pitt is quoted in Cardwell, *Arts and arms*, p. 266. Newcastle to Bentinck, 24 February 1763, Newcastle House (BL Add Mss 32947, fos. 81–2).

18 Imperial Retrenchments, 1763–1765

1. Quoted in Crout, 'In search', p. 373.
2. Quoted in Black, 'Crown, Hanover', p. 130.
3. Varsori, 'Is Britain part of Europe?', p. 156. Kippis is quoted in Bob Harris, *Politics and the nation*, p. 324.

4. Stourzh, *Benjamin Franklin*, p. 81. Rashed, *Peace of Paris*, p. 204. On the transformations of 1763 in America, see most recently Calloway, *Scratch of a pen*.

5. Vergennes is quoted in Gould, *Persistence of empire*, pp. 106–7, and in Crout, 'In search', p. 373. Voltaire/Walpole is quoted in Grafton, *Autobiography*, pp. 11–12. The Irish priest is quoted in Morley, *Irish opinion*, p. 46. The Shawnees are quoted in Matthew C. Ward, *Breaking the backcountry*, p. 216.

6. Thomas Walpole to Newcastle, 25 March 1763 (BL Add Mss 32947, fo. 309).

7. The pamphleteer is quoted in Bob Harris, *Politics and the nation*, p. 145. On Hume, see Hont, *Jealousy of trade*, pp. 85, 340–41. On British fears of 'over-expansion', see also Koehn, *Power of commerce*, pp. 180–81.

8. See Forbes, *Hume's philosophical politics*, p. 174.

9. See Bowen, 'British conceptions', on the shift to a territorial empire. A good sense of the military implications of the new perimeter line is given in McConnell, *Army and Empire*, esp. chapter 2, 'Frontier fortresses', pp. 32–52 (with maps on pp. 29–31).

10. See Matthew C. Ward, *Breaking the backcountry*, pp. 220, 203, 211–12; p. 229 for quotations; pp. 186–7 on penny-pinching. On the Pontiac revolt as a failure of Indian diplomacy, see Jacobs, *Diplomacy and Indian gifts*, pp. 181–5.

11. Matthew C. Ward, *Breaking the backcountry*, pp. 227, 234 5. Peter J. Marshall, 'Nation defined by empire', p. 209.

12. Doll, *Revolution, religion*, p. 61.

13. Cabinet memorandum, 9 February 1764, London, in Grenville, *Additional papers*, p. 320. On anxieties in India after 1763, see Peter J. Marshall, *Making and unmaking*, pp. 207–28, esp. p. 211.

14. Morley, *Irish opinion*, pp. 1–4, 48–50, *et passim*. Leighton, *Catholicism*, passim.

15. Morley, *Irish opinion*, pp. 7–8, 11, 48.

16. Hamish M. Scott, 'Importance', p. 18. Hamish M. Scott, 'Britain's emergence', p. 10. Baugh, 'Withdrawing from Europe', p. 20. Hamish M. Scott 'Importance', p. 29, and 'Le Duc de Choiseul'. On the colonial dimension to French strategy, see Singh, *French diplomacy*, pp. 6–8, 61–108.

17. Details and figures on the naval situation are in Hamish M. Scott, 'Importance', pp. 19–28, and the tables in Richard Harding, *Sea power*, pp. 291–2. For fears of French intentions see Bullion, 'Securing the peace', p. 21, and Rashed, *Peace of Paris*, p. 209.

18. See Grenville, *Additional papers*, p. 321; 'At Lord Sandwich's at the Pay Office', Whitehall, 12 December 1764, p. 332.

19. Cobbett, *Parliamentary history*, XVI, 22 November 1770, col. 1102.

20. Grenville to the Earl of Egmont, 16 April 1764, Downing Street, in Grenville, *Grenville papers*, vol. II, p. 293.

21. On this, see Hamish M. Scott, *British foreign policy*, p. 160, *et passim*; and Hamish M. Scott, 'Britain's emergence'. The perplexed diplomats were Joseph Yorke to Earl of Hardwicke, 1 September 1772 (BL Add Mss 35370, fo. 46); and Stormont to R. M. Keith, 24 April 1773, Paris (BL Add Mss 35505, fo. 206).

22. Pitt's remarks are recounted in Grenville's diary of 28 August 1763, in *Grenville papers*, vol. II, pp. 197–9. Brewer, *Party ideology*, pp. 39–44, tends to stress ideological and domestic reasons for new polarities after 1760.

23. Most of the *North Briton* no. 45, 23 April 1763, is devoted to foreign policy failures and their domestic causes and implications. For the attack on Bute more generally, see Kathleen Wilson, *Sense of the people*, pp. 213–16, and Brewer, 'Misfortunes of Lord Bute', esp. pp. 9, 113. Rudé, *Wilkes and liberty*, pp. 22–3, ignores the foreign policy context and is consequently puzzled as to what all the fuss was about: 'There was nothing in this latest number of the *North Briton* that would seem to our generation to warrant a charge of seditious libel!' The latest account, Cash, *John Wilkes*, pp. 99–100, makes no mention of foreign policy in its short account of issue no. 45.

24. Wilkes to Earl Temple, 15 July 1763, Aylesbury; Earl Temple to Michell, 18 October

1764, Stowe, in Grenville, *Grenville papers*, vol. II, pp. 77, 450–52. Brewer, 'Misfortunes of Lord Bute', p. 37.

25. Hamish M. Scott, 'Britain's emergence', p. 137. Sandwich to Sir Joseph Yorke, 31 May 1765, Whitehall, in Sandwich, *Fourth Earl*, p. 314. Conway to Stormont, 23 August 1767, St James's (NA SP 80/204, unfoliated). For Frederick on British ministers, see Hamish M. Scott, 'Britain as a European Great Power', p. 186.

26. Goldsmith is quoted in Gould, *Persistence of empire*, p. 106; see also his chapter 'The blue water vision', pp. 36–71, more generally. For the press, see Peters, 'Names and cant', p. 120; Schweizer, 'Newspapers', p. 35, and Brewer, *Party ideology*, pp. 139–60. On the growing importance of the press after the Seven Years War, see Barker, 'England', esp. pp. 93–7.

27. Bob Harris, *Politics and the nation*, p. 240. Schumpeter, *English overseas trade statistics*. On empire and virtue see Kathleen Wilson, *Sense of the people*, pp. 201–2. On British 'national self-congratulation and show', see Colley, 'Apotheosis', pp. 98–9. On British interest in the colonies, see Price, 'Who cared', esp. p. 404. For a slightly contrary view, see Peter J. Marshall, 'Who cared'.

28. Lord Clive to Grenville, October 1764, Rio de Janeiro, in Grenville, *Grenville papers*, p. 446.

29. My view of Sandwich differs somewhat from that of Rodger, *Insatiable earl*, pp. xvii–xviii, 105–6, *et passim*, who sees him much more within the classic Continentalist tradition.

30. Sandwich to Buckingham, 20 November 1764, Whitehall, in Sandwich, *Fourth Earl*, p. 240. Black, 'Crown, Hanover', p. 129. On Britain's 'reserved' attitude towards alliances more generally, see Hamish M. Scott, *British foreign policy*. Sandwich to Goodricke, 30 November 1764, Whitehall; Sandwich to Dudley Cosby, 11 December 1764; Sandwich to Macartney, 15 February 1765, Whitehall; Sandwich to Stormont, 31 January 1764, Whitehall, in Sandwich, *Fourth Earl*, pp. 247, 253, 282, 130.

31. Horn, *Great Britain and Europe*, p. 198. Black, 'Crown, Hanover', p. 130. Grenville is from his own account of a conversation with the more conciliatory Duke of Bedford: diary entry of 26 July 1764, in *Grenville papers*, p. 510. See also Lawson, *George Grenville*, pp. 203–10.

32. Buckingham to Sandwich, 23 November 1763, St Petersburg; Sandwich to Bedford, 8 September 1764, Belvedere; Sandwich to Macartney, 15 January 1765, in Sandwich, *Fourth Earl*, pp. 108, 214, 219–20, 273. Black, 'Crown, Hanover', p. 130.

33. Tracy, *Navies, deterrence*. Cabinet minute 'At Lord Halifax's in Great George's Street', 4 October 1764, in Grenville, *Additional papers*, p. 331. Sir Edward Hawke, 1770, Cobbett, *Parliamentary history*, XVI, 9 January 1770, col. 706. Hamish M. Scott, *British foreign policy*, p. 169.

34. Joseph Yorke to James Harris, 22 December 1773, The Hague (BL Add Mss 35434, fo. 41).

35. Brooke, *Chatham administration* pp. 49–50. Peters, 'Names and cant', p. 122.

36. Brooke, *Chatham administration*, pp. 35–7. See diary entry of 25 March 1767, in Grenville, *Grenville papers*, vol. IV, pp. 216–17.

37. On levels of representation at the smaller German courts, see Horn, *Great Britain and Europe*, pp. 184–5.

38. Sandwich, *Fourth Earl*, p. 241.

39. On the Duke of Richmond, see Brooke, *Chatham administration*, p. 143. Hamish Scott, 'Great Britain, Poland', p. 59.

40. Black, *Continental commitment*, p. 151. Sandwich to Bedford, 15 August 1764, Whitehall, in Sandwich, *Fourth Earl*, pp. 198–9. On Sandwich and the primacy of home waters, see Rodger, *Insatiable Earl*.

41. Bedford to Sandwich, 7 September 1764, Woburn Abbey, in Sandwich, *Fourth Earl*, pp. 211–12.

42. Dippel, 'Prussia's English policy'. Hamish M. Scott, 'Britain's emergence', p. 108. Sand-

wich to Stormont, 8 January 1765; Stormont to Sandwich, 26 January 1765, Vienna, in Sandwich, *Fourth Earl*, pp. 265, 277. For Frederick's views on British perfidy in the 1760s, see Schmidt, 'Idea and slogan', pp. 607–8. The diplomatic afterlife of the Anglo-Prussian breach is described in Dorn, 'Frederick the Great', p. 529.

43. For British fears in this regard, see Stormont to Sandwich, 26 January and 6 March 1765, Vienna; Sandwich to Stormont, 27 December 1763, Whitehall, in ibid., pp. 277–8, 286, 278, 102, 122.

44. Sandwich to Stormont, 27 December 1763, Whitehall, ibid., p. 121; see also p. 123. Stormont to Sandwich, 17 January 1764, Vienna, 'most secret' (NA SP 80/200, unfoliated). See also the account in Grenville's diary entries of 24 and 25 December, in *Grenville papers*, pp. 240–41.

45. Stormont to Sandwich, 17 January 1764, Vienna, 'most secret' (NA SP 80/200, unfoliated).

46. Münchhausen is quoted in Riotte, 'George III', p. 63. See the text of the treaty in Rashed, *Peace of Paris*, p. 25. Thomas Walpole to Newcastle, 25 March 1763 (BL Add Mss 32947, fo. 309).

47. Thus Sandwich to Cressener, 6 January 1764, Whitehall (NA SP 81/144, unfoliated). *Owen's Weekly Chronicle* 17 and 13 March 1764, quoted in Black, 'Crown, Hanover', p. 126.

48. Instructions for Fulke Greville, 31 December 1765, St James's (NA SP 104/240, Foreign Entry Book, p. 8). Cressener to Halifax, 12 February 1763, Regensburg (NA SP 81/143, unfoliated). On the complications of Osnabrück, see von Aretin, *Das alte Reich*, pp. 136–9.

49. Stormont to Sandwich, 4 January, 17 January and 18 February 1764, Vienna (NA SP 80/200, unfoliated). Re Pompadour, see ibid., 4 April 1764.

50. On this, see Hamish M. Scott, 'True principles'.

51. Sandwich to Stormont, 8 January 1765, in Sandwich, *Fourth Earl*, p. 265. Reddaway, 'Macartney', p. 263. On British attempts to bribe Tsarist officials, see (in some detail) Hamish M. Scott, 'Britain's emergence', pp. 152–4.

52. Cabinet minute, 16 September 1763, St James's, in Sandwich, *Fourth Earl*, p. 71; in a similar vein, see the comments of Buckinghamshire on p. 170. Hamish M. Scott, 'Britain, Poland', p. 68.

53. Cabinet minute, 16 September 1763, St James's, in Sandwich, *Fourth Earl*, p. 71. Also see, e.g., Sandwich to Macartney, 15 January 1765, ibid., p. 273. For the Russian perspective, see Griffiths, 'Rise and fall', pp. 551–3. George Macartney to Sandwich, 12 March 1765, St Petersburg, ibid., p. 295.

54. Sandwich to Sir John Goodricke, 22 May 1764, Whitehall, ibid., p. 161. In the same vein, see also the dispatch to the ambassador at St Petersburg: Sandwich to Macartney, 15 February 1765, Whitehall, ibid., p. 282; and also p. 176. Sandwich to Walter Titley and Dudley Cosby, 30 November 1764, Whitehall, ibid., p. 245. On the centrality of naval concerns in British policy towards Sweden, see Michael Roberts, *British diplomacy*, pp. 79, 243–5, and Metcalf, *Russia, England*, pp. 64, 70, 83–5.

55. Roberts, *British diplomacy*. Metcalf, *Russia, England*.

56. On the 'designs of France' see Stormont to Sandwich, 18 February 1764, Vienna (NA SP 80/200, unfoliated), and Sandwich, *Fourth Earl*, pp. 78, 82. The British ambassador, Buckinghamshire is quoted in Sandwich, *Fourth Earl*, p. 169. London was kept well informed of the situation in Poland: e.g. Stormont to Sandwich, 7 January 1764, Vienna; Stormont to Sandwich, 'separate & private', 17 January 1764, Vienna (NA SP 80/200, unfoliated). On Britain's 'basic indifference' to eastern Europe, see Hamish M. Scott, 'Britain's emergence', p. 106, and especially, 'Great Britain, Poland', p. 55, *et passim*. Sandwich, *Fourth Earl*, p. 167. See NA SP/200 unfoliated, *passim*.

19 Imperial Pre-emptions, 1765–1767

1. Quoted in Stourzh, *Benjamin Franklin*, p. 114.
2. Quoted in Black, *George III*, pp. 313–14.
3. Quoted in Reddaway, 'Macartney', p. 261.
4. On this see Fred Anderson, *Crucible of war*, pp. 617–37 (esp. pp. 633–7, 'The lessons of Pontiac's War'). Gould, *Persistence of empire*, p. 113; on the legacy of Albany, see p. 67.
5. Stourzh, *Benjamin Franklin*, p. 89. Peter J. Marshall, 'Nation defined by empire', p. 209. Doll, *Revolution, religion*, p. 98.
6. Bullion, 'Securing the peace', pp. 18–20. The best account of the problems of imperial defence after the Seven Years War is Tucker and Hendricksen, *Fall of the first British empire*, esp. pp. 76–107. On thinking in London, see also Fred Anderson, *Crucible of war*, pp. 560–71.
7. See 'Royal Proclamation', 7 October 1763, in Madden and Fieldhouse, *Classical period*, pp. 520–23. The standard account of British 'wilderness' policy after 1763 is Sosin, *Whitehall and the wilderness*, esp. pp. 52–78. On the relative success of British diplomacy with the Indians, see Bickham, *Savages*, pp. 134–67, esp. pp. 134–6. For the figures, see 'Mr West's paper' for Newcastle, 23 March 1763 (BL Add Mss 32947, fo. 265).
8. For Pitt's warning of an 'armed truce', see Gould, 'Zones of law'. Pitt's remarks in committee are reported in 'Mr West's paper' for Newcastle, 23 March 1763 (BL Add Mss 32947, fo. 265). Whately is quoted in Draper, *Struggle for power*, p. 345.
9. For contemporary thinking on the economic potential of North America, see Draper, *Struggle for power*, pp. 103, 108. See also Judith Blow Williams, *British commercial policy*, pp. 6–22, on the shift from the sugar islands to the thirteen colonies.
10. Draper, *Struggle for power*, p. 354. Morley, *Irish opinion*, p. 79.
11. Draper, *Struggle for power*, p. 275. 'Israel Mauduit's account of a conference between Mr Grenville and the several colony agents', in *Jenkinson papers*, pp. 306–7. See also Thomas, *British politics*, esp. pp. 69–94, and Lawson, *George Grenville*, pp. 193–201.
12. On this, see Lees, 'Retrenchment', p. 1, *et passim*. I thank Mr Lees for kindly letting me have a copy of his unpublished paper. See also Peter J. Marshall, *Making and unmaking*, pp. 1–3, 59–60, 273–310, *et passim*, and Koehn, *Power of commerce*.
13. For Russia, Prussia and Austria, see most recently Hamish M. Scott, 'Britain's emergence'. On the Spanish reforms, with a comparative look at Britain, see Elliott, *Empires of the Atlantic*, chapter 10, 'War and reform', pp. 292–324, esp. pp. 295, 301, 310. A comparative look at Britain and the German states in this period can be found in Hellmuth, 'Why does corruption matter?'
14. See Draper, *Struggle for power*, p. 204, and Fred Anderson, *Crucible of war*, pp. 604–51. On America and Hanover, see Nicholas B. Harding, 'Dynastic union', p. 316, and Peter J. Marshall, 'Nation defined by empire', p. 215.
15. *Brief state*, pp. 12–13. Bollan, *Succinct view*, pp. 7, 33–6. On the idea of a colonial bargain, see LaFeber, 'Foreign policies', p. 12.
16. Dickinson, *Speech*, p. 5. Draper, *Struggle for power*, p. 205. Bollan, *Succinct view*, p. 16. *Grievances of the American colonies*, p. 19.
17. Both quotations are from Stourzh, *Benjamin Franklin*, pp. 198–9, the latter being a description of Franklin's meeting with Shelburne in a letter to his son.
18. Egnal, *Mighty empire*, p. 190; on the role of the expansionists generally, see pp. 1–3, 6–7, *et passim*. On the role of imperialism in the making of the revolution, see William A. Williams, 'Age of mercantilism', p. 420; Darling, *Our rising empire*; and Rostow, *Breakfast for Bonaparte*, chapter 4, 'From sea to shining sea', pp. 72–85, which discusses the period before 1776. The most recent account of colonists as English imperialists is Kagan, *Dangerous nation*, pp. 12–16, 18.

19. *Grievances of the American colonies*, p. 41. On westward expansion as a pre-emptive move, see Kagan, *Dangerous nation*, pp. 23–5.
20. Matthew C. Ward, *Breaking the backcountry*, p. 257. Egnal, *Mighty empire*, p. 226. Van Alstyne, 'Significance of the Mississippi Valley', p. 222. Egnal, *Mighty empire*, p. 225.
21. Draper, *Struggle for power*, pp. 336–7. *Considerations relative to the North American colonies*, p. 8. Savelle, 'Appearance of an American attitude', p. 663. Stourzh, *Benjamin Franklin*, pp. 101, 116. I disagree with the otherwise persuasive van Alstyne, *Rising American empire*, p. 22, on the significance of the naming of wars. On the eurocentricity of early American strategic ideas, see Hutson, *John Adams*, pp. 1–12, and 'Intellectual foundations' (Adams quotation on p. 14).
22. Savelle, 'Appearance of an American attitude', p. 663.
23. Draper, *Struggle for power*, pp. 220, 340. On the advance of the expansionists, see Egnal, *Mighty empire, passim*, esp. pp. 150, 229.
24. *Considerations relative to the North American colonies*, p. 14. Conway is quoted in Conway, *British Isles*, p. 330. Stourzh, *Benjamin Franklin*, p. 114.
25. Bollan, *Succinct view*, p. 10. See in the same vein, *Grievances of the American colonies*, p. 24. Ray is quoted in Van Alstyne, *Empire and independence*, p. 29, and Livingston in Egnal, *Mighty empire*, p. 190.
26. Hamish M. Scott, 'Britain's emergence', p. 138, and 'Importance', p. 35. Langford, *First Rockingham administration*. Hamish M. Scott, 'Britain's emergence', pp. 166–7.
27. See Newcastle to Rockingham, 17 September 1766, Claremont; and Newcastle, 'Memo for General Conway, Foreign Affairs [1766]' (BL Add Mss 32977, fos. 91–3, 85). Albemarle is quoted in Black, *George III*, pp. 313–14, where his claims are treated with some scepticism.
28. Pitt to Duke of Brunswick, 23 July 1764, Hayes (NStAH Hann. 9e Nr. 1098, fo. 150). Conway is quoted in Reddaway, 'Macartney', p. 261; for examples of arrogance, see pp. 288–9. Pitt on the North is quoted in Brooke, *Chatham administration*, pp. 39–40. Conway to Mitchell, 8 August 1766, St James's, in Pitt, *Correspondence of William Pitt, Earl of Chatham*, vol. III, p. 29. The observations on Stanley's mission are in Alexander Wedderburn to George Grenville, 9 September 1766, London, in Grenville, *Grenville papers*, p. 320.
29. Conway to Stormont, 23 August 1767, St James's (NA SP 80/204, unfoliated). Reddaway, 'Macartney', p. 265. Conway to Stormont, 27 October and 5 May 1767, St James's (NA SP 80/204, unfoliated).
30. Conway to Stormont, 13 January 1767, St James's, ibid. Frederick's complaints are quoted in Hamish M. Scott, *British foreign policy*, p. 110. Conway to Mitchell, 8 August 1766, St James's, in Pitt, *Correspondence of William Pitt, Earl of Chatham*, vol. III, pp. 29–30. The British ambassador to St. Petersburg is quoted in Hamish M. Scott, *British foreign policy*, p. 100.
31. Charles Jenkinson, 'Heads of Defence of the extra estimate of the Navy', [1767] (BL Add Mss 38336, fos. 366–7).
32. Ibid., p. 366.
33. Bullion, 'Securing the peace', p. 35. In the same vein, see the disjointed notes in Charles Jenkinson, 'Heads of Defence of the extra estimate of the Navy', [1767] (BL Add Mss 38336, fo. 359).
34. For India, see Bowen, *Revenue and reform*, pp. 84–118, and Sutherland, *East India Company in eighteenth-century politics*, pp. 138–76. On Ireland, see Morley, *Irish opinion*, p. 58; and Conway, *British Isles*, pp. 188–9. On the rapprochement with the Catholic elite in Ireland, see Conway, 'War, expansion'.
35. Draper, *Struggle for power*, p. 106.
36. I have been influenced by Kathleen Wilson's graphic and persuasive account in *Sense of the people*, p. 223.

37. Stourzh, *Benjamin Franklin*, p. 98. On the rise of the expansionists, see Egnal, *Mighty empire*, pp. 160–61.
38. Van Alstyne, *Empire and independence*, p. 43. Stourzh, *Benjamin Franklin*, p. 115. Van Alstyne, *Empire and independence*, p. 43. Draper, *Struggle for power*, pp. 107, 409.
39. Draper, *Struggle for power*, pp. 319, 408.

20 Empire Adrift, 1768–1772

1. Quoted in Hamish M. Scott, 'True principles', p. 56.
2. Rochford to Shelburne, 21 April 1768, Paris; Shelburne to Rochford, 29 April 1768, Whitehall (NA SP 78/274, fos. 206, 210). See also Rice, 'Deceit and distraction', and Hall, *France*, pp. 156–214.
3. Panin is quoted in Hamish M. Scott, 'Britain's emergence', p. 137. For many examples of the view that Britain was now only interested in America, see Hamish M. Scott, *British foreign policy*, pp. 122–3.
4. Joseph Yorke to Lord Rochford, 8 December 1769, The Hague; Stormont to Rochford, 10 March 1770, Vienna (BL Add Mss 35434, fos. 8, 10).
5. Whately to Earl Temple, 22 September 1769, in Grenville, *Grenville papers*, p. 461.
6. See M. S. Anderson, 'Great Britain and the Russo-Turkish War', pp. 39–41, 49.
7. [Joseph II] 'Beschreibung der Österreichischen Monarchie', [Tableau Générale] dated c.1767-8 (HHStA Hausarchiv Sammelbände, 88, fos. 72–4). See Scott, Elliott and Hufton, *Emergence of the eastern powers*, p. 164, and esp. p. 194. Dann, *Hanover and Great Britain*, p. 146.
8. I was innocent of all knowledge of this fascinating subject until I read *The King's silver: George III's service in Hanover and England*, a leaflet produced by the Rothschild Collection at Waddesdon Manor in 2003. I am most grateful to the academic director of Waddesdon, Dr Philippa Glanville, for drawing this to my attention.
9. Thus 'Instruction for Lewis de Visme', 31 January 1770, St James's, where he was told to 'take the advice' of the Hanoverian minister; see also 'Particular instructions' for John Osborn, 'Envoy Extraordinary' to Electoral Saxony, 30 March 1771 (NA SP 104/240, pp. 47, 76–8). [Joseph II] 'Beschreibung der Österreichischen Monarchie', [Tableau Générale] dated c.1767-8 (HHStA Hausarchiv Sammelbände, 88, fo. 126).
10. For Chatham's role, see Black, *Parliament and foreign policy in the eighteenth century*, p. 103. For North and the crisis generally, see Goebel, *Struggle*, pp. 270–410, esp. 306–8, 368–71. See also Rice, 'Great Britain'.
11. Thomas Coleman to Grenville, Port Egmont, 4 March 1770, in Grenville, *Grenville papers*, pp. 505–6. Cobbett, *Parliamentary history*, XVI, 25 January 1771, col. 1345.
12. See M. S. Anderson, 'Great Britain and the Russo-Turkish War', p. 41. Rodger, *Insatiable earl*, p. 194. Black, *Parliament and foreign policy in the eighteenth century*, p. 179. Nicholas Tracy takes a more robust view in 'Falkland Islands crisis'.
13. See letters of 30 May, 12 and 22 June 1769, and 30 January 1771, in 'Junius', *Letters*, pp. 72–3, 76, 79, 222.
14. Cobbett, *Parliamentary history*, XVI, 22 January 1771, cols. 749, 680–81.
15. Ibid., 9 January 1771, cols. 682, 1096, 1094.
16. Hamish M. Scott, *British foreign policy*, p. 176.
17. See Roberts, *British diplomacy*, esp. pp. 349–403. Walpole is quoted in Horn, *British public opinion*, p. 14. Rochford memorandum for Lord Sandwich, November 1772, in Sandwich, *Sandwich papers*, vol. I, pp 31–2. Joseph Yorke to Earl of Hardwicke, 1 September 1772 (BL Add Mss 35370, fo. 46).
18. North to Sandwich, 5 September 1772, Compton, in Sandwich, *Sandwich papers*, vol. I, p. 20. For indifference of Britain to the partition of Poland, see Brooks, 'British political culture'; Horn, *British public opinion*, esp. p. iii; and Michael, *Englands Stellung*, esp. pp. 2–9, 90–91.

19. Joseph Yorke to James Harris, 22 December 1773, The Hague (BL Add Mss 35434, fo. 41). Horn, *British public opinion*, pp. 10, 60–61.

20. Ibid., pp. 62, 63, 65. Joseph Yorke to James Harris, 22 December 1773, The Hague (BL Add Mss 35434, fo. 41). The *Bristol Gazette and Public Advertiser* is quoted in Black, *George III*, p. 314.

21. Horn, *British public opinion*, pp. 9, 1–2.

22. Quotations ibid., pp. 50, 45, 56.

23. The engraving serves as the jacket illustration for Scott, Elliott and Hufton's *Emergence of the eastern powers*. Horn, *British public opinion*, p. 15; see also pp. 46, 7, 65.

24. Horn, *British public opinion*, pp. 63, 60, 49.

25. Ibid., pp. 48, 25, 36–7. See also Vincitorio, 'Edmund Burke', esp. pp. 33, 37 and 42 for quotations.

26. Horn, *British public opinion*, pp. 26, 36–7. The *Annual Register* is quoted in Vincitorio, 'Edmund Burke'.

27. On Americans and Corsica, see George P. Anderson, 'Pascal Paoli', esp. pp. 189–91, 202–3 (for quotation). For the impact of the Polish partition on the constitutional convention, see Marks, *Independence on trial*, chapter 2, 'The problem of national defense', pp. 3–51, esp. p. 33. Madison is quoted in Ciencala, 'American founding fathers', p. 112. Wandycz, 'American Revolution', deals mainly with the period after 1775. On the British imperial retreat in the west, see Sosin, *Whitehall and the wilderness*, pp. 211–38.

28. Rochford memorandum for Lord Sandwich, November 1772, in Sandwich, *Sandwich papers*, vol. I, pp. 30–31. 'Separate and secret instructions' for Keith, 10 October 1772, St James's (NA SP 104/240, p. 112).

29. 'Copy of a military dispatch of Lord Townshend's at a time when the seizure of the Falkland Islands made a rupture with France and Spain hourly expected', 16 October 1770, Dublin Castle (BL Add Mss 33118, fos. 1–2, 5, 13, 20). For warnings re England, see Captain Guy Carleton, 'Observation', 22 October 1771, and (for quotation) 'Memorandum by Captain Guy Carleton: The probability of an intended invasion, its practicableness, the dangers that must ensue, the means of guarding against them', in George III, *Correspondence*, vol. II, pp. 287, 294.

30. Rodger, *Insatiable earl*, p. 194. Sandwich to North, 10 September 1772, Hinchingbroke; report 'Relative to the state of the French navy', by Durnford to Rochford, 14 December 1772, Dunkirk, in Sandwich, *Sandwich papers*, vol. I, pp. 24, 33–4.

31. Glete, *Navies and nations*, vol. I, tables on pp. 271–2.

32. Cobbett, *Parliamentary history*, XVI, 13 November 1770, cols. 1038, 1046, 1069, 1093. For foreign policy attacks on Lord North before the American Revolution, see Whiteley, *Lord North*, pp. 98–100.

21 Fighting for Europe in America, 1773–1777

1. Chatham to Baron Bridport (Admiral Hood), 6 June 1773, Burton Pynsent (BL Add Mss 35192, fo. 15).

2. Quoted in Stourzh, *Benjamin Franklin*, p. 88.

3. 'Debate in the Lords on employing foreign troops without the consent of Parliament', 1 November 1775, Cobbett, *Parliamentary history*, XVIII, cols. 798–9.

4. Quoted in Gould, 'Zones of law', p. 489.

5. Burwell is quoted in Bowen, *Revenue and reform*, pp. 131–2. Chatham to Shelburne, 20 October 1773, Burton Pynsent, in Pitt, *Correspondence of William Pitt, Earl of Chatham*, vol. IV, p. 299. Burke's remarks are in Cobbett, *Parliamentary history*, XVII, 2 December 1772, col. 548. See also Bayly, *Imperial meridian*, pp. 96–9.

6. Richard B. Sheridan, 'British credit crisis', provides background but concentrates on the economic rather than the fiscal and strategic dimensions. Tucker is quoted in van Alstyne,

Empire and independence, p. 7. On reform in the Habsburg monarchy, see Beales, *Joseph II*, and Brendan Simms, *Struggle for mastery*, pp. 23–44.

7. On the Falklands see Goebel, *Struggle*, pp. 408–10.

8. Conway, *War of American independence*, pp. 15–16. See Greene, *Peripheries and centre*, pp. 117–18 for the Hanover comparison, and pp. 129–50 for the final stages of disintegration.

9. John Cannon takes a witty and waspish look at the issues in 'George III and America', though without mentioning strategy. On ideological divides see Bailyn, *Ideological origins*. For Quebec see Philip Lawson, *Taste for empire*, pp. 301–23. Doll, *Revolution, religion*, pp. 198, 94, 153.

10. Stourzh, *Benjamin Franklin*, p. 199. See also Doll, *Revolution, religion*, p. 149, and van Alstyne, *Empire and independence*, p. 38.

11. Lawson, *Taste for empire*, p. 314. See James Duane, 'Notes of debates', *c.* 17 October 1774, in Burnett, *Letters of members of the Continental Congress*, vol. I, p. 77. Lawson, *Taste for empire*, pp. 314–15, is a bit more sceptical about the importance of the strategic dimensions. Jefferson is quoted in Kagan, *Dangerous nation*, p. 36. For the west see Sosin, *Whitehall and the wilderness*, chapter 10, 'The Quebec Act: the final decision', pp. 239–58. Bernard Donoughue's chapter on the Quebec Act in his *British Politics*, pp. 105–26, shows that the House of Commons was worried about the boundaries as well as the religious issues.

12. Franklin as quoted in van Alstyne, *Empire and independence*, p. 44; Stourzh, *Benjamin Franklin*, p. 110; and Black, *Pitt the Elder*, p. 290. On the link between expansionism and revolution see Reginald C. Stuart, *United States expansionism*, pp. 8–27.

13. M. S. Anderson, 'Great Britain and the Russo-Turkish War', pp. 54, 51. Joseph Yorke to James Harris, 22 December 1773, The Hague (BL Add Mss 35434, fo. 41).

14. Vincitorio, 'Edmund Burke', p. 37.

15. Von Aretin, *Das alte Reich*, vol. III, p. 148. Additional 'Secret instructions' for de Visme, 31 January 1770, St James's; 'Particular instructions' for John Osborn, 'Envoy Extraordinary' to Electoral Saxony, 30 March 1771 (NA SP 104/240, pp. 52, 78). Von Aretin, *Das alte Reich*, vol. III, pp. 108, 114, 148. Joseph Yorke to James Harris, 22 December 1773, The Hague (BL Add Mss 35434, fo. 41). On Joseph's relations with George see also Beales, *Joseph II*, p. 304.

16. Instructions for Hugh Elliot [envoy to the Reichstag and also to Bavaria], 29 April 1774, St James's (NA SP 104/240, p. 14). Von Aretin, *Das alte Reich*, vol. III, pp. 144–8. Belgioso to Kaunitz, 30 August 1774, London (HHStA England Korrespondenz, Berichte Karton 117). Instruction for Belgioso, 12 September 1774, Vienna (ibid., Karton 128). Black, *British foreign policy in an age of revolution*, p. 86. R. M. Keith to Anthony Chamier, 17 December 1774, Vienna, in Keith, *Memoirs*, vol. II, pp. 34–5.

17. See Egnal, 'The expansionists prevail', in *Mighty empire*, p. 14. For loyalist fears of partition, see Hutson, *John Adams*, pp. 13–14, 19–20.

18. Draper, *Struggle for power*, p. 509. Egnal, *Mighty empire*, p. 326.

19. See Gilbert, 'English background', pp. 151–2. A study of this particular afterlife of Bolingbroke would be useful. Stourzh, *Benjamin Franklin*, p. 120.

20. Hamish M. Scott, *British foreign policy in the age of the American Revolution*, p. 195. Joseph Yorke to James Harris, 13 December 1774, The Hague (BL Add Mss 35434, fo. 44). Cobbett, *Parliamentary history*, XVIII, 26 October 1775, col. 789. See the trenchant remarks of Rodger, *Command of the ocean*, p. 327. Cobbett, *Parliamentary history*, XVIII, 26 October 1775, col. 727. See also Tucker and Hendrickson, *Fall of the first British empire*, p. 356.

21. On this see O'Shaughnessy, *Empire divided*, and the very useful discussion in Cotlar, 'American Revolution'. Memorandum by Charles Jenkinson, *c.*1775 (BL Add Mss 38210, fos. 187, 190).

22. Draper, *Struggle for power*, p. 129. Van Alstyne, *Empire and independence*, p. 75.

23. Draper, *Struggle for power*, p. 393. Van Alstyne, *Empire and independence*, pp. 46–7, 69, 67.

24. Keith to Chamier, 5 February 1775, Vienna, in Keith, *Memoirs*, vol. II, pp. 39–40. Cobbett, *Parliamentary history*, XVIII, 16 March and 15 December 1775, cols. 446, 1072, 1102.

25. See the advertisement for troops to serve in India by Christian Ludewig von Hardenberg, Hanover, 15 June 1781, in Oberschelp, *Niedersächsische Texte*, pp. 22–5. Conway, *British Isles*, pp. 16, 150. 'Précis of treaties with the several German princes whose troops are in His Majesty's service', 1776, 1777, 1778 (re Brunswick, Hesse, Waldeck, Ansbach and Anhalt) (NA 30/8/89, fos. 313–14). See also the documents in NA SP 90/101, which date from 1777 and relate entirely to the question of the hire and movement of German mercenaries for the American War; the unhelpful role of Frederick is clearly apparent. See the activities of Colonel William Fawcitt: 'Instruction', 21 January 1776, St James's; and 21 February 1777 (NA SP 104/240, pp. 165–67, 170–71); and for liaison with Hanover, see 'Instructions for Major-General William Fawcitt', 21 October 1777, St James's (p. 198). See also 'Instructions for the British minister to the Reichstag, Morton Eden', 29 November 1776, St James's (pp. 161–3); Yorke to Harris, 22 March 1776 (BL Add Mss 35434, fo. 49); and Dippel, *Germany and the American Revolution*, pp. 118–30 (re recruitment), and Atwood, *The Hessians*, pp. 17–36, which places them in the context of broader relations with Hesse-Kassel stretching back to the Seven Years War and beyond.

26. See 'Translation of a treaty between His Majesty and the Landgrave of Hesse Cassel, signed at Cassel', 15 January 1776, in Cobbett, *Parliamentary history*, XVIII, cols. 1164, 1206–7.

27. Weintraub, *Iron tears*, p. 9. Lawson, *Taste for empire*, p. 314. I am grateful to Gideon Mailer of St John's College, Cambridge, for elucidation on the matters discussed in this paragraph. For the American War as the 'second British – or perhaps the first American – Civil War', see Ferguson, *Empire*, pp. 94–6. Cobbett, *Parliamentary history*, XVIII, 16 March and 26 October 1775, cols. 432, 727.

28. Cobbett, *Parliamentary history*, XIX, 28 May 1777, col. 318, XX, 29 March 1779, col. 363; XXII, 27 November 1781, cols. 690–91. Conway, *British Isles*, p. 145.

29. Burke is quoted in Conor Cruise O'Brien, *Great melody*, p. 158. Cobbett, *Parliamentary history*, XIX, 18 November 1777, cols. 403, 424.

30. Ibid., XVIII, 26 October 1775, col. 728; see in the same vein the Duke of Richmond, cols. 721, 736, 822, 827.

31. Ibid., 16 December 1774, col. 60. Keith to Chamier, 21 January 1775, Vienna, in Keith, *Memoirs*, vol. II, pp. 35–6. Van Alstyne, 'Parliamentary supremacy', p. 211. Cobbett, *Parliamentary history*, XVIII, 26 October 1775, col. 728; 16 November 1775, col. 229. Van Alstyne, 'Parliamentary supremacy', p. 220.

32. See also Cobbett, *Parliamentary history*, XVIII, 16 March, 8 and 1 November 1775, cols. 442, 886, 813. Van Alstyne, 'Great Britain', pp. 311–12.

33. Van Alstyne, 'Parliamentary supremacy', p. 202. Cobbett, *Parliamentary history*, XVIII, 20 January 1775, col. 156. Van Alstyne, 'Parliamentary supremacy', pp. 212, 220, and 'Europe'. The idea of bringing back Chatham rumbled on well into the war: see the banker Thomas Coutts to Chatham, 21 January 1778, in Pitt, *Correspondence of William Pitt, Earl of Chatham*, vol. IV, p. 485. For Burke see Conor Cruise O'Brien, *Great melody*, pp. 150–53.

34. Conway, *British Isles*, p. 129. Kathleen Wilson, *Sense of the people*, pp. 238–9. Van Alstyne, 'Parliamentary supremacy', pp. 230–31. Kathleen Wilson, *Sense of the people*, p. 241; but see van Alstyne, *Empire and independence*, p. 158 re Mauduit.

35. Conway, *British Isles*, p. 13. Memorandum of Sandwich for Lord North, 7 December 1777, Admiralty, in Sandwich, *Sandwich papers*, pp. 327–8. Van Alstyne, *Empire and independence*, p. 122.

36. Joseph Yorke to James Harris, 26 May 1775. The Hague (BL Add Mss 35434, fo. 46). For British–Dutch commercial tensions in the first half of the war, see Miller, *Sir Joseph Yorke*, pp. 37–59. For the treatment of Swedish shipping in the early years of the Revolution, see Barton, 'Sweden', pp. 410–12.

37. On the success of British commercial warfare, see Buel, *In irons*. British logistical difficulties are discussed in Syrett, *Shipping*, esp. pp. 121–38, 243. Richmond's remarks are in Cobbett, *Parliamentary history*, XIX, 18 November 1777, cols. 400–401.

38. Van Alstyne, *Empire and independence*, pp. 67, 79. See also Schiff, *Benjamin Franklin*. Stourzh, *Benjamin Franklin*, p. 138. Crout, 'In search', p. 374. See Baugh, 'Withdrawing from Europe', p. 20; and Murphy, *Charles Gravier*, pp. 253–5. On the French need to complete naval preparations, see Dull, *French navy and American Independence*, pp. 56–68.

39. Gilbert 'New diplomacy'. Van Alstyne, *Empire and independence*, p. 106. See also Stourzh, *Benjamin Franklin*, p. 123. Van Alstyne, *Rising American empire*, p. 34. Paine, 'Common Sense' in *Selected work*, p. 28; in the same vein, see p. 47.

40. Armitage, 'Declaration of Independence and international law', p. 4; and *Declaration of Independence: A global history*, p. 45. The tenacious if unfounded American belief in an imminent partition by the Great Powers is traced in Hutson, 'Partition Treaty', esp. pp. 886, 892, 894. Fear of partition lived on not least in the mind of a patriot historian: see Morris, *Peacemakers*, pp. 173–190 ('The plot to partition America').

41. Cobbett, *Parliamentary history*, XVIII, 20 February 1776, col. 1154; XIX, 21 November and 5 December 1777, cols. 442, 493–4.

42. LaFeber, 'Foreign policies', p. 18. Egnal, *Mighty empire*, p. xiii.

43. Paine, 'Common Sense' in *Selected work*, pp. 28, 30, 33. See also Gilbert, *To the farewell address*, pp. 19–75.

44. Van Alstyne, *Rising American empire*, p. 41.

45. See Stourzh, *Benjamin Franklin*, p. 126. Van Alstyne, *Empire and independence*, p. 94; *Rising American empire*, p. 44. On US diplomatic missions to the Continent, see (most authoritatively) Dull, *Diplomatic history*, pp. 75–81.

46. Weintraub, *Iron tears*, p. 110. Stourzh, *Benjamin Franklin*, p. 131.

47. Yorke to Harris, 16 September 1777, The Hague (BL Add Mss 35434, fo. 53). See van Alstyne, 'Great Britain', p. 332.

48. Cobbett, *Parliamentary history*, XVIII, 31 October 1776, cols. 1415–16. Van Alstyne, *Rising American empire*, pp. 65–6. Cobbett, *Parliamentary history*, XIX, 18 November 1777, cols. 365, 399.

49. Ibid., XVIII, 26 October and 7 February 1775, cols. 710, 285. Yorke to Harris, 19 June 1778, The Hague (BL Add Mss 35434, fo. 61).

50. Cobbett, *Parliamentary history*, XIX, 13 and 19 February 1778, cols. 46–7, 753. Yorke to Harris, 13 January 1778, The Hague (BL Add Mss 35434, fo. 55).

51. Cobbett, *Parliamentary history*, XIX, 26 November 1777, cols. 458–9; 30 May 1777, cols. 316–18; 18 November 1777, cols. 363, 371; 2 December 1777, col. 476; 5 December 1777, col. 489; 18 November 1777, col. 371.

52. Van Alstyne, 'Europe', p. 24.

53. Cobbett, *Parliamentary history*, XIX, 4, 5, 11 December, 30 May, 18 November, 5 December 1777, cols. 544, 549, 597, 316, 372, 492. Chatham to Earl Temple, 24 September 1777, Hayes, in Grenville, *Grenville papers*, vol. IV, p. 573.

54. *British diplomatic instructions*, vol. 7, pp. 164–71. Patterson, *The other Armada*, p. 37. Van Alstyne, *Empire and independence*, p. 139, and Dull, *French navy and American Independence*, pp. 89–94.

55. Corwin, *French policy*, pp. 142–4.

56. Black, *Pitt the Elder*, p. 300. Kathleen Wilson, *Sense of the people*, pp. 204–5.

57. Yorke to Harris, 13 January 1778, The Hague (BL Add Mss 35434, fo. 57). Cobbett, *Parliamentary history*, XIX, 18 November 1777, col. 378; and in the same vein, 2 December and 26 November 1777, 2 February 1778, cols. 479–80, 455, 659. Black, *Parliament and foreign policy in the eighteenth century*, p. 193.

58. Cobbett, *Parliamentary history*, XIX, 26 November 1778, col. 1296. Sandwich to North, 7 May 1778, Portsmouth; Keppel to Sandwich, 9 May 1778, off Spithead, and 20 May 1778, Portsmouth; in the same vein, Keppel to Sandwich, 26 May 1778, Spithead;

Palliser to Sandwich, 6 July 1778, St Helen's, in Sandwich, *Sandwich papers*, vol. II, pp. 49, 54–5, 69, 78, 112.

59. Cobbett, *Parliamentary history*, XX, 7 December 1778, cols. 8, 19. Sandwich to Keppel, 8 July 1778, Admiralty, in Sandwich, *Sandwich papers*, vol. II, pp. 114–15.
60. Vergennes is quoted in Stockley, *Britain and France*, p. 132.

22 Losing America in Europe, 1778–1779

1. North to Eden, 'Tuesday night', undated but probably written at the very end of January 1778 (BL Add Mss 34415, fo. 92).
2. 'Considerations with regard to the invasion, and defence of Ireland in case of a rupture with France', 27 March 1778 (BL Add Mss 33118, fo. 35).
3. Quoted in van Alstyne, *Rising American empire*, p. 53.
4. Cobbett, *Parliamentary history*, XX, 7 December 1778, cols. 27–8.
5. Morley, *Irish opinion*, p. 109.
6. See O'Brien, *Great melody*, pp. 176–201. For the fear of French invasion, see Beresford, 'Ireland in French strategy'.
7. On this and other aspects of Gaelic interest in the European state system, see the remarkable work of Vincent Morley: *Irish opinion*, pp. 177–8, 199.
8. 'Considerations with regard to the invasion, and defence of Ireland in case of a rupture with France', 27 March 1778 (BL Add Mss 33118, fo. 33). For fears about Hanover, see: Elliot to Suffolk, 22 February 1778, Berlin, and 28 March 1778, Berlin (NA SP 90/102, unfoliated); Suffolk to Keith, 1 May 1778, St James's (BL Add Mss 35514, fo. 1); Elliot to Suffolk, 28 March 1778, Berlin, 'private' (NA SP 90/102); King to Lord North, 6 April 1778, Queen's House, in George III, *Correspondence*, vol. IV, p. 98.
9. On Britain generally, see Conway, *British Isles*, pp. 16, 17 (for figures), 350. On Ireland, see Morley, *Irish opinion*, pp. 186, 233, 235, 251; Bartlett, 'Weapon of war'; and Donovan, 'Military origins'.
10. Palliser to Sandwich, 15 May 1778, in Sandwich, *Sandwich papers*, vol. II, p. 62. Joseph Yorke to William Eden, 13 January 1778, The Hague (BL Add Mss 34415, fo. 73). Ainslie to Keith, 4 January 1779, Constantinople (BL Add Mss 35515, fo. 178).
11. Cobbett, *Parliamentary history*, XIX, 25 February 1777, cols. 65–66. Sandwich to North, 15 October 1778, in Sandwich, *Sandwich papers*, vol. II, p. 180.
12. I have profited here from Melkonian, 'Franco-Spanish relations'. Richmond's remarks are in Cobbett, *Parliamentary history*, XIX, 2 December 1777, col. 482.
13. 'Considerations', 27 March 1778 (BL Add Mss 33118, fo. 35). Yorke to Keith, 14 April 1778, The Hague (BL Add Mss 35513, fo. 242). Cobbett, *Parliamentary history*, XX, 14 December 1778, col. 79.
14. On this issue generally, see Scott, Elliot and Hufton, *Emergence of the eastern powers* (p. 1 for quotation). Harris to Sir Robert Keith, 15 December 1778, St Petersburg, in Malmesbury, *Diaries and correspondence*, vol. I, p. 218. Fichtner, 'Viennese perspectives', pp. 11–29.
15. Elliot to Suffolk, 11 April 1778, no. 25, Berlin (NA SP 90/102, unfoliated). Murphy, *Charles Gravier*, p. 304. Joseph Yorke to Sir Robert Murray Keith, 9 October 1778, The Hague (BL Add Mss 35515, fo. 54).
16. Elliot to Suffolk, 22 February 1778, no. 8, Berlin; Suffolk to Elliot, 7 April 1778, St James's; Elliot to Suffolk, 28 February 1778, Berlin; Suffolk to Elliot, 8 May 1778, St James's (NA SP 90/102, unfoliated).
17. Ainslie to Keith, 4 January 1779, Constantinople (BL Add Mss 35515, fo. 178). North to Eden, 'Tuesday night', undated but probably written at the very end of January (BL Add Mss 34415, fo. 92). Joseph Yorke to James Harris, 13 January 1778, The Hague (BL Add Mss 35434, fo. 56). Joseph Yorke to William Eden, 16 January 1778, The Hague (BL Add Mss 34415, fo. 73). As reported in Hugh Elliot to William Eden, 12 January 1778, Berlin (BL Add Mss 34415, fo. 70). Re regional newspapers, see the examples quoted by Kathleen Wilson in *Sense of the people*, p. 254.

18. Van Alstyne, *Rising American empire*, p. 46.

19. W. Lee to the President of Congress, 28 February 1778, Paris; Arthur Lee to Committee of Foreign Affairs, 28 February 1778, Paris (Lee was convinced that Britain's optimism was misplaced); Ralph Izzard to Henry Laurens, President of Congress, 16 February 1778, Paris, in Wharton, *Revolutionary diplomatic correspondence*, vol. II, pp. 510–11, 501.

20. Arthur Lee to Committee of Foreign affairs, 9 June 1778, Paris, ibid., p. 609; John Adams to Lovell, 9 July 1778, Passy (p. 642); see also pp. 715, 788. It has to be said that Adams appeared unconcerned by this; William Lee to the Committee for Foreign Affairs, Frankfurt, 28 September 1779 (p. 348).

21. Elliot to Suffolk, 28 April 1778, no. 29, Berlin (NA SP 90/102, unfoliated). De Madariaga, *Britain, Russia*, p. 43.

22. Suffolk to Elliot, 7 April 1778, St James's; see also Elliot to Suffolk, 4 May 1778, Berlin (NA SP 90/102, unfoliated).

23. Buddruss, *Die Französische Deutschlandpolitik*, pp. 227, 73. Murphy, *Charles Gravier*, *passim*. See Vergennes to Gerard, 28 July 1778, Versailles; also 26 January, 6 and 26 December 1778, in Meng, *Comte de Vergennes*, pp. 192, 145, 362.

24. Ralph Heathcote to Keith, 7 December 1778, Ratisbon; Suffolk to Keith, 27 November 1778, St James's (BL Add Mss 35515, fos. 115, 103). George Cressener to Charles Jenkinson, 5 November 1778, Bonn (BL Add Mss 38210, fo. 108). This theme became something of an *idée fixe* with Cressener: see his further letters to Jenkinson of 9 November, 14 December, 21 December 1778, and 11 January 1779 (fos. 111, 134, 151, 214).

25. Keith to Drummond, 12 June 1779, Vienna, in Keith, *Memoirs*, vol. II, p. 80.

26. Mahan, *Influence of sea power*, p. 510. Crout, 'In search', p. 380. On the Franco-Spanish alliance, see Dull, *Diplomatic history*, pp. 107–13.

27. See Baugh, 'Withdrawing from Europe', p. 20. Butterfield, *George III*, p. 67. Cobbett, *Parliamentary history*, XX, 23 April 1779, col. 429.

28. Ibid., 11 May 1779, col. 648. See Patterson, *The other Armada*, *passim*; Butterfield, *George III*, p. 69. Dull, *French navy and American Independence*, pp. 143–58, thinks this is just as well because it would have been defeated. For British naval distress and the shortage of ships, see Syrett, *Royal Navy in European waters*, pp. 61–82, 133.

29. Cannon, 'George III and America', p. 25. George III to Sandwich, 13 September 1779, Windsor, in Sandwich, *Sandwich papers*, vol. III, pp. 163–4.

30. Cobbett, *Parliamentary history*, XX, 22 June 1779, cols. 931–2. Conway, *British Isles*, pp. 199, 100.

31. 'Protest against the rejection of an amendment to the address on the Spanish manifesto', Cobbett, *Parliamentary history*, XX, 17 June 1779, col. 894.

32. Sandwich, Memorandum for cabinet, September 1779, in Sandwich, *Sandwich papers*, vol. III, p. 170. In a similar vein, see the remarks of the pro-government Earl of Westmorland: Cobbett, *Parliamentary history*, XXI, 1 November 1780, col. 813. North's remarks are in ibid., XX, 21 June and 25 November 1779, cols. 949, 1109–10.

33. Ibid., 7 December 1778, cols. 24–5.

34. Commodore Johnstone to Sandwich, 10 December 1779, at sea, in Sandwich, *Sandwich papers*, vol. III, p. 190.

35. On the perceived link between domestic corruption and internal crisis, see Armitage, 'A patriot for whom?', p. 411. The crisis of the British state in 1779–80 is discussed in Butterfield, *George III*. See also Haydon, *Anti-Catholicism*, pp. 204–44, esp. p. 206 on the context of war.

36. 'Debate on the Duke of Richmond's motion for an economical reform of the Civil List establishment', 7 December 1779, Cobbett, *Parliamentary history*, XX, cols. 1256–7. He had anticipated some of these themes on 7 December 1778, col. 21. 'Mr Burke's speech on presenting his plan for the better security of the independence of Parliament and the economical reformation of the civil and other establishments', 11 February 1780, ibid., XXI, cols. 1, 6, 9. On economical reform, see Binney, *British public finance*, esp. pp. 7–14 re the American War as a driving factor.

37. John Robinson to Sandwich, 18 August 1777, in Sandwich, *Sandwich papers*, vol. II, p. 240. 'Debate on the clause of Mr Burke's Establishment Bill, for abolishing the office of third secretary of state', Cobbett, *Parliamentary history*, XXI, 8 March 1780, col. 196.

38. Conway, *British Isles*, p. 260. Armitage, 'A patriot for whom?', pp. 410–11.

39. Hamish M. Scott, 'Britain's emergence', p. 1.

23 The Partition of Britain, 1780–1783

1. Stormont to Keith, 'most confidential', 12 December 1780, St James's (NA SP 80/223, fo. 206).

2. Sandwich remarks to cabinet 19 January 1781, Queens' House, in the presence of the King, in Sandwich, *Sandwich Papers*, vol. IV, p. 24.

3. Cobbett, *Parliamentary history*, XXI, 26 February 1781, col. 1273.

4. Stormont to Keith, 12 December 1780, St James's (NA SP 80/223, fo. 200). See Harris to Stormont, 26 June 1780, St Petersburg; Harris to Keith, 29 November 1780, St Petersburg, in Malmesbury, *Diaries and correspondence*, vol. I, pp. 319, 345.

5. Keith to Chamier, 11 April 1777; Richard Rigby to Keith, 21 January 1781, Pay Office; Keith to Philip Yorke, 20 January 1781, Vienna, in Keith, *Memoirs*, vol. II, pp. 77, 119, 116. Stormont to Keith, 25 August 1780, St James's; Stormont to Keith, 'most confidential', 12 December 1780, St James's; Stormont to Keith, 'most secret', 12 December 1780, St James's (NA SP 80/223 Germany/Empire, fos. 31, 204, 200).

6. Keith to Stormont, 12 August 1780, Vienna; Stormont to Keith, 8 August, 19 September and 26 December 1780, St James's; see also Keith to Stormont, 6 September 1780, Vienna (ibid., fos. 14, 4, 60, 235, 40). See also Bindoff, *Scheldt question*, pp. 138–9.

7. Black, 'British foreign policy in the eighteenth century: A survey', p. 44. Suffolk to Elliot, 8 May 1779, St James's (NA SP 90/102, unfoliated).

8. See von Aretin, *Das alte Reich*, vol. III, p. 214. Keith to Stormont, 9 August 1780, Vienna; Stormont to Keith, 22 August 1780, St James's (NA SP 80/223, fos. 12, 21).

9. See von Aretin, *Das alte Reich*, vol. III, pp. 213–14, 219–21, who sees this as part of a British attempt to split the Austro-French alliance. Keith to Stormont, 13 September 1780, Vienna (NA SP 80/223, fo. 59).

10. 'Debate on General Conway's Bill for quieting the troubles in America', 5 May 1780, Cobbett, *Parliamentary history*, XXI, col. 577. Henry Seymour Conway to Keith, 30 August 1780, Park Place, in Keith, *Memoirs*, vol. II, p. 108. 'Debate on General Conway's Bill for quieting the troubles in America', 5 May 1780, Cobbett, *Parliamentary history*, XXI, col. 573.

11. Keith to A. B. Drummond, 14 October 1780, Vienna, in Keith, *Memoirs*, vol. II, p. 109.

12. Stormont to Keith, 8 September, 12 December 1780; and 12 September 1780, St James's (NA SP 80/223, fos. 46, 206, 56).

13. Creutz is quoted in Barton, 'Sweden', p. 422.

14. Keith to Stormont, 9 August 1780, Vienna; Stormont to Keith, 20 October 1780, St James's (NA SP 80/223, fos. 10, 93). 'The Earl of Shelburne's motion respecting the Armed Neutrality', 1 June 1780, Cobbett, *Parliamentary history*, XXI, col. 631. 'Instruction for Belgioso', 23 November 1780, Vienna (HHStA England Korrespondenz, Berischte Karton 128). Keith to Stormont, 16 December 1780, Vienna (NA SP 80/223, fo. 214).

15. 'The Earl of Shelburne's motion respecting the Armed Neutrality', 1 June 1780, Cobbett, *Parliamentary history*, XXI, col. 633.

16. Yorke to Harris, 8 October 1779, The Hague (BL Add Mss, fo. 73). 'The Earl of Shelburne's motion respecting the Armed Neutrality', 1 June 1780, Cobbett, *Parliamentary history*, XXI, col. 633. See Hamish M. Scott, 'Sir Joseph Yorke', esp. pp. 575–6, 582–3.

17. See the maps in Conway, *British Isles*, p. 197.

18. Cobbett, *Parliamentary history*, XXI, 1 June 1780, col. 640; 25 January 1781, col. 1024.

19. Sandwich remarks to cabinet 19 January 1781, Queens' House, in the presence of the King, in Sandwich, *Sandwich papers*, vol. IV, p. 24.

20. Sir James Harris to Sir Robert M. Keith, 29 November 1780, St Petersburg; and 21 April 1781, in Malmesbury, *Diaries and correspondence*, vol. I, pp. 345, 414. Morley, *Irish opinion*, p. 268. Cobbett, *Parliamentary history*, XXI, 6 November 1780, col. 828. P.S. to Rigby to Keith, 29 January 1781, Pay Office, in Keith, *Memoirs*, vol. II, p. 122.

21. Cobbett, *Parliamentary history*, XXI, 6 November 1780, cols. 829, 835, 837.

22. Ibid., 25 January 1781, col. 1092.

23. Ibid., 1 June 1780, col. 652.

24. Harris to Stormont, 13/24 December 1780, St Petersburg, in Malmesbury, *Diaries and correspondence*, vol. I, p. 367. Cobbett, *Parliamentary history*, XXI, 25 January 1781, cols. 1031, 1102, 1104.

25. Stockley, *Britain and France* p. 14. See 'Narrative of a secret negotiation in Spain', by Richard Cumberland. Addressed to the Earl of Shelburne, 20 May 1782, London (BL Add Mss 28851, esp. fos. 6–42).

26. Black, *British foreign policy in an age of revolution*, p. 59. Harris to Malmesbury, 24 December 1780, St Petersburg, in Malmesbury, *Diaries and correspondence*, vol. I, p. 363.

27. Harris to Stormont, 24 December 1780, St Petersburg, ibid., pp. 364–8.

28. Stormont to Harris, 20 January 1780, St James's, ibid., p. 373.

29. Stormont to Keith, 14 November 1780, St James's (NA SP 80/223, fo. 122).

30. 'Debate on General Conway's Bill for quieting the troubles in America', 5 May 1780, Cobbett, *Parliamentary history*, XXI, col. 574; see also 6 November 1780, col. 837. Earlier in the same vein, see Burke in ibid., XX, 31 May 1779, cols. 826–7; Richmond, 17 June 1779, col. 884; XXI, 3 June 1779, col. 841. George III to Sandwich, 13 September 1779, Windsor, in Sandwich, *Sandwich papers*, vol. III, p. 164.

31. As related in Harris to Stormont, 24 December 1780, St Petersburg, in Malmesbury, *Diaries and correspondence*, vol. I, p. 363. Cobbett, *Parliamentary history*, XXI, 15 and 26 February 1781, cols. 1236, 1273.

32. See Schiff, *Benjamin Franklin*. Stourzh, *Benjamin Franklin*, p. 164.

33. Stockley, *Britain and France*, p. 33. For the abandonment of the Mediterranean, see Syrett, *Royal Navy in European waters*, pp. 165–6. On the French naval contribution to the war in North America itself, see Dull, *French navy and American Independence*, pp. 240–48.

34. Cobbett, *Parliamentary history*, XXII, 27 November 1781, col. 726. Stockley, *Britain and France*, p. 53. Cobbett, *Parliamentary history*, XXII, 27 November 1781, cols. 716, 669. On the impact of Yorktown, see Christie, *End of North's ministry*, pp. 267–98.

35. Memorandum by Lord Sandwich, 'Observations upon the points which it is supposed will be the subject of the Naval Enquiry in the House of Commons', in Sandwich, *Sandwich papers*, vol. IV, pp. 281–301. See Rodger's persuasive rehabilitation in *Insatiable earl*. Sandwich's arguments were a common currency of strategic debate in 1780–81: e.g. the remarks of Lord Mulgrave in Cobbett, *Parliamentary history*, XXII, 27 November 1781, cols. 710–11; in the same vein, see 24 January 1782, cols. 884 and 887–8. For details on how the massive French fiscal effort in the American War and the resulting naval expansion would not have been possible with the distractions of a European war, see Dull, *French navy and American Independence*, appendix A, 'The naval and colonial budget, 1776–1783', pp. 345–50.

36. Sandwich's remarks are in ibid., 5 December 1781, col. 801. On the Sandwich debates, see Christie, *End of North's ministry*, pp. 304–19.

37. See Ritcheson, 'Earl of Shelburne', esp. p. 325 re Cromwell. 'Instruction for Belgioso', 20 May 1781, Vienna (HHStA England Korrespondenz, Berichte Karton 128, fos. 46–7).

38. Dispatch of Harris to Fox, 30 April 1782, St Petersburg, in Malmesbury, *Diaries and correspondence*, p. 505. Shelburne is quoted in Stockley, *Britain and France*, p. 55.

39. The centrality of Europe to British foreign policy in 1782–3 emerges very clearly from Stockley, *Britain and France*. For the new dispensation at the Foreign Office, see Fox to Sir Robert Murray Keith, 29 March 1782, St James's (BL Add Mss 35525, fo. 39). See

also Middleton, *Administration*, p. 10. 'Debate in the Commons on the Earl of Shelburne's plan for arming the people', 10 May 1782, Cobbett, *Parliamentary history*, XXIII, cols. 1–16; King's Speech on opening the session, 5 December 1782, cols. 206–7.

40. Translations of these treaties are printed in ibid., cols. 346–58. Stockley, *Britain and France*, pp. 65, 206.

41. See Black, *Parliament and foreign policy in the eighteenth century*, p. 107.

42. Cobbett, *Parliamentary history*, XXIII, 19 February 1783, cols. 504–5.

43. See Schweizer, 'Newspapers', p. 39. Black, *British foreign policy in an age of revolution*, p. 61. Stockley, *Britain and France*, p. 47. Cobbett, *Parliamentary history*, XXIII, 21 February 1783, cols. 548–9.

44. 'Debate in the Lords on the Preliminary articles of peace', 17 February 1783, ibid., col. 375; see also col. 457.

45. Crout, 'In search', p. 398. Weintraub, *Iron tears*, p. 324.

Conclusion

1. Cobbett, *Parliamentary history*, XXII, 27 November 1781, col. 695.

2. Ibid., XXIII, 10 July 1782, cols. 193–4; 5 December 1782, col. 29. Black, *Parliament and foreign policy in the eighteenth century*, p. 109.

3. Grafton, *Autobiography*, p. 13.

4. *Newcastle Chronicle*, 19 August 1786, quoted in Kathleen Wilson, *Sense of the people*, p. 435.

5. Conway, *British Isles*, p. 318. Cobbett, *Parliamentary history*, XXI, 25 January 1781, col. 1031.

6. Conway, *British Isles*, p. 89. 'Debate in the Lords on the Address of Thanks', 27 November 1781, Cobbett, *Parliamentary history*, XXII, col. 655.

7. Morley, *Irish opinion*, p. 281.

8. The relevant figures are in Conway, *British Isles*, pp. 17, 28–9, 13.

9. The problem of 'imperial overstretch' was expounded in Paul Kennedy's classic *Rise and fall of the Great Powers*. Kennedy's necessarily short account of the American War, pp. 149–54, it should be stressed, still reads very well eighteen years on. The concept of 'imperial attention deficit' was developed by Niall Ferguson in his studies of British and American empires. His account of the American War is in *Empire*, pp. 84–101. Mahan, *Influence of sea power*, pp. 528–9.

10. Conway, *British Isles*, p. 352. Keith to Andrew Drummond, 3 November 1781, Vienna, in Keith, *Memoirs*, vol. II, p. 126. Cobbett, *Parliamentary history*, XXIII, 17 February 1783, col. 437.

11. See Stourzh, *Benjamin Franklin*, p. 61.

12. For a well-argued sceptical view, see Rodger, 'Continental commitment'. Black, *America or Europe?*, pp. 68–9, 79, 143.

13. See Conway, 'Continental connections', pp. 373–4.

14. Hamish M. Scott, *British foreign policy, passim*. See Black, *America or Europe?*, p. 102.

15. Baugh, 'Why did Britain lose command of the sea?', p. 151.

16. Conway, *British Isles*, p. 202.

17. Black, *Parliament and foreign policy in the eighteenth century*, p. 109. Cobbett, *Parliamentary history*, XXIII, 7 May and 11 November 1783, cols. 827ff, 1141, on economical reform to preserve European position.

18. One recent historian speaks of the lack of a 'coherent debate' after 1783: Black, *Parliament and foreign policy in the eighteenth century*, p. 107. 'Debate in the Lords on the address of thanks', 27 November 1781, Cobbett, *Parliamentary history*, XXII, col. 655.

19. Ibid., XXIII, 10 July 1782, col. 194.

Index

Page references in italics refer to illustrations. An individual's position or job is indicated parenthetically only where it is necessary for clarity or for locating the reference in the text.

Abercromby, James 356, 367–8, 442–3
Acadia and Acadians 93, 178–9, 244, 359, 395, 506
Act of Settlement (1701) 49, 52, 83, 111, 113–14, 131, 325
Act of Union (1707) 1, 51–3, 675
acts and bills
  Act of Settlement (1701) 49, 52, 83, 111, 113–14, 131, 325
  Act of Union (1707) 1, 51–3, 675
  Black Acts (1722–3) 177
  Catholic Relief Act (1778) 618–19
  Declaratory Act (1766) 545
  Dissenters Relief Act (1779) 635
  India Recruitment Bill (1771) 550
  Licensing of the Press Act (1662) 39
  Massachusetts Government Act (1774) 582, 611
  Militia Bill (1756) 414–15
  Mutiny Bill debates 103, 188, 222, 234, 259, 670
  Navigation Acts 28, 458, 538, 584
  Peerage Bill (1718–19) 148, 152–3
  Quebec Act (1774) 582–4
  Recruitment Acts (1778; 1779) 618
  Regulating Act (1773) 580

  Renunciation Act (1778) 611
  Riot Act (1715) 101
  Septennial Act (1716) 102–3
  Stamp Act (1765) 536, 537–8, 553
  Sugar Act (1764) 536, 537–8
  Tea Act (1773) 581–2
  Triennial Act (1694) 39
Adair, Sergeant 597
Adams, Amos 542
Adams, John 387, 542, 572, 572, 588, 624–5
Addison, Joseph 87, 120, 127, 466
Africa 502, 510
Aiguillon, Emmanuel Armand de Richelieu, Duc d' 568–9
Ainslie, Sir Robert 623
Aix-la-Chapelle, Treaty of (1748) 350–52, 358–9, 403, 458, 516, 542, 661
Alba, Fernando Alvarez de Toledo, 3rd Duke of 14
Albany Congress (1754) 394–5, 533, 587
Albemarle, George Keppel, 3rd Earl of 532, 546
Alberoni, Giulio, Cardinal 136, 137, 139
Almanza, Battle of (1707) 56
Alsace 56–7
Altona 230
Altranstädt, Treaty of (1706) 55, 109
Amboyna, massacre of 25
Amelia Sophia, Princess 215, 230
American colonies, British

Albany Congress 394–5, 533, 587
Continental Congresses 587, 588, 591, 597, 600, 601–2
Declaration of Independence 602–4, 661
defence of 504–6, 533–6, 539–40, 571
expansionism 392–3, 540–42, 544, 552, 679
and French North America 92–4, 244–5, 346–7, 352, 368, 583–4
and Hanoverian succession 87–8
under James I 25, 179–80
under James II 35–6
population 535–6, 550–51
under Queen Anne 53, 62–3
Seven Years War 389–96, 426, 431–2, 435, 442–3
taxation 536, 537–8, 543–5, 551–3, 581–2, 597–8, 679–80
trade with Britain 366–8, 535–6, 538–40, 681
see also individual settlements and colonies/states; United States of America
American War of Independence 584, 587–601, 606, 610–11, 616–22, 652–9, 664–8, 677–8
Amherst, Jeffrey, Baron 443, 505, 533
Anglo-Dutch Wars
  (1664–7; 1672–4) 31–2
  (1780–83) 645–7, 651–2

Anglo-French War (1557–9)
    12–13
Anglo-Russian subsidy treaty
    (1755) 402–5
Anglo-Spanish War (1654–60)
    28–9
Anjou, François, Duke of 18
Anna Ivanova, Tsarina of Russia
    243
Anna Petrovna, Grand Duchess
    of Russia 200
Annandale, William Johnstone,
    1st Marquess of 84
Anne, Princess Royal (later
    Princess of Orange) 178,
    209, 229–30, 230, 364
Anne, Queen 49, 58, 67, 69–70,
    80, 470
Anson, George, Admiral 281–2,
    353, 373, 381, 398, 413,
    482, 516, 561
Anti-Gallican Society 365
Antigua 429
Antwerp 105, 638, 658
Aranjuez, Treaty of (1752) 382,
    400, 434, 511, 556
Aranjuez, Treaty of (1779) 628
Archer, Henry 275
Argyll, John Campbell, 2nd
    Duke of 223, 269, 271,
    283, 294, 301
Armed Neutrality, League of
    (1780) 459, 643–5, 657
Armitage, David 3
Armstrong, Lawrence 244
Army, British
    and Duke of Cumberland
        365, 425
    Militia Bill (1756) 414–15
    Mutiny Bill debates 103, 188,
        222, 234, 259
    overseas deployment 429–30,
        442, 451
    Recruitment Acts (1778;
        1779) 618
    size 71, 103–4, 171–2, 199,
        336, 340, 451, 666
    standing army 222–3, 259,
        327–8
Army of Observation 425–6,
    435–6, 437–40, 442,
    445–6, 471–2
Ash, John 93
Ashton, Sir Thomas 228
Asiento 47, 66, 68, 136, 160,
    202, 212, 249, 381

Astrakhan 197
Atterbury, Francis, Bishop of
    Rochester 85, 176
Augsburg, League of 35, 36, 40
Augusta, Princess, Duchess of
    Brunswick 257, 468, 474,
    546
Auguste, Robert-Joseph 559
Augustus II, King of Poland and
    Elector of Saxony 55, 149,
    181, 231
Augustus III, King of Poland
    and Elector of Saxony 231,
    241, 337, 380, 531
Austria
    Armed Neutrality 643–4, 645
    Austro-Russian treaty (1781)
        651
    Austro-Spanish alliance
        184–90, 192–4, 198–202,
        205, 210–12
    'blood justice of Thorn' 181
    and France 548, 557
    and Great Northern War 146
    and Imperial Election Scheme
        377
    and investitures 165–6
    and Italy 69, 116, 136–8,
        189–90, 213–14, 221, 228,
        241
    Pragmatic Sanction 168–9,
        184–5, 211, 212, 216–19,
        281
    Protestant enclaves 220
    and Prussia 214–15, 289,
        300, 310, 363, 370–71,
        377, 396, 401, 559
    reforms 537
    relations with Britain after
        Seven Years War 517,
        524–5, 528–9, 560, 566,
        572, 586–7, 617, 622,
        637–40, 650
    Seven Years War 435–6, 437,
        442, 455, 464–5
    territorial expansion 105–6,
        167–71, 210
    and Thirty Years War 20, 29
    Treaty of St Petersburg (1757)
        435
    Treaty of Versailles (1756)
        409–10
    Treaty of Vienna (1731)
        218–19, 396
    Treaty of Westminster (1716)
        116

Treaty of Worms (1743) 310
Turkish wars 37, 106, 118,
    137–8, 168, 243, 261–2,
    269
    and War of Polish Succession
        231–2, 241–2, 261
    and War of Spanish
        Succession 56, 65, 67, 68
Austrian Netherlands
    awarded to Charles VI 68,
        137, 159, 167, 168, 188–9
    Dutch defence of 261, 652
    French threats to 200, 201,
        217, 221–2, 291, 411, 437,
        459, 557
    neutrality 344
    see also Flanders; Spanish
        Netherlands
Austrian Succession, War of
    (1740–48) 289–301,
    309–19, 329–39, 341–4,
    347–50, 542, 670

Bacon, Sir Francis, 1st Viscount
    St Albans 22
Bagot, Lewis 635
Bahamas 507, 659
Baker, Sir William 477
Baltic Sea
    George I's policy 109–10,
        118, 135, 139, 142–5,
        153–4, 165
    George II's policy 229–30
    George III's policy 530,
        564–5
Baltic states 108, 110, 142
Bank of England 58, 62, 71,
    160, 414
Bar, Duchy of 477
Barbados 139
Barnard, Sir John 250, 252,
    258, 259, 282, 288,
    290–91, 315
Barré, Isaac 486, 603
Barrier treaties
    (1709) 56–7, 68, 96, 105
    (1715) 106, 147, 170–71,
        370
Barrington, Samuel 629
Barrington, William, 2nd
    Viscount 320, 326, 443
Bassett, Henry 533
Bassewitz, Count 145
Bathurst, Allen, 1st Earl 213,
    251, 258, 267, 286–7, 300,
    331

Baugh, Daniel 3
Bavaria, Electorate of 106, 169,
    195, 208, 215, 310-11,
    337, 374
Bavarian Succession, War of
    (1778-9) 622, 624-5, 627
Beckford, Richard 398
Beckford, William
    military policy 445-6, 454,
    509-10, 563
    and North America 460, 476,
    534
    and Pitt the Elder 398, 428,
    443-4, 465
    on Treaty of Paris 496
Bedford, John Russell, 4th Duke
    of
    First Lord of Admiralty 349
    and Hanoverians 320, 324,
    404, 407
    on militarization 414, 503,
    523
    Secretary of State 358, 373
    and Seven Years War 478,
    479-80, 487, 490
Belgioso, Count Ludovico 587
Belle Ile 479, 481
Bengal 537
Bentinck, Hans Wilhelm, 1st
    Earl of Portland 81
Bentinck, William, Count 322,
    375, 396, 498
Berkeley, George 179-80
Berkeley, James, 3rd Earl of 84
Bernis, François de 454-5
Bernstorff, Andreas Gottlieb von
    119
    and accession of George I 84,
    88, 122
    and Baltic crisis 109, 111,
    117, 135, 145-51
    and Duchy of Mecklenburg
    119, 149
    mediates royal split 128
    and St Saphorin 92
    and Walpole's rise to power
    161
Berwick, James FitzJames, Duke
    of 204
Bestuzhev, Count Alexis 313,
    529
Beverley, Robert 588
Bigot, François 179
Bingley, Robert Benson, Baron
    192
Black Acts (1722-3) 177

Blair, John 541
Blenheim, Battle of (1704)
    44-5, 50-51, 55, 55, 217
Blenheim Palace 44, 217
Bligh, Thomas 468
Bohemia 20-21
Bolingbroke, Henry St John, 1st
    Viscount 254
    and Hanoverian succession
    79, 95, 96, 97-8, 99, 101
    pardon 180
    The Patriot King 253-4, 588
    Secretary at War 62, 63-5,
    67, 69, 70, 109
    and Swift 58
    and Walpole 217
Bollan, William 347, 539, 542,
    544
Bombay 30, 33
Boston 551, 553, 600
    'Tea Party' 582
Bothmer, Hans Caspar von 67,
    80, 81, 81, 83-4, 95, 96,
    122, 128
Bourbon family compacts 221,
    241, 244, 278, 312, 555,
    562-3, 611
Braddock, Edward 388, 405,
    412
Brandenburg, Frederick
    William, Great Elector of
    31, 37
Brazil 516
Breda, congress of (1746-8)
    344, 350, 516
Bremen, Duchy of
British-Hanoverian
    annexation 100, 109, 110,
    115, 116, 124, 144-5, 325
    investitures 116, 164-5, 193,
    219
    Treaty of Westphalia (1648)
    108
Breslau, Treaty of (1742) 310
Brest 42, 503
Brihuega, Battle of (1710) 58
Bristol, Augustus Hervey, 3rd
    Earl of 629
British South Sea Company 249
Briton 488, 493, 533-4
Broglie, François-Marie, Duc de
    216
Brown, John 435
Bruges 189
Brühl, Heinrich, Count von
    374-5

Bryant, Arthur 2
Buckingham, George Villiers,
    1st Duke of 23, 24, 26, 675
Buckingham and Normanby,
    John Sheffield, 1st Duke of
    80, 128
Buckinghamshire, John Hobart,
    2nd Earl of 528, 529,
    663-4, 682
Bunbury, Sir Charles 610
Bunker Hill, Battle of (1775)
    587
Burchett, Sir Josiah 154
Burgh, James 588
Burghley, William Cecil, 1st
    Baron 14, 15, 16
Burgoyne, John 610
Burke, Edmund 536, 561,
    569-71, 574-5, 580, 585,
    594, 597, 609, 634, 649,
    653
Burke, William 476-7
Burnet, Gilbert, Bishop of
    Salisbury 84
Burrish, Onslow 375
Burwell, Lewis 392
Burwell, William 580
Bussy, François de 296, 493-4
Bute, John Stuart, 3rd Earl of
    and Pitt the Elder 444
    resignation 512-13, 551
    and Seven Years War 468,
    470, 474, 475, 478, 483,
    487-9, 493-4, 496
Byng, Sir George (later 1st
    Viscount Torrington) 139,
    140, 141, 679
Byng, John, Admiral 412,
    413-14, 416
Byrd, William 245

Cadiz 24
Cadogan, William, 1st Earl 84,
    151, 169
Calais 12, 13
Cambrai, Congress of (1724)
    141, 181
Camden, Charles Pratt, 1st Earl
    593, 598, 655
Camisards 50
Campbell of Cawdor, John 319
Canada
    and American War of
    Independence 600, 659
    and British American colonies
    392, 463

Canada – *cont.*
British rule 506, 533, 672
French expansion in 62–4,
216, 244–6, 368–9
Seven Years War 459–60,
464, 475–8, 495
see also French North
America; *individual
provinces/cities*
Cape Breton 93, 344–7,
349–52, 478, 542
Cape Colony 645
Cape Passaro, Battle of (1718)
139–40, *140*, 679
Capel, Sir Henry 32
Cardiff, John Stuart, Baron
(*later* 1st Marquess of Bute)
607
Carlisle, Frederick Howard, 5th
Earl of 611
Carlos II, King of Spain 45, 46
Carlyle, Alexander 580
Carmarthen, Francis Osborne,
Marquess of (*later* 5th
Duke of Leeds) 661
Carolinas 87, 139, 246, 544,
653
Caroline of Ansbach, Queen
accession 207
death 256
as Princess of Wales 80, 83,
100, 125–6, 127, 144, 148,
152–3
Caroline of Brunswick-
Wolfenbüttel, Princess 468
Caroline Mathilda, Queen of
Denmark 564
Carrickfergus 455
Cartagena 278, 284–6, *285*,
288, 301, 675
Carter, Landon 389
Carteret, John, 2nd Baron (*later*
2nd Earl Granville)
Ambassador to Sweden
143–5, 153
death 519
in George I's first ministry
95
on Imperial Election Scheme
372
Lord Lieutenant of Ireland
169
and North American
expansion 360
in opposition 229, 251, 252,
257, 270, 271–2

Secretary of State (first
ministry) 171, 175
Secretary of State (second
ministry) 308–11, 313–15,
317, 320–21, 327, 330–31,
334–5
and Walpole's resignation
301–2
on War of Jenkins' Ear 275,
289
Carvajal, Don Joseph 380, 400
Casanova, Giacomo 501
Castlecomer, Christopher
Wandesford, 2nd Viscount
87
Catalans 50, 68, 136, 152
Catawba, tribe 433
Cathcart, Charles, 9th Lord 558
Catherine I, Tsarina of Russia
186–7, 196
Catherine II, 'the Great', Tsarina
of Russia 530, 537, 548,
557–8, 562, 627, 643,
650–51
Catherine of Aragon, Queen 11
Catherine of Braganza, Queen
30
Catholic League 14, 150
Catholic Relief Act (1778)
618–19
Cecil, William, 1st Baron
Burghley 14, 15, 16
Ceylon 645
Chamier, Anthony 587
Chandernagore 507
Charles, Duke of Wolfenbüttel
437
Charles I, King 20, 23–8, 29
Charles II, King 30–34, 39
Charles II, King of Spain 45, 46
Charles III, King of Spain
accession 457–8, 676
as Don Carlos, Duke of
Parma 137, 184, 186, 210,
212–13, 219, 231, 232,
241
as King of Sicily and Naples
312, 433–4
Charles V, Holy Roman
Emperor 11, 16, 185
Charles VI, Holy Roman
Emperor *161*
accession 64
and Austro-Spanish alliance
184–5, 189, 194–5
claims to Spanish throne 46,

49–50, 68, 92, 116, 136–7,
168
death 274, 275, 280–81
imperial policy 150, 159–61,
172–4, 184
and investitures 165–6
Pragmatic Sanction 168–9,
184–5, 211
and Quadruple Alliance 139
and Turkish wars 261–2
and War of Polish Succession
231
and War of Spanish
Succession 56, 58, 70
Charles VII, Holy Roman
Emperor
death 333, 337
as Elector of Bavaria 215,
289, 294, 302
as Emperor 309, 310, 311,
318, 335
Charles XII, King of Sweden 44,
55, 101, 108, 123, 133,
143
Charles Edward, Prince ('Bonnie
Prince Charlie') 70, 176,
232, 279, 334, 339–41,
362, 507
Charles Leopold, Duke of
Mecklenburg-Schwerin
117, 146, 165, 229, 240
Charles Philip, Elector Palatine
149
Charles William Frederick,
Duke of Brunswick 474,
546
Charles William Frederick,
Margrave of Ansbach 402
Charleston 653
Charlotte of Mecklenburg-
Strelitz, Queen 474
Charlottenburg, Treaty of
(1723) 174–5
Chatham, William Pitt, Earl of
see Pitt, William, the Elder
Chauvelin, Germain-Louis de
217
Cherbourg 445
Cherokee, tribe 433, 458
Chesme, Battle of (1770) 558
Chesterfield, Philip Stanhope,
3rd Earl of 192
Chesterfield, Philip Stanhope,
4th Earl of
on Hanover 307, 317–18,
320, 321–2, 324, 325

on Jacobite rebellion 340
on Prussia 335, 336–7, 456
and Seven Years War 419–20,
  449
and Walpole's government
  257, 264, 271, 288, 301
and War of Austrian
  Succession 342–4, 348,
  350, 351
Chevalier, Jean-Baptiste 507
Chile 198
Choiseul, Étienne François, Duc
  de 455, 457, 480, 481, 491,
  496, 508–9, 532, 544, 561
Cholmondeley, George, 3rd Earl
  of 251, 317
Christian IV, King of Denmark
  24
Christian VII, King of Denmark
  564
Churchill, General Charles 127
Churchill, Sir Winston 356
Churchman, John 389
Civil List 82, 634
Civil War (English) 28–9
Clarendon, Edward Hyde, 1st
  Earl of 31
Clarendon, Edward Hyde, 3rd
  Earl of 82
Clarke, William 391, 393
Clemens August, Elector of
  Cologne 374
Clement VII, Pope 11
Clementina Sobieska, Princess
  232, 233
Cleves-Mark, Duchy of 262
Clive, Robert, Baron 516
Clutterbuck, Thomas 293
Cobham, Richard Temple, 1st
  Viscount 257–8, 259, 515
Colley, Linda 675
Colloredo, Count Hieronymus
  von 528
Cologne, Archbishopric and
  Electorate of 374, 375,
  474
Connecticut Courant 615
conventions
  Hanover (1745) 337
  Kloster-Zeven (1757)
    436–41, 467
  Pardo (1728) 211
  Pardo (1739) 267–8, 273
  Westminster (1756) 403–6,
    408–9, 419, 420, 626
Conway, Henry Seymour 514,

532, 544, 545, 546–7, 548,
  608, 640–41, 652, 657
Cornewall, Velters 352
Cornwallis, Charles, 1st
  Marquess 654
Corpus Catholicorum 90
Corpus Evangelicorum 90, 149,
  172–3, 194, 195, 255, 262,
  527, 640
Corsica 556–7, 562–3, 571,
  676
Cotton, Sir John Hynde 239,
  275, 318, 319, 362
Coventry, George William, 6th
  Earl of 609
Cowper, William, 1st Earl 95,
  96, 177
Cowper, William (poet) 665
Craftsman 217, 256, 259
Craggs, James 87, 103–4, 110,
  119, 120
Cressener, George 494, 627
Creutz, Count Gustaf Philip 643
Crimea 201, 659
Cromwell, Oliver 28–30, 107
Cronhielm, Count 144
crusades 10
Cuba 164, 284, 486, 507, 540
Culloden, Battle of (1746) 341,
  362
Cumberland, Prince William
  Augustus, Duke of 132,
  342, 348, 362, 365, 398,
  425, 428, 438
Cumberland, Richard 649

Danby, Thomas Osborne, Earl
  of (later 1st Duke of Leeds)
  32, 675
Daniel, Shamokin 432
Danvers, John 247, 251
Danzig 231, 233, 585
Darlington, Sophia, Countess of
  169
Dashwood, Sir Francis 470
Davenant, Charles 41, 48
Davies, Sir John 22
de Ruyter, Michiel 32
Deane, Silas 605, 624
debt, British national 361, 510,
  535, 667
Declaratory Act (1766) 545
Defoe, Daniel 43, 46, 65,
  138–9, 142, 205
Delavall, Sir Ralph 41
Delaware 33

Denain, Battle of (1712) 66, 67
Denmark
  Armed Neutrality 459, 643
  and Elizabethan England 14
  and France 262, 270
  and Great Northern War
    108–9, 110, 117, 118, 153,
    165
  Lord Sandwich on 517
  palace revolution (1770) 564
  and Russia 186, 530
  and Sweden 230
  and Thirty Years War 24
  treaty with Britain (1739) 270
  and Treaty of Hanover (1725)
    193, 200–201, 209
Dettingen, Battle of (1743) 308,
  315, 318–19, 333, 452–3
Devolution, War of (1667–8)
  30–31
Devonshire, William Cavendish,
  2nd Duke of 103
Dickens, Guy (ambassador to
  Prussia) 263
Dickinson, John 539, 543
Digby, Henry 422
Digges, Sir Dudley 28
Dinwiddie, Robert 395
Diplomatic Revolution (1756)
  354, 508
Dissenters Relief Act (1779) 635
Dodington, George (later 1st
  Baron Melcombe) 321
Dolgorouky, Prince Vasily 176
Dominica 388, 502, 629, 654
Dongan, Thomas 35
Donne, John 9–10
Douglass, William 368
Downing, Sir George 31
Drake, Sir Francis 12, 15, 18
Drayton, William Henry 605
Dresden 419
Dresden, Treaty of (1745) 338
Dubois, Abbé 113
Dulany, Daniel 542
Dummer, Jeremiah 62–3
Dundas, Henry (later 1st
  Viscount Melville) 655
Dunes, Battle of the (1658) 29
Dunkirk 29, 31, 92, 216–17,
  413, 509–10, 523
Dutch United Provinces (Dutch
  Republic)
  Anglo-Dutch Wars: (1664–7;
    1672–4) 31–2; (1780–84)
    645–7, 651–2

Dutch United Provinces – *cont.*
Armed Neutrality 459, 643, 644–5
and Austro-Spanish alliance 188
and English Commonwealth 28, 29
and Great Northern War 111, 118
and Imperial Election Scheme 375
Orangist coup (1747) 348
and reign of George I 105
and Restoration England 31–3, 36
Scots Brigade 599–600
and Seven Years War 417, 450, 458–9
and Stuart England 25–6
Triple Alliance (1788) 683
and War of Austrian Succession 322, 343–4, 347–8
and War of Polish Succession 232, 234, 235, 239, 261
and War of Spanish Succession 49, 56–7, 59, 66–7
weakness 268–9, 348, 364, 396–7, 585
Dutch West India Company 33

East Friesland 219, 334
East India Company 33, 62, 160, 507, 537, 550, 580–81, 672
East Indies 429
Eastern Question 175
Eden, William (*later* 1st Baron Auckland) 611, 641
Edict of Nantes 34
Effingham, Thomas Howard, 3rd Earl of 593
Egmont, John Perceval, 2nd Earl of 326–7, 365
Egremont, Charles Wyndham, 2nd Earl of 494–5, 506, 512
Eichsfeld 441
Elba 204
elections, British: (1741) 293–4; (1760) 465
Elizabeth I, Queen 12–19, 107
Elizabeth, Electress Palatine 9–10, 20, 49, 438

Elizabeth, Tsarina of Russia 312–13, 363, 408
Elizabeth Farnese, Queen of Spain 136–7, 163–4, 181, 184, 207, 264–5, 267
Elliot, Hugh, British envoy in Berlin 622, 623, 625
Ellis, Welbore (*later* 1st Baron Mendip) 534, 655
Emden 361–2, 435, 442, 645
Estonia 110, 142, 164
Eugene, Prince of Savoy 54, 67, 86, 168, 219, 240, 243

Fairfax, Sir Thomas 28
Falkland Islands 560–61, 572–3, 581, 620
Farinelli 266, 267
Favier, Jean-Louis 626–7
Ferdinand, Duke of Brunswick 438, 439, 442, 446, 451–2, 493
Ferdinand I, King of Two Sicilies 458
Ferdinand II, Holy Roman Emperor 20
Ferdinand VI, King of Spain 380, 457
Finland 142, 565
Firmian, Leopold von, Archbishop of Salzburg 220
fisheries 98, 478, 480, 495, 496, 510, 679
FitzHerbert, Alleyne (*later* Baron St Helens) 659
Flanders
and Austro-Spanish alliance 184–5, 189
and Barrier treaties 370, 557
and Elizabethan and Stuart England 4, 16, 22, 37
and Joseph II 638
and War of Austrian Succession 334, 341–3, 347
and War of Spanish Succession 56, 60, 64, 66
see also Austrian Netherlands; Spanish Netherlands
Fleury, André-Hercule, Cardinal de
Austrian policy 204, 215, 217–18
Catholicism 195
and Spain 202, 220–21, 263, 265, 278–9

and War of Austrian Succession 295, 313
Florida 164, 245–6, 281, 481, 495, 502, 628, 649, 653, 654, 659
Fontenoy, Battle of (1745) 338, 341, 347
Forbes, John 433, 443
Fort Duquesne 443
Fox, Charles James 594, 621, 647, 657, 660, 662, 665–6
Fox, Henry (*later* 1st Baron Holland) 259, 353, 398, 417, 446
France
African territories 502, 510, 518–19
and American War of Independence 600–601, 605, 607–8, 610–14, 616–17, 621–2, 626–7, 628–9, 649, 653–4, 661
Anglo-French War (1557–9) 12–13
annexation of Corsica 556–7, 562–3
Caribbean territories 216, 359, 388, 451, 476, 495, 504, 507, 509, 629, 654
and Great Northern War 108–9, 110
Jacobitism 48, 92, 99–100, 101–2, 133, 176, 181–2, 279, 341, 362, 514
under Louis XIV 30–32, 34, 37–8, 47–8, 50, 52, 56, 70, 71, 92
navy 230, 244, 279, 312, 332, 360–61, 368–9, 393, 409, 426, 447, 503, 508–9, 561, 573–4, 627
and Polish partition 568–70
Revolution 681–2, 683–4
Seven Years War 412–13, 434–6, 442, 445–7, 451–2, 454–5, 464, 472, 477–81, 493–5
and Sweden 262, 530, 545, 564–5
territories in India 347, 502, 504, 507
and Thirty Years War 24, 28–9
transatlantic trade 359–60
Treaty of Hanover (1725)

191, 192, 195, 199–200,
202, 204, 210
Treaty of Paris (1763) 495,
501, 502, 503
Treaty of Versailles (1756)
408–12
Triple Alliance (1716–17)
112–16, 120, 137, 168,
170, 217
and War of Austrian
Succession 289, 294, 296,
309, 310, 314–15, 330,
332, 334, 341–2, 347–50
and War of Jenkins' Ear
278–9
and War of Polish Succession
228, 231–4, 240, 241–3,
261
wars of religion 13, 14
see also French North
America
Francis, Philip 471
Francis I, Holy Roman Emperor
292, 334, 337–8, 371
Francis I, King of France 11
Francis II, King of France 12
Frankfurt, Union of (1744) 334
Franklin, Benjamin 604
and American independence
588–9, 603, 653–4
on defence of colonies 533,
539, 579
early policy for Pennsylvania
245
and Edward Vernon 276
expansionism 552–3, 668
and French North America
388, 391–5, 463, 478
and Hanover 538
on Navigation Acts 584
on Treaty of Paris 502
Frederick, Prince of Wales (son
of George II) 80, 130, 132,
175, 196, 209, 215, 250,
256–7, 294, 364, 466
Frederick II, 'the Great', King of
Prussia 448
accession 279–80
annexation of Silesia 275,
289, 291–2, 362
and Armed Neutrality 643
on British foreign policy 521
and British missions to Prussia
378–9
Convention of Westminster
(1755) 408–9

and German armies 592
on Hanoverian succession 91
invasion of Saxony 419–20
Jacobitism 362–3, 371
and Joseph II 559
on King of England 400, 514
marriage projects 175, 209,
215
Polish policy 531
reforms 537
Seehandlung 585
and Seven Years War 431,
434, 436–7, 441–2,
447–9, 460–61, 463–5,
467, 471–2, 488, 492
and Treaty of Paris 513,
523–4, 548
and War of Austrian
Succession 310, 313–14,
334–5, 337–8, 342–4
and War of Bavarian
Succession 622, 625–6
Frederick II, Landgrave of
Hesse-Kassel 230, 401,
402, 592–3
Frederick V, Elector Palatine
9–10, 20–22, 21, 49
Frederick V, King of Denmark
230
Frederick Augustus II, Elector of
Saxony see Augustus III,
King of Poland
Frederick Christian, Elector of
Saxony (son of King of
Poland) 380
Frederick William I, King of
Prussia
death 279
and France 217
and George I 174–5, 188, 196
and George II 214–15
and Hanover 112, 118–19,
209–10, 262–3
and Russia 147, 154
Free, John 415
French and Indian War see
Seven Years War
French North America 92–4,
178–9, 216, 244–6,
368–9, 387–96, 423, 452,
481, 502, 506
see also Canada; individual
provinces/cities
Frobisher, Martin 12
fur trade 359–60
Füssen, Treaty of (1745) 337

Galissonière, Roland-Michel
Barrin, Marquis de la
368–9
Gallipoli 139
Gambia 518–19
Gates, Horatio 610
Gazetteer and London Daily
Advertiser 422, 443–4
Gemmingen, Baron 494
Gemmingen, Miss (governess)
130
Genoa, Republic of 556
Gentlemen's Magazine 271,
333, 345, 448, 513
George, Prince of Wales (later
King George IV) 526–7
George I, King
accession 70, 79–82
anglicization of family 130
and British Army 188
and Charles VI's territorial
ambitions 159, 172–4
coronation 100–101
his Court 81–6, 121–3
death 205
foreign policy 89–91, 94–7,
107–8, 135, 138, 141,
149–50, 162–3, 172–4
and Great Northern War
109–10, 112–15, 117–19,
197
and investitures 165–7
and Jacobites 101–2, 177,
187, 191
relations with Prince of Wales
125–7
visits Hanover 74, 113–14,
120, 151, 163, 173
and War of Spanish
Succession 67, 68–9
George II, King (earlier Prince of
Wales) 206, 316, 399
accession 205–6
and accession of George I
80–81, 83, 85
and Countess Walmoden 254
death 466
foreign policy 207, 210, 228,
366, 683
and Frederick II of Prussia
279, 291–2, 361
and Imperial Election Scheme
375–6
and Peerage Bill 148, 152–3
and Pitt the Elder 421, 428–9,
456, 461

George II, King – *cont.*
Prussian policy 262–3,
291–2, 420
and Queen Anne 67
relations with Frederick,
Prince of Wales 256–7
relations with George I
125–7
and separation of Hanover
from British Crown 330,
440–41, 461–2, 467
and Seven Years War 436–8,
440, 461
visits Hanover 255–6, 280,
295–6, 311, 314, 344, 398,
400–401
and War of Austrian
Succession 313–16,
318–19, 337–8, 342–3
and War of Polish Succession
232, 234, 237, 239–40
and war with Spain 267, 273,
300
George III, King 522
accession 466–7, 470
and American War of
Independence 629–30, 649,
655
foreign policy 555, 567,
586–7, 629–30, 664, 677,
682
and Hanover 473–5, 521–2,
526–7, 559–60
and Pitt the Elder 467–8, 482,
511–12, 546
as Prince of Wales 364, 402,
406, 440, 444, 452, 454,
467–9
rivalry with Joseph II 622,
638–40
and Seven Years War 490,
493
Georgia 245–6, 250, 267, 268
Germain, Lord George *see*
Sackville, Lord George
Germany
and American War of
Independence 592–3,
595–6, 609–10, 617–18,
623–4
Army of Observation 425–6,
435–6, 437–40, 442,
445–7, 471–2
and France 289, 370–71
George I's foreign policy
172–3

George II's foreign policy 210,
215, 219–20, 228
George III's foreign policy
474, 521
and Great Northern War 108,
109
and Hanoverian succession
79–83
Imperial Election Scheme
371–8
mercenaries 212, 213, 294,
309, 342, 417–18, 592–3,
596, 609, 617–18, 666–7
and 17th-century English
foreign policy 4, 20–22,
32–3
and Spanish Netherlands 17,
20–21
and Treaty of Hanover (1725)
193–5, 199–200
and War of Austrian
Succession 315
and War of Polish Succession
231, 242
and War of Spanish
Succession 49, 51, 57
Gertruydenberg, peace
negotiations (1709–10) 56,
60, 674
Gibbon, Edward 665
Gibraltar
and Austro-Spanish alliance
194
British defence of 136, 137,
412, 557, 592
British rule 74, 137, 164,
170–71, 181, 349–50, 433
English capture 50, 54, 68
Spanish attacks on 184, 198,
199, 211, 212, 218
Spanish claims to 482,
620–21, 628, 632–3, 649,
657
Glorious Revolution (1688)
36–40, 57, 328
Gloucester, Prince William,
Duke of 49
gold 12, 22–3, 198, 211–12,
373
Goldsmith, Oliver 515
Goodricke, Sir John 530
Gordon, Lord George 633
Gordon, Thomas 233
Gordon, William 517
Gordon Riots (1780) 633, 640
Görtz, Baron Friedrich Wilhelm

von 84, 88, 95, 138, 144,
151, 160, 165, 174
Görtz, Baron Georg von 133
Grafton, Augustus FitzRoy, 3rd
Duke of 545, 555–6, 664
Grand Alliance, Treaty of
(1701) 48–9, 50, 55, 98
Grand Alliance, War of *see* Nine
Years War
Grand Remonstrance (1641) 27
Grand Tour 358, 516
Granville, John Carteret, 2nd
Earl *see* Carteret, John, 2nd
Baron
Grave, Captain 118
Gray, Sir James 520
Great Northern War 55,
108–12, 117–20, 142–5,
153–4, 164–5
Grenada 502, 629, 654
Grenville, George
American policy 536
chief minister 510, 512, 516,
517–18, 520, 529
fall from power 545
Secretary of State 492, 495
and Seven Years War 438,
471, 480, 483
and War of Austrian
Succession 338, 341
Grenville, James 423
Grenville, Richard *see* Temple,
Richard Grenville-Temple,
2nd Earl
Grub Street Journal 417
Grumbkow, Friedrich Wilhelm
von 262–3
Guadaloupe 359, 451, 475–7,
495, 503, 672
Gustavus III, King of Sweden
564
Gustavus Adolphus, King of
Sweden 25
Gyllenborg, Count 133

Haddock, Nicholas 273, 286,
287
Haiti 359, 507
Hakluyt, Richard 16
Halifax, Charles Montagu, Earl
of 84, 96
Halifax, George Montagu-
Dunk, 2nd Earl of
in opposition 288, 323–4
President of Board of Trade
358, 360, 390, 404, 414

Secretary of State for North
474–5, 493
Hamburg 108
Hanau, 'treaty' of 310–11, 335
Hanbury Williams, Sir Charles
370, 375, 378, 379, 396,
402, 447
Handel, George Frideric 435
Hanmer, Sir Thomas 104
Hanover, Convention of (1745)
337
Hanover, Electorate of
and American War of
Independence 617–18,
622–3
Army of Observation 425–6,
435–6, 437–40, 442,
445–7, 471–2
Benjamin Franklin visits 538
and British national identity
324–6, 670–71
and Charles VI 212–13
Convention of Kloster-Zeven
(1757) 436–41, 467
George I visits 113–14, 120,
151, 163, 173
and George II 208, 240, 255,
295, 398, 400–401
and George III 521, 526–7,
559–60, 586–7, 638–9
and Great Northern War 108,
109–12, 117, 145
and Imperial Election Scheme
374–5
mercenaries 592, 596, 609,
617–18
Neutrality Convention (1741)
295–300, 313
'Pragmatic Army' 308, 313,
314–17
Prussian threats to 209–10,
262–3, 293, 294, 361–2,
400, 402–3, 525–6, 546,
566–7, 625–7
schemes for separation from
British crown 130–32, 330,
339, 440–41, 461–2, 467,
526–7, 671
and Seven Years War 417–18,
420–21, 431, 435–41, 447,
450, 473–4, 484–6, 487,
493–4
and subsidy treaties (1755)
404–7
and War of Austrian
Succession 313–32, 337–8

Hanover, Treaty of (1725)
191–6, 200–202, 209, 239,
290, 303, 375
Hardenberg, Christian Ludwig
von 295–6, 299–300
Hardwicke, Philip Yorke, 1st
Earl of
and American colonies 395
on British foreign policy
270–71, 272, 274, 311,
315, 379, 399, 407, 416
fall from power 520
and George III 470–71
and Imperial Election Scheme
373, 374, 377–8
loss of Minorca 413, 416
on Militia Bill (1756) 415
and separation of Hanover
from British crown 462
and Seven Years War 436,
438, 456–7, 459–60, 466,
489, 492, 493, 496
and Walpole's government
257
Hare, Francis 54, 61–2, 65, 68
Harley, Robert see Oxford and
Mortimer, Robert Harley,
1st Earl of
Harper, William 340
Harrington, William Stanhope,
1st Earl of
on Austro-Spanish alliance
198
and George I 84
and Prussia 262
relations with Hanoverian
chancellery 255–6, 280,
295, 296, 297
and War of Austrian
Succession 349
and War of Polish Succession
227, 231–2, 234
Harris, James, (later 1st Earl of
Malmesbury) (ambassador
to Russia) 607, 622, 626,
637, 646, 648, 650–51,
653, 658
Hartley, David 596, 610
Haslang, Joseph, Baron 439
Hattorf, Johann Philip von 151,
240
Havana 50, 486, 495
Hawke, Edward, Admiral 399,
452
Hawkins, Sir John 12, 15
Heathcote, George 213, 235

Heathcote, Ralph 627
Heidelberg 149
Henri IV, King of France 18
Henrietta Maria, Queen of
France 23
Henry, Prince of Wales 20
Henry I, King 10
Henry VIII, King 10–11
Hervey, John, 2nd Baron 254,
260, 268, 269, 271
Hesse-Kassel, Electorate of 193,
195, 208, 209, 402, 404,
442
Hessian mercenaries 212, 213,
294, 309, 342, 417, 592–3,
596, 609
Heusch, Baron 112
Hildesheim, Bishopric of 441,
461, 473, 474, 559
Hill, John 64
Hillsborough, Wills Hill, Earl of
(later 1st Marquess of
Downshire) 562
Hinton, John Poulett, Viscount
(later 2nd Earl Poulett) 227
Hoadley, Benjamin, Bishop of
Salisbury 251
Hohenfriedberg, Battle of
(1745) 337–8
Holdernesse, Robert Darcy, 4th
Earl of
Secretary of State for North
403, 408, 427, 438, 464,
470, 472
Secretary of State for South
373–4
Holland see Dutch United
Provinces
Holstein-Gottorp, Charles
Frederick, Duke of 153,
165, 187, 200
Holy Roman Empire
of Charles V 11, 16, 184
and George I's foreign policy
118, 159, 167–8, 172–3
and George III's foreign policy
586
and Habsburg succession
371–2
and Hanoverian succession
89–90
Imperial Election Scheme
371–8
Pragmatic Sanction 168–9,
184–5, 211, 212, 216–21,
281

Honduras 481, 518, 628
Hopson, Edward 112
Hosier, Francis 198
Hotham, Sir John 214–15
Hudson Bay 92
Huguenots 11, 13, 24, 34, 42
Hume, David 361, 364, 370, 504, 516, 520
Hundred Years War 10
Hungary 56, 72, 168, 198
Hungerford, John (MP for Scarborough) 137, 191
Hunter, Robert 63
Hussey, Thomas 649
Hyder Ali 507
Hyndford, John Carmichael, 3rd Earl of 274, 281, 291, 300, 309–10, 314, 376–7

Iberville, Charles d' 114
Imperial Election Scheme 371–8, 674, 677
India 30, 33, 347, 351, 423, 502, 504, 507, 537
India Recruitment Bill (1771) 550
'Indian Diplomacy' 534
Indians, North American 388–9, 432–3, 503, 504–6, 534
Ingoldsby, James 338
Ingul 403
Interest of Hanover steadily pursued, The 323
investitures 116, 164–7, 193, 218, 219
Ireland
    Catholic Relief Act (1778) 618–19
    Cromwell in 29
    defence of 572–3, 583, 615
    Elizabethan policy towards 18–19
    French landing 455
    Jacobitism 37, 187, 502–3, 507–8, 573, 616–17, 629, 654
    military establishment 550
    parliament 53, 538, 550, 658
    and William III 37
Iroquois 360
Isla, Archibald Campbell, Earl of (later 3rd Duke of Argyll) 269, 362–3

Italy
    and Austria 69, 116, 136, 189–90, 213–14, 221, 228, 241, 382
    Spanish claims in 137, 184, 186, 210, 212–13, 214, 219, 300–301, 382
    and War of Polish Succession 231, 241
Izzard, Ralph 625

Jacobites and Jacobitism
    Austria and 176, 184, 187, 191–2
    and British foreign policy 41, 142–3, 187
    France and 48, 92, 99–100, 101–2, 133, 176, 181–2, 279, 341, 362, 514
    Irish 37, 187, 502–3, 507–8, 616–17, 654
    Prussia and 363
    rebellions 99–102, 129, 187, 339–41, 342
    Russia and 142–3, 176–7, 196, 312
    Scottish 101–2, 187, 339–41, 362–3, 507
    Spain and 101, 181–2, 184, 187, 191–2, 198–9
    Sweden and 132–3, 143
    and Walpole 183, 192, 264–5
    and War of Polish Succession 232–3
Jamaica 29, 139, 429, 476, 506–7, 629, 654
James I, King 9, 19–23, 25, 81
James II, King (earlier Duke of York) 32, 34–7, 47
James Francis Edward, Prince of Wales 233
    birth 36
    as Pretender 70, 82, 99–102, 115, 133, 141, 142–3, 176, 187–8, 264
Jamestown, Virginia 25
Jefferies, Edward 104
Jefferson, Thomas 591, 603
    Summary of the rights of British America 584
Jefferys, James 142
Jenkins, Robert 247
Jenkins' Ear, War of (1739–42) 247–8, 248, 273–9, 281–8, 308, 312
Jenkinson, Charles (later 1st

Earl of Liverpool) 442, 548–9, 574, 589–90, 621, 628, 629
Jennings, Sir John 198
Jesuits 32
Johnson, Samuel 254–5, 405, 432, 598
Johnson, Sir William 505
Johnstone, George 596, 611, 620, 633
Joseph I, Holy Roman Emperor 64, 168
Joseph II, Holy Roman Emperor as Emperor 537, 558–9, 560, 586, 617, 622, 637–8, 639–40, 651, 659, 682
    as 'King of the Romans' 371, 374, 376, 377
Joseph Ferdinand, Prince of Bavaria 46
Jülich-Berg, Duchy of 174, 262, 279, 280, 291
'Junius' (correspondent) 562–3

Karelia 110, 164
Karl Leopold, Duke of Mecklenburg-Schwerin 117, 146, 165, 229, 240
Karl Theodor, Elector Palatine and Elector of Bavaria 334, 622
Kaunitz, Wenzel Anton 396, 397, 401, 429, 528, 622, 637, 638, 644
Keene, Sir Benjamin (ambassador to Spain) 249, 261, 266, 341, 380–81, 412
Keith, James 363
Keith, Sir Robert Murray (ambassador to Vienna) 591, 596, 628, 637–9, 641–2, 644, 667
Keith, Sir William 246, 271
Kennedy, Archibald 391
Keppel, Augustus (later 1st Viscount Keppel) 613, 614
Killigrew, Henry 41
Kinsky, Count 218
Kippis, Andrew 501–2
Kloster-Zeven, Convention of (1757) 436–41, 467
Königs Wusterhausen, Treaty of (1726) 196
Krefeld, Battle of (1758) 423, 442, 444

Kunersdorf, Battle of (1759) 464

La Rochelle 24
Lacy, Peter 233
Lagos, Battle of (1759) 423, 452
Latvia 142, 164
Laurens, Henry 587
Lawless, Sir Patrick 182
Le Havre 13
Lee, Arthur 584, 590, 593, 606, 624–5
Lee, Richard Henry 601–2
Lee, William 624, 625
Legge, Henry 378, 486
Leheup, Isaac 194
Leicester, Robert Dudley, Earl of 15, 16
Leicester House 364, 406, 444, 445, 452, 466, 467–8
Leigh, Egerton 590
Leonard, Daniel 602
Lepanto, Battle of (1571) 14, 17
Lestocq, Jean Armand de 342
Leszczyński, Stanislas, King of Poland 184, 231, 477, 545
Leuthen, Battle of (1757) 442, 467
Lewis, Erasmus 132
Licensing of the Press Act (1662) 39
Lichfield, George Lee, 3rd Earl of (earlier Viscount Quarendon) 316, 321
Lincoln, Henry Clinton, 7th Earl of 87
Lind, John 570
literacy 53
Literary Magazine 405
Littleton, Sir Thomas 32
Livingston, Robert 545
Livingston, William 392, 449
Locke, John 38
Lockhart, Sir William 31
Lodge, John, The Polish plum cake 568
Logan, James 245, 246
London, Hanoverian street names 87
London Evening Post 459, 496
Lonsdale, Henry Lowther, 3rd Viscount 318, 325
Lorraine, Duchy of 204, 218, 228, 241–2, 261, 311, 477, 545, 563

Loudoun, John Campbell, 4th Earl of 395, 431–2
Louis, Dauphin of France 215–16
Louis, Margrave of Baden 54, 86
Louis XIV, King of France
and Charles II 30–32, 34
death 101, 112
and George I 92, 101
and Lorraine 242
and War of Spanish Succession 46, 49, 56–7, 59, 61, 62–3, 66
and William III 37–8, 40, 43
Louis XV, King of France 175, 178, 180, 561
Louis XVI, King of France 627, 661, 682
Louis of Bourbon, Duke of Orleans 170
Louis of Brunswick, Prince 474
Louisburg 334, 344–7, 349–52, 435, 443, 450–51, 460, 542, 672
Louise, Princess, and Queen of Denmark 230
Louisiana 93, 94, 178, 392, 393, 481, 502
Lowther, Sir James 364
Lutheranism 123
Lutwyche, Thomas 159, 177–8
Luxembourg, Duchy of 241, 658
Lyttelton, George, 1st Baron 254, 258, 259, 320, 482, 591
Lyttelton, Thomas, 2nd Baron 603, 611

Macartney, Sir George (later Earl Macartney) 502, 529–30, 536
McDomhnaill, Séan Clarach 294
Madison, James 571
Madras 347, 351, 423
Mahan, Alfred Thayer 3, 139, 455, 667
Maillebois, Marshal 343
Mallett, David 417
Malplaquet, Battle of (1709) 57
Manchester, George Montagu, 4th Duke of 580, 629
Manila 486, 502, 555, 561

Mann, Sir Horace 632, 646
Mansfield, William Murray, 1st Earl of 591
Mar, John Erskine, 22nd Earl of 101, 141
Mardyk 92, 115
Maria Leszczyńska, Queen of France 184
Maria Theresa of Austria, Holy Roman Empress
death 637
and Flanders 370, 396
and Habsburg succession 371
marriage projects 185, 186, 210, 211, 218
on Polish partition 566
and Silesia 404
succession claims 168, 204, 211, 281
and War of Austrian Succession 292–3, 297–9, 307–11, 313, 314, 336, 337–8, 343
Mariana Victoria of Spain, Princess 175, 184
Marlborough, Charles Spencer, 3rd Duke of 331, 445, 446
Marlborough, John Churchill, 1st Duke of 51
Battle of Blenheim 50–51, 54–5
Blenheim Palace 44, 217
his army 49
as strategist 44, 55–6, 109
and Tories 58, 62, 64, 66–7
Marlborough, Sarah, Duchess of 68
Marshall, Henrietta 2
Marshall, Peter 3
Martin, William 312, 676
Martinique 359, 451, 495, 503
Mary, Princess, Landgravine of Hesse 230, 401–2, 438
Mary, Queen of Scots 12–13, 18
Mary I, Queen 12
Mary II, Queen 36, 37, 49
Maryland 390
Massachusetts 538, 587
Assembly 346, 544, 552, 590
Massachusetts Government Act (1774) 582, 611
Mathews, Thomas 342
Matthias, Holy Roman Emperor 20

Mauduit, Israel 471, 598
  Considerations on the present German war 469–70, 489, 515, 588
Maurepas, Jean-Frédéric, Comte de 178
Mauritius 507
Maximilian I, Elector of Bavaria 21
Maximilian II, Elector of Bavaria 50
Maximilian III Joseph, Elector of Bavaria 33
Maximilian Franz of Austria, Archduke 639–40
Mecklenburg, Duchy of
  and Austria 210, 218, 219
  Bernstorff's views on 119, 145, 149
  and Duke Charles Leopold 229, 240
  Russian occupation 107, 108, 117–18, 125, 142, 145–6
Mehmet (servant of George I) 83, 86
Meredith, Sir William 574
Methuen, Sir Paul 87
Methuen Treaty (1703) 50
Mexico 198, 540, 620
Milan 168, 189–90
Militia Bill (1756) 414–15
Minden, Battle of (1759) 423, 452–4, 456, 467, 522
Minorca
  Admiralty Court 643–4
  British rule 68, 74, 136, 164, 170, 181, 184, 350, 433, 557, 583, 592
  French capture 412–13, 416
  Russian claims to 650–51
  Spanish claims to 482, 628, 657, 659
Mississippi River 244, 245, 494, 495
Mitchell, Andrew 437, 469, 488, 513, 524, 547
Mitchell, John 449, 550–51
Mohawks 64
Moldavia 243
Monitor 398, 428–9, 434, 444, 453, 454, 459, 473, 488, 489, 495
Monongahela, Battle of (1755) 388, 405, 412
Montagu, Edward Wortley 266
Montagu, Elizabeth 463

Montmorin, Armand Marc, Comte de 611
Montreal 443, 464
Montrose, James Graham, 1st Duke of 114
Morning Post and Daily Advertiser 630
Morris, Robert 605–6
Mosquito Shore 249
Mulgrave, Constantine Phipps, 2nd Baron 613
Münchhausen, Baron Gerlach Adolf von
  Austrian strategy 194
  Convention of Kloster-Zeven 436, 438–9, 440
  and Duke of Newcastle 375–6, 431
  and France 447
  'Neustadt Protocol' 296
  and Prussia 280, 400, 404, 431, 441, 464
Münchhausen, Philip Adolf von 375–6, 376, 526
Münster, Bishopric of 123–4, 474, 639
Mustafa (servant of George I) 83, 86
Mustapha III, Sultan 585
Mutiny Bill debates 103, 188, 222, 234, 259, 670
Mysore War (1767–9) 507

Naples 17, 139, 168, 204, 231, 241, 312, 458, 676
  see also Two Sicilies, Kingdom of
Napoleon I 684
national identity, British 324–6, 675
naval strategy, British
  under George II 205–7, 211, 223, 229–30, 258–9, 270–73, 275, 284–6, 312, 323, 352–3, 366–7, 397–9, 434–5
  under George III 510–11, 518–19, 523, 548–9, 561–2, 573–4, 607–8, 612–14, 627–8, 631–2, 667, 672–3, 676, 678
Navigation Acts 28, 458, 538, 584
navy
  Elizbethan 15, 17–18
  Stuart 26, 33, 35–6, 40

Navy, Royal
  Baltic fleet 118, 188, 200
  deployment 429–30, 449, 518–19, 560–61
  financing of 361, 510, 667
  impressment 618
  Mediterranean fleet 75, 136, 138, 139–41, 188, 202, 311–12, 412–13, 561, 654
  and Samuel Pepys 33
  and Sir Robert Walpole 244
  size 261, 271, 312, 335–6, 447, 548–9, 574, 608, 618, 666
  supplies 110–11, 128, 138, 165, 230, 284–5, 672
Navy Act (1779) 618
Necker, Jacques 649, 653
Neisse 559
Netherlands, independence of 16–17, 19–20, 342, 411
  see also Austrian Netherlands; Dutch United Provinces; Spanish Netherlands
'Neustadt Protocol' (1741) 296
New Brunswick 87
New Jersey 33, 87, 600
New Orleans 93
New Spain
  conflicts with Britain in North America 139, 178, 245, 250, 267, 458, 507
  gold 12, 22–3, 198, 211–12
  illegal trade with Britain 228, 247–8, 260
  16th-century expansion 12, 15–16, 22–3
  see also individual territories
New York 33, 600
Newcastle, John Holles, Duke of 84, 86
Newcastle, Thomas Pelham-Holles, Duke of
  Austrian policy 169, 218, 371–9, 396–7, 401, 410–11
  and Austro-Spanish alliance 187, 190, 194–5
  and Caribbean colonies 249
  on Lord Carteret 321
  defection 302
  and Dutch Republic 396
  fall from power 520, 681
  and Frederick, Prince of Wales 257

on Frederick William I of
Prussia 196
French policy 175, 191,
199–200, 202, 217–18,
359, 399, 400, 672–3
and French expansion in
Canada 244
and Hanover 151–2, 280,
296, 297, 400–402, 675,
676
Imperial Election Scheme
371–8, 674, 677
and Jacobites 180–81, 182,
340, 362–3
naval policy 355, 366–7, 400,
409–10
and Pitt the Elder 405, 429,
444
and Polish succession 379
Prussian policy 408, 546
resignation of first ministry
415–17, 419, 420–21
on Septennial Bill 103
on Seven Years War 388,
390, 431, 436–7, 438–9,
443, 455–6, 457, 459–62,
464, 473, 475, 482, 483,
489–92, 496, 497–8
Spanish policy 212, 218,
263–4, 265, 272–3,
379–82, 400
as strategist 229, 369–70
on Viscount Townshend 209
and War of Austrian
Succession 289, 292–3,
295, 298–9, 311, 315,
335–7, 338, 341, 342, 344,
350, 351
and War of Jenkins' Ear
278–9, 282, 286
and War of Polish Succession
231, 232, 233–4, 243
and Whig party 126–7, 141
Newfoundland 92–3, 244
fisheries 98, 478, 480, 495,
496, 510, 679
newspapers 39, 53–4, 74, 181,
251, 346, 365, 390–91
Nieuport 189, 437
Nine Years War (War of Grand
Alliance) 39, 40, 43, 61,
138, 542, 675
Nineteen Propositions (1642) 27
Norris, Sir John 111–12, 118,
120, 144, 151, 153, 200,
216, 675

North, Frederick, Lord (later
2nd Earl of Guilford) 556,
565, 580–82, 613, 615,
624, 631–2, 654–5, 657,
682
North Briton 489, 496, 512–13
North Carolina 87
Northampton Mercury 181
Norway 117, 133
Nottingham, Daniel Finch, 2nd
Earl of 41, 96
Nova Scotia 360, 390, 395
Nugent, Robert, 1st Earl 603,
630–31
Nystad, Treaty of (1721) 164–5

O'Brien, Daniel 176
O'Dalaigh, Seamus 617
Ohio Company of Virginia
359–60
Ohio Valley 359, 369, 387, 541
o'hIrlarhaithe, Liam 502–3
oil 139
Old England, or the
Constitutional Journal 317,
321–2, 325–6, 339
Onslow, Arthur 317
Orford, Edward Russell, Earl of
(First Lord of Admiralty)
119
Ormonde, James Butler, 2nd
Duke of 67, 98, 99
Orrery, Charles Boyle, 4th Earl
of 177
Osnabrück, Bishopric of 441,
461, 473, 474, 527, 640
Ostend 167, 185, 187, 189,
193, 340, 437
Ostend Company 167, 169,
184–5, 188, 193–4, 212,
219, 363, 638
Ostermann, Count Ivan 530
O'Suillebhain, Eoghan Rua 617
Otis, James 541
Ottoman Empire
and Habsburgs 17, 243
navy 558
and Russia 175, 196–7, 243,
518, 651
see also Turkey
Oudenaarde, Battle of (1708)
56, 319
Oxford and Mortimer, Robert
Harley, 1st Earl of
and accession of George I 62,
96, 97–9, 675, 679

reign of Queen Anne 58, 62,
65–6, 67, 69–70
and South Sea Company 160
trial 128–9

Paderborn, Bishopric of 441,
461, 474
Paine, Tom 602, 603–5
Palliser, Sir Hugh 613, 619–20
pamphleteers 53–4, 85, 92,
283–4, 315, 398, 407, 412,
420, 459, 471–2, 515
Panama 45, 52, 198, 276
Panin, Count Nikita 557, 626,
637
Pardo, Convention of (1728) 211
Pardo, Convention of (1739)
267–8, 273
Paris, Treaty of (1763) 495,
501, 502, 503, 526, 535
Paris, Treaty of (1783) 683
Parker, Thomas (later 1st Earl
of Macclesfield) 131
Parma, Alexander Farnese,
Duke of 14, 16, 40
Parma, Don Carlos, Duke of see
Charles III, King of Spain
Parma, Duchy of 212, 219, 231
Parma, Francesco Farnese, Duke
of 137
Parma, Philip of Bourbon, Duke
of 411, 434, 458
Passarowitz, Peace of (1718)
138
Patino, Don José 240
patriotism, British 364–5,
414–15, 678
Payne, John 394
Peerage Bill (1718–19) 148,
152–3
Pelham, Henry
on Lord Carteret 372
First Lord of Treasury 311,
335, 361, 370
on Germany 274, 293
and Imperial Election Scheme
373, 374, 378
and Walpole's government
257, 260
and War of Austrian
Succession 342, 350–51
Pelham, Thomas 219
Pennsylvania 87, 245
Assembly 539, 544
Seven Years War 389–90,
443, 505

Penny London Post 365
Pepys, Samuel 33
Perceval, John, Viscount (*later* 2nd Earl of Egmont) 326–7, 365
Perry, Micajah 250
Peru 198, 620
Peter I, 'the Great', Tsar
  death 180
  and Great Northern War 117–18, 135, 142–7, 153, 164–5
  and Jacobites 176
  and Ottoman Empire 175
Peterborough, Charles Mordaunt, 3rd Earl of 114
Petty, Sir William 36
Pfalz-Sulzbach Palatinate 262
Phelps, Richard 517
Philadelphia 587, 600
Philip II, King of Spain 12, 14, 15–18
Philip V, King of Spain, and Duke of Anjou
  and Austro-Spanish alliance 184, 202
  claims to French throne 45, 92, 115, 163
  his Court 267
  and Jacobites 102
  and War of Spanish Succession 45, 46, 47, 50, 56, 59, 65, 66, 68
Philippe II, Duke of Orleans (Regent of France) 101, 112–13, 170
Phillips, John 326
Piacenza, Duchy of 212, 219
Pitt, Robert 'Diamond' 257
Pitt, Thomas (*later* 1st Baron Camelford) 667
Pitt, William, the Elder (*later* 1st Earl of Chatham) 472
  chief minister 546–7, 548
  death 612
  early career 257–8, 267
  and end of Newcastle's first ministry 414, 417–21
  and George III 467–8, 512, 546
  in Lords 563–4, 569, 575, 579, 594, 597–8, 609–11
  out of power (1761–6) 510, 524, 534–5, 544
  Paymaster General 355, 372, 381–2, 405–7

  resignation as Secretary of State 483–6, 490–91, 496, 497
  Secretary of State 423–39, 441–5, 447–9, 450–54, 456–7, 459–62, 465–6, 471–3, 480–82, 673, 676
  and Sir Robert Walpole 301, 303
  and War of Austrian Succession 288, 290, 300, 317–18, 336, 348
Pitt, William, the Younger 660–61, 683
Plain reasoner 329–30
Plumb, J. H. 122
Poland
  and Austria 181
  and Great Northern War 108, 109, 145–6, 153–4
  and Holy Roman Empire 169
  partition 565–71, 681
  reforms 547–8
  succession schemes 379–80, 531
  and Treaty of Hanover (1725) 194–5
  War of Polish Succession 227–8, 231–42, 261, 477
Political maxims (1744) 322
Political Register 551
Polwarth, Alexander Hume-Campbell, Lord (*later* 2nd Earl of Marchmont) 112
Pompadour, Madame de 399, 528
Pondicherry 507
Poniatowski, Stanislas August, King of Poland 531
Pontiac (chief) 505, 506
Pontpietin, General du 319
population statistics 535–6
Porter, James 522–3
Porteus, Beilby, Bishop of Chester 665
Portland, Hans Wilhelm Bentinck, 1st Earl of 81
Portland, William Bentinck, 2nd Duke of 268
Portland, Elizabeth, Dowager Duchess of 130
Porto Bello 198, 276–7, 277, 284
Portugal
  alliance with Britain 50, 207, 263, 516

  and France 31
  and Seven Years War 487, 492
  under Spanish monarchy 14, 17
  and Treaty of Vienna (1725) 193
Postlethwayt, Malachy 449–50
Potemkin, Prince Gregori Alexandrovich 650–51, 653
Potenger, Richard 456
Poulett, John, 2nd Earl 398
Pownall, Thomas 536
Powys, Thomas (*later* 1st Baron Lilford) 661
Poyntz, Stephen 211, 218
'Pragmatic Army' 308, 313, 314–17
Pragmatic Sanction (1713) 168–9, 184–5, 211, 212, 216–21, 281, 336
Prince, Thomas 346
Prior, Matthew 69
privateers 362, 399, 458–9, 642, 643–4, 654
Proclamation Line (1763) 540–41, 543, 583–4, 668
Propositions of Uxbridge 27–8
Protestantism 17–18, 20, 24–5, 43, 71–2, 149–50, 220
Prussia, Kingdom of
  annexation of Silesia 275, 289, 291–2, 362
  Armed Neutrality 643
  and Austro-Spanish alliance 184, 194–5
  British missions to 378–9
  Convention of Westminster (1756) 403–4, 406, 408–9, 626
  and Great Northern War 109, 117, 139, 146–7, 154
  invasion of Saxony 419–20
  Jacobitism 363
  relations with Austria 214–15, 300, 310, 333, 334–6, 342–4, 359, 559
  and Russia 379–80, 402–3, 408–9, 511, 523–4
  Seven Years War 431, 434, 435–7, 439, 441–2, 447–9, 454, 460–61, 463–5, 471–2, 474–5, 490–92
  subsidy treaties 404–5, 442,

454, 456, 470, 489–90, 492
  threats to Hanover 209–10,
    262–3, 280, 293, 294,
    361–3, 400, 402–3,
    525–6, 546, 566–7, 625–7
  Treaty of Charlottenburg
    (1723) 174–5
  Treaty of Hanover (1725)
    191, 193, 196, 202, 209
  Triple Alliance (1788) 683
Public Ledger 478
Pufendorf, Samuel von 427
Pulteney, William (*later* 1st Earl
  of Bath)
  and Frederick, Prince of Wales
    257
  and Hanoverian succession
    87, 96, 97, 227
  on Treaty of Hanover (1725)
    193
  on Treaty of Seville (1729)
    239
  and Walpole 216–17, 251–2,
    271–2, 301–2
  and War of Austrian
    Succession 290, 309, 311,
    321
  and War of Jenkins' Ear 266,
    275, 282, 283–4
  and War of Polish Succession
    235–6, 237, 238
  and Whig split 120, 121,
    123–4
Pyle, Edmund 483

Quadruple Alliance (1718)
  139–41, 163, 175, 213,
  382
Quadruple Alliance, War of
  (1718–20) 138–41
Quakers 389–90
Quebec
  and British American colonies
    392
  British capture (1759) 423,
    443, 452
  British rule 506, 541
  English/British expeditions:
    (1690) 41; (1711) 62–4,
    66, 73, 98; (1746) 344–5,
    347
  French settlement 62–4, 93
Quebec Act (1774) 582–4, 600
Quiberon Bay, Battle of (1759)
  423, 452, 455
Rakoczy rising 56

Raleigh, Sir Walter 23
Ralph, James 326
Rastadt, Treaty of (1714) 70, 167
Ray, Nicholas 545
Raymond, Robert, 2nd Baron
  331–2
Recruitment Acts (1778; 1779)
  618
Reed, Joseph 413
Reformation, The 11
Regency Councils 95–6, 114,
  311
Regulating Act (1773) 580
Renunciation Act (1778) 611
Réunion 507
Review 65
Rhode Island 543, 551, 654
Richard I, 'the Lionheart', King
  10
Richecourt, Emmanuel, Count
  363
Richmond, Charles Lennox, 3rd
  Duke of 521–2, 594, 600,
  607–8, 614, 633–4
Rigby, Richard 373, 378, 398,
  478–9, 486, 487, 637, 646
Rio de Janeiro 516
Riot Act (1715) 101
Robethon, Jean de 84, 111, 112,
  122, 151
Robinson, John 634
Robinson, Thomas (*later* 1st
  Baron Grantham) 198, 229,
  241–2, 255–6, 403
Robson, Joseph 368
Rochester, Francis Atterbury,
  Bishop of 86
Rochester, Laurence Hyde, 1st
  Earl of 41
Rochford, William Nassau de
  Zuylestein, 4th Earl of
  representative in Turin 382
  Secretary of State for North
    521, 555
  Secretary of State for South
    519, 521, 558, 565, 569,
    571–2, 608
Rockingham, Charles Watson-
  Wentworth, 2nd Marquess
  of 520, 545, 563, 594, 657,
  666, 683
Rocoux, Battle of (1746) 347
Rodger, Nicholas 3
Rodney, George, 1st Baron 657,
  658
Role, Sebastian 179

Romania 168
Rooke, Sir George 54
Rossbach, Battle of (1757) 442,
  448, 467
Rowse, A. L. 81–2
Roxburghe, John Ker, 1st Duke
  of 84
Royal Africa Company 178
Rudyerd, Sir Benjamin 23
'Rule Britannia' (Thomson) 3,
  206–7
Russia
  Armed Neutrality 643, 646
  Austro-Russian treaty (1781)
    651
  conflicts with Turkey 403,
    518, 530, 557–8, 585, 677
  death of Peter the Great 180
  and Great Northern War 69,
    108–10, 113, 117–18, 135,
    139, 142–6, 153–4, 164–5
  Jacobitism 176, 200, 312,
    363
  and Ottoman Empire 175,
    243, 558, 651
  Polish partition 565
  proposed alliances with
    Britain 528–31, 547–8,
    621–2, 636–7, 650–51
  relations with Prussia
    379–80, 402–3, 408–9,
    511, 523–4
  Seven Years War 463–4
  subsidy treaty (1755) 402–5
  Treaty of St Petersburg (1757)
    435
  Treaty of Vienna (1725) 184,
    186–7, 190, 193, 196
  and War of Austrian
    Succession 312–13
  and War of Polish Succession
    231
Ryalton, William Godolphin,
  Viscount 114
Ryswick, Treaty of (1697) 43,
  48, 169

Sacheverell, Henry 57
Sackville, Sir Edward, (*later* 4th
  Earl of Dorset) 9–10
Sackville, Lord George (*later*
  Germain, *afterwards* 1st
  Viscount Sackville) 446,
  452–4, 467, 513, 594, 608,
  635, 652, 654–5

St Albans, Sir Francis Bacon, 1st Viscount 22
St Aubyn, Sir John 301, 320, 325
Saint Contest, François Dominique de Barberie, Comte de 369
St Eustatius 599, 646
St James's Chronicle 501
St John, Henry *see* Bolingbroke, Henry St John, 1st Viscount
St John, Oliver 27
St John, St Andrew 660
St Lucia 388, 503
St Malo 443, 445, 468
St Petersburg, Treaty of (1757) 435
St Pierre and Miquelon 495, 502, 503, 506
St Saphorin, François Louis de Pesme, Seigneur de 92, 166, 173, 175, 188, 195, 199
St Tropez 312
St Vincent 388, 502, 629, 654
Saints, Battle of the (1782) 658
Salisbury, Benjamin Hoadley, Bishop of 251
Salisbury, Gilbert Burnet, Bishop of 84
Salzburg, Leopold von Firmian, Archbishop of 220
Samuel, Raphael 2–3
Sanderson, Sir Thomas 238, 267
Sandwich, John Montagu, 4th Earl of
  First Lord of Admiralty 358, 373, 562, 573, 676
  and American War of Independence 591, 599, 608, 612–13, 620, 629, 631, 636, 641, 646, 655–7
  on Hanoverians 317, 318, 319, 320
  Secretary of State 514, 516–17, 518, 523–5, 529
  and War of Austrian Succession 322, 325, 341, 349, 351
Sandys, Samuel, 1st Baron 257, 327, 328
Santo Domingo 507
Saratoga, Battle of (1777) 610, 611
Sardinia 137, 231, 311, 382
Sartine, Antoine de 601

Savoy, House of 69, 70, 137, 189, 230, 310–11, 382
Sawbridge, John 648–9
Saxe-Gotha, Duchy of 123–4, 208
Saxony, Electorate of 168, 169, 336, 374, 419–20, 560
Schaub, Sir Luke 115–16
Schleswig, Duchy of 153
Schulenburg, Count Friedrich Wilhelm von der
  and accession of George I 84, 87–8
  and Baltic crisis 141–2, 151
  and defeat of Spain 138, 139
  and George I's first ministry 95
  on 'German' ministers 129–30
  and Hanoverian chancellery 114
  on Earl of Sunderland 126
  on Viscount Townshend 120
  on Whig split 127–8
Schulenburg, Melusine von der, (*later* Duchess of Kendal and Munster) 83, 122
Schwicheldt, August Wilhelm von 440
Scotland
  Act of Union (1707) 1, 51–3
  'Auld Alliance' 11, 13
  Darien scheme 45, 52
  Elizabethan policy towards 18–19
  Highlands 365
  Jacobite revolts 101–2, 187, 339–41, 362–3, 507
  Scots Brigade 599–600
Seehandlung 585
Seeley, John Robert 1
Seilern, Count (Austrian ambassador) 517, 524
Sellar, W. C. 677
Senegal 502, 510
Septennial Act (1716) 102–3
Serbia 168
Seven Years War 356, 388–90, 412, 419–21, 423–4, 431–61, 471–3, 478–97, 518, 542, 670
Seville, Treaty of (1729) 212–13, 239, 303
Seymour, Sir Edward 41
Seymour, Sir Henry 16

Shaftesbury, Anthony Ashley-Cooper, 1st Earl of 33
Shawnees 360, 503
Shebbeare, John 412, 416, 598
Shelburne, William Petty, 2nd Earl of
  on American independence 658, 663
  on British military success 665
  and League of Armed Neutrality 643–4, 645, 648, 657
  President of Board of Trade 502, 520
  Prime Minister 659–60, 683
  Secretary of State 556
  on Seven Years War 487, 502
Shippen, William 104, 123–4, 127, 129, 192
Shirley, William 344–5, 346, 352, 367, 394–5
Shovell, Sir Cloudesley 41, 54
Sicily 45, 69, 137, 138–9, 189, 204, 241, 458
  see also Two Sicilies, Kingdom of
Silesia, Electorate of 199, 275, 289, 300, 310–11, 343, 359, 362, 404, 435, 559
silk 19
silver 12, 50, 563
slavery
  Asiento 47, 66, 68, 136, 160, 202, 212, 249, 381
  French slave imports 359
  in North America 653
Smith, William 540
Society for the Encouragement of Arts, Manufactures and Commerce 365
Soissons, congress of (1728) 211, 215
Somers, John, Baron 56, 96
Sophia, Electress of Hanover 49, 70, 83
Sophia Caroline of Wolfenbüttel, Princess 402, 474
Sophia Dorothea of Celle 80, 125
Sophia Dorothea, Queen in Prussia 174, 209, 279
South Carolina 544, 653
'South Sea Bubble' 159, 160–61, 176, 205

South Sea Company 62, 160, 381, 672
Spain
  and American War of Independence 601, 606, 619–21, 628–9, 630–31, 632–3, 649, 654
  Anglo-Spanish trade treaty (1750) 381–2
  Anglo-Spanish War (1654–60) 28–9
  Asiento 47, 66, 68, 136, 160, 202, 212, 249
  Austro-Spanish alliance 184–90, 193, 198–9, 210–12
  British naval strategy 205–7, 261, 263–5
  Convention of Pardo (1728) 211
  Convention of Pardo (1739) 267–8, 273
  and Elizabethan England 14–19, 40
  Falkland Islands crisis 560–61, 572–3
  Habsburg monarchy 11, 24
  Manila Ransom 486, 502, 555
  Mediterranean expansion 136–7, 138–40, 163–4, 181, 300–301, 312
  navy 509, 561, 574
  reforms 537
  and Seven Years War 433, 457–8, 481–3, 486–7, 492, 495, 502
  and Thirty Years War 22–3, 24
  trade 'depredations' 247–52, 256, 260, 266–7
  and War of Devolution 30–31
  War of Jenkins' Ear 247–8, 273–9, 281–8, 308, 312
  and War of Polish Succession 231
  and War of Quadruple Alliance 138–41
Spanish America *see* New Spain
Spanish Netherlands 14–15, 17–18, 20, 21–2, 26, 30, 43, 48, 68
  see also Austrian Netherlands; Flanders
Spanish Partition Treaty (1698) 675

Spanish Succession, War of (1701–14) 44, 48–51, 55–68, 71, 73, 79, 107–8, 329, 669–70
Spotswood, Alex 93–4
Stair, John Dalrymple, 2nd Earl of 192, 257, 309, 313, 319, 321, 452–3
Stamp Act (1765) 536, 537–8, 543–4, 553
Stanhope, James (*later* 1st Earl Stanhope)
  on Austro-Spanish alliance 185, 190
  and Baltic crisis 113, 118, 120–21, 132, 135–6, 143, 677
  on British Army 103–4, 124
  chief minister 88, 680
  death 162, 169
  and defeat of Spain 137, 140–41
  in George I's first ministry 96
  on 'German' ministers 151
  and Gibraltar 164
  and Holy Roman Empire 124–5, 169
  and Prussia 147–9, 154
  and rise of Walpole 161–2
  and War of Spanish Succession 58, 96, 97
  and Whig split 125–6, 127, 128
Stanhope, William *see* Harrington, William Stanhope, 1st Earl of
Stanislas I, King of Poland 184, 231, 477, 545
Stanislas August, King of Poland 531, 547
Stanley, Hans 547
Stanyan, Abraham 196–7, 197
Starkey, David 3
Steele, Sir Richard 87
Stone, Andrew 294
Stormont, David Murray, 7th Viscount (*later* 2nd Earl of Mansfield)
  Ambassador to Austria 524–5, 528, 566
  Ambassador to France 607, 616
  Secretary of State 636, 637–8, 639, 642, 651–2, 663
Stourzh, Gerald 668

Stowe, Temple of British Worthies 259, 515
Strafford, Thomas Wentworth, 1st Earl of 140, 222, 675
Strange, James Murray, Baron 339
strategy, British foreign policy 670–84
Strube, David Georg 441
Struensee, Count Johann Friedrich 564
Stuart, Henry Benedikt, Cardinal Duke of York 176
subsidy treaties 518
  (1755) 402–8, 427
  (1758) 442, 454, 456
Suffolk, Henry Howard, 12th Earl of 564, 566, 606, 613, 614, 623, 626, 627
sugar 359, 451, 476, 503, 535, 589, 629
Sugar Act (1764) 536, 537–8, 543
Sumatra 645
Sunderland, Charles Spencer, 3rd Earl of
  on Battle of Blenheim 50
  death 169
  First Lord of Treasury 148, 151
  in George I's first ministry 94–5, 96, 113
  and Hanoverian chancellery 84, 88
  and rise of Walpole 161–2
  Secretary of State 120–21, 126, 128, 132, 139
Sweden
  Armed Neutrality 643
  conflicts with Russia 186–7, 196, 312, 564–5
  and Elizabethan England 14
  and France 262, 530, 545, 564–5
  friendship treaty 530–31
  Great Northern War 55, 69, 70, 108–12, 117–18, 139, 142–5, 153, 164
  Jacobite plot 132–3
  and Thirty Years War 25
  Treaty of Hanover (1725) 193, 200–201, 209
  Treaty of St Petersburg (1757) 435
Swedish East India Company 230

Swift, Jonathan 84, 132
  The conduct of the allies
    58–61, 64–5, 272–3

Tangier 30, 33
Tea Act (1773) 581–2
Temple, Richard Grenville-
  Temple, 2nd Earl 324, 405,
  414, 456
Teschen, Treaty of (1779) 627,
  643
Test, The 422, 424, 426–7
Thirty Years War 9, 20–25,
  108
Thompson, E. P. 177
Thomson, James 3, 206–7
Thorn, Poland 181, 195
Thurloe, John 28
Ticonderoga, Battle of (1758)
  445
Ticonderoga, Battle of (1777)
  606
Tilly, Johann Tserclaes, Count
  of 22
Tilson, George 154, 255
tobacco 235
Tobago 388, 502, 654
Toulon, Battle of (1744) 342
Townshend, Charles, 2nd
  Viscount *121*
  appointed Secretary of State
    162
  Austrian policy 159, 165–6,
    167, 169, 172–4, 218–19
  and Austro-Spanish alliance
    183, 185–7, 189, 193, 195
  and Barrier Treaty (1709) 68,
    96
  on British Army 171
  German policy 204–5,
    208–9, 210, 214
  and Great Northern War 112,
    118–22, 133, 164–5
  and Jacobites 181, 183
  and Peerage Bill 148
  and Prussia 210
  resignation 219
  and Russian threat 175, 190,
    196–7
  and Seven Years War 486
  Spanish policy 211, 212
  and Whig split 125, 127, 128,
    680
Townshend, Charles
  (Chancellor of Exchequer)
  551–2

Townshend, Dorothy,
  Viscountess 219
Townshend, George, 4th
  Viscount (*later* 1st
  Marquess) 414, 572–3
Townshend, Thomas (*later* 1st
  Viscount Sydney) 607, 609,
  647
trade
  with American colonies
    366–8, 535–6, 538–40,
    681
  Anglo-Spanish treaty (1750)
    381–2
  with Spain 247–52, 256, 260,
    266–7, 482
  statistics 74–5
treaties
  Aix-la-Chapelle (1748)
    350–52, 358–9, 403, 458,
    516, 542, 661
  Aranjuez (1752) 382, 400,
    434, 511, 556
  Aranjuez (1779) 628
  Austro-Russian (1781) 651
  Barrier treaties: (1709) 56–7
    68 96: 105; (1715) 106,
    147, 170–71, 370
  Breslau (1742) 310
  Britain and Denmark (1739)
    270
  Charlottenburg (1723) 174–5
  Dresden (1745) 338
  Füssen (1745) 337
  Grand Alliance (1701) 48–9,
    50, 55, 97–8
  Hanover (1725) 191–6,
    200–202, 209, 239, 290,
    303, 375
  Königs Wusterhausen (1726)
    196
  Methuen (1703) 50
  Nystad (1721) 164–5
  Paris (1763) 495, 501, 502,
    503, 526, 535
  Paris (1783) 683
  Rastadt (1714) 70, 167
  Ryswick (1697) 43, 48, 169
  St Petersburg (1757) 435
  Seville (1729) 212–13, 239,
    303
  Spanish Partition (1698) 675
  subsidy treaties: (1755)
    402–8, 427; (1758) 442,
    454, 456
  Teschen (1779) 627, 643

Two Empresses (1746) 313
Utrecht (1713) 68–70, 79, 92,
  95, 97, 99, 115, 154, 160,
  167, 170–71, 188, 217,
  263–4, 290, 346, 461, 674
Versailles (1756) 409–11
Versailles (1757) 435
Versailles (1783) 660–61
Vienna (1725) 184–7, 190,
  193, 198, 202
Vienna (1731) 219–21, 231,
  396
Vienna (1738) 243
Warsaw (1745) 336
Westminster (1716) 116
Westminster (1742) 310, 403
Westphalia (1648) 29, 108,
  150, 191, 401, 527
Worms (1743) 310, 334
Trenton, Battle of (1776) 600
Trevor, Robert 268–9, 296, 297
Triennial Act (1694) 39
Triple Alliance (1716–17)
  115–16, 120, 137, 139,
  168, 170, 175–6, 217
Triple Alliance (1788) 683
Tromp, Maarten 26
'Troop Society' 454
True Briton 166
Tucker, John 324
Tucker, Josiah 581
Turgot, Roger-Jacques 601
Turkey
  Austrian wars 37, 106, 118,
    137–8, 168, 243, 261–2
  conflicts with Russia 403,
    518, 530, 557–8, 585, 677
  see also Ottoman Empire
Turkish Society 516
Turks and Caicos Islands 518,
  523, 563
Turner, Edward 339
Tuscany, Duchy of 212, 219
Tweeddale, John Hay, 4th
  Marquess of 314
Two Empresses, Treaty of
  (1746) 313
Two Sicilies, Kingdom of 312,
  643
  see also Naples; Sicily
Tyrawly, James O'Hara, 2nd
  Baron 207, 412, 414
Tyrconnel, John Brownlow,
  Viscount 352
Tyrconnell, Richard Talbot,
  Duke of 36

Ulrica Eleonora, Queen of
  Sweden 143
United States of America
  Declaration of Independence
    602–4, 661
  European delegations 605–6
  frontier 659
  trade with Britain 681
  Treaty of Versailles (1783)
    660–61
Universal Spectator 345–6
Utrecht, Treaty of (1713)
  68–70, 79, 92, 95, 97, 99,
  115, 154, 160, 167,
  170–71, 188, 217, 263–4,
  290, 346, 461, 674

'Vandalia' 581
Venice 264
Veracruz 198
Verden, Duchy of
  British–Hanoverian
    annexation 109, 110, 115,
    116, 124, 144–5, 325
  investitures 116, 164–5, 193,
    219
  Treaty of Westphalia (1648)
    108
Vergennes, Charles Gravier,
  Comte de 501, 502,
  600–601, 606, 611–12,
  614, 626–8, 659, 661
Vernon, Edward 216, 276–7,
  281, 283, 284–6, 288, 312,
  360, 365, 413–15
Versailles, Treaty of (1756)
  409–11
Versailles, Treaty of (1757) 435
Versailles, Treaty of (1783)
  660–61
Vetch, Samuel 62–3
Victor Amadeus III of Savoy,
  King of Sardinia 382
Vienna, Treaty of (1725) 184–7,
  190, 193, 198, 202
Vienna, Treaty of (1731)
  219–21, 231, 396
Vienna, Treaty of (1738) 243
Vigo 50
Virginia 87, 93, 245, 551
  'Mount Vernon' 276–7
  Seven Years War 389, 390,
    432, 443, 505
Volkra, Count 114
Voltaire 416, 502
Vorpommern 108, 109

Wager, Sir Charles 196, 200,
  201, 202, 261
Waldeck, Principality of 592, 609
Waldegrave, James, 1st Earl
  208, 253, 406, 419, 424
Walker, Sir Hovenden 64
Wall, Don Riccardo 381, 400
Wallachia 168, 243
Waller, Edmund 307, 317, 322,
  323–4, 326
Walmoden, Amalie von,
  Countess of Yarmouth 254,
  420
Walpole, Horace (*later* 4th Earl
  of Orford) 378, 420,
  423–4, 438, 447–8, 456,
  469, 502, 564, 567, 661
Walpole, Horatio (*later* 1st
  Baron Walpole) 220
  on Austrian succession 204
  and Austro-Spanish alliance
    186, 189–90, 193, 194,
    202, 219
  on British Army 223
  death 520
  and Dutch United Provinces
    105
  and George II 255, 256, 257
  on Hanoverian politics 280
  and Imperial Election Scheme
    373, 378
  on Mecklenburg 119–20
  on Duke of Newcastle 126,
    249
  and Seven Years War 388,
    390
  as strategist 229, 355–6
  on Viscount Townshend 209
  and War of Austrian
    Succession 291, 319–20,
    328–9, 331, 339, 341
  and War of Jenkins' Ear 261,
    266, 269–70, 272, 283
  and War of Polish Succession
    231, 240–41, 243
Walpole, Horatio (son of Sir
  Robert Walpole) 348
Walpole, Sir Robert (*later* 1st
  Earl of Orford)
  Austrian policy 218–19
  becomes 'prime minister' 159,
    161–2
  on British Army 222–3
  Chancellor of Exchequer
    96–8, 99, 113
  and *Craftsman* journal 217

elections (1741) 294–5
impeachment attempts 220,
  271–2, 289–90, 675, 679
and Jacobites 183, 192,
  264–5
on ministerial role 73, 212,
  673–4
in opposition 120–22, 128,
  129, 132, 138, 140, 148,
  152
resignation 301–4, 680
and Russian expansion 165,
  188
Spanish policy 247, 260–61,
  265–6, 269–71
taxation policy 235, 246
and War of Austrian
  Succession 293, 299
and War of Jenkins' Ear 275,
  282–3
and War of Polish Succession
  228, 233–4, 236–7, 239,
  240, 242–3
Walsingham, Sir Francis 15, 17
Ward, John 97
Warren, (Sir) Peter 344
wars
  American Independence 584,
    587–601, 606, 610–11,
    616–22, 652–9, 664–8,
    677–8
  Anglo-Dutch (1664–7,
    1672–4) 31–2; (1780–84)
    645–7, 651–2
  Anglo-French (1557–9)
    12–13
  Anglo-Spanish (1654–60)
    28–9
  Austrian Succession 289–301,
    309–19, 329–39, 341–4,
    347–50, 670
  Bavarian Succession 622,
    624–5, 627
  Devolution 30–31
  English Civil 28–9
  Great Northern 55, 108–12,
    117–20, 142–5, 153–4,
    164–5
  Hundred Years 10
  Jenkins' Ear 247–8, 273–9,
    281–8, 308, 312
  Mysore (1767–9) 507
  Nine Years 39, 40, 43, 61,
    138, 542, 675
  Polish Succession 227–8,
    231–42, 261, 477

wars – *cont.*
  Quadruple Alliance 138–41
  Seven Years 356, 388–90,
    412, 419–21, 423–4,
    431–61, 471–3, 478–97,
    518, 542, 670
  Spanish Succession 44,
    48–51, 55–68, 71, 73, 79,
    107–8, 329, 542, 669–70
  Thirty Years 9, 20–25, 108
Warsaw, Treaty of (1745) 336
Washington, George 277, 388,
    389, 541, 593–4, 600, 603
Washington, Lawrence 276
Wesley, John 598
Westminster, Convention of
    (1756) 403–6, 408–9, 419,
    420, 626
Westminster, Treaty of (1716)
    116
Westminster, Treaty of (1742)
    310, 403
Westminster Journal 326, 339,
    346
Westmorland, John Fane, 7th
    Earl of 316–17
Westphalia, Treaty of (1648) 29,
    108, 150, 191, 402, 527
Wetstein, Caspar 314
Weymouth, Thomas Thynne,
    3rd Viscount (*later* 1st
    Marquess of Bath) 562, 606
Wharton, Philip, Duke of 96
Whately, Thomas 535
White Mountain, Battle of
    (1620) 20
Whitworth, Charles, Baron 69,
    118, 162

'Wild Geese' (Irish Jacobite
    soldiers) 507–8
Wilhelmina of Prussia, Princess
    175, 196, 209, 215
Wilkes, John 416, 489, 512–13,
    529, 594–5, 596
Willes, Edward, Bishop of Bath
    and Wells 163
William I, 'the Conqueror', King
    10, 39
William III, King, and Prince of
    Orange 4, 36–7, 39–43,
    45–7, 49, 81, 83, 86–7
William IV, Prince of Orange
    (Stadtholder of
    Netherlands) 229–30, 364
William VIII, Landgrave of
    Hesse 309, 310, 334–5,
    437, 438
Williams, Ephraim 392
Willimot, Robert 252
Wilmington, Spencer Compton,
    1st Earl of 311
Wilson, Kathleen 3
Winchelsea, Daniel Finch, 8th
    Earl of 123, 222, 237
wine 52, 235, 250
Winnington, Thomas 327–8
Wolfe, James 432, 443, 446,
    452
Wootton, John 319
Worms, Treaty of (1743) 310,
    334
Wortley Montagu, Edward 266
Wraxall, Sir Nathaniel 636,
    647–8, 653
Wroughton, Thomas 531
Würzburg, Bishopric of 208

Wyndham, Sir William 192,
    204, 216, 237, 238,
    239–40, 251, 264
Wyvill, Christopher 633

Yarmouth, Amalie, Countess of
    254, 420
Yeatman, R. J. 677
Yonge, Sir William 223, 236,
    307, 328, 331
York, Prince Edward, Duke of
    468
York, Prince Frederick, Duke of
    527, 640, 684
Yorke, Joseph (*later* Baron
    Dover)
  envoy to Dutch United
    Provinces 396, 585, 599,
    621, 645
  on European role of Britain
    416, 493, 519, 522, 565,
    586, 589, 608–9
  and French policy 430–31,
    464, 621
  and Hanoverian policy
    622–3, 624
  and Hessian mercenaries 592
  and Polish policy 566
  and Prussian policy 436, 489
  and Russian policy 607
  and Spanish policy 482, 520,
    620
Yorkshire Association 633, 635
Yorktown, Siege of (1781)
    654–5, 657
Ypres 357, 357, 557

Zealand 651–2